W9-BRF-321

PRESCHOOL PERIOD (3 to 6 years)	MIDDLE CHILDHOOD (6 to 12 years)
• Height and weight continue to increase rapidly. • The body becomes less rounded and more muscular. • The brain grows larger, neural interconnections continue to develop, and lateralization emerges. • Gross and fine motor skills advance quickly. Children can throw and catch balls, run, use forks and spoons, and tie shoelaces. • Children begin to develop handedness.	• Growth becomes slow and steady. Muscles develop, and "baby fat" is lost. • Gross motor skills (biking, swimming, skating, ball handling) and fine motor skills (writing, typing, fastening buttons) continue to improve.
• Children show egocentric thinking (viewing world from their own perspective) and "centration," a focus on only one aspect of a stimulus. • Memory, attention span, and symbolic thinking improve, and intuitive thought begins. • Language (sentence length, vocabulary, syntax, and grammar) improves rapidly.	• Children apply logical operations to problems. • Understanding of conservation (that changes in shape do not necessarily affect quantity) and transformation (that objects can go through many states without changing) emerge. • Children can "decenter"—take multiple perspectives into account. • Memory encoding, storage, and retrieval improve, and control strategies (meta-memory) develop. • Language pragmatics (social conventions) and metalinguistic awareness (self-monitoring) improve.
• Children develop self-concepts, which may be exaggerated. • A sense of gender and racial identity emerges. • Children begin to see peers as individuals and form friendships based on trust and shared interests. • Morality is rule-based and focused on rewards and punishments. • Play becomes more constructive and cooperative, and social skills become important.	• Children refer to psychological traits to define themselves. Sense of self becomes differentiated. • Social comparison is used to understand one's standing and identity. • Self-esteem grows differentiated, and a sense of self-efficacy (an appraisal of what one can and cannot do) develops. • Children approach moral problems intent on maintaining social respect and accepting what society defines as right. • Friendship patterns of boys and girls differ. Boys mostly interact with boys in groups, and girls tend to interact singly or in pairs with other girls.
Preoperational stage	Concrete operational stage
Initiative-versus-guilt stage	Industry-versus-inferiority stage
Phallic stage	Latency period
Preconventional morality level	Conventional morality level

	ADOLESCENCE (12 to 20 years)	YOUNG ADULTHOOD (20 to 40 years)
PHYSICAL DEVELOPMENT	• Girls begin the adolescent growth spurt around age 10, boys around age 12. • Girls reach puberty around age 11 or 12, boys around age 13 or 14. • Primary sexual characteristics develop (affecting the reproductive organs), as do secondary sexual characteristics (pubic and underarm hair in both sexes, breasts in girls, deep voices in boys).	• Physical capabilities peak in the 20's, including strength, senses, coordination, and reaction time. • Growth is mostly complete, although some organs, including the brain, continue to grow. • For many young adults, obesity becomes a threat for the first time, as body fat increases. • Stress can become a significant health threat. • In the mid-30's, disease replaces accidents as the leading cause of death.
COGNITIVE DEVELOPMENT	• Abstract thought prevails. Adolescents use formal logic to consider problems in the abstract. • Relative, not absolute, thinking is typical. • Verbal, mathematical, and spatial skills improve. • Adolescents are able to think hypothetically, divide attention, and monitor thought through meta-cognition. • Egocentrism develops, with a sense that one is always being observed. Self-consciousness and introspection are typical. • A sense of invulnerability can lead adolescents to ignore danger.	• As world experience increases, thought becomes more flexible and subjective, geared to adept problem solving. • Intelligence is applied to long-term goals involving career, family, and society. • Significant life events of young adulthood may shape cognitive development.
SOCIAL/ PERSONALITY DEVELOPMENT	• Self-concept becomes organized and accurate and reflects others' perceptions. Self-esteem grows differentiated. • Defining identity is a key task. Peer relationships provide social comparison and help define acceptable roles. Popularity issues become acute; peer pressure can enforce conformity. • Adolescents' quest for autonomy can bring conflict with parents as family roles are renegotiated. • Sexuality assumes importance in identity formation. Dating begins.	• Forming intimate relationships becomes highly important. Commitment may be partly determined by the attachment style developed in infancy. • Marriage and children bring developmental changes, often stressful. Divorce may result, with new stresses. • Identity is largely defined in terms of work, as young adults consolidate their careers.
THEORIES & THEORISTS		
Jean Piaget	Formal operations stage	
Erik Erikson	Identity-versus-confusion stage	Intimacy-versus-isolation stage
Sigmund Freud	Genital stage	
Lawrence Kohlberg	Postconventional morality level may be reached	

MIDDLE ADULTHOOD (40 to 65 years)	LATE ADULTHOOD (65 years to death)
• Physical changes become evident. Vision declines noticeably, as does hearing, but less obviously. • Height reaches a peak and declines slowly. Osteoporosis speeds this process in women. Weight increases, and strength decreases. • Reaction time slows, but performance of complex tasks is mostly unchanged due to lifelong practice. • Women experience menopause, with unpredictable effects. The male climacteric brings gradual changes in men's reproductive systems.	• Wrinkles and gray or thinning hair are marks of late adulthood. Height declines as backbone disk cartilage thins. Women are especially susceptible to osteoporosis. • The brain shrinks, and the heart pumps less blood through the body. Reactions slow, and the senses become less acute. Cataracts and glaucoma may affect the eyes, and hearing loss is common. • Chronic diseases, especially heart disease, grow more common. Mental disorders, such as depression and Alzheimer's disease, may occur.
• Some loss of cognitive functioning may begin in middle adulthood, but overall cognitive competence holds steady because adults use life experience and effective strategies to compensate. • Slight declines occur in the efficiency of retrieval from long-term memory.	• Cognitive declines are minimal until the 80's. Cognitive abilities can be maintained with training and practice, and learning remains possible throughout the life span. • Short-term memory and memory of specific life episodes may decline, but other types of memory are largely unaffected.
• People in middle adulthood take stock, appraising accomplishments against a "social clock" and developing a consciousness of mortality. • Middle adulthood, despite the supposed "midlife crisis," usually is tranquil and satisfying. Individuals' personality traits are generally stable over time. • While marital satisfaction is usually high, family relationships can present challenges. • The view of one's career shifts from outward ambition to inner satisfaction or, in some cases, dissatisfaction. Career changes are increasingly common.	• Basic personality traits remain stable, but changes are possible. "Life review," a feature of this period, can bring either fulfillment or dissatisfaction. • Retirement is a major event of late adulthood, causing adjustments to self-concept and self-esteem. • A healthy lifestyle and continuing activity in areas of interest can bring satisfaction in late adulthood. • Typical circumstances of late adulthood (reduced income, the aging or death of a spouse, a change in living arrangements) cause stress.
Generativity-versus-stagnation stage	Ego-integrity-versus-despair stage

DISCOVERING THE LIFE SPAN

THIRD EDITION

ROBERT S. FELDMAN
University of Massachusetts, Amherst

PEARSON

Boston Columbus Indianapolis New York San Francisco Upper Saddle River
Amsterdam Cape Town Dubai London Madrid Milan Munich Paris Montréal Toronto
Delhi Mexico City São Paulo Sydney Hong Kong Seoul Singapore Taipei Tokyo

Acquisitions Editor: Amber Chow
Editorial Assistant: Alex Stavrakas
VP, Director of Marketing: Brandy Dawson
Senior Marketing Manager: Jeremy Intal
Marketing Assistant: Frank Alarcon
Director of Production: Lisa Iarkowski
Senior Managing Editor: Linda Behrens
Project Manager: Maria Piper
Program Manager: Diane Szulecki
Operations Supervisor: Mary Fischer
Operations Specialist: Diane Peirano
Creative Design Director: Blair Brown
Interior/Cover Design: Kathryn Foot
Digital Media Editor: Lisa Dotson
Digital Media Project Manager: Caitlin Smith
Full-Service Project Management: PreMediaGlobal
Printer/Binder: Courier Kendallville
Cover Printer: Lehigh-Phoenix Color/Hagerstown
Cover Image: © Robert Adrian Hillman / Alamy; © Oleksii Telnov / Alamy; © Oleksii Telnov / Alamy
Text Font: Minion 10/12

To Alex and Miles

Credits and acknowledgments borrowed from other sources and reproduced, with permission, in this textbook appear on the appropriate page within text or on page C-1.

Copyright © 2015, 2012, 2009 Pearson Education, Inc. All rights reserved. Manufactured in the United States of America. This publication is protected by Copyright, and permission should be obtained from the publisher prior to any prohibited reproduction, storage in a retrieval system, or transmission in any form or by any means, electronic, mechanical, photocopying, recording, or likewise. To obtain permission(s) to use material from this work, please submit a written request to Pearson Education, Inc., Permissions Department, One Lake Street, Upper Saddle River, New Jersey 07458, or you may fax your request to 201-236-3290.

Many of the designations by manufacturers and sellers to distinguish their products are claimed as trademarks. Where those designations appear in this book, and the publisher was aware of a trademark claim, the designations have been printed in initial caps or all caps.

Library of Congress Cataloging-in-Publication Data
Feldman, Robert S. (Robert Stephen)
Discovering the life span / Robert S. Feldman, University of Massachusetts Amherst Pearson. — THIRD EDITION.
pages cm
Includes bibliographical references and index.
ISBN-13: 978-0-205-99231-7
ISBN-10: 0-205-99231-5
1. Developmental psychology—Textbooks. 2. Life cycle, Human—Textbooks. 3. Human growth—Textbooks. I. Title.
BF713.F46 2013
155—dc23
2013037104

10 9 8 7 6 5 4 3 2 1

Student Version
ISBN 10: 0-205-99231-5
ISBN 13: 978-0-205-99231-7

Books à la Carte
ISBN 10: 0-205-98318-9
ISBN 13: 978-0-205-98318-6

PEARSON

Brief Contents

CHAPTER 1 **Introduction** 2

Module 1.1 Beginnings 4
Module 1.2 Theoretical Perspectives on Lifespan Development 12
Module 1.3 Research Methods 24

CHAPTER 2 **The Start of Life** 38

Module 2.1 Prenatal Development Difficult Decisions 40
Module 2.2 Prenatal Growth and Change 57
Module 2.3 Birth and the Newborn Infant 68

CHAPTER 3 **Infancy** 90

Module 3.1 Physical Development in Infancy 92
Module 3.2 Cognitive Development in Infancy 112
Module 3.3 Social and Personality Development in Infancy 131

CHAPTER 4 **The Preschool Years** 150

Module 4.1 Physical Development in the Preschool Years 152
Module 4.2 Cognitive Development in the Preschool Years 159
Module 4.3 Social and Personality Development in the Preschool Years 174

CHAPTER 5 **Middle Childhood** 196

Module 5.1 Physical Development in Middle Childhood 198
Module 5.2 Cognitive Development in Middle Childhood 208
Module 5.3 Social and Personality Development in Middle Childhood 229

CHAPTER 6 **Adolescence** 252

Module 6.1 Physical Development in Adolescence 254
Module 6.2 Cognitive Development in Adolescence 268
Module 6.3 Social and Personality Development in Adolescence 278

CHAPTER 7 **Early Adulthood** 304

Module 7.1 Physical Development in Early Adulthood 306
Module 7.2 Cognitive Development in Early Adulthood 317
Module 7.3 Social and Personality Development in Early Adulthood 330

CHAPTER 8 **Middle Adulthood** 354

Module 8.1 Physical Development in Middle Adulthood 356
Module 8.2 Cognitive Development in Middle Adulthood 369
Module 8.3 Social and Personality Development in Middle Adulthood 376

CHAPTER 9 **Late Adulthood** 398

Module 9.1 Physical Development in Late Adulthood 400
Module 9.2 Cognitive Development in Late Adulthood 416
Module 9.3 Social and Personality Development in Late Adulthood 421

CHAPTER 10 **Death and Dying** 444

Module 10.1 Dying and Death Across the Life Span 446
Module 10.2 Confronting Death Deciding to Say Good-Bye 453
Module 10.3 Grief and Bereavement Facing the Void 460

Contents

Preface xii
Ancillaries xviii
About the Author xxv

CHAPTER 1 **Introduction** 2

- Module 1.1 Beginnings 4
  - An Orientation to Lifespan Development 5
    - **Cultural Dimensions: How Culture, Ethnicity, and Race Influence Development 7**
  - Key Issues and Questions: Determining the Nature—and Nurture—of Lifespan Development 9
- Module 1.2 Theoretical Perspectives on Lifespan Development 12
  - The Psychodynamic, Behavioral, and Cognitive Perspectives 13
  - The Humanistic, Contextual, and Evolutionary Perspectives 19
- Module 1.3 Research Methods 24
  - Theories, Hypotheses, and Correlational Studies 25
  - Experiments: Determining Cause and Effect 29
    - **From Research to Practice 32**
    - **Becoming an Informed Consumer of Development: Thinking Critically About "Expert" Advice 34**

CHAPTER 2 **The Start of Life** 38

- Module 2.1 Prenatal Development Difficult Decisions 40
  - Earliest Development 40
  - The Interaction of Heredity and Environment 49
    - **From Research to Practice: When Nurture Becomes Nature 51**
    - **Cultural Dimensions: Cultural Differences in Physical Arousal: Might a Culture's Philosophical Outlook Be Determined by Genetics? 55**
- Module 2.2 Prenatal Growth and Change 57
  - The Prenatal Period 58
  - The Prenatal Environment: Threats to Development 63
    - **Becoming an Informed Consumer of Development: Optimizing the Prenatal Environment 67**
- Module 2.3 Birth and the Newborn Infant 68
  - Birth 69
    - **Becoming an Informed Consumer of Development: Dealing With Labor 74**
  - Birth Complications 75
    - **Cultural Dimensions: Overcoming Racial and Cultural Differences in Infant Mortality 80**
  - The Competent Newborn 82

CHAPTER 3 **Infancy** 90

- Module 3.1 Physical Development in Infancy 92
  - Growth and Stability 92
  - Motor Development 100
    - **Cultural Dimensions: Motor Development Across Cultures 104**
  - The Development of the Senses 107
    - **Becoming an Informed Consumer of Development: Exercising Your Infant's Body and Senses 111**
- Module 3.2 Cognitive Development in Infancy 112
  - Piaget's Approach to Cognitive Development 112
  - Information Processing Approaches to Cognitive Development 118
    - **From Research to Practice: Infants Learn From Adults, Not Videos 119**

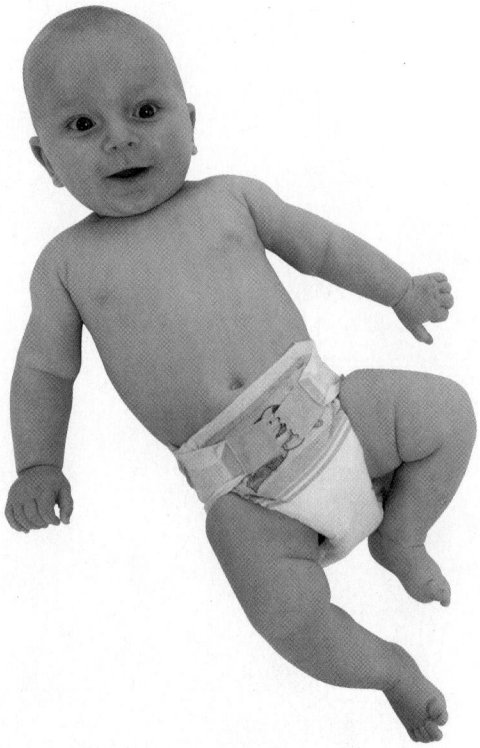

The Roots of Language 124
Cultural Dimensions: Is Infant-Directed Speech Similar Across All Cultures? 130
Becoming an Informed Consumer of Development: What Can You Do to Promote Infants' Cognitive Development? 131

■ Module 3.3 Social and Personality Development in Infancy 131
Developing the Roots of Sociability 132
Forming Relationships 137
Cultural Dimensions: Does Attachment Differ Across Cultures? 140
Differences Among Infants 141
Becoming an Informed Consumer of Development: Choosing the Right Infant Care Provider 147

CHAPTER 4 **The Preschool Years** 150

■ Module 4.1 Physical Development in the Preschool Years 152
The Growing Body 152
The Growing Brain 155
Motor Development 156
Becoming an Informed Consumer of Development: Keeping Preschoolers Healthy 158

■ Module 4.2 Cognitive Development in the Preschool Years 159
Piaget's Approach to Cognitive Development 160
Information Processing and Vygotsky's Approach to Cognitive Development 164
The Growth of Language and Learning 169
Cultural Dimensions: Preschools Around the World: Why Does the United States Lag Behind? 173

■ Module 4.3 Social and Personality Development in the Preschool Years 174
Forming a Sense of Self 174
Cultural Dimensions: Developing Racial and Ethnic Awareness 175
Friends and Family: Preschoolers' Social Lives 178
Becoming an Informed Consumer of Development: Disciplining Children 185
Moral Development and Aggression 186
From Research to Practice: Do Violent Video Games Make Children Violent? 191
Becoming an Informed Consumer of Development: Increasing Moral Behavior and Reducing Aggression in Preschool-Age Children 192

CHAPTER 5 **Middle Childhood** 196

■ Module 5.1 Physical Development in Middle Childhood 198
The Growing Body 198
Motor Development and Safety 201
Children With Special Needs 205
Becoming an Informed Consumer of Development: Keeping Children Fit 207

■ Module 5.2 Cognitive Development in Middle Childhood 208
Intellectual and Language Development 209
Schooling: The Three Rs (and More) of Middle Childhood 215
Cultural Dimensions: Multicultural Education 219
Intelligence: Determining Individual Strengths 219

■ Module 5.3 Social and Personality Development in Middle Childhood 229
The Developing Self 230
Cultural Dimensions: Are Children of Immigrant Families Well Adjusted? 233
Relationships: Building Friendship in Middle Childhood 237
Becoming an Informed Consumer of Development: Increasing Children's Social Competence 242

Family Life in Middle Childhood 243
From Research to Practice: Closing the Digital Divide: Some Unintended Consequences 248

CHAPTER 6 **Adolescence** 252

■ Module 6.1 Physical Development in Adolescence 254
Physical Maturation 254
Threats to Adolescents' Well-Being 262
Becoming an Informed Consumer of Development: Hooked on Drugs or Alcohol? 265
Cultural Dimensions: Selling Death: Pushing Smoking to the Less Advantaged 266

■ Module 6.2 Cognitive Development in Adolescence 268
Cognitive Development 269
School Performance 274

■ Module 6.3 Social and Personality Development in Adolescence 278
Identity: Asking "Who Am I?" 279
Becoming an Informed Consumer of Development: Preventing Adolescent Suicide 287
Relationships: Family and Friends 288
Cultural Dimensions: Race Segregation: The Great Divide of Adolescence 293
From Research to Practice: R U Friends 4 Real?: Are Digital Communications Changing Teenagers' Friendships? 295
Dating, Sexual Behavior, and Teenage Pregnancy 297

CHAPTER 7 **Early Adulthood** 304

■ Module 7.1 Physical Development in Early Adulthood 306
Physical Development 306
Cultural Dimensions: How Cultural Beliefs Influence Health and Health Care 309
Physical Limitations and Challenges 310
Stress and Coping: Dealing With Life's Challenges 312
Becoming an Informed Consumer of Development: Coping With Stress 316

■ Module 7.2 Cognitive Development in Early Adulthood 317
Cognitive Development 318
Intelligence: What Matters in Early Adulthood? 321
College: Pursuing Higher Education 323
Becoming an Informed Consumer of Development: When Do College Students Need Professional Help With Their Problems? 327

■ Module 7.3 Social and Personality Development in Early Adulthood 330
Forging Relationships: Intimacy, Liking, and Loving During Early Adulthood 331
From Research to Practice: Emerging Adulthood: A New Stage of Life? 332
Cultural Dimensions: Gay and Lesbian Relationships: Men With Men and Women With Women 338
The Course of Relationships 339
Work: Choosing and Embarking on a Career 346
Becoming an Informed Consumer of Development: Choosing a Career 350

CHAPTER 8 **Middle Adulthood** 354

■ Module 8.1 Physical Development in Middle Adulthood 356
Physical Development 356
Sexuality in Middle Adulthood 359
Health 363
Cultural Dimensions: Individual Variation in Health: Ethnic and Gender Differences 366

■ Module 8.2 Cognitive Development in Middle Adulthood 369
Cognitive Development 369

From Research to Practice: What Is Multitasking Doing to Our Brains? 373
Memory 374
Becoming an Informed Consumer of Development: Effective Strategies for Remembering 375
■ Module 8.3 Social and Personality Development in Middle Adulthood 376
Personality Development 376
Cultural Dimensions: Middle Age: In Some Cultures It Doesn't Exist 380
Relationships: Family in Middle Age 382
Becoming an Informed Consumer of Development: Dealing With Spousal Abuse 390
Work and Leisure 392
Cultural Dimensions: Immigrants on the Job: Making It in America 395

CHAPTER 9 **Late Adulthood** 398

■ Module 9.1 Physical Development in Late Adulthood 400
Physical Development in Late Adulthood 401
Health and Wellness in Late Adulthood 407
From Research to Practice: Alzheimer's Disease: A Step Toward Prevention? 409
Becoming an Informed Consumer of Development: Caring for People With Alzheimer's Disease 410
Cultural Dimensions: Gender, Race, and Ethnic Differences in Average Life Expectancy: Separate Lives, Separate Deaths 415
■ Module 9.2 Cognitive Development in Late Adulthood 416
Intelligence 417
Memory 419
■ Module 9.3 Social and Personality Development in Late Adulthood 421
Personality Development and Successful Aging 422
Cultural Dimensions: How Culture Shapes the Way We Treat People in Late Adulthood 426
The Daily Life of Late Adulthood 430
Becoming an Informed Consumer of Development: Planning for—and Living—a Good Retirement 434
Relationships: Old and New 435

CHAPTER 10 **Death and Dying** 444

■ Module 10.1 Dying and Death Across the Life Span 446
Defining Death: Determining the Point at Which Life Ends 446
Death Across the Life Span: Causes and Reactions 447
Cultural Dimensions: Differing Conceptions of Death 451
Death Education: Preparing for the Inevitable? 451
■ Module 10.2 Confronting Death Deciding to Say Good-Bye 453
Understanding the Process of Dying: Taking Steps Toward Death 453
Choosing the Nature of Death: Is DNR the Way to Go? 456
Caring for the Terminally Ill: The Place of Death 459
■ Module 10.3 Grief and Bereavement Facing the Void 460
Mourning and Funerals: Final Rites 461
Bereavement and Grief: Adjusting to the Death of a Loved One 462
From Research to Practice: How Helpful Is Grief Counseling? 464
Becoming an Informed Consumer of Development: Helping a Child Cope With Grief 465

References R–1
Glossary G–1
Credits C–1
Name Index NI–1
Subject Index SI–1

Preface

TO THE STUDENT

Welcome to the field of lifespan development! It's a discipline that's about you, about your family and those who came before you, and about those who may follow in your footsteps. It's about your genetic heritage, and it's about the world in which you were raised.

Lifespan development is a field that will speak to you in a very personal way. It covers the range of human existence from its beginnings at conception to its inevitable ending at death. It is a discipline that deals with ideas and concepts and theories, but one that above all has at its heart people—our fathers and mothers, our friends and acquaintances, and our very selves.

But before we jump into the world of lifespan development, let's spend a little time getting to know this book and the way it presents the material. Knowing how the book is constructed will pay off in big ways.

Getting to Know the Book

You've probably already read a fair number of textbooks over the course of your college career. This one is different.

Why? Because it's written from your perspective as a student. Every word, sentence, paragraph, and feature in this book is included because it's meant to explain the field of lifespan development in a way that excites you, engages you with the content, and facilitates the study of the material. And by doing that, it maximizes your chances for not only learning the material and getting a good grade in your class, but also applying the material in a way that will improve your life.

The very organization of the book is based on what psychologists know about how students study most effectively. The text is divided into short modules, nestled within chapters, with each module having several clearly demarcated subsections. By focusing your study in short sections, you're much more likely to master the material.

Similarly, the material is organized into *learning objectives*, abbreviated as *LO*. At the start of every major section, you'll find them in the form of questions. It makes sense to pay particular attention to the learning objectives, because they indicate the material that instructors most want you to learn and that they use to develop test questions.

The book also has a way of indicating which terms are most critical to your understanding of lifespan development. Key terms and concepts are printed in **boldface type**, and are defined in the margins. Less-critical terms and concepts are printed in *italics* and defined within the paragraph where they first appear, but not in the margin.

To further help you study, modules end with a "Review, Check, and Apply" section. The "Review" section includes a summary of the material in the module, organized by learning objective. There are also several "Check Yourself" questions, which require that you recall and understand the material in order to answer correctly. Finally, there's a question that requires you to apply the material in the chapter to some real-world issue. By answering the "Applying Lifespan Development" question, you're demonstrating a higher-order understanding related to critical thinking.

You'll also find several recurring features in every chapter. There are opening vignettes designed to illustrate how lifespan development is relevant to everyday life. There are boxes, called "From Research to Practice," which include recent research that is applied to current social issues, and "Cultural Dimensions" sections that highlight multicultural issues related to lifespan development.

Ever wish you could apply the theoretical material you're reading about in a textbook to your own life? The section called, "Becoming an Informed Consumer of Development," offers a variety of tips and guidelines, based on the chapter's theme, ranging from child-rearing tips to choosing a career and planning your retirement. By applying these to your life, you'll learn the diversity of what the field of lifespan development has to offer.

Finally, there are several features illustrating how the material is relevant from the perspectives of people in different roles and professions, including parents, educators, health care providers, and social workers. "From the Perspective of..." asks you questions designed to help you think critically about how lifespan development applies to someone working in a specific field, and "Putting It All Together"—a summary at the end of each chapter—will help you integrate the material in the modules and learn how it applies across a variety of dimensions.

And That's Not All...

In addition to the features of the book described above, there are a variety of superb online materials that will help you learn and master the material in the text. (Indeed, the entire book can be found online in an e-book format.) These materials include MyPsychLab and MyVirtualLife. MyPsychLab provides quizzes and tests that offer an individualized study plan, as well as videos and interactivities that allow a hands-on introduction to the material. MyVirtualLife is a unique, interactive online tool that allows you to virtually "raise" a child through adolescence by asking key questions about parenting practices, and then forecast your own life from adolescence through late adulthood. You'll see how the decisions you make—based on the material you're studying—play out in the life of your virtual child as well as your own.

Use these online materials! They are wonderful interactive tools that can help you learn the material in a way that can't occur from reading the textbook alone.

A Last Word...

I wrote this book for you. Not for your instructor, not for my colleagues, and not to see it sitting on my own bookshelf. I wrote this book as an opportunity to extend what I do in my own classes at the University of Massachusetts Amherst, and to reach a wider, and more diverse, set of students. For me, there's nothing more exciting as a college professor than to share my teaching and knowledge with as many students as possible.

I hope this book grabs your interest in lifespan development and shows you how it can apply to your own life and improve it. Let me know if it does, or anything else you'd like to convey to me. I'd love to hear from you, and you can easily reach me at feldman@psych.umass.edu. In the meantime, enjoy your introduction to lifespan development.

TO THE INSTRUCTOR

I've never met an instructor of a lifespan development course who didn't feel that he or she was fortunate to teach the course. The subject matter is inherently fascinating, and there is a wealth of information to convey that is at once intriguing and practical. Students come to the course with anticipation, motivated to learn about a topic that, at base, is about their own lives and the lives of every other human being.

At the same time, the course presents unique challenges. For one thing, the breadth of lifespan development is so vast that it is difficult to cover the entire field within the confines of a traditional college term. In addition, many instructors find traditional lifespan development texts too long. Students are concerned about the length of the texts and have trouble completing the entire book. As a result, instructors are often reluctant to assign the complete text and are forced to drop material, often arbitrarily.

Finally, instructors often wish to incorporate into their classes computer-based electronic media that promote understanding of key concepts and take advantage of students' capabilities using electronic media. Yet traditional lifespan development textbooks do little to integrate the electronic media with the book. Consequently, in most courses, the book and accompanying electronic media stand largely in isolation to one another. This lack of integration diminishes the potential impact of both traditional and electronic media and the advantages that an integration of the two could produce in terms of helping students engage with and learn the subject matter.

Discovering the Life Span, **Third Edition,** directly addresses these challenges. The book, which is based on the highly popular ***Development Across the Life Span,*** is some 25 percent shorter than traditional lifespan books. At the same time, it maintains the student friendliness that has been the hallmark of the original. It is rich in examples and illustrates the applications that can be derived from the research and theory of lifespan developmentalists.

The book uses a modular approach to optimize student learning. Each chapter is divided into two or three modules, and in turn each module is divided into several smaller sections. Consequently, rather than facing long, potentially daunting chapters, students encounter material that is divided into smaller, more manageable chunks. Of course, presenting material in small chunks represents a structure that psychological research long ago found to be optimum for promoting learning.

The modular approach has another advantage: It allows instructors to customize instruction by assigning only those modules that fit their course. Each of the book's chapters focuses on a particular period of the life span, and within each chapter separate modules address the three main conceptual approaches to the period: physical development, cognitive development, and social and personality development. Because of the flexibility of this structure, instructors who wish to highlight a particular theoretical or topical approach to lifespan development can do so easily.

Finally, ***Discovering the Life Span,* third edition,** provides complete integration between the book and a huge array of electronic media in MyVirtualLife and MyPsychLab, comprising online electronic exercises, videos, sample tests, and literally hundreds of activities that extend the text and make concepts come alive. The online material is referenced throughout the book in an engaging way, enticing students to go online to make use of the electronic materials that will help them understand the material in the book more deeply.

AN INTRODUCTION TO *DISCOVERING THE LIFE SPAN,* THIRD EDITION

Discovering the Life Span, third edition—like its predecessor—provides a broad overview of the field of human development. It covers the entire range of the human life, from the moment of conception through death. The text furnishes a broad, comprehensive introduction to the field, covering basic theories and research findings, as well as highlighting current applications outside the laboratory. It covers the life span chronologically, encompassing the prenatal period, infancy and toddlerhood, the preschool years, middle childhood, adolescence, early and middle adulthood, and late adulthood. Within these periods, it focuses on physical, cognitive, and social and personality development.

In a unique departure from traditional lifespan development texts, each chapter integrates the physical, cognitive, and social and personality domains within each chronological period. Chapters begin with a compelling story about an individual representing the age period covered by the chapter, and the chapter ends by refocusing on that individual and integrating the three domains. At the same time, chapters drive students to MyPsychLab through marginal queries and reminders about the rich media content available to them.

The book also blends and integrates theory, research, and applications, focusing on the breadth of human development. Furthermore, rather than attempting to provide a detailed historical record of the field, it focuses on the here-and-now, drawing on the past where appropriate, but with a view toward delineating the field as it now stands and the directions toward which it is evolving. Similarly, while providing descriptions of classic studies, the emphasis is more on current research findings and trends.

The book is designed to be user-friendly. Written in a direct, conversational voice, it replicates as much as possible a dialogue between author and student. The text is meant to be understood and mastered on its own by students of every level of interest and motivation. To that end, it includes a variety of pedagogical features that promote mastery of the material and encourage critical thinking. These features include:

- **CHAPTER-OPENING PROLOGUES.** Each of the chapters starts with an attention-grabbing account of an individual who is at the developmental stage covered by the chapter. The material in the prologue sets the stage for the chapter, and the material is addressed in the end of the chapter when the physical, cognitive, and social and personality aspects are integrated.
- **LEARNING OBJECTIVES.** Every module begins with a set of learning objectives, clearly specifying what students are expected to master after reading and studying the material. The learning objectives are couched in the form of engaging questions meant to intrigue students and motivate learning.

- **MODULE-OPENING VIGNETTE.** Modules (which are nestled within chapters) begin with short vignettes, describing an individual or situation that is relevant to the basic developmental issues being addressed in the module.
- **FROM RESEARCH TO PRACTICE.** Each chapter includes a box that describes current developmental research or research issues, applied to everyday problems.
- **CULTURAL DIMENSIONS.** Every chapter includes several "Cultural Dimensions" sections incorporated into the text. These sections highlight issues relevant to today's multicultural society. Examples of these sections include discussions about preschools around the world, gay and lesbian relationships, the marketing of cigarettes to the less advantaged, and race, gender, and ethnic differences in life expectancy.
- **BECOMING AN INFORMED CONSUMER OF DEVELOPMENT.** Every chapter includes information on specific uses that can be derived from research conducted by developmental investigators. For instance, the text provides concrete information on how to encourage children to become more physically active, help troubled adolescents who might be contemplating suicide, and planning and living a good retirement.
- **REVIEW, CHECK, AND APPLY SECTIONS.** Each module is divided into several subsections. At the end of each section are a series of questions on the chapter content, short recaps of the chapters' main points, and an question oriented to apply the chapter content to the real world, keyed to the learning objectives. In addition, students are encouraged to use the MyPsychLab assessment resources associated with the chapter.
- **"FROM THE PERSPECTIVE OF..." QUESTIONS.** Students will encounter frequent questions throughout the text designed to show the applicability of the material to a variety of professions, including education, nursing, social work, and healthcare providers.
- **RUNNING GLOSSARY.** Key terms are defined in the margins of the page on which the term is presented.
- **END-OF-CHAPTER INTEGRATIVE MATERIAL.** At the end of each chapter, the chapter-opening prologue is recapped and addressed from the three domains of physical, cognitive, and social and personality development. In addition, questions address the prologue from the perspective of people such as parents, professional caregivers, nurses, and educators.

WHAT'S NEW IN THE THIRD EDITION?

The third edition of ***Discovering the Life Span*** has been extensively revised in response to the comments of dozens of reviewers. Among the major changes are the following:

Additions of New and Updated Material. The revision incorporates a significant amount of new and updated information. For instance, advances in areas such as behavioral genetics, brain development, evolutionary perspectives, and cross-cultural approaches to development receive expanded and new coverage. In addition, this new edition reflects the recently-published new edition of DSM-5. Overall, hundreds of new citations have been added, with most of those from articles and books published in the last 2 years.

New topics were added to every chapter. The following sample of new and revised topics featured in this edition provides a good indication of the currency of the revision:

Chapter 1

Update on first person conceived in *in vitro*
New examples of police issues by lifespan development research
Debunking relationship between vaccination and autism
Research on same-sex parenting efficacy
Emerging adulthood

Chapter 2

Transgenerational epigenetic inheritance
Placental role in brain development
Down syndrome treatment
In vitro fertilization success rates
In vitro fertilization live birth rates
Psychological consequences of miscarriage
Statistics on international abortion incidence
Incidence of hunger worldwide
Miscarriage and postpartum depression
Controversy regarding routine screening
Statistics on infant mortality
Water birthing

Costs of caring for premature infants
Increase in cesarean deliveries
Higher risk of mental illness in preterm infants

Chapter 3

Reduced rates of infection in breastfed infants
Shaken baby syndrome incidence
Brain scan showing shaken baby syndrome damage
Line between Cesarean delivery and infant obesity
New statistics on incidence of SIDS
Efficacy of educational media for children
Parent responsiveness to infants' babbling
Infant understanding of movement trajectories
Infant understanding of gravity
Evidence of infants' theory of mind at 18 months
Research showing 10 and 13-month olds mentally represent social dominance
Infant preferences for helpful versus antisocial behavior

Chapter 4

Lack of link between vaccination and autism
Importance of serving food with low sodium and fat content
Preschool benefits 25 years after participation
Additional characteristics of high quality child care
Effect of violent video games
Incidence of autism
Spanking as a violation of human rights
Genetic roots of generosity and selfishness

Chapter 5

Autistic spectrum disorders
Asthma
Cost of psychological disorders in children
ADHD incidence and treatment
Changes in brain due to reading
Change in term "mental retardation" to "intellectual disability"
Decreasing digital divide between poor and affluent children
Unmonitored digital use in children raised in poverty
Immigrant children's physical health
Sibling experiences in different cultural contexts
Anti-bullying programs

Chapter 6

Brain damage due to binge drinking in teenagers
Cyberbullying
Risky behavior caused by overestimation of rewards
Media use supplants other forms of social interaction
New figure on teens and cell phone use
Waivers for "No Child Left Behind" law
Use of Adderall to increase academic performance
New AIDS statistics
Friendship and social networks
Sexting
Teenage pregnancy rates at historic lows
Declines in rates of adolescent sexual intercourse
Increase in use of condoms
Religion as viewing the world in terms of intentional design
Gender-nonconforming gays and lesbian adjustment
More positive societal attitudes towards homosexuality: majority support of gay and lesbian marriage
Increase in bicultural identity

Chapter 7

College completion for blacks
Future orientation personality variable
Sex discrimination in math intensive fields
Average weight cross-culturally
Emerging adulthood
Total costs of raising children
New figure on ideal family size
Fertility rate in the United States, Afghanistan, and Zambia
Increase in cohabitation
New data on husband/wife division of labor
Majority of births occur outside of marriage for women under 30

Chapter 8

Multitasking and thinking quality
Driving and texting
Sexual activity in middle age
Differences in brain activity in older adults
Decline in percentage of post-menopausal women taking hormone therapy
Coping mechanisms in successful marriages
Disengagement from work during leisure time
Boomerang generation statistics/figures
Helicopter parenting
Divorce rate increase for people 50 and older (statistics and graph)

Chapter 9

Discovery of gene mutation that prevents Alzheimer's disease
Updated statistics on life expectancy
Drug therapy with mTOR to extend life
Maximum aging possibilities
Increase in sexually transmitted diseases in late adulthood
Dwindling confidence in ability to retire comfortably
Grandchildren as part of grandparents' social networks
Health improvements lead to greater involved of great-grandparents in the lives of their great-grandchildren
Elder abuse prevalence
Changes in theory of mind in late adulthood
Light/dark adaptation changes
Selective optimization with compensation term changed
Health screenings table condensed

Chapter 10

Effectiveness of grief counseling
Efficacy of encouraging people o express negative emotions following grief
Criticisms of Kubler-Ross

A FINAL NOTE

I am very excited about this new edition of ***Discovering the Life Span***. I believe its length, structure, and media and text integration will help students learn the material in a highly effective way. Just as important, I hope it will nurture an interest in the field that will last a lifetime.

Ancillaries

Discovering the Life Span is accompanied by a superb set of teaching and learning materials.

FOR THE INSTRUCTOR:

- ***Instructor's Resource Manual*** **(ISBN: 0205994059).** Designed to make your lectures more effective and save you preparation time, this extensive resource gathers together the most effective activities and strategies for teaching your course. The *Instructor's Resource Manual* includes learning objectives, key terms and concepts, self-contained lecture suggestions, and class activities for each chapter with handouts, supplemental reading suggestions, and an annotated list of additional multimedia resources.

  The *Instructor's Resource Manual* is available for download via the Pearson Instructor's Resource Center (www.pearsonhighered.com) or in MyPsychLab (www.mypsychlab.com).
- ***PowerPoint Lecture Slides*** **(ISBN: 0205994040).** The PowerPoints provide an active format for presenting concepts from each chapter and feature prominent figures and tables from the text. The PowerPoint Lecture Slides are available for download via the Pearson Instructor's Resource Center (www.pearsonhighered.com) or in MyPsychLab (www.mypsychlab.com).
- ***Test Item File*** **(ISBN: 0133802191).** For the third edition, each question was checked to ensure that the correct answer was marked and the page reference was accurate. The test bank contains multiple-choice, true/false, and essay questions, each referenced to the relevant page in the book and correlated to chapter learning objectives and APA learning outcomes. An additional feature for the test bank is the identification of each question as factual, conceptual, or applied. This allows professors to customize their tests and to ensure a balance of question types. Each chapter of the test item file begins with the Total Assessment Guide: an easy to reference grid that makes creating tests easier by organizing the test questions by text section, question type, and whether it is factual, conceptual, or applied. The Test Item File is available for download via the Pearson Instructor's Resource Center (www.pearsonhighered.com) or in MyPsychLab (www.mypsychlab.com).
- ***MyTest*** **(ISBN: 0133802183).** This powerful assessment-generation program helps instructors easily create and print quizzes and exams. Questions and tests can be authored online, allowing instructors ultimate flexibility and the ability to efficiently manage assessments anytime, anywhere. For more information, go to www.PearsonMyTest.com or MyPsychLab (www.mypsychlab.com).
- ***My Virtual Life.*** Raise your child. Live your life. MyVirtualLife is two simulations in one. The first simulation allows students to raise a child from birth to age 18 and monitor the effects of their parenting decisions over time. In the second simulation students make first-person decisions and see the impact of those decisions on their simulated future self over time. By incorporating physical, social, emotional, and cognitive development throughout the entire life span, MyVirtualLife helps students think critically as they apply their course work to their own virtual life. You can access MyVirtualLife within MyPsychLab (www.mypsychlab.com) or as a standalone product.
- ***MyPsychLab*** **(ISBN: 0205982492).** Available at www.mypsychlab.com, **MyPsychLab** is an online homework, tutorial, and assessment program that truly engages students in learning. It helps students better prepare for class, quizzes, and exams—resulting in better performance in the course. It provides educators a dynamic set of tools for gauging individual and class performance:
  - ***Customizable*** MyPsychLab is customizable. Instructors choose what students' course looks like. Homework, applications, and more can easily be turned on and off.
  - ***Blackboard Single Sign-On*** MyPsychLab can be used by itself or linked to any course management system. Blackboard single sign-on provides deep linking to all new MyPsychLab resources.

- ***Pearson eText and Chapter Audio*** Like the printed text, students can highlight relevant passages and add notes. The Pearson eText can be accessed through laptops, iPads, and tablets. Download the free Pearson eText app to use on tablets. Students can also listen to their text with the Audio eText.
- ***Assignment Calendar & Gradebook*** A drag and drop assignment calendar makes assigning and completing work easy. The automatically graded assessment provides instant feedback and flows into the gradebook, which can be used in the MyPsychLab or exported.
- ***Personalized Study Plan*** Students' personalized plans promote better critical thinking skills. The study plan organizes students' study needs into sections, such as Remembering, Understanding, Applying, and Analyzing.
- ***MyPsychLab Margin Icons*** Margin icons guide students from their reading material to relevant videos and activities. To package MyPsychLab with the student text, use ISBN 0133814912.
- ***Class Preparation Tool.*** Available for instructors within MyPsychLab, this exciting instructor resource makes lecture preparation easier and less time consuming. MyClassPrep collects the very best class preparation resources—art and figures from our leading texts, videos, lecture activities, classroom activities, demonstrations, and much more—in one convenient online destination. You can search through MyClassPrep's extensive database of tools by content topic or by content type. You can select resources appropriate for your lecture, many of which can be downloaded directly; or you can build your own folder of resources and present from within MyClassPrep.

Video Resources for Instructors

- **The Development Video Series in MyPsychLab.** This video collection contains a rich assortment of updated video clips for each chapter, including new sketchnote-style tutorials as well as cross-cultural footage and applied segments featuring real students sharing their experiences. Many of these video segments are tied to quizzes or writing prompts and can be assigned through MyPsychLab.
- ***Pearson Teaching Films Lifespan Development Video,*** **ISBN: 0205656021.**

FOR THE STUDENT:

Media Supplements for the Student

- **NEW Interactive eText.** For the 3rd edition of *Discovering the Life Span,* Pearson is proud to offer a fully interactive eText version of the book to enliven the learning experience for students. Each chapter contains interactive experiences, rich video content, and assessments that provide students with immediate feedback on their progress. Pearson offers its titles on the devices students love through Pearson's MyLab products, CourseSmart, Amazon, and more. To learn more about pricing options and customization, visit www.pearsonhighered.com.
- ***MyPsychLab.*** With this exciting new tool students are able to self-assess using embedded diagnostic tests and instantly view results along with a customized study plan.

  The customized study plan will focus on the student's strengths and weaknesses, based on the results of the diagnostic testing, and present a list of activities and resources for review and remediation, organized by chapter section. Some study resources intended for use with portable electronic devices are made available exclusively through the MyPsychLab, such as key terms, flashcards, and optimized video clips. Students will be able to quickly and easily analyze their own comprehension level of the course material, and study more efficiently, leading to exceptional exam results! An access code is required and can be purchased at www.pearsonhighered.com or at www.mypsychlab.com.

- ***CourseSmart eTextbook* (ISBN: 0205994253).** CourseSmart offers students an online subscription to *Discovering the Life Span,* third edition at up to 60 percent savings. With the CourseSmart eTextbook, students can search the text, make notes online, print our reading assignments that incorporate lecture notes, and bookmark important passages. Ask your Pearson sales representative for details or visit www.coursesmart.com.

SUPPLEMENTARY TEXTS

Contact your Pearson representative to package any of these supplementary texts with *Discovering the Life Span*, third edition.

- ***Current Directions in Developmental Psychology* (ISBN: 0205597505).** Readings from the American Psychological Society. This exciting reader includes over 20 articles that have been carefully selected for the undergraduate audience, and taken from the very accessible *Current Directions in Psychological Science* journal. These timely, cutting-edge articles allow instructors to bring their students a real-world perspective about today's most current and pressing issues in psychology. The journal is discounted when packaged with this text for college adoptions.
- ***Twenty Studies That Revolutionized Child Psychology* by Wallace E. Dixon Jr. (ISBN: 0130415723).** Presenting the seminal research studies that have shaped modern developmental psychology, this brief text provides an overview of the environment that gave rise to each study, its experimental design, its findings, and its impact on current thinking in the discipline.
- ***Human Development in Multicultural Contexts: A Book of Readings* (ISBN: 0130195235).** Written by Michele A. Paludi, this compilation of readings highlights cultural influences in developmental psychology.
- ***The Psychology Major: Careers and Strategies for Success* (ISBN: 0205684688)**. Written by Eric Landrum (Idaho State University), Stephen Davis (Emporia State University), and Terri Landrum (Idaho State University), this 160-page paperback provides valuable information on career options available to psychology majors, tips for improving academic performance, and a guide to the APA style of research reporting.

Acknowledgments

I am grateful to the following reviewers who provided a wealth of comments, constructive criticism, and encouragement:

Lola Aagaard, Morehead State University
Glen Adams, Harding University
Sharron Adams, Wesleyan College
Carolyn Adams-Price, Mississippi State University
Leslie Adams Lariviere, Assumption
Judi Addelston, Valencia Community College
Bill Anderson, Illinois State University
Carrie Andreoletti, Central Connecticut State University
Harold Andrews, Miami Dade College–Wolfson
Ivan Applebaum, Valencia Community College
Sally Archer, The College of New Jersey
Janet Arndt, Gordon College
Christine Bachman, University of Houston–Downtown
Harriet Bachner, Pittsburg State University
Nannette Bagstad, Mayville State University
Mary Ballard, Appalachian State University
Michelle Bannoura, Hudson Valley Community College
Daniel Barajas, Community Collge of Denver
Ted Barker, Okaloosa-Walton College
Catherine Barnard, Kalamazoo Valley Community College
Gena Barnhill, Lynchburg College
Sue Barrientos, Butler Community College
Sandra Barrueco, The Catholic University of America
Carolyn Barry, Loyola College in Maryland
Chris Barry, University of Southern Mississippi
Robin Bartlett, Northern Kentucky University
Shirley Bass-Wright, St. Philip's College
Kellie Bassell, Palm Beach Community College
Sherry Black, Western Nevada College
Bette Beane, The University of North Carolina at Greensboro
Dan Bellack, Trident Technical College
Amy Bender, University of Milwaukee
Marshelle Bergstrom, University of Wisconsin–Oshkosh
Doreen Berman, Queens College
Debra Berrett, Solano Community College
Irene Bersola-Nguyen, Sacramento State University
Wendy Bianchini, Montana State University
John Bicknell, Temple College
Robert Birkey, Goshen College
Carol Bishop, Solano Community College
Sherry Black, Western Nevada College
Angela Blankenship, Nash Community College
Cheryl Bluestone, Queensborough Community (CUNY)
Tracie Blumentritt, University of Wisconsin–La Crosse
Kathy Bobula, Clark College
Denise Ann Bodman, Arizona State University
Kathleen Bonnelle, Lansing Community College
Janet Boseovski, The University of North Carolina at Greensboro
Teri Bourdeau, University of Tulsa
Sarah Boysen, The Ohio State University
Nicole Bragg, Mt. Hood Community College
Gregory Braswell, Illinois State University
Judith Breen, College of DuPage
Alaina Brenick, University of Maryland
Jennifer Brennom, Kirkwood Community College
Barbara Briscoe, Kapiolani Community College
Caralee Bromme, San Joaquin Delta Community College
Brookover, Betty Cecile, Xavier University of Louisiana
Veda Brown, Prairie View A&M University
Janine Buckner, Seton Hall University
Sharon Burson, Temple College
Cathy Bush, Carson-Newman College
Jean Cahoon, Pitt Community College
Cheryl Camenzuli, Molloy College
Angela Campbell, Harrisburg Area Community College
Debb Campbell, College of the Sequoias
Lillian Campbell, Humber College
Diane Caulfield, Honolulu Community College
Rick Caulfield, University of Hawaii at Manoa
Lisa Caya, University of Wisconsin–La Crosse
Laura Chapin, Colorado State University
Jing Chen, Grand Valley State University
John Childers, East Carolina University
Saundra Ciccarelli, Gulf Coast Community College
Diana Ciesko, Valencia Community College
Cherie Clark, Queens University of Charlotte
Wanda Clark, South Plains College
J. B Clement, Daytona College
Kimberly Cobb, Edgecombe Community College
Margaret Coberly, University of Hawaii–Windward
Lawrence Cohn, University of Texas at El Paso
Barbara Connolly, University of Tennessee Health Sciences Center
Deborah Copeland, Palm Beach Community College
Kristi Cordell-McNulty, Angelo State University
Ellen Cotter, Georgia Southwestern State University
Trina Cowan, Northwest Vista College
Jodi Crane, Lindsey Wilson College
Pat Crane, Santa Ana College
Amanda Creel, Sowela Technical Community College
Jeanne Cremeans, Hillsborough Community College
Don Crews, Southwest Georgia Technical College
Geraldine Curley, Bunker Hill Community College
Gregory Cutler, Bay de Noc Community College
Chris Daddis, The Ohio State University at Marion
Anne Dailey, Community College of Allegheny County
Billy Daley, Fort Hays State University
Dianne Daniels, UNC Charlotte
Karen Davis, Southwest Georgia Technical College
Dora Davison, Southern State Community College
Paul Dawson, Weber State University
Barbara DeFilippo, Lansing Community College
Tara Dekkers, Northwestern College
J DeSimone, William Paterson University
Michael Devoley, Montgomery College
David Devonis, Graceland University
Ginger Dickson, The University of Texas at El Paso
Trina Diehl, Northwest Vista College
Darryl Dietrich, The College of St. Scholastica
Jennie Dilworth, Georgia Southern University
Stephanie Ding, Del Mar College
Betsy Diver, Lake Superior College
Delores Doench, Southwestern Community College
Margaret Dombrowski, Harrisburg Area Community College–Lancaster
Heather Dore, Florida Community College at Jacksonville
Jackie Driskill, Texas Tech University
Victor Duarte, North Idaho College
Susan Dubitsky, Florida International University
Shelley Dubkin-Lee, Oregon State University
Beryl Dunsmoir, Concordia University at Austin
Paula Dupuy, The University of Toledo
Kathleen Dwinnells, Kent State University–Trumbull Campus
Darlene Earley-Hereford Southern Union State Community College
Y. van Ecke, College of Marin
David Edgerly, Quincy University
Jean Egan, Asnuntuck Community College
Trish Ellerson, Miami University
Kelley Eltzroth, Mid-Michigan Community College
Laurel End, Mount Mary College
Dale Epstein, University of Maryland
Diana E., Espinoza Laredo Community College
Melissa Essman, California State University, Fullerton
Deborah Evans, Stipp Ivy Tech Community College
Jenni Fauchier, Metropolitan Community College
Nancy Feehan, University of San Francisco
Jef Feldman, Los Angeles Pierce College
Pamela Fergus, MCTC and IHCC
Ric Ferraro, University of North Dakota
Donna Fletcher, Florida State University
Christine Floether, Centenary College
June Foley, Clinton Community College
Jeanene Ford, Holmes Community College
Lee Fournet, Central Arizona College
Jody Fournier, Capital University
Tony Fowler, Florence-Darlington Technical College
James Francis, San Jacinto College
Inoke Funaki, Brigham Young University Hawaii
Sonia Gaiane, Grossmont College
Donna Gainer, Mississippi State University
Teresa Galyean, Wytheville Community College
Mary Garcia-Lemus, California Polytechnic State University, San Luis Obispo
Laura Garofoli, Fitchburg State College
Andy Gauler Florida, Community College at Jacksonville
C. Ray Gentry, Lenior-Rhyne College
Jarilyn Gess, Minnesota State University Moorhead

Sharon Ghazarian, The University of North
Pam Gingold, Merced College
Shery Ginn, Rowan Cabarrus Community College
Drusilla Glascoe, Salt Lake Community College
Donna Goetz, Elmhurst College
Rob Goralewicz, Dabney Lancaster Community College
Christina Gotowka, Tunxis Community College
Thomas Grady, Neosho County Community College
Donna Gray, Irvine Valley College
Troianne Grayson, Florida Community College at Jacksonville–South Campus
Jo Greathouse, Brazosport College
Jerry Green, Tarrant County College
Janelle Grellner, University of Central Oklahoma
Kristi Guest, University of Alabama at Birmingham
James Guinee, University of Central Arkansas
Jill Haasch, Glenville State College
Sharon Habermann, Providence Theological Seminary
Helen Hagens, Central Michigan University
Lisa Hager, Spring Hill College
Carolyn Halliburton, Dallas Baptist University
Sam Hardy, Brigham Young University
Mark Harmon, Reedley College–North Centers
Dyan W., Harper University of Missouri–St. Louis
Melody Harrington, St. Gregory's University
Nancy Hartshorne, Central Michigan University
Loretta Hauxwell, McCook Community College
Christina Hawkey, Arizona Western College
Lora Haynes, University of Louisville
Sam Heastie, Fayetteville State University
Patti Heer, Clarke College
Steve Hendrix, James Sprunt Community College
Sarah Herald, Arizona State University
Mary Hetland, Minnesota State Community
Carolyn Hildebrandt, University of Northern Iowa
Pamela Hill, San Antonio College
Sharon Hogan, Cuyahoga Community College
Frank Holiwski, South Georgia College
Debra Hollister, Valencia Community College
Sachi Horback, Baltimore City Community College
Scott Horton, Mitchell College
Julie Howard, Vanguard University
Herman Huber, College of Saint Elizabeth
Martha Hubertz, Florida Atlantic University
Heidi Humm, Mercy College
Bob Humphries, Walsh University
David Hurford, Pittsburg State University
MaryLu Hutchins, West Liberty State College
Cynthia Ingle, Bluegrass Community and Technical College
Nicolle Ionascu, Queen's University
Jessica Jablonski, Richard Stockton College of New Jersey
Sabra Jacobs, Big Sandy Community and Technical College
Alisha Janowsky, University of Central Florida
Debbra Jennings, Richland College
Sybillyn Jennings, Russell Sage College
Daphne Johnson, Sam Houston State University
Margaret Johnson, Bridgewater State College
Stephanie Johnson, Southeast Community College
Deborah Jones, Florida Community College
Katherine Jones, Mississippi College
James Jordan, Lorain County Community College
Linda G.Jordan, Skagit Valley College
Terri Joseph, Kent State University East Liverpool
Diana Joy, Community College of Denver
Carl Jylland-Halverson, University of Saint Francis
Louise Kahn, University of New Mexico
Susan Kamphaus, Tulsa Community College West Campus
Richard Kandus, Mt. San Jacinto College
Paul Kaplan, SUNY at Stony Brook
Michele Karpathian, Waynesburg College
Mark Kavanaugh, Kennebec Valley Community College
Henry Keith, Delaware Technical & Community College
Debbie Keller, College of the Ozarks
Jeffrey Kellogg, Marian College
Colleen Kennedy, Roosevelt University
Rosalie Kern, Michigan Tech University
Lisa Kiang, Wake Forest
Tim Killian, University of Arkansas
William Kimberlin, Lorain County Community College
Michalene King, Kent State Tuscarawas
Jennifer King-Cooper, Sinclair Community College
Kenyon Knapp, Troy University, Montgomery Campus
Don Knox, Midwestern State University
Larry Kollman, North Iowa Area Community College
Leslee Koritzke, Los Angeles Trade Tech College
Nicole Korzetz, Lee College
Holly Krogh, Mississippi University for Women
August Lageman, Virginia Intermont College
Carol Laman, Houston Community College
Warren Lambert, Somerset Community College
Jonathan Lang, Borough of Manhattan C. College
Rich Lanthier, George Washington University
Leslie Lariviere, Adams Assumption
Larkan-Skinner, Kara, Amarillo College
Yvonne Larrier, Indiana University South Bend
Richard Lazere, Portland Community College
Jennifer Leaver, Eastern Arizona College
Maria LeBaron, Randolph Community College
Gary Leka, University of Texas–Pan American
Diane Lemay, University of Maine at Augusta
Elizabeth Lemerise, Western Kentucky University
Cynthia Lepley, Thomas College
Norma Lestikow, Highland Community College
Blue Levin, Ridge Community College
Lawrence Lewis, Loyola University New Orleans
Mary B Lewis. Eberly, Oakland University
Linda Liptok, McIntosh Kent State University–Tuscarawas
Nancey Lobb, Alvin Community College
R. Martin Lobdell, Pierce College
Janet Lohan, Washington State University
Don Lucas Northwest Vista College
Joe Lund, Taylor University
Salvador Macias, University of South Carolina Sumter
Grace Malonai, Saint Mary's College of California
Donna Mantooth, Georgia Highlands College
Deborah Marche, Van Glendale Community College
Rebecca Marcon, University of North Florida
T. Darin Matthews, The Citadel
Kelly McCabe, University of Mary Hardin Baylor
William McCracken, Delaware Technical & Community College
Jim McDonald, California State University, Fresno
Cathy Mcelderry, University of Alabama at Birmingham
Jim McElhone, The University of Texas of the Permian Basin
Cathy McEvoy, University of South Florida
Annie McManus, Parkland College at Jacksonville
Beth McNulty, Lake Sumter Community College
Marcia McQuitty, Southwestern Theological Seminary
Dixie Cranmer McReynolds, St. Vincent's College
Joan Means, Solano Community College
Omar Mendez, William Paterson University of New Jersey
K.Mentink, Chippewa Valley Technical College
Peter Metzner, Vance Granville Community College
LeeAnn Miner, Mount Vernon Nazarene University
Ellen Mink, Elizabethtown Community and Technical College
Michael Miranda, Kingsborough Community College/CUNY
Steve Mitchell, Somerset Community College
Yvonne Montgomery, Langston University
Beverly Moore, Sullivan County Community College
Brad Morris, Grand Valley State University
Dolly Morris, University Alaska Fairbanks, TVC Campus
AudreyAnn C Moses, Hampton University
Jean Mosley, Oral Roberts University
Carol Mulling, Des Moines Area Community College
Jeannette Murphey, Meridian Community College
Sylvia Murray, University of South Carolina Upstate
Ron Naramore, Angelina College
Lisa Newell, Indiana, University of Pennsylvania
Glenda Nichols, Tarrant County College–South
David Nitzschke, Western Iowa Tech Community College
Harriett Nordstrom, University of Michigan–Flint
Meghan Novy, Palomar College
Elleen O'Brien, UMBC
Valerie O'Krent, California State University–Fullerton
Shirley Ogletree, Texas State–San Marcos
Jennifer Oliver, Rockhurst University
Leanne Olson, Wisconsin Lutheran College
Rose Olver, Amherst College
Sharon Ota, Honolulu Community College
John Otey, Southern Arkansas University
Karl Oyster, Tidewater Community College
Gwynne Pacheco, Hawaii Community College
Roger Page, Ohio State University–Lima

Joseph Panza, Southern Connecticut State University
Jennifer Parker, University of South Carolina Upstate
Brian Parry, San Juan College
Joan Paterna, Manchester Community College
Julie Patrick, West Virginia University
Sue Pazynski, Glen Oaks Community College
Carola Pedreschi, Miami Dade College
Colleen Peltz, Iowa Lakes Community College
John Phelan, Western Oklahoma State College
Peter Phipps, Dutchess Community College
Michelle Pilati, Rio Hondo College
Laura Pirazzi, San Jose State University
Diane Pisacreta, St. Louis Community College
Deanna Pledge, Stephens College
Leslee Pollina, Southeast Missouri State University
Yuly Pomares, Miami Dade College
Jean Poppei, The Sage Colleges/Russell Sage College
Lydia Powell, Vance-Granville Community College
Sherri Restauri, Jacksonville State University
Kate Rhodes, Dona Ana Community College
Shannon Rich Texas Woman's University
Cynthia Riedi, Morrisville State College, Norwich Campus
Laura Rieves, Tidewater Community College
Jane Roda, Penn State–Hazleton Campus
Keith Rosenbaum, Dallas Baptist University
Karl Rosengren, University of Illinois at Urbana-Champaign
Renda Ross, Capital University
Willow Rossmiller, Montana State University–Great Falls College of Technology
Melinda Rouse, Alamance Community College
Marlo Rouse-Arnett, Georgia Southern
Lisa Routh, Pikes Peak Community College
Loretta Rudd, Texas Tech University
Robert Rycek, University of Nebraska at Kearney
Brooke Saathoff, Labette Community College
James Sapp, Kentucky Christian University
Marie Saracino, Stephen F. Austin State University
Al Sarno, Hannibal-LaGrange College
Patricia Sawyer, Middlesex Community College
Linda Schaefer, Minot State University
Troy Schiedenhelm, Rowan Cabarrus Community College
Celeste Schneider, Saint Mary's College
Pamela Schuetze, Buffalo State College
Joe Schuh, Northern Kentucky University
Candace Schulenburg, Cape Cod Community College
Eric Seemann, University of Alabama in Huntsville
Nancy Segal, California State University–Fullerton
Sandy Sego, American International College
Zewelanji Serpell, James Madison University
Nitya Sethuraman, Indiana University
Virginia Shipman, University of New Mexico
Beth Sigmon, Robeson Community College
Denise Simonsen, Fort Lewis College
Julie Singer, University of Nevada, Reno
Peggy Skinner, South Plains College
Tara Smith, Elizabethtown College
Todd Smith, Lake Superior State University
Jerry Snead, Coastal Carolina Community College
James Snowden, Midwestern State University
Le'Ann Solmonson, Stephen F. Austin State University
Brooke Spatta, Lynn University
Tracy Spinrad, School of Social and Family Dynamics
Melinda Spohn, Spokane Falls Community College
Jill Steinberg, University of Wisconsin–Madison
Robby Stewart, Oakland University
Nancy Stinnett, University of Alabama
Mary Hughes Stone, San Francisco State University
Julia Stork, Jefferson State Community College
Amy Strimling, Sacramento City College
Rose Suggett, Southeast Community College
Terre Sullivan, Chippewa Valley Technical College
Cyril Svoboda, University of Maryland University College
Peter Talty, Keuka College
Amber Tatnall, SUNY Delhi
Becky Taylor, Texas Christian University
Marianne Taylor, Pacific Lutheran University
Luis Terrazas, California State University–San Marcos
Thomas Thieman, College of St. Catherine
Linda EagleHeart Thomas, The University of Montana–COT
Mojisola Tiamiyu, University of Toledo
Vicki Tinsley, Brescia University
Ed Titus, Troy University
Ivonne Tjoefat, Rochester Community & Technical College
Adrian Tomer, Shippensburg University
Barbara Townsend, Gannon University
Jeannine Turner, Florida State University
Jeffrey Turner, Mitchell College
Dave Urso, Lord Fairfax Community College
Cecelia Valrie, East Carolina University
Michael Vandehey, Midwestern State University
Marina Vera, Southwestern College
Monica Vines, Central Oregon Community College
Steven Voss, Moberly Area Community College
John Wakefield, University of North Alabama
Rebecca Walker-Sands, Central Oregon Community College
James Wallace, St. Lawrence University
Todd Walter, D'Youville College
Mark Wasicsko, Northern Kentucky University
Debbie Watson, Shawnee State University
Sheree Watson, University of Southern Mississippi
Nancy Wedeen, Los Angeles Valley College
Glenn Weisfeld, Wayne State University
Orville Weiszhaar, Minneapolis Community and Technical College
Lori Werdenschlag, Lyndon State College
Laurie Westcott, New Hampshire Community Technical College
Linda Whitney, Houston Community College Northwest
Robert Wiater, Bergen Community College
Sharon Wiederstein, Blinn College
Jacqueline Williams, ,Moorpark College
June Williams, Southeastern Louisiana University
Kay Williams, Tidewater Community College
Patti Williams, Tidewater Community College
Lois Willoughby, Miami Dade College
Stephen Wills, Mercer University
Cynthia Wilson, University of South Alabama–Baldwin County
Christy Wolfe, University of Louisville
Peter Wooldridge, Durham Technical Community College
Shelly Wooldridge, University of Arkansas Community College at Batesville
Bonnie Wright, Gardner-Webb University
Kent Yamauchi, Pasadena City College
Robin Yaure, Penn State Mont Alto
Ani Yazedjian, Texas State University–San Marcos
Mahbobeh Yektaparast, Central Piedmont Community College
Susan Zandrow, Bridgewater State College
Rowan Zeiss, Blue Ridge Community College
Laura Zettel-Watson, California State University–Fullerton
Elizabeth Zettler, Rellinger Illinois College
Ginny Zhan, Kennesaw State University
Ling-Yi Zhou, University of St. Francis
Renee Zucchero, Xavier University

Many others deserve a great deal of thanks. I am indebted to the numerous people who provided me with a superb education, first at Wesleyan University and later at the University of Wisconsin. Specifically, Karl Scheibe played a pivotal role in my undergraduate education, and the late Vernon Allen acted as mentor and guide through my graduate years. It was in graduate school that I learned about development, being exposed to such experts as Ross Parke, John Balling, Joel Levin, Herb Klausmeier, and many others. My education continued when I became a professor. I am especially grateful to my colleagues at the University of Massachusetts, who make the university such a wonderful place in which to teach and do research.

Several people played important roles in the development of this book. Edward Murphy and Christopher Poirier provided significant research and editorial support. In addition, John Graiff was essential in juggling and coordinating the multiple aspects of writing a book. I am very grateful for his help.

I am also thankful to the superb Pearson team that was instrumental in the inception and development of this book. Jeff Marshall, the original Executive Editor, conceived of the format of this book. Now Amber Chow has taken over, and she has brought creativity and a wealth of good ideas to the project. I'm also extremely grateful to Program Manager Diane Szulecki, who stayed on top of every aspect of the project and brought inventiveness and imagination to the book. I can't thank her enough for her way-beyond-the-call-of duty efforts and patience with me.

Editor-in-Chief Dickson Musslewhite stood behind the project, and I'm very grateful for his support. On the production end of things, Maria Piper, the project manager, and Kathryn Foot, the designer, helped in giving the book its distinctive look. Finally, I'd like to thank (in advance) marketing manager Jeremy Intal, on whose skills I'm counting.

I also wish to acknowledge the members of my family, who play such an essential role in my life. My brother, Michael, my sisters-in-law and brother-in-law, my nieces and nephews, all make up an important part of my life. In addition, I am always indebted to the older generation of my family, who led the way in a manner I can only hope to emulate. I will always be obligated to the late Harry Brochstein, Mary Vorwerk, and Ethel Radler. Most of all, the list is headed by my father, the late Saul Feldman, and my mother, Leah Brochstein.

In the end, it is my immediate family who deserve the greatest thanks. My son, Jon, his wife, Leigh, and my grandsons Alex and Miles; my son, Josh, and his wife, Julie; and my daughter, Sarah, and her husband, Jeff, not only are nice, smart, and good-looking, but my pride and joy. And ultimately my wife, Katherine Vorwerk, provides the love and grounding that makes everything worthwhile. I thank them, with all my love.

Robert S. Feldman
University of Massachusetts Amherst

About the Author

Robert S. Feldman is Professor of Psychology and Dean of the College of Social and Behavioral Sciences at the University of Massachusetts at Amherst. A recipient of the College Distinguished Teacher Award, he teaches psychology classes ranging in size from 15 to nearly 500 students. During the course of more than 2 decades as a college instructor, he has taught both undergraduate and graduate courses at Mount Holyoke College, Wesleyan University, Virginia Commonwealth University, in addition to the University of Massachusetts.

Professor Feldman, who initiated the Minority Mentoring Program at the University of Massachusetts, also has served as a Hewlett Teaching Fellow and Senior Online Teaching Fellow. He initiated distance learning courses in psychology at the University of Massachusetts.

Professor Feldman also is actively involved in promoting the field of psychology. He is President of the Federation of Associations of the Behavioral and Brain Sciences Foundation, and he is on the Board of Directors of the Social Psychology Network.

A Fellow of both the American Psychological Association and the Association for Psychological Science, Professor Feldman received a B.A. with High Honors from Wesleyan University and an M.S. and Ph.D. from the University of Wisconsin-Madison.

Professor Feldman is a winner of a Fulbright Senior Research Scholar and Lecturer award, and he has written more than 200 books, book chapters, and scientific articles. He has edited *Development of Nonverbal Behavior in Children* (Springer-Verlag), *Applications of Nonverbal Behavioral Theory and Research* (Erlbaum), and co-edited *Fundamentals of Nonverbal Behavior* (Cambridge University Press). He is also author of *Child Development, Understanding Psychology,* and *P.O.W.E.R. Learning: Strategies for Success in College and Life.* His books have been translated into a number of languages, including Spanish, French, Portuguese, Dutch, Chinese, and Japanese.

His research interests include honesty and deception in everyday life and the use of nonverbal behavior in impression management, and his research has been supported by grants from the National Institute of Mental Health and the National Institute on Disabilities and Rehabilitation Research.

Professor Feldman loves music, is an enthusiastic, if not-exactly-expert, pianist, and enjoys cooking and traveling. He has three children, and he and his wife, a psychologist, live in western Massachusetts, in a home overlooking the Holyoke mountain range.

1 INTRODUCTION

The Ruiz "Happy Birthday Family Reunion" was a big success. Marco Ruiz's grandfather, Geraldo, who would turn 90 tomorrow, was in his glory at the center of the festivities.

Marco's wife, Louise, had hatched the reunion idea while planning next summer's wedding of their youngest daughter Eva. Eva's husband-to-be, Peter, would be the first African American in the family, and Louise's idea was to introduce him early so his ethnicity would be old news by the wedding day.

Louise's brainstorm was apparently working, given the happy din of the huge throng in attendance. Marco took a quiet census: his father, Damiano, and Louise's mom and dad, plus a gaggle of uncles, aunts, siblings, and cousins from his and Louise's families. One generation down, he counted his children and their families, and virtual busloads of nieces and nephews with their families, down to the youngest child, the daughter of Marco's niece Terri and her husband Tony, 4-year-old Alicia Wei-Li Saucedo, Geraldo's great-great-granddaughter, who had been adopted from China.

Marco watched as Grandpa Geraldo hugged and chatted happily with Alicia. There in one small picture frame was the story of the five generations of Grandpa's family, from 4 to 90.

Marco thought to himself: What is Grandpa making of all this? Is he wondering how he spawned all these different personalities? Is he speculating about their careers, their futures? Is he looking for traces of his stubbornness and short temper, his generosity and open-mindedness? Does he find in this gathering the vast ambitions that he had as a boy? Will any of them be—at last—the athlete that he never was, or will they be writers and thinkers like him and his children?

Marco smiled at Louise's idea of "integrating" Peter into the family. Peter's skin color wasn't even an issue. The main stories were that Marco's nephew Ted was here with his fiancé Tom, and his niece Clarissa had her fiancée Rosa on her arm. Marco's smile grew broader. Let Grandpa wonder where this latest family trend came from.

Lifespan development is a diverse and growing field with a broad focus and wide applicability. It covers the entire life span of the individual from birth to death as it examines the ways in which people develop physically, intellectually, and socially. It asks and attempts to answer questions about the ways in which people change and remain the same over their years of life.

Many of the questions that developmentalists ask are, in essence, the scientist's version of the questions that parents ask about their children and themselves: How the genetic legacy of parents plays out in their children; how children learn; why they make the choices they make; whether personality characteristics are inherited and whether they change or are stable over time; how a stimulating environment affects development; and many others. To pursue these answers, of course, developmentalists use the highly structured, formal scientific method, while parents mostly use the informal strategy of waiting, observing, engaging with, and loving their kids.

In this chapter, we will introduce the field of lifespan development. We first discuss the breadth of the field, both in the range of years it covers and in the topics it addresses, and we look at the major theoretical perspectives that have examined those topics. We also describe the key features of the scientific method, the main approach that scientists take to answering questions of interest.

MODULE 1.1

BEGINNINGS

Nature vs. nurture: Which has the greater influence?

MODULE 1.2

THEORETICAL PERSPECTIVES ON LIFESPAN DEVELOPMENT

Is one right and one wrong?

MODULE 1.3

RESEARCH METHODS

What kind of research could you conduct using Marco's five-generation family?

MyVirtualLife

If you are currently using MyVirtualLife, consider how you will navigate your journey through the lifespan. What decisions will you make?

Access MyVirtualLife for a chance to live your own virtual life.

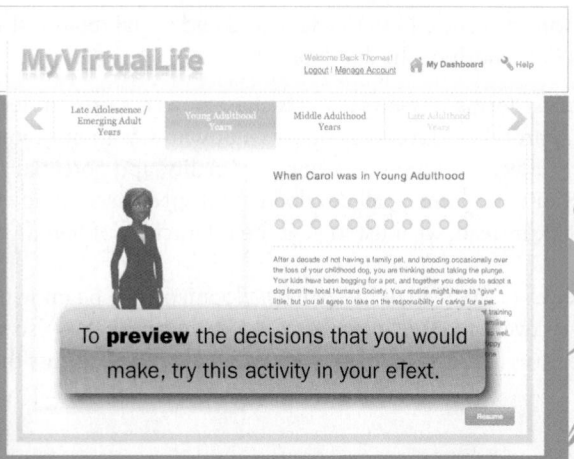

To **preview** the decisions that you would make, try this activity in your eText.

MODULE 1.1

BEGINNINGS

New Conceptions

In July 1978, Louise Brown became the world's first "test tube baby"—the first baby conceived through in vitro fertilization (IVF), a medical procedure in which fertilization of the mother's egg with the father's sperm occurs outside the mother's body.

Louise's parents told her the story of her conception when she was in preschool, explaining exactly what had happened and answering all her questions. Even so, she was ill-prepared for the years of questions from curious schoolmates about her supposed birth in a bottle in a science lab.

She did her best to minimize differences between herself and her schoolmates, but in those early years, she often felt alone. Gradually her sense of isolation diminished as she was joined by literally millions of other children conceived the same way. Today, IVF is essentially a routine procedure practiced all over the world.

And there's a happy ending: At age 28, Louise gave birth to a son, Cameron, conceived—she is pleased to say—the old-fashioned way (Falco, 2012; ICMRT, 2012).

Louise Brown's conception may have been novel, but her development since then has followed a predictable pattern. While the specifics of our development vary, the broad strokes set in motion in that test tube more than three decades ago are remarkably similar for all of us. Shaquille O'Neal, Donald Trump, the Queen of England—all are traversing the territory known as lifespan development.

Louise Brown's conception is just one of the brave new worlds of the day. Issues that affect human development range from cloning to poverty to the prevention of AIDS. Underlying these are even more fundamental issues: How do we develop physically? How does our understanding of the world change throughout our lives? And how do our personalities and social relationships develop as we move through the life span?

These questions and many others are central to lifespan development. The field encompasses a broad span of time and a wide range of areas. Consider the range of interests that different specialists might focus on when considering Louise Brown:

- Lifespan development researchers who investigate behavior at the biological level might ask if Louise's functioning before birth was affected by her conception outside the womb.
- Specialists in lifespan development who study genetics might examine how the genetic endowment from Louise's parents affects her later behavior.
- Lifespan development specialists who investigate thinking processes might examine how Louise's understanding of the circumstances of her conception changed as she grew older.
- Other researchers in lifespan development, who focus on physical growth, might consider whether her growth rate differed from children conceived more traditionally.
- Lifespan development experts who specialize in the social world and social relationships might look at the ways that Louise interacted with others and the kinds of friendships she developed.

Although their interests take many forms, these specialists share one concern: understanding the growth and change that occur during life. Taking many different approaches, developmentalists study how both our biological inheritance from our parents and the environment in which we live jointly affect our future behavior, personality, and potential as human beings.

Whether they focus on heredity or environment, all developmental specialists acknowledge that neither one alone can account for the full range of human development. Instead, we must look at the interaction of heredity and environment, attempting to grasp how both underlie human behavior.

In this module, we orient ourselves to the field of lifespan development. We begin with a discussion of the scope of the discipline, illustrating the wide array of topics it covers and the full range of ages it examines. We also survey the key issues and controversies of the field and consider the broad perspectives that developmentalists take. Finally, we discuss the ways developmentalists use research to ask and answer questions.

AN ORIENTATION TO LIFESPAN DEVELOPMENT

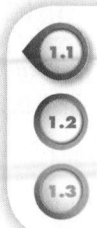

LO1 What is the scope of the field of lifespan development?
LO2 What are cohorts, and how do they influence development?

Have you ever wondered at the way an infant tightly grips your finger with tiny, perfectly formed hands? Or marveled at how a preschooler methodically draws a picture? Or at the way an adolescent can make involved decisions about whom to invite to a party or the ethics of downloading music files? Or the way a middle-aged politician can deliver a long, flawless speech from memory? Or what makes a grandfather at 80 so similar to the father he was at 40?

If you've ever wondered about such things, you are asking the kinds of questions that scientists in the field of lifespan development pose. **Lifespan development** is the field of study that examines patterns of growth, change, and stability in behavior that occur throughout the life span.

In its study of growth, change, and stability, lifespan development takes a *scientific* approach. Like members of other scientific disciplines, researchers in lifespan development test their assumptions by applying scientific methods. They develop theories about development and use methodical, scientific techniques to validate the accuracy of their assumptions systematically.

Lifespan development focuses on *human* development. Although there are developmentalists who study nonhuman species, the vast majority study people. Some seek to understand universal principles of development, while others focus on how cultural, racial, and ethnic differences affect development. Still others aim to understand the traits and characteristics that differentiate one person from another. Regardless of approach, however, all developmentalists view development as a continuing process throughout the life span.

As developmental specialists focus on change during the life span, they also consider stability. They ask in which areas, and in what periods, people show change and growth, and when and how their behavior reveals consistency and continuity with prior behavior.

Finally, developmentalists assume that the process of development persists from the moment of conception to the day of death, with people changing in some ways right up to the end of their lives and in other ways exhibiting remarkable stability. They believe that no single period governs all development, but instead that people maintain the capacity for substantial growth and change throughout their lives.

Characterizing Lifespan Development: The Scope of the Field

Clearly, the definition of lifespan development is broad and the scope of the field is extensive. Typically, lifespan development specialists cover several diverse areas, choosing to specialize in both a topical area and an age range.

Topical Areas in Lifespan Development. Some developmentalists focus on **physical development**, examining the ways in which the body's makeup—the brain, nervous system, muscles, and senses, and the need for food, drink, and sleep—helps determine behavior. For example, one specialist in physical development might examine the effects of malnutrition on the pace of growth in children, while another might look at how athletes' physical performance declines during adulthood (Fell & Williams, 2008).

Other developmental specialists examine **cognitive development**, seeking to understand how growth and change in intellectual capabilities influence a person's behavior. Cognitive developmentalists examine learning, memory, problem solving, and intelligence. For example, specialists in cognitive development might want to see how problem-solving skills change over the course of life, or if cultural differences exist in the way people explain their academic successes and failures, or how traumatic events experienced early in life are remembered later in life (Penido et al., 2012; Feldman, 2013).

lifespan development the field of study that examines patterns of growth, change, and stability in behavior that occur throughout the entire life span

physical development development involving the body's physical makeup, including the brain, nervous system, muscles, and senses, and the need for food, drink, and sleep

cognitive development development involving the ways that growth and change in intellectual capabilities influence a person's behavior

TABLE 1-1 APPROACHES TO LIFESPAN DEVELOPMENT

Orientation	Defining Characteristics	Examples of Questions Asked*
Physical development	Emphasizes how brain, nervous system, muscles, sensory capabilities, and needs for food, drink, and sleep affect behavior	• What determines the sex of a child? (2.1) • What are the long-term results of premature birth? (2.3) • What are the benefits of breast milk? (3.1) • What are the consequences of early or late sexual maturation? (6.1) • What leads to obesity in adulthood? (7.1) • How do adults cope with stress? (8.1) • What are the outward and internal signs of aging? (9.1) • How do we define death? (10.1)?
Cognitive development	Emphasizes intellectual abilities, including learning, memory, problem solving, and intelligence	• What are the earliest memories that can be recalled from infancy? (3.2) • What are the intellectual consequences of watching television? (4.2) • Do spatial reasoning skills relate to music practice? (4.2) • Are there benefits to bilingualism? (5.2) • How does an adolescent's egocentrism affect his or her view of the world? (6.2) • Are there ethnic and racial differences in intelligence? (5.2) • How does creativity relate to intelligence? (7.2) • Does intelligence decline in late adulthood? (9.2)?
Personality and social development	Emphasizes enduring characteristics that differentiate one person from another, and how interactions with others and social relationships grow and change over the lifetime	• Do newborns respond differently to their mothers than to others? (2.3) • What is the best procedure for disciplining children? (4.3) • When does a sense of gender identity develop? (4.3) • How can we promote cross-race friendships? (5.3) • What are the causes of adolescent suicide? (6.3) • How do we choose a romantic partner? (7.3) • Do the effects of parental divorce last into old age? (9.3) • Do people withdraw from others in late adulthood? (9.3) • What are the emotions involved in confronting death? (10.1)?

*Numbers in parentheses indicate in which chapter and module the question is addressed.

Finally, some developmental specialists focus on personality and social development. **Personality development** is the study of stability and change in the characteristics that differentiate one person from another over the life span. **Social development** is the way in which individuals' interactions and relationships with others grow, change, and remain stable over the course of life. A developmentalist interested in personality development might ask whether there are stable, enduring personality traits throughout the life span, while a specialist in social development might examine the effects of racism or poverty or divorce on development. These four major topic areas—physical, cognitive, social, and personality development—are summarized in Table 1-1.

Age Ranges and Individual Differences. In addition to choosing a particular topical area, developmentalists also typically look at a particular age range. The life span is usually divided into broad age ranges: the prenatal period (from conception to birth); infancy and toddlerhood (birth to 3); the preschool period (3 to 6); middle childhood (6 to 12); adolescence (12 to 20); young adulthood (20 to 40); middle adulthood (40 to 60); and late adulthood (60 to death).

personality development development involving the ways that the enduring characteristics that differentiate one person from another change over the lifes pan

social development the way in which individuals' interactions with others and their social relationships grow, change, and remain stable over the course of life

It's important to keep in mind that these periods are social constructions. A *social construction* is a shared notion of reality that is widely accepted but is a function of society and culture at a given time. Thus, the age ranges within a period—and even the periods themselves—are in many ways arbitrary and culturally derived. For example, we'll see how the concept of childhood as a special period did not even exist during the seventeenth century—children were seen then simply as miniature adults. Furthermore, while some periods have a clear-cut boundary (infancy begins with birth, the preschool period ends with entry into public school, and adolescence starts with sexual maturity), others don't.

For instance, consider the period of young adulthood, which at least in Western cultures is typically assumed to begin at age 20. That age, however, is notable only because it marks the end of the teenage period. In fact, for many people, such as those enrolled in higher education, the age change from 19 to 20 has little special significance, coming as it does in the middle of college. For them, more substantial changes are likely to occur when they leave college around age 22. Furthermore, in some cultures adulthood starts much earlier, as soon as a child can begin full-time work.

In fact, some developmentalists have proposed entirely new developmental periods. For instance, psychologist Jeffrey Arnett argues that adolescence extends into *emerging adulthood*, a period beginning in the late teenage years and continuing into the mid-20s. During emerging adulthood, people are no longer adolescents, but they haven't fully taken on the responsibilities of adulthood. Instead, they are still trying out different identities and engaging in self-focused exploration (Arnett, 2010, 2011; de Dios, 2012; Syed & Seiffge-Krenke, 2013).

In short, there are substantial *individual differences* in the timing of events in people's lives. In part, this is a biological fact of life: People mature at different rates and reach developmental milestones at different points. However, environmental factors also play a significant role; for example, the typical age of marriage varies from one culture to another, depending in part on the functions that marriage plays.

This wedding of two children in India is an example of how environmental factors can play a significant role in determining the age when a particular event is likely to occur.

The Links Between Topics and Ages. Each of the broad topical areas of lifespan development—physical, cognitive, social, and personality development—plays a role throughout

Cultural Dimensions

How Culture, Ethnicity, and Race Influence Development

Mayan mothers in Central America are certain that almost constant contact between themselves and their infant children is necessary for good parenting, and they are physically upset if contact is not possible. They are shocked when they see a North American mother lay her infant down, and they attribute the baby's crying to the poor parenting of the North American (Morelli et al., 1992).

What are we to make of the two views of parenting depicted in this passage? Is one right and the other wrong? Probably not, if we take cultural context into consideration. Different cultures and subcultures have their own views of appropriate and inappropriate childrearing, just as they have different developmental goals for children (Feldman & Masalha, 2007; Huijbregts et al., 2009; Chen, Chen, & Zheng, 2012).

Clearly, to understand development, developmentalists must take into consideration broad cultural factors, such as an orientation toward individualism or collectivism, as well as finer ethnic, racial, socioeconomic, and gender differences. If they succeed in doing this, not only can they achieve a better understanding of human development, but they may be able to derive more precise applications for improving the human social condition.

To complicate the study of diverse populations, the terms *race* and *ethnic group* are often used inappropriately. *Race* is a biological concept, which should refer to classifications based on physical and structural characteristics of species. In contrast, *ethnic group* and *ethnicity* are broader, referring to cultural background, nationality, religion, and language.

The concept of race has proven particularly problematic. It has inappropriately taken on nonbiological meanings ranging from skin color to religion to culture. Moreover, as a concept it is exceedingly imprecise; depending on how it is defined, there are between 3 and 300 races, and no race is genetically distinct. The fact that 99.9 percent of humans' genetic makeup is identical in all humans makes the question of race seem insignificant (Helms, Jernigan, & Mascher, 2005; Smedley & Smedley, 2005; Alfred & Chlup, 2010).

In addition, there is little agreement about which names best reflect different races and ethnic groups. Should the term *African American*—which has geographical and cultural implications—be preferred over *black*, which focuses primarily on race and skin color? Is *Native American* preferable to *Indian*? Is *Hispanic* more appropriate than *Latino*? And how can researchers accurately categorize people with multiracial backgrounds?

In order to fully understand development, then, we need to take the complex issues associated with human diversity into account. In fact, it is only by looking for similarities and differences among various ethnic, cultural, and racial groups that developmental researchers can distinguish principles of development that are universal from ones that are culturally determined. In the years ahead, then, it is likely that lifespan development will move from a discipline that primarily focuses on North American and European development to one that encompasses development around the globe (Fowers & Davidov, 2006; Matsumoto & Yoo, 2006; Kloep et al., 2009).

the life span. Consequently, some developmental experts may focus on physical development during the prenatal period, and others during adolescence. Some might specialize in social development during the preschool years, while others look at social relationships in late adulthood. And still others might take a broader approach, looking at cognitive development through every period of life.

In this book, we'll take a comprehensive approach, proceeding chronologically from the prenatal period through late adulthood and death. Within each period, we'll look at physical, cognitive, social, and personality development.

Cohort and Other Influences on Development: Developing With Others in a Social World

Bob, born in 1947, is a baby boomer; he was born soon after the end of World War II, when returning soldiers caused an enormous bulge in the birth rate. He was an adolescent at the height of the Civil Rights movement and protested against the Vietnam War. His mother, Leah, was born in 1922; her generation passed its childhood and teenage years in the shadow of the Depression. Bob's son, Jon, was born in 1975. Now building a career and starting a family, he is a member of what has been called Generation X. Jon's younger sister, Sarah, who was born in 1982, is part of the next generation, which sociologists have called the Millennial Generation.

These people are in part products of the social times in which they live. Each belongs to a particular **cohort**, a group of people born at around the same time in the same place. Such major social events as wars, economic upturns and depressions, famines, and epidemics (like the one due to the AIDS virus) work similar influences on members of a particular cohort (Mitchell, 2002; Dittman, 2005).

Cohort effects are an example of *history-graded influences*, biological and environmental influences associated with a particular historical moment. For instance, people who lived in New York City during the 9/11 terrorist attack on the World Trade Center experienced shared biological and environmental challenges due to the attack. In fact, the specter of terrorism is a history-graded influence that is common to people living in the United States today (Bonanno, Galea, Bucciarelli, & Vlahov, 2006; Breslau, Bohnert, & Koenen, 2010; Park, Riley, & Snyder, 2012).

From an educator's perspective: How would a student's cohort membership affect his or her readiness for school? For example, what would be the benefits and drawbacks of coming from a cohort in which Internet use was routine, compared with earlier cohorts before the appearance of the Internet?

In contrast, *age-graded influences* are biological and environmental influences that are similar for individuals in a particular age group, regardless of when or where they are raised. For example, biological events such as puberty and menopause are universal events that occur at about the same time in all societies. Similarly, a sociocultural event such as entry into formal education can be considered an age-graded influence because it occurs in most cultures around age 6.

Development is also affected by *sociocultural-graded influences*, the social and cultural factors present at a particular time for a particular individual, depending on such variables as ethnicity, social class, and subcultural membership. For example, sociocultural-graded influences will be considerably different for white and nonwhite children, especially if one lives in poverty and the other in affluence (Rose et al., 2003).

Finally, *non-normative life events* are specific, atypical events that occur in a particular person's life at a time when such events do not happen to most people. For example, a child whose parents die in an automobile accident when she is 6 has experienced a significant non-normative life event.

cohort a group of people born at around the same time in the same place

REVIEW, CHECK, AND APPLY

1.1
1.2
1.3

REVIEW

L01 What is the scope of the field of lifespan development?

- Lifespan development is a scientific approach to understanding human growth and change throughout life.
- The field covers a broad range of ages and topical areas. Its chief aim is to examine the links between human age groups and the areas of physical, cognitive, social, and personality development.

L02 What are cohorts, and how do they influence development?

- Membership in a cohort, based on age and place of birth, subjects people to influences based on historical events (history-graded influences).
- People are also subject to age-graded influences, sociocultural-graded influences, and non-normative life events.

CHECK YOURSELF

1. Three assumptions made by lifespan developmentalists are: (1) a focus on human development, (2) an understanding of stability in addition to growth and change, and (3) _____.
   - a the perception that development persists throughout our entire lives
   - b the perception that childhood developmental changes are the only changes worth studying
   - c the idea that some periods of the life span are more important than others
   - d the perception that development is a stagnant process
2. Stages of the life span such as adolescence and middle age are universal across cultures and stable across history.
   - True
   - False
3. The time when children utter their first complete sentence is an example of _____.
   - a a history-graded influence
   - b an age-graded influence
   - c a sociocultural-graded influence
   - d a non-normative life event

APPLYING LIFESPAN DEVELOPMENT

- What are some examples in your life of events and experiences that have affected your age cohort differently from other cohorts?

✓ **Study** and **Review** on **MyPsychLab.com**

KEY ISSUES AND QUESTIONS: DETERMINING THE NATURE—AND NURTURE—OF LIFESPAN DEVELOPMENT

L03 What are the key issues in the field of development?
L04 How have developmental researchers resolved these issues?

Lifespan development is a decades-long journey through shared milestones, with many individual routes along the way. For developmentalists, the variations in lifespan development raise many questions. What are the best ways to think about the enormous changes that a person undergoes from before birth to death? How important is chronological age? Is there a clear timetable for development? How can one begin to find common threads and patterns?

These questions have been debated since lifespan development became established as a separate field in the late nineteenth and early twentieth centuries, though a fascination with the nature and course of humans' development can be traced back to the ancient Egyptians and Greeks.

In this section we examine four of the most important—and continuously argued—issues in the field of lifespan development. We also consider the resolutions to which researchers have come regarding these issues.

Continuous Change Versus Discontinuous Change

One of the primary issues challenging developmentalists is whether development proceeds in a continuous or discontinuous fashion. In **continuous change**, development is gradual, with achievements at one level building on those of previous levels. Continuous change is quantitative; the underlying developmental processes remain the same over the life span. In this view

continuous change gradual development in which achievements at one level build on those of previous levels changes are a matter of degree, not of kind—like changes in a person's height. Some theorists suggest that changes in people's thinking abilities are also continuous, building on gradual improvements rather than developing entirely new processing capabilities.

In contrast, others see development as primarily a matter of **discontinuous change**, occurring in distinct stages. Each stage brings about behavior that is assumed to be qualitatively different from behavior at earlier stages. Consider cognitive development again. Some cognitive developmentalists suggest that our thinking changes in fundamental ways as we develop, not just quantitatively but qualitatively.

Most developmentalists agree that it makes little sense to take an either/or position on this issue. While many types of developmental change are continuous, others are clearly discontinuous (Flavell, 1994; Heimann, 2003; Gumz et al., 2010).

Critical and Sensitive Periods: Gauging the Impact of Environmental Events

If a woman comes down with a case of rubella (German measles) in the 11th week of pregnancy, the consequences for the child she is carrying—possible blindness, deafness, and heart defects—can be devastating. However, if she comes down with the same strain of rubella in the 30th week of pregnancy, damage to the child is unlikely.

The differing outcomes demonstrate the concept of critical periods. A **critical period** is a specific time during development when a particular event has its greatest consequences. Critical periods occur when the presence of certain kinds of environmental stimuli are necessary for development to proceed normally (Uylings, 2006).

Although early specialists in lifespan development placed great emphasis on critical periods, recent thinking suggests that individuals are more malleable, particularly in the domain of personality and social development. For instance, rather than suffering permanent damage from a lack of certain early social experiences, there is increasing evidence that people can use later experiences to help overcome earlier deficits.

Consequently, developmentalists are now more likely to speak of **sensitive periods** rather than critical periods. In a sensitive period, organisms are particularly susceptible to certain kinds of stimuli in their environments. In contrast to a critical period, however, the absence of those stimuli during a sensitive period does not always produce irreversible consequences.

It is important to understand the difference between the concepts of critical periods and sensitive periods: In critical periods, it is assumed that the absence of certain kinds of environmental influences is likely to produce permanent, irreversible consequences for the developing individual. In contrast, although the absence of particular environmental influences during a sensitive period may hinder development, it is possible for later experiences to overcome the earlier deficits. In other words, the concept of sensitive period recognizes the plasticity of developing humans (Armstrong et al., 2006; Hooks & Chen, 2008; Steele et al., 2013).

discontinuous change development that occurs in distinct steps or stages, with each stage bringing about behavior that is assumed to be qualitatively different from behavior at earlier stages

critical period a specific time during development when a particular event has its greatest consequences and the presence of certain kinds of environmental stimuli are necessary for development to proceed normally

sensitive period a point in development when organisms are particularly susceptible to certain kinds of stimuli in their environments, but the absence of those stimuli does not always produce irreversible consequences

Lifespan Approaches Versus a Focus on Particular Periods

Early developmentalists tended to focus their attention on infancy and adolescence, largely to the exclusion of other parts of the life span. Today, however, developmentalists believe the entire life span is important, largely because developmental growth and change continue during every part of life—as we'll discuss throughout this book.

Furthermore, to fully understand the social influences on a person of a given age, we need to understand the person's social environment—the people who in large measure provide those influences. For instance, to understand development in infants, we need to unravel the effects of their parents' ages on their social environments. A 15-year-old, first-time mother and an experienced 37-year-old mother will provide parental influences of very different sorts. Consequently, infant development is in part an outgrowth of adult development.

Additionally, as lifespan developmentalist Paul Baltes points out, development across the life span involves both gains and losses. With age, certain capabilities become more refined and sophisticated, while others decline. For example, vocabulary tends to grow throughout childhood and continue through most of adulthood, but certain physical abilities, like reaction time, improve until early and middle adulthood, and then begin to decline (Baltes, Staudinger, & Lindenberger, 1999; Baltes, 2003; Ghisletta et al., 2010).

The Relative Influence of Nature and Nurture on Development

One of the enduring questions of development involves how much of people's behavior is due to genetics (nature) and how much to the physical and social environment (nurture) (Wexler, 2006).

Nature refers to traits, abilities, and capacities that are inherited from one's parents. It encompasses any factor that is produced by the predetermined unfolding of genetic information—a process known as **maturation**. These genetic, inherited influences are at work as we move from the one-cell organism created at conception to the billions of cells that make up a fully formed human. Nature influences whether our eyes are blue or brown, whether we have thick hair throughout life or eventually go bald, and how good we are at athletics. Nature allows our brains to develop in such a way that we can read the words on this page.

In contrast, *nurture* refers to the environmental influences that shape behavior. Some influences may be biological, such as the impact of a pregnant mother's use of cocaine on her unborn child or the amount and kind of food available to children. Other influences are more social, such as the ways parents discipline their children and the effects of peer pressure on an adolescent. Finally, some influences are a result of societal factors, such as the socioeconomic circumstances in which people find themselves.

Although developmentalists reject the notion that behavior is the sole result of either nature or nurture, the nature–nurture question can cause heated debate. Take, for instance, intelligence. If intelligence is primarily determined by heredity and is largely fixed at birth, then efforts to improve intellectual performance later in life may be doomed to failure. In contrast, if intelligence is primarily a result of environmental factors, such as the amount and quality of schooling and home stimulation, then an improvement in social conditions could cause intelligence to increase.

Clearly, neither nature nor nurture stands alone in most developmental matters. The interaction of genetic and environmental factors is complex, in part because certain genetically determined traits have not only a direct influence on children's behavior, but an indirect influence in shaping children's *environments*. For example, children who cry a great deal—a trait that may be produced by genetic factors—may influence their environment by making their parents rush to comfort them whenever they cry. The parents' responsivity to their children's genetically determined behavior becomes an environmental influence on the children's subsequent development.

Similarly, although our genetic background orients us toward particular behaviors, those behaviors will not necessarily occur without an appropriate environment. People with similar genetic backgrounds (such as identical twins) may behave in very different ways; and people with highly dissimilar genetic backgrounds can behave quite similarly to one another in certain areas (Kato & Pedersen, 2005; Gangestad, 2010; Barnes & Boutwell, 2013).

In sum, the nature–nurture question is challenging. Ultimately, we should consider the two sides of the issue as ends of a continuum, with particular behaviors falling somewhere between the ends. The same can be said of the other controversies that we have considered. For instance, continuous versus discontinuous development is not an either/or proposition; some forms of development fall toward the continuous end of the continuum, while others lie closer to the discontinuous end. In short, few statements about development involve either/or absolutes (Deater-Deckard & Cahill, 2006; Rutter, 2006).

maturation the predetermined unfolding of genetic information

REVIEW, CHECK, AND APPLY

REVIEW

L03 What are the key issues in the field of development?

- Four important issues in lifespan development are continuity versus discontinuity in development, the importance of critical periods, whether to focus on certain periods or on the entire life span, and the nature–nurture controversy.
- These issues have been the subject of research and discussions since the field of development began.

L04 How have developmental researchers resolved these issues?

- Research and discussions on these issues have led to the conclusion that for three of them, no either–or answer makes sense.
- For the "focus on certain periods" issue, however, there is general agreement that development is not limited to childhood and adolescence, but continues through the life span.

CHECK YOURSELF

1. Grady believes that human development occurs in small, measurable amounts. His sister Andrea disagrees and suggests that human development is more distinct and steplike. Their argument is most reflective of the _____ issue.
   - a critical and sensitive period
   - b nature and nurture
   - c continuous and discontinuous
   - d lifespan approach and particular period
2. A _____ is a specific time during development when a particular event has its greatest consequence.
   - a critical period
   - b sensitive period
   - c genetic period
   - d embryo period
3. Nurture refers to traits, abilities, and capacities that are inherited from one's parents.
   - True
   - False

APPLYING LIFESPAN DEVELOPMENT

- What are some examples of the ways culture (either broad culture or aspects of culture) affects human development?

✓ **Study** and **Review** on **MyPsychLab.com**

MODULE 1.2

THEORETICAL PERSPECTIVES ON LIFESPAN DEVELOPMENT

In Europe, there was no concept of "childhood" until the seventeenth century. Instead, children were simply thought of as miniature adults. They were assumed to be subject to the same needs and desires as adults, to have the same vices and virtues, and to warrant no more privileges. They were dressed the same as adults, and their work hours were the same. Children also received the same punishments for misdeeds. If they stole, they were hanged; if they did well, they could achieve prosperity, at least so far as their station in life or social class would allow.

Society's view of childhood, and what is appropriate to ask of children, has changed through the ages. These children worked full time in mines in the early 1900s.

This view of childhood seems wrongheaded now, but at the time it was society's understanding of lifespan development. From this perspective, there were no differences due to age; except for size, people were assumed to be virtually unchanging, at least on a psychological level, throughout most of the life span (Aries, 1962; Acocella, 2003; Hutton, 2004; Wines, 2006).

It is easy to reject the medieval view but less clear how to formulate a contemporary substitute. Should our view of development focus on the biological aspects of change, growth, and stability over the life span? The cognitive or social aspects? Or some other factors?

In fact, people who study lifespan development approach the field from different perspectives. Each perspective encompasses one or more **theories**: broad, organized explanations and predictions concerning phenomena of interest. A theory provides a framework for understanding the relationships among a seemingly unorganized set of facts or principles.

We all develop theories about development, based on our experience, folklore, and stories in the media. However, theories in lifespan development are different. Whereas our own personal theories are haphazardly built on unverified observations, developmentalists' theories are more formal, based on a systematic integration of prior findings and theorizing. Theories allow developmentalists to summarize and organize prior observations, and they allow them to move beyond existing observations to draw deductions that may not be immediately apparent. In addition, theories are subject to rigorous testing through research. By contrast, the developmental theories of individuals are not subject to testing and may never be questioned at all (Thomas, 2001).

We'll consider the six major theoretical perspectives used in lifespan development—the psychodynamic, behavioral, cognitive, humanistic, contextual, and evolutionary perspectives—and discuss them in greater detail in later chapters. Each perspective emphasizes somewhat different aspects of development and steers developmentalists in particular directions. Furthermore, each continues to evolve, as befits a dynamic discipline.

THE PSYCHODYNAMIC, BEHAVIORAL, AND COGNITIVE PERSPECTIVES

LO5 Which theoretical perspectives have guided lifespan development?
LO6 What are the main characteristics of the psychodynamic, behavioral, and cognitive perspectives?

The Psychodynamic Perspective: Focusing on the Inner Person

When Marisol was 6 months old, she was involved in a bloody automobile accident—or so her parents tell her, since she has no recollection of it. Now, however, at age 24, she is having difficulty maintaining relationships, and her therapist is seeking to determine whether her current problems are a result of the earlier accident.

Looking for such a link might seem a bit far-fetched—but not to proponents of the **psychodynamic perspective**. Advocates believe that much behavior is motivated by inner forces, memories, and conflicts of which a person has little awareness or control. The inner forces, which may stem from childhood, influence behavior throughout the life span.

Sigmund Freud

Freud's Psychoanalytic Theory. The psychodynamic perspective is most closely associated with Sigmund Freud. Freud, who lived from 1856 to 1939, was a Viennese physician whose revolutionary ideas had a profound effect not only on psychology and psychiatry, but on Western thought in general (Masling & Bornstein, 1996; Greenberg, 2012).

Freud's **psychoanalytic theory** suggests that unconscious forces act to determine personality and behavior. To Freud, the *unconscious* is a part of the personality about which a person is unaware. It contains infantile wishes, desires, demands, and needs that are hidden, because of their disturbing nature, from conscious awareness. Freud suggested that the unconscious is responsible for a good part of our everyday behavior.

According to Freud, everyone's personality has three aspects: id, ego, and superego. The *id* is the raw, unorganized, inborn part of personality that is present at birth. It represents primitive drives related to hunger, sex, aggression, and irrational impulses. The id operates according to the *pleasure principle*, in which the goal is to maximize satisfaction and reduce tension.

The *ego* is the part of personality that is rational and reasonable. The ego acts as a buffer between the external world and the primitive id. The ego operates on the *reality principle*, in which instinctual energy is restrained in order to maintain the safety of the individual and help integrate the person into society.

Finally, Freud proposed that the *superego* represents a person's conscience, incorporating distinctions between right and wrong. It begins to develop from age 5 or 6 and is learned from an individual's parents, teachers, and other significant figures.

Freud also addressed personality development during childhood. He argued that **psychosexual development** occurs as children pass through distinct stages in which pleasure, or gratification, is focused on a particular biological function and body part. As illustrated in Table 1-2, he suggested that pleasure shifts from the mouth (the *oral stage*) to the anus (the *anal stage*) and eventually to the genitals (the *phallic stage* and the *genital stage*).

According to Freud, if children are unable to gratify themselves sufficiently during a particular stage, or if they receive too much gratification, fixation may occur. *Fixation* is behavior reflecting an earlier stage of development due to an unresolved conflict. For instance, fixation at the oral stage might produce an adult unusually absorbed in oral activities—eating, talking, or chewing gum. Freud also argued that fixation is represented through symbolic oral activities, such as the use of "biting" sarcasm.

Erikson's Psychosocial Theory. Psychoanalyst Erik Erikson, who lived from 1902 to 1994, provided an alternative psychodynamic view, emphasizing our social interaction with other people. In Erikson's view, society and culture both challenge and shape us. **Psychosocial development** encompasses changes in our interactions with and understandings of one another, as well as in our knowledge and understanding of us as members of society (Erikson, 1963; Dunkel, Kim, & Papini, 2012).

Erikson's theory suggests that development proceeds throughout our lives in eight stages (see Table 1-2), which emerge in a fixed pattern and are similar for all people.

theories broad explanations, and predictions about phenomena of interest

psychodynamic perspective the approach that states behavior is motivated by inner forces, memories, and conflicts that are generally beyond people's awareness and control

psychoanalytic theory the theory proposed by Freud that suggests that unconscious forces act to determine personality and behavior

psychosexual development according to Freud, a series of stages that children pass through in which pleasure, or gratification, is focused on a particular biological function and body part

psychosocial development according to Erikson, development that encompasses changes both in the understandings individuals have of themselves as members of society and in their comprehension of the meaning of others' behavior.

TABLE 1-2 FREUD'S AND ERIKSON'S THEORIES

Approximate Age	Freud's Stages of Psychosexual Development	Major Characteristics of Freud's Stages	Erikson's Stages of Psychosocial Development	Positive and Negative Outcomes of Erikson's Stages
Birth to 12–18 months	Oral	Interest in oral gratification from sucking, eating, mouthing, biting	Trust vs. mistrust	*Positive*: Feelings of trust from environmental support *Negative*: Fear and concern regarding others
12–18 months to 3 years	Anal	Gratification from expelling and withholding feces; coming to terms with society's controls relating to toilet training	Autonomy vs. shame and doubt	*Positive*: Self-sufficiency if exploration is encouraged *Negative*: Doubts about self, lack of independence
3 to 5–6 years	Phallic	Interest in the genitals; coming to terms with Oedipal conflict, leading to identification with same-sex parent	Initiative vs. guilt	*Positive*: Discovery of ways to initiate actions *Negative*: Guilt from actions and thoughts
5–6 years to adolescence	Latency	Sexual concerns largely unimportant	Industry vs. inferiority	*Positive*: Development of sense of competence *Negative*: Feelings of inferiority, no sense of mastery
Adolescence to adulthood (Freud) Adolescence (Erikson)	Genital	Reemergence of sexual interests and establishment of mature sexual relationships	Identity vs. role diffusion	*Positive*: Awareness of uniqueness of self, knowledge of role to be followed *Negative*: Inability to identify appropriate roles in life
Early adulthood (Erikson)			Intimacy vs. isolation	*Positive*: Development of loving, sexual relationships and close friendships *Negative*: Fear of relationships with others
Middle adulthood (Erikson)			Generativity vs. stagnation	*Positive*: Sense of contribution to continuity of life *Negative*: Trivialization of one's activities
Late adulthood (Erikson)			Ego-integrity vs. despair	*Positive*: Sense of unity in life's accomplishments *Negative*: Regret over lost opportunities of life

Each stage presents a crisis or conflict that the individual must resolve. Although no crisis is ever fully resolved, the individual must at least address the crisis of each stage sufficiently to deal with demands made during the next stage of development. Unlike Freud, who regarded development as relatively complete by adolescence, Erikson suggested that growth and change continue throughout the life span (de St. Aubin, McAdams, & Kim, 2004).

Assessing the Psychodynamic Perspective. Freud's insight that unconscious influences affect behavior was a monumental accomplishment, and the fact that it seems at all reasonable to us shows how extensively the idea of the unconscious has pervaded thinking in Western cultures. In fact, work by contemporary researchers studying memory and learning suggests that we unconsciously carry with us memories that have a significant impact on our behavior.

Some of the most basic principles of Freud's psychoanalytic theory have been questioned, however, because they have not been validated by research. In particular, the notion that childhood stages determine adult personalities has little research support. In addition, because much of Freud's theory was based on a limited population of upper-middle-class Austrians living during a strict, puritanical era, its application to broad, multicultural populations is questionable. Finally, because Freud's theory focuses primarily on male development, it has been criticized as sexist and interpreted as devaluing women (Messer & McWilliams, 2003; Schachter, 2005; Gillham, Law, & Hickey, 2010).

Erikson's view that development continues throughout the life span is highly important—and has received considerable support. However, the theory also has its drawbacks. Like Freud's theory, it focuses more on men than women. Further, its vagueness makes it difficult to test rigorously. And, as with psychodynamic theories in general, it is difficult to make definitive predictions about a given individual's behavior using the theory (Zauszniewski & Martin, 1999; De St. Aubin & McAdams, 2004; Balsam, 2013).

Erik Erikson

The Behavioral Perspective: Focusing on Observable Behavior

When Elissa Sheehan was 3, a large brown dog bit her, and she needed dozens of stitches and several operations. From the time she was bitten, she broke into a sweat whenever she saw a dog, and in fact never enjoyed being around any pet.

To a lifespan development specialist using the behavioral perspective, the explanation for Elissa's behavior is straightforward: She has a learned fear of dogs. Rather than looking inside the organism at unconscious processes, the **behavioral perspective** suggests that the keys to understanding development are observable behavior and environmental stimuli. If we know the stimuli, we can predict the behavior. In this respect, the behavioral perspective reflects the view that nurture is more important to development than nature.

Behavioral theories reject the notion that people universally pass through a series of stages. Instead, people are affected by the environmental stimuli to which they happen to be exposed. Developmental patterns, then, are personal, reflecting a particular set of environmental stimuli, and behavior is the result of continuing exposure to specific factors in the environment. Furthermore, developmental change is viewed in quantitative, rather than qualitative, terms. For instance, behavioral theories hold that advances in problem-solving capabilities as children age are largely a result of greater mental *capacities*, rather than changes in the *kind* of thinking that children can bring to bear on a problem.

Classical Conditioning: Stimulus Substitution.

> *Give me a dozen healthy infants, well-formed, and my own specified world to bring them up in and I'll guarantee to take any one at random and train him to become any type of specialist I might select—doctor, lawyer, artist, merchant-chief, and yes, even beggar-man and thief, regardless of his talents, penchants, tendencies, abilities. (Watson, 1925)*

With these words, John B. Watson, one of the first American psychologists to advocate a behavioral approach, summed up the behavioral perspective. Watson, who lived from 1878 to 1958, believed strongly that we could gain a full understanding of development by carefully studying the stimuli that composed the environment. In fact, he argued that by effectively controlling—or *conditioning*—a person's environment, it was possible to produce virtually any behavior.

Classical conditioning occurs when an organism learns to respond in a particular way to a neutral stimulus. For instance, if the sound of a bell is paired with the arrival of meat, a dog will learn to react to the bell alone in the same way it reacts to the meat—by salivating and wagging its tail. The behavior is a result of conditioning, a form of learning in which the response associated with one stimulus (food) comes to be connected to another—in this case, the bell.

The same process of classical conditioning explains how we learn emotional responses. In the case of dog-bite victim Elissa Sheehan, for instance, Watson would say that one stimulus has been substituted for another: Elissa's unpleasant experience with a particular dog (the initial stimulus) has been transferred to other dogs and to pets in general.

behavioral perspective the approach that suggests that the keys to understanding development are observable behavior and outside stimuli in the environment

classical conditioning a type of learning in which an organism responds in a particular way to a neutral stimulus that normally does not bring about that type of response

John B. Watson

Operant Conditioning. In addition to classical conditioning, the behavioral perspective accounts for other types of learning, especially what behavioralists call operant conditioning. **Operant conditioning** is a form of learning in which a voluntary response is strengthened or weakened by its association with positive or negative consequences. It differs from classical conditioning in that the response being conditioned is voluntary and purposeful rather than automatic (such as salivating). In operant conditioning, formulated and championed by psychologist B. F. Skinner (1904–1990), individuals learn to *operate* on their environments in order to bring about desired consequences (Skinner, 1975).

Whether or not children and adults will seek to repeat a behavior depends on whether it is followed by reinforcement. *Reinforcement* is the process by which a behavior is followed by a stimulus that increases the probability that the behavior will be repeated. Hence, a student is apt to work harder if he or she receives good grades; workers are likely to labor harder if their efforts are tied to pay increases; and people are more apt to buy lottery tickets if they are reinforced by winning occasionally. In addition, *punishment*, the introduction of an unpleasant or painful stimulus or the removal of a desirable stimulus, will decrease the probability that a preceding behavior will occur in the future.

Behavior that is reinforced, then, is more likely to be repeated, while behavior that receives no reinforcement or is punished is likely to be *extinguished* in the language of operant conditioning. Principles of operant conditioning are used in **behavior modification**, a formal technique for promoting the frequency of desirable behaviors and decreasing the incidence of unwanted ones. Behavior modification has been used in situations ranging from teaching people with severe retardation basic language to helping people with self-control problems stick to diets (Matson & LoVullo, 2008; Wupperman et al., 2012).

Social-Cognitive Learning Theory: Learning Through Imitation. A 5-year-old boy seriously injures his 22-month-old cousin while imitating a violent wrestling move he has seen on television. Although the baby sustained spinal cord injuries, he improved and was discharged 5 weeks after his hospital admission (Reuters Health eLine, 2002).

Cause and effect? We can't know for sure, but it certainly seems possible, especially to social-cognitive learning theorists. According to developmental psychologist Albert Bandura and colleagues, a significant amount of learning is explained by **social-cognitive learning theory**, an approach that emphasizes learning by observing the behavior of another person, called a *model* (Bandura, 1994, 2002).

From a social worker's perspective: How do the concepts of social learning and modeling relate to the mass media, and how might exposure to mass media influence a child's family life?

According to social-cognitive learning theory, behavior is learned primarily through observation and not through trial and error, as it is with operant conditioning. We don't need to experience the consequences of a behavior ourselves to learn it. Social-cognitive learning theory holds that when we see the behavior of a model being rewarded, we are likely to imitate that behavior. For instance, in one classic experiment, children who were afraid of dogs were exposed to a model, nicknamed the "Fearless Peer," who was seen playing happily with a dog (Bandura, Grusec, & Menlove, 1967). After exposure, the children who previously had been afraid were more likely to approach a strange dog than children who had not seen the model.

Assessing the Behavioral Perspective. Research using the behavioral perspective has made significant contributions, ranging from the education of children with severe mental retardation to the development of procedures for curbing aggression. At the same time, the perspective has experienced internal disagreements. For example, although part of the same behavioral perspective, classical and operant conditioning and social learning theory disagree in some basic ways. Classical and operant conditioning consider learning in terms of external stimuli and responses, in which the only important factors are the observable features of the environment. People and other organisms are like inanimate "black boxes"; nothing that occurs inside the box is understood—nor much cared about, for that matter.

operant conditioning a form of learning in which a voluntary response is strengthened or weakened by its association with positive or negative consequences

behavior modification a formal technique for promoting the frequency of desirable behaviors and decreasing the incidence of unwanted ones

social-cognitive learning theory learning by observing the behavior of another person, called a model

To social learning theorists, such an analysis is an oversimplification. They argue that what makes people different from rats and pigeons is the mental activity, in the form of thoughts and expectations. We cannot derive a full understanding of people's development without moving beyond external stimuli and responses.

In many ways, social learning theory has won this argument in recent decades. In fact, another perspective that focuses explicitly on internal mental activity—the cognitive perspective—has become enormously influential.

The Cognitive Perspective: Examining the Roots of Understanding

When 3-year-old Jake is asked why it sometimes rains, he answers "so the flowers can grow." When his 11-year-old sister Lila is asked the same question, she responds "because of evaporation from the surface of the Earth." And when their cousin Ajima, who is studying meteorology in graduate school, considers the same question, her extended answer includes a discussion of cumulo-nimbus clouds, the Coriolis Effect, and synoptic charts.

To a developmental theorist using the cognitive perspective, the difference in the sophistication of the answers is evidence of a different degree of knowledge and understanding, or cognition. The **cognitive perspective** focuses on the processes that allow people to know, understand, and think about the world.

The cognitive perspective emphasizes how people internally represent and think about the world. By using this perspective, developmental researchers hope to understand how children and adults process information and how their ways of thinking and understanding affect their behavior. They also seek to learn how cognitive abilities change as people develop, the degree to which cognitive development represents quantitative and qualitative growth in intellectual abilities, and how different cognitive abilities are related to one another.

On the reality show *Survivor*, contestants often must learn new survival skills in order to be successful. What form of learning is prevalent?

Piaget's Theory of Cognitive Development. No one has had a greater impact on the study of cognitive development than Jean Piaget, a Swiss psychologist who lived from 1896 to 1980. Piaget proposed that all people pass through a fixed sequence of universal stages of cognitive development—and not only does the *quantity* of information increase in each stage, but the *quality* of knowledge and understanding changes as well. His focus was on the change in cognition that occurs as children move from one stage to the next (Piaget, 1952, 1962, 1983). Broadly speaking, Piaget suggested that human thinking is arranged into *schemes*, organized mental patterns that represent behaviors and actions. In infants, schemes represent concrete behavior—a scheme for sucking, for reaching, and for each separate behavior. In older children, the schemes become more sophisticated and abstract, such as the skills involved in riding a bike or playing an interactive video game. Schemes are like intellectual computer software programs that direct and determine how data from the world are looked at and handled (Parker, 2005).

Piaget suggested that the growth in children's understanding of the world could be explained by two basic principles: assimilation and accommodation. *Assimilation* is the process in which people understand a new experience in terms of their current stage of cognitive development and existing ways of thinking. In contrast, *accommodation* refers to changes in existing ways of thinking in response to encounters with new stimuli or events. Assimilation and accommodation work in tandem to bring about cognitive development.

Assessing Piaget's Theory. Piaget has profoundly influenced our understanding of cognitive development and is one of the towering figures in lifespan development. He provided masterly descriptions of intellectual growth during childhood—descriptions that have stood the test of literally thousands of investigations. Broadly, then, Piaget's view of cognitive development is accurate.

However, the specifics of the theory have been questioned. For instance, some cognitive skills clearly emerge earlier than Piaget suggested. Furthermore, the universality of Piaget's stages has been disputed. Growing evidence suggests that particular cognitive skills emerge on a different timetable in non-Western cultures. And in every culture, some people never seem to reach Piaget's highest level of cognitive sophistication: formal, logical thought

cognitive perspective the approach that focuses on the processes that allow people to know, understand, and think about the world

(Kesselring & Müller, 2010; De Jesus-Zayas, Buigas, & Denney, 2012; Müller, Burman, & Hutchison, 2013).

Ultimately, the greatest criticism is that cognitive development is not necessarily as discontinuous as Piaget's stage theory suggests. Many developmental researchers argue that growth is considerably more continuous. These critics have suggested an alternative perspective, known as the information processing approach, that focuses on the processes that underlie learning, memory, and thinking throughout the life span.

Information Processing Approaches. Information processing approaches have become an important alternative to Piagetian approaches. **Information processing approaches** to cognitive development seek to identify the ways individuals take in, use, and store information.

Information processing approaches grew out of developments in computers. They assume that even complex behavior such as learning, remembering, categorizing, and thinking can be broken down into a series of individual, specific steps.

Like computers, children are assumed by information processing approaches to have limited capacity for processing information. As they develop, though, they employ increasingly sophisticated strategies that allow them to process information more efficiently.

In stark contrast to Piaget's view, information processing approaches assume that development is marked more by quantitative advances than qualitative ones. Our capacity to handle information changes with age, as does our processing speed and efficiency. Furthermore, information processing approaches suggest that as we age, we are better able to control the nature of processing and the strategies we choose to process information.

An information processing approach that builds on Piaget's research is known as neo-Piagetian theory. In contrast to Piaget's original work, which viewed cognition as a single system of increasingly sophisticated general cognitive abilities, *neo-Piagetian theory* considers cognition as made up of different types of individual skills. Using the terminology of information processing approaches, neo-Piagetian theory suggests that cognitive development proceeds quickly in certain areas and more slowly in others. For example, reading ability and the skills needed to recall stories may progress sooner than the abstract computational abilities used in algebra or trigonometry. Furthermore, neo-Piagetian theorists believe that experience plays a greater role in advancing cognitive development than traditional Piagetian approaches claim (Case, Demetriou, & Platsidou, 2001; Yan & Fischer, 2002; Loewen, 2006).

Assessing Information Processing Approaches. As we'll see in future chapters, information processing approaches have become a central part of our understanding of development. At the same time, they do not offer a complete explanation of behavior. For example, they have paid little attention to behavior such as creativity, in which the most profound ideas often are developed in a seemingly nonlogical, nonlinear manner. In addition, they do not take into account the social context in which development takes place—and theories that do this have become increasingly popular.

Cognitive Neuroscience Approaches. One of the most recent additions to the array of approaches are **cognitive neuroscience approaches**, which look at cognitive development at the level of brain processes. Like other cognitive perspectives, cognitive neuroscience approaches consider internal, mental processes, but they focus specifically on the neurological activity that underlies thinking, problem solving, and other cognitive behavior.

Cognitive neuroscientists seek to identify actual locations and functions within the brain that are related to different types of cognitive activities. For example, using sophisticated brain scanning techniques, cognitive neuroscientists have demonstrated that thinking about the meaning of a word activates different areas of the brain than thinking about how the word sounds when spoken.

Cognitive neuroscientists are also providing clues to the cause of *autism spectrum disorder*, a major developmental disability that can produce profound language deficits and self-injurious behavior in young children. For example, neuroscientists have found that the brains of children with the disorder show explosive, dramatic growth in the first year of life, making their heads significantly larger than those of children without the disorder (see Figure 1-1). By identifying children with the disorder very early in their lives, health care providers can

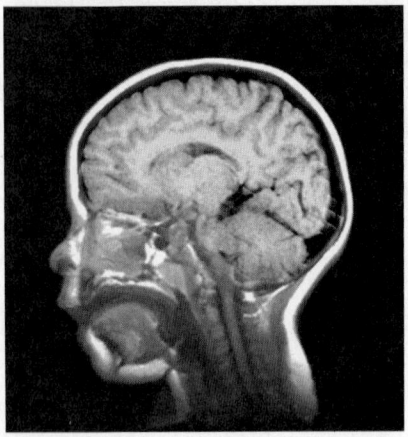

FIGURE 1-1 Brain Size Matters
Neuroscientists found evidence that the brains of children with autism spectrum disorder are somewhat larger than those of children without the disorder. This finding might help identify cases of autism spectrum disorder early, allowing for more effective intervention and treatment.

information processing approaches the model that seeks to identify the ways individuals take in, use, and store information

cognitive neuroscience approaches the approach that examines cognitive development through the lens of brain processes provide crucial early intervention (Akshoomoff, 2006; Nadel & Poss, 2007; Lewis & Elman, 2008; Bal et al., 2010).

Cognitive neuroscience approaches are also on the forefront of cutting-edge research that has identified genes associated with disorders ranging from physical problems such as breast cancer to psychological disorders such as schizophrenia. Identifying the genes that make one vulnerable to such disorders is the first step in genetic engineering in which gene therapy can reduce or even prevent the disorder from occurring (DeLisi & Fleischhaker, 2007; Strobel et al., 2007; Ranganath, Minzenberg, & Ragland, 2008; Rodnitzky, 2012).

REVIEW, CHECK, AND APPLY

REVIEW

L05 Which theoretical perspectives have guided lifespan development?

- Lifespan development has been viewed from six major theoretical perspectives: the psychodynamic, behavioral, cognitive, humanistic, contextual, and evolutionary perspectives. Each emphasizes somewhat different aspects of development and steers developmentalists in particular directions.

L06 What are the main characteristics of the psychodynamic, behavioral, and cognitive perspectives?

- The psychodynamic perspective looks primarily at the influence of internal, unconscious forces on development.
- In contrast, the behavioral perspective focuses on external, observable behaviors as the key to development.
- The cognitive perspective focuses on mental activity, holding that individuals pass through stages in which their ways of thinking change both qualitatively and quantitatively.

CHECK YOURSELF

1. _____ are organized explanations and predictions concerning phenomena of interest and provide frameworks for understanding the relationships across variables.
   - a Evaluations
   - b Constitutions
   - c Intuitions
   - d Theories
2. The _____ perspective suggests that the key to understanding one's actions involves observation of those actions and the outside stimuli in the environment.
   - a psychodynamic
   - b cognitive
   - c behavioral
   - d operant conditioning
3. Which of the following is NOT a concern with Piaget's cognitive perspective?
   - a Everyone reaches Piaget's highest level of thought, suggesting that it isn't much of an achievement.
   - b Some cognitive skills appear much earlier than Piaget originally thought.
   - c The timing of cognitive skills differs as a function of culture.
   - d Cognitive development does not appear to be as discontinuous as Piaget suggested.

APPLYING LIFESPAN DEVELOPMENT

- Can you think of examples of human behavior that may have been inherited from our ancestors because they helped survival and adaptation? Explain why you think this.

✓ **Study** and **Review** on **MyPsychLab.com**

THE HUMANISTIC, CONTEXTUAL, AND EVOLUTIONARY PERSPECTIVES

L07 What are the main characteristics of the humanistic, contextual, and evolutionary perspectives?

L08 Why is there no "right" approach to development?

The Humanistic Perspective: Concentrating on Uniquely Human Qualities

The unique qualities of humans are the central focus of the humanistic perspective, the fourth of the major theories used by lifespan developmentalists. Rejecting the notion that behavior is largely determined by unconscious processes, the environment, or cognitive processing, the **humanistic perspective** contends that people have a natural capacity to make decisions about their lives and to control their behavior. According to this approach, each individual has the ability and motivation to reach more advanced levels of maturity, and people naturally seek to reach their full potential.

humanistic perspective the theory that contends that people have a natural capacity to make decisions about their lives and control their behavior

The humanistic perspective emphasizes *free will*, the ability of humans to make choices and come to decisions about their lives. Instead of relying on societal standards, then, people are assumed to be motivated to make their own decisions about what they do with their lives.

Carl Rogers, one of the major proponents of the humanistic perspective, suggests that people need positive regard, which results from an underlying wish to be loved and respected. Because positive regard comes from other people, we become dependent on them. Consequently, our view of ourselves and our self-worth is a reflection of how we think others view us (Rogers, 1971; Motschnig & Nykl, 2003; Cornforth, 2010).

Rogers, along with another key figure in the humanistic perspective, Abraham Maslow, suggests that self-actualization is a primary goal in life. *Self-actualization* is a state of self-fulfillment in which people achieve their highest potential in their own unique way (Maslow, 1970; Jones & Crandall, 1991; Sheldon, Joiner, & Pettit, 2003; Malchiodi, 2012).

Assessing the Humanistic Perspective. Despite its emphasis on important and unique human qualities, the humanistic perspective has not had a major impact on the field of lifespan development. This is primarily due to its inability to identify any sort of broad developmental change that is the result of increasing age or experience. Still, some of the concepts drawn from the humanistic perspective, such as self-actualization, have helped describe important aspects of human behavior and are widely discussed in areas ranging from health care to business (Laas, 2006; Zalenski & Raspa, 2006; Elkins, 2009).

The Contextual Perspective: Taking a Broad Approach to Development

Although lifespan developmentalists often consider physical, cognitive, personality, and social factors separately, such a categorization has one serious drawback: In the real world, none of these broad influences occurs in isolation from any other. Instead, there is a constant, ongoing interaction between the different types of influence.

The **contextual perspective** considers the relationship between individuals and their physical, cognitive, personality, and social worlds. It suggests that a person's unique development cannot be properly viewed without seeing how that person is enmeshed within a rich social and cultural context. We'll consider two major theories that fall under this category, Bronfenbrenner's bioecological approach and Vygotsky's sociocultural theory.

The Bioecological Approach to Development. In acknowledging the problem with traditional approaches to lifespan development, psychologist Urie Bronfenbrenner (1989; 2000; 2002) has proposed an alternative perspective, the bioecological approach. The **bioecological approach** suggests that there are five levels of the environment that simultaneously influence individuals. Bronfenbrenner suggests that we cannot fully understand development without considering how a person is influenced by each of these levels.

- The *microsystem* is the everyday, immediate environment of children's daily lives. Homes, caregivers, friends, and teachers all are influences, but the child is not just a passive recipient. Instead, children actively help construct the microsystem, shaping their immediate world. The microsystem is the level to which most traditional work in child development has been directed.
- The *mesosystem* connects the various aspects of the microsystem. The mesosystem binds children to parents, students to teachers, employees to bosses, friends to friends. It acknowledges the direct and indirect influences that bind us to one another, such as those that affect a mother who has a bad day at the office and then is short-tempered with her son or daughter at home.
- The *exosystem* represents broader influences: societal institutions such as local government, the community, schools, places of worship, and the local media. Each of these institutions can have an immediate and major impact on personal development, and each affects how the microsystem and mesosystem operate. For example, the quality of a school will affect a child's cognitive development and potentially can have long-term consequences.
- The *macrosystem* represents the larger cultural influences on an individual, including society in general, types of governments, religious and political value systems, and other broad, encompassing factors. For example, the value a culture places on education affects

contextual perspective the theory that considers the relationship between individuals and their physical, cognitive, personality, and social worlds

bioecological approach the perspective suggesting that levels of the environment simultaneously influence individuals the values of the people who live in that culture. Children are part of both a broader culture (such as Western culture) and members of one or more subcultures (for instance, Mexican American subculture).

- Finally, the *chronosystem* underlies each of the previous systems. It involves the way the passage of time—including historical events (such as the terrorist attacks in September of 2001) and more gradual historical changes (such as changes in the number of women who work outside the home)—affects children's development.

The bioecological approach emphasizes the *interconnectedness of the influences on development.* Because the various levels are related to one another, a change in one part of the system affects other parts. For instance, a parent's loss of a job (involving the mesosystem) has an impact upon a child's microsystem.

Conversely, changes on one environmental level may make little difference if other levels are not also changed. For instance, improving the school environment may have a negligible effect on academic performance if children receive little support for academic success at home. Similarly, the influences among family members are multidirectional. Parents don't just influence their child's behavior—the child also influences the parents' behavior.

Finally, the bioecological approach stresses the importance of broad cultural factors that affect development. Researchers in lifespan development increasingly look at how membership in cultural groups influences behavior.

Consider, for instance, whether you agree that children should be taught that their classmates' assistance is essential to getting good grades in school, or that they should plan to continue their fathers' businesses, or that they should take their parents' advice in choosing a career. If you have been raised in the most widespread North American culture, you would likely disagree with all three statements, since they violate the premises of *individualism*, the dominant Western philosophy that emphasizes personal identity, uniqueness, freedom, and the worth of the individual.

On the other hand, if you were raised in a traditional Asian culture, your agreement with the three statements is considerably more likely because the statements reflect the value orientation known as collectivism. *Collectivism* is the notion that the well-being of the group is more important than that of the individual. People raised in collectivistic cultures sometimes emphasize the welfare of the group at the expense of their own personal well-being.

According to Vygotsky, children can develop cognitively in their understanding of the world and learn what is important in society, through play and cooperation with others.

The individualism–collectivism spectrum is one of several dimensions along which cultures differ, and it illustrates differences in the cultural contexts in which people operate. Such broad cultural values play an important role in shaping the ways people view the world and behave (Garcia & Saewyc, 2007; Yu & Stiffman, 2007; Boles, Le, & Nguyen, 2010).

Assessing the Bioecological Approach. Although Bronfenbrenner regards biological influences as an important component of the bioecological approach, ecological influences are central to the theory. In fact, some critics argue that the perspective pays insufficient attention to biological factors. Still, the bioecological approach is important because it suggests the multiple levels at which the environment affects children's development.

Vygotsky's Sociocultural Theory. To Russian developmentalist Lev Semenovich Vygotsky, a full understanding of development is impossible without taking into account the culture in which people develop. Vygotsky's **sociocultural theory** emphasizes how cognitive development proceeds as a result of social interactions between members of a culture (Vygotsky, 1979, 1926/1997; Ferholt & Lecusay, 2010; Göncü, 2012).

Vygotsky, who lived a brief life, from 1896 to 1934, argued that children's understanding of the world is acquired through their problem-solving interactions with adults and other children. As children play and cooperate with others, they learn what is important in their society and, at the same time, advance cognitively. Consequently, to understand development, we must consider what is meaningful to members of a given culture.

sociocultural theory the approach that emphasizes how cognitive development proceeds as a result of social interactions between members of a culture

More than most other theories, sociocultural theory emphasizes that development is a *reciprocal transaction* between the people in a child's environment and the child. Vygotsky believed that people and settings influence the child, who in turn influences the people and settings. This pattern continues in an endless loop, with children being both recipients of socialization influences and sources of influence. For example, a child raised with his or her extended family nearby will grow up with a different sense of family life than a child whose relatives live far away. Those relatives, too, are affected by that situation and that child, depending upon how close and frequent their contact is with the child.

Assessing Vygotsky's Theory. Sociocultural theory has become increasingly influential, despite Vygotsky's death almost 8 decades ago. The reason is the growing acknowledgment of the central importance of cultural factors in development. Children do not develop in a cultural vacuum. Instead, their attention is directed by society to certain areas, and as a consequence, they develop particular kinds of skills. Vygotsky was one of the first developmentalists to recognize and acknowledge the importance of the cultural environment, and—as today's society becomes increasingly multicultural—sociocultural theory helps us to understand the rich and varied influences that shape development (Koshmanova, 2007; Rogan, 2007; Mahn & John-Steiner, 2013).

Sociocultural theory is not without its critics, however. Some suggest that Vygotsky's strong emphasis on the role of culture and social experience led him to ignore the effects of biological factors on development. In addition, his perspective seems to minimize the role that individuals play in shaping their environment.

Evolutionary Perspectives: Our Ancestors' Contributions to Behavior

One increasingly influential approach is the evolutionary perspective, the sixth and final developmental perspective that we will consider. The **evolutionary perspective** seeks to identify behavior that is the result of our genetic inheritance from our ancestors (Buss & Reeve, 2003; Bjorklund, 2005; Goetz & Shackelford, 2006). **Watch** the **Video** *Thinking Like a Psychologist: Evolutionary Psychology* in **MyPsychLab.**

Konrad Lorenz, seen here with geese who from their birth have followed him, considered the ways in which behavior reflects inborn genetic patterns.

Evolutionary approaches grow out of the groundbreaking work of Charles Darwin. In 1859, Darwin argued in *On the Origin of Species* that a process of natural selection creates traits in a species that are adaptive to its environment. Using Darwin's arguments, evolutionary approaches contend that our genetic inheritance not only determines such physical traits as skin and eye color, but certain personality traits and social behaviors as well. For instance, some evolutionary developmentalists suggest that behaviors such as shyness and jealousy are produced in part by genetic causes, presumably because they helped in increasing survival rates of humans' ancient relatives (Buss, 2003, 2012; Easton, Schipper, & Shackelford, 2007).

The evolutionary perspective draws heavily on the field of *ethology*, which examines the ways in which our biological makeup influences our behavior. A primary proponent of ethology was Konrad Lorenz (1903–1989), who discovered that newborn geese are genetically preprogrammed to become attached to the first moving object they see after birth. His work, which demonstrated the importance of biological determinants in influencing behavior patterns, led developmentalists to consider the ways in which human behavior might reflect inborn genetic patterns.

The evolutionary perspective encompasses one of the fastest growing areas within the field of lifespan development: behavioral genetics. *Behavioral genetics* studies the effects of heredity on behavior. Behavioral geneticists seek to understand how we might inherit certain behavioral traits and how the environment influences whether we actually display those traits. It also considers how genetic factors may produce psychological disorders such as schizophrenia (Li, 2003; Bjorklund & Ellis, 2005; Rembis, 2009).

Assessing the Evolutionary Perspective. There is little argument among lifespan developmentalists that Darwin's evolutionary theory provides an accurate description of basic genetic processes, and the evolutionary perspective is increasingly visible in the field of lifespan development. However, applications of the evolutionary perspective have been subjected to considerable criticism.

evolutionary perspective the theory that seeks to identify behavior that is a result of our genetic inheritance from our ancestors

Some developmentalists are concerned that because of its focus on genetic and biological aspects of behavior, the evolutionary perspective pays insufficient attention to the environmental and social factors involved in producing children's and adults' behavior. Other critics argue that there is no good way to experimentally test theories derived from this approach because humans evolved so long ago. For example, it is one thing to say that jealousy helped individuals to survive more effectively and another thing to prove it. Still, the evolutionary approach has stimulated research on how our biological inheritance influences at least partially our traits and behaviors (Buss & Reeve, 2003; Bjorklund, 2006; Baptista et al., 2008).

Why "Which Approach Is Right?" Is the Wrong Question

We have considered the six major perspectives on development—psychodynamic, behavioral, cognitive, humanistic, contextual, and evolutionary—summarized in Table 1-3 and applied to a specific case. It would be natural to wonder which of the six provides the most accurate account of human development.

For several reasons, this is not an appropriate question. For one thing, each perspective emphasizes different aspects of development. For instance, the psychodynamic approach emphasizes unconscious determinants of behavior, while behavioral perspectives emphasize overt behavior. The cognitive and humanistic perspectives look more at what people *think* than at what they do. The contextual perspective examines social and cultural influences on development, and the evolutionary perspective focuses on how inherited biological factors underlie development.

For example, a developmentalist using the psychodynamic approach might consider how the 9/11 terrorist attacks on the World Trade Center and Pentagon might affect children, unconsciously, for their entire life span. A cognitive approach might focus on how children perceived and came to interpret and understand terrorism, while a contextual approach might consider what personality and social factors led the perpetrators to adopt terrorist tactics.

Clearly, each perspective is based on its own premises and focuses on different aspects of development. Furthermore, the same developmental phenomenon can be looked at from a number of perspectives simultaneously. In fact, some lifespan developmentalists use an *eclectic* approach, drawing on several perspectives simultaneously.

TABLE 1-3 MAJOR PERSPECTIVES ON LIFESPAN DEVELOPMENT

Perspective	Key Ideas About Human Behavior and Development	Major Proponents	Example
Psychodynamic	Behavior throughout life is motivated by inner, unconscious forces, stemming from childhood, over which we have little control.	Sigmund Freud, Erik Erikson	This view might suggest that a young adult who is overweight has a fixation in the oral stage of development.
Behavioral	Development can be understood through studying observable behavior and environmental stimuli.	John B. Watson, B. F. Skinner, Albert Bandura	In this perspective, a young adult who is overweight might be seen as not being rewarded for good nutritional and exercise habits.
Cognitive	Emphasis on how changes or growth in the ways people know, understand, and think about the world affect behavior.	Jean Piaget	This view might suggest that a young adult who is overweight hasn't learned effective ways to stay at a healthy weight and doesn't value good nutrition.
Humanistic	Behavior is chosen through free will and motivated by our natural capacity to strive to reach our full potential.	Carl Rogers, Abraham Maslow	In this view, a young adult who is overweight may eventually choose to seek an optimal weight as part of an overall pattern of individual growth.
Contextual	Development should be viewed in terms of the interrelationship of a person's physical, cognitive, personality, and social worlds.	Urie Bronfenbrenner, Lev Vygotsky	In this perspective, being overweight is caused by a number of interrelated factors in that person's physical, cognitive, personality, and social worlds.
Evolutionary	Behavior is the result of genetic inheritance from our ancestors; traits and behavior that are adaptive for promoting the survival of our species have been inherited through natural selection.	Influenced by early work of Charles Darwin, Konrad Lorenz	This view might suggest that a young adult might have a genetic tendency toward obesity because extra fat helped his or her ancestors to survive in times of famine.

In the same way, the various theoretical perspectives provide different ways of looking at development. Considering them together paints a fuller portrait of the myriad ways human beings change and grow over the course of their lives. However, not all theories and claims derived from the various perspectives are accurate. How do we choose among competing explanations? The answer can be found through *research*, which we consider in the final part of this chapter.

REVIEW, CHECK, AND APPLY

REVIEW

LO7 What are the main characteristics of the humanistic, contextual, and evolutionary perspectives?

- The humanistic perspective maintains that individuals have the ability and motivation to reach advanced levels of maturity and that people naturally seek to reach their full potential.
- The contextual perspective considers the relationship between individuals and their physical, cognitive, personality, and social worlds. Bronfenbrenner's bioecological approach and Vygotsky's sociocultural theory fall into this category.
- The evolutionary perspective attempts to identify behavior that is a result of our genetic inheritance.

LO8 Why is there no "right" approach to development?

- The theoretical perspectives provide different ways of looking at development. Considering them together paints a fuller portrait of the myriad ways human beings change and grow over the course of their lives.
- However, not all theories and claims derived from the various perspectives are accurate.

CHECK YOURSELF

1. According to the humanistic perspective, people reject the urge to seek love and respect from others and strive to achieve personal independence free of societal interconnections.
   - True
   - False
2. Bronfenbrenner's bioecological approach and Vygotsky's sociocultural theory fall under the category of the _____ perspective.
   - a humanistic
   - b ethnological
   - c contextual
   - d evolutionary
3. The researcher most closely associated with the evolutionary perspective is _____.
   - a Konrad Lorenz
   - b Jean Piaget
   - c Carl Rogers
   - d B. F. Skinner

APPLYING LIFESPAN DEVELOPMENT

- Can you think of people you have known who exhibited distinct signs of being in a stage of psychosocial development discussed by Erikson? What stage were they in and what were the signs?

✓ **Study** and **Review** on **MyPsychLab.com**

MODULE 1.3

RESEARCH METHODS

The Greek historian Herodotus wrote of an experiment conducted by Psamtik, the King of Egypt in the seventh century B.C. Psamtik was eager to prove a cherished Egyptian belief, that his people were the oldest race on earth. To test this notion, he developed a hypothesis: If a child was never exposed to the language of his elders, he would instinctively adopt the primal language of humanity—the original language of the first people. Psamtik was certain this would be Egyptian.

For his experiment, Psamtik entrusted two Egyptian infants to the care of a herdsman in an isolated area. They were to be well looked after, but not allowed to leave their cottage. And they were never to hear anyone speak a single word.

When Herodotus investigated the story, the priests of Hephaestus in Memphis told him that Psamtik's quest "was to know, after the indistinct babblings of infancy were over, what word [the children] would first articulate." Herodotus claims the experiment worked, but not as Psamtik had hoped. One day, when the children were 2 years old, they greeted the herdsman with the word "Becos!" The herdsman didn't know this word but when the children continued to use it, he contacted Psamtik. The king sent for the children who repeated the strange word to him. Psamtik did some research. Becos, it evolved, was "bread" in Phrygian. Psamtik had to conclude the Phrygians had preceded the Egyptians.

With the perspective of several thousand years, we can easily see the shortcomings—both scientific and ethical—in Psamtik's approach. Yet his procedure represents an improvement over mere speculation, and as such is sometimes looked upon as the first developmental experiment in recorded history (Hunt, 1993).

THEORIES, HYPOTHESES, AND CORRELATIONAL STUDIES

LO9 What roles do theories and hypotheses play in the study of development?
LO10 What sorts of studies and methods are used in correlational research?

Theories and Hypotheses: Posing Developmental Questions

Questions such as those raised by Psamtik drive the study of development. In fact, developmentalists are still studying how children learn language. Others are working on such questions as, What are the effects of malnutrition on intellectual performance? How do infants form relationships with their parents, and does day care disrupt such relationships? Why are adolescents particularly susceptible to peer pressure? Can mentally challenging activities reduce the declines in intellectual abilities related to aging? Do any mental faculties improve with age?

To answer such questions, developmentalists, like all psychologists and other scientists, rely on the scientific method. The **scientific method** is the process of posing and answering questions using careful, controlled techniques that include systematic, orderly observation and the collection of data. The scientific method involves three major steps: (1) identifying questions of interest, (2) formulating an explanation, and (3) carrying out research that either lends support to the explanation or refutes it.

The scientific method involves the formulation of theories, broad explanations, and predictions about phenomena of interest. For instance, the idea that there is a crucial bonding period between parent and child immediately after birth is a theory.

Developmental researchers use theories to form hypotheses. A **hypothesis** is a prediction stated in a way that permits it to be tested. For instance, someone who subscribes to the general theory that bonding is crucial might derive the hypothesis that effective bonding occurs only if it lasts for a certain length of time.

Choosing a Research Strategy: Answering Questions

Once researchers have formed a hypothesis, they must develop a research strategy to test its validity. There are two major categories of research: correlational research and experimental research. Correlational research seeks to identify whether an association or relationship between two factors exists. As we'll see, **correlational research** cannot determine whether one factor *causes* changes in the other. For instance, correlational research could tell us if there is an association between the number of minutes a mother and her newborn child are together immediately after birth and the quality of the mother–child relationship when the child reaches age 2. Such correlational research indicates whether the two factors are *associated* or *related* to one another, but not whether the initial contact caused the relationship to develop in a particular way (Schutt, 2001).

In contrast, **experimental research** is designed to discover *causal* relationships between various factors. In experimental research, researchers deliberately introduce a change in a carefully structured situation in order to see the consequences of that change. For instance, a researcher conducting an experiment might vary the number of minutes that mothers and children interact immediately following birth, in an attempt to see whether the bonding time affects the mother–child relationship.

Because experimental research is able to answer questions of causality, it is fundamental to finding answers to various developmental hypotheses. However, some research questions cannot be answered through experiments, for either technical or ethical reasons (e.g., it would be unethical to design an experiment in which a group of infants was offered no chance to bond with a caregiver at all). In fact, a great deal of pioneering developmental research—such as that conducted by Piaget and Vygotsky—employed correlational techniques. Consequently, correlational research remains an important tool for developmental researchers.

scientific method the process of posing and answering questions using careful, controlled techniques that include systematic, orderly observation and the collection of data

hypothesis a prediction stated in a way that permits it to be tested

correlational research research that seeks to identify whether an association or relationship between two factors exists

experimental research research designed to discover causal relationships between various factors

Correlational Studies

As we've noted, correlational research examines the relationship between two variables to determine whether they are associated, or *correlated*. For instance, researchers interested in the relationship between televised aggression and subsequent behavior have found that children who watch a good deal of aggression on television—murders, crime shows, shootings, and the like—tend to be more aggressive than those who watch only a little. In other words, viewing aggression and actual aggression are strongly associated, or correlated (Center for Communication & Social Policy, 1998; Singer & Singer, 2000; Feshbach & Tangney, 2008; Coyne et al., 2009).

But can we conclude that the viewing of televised aggression *causes* the more aggressive behavior? Not at all. Consider some of the other possibilities: It might be that being aggressive in the first place makes children more likely to choose to watch violent programs. In this case, the aggressive tendency causes the viewing behavior, not the other way around.

Or consider that there may be a *third* factor operating on both the viewing and the aggression. Suppose, for example, that children of lower socioeconomic status are more likely to behave aggressively *and* to watch higher levels of aggressive television than those raised in more affluent settings. In this case, the third variable—socioeconomic status—causes *both* the aggressive behavior and the television viewing. (The various possibilities are illustrated in Figure 1-2.)

In short, finding that two variables are correlated proves nothing about causality. Although the variables may be linked causally, this is not necessarily the case.

Correlational studies do provide important information, however. For instance, as we'll see in later chapters, we know from correlational studies that the closer the genetic link between two people, the more highly associated is their intelligence. We have learned that the more parents speak to their young children, the more extensive are the children's vocabularies. And we know from correlational studies that the better the nutrition that infants receive, the

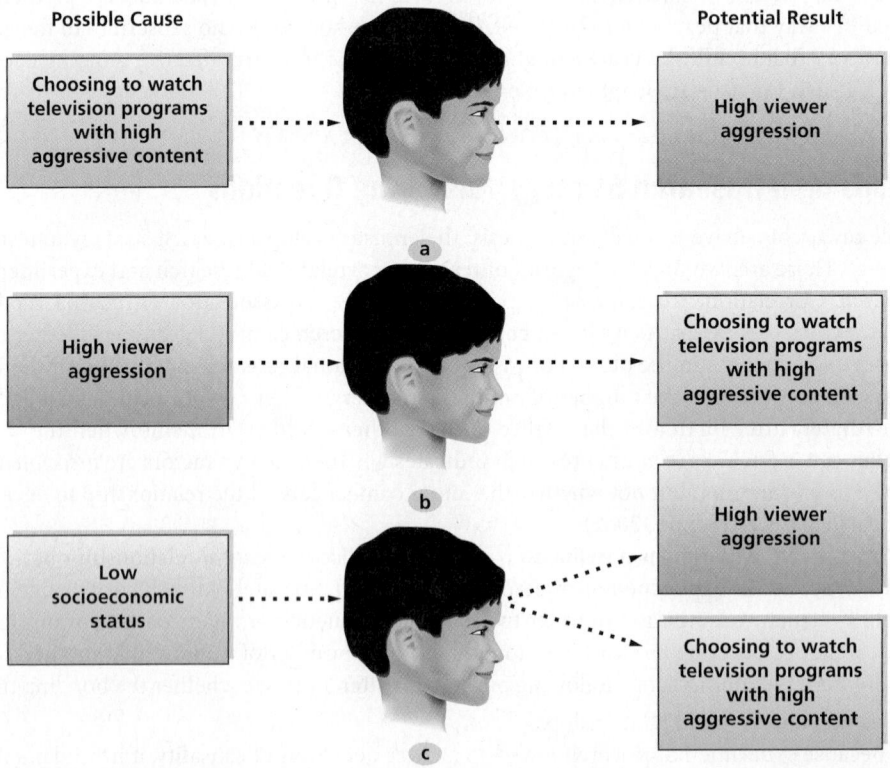

FIGURE 1-2 Finding a Correlation
Finding a correlation between two factors does not imply that one factor *causes* the other factor to vary. For instance, suppose a study found that viewing television shows with high levels of aggression is correlated with actual aggression in children. The correlation may reflect at least three possibilities: (a) watching television programs containing high levels of aggression causes aggression in viewers; (b) children who behave aggressively choose to watch TV programs with high levels of aggression; or (c) some third factor, such as a child's socioeconomic status, leads both to high viewer aggression and to choosing to watch television programs with high viewer aggression. What other factors, besides socioeconomic status, might be plausible third factors?

fewer the cognitive and social problems they experience later (Hart, 2004; Colom, Lluis-Font, & Andrés-Pueyo, 2005; Robb, Richert, & Wartella, 2009).

The Correlation Coefficient. The strength and direction of a relationship between two factors is represented by a mathematical score, called a *correlation coefficient*, that ranges from +1.0 to −1.0. A *positive* correlation indicates that as the value of one factor increases, it can be predicted that the value of the other will also increase. For instance, if we administer a job satisfaction survey and find that the more money people make in their first job, the higher their job satisfaction, and the less money they make the lower their job satisfaction, we have found a positive correlation The correlation coefficient would be indicated by a positive number, and the stronger the association between salary and job satisfaction, the closer the number would be to +1.0.

In contrast, a correlation coefficient with a *negative* value informs us that as the value of one factor increases, the value of the other factor declines. For example, suppose we found that the more time adolescents spend using instant messaging on their computers, the worse their academic performance is. This would produce a negative correlation, a number between 0 and −1. More instant messaging would be associated with lower performance, and less instant messaging with higher performance. The stronger the association between instant messaging and school performance, the closer the correlation coefficient will be to −1.0.

Finally, it may be that two factors are unrelated to one another. For example, it is unlikely that we would find a correlation between school performance and shoe size. In this case, the lack of a relationship would be indicated by a correlation coefficient close to 0.

It is important to repeat that, even if a correlation coefficient is very strong, there is no way we can know whether one factor *causes* the other factor to vary. It simply means that the two factors are associated with one another in a predictable way.

Types of Correlational Studies. There are several types of correlational studies. **Naturalistic observation** is the observation of a naturally occurring behavior without intervention. For instance, an investigator who wishes to learn how often preschool children share toys might observe a classroom over a 3-week period, recording how often the preschoolers spontaneously share with one another. The key point is that the investigator observes without interfering (e.g., Prezbindowski & Lederberg, 2003; Mortensen & Cialdini, 2010; Fanger, Frankel, & Hazen, 2012).

Though naturalistic observation has the advantage of identifying what children do in their "natural habitat," there is an important drawback to the method: Researchers are unable to exert control over factors of interest. For instance, in some cases researchers might find so few naturally occurring instances of the behavior of interest that they are unable to draw any conclusions at all.

Ethnography and qualitative research. Increasingly, naturalistic observation employs *ethnography*, a method that borrows from anthropology and is used to investigate cultural questions. In ethnography, the goal is to understand a culture's values and attitudes through careful, extended examination. Typically, researchers act as participant observers, living for a period of weeks, months, or even years in another culture. By carefully observing everyday life and conducting in-depth interviews, researchers can obtain a deep understanding of life within another culture (Dyson, 2003).

Ethnographic studies are an example of a broader category of research known as qualitative research. In *qualitative research*, researchers choose particular settings of interest and seek to carefully describe, in narrative fashion, what is occurring, and why. Qualitative research can be used to generate hypotheses that can later be tested using more objective, quantitative methods.

Although ethnographic and qualitative studies provide a fine-grained view of behavior in particular settings, they suffer from several drawbacks. As mentioned, the presence of a participant observer may influence the behavior of the individuals being studied. Furthermore, because only a small number of individuals are studied, it may be hard to generalize the findings to other settings. Finally, ethnographers carrying out cross-cultural research may misinterpret and misconceive what they are observing, particularly in cultures that are very different from their own (Polkinghorne, 2005).

Case studies involve extensive, in-depth interviews with a particular individual or small group of individuals. They often are used not just to learn about the individual being interviewed, but to derive broader principles or draw tentative conclusions that might apply to others. For example, case studies have been conducted on children who display unusual genius

naturalistic observation a type of correlational study in which some naturally occurring behavior is observed without intervention in the situation

case studies studies that involve extensive, in-depth interviews with a particular individual or small group of individuals

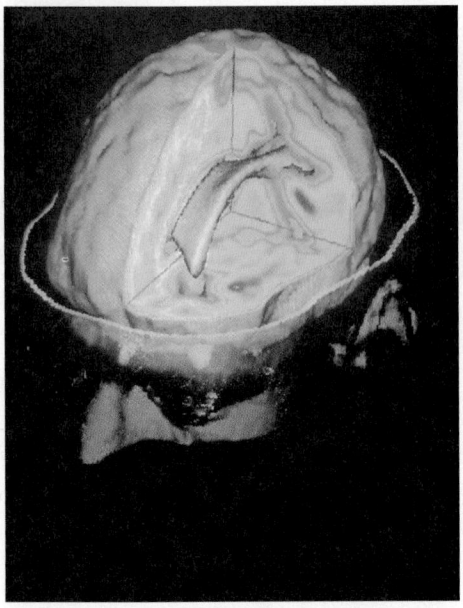

This fMRI shows activity in different regions of the brain.

and on children who have spent their early years in the wild, apparently without human contact. These case studies have provided important information to researchers and have suggested hypotheses for future investigation (Wilson, 2003; Ng & Nicholas, 2010; Halkier, 2013).

Using *diaries*, participants are asked to keep a record of their behavior on a regular basis. For example, a group of adolescents may be asked to record each time they interact with friends for more than 5 minutes, thereby providing a way to track their social behavior.

Surveys represent another sort of correlational research. In **survey research**, a group of people chosen to represent some larger population are asked questions about their attitudes, behavior, or thinking on a given topic. For instance, surveys have been conducted about parents' use of punishment on their children and on attitudes toward breastfeeding. From the responses, inferences are drawn regarding the larger population represented by the individuals being surveyed.

Psychophysiological Methods. Some developmental researchers, particularly those using a cognitive neuroscience approach, make use of psychophysiological methods. **Psychophysiological methods** focus on the relationship between physiological processes and behavior. For instance, a researcher might examine the relationship between blood flow in the brain and problem-solving ability. Similarly, some studies use infants' heart rate as a measure of their interest in stimuli to which they are exposed (Santesso, Schmidt, & Trainor, 2007; Field, Diego, & Hernandez-Reif, 2009; Mazoyer et al., 2009).

Among the most frequently used psychophysiological measures:

- **Electroencephalogram (EEG).** The EEG uses electrodes placed on the skull to record electrical activity in the brain. The brain activity is transformed into a pictorial representation of brain wave patterns, permitting the diagnosis of disorders such as epilepsy and learning disabilities.
- **Computerized axial tomography (CAT) scan.** In a CAT scan, a computer constructs an image of the brain by combining thousands of individual x-rays taken at slightly different angles. Although it does not show brain activity, it does illuminate the structure of the brain.
- **Functional magnetic resonance imaging (fMRI) scan.** An fMRI provides a detailed, three-dimensional computer-generated image of brain activity by aiming a powerful magnetic field at the brain. It offers one of the best ways of learning about the operation of the brain, down to the level of individual nerves.

survey research a type of study where a group of people chosen to represent some larger population are asked questions about their attitudes, behavior, or thinking on a given topic

psychophysiological methods research that focuses on the relationship between physiological processes and behavior

REVIEW, CHECK, AND APPLY

REVIEW

L09 What roles do theories and hypotheses play in the study of development?

- Theories are systematically derived explanations of facts or phenomena.
- Theories suggest hypotheses, which are predictions that can be tested.

L010 What sorts of studies and methods are used in correlational research?

- Correlational studies examine the relationship, or correlation, between two factors without demonstrating causality.
- Correlational methods include naturalistic observation, ethnography, case studies, survey research, and psychophysiological methods.

CHECK YOURSELF

1. Consider the following steps of the scientific method and rank them from first to last.

   a 3 Formulating an explanation.

   b 2 Carrying out research that either lends support to the explanation or refutes it.

   c 1 Identifying questions of interest.

2. In order to make a prediction in such a way that permits it to be tested, one must make a(n) _____.

   a theory

   b hypothesis

   c analysis

   d judgment

3. A researcher stands near an intersection and writes down the time it takes for the lead driver to start up after the light turns green. The researcher records the gender and approximate age of the driver. This researcher is most likely engaged in _____.

   a a case study

   b naturalistic observation

   c an ethnography

   d survey research

4. Researchers using correlational methods typically use a study group and a control group to isolate cause-and-effect relationships.

   True

   False

APPLYING LIFESPAN DEVELOPMENT

- Formulate a theory about one aspect of human development and a hypothesis that relates to it.

✓ **Study** and **Review** on **MyPsychLab.com**

EXPERIMENTS: DETERMINING CAUSE AND EFFECT

LO11 What are the characteristics of experimental research?
LO12 Why is it important to think critically about "expert" advice?

In an **experiment**, an investigator or experimenter typically devises two different conditions (or *treatments*) and then compares how the behavior of the participants exposed to each condition is affected. One group, the *treatment* or *experimental group*, is exposed to the treatment variable being studied; the other, the *control group*, is not.

For instance, suppose you want to see if exposure to movie violence makes viewers more aggressive. You might show a group of adolescents a series of movies with a great deal of violent imagery. You would then measure their subsequent aggression. This group would constitute the treatment group. For the control group you might show a second group of adolescents movies that contain no violent imagery, and measure their subsequent aggression. By comparing the amount of aggression displayed by members of the treatment and control groups, you would be able to determine if exposure to violent imagery produces aggression in viewers. In fact, this describes an experiment conducted at the University of Louvain in Belgium. Psychologist Jacques-Philippe Leyens and colleagues found that the level of aggression rose significantly for the adolescents who had seen the movies containing violence (Leyens et al., 1975).

The central feature of this experiment—and all experiments—is the comparison of the consequences of different treatments. The use of both treatment and control groups allows researchers to rule out the possibility that something other than the experimental manipulation produced the results found in the experiment. For instance, if a control group was not used, experimenters could not be certain that some other factor, such as the time of day the movies were shown or even the mere passage of time, produced the observed changes. By using a control group, experimenters can draw accurate conclusions about causes and effects.

Independent and Dependent Variables. The **independent variable** is the variable that researchers manipulate in the experiment (in our example, it is the type of movie participants saw—violent or non-violent). In contrast, the **dependent variable** is the variable that researchers measure to see if it changes as a result of the experimental manipulation. In our example, the degree of aggressive behavior shown by the participants after viewing violent or nonviolent films is the dependent variable. (One way to remember the difference: A hypothesis predicts how a dependent variable *depends* on the manipulation of the independent variable.) Every experiment has an independent and dependent variable.

Experimenters must make sure their studies are not influenced by factors other than those they are manipulating. For this reason, they take great care to make sure that the participants in both the treatment and control groups are not aware of the purpose of the experiment (which could affect their responses or behavior) and that the experimenters do not influence who is chosen for the control and treatment groups. The procedure that is used for this is known as random assignment. In *random assignment*, participants are assigned to different experimental groups or "conditions" purely on the basis of chance. This way the laws of statistics ensure that personal characteristics that might affect the outcome of the experiment are divided proportionally among the participants in the different groups, making the groups equivalent. Equivalent groups achieved by random assignment allow an experimenter to draw conclusions with confidence.

Figure 1-3 illustrates the Belgian experiment on adolescents exposed to films containing violent or non-violent imagery, and the effects of such imagery on subsequent aggressive behavior. As you can see, it contains each of the elements of an experiment:

- An independent variable (the assignment to a violent or nonviolent film condition)
- A dependent variable (measurement of the adolescents' aggressive behavior)
- Random assignment to condition (viewing a film with violent imagery versus a film with nonviolent imagery)
- A hypothesis that predicts the effect the independent variable will have on the dependent variable (that viewing a film with violent imagery will produce subsequent aggression)

experiment a process in which an investigator, called an experimenter, devises two different experiences for participants

independent variable the variable that researchers manipulate in an experiment

dependent variable the variable that researchers measure to see if it changes as a result of the experimental manipulation

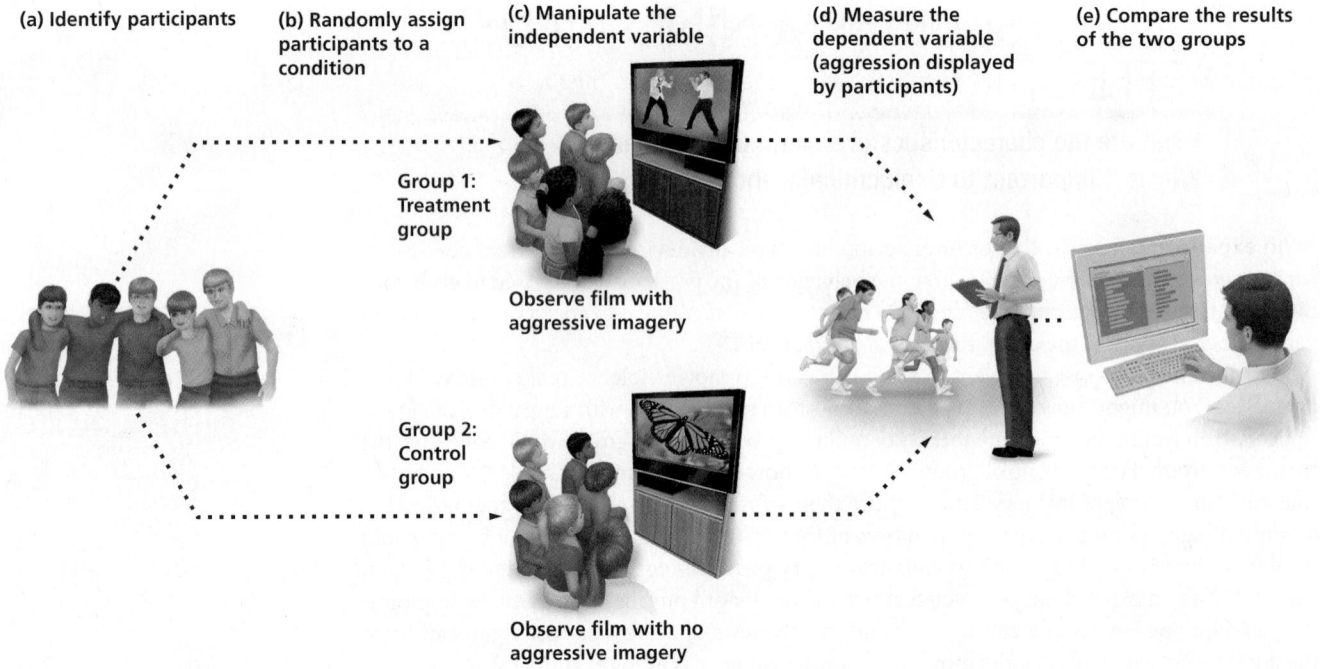

FIGURE 1-3 Elements of an Experiment
In this experiment, researchers randomly assigned a group of adolescents to one of two conditions: viewing a film that contained violent imagery or viewing a film that lacked violent imagery (manipulation of the independent variable). Then participants were observed later to determine how much aggression they showed (the dependent variable). Analysis of the findings showed that adolescents exposed to aggressive imagery showed more aggression later (based on an experiment by Leyens et al., 1975).

Given the advantage of experiments—that they provide a means of determining causality—why aren't experiments always used? The answer is that there are some situations that a researcher, no matter how ingenious, simply cannot control. And there are some situations in which control would be unethical, even if it were possible. For instance, no researcher would be able to assign different groups of infants to parents of high and low socioeconomic status in order to learn the effects of such status on subsequent development. In situations in which experiments are logistically or ethically impossible, developmentalists employ correlational research.

Furthermore, keep in mind that a single experiment is insufficient to answer a research question definitively. Before complete confidence can be placed in a conclusion, research must be *replicated*, or repeated, sometimes using other procedures and techniques with other participants. Sometimes developmentalists use a procedure called *meta-analysis*, which permits the combination of results of many studies into one overall conclusion (Peterson & Brown, 2005; Le et al., 2010). **Watch** the **Video** *The Basics: Scientific Research Methods* in **MyPsychLab**.

Choosing a Research Setting. Deciding *where* to conduct a study may be as important as determining *what* to do. In the Belgian experiment on the influence of exposure to media aggression, the researchers used a real-world setting—a group home for boys who had been convicted of juvenile delinquency. They chose this **sample**, the group of participants chosen for the experiment, because it was useful to have adolescents whose normal level of aggression was relatively high, and because they could incorporate the films into the everyday life of the home with minimal disruption.

Using a real-world setting (as in the aggression experiment) is the hallmark of a field study. A **field study** is a research investigation carried out in a naturally occurring setting. Field studies capture behavior in real-life settings, where research participants may behave more naturally than in a laboratory.

Field studies may be used in both correlational studies and experiments. They typically employ naturalistic observation, the technique in which researchers observe a naturally occurring behavior without intervening or changing the situation. A researcher might examine behavior in a child-care center, view the groupings of adolescents in high school corridors, or observe elderly adults in a senior center.

sample the group of participants chosen for the experiment

field study a research investigation carried out in a naturally occurring setting

Because it is often difficult to control the situation and environment enough to run an experiment in a real-world setting, field studies are more typical of correlational designs than experimental designs. Most developmental research experiments are conducted in laboratory settings. A **laboratory study** is a research investigation conducted in a controlled setting explicitly designed to hold events constant. The laboratory may be a room or building designed for research, as in a university psychology department. Their ability to control the settings in laboratory studies enables researchers to learn more clearly how their treatments affect participants.

Theoretical and Applied Research: Complementary Approaches

In experimental research, developmentalists use controlled conditions to discover causal relationships between various factors.

Developmental researchers typically focus on either theoretical research or applied research. **Theoretical research** is designed to test some developmental explanation and expand scientific knowledge, while **applied research** is meant to provide practical solutions to immediate problems. For instance, if we were interested in the processes of cognitive change during childhood, we might carry out a study of how many digits children of various ages can remember after one exposure to multidigit numbers—a theoretical approach. Alternatively, we might focus on the more practical question of how teachers can help children to remember information more easily. Such a study would represent applied research, because the findings are applied to a particular setting and problem.

There is not always a clear distinction between theoretical and applied research. For instance, is a study that examines the consequences of ear infections in infancy on later hearing loss theoretical or applied? Because such a study may help illuminate the basic processes involved in hearing, it can be considered theoretical. But if it helps to prevent hearing loss, it may be considered applied (Lerner, Fisher, & Weinberg, 2000).

In fact, as we discuss in the accompanying "From Research to Practice" box, research of both a theoretical and an applied nature has played a significant role in shaping and resolving a variety of public policy questions.

Measuring Developmental Change

How people grow and change through the life span is central to the work of all developmental researchers. Consequently, one of the thorniest research issues they face concerns the measurement of change and differences over age and time. To solve this problem, researchers have developed three major research strategies: longitudinal research, cross-sectional research, and sequential research.

Longitudinal Studies: Measuring Individual Change. If you were interested in learning how a child develops morally between 3 and 5, the most direct approach would be to take a group of 3-year-olds and follow them until they were 5, testing them periodically.

This strategy illustrates longitudinal research. In **longitudinal research**, the behavior of one or more study participants is measured as they age. Longitudinal research measures change over time. By following many individuals over time, researchers can understand the general course of change across some period of life.

The granddaddy of longitudinal studies, which has become a classic, is a study of gifted children begun by Lewis Terman about 80 years ago. In the study—which has yet to be concluded—a group of 1,500 children with high IQs were tested about every 5 years. Now in their 80s, the participants—who call themselves "Termites"—have provided information on everything from intellectual accomplishment to personality and longevity (Feldhusen, 2003; McCullough, Tsang, & Brion, 2003; Subotnik, 2006).

Longitudinal research has also provided insight into language development. For instance, by tracing how children's vocabularies increase on a day-by-day basis, researchers have been able to understand the processes that underlie the human ability to become competent in using language (Gershkoff-Stowe & Hahn, 2007; Oliver & Plomin, 2007; Childers, 2009; Fagan, 2009).

laboratory study a research investigation conducted in a controlled setting explicitly designed to hold events constant

theoretical research research designed specifically to test some developmental explanation and expand scientific knowledge

applied research research meant to provide practical solutions to immediate problems

longitudinal research research in which the behavior of one or more participants in a study is measured as they age

Longitudinal studies can provide a wealth of information about change over time, but they have drawbacks. For one thing, they require a tremendous investment of time, because researchers must wait for participants to become older. Furthermore, participants often drop out over the course of the research. Participants may drop out of a study, move away, or become ill or even die as the research proceeds.

Finally, participants who are observed or tested repeatedly may become "test-wise" and perform better each time they are assessed as they become more familiar with the procedure. Even if the observations of participants in a study are not terribly intrusive (such as simply recording, over a lengthy period of time, vocabulary increases in infants and preschoolers), experimental participants may be affected by the repeated presence of an experimenter or observer.

Consequently, despite the benefits of longitudinal research, particularly its ability to look at change within individuals, developmental researchers often turn to other methods. The alternative they choose most often is the cross-sectional study.

From Research to Practice

Does the Head Start preschool program actually work?

Are there drawbacks to using infant day care?

What are some effective ways to bolster schoolgirls' confidence in their math and science aptitude?

Are children better off with a mother and a father than they are with two mothers or two fathers?

Should children with developmental disabilities be schooled in regular classrooms, or are they better off in special classrooms with other children who are similarly disabled?

Each of these questions represents a national policy issue that can be answered only by considering the results of relevant research studies. By conducting controlled studies, developmental researchers have made a number of important contributions affecting education, family life, and health on a national scale. Consider, for instance, the variety of ways that public policy issues have been informed by various types of research findings (Brooks-Gunn, 2003; Maton et al., 2004; Mervis, 2004; Aber et al., 2007):

- *Research findings can provide policymakers a means of determining what questions to ask in the first place.* For example, studies of children's caregivers (some of which we'll consider in Chapter 10) have led policymakers to question whether the benefits of infant day care are outweighed by possible deterioration in parent–child bonds. Research has also disconfirmed the widespread belief that childhood vaccinations are linked to autism spectrum disorder, contributing invaluable evidence to the controversy over the risks and benefits of mandatory child immunization (Price et al., 2010).
- *Research findings and the testimony of researchers are often part of the process by which laws are drafted.* A good deal of legislation has been passed based on findings from developmental researchers. For example, research revealed that children with developmental disabilities benefit from exposure to children without special needs, ultimately leading to passage of national legislation mandating that children with disabilities be placed in regular school classes as often as possible. Research showing that children raised by same-sex couples fare just as well as children raised by a mother and father has undermined an often-used but baseless argument that same-sex marriage is harmful to children (Gartrell & Bos, 2010).
- *Policymakers and other professionals use research findings to determine how best to implement programs.* Research has shaped programs designed to reduce the incidence of unsafe sex among teenagers, to increase the level of prenatal care for pregnant mothers, to encourage and support women in the pursuit of math and science studies, and to promote flu shots for older adults. The common thread among such programs is that many of the details of the programs are built on basic research findings.
- *Research techniques are used to evaluate the effectiveness of existing programs and policies.* Once a public policy has been implemented, it is necessary to determine whether it has been effective and successful in accomplishing its goals. To do this, researchers employ formal evaluation techniques, developed from basic research procedures. For instance, researchers have continually scrutinized the Head Start preschool program, which has received massive federal funding, to ensure that it really does what it is supposed to do—improve children's academic performance.

  Similarly, careful studies of DARE, a popular program meant to reduce children's use of drugs, began to find that it was ineffective. Using the research findings of developmentalists, DARE instigated new techniques, and preliminary findings suggest that the revised program is more effective (Rhule, 2005; University of Akron, 2006).

By building on research findings, developmentalists have worked hand in hand with policymakers, and research has a substantial impact on public policies that can benefit us all.

- *What are some policy issues affecting children and adolescents that are currently being debated nationally?*
- *Despite the existence of research data that might inform policy about development, politicians rarely discuss such data in their speeches. Why do you think that is the case?*

Cross-Sectional Studies. Suppose again that you want to consider how children's moral development, their sense of right and wrong, changes from ages 3 to 5. Instead of following the same children over several years, we might look simultaneously at three groups of children: 3-year-olds, 4-year-olds, and 5-year-olds, perhaps presenting each group with the same problem and then seeing how they respond to it and explain their choices.

Such an approach typifies cross-sectional research. In **cross-sectional research**, people of different ages are compared at the same point in time. Cross-sectional studies provide information about differences in development between different age groups.

Cross-sectional research takes far less time than longitudinal research: Participants are tested at just one point in time. Terman's study might have been completed 75 years ago if Terman had simply looked at a group of gifted 15-year-olds, 20-year-olds, 25-year-olds, and so forth, up to 80-year-olds. Because the participants would not be periodically tested, there would be no chance that they would become test-wise, and problems of participant attrition would not occur. Why, then, would anyone choose to use a procedure other than cross-sectional research?

The answer is that cross-sectional research brings its own set of difficulties. Recall that every person belongs to a particular *cohort*, the group of people born at around the same time in the same place. If we find that people of different ages vary along some dimension, it may be due to differences in cohort membership, not age per se.

Consider a concrete example: If we find in a correlational study that people who are 25 perform better on a test of intelligence than those who are 75, there are several possible explanations other than that intelligence declines in old age. Instead, the finding may be attributable to cohort differences. The 75-year-olds may have had less formal education than the 15-year-olds because members of the older cohort were less likely to finish high school and attend college than members of the younger one. Or perhaps the older group received less adequate nutrition as infants than the younger group. In short, we cannot rule out the possibility that age-related differences in cross-sectional studies are actually cohort differences.

Cross-sectional studies may also suffer from *selective dropout*, in which participants in some age groups are more likely to stop participating than others. For example, suppose a study of cognitive development in preschoolers includes a long test of cognitive abilities, which young preschoolers find more difficult than older preschoolers. If more young children quit than the older preschoolers and if it is the least competent young preschoolers who drop out, then the remaining sample of that age group will consist of the more competent young preschoolers—together with a broader and more representative sample of older preschoolers. The results of such a study would be questionable (Miller, 1998).

Finally, cross-sectional studies have an additional, and more basic, disadvantage: They are unable to inform us about changes in individuals or groups. If longitudinal studies are like videos taken of a person at various ages, cross-sectional studies are like snapshots of entirely different groups. Although we can establish differences related to age, we cannot fully determine if such differences are related to change over time. **Explore** the **Concept** *Cross-Sectional and Longitudinal Research Designs* in **MyPsychLab**.

Sequential Studies. Because both longitudinal and cross-sectional studies have drawbacks, researchers have turned to some compromise techniques. Among the most frequently employed are sequential studies, which are essentially a combination of longitudinal and cross-sectional studies.

In **sequential studies**, researchers examine a number of different age groups at several points in time. For instance, an investigator interested in children's moral behavior might begin a sequential study by examining the behavior of three groups of children, who are either 3, 4, or 5 years old at the time the study begins.

The study continues for the next several years, with each participant tested annually. Thus, the 3-year-olds would be tested at ages 3, 4, and 5; the 4-year-olds at ages 4, 5, and 6; and the 5-year-olds at ages 5, 6, and 7. By combining the advantages of longitudinal and cross-sectional research, this approach permits developmental researchers to tease out the consequences of age *change* versus age *difference*. The major research techniques for studying development are summarized in Figure 1-4.

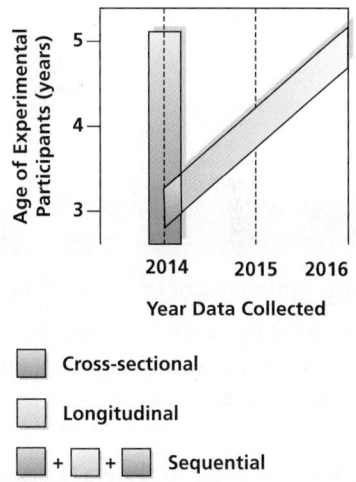

FIGURE 1-4 Research Techniques for Studying Development
In a *cross-sectional study*, 3-, 4-, and 5-year-olds are compared at a similar point in time (in 2014). In *longitudinal research*, a set of participants who are 3 years old in 2014 are studied when they are 4 years old (in 2015) and when they are 5 years old (in 2016). Finally, a *sequential study* combines cross-sectional and longitudinal techniques; here, a group of 3-year-olds would be compared initially in 2014 with 4- and 5-year-olds, but would also be studied 1 and 2 years later, when they themselves were 4 and 5 years old. Although the graph does not illustrate this, researchers carrying out this sequential study might also choose to retest the children who were 4 and 5 in 2014 for the next 2 years. What advantages do the three kinds of studies offer?

cross-sectional research research in which people of different ages are compared at the same point in time

sequential studies research in which researchers examine a number of different age groups over several points in time

Ethics and Research

In the "study" conducted by Egyptian King Psamtik, two children were removed from their mothers and held in isolation in an effort to learn about the roots of language. If you found yourself thinking this was extraordinarily cruel, you are in good company. Clearly, such an experiment raises blatant ethical concerns, and nothing like it would ever be done today.

But sometimes ethical issues are more subtle. For instance, U.S. government researchers proposed a conference to examine possible genetic roots of aggression. Some researchers had begun to raise the possibility that genetic markers might be found that would identify particularly violence-prone children. If so, it might be possible to track these children and provide interventions to reduce the likelihood of later violence.

Critics objected strenuously, however, arguing that identification might lead to a self-fulfilling prophecy. Children labeled as violence-prone might be treated in a way that would actually *cause* them to be more aggressive. Ultimately, under intense political pressure, the conference was canceled (Wright, 1995).

In order to help researchers deal with ethical problems, the major organizations of developmentalists, including the Society for Research in Child Development and the American Psychological Association, have developed ethical guidelines for researchers. Among the principles are those involving freedom from harm, informed consent, the use of deception,

Becoming an Informed Consumer of Development

Thinking Critically About "Expert" Advice

If you immediately comfort crying babies, you'll spoil them.

If you let babies cry without comforting them, they'll be untrusting and clingy as adults.

***

Spanking is one of the best ways to discipline your child.

Never hit your child.

***

If a marriage is unhappy, children are better off if their parents divorce than if they stay together.

No matter how difficult a marriage is, parents should avoid divorce for the sake of their children.

There is no lack of advice on the best way to raise a child or, more generally, to lead one's life. From bestsellers such as *Chicken Soup for the Soul: On Being a Parent,* to magazine and newspaper columns that provide advice on every imaginable topic, to a myriad of websites and blogs, each of us is exposed to tremendous amounts of information.

Yet not all advice is equally valid. The mere fact that something is in print, on television, or on the Web does not make it legitimate or accurate. Fortunately, some guidelines can help distinguish when recommendations and suggestions are reasonable and when they are not:

- Consider the source of the advice. Information from established, respected organizations such as the American Medical Association, the American Psychological Association, and the American Academy of Pediatrics reflects years of study and is usually accurate. If you don't know the organization, investigate it further to find out more about its goals and philosophy.
- Evaluate the credentials of the person providing advice. Trustworthy information tends to come from established, acknowledged researchers and experts, not from persons with obscure credentials. Consider where the author is employed and whether he or she has a particular political or personal agenda.
- Understand the difference between anecdotal evidence and scientific evidence. Anecdotal evidence is based on one or two instances of a phenomenon, haphazardly discovered or encountered; scientific evidence is based on careful, systematic procedures. If an aunt tells you that all her children slept through the night by 2 months of age and therefore your child will too, that is quite different from reading a report that 75 percent of children sleep through the night by 9 months. Of course, even with such a report, it would be a good idea to find out how large the study was or how this number was arrived at.
- If advice is based on research findings, there should be a clear, transparent description of the studies on which the advice is based. Who were the participants? What methods were used? What do the results show? Think critically about the way the findings were obtained before accepting them.
- Don't overlook the cultural context of the information. An assertion may be valid in some contexts, but not in all. For example, it is typically assumed that providing infants the freedom to move about and exercise their limbs facilitates their muscular development and mobility. Yet in some cultures, infants spend most of their time closely bound to their mothers—with no apparent long-term damage (Kaplan & Dove, 1987; Tronick, 1995).
- Don't assume that because many people believe something, it is necessarily true. Scientific evaluation has often proved that some of the most basic presumptions about the effectiveness of various techniques are invalid.

In short, the key to evaluating information relating to human development is to maintain a healthy dose of skepticism. No source of information is invariably, unfailingly accurate. By keeping a critical eye on the statements you encounter, you'll be in a better position to determine the very real contributions made by developmentalists to understanding how humans develop over the course of the life span.

and maintenance of participants' privacy (Sales & Folkman, 2000; American Psychological Association, 2002; Fisher, 2003, 2004, 2005; Curlette & Kern, 2010; Toporek, Kwan, & Williams, 2012):

- **Researchers must protect participants from physical and psychological harm.** Their welfare, interests, and rights come before those of researchers. In research, participants' rights always come first (Sieber, 2000; Fisher, 2004).
- **Researchers must obtain informed consent from participants before their involvement in a study.** If they are over the age of 7, participants must voluntarily agree to be in a study. If under 18, parents or guardians must also provide consent.

  Informed consent can be a sensitive requirement. Suppose, for instance, researchers want to study the psychological effects of abortion on adolescents. To obtain the consent of an adolescent minor who has had an abortion, the researchers would need to get her parents' permission as well. But if the adolescent hasn't told her parents about the abortion, the request for parental permission would violate her privacy—leading to a breach of ethics.
- **The use of deception in research must be justified and cause no harm.** Although deception to disguise the true purpose of an experiment is permissible, any experiment that uses deception must undergo careful scrutiny by an independent panel before it is conducted. Suppose, for example, we want to know the reaction of participants to success and failure. It is ethical to tell participants that they will be playing a game when the true purpose is actually to observe how they respond to doing well or poorly on the task. However, this is ethical only if it causes no harm to participants, has been approved by a review panel, and includes a full explanation for participants when the study is over (Underwood, 2005).
- **Participants' privacy must be maintained.** If participants are videotaped during a study, for example, they must give their permission for the videotapes to be viewed. Furthermore, access to the tapes must be carefully restricted.

From the perspective of a health care provider: Do you think there are some special circumstances involving adolescents, who are not legally adults, that would justify allowing them to participate in a study without obtaining their parents' permission? What might such circumstances involve?

REVIEW, CHECK, AND APPLY

REVIEW

L011 What are the characteristics of experimental research?

- Experimental research seeks to discover cause-and-effect relationships.
- Experiments typically create two different conditions and use an experimental group and a control group.
- Researchers measure age-related change by longitudinal studies, cross-sectional studies, and sequential studies.

L012 Why is it important to think critically about "expert" advice?

- Scientific evaluation has shown that some practices supposedly based on developmental research are at best dubious and at worst invalid.
- The key to evaluating information relating to human development is to maintain a healthy dose of skepticism.

CHECK YOURSELF

1. If a control group is not used in an experiment, the researcher cannot rule out the possibility that something other than the treatment produced the observed outcome.
   - True
   - False
2. In a(n) _____, an investigator devises two conditions (treatment or control) and compares the outcomes of the participants exposed to those two different conditions in order to see how behavior is affected.
   - a experiment
   - b correlational study
   - c interview
   - d naturalistic observation
3. In a _____research study, researchers are interested in measuring change in a single group of subjects over time.
   - a correlational
   - b cross-sectional
   - c longitudinal
   - d sequential

APPLYING LIFESPAN DEVELOPMENT

- High school students who routinely do their homework while writing text messages to friends, watching a program on television, and playing an electronic game in a window of their computer often claim that they are "multitasking" and are able to study more quickly and effectively this way. How might you design a basic experiment to test this claim?

Study and **Review** on **MyPsychLab.com**

SUMMARY

1 PUTTING IT ALL TOGETHER INTRODUCTION

MARCO RUIZ, watching the large, multigenerational reunion we encountered in the chapter opener, found himself pondering many of the questions that developmentalists study formally. Putting himself into his Grandpa's mind, he thought about how the traits for which his grandfather was noted might show up—or not—in the members of the generations at the reunion. He considered both inherited characteristics and personality traits and habits potentially acquired from social and environmental interactions. Marco's "thought experiment" on five generations of his grandfather's extended family gave him a lot to ponder, given the size and diversity of his experimental "sample."

MODULE 1.1 BEGINNINGS

- Marco's consideration of his five-generation household mirrors the work of developmentalists with a wide range of interests, including those who focus on genetic versus environmental influences, cognitive changes across the life span, and social and personality development. *(pp. 4–5)*
- The age range of Marco's family mirrors the full range that developmentalists cover, from before birth to old age. *(pp. 5–7)*
- Each family member naturally experiences different cohort influences, which interact with their shared genetic heritage. *(pp. 8–9)*
- Key issues in development are reflected in Marco's thoughts, including the nature–nurture issue and continuity versus discontinuity. *(pp. 8–12)*

MODULE 1.2 THEORETICAL PERSPECTIVES ON LIFESPAN DEVELOPMENT

- Developmentalists with different perspectives might guide Marco's musings. Erikson might help Marco interpret generational differences in his family in terms of stages along the life span; Piaget might illuminate little Alicia's developing thought processes; and Vygotsky might underscore the importance of social interactions in cognitive, social, and physical development. *(pp. 13–23)*
- Marco is likely to understand that it is best to avoid considering any particular theoretical perspective either all wrong or all right. *(pp. 23–24)*

MODULE 1.3 RESEARCH METHODS

- Marco reveals an instinctive knack for constructing theories about development and considering informal hypotheses to test them. *(pp. 25–27)*
- Marco asks questions about the development of his family members and himself through a combination of a sort of "life experiment" and naturalistic observation. *(pp. 27–28)*
- In a sense, Marco's curiosity about development contains elements of the case study (i.e., observing his family's life), longitudinal research (i.e., reflecting on and interpreting generational traits in his family), and the cross-sectional study (i.e., the family reunion) is a cross-section of development across the life span). *(pp. 29–34)*

What would an EDUCATOR do?

How could you prepare Terri and Tony, little Alicia's parents, for the changes in educational practice that may have occurred since they were in school? What might you tell them to look for in gauging young Alicia's cognitive, physical, and social readiness for school? What ideas could you give them to help Alicia prepare for school? Do you think Alicia's parents may need to be cautioned against taking Alicia's learning for granted, given their extended family's history of successful school experiences?

What would a PARENT do?

Marco is a parent and grandparent who is also a son and grandson. How would you suggest he balance his "upward" responsibilities toward his father and grandfather with his "downward" responsibilities toward his children and their children? Marco and Louise's children themselves represent a range of developmental stages and ages. How would you help them deal differently with the needs and potential sources of support that such a variety of children offers?

What would YOU do?

How would you help Marco understand his varying roles as a father, son, grandson, and grandfather? What things would you suggest that Marco's father and grandfather could help him with or advise him about? Has the role of father and grandfather changed too much for cross-generational wisdom to be shared helpfully?

What would a HEALTH CARE PROVIDER do?

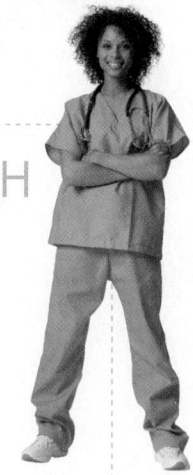

How would you help Marco and Louise understand the different stages of development, with all their varying states of physical, cognitive, and emotional health, represented in their family? How could you help them accept their power and limitations in perceiving and responding to their family's varied physical and emotional needs? How could you help Marco and Louise prepare for a death in their family (e.g., grandparent, parent, spouse, children, grandchildren)?

Explore on MyPsychLab

To read how real-life educators, health care providers, and parents responded to these questions, log on to MyPsychLab.com.

Do you agree or disagree with their responses? Why? What concepts that you've read about back up their opinion?

2 THE START OF LIFE

Dawn drove home in a state of shock. Her midwife had just confirmed that the baby Dawn was carrying was actually two babies. How would she ever juggle two infants? In contrast, her husband Lyle greeted the news with enthusiasm. Twins! He wondered if they were identical or fraternal. Would they both have sunny dispositions like Dawn or turn out to be worry-warts like his dad? Perhaps one of them would be adventurous while the other was cautious. He promised to cut back on the hours of his consulting business after the twins' birth to help with child care. In the meantime, they could knock down the wall between the two small rooms upstairs to make one good-sized nursery. And they would fence in a safe play yard.

In the following months, Dawn ate nutritious meals and joined an exercise class for pregnant women. She made friends in the group. Her midwife said it would help to know other new moms. Dawn also asked her sister Megan to be part of her birthing team. While Lyle was coaching her through labor, Megan could film the event.

In the 30th week, Dawn experienced weak, intermittent contractions. At the hospital, the doctor said the babies were fine, their heartbeats strong, but that twins were more susceptible to premature birth. The doctor ordered complete bed rest for the next 8 weeks. Dawn took her maternity leave early. She was often bored but 2 months later her twins—identical, girls—were born healthy.

In this chapter, we start our voyage through the life span at its logical beginning: conception. We discuss genetics and the ways in which genetic information is transmitted from parents to child. We then introduce a topic that receives a great deal of attention from developmentalists: the comparative roles of heredity and environment (or nature versus nurture) in forming the individual.

Next, we proceed through the stages of the prenatal period, from fertilization to the fetal stage. We look at factors that can affect the health and development of the fetus before birth.

We finish the chapter with a discussion of the process of birth, including the ways women experience labor and the choices that parents have available for care before and during childbirth. We touch on some of the complications that can attend birth, including infants born significantly before or after their due date. We end with a discussion of the considerable abilities that newborns possess from the moment they enter the world.

MODULE 2.1

PRENATAL DEVELOPMENT

What role is genetics playing in the prenatal development of Dawn and Lyle's babies?

MODULE 2.2

PRENATAL GROWTH AND CHANGE

What can Dawn and Lyle do, or avoid, to help their babies develop normally?

MODULE 2.3

BIRTH

What can Dawn and Lyle expect during each stage of labor?

MyVirtualLife

If you are currently using MyVirtualLife, consider how you will navigate the pregnancy and birth processes. What decisions will you make?

Access MyVirtualLife for a chance to live your own virtual life.

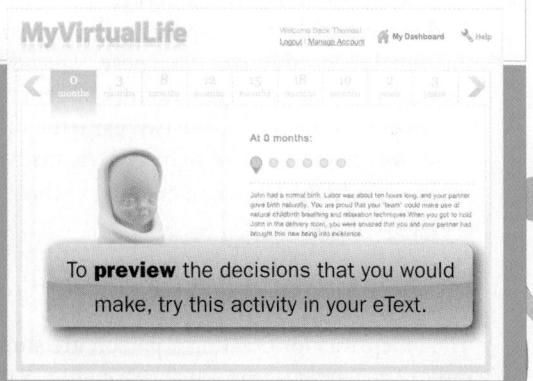

To **preview** the decisions that you would make, try this activity in your eText.

MODULE 2.1

PRENATAL DEVELOPMENT DIFFICULT DECISIONS

Leah and John Howard's joy at learning Leah was pregnant turned to anxiety when Leah's doctor discovered that her brother had died from Duchenne muscular dystrophy (DMD) at age 12. The disease, the doctor explained, was an X-linked inherited disorder. There was a chance Leah was a carrier. If so, there was a 50 percent chance that the baby would inherit the disease if it were a boy. The doctor advised them to have an ultrasound to determine the baby's sex. It turned out to be a boy.

The Howards faced new options. The doctor could take a chorion villus sampling now or wait a month and perform an amniocentesis. Both carried a very low risk for miscarriage. Leah chose amniocentesis, but the results were inconclusive. The doctor then suggested a fetal muscle biopsy to confirm the presence or lack of the muscle protein dystrophin. No dystrophin signaled DMD. The risk of miscarriage, however, was not inconsiderable.

Four months pregnant at this point and tired of the worries and tears, Leah and John decided to take their chances and look forward to their baby's birth.

The Howards' decision to forego a fetal muscle biopsy does not change the outcome. They did not wish to consider a late-term abortion and DMD has no cure.

But their case illustrates the difficult decisions that parents sometimes face because of advances in the identification of inherited disorders and our understanding of genetics.

In this chapter, we'll examine what developmental researchers and other scientists have learned about ways that heredity and the environment work in tandem to create and shape human beings, and how that knowledge is being used to improve people's lives. We begin with the basics of heredity, the genetic transmission of characteristics from biological parents to their children, by examining how we receive our genetic endowment. We'll consider an area of study, behavioral genetics, that specializes in the consequences of heredity on behavior. We'll also discuss what happens when genetic factors cause development to go off track, and how such problems are dealt with through genetic counseling and, in some cases, manipulation of a child's genes.

But genes are only one part of the story of prenatal development. We'll also consider the ways in which a child's genetic heritage interacts with the environment in which he or she grows up—how one's family, socioeconomic status, and life events can affect a variety of characteristics, including physical traits, intelligence, and even personality.

EARLIEST DEVELOPMENT

LO1 What is our basic genetic endowment?
LO2 What are the major genetic threats to normal development?
LO3 What is the role of behavioral genetics?

We humans begin the course of our lives simply.

Like individuals from tens of thousands of other species, we start as a single tiny cell weighing no more than one 20-millionth of an ounce. But from this humble beginning, in a matter of a few months, a living, breathing individual infant is born. That first cell is created when a male reproductive cell, a *sperm*, pushes through the membrane of the *ovum*, the female reproductive cell. These *gametes*, as the male and female reproductive cells are also called, contain huge amounts of genetic information. About an hour or so after the sperm enters the ovum, the two gametes suddenly fuse, becoming one cell, a **zygote**. The resulting combination of their genetic instructions—over 2 billion chemically coded messages—is sufficient to begin creating a whole person. **Watch** the **Video** *Period of the Zygote* in **MyPsychLab**.

zygote the new cell formed by the process of fertilization

genes the basic unit of genetic information

Genes and Chromosomes: The Code of Life

The blueprints for creating a person are stored and communicated in our **genes**, the basic units of genetic information. The roughly 25,000 human genes are the biological equivalent of "software" that programs the future development of all parts of the body's "hardware."

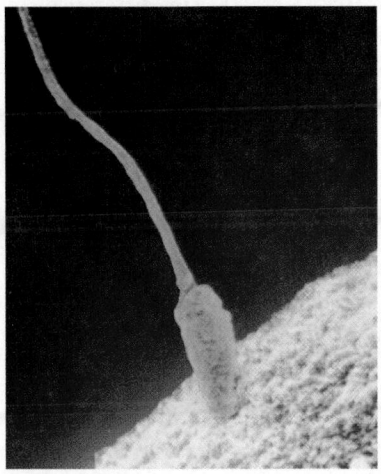
(a)

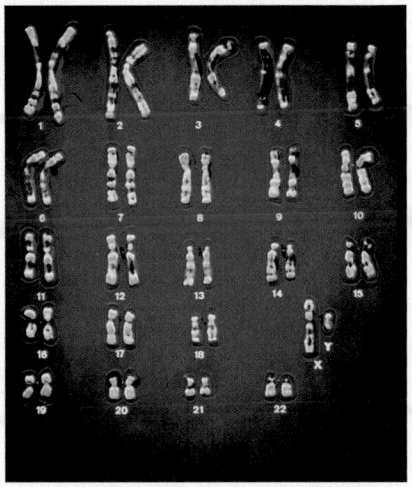
(b)

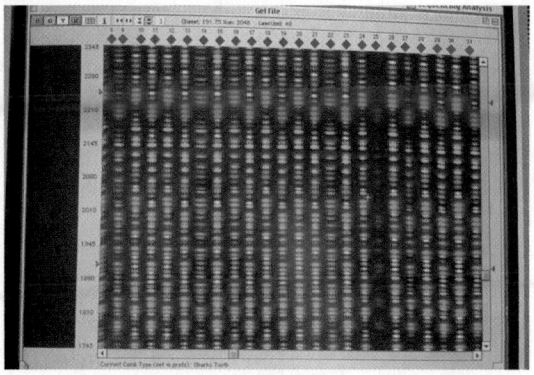
(c)

At the moment of conception (a), humans receive 23 pairs of chromosomes (b), half from the mother and half from the father. These chromosomes contain thousands of genes, shown in the computer-generated map (c).

All genes are composed of specific sequences of **DNA (deoxyribonucleic acid) molecules**. The genes are arranged in specific locations and in a specific order along 46 **chromosomes**, rod-shaped portions of DNA that are organized in 23 pairs. Each of the sex cells—ovum and sperm—contains half this number, so that a child's mother and father each provide one of the two chromosomes in each of the 23 pairs. The 46 chromosomes (in 23 pairs) in the new zygote contain the genetic blueprint that will guide cell activity for the rest of the individual's life (Pennisi, 2000; International Human Genome Sequencing Consortium, 2001) (see Figure 2-1). Through a process called *mitosis*, which accounts for the replication of most types of cells, nearly all the cells of the body will contain the same 46 chromosomes as the zygote.

DNA (deoxyribonucleic acid) molecules the substance that genes are composed of that determines the nature of every cell in the body and how it will function

chromosomes rod-shaped portions of DNA that are organized in 23 pairs

Genes determine the nature and function of every cell in the body. For instance, they determine which cells will become part of the heart and which will become part of the muscles of the leg. Genes also establish how different parts of the body will function: how rapidly the heart will beat, or how much strength a muscle will have.

If each parent provides just 23 chromosomes, where does the vast diversity of human beings come from? The answer resides primarily in the processes that underlie the cell division of the gametes. When gametes—the sex cells, sperm and ova—are formed in the adult body in a process called *meiosis*, each gamete receives one of the two chromosomes that make up each of the 23 pairs. Because for each pair the chromosome that is chosen is largely a matter of chance, there are 223, or some 8 million, different combinations possible. Furthermore, other processes, such as random transformations of particular genes, add to the variability of the genetic brew. The ultimate outcome: tens of *trillions* of possible genetic combinations.

With so many possible genetic mixtures, there is no likelihood that someday you'll bump into a genetic duplicate—with one exception: an identical twin.

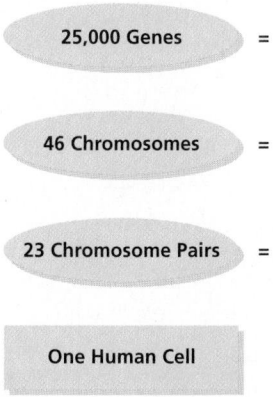

FIGURE 2-1 The Contents of a Single Human Cell
At the moment of conception, humans receive about 25,000 genes, contained of 46 chromosomes in 23 pairs.

Multiple Births: Two—or More—for the Genetic Price of One

Although it is routine for dogs and cats to give birth to several offspring at one time, in humans multiple births are cause for comment. They should be: Less than 3 percent of all pregnancies produce twins, and the odds are even slimmer for pregnancies of three or more children.

Why do multiple births occur? Some occur when a cluster of cells in the ovum splits off within the first 2 weeks after fertilization. The result is two genetically identical zygotes, which, because they come from the same original zygote, are called monozygotic.

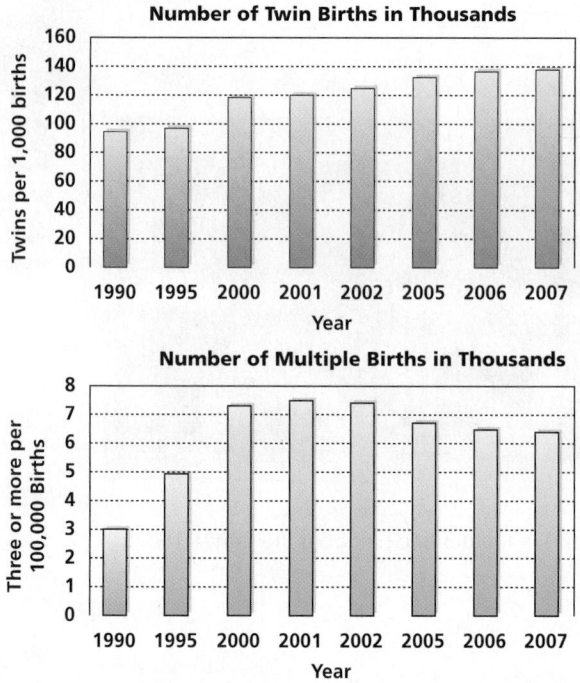

FIGURE 2-2 Rising Multiples
Multiple births have increased significantly over the last 25 years. What are some of the reasons for this phenomenon?
Source: Martin et al. 2010.

Monozygotic twins are twins who are genetically identical. Any differences in their future development can be attributed only to environmental factors.

However, multiple births are more commonly the result of two separate sperm fertilizing two separate ova at roughly the same time. Twins produced in this fashion are known as **dizygotic twins**. Because they are the result of two separate ovum–sperm combinations, they are no more genetically similar than two siblings born at different times. Triplets, quadruplets, and even more births are produced by either (or both) of the mechanisms that yield twins. Thus, triplets may be some combination of monozygotic, dizygotic, or trizygotic.

Of course, not all multiple births produce only two babies. Triplets, quadruplets, and even more births are produced by either (or both) of the mechanisms that yield twins. Thus, triplets may be some combination of monozygotic, dizygotic, or trizygotic.

Although the chances of having a multiple birth are typically slim, the odds rise considerably when fertility drugs are used before conception. Older women, too, are more likely to have multiple births, and multiple births are also more common in some families than in others. The increased use of fertility drugs and the rising average age of mothers giving birth means that multiple births have increased in the last 25 years (see Figure 2-2) (Martin et al., 2005, 2010).

There are also racial, ethnic, and national differences in the rate of multiple births, probably due to inherited differences in the likelihood that more than one ovum will be released at a time. For example, 1 out of 70 African American couples have dizygotic births, compared with 1 out of 86 white American couples (Vaughan, McKay, & Behrman, 1979; Wood, 1997).

Boy or Girl? Establishing the Sex of the Child. In 22 of the 23 matched chromosome pairs, each chromosome is similar to the other member of its pair. The one exception is the 23rd pair—the one that determines the sex of the child. In females, the 23rd pair consists of two matching, relatively large X-shaped chromosomes, identified as XX. In males, on the other hand, one member of the pair is an X-shaped chromosome, but the other is a shorter, smaller Y-shaped chromosome. This pair is identified as XY.

Because a female's 23rd pair of chromosomes are both Xs, an ovum will always carry an X chromosome. A male's 23rd pair is XY, so each sperm could carry either an X or a Y chromosome. If the sperm contributes an X chromosome when it meets an ovum, the child will have an XX pairing on the 23rd chromosome—and will be a female. If the sperm contributes a Y chromosome, the result will be an XY pairing—a male (see Figure 2-3).

Because the father's sperm determines the gender of the child, new techniques are being developed to help specify in advance the gender of the child. In one new technique, lasers measure the DNA in sperm. Discarding sperm that harbor the unwanted sex chromosome dramatically increases the chances of having a child of the desired sex (Hayden, 1998; Belkin, 1999; Van Balen, 2005).

Sex selection raises ethical and practical issues. For example, in cultures that value one gender over the other, might there be a kind of gender discrimination before birth? And could there ultimately be a shortage of children of the less-preferred sex? Many questions of this type will have to be addressed before sex selection can ever become routine (Sleeboom-Faulkner, 2010; Bhagat, Laskar, & Sharma, 2012).

The Basics of Genetics: The Mixing and Matching of Traits

What determined the color of your hair? Why are you tall or short? What made you susceptible to hay fever? And why do you have so many freckles? To answer these questions, we need to consider the basic mechanisms through which the genes we inherit from our parents transmit information.

We can start by examining the discoveries of an Austrian monk, Gregor Mendel, in the mid-1800s. In a series of simple yet convincing experiments, Mendel cross-pollinated pea plants that always produced yellow seeds with pea plants that always produced green seeds. The result was not, as one might guess, a plant with a combination of yellow and green seeds.

monozygotic twins twins who are genetically identical

dizygotic twins twins who are produced when two separate ova are fertilized by two separate sperm at roughly the same time

Instead, all of the resulting plants had yellow seeds. At first it appeared that the green-seeded plants had had no influence.

However, additional research on Mendel's part proved this was not true. He bred together plants from the new, yellow-seeded generation that had resulted from his original crossbreeding of the green-seeded and yellow-seeded plants. The consistent result was a ratio of three-quarters yellow seeds to one-quarter green seeds.

It was Mendel's genius to figure out why this ratio appeared so consistently. Based on his experiments with pea plants, he argued that when two competing traits, such as green or yellow coloring, were both present, only one could be expressed. The one that was expressed was called a **dominant trait**. Meanwhile, the other trait remained present in the organism, although unexpressed (displayed). This was called a **recessive trait**. In the case of the pea plants, the offspring plants received genetic information from both the green-seeded and yellow-seeded parents. However, the yellow trait was dominant, and consequently the recessive green trait did not assert itself.

Keep in mind, though, that genetic material from both parent plants is present in the offspring, even if unexpressed. The genetic information is known as the organism's genotype. A **genotype** is the underlying combination of genetic material present (but outwardly invisible) in an organism. In contrast, a **phenotype** is the observable trait—the trait that is actually seen.

Although the offspring of the yellow-seeded and green-seeded pea plants all have yellow seeds (i.e., they have a yellow-seeded phenotype), the genotype consists of genetic information relating to both parents.

And what is the nature of the information in the genotype? To answer that question, let's turn from peas to people. In fact, the principles are the same not just for plants and humans, but for the majority of species.

Recall that parents transmit genetic information to their offspring via the chromosomes they contribute through the gamete they provide during fertilization. Some of the genes form pairs called *alleles*, genes governing traits that may take alternate forms, such as hair or eye color. For example, brown eye color is a dominant trait (B); blue eyes are recessive (b). A child's allele may contain similar or dissimilar genes from each parent. If the child receives similar genes, he or she is said to be **homozygous** for the trait. On the other hand, if the child receives different forms of the gene from its parents, he or she is said to be **heterozygous**. In the case of heterozygous alleles (Bb), the dominant characteristic (brown eyes) is expressed. However, if the child happens to receive a recessive allele from each of its parents, and therefore lacks a dominant characteristic (bb), it will display the recessive characteristic (in this case, blue eyes).

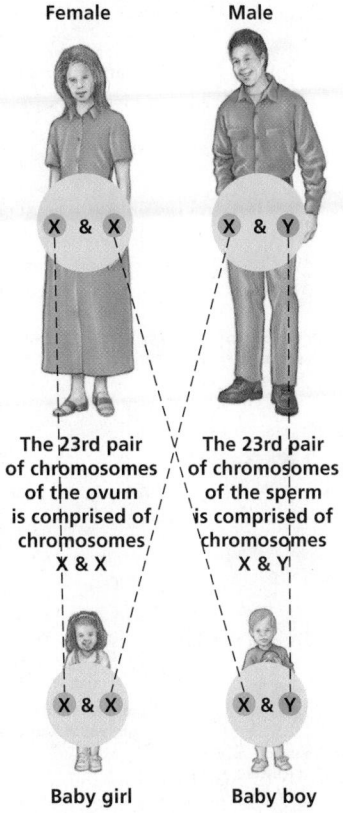

FIGURE 2-3 Determining Sex
When an ovum and sperm meet at the moment of fertilization, the ovum is certain to provide an X chromosome, while the sperm will provide either an X or a Y chromosome. If the sperm contributes its X chromosome, the child will have an XX pairing on the 23rd chromosome and will be a girl. If the sperm contributes a Y chromosome, the result will be an XY pairing—a boy. Does this mean that girls are more likely to be conceived than boys?

Transmission of Genetic Information

One example of this process at work is the transmission of *phenylketonuria (PKU)*, an inherited disorder in which a child is unable to make use of phenylalanine, an essential amino acid present in proteins found in milk and other foods. If untreated, PKU allows phenylalanine to build to toxic levels, causing brain damage and mental retardation (Widaman, 2009; McCabe & Shaw, 2010; Waisbren & Antshel, 2013).

PKU is produced by a single allele, or pair of genes. As shown in Figure 2-4, we can label each gene of the pair with a *P* if it carries a dominant gene, which causes the normal production of phenylalanine, or a *p* if it carries the recessive gene that produces PKU. In cases in which neither parent is a PKU carrier, both the mother's and the father's pairs of genes are the dominant form, symbolized as *PP*, in which case the child's genes will be *PP*, and the child will not have PKU.

Imagine what happens if one parent has the recessive *p* gene. In this case, symbolized as *Pp*, the parent will not have PKU, because the normal *P* gene is dominant. But the recessive gene can be passed down to the child. This is not so bad: If the child has only one recessive gene, it will not suffer from PKU. But what if both parents carry a recessive *p* gene? In this case, although neither parent has the disorder, it is possible for the child to receive a recessive gene from both parents. The child will have the *pp* genotype for PKU and will have the disorder.

dominant trait the one trait that is expressed when two competing traits are present

recessive trait a trait within an organism that is present, but is not expressed

genotype the underlying combination of genetic material present (but not outwardly visible) in an organism

phenotype an observable trait; the trait that is actually seen

homozygous inheriting from parents similar genes for a given trait

heterozygous inheriting from parents different forms of a gene for a given trait

FIGURE 2-4 PKU Probabilities
PKU, a disease that causes brain damage and mental retardation, is produced by a single pair of genes inherited from one's mother and father. If neither parent carries a gene for the disease (a), a child cannot develop PKU. Even if one parent carries the recessive gene, but the other doesn't (b), the child cannot inherit the disease. However, if both parents carry the recessive gene (c), there is a one in four chance that the child will have PKU.

Remember, though, that even children whose parents both have the recessive gene for PKU have only a 25 percent chance of inheriting the disorder. Due to the laws of probability, 25 percent of children with *Pp* parents will receive the dominant gene from each parent (these children's genotype would be *PP*), and 50 percent will receive the dominant gene from one parent and the recessive gene from the other (their genotypes would be either *Pp* or *pP*). Only the unlucky 25 percent who receive the recessive gene from each parent and end up with the genotype *pp* will suffer from PKU.

Polygenic Traits. PKU illustrates the basic principles of genetic transmission, although PKU transmission is simpler than most cases. Relatively few traits are governed by a single pair of genes. Instead, most traits are the result of polygenic inheritance. In **polygenic inheritance**, a combination of multiple gene pairs is responsible for the production of a particular trait.

Furthermore, some genes come in several alternate forms, and still others act to modify the way that particular genetic traits (produced by other alleles) are displayed. Genes also vary in terms of their *reaction range*, the potential degree of variability in the expression of a trait due to environmental conditions. And some traits, such as blood type, are produced by genes in which neither member of a pair of genes can be classified as purely dominant or recessive. Instead, the trait is expressed in terms of a combination of the two genes—such as type AB blood.

A number of recessive genes, called **X-linked genes**, are located only on the X chromosome. Recall that in females, the 23rd pair of chromosomes is an XX pair, while in males it is an XY pair. One result is that males have a higher risk for a variety of X-linked disorders—as the Howards' unborn son did in the story at the beginning of this module—because males lack a second X chromosome that can counteract the genetic information that produces the disorder. For example, males are significantly more apt to have red-green color blindness, a disorder produced by a set of genes on the X chromosome. Similarly, *hemophilia*, a blood disorder, is produced by X-linked genes, a recurrent problem in the royal families of Europe.

The Human Genome and Behavioral Genetics: Cracking the Genetic Code. Mendel's trailblazing achievements mark only the beginning of our understanding of genetics. The most recent milestone was reached in early 2001, when molecular geneticists succeeded in mapping the sequence of genes on each chromosome. This is one of the most important accomplishments in the history of genetics (International Human Genome Sequencing Consortium, 2001; Oksenberg & Hauser, 2010; Maxson, 2013).

Already, the mapping of the gene sequence has significantly advanced our understanding of genetics. For instance, the number of human genes, long thought to be 100,000, has been revised downward to 25,000—not many more than organisms that are far less complex (see Figure 2-5). Furthermore, scientists have discovered that 99.9 percent of the gene sequence is shared by all humans—meaning that many of the differences that seemingly separate people—such as race—are, literally, only skin-deep. Genome mapping will also help in the identification of disorders to which a given individual is susceptible (Gupta & State, 2007; Levinson, 2012; Serretti & Fabbri, 2013).

The mapping of the human gene sequence is supporting the field of behavioral genetics. As the name implies, **behavioral genetics** studies the effects of heredity on behavior and psychological characteristics. Rather than simply examining stable, unchanging characteristics such as hair or eye color, behavioral genetics takes a broader approach, considering how

polygenic inheritance inheritance in which a combination of multiple gene pairs is responsible for the production of a particular trait

X-linked genes genes that are considered recessive and located only on the X chromosome

behavioral genetics the study of the effects of heredity on behavior our personality and behavioral habits are affected by genetic factors (Li, 2003; McGue, 2010; Judge, Ilies, & Zhang, 2012).

Personality traits such as shyness or sociability, moodiness, and assertiveness are among the areas being studied. Other behavior geneticists study psychological disorders, such as depression, attention deficit hyperactivity disorder, and schizophrenia, looking for possible genetic links (DeYoung, Quilty, & Peterson, 2007; Haeffel et al., 2008; Wang et al., 2012) (see Table 2-1). **Watch** the **Video** *Genetic Mechanisms and Behavioral Genetics* in **MyPsychLab.**

Inherited and Genetic Disorders: When Development Deviates From the Norm

As we saw with PKU, a recessive gene responsible for a disorder may be passed on unknowingly from one generation to the next, revealing itself only when, by chance, it is paired with another recessive gene. When this happens, the gene will express itself and the unsuspected genetic disorder will be inherited.

Another way that genes are a source of concern is that they may become physically damaged. Genes may break down due to wear-and-tear or chance events occurring during the cell division processes of meiosis and mitosis. Sometimes genes, for no known reason, spontaneously change their form, a process called *spontaneous mutation*. Also, certain environmental factors, such as x-rays or even highly polluted air, may produce a malformation of genetic material. When damaged genes are passed on to a child, the results can be disastrous for physical and cognitive development (Samet, DeMarini, & Malling, 2004; Barnes & Jacobs, 2013).

In addition to PKU, which occurs once in 10- to 20-thousand births, other inherited and genetic disorders include the following:

- **Down syndrome.** Instead of 46 chromosomes in 23 pairs, individuals with **Down syndrome** have an extra chromosome on the 21st pair. Once referred to as mongolism, Down syndrome is the most frequent cause of intellectual deficit. It occurs in about 1 out of 500 births, although the risk is much greater in mothers who are unusually young or old (Crane & Morris, 2006; Sherman et al., 2007; Davis, 2008).
- **Fragile X syndrome. Fragile X syndrome** occurs when a particular gene is injured on the X chromosome. The result is mild to moderate mental retardation (Cornish, Turk, & Hagerman, 2008; Hocking, Kogan, & Cornish, 2012).

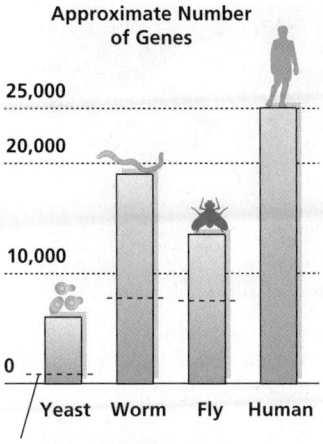

FIGURE 2-5 Uniquely Human?
Humans have about 25,000 genes, making them not much more genetically complex than some primitive species.
Source: Celera Genomics: International Human Genome Sequencing Consortium, 2001.

TABLE 2-1 CURRENT UNDERSTANDING OF THE GENETIC BASIS OF SELECTED BEHAVIORAL DISORDERS AND TRAITS

Behavioral Trait	Current Ideas of Genetic Basis
Huntington's disease	Huntington gene localized to the terminal portion of the short arm of chromosome 4.
Early onset (familial) Alzheimer's disease	Three distinct genes identified. Most cases caused by single-gene mutation on chromosomes 21, 14, and 1.
Fragile X mental retardation	Two genes identified.
Attention deficit hyperactivity disorder (ADHD)	Evidence in some studies has linked ADHD with the dopamine D4 and D5 genes, but the complexity of the disease makes it difficult to identify an specific gene beyond reasonable doubt.
Alcoholism	Research suggests that genes which affect the activity of neurotransmitters serotonin and GABA likely are involved in risk for alcoholism.
Schizophrenia	There is no agreement, but links to chromosomes 1, 5, 6, 10, 13, 15, and 22 have been reported.

Source: Based on McGuffin, Riley, & Plomin, 2001.

Down syndrome a disorder produced by the presence of an extra chromosome on the 21st pair; once referred to as mongolism

fragile X syndrome a disorder produced by injury to a gene on the X chromosome, producing mild to moderate mental retardation

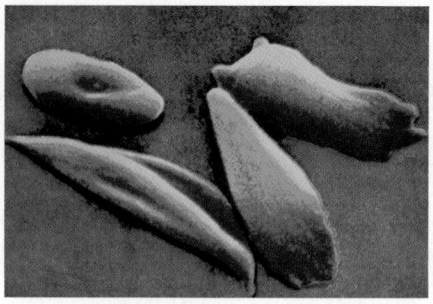

Sickle-cell anemia, named for the presence of misshapen red blood cells, is carried in the genes of one in ten African Americans.

- **Sickle-cell anemia.** Around one-tenth of people of African descent carry genes that produce sickle-cell anemia, and 1 individual in 400 actually has the disease. **Sickle-cell anemia** is a blood disorder named for the shape of the red blood cells. Symptoms include poor appetite, stunted growth, swollen stomach, and yellowish eyes. People afflicted with the most severe form rarely live beyond childhood. However, for those with less severe cases, medical advances have produced significant increases in life expectancy (Ballas, 2010).
- **Tay-Sachs disease.** Occurring mainly in Jews of eastern European ancestry and in French-Canadians, **Tay-Sachs disease** usually causes death before its victims reach school age. There is no treatment for the disorder, which produces blindness and muscle degeneration prior to death.
- **Klinefelter's syndrome.** One male out of every 400 is born with **Klinefelter's syndrome**, the presence of an extra X chromosome. The resulting XXY complement produces underdeveloped genitals, extreme height, and enlarged breasts. Klinefelter's syndrome is one of a number of genetic abnormalities that result from receiving the improper number of sex chromosomes. For instance, there are disorders produced by an extra Y chromosome (XYY), a missing second chromosome (X0, called *Turner's syndrome*), and three X chromosomes (XXX). Such disorders are typically characterized by problems relating to sexual characteristics and by intellectual deficits (Ross, Stefanatos, & Roeltgen, 2007; Murphy & Mazzocco, 2008; Murphy, 2009).

It is important to keep in mind that the mere fact that a disorder has genetic roots does not mean that environmental factors do not also play a role. Consider sickle-cell anemia. Because the disease can be fatal in childhood, we'd expect that those who suffer from it would be unlikely to live long enough to pass it on. And this does seem to be true in the United States: Compared with parts of West Africa, the incidence in the United States is much lower.

But why the difference between the United States and West Africa? Ultimately, scientists determined that carrying the sickle-cell gene raises immunity to malaria, a common disease in West Africa. This heightened immunity meant that people with the sickle-cell gene had a genetic advantage (in terms of resistance to malaria) that offset, to some degree, the disadvantage of being a carrier of the gene.

Genetic Counseling: Predicting the Future From the Genes of the Present

If you knew that your mother and grandmother had died of Huntington's disease—a devastating, always fatal inherited disorder marked by tremors and intellectual deterioration—how could you learn your own chances of getting the disease? The best way is a field that, just a few decades ago, was nonexistent: genetic counseling. **Genetic counseling** focuses on helping people deal with issues relating to inherited disorders.

Genetic counselors use a variety of data in their work. For instance, couples thinking about having a child may want to know the risks involved in a pregnancy. The counselor will take a thorough family history, looking for a familial incidence of birth defects that might indicate a pattern of recessive or X-linked genes. In addition, the counselor will take into account factors such as the age of the mother and father and any previous abnormalities in other children they may have already had (Resta et al., 2006; Lyon, 2012).

Typically, genetic counselors suggest a thorough physical examination to identify physical abnormalities that the potential parents may be unaware of. In addition, samples of blood, skin, and urine may be used to isolate and examine specific chromosomes. Possible genetic defects, such as the presence of an extra sex chromosome, can be identified by assembling a *karyotype*, a chart containing enlarged photos of each of the chromosomes. **Watch** the **Video** *Genetic Counseling* in **MyPsychLab**.

Prenatal Testing. If the woman is already pregnant, there are a variety of techniques to assess the health of her unborn child (see Table 2-2 for a list of currently available tests). The earliest is a *first-trimester screen*, which combines a blood test and ultrasound sonography in the 11th to 13th week of pregnancy and can identify chromosomal abnormalities and other disorders, such as heart problems. In **ultrasound sonography**, high-frequency sound waves

sickle-cell anemia a blood disorder that gets its name from the shape of the red blood cells

Tay-Sachs disease a disorder that produces blindness and muscle degeneration prior to death; there is no treatment

Klinefelter's syndrome a disorder resulting from the presence of an extra X chromosome that produces underdeveloped genitals, extreme height, and enlarged breasts

genetic counseling the discipline that focuses on helping people deal with issues relating to inherited disorders

ultrasound sonography a process in which high-frequency sound waves scan the mother's womb to produce an image of the unborn baby, whose size and shape can then be assessed

TABLE 2-2 FETAL DEVELOPMENT MONITORING TECHNIQUES

Technique	Description
Amniocentesis	Done between the 15th and 20th week of pregnancy, this procedure examines a sample of the amniotic fluid, which contains fetal cells. Recommended if either parent carries Tay-Sachs, spina bifida, sickle-cell, Down syndrome, muscular dystrophy, or Rh disease.
Chorionic villus sampling (CVS)	Done at 8 to 11 weeks, either transabdominally or transcervically, depending on where the placenta is located. Involves inserting a needle (abdominally) or a catheter (cervically) into the substance of the placenta but staying outside the amniotic sac and removing 10 to 15 milligrams of tissue. This tissue is manually cleaned of maternal uterine tissue and then grown in culture, and a karyotype is made, as with amniocentesis.
Embryoscopy	Examines the embryo or fetus during the first 12 weeks of pregnancy by means of a fiber-optic endoscope inserted through the cervix. Can be performed as early as week 5. Access to the fetal circulation may be obtained through the instrument, and direct visualization of the embryo permits the diagnosis of malformations.
Fetal blood sampling (FBS)	Performed after 18 weeks of pregnancy by collecting a small amount of blood from the umbilical cord for testing. Used to detect Down syndrome and most other chromosome abnormalities in the fetuses of couples who are at increased risk of having an affected child. Many other diseases can be diagnosed using this technique.
Sonoembryology	Used to detect abnormalities in the first trimester of pregnancy. Involves high-frequency transvaginal probes and digital image processing. In combination with ultrasound, can detect more than 80 percent of all malformations during the second trimester.
Sonogram	Uses ultrasound to produce a visual image of the uterus, fetus, and placenta.
Ultrasound sonography	Uses very-high-frequency sound waves to detect structural abnormalities or multiple pregnancies, measure fetal growth, judge gestational age, and evaluate uterine abnormalities. Also used as an adjunct to other procedures such as amniocentesis.

chorionic villus sampling (CVS) a test used to find genetic defects that involves taking samples of hairlike material that surrounds the embryo

amniocentesis the process of identifying genetic defects by examining a small sample of fetal cells drawn by a needle inserted into the amniotic fluid surrounding the unborn fetus

bombard the mother's womb, producing an image of the unborn baby, whose size and shape can then be assessed. Repeated use of ultrasound sonography can reveal developmental patterns.

A more invasive test, **chorionic villus sampling (CVS)**, can be employed in the 10th to 13th week of the first trimester, if blood tests and ultrasound have identified a potential problem or if there is a family history of inherited disorders. CVS involves inserting a thin needle into the placenta and taking small samples of hair-like material that surrounds the embryo. The test can be done between the 8th and 11th week of pregnancy. However, it produces a risk of miscarriage of 1 in 100 to 1 in 200. Because of the risk, its use is relatively infrequent.

In **amniocentesis**, a small sample of fetal cells is drawn by a tiny needle inserted into the amniotic fluid surrounding the unborn fetus. Carried out 15 to 20 weeks into the pregnancy, amniocentesis allows the analysis of the fetal cells that can identify a variety of genetic defects with nearly 100 percent accuracy. In addition, the sex of the child can be determined. Although there is always a danger to the fetus in an invasive procedure such as amniocentesis, it is generally safe.

After the various tests are complete, the couple will meet with the genetic counselor again. Typically, counselors avoid giving recommendations. Instead, they lay out the facts and present options for the parents, which typically range from doing nothing to taking more drastic steps, such as an abortion.

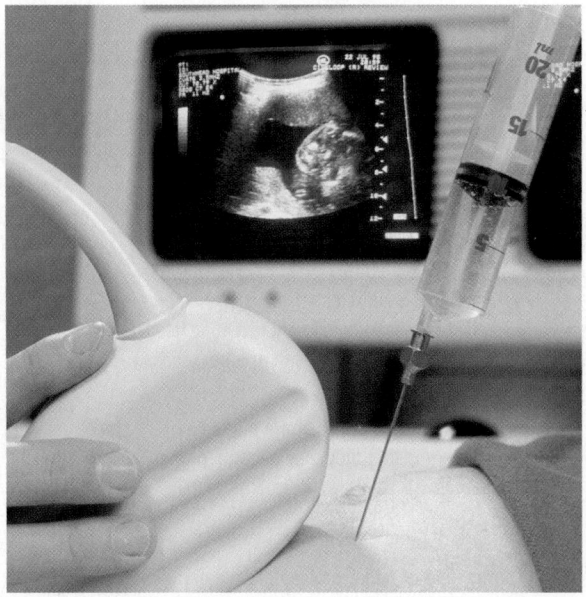

In amniocentesis, a sample of fetal cells is withdrawn from the amniotic sac and used to identify a number of genetic defects.

Screening for Future Problems. The newest role of genetic counselors involves testing people to identify whether they themselves, rather than their children, are susceptible to future disorders because of genetic abnormalities.

For instance, Huntington's disease typically does not appear until people reach their 40s. However, genetic testing can identify much earlier the flawed gene that produces Huntington's. Presumably, knowing that they carry the gene can help people prepare for the future (van't Spijker & ten Kroode, 1997; Ensenauer, Michels, & Reinke, 2005).

In addition to Huntington's disease, more than a thousand disorders can be predicted on the basis of genetic testing, ranging from cystic fibrosis to ovarian cancer. Negative results can bring welcome relief, but positive results may produce just the opposite effect. In fact, genetic testing raises difficult practical and ethical questions (Human Genome Project, 2006; Wilfond & Ross, 2009; Klitzman, 2012).

Suppose, for instance, a woman is tested in her 20s for Huntington's and finds that she does not carry the defective gene. Obviously, she would be relieved. But suppose she finds that she does carry the flawed gene and will therefore get the disease. In this case, she might well experience depression and remorse. In fact, some studies show that 10 percent of people who find they have the flawed gene that leads to Huntington's disease never recover fully on an emotional level (Myers, 2004; Wahlin, 2007; Richmond-Rakerd, 2013).

Genetic testing is a complicated issue. It rarely provides a simple yes/no answer, typically presenting a range of probabilities instead. In some cases, the likelihood of becoming ill depends on the stressors in a person's environment. Personal differences also affect susceptibility to a disorder (Bonke et al., 2005; Martin, Greenwood, & Nisker, 2010; Lucassen, 2012).

From the perspective of a health care provider: What are some ethical and philosophical questions that surround the issue of genetic counseling? Might it sometimes be unwise to know ahead of time about possible disorders that might affect your child or yourself?

Today, many researchers and medical practitioners have moved beyond testing and counseling to actually modifying flawed genes. For example, in *germ line therapy*, cells with defective genes are taken from an embryo, repaired, and replaced.

REVIEW, CHECK, AND APPLY

REVIEW

LO1 What is our basic genetic endowment?

- In humans, the male sex cell (the sperm) and the female sex cell (the ovum) provide the developing baby with 23 chromosomes each, making up roughly 25,000 genes, the basic units of genetic information.

LO2 What are the major genetic threats to normal development?

- A recessive gene responsible for a disorder may be passed on silently, revealing itself only when it is paired with another recessive gene.
- Another way that genes are a source of concern is that they may become physically damaged.

LO3 What is the role of behavioral genetics?

- The field of behavioral genetics, a combination of psychology and genetics, studies the effects of heredity on personality and behavioral characteristics.

CHECK YOURSELF

1. Sex cells (the ova and the sperm) are different from other cells because they:
   - a have twice the 46 chromosomes necessary so that when the cells combine and material is "spilled," the appropriate number of chromosomes will still be there.
   - b each has half of the 46 chromosomes so that when they combine, the new zygote will have all the genetic information necessary.
   - c are younger than all other cells in the developing human body.
   - d are the only cells with chromosomal information.
2. According to Mendel, when competing traits are both present, only one trait, also known as the _____ trait, can be expressed.
   - a homozygous
   - b recessive
   - c polygenic
   - d dominant
3. Just because a disorder has genetic roots does not mean that environmental factors do not also play a role.
   - True
   - False

APPLYING LIFESPAN DEVELOPMENT

- How can the study of identical twins who were separated at birth help researchers determine the effects of genetic and environmental factors on human development?

Study and **Review** on **MyPsychLab.com**

THE INTERACTION OF HEREDITY AND ENVIRONMENT

L04 How do the environment and genetics work together?
L05 What is the role of genetics and the environment in determining specific major human characteristics?

Like many other parents, Jared's mother, Leesha, and his father, Jamal, tried to figure out which of them their new baby resembled more. He seemed to have Leesha's big, wide eyes, and Jamal's generous smile. As he grew, they noticed that his hairline was just like Leesha's, and his teeth made his smile resemble Jamal's. He also seemed to act like his parents. For example, he was a charming little baby, always ready to smile at people who visited the house—just like his friendly, jovial dad. He seemed to sleep like his mom, which was lucky because Jamal was an extremely light sleeper who could do with as little as 4 hours a night, while Leesha liked a regular 7 or 8 hours.

Were Jared's ready smile and regular sleeping habits something he just luckily inherited from his parents? Or did Jamal and Leesha provide a happy and stable home that encouraged these welcome traits? What causes our behavior? Nature or nurture? Is behavior produced by genetic influences or factors in the environment?

The simple answer is: There is no simple answer.

The Role of the Environment in Determining the Expression of Genes: From Genotypes to Phenotypes

As developmental research accumulates, it is becoming increasingly clear that to view behavior as due to *either* genetic *or* environmental factors is inappropriate, because behavior is the product of some combination of the two.

For instance, consider **temperament**, patterns of arousal and emotionality that represent consistent and enduring characteristics in an individual. Suppose we found, as increasing evidence suggests, that a small percentage of children are born with an unusual degree of physiological reactivity—a tendency to shrink from anything unusual. Such infants react to novel stimuli with a rapid increase in heartbeat and unusual excitability of the limbic system of the brain. By age 4 or 5, children with heightened reactivity to stimuli are often considered shy by their parents and teachers. But not always: Some of them behave indistinguishably from their peers at the same age (Kagan & Snidman, 1991; McCrae et al., 2000; Gerken, 2010; Lemery-Chalfant et al., 2013).

What makes the difference? The answer seems to be the children's environment. Children whose parents encourage them to be outgoing by arranging new opportunities for them may overcome their shyness. In contrast, children raised in a stressful environment marked by marital discord or a prolonged illness may be more likely to retain their shyness later in life (Kagan, Arcus, & Snidman, 1993; Propper & Moore, 2006; Bridgett et al., 2009; Casalin et al., 2012). Jared, described earlier, may have been born with an easy temperament, which was easily reinforced by his caring parents.

Interaction of Factors. Such findings illustrate that many traits reflect **multifactorial transmission**, meaning that they are determined by a combination of both genetic and environmental factors. In multifactorial transmission, a genotype provides a range within which a phenotype may be expressed. For instance, people with a genotype that permits them to gain weight easily may vary in their actual body weight. They may be *relatively* slim, given their genetic heritage, but never able to get beyond a certain degree of thinness (Faith, Johnson, & Allison, 1997). In many cases, then, the environment determines how a particular genotype will be expressed as a phenotype (Wachs, 1992, 1993, 1996; Plomin, 1994a).

On the other hand, certain genotypes are relatively unaffected by environmental factors. For instance, pregnant women who were severely malnourished during famines caused by World War II had children who were, on average, unaffected physically or intellectually as adults (Stein et al., 1975). Similarly, people will never grow beyond certain genetically imposed

temperament patterns of arousal and emotionality that represent consistent and enduring characteristics in an individual

multifactorial transmission the determination of traits by a combination of both genetic and environmental factors in which a genotype provides a range within which a phenotype may be expressed

Michael Shaw/The New Yorker Collection/www.cartoonbank.com

"The title of my science project is 'My Little Brother: Nature or Nurture.'"

limitations in height, no matter how well or how much they eat. And the environment had little to do with Jared's hairline.

Although we can't attribute specific behaviors exclusively to nature or nurture, we can ask how much of a behavior is caused by genetic factors and how much by environmental factors. We'll turn to this question next.

Studying Development: How Much Is Nature? How Much Is Nurture?

Developmental researchers use several strategies to study the relative influence of genetic and environmental factors on traits, characteristics, and behavior. Their studies involve both nonhuman species and humans.

Nonhuman Animal Studies: Controlling Both Genetics and Environment. It is relatively simple to develop breeds of animals with genetically similar traits. The Butterball people do it all the time, producing Thanksgiving turkeys that grow especially rapidly so that they can be brought to market inexpensively. Similarly, strains of laboratory animals can be bred to share similar genetic backgrounds.

By observing genetically similar animals in different environments, scientists can determine, with reasonable precision, the effects of specific kinds of environmental stimulation. For example, to examine the effects of different environmental settings, researchers can raise some of the genetically similar animals in unusually stimulating environments, with lots of items to climb over or through, and others in relatively barren environments. Conversely, by exposing groups of genetically *dissimilar* animals to *identical* environments, researchers can examine in a different way the role that genetic background plays. (Also see the "From Research to Practice" box.)

Animal research offers substantial opportunities, but the drawback is that we can't be sure how well our findings can be generalized to people.

Contrasting Relatedness and Behavior: Adoption, Twin, and Family Studies. Obviously, researchers can't control either the genetic backgrounds or the environments of humans as they can with nonhumans. However, nature conveniently has provided ideal subjects for carrying out various kinds of "natural experiments"—twins.

From Research to Practice

When Nurture Becomes Nature

A fundamental assumption about genetic inheritance has long been that environmental alterations of an organism's health cannot be passed down to future generations; if we cut off a mouse's tail, we do not expect its offspring to be tailless. Only genetic mutations—neither lifestyle choices such as poor diet nor environmental insults such as exposure to toxins—were thought to be heritable. But recent research finds that an individual's life experiences can be passed down to children, grandchildren, and subsequent generations.

It's a phenomenon called *transgenerational epigenetic inheritance*, and it works a bit differently from usual inheritance. Instead of changing the genetic code itself, life experiences change the parts of DNA that switch individual genes on or off. Not every gene is active everywhere in the body; the DNA that is responsible for making insulin, for example, is only "switched on" in certain cells of the pancreas. When an event such as malnourishment or drug use affects the DNA "switches" in sperm or eggs, the alterations can be passed on to future generations (Begley, 2010; Daxinger & Whitelaw, 2012).

In one study, healthy male rats were fed a high-fat diet that caused them to put on weight and develop symptoms consistent with type 2 diabetes such as insulin resistance. Although these rats did not have a preexisting genetic tendency to be diabetic, their daughters also developed symptoms of type 2 diabetes as adults—even though they ate normal diets. Some researchers think that transgenerational epigenetic inheritance could partly explain the epidemic of childhood obesity: Our high fat diets may not only put us at risk, but perhaps our children as well (Skinner, 2010).

Happily, it's not just harmful effects that can be passed on this way. One study showed that mice developed better memory after being exposed to an enriched and stimulating environment, as previous research showed would be the case, and that the mice's offspring also showed the beneficial memory effect even though they didn't experience the same enriched environment.The implications of this research are astounding—it may well be the case that the poor life choices we make in our youth have consequences for our progeny as well as ourselves (Arai, Li, Hartley, & Feig, 2009; Nestler, 2011).

- *Why would the poor life choices we make in our youth, rather than those we might make later in life, have possible consequences for our children?*
- *How would you explain the principle of transgenerational epigenetic inheritance to a friend?*

Recall that identical, monozygotic twins are *genetically* identical. Because their inherited backgrounds are precisely the same, any variations in their behavior must be due entirely to environmental factors.

Theoretically, identical twins would make great subjects for experiments about the roles of nature and nurture. For instance, by separating identical twins at birth and placing them in totally different environments, researchers could assess the impact of environment unambiguously. Of course, ethical considerations make this impossible.

What researchers can—and do—study, however, are cases in which identical twins have been put up for adoption at birth and are raised in substantially different environments. Such instances allow us to draw fairly confident conclusions about the relative contributions of genetics and environment (Richardson & Norgate, 2007; Agrawal & Lynskey, 2008; Nikolas, Klump, & Burt, 2012).

The data from such studies of identical twins raised in different environments are not always without bias. Adoption agencies typically take the characteristics (and wishes) of birth mothers into account when they place babies in adoptive homes. For instance, children tend to be placed with families of the same race and religion. Consequently, even when monozygotic twins are placed in different adoptive homes, there are often similarities between the two home environments. As a result, researchers can't always be certain that differences in behavior are due to differences in the environment.

Studies of nonidentical, dizygotic twins also present opportunities to learn about nature and nurture. Recall that dizygotic twins are genetically no more similar than siblings in a family born at different times. By comparing the behavior of dizygotic twins with that of monozygotic twins (who are genetically identical) researchers can determine if monozygotic twins tend to be more similar on a particular trait than dizygotic twins. If so, they can assume that genetics plays an important role in determining the expression of that trait.

Still another approach is to study people who are totally unrelated and therefore have dissimilar genetic backgrounds, but who share an environmental background. For instance, a family that adopts, at the same time, two very young unrelated children probably will provide them with similar environments. In this case, similarities in the children's characteristics and behavior can be attributed with some confidence to environmental influences (Segal, 1993, 2000).

Finally, developmental researchers have examined groups of people in light of their degree of genetic similarity. For instance, if we find a high association on a particular trait between biological parents and their children but a weaker association between adoptive parents and their children, we have evidence for the importance of genetics in determining the expression of that trait. On the other hand, if there is a stronger association on a trait between adoptive parents and their children than between biological parents and their children, we have evidence for the importance of the environment in determining that trait. If a particular trait tends to occur at similar levels among genetically similar individuals, but at different levels among genetically distant individuals, genetics probably plays a major role in the development of that trait.

Developmental researchers using all these approaches, and more, for decades have come to a general conclusion: Virtually all traits, characteristics, and behaviors result from the combination and interaction of nature and nurture (Robinson, 2004; Waterland & Jirtle, 2004; Jaworski & Accardo, 2010).

Physical Traits: Family Resemblances

When patients entered the examining room of Dr. Cyril Marcus, they didn't realize that sometimes they were actually being treated by his identical twin brother, Dr. Stewart Marcus. So similar in appearance and manner were the twins that even long-time patients were fooled by this admittedly unethical behavior, which occurred in a bizarre case made famous in the film *Dead Ringers*.

Monozygotic twins are merely the most extreme example of the fact that the more genetically similar two people are, the more likely they are to share physical characteristics. Tall parents tend to have tall children and short parents short children. Obesity also has a strong genetic component. For example, in one study, pairs of identical twins were put on diets that contained an extra 1,000 calories a day—and ordered not to exercise. Over a three-month period, the twins gained almost identical amounts of weight. Moreover, different pairs of twins varied substantially in how much weight they gained, with some pairs gaining almost three times as much weight as other pairs (Bouchard et al., 1990).

Other, less obvious physical characteristics also show strong genetic influences. For instance, blood pressure, respiration rates, and even the age at which life ends are more similar in closely related individuals than in those who are less genetically alike (Price & Gottesman, 1991; Melzer, Hurst, & Frayling, 2007).

Intelligence: More Research, More Controversy

No other nature–nurture issue has generated more research than intelligence. The reason is that intelligence, generally measured as an IQ score, is a central human characteristic that differentiates humans from other species. In addition, intelligence is strongly related to scholastic success and, somewhat less strongly, to other types of achievement.

Genetics plays a significant role in intelligence. In studies of both overall or general intelligence and of specific subcomponents of intelligence (such as spatial skills, verbal skills, and memory), as can be seen in Figure 2-6, the closer the genetic link between two individuals, the greater the correspondence of their overall IQ scores.

Not only is genetics an important influence on intelligence, but the impact increases with age. For instance, as fraternal (i.e., dizygotic) twins move from infancy to adolescence, their IQ scores become less similar. Not so with identical (monozygotic) twins, who become increasingly similar as they age (Brody, 1993; Chamorro-Premuzic et al., 2010; Silventoinen et al., 2012).

Clearly, heredity plays an important role in intelligence, but to what degree is it inherited? Perhaps the most extreme view is held by psychologist Arthur Jensen (2003), who argues that as much as 80 percent of intelligence is a result of heredity. Others suggest more modest figures, ranging from 50 to 70 percent. It is critical to recall that these figures are averages across

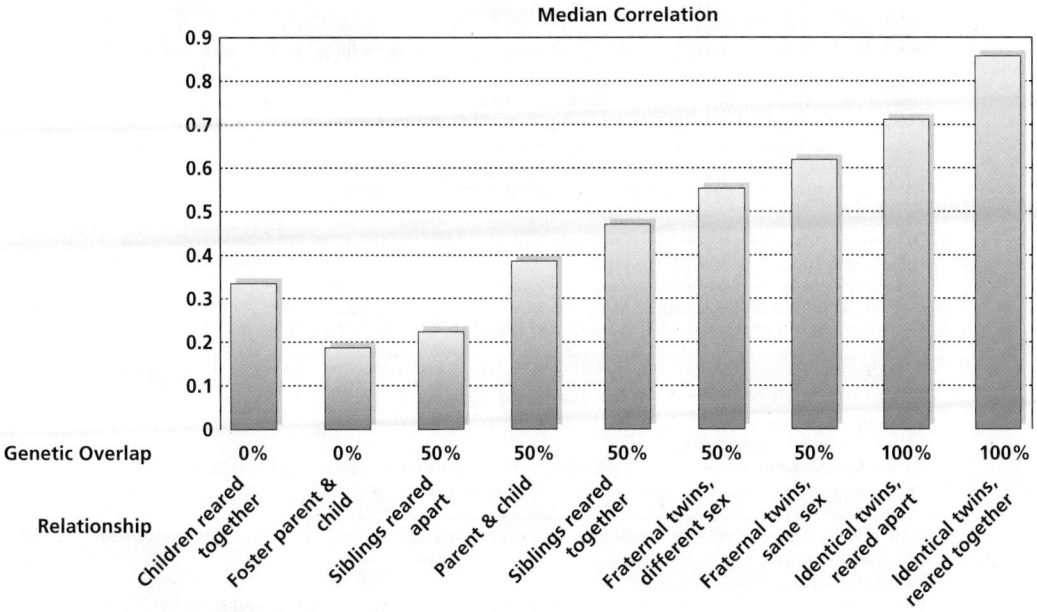

FIGURE 2-6 Genetics and IQ
The closer the genetic link between two individuals, the greater the correspondence between their IQ scores. Why do you think there is a sex difference in the fraternal twins' figures? Might there be other sex differences in other sets of twins or siblings, not shown on this chart?
Source: Based on Bouchard & McGue, 1981.

many people and say nothing about any individual's degree of inheritance (e.g., Herrnstein & Murray, 1994; Devlin, Daniels, & Roeder, 1997; Richardson, 2013).

It is important to keep in mind that, whatever role heredity plays, environmental factors such as exposure to books, good educational experiences, and intelligent peers are profoundly influential. In fact, in terms of public policy, environmental influences are the focus of efforts geared toward maximizing people's intellectual success. As developmental psychologist Sandra Scarr suggests, we should be asking what can be done to maximize the intellectual development of each individual (Scarr & Carter-Saltzman, 1982; Storfer, 1990; Bouchard, 1997).

From an educator's perspective: Some people have used the proven genetic basis of intelligence to argue against strenuous educational efforts on behalf of individuals with below-average IQs. Does this viewpoint make sense based on what you have learned about heredity and environment? Why or why not?

Genetic and Environmental Influences on Personality: Born to Be Outgoing?

Do we inherit our personality?

At least in part. Evidence suggests that some of our most basic personality traits have genetic roots. For example, two of the "Big Five" personality traits, neuroticism and extroversion, have been linked to genetic factors. *Neuroticism*, as used by personality researchers, is the degree of emotional stability an individual characteristically displays. *Extroversion* is the degree to which a person seeks to be with others, to behave in an outgoing manner, and generally to be sociable. For instance, Jared, the baby described earlier, may have inherited an outgoing personality from his extroverted father, Jamal (Zuckerman, 2003; Horwitz, Luong, & Charles, 2008; Veselka et al., 2012).

Are some children born to be outgoing and extroverted? The answer seems to be "yes."

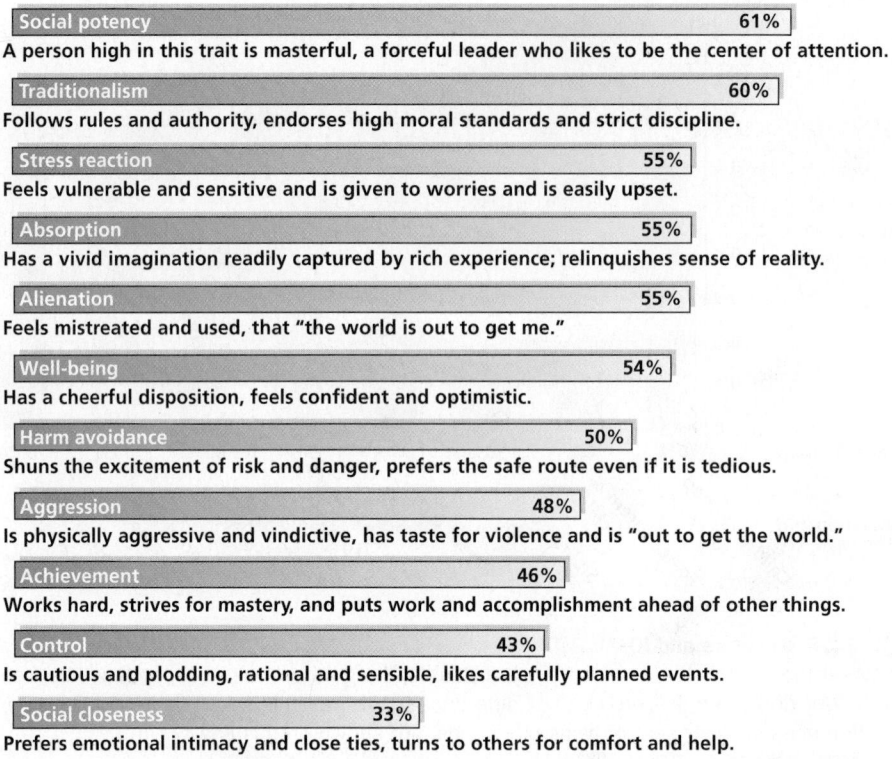

FIGURE 2-7 Inheriting Traits
These traits are among the personality factors that are related most closely to genetic factors. The higher the percentage, the greater the degree to which the trait reflects the influence of heredity. Do these figures mean that "leaders are born, not made"? Why or why not?
Source: Adapted from Tellegen et al., 1988.

How do we know which personality traits reflect genetics? Some evidence comes from direct examination of genes themselves. For instance, it appears that a specific gene is very influential in determining risk-taking behavior. This novelty-seeking gene affects the production of the brain chemical dopamine, making some people more prone than others to seek out novel situations and to take risks (Gillespie et al., 2003; Serretti et al., 2007; Ray et al., 2009).

Other evidence comes from studies of twins. In one major study, researchers looked at the personality traits of hundreds of pairs of twins. Because a good number of the twins were genetically identical but had been raised apart, it was possible to determine with some confidence the influence of genetic factors (Tellegen et al., 1988). The researchers found that certain traits reflected the contribution of genetics considerably more than others. As you can see in Figure 2-7, social potency (the tendency to be a masterful, forceful leader who enjoys being the center of attention) and traditionalism (strict endorsement of rules and authority) are strongly associated with genetic factors (Harris, Vernon, & Jang, 2007).

Even less basic personality traits are linked to genetics. For example, political attitudes, religious interests and values, and even attitudes toward human sexuality have genetic components (Bouchard, 2004; Koenig et al., 2005; Bradshaw & Ellison, 2008).

Clearly, genetic factors play a role in determining personality—but so does the environment in which a child is raised. For example, some parents encourage high activity levels as a manifestation of independence and intelligence. Other parents may encourage lower levels of activity, feeling that more passive children will get along better in society. In part, these parental attitudes are culturally determined: U.S. parents may encourage higher activity levels, while parents in Asian cultures may encourage greater passivity. In both cases, children's personalities will be shaped in part by their parents' attitudes (Cauce, 2008).

Cultural Dimensions

Cultural Differences in Physical Arousal: Might a Culture's Philosophical Outlook Be Determined by Genetics?

The Buddhist philosophy of many Asian cultures emphasizes harmony and peace. In contrast, many Western philosophies accentuate the control of anxiety, fear, and guilt, which are assumed to be basic parts of the human condition.

Could such philosophical approaches reflect, in part, genetic factors? That is the controversial suggestion made by developmental psychologist Jerome Kagan and his colleagues. They speculate that the underlying temperament of a given society, determined genetically, may predispose people in that society toward a particular philosophy (Kagan, Arcus, & Snidman, 1993; Kagan, 2003, 2010).

Kagan bases his admittedly speculative suggestion on well-confirmed findings that show clear differences in temperament between Caucasian and Asian children. For instance, one study that compared 4-month-old infants in China, Ireland, and the United States found several relevant differences. In comparison to the Caucasian American babies and the Irish babies, the Chinese babies had significantly lower motor activity, irritability, and vocalization.

Kagan suggests that the Chinese, who enter the world temperamentally calmer, may find Buddhist notions of serenity more in tune with their nature. In contrast, Westerners, who are emotionally more volatile, tense, and prone to guilt, may be attracted to philosophies that focus on the control of unpleasant feelings, which are usual features of everyday experience (Kagan et al., 1994; Kagan, 2003, 2010).

Of course, neither philosophical approach is better or worse than the other; that's a matter of personal values. Also, any individual within a culture can be more or less temperamentally volatile and the range of temperaments even within a single culture is vast. Finally, environmental conditions can have a significant effect on the portion of a person's temperament that is not genetically determined. But what this speculation does reflect is the complex interaction between culture and temperament. Religion may help mold temperament; temperament may make certain religious ideals more attractive.

To validate this intriguing notion would require additional research to determine just how the unique interaction of heredity and environment within a given culture may produce a framework for viewing and understanding the world.

The Buddhist philosophy emphasizes harmony and peacefulness. Could this decidedly non-Western philosophy be a reflection, in part, of genetic causes?

Because both genetic and environmental factors have consequences for a child's personality, personality development is a perfect example of the interplay between nature and nurture. Furthermore, it is not only individuals who reflect the interaction of nature and nurture, but even entire cultures, as we see above.

Psychological Disorders: The Role of Genetics and Environment

Dana Horowitz started hearing voices when she was waiting tables one summer during high school. "A customer was giving me his order and I suddenly heard him whispering, 'I'm going to kill you,' " she remembers. Co-workers recall her screaming and attacking the customer for "no reason." Several described her as "possessed."

In a sense, she *was* possessed—possessed with schizophrenia, one of the severest types of psychological disorder. Horowitz's world, normal and happy through childhood, took a tumble during adolescence as she increasingly lost her hold on reality. For the next two decades, she would be in and out of institutions.

What was the cause of Horowitz's mental disorder? Evidence suggests that schizophrenia is brought about by genetic factors and runs in families. Moreover, the closer the genetic links between family members, the more likely it is that if one person develops schizophrenia, the other will too. For instance, a monozygotic twin has close to a 50 percent risk of developing schizophrenia when the other twin develops the disorder (see Figure 2-8). On the other hand, a niece or nephew of a person with schizophrenia has less than a 5 percent chance

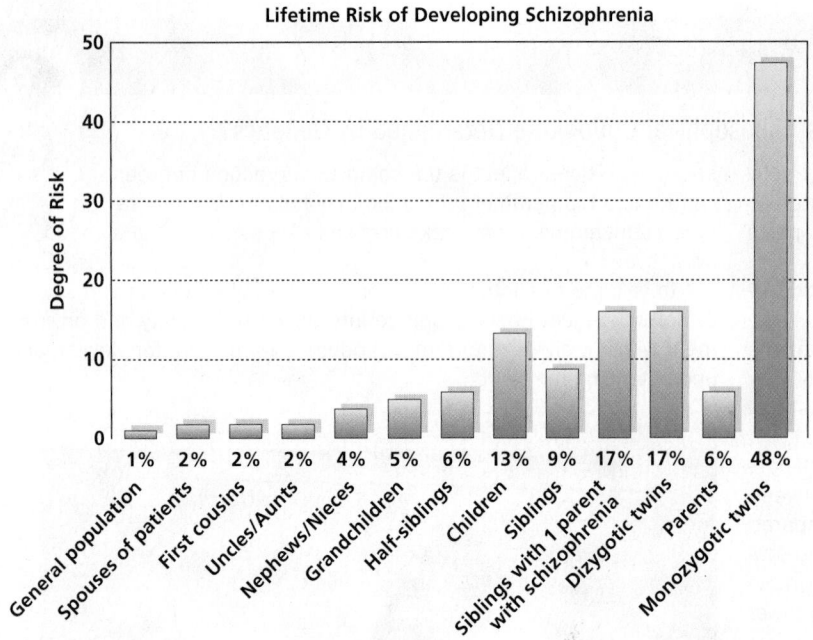

FIGURE 2-8 The Genetics of Schizophrenia
The psychological disorder of schizophrenia has clear genetic components. The closer the genetic links between someone with schizophrenia and another family member, the more likely it is that the other person will also develop schizophrenia.
Source: Based on Gottesman, 1991.

of developing the disorder (Prescott & Gottesman, 1993; Hanson & Gottesman, 2005; van Haren et al., 2012).

These data also illustrate that genetics alone does not influence the development of the disorder. If genetics were the sole cause, the risk for an identical twin would be 100 percent. Consequently, other factors account for the disorder, ranging from structural abnormalities in the brain to a biochemical imbalance (e.g., Hietala, Cannon, & van Erp, 2003; Howes & Kapur, 2009; Wada et al., 2012).

It also seems that even if individuals harbor a genetic predisposition toward schizophrenia, they are not destined to develop the disorder. Instead, they may inherit an unusual sensitivity to stress in the environment. If stress is low, schizophrenia will not occur. But if stress is sufficiently strong, schizophrenia will result. On the other hand, for someone with a strong genetic predisposition toward the disorder, even relatively weak environmental stressors may lead to schizophrenia (Mittal, Ellman, & Cannon, 2008; Francis et al., 2013).

Several other psychological disorders have been shown to be related, at least in part, to genetic factors. For instance, major depression, alcoholism, autism spectrum disorder, and attention-deficit hyperactivity disorder have significant inherited components (Dick, Rose, & Kaprio, 2006; Monastra, 2008; Burbach & van der Zwaag, 2009).

These disorders, which are genetic but far from preordained, illustrate a fundamental principle regarding the relationship between heredity and environment. Genetics often produces a tendency toward a future course of development, but when and whether the characteristic will be displayed depends on the environment. Thus, although a predisposition for schizophrenia may be present at birth, typically people do not show the disorder until adolescence—if at all.

Similarly, other traits are more likely to be displayed as the influence of parents and other socializing factors declines. For example, young adopted children may display traits that are relatively similar to those of their adoptive parents. As they get older and their parents' day-to-day influence declines, genetically influenced traits may begin to manifest themselves as unseen genetic factors (Caspi & Moffitt, 1993; Arsenault et al., 2003; Poulton & Caspi, 2005).

Can Genes Influence the Environment?

According to developmental psychologist Sandra Scarr (1993, 1998), the genetic endowment provided to children by their parents not only determines their genetic characteristics but also actively influences their environment. Scarr suggests three ways a child's genetic predisposition might influence his or her environment.

First, children tend to focus on aspects of their environment that are most in tune with their genetic abilities. For example, an active, aggressive child may gravitate toward sports, while a reserved child may be more engaged by academics or solitary pursuits like computer games or drawing. Or, one girl reading the school bulletin board may notice the upcoming tryouts for Little League baseball, while her less coordinated but more musically endowed friend might spot a poster recruiting students for an after-school chorus. In these examples the children are attending to those aspects of the environment in which their genetically determined abilities can flourish.

Second, the gene–environment influence may be more passive and less direct. For example, a particularly sports-oriented parent, who has genes that promote good physical coordination, may provide many opportunities for a child to play sports.

Finally, the genetically driven temperament of a child may *evoke* certain environmental influences. For instance, an infant's demanding behavior may cause parents to be more

attentive to the infant's needs than they would be otherwise. Or, a child who is genetically well coordinated may play ball with anything in the house so often that her parents notice and decide to give her some sports equipment.

In sum, determining whether behavior is primarily attributable to nature or nurture is like shooting at a moving target. Not only are behaviors and traits a joint outcome of genetic and environmental factors, but the relative influence of genes and environment for specific characteristics shifts over the life span. Although the genes we inherit at birth set the stage for our future development, the constantly shifting scenery and the other characters in our lives determine just how our development eventually plays out. The environment both influences our experiences and is molded by the choices we are temperamentally inclined to make.

REVIEW, CHECK, AND APPLY

REVIEW

LO4 How do the environment and genetics work together?

- Using a variety of approaches, developmental researchers have come to the general conclusion that virtually all traits, characteristics, and behaviors result from a combination and interaction of nature and nurture.

LO5 What is the role of genetics and the environment in determining specific major human characteristics?

- Genetic influences have been identified in physical characteristics, intelligence, personality traits and behaviors, and psychological disorders.
- There is speculation that entire cultures may be predisposed genetically toward certain types of philosophical viewpoints and attitudes.

CHECK YOURSELF

1. Most behavioral traits are a product of genetic influence and environmental factors. This is also known as _____.
   - a systematic desensitization
   - b creative orientation
   - c genetic predetermination
   - d multifactorial transmission
2. Instead of asking if behavior is caused by genetic *or* environmental influence, we should be asking *how much* of the behavior is caused by genetic factors and *how much* is caused by environmental factors.
   - True
   - False
3. According to psychologist Jerome Kagan, differences in temperament between Chinese and American children suggest a culture's philosophical outlook may be related to _____ factors.
   - a environmental
   - b genetic
   - c cultural
   - d social

APPLYING LIFESPAN DEVELOPMENT

- How might an environment different from the one you experienced have affected the development of personality characteristics that you believe you inherited from one or both of your parents?

✓ **Study** and **Review** on **MyPsychLab.com**

MODULE 2.2

PRENATAL GROWTH AND CHANGE

Jill and Casey Adams own a small New York advertising firm. When Jill found out she was pregnant, the couple knew they'd need to make radical changes in their lifestyle. Donut breakfasts and fast food lunches would have to give way to healthier meals with lots of protein and veggies. Gone too were late night parties and clubbing with clients. "No alcohol," their midwife stressed. They would also need to give up smoking. Near her due date now, Jill says the changes were tough but good. "And we use our new lifestyle to connect with health-conscious companies. Instead of clubbing until dawn with clients, we now go jogging at dawn with them."

From the moment of conception, development proceeds relentlessly. Much of it is guided by the complex set of genetic guidelines inherited from the parents, but much is also influenced from the start by environmental factors (Leavitt & Goldson, 1996). And both parents, like Jill and Casey Adams, will have the chance to provide a good prenatal environment.

In this module, we trace the first stirrings of life, when the father's sperm meets the mother's egg. We consider the stages of prenatal development, as the fertilized egg rapidly grows and differentiates into the vast variety of cells that make up the human body. We also look at how pregnancy can go awry, and conclude with a discussion of the factors that present threats to normal development.

THE PRENATAL PERIOD

LO6 What are the major milestones during the prenatal stages of development?
LO7 What are some of the problems that can arise during a pregnancy?

When most of us think about the facts of life, we tend to focus on the events that cause a male's sperm cells to begin their journey toward a female's ovum. Yet the act of sex that brings about the potential for conception is both the consequence and the start of a long string of events that precede and follow conception.

Fertilization: The Moment of Conception

Fertilization, or conception, is the joining of sperm and ovum to create the single-celled zygote from which all of us began our lives. Both the male's sperm and the female's ovum come with a history of their own. Females are born with around 400,000 ova located in the two ovaries (see Figure 2-9 for the basic anatomy of the female reproductive organs). However, the ova do not mature until the female reaches puberty. From that point until she reaches menopause, the female will ovulate about every 28 days. During ovulation, an egg is released from one of the ovaries and pushed by minute hair cells through the fallopian tube toward the uterus. If the ovum meets a sperm in the fallopian tube, fertilization takes place (Aitken, 1995).

Sperm, which look a little like microscopic tadpoles, have a shorter life span. They are created by the testicles at a rapid rate: An adult male typically produces several hundred million sperm a day. Consequently, the sperm ejaculated during sexual intercourse are of considerably more recent origin than the ovum to which they are heading.

When sperm enter the vagina, they begin a winding journey through the cervix—the opening into the uterus—and into the fallopian tube, where fertilization may take place. However, only a tiny fraction of the 300 million cells that are typically ejaculated during sexual intercourse ultimately survive the arduous journey. That's usually okay, though: It takes only one sperm to fertilize an ovum, and each sperm and ovum contains all the genetic data necessary to produce a new human. **Explore** the **Concept** *Female Reproductive Organs* in **MyPsychLab**.

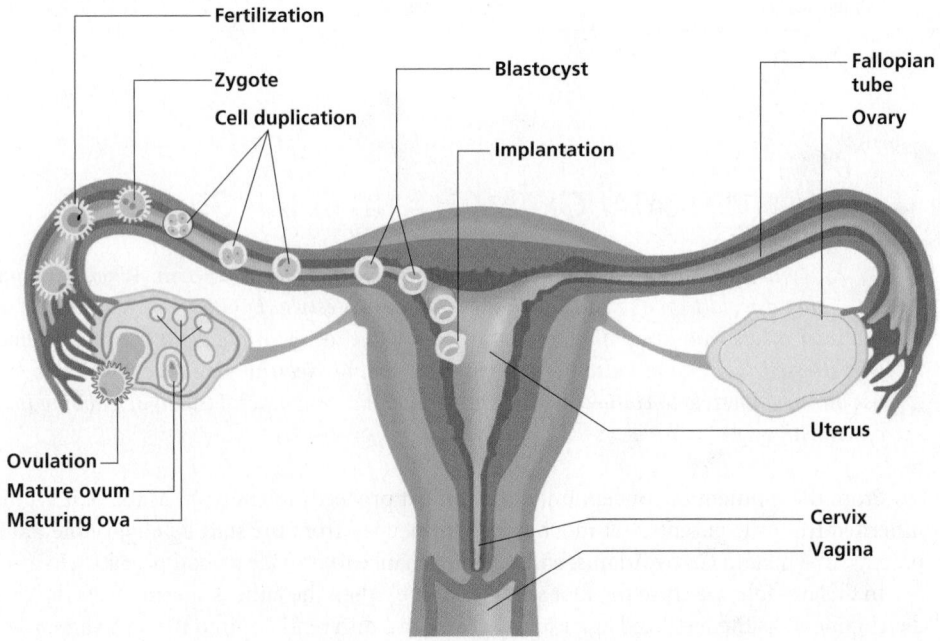

FIGURE 2-9 Anatomy of the Female Reproductive Organs
The basic anatomy of the female reproductive organs is illustrated in this cutaway view.
Source: Based on Moore & Persaud, 2003.

fertilization the process by which a sperm and an ovum—the male and female gametes, respectively—join to form a single new cell

The Stages of the Prenatal Period: The Onset of Development

The prenatal period consists of three phases: the germinal, embryonic, and fetal stages.

The Germinal Stage: Fertilization to 2 Weeks. During the **germinal stage,** the first—and shortest—stage of the prenatal period, the zygote begins to divide and grow in complexity. The fertilized egg (now called a *blastocyst*) travels toward the *uterus*, where it becomes implanted in the uterus's wall, which is rich in nutrients. The germinal stage is characterized by methodical cell division, which gets off to a quick start: Three days after fertilization, the organism consists of some 32 cells, and by the next day the number doubles. Within a week, it comprises of 100 to 150 cells, and the number rises with increasing rapidity.

In addition to increasing in number, the cells of the organism become increasingly specialized. For instance, some cells form a protective layer around the mass of cells, while others begin to establish the rudiments of a placenta and umbilical cord. When fully developed, the **placenta** serves as a conduit between the mother and fetus, providing nourishment and oxygen via the *umbilical cord*, which also removes waste materials from the developing child. The placenta also plays a role in fetal brain development (Kalb, 2012).

The Embryonic Stage: 2 to 8 Weeks. By the end of the germinal period—just 2 weeks after conception—the organism is firmly secured to the wall of the mother's uterus. At this point, the child is called an *embryo*. The **embryonic stage** is the period from 2 to 8 weeks following fertilization. One of the highlights of this stage is the development of the major organs and basic anatomy.

At the beginning of this stage, the developing child has three distinct layers, each of which will form a different set of structures that eventually make up every part of the body. The outer layer of the embryo, the *ectoderm*, will form skin, hair, teeth, sense organs, and the brain and spinal cord. The *endoderm*, the inner layer, produces the digestive system, liver, pancreas, and respiratory system. Sandwiched between the ectoderm and endoderm is the *mesoderm*, from which the muscles, bones, blood, and circulatory system are forged.

If you were looking at an embryo at the end of the embryonic stage, you might be hard-pressed to identify it as human. Only an inch long, an 8-week-old embryo has what appear to be gills and a tail-like structure. On the other hand, a closer look reveals several familiar features. Rudimentary eyes, nose, lips, and even teeth can be recognized, and the embryo has stubby bulges that will form arms and legs.

The head and brain undergo rapid growth during the embryonic period. The head begins to represent a significant proportion of the embryo's size, encompassing about 50 percent of its total length. The growth of nerve cells, called *neurons*, is astonishing: As many as 100,000 neurons are produced every minute during the second month of life! The nervous system begins to function around the fifth week, emitting weak brain waves (Lauter, 1998; Nelson & Bosquet, 2000).

The Fetal Stage: 8 Weeks to Birth. It is not until the final period of prenatal development, the fetal stage, that the developing child becomes easily recognizable. The **fetal stage** starts about 8 weeks after conception and continues until birth. The fetal stage formally starts when the major organs have differentiated.

germinal stage the first—and shortest—stage of the prenatal period, which takes place during the first 2 weeks following conception

placenta a conduit between the mother and fetus, providing nourishment and oxygen via the umbilical cord

embryonic stage the period from 2 to 8 weeks following fertilization during which significant growth occurs in the major organs and body systems

fetal stage the stage that begins at about 8 weeks after conception and continues until birth

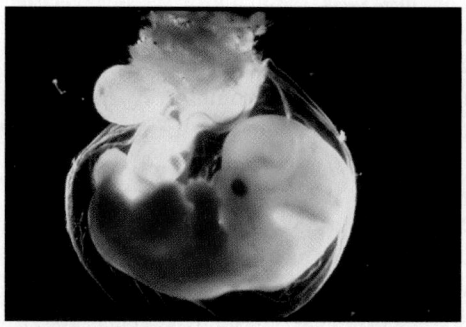

(a) Embyro at 5-6 weeks

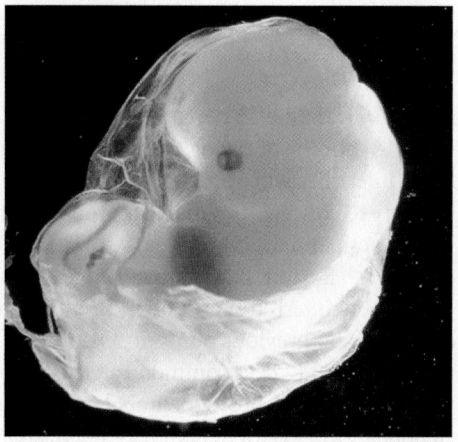

(b) Fetus at 8 weeks

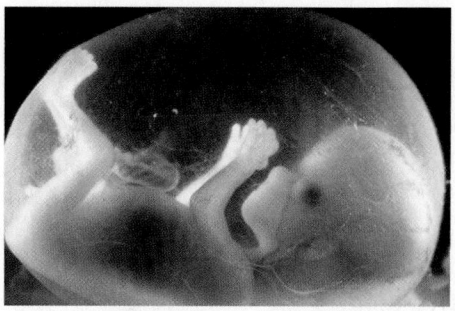

(c) Fetus at 14 weeks

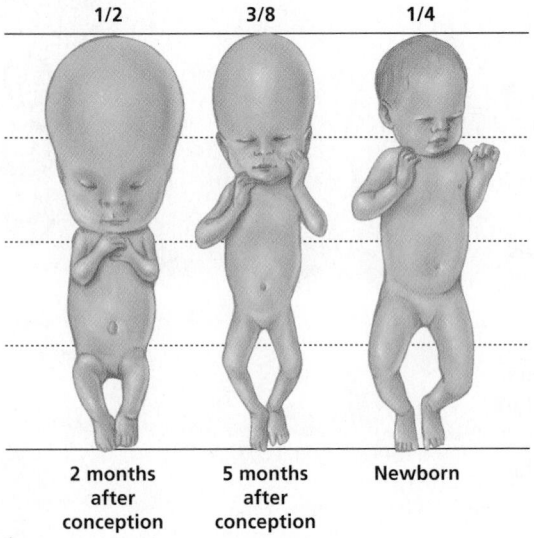

FIGURE 2-10 Body Proportions
During the fetal period, the proportions of the body change dramatically. At 2 months, the head represents about half the fetus, but by the time of birth, it is one-quarter of its total size.

Now called a **fetus**, the developing child undergoes astoundingly rapid change. It increases in length some 20 times, and its proportions change dramatically. At 2 months, around half the fetus is what will ultimately be its head; by 5 months, the head accounts for just over a quarter of its total size (see Figure 2-10). The fetus also substantially increases in weight. At 4 months, the fetus weighs an average of about 4 ounces; at 7 months, it weighs about 3 pounds; and at the time of birth, the average child weighs just over 7 pounds.

At the same time, the developing child is rapidly becoming more complex. Organs become more differentiated and start to work. By 3 months, for example, the fetus swallows and urinates. In addition, the interconnections between the different parts of the body become more complex and integrated. Arms develop hands; hands develop fingers; fingers develop nails.

As this is happening, the fetus makes itself known to the outside world. In the earliest stages of pregnancy, mothers may be unaware that they are, in fact, pregnant. As the fetus becomes increasingly active, however, most mothers take notice. By 4 months, a mother can feel the movement of her child, and several months later others can feel the baby's kicks through the mother's skin. In addition, the fetus can turn, do somersaults, cry, hiccup, clench its fist, open and close its eyes, and suck its thumb.

The brain, too, becomes increasingly sophisticated. The symmetrical left and right halves of the brain, known as *hemispheres*, grow rapidly, and the interconnections between neurons become more complex. The neurons become coated with an insulating material called *myelin*, which helps speed the transmission of messages from the brain to the rest of the body.

By the end of the fetal period, brain waves indicate that the fetus passes through different stages of sleep and wakefulness. The fetus is able to hear (and feel the vibrations of) sounds to which it is exposed. Researchers Anthony DeCasper and Melanie Spence (1986) asked a group of pregnant mothers to read aloud the Dr. Seuss story *The Cat in the Hat* two times a day during the latter months of pregnancy. Three days after the babies were born, they appeared to recognize the story, responding more to it than to another story with a different rhythm.

In weeks 8 to 24 following conception, hormones are released that lead to the increasing differentiation of male and female fetuses. For example, high levels of androgen are produced in males that affect the size of brain cells and the growth of neural connections. Some scientists speculate that this may ultimately lead to differences in male and female brain structure and even to later variations in gender-related behavior (Knickmeyer & Baron-Cohen, 2006; Burton et al., 2009; Jordan-Young, 2012).

Just as no two adults are alike, no two fetuses are the same. Some fetuses are exceedingly active (a trait that will probably remain with them after birth), while others are more sedentary. Some have relatively quick heart rates, while others have slower rates. Such differences are due in part to genetic characteristics inherited at the moment of fertilization. Other differences, though, are caused by the nature of the environment in which the child spends its first 9 months. The prenatal environment can affect infants' development in many ways—for good or ill (Niederhofer, 2004; Tongsong et al., 2005; Monk, Georgieff, & Osterholm, 2013).

Pregnancy Problems

For some couples, conception presents challenges—both physical and ethical—that relate to pregnancy.

Infertility. Some 15 percent of couples suffer from **infertility**, the inability to conceive after 12 to 18 months of trying. Infertility is correlated with age: The older the parents, the more likely infertility will occur (see Figure 2-11). Regardless of when it occurs in the life span, the inability to conceive is a difficult problem for couples, who may feel a combination of sadness, frustration, and even guilt, particularly on the part of the individual who is infertile (Miles et al., 2009; Sexton, Byrd, & von Kluge, 2010).

In men, infertility most often results from producing too few sperm. Use of illicit drugs or cigarettes and previous bouts of sexually transmitted infections (STIs) also increase infertility. For women, the most common cause is failure to release an egg through ovulation. This may occur because of a hormone imbalance, a damaged fallopian tube or uterus, stress, or abuse of alcohol or drugs (Lewis, Legato, & Fisch, 2006; Kelly-Weeder & Cox, 2007; Wilkes et al., 2009).

Several treatments for infertility exist. Some difficulties can be corrected through the use of drugs or surgery. Another option may be **artificial insemination**, a procedure in which a

fetus a developing child, from 8 weeks after conception until birth

infertility the inability to conceive after 12 to 18 months of trying to become pregnant

artificial insemination a process of fertilization in which a man's sperm is placed directly into a woman's reproductive tract by a physician

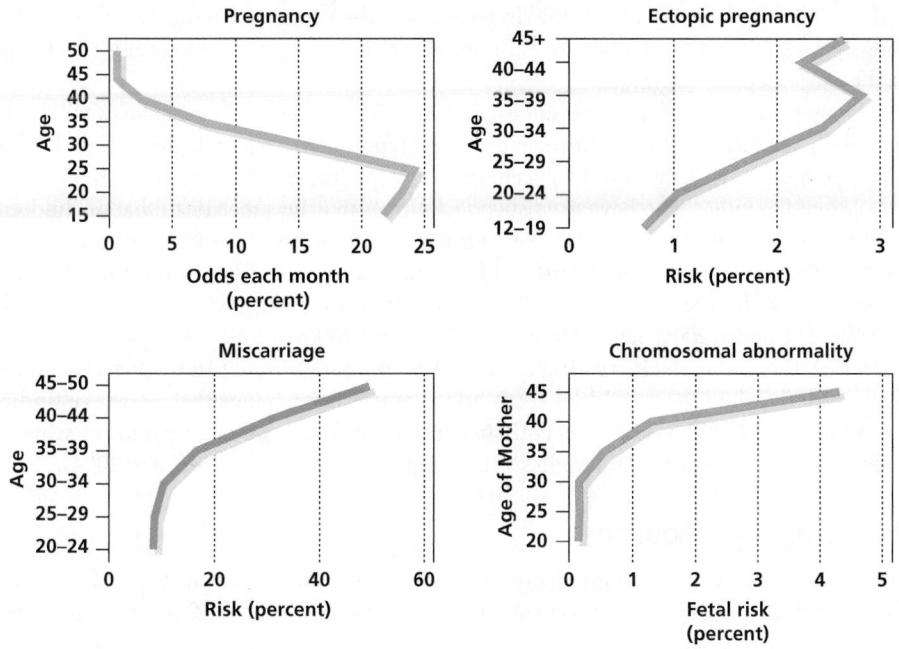

FIGURE 2-11 Older Women and Risks of Pregnancy
Not only does the rate of infertility increase as women get older, but the risk of chromosomal abnormality increases as well.
Source: Reproductive Medicine Associates of New Jersey, 2002.

man's sperm is placed directly into a woman's reproductive tract by a physician. In some situations, the woman's husband provides the sperm, while in others the source is an anonymous donor from a sperm bank.

The most common type of artificial insemination is *intracervical insemination* (*ICI*), in which sperm is placed directly into a woman's cervix. In *intrauterine insemination* (*IUI*), sperm is deposited into the uterus after being "washed," a process that concentrates sperm in a small amount of fluid.

In other cases, fertilization takes place outside the mother's body. **In vitro fertilization (IVF)** is a procedure in which a woman's ova are removed from her ovaries, and a man's sperm is used to fertilize the ova in a laboratory. The fertilized egg is then implanted in the uterus. Similarly, *gamete intrafallopian transfer (GIFT)* and *zygote intrafallopian transfer* (*ZIFT*) are procedures involving the implantation of an egg and sperm or a fertilized egg in a woman's fallopian tubes. In IVF, GIFT, and ZIFT, implantation is usually done in the woman who provided the donor eggs. More rarely, a *surrogate mother* is used. The surrogate mother is artificially inseminated by the biological father or some other male, brings the baby to term, and gives up rights to it (Frazier et al., 2004; Kolata, 2004; Aydiner, Yetkin, & Seli, 2010).

IVF is increasingly successful, with pregnancy rates as high as 48 percent for women under 35 (but with lower rates for older women). (Actual live birth rates are lower, because not all pregnancies ultimately result in birth.) It is also becoming more commonplace, with the procedure being used and publicized by women such as actresses Marcia Cross and Nicole Kidman. Worldwide, more than 3 million babies have been created through IVF (SART, 2012).

Furthermore, reproductive technologies are becoming increasingly sophisticated, permitting parents to choose the sex of their baby. One technique is to separate sperm carrying the X and Y chromosome and implant the desired type into a woman's uterus. In another technique, eggs are removed from a woman and fertilized with sperm through IVF. Three days after fertilization, the embryos are tested to determine their sex. If they are the desired gender, they are then implanted into the mother (Duenwald, 2003, 2004; Kalb, 2004).

"I'm their real child, and you're just a frozen embryo thingy they bought from some laboratory."

William Hamilton/The New Yorker Collection/www.cartoonbank.com

in vitro fertilization (IVF) a procedure in which a woman's ova are removed from her ovaries, and a man's sperm are used to fertilize the ova in a laboratory

The use of surrogate mothers, IVF, and sex selection techniques present a web of ethical and legal issues, as well as many emotional concerns. In some instances, surrogate mothers have refused to give up the child after its birth, while in others the surrogate mother has sought to have a role in the child's life. In such cases, the rights of the mother, the father, the surrogate mother, and ultimately the baby are in conflict. Even more troubling are concerns raised by sex selection techniques.

Although these ethical and legal questions are difficult to resolve, we can answer one question: How do children conceived through emerging reproductive technologies such as IVF fare?

Research shows that they do quite well. In fact, some studies find that the quality of life for the children of families who have used such techniques may be superior to that of children in families who used natural conception. Furthermore, the later psychological adjustment of children conceived through IVF and artificial insemination is no different from that of children conceived through natural techniques (DiPietro, Costigan, & Gurewitsch, 2005; Hjelmstedt, Widström, & Collins, 2006; Siegel, Dittrich, & Vollmann, 2008).

On the other hand, the increasing use of IVF techniques by older individuals (who might be quite elderly when their children reach adolescence) may change these positive findings. Because the use of IVF has only recently become widespread, we don't yet know what outcomes will be most common in families with aging parents (Colpin & Soenen, 2004).

Miscarriage and Abortion

A *miscarriage—known* as a spontaneous abortion—occurs when pregnancy ends before the developing child is able to survive outside the mother's womb. The embryo detaches from the wall of the uterus and is expelled.

Some 15 to 20 percent of all pregnancies end in miscarriage, usually in the first several months of pregnancy. Many occur so early that the mother is not even aware she was pregnant and may not even know she has suffered a miscarriage. Typically, miscarriages are attributable to some sort of genetic abnormality. Whatever the cause, women who suffer miscarriage frequently experience anxiety, depression, and grief. Even after subsequently having a healthy child, women who have had a miscarriage in the past still have a higher risk for depression and may have difficulty caring for their healthy child (Leis-Newman, 2012; Murphy, Lipp, & Powles, 2012).

About one in five pregnancies worldwide end in *abortion*, in which a mother voluntarily chooses to terminate pregnancy. Involving a complex set of physical, psychological, legal, and ethical issues, abortion is a difficult choice for every woman. A task force of the American Psychological Association, which looked at the aftereffects of abortion, found that, following an abortion, most women experienced a combination of relief over terminating an unwanted pregnancy and regret and guilt. However, in most cases, the negative psychological after-effects did not last, except for a small proportion of women who already had serious emotional problems (APA Reproductive Choice Working Group, 2000; Sedgh et al., 2012).

Other research finds that abortion may be associated with an increased risk of future psychological problems; however, the findings are mixed, and there are significant individual differences in how women respond to the experience of abortion. What is clear is that in all cases, abortion is a difficult decision (Fergusson, Horwood, & Ridder, 2006; Cockrill & Gould, 2012).

REVIEW, CHECK, AND APPLY

REVIEW

L06 What are the major milestones during the prenatal stages of development?

- Fertilization joins the sperm and ovum to start prenatal development.
- The prenatal period consists of three stages: germinal, embryonic, and fetal.

L07 What are some of the problems that can arise during a pregnancy?

- In addition to difficulties in conceiving due to infertility, some 15 to 20 percent of all pregnancies end in miscarriage, usually in the first several months of pregnancy.

CHECK YOURSELF

1. The fertility treatment in which fertilization is induced inside the mother's body is known as_____.
   - a artificial insemination
   - b intracervical insemination
   - c intrauterine insemination
   - d in vitro fertilization
2. Fertilization that occurs outside the mother's body is called _____.
   - a artificial insemination
   - b infertility
   - c in vitro fertilization (IVF)
   - d intracervical insemination

APPLYING LIFESPAN DEVELOPMENT

- In your opinion, is it wiser for a woman to ask a friend or a stranger to be the surrogate mother for her child? Why?

✓ **Study** and **Review** on **MyPsychLab.com**

THE PRENATAL ENVIRONMENT: THREATS TO DEVELOPMENT

LO8 What are the major threats to the fetal environment and what can be done about them?

According to the Siriono people of South America, a pregnant woman who eats the meat of certain animals risks having a child who acts and looks like those animals. According to opinions on TV talk shows, a pregnant mother should never lose her temper or else her child may enter the world angry (Cole, 1992).

While these views are largely the stuff of folklore, there is some evidence that a mother's feelings and emotions may have an effect on her fetus. For example, a mother's anxiety during pregnancy may affect the sleeping patterns of the fetus prior to birth. There are even aspects of a mother's and father's behavior, both before and after conception, that can produce lifelong consequences for the child. Some effects show up immediately, but others don't appear until years later (Groome et al., 1995; Couzin, 2002). Among the most profound negative effects are those caused by teratogenic agents. A **teratogen** is an environmental agent such as a drug, chemical, virus, or other factor that produces a birth defect. Although the placenta is responsible for keeping teratogens from the fetus, it is not 100 percent successful and probably every fetus is exposed to some teratogens.

The timing and quantity of exposure to a teratogen are crucial. At some phases of prenatal development, a certain teratogen may have only a minimal impact, while at others the consequences may be profound. Generally, teratogens have their severest effects during periods of especially rapid prenatal development. Sensitivity to specific teratogens is also related to racial and cultural background. For example, Native American fetuses are more susceptible to the effects of alcohol than European American fetuses (Kinney et al., 2003; Winger & Woods, 2004).

Furthermore, different organ systems are vulnerable to teratogens at different times. For example, the brain is most susceptible 15 to 25 days after conception, while the heart is most vulnerable 20 to 40 days after conception (Needleman & Bellinger, 1994; Bookstein et al., 1996; Pajkrt et al., 2004) (see Figure 2-12).

Mothers' Diet

A mother's diet clearly plays an important role in fetal development. A mother who eats a varied diet high in nutrients is apt to have fewer complications during pregnancy, an easier labor, and a generally healthier baby than a mother whose diet is restricted in nutrients (Kaiser & Allen, 2002; Guerrini, Thomson, & Gurling, 2007).

With 925 million hungry people in the world, the problem of diet is of immense global concern. Even worse, the number of people vulnerable to hunger is close to one *billion*. Clearly, restrictions in diet that bring about hunger on such a massive scale affect millions of children born to women living in those conditions (United Nations, 2010).

Fortunately, there are ways to counteract maternal malnutrition. Dietary supplements for mothers can reverse some of the problems produced by a poor diet. Furthermore, research shows that babies who were malnourished as fetuses, but who are subsequently raised in enriched environments, can overcome some of the effects of early malnutrition. However, the reality is that few of the world's children whose mothers were malnourished *before* their birth are apt to find themselves in enriched environments after birth (Grantham-McGregor, Ani, & Fernold, 1994; Kramer, 2008; Olness, 2003).

Mothers' Age

More women are giving birth later in life than was true just 2 or 3 decades ago. This change is largely due to transformations in society, as more women choose to continue their education by seeking advanced degrees and to defer child rearing until they have started careers (Gibbs, 2002; Wildberger, 2003; Bornstein et al., 2006).

Consequently, the number of women in their 30s and 40s who give birth has grown considerably since the 1970s—a situation that may have consequences for both mothers' and

teratogen a factor that produces a birth defect

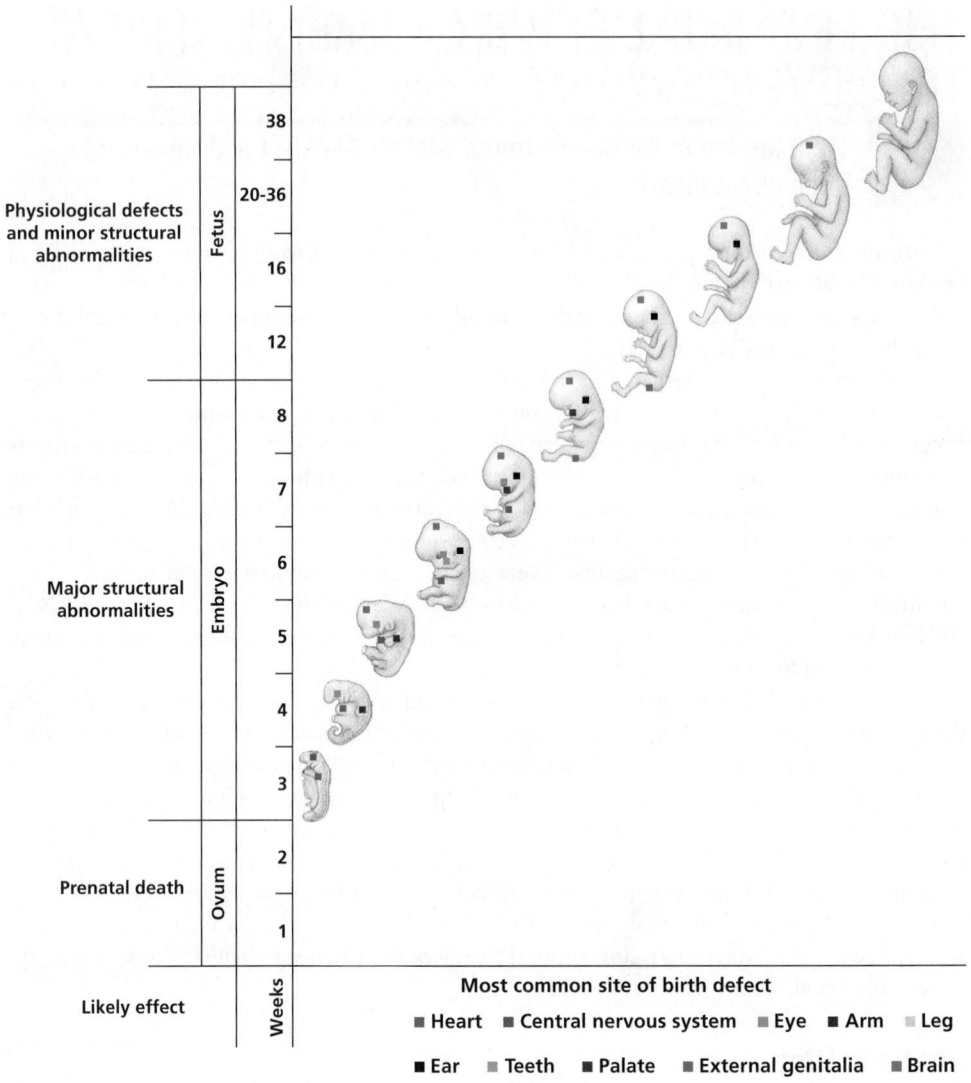

FIGURE 2-12 Teratogen Sensitivity
Depending on their state of development, some parts of the body vary in their sensitivity to teratogens.
Source: Moore, 1974.

children's health. Women over 30 who give birth are at greater risk for a variety of pregnancy and birth complications than younger women. They are more apt to give birth prematurely and to have children with low birthweights. This occurs in part because of a decline in the condition of a woman's eggs. By the time women reach age 42, 90 percent of their eggs are no longer normal (Cnattingius, Berendes, & Forman, 1993; Gibbs, 2002). Older mothers are also considerably more likely to give birth to children with Down syndrome, a form of mental retardation. About 1 in 100 babies born to mothers over 40 has Down syndrome; for mothers over 50, the incidence increases to 1 in 4 (Gaulden, 1992). On the other hand, some research show that older mothers are not automatically at risk. For instance, one study found that when women in their 40s who have not experienced health difficulties are considered, they are no more likely to have prenatal problems than those in their 20s (Ales, Druzin, & Santini, 1990; Dildy et al., 1996).

The risks involved in pregnancy are greater not only for older mothers, but for atypically young women as well. Women who become pregnant during adolescence—and such pregnancies actually encompass 20 percent of all pregnancies—are more likely to have premature deliveries. Furthermore, the mortality rate of infants born to adolescent mothers is double that for mothers in their 20s (Kirchengast & Hartmann, 2003).

Keep in mind that the higher mortality rate for babies of adolescent mothers reflects more than just physiological problems related to the mothers' young age. Young mothers often face adverse social and economic factors that can affect infant health. Many teenage mothers do not have adequate financial or social support, a situation that prevents them from getting good prenatal care and parenting support after the baby is born. Poverty or social circumstances, such as a lack of parental involvement or supervision, may even have set the stage for the adolescent to become pregnant in the first place (Huizink, Mulder, & Buitelaar, 2004; Langille, 2007; Meade, Kershaw, & Ickovics, 2008). **Watch** the **Video** *Pregnancy and Prenatal Care Across Cultures* in **MyPsychLab.**

Mothers' Health

Mothers who eat the right foods, maintain an appropriate weight, and exercise appropriately maximize the chances of having a healthy baby. Furthermore, they can reduce the lifetime risk of obesity, high blood pressure, and heart disease in their children by maintaining a healthy lifestyle (Walker & Humphries, 2005, 2007).

Depending on when it strikes, an illness in a pregnant woman can have devastating consequences. For instance, the onset of *rubella* (German measles) before the 11th week of pregnancy can cause blindness, deafness, heart defects, or brain damage in the baby. In later stages of a pregnancy, however, rubella has less serious effects.

Several other diseases may affect a developing fetus, depending on when they are contracted. For instance, *chicken pox* may produce birth defects, while *mumps* may increase the risk of miscarriage.

Some STIs such as *syphilis* can be transmitted directly to the fetus, who will be born with the disease. Some STIs such as *gonorrhea* are communicated to the child as it passes through the birth canal to be born.

AIDS (acquired immune deficiency syndrome) is the newest of the diseases to affect a newborn. Mothers who have the disease or who merely are carriers of the virus may pass it on to their fetuses through the blood that reaches the placenta. However, if mothers with AIDS are treated with antiviral drugs such as AZT during pregnancy, less than 5 percent of infants are born with the disease. Those infants who are born with AIDS must remain on antiviral drugs their entire lives (Nesheim et al., 2004).

A mother's mental health status can also affect her children. For example, if the mother suffers from clinical depression while she is pregnant, the development of her children may be negatively affected.

Mothers' Drug Use

The use of many kinds of drugs—both legal and illegal—poses serious risks to the unborn child. Even over-the-counter remedies for common ailments can have surprisingly injurious consequences. For instance, aspirin taken for a headache can lead to fetal bleeding and growth impairments (Griffith, Azuma, & Chasnoff, 1994).

Some drugs taken by mothers cause problems for their children decades after they were taken. As recently as the 1970s, the artificial hormone *DES (diethylstilbestrol)* was frequently prescribed to prevent miscarriage. Only later was it found that the daughters of mothers who took DES stood a much higher than normal chance of developing a rare form of vaginal or cervical cancer and had more difficulties during their pregnancies. Sons of the mothers who had taken DES had their own problems, including a higher than average rate of reproductive difficulties (Adams Hillard, 2001; Schecter, Finkelstein, & Koren, 2005).

Birth control or fertility pills taken by pregnant women before they are aware of their pregnancy can also cause fetal damage. Such medicines contain sex hormones which, when produced naturally, are related to sexual differentiation in the fetus and gender differences after birth. These medicines can cause significant damage to developing brain structures (Miller, 1998; Brown, Hines, & Fane, 2002).

Illicit drugs may pose equally great, and sometimes even greater, risks for the environments of prenatal children. For one thing, the purity of drugs purchased illegally varies significantly, so drug users can never be quite sure what specifically they are ingesting. Furthermore, the effects of some commonly used illicit drugs can be particularly devastating.

Consider, for instance, the use of *marijuana*. Certainly one of the most commonly used illegal drugs—millions of people in the United States have admitted trying it—marijuana used during pregnancy can restrict the oxygen that reaches the fetus. Its use can lead to infants who are irritable, nervous, and easily disturbed. Children exposed to marijuana prenatally show learning and memory deficits at the age of 10 (Mayes et al., 2007; Williams & Ross, 2007; Goldschmidt et al., 2008; Willford, Richardson, & Day, 2012).

During the early 1990s, *cocaine* use by pregnant women led to the birth of thousands of so-called crack babies. Cocaine restricts the arteries leading to the fetus, significantly reducing the flow of blood and oxygen and increasing the risk of fetal death, birth defects, and disabilities (Schuetze, Eiden, & Coles, 2007).

Children whose mothers were addicted to cocaine may themselves be born addicted and have to undergo painful withdrawal. Even if not addicted, they are often shorter and weigh less than average, and they may have serious respiratory problems, visible birth defects, or seizures. They behave quite differently from other infants: Their reactions to stimulation are muted, but once they start to cry, they may be hard to soothe (Eiden, Foote, & Schuetze, 2007; Richardson, Goldschmidt, & Willford, 2009; Richardson et al., 2013).

It is difficult to determine the long-term effects of mothers' cocaine use in isolation, because such drug use is often accompanied by poor prenatal care and impaired nurturing after birth. In many cases it is neglectful caregiving by mothers who use cocaine that causes the children's problems, and not exposure to the drug. Treatment of such children requires not only that the mother stop using the drug, but that she or other caregivers provide improved care to the infant (Brown et al., 2004; Jones, 2006).

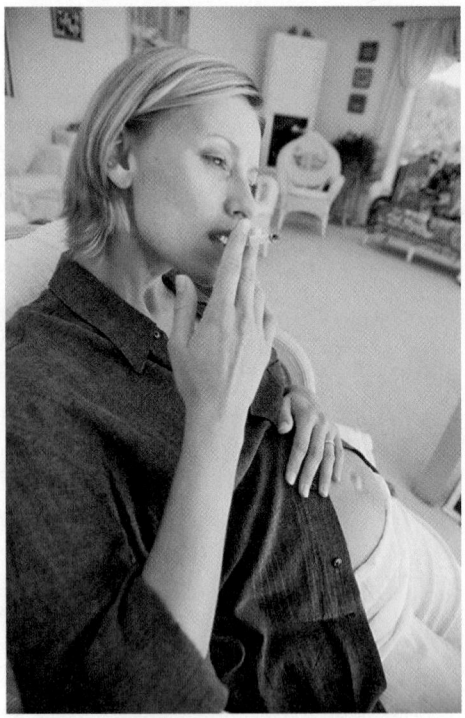

Pregnant women who use tobacco place their unborn children at significant risk.

Mothers' Use of Alcohol and Tobacco

Evidence strongly suggests that pregnant women who take even small amounts of alcohol or nicotine can disrupt the development of the fetus.

The children of alcoholics, who consume substantial quantities of alcohol during pregnancy, are at the greatest risk. Approximately 1 out of every 750 infants is born with **fetal alcohol syndrome (FAS)**, a disorder that may include below-average intelligence and sometimes mental retardation, delayed growth, and facial deformities. FAS is now the primary preventable cause of mental retardation (Steinhausen & Spohr, 1998; Burd et al., 2003; Calhoun & Warren, 2007).

Even mothers who use smaller amounts of alcohol during pregnancy place their child at risk. **Fetal alcohol effects (FAE)** is a condition in which children display some, but not all, of the problems of FAS due to their mother's consumption of alcohol during pregnancy (Streissguth, 1997; Baer, Sampson, & Barr, 2003; Molina et al., 2007).

Children who do not have FAE may still be affected by their mothers' use of alcohol. Studies have found that maternal consumption of an average of just two alcoholic drinks a day during pregnancy is associated with lower intelligence in their offspring at age 7. Other research concurs, suggesting that relatively small quantities of alcohol taken during pregnancy can have future adverse effects on children's behavior and psychological functioning. Furthermore, the consequences of alcohol ingestion during pregnancy are long lasting. For example, one study found that the success of 14-year-olds on a test involving spatial and visual reasoning was related to their mothers' alcohol consumption during pregnancy. The more the mothers reported drinking, the less accurately their children responded (Lynch et al., 2003; Mattson, Calarco, & Lang, 2006; Streissguth, 2007; Chiodo et al., 2012).

Because of these risks, physicians today counsel pregnant women and women who are trying to become pregnant to stop drinking alcohol entirely. They also caution against another practice proven to have an adverse effect on an unborn child: smoking.

Like alcohol consumption, smoking has many consequences, none good. For starters, it reduces the oxygen content and increases the carbon monoxide of the mother's blood, which quickly restricts the oxygen available to the fetus. In addition, the nicotine and other toxins in cigarettes slow the respiration rate of the fetus and speed up its heart.

The ultimate result is an increased possibility of miscarriage and a higher likelihood of death during infancy. In fact, estimates suggest that smoking by pregnant women leads to more than 100,000 miscarriages and the deaths of 5,600 babies in the United States alone each year (Triche & Hossain, 2007; Geller, Nelson, & Bonacquisti, 2013).

fetal alcohol syndrome (FAS) a disorder caused by the pregnant mother consuming substantial quantities of alcohol during pregnancy, potentially resulting in mental retardation and delayed growth in the child

fetal alcohol effects (FAE) a condition in which children display some, but not all, of the problems of FAS due to the mother's consumption of alcohol during pregnancy

Smokers are two times as likely as nonsmokers to have babies with an abnormally low birthweight, and smokers' babies are shorter, on average, than those of nonsmokers. Furthermore, women who smoke during pregnancy are 50 percent more likely to have mentally retarded children. Finally, mothers who smoke are more likely to have children who exhibit disruptive behavior during childhood (Wakschlag et al., 2006; McCowan et al., 2009).

Do Fathers Affect the Prenatal Environment?

It would be easy to believe that fathers, having done their part to cause conception, have no further effect on the *prenatal* environment of the fetus, but it turns out that a father's behavior may well have an influence. In fact, health practitioners are applying new research to suggest ways fathers can support healthy prenatal development.

For instance, fathers-to-be should avoid smoking. Secondhand smoke may affect the health of the mother and her unborn child. The more the father smokes, the lower the birthweight of his children (Hyssaelae, Rautava, & Helenius, 1995; Tomblin, Hammer, & Zhang, 1998).

Similarly, alcohol and drug use by a father can have significant effects on the fetus. Alcohol and drugs impair sperm and may lead to chromosomal damage, which may affect the fetus at conception. In addition, alcohol and drug use may create stress in the mother and generally produce an unhealthy environment. In addition, workplace toxins such as lead or mercury may bind to sperm and cause birth defects (Wakefield et al., 1998; Choy et al., 2002; Dare et al., 2002).

Finally, fathers who are physically or emotionally abusive to their pregnant wives can harm their unborn children by increasing maternal stress or causing actual physical damage. In fact, 4 to 8 percent of women face physical abuse during pregnancy (Gilliland & Verny, 1999; Gazmararian et al., 2000; Bacchus, Mezey, & Bewley, 2006; Martin et al., 2006).

From the perspective of a health care provider: In addition to avoiding smoking, what other sorts of things might fathers-to-be do to help their unborn children develop normally in the womb?

Becoming an Informed Consumer of Development

Optimizing the Prenatal Environment

If you are contemplating ever having a child, you may be overwhelmed, at this point in the chapter, by the number of things that can go wrong. Don't be. Although both genetics and the environment pose their share of risks, in the vast majority of cases, pregnancy and birth proceed without mishap. Moreover, there are several things that women can do—both before and during pregnancy—to optimize the probability that pregnancy will progress smoothly (Massaro, Rothbaum, & Aly, 2006). Among them:

- **For women who are planning to become pregnant, several precautions are in order.** First, schedule any necessary nonemergency x-rays only during the first 2 weeks after your menstrual periods. Second, be sure you are vaccinated against rubella (German measles) at least 3, and preferably 6, months before getting pregnant. Finally, discontinue birth control pills, which disrupt hormone production, at least 3 months before trying to conceive.
- **Eat well before and during pregnancy.** As the saying goes, pregnant mothers are eating for two. It is more essential than ever to eat regular, well-balanced meals. In addition, take prenatal vitamins, including folic acid, which can decrease the likelihood of birth defects (Amitai et al., 2004).
- **Don't use alcohol or other drugs.** The evidence is clear that many drugs pass directly to the fetus and may cause birth defects. It is also clear that the more one drinks, the greater the risk to the fetus. The best advice: Don't use *any* drug unless directed by a physician. If you are planning to get pregnant, encourage your partner to avoid using alcohol or other drugs too (O'Connor & Whaley, 2006).
- **Monitor caffeine intake.** Although it is not clear that caffeine produces birth defects, it is known that the caffeine in coffee, tea, and chocolate can pass to the fetus, acting as a stimulant. Because of this, you probably shouldn't drink more than a few cups of coffee a day (Wisborg et al., 2003; Diego et al., 2007).
- **Whether pregnant or not, don't smoke.** This holds true for mothers, fathers, and anyone else in the vicinity of the pregnant mother, because research suggests that smoke in the fetal environment can affect birthweight.
- **Exercise regularly.** In most cases, pregnant women can continue with low-impact exercise, but should avoid extreme exercise, especially on very hot or cold days. "No pain, no gain" isn't applicable during pregnancy (O'Toole & Sawicki, 2003; Paisley, Joy, & Price, 2003; Schmidt et al., 2006; DiNallo, Downs, & Le Masurier, 2012).

REVIEW, CHECK, AND APPLY

REVIEW

L08 What are the major threats to the fetal environment and what can be done about them?

- The prenatal environment significantly influences the development of the baby. The diet, age, prenatal support, and illnesses of mothers can affect their babies' health and growth.
- Mothers' use of drugs, alcohol, tobacco, and caffeine can adversely affect the health and development of the unborn child. The behavior of fathers and others can also affect the child.
- Eating well and nutritiously, exercising regularly, avoiding alcohol and tobacco, and controlling caffeine intake are sound strategies for averting threats to the fetal environment.

CHECK YOURSELF

1. Match the following descriptions of prenatal development to their appropriate labels: germinal, embryonic, and fetal.

   a. This stage lasts from 8 weeks until birth and involves the differentiation of major organs. _____

   b. From 2 to 8 weeks following fertilization, when the major organs and basic anatomy begin developing. _____

   c. The first and shortest stage, where the zygote begins to divide and grow in complexity during the first 2 weeks following conception. _____

2. A _____ is an environmental agent such as a drug, chemical, virus, or other factor that produces a birth defect.

   a. terminal button
   b. teratogen
   c. terrapin
   d. chromosome

APPLYING LIFESPAN DEVELOPMENT

- Studies show that "crack babies" who are starting school have significant difficulty dealing with multiple stimuli and forming close attachments. How might both genetic and environmental influences have combined to produce these results?

✓ **Study** and **Review** on **MyPsychLab.com**

MODULE 2.3

BIRTH AND THE NEWBORN INFANT

Tania and Lou Kerry hadn't planned to have a second child so soon, but 3 months after their son Caleb was born, Tania became pregnant again. Tania's midwife referred her to an obstetrician for the second birth. The reason? Women who become pregnant within months of giving birth are more likely to deliver prematurely. The midwife wanted a doctor on board in case Tania went into labor early.

Despite help from both her mother and Lou, Tania was exhausted most of the pregnancy. And worried the new baby would come too soon. "Take it one day at a time," her doctor advised. "Every day that baby stays in the womb, its chances of survival increase."

Tania was almost in the home stretch at 35 weeks when her water broke. Because the baby was early, she came very fast. Tania gave birth in the ambulance on the way to the hospital, but the medics knew what to do for her daughter who weighed under five pounds. After a month in an incubator, Gemma Kerry is home with her family. "We were lucky," Tania says. "Not every preemie survives."

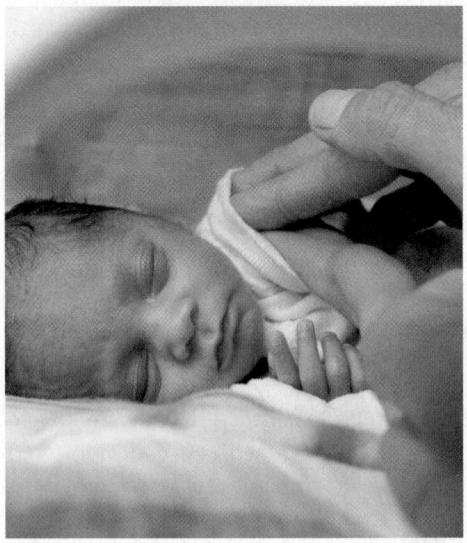

Infants were not meant to be born as early as Gemma. Yet, for a variety of reasons, more than 10 percent of all babies today are born early, and the odds of their leading a normal life are improving dramatically.

All births, even those that reach full term, are a combination of excitement and anxiety. In the vast majority of cases delivery goes smoothly, and it is an amazing and joyous moment when a new being enters the world. The excitement of birth is soon replaced by wonder at the extraordinary nature of newborns themselves. Babies enter the world with a surprising array of abilities, ready from the first moments of life outside the womb to respond to the world and the people in it.

In this module we'll examine the events that lead to the delivery and birth of a child, and take an initial look at the newborn. We first consider labor and delivery, exploring how the process usually proceeds, as well as several alternative approaches.

We next examine some of the possible complications of birth. Problems that can occur range from premature births to infant mortality. Finally, we consider the extraordinary range of capabilities of newborns. We'll look not only at their physical and perceptual abilities, but at the way they enter the world with the ability to learn and with skills that help form the foundations of their future relationships with others.

BIRTH

LO9 What is the normal process of labor?

I wasn't completely naïve. I mean, I knew that it was only in movies that babies come out of the womb all pink, dry, and beautiful. But still, I was initially taken aback by my son's appearance. Because of his passage through the birth canal, his head was cone-shaped, a bit like a wet, partly-deflated football. The nurse must have noticed my reaction because she hastened to assure me that this would change in a matter of days. She then moved quickly to wipe off the whitish sticky substance all over his body, informing me as she did so that the fuzzy hair on his ears was only temporary. I leaned in and put my finger into my boy's hand. He rewarded me by closing his hand around it. I interrupted the nurse's assurances. "Don't worry," I stammered, tears suddenly filling my eyes. "He's absolutely the most beautiful thing I've ever seen."

For those of us accustomed to thinking of newborns in the images of baby food commercials, this portrait of a typical newborn may be surprising. Yet most **neonates**—the term used for newborns—resemble this one. Make no mistake, however: Babies are a welcome sight to their parents from the moment of birth.

The neonate gains its odd appearance during its journey from the uterus, down the birth canal, and into the world. We can trace this journey, beginning with the release of the chemicals that initiate labor.

Labor: The Process of Birth Begins

About 266 days after conception, a protein called *corticotropin-releasing hormone (CRH)* triggers the release of various hormones, and the process that leads to birth begins. One critical hormone is *oxytocin*, from the mother's pituitary gland. When the concentration of oxytocin becomes high enough, the uterus begins periodic contractions (Hertelendy & Zakar, 2004; Terzidou, 2007; Tattersall et al., 2012).

During the prenatal period, the uterus, which is composed of muscle tissue, slowly expands as the fetus grows. For most of the pregnancy it is inactive, but after the fourth month it occasionally contracts to ready itself for the delivery. These *Braxton-Hicks contractions* are sometimes called "false labor" because they can fool eager and anxious parents.

When birth is imminent, the uterus begins to contract intermittently. The increasingly intense contractions force the head of the fetus against the *cervix*, the neck of the uterus that separates it from the vagina. Eventually, the contractions become strong enough to propel the fetus slowly down the birth canal until it enters the world (Mittendorf et al., 1990). This exertion and the narrow birth passageway often give newborns a battered, conehead appearance.

Labor proceeds in three stages (see Figure 2-13). In the *first stage of labor*, the uterine contractions initially occur around every 8 to 10 minutes and last about 30 seconds. As labor proceeds, the contractions occur more frequently and last longer. Toward the end of labor, the contractions may occur every 2 minutes and last almost 2 minutes. As the first stage of labor ends, the contractions reach their greatest intensity, a period known as *transition*. The mother's cervix fully opens, eventually expanding enough (usually to around 10 centimeters) to allow the baby's head to pass through.

During the *second stage of labor*, which typically lasts around 90 minutes, the baby's head proceeds further with each contraction, increasing the size of the vaginal opening. Because the area between the vagina and rectum must stretch, an incision called an **episiotomy** is sometimes made to increase the size of the opening of the vagina. However, this practice is now seen as potentially harmful, and the number of episiotomies has fallen drastically in the last decade (Goldberg et al., 2002; Graham et al., 2005; Dudding, Vaizey, & Kamm, 2008).

The second stage of labor ends when the baby has completely left the mother's body. Finally, in the *third stage of labor* the child's umbilical cord (still attached to the neonate) and the placenta are expelled from the mother. This stage is the quickest and easiest, taking just a few minutes.

The nature of a woman's reactions to labor reflects, in part, cultural factors. Although there is no evidence that the physiological aspects of labor differ among women of different

neonates the term used for newborns

episiotomy an incision sometimes made to increase the size of the opening of the vagina to allow the baby to pass

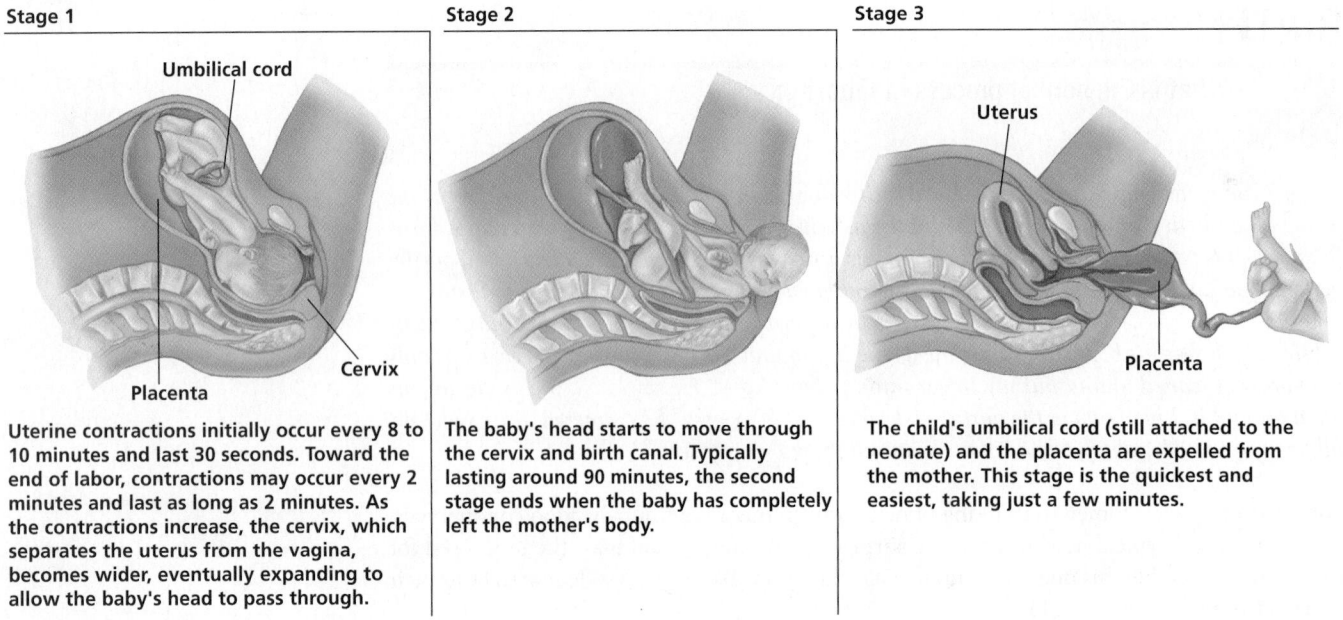

FIGURE 2-13 The Three Stages of Labor

cultures, expectations about labor and interpretations of its pain do vary significantly from one culture to another (Callister et al., 2003; Fisher, Hauck, & Fenwick, 2006). For instance, there is a kernel of truth to popular stories of women in some societies putting down their tools, giving birth, and immediately returning to work with their neonates on their backs. Accounts of the !Kung people in Africa describe women giving birth without much ado—or assistance—and quickly recovering. On the other hand, many societies regard childbirth as dangerous or even as essentially an illness.

Birth: From Fetus to Neonate

Birth occurs when the fetus emerges fully from its mother's body. In most cases, babies automatically make the transition for their oxygen needs from the placenta to their lungs. Consequently, most newborns spontaneously cry, which helps them clear their lungs and breathe on their own.

What happens next varies from situation to situation and from culture to culture. In Western cultures, health care workers are almost always on hand to assist with the birth. In the United States, 99 percent of births are attended by professional health care workers, but in many less-developed countries less than half of births have professional health care workers in attendance (United Nations Statistics Division, 2012).

The Apgar Scale. In most cases, the newborn undergoes a quick visual inspection. While parents lovingly count fingers and toes, health care workers use the **Apgar scale**, a standard measurement system that looks for a variety of indications of good health (see Table 2-3). Developed by physician Virginia Apgar, the scale directs attention to five basic qualities, recalled most easily by using Apgar's name as a guide: *a*ppearance (color), *p*ulse (heart rate), *g*rimace (reflex irritability), *a*ctivity (muscle tone), and *r*espiration (respiratory effort).

The newborn receives a score ranging from 0 to 2 on each of the five qualities, for an overall score between 0 and 10. Most score 7 or above; the 10 percent who score under 7 require help to start breathing. Newborns who score under 4 need immediate, life-saving intervention.

In addition to problems or defects already present in the fetus, the process of birth itself may sometimes cause difficulties. Oxygen deprivation is one of the most profound. At times during labor, the umbilical cord may get wrapped around the neck or pinched during a prolonged contraction, thereby cutting off the supply of oxygen. Lack of oxygen for a few seconds is not harmful, but if it lasts longer it may cause serious harm. A restriction of oxygen, or **anoxia**, lasting a few minutes can produce cognitive deficits such as language delays and even mental retardation due to brain cell death (Hopkins-Golightly, Raz, & Sander, 2003; Rossetti, Carrera, & Oddo, 2012).

Apgar scale a standard measurement system that looks for a variety of indications of good health in newborns

anoxia a restriction of oxygen to the baby, lasting a few minutes during the birth process, which can produce cognitive defects

TABLE 2-3 APGAR SCALE

A score is given for each sign at 1 minute and 5 minutes after the birth. If there are problems with the baby, an additional score is given at 10 minutes. A score of 7–10 is considered normal, whereas 4–7 might require some resuscitative measures, and a baby with an Apgar score under 4 requires immediate resuscitation.

	Sign	0 Points	1 Point	2 Points
A	Appearance (skin color)	Blue-gray, pale all over	Normal, except for extremities	Normal over entire body
P	Pulse	Absent	Below 100 bpm	Above 100 bpm
G	Grimace (reflex irritability)	No response	Grimace	Sneezes, coughs, pulls away
A	Activity (muscle tone)	Absent	Arms and legs flexed	Active movement
R	Respiration	Absent	Slow, irregular	Good, crying

Source: Apgar, 1953.

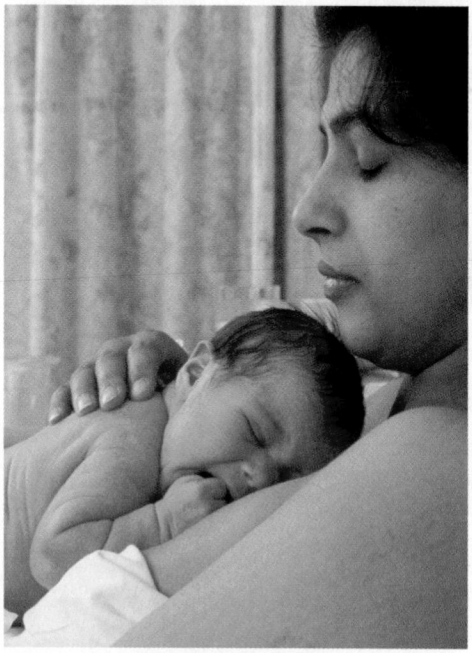

Physical Appearance and Initial Encounters. After assessing the newborn's health, health care workers deal with the remnants of the child's passage through the birth canal. They clean away the *vernix*, the thick, greasy substance (like cottage cheese) that covers the newborn and smoothes the passage through the birth canal. The fine, dark fuzz known as *lanugo* that covers the newborn's body soon disappears. The newborn's eyelids may be puffy from fluids that accumulated during labor, and blood or other fluids may remain on parts of his or her body.

The clean newborn is then handed to the parent or parents for their first, miraculous encounter with their child. The importance of this initial encounter has become a matter of controversy. Some psychologists and physicians argued in the 1970s that **bonding**, the close physical and emotional contact between parent and child during the period immediately following birth, was crucial for lasting parent–child relationships. More recent research suggests otherwise, however: Although it does appear that mothers who have early physical contact with their babies are more responsive to them than those who don't have such contact, the difference lasts only a few days. Such news is reassuring to parents whose children must receive immediate, intensive medical attention just after birth (Weinberg, 2004; Miles et al., 2006; Bigelow & Power, 2012; Stikes & Barbier, 2013).

Although observation of nonhuman animals highlights the importance of contact between mother and offspring following birth, research on humans suggests that immediate physical contact is less critical.

Approaches to Childbirth: Where Medicine and Attitudes Meet

In her second pregnancy, Alma Juarez knew she wanted something other than traditional obstetrics. No drugs. No lying flat on her back for the delivery (which had slowed her contractions and made an oxygen mask necessary). This time, Juarez took control. She joined an exercise class for pregnant women and read books on childbirth. She also chose a nurse-midwife instead of an obstetrician. She wanted someone to work with her, not dictate to her.

When Juarez went into labor, she called the midwife who met her at the hospital. Juarez was determined to stay on her feet, making use of gravity to hasten the birth. Her husband and the midwife took turns walking with her as the contractions got stronger. When she was fully dilated, she got on her hands and knees, a posture she knew would minimize the effort of pushing. Thirty minutes later, her daughter was born. No drugs, no extra oxygen. Juarez says, "The first birth, I was exhausted. The second birth, I was elated."

Parents in the Western world have developed a variety of strategies—and some very strong opinions—to help them deal with something as natural as giving birth, which occurs apparently without much thought throughout the nonhuman animal world. Today parents need to decide, should the birth take place in a hospital or in the home? Should a physician, a nurse, or a midwife assist? Is the father's presence desirable? Should siblings and other family members be on hand to participate in the birth?

Most of these questions, of course, are matters not of fact but of values and opinions. No single approach will be effective for everyone, and no conclusive research indicates that one procedure is significantly more effective than another. And not only are personal preferences involved, culture also plays a role in the choice of birthing procedures.

bonding close physical and emotional contact between parent and child during the period immediately following birth

In Lamaze classes, parents are taught relaxation techniques to prepare for childbirth and to reduce the need for anesthetics.

The abundance of choices is largely due to a reaction to traditional medical practices that had been common in the United States until the early 1970s. Before that time, the typical birth went something like this: A woman in labor was placed in a room with many other women, all of whom were in various stages of childbirth, and some of whom were screaming in pain. Fathers and other family members were not allowed to be present. Just before delivery, the woman was rolled into a delivery room, where the birth took place. Often she was so drugged that she was not aware of the birth at all.

Alternative Birthing Procedures. Now not all mothers give birth in hospitals, and not all births follow the traditional course. Among the alternatives:

- **Lamaze birthing techniques.** Based on the writings of Dr. Fernand Lamaze, this method uses breathing techniques and relaxation training (Lamaze, 1970). Typically, mothers-to-be attend weekly training sessions to learn to relax various parts of the body on command. A "coach," usually the father, is trained at the same time. Through the training, women learn how to deal positively with pain and to relax at the onset of a contraction. Part of the method is to build self-confidence in parents-to-be, demystifying the process of birth.

  Does it work? Most mothers, as well as fathers, report that a Lamaze birth is a very positive experience. On the other hand, we can't be sure that parents who choose the Lamaze method aren't already more highly motivated about the experience of childbirth than parents who do not choose the technique. Furthermore, there is a lack of definitive research on the benefits of Lamaze techniques. Still, Lamaze remains one of the most popular childbirth methods in the United States (Larsen et al., 2001; Zwelling, 2006).
- **Bradley Method.** The Bradley Method, which is sometimes known as "husband-coached childbirth," is based on the principle that childbirth should be natural, without medication or medical interventions. To prepare for childbirth, mothers-to-be are taught muscle relaxation, breathing techniques, techniques for "trusting their bodies," and practices to promote good nutrition and exercise. Parents are urged to take responsibility for childbirth and the use of physicians is viewed as unnecessary and sometimes even dangerous. As you might expect, the discouragement of traditional medical interventions is highly controversial (McCutcheon-Rosegg, Ingraham, & Bradley, 1996; Reed, 2005).
- **Hypnobirthing.** Hypnobirthing is a relatively new technique involving a form of self-hypnosis during delivery that produces a sense of peace and calm, thereby reducing pain. The basic concept is to produce a state of focused concentration in which a mother relaxes her body while focusing inward. Increasing research evidence shows the technique can be effective in reducing pain (Olson, 2006; White, 2007; Alexander, Turnball, & Cyna, 2009).
- **Water Birthing.** Still relatively uncommon in the United States, water birthing is a practice in which a woman enters a pool of warm water to give birth. The theory is that the warmth and buoyancy of the water is soothing, easing the length and pain of labor and childbirth, and the entry into the world is soothed for the infant, who moves from the watery environment of the womb to the birthing pool. Although there is some evidence that water birthing reduces pain and the length of labor, there is a risk of infection from the unsterile water (Thöni, Mussner, & Ploner, 2010; Jones et al., 2012).

Childbirth Attendants: Who Delivers? Traditionally, *obstetricians*, physicians who specialize in delivering babies, have been the childbirth attendants of choice. In the last few decades, more mothers have chosen to use a *midwife*, a childbirth attendant who stays with the mother throughout labor and delivery. Midwives—most often nurses specializing in childbirth—are used primarily for pregnancies in which no complications are expected. The use of midwives has increased steadily in the United States—there are now 7,000 of them—and they are employed in 10 percent of births. Midwives help deliver some 80 percent of babies in other parts of the world, often at home. Home birth is common in countries at all levels of economic development. For instance, a third of all births in the Netherlands occur at home (Ayoub, 2005; Klein, 2012).

The newest trend is also one of the oldest: the doula (pronounced *doo-lah*). A *doula* provides emotional, psychological, and educational support during birth. A doula does not replace an obstetrician or midwife, and does not do medical exams. Instead, doulas provide the mother with support and suggest consideration of birthing alternatives. This represents a return to a centuries-old tradition in which supportive, experienced older women serve as birthing assistants and guides. A growing body of research indicates that the presence of a doula is beneficial to the birth process, speeding deliveries and reducing reliance on drugs. Yet concerns remain about their use. Unlike certified midwives, who are nurses and receive an additional year or two of training, doulas do not need to be certified or have any particular level of education (Campbell et al., 2007; Mottl-Santiago et al., 2008; Humphries & Korfmacher, 2012).

From the perspective of a health care provider: While 99 percent of U.S. births are attended by professional medical workers or birthing attendants, this is the case in only about half of births worldwide. What do you think are some reasons for this, and what are the implications of this statistic?

Use of Anesthesia and Pain-Reducing Drugs. Certainly the ongoing discovery of pain-reducing drugs is one of the greatest advances of modern medicine, but the use of medication during childbirth has both benefits and pitfalls. About a third of women who choose anesthesia receive *epidural anesthesia*, which produces numbness from the waist down. Traditional epidurals immobilize women and can prevent them from helping to push the baby. A newer form—a *walking epidural* or *dual spinal-epidural*—uses smaller needles and administers doses continuously. This permits women to move more freely and has fewer side effects (Simmons et al., 2007).

It is important to remember that pain reduction comes at a cost. Drugs reach not just the mother but the fetus as well, and the stronger the drug, the greater its effects on the fetus and neonate. For example, anesthetics may temporarily depress the flow of oxygen to the fetus and slow labor. In addition, newborns whose mothers have been anesthetized are less physiologically responsive, show poorer motor control during the first days after birth, cry more, and may have more difficulty breastfeeding. Further, because of the size difference, doses that might have a minimal effect on the mother can have a magnified effect on the fetus (Ransjö-Arvidson, 2001; Torvaldsen et al., 2006; Irland, 2010).

However, most research suggests that drugs as currently used produce only minimal risks. The American College of Obstetricians and Gynecologists suggests that a woman's request for pain relief at any stage of labor should be honored, and that the proper use of minimal amounts of drugs for pain relief is reasonable and has no significant effect on a child's later well-being (Shute, 1997; ACOG, 2002; Alberst et al., 2007).

Postdelivery Hospital Stay: Deliver, Then Depart? When Diane Mensch was sent home from the hospital just a day after the birth of her third child, she still felt exhausted. But her insurance company insisted that 24 hours was sufficient time to recover, and it refused to pay for more. Three days later, her newborn was back in the hospital with jaundice. Mensch is convinced the problem would have been discovered and treated sooner had she and her newborn been allowed to remain in the hospital longer (Begley, 1995).

Mensch's experience is not unusual. In the 1970s the average hospital stay for a normal birth was 3.9 days. By the 1990s, it was 2 days. The change was prompted in large part by medical insurance companies focused on reducing costs.

Medical providers have fought this trend, citing definite risks for mothers and newborns. For instance, mothers may experience bleeding from tissues torn during childbirth, and newborns may require the intensive medical care that hospitals uniquely provide. Furthermore, mothers are better rested and more satisfied with their care when they stay longer (Finkelstein, Harper, & Rosenthal, 1998).

Accordingly, the American Academy of Pediatrics states that women should stay in the hospital no less than 48 hours after giving birth, and the U.S. Congress passed legislation mandating a minimum insurance coverage of 48 hours for childbirth (American Academy of Pediatrics Committee on Fetus and Newborn, 2004).

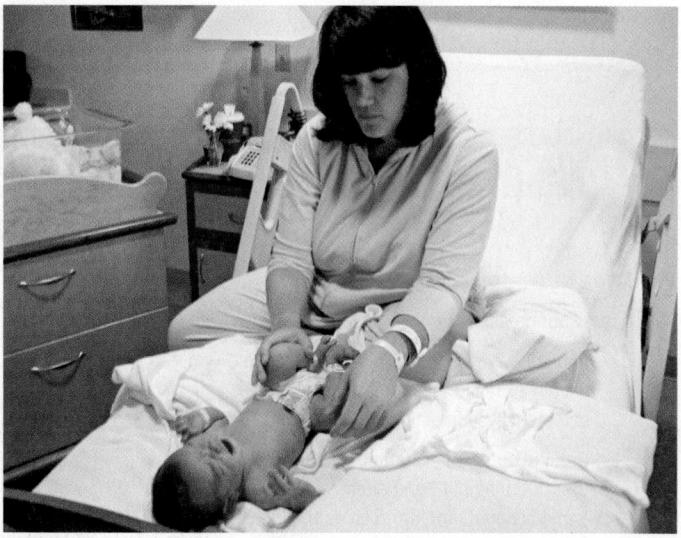

Mothers who spend more time in the hospital following the birth of a child do better than those discharged after a shorter period.

Newborn Medical Screening

Just after birth, newborns typically are tested for a variety of diseases and genetic conditions. The American College of Medical Genetics recommends that all newborns be screened for 29 disorders, ranging from hearing difficulties and sickle-cell anemia to extremely rare conditions such as isovaleric acidemia (IVA), a disorder that interferes with the normal metabolism of leucine, an important amino acid. IVA and other disorders can be detected from a tiny quantity of blood drawn from an infant's heel (American College of Medical Genetics, 2006).

The advantage of newborn screening is that it permits early treatment of problems that might go undetected for years. In some cases, devastating conditions can be prevented through early treatment of the disorder, such as the implementation of a particular kind of diet (Goldfarb, 2005; Kayton, 2007; Timmermans & Buchbiner, 2012).

The exact number of tests that a newborn experiences varies drastically from state to state. In some states, only three tests are mandated, while in others over 30 are required. In jurisdictions with only a few tests, many disorders go undiagnosed. In fact, each year around 1,000 infants in the United States suffer from disorders that could have been detected at birth if appropriate screening had been conducted (American Academy of Pediatrics, 2005).

As advances in medical science give rise to newer and better screening procedures, the question of how many and which diseases to screen for in newborn infants will continue to be a matter for debate. Clearly, more research is needed in order to determine the need for early testing (Hertzberg et al., 2011).

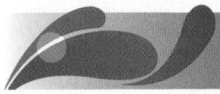

Becoming an Informed Consumer of Development

Dealing with Labor

Every woman who is soon to give birth has some fear of labor. Most have heard gripping tales of extended, 48-hour labors. Still, few mothers would deny that the rewards of giving birth are worth the effort.

There is no right or wrong way to deal with labor. However, several strategies can help make the process as positive as possible:

- **Be flexible.** Although you may have carefully planned your labor, don't feel obliged to follow through exactly. If one strategy is ineffective, try another.
- **Communicate with your health care providers.** Let them know what you are experiencing and ask for help and information. They should be able to give you an indication of how much longer you will be in labor, which may help you feel you can handle it.
- **Remember that labor is ... laborious.** Expect to become fatigued, but realize that toward the end you may well get a second wind.
- **Accept your partner's support.** If a spouse or other partner is present, allow that person to make you comfortable and provide support. Research has shown that women who are supported by a spouse or partner have a more comfortable birth experience (Bader, 1995; Kennell, 2002).
- **Be realistic and honest about your reactions to pain.** Even if you had planned an unmedicated delivery, realize that you may find the pain hard to bear. At that point, consider drugs. Asking for pain medication is not a sign of failure.
- **Focus on the big picture.** Keep in mind that labor is part of a process that leads to an event unmatched in the joy it can bring.

REVIEW, CHECK, AND APPLY

REVIEW

L09 What is the normal process of labor?

- Labor proceeds through three stages.
- Immediately after birth, birthing attendants usually examine the neonate using a measurement system such as the Apgar scale.
- Birthing options include the use of anesthetics during birth and alternatives to traditional hospital birthing, such as the Lamaze method, the use of a birthing center, and the use of a midwife.

CHECK YOURSELF

1. Labor proceeds in three stages. The longest stage of labor is _____.
   - a the first stage
   - b the second stage
   - c the third stage
   - d hard to determine
2. Women appear to respond differently to labor as a function of culture.
   - True
   - False
3. The _____ scale measures infant health by assessing appearance (color), pulse (heart rate), grimace (reflex irritability), activity (muscle tone), and respiration (respiratory effort).
   - a Bronfenbrenner
   - b Brazelton
   - c Anoxia
   - d Apgar
4. Which of the following factors influence a woman's delivery? (Check all that apply.)
   - a her preparation for childbirth
   - b the support she has before and during delivery
   - c her culture's view of pregnancy and delivery
   - d all of the above

APPLYING LIFESPAN DEVELOPMENT

- Why might cultural differences exist in expectations and interpretations of labor?

✓ **Study** and **Review** on **MyPsychLab.com**

BIRTH COMPLICATIONS

LO10 **What complications can occur at birth, and what are their causes, effects, and treatments?**

LO11 **How can infant mortality rates be lowered?**

When Ivy Brown's son was born dead, a nurse told her that sad as it was, she was not alone: A surprisingly high number of births in her city, Washington, D.C., ended with the death of the child. That fact spurred Brown to become a grief counselor, specializing in infant mortality. She formed a committee of physicians and city officials to study the capital's high infant mortality rate and find solutions to lower it. "If I can spare one mother this terrible grief, my loss will not be in vain," Brown says.

The infant mortality rate in Washington, D.C., capital of the richest country in the world, is 13.7 deaths per 1,000 births, exceeding the rate of countries such as Hungary, Cuba, Kuwait, and Costa Rica. Overall, 44 countries have better birth rates than the United States, which has 6.26 deaths for every 1,000 live births (U.S. Department of Health and Human Services, 2009; The World Factbook, 2009; Sun 2012) (see Figure 2-14).

Why do infants have less chance of survival in the United States than in other, less developed countries? To answer this question, we need to consider the problems that can occur during labor and delivery.

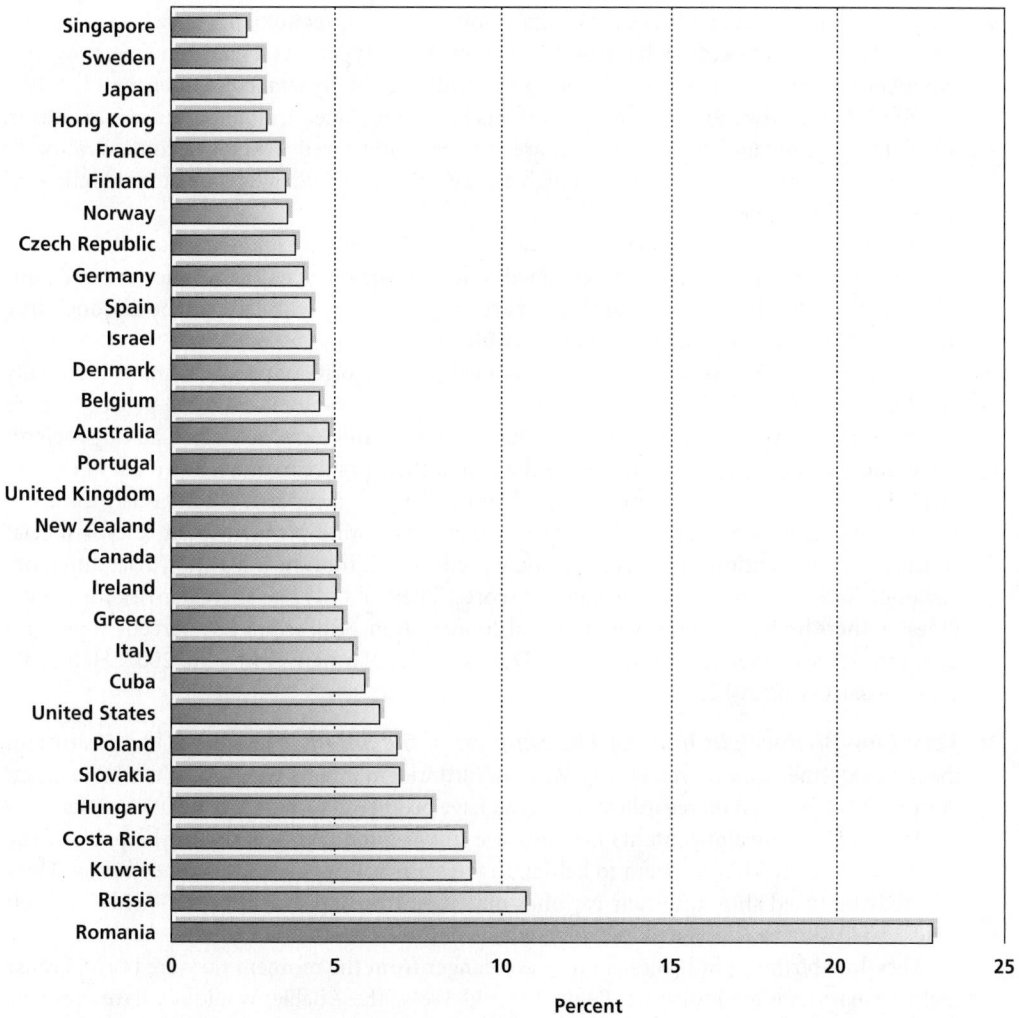

FIGURE 2-14 International Infant Mortality
Infant mortality rates in selected countries. While the United States has greatly reduced its infant mortality rate in the past 25 years, it ranks only 23rd among industrialized countries as of 2009. What are some of the reasons for this?
Source: The World Factbook, 2009.

Preterm Infants: Too Soon, Too Small

Like Tamera Dixon, whose birth was described in the module prologue, 11 percent of infants are born early. **Preterm infants**, or premature infants, are born prior to 38 weeks after conception. Because they have not had time to develop fully, preterm infants are at high risk for illness and death.

The extent of danger faced by preterm babies largely depends on the child's weight at birth, which has great significance as an indicator of the extent of the baby's development. Although the average newborn weighs around 3,400 grams (about 7 1/2 pounds), **low-birthweight infants** weigh less than 2,500 grams (around 5 1/2 pounds). Although only 7 percent of U.S. newborns are in the low-birthweight category, they account for most newborn deaths (Gross, Spiker, & Haynes, 1997; DeVader et al., 2007).

Although most low-birthweight infants are preterm, some are small-for-gestational-age babies. **Small-for-gestational-age infants** are infants who, because of delayed fetal growth, weigh 90 percent (or less) of the average weight of infants of the same gestational age. Small-for-gestational-age infants are sometimes also preterm, but may not be. The syndrome may be caused by inadequate nutrition during pregnancy (Bergmann, Bergmann, & Dudenhausen, 2008; Karagianni et al., 2010).

If the baby is not very premature and the weight at birth is not extremely low, the threat is relatively minor. In such cases, the best treatment may be to keep the baby in the hospital to gain weight. Additional weight is critical because fat layers help prevent chilling in neonates, who are not very efficient at regulating body temperature.

Newborns who are born more prematurely and who have birthweights significantly below average face a tougher road. They are highly vulnerable to infection and, because their lungs are not fully developed, they have problems taking in oxygen. As a consequence, they may experience *respiratory distress syndrome (RDS)*, with potentially fatal consequences.

To deal with RDS, low-birthweight infants are often placed in incubators, enclosures in which temperature and oxygen content are carefully monitored. Too low a concentration of oxygen will not provide relief, and too high a concentration can damage the delicate retinas of the eyes, leading to permanent blindness.

Preterm neonates are unusually sensitive to the sights, sounds, and sensations they experience, and their breathing may be interrupted or their heart rates may slow. They are often unable to move smoothly, with uncoordinated arm and leg movements that can be disconcerting to parents (Doussard-Roosevelt et al., 1997; Miles et al., 2006).

Despite the difficulties they experience at birth, the majority of preterm infants eventually develop normally in the long run. However, the tempo of development often proceeds more slowly for preterm children compared to children born at full term, and more subtle problems sometimes emerge later. For example, by the end of their first year, only 10 percent of prematurely born infants display significant problems, and only 5 percent are seriously disabled. By the age of 6, however, approximately 38 percent have mild problems that call for special educational interventions. For instance, some preterm children show learning disabilities, behavior disorders, or lower-than-average IQ scores. They may also be at greater risk for mental illness. Others have difficulties with physical coordination. Still, around 60 percent of preterm infants are free of even minor problems (Dombrowski, Noonan, & Martin, 2007; Hall et al., 2008; Nosarti et al., 2012).

preterm infants infants who are born prior to 38 weeks after conception (also known as premature infants)

low-birthweight infants infants who weigh less than 2,500 grams (around 5 1/2 pounds) at birth

small-for-gestational-age infants infants who, because of delayed fetal growth, weigh 90 percent (or less) of the average weight of infants of the same gestational age

very-low-birthweight infants infants who weigh less than 1,250 grams (around 2.25 pounds) or, regardless of weight, have been in the womb less than 30 weeks

Very-Low-Birthweight Infants: The Smallest of the Small. The story is less positive for the most extreme cases of prematurity. **Very-low-birthweight infants** weigh less than 1,250 grams (around 2 1/4 pounds) or, regardless of weight, have been in the womb less than 30 weeks.

Very-low-birthweight infants not only are tiny—some fitting easily in the palm of the hand at birth—they hardly seem to belong to the same species as full-term newborns. Their eyes may be fused shut and their earlobes may look like flaps of skin on the sides of their heads. Their skin is a darkened red color, whatever their race.

Very-low-birthweight babies are in grave danger from the moment they are born because their organ systems are immature. Before the mid-1980s, these babies would not have survived; recent medical advances have pushed the *age of viability*, the point at which an infant can survive prematurely, to about 22 weeks—some 4 months earlier than the normal term. Of course, the longer the baby develops after conception, the higher the chance of survival. A baby born earlier than 25 weeks has less than a 50–50 chance of survival (see Figure 2-15) (Seaton et al., 2012).

	United States	Austria	Denmark	England and Wales[2]	Finland	Northern Ireland	Norway	Poland	Scotland	Sweden
22–23 weeks[1]	707.7	888.9	947.4	880.5	900.0	1,000.0	555.6	921.1	1,000.0	515.2
24–27 weeks	236.9	319.6	301.2	298.2	315.8	268.3	220.2	530.6	377.0	197.7
28–31 weeks	45.0	43.8	42.2	52.2	58.5	54.5	56.4	147.7	60.8	41.3
32–36 weeks	8.6	5.8	10.3	10.6	9.7	13.1	7.2	23.1	8.8	12.8
37 weeks or more	2.4	1.5	2.3	1.8	1.4	1.6	1.5	2.3	1.7	1.5

1 Infant mortality rates at 22–23 weeks of gestation may be unreliable due to reporting differences.
2 England and Wales provided 2005 data.
NOTE: Infant mortality rates are per 1,000 live births in specified group.
SOURCE: NCHS linked birth/infant death data set (for U.S. data), and *European Perinatal Health Report* (for European data).

FIGURE 2-15 Survival and Gestational Age
Chances of a fetus surviving greatly improve after 28 to 32 weeks. Rates shown are the number per 1,000 babies born in the United States after specified lengths of gestation who survive the first year of life.
Source: Based on MacDorman & Mathews, 2009.

If a very-low-birthweight preterm infant survives, the medical costs can be astonishing—between 3 and 50 times higher than the medical costs for a full-term child during the first 3 years of life. This fact has engendered ethical debates about the expenditure of substantial financial and human resources in cases in which a positive outcome may be unlikely (Prince, 2000; Doyle, 2004a; Petrou, 2006). Still, emerging evidence suggests that high-quality care can provide protection from some of the risks of prematurity, and that by the time they reach adulthood, premature babies may be little different from other adults. Still, the costs of caring for preterm infants are enormous: The U.S. government estimates that caring for premature infants costs $26 million a year (Hack et al., 2002; Saul, 2009).

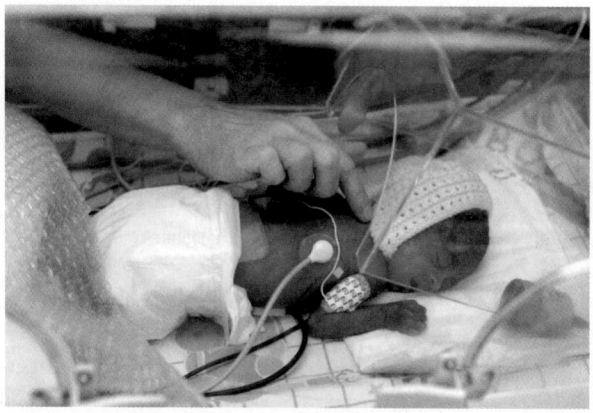

Preterm infants stand a much greater chance of survival today than they did even a decade ago.

Research also shows that preterm infants who receive more responsive, stimulating, and organized care are apt to show more positive outcomes than those children whose care is not as good. Some of these interventions are quite simple. For example, "Kangaroo Care," in which infants are held skin-to-skin against their parents' chests, appears to be effective in helping preterm infants develop. Massaging preterm infants several times a day triggers the release of hormones that promote weight gain, muscle development, and abilities to cope with stress (Tallandini & Scalembra, 2006; Erlandsson et al., 2007; Field et al., 2008).

What Causes Preterm and Low-Birthweight Deliveries? About half of preterm and low-birthweight births are unexplained, but several known causes account for the remainder. In some cases, the cause arises from difficulties in the mother's reproductive system. For instance, twins place unusual stress on their mothers, which can lead to early labor. In fact, most multiple births are preterm to some degree (Tan et al., 2004; Luke & Brown, 2008).

In other cases, preterm and low-birthweight babies are a result of the immaturity of the mother's reproductive system. Young mothers—under age 15—are more prone to deliver prematurely than older ones. In addition, a woman who becomes pregnant within 6 months of her previous delivery is more likely to have a preterm or low-birthweight infant than a woman whose reproductive system has had a chance to recover. The father's age matters, too: Wives of older fathers are more likely to have preterm deliveries (Zhu, 2005; Branum, 2006; Chen et al., 2010). Finally, factors that affect the general health of the mother, such as nutrition, level of medical care, amount of stress in the environment, and economic support, are all related to prematurity and low birthweight. Rates of preterm births differ between racial groups, not because of race per se, but because members of racial minorities have disproportionately lower incomes and higher stress as a result. For instance, the percentage of low-birthweight infants born to African American mothers is double that for Caucasian American mothers. (A summary of the

TABLE 2-4 FACTORS ASSOCIATED WITH INCREASED RISK OF LOW BIRTHWEIGHT

I. **Demographic Risks**
- A. Age (less than 17; over 34)
- B. Race (minority)
- C. Low socioeconomic status
- D. Unmarried
- E. Low level of education

II. **Medical Risks Predating Pregnancy**
- A. Number of previous pregnancies (0 or more than 4)
- B. Low weight for height
- C. Genitourinary anomalies/surgery
- D. Selected diseases such as diabetes, chronic hypertension
- E. Nonimmune status for selected infections such as rubella
- F. Poor obstetric history, including previous low-birthweight infant, multiple spontaneous abortions
- G. Maternal genetic factors (such as low maternal weight at own birth)

III. **Medical Risks in Current Pregnancy**
- A. Multiple pregnancy
- B. Poor weight gain
- C. Short interpregnancy interval
- D. Low blood pressure
- E. Hypertension/preeclampsia/toxemia
- F. Selected infections such as asymptomatic bacteriuria, rubella, and cytomegalovirus
- G. First- or second-trimester bleeding
- H. Placental problems such as placenta previa, abruptio placentae
- I. Severe morning sickness
- J. Anemia/abnormal hemoglobin
- K. Severe anemia in a developing baby
- L. Fetal anomalies
- M. Incompetent cervix
- N. Spontaneous premature rupture of membrane

IV. **Behavioral and Environmental Risks**
- A. Smoking
- B. Poor nutritional status
- C. Alcohol and other substance abuse
- D. DES exposure and other toxic exposure, including occupational hazards
- E. High altitude

V. **Health Care Risks**
- A. Absent or inadequate prenatal care
- B. Iatrogenic prematurity

VI. **Evolving Concepts of Risks**
- A. Stress, physical and psychosocial
- B. Uterine irritability
- C. Events triggering uterine contractions
- D. Cervical changes detected before onset of labor
- E. Selected infections such as mycoplasma and chlamydia trachomatis
- F. Inadequate plasma volume expansion
- G. Progesterone deficiency

Source: Reprinted with permission from Committee to Study the Prevention of Low Birth Weight, 1985 by the National Academy of Sciences, Courtesy of the National Academies Press, Washington, D.C.

factors associated with increased risk of low birthweight is shown in Table 2-4; Field, Diego, & Hernandez-Reif, 2006, 2008; Bergmann et al., 2008; Butler, Wilson, & Johnson, 2012.)

Postmature Babies: Later, Larger

One might imagine that a baby who spends extra time in the womb might have some advantages, given the opportunity to continue growth undisturbed by the outside world. Yet **postmature infants**—those still unborn 2 weeks after the mother's due date—face several risks.

For example, the blood supply from the placenta may become insufficient to nourish the still-growing fetus. A decrease in blood to the brain may lead to brain damage. Similarly, labor is riskier (for both mother and child) if a fetus nearly the size of a 1-month-old infant has to make its way through the birth canal (Shea, Wilcox, & Little, 1998; Fok, 2006).

Postmature infants are less of a problem than preterm babies because medical practitioners can induce labor artificially through drugs or a cesarean delivery.

postmature infants infants still unborn 2 weeks after the mother's due date

cesarean delivery a birth in which the baby is surgically removed from the uterus, rather than traveling through the birth canal

fetal monitor a device that measures the baby's heartbeat during labor

stillbirth the delivery of a child who is not alive, occurring in fewer than 1 delivery in 100

infant mortality death within the first year of life

Cesarean Delivery: Intervening in the Process of Birth

As Elena entered her 18th hour of labor, her obstetrician began to look concerned. She told Elena and her husband, Pablo, that the fetus's heart rate had begun to fall after each contraction. After trying some simple remedies, such as repositioning Elena on her side, the obstetrician came to the conclusion that the fetus was in distress. She told them that the baby should be delivered immediately by cesarean delivery.

Elena became one of the more than 1 million mothers in the United States who have a cesarean delivery each year. In a **cesarean delivery** (sometimes known as a *c-section*), the baby is surgically removed from the uterus, rather than traveling through the birth canal.

Cesarean deliveries occur most frequently when the fetus shows distress of some sort. For instance, if the fetus appears to be in danger, as indicated by a sudden rise in its heart rate or if blood is seen coming from the mother's vagina during labor, a cesarean may be performed. In addition, mothers over the age of 40 are more likely to have cesarean deliveries than younger ones (Tang, Wu, Liu, Lin, & Hsu, 2006; Romero, Coulson, & Galvin, 2012).

Cesarean deliveries are sometimes used when the baby is in *breech position*, feet first in the birth canal. Breech position births, which occur in about 1 of 25 births, place the baby at risk because the umbilical cord is more likely to be compressed, depriving the baby of oxygen. Cesarean deliveries are also more likely in *transverse position* births, in which the baby lies crosswise in the uterus, or when the baby's head is so large it has trouble moving through the birth canal.

The routine use of **fetal monitors**, which measure the baby's heartbeat during labor, has contributed to a soaring rate of cesarean deliveries. Some 25 percent of children in the United States are born in this way, up some 500 percent from the early 1970s (National Center for Health Statistics, 2003).

Are cesareans an effective medical intervention? Other countries have substantially lower rates of cesarean deliveries (see Figure 2-16), and there is no association between successful birth consequences and the rate of cesarean deliveries. In addition, cesarean deliveries are major surgeries that carry dangers. The mother's recovery can be relatively lengthy, particularly when compared to a normal delivery. In addition, the risk of maternal infection is higher with cesarean deliveries (Koroukian, Trisel, & Rimm, 1998; Miesnik & Reale, 2007).

Finally, a cesarean delivery presents some risks for the baby. Because cesarean babies are spared the stresses of passing through the birth canal, their relatively easy passage into the world may deter the normal release of certain stress-related hormones, such as catecholamines, into the newborn's bloodstream. These hormones help prepare the neonate to deal with the stress of the world outside the womb, and their absence may be detrimental to the newborn child. In fact, research indicates that babies born by cesarean delivery who have not experienced labor are more likely to experience breathing problems upon birth than those who experience at least some labor prior to being born via a cesarean delivery. Finally, mothers who deliver by cesarean are less satisfied with the birth experience, although their dissatisfaction does not influence the quality of mother–child interactions (Porter et al., 2007; MacDorman et al., 2008; Janevic et al., 2013).

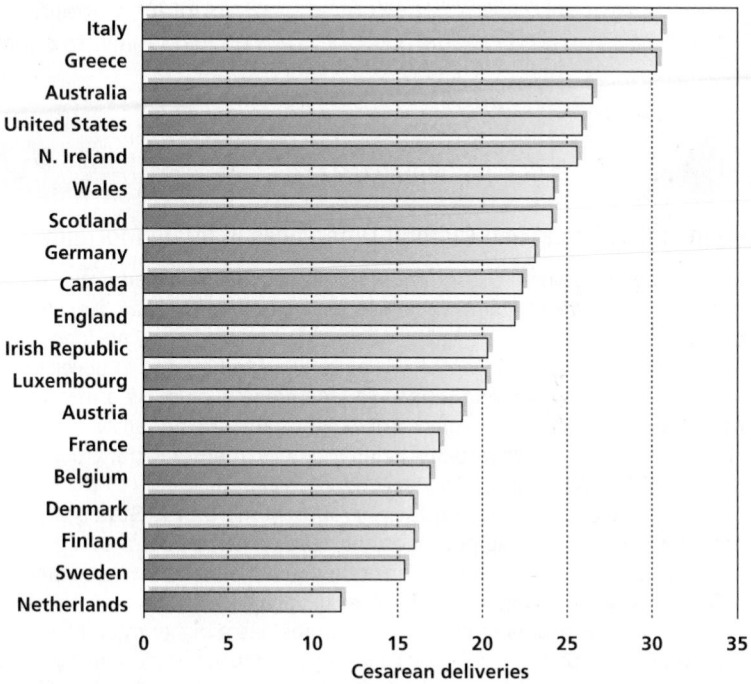

FIGURE 2-16 Cesarean Deliveries
The rate at which cesarean deliveries are performed varies substantially from one country to another. Why do you think the United States has one of the highest rates?
Source: International Cesarean Awareness Network, 2004.

Because the increase in cesarean deliveries is, as we have said, connected to the use of fetal monitors, medical authorities now recommend that they not be used routinely. There is evidence that outcomes are no better for newborns who have been monitored than for those who have not been monitored. In addition, monitors tend to indicate fetal distress when there is none—false alarms—with disquieting regularity. Monitors do, however, play a critical role in high-risk pregnancies and in cases of preterm and postmature babies (Albers & Krulewitch, 1993; Freeman, 2007).

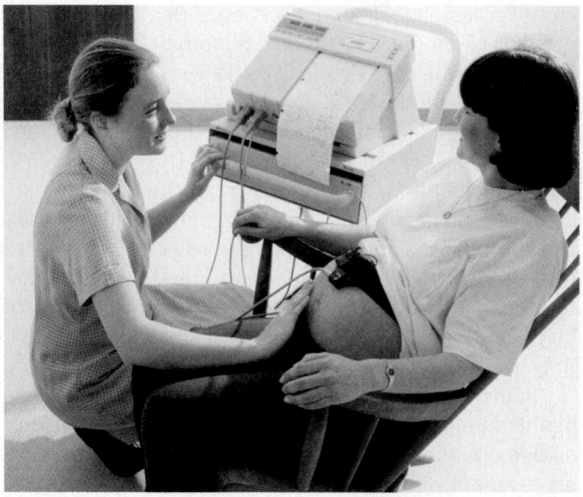

The use of fetal monitoring has contributed to a sharp increase of cesarean deliveries in spite of evidence showing few benefits from the procedure.

Mortality and Stillbirth: The Tragedy of Premature Death

Sometimes a child does not live to pass through the birth canal. **Stillbirth**, the delivery of a child who is not alive, occurs in less than 1 delivery out of 100. If the death is detected before labor begins, labor is typically induced, or physicians may perform a cesarean to remove the body as soon as possible. In other cases of stillbirth, the baby dies during its travels through the birth canal.

The overall rate of **infant mortality** (defined as death within the first year of life) is 7.0 deaths per 1,000 live births. Infant mortality generally has been declining since the 1960s (MacDorman et al., 2005).

Whether the death is a stillbirth or occurs after the child is born, the loss of a baby is tragic, and the impact on parents is enormous. The loss and grief parents feel, and their passage through it, is similar to that experienced when an older loved one dies (discussed in Chapter 10). In fact, the juxtaposition of the first dawning of life and an unnaturally early death may make the death particularly difficult to accept and deal with. Depression is common, and it is often intensified due to a lack of support. Some parents even experience posttraumatic stress disorder (Badenhorst et al., 2006; Cacciatore & Bushfield, 2007; Turton, Evans, & Hughes, 2009).

From an educator's perspective: Why do you think the United States has for so long lacked national educational and health care policies that could reduce infant mortality rates overall and among poorer people? What arguments would you make to change this situation?

Cultural Dimensions

Overcoming Racial and Cultural Differences in Infant Mortality

Even though the overall U.S. infant mortality rate has declined over the past decades, African American babies are more than twice as likely to die before age 1 than white babies. This difference is largely socioeconomic: African American women are more likely to be living in poverty than Caucasian women and to receive less prenatal care. As a result, they are more likely to have low-birthweight babies—the factor most closely linked to infant mortality—than mothers of other racial groups (Duncan & Brooks-Gunn, 2000) (see Figure 2-17).

But members of particular racial groups in the United States are not alone in experiencing poor mortality rates. The overall rate in the United States is higher than in many other countries. For example, the U.S. mortality rate is almost double that of Japan.

Why? One answer is that the United States has a higher rate of low-birthweight and preterm deliveries than many other countries. In fact, when U.S. infants are compared to infants of the same weight who are born in other countries, the mortality rate differences disappear (Wilcox et al., 1995; MacDorman et al., 2005; Davis & Hofferth, 2012).

Another reason relates to economic diversity. Compared to many other countries, the United States has a higher proportion of people living in poverty, who are less likely to have adequate medical care and to be healthy. This has an impact on the overall mortality rate (Terry, 2000; Bremner & Fogel, 2004; MacDorman et al., 2005).

Also, many countries do a much better job in providing prenatal care. For instance, low-cost and even free care, both before and after delivery, is often available. Paid maternity leave is frequently provided, lasting in some cases as long as 51 weeks. The opportunity to take an extended maternity leave can lead to better mental health for mothers and higher quality interactions with their infants (Clark et al., 1997; Waldfogel, 2001; Ayoola et al., 2010).

Better health care is only part of the story. In certain European countries, pregnant women receive many additional privileges, such as transportation benefits for medical visits. In Norway, pregnant women may be given living expenses for up to 10 days so they can be close to a hospital when it is time to give birth. And when their babies are born, new mothers receive, for just a small payment, the assistance of trained home helpers (Morice, 1998; DeVries, 2005).

In the United States, the story is very different. The lack of national health care insurance or a national health policy means that prenatal care is often haphazardly provided to the poor. About one out of every six pregnant women has insufficient prenatal care. Some 20 percent of white women and close to 40 percent of African American women receive no prenatal care early in their pregnancies. Five percent of white mothers and 11 percent of African American mothers do not see a health care provider until the last 3 months of pregnancy; some never see a health care provider at all (Hueston, Geesey, & Diaz, 2008; Friedman, Heneghan, & Rosenthal, 2009; Cogan et al., 2012).

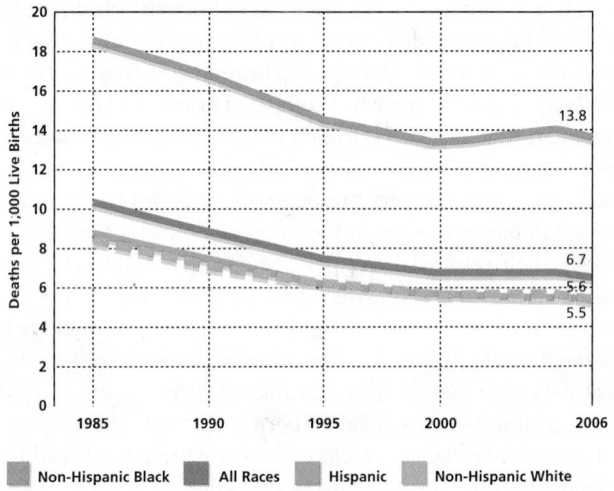

FIGURE 2-17 Race and Infant Mortality
Although infant mortality is dropping for both African American and white children, the death rate is still more than twice as high for African American children. These figures show the number of deaths in the first year of life for every 1,000 live births.
Source: Child Health USA, 2009.

Ultimately, the lack of prenatal services results in a higher mortality rate. Yet this situation can be changed if greater support is provided. A start would be to ensure that all economically disadvantaged pregnant women have access to free or inexpensive high-quality medical care from the very beginning of pregnancy. Furthermore, barriers that prevent poor women from receiving such care should be reduced. For instance, programs can be developed that help pay for transportation to a health facility or for the care of older children while the mother is making a health care visit. The cost of these programs is likely to be offset by the savings they make possible—healthy babies cost less than infants with chronic problems as a result of poor nutrition and prenatal care (Cramer et al., 2007; Edgerley et al., 2007; Barber & Gertler, 2009; Hanson, 2012).

Postpartum Depression: Moving From the Heights of Joy to the Depths of Despair

Renata had been overjoyed when she found out that she was pregnant and had spent the months of her pregnancy happily preparing for her baby's arrival. The birth was routine, the baby a healthy, pink-cheeked boy. But a few days after her son's birth, she sank into the depths of depression. Constantly crying, confused, feeling incapable of caring for her child, she was experiencing unshakable despair.

The diagnosis: postpartum depression. *Postpartum depression*, a period of deep depression following the birth of a child, affects some 10 percent of new mothers. The deep sadness that is its main symptom may last for months or even years. In about 1 in 500 cases, the symptoms evolve into a total break with reality. In extremely rare instances, postpartum depression may turn deadly. For example, Andrea Yates, a mother in Texas who was charged with drowning all five of her children in a bathtub, said that postpartum depression led to her actions (Yardley, 2001; Oretti et al., 2003; Misri, 2007).

The onset of depression usually comes as a complete surprise. Certain mothers seem more likely to become depressed, such as those who have been clinically depressed at some point in the past or who have depressed family members. Furthermore, women who are unprepared for the range of emotions that follow birth—some positive, some negative—may be more prone to depression (Kim et al., 2008; Howell et al., 2010; LaCoursiere, Hirst, & Barrett-Connor, 2012).

Finally, postpartum depression may be triggered by the pronounced swings in hormone production that occur after birth. During pregnancy, the production of estrogen and progesterone increases significantly. However, 24 hours after birth they plunge to normal levels. This rapid change may result in depression (Klier et al., 2007; Yim et al., 2009; Anderson & Maes, 2013).

Whatever the cause, maternal depression leaves its marks on the infant. As we'll see later in the chapter, babies are born with impressive social capacities, and they are highly attuned to the moods of their mothers. When depressed mothers interact with their infants, they are likely to display little emotion and to act detached and withdrawn. This lack of responsiveness leads infants to display fewer positive emotions and to withdraw from contact not only with their mothers but with other adults as well. In addition, children of depressed mothers are at risk for depression and other negative emotional and cognitive outcomes continuing into adulthood (Nylen et al., 2006; Goodman et al., 2008; Tompson et al., 2010).

REVIEW, CHECK, AND APPLY

REVIEW

L010 What complications can occur at birth, and what are their causes, effects, and treatments?

- Preterm infants may have substantial difficulties after birth and later in life.
- Preterm and low-birthweight deliveries can be caused by health, age, and pregnancy-related factors in the mother. Income (and, because of its relationship with income, race) is also an important factor.

L011 How can infant mortality rates be lowered?

- Infant mortality rates can be lowered by the availability of inexpensive health care and good education programs for mothers-to-be.

CHECK YOURSELF

1. The amount of danger facing preterm infants largely depends on the child's _____ at birth.
   - a weight
   - b intelligence
   - c eye color
   - d movements
2. The point at which an infant can survive prematurely is also known as the age of survivability.
   - True
   - False
3. _____, defined as death within the first year of life, has been declining since the 1960s.
   - a Infant decline
   - b Infant mortality
   - c Life expectancy
   - d Age of viability

APPLYING LIFESPAN DEVELOPMENT

- What are some ethical considerations relating to providing intensive medical care to very-low-birth-weight babies? Do you think such interventions should be routine practice? Why or why not?

✓ **Study** and **Review** on **MyPsychLab.com**

THE COMPETENT NEWBORN

LO12 What capabilities does the newborn have?

Relatives gathered around the infant car seat and its occupant, Kaita Castro, born just two days ago. This is Kaita's first day home from the hospital. Kaita's nearest cousin, 4-year-old Tabor, seems uninterested in the new arrival. "Babies can't do anything fun. They can't even do anything at all," he says.

Kaita's cousin, Tabor, is partly right. There are many things babies cannot do. Neonates arrive in the world quite incapable of successfully caring for themselves, for example. Why are human infants born so dependent, while members of other species seem to arrive much better equipped for their lives?

One reason is that, in a sense, humans are born too soon. The brain of the average newborn is just one-quarter what it will be at adulthood. In comparison, the brain of the macaque monkey, which is born after just 24 weeks of gestation, is 65 percent of its adult size. Because of the relative puniness of the infant human brain, some have suggested that we emerge from the womb 6 to 12 months early.

In reality, evolution knew what it was doing: If we stayed inside our mothers' bodies an additional half-year to a year, our heads would be so large that we'd never manage to get through the birth canal (Schultz, 1969; Gould, 1977; Kotre & Hall, 1990).

The relatively underdeveloped brain of the human newborn helps explain the infant's apparent helplessness. But developmental researchers are coming to realize that infants enter this world with an astounding array of capabilities in all domains of development: physical, cognitive, and social.

Physical Competence: Meeting the Demands of a New Environment

The world the neonate faces is markedly different from the "womb world." Consider, for instance, the significant changes that Kaita Castro encountered as she began the first moments of life in her new environment.

Kaita's first task was to bring air into her body. Inside her mother, the umbilical cord delivered air and removed carbon dioxide. The outside world was different: Once the umbilical cord was cut, Kaita's respiratory system had to start its lifetime's work.

For Kaita, the task was automatic. Most newborn babies begin to breathe on their own as soon as they are exposed to air. The ability to breathe immediately indicates that the respiratory system is reasonably well developed, despite its lack of rehearsal in the womb.

Neonates emerge from the uterus more practiced in other types of physical activities. For example, newborns such as Kaita have **reflexes**—unlearned, organized involuntary responses that occur automatically in the presence of certain stimuli. Some reflexes have been rehearsed for several months before birth. The *sucking reflex* and the *swallowing reflex* permit Kaita to ingest food right away. The *rooting reflex*, which involves turning in the direction of a stimulus (such as a light touch) near the mouth, is also related to eating. It guides Kaita toward nearby sources of food, such as a mother's nipple.

Other reflexes that present themselves at birth—such as coughing, sneezing, and blinking—help the infant avoid stimuli that are potentially bothersome or hazardous. Kaita's sucking and swallowing reflexes, which help her to consume her mother's milk, are coupled with the newfound ability to digest nutriments. The newborn's digestive system initially produces feces in the form of *meconium*, a greenish-black material that is a remnant of the neonate's days as a fetus.

Because the liver, a critical component of the digestive system, does not always work effectively at first, almost half of newborns develop a yellowish tinge to their bodies and eyes. This *neonatal jaundice* is most prevalent in preterm and low-weight neonates and is typically not dangerous. Treatment involves placing the baby under fluorescent lights or administering medicine.

reflexes unlearned, organized involuntary responses that occur automatically in the presence of certain stimuli

Sensory Capabilities: Experiencing the World

Just after Kaita was born, her father was certain that she looked directly at him. Did she, in fact, see him?

This is a hard question to answer. When sensory experts talk of "seeing," they mean both a sensory reaction to stimulation and an interpretation of that stimulation (the distinction between sensation and perception). Furthermore, it is tricky to pinpoint the specific sensory skills of newborns who can't explain what they are experiencing.

Still, it is clear that neonates such as Kaita can see to some extent. Although their visual acuity is not fully developed, newborns actively pay attention to certain types of information in their environment.

For instance, they attend to high-information elements in their field of vision, such as objects that sharply contrast with the rest of the environment. Furthermore, they can discriminate levels of brightness. There is even evidence that they may have a sense of size constancy—the awareness that objects stay the same size even though the size of the image on the retina varies with distance (Slater, Mattock, & Brown, 1990; Slater & Johnson, 1998; Chien et al., 2006).

In addition, not only can newborn babies distinguish different colors, they seem to prefer particular ones. For example, they can distinguish between red, green, yellow, and blue, and they take more time staring at blue and green objects (Dobson, 2000; Alexander & Hines, 2002; Zemach, Chang, & Teller, 2007).

Newborns can also hear. They react to certain sounds, showing startle reactions to loud, sudden noises, for instance. They also recognize sounds. For example, a crying newborn, hearing other newborns crying, will continue to cry. But on hearing a recording of its own crying, the newborn is more likely to stop crying, as if recognizing a familiar sound (Dondi, Simion, & Caltran, 1999; Fernald, 2001).

Starting at birth, infants are able to distinguish colors and even show preferences for particular ones.

The auditory system is not completely developed, however, and auditory acuity is not as great as it will be. Moreover, amniotic fluid, which is initially trapped in the middle ear, must drain before the newborn can fully hear.

In addition to sight and hearing, the other senses also function quite adequately in the newborn. It is obvious that newborns are sensitive to touch. For instance, they respond to stimuli such as the hairs of a brush, and they are aware of puffs of air so weak that adults cannot notice them.

The senses of smell and taste are also well developed. Newborns suck and increase other physical activity when the odor of peppermint is placed near the nose. They also pucker their lips when a sour taste is placed on them, and respond with suitable facial expressions to other tastes as well. Such findings clearly indicate that the senses of touch, smell, and taste are not only present at birth, but are reasonably sophisticated (Cohen & Cashon, 2003; Armstrong et al., 2007).

In one sense, the sophistication of the sensory systems of newborns such as Kaita is not surprising. After all, the typical neonate has had 9 months to prepare for his or her encounter with the outside world. Human sensory systems begin their development well before birth. Furthermore, the passage through the birth canal may place babies in a state of heightened sensory awareness, preparing them for the world that they are about to encounter for the first time.

This infant is imitating the happy expressions of the adult. Why is this important?

Circumcision of Newborn Male Infants: The Unkindest Cut?

An estimated three-quarters of males in the United States are circumcised, and worldwide the prevalence is around 30 percent. *Circumcision* is the surgical removal of part or all of the foreskin from the penis, most commonly performed shortly after birth (National Center for Health Statistics, 2006; World Health Organization, 2007).

Parents usually choose circumcision for a combination of health, religious, cultural, and traditional reasons. But although it is one of the most common surgical procedures in the United States, the American Medical Association, the American

Academy of Pediatrics, and the American Academy of Family Physicians have long denied that it is medically necessary and recommended against its routine use (American Academy of Pediatrics, 1999; American Academy of Family Physicians, 2002).

But new research has added a twist: Circumcision provides protection against sexually transmitted diseases. A number of studies in Africa have found that circumcised men are less likely to become infected with HIV, even when other factors such as hygiene are controlled. In fact, when large experimental studies in Kenya and Uganda found compelling evidence that circumcision cut the risk of HIV infection nearly in half, researchers stopped the studies early to allow the uncircumcised men in the control groups to be circumcised and gain the same protective benefits (American Academy of Family Physicians, 2002; Mills & Siegfried, 2006; National Institutes of Health, 2006; Castro et al., 2010).

Circumcision may produce other medical benefits. The risk of urinary tract infections is reduced in circumcised males, especially during the first year of life, and the risk of penile cancer is about three times higher in uncircumcised men than in men who were circumcised at birth (Frisch et al., 1995; American Academy of Pediatrics, 1999).

On the other hand, circumcision is not without complications. The most common are bleeding and infection, both of which are easily treated. The procedure is also painful and stressful to the infant, as it is typically done without general anesthesia. Further, some experts believe that circumcision reduces sensation and sexual pleasure later in life, while others argue that it is unethical to remove a healthy body part without a person's consent when there is no medical need to do so (American Academy of Pediatrics, 1999; American Academy of Family Physicians, 2002).

One thing is clear: Circumcision is highly controversial and evokes strong emotions. The decision ultimately comes down to the parents' personal preferences and values (Goldman, 2004).

Early Learning Capabilities

One-month-old Michael Samedi was on a car ride with his family when a violent thunderstorm suddenly began. Flashes of lightning were quickly followed by loud thunderclaps. Michael, clearly disturbed, began to sob. With each new thunderclap, the pitch and fervor of his crying increased. Unfortunately, before very long it wasn't just the thunder that would raise Michael's anxiety; the lightning alone was enough to make him cry out. In fact, even as an adult, Michael feels his chest tighten and his stomach churn at the mere sight of lightning.

Classical Conditioning. The source of Michael's fear is classical conditioning, a type of learning first identified by Ivan Pavlov, a Russian scientist. In **classical conditioning** an organism learns to respond in a particular way to a neutral stimulus that normally does not bring about that type of response.

Pavlov discovered that by repeatedly pairing two stimuli, such as the sound of a bell and the arrival of meat, he could make hungry dogs learn to respond (in this case by salivating) not only when the meat was presented, but even when the bell was sounded without the meat (Pavlov, 1927).

The key feature of classical conditioning is stimulus substitution, in which a stimulus that doesn't naturally bring about a particular response is paired with a stimulus that does evoke that response. Repeatedly presenting the two stimuli together results in the second stimulus taking on the properties of the first. In effect, the second stimulus is substituted for the first.

One of the earliest examples of classical conditioning shaping human emotions was the case of 11-month-old "Little Albert" (Watson & Rayner, 1920; Fridlund et al., 2012). Although he initially adored furry animals and showed no fear of rats, Little Albert learned to fear them when, during a laboratory demonstration, a loud noise was sounded every time he played with a cute and harmless white rat. In fact, the fear generalized to other furry objects, including rabbits and even a Santa Claus mask. (By the way, this demonstration would be considered unethical today and would never be conducted.) **Explore** the **Concept** *The Classical Conditioning of Little Albert* in **MyPsychLab**.

classical conditioning a type of learning in which an organism responds in a particular way to a neutral stimulus that normally does not bring about that type of response

Clearly, classical conditioning is in operation from the time of birth. One- and two-day-old newborns who are stroked on the head just before receiving a drop of sweet-tasting liquid soon learn to turn their heads and suck at the head-stroking alone (Blass, Ganchrow, & Steiner, 1984; Dominguez, Lopez, & Molina, 1999).

Operant Conditioning. Infants also respond to operant conditioning. **Operant conditioning** is a form of learning in which a *voluntary* response is strengthened or weakened, depending on its association with positive or negative consequences. In operant conditioning, infants learn to act deliberately on their environments in order to bring about a desired consequence. An infant who learns that crying in a certain way attracts her parents' attention is displaying operant conditioning.

Like classical conditioning, operant conditioning functions from the earliest days of life. For instance, researchers have found that even newborns readily learn through operant conditioning to keep sucking on a nipple when it permits them to continue hearing their mothers read a story or to listen to music (DeCasper & Fifer, 1980; Lipsitt, 1986).

Habituation. Probably the most primitive form of learning is habituation. **Habituation** is the decrease in the response to a stimulus that occurs after repeated presentations of the same stimulus.

Habituation in infants relies on the fact that when newborns are presented with a new stimulus, they produce an *orienting response*, in which they become quiet and attentive and experience a slowed heart rate as they take in the novel stimulus. When the novelty wears off, the infant no longer reacts. If a new and different stimulus is presented, the infant once again reacts with an orienting response. When this happens, we can say that the infant recognizes the original stimulus and can distinguish it from others.

Habituation occurs in every sensory system, and researchers have studied it in several ways. One is to examine changes in sucking, which stops temporarily when a new stimulus is presented. This reaction is not unlike that of an adult who temporarily puts down her knife and fork when a dinner companion makes an interesting statement to which she wishes to pay particular attention. Other measures of habituation include changes in heart rate, respiration rate, and the length of time an infant looks at a particular stimulus (Farroni et al., 2007; Colombo & Mitchell, 2009; Domsch, Thomas, & Hoben, 2010; Macchi et al., 2012).

The development of habituation is linked to physical and cognitive maturation. It is present at birth and becomes more pronounced over the first 12 weeks of infancy. Difficulties involving habituation represent a signal of developmental problems such as mental retardation (Moon, 2002). The three basic processes of learning that we've considered—classical conditioning, operant conditioning, and habituation—are summarized in Table 2-5. **Watch** the **Video** *Habituation* in **MyPsychLab**.

operant conditioning a form of learning in which a voluntary response is strengthened or weakened, depending on its association with positive or negative consequences

habituation the decrease in the response to a stimulus that occurs after repeated presentations of the same stimulus

Social Competence: Responding to Others

Soon after Kaita was born, her older brother looked into her crib and opened his mouth wide, pretending to be surprised. Kaita's mother was amazed when Kaita imitated his expression, opening her mouth as if *she* were surprised.

TABLE 2-5 THREE BASIC PROCESSES OF LEARNING

Type	Description	Example
Classical conditioning	A situation in which an organism learns to respond in a particular way to a neutral stimulus that normally does not bring about that type of response.	A hungry baby stops crying when her mother picks her up because she has learned to associate being picked up with subsequent feeding.
Operant conditioning	A form of learning in which a voluntary response is strengthened or weakened, depending on its positive or negative consequences.	An infant who learns that smiling at his or her parents brings positive attention may smile more often.
Habituation	The decrease in the response to a stimulus that occurs after repeated presentations of the same stimulus.	A baby who showed interest and surprise at first seeing a novel toy may show no interest after seeing the same toy several times.

Researchers registered surprise of their own when they found that newborns could apparently imitate others' behavior. Although infants have all the facial muscles needed to express basic emotions, the appearance of such expressions was assumed to be random.

However, research beginning in the late 1970s began to suggest a different conclusion. For instance, developmental researchers found that, when exposed to an adult modeling a behavior that the infant already performed spontaneously, such as opening the mouth or sticking out the tongue, the newborn appeared to imitate the behavior (Meltzoff & Moore, 1977, 2002; Nagy, 2006).

Even more exciting were findings from studies conducted by developmental psychologist Tiffany Field and her colleagues. They first showed that infants could discriminate between such basic facial expressions as happiness, sadness, and surprise. They then exposed newborns to an adult model with a happy, sad, or surprised facial expression. The results suggested that newborns produced a reasonably accurate imitation of the adult's expression (Field & Walden, 1982; Field et al., 1984; Field, 2010).

This result was questioned, however, when subsequent research found consistent evidence for only one movement: sticking out the tongue. And even that seemed to disappear around the age of 2 months. Because it seems unlikely that imitation would be limited to a single gesture of only a few months' duration, researchers began to question the earlier findings. In fact, some researchers suggested that sticking out the tongue was not imitation, but merely an exploratory behavior (Anisfeld, 1996; Bjorklund, 1997; Jones, 2006, 2007; Tissaw, 2007; Huang, 2012). The jury is still out on exactly when true imitation begins, although it seems clear that some forms of imitation begin early. Imitative skills are important because effective social interactions rely in part on the ability to react to other people in an appropriate way and to understand the meaning of others' emotional states. Consequently, newborns' ability to imitate provides them with an important foundation for social interaction later in life (Heimann, 2001; Meltzoff, 2002; Rogers & Williams, 2006; Zeedyk & Heimann, 2006; Legerstee & Markova, 2008; Beisert, 2012).

Several other aspects of newborns' behavior also act as forerunners for more formal types of social interaction that develop later. As shown in Table 2-6, certain characteristics of neonates mesh with parental behavior to help produce a social relationship between child and parent, as well as relationships with others (Eckerman & Oehler, 1992).

For example, newborns cycle through various **states of arousal**, different degrees of sleep and wakefulness, that range from deep sleep to great agitation. Caregivers become involved in easing the baby through transitions from one state to another. For instance, a father who rhythmically rocks his crying daughter to calm her is engaged with her in a joint activity that is a prelude to future social interactions of different sorts. Similarly, newborns pay particular attention to their mothers' voices, in part because they have become familiar with them after months in the womb. In turn, parents and others modify their speech when talking to infants to gain their attention and encourage interaction, using a different pitch and tempo than they use with older children and adults (DeCasper & Fifer, 1980; Trainor, Austin, & Desjardins, 2000; Kisilevsky et al., 2003; Newman & Hussain, 2006; Smith & Trainor, 2008).

TABLE 2-6 FACTORS THAT ENCOURAGE SOCIAL INTERACTION BETWEEN FULL-TERM NEWBORNS AND THEIR PARENTS

Full-Term Newborn	Parent
Shows a preference for particular stimuli	Offers those stimuli more than others
Begins to show a predictable cycle of arousal states	Uses the observed cycle to achieve more regulated states
Shows some consistency in time patterns	Conforms to and shapes the newborn's patterns
Shows awareness of parent's actions	Helps newborn grasp intent of actions
Reacts and adapts to actions of parent	Acts in predictable, consistent ways
Shows evidence of a desire to communicate	Works to comprehend the newborn's communicative efforts

Source: Based on Eckerman & Oehler, 1992.

states of arousal different degrees of sleep and wakefulness through which newborns cycle, ranging from deep sleep to great agitation

The ultimate outcome of the social interactive capabilities of the newborn infant, and the responses from parents, is a paved path for future social interactions. In sum, then, neonates display remarkable physical, perceptual, *and* social capabilities.

From a child care worker's perspective: Developmental researchers no longer view the neonate as a helpless, incompetent creature, but rather as a remarkably competent, developing human being. What do you think are some implications of this change in viewpoint for methods of child rearing and child care?

REVIEW, CHECK, AND APPLY

REVIEW

L012 What capabilities does the newborn have?

- Newborns' respiratory and digestive systems begin to function at birth. They have an array of reflexes to help them eat, swallow, find food, and avoid unpleasant stimuli.
- Newborns' sensory competence includes the ability to distinguish objects in the visual field and to see color differences; the ability to hear and to discern familiar sounds; and sensitivity to touch, odors, and tastes.
- The processes of classical conditioning, operant conditioning, and habituation demonstrate infants' learning capabilities.

CHECK YOURSELF

1. In order to survive the first few minutes or even days, infants are born with _____, or unlearned, organized, involuntary responses that occur automatically in the presence of certain stimuli.
   - a sensory capabilities
   - b acute hearing
   - c narrow vision
   - d reflexes
2. Evidence suggests that infants have size constancy, meaning that they are aware that objects stay the same size even though the size of the image on the retina varies with distance.
   - True
   - False
3. An infant learning through _____ learns to respond in a particular way to a neutral stimulus that normally does not bring about that type of response.
   - a reward
   - b classical conditioning
   - c operant conditioning
   - d social learning

APPLYING LIFESPAN DEVELOPMENT

- Can you think of examples of the use of classical conditioning on adults in everyday life, in such areas as entertainment, advertising, or politics?

Study and **Review** on **MyPsychLab.com**

SUMMARY 2

PUTTING IT ALL TOGETHER BEGINNINGS

DAWN AND LYLE, the parents we met in the chapter opener, looked forward to the birth of their twins. They speculated—just as lifespan developmentalists do—about the role of genetics in their children's development. They planned to create a loving and safe environment, with both parents involved in childcare, a comfortable nursery, and a safe outdoor play space. For the birth itself, they had many options available. Dawn and Lyle chose to use a midwife rather than an obstetrician and to involve Dawn's sister in the delivery. When their babies were born, both felt pride and relief that their twins had been born healthy.

MODULE 2.1

PRENATAL DEVELOPMENT

- Like all parents, Dawn and Lyle contributed 23 chromosomes to each child at conception. Their babies' sex was determined from the particular mix of one pair of chromosomes. *(pp. 40–42)*
- Even before their baby's birth, Dawn and Lyle had a range of options for checking for gender, possible genetic defects, and fetal growth. Measures available to them included procedures such as ultrasound sonography, amniocentesis, and fetal blood sampling. *(pp. 46–48)*
- Many of the twins' characteristics will have a strong genetic component, but virtually all will represent some combination of genetics and environment. *(pp. 49–57)*

MODULE 2.2

PRENATAL GROWTH AND CHANGE

- In the prenatal period, Dawn's babies showed a multistage pattern of development, starting with the germinal stage, progressing to the embryonic stage, and completing the prenatal period in the fetal stage. *(pp. 59–60)*
- Dawn was comparatively young, watched her diet, exercised regularly, and relied on her husband's strong support. Consequently, there were few potential threats to her babies' health and development. *(pp. 63–65)*
- Because Dawn ate a nutritious diet, exercised and abstained from alcohol during the pregnancy, she had relatively few worries about teratogenic agents harming the fetuses. *(pp. 66–68)*

MODULE 2.3

BIRTH

- Dawn's labor was relatively easy but women experience labor in different ways due to individual and cultural differences. *(pp. 69–74)*
- Dawn chose to use a midwife, one of several alternative birthing methods. *(p. 72)*
- Like the vast majority of births, Dawn's was completely normal and successful. *(p. 73)*
- Although the twins seemed utterly helpless and dependent, they actually possessed from birth an array of useful capabilities and skills. *(pp. 82–83)*

What would a PARENT do?

What strategies would you use to prepare yourself for the birth of twins? How would you evaluate the different options for prenatal care and delivery? How would you prepare an older child for the birth of a new baby?

What would a HEALTH CARE PROVIDER do?

How would you prepare Dawn and Lyle for the birth of their twins ? How would you respond to their concerns and anxieties? What would you tell them about the different options they have for giving birth?

What would an EDUCATOR do?

What strategies might you use to teach Dawn and Lyle about the stages of pregnancy and the process of birth? What might you tell them about infancy to prepare them for caring for their children?

What would YOU do?

What would you say to Dawn and Lyle about the impending birth of their twins ? What advice would you give to Dawn and Lyle about prenatal care and their decision to use a midwife?

Explore on MyPsychLab

To read how real-life educators, health care providers, and parents responded to these questions, log onto MyPsychLab.com.

Do you agree or disagree with their responses? Why? What concepts that you've read about back up their opinion?

3 INFANCY

Although they welcomed their adopted daughter Jenna to their family when she was 4 months old, she was still an infant and, to new parents Malia and Tom Turin, a complete mystery. They had by then read what they felt was every baby book ever published, listened intently to tons of advice from experienced friends, and attended a series of training sessions designed, it seemed, to bewilder rather than clarify.

They felt like total amateurs as they drove Jenna home from the airport. Every movement or sound she made was greeted by a diaper change and a bottle in the mouth. Although weary after the long drive home, they barely slept that night from listening for sounds from her crib, which might signal distress.

But they soon understood that Jenna was a healthy, cheerful baby. They learned when she needed feeding and changing, and they responded to her nighttime crying by rocking and soothing her until she quieted. They learned to talk and play with her and to be comfortable around her. They learned, in short, to be parents.

It took a while, but they had arrived. Still, they knew not to be too relaxed, for theirs would be a long journey of many uncertain steps.

All infants, whether they have basically good dispositions like Jenna or are fussy and demanding, are engaging, energetic, and challenging. And they are constantly changing as they develop physically, cognitively, socially, and in terms of developing their own unique personality.

In this chapter, we examine infancy, the period of the life span that starts at birth and continues through the first 2 years of life. We'll first discuss the ways in which infants grow physically, examining their remarkably rapid progress from largely instinctual beings to individuals with a range of complex physical abilities.

Turning to infants' cognitive development, we'll discuss the notion of stages of development, as well as some alternative views. We'll consider the amazing growth in learning, memory, and language that infants experience—and adults witness with awe.

Finally, we will examine social and personality development. We will look at personality and temperament and observe how gender differences are a matter of both genes and environment. We'll see how infants begin to develop as social beings, moving from interactions with their parents to relations with other adults and children.

Above all, we'll marvel at the rate of infants' progress, and we will get a preview of the ways in which characteristics that date from infancy continue to influence the individual into adulthood. As we proceed, keep in mind how the seeds of our futures appear in our earliest beginnings.

MODULE 3.1

PHYSICAL DEVELOPMENT IN INFANCY

What basic reflexes are we born with?

MODULE 3.2

COGNITIVE DEVELOPMENT IN INFANCY

Do infants have a memory?

MODULE 3.3

SOCIAL AND PERSONALITY DEVELOPMENT IN INFANCY

Do infants know who they are?

MyVirtualLife

If you are currently using MyVirtualLife, consider how you will raise your virtual child during infancy. What decisions will you make?

Access MyVirtualLife for a chance to help your virtual child navigate infancy.

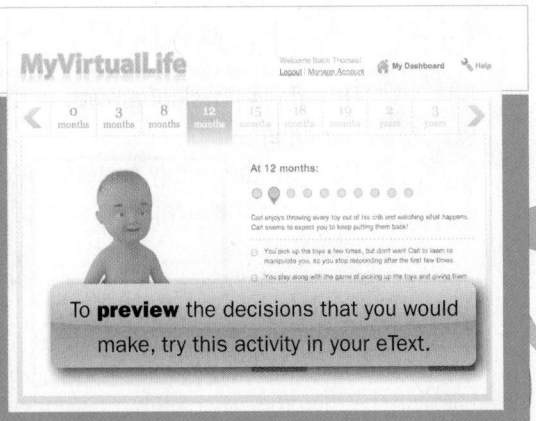

To **preview** the decisions that you would make, try this activity in your eText.

MODULE 3.1

PHYSICAL DEVELOPMENT IN INFANCY

Milestones

At first the infant play group seemed like a good idea. Six sets of first-time parents from the area would meet alternately at each other's houses and let their infants play together.

The first few months were great, with parents eagerly swapping baby stories and parental mishaps, but gradually a competition developed. The play group became a contest of infant accomplishments, and Linda and Sam found themselves stuck in a kind of Developmental Milestone Olympics.

Maybe they wouldn't have minded so much if their son Tad had been a gold medalist, but he seemed never to be in the running for even a bronze. When the prestigious First Steps event rolled around, all the other infants were jetting around from X to Y to Z, while Tad was content to sit and watch, not even trying to get up and walk.

Linda and Sam had to quit the play group because they were starting to resent the other parents, worry about Tad, and feel like losers in a game they had never signed up for.

Two weeks after they quit, Tad used the sofa to pull himself up and, before his parents' moist eyes, took his first happy steps all the way across the room.

The reactions of Tad's parents in the lead-up to their son's first steps, and their elation at the steps themselves, were typical. Modern parents frequently scrutinize their children's behavior, worrying over what they see as potential abnormalities (for the record, the range at which developmentally healthy children start to walk is quite large) and celebrating important milestones. In this module, we consider the nature of the astonishing physical development that occurs during infancy, a period that starts at birth and continues until the second birthday. We begin by discussing the pace of growth during infancy, noting obvious changes in height and weight as well as less apparent changes in the nervous system. We also consider how infants quickly develop increasingly stable patterns in such basic activities as sleeping, eating, and attending to the world.

Our discussion then turns to infants' thrilling gains in motor development as skills emerge that eventually will allow an infant to roll over, take the first step, and pick up a cookie crumb from the floor—skills that ultimately form the basis of later, even more complex behaviors. We start with basic, genetically determined reflexes and consider how even these may be modified through experience. We also discuss the nature and timing of the development of particular physical skills, look at whether their emergence can be speeded up, and consider the importance of early nutrition to their development.

Finally, we explore how infants' senses develop. We investigate how sensory systems like hearing and vision operate, and how infants sort through the raw data from their sense organs and transform it into meaningful information.

GROWTH AND STABILITY

LO1 How does physical growth in the body and nervous system proceed during infancy?
LO2 How are the bodily systems integrated during infancy?
LO3 What are the sleep patterns of infants?

The average newborn weighs just over 7 pounds, which is less than the weight of the average Thanksgiving turkey. Its length is about 20 inches, shorter than a loaf of French bread. It is helpless; if left to fend for itself, it could not survive.

Yet after just a few years, the story is very different. Babies become much larger, they are mobile, and they become increasingly independent. How does this growth happen? We can answer this question first by describing the changes in weight and height that occur over the first 2 years of life, and then by examining some of the principles that underlie and direct that growth.

Physical Growth: The Rapid Advances of Infancy

Infants grow at a rapid pace over the first 2 years of their lives (see Figure 3-1). By the age of 5 months, the average infant's birthweight has doubled to around 15 pounds. By the first birthday, the baby's weight has tripled to about 22 pounds. Although the pace of weight gain slows during the second year, it still continues to increase. By the end of his or her second year, the average child weighs around four times as much as he or she did at birth. Of course, there is a good deal of variation among infants. Height and weight measurements, which are taken regularly during physical exams in a baby's first year, provide a way to spot problems in development.

The weight gains of infancy are matched by increased length. By the end of the first year, the typical baby grows almost a foot and is about 30 inches tall. By their second birthdays, children average a height of 3 feet.

Not all parts of an infant's body grow at the same rate. For instance, at birth the head accounts for one-quarter of the newborn's entire body size. During the first 2 years of life, the rest of the body begins to catch up. By the age of 2, the baby's head is only one-fifth of its body length, and by adulthood it is only one-eighth (see Figure 3-2).

There also are gender and ethnic differences in weight and length. Girls generally are slightly shorter and weigh slightly less than boys, and these differences remain throughout childhood (and, as we will see later in the book, the disparities become considerably greater during adolescence). Furthermore, Asian infants tend to be slightly smaller than North American Caucasian infants, and African American infants tend to be slightly bigger than North American Caucasian infants.

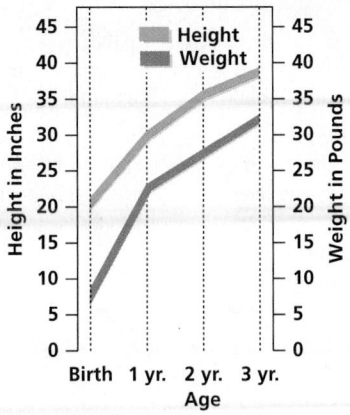

FIGURE 3-1 Height and Weight Growth
Although the greatest increase in height and weight occurs during the first year of life, children continue to grow throughout infancy and toddlerhood.
Source: Cratty, 1979.

Four Principles of Growth. The disproportionately large size of infants' heads at birth is an example of one of four major principles (summarized in Table 3-1) that govern growth.

- The **cephalocaudal principle** states that growth follows a direction and pattern that begins with the head and upper body parts and then proceeds to the rest of the body. The cephalocaudal growth principle means that we develop visual abilities (located in the head) well before we master the ability to walk (closer to the end of the body).
- The **proximodistal principle** states that development proceeds from the center of the body outward. The proximodistal principle means that the trunk of the body grows before the extremities of the arms and legs. Furthermore, the development of the ability to use various parts of the body also follows the proximodistal principle. For instance, effective use of the arms precedes the ability to use the hands.

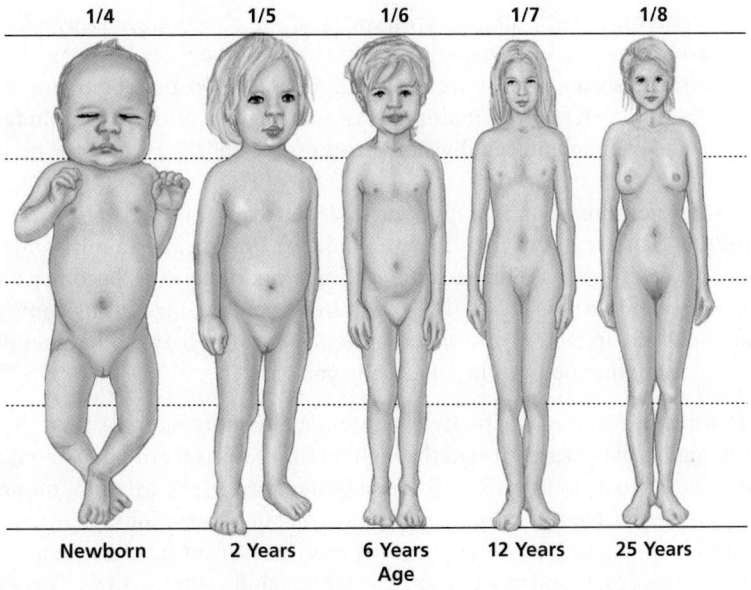

FIGURE 3-2 Decreasing Proportions
At birth, the head represents one-quarter of the neonate's body. By adulthood, the head is only one-eighth the size of the body. Why is the neonate's head so large?

cephalocaudal principle the principle that growth follows a pattern that begins with the head and upper body parts and then proceeds down to the rest of the body

proximodistal principle the principle that development proceeds from the center of the body outward

TABLE 3-1 THE MAJOR PRINCIPLES GOVERNING GROWTH

Cephalocaudal Principle	Proximodistal Principle	Principle of Hierarchical Integration	Principle of the Independence of Systems
Growth follows a pattern that begins with the head and upper body parts and then proceeds to the rest of the body. Based on Greek and Latin roots meaning "head-to-tail."	Development proceeds from the center of the body outward. Based on the Latin words for "near" and "far."	Simple skills typically develop separately and independently. Later they are integrated into more complex skills.	Different body systems grow at different rates.

- The **principle of hierarchical integration** states that simple skills typically develop separately and independently, but that these simple skills are integrated into more complex ones. Thus, the relatively complex skill of grasping something in the hand cannot be mastered until the developing infant learns how to control—and integrate—the movements of the individual fingers.
- Finally, the **principle of the independence of systems** suggests that different body systems grow at different rates. For instance, the patterns of growth for body size, the nervous system, and sexual maturation are quite different.

The Nervous System and Brain: The Foundations of Development

When Rina was born, she was the first baby among her parents' circle of friends. These young adults marveled at the infant, oohing and aahing at every sneeze and smile and whimper, trying to guess at their meaning. Whatever feelings, movements, and thoughts Rina was experiencing, they were all brought about by the same complex network: the infant's nervous system. The *nervous system* comprises the brain and the nerves that extend throughout the body.

Neurons are the basic cells of the nervous system. Figure 3-3 shows the structure of an adult neuron. Like all cells in the body, neurons have a cell body containing a nucleus. But unlike other cells, neurons have a distinctive ability: They can communicate with other cells, using a cluster of fibers called *dendrites* at one end. Dendrites receive messages from other cells. At their opposite end, neurons have a long extension called an *axon*—the part of the neuron that carries messages destined for other neurons. Neurons do not actually touch one another. Rather, they communicate with other neurons by means of chemical messengers, *neurotransmitters*, that travel across the small gaps, known as **synapses**, between neurons.

Although estimates vary, infants are born with between 100 and 200 billion neurons. In order to reach this number, neurons multiply at an amazing rate prior to birth. In fact, at some points in prenatal development, cell division creates some 250,000 additional neurons every minute.

At birth, most neurons in an infant's brain have relatively few connections to other neurons. During the first 2 years of life, however, a baby's brain will establish billions of new connections between neurons. Furthermore, the network of neurons becomes increasingly complex, as illustrated in Figure 3-4. The intricacy of neural connections continues to increase throughout life. In fact, in adulthood a single neuron is likely to have a minimum of 5,000 connections to other neurons or other body parts.

principle of hierarchical integration the principle that simple skills typically develop separately and independently but are later integrated into more complex skills

principle of the independence of systems the principle that different body systems grow at different rates

neuron the basic nerve cell of the nervous system

synapse the gap at the connection between neurons, through which neurons chemically communicate with one another

Synaptic Pruning. Babies are actually born with many more neurons than they need. In addition, although synapses are formed throughout life, based on our changing experiences, the billions of new synapses infants form during the first 2 years are more numerous than necessary. What happens to the extra neurons and synaptic connections?

Like a farmer who, in order to strengthen the vitality of a fruit tree, prunes away unnecessary branches, brain development enhances certain capabilities in part by a "pruning down" of unnecessary neurons. Neurons that do not become interconnected with other neurons as the infant's experience of the world increases become unnecessary. They eventually die out, increasing the efficiency of the nervous system.

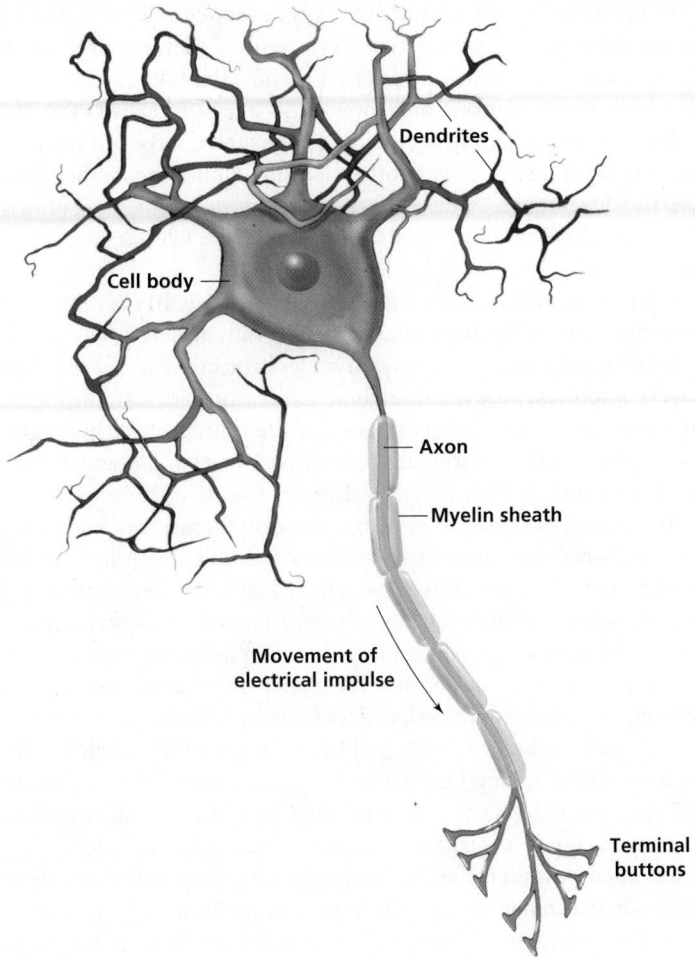

FIGURE 3-3 The Neuron
The basic element of the nervous system, the neuron is comprised of a number of components.
Source: Van de Graaff, 2000.

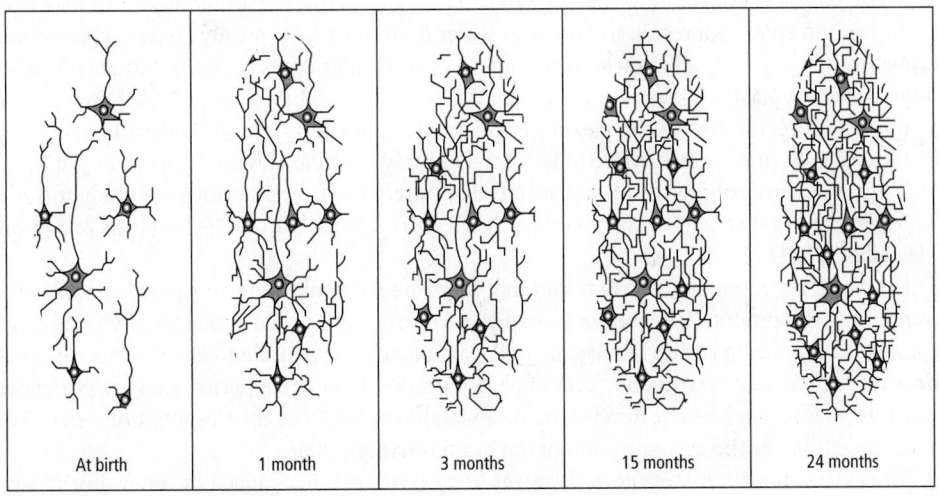

FIGURE 3-4 Neuron Networks
Over the first 2 years of life, networks of neurons become increasingly complex and interconnected. Why are these connections important?
Source: Conel, 1930/1963.

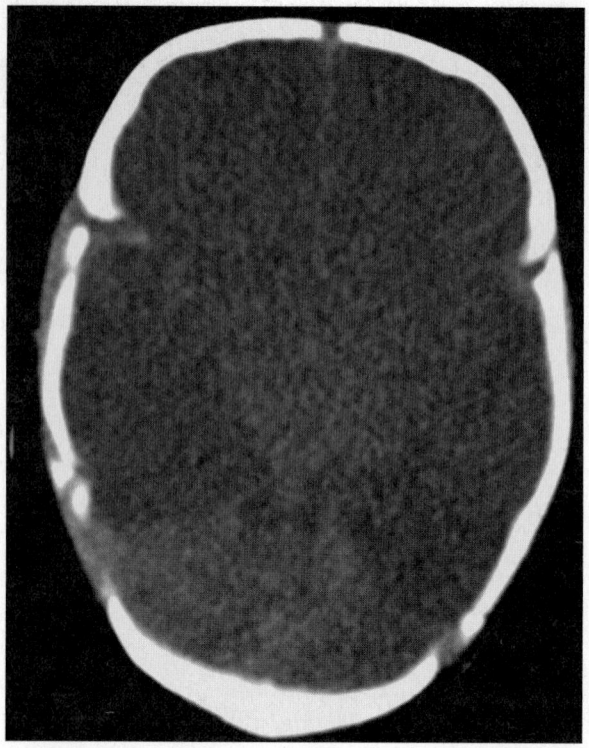

FIGURE 3-5 Shaken Baby
This CAT scan shows severe brain injury in an infant suspected of being abused by caretaker shaking.
Source: Malung, Bilo, Kuba & van Rijn, 2011.

As unnecessary neurons are being reduced, connections between remaining neurons are expanded or eliminated as a result of their use or disuse during the baby's experiences. If a baby's experiences do not stimulate certain nerve connections, these, like unused neurons, are eliminated—a process called **synaptic pruning**. The result of synaptic pruning is to allow established neurons to build more elaborate communication networks with other neurons. Unlike most other aspects of growth, then, the development of the nervous system proceeds most effectively through the loss of cells (Mimura, Kimoto, & Okada, 2003; Iglesias et al., 2005; Lourenco & Casey, 2013).

After birth, neurons continue to increase in size. In addition to growth in dendrites, the axons of neurons become coated with **myelin**, a fatty substance that, like the insulation on an electric wire, provides protection and speeds the transmission of nerve impulses. So, even though many neurons are lost, the increasing size and complexity of the remaining ones contribute to impressive brain growth. A baby's brain triples its weight during his or her first 2 years of life, and it reaches more than three-quarters of its adult weight and size by the age of 2.

As the neurons grow, they also reposition themselves, becoming arranged by function. Some move into the **cerebral cortex**, the upper layer of the brain, while others move to *subcortical levels*, which are below the cerebral cortex. The subcortical levels, which regulate such fundamental activities as breathing and heart rate, are the most fully developed at birth. As time passes, however, the cells in the cerebral cortex, which are responsible for higher-order processes such as thinking and reasoning, become more developed and interconnected.

Although the brain is protected by the bones of the skull, it is highly sensitive to some forms of injury. One particularly devastating injury comes from a form of child abuse called *shaken baby syndrome*, in which an infant is shaken by a caretaker, usually out of frustration or anger due to a baby's crying. Shaking can lead the brain to rotate within the skull, causing blood vessels to tear and destroying the intricate connections between neurons, producing severe medical problems, long-term physical and learning disabilities, and often death. Estimates of the incidence of shaken baby syndrome range from 600 to 1400 cases a year in the United States (Runyan, 2008; American Association of Neurological Surgeons, 2012; Hitchcock, 2012) (also see Figure 3-5).

Environmental Influences on Brain Development. Brain development, much of which unfolds automatically because of genetically predetermined patterns, is also strongly susceptible to environmental influences. In fact, the brain's **plasticity**, the degree to which a developing structure or behavior is modifiable due to experience, is relatively great.

The brain's plasticity is greatest during the first several years of life. Because many areas of the brain are not yet devoted to specific tasks, if one area is injured, other areas can take over for the injured area. As a result, infants who suffer brain injuries typically are less affected and recover more fully than adults who have experienced similar types of brain injuries, showing a high degree of plasticity (Vanlierde, Renier, & DeVolder, 2008; Mercado, 2009; Stiles, 2012).

Furthermore, infants' sensory experience affects both the size of individual neurons and the structure of their interconnections. Consequently, compared with those brought up in more enriched environments, infants raised in severely restricted settings are likely to show differences in brain structure and weight (Cirulli, Berry, & Alleva, 2003; Couperus & Nelson, 2006; Glaser, 2012).

Furthermore, researchers have found that there are particular sensitive periods during the course of development. A **sensitive period** is a specific but limited time, usually early in an organism's life, during which the organism is particularly susceptible to environmental influences relating to some particular facet of development. A sensitive period may be associated with a behavior—such as the development of vision—or with the development of a structure of the body, such as the configuration of the brain (Uylings, 2006).

The existence of sensitive periods raises several important issues. For one thing, it suggests that unless an infant receives a certain level of early environmental stimulation during a sensitive period, the infant may suffer damage or fail to develop capabilities that can never be fully remedied. If this is true, providing successful later intervention for such children may prove to be particularly challenging (Zeanah, 2009; Steele et al., 2013).

synaptic pruning the elimination of neurons as the result of nonuse or lack of stimulation

myelin protective insulation that surrounds parts of neurons—which speeds the transmission of electrical impulses along brain cells but also adds to brain weight

cerebral cortex the upper layer of the brain

plasticity the degree to which a developing structure or behavior is modifiable due to experience

sensitive period a point in development when organisms are particularly susceptible to certain kinds of stimuli in their environments, but the absence of those stimuli does not always produce irreversible consequences

The opposite question also arises: Does an unusually high level of stimulation during sensitive periods produce developmental gains beyond what a more commonplace level of stimulation would provide?

Such questions have no simple answers. Determining how unusually impoverished or enriched environments affect later development is one of the major questions addressed by developmental researchers as they try to find ways to maximize opportunities for developing children.

In the meantime, many developmentalists suggest that there are many simple ways parents and caregivers can provide a stimulating environment that will encourage healthy brain growth. Cuddling, talking and singing to, and playing with babies all help enrich their environment (Lafuente et al., 1997; Garlick, 2003).

From a social worker's perspective: What are some cultural or subcultural influences that might affect parents' childrearing practices?

Integrating the Bodily Systems: The Life Cycles of Infancy

If you happen to overhear new parents discuss their newborns, chances are one or several bodily functions will be the subject. In the first days of life, infants' body rhythms—waking, eating, sleeping, and eliminating waste—govern the infant's behavior, often at seemingly random times.

These most basic activities are controlled by a variety of bodily systems. Although each of these individual behavioral patterns probably is functioning quite effectively, it takes some time and effort for infants to integrate the separate behaviors. In fact, one of the neonate's major missions is to make its individual behaviors work in harmony, helping it, for example, to sleep through the night (Ingersoll & Thoman, 1999; Waterhouse & DeCoursey, 2004).

Rhythms and States. One of the most important ways that behavior becomes integrated is through the development of various **rhythms**, which are repetitive, cyclical patterns of behavior. Some rhythms are immediately obvious, such as the change from wakefulness to sleep. Others are more subtle, but still easily noticeable, such as breathing and sucking patterns. Still other rhythms may require careful observation to be noticed. For instance, newborns may go through periods in which they jerk their legs in a regular pattern every minute or so. Although some of these rhythms are apparent just after birth, others emerge slowly over the first year as the neurons of the nervous system become increasingly integrated (Thelen & Bates, 2003).

One of the major body rhythms is that of an infant's **state**, the degree of awareness he or she displays to both internal and external stimulation. As can be seen in Table 3-2, such states include various levels of wakeful behaviors, such as alertness, fussing, and crying, and different levels of sleep as well. Each change in state brings about an alteration in the amount of stimulation required to get the infant's attention (Diambra & Menna-Barreto, 2004).

Infants sleep in spurts, often making them out of sync with the rest of the world.

Sleep: Perchance to Dream? At the beginning of infancy, the major state that occupies a baby's time is sleep—much to the relief of exhausted parents, who often regard sleep as a welcome respite from caregiving responsibilities. On average, newborn infants sleep some 16 to 17 hours a day. However, there are wide variations. Some sleep more than 20 hours, while others sleep as little as 10 hours a day (Buysse, 2005; Tikotzky & Sadeh, 2009; de Graag et al., 2012).

Infants sleep a lot, but you shouldn't wish to "sleep like a baby." The sleep of infants comes in fits and starts. Rather than covering one long stretch, sleep initially comes in spurts of around 2 hours, followed by periods of wakefulness. Because of this, infants—and their sleep-deprived parents—are "out of sync" with the rest of the world, for whom sleep comes at night and wakefulness during the day (Groome et al., 1997; Burnham et al., 2002). Most babies do not sleep through the night for several months. Parents' sleep is interrupted, sometimes several times a night, by the infant's cries for food and physical contact.

rhythms repetitive, cyclical patterns of behavior

state the degree of awareness an infant displays to both internal and external stimulation

TABLE 3-2 PRIMARY BEHAVIORAL STATES

States	Characteristics	Percentage of Time When Alone in State
Awake States		
Alert	Attentive or scanning, the infant's eyes are open, bright, and shining.	6.7
Nonalert waking	Eyes are usually open, but dull and unfocused. Varied, but typically high motor activity.	2.8
Fuss	Fussing is continuous or intermittent, at low levels.	1.8
Cry	Intense vocalizations occurring singly or in succession.	1.7
Transition States Between Sleep and Waking		
Drowse	Infant's eyes are heavy-lidded, but opening and closing slowly. Low level of motor activity.	4.4
Daze	Open, but glassy and immobile eyes. State occurs between episodes of alert and drowse. Low level of activity.	1.0
Sleep–wake transition	Behaviors of both wakefulness and sleep are evident. Generalized motor activity; eyes may be closed, or they open and close rapidly. State occurs when baby is awakening.	1.3
Sleep States		
Active sleep	Eyes closed; uneven respiration; intermittent rapid eye movements. Other behaviors: smiles, frowns, grimaces, mouthing, sucking, sighs, and sigh sobs.	50.3
Quiet sleep	Eyes are closed and respiration is slow and regular. Motor activity limited to occasional startles, sighs, sobs, or rhythmic mouthing.	28.1
Transitional Sleep States		
Active-quiet transition sleep	During this state, which occurs between periods of active sleep and quiet sleep, the eyes are closed and there is little motor activity. Infant shows mixed behavioral signs of active sleep and quiet sleep.	1.9

Source: Based on Thoman & Whitney, 1990.

Luckily for their parents, infants gradually settle into a more adultlike pattern. After a week, babies sleep a bit more at night and are awake for slightly longer periods during the day. Typically, by the age of 16 weeks infants begin to sleep as much as 6 continuous hours at night, and daytime sleep falls into regular naplike patterns. Most infants sleep through the night by the end of the first year, and the total amount of sleep they need each day is down to about 15 hours (Mao, 2004).

Hidden beneath the supposedly tranquil sleep of infants is another cyclic pattern. During periods of sleep, infants' heart rates increase and become irregular, their blood pressure rises, and they begin to breathe more rapidly (Montgomery-Downs & Thomas, 1998). Sometimes, although not always, their closed eyes begin to move in a back-and-forth pattern, as if they were viewing an action-packed scene. This period of active sleep is similar, although not identical, to the **rapid eye movement (REM) sleep** that is found in older children and adults and is associated with dreaming.

At first, this active, REM-like sleep takes up around one-half of an infant's sleep, compared with just 20 percent of an adult's sleep (see Figure 3-6). However, the quantity of active sleep quickly declines, and by the age of 6 months, amounts to just one-third of total sleep time (Burnham et al., 2002; Staunton, 2005).

The appearance of active sleep periods that are similar to REM sleep in adults raises the intriguing question of whether infants dream during those periods. No one knows the answer, although it seems unlikely. First of all, young infants do not have much to dream about, given their relatively limited experiences. Furthermore, the brain waves of sleeping infants appear to be qualitatively different from those of adults who are dreaming. It is not until the baby reaches 3 or 4 months of age that the wave patterns become similar to those of dreaming adults, suggesting that young infants are not dreaming during active sleep—or at least are not doing so in the same way as adults do (McCall, 1979; Parmalee & Sigman, 1983; Zampi et al., 2002).

rapid eye movement (REM) sleep the period of sleep that is found in older children and adults and is associated with dreaming

Then what is the function of REM sleep in infants? Although we don't know for certain, some researchers think it provides a means for the brain to stimulate itself—a process called *autostimulation* (Roffwarg, Muzio, & Dement, 1966). Stimulation of the nervous system would be particularly important in infants, who spend so much time sleeping and relatively little in alert states.

Infants' sleep cycles seem largely preprogrammed by genetic factors, but environmental influences also play a part. For instance, cultural practices affect infants' sleep patterns. For example, among the Kipsigis of Africa, infants sleep with their mothers at night, a practice known as *co-sleeping* that is typical in most non-Western cultures. Infants are allowed to nurse whenever they wake. In the daytime, they accompany their mothers during daily chores, often napping while strapped to their mothers' backs. Because they are often out and on the go, Kipsigis infants do not sleep through the night until much later than babies in Western societies, and for the first 8 months of life, they seldom sleep longer than 3 hours at a stretch. In comparison, 8-month-old infants in the United States may sleep as long as 8 hours at a time (Super & Harkness, 1982; Anders & Taylor, 1994; Gerard, Harris, & Thach, 2002).

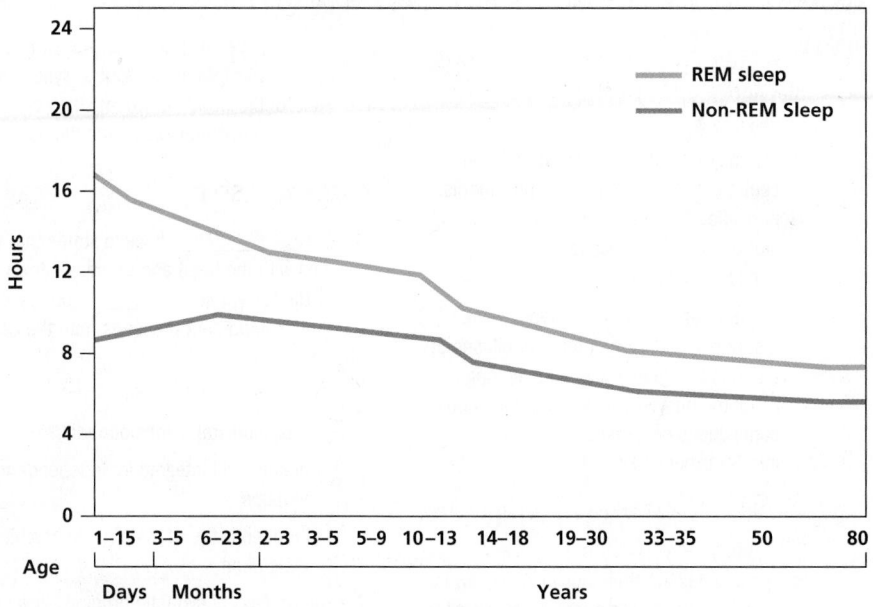

FIGURE 3-6 REM Sleep Through the Life Span
As we age, the proportion of REM sleep increases as the proportion of non-REM sleep declines. In addition, the total amount of sleep falls as we get older.
Source: Based on Roffwarg, Muzio, & Dement, 1966.

SIDS: The Unanticipated Killer

For a tiny percentage of infants, the rhythm of sleep is interrupted by a deadly affliction: sudden infant death syndrome, or SIDS. **Sudden infant death syndrome (SIDS)** is a disorder in which seemingly healthy infants die in their sleep. Put to bed for a nap or for the night, an infant simply never wakes up.

SIDS strikes about 2,500 infants in the United States each year. Although it seems to occur when the normal patterns of breathing during sleep are interrupted, scientists have been unable to discover why that might happen. It is clear that infants don't smother or choke; they die a peaceful death, simply ceasing to breathe.

While no reliable means for preventing the syndrome has been found, the American Academy of Pediatrics now suggests that babies sleep on their backs rather than on their sides or stomachs—called the *back-to-sleep* guideline. In addition, they suggest that parents consider giving their babies a pacifier during naps and bedtime (Task Force on Sudden Infant Death Syndrome, 2005).

The number of deaths from SIDS has decreased significantly since these guidelines were developed (see Figure 3-7). Still, SIDS is the leading cause of death in children under the age of 1 year (Daley, 2004; Blair et al., 2006).

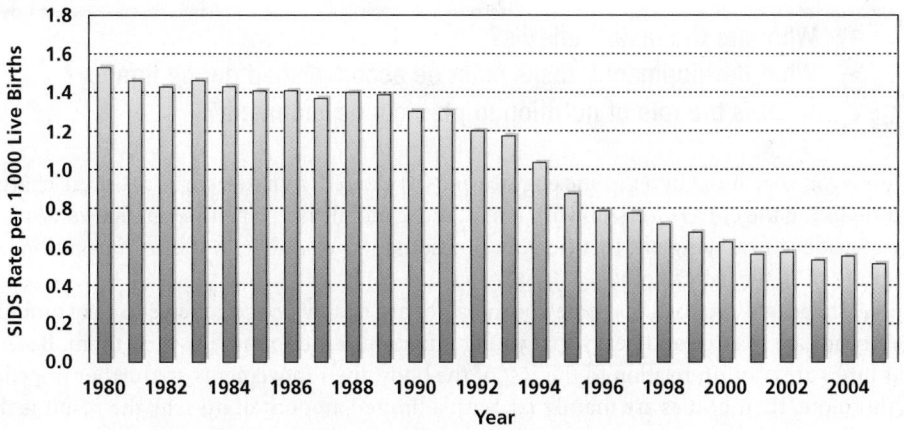

FIGURE 3-7 Declining Rates of SIDS
In the United States, SIDS rates have dropped dramatically as parents have become more informed and put babies to sleep on their backs instead of their stomachs.
Source: American SIDS Institute, based on data from the Center for Disease Control and the National Center for Health Statistics, 2004.

sudden infant death syndrome (SIDS) the unexplained death of a seemingly healthy baby

Many hypotheses have been suggested to explain why infants die from SIDS. These include problems such as undiagnosed sleep disorders, suffocation, nutritional deficiencies, problems with reflexes, brainstem abnormalities, and undiagnosed illness. Still, the actual cause of SIDS remains elusive (Kinney & Thach, 2009; Mitchell, 2009; Duncan et al., 2010; Lavezzi, Corna, & Matturri, 2013).

REVIEW, CHECK, AND APPLY

REVIEW

L01 How does physical growth in the body and nervous system proceed during infancy?

- The major principles of growth are the cephalocaudal principle, the proximodistal principle, the principle of hierarchical integration, and the principle of the independence of systems.
- The development of the nervous system first entails the development of billions of neurons and interconnections among them. Later, the numbers of both neurons and connections decrease as a result of the infant's experiences.

L02 How are the bodily systems integrated during infancy?

- Infants integrate their individual behaviors by developing rhythms, which are repetitive, cyclical patterns of behavior.

L03 What are the sleep patterns of infants?

- The sleep of infants comes in fits and starts initially coming in spurts of around 2 hours, followed by periods of wakefulness. Because of this infants are "out of sync" with the rest of the world, for whom sleep comes at night and wakefulness during the day.

CHECK YOURSELF

1. The _____ principle states that growth begins with the head and proceeds down to the rest of the body; the _____ principle states that development proceeds from the center of the body outward.
   - a cephalocaudal; proximodistal
   - b proximodistal; cephalocaudal
   - c hierarchical integration; independence of systems
   - d independence of systems; hierarchical integration
2. The process of synaptic pruning allows established neurons to build stronger networks and reduces unnecessary neurons during the first 2 years of life.
   - True
   - False
3. Although brain development is largely genetically predetermined, it is also susceptible to environmental experiences; the ability of the brain to be modifiable by the environment is called _____.
   - a plasticity
   - b synaptic pruning
   - c sensitive period
   - d critical period

APPLYING LIFESPAN DEVELOPMENT

- What evolutionary advantage could there be for infants to be born with more nerve cells than they actually need or use? How might our understanding of synaptic "pruning" affect the way we treat infants?

✓ **Study** and **Review** on **MyPsychLab.com**

MOTOR DEVELOPMENT

L04 What are the major reflexes?
L05 What developmental tasks must be accomplished during infancy?
L06 What is the role of nutrition in physical development?

Suppose you were hired by a genetic engineering firm to redesign newborns and were charged with replacing the current version with a new, more mobile one. The first change you'd probably consider in carrying out this (luckily fictitious) job would be in the conformation and composition of the baby's body.

The shape and proportions of newborn babies are simply not conducive to easy mobility. Their heads are so large and heavy that young infants lack the strength to raise them. Because their limbs are short in relation to the rest of the body, their movements are further impeded. Furthermore, their bodies are mainly fat, with a limited amount of muscle; the result is that they lack strength.

Fortunately, it doesn't take too long before infants begin to develop a remarkable amount of mobility. In fact, even at birth they have an extensive repertoire of behavioral possibilities brought about by innate reflexes, and their range of motor skills grows rapidly during the first 2 years of life.

Reflexes: Our Inborn Physical Skills

When her father pressed 3-day-old Christina's palm with his finger, she responded by tightly winding her small fist around his finger and grasping it. When he moved his finger upward, she held on so tightly that it seemed he might be able to lift her completely off her crib floor.

The Basic Reflexes. In fact, her father was right: Christina probably could have been lifted in this way. The reason for her resolute grip was activation of one of the dozens of reflexes with which infants are born. **Reflexes** are unlearned, organized, involuntary responses that occur automatically in the presence of certain stimuli. Newborns enter the world with a repertoire of reflexive behavioral patterns that help them adapt to their new surroundings and serve to protect them.

As we can see from the list of reflexes in Table 3-3, many reflexes clearly represent behavior that has survival value, helping to ensure the well-being of the infant. For instance, the *swimming reflex* makes a baby who is lying face down in a body of water paddle and kick in a sort of swimming motion. The obvious consequence of such behavior is to help the baby move from danger and survive until a caregiver can come to its rescue. Similarly, the *eye-blink reflex* seems designed to protect the eye from too much direct light, which might damage the retina.

Given the protective value of many reflexes, it might seem beneficial for them to remain with us for our entire lives. In fact, some do: The eye-blink reflex remains functional throughout the full life span. On the other hand, quite a few reflexes, such as the swimming reflex, disappear after a few months. Why should this be the case?

Researchers who focus on evolutionary explanations of development attribute the gradual disappearance of reflexes to the increase in voluntary control over behavior that occurs as infants become more able to control their muscles. In addition, it may be that reflexes form the foundation for future, more complex behaviors. As these more intricate behaviors become well learned, they encompass the earlier reflexes. Finally, it is possible that reflexes stimulate parts of the brain responsible for more complex behaviors, helping them develop (Myklebust & Gottlieb, 1993; Zelazo, 1998; Lipsitt, 2003).

Ethnic and Cultural Differences and Similarities in Reflexes. Although reflexes are, by definition, genetically determined and universal throughout all infants, there are actually some cultural variations in the ways they are displayed. For instance, consider the *Moro reflex* that is activated when support for the neck and head is suddenly removed. The Moro reflex consists of the infant's arms thrusting outward and then appearing to seek to grasp onto something. Most scientists feel that the Moro reflex represents a leftover response that we humans have inherited from our nonhuman ancestors. The Moro reflex is an extremely useful

reflexes unlearned, organized involuntary responses that occur automatically in the presence of certain stimuli

TABLE 3-3 SOME BASIC REFLEXES IN INFANTS

Reflex	Approximate Age of Disappearance	Description	Possible Function
Rooting reflex	3 weeks	Neonate's tendency to turn its head toward things that touch its cheek.	Food intake
Stepping reflex	2 months	Movement of legs when held upright with feet touching the floor.	Prepares infants for independent locomotion
Swimming reflex	4–6 months	Infant's tendency to paddle and kick in a sort of swimming motion when lying face down in a body of water.	Avoidance of danger
Moro reflex	6 months	Activated when support for the neck and head is suddenly removed. The arms of the infant are thrust outward and then appear to grasp onto something.	Similar to primate's protection from falling
Babinski reflex	8–12 months	An infant fans out its toes in response to a stroke on the outside of its foot.	Unknown
Startle reflex	Remains in different form	An infant, in response to a sudden noise, flings out arms, arches its back, and spreads its fingers.	Protection
Eye-blink reflex	Remains	Rapid shutting and opening of eye on exposure to direct light.	Protection of eye from direct light
Sucking reflex	Remains	Infant's tendency to suck at things that touch its lips.	Food intake
Gag reflex	Remains	An infant's reflex to clear its throat.	Prevents choking

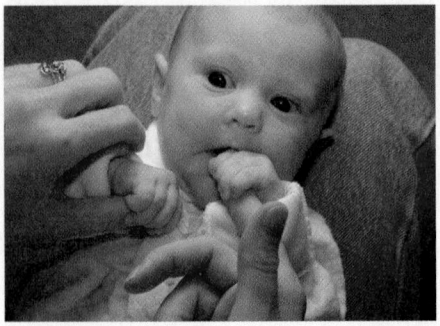

(a)

(b)

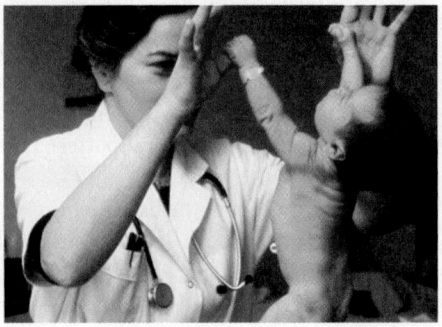

(c)

Infants showing (a) the rooting reflex, (b) the startle reflex, and (c) the Moro reflex.

behavior for monkey babies, who travel about by clinging to their mothers' backs. If they lose their grip, they fall down unless they are able to grasp quickly onto their mother's fur—using a Moro-like reflex (Prechtl, 1982; Zafeiriou, 2004).

The Moro reflex is found in all humans, but it appears with significantly different vigor in different children. Some differences reflect cultural and ethnic variations (Freedman, 1979). For instance, Caucasian infants show a pronounced response to situations that produce the Moro reflex. Not only do they fling out their arms, but they also cry and respond in a generally agitated manner. In contrast, Navajo babies react to the same situation much more calmly. Their arms do not flail out as much, and they cry only rarely. **Watch** the **Video** *Reflexes* in **MyPsychLab.**

Motor Development in Infancy: Landmarks of Physical Achievement

Probably no physical changes are more obvious—and more eagerly anticipated—than the increasing array of motor skills that babies acquire during infancy. Most parents can remember their child's first steps with a sense of pride and awe at how quickly she or he changed from a helpless infant, unable even to roll over, into a person who could navigate quite effectively in the world.

Gross Motor Skills. Even though the motor skills of newborn infants are not terribly sophisticated, at least compared with attainments that will soon appear, young infants still are able to accomplish some kinds of movement. For instance, when placed on their stomachs they wiggle their arms and legs and may try to lift their heavy heads. As their strength increases, they are able to push hard enough against the surface on which they are resting to propel their bodies in different directions. They often end up moving backward rather than forward, but by the age of 6 months they become rather accomplished at moving themselves in particular directions. These initial efforts are the forerunners of crawling, in which babies coordinate the motions of their arms and legs and propel themselves forward. Crawling appears typically between 8 and 10 months. (Figure 3-8 provides a summary of some of the milestones of normal motor development.)

Walking comes later. At around the age of 9 months, most infants are able to walk by supporting themselves on furniture, and half of all infants can walk well by the end of their first year of life.

At the same time infants are learning to move around, they are perfecting the ability to remain in a stationary sitting position. At first, babies cannot remain seated upright without support. But they quickly master this ability, and most are able to sit without support by the age of 6 months.

TABLE 3-4 MILESTONES OF FINE MOTOR DEVELOPMENT

Age (months)	Skill
3	Opens hand prominently
3	Grasps rattle
8	Grasps with thumb and finger
11	Holds crayon adaptively
14	Builds tower of two cubes
16	Places pegs in board
24	Imitates strokes on paper
33	Copies circle

Source: From Frankenburg, W. K., Dodds, J., Archer, P., Shapiro, H., and Brunsneck, B., The Denver II: A Major Revision and Restandardization of the Denver Developmental Screening Test, Pediatrics, 89, pp. 91–97, 1992. Reprinted with permission from Dr. William K. Frankenburg.

Fine Motor Skills. As infants are perfecting their gross motor skills, such as sitting upright and walking, they are also making advances in their fine motor skills (see Table 3-4). For instance, by the age of 3 months, infants show some ability to coordinate the movements of their limbs.

Furthermore, although infants are born with a rudimentary ability to reach toward an object, this ability is neither very sophisticated nor very accurate, and it disappears around

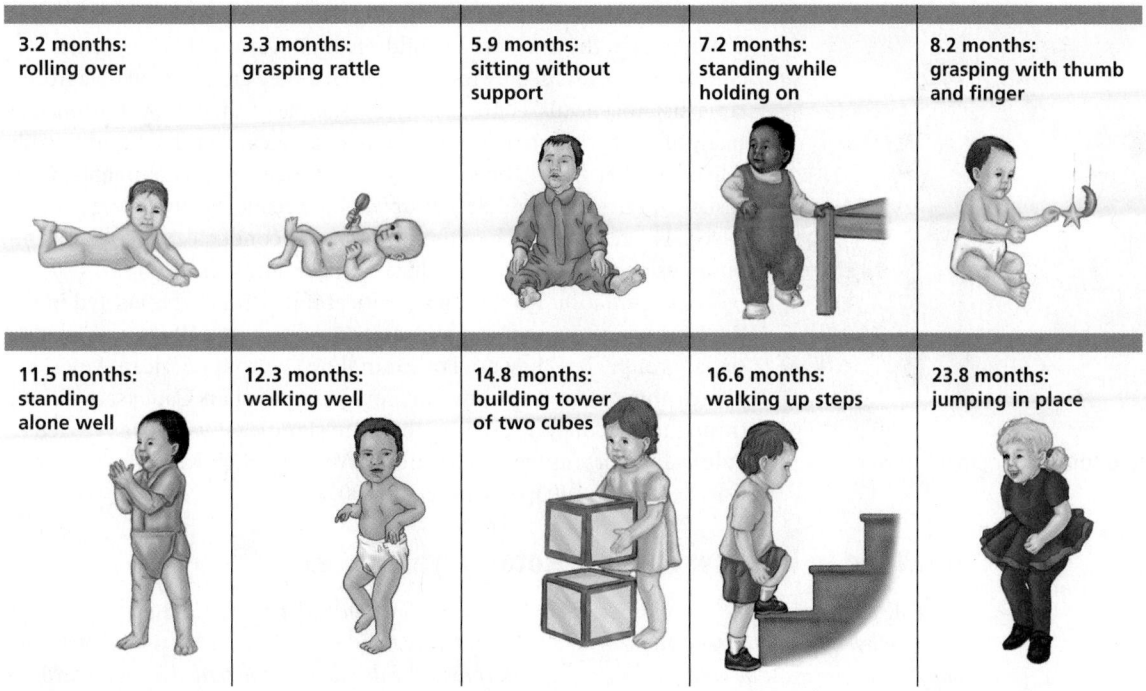

FIGURE 3-8 Milestones of Motor Development
Fifty percent of children are able to perform each skill at the month indicated in the figure. However, the specific timing at which each skill appears varies widely. For example, one-quarter of children are able to walk well at 11.1 months; by 14.9 months, 90 percent of children are walking well. Is knowledge of such average benchmarks helpful or harmful to parents?
Source: Adapted from Frankenburg et al., 1992.

the age of 4 weeks. A different, more precise, form of reaching reappears at 4 months. It takes some time for infants to coordinate successful grasping after they reach out, but in fairly short order they are able to reach out and hold onto an object of interest (Claxton, McCarty, & Keen, 2009; Grissmer et al., 2010; Foroud & Whishaw, 2012).

The sophistication of fine motor skills continues to grow. By the age of 11 months, infants are able to pick up off the ground objects as small as marbles—something caregivers need to be concerned about, because the next place such objects often go is the mouth. By the time they are 2 years old, children can carefully hold a cup, bring it to their lips, and take a drink without spilling a drop.

Grasping, like other motor advances, follows a sequential developmental pattern in which simple skills are combined into more sophisticated ones. For example, infants first begin picking things up with their whole hand. As they get older, they use a *pincer grasp*, where thumb and index finger meet to form a circle. The pincer grasp allows for considerably more precise motor control (Barrett & Needham, 2008).

Developmental Norms: Comparing the Individual to the Group. Keep in mind that the timing of the milestones in motor development that we have been discussing is based on norms. **Norms** represent the average performance of a large sample of children of a given age. They permit comparisons between a particular child's performance on a particular behavior and the average performance of the children in the norm sample.

For instance, one of the most widely used techniques to determine infants' normative standing is the **Brazelton Neonatal Behavioral Assessment Scale (NBAS)**, a measure designed to determine infants' neurological and behavioral responses to their environment.

Taking about 30 minutes to administer, the NBAS includes 27 separate categories of responses that constitute four general aspects of infants' behavior: interactions with others (such as alertness and cuddliness), motor behavior, physiological control (such as the ability to be soothed after being upset), and responses to stress (Brazelton, 1990; Canals et al., 2003; Ohta & Ohgi, 2013).

Although the norms provided by scales such as the NBAS are useful in making broad generalizations about the timing of various behaviors and skills, they must be interpreted with

norms the average performance of a large sample of children of a given age

Brazelton Neonatal Behavioral Assessment Scale (NBAS) a measure designed to determine infants' neurological and behavioral responses to their environment

Cultural influences affect the rate of the development of motor skills.

caution. Because norms are averages, they mask substantial individual differences in the times when children attain various achievements.

Norms are useful only to the extent that they are based on data from a large, heterogeneous, culturally diverse sample of children. Unfortunately, many of the norms on which developmental researchers have traditionally relied have been based on groups of infants who are predominantly Caucasian and from the middle and upper socioeconomic strata (e.g., Gesell, 1946). The reason: Much of the research was conducted on college campuses, using the children of graduate students and faculty.

This limitation would not be critical if no differences existed in the timing of development in children from different cultural, racial, and social groups. But they do. For example, as a group, African American babies show more rapid motor development than Caucasian babies throughout infancy. Moreover, there are significant variations related to cultural factors, as we discuss next (Werner, 1972; Keefer et al., 1991; Gartstein et al., 2003; de Onis et al., 2007).

Nutrition in Infancy: Fueling Motor Development

Rosa sighed as she sat down to nurse the baby—again. She had fed 4-week-old Juan about every hour today, and he still seemed hungry. Some days, it seemed like all she did was breastfeed her baby. "Well, he must be going through a growth spurt," she decided, as she settled into her favorite rocking chair and put the baby to her nipple.

The rapid physical growth that occurs during infancy is fueled by the nutrients that infants receive. Without proper nutrition, infants cannot reach their physical potential, and they may suffer cognitive and social consequences as well (Tanner & Finn-Stevenson, 2002; Costello et al., 2003; Gregory, 2005).

Cultural Dimensions

Motor Development Across Cultures

Among the Ache people, who live in the rain forest of South America, infants face an early life of physical restriction. Because the Ache lead a nomadic existence, living in a series of tiny camps in the rain forest, open space is at a premium. Consequently, for the first few years of life, infants spend nearly all their time in direct physical contact with their mothers. Even when they are not physically touching their mothers, they are permitted to venture no more than a few feet away.

Infants among the Kipsigis people, who live in a more open environment in rural Kenya, Africa, lead quite a different existence. Their lives are filled with activity and exercise. Parents seek to teach their children to sit up, stand, and walk from the earliest days of infancy. For example, very young infants are placed in shallow holes in the ground designed to keep them in an upright position. Parents begin to teach their children to walk starting at the eighth week of life. The infants are held with their feet touching the ground, and they are pushed forward.

Clearly, the infants in these two societies lead very different lives (Super, 1976; Kaplan & Dove, 1987). But do the relative lack of early motor stimulation for Ache infants and the efforts of the Kipsigis to encourage motor development really make a difference?

The answer is both yes and no. It's yes, in that Ache infants tend to show delayed motor development, relative both to Kipsigis infants and to children raised in Western societies. Although their social abilities are no different, Ache children tend to begin walking at around 23 months, about a year later than the typical child in the United States. In contrast, Kipsigis children, who are encouraged in their motor development, learn to sit up and walk several weeks earlier, on average, than U.S. children.

In the long run, however, the differences between Ache, Kipsigis, and Western children disappear. By late childhood, about age 6, there is no evidence of differences in general, overall motor skills among Ache, Kipsigis, and Western children.

As we see with the Ache and Kipsigis babies, variations in the timing of motor skills seem to depend in part on parental expectations of what is the "appropriate" schedule for the emergence of specific skills. For instance, one study examined the motor skills of infants who lived in a single city in England, but whose mothers varied in ethnic origin. In the research, English, Jamaican, and Indian mothers' expectations were first assessed regarding several markers of their infants' motor skills. The Jamaican mothers expected their infants to sit and walk significantly earlier than the English and Indian mothers, and the actual emergence of these activities was in line with their expectations. The source of the Jamaican infants' earlier mastery seemed to lie in the treatment of the children by their parents. For instance, Jamaican mothers gave their children practice in stepping quite early in infancy (Hopkins & Westra, 1989, 1990).

In sum, cultural factors help determine the time at which specific motor skills appear. Activities that are an intrinsic part of a culture are more apt to be purposely taught to infants in that culture, leading to the potential of their earlier emergence (Nugent, Lester, & Brazelton, 1989).

Although there are vast individual differences in what constitutes appropriate nutrition—infants differ in terms of growth rates, body composition, metabolism, and activity levels—some broad guidelines do hold. In general, infants should consume about 50 calories per day for each pound they weigh—an allotment that is twice the suggested caloric intake for adults (Dietz & Stern, 1999; Skinner et al., 2004).

Typically, though, it's not necessary to count calories for infants. Most infants regulate their caloric intake quite effectively on their own. If they are allowed to consume as much they seem to want, and not pressured to eat more, they will do fine.

Malnutrition. *Malnutrition*, the condition of having an improper amount and balance of nutrients, produces several results, none good. For instance, malnutrition is more common among children living in many developing countries than among children who live in more industrialized, affluent countries. Malnourished children in these countries begin to show a slower growth rate by the age of 6 months. By the time they reach the age of 2 years, their height and weight are only 95 percent the height and weight of children in more industrialized countries.

Children who have been chronically malnourished during infancy later score lower on IQ tests and tend to do less well in school. These effects may linger even after the children's diet has improved substantially (Grantham-McGregor, Ani, & Fernald, 2001; Ratanachu-Ek, 2003).

The problem of malnutrition is greatest in underdeveloped countries, where overall 10 percent of infants are severely malnourished. In some countries the problem is especially severe. For example, over a third of North Korean children are chronically malnourished, suffering moderate to severe malnutrition (United Nations World Food Programme, 2008; Chaudhary & Sharma, 2012).

Severe malnutrition during infancy may lead to several disorders. Malnutrition during the first year can produce *marasmus*, a disease in which infants stop growing. Marasmus, attributable to a severe deficiency in proteins and calories, causes the body to waste away and ultimately results in death. Older children are susceptible to *kwashiorkor*, a disease in which a child's stomach, limbs, and face swell with water. To a casual observer, it appears that a child with kwashiorkor is actually chubby. However, this is an illusion: The child's body is in fact struggling to make use of the few nutrients that are available (Douglass & McGadney-Douglass, 2008; Galler et al., 2010).

From an educator's perspective: What might be some of the reasons that malnourishment, which slows physical growth, harms IQ scores and school performance? How might malnourishment affect education in third-world countries?

In some cases, infants who receive sufficient nutrition act as though they have been deprived of food. Looking as though they suffer from marasmus, they are underdeveloped, listless, and apathetic. The real cause, though, is emotional: They lack sufficient love and emotional support. In such cases, known as **nonorganic failure to thrive**, children stop growing not for biological reasons but due to a lack of stimulation and attention from their parents. Usually occurring by the age of 18 months, nonorganic failure to thrive can be reversed through intensive parent training or by placing children in a foster home where they can receive emotional support.

Obesity. It is clear that malnourishment during infancy has potentially disastrous consequences for an infant. Less clear, however, are the effects of *obesity*, defined as weight greater than 20 percent above the average for a given height. While there is no clear correlation between obesity during infancy and obesity at the age of 16 years, some research suggests that overfeeding during infancy may lead to the creation of an excess of fat cells, which remain in the body throughout life and may predispose a person to be overweight. In fact, weight gains during infancy are associated with weight at age 6. Other research shows an association between obesity after the age of 6 and adult obesity, suggesting that obesity in babies ultimately may be found to be associated with adult weight problems. A clear link between overweight babies and overweight adults, however, has not yet been found (Adair, 2008; Taveras et al., 2009; Carnell et al., 2013).

Although the evidence linking infant obesity to adult obesity is inconclusive, it's plain that the societal view that "a fat baby is a healthy baby" is not necessarily correct. Indeed, cultural

nonorganic failure to thrive a disorder in which infants stop growing due to a lack of stimulation and attention as the result of inadequate parenting

"I forgot to say I was breast-fed."

Mike Twohy/The New Yorker Collection/www.cartoonbank.com.

myths about food clearly lead to overfeeding. But other factors are related to obesity in infants. For example, infants delivered via Cesarean section are twice as likely to become obese as infants born vaginally (Huh et al., 2011).

Parents should concentrate, then, on providing appropriate nutrition. But just what constitutes proper nutrition? Probably the biggest question revolves around whether infants should be breastfed or given a formula of commercially processed cow's milk with vitamin additives, as we consider next.

Breast or Bottle?

Fifty years ago, if a mother asked her pediatrician whether breastfeeding or bottlefeeding was better, she would have received a simple and clear-cut answer: Bottle-feeding was the preferred method. Starting around the 1940s, the general belief among child-care experts was that breastfeeding was an obsolete method that put children unnecessarily at risk.

With bottle-feeding, the argument went, parents could keep track of the amount of milk their baby was receiving and could thereby ensure that the child was taking in sufficient nutrients. In contrast, mothers who breastfed their babies could never be certain just how much milk their infants were getting. Use of the bottle was also supposed to help mothers keep their feedings to a rigid schedule of one bottle every 4 hours, the recommended procedure at that time.

Today, however, a mother would get a very different answer to the same question. Child-care authorities agree: For the first 12 months of life, there is no better food for an infant than breast milk. Breast milk not only contains all the nutrients necessary for growth, but it also seems to offer some degree of immunity to a variety of childhood diseases, such as respiratory illnesses, ear infections, diarrhea, and allergies. Breast milk is more easily digested than cow's milk or formula, and it is sterile, warm, and convenient for the mother to dispense. There is even some evidence that breast milk may enhance cognitive growth, leading to high adult intelligence (American Academy of Pediatrics, 2005; Tanaka et al., 2009; Duijts et al., 2010).

Breastfeeding is not a cure-all for infant nutrition and health, and the millions of mothers who must use formula (either because they are physically unable to produce milk or because of social factors such as work schedules) should not be concerned that their children are suffering significant harm. (In fact, recent research suggests that infants fed enriched formula show better cognitive development than those using traditional formula.) But it does continue to be clear that the popular slogan used by groups advocating the use of breastfeeding is right on target: "Breast Is Best" (Rabin, 2006; Sloan, Stewart, & Dunne, 2010; Ludlow et al., 2012).

Introducing Solid Foods: When and What?

Although pediatricians agree that breast milk is the ideal initial food, at some point infants require more nutriments than breast milk alone can provide. The American Academy of Pediatrics and the American Academy of Family Physicians suggest that babies can start solids at around 6 months, although they aren't needed until 9 to 12 months of age (American Academy of Pediatrics, 1997).

Solid foods are introduced into an infant's diet gradually, one at a time, in order to be able to be aware of preferences and allergies. Most often cereal comes first, followed by strained fruits. Vegetables and other foods typically are introduced next, although the order varies significantly from one infant to another.

The timing of *weaning*, the gradual cessation of breast- or bottle-feeding, varies greatly. In developed countries such as the United States, weaning frequently occurs as early as 3 or 4 months. On the other hand, some mothers continue breastfeeding for 2 or 3 years or beyond. The American Academy of Pediatrics recommends that infants be fed breast milk for the first 12 months (American Academy of Pediatrics, 1997; Sloan et al., 2008).

REVIEW, CHECK, AND APPLY

REVIEW

L04 What are the major reflexes?

- Reflexes are universal, genetically determined physical behaviors.
- Among the major reflexes are the rooting reflex, the Moro reflex, and the startle reflex.

L05 What developmental tasks must be accomplished during infancy?

- During infancy, children reach a series of milestones in their physical development on a fairly consistent schedule, with some individual and cultural variations.
- Gross motor skills include rolling over, sitting, and walking. Later, fine motor skills appear, such as grasping.

L06 What is the role of nutrition in physical development?

- Nutrition strongly affects physical development.
- Without proper nutrition, infants cannot reach their physical potential and may suffer cognitive and social consequences as well.
- Breastfeeding has numerous advantages.

CHECK YOURSELF

1. Behavior becomes integrated through the development of _____, which are repetitive, cyclical patterns of behaviors.
   - a states
   - b rhythms
   - c REM sleep
   - d reflexes
2. Which of the following is NOT one of the consequences of malnutrition during infancy?
   - a Malnourished children sleep, on average, 6 to 8 hours less than nonmalnourished children of the same age.
   - b Malnourished children show a slower growth rate by the age of 6 months.
   - c Malnourished children score lower on IQ tests later in life.
   - d Malnourished children have a lower height and weight by age 2 than nonmalnourished children.
3. Breastfeeding has been associated with enhanced cognitive growth.
   - True
   - False

APPLYING LIFESPAN DEVELOPMENT

- What advice might you give a friend who is concerned that her infant is still not walking at 14 months, when every other baby she knows started walking by the first birthday?

✓ **Study** and **Review** on **MyPsychLab.com**

THE DEVELOPMENT OF THE SENSES

L07 What sensory capabilities do infants possess?
L08 How does multisensory perception function?

William James, one of the founding fathers of psychology, believed the world of the infant is a "blooming, buzzing confusion" (James, 1890/1950). Was he right?

In this case, James's wisdom failed him. The newborn's sensory world does lack the clarity and stability that we can distinguish as adults, but day by day the world grows increasingly

While an infant's distant vision is 10 to 30 times poorer than the average adult's, the vision of newborns provides the same degree of distance acuity as the uncorrected vision of many adults who wear eyeglasses or contact lenses.

comprehensible as the infant's ability to sense and perceive the environment develops. In fact, babies appear to thrive in an environment enriched by pleasing sensations.

The processes that underlie infants' understanding of the world around them are sensation and perception. **Sensation** is the physical stimulation of the sense organs, and **perception** is the mental process of sorting out, interpreting, analyzing, and integrating stimuli from the sense organs and brain.

The study of infants' capabilities in the realm of sensation and perception challenges the ingenuity of investigators. As we'll see, researchers have developed a number of procedures for understanding sensation and perception in different realms.

Visual Perception: Seeing the World

From the time of Lee Eng's birth, everyone who met him felt that he gazed at them intently. His eyes seemed to meet those of visitors. They seemed to bore deeply and knowingly into the faces of people who looked at him.

How good, in fact, was Lee's vision, and what, precisely, could he make out of his environment? Quite a bit, at least up close. According to some estimates, a newborn's distance vision ranges from 20/200 to 20/600, which means that an infant can only see with accuracy visual material up to 20 feet that an adult with normal vision is able to see with similar accuracy from a distance of between 200 and 600 feet (Haith, 1991).

These figures indicate that infants' distance vision is one-tenth to one-third that of the average adult's. This isn't so bad, actually: The vision of newborns provides the same degree of distance acuity as the uncorrected vision of many adults who wear eyeglasses or contact lenses. Furthermore, infants' distance vision grows increasingly acute. By 6 months of age, the average infant's vision is already 20/20—in other words, identical to that of adults (Cavallini et al., 2002; Corrow et al., 2012).

Depth perception is a particularly useful ability, helping babies acknowledge heights and avoid falls. In a classic study, developmental psychologists Eleanor Gibson and Richard Walk (1960) placed infants on a sheet of heavy glass. A checkered pattern appeared under one-half of the glass sheet, making it seem that the infant was on a stable floor. However, in the middle of the glass sheet, the pattern dropped down several feet, forming an apparent "visual cliff." The question Gibson and Walk asked was whether infants would willingly crawl across the cliff when called by their mothers (see Figure 3-9).

sensation the physical stimulation of the sense organs

perception the sorting out, interpretation, analysis, and integration of stimuli involving the sense organs and brain

The results were clear: Most of the infants in the study, who ranged in age from 6 to 14 months, could not be coaxed over the apparent cliff. Clearly most of them had already developed the ability to perceive depth by that age (Campos, Langer, & Krowitz, 1970; Kretch & Adolph, 2013).

FIGURE 3-9 Visual Cliff
The "visual cliff" experiment examines the depth perception of infants. Most infants in the age range of 6 to 14 months cannot be coaxed to cross the cliff, apparently responding to the fact that the patterned area drops several feet.

Infants also show clear visual preferences, preferences that are present from birth. Given a choice, infants reliably prefer to look at stimuli that include patterns than to look at simpler stimuli (see Figure 3-10). How do we know? Developmental psychologist Robert Fantz (1963) created a classic test. He built a chamber in which babies could lie on their backs and see pairs of visual stimuli above them. Fantz could determine which of the stimuli the infants were looking at by observing the reflections of the stimuli in their eyes.

Fantz's work was the impetus for a great deal of research on the preferences of infants, most of which points to a critical conclusion: Infants are genetically preprogrammed to prefer particular kinds of stimuli. For instance, just minutes after birth they show preferences for certain colors, shapes, and configurations of various stimuli. They prefer curved over straight lines, three-dimensional figures to two-dimensional ones, and human faces to nonfaces. Such capabilities may be a reflection of the existence of highly specialized cells in the brain that react to stimuli of a particular pattern, orientation, shape, and direction of movement (Hubel & Wiesel, 1979, 2004; Gliga et al., 2009; Soska, Adolph, & Johnson, 2010).

However, genetics is not the sole determinant of infant visual preferences. Just a few hours after birth, infants have already learned to prefer their own mother's face to other faces. Similarly, between the ages of 6 and 9 months, infants become more adept at distinguishing between the faces of humans, while they become less able to distinguish faces of members of other species. They also distinguish between male and female faces. Such findings provide another clear piece of evidence of how heredity and environmental experiences are woven together to determine an infant's capabilities (Valenti, 2006; Quinn et al., 2008; Otsuka et al., 2012).

Auditory Perception: The World of Sound

What is it about a mother's lullaby that helps soothe crying babies, like Jenna, whom we discussed in the chapter opener? Some clues emerge when we look at the capabilities of infants in the realm of auditory sensation and perception.

Infants hear from the time of birth—and even before, as the ability to hear begins prenatally. Even in the womb, the fetus responds to sounds outside of its mother. Furthermore, infants are born with preferences for particular sound combinations (Trehub, 2003).

Because they have had some practice in hearing before birth, it is not surprising that infants have reasonably good auditory perception after they are born. In fact, infants actually are more sensitive to certain very high and very low frequencies than adults—a sensitivity that seems to increase during the first 2 years of life. On the other hand, infants are initially less sensitive than adults to middle-range frequencies. Eventually, however, their capabilities within the middle range improve (Fenwick & Morongiello, 1991; Werner & Marean, 1996; Frenald, 2001).

In addition to the ability to detect sound, infants need several other abilities in order to hear effectively. For instance, *sound localization* permits us to pinpoint the direction from which a sound is emanating. Compared to adults, infants have a slight handicap in this task because effective sound localization requires the use of the slight difference in the times at which a sound reaches our two ears. Sound that we hear first in the right ear tells us that the source of the sound is to our right. Because infants' heads are smaller than those of adults, the difference in timing of the arrival of sound at the two ears is less than it is in adults, so they have difficulty determining from which direction sound is coming.

Despite the potential limitation brought about by their smaller heads, infants' sound localization abilities are actually fairly good even at birth, and they reach adult levels of success by the age of 1 year. Furthermore, young infants are capable of making the fine discriminations that their future understanding of language will require (Fenwick, Kimberley, & Morrongiello, 1998; van Heugten, & Johnson, 2010; Purdy et al., 2013).

Smell and Taste

What do infants do when they smell a rotten egg? Pretty much what adults do—crinkle their noses and generally look unhappy. On the other hand, the scents of bananas and butter produce a pleasant reaction on the part of infants (Steiner, 1979; Pomares, Schirrer, & Abadie, 2002).

The sense of smell is so well developed, even among very young infants, that at least some 12- to 18-day-old babies can distinguish their mothers on the basis of smell alone. For instance, in one experiment infants were exposed to the smell of gauze pads worn under the arms of adults the previous evening. Infants who were being breastfed were able to distinguish their mothers' scent from those of other adults. However, not all infants could do this: Those who were being bottle-fed were unable to make the distinction. Moreover, both breastfed and bottle-fed infants were unable to distinguish their fathers on the basis of odor (Allam, Marlier, & Schaal, 2006; Lipsitt & Rovee-Collier, 2012).

Infants seem to have an innate sweet tooth (even before they have teeth!), and they show facial expressions of disgust when they taste something bitter. Very young infants smile when a sweet-tasting liquid is placed on their tongues. They also suck harder at a bottle if it is sweetened. Because breast milk has a sweet taste, it is possible that this preference may be part of our evolutionary heritage, retained because it offered a survival advantage (Porges, Lipsitt, & Lewis, 1993; Silveira et al., 2007).

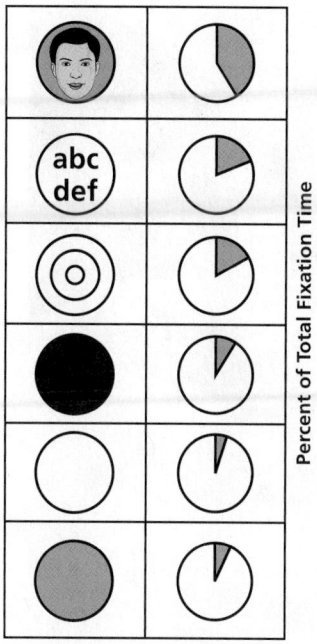

FIGURE 3-10 Preferring Complexity
In a classic experiment, researcher Robert Fantz found that 2- and 3-month-old infants preferred to look at more complex stimuli than simple ones.
Source: Based on Fantz, 1961.

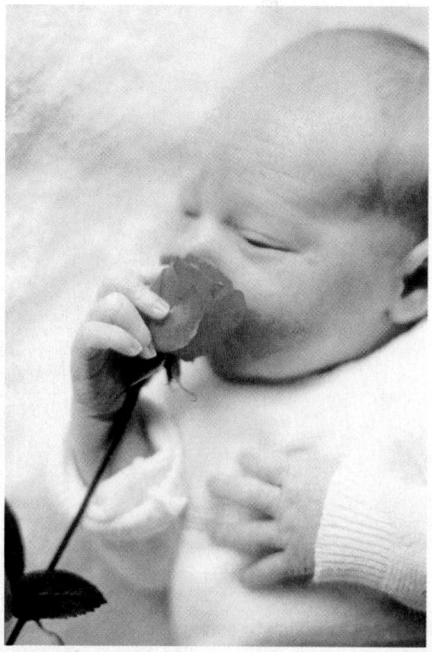

Infants' sense of smell is so well developed they can distinguish their mothers on the basis of smell alone.

By the age of 4 months infants are able to discriminate their own names from other, similar sounding words. What are some ways an infant is able to discriminate his or her name from other words?

Sensitivity to Pain and Touch

Infants are born with the capacity to experience pain. Obviously, no one can be sure if the experience of pain in children is identical to that in adults, any more than we can tell if an adult friend who complains of a headache is experiencing pain that is more or less severe than our own pain when we have a headache.

What we do know is that pain produces distress in infants. Their heartbeat increases, they sweat, show facial expressions of discomfort, and change the intensity and tone of crying when they are hurt (Simons et al., 2003; Warnock & Sandrin, 2004; Kohut & Riddell, 2009).

There appears to be a developmental progression in reactions to pain. For example, a newborn infant who has her heel pricked for a blood test responds with distress, but it takes her several seconds to show the response. In contrast, only a few months later, the same procedure brings a much more immediate response. It is possible that the delayed reaction in infants is produced by the relatively slower transmission of information within the newborn's less-developed nervous system (Anand & Hickey, 1992; Axia, Bonichini, & Benini, 1995; Puchalski & Hummel, 2002).

Responding to Touch. Touch is one of the most highly developed sensory systems in a newborn. It is also one of the first to develop; there is evidence that by 32 weeks after conception, the entire body is sensitive to touch. Furthermore, several of the basic reflexes present at birth, such as the rooting reflex, require touch sensitivity to operate: An infant must sense a touch near the mouth in order to seek automatically a nipple to suck (Haith, 1986).

Infants' abilities in the realm of touch are particularly helpful in their efforts to explore the world. Several theorists have suggested that one of the ways children gain information about the world is through touching. As mentioned earlier, at the age of 6 months, infants are apt to place almost any object in their mouths, apparently taking in data about its configuration from their sensory responses to the feel of it in their mouths (Ruff, 1989).

Touch also plays an important role in an organism's future development, for it triggers a complex chemical reaction that assists infants in their efforts to survive. For example, gentle massage stimulates the production of certain chemicals in an infant's brain that instigate growth (Field, Hernandez-Reif, & Diego, 2006; Diego, Field, & Hernandez-Reif, 2008, 2009).

Multimodal Perception: Combining Individual Sensory Inputs

When Eric Pettigrew was 7 months old, his grandparents presented him with a squeaky rubber doll. As soon as he saw it, he reached out for it, grasped it in his hand, and listened as it squeaked. He seemed delighted with the gift.

One way of considering Eric's sensory reaction to the doll is to focus on each of the senses individually: what the doll looked like to Eric, how it felt in his hand, and what it sounded like. In fact, this approach has dominated the study of sensation and perception in infancy.

However, let's consider another approach: We might examine how the various sensory responses are integrated with one another. Instead of looking at each individual sensory response, we could consider how the responses work together and are combined to produce Eric's ultimate reaction. The **multimodal approach to perception** considers how information that is collected by various individual sensory systems is integrated and coordinated (Farzin, Charles, & Rivera, 2009).

From a health care worker's perspective: Persons who are born without the use of one sense often develop unusual abilities in one or more other senses. What can health care professionals do to help infants who are lacking in a particular sense?

Although the multimodal approach is a relatively recent innovation in the study of how infants understand their sensory world, it raises some fundamental issues about the development of sensation and perception. For instance, some researchers argue that sensations are initially integrated with one another in the infant, while others maintain that the infant's sensory systems are initially separate and that brain development leads to increasing integration (Lickliter & Bahrick, 2000; Lewkowicz, 2002; Flom & Bahrick, 2007).

We do not know yet which view is correct. However, it does appear that by an early age infants are able to relate what they have learned about an object through one sensory channel to

multimodal approach to perception the approach that considers how information that is collected by various individual sensory systems is integrated and coordinated

affordances the action possibilities that a given situation or stimulus provides

Becoming an Informed Consumer of Development

Exercising Your Infant's Body and Senses

Recall how cultural expectations and environments affect the age at which various physical milestones, such as the first step, occur. While most experts feel attempts to accelerate physical and sensory-perceptual development yield little advantage, parents should ensure that their infants receive sufficient physical and sensory stimulation. There are several specific ways to accomplish this goal:

- Carry a baby in different positions—in a backpack, in a frontpack, or in a football hold with the infant's head in the palm of your hand and its feet lying on your arm. This lets the infant view the world from several perspectives.
- Let infants explore their environment. Don't contain them too long in a barren environment. Let them crawl or wander around—after first making the environment "childproof" by removing dangerous objects.
- Engage in "rough-and-tumble" play. Wrestling, dancing, and rolling around on the floor—if not violent—are activities that are fun and that stimulate older infants' motor and sensory systems.
- Let babies touch their food and even play with it. Infancy is too early to start teaching table manners.
- Provide toys that stimulate the senses, particularly toys that can stimulate more than one sense at a time. For example, brightly colored, textured toys with movable parts are enjoyable and help sharpen infants' senses.

what they have learned about it through another. For instance, even 1-month-old infants are able to recognize by sight objects that they have previously held in their mouths but never seen (Meltzoff, 1981; Steri & Spelke, 1988). Clearly, some cross-talk between various sensory channels is already possible a month after birth.

Infants' abilities in multimodal perception showcase the sophisticated perceptual abilities of infants, which continue to grow throughout the period of infancy. Such perceptual growth is aided by infants' discovery of **affordances**, the options that a given situation or stimulus provides. For example, infants learn that they might potentially fall when walking down a steep ramp—that is, the ramp *affords* the possibility of falling. Such knowledge is crucial as infants make the transition from crawling to walking. Similarly, infants learn that an object shaped in a certain way can slip out of their hands if not grasped correctly. For example, Eric is learning that his toy has several affordances: He can grab it and squeeze it, listen to it squeak, and even chew comfortably on it if he is teething (Wilcox et al., 2007; Huang, C-T, 2012; Walker-Andrews et al., 2013).

The senses of sight and touch are integrated by infants through multimodal perception.

REVIEW, CHECK, AND APPLY

REVIEW

LO7 What sensory capabilities do infants possess?

- Infants' sensory abilities are surprisingly well developed at or shortly after birth. Their perceptions help them explore and begin to make sense of the world.
- Very early on, infants can see depth and motion, distinguish colors and patterns, localize and discriminate sounds, and recognize the sound and smell of their mothers.
- Infants are sensitive to pain and touch, and most medical authorities now advocate for procedures, including anesthesia, that minimize infants' pain.

LO8 How does multisensory perception function?

- The multimodal approach to perception considers how information that is collected by individual sensory systems is integrated and coordinated.

CHECK YOURSELF

1. _____ is the physical stimulation of the sense organs.
   - a Perception
   - b Crying
   - c Crawling
   - d Sensation
2. We know that infants experience pain because their heartbeat increases, they sweat, they show discomfort, and their crying changes tone.
   - True
   - False
3. The _____ considers how information that is collected by various individual sensory systems is integrated and coordinated.
   - a multimodal approach to perception
   - b affordance theory
   - c multidisciplinary motor development cycle
   - d macrosystem

APPLYING LIFESPAN DEVELOPMENT

- If you were selecting a mobile as a gift for a young infant, what features would you look for to make the mobile as interesting as possible to the baby?

✓ **Study** and **Review** on **MyPsychLab.com**

MODULE 3.2

COGNITIVE DEVELOPMENT IN INFANCY

High-IQ DVDs?

Luisa Roman, 2, and her 10-month-old brother Tino just love TV. If they were allowed to, they'd sit in front of the television for hours at a time. But Mariela Roman, their mother, limits their viewing to around an hour a day, and for most of this time she puts on DVDs of a show called Eebee's Adventures that Mariela approves of. She reasons that she can't be interacting with her children every minute of the day, and the times when she can't should be spent on something worthwhile.

She knows that Eebee's Adventures involves singing, dancing, and playing, and that it presents interesting situations that her children, especially Luisa, can understand. It also uses a lot of good, varied language spoken at a reasonable pace, so that both of her kids can follow it. She is confident that the DVDs are giving her children a jump start on important skills that they will need in school.

Looking Ahead

Can infants really become miniature Einsteins by watching educational media? What concepts are babies as young as 10-month-old Tino Roman actually grasping, and what intellectual abilities remain undeveloped at that age? Can an infant's cognitive development really be accelerated through intellectual stimulation, or does the process unfold on its own timetable despite the best efforts of parents to hasten it?

We address these questions in this module as we consider cognitive development during the first years of life, focusing on how infants develop their knowledge and understanding of the world. We first discuss the work of Swiss psychologist Jean Piaget, whose theory of developmental stages served as a highly influential impetus for a considerable amount of work on cognitive development.

We then cover more contemporary views of cognitive development, examining information processing approaches that seek to explain how cognitive growth occurs. We also examine memory in infants and address individual differences in intelligence.

Finally, we consider language, the cognitive skill that permits infants to communicate with others. We look at the roots of language in prelinguistic speech and trace the milestones indicating the development of language skills in the progression from the baby's first words to phrases and sentences.

PIAGET'S APPROACH TO COGNITIVE DEVELOPMENT

LO9 **What are the fundamental features of Piaget's theories of cognitive development?**

LO10 **How has Piaget's theory been supported and challenged?**

Olivia's dad is wiping up the mess around the base of her high chair—for the third time today! It seems to him that 14-month-old Olivia takes great delight in dropping food from the high chair. She also drops toys, spoons, anything it seems, just to watch how it hits the floor. She almost appears to be experimenting to see what kind of noise or what size of splatter is created by each different thing she drops.

Swiss psychologist Jean Piaget (1896–1980) probably would have said that Olivia's dad is right in theorizing that Olivia is conducting her own series of experiments to learn more about the workings of her world. Piaget's views of the ways infants learn could be summed in a simple equation: *Action = Knowledge*.

Piaget argued that infants do not acquire knowledge from facts communicated by others, nor through sensation and perception. Instead, Piaget suggested that knowledge is the product of direct motor behavior. Although many of his basic explanations and propositions have been challenged by subsequent research, as we'll discuss later, the view that in significant ways infants learn by doing remains unquestioned (Piaget, 1952, 1962, 1983; Bullinger, 1997).

Key Elements of Piaget's Theory

As we first noted in Module 1.1, Piaget's theory is based on a stage approach to development. He assumed that all children pass through a series of four universal stages in a fixed order from birth through adolescence: sensorimotor, preoperational, concrete operational, and formal operational. He also suggested that movement from one stage to the next occurs when a child reaches an appropriate level of physical maturation *and* is exposed to relevant experiences. Without such experience, children are assumed to be incapable of reaching their cognitive potential. Some approaches to cognition focus on changes in the *content* of children's knowledge about the world, but Piaget argued that it was critical to also consider the changes in the *quality* of children's knowledge and understanding as they move from one stage to another.

For instance, as they develop cognitively, infants experience changes in their understanding about what can and cannot occur in the world. Consider a baby who participates in an experiment during which she is exposed to three identical versions of her mother all at the same time, thanks to some well-placed mirrors. A 3-month-old infant will interact happily with each of these images of mother. However, by 5 months of age, the child becomes quite agitated at the sight of multiple mothers. Apparently, by this time the child has figured out that he or she has but one mother, and viewing three at a time is thoroughly alarming (Bower, 1977). To Piaget, such reactions indicate that a baby is beginning to master principles regarding the way the world operates, indicating that he or she has begun to construct a mental sense of the world that he or she didn't have 2 months earlier.

Swiss psychologist Jean Piaget.

Piaget believed that the basic building blocks of the way we understand the world are mental structures called **schemes**, organized patterns of functioning, that adapt and change with mental development. At first, schemes are related to physical, or sensorimotor, activity, such as picking up or reaching for toys. As children develop, their schemes move to a mental level, reflecting thought. Schemes are similar to computer software: They direct and determine how data from the world, such as new events or objects, are considered and dealt with (Rakison & Oakes, 2003; Rakison & Krogh, 2012).

If you give a baby a new cloth book, for example, he or she will touch it, mouth it, perhaps try to tear it or bang it on the floor. To Piaget, each of these actions represents a scheme, and they are the infant's way of gaining knowledge and understanding of this new object.

Piaget suggested that two principles underlie the growth in children's schemes: assimilation and accommodation. **Assimilation** is the process by which people understand an experience in terms of their current stage of cognitive development and way of thinking. Assimilation occurs, then, when a stimulus or event is acted upon, perceived, and understood in accordance with existing patterns of thought. For example, an infant who tries to suck on any toy in the same way is assimilating the objects to her existing sucking scheme. Similarly, a child who encounters a flying squirrel at a zoo and calls it a "bird" is assimilating the squirrel to his or her existing scheme of bird.

In contrast, when we change our existing ways of thinking, understanding, or behaving in response to encounters with new stimuli or events, **accommodation** takes place. For instance, when a child sees a flying squirrel and calls it "a bird with a tail," he or she is beginning to *accommodate* new knowledge, modifying his or her scheme of bird.

Piaget believed that the earliest schemes are primarily limited to the reflexes with which we are all born, such as sucking and rooting. Infants start to modify these simple early schemes almost immediately, through the processes of assimilation and accommodation, in response to their exploration of the environment. Schemes quickly become more sophisticated as infants become more advanced in their motor capabilities—to Piaget, a signal of the potential for more advanced cognitive development. Because Piaget's sensorimotor stage of development begins at birth and continues until the child is about 2 years old, we consider it here in detail.

scheme an organized patterns of functioning that adapt and change with mental functioning

assimilation the process in which people understand an experience in terms of their current stage of cognitive development and way of thinking

accommodation changes in existing ways of thinking that occur in response to encounters with new stimuli or events

The Sensorimotor Period: The Earliest Stage of Cognitive Growth

Piaget suggests that the **sensorimotor stage**, the initial major stage of cognitive development, can be broken down into six substages. These are summarized in Table 3-5. It is important to keep in mind that although the specific substages of the sensorimotor period may at first appear to unfold with great regularity, as though infants reach a particular age and smoothly proceed into the next substage, the reality of cognitive development is somewhat different. First, the ages at which infants actually reach a particular stage vary a good deal among different children. The exact timing of a stage reflects an interaction between the infant's level of physical maturation and the nature of the social environment in which the child is being raised. Consequently, although Piaget contended that the order of the substages does not change from one child to the next, he admitted that the timing can and does vary to some degree.

Piaget viewed development as a more gradual process than the notion of different stages might seem to imply. Infants do not go to sleep one night in one substage and wake up the next morning in the next one. Instead, there is a rather steady shifting of behavior as a child moves toward the next stage of cognitive development. Infants also pass through periods of transition, in which some aspects of their behavior reflect the next higher stage, while other aspects indicate their current stage (see Figure 3-11 on page 115).

sensorimotor stage (of cognitive development) Piaget's initial major stage of cognitive development, which can be broken down into six substages

Substage 1: Simple Reflexes. The first substage of the sensorimotor period is *Substage 1: Simple reflexes*, encompassing the first month of life. During this time, the various inborn reflexes, described in Module 3.1, are at the center of a baby's physical and cognitive life, determining the nature of his or her interactions with the world. At the same time, some of the reflexes begin to accommodate the infant's experience with the nature of the world. For instance,

TABLE 3-5 PIAGET'S SIX SUBSTAGES OF THE SENSORIMOTOR STAGE

Substage	Age	Description	Example
Substage 1: Simple reflexes	First month of life	During this period, the various reflexes that determine the infant's interactions with the world are at the center of its cognitive life.	The sucking reflex causes the infant to suck at anything placed in his or her lips.
Substage 2: First habits and primary circular reactions	From 1 to 4 months	At this age infants begin to coordinate what were separate actions into single, integrated activities.	An infant might combine grasping an object with sucking on it, or staring at something with touching it.
Substage 3: Secondary circular reactions	From 4 to 8 months	During this period, infants take major strides in shifting their cognitive horizons beyond themselves and begin to act on the outside world.	A child who repeatedly picks up a rattle in her crib and shakes it in different ways to see how the sound changes is demonstrating her ability to modify her cognitive scheme about shaking rattles.
Substage 4: Coordination of secondary circular reactions	From 8 to 12 months	In this stage infants begin to use more calculated approaches to producing events, coordinating several schemes to generate a single act. They achieve object permanence during this stage.	An infant will push one toy out of the way to reach another toy that is lying, partially exposed, under it.
Substage 5: Tertiary circular reactions	From 12 to 18 months	At this age infants develop what Piaget regards as the deliberate variation of actions that bring desirable consequences. Rather than just repeating enjoyable activities, infants appear to carry out miniature experiments to observe the consequences.	A child will drop a toy repeatedly, varying the position from which he drops it, carefully observing each time to see where it falls.
Substage 6: Beginnings of thought	From 18 months to 2 years	The major achievement of Substage 6 is the capacity for mental representation or symbolic thought. Piaget argued that only at this stage can infants imagine where objects that they cannot see might be.	Children can even plot in their heads unseen trajectories of objects, so that if a ball rolls under a piece of furniture, they can figure out where it is likely to emerge on the other side.

an infant who is being breastfed but who also receives supplemental bottles may start to change the way he or she sucks, depending on whether a nipple is on a breast or a bottle.

Substage 2: First Habits and Primary Circular Reactions. *Substage 2: First habits and primary circular reactions*, the second substage of the sensorimotor period, occurs from 1 to 4 months of age. In this period, infants begin to coordinate what were separate actions into single, integrated activities. For instance, an infant might combine grasping an object with sucking on it, or staring at something while touching it.

If an activity engages a baby's interests, he or she may repeat it over and over, simply for the sake of continuing to experience it. This repetition of a chance motor event helps the baby start building cognitive schemes through a process known as a *circular reaction*. *Primary circular reactions* are schemes reflecting an infant's repetition of interesting or enjoyable actions, just for the enjoyment of doing them, which focus on the infant's own body.

Substage 3: Secondary Circular Reactions. *Substage 3: Secondary circular reactions* are more purposeful. According to Piaget, this third stage of cognitive development in infancy occurs from 4 to 8 months of age. During this period, a child begins to act upon the outside world. For instance, infants now seek to repeat enjoyable events in their environments if they happen to produce them through chance activities. A child who repeatedly picks up a rattle in her crib and shakes it in different ways to see how the sound changes is demonstrating her ability to modify her cognitive scheme about shaking rattles. She is engaging in what Piaget calls *secondary circular reactions*, which are schemes regarding repeated actions that bring about a desirable consequence.

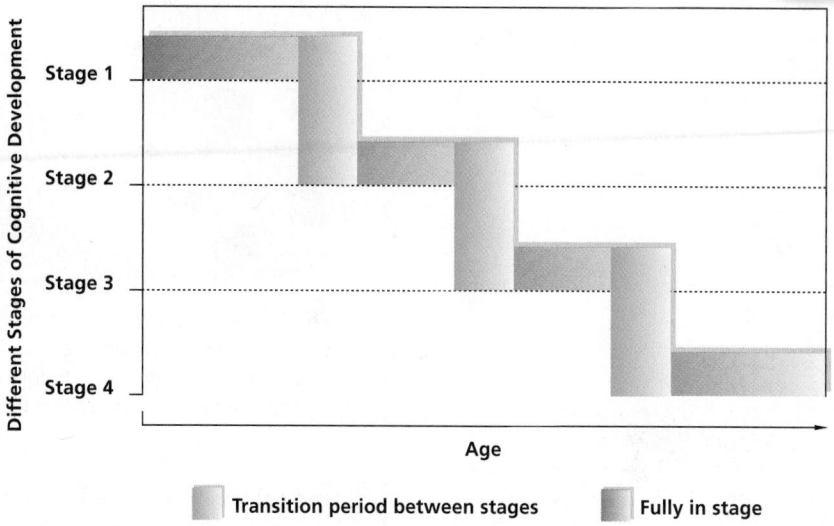

FIGURE 3-11 Transitions
Infants do not suddenly shift from one stage of cognitive development to the next. Instead, Piaget argues that there is a period of transition in which some behavior reflects one stage, while other behavior reflects the more advanced stage. Does this gradualism argue against Piaget's interpretation of stages?

Substage 4: Coordination of Secondary Circular Reactions. Some major leaps forward occur in *Substage 4: Coordination of secondary circular reactions*, which lasts from 8 months to 12 months. In Substage 4, infants begin to employ *goal-directed behavior*, in which several schemes are combined and coordinated to generate a single act to solve a problem. For instance, they will push one toy out of the way to reach another toy that is lying, partially exposed, under it.

Infants' newfound purposefulness, their ability to use means to attain particular ends, and their skill in anticipating future circumstances owe their appearance in part to the developmental achievement of object permanence that emerges in Substage 4. **Object permanence** is the realization that people and objects exist even when they cannot be seen. It is a simple principle, but its mastery has profound consequences.

Consider, for instance, 7-month-old Chu, who has yet to learn the idea of object permanence. Chu's mother shakes a rattle in front of him, then takes the rattle and places it under a blanket. To Chu, who has not mastered the concept of object permanence, the rattle no longer exists. He will make no effort to look for it.

Several months later, when he reaches Substage 4, the story is quite different (see Figure 3-12). This time, as soon as his mother places the rattle under the blanket, Chu tries to toss the cover aside, eagerly searching for the rattle. Chu clearly has learned that the object continues to exist even when it cannot be seen. For the infant who achieves an understanding of object permanence, then, out of sight is decidedly not out of mind.

The attainment of object permanence extends not only to inanimate objects, but to people, too. It gives Chu the security that his father and mother still exist even when they have left the room.

Substage 5: Tertiary Circular Reactions. *Substage 5: Tertiary circular reactions* is reached at around the age of 12 months and extends to 18 months. As the name of the stage indicates, during this period infants develop these reactions, which are schemes regarding the deliberate variation of actions that bring desirable consequences. Rather than just repeating

object permanence the realization that people and objects exist even when they cannot be seen

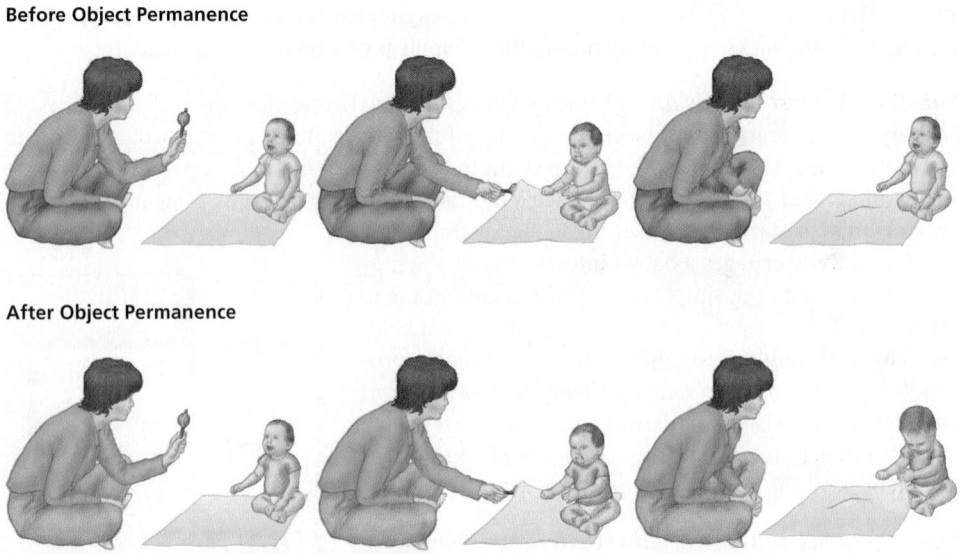

FIGURE 3-12 Object Permanence
Before an infant has understood the idea of object permanence, he will not search for an object that has been hidden right before his eyes. But several months later, he will search for it, illustrating that he has attained object permanence. Why is the concept of object permanence important?

enjoyable activities, as they do with secondary circular reactions, infants appear to carry out miniature experiments to observe the consequences.

For example, Piaget observed his son Laurent dropping a toy swan repeatedly, varying the position from which he dropped it, carefully observing each time to see where it fell. Instead of just repeating the action each time, Laurent made modifications in the situation to learn about their consequences. As you may recall from our discussion of research methods in Module 1.1, this behavior represents the essence of the scientific method: An experimenter varies a situation in a laboratory to learn the effects of the variation. To infants in Substage 5, the world is their laboratory, and they spend their days leisurely carrying out one miniature experiment after another.

Substage 6: Beginnings of Thought. The final stage of the sensorimotor period is *Substage 6: Beginnings of thought*, which lasts from 18 months to 2 years. The major achievement of Substage 6 is the capacity for mental representation, or symbolic thought. A *mental representation* is an internal image of a past event or object. Piaget argued that by this stage infants can imagine where objects might be that they cannot see. They can even plot in their heads unseen trajectories of objects, so if a ball rolls under a piece of furniture, they can figure out where it is likely to emerge on the other side.

With the attainment of the cognitive skill of deferred imitation, children are able to imitate people and scenes they have witnessed in the past.

From a caregiver's perspective: What are some implications for childrearing practices of Piaget's observations about the ways children gain an understanding of the world? Would you use the same approaches in childrearing for a child growing up in a non-Western culture?

Appraising Piaget: Support and Challenges

Most developmental researchers would probably agree that in many significant ways, Piaget's descriptions of how cognitive development proceeds during infancy are quite accurate (Harris, 1987; Marcovitch, Zelazo, & Schmuckler, 2003). Yet, there is substantial disagreement over the validity of the theory and many of its specific predictions.

Let's start with what is clearly accurate about the Piagetian approach. Piaget was a masterful reporter of children's behavior, and his descriptions of growth during infancy remain a monument to his powers of observation. Furthermore, literally thousands of studies have supported Piaget's view that children learn much about the world by acting on objects in their environment. Finally, the broad outlines sketched out by Piaget of the sequence of cognitive development and the increasing cognitive accomplishments that occur during infancy are generally accurate (Schlottmann & Wilkening, 2012; Müller et al., 2013).

On the other hand, specific aspects of the theory have come under increasing scrutiny—and criticism—in the decades since Piaget carried out his pioneering work. For example, some researchers question the stage conception that forms the basis of Piaget's theory. Although, as we noted earlier, even Piaget acknowledged that children's transitions between stages are gradual, critics contend that development proceeds in a much more continuous fashion. Rather than showing major leaps of competence at the end of one stage and the beginning of the next, improvement comes in more gradual increments, growing step by step in a skill-by-skill manner.

For instance, developmental researcher Robert Siegler suggests that cognitive development proceeds not in stages but in "waves." According to Siegler, children don't one day drop a mode of thinking and the next take up a new form. Instead, there is an ebb and flow of cognitive approaches that children use to understand the world (Siegler, 2007; Siegler & Lin, 2010; Siegler, 2012).

Other critics dispute Piaget's notion that cognitive development is grounded in motor activities. They charge that Piaget overlooked the importance of the sensory and perceptual systems that are present from a very early age in infancy—systems about which Piaget knew little, because so much of the research illustrating how sophisticated they are even in infancy was done relatively recently (Decarrie, 1969; Butterworth, 1994).

To bolster their views, Piaget's critics also point to more recent studies that cast doubt on Piaget's view that infants are incapable of mastering the concept of object permanence until they are close to a year old. For instance, some work suggests that younger infants did not appear to understand object permanence because the techniques used to test their abilities were not sensitive enough to their true capabilities (Krojgaard, 2005; Walden et al., 2007; Baillargeon, 2004, 2008).

It may be that a 4-month-old doesn't search for a rattle hidden under a blanket because she hasn't learned the motor skills necessary to do the searching—not because she doesn't understand that the rattle still exists. Similarly, the apparent inability of young infants to comprehend object permanence may reflect more about their memory deficits than their lack of understanding of the concept: The memories of young infants may be poor enough that they simply do not recall the earlier concealment of the toy. In fact, when more age-appropriate tasks are employed, some researchers have found indications of object permanence in children as young as 3 1/2 months (Wang, Baillargeon, & Paterson, 2005; Ruffman, Slade, & Redman, 2006; Luo, Kaufman, & Baillargeon, 2009).

Piaget's work also seems to describe children from developed, Western countries better than those in non-Western cultures. For instance, some evidence suggests that cognitive skills emerge on a different timetable for children in non-Western cultures than for children living in Europe and the United States. Infants raised in the Ivory Coast of Africa, for example, reach the various substages of the sensorimotor period at an earlier age than infants reared in France (Dasen et al., 1978; Mistry & Saraswathi, 2003; Tamis-LeMonda et al., 2012).

However, even Piaget's most passionate critics concede that he has provided us with a masterful description of the broad outlines of cognitive development during infancy. His failings seem to be in underestimating the capabilities of younger infants and in his claims that sensorimotor skills develop in a consistent, fixed pattern. Still, his influence has been enormous and, although the focus of many contemporary developmental researchers has shifted to newer information processing approaches that we discuss next, Piaget remains a towering and pioneering figure in the field of development (Fischer & Hencke, 1996; Roth, Slone, & Dar, 2000; Kail, 2004; Maynard, 2008).

Appraising Piaget: Research on babies in non-Western cultures suggests that Piaget's stages are not universal, but are to some degree culturally derived.

REVIEW, CHECK, AND APPLY

REVIEW

L09 What are the fundamental features of Piaget's theories of cognitive development?

- Piaget's theory of human cognitive development involves a succession of stages through which children progress from birth to adolescence.
- As infants move from one stage to another, the way they understand the world changes.
- The sensorimotor stage has six substages. The sensorimotor stage, from birth to about 2 years, involves a gradual progression through simple reflexes, single coordinated activities, interest in the outside world, purposeful combinations of activities, manipulation of actions to produce desired outcomes, and symbolic thought.

L010 How has Piaget's theory been supported and challenged?

- Although Piaget's theory accurately describes cognitive development in a broad sense, many specifics of the theory, particularly the age at which various skills develop, has been challenged.

CHECK YOURSELF

1. According to Piaget, children can move from one cognitive stage to another only when a child _____ and is exposed to relative experiences.
   - a is adequately nourished
   - b is born with an adequate genetic predisposition for learning
   - c has remembered his or her goal of learning
   - d reaches an appropriate level of physical maturation
2. Infants' schemes for understanding the world usually involve their physical or sensorimotor activities.
   - True
   - False
3. In general, when it comes to infant cognitive development, it appears that Piaget_____.
   - a overestimated infants and what they could do
   - b underestimated infants and what they could do
   - c was more accurate about adolescent cognitive development
   - d overestimated the role of culture

APPLYING LIFESPAN DEVELOPMENT

- Think of a common young children's toy with which you are familiar. How might its use be affected by the principles of assimilation and accommodation?

✓ **Study** and **Review** on **MyPsychLab.com**

INFORMATION PROCESSING APPROACHES TO COGNITIVE DEVELOPMENT

L011 How do infants process information?
L012 How is infant intelligence measured?

Amber Nordstrom, 3 months old, breaks into a smile as her brother Marcus stands over her crib, picks up a doll, and makes a whistling noise through his teeth. In fact, Amber never seems to tire of Marcus's efforts at making her smile and, soon, whenever Marcus appears and simply picks up the doll, her lips begin to curl into a smile.

Clearly, Amber remembers Marcus and his humorous ways. But how does she remember him? And how much else can Amber remember?

To answer questions such as these, we need to diverge from the road that Piaget laid out for us. Rather than seeking to identify the universal, broad milestones in cognitive development through which all infants pass, as Piaget tried to do, we must consider the specific processes by which individual babies acquire and use the information to which they are exposed. We need, then, to focus less on the qualitative changes in infants' mental lives and consider more closely their quantitative capabilities.

Information processing approaches to cognitive development seek to identify the way that individuals take in, use, and store information. According to this approach, the quantitative changes in infants' abilities to organize and manipulate information represent the hallmarks of cognitive development.

Taking this perspective, cognitive growth is characterized by increasing sophistication, speed, and capacity in information processing. Earlier, we compared Piaget's idea of schemes to computer software, which directs the computer in how to deal with data from the world. We might compare the information processing perspective on cognitive growth to the improvements that come from the use of more efficient programs that lead to increased speed

information processing approaches the model that seeks to identify the way that individuals take in, use, and store information and sophistication in the processing of information. Information processing approaches, then, focus on the types of "mental programs" that people use when they seek to solve problems (Cohen & Cashon, 2003; Hugdahl & Westerhausen, 2010).

Ultimately, both Piagetian and information processing approaches are critical in providing an account of cognitive development in infancy. Coupled with advances in the biochemistry of the brain and theories that consider the effects of social factors on learning and cognition, the two help us paint a full picture of cognitive development. (Also see the "*From Research to Practice*" box.)

From Research to Practice

Infants Learn From Adults, Not Videos

The advertisements are certainly compelling—proud parents giving gushing testimonials about the effectiveness of the latest "baby genius" DVD and how it helped their toddler's vocabulary "blossom." The word has gotten out that an intellectually stimulating environment best supports young children's rapidly developing cognitive abilities, and many parents are drawn to the idea of providing such enrichment even during downtimes when they themselves are unavailable for interaction. But are such baby media products really beneficial?

Quite a bit of research shows that they're not. One recent study examined the effectiveness of a baby DVD that teaches vocabulary by having groups of parents use the product in their homes for 4 weeks, either while actively engaging their children or while just passively watching. The researchers intentionally chose a best-selling DVD, allowed a lengthy exposure time, created real-world conditions by doing the study in people's homes, ensured that parents followed the directions closely, and monitored for compliance, all to give the DVD the best possible chance of actually working.

Another group of parents attempted to teach their children the same vocabulary words themselves without the DVD, and a control group used no vocabulary training at all. The findings were clear: whether parents actively engaged their children with the DVD or just passively watched it, those children didn't learn the words significantly better than the control group. Only the children who were learning the words from their parent (with no DVD) learned them better than the control group (DeLoache et al., 2010).

Other research on infants' early language production helps explain this finding: Infants learn vocabulary best in an interactive setting where adults are responding to the sounds the infant is making. According to research by Michael Goldstein, babies learn vocabulary best when they initiate the learning and when they choose the object to be labeled. For instance, if an infant babbles while looking at an object, the best approach is to name the object (even if the babbling sounds like a different word). In this way, the "lesson" coincides with the infant's natural exploration of the world rather than trying to impose an experience on the child, as videos do (Goldstein et al., 2010; Klass, 2010; Bergelson & Swingley, 2012).

- *According to Goldstein, if an infant is looking at an apple and saying "ba-ba-ba," it's better for parents to name the apple rather than find a word that fits the babble (such as banana or bottle). Why do you think this is so?*
- *Goldstein's research shows that parents who liked educational DVDs best believed that it improved their child's vocabulary significantly, even though that was rarely the case. Why might parents acquire this false belief?*

Encoding, Storage, and Retrieval: The Foundations of Information Processing

Information processing has three basic aspects: encoding, storage, and retrieval (see Figure 3-13). *Encoding* is the process by which information is initially recorded in a form usable to memory. Infants and children—indeed, all people—are exposed to a massive amount of information; if they tried to process it all, they would be overwhelmed. Consequently, they encode selectively, picking and choosing the information to which they will pay attention.

Even if someone has been exposed to the information initially and has encoded it in an appropriate way, there is still no guarantee that he or she will be able to use it in the future. Information must also have been stored in memory adequately. *Storage* refers to the placement of material into memory. Finally, success in using the material in the future depends on retrieval processes. *Retrieval* is the process by which material in memory storage is located, brought into awareness, and used.

FIGURE 3-13 Information Processing
The process by which information is encoded, stored, and retrieved.

We can use our comparison to computers again here. Information processing approaches suggest that the processes of encoding, storage, and retrieval are analogous to different parts of a computer. Encoding can be thought of as a computer's keyboard, through which one inputs information; storage is the computer's hard drive, where information is stored; and retrieval is analogous to software that accesses the information for display on the screen. Only when all three processes are operating—encoding, storage, and retrieval—can information be processed. **Explore** the **Concept** *Encoding, Storage, and Retrieval in Memory* in **MyPsychLab.**

Automatization. In some cases, encoding, storage, and retrieval are relatively automatic, while in other cases they are deliberate. *Automatization* is the degree to which an activity requires attention. Processes that require relatively little attention are automatic; processes that require relatively large amounts of attention are controlled. For example, some activities such as walking, eating with a fork, or reading may be automatic for you, but at first they required your full attention.

Automatic mental processes help children in their initial encounters with the world by enabling them to easily and "automatically" process information in particular ways. For instance, by the age of 5, children automatically encode information in terms of frequency. Without a lot of attention to counting or tallying, they become aware, for example, of how often they have encountered various people, permitting them to differentiate familiar from unfamiliar people (Homae et al., 2012).

Some of the things we learn automatically are unexpectedly complex. For example, infants have the ability to learn subtle statistical patterns and relationships. The existence of basic mathematical skills in infants has been supported by findings that nonhumans are born with some basic numeric proficiency. Even newly hatched chicks show some counting abilities. And it is not too long into infancy that children demonstrate an understanding of such basic physics as movement trajectories and gravity (Gopnik, 2010; vanMarle & Wynn, 2011; Hespos & vanMarle, 2012).

The result of this growing body of research suggests that infants have an innate grasp of certain basic mathematical functions and statistical patterns. This inborn proficiency is likely to form the basis for learning more complex mathematics and statistical relationships later in life (Gelman & Gallistel, 2004; McCrink & Wynn, 2004, 2007, 2009; van Marle & Wynn, 2006, 2009).

Memory During Infancy: They Must Remember This ...

Arif Terzić was born during the war in Bosnia. He spent his first 2 years hiding in a basement with his mother. The only light he saw came from a kerosene lamp. The only sounds he heard were his mother's hushed lullabies and the explosion of shells. Someone he never saw who left food for them. There was a tap, but sometimes the water was too filthy to drink. At one point, his mother suffered a kind of breakdown. She fed him when she remembered. But she didn't speak. Or sing.

Arif was lucky. His family emigrated to the United States when he was 2. His father found work. They rented a little house. Arif went to preschool and then kindergarten. Today, he has friends, toys, a dog, and loves soccer. "He doesn't remember Bosnia," his mother says. "It's like it never happened."

How likely is it that Arif truly remembers nothing of his infancy? And if he ever does recall his first 2 years of life, how accurate will his memories be? To answer these questions, we need to consider the qualities of memory that exist during infancy.

Memory Capabilities in Infancy. Certainly, infants have **memory** capabilities, defined as the process by which information is initially recorded, stored, and retrieved. As we've seen, infants can distinguish new stimuli from old, and this implies that some memory of the old must be present. Unless the infants had some memory of an original stimulus, it would be impossible for them to recognize that a new stimulus differed from the earlier one.

Infants' capability to recognize new stimuli from old tells us little about how age brings about changes in the capacities of memory and in its fundamental nature. Do infants' memory capabilities increase as they get older? The answer is clearly affirmative. In one study, infants were taught that they could move a mobile hanging over the crib by kicking their legs. It took only a few days for 2-month-old infants to forget their training, but 6-month-old infants still remembered for as long as 3 weeks (Rovee-Collier, 1993, 1999; Haley et al., 2010).

Furthermore, infants who were later prompted to recall the association between kicking and moving the mobile showed evidence that the memory continued to exist even longer. Infants who had received just two training sessions lasting 9 minutes each still recalled about a week later, as illustrated by the fact that they began to kick when placed in the crib with the mobile. Two weeks later, however, they made no effort to kick, suggesting that they had forgotten entirely.

memory the process by which information is initially recorded, stored, and retrieved

But they hadn't forgotten: When the babies saw a reminder—a moving mobile—their memories were apparently reactivated. In fact, the infants could remember the association, following prompting, for as long as an additional month. Other evidence confirms these results, suggesting that hints can reactivate memories that at first seem lost, and that the older the infant, the more effective such prompting is (Sullivan, Rovee-Collier, & Tynes, 1979; Bearce & Rovee-Collier, 2006; DeFrancisco & Rovee-Collier, 2008; Moher, Tuerk, & Feigenson, 2012).

The Duration of Memories. Although the processes that underlie memory retention and recall seem similar throughout the life span, the quantity of information stored and recalled does differ markedly as infants develop. Older infants can retrieve information more rapidly and they can remember it longer. But just how long? Can memories from infancy be recalled, for example, after babies grow up?

Researchers disagree on the age from which memories can be retrieved. Although early research supported the notion of **infantile amnesia**, the lack of memory for experiences occurring prior to 3 years of age, more recent research shows that infants do retain memories. For example, 6-month-old children exposed to an unusual series of events, such as intermittent periods of light and dark and unusual sounds, have some memories of their participation in the earlier experience 2 years later (Neisser, 2004; Ribordy et al., 2013).

Still, although it is at least theoretically possible for memories to remain intact from a very young age—if subsequent experiences do not interfere with their recollection—in most cases memories of personal experiences in infancy do not last into adulthood. Memories of personal experience seem not to become accurate before age 18 to 24 months (Howe, 2003; Howe, Courage, & Edison, 2004; Bauer, 2007).

The Cognitive Neuroscience of Memory. Some of the most exciting research on the development of memory is coming from studies of the neurological basis of memory. Advances in brain scan technology, as well as studies of adults with brain damage, suggest that there are two separate systems involved with long-term memory. These two systems, called explicit memory and implicit memory, retain different sorts of information.

Explicit memory is memory that is conscious and that can be recalled intentionally. When we try to recall a name or phone number, we're using explicit memory. In comparison, *implicit memory* consists of memories of which we are not consciously aware, but that affect performance and behavior. Implicit memory consists of motor skills, habits, and activities that can be remembered without conscious cognitive effort, such as how to ride a bike or climb a stairway.

Explicit and implicit memories emerge at different rates and involve different parts of the brain. The earliest memories seem to be implicit, and they involve the cerebellum and brain stem. The forerunner of explicit memory involves the hippocampus, but true explicit memory doesn't emerge until the second half of the first year. When explicit memory does emerge, it involves an increasing number of areas of the cortex of the brain (Squire & Knowlton, 2005; Bauer, 2007; Low & Perner, 2012).

Individual Differences in Intelligence: Is One Infant Smarter Than Another?

Maddy Rodriguez is a bundle of curiosity and energy. At 6 months of age, she cries heartily if she can't reach a toy, and when she sees a reflection of herself in a mirror, she gurgles and seems, in general, to find the situation quite amusing.

Jared Lynch, at 6 months, is a good deal more inhibited than Maddy. He doesn't seem to care much when a ball rolls out of his reach, losing interest in it rapidly. And, unlike Maddy, when he sees himself in a mirror, he pretty much ignores the reflection.

As anyone who has spent any time at all observing more than one baby can tell you, not all infants are alike. Some are full of energy and life, apparently displaying a natural-born curiosity, while others seem, by comparison, somewhat less interested in the world around them. Does this mean that such infants differ in intelligence?

Answering questions about how and to what degree infants vary in their underlying intelligence is not easy. Although it is clear that different infants show significant variations in their behavior, the issue of just what types of behavior may be related to cognitive ability is complicated. Interestingly, the examination of individual differences between infants was the initial approach taken by developmental specialists to understand cognitive development, and such issues still represent an important focus within the field.

infantile amnesia the lack of memory for experiences that occurred prior to 3 years of age

TABLE 3-6 APPROACHES USED TO DETECT DIFFERENCES IN INTELLIGENCE DURING INFANCY

Developmental quotient	Formulated by Arnold Gesell, the developmental quotient is an overall development score that relates to performance in four domains: motor skills (balance and sitting), language use, adaptive behavior (alertness and exploration), and personal–social behavior.
Bayley Scales of Infant Development	Developed by Nancy Bayley, the Bayley Scales of Infant Development evaluate an infant's development from 2 to 42 months. The Bayley Scales focus on two areas: mental (senses, perception, memory, learning, problem solving, and language) and motor abilities (fine and gross motor skills).
Visual-recognition memory measurement	Measures of visual-recognition memory, the memory of and recognition of a stimulus that has been previously seen, also relate to intelligence. The more quickly an infant can retrieve a representation of a stimulus from memory, the more efficient, presumably, is that infant's information processing.

A developmental quotient provides a measure of infant intelligence.

What Is Infant Intelligence? Developmental specialists have devised several approaches (summarized in Table 3-6) to illuminate the nature of individual differences in intelligence during infancy.

Developmental Scales. Developmental psychologist Arnold Gesell formulated the earliest measure of infant development, which was designed to distinguish between normally developing and atypically developing babies (Gesell, 1946). Gesell based his scale on examinations of hundreds of babies. He compared their performance at different ages to learn what behaviors were most common at a particular age. If an infant varied significantly from the norms of a given age, he or she was considered to be developmentally delayed or advanced.

Following the lead of researchers who sought to quantify intelligence through a specific score (known as an intelligence quotient, or IQ, score), Gesell developed a developmental quotient (DQ). The **developmental quotient** is an overall developmental score that relates to performance in four domains: motor skills (e.g., balance and sitting), language use, adaptive behavior (such as alertness and exploration), and personal–social (e.g., adequately feeding and dressing oneself).

developmental quotient an overall developmental score that relates to performance in four domains: motor skills, language use, adaptive behavior, and personal–social

Bayley Scales of Infant Development a measure that evaluates an infant's development from 2 to 42 months

Later researchers have created other developmental scales. For instance, Nancy Bayley developed one of the most widely used measures for infants. The **Bayley Scales of Infant Development** evaluate an infant's development from 2 to 42 months. The Bayley Scales focus on two areas: mental and motor abilities. The mental scale focuses on the senses, perception, memory, learning, problem solving, and language, while the motor scale evaluates fine and gross motor skills (see Table 3-7). Like Gesell's approach, the Bayley yields a DQ.

TABLE 3-7 SAMPLE ITEMS FROM THE BAYLEY SCALES OF INFANT DEVELOPMENT

Age	**2 months**	**6 months**	**12 months**	**17–19 months**	**23–25 months**	**38-42 months**
Mental Scale	Turns head to locate origin of sound; Visibly responds to disappearance of face	Picks up cup by handle; Notices illustrations in a book	Constructs tower of 2 cubes; Can turn pages in a book	Mimics crayon stroke; Labels objects in photo	Pairs up pictures; Repeats a 2-word sentence	Can identify 4 colors; Past tense evident in speech; Distinguishes gender
Motor Scale	Can hold head steady and erect for 15 seconds; Sits with assistance	Sits up without aid for 30 seconds; Grasps foot with hands	Walks when holding onto someone's hand or furniture; Holds pencil in fist	Stands on right foot without help; Remains upright climbing stairs with assistance	Strings 3 beads; Jumps length of 4 inches	Can reproduce drawing of a circle; Hops two times on one foot; Descends stairs, alternating feet

Source: Based on *Bayley, N. 7 1993. Bayley scales of infant development* [BSID-II] 2nd ed., San Antonio, IX: The Psychological Corporation.

A child who scores at an average level—meaning average performance for other children at the same age—receives a score of 100 (Bayley, 1969; Black & Matula, 1999; Gagnon & Nagle, 2000; Lynn, 2009).

The virtue of approaches such as those taken by Gesell and Bayley is that they provide a good snapshot of an infant's current developmental level. Using these scales, we can tell in an objective manner whether a particular infant falls behind or is ahead of his or her same-age peers. They are particularly useful in identifying infants who are substantially behind their peers, and who therefore need immediate special attention (Aylward & Verhulst, 2000; Sonne, 2012).

What such scales are *not* useful for is predicting a child's future course of development. A child whose development is identified by these measures as relatively slow at the age of 1 year will not necessarily display slow development at age 5, or 12, or 25. The association between most measures of behavior during infancy and adult intelligence, then, is minimal (Molfese & Acheson, 1997; Murray et al., 2007).

From a nurse's perspective: In what ways is the use of such developmental scales as Gesell's or Bayley's helpful? In what ways is it dangerous? How would you maximize the helpfulness and minimize the danger if you were advising a parent?

Information Processing Approaches to Individual Differences in Intelligence. Contemporary approaches to infant intelligence suggest that the speed with which infants process information may correlate most strongly with later intelligence, as measured by IQ tests administered during adulthood (Rose & Feldman, 1997; Sigman, Cohen, & Beckwith, 1997).

How can we tell if a baby is processing information quickly or not? Most researchers use habituation tests. Infants who process information efficiently ought to be able to learn about stimuli more quickly. Consequently, we would expect that they would turn their attention away from a given stimulus more rapidly than those who are less efficient at information processing, leading to the phenomenon of habituation. Similarly, measures of *visual-recognition memory*, the memory and recognition of a stimulus that has been previously seen, also relate to IQ. The more quickly an infant can retrieve a representation of a stimulus from memory, the more efficient, presumably, is that infant's information processing (Robinson & Pascalis, 2005; Karmiloff-Smith et al., 2010; Trainor, 2012).

Research using an information processing framework clearly suggests a relationship between information processing efficiency and cognitive abilities: Measures of how quickly infants lose interest in stimuli that they have previously seen, as well as their responsiveness to new stimuli, correlate moderately well with later measures of intelligence. Infants who are more efficient information processors during the 6 months following birth tend to have higher intelligence scores between 2 and 12 years of age, as well as higher scores on other measures of cognitive competence (Fagan, Holland, & Wheeler, 2007; Domsch, Lohaus, & Thomas, 2009; Rose, Feldman, & Jankowski, 2004, 2009).

Although information processing efficiency during infancy relates moderately well to later IQ scores, we need to keep in mind two qualifications. Even though there is an association between early information processing capabilities and later measures of IQ, the correlation is only moderate in strength. Consequently, we should not assume that intelligence is somehow permanently fixed in infancy.

Assessing Information Processing Approaches. The information processing perspective on cognitive development during infancy is very different from Piaget's. Rather than focusing on broad explanations of the *qualitative* changes that occur in infants' capabilities, as Piaget does, information processing looks at *quantitative* change. Piaget sees cognitive growth occurring in fairly sudden spurts; information processing sees more gradual, step-by-step growth. (Think of the difference between a track-and-field runner leaping hurdles versus a slow-but-steady marathon racer.)

Because information processing researchers consider cognitive development in terms of a collection of individual skills, they are often able to use more precise measures of cognitive ability, such as processing speed and memory recall, than proponents of Piaget's approach. Still, the very precision of these individual measures makes it harder to get an overall sense of the nature of cognitive development, something at which Piaget was a master. It's as if information processing approaches focus more on the individual pieces of the puzzle of cognitive development, while Piagetian approaches focus more on the whole puzzle (Kagan, 2008; Quinn, 2008).

Ultimately, both Piagetian and information processing approaches provide an account of cognitive development in infancy. Coupled with advances in understanding the biochemistry of the brain and theories that consider the effects of social factors on learning and cognition, the two help us paint a full picture of cognitive development.

REVIEW, CHECK, AND APPLY

REVIEW

L011 How do infants process information?

- Information processing approaches consider quantitative changes in children's abilities to organize and use information. Cognitive growth is regarded as the increasing sophistication of encoding, storage, and retrieval.
- Infants clearly have memory capabilities from a very early age, although the duration and accuracy of such memories are unresolved questions.

L012 How is infant intelligence measured?

- Traditional measures of infant intelligence focus on behavioral attainments, which can help identify developmental delays or advances.

CHECK YOURSELF

1. The information processing approach to cognitive development emphasizes the increased sophistication, speed, and _____ associated with cognitive growth.

   a capacity
   b circular reactions
   c categorization
   d analysis

2. Infants have memory capabilities from a very early age, although the duration and accuracy of such memories are unresolved questions.

   - True
   - False

3. When Justin first learned to drive a stick shift he had a difficult time coordinating the movements associated with the clutch, the gas, and the gear shift. After much practice the motions became more fluid and each component of the process required less attention. According to the information processing model, this would be an example of _____.

   a encoding
   b crystalized intelligence
   c automatization
   d retrieval

APPLYING LIFESPAN DEVELOPMENT

- What information from this module could you use to refute the claims of books or educational programs that promise to help parents increase their babies' intelligence or instill advanced intellectual skills in infants? Based on valid research, what approaches would you use for intellectual development of infants?

✓ **Study** and **Review** on **MyPsychLab.com**

THE ROOTS OF LANGUAGE

L013 How do children learn to use language?
L014 How do infants influence adults' language?

Vicki and Dominic were engaged in a friendly competition over whose name would be the first word their baby, Maura, said. "Say 'mama,' " Vicki would coo before handing Maura over to Dominic for a diaper change. Grinning, he would take her and coax, "No, say 'daddy.' " Both parents ended up losing—and winning—when Maura's first word sounded more like "baba," and seemed to refer to her bottle.

Mama. No. Cookie. Dad. Jo. Most parents can remember their baby's first word, and no wonder. It's an exciting moment, this emergence of a skill that is, arguably, unique to human beings.

But those initial words are just the first and most obvious manifestations of language. Many months earlier, infants began to understand the language used by others to make sense of the world around them. How does this linguistic ability develop? What is the pattern and sequence of language development? And how does the use of language transform the cognitive world of infants and their parents? We consider these questions, and others, as we address the development of language during the first years of life.

The Fundamentals of Language: From Sounds to Symbols

Language, the systematic, meaningful arrangement of symbols, provides the basis for communication. But it does more than this: It is closely tied to the way we think and understand the world. It enables us to reflect on people and objects and to convey our thoughts to others.

Language has several formal characteristics that must be mastered as linguistic competence is developed. They include the following:

- **Phonology.** Phonology refers to the basic sounds of language, called *phonemes*, that can be combined to produce words and sentences. For instance, the "a" in "mat" and the "a" in "mate" represent two different phonemes in English. Although English employs just 40 phonemes to create every word in the language, other languages have as many as 85 phonemes—and some as few as 15 (Akmajian, Demers, & Harnish, 1984).
- **Morphemes.** A morpheme is the smallest language unit that has meaning. Some morphemes are complete words, while others add information necessary for interpreting a word, such as the endings "-s" for plural and "-ed" for past tense.
- **Semantics.** Semantics are the rules that govern the meaning of words and sentences. As their knowledge of semantics develops, children are able to understand the subtle distinction between "Ellie was hit by a ball" (an answer to the question of why Ellie doesn't want to play catch) and "A ball hit Ellie" (used to announce the current situation).

Although we tend to think of language in terms of the production of words and then groups of words, infants can begin to communicate linguistically well before they say their first word.

In considering the development of language, we need to distinguish between linguistic *comprehension*, the understanding of speech, and linguistic *production*, the use of language to communicate. One principle underlies the relationship between the two: Comprehension precedes production. An 18-month-old may be able to understand a complex series of directions ("Pick up your coat from the floor and put it on the chair by the fireplace") but may not yet have strung more than two words together when speaking for herself. Throughout infancy, comprehension also outpaces production. For example, during infancy, comprehension of words expands at a rate of 22 new words a month, while production of words increases at a rate of about 9 new words a month, once talking begins (Tincoff & Jusczyk, 1999; Rescorla, Alley, & Christine, 2001; Cattani, 2010; Shafto et al., 2012) (see Figure 3-14 on page 126).

Early Sounds and Communication. Spend 24 hours with even a very young infant and you will hear a variety of sounds: cooing, crying, gurgling, murmuring, and assorted types of other noises. These sounds, although not meaningful in themselves, play an important role in linguistic development, paving the way for true language (O'Grady & Aitchison, 2005; Martin, Onishi, & Vouloumanos, 2012).

Prelinguistic communication is communication through sounds, facial expressions, gestures, imitation, and other nonlinguistic means. When a father responds to his daughter's "ah" with an "ah" of his own, and then the daughter repeats the sound, and the father responds once again, they are engaged in prelinguistic communication. Clearly, the "ah" sound has no particular meaning. However, its repetition, which mimics the give-and-take of conversation, teaches the infant something about turn-taking and the back-and-forth of communication (Reddy, 1999).

The most obvious manifestation of prelinguistic communication is babbling. **Babbling**, making speechlike but meaningless sounds, starts at the age of 2 or 3 months and continues until around the age of 1 year. When they babble, infants repeat the same vowel sound over and over, changing the pitch from high to low (as in "ee-ee-ee," repeated at different pitches). After the age of 5 months, the sounds of babbling begin to expand, reflecting the addition of consonants (such as "bee-bee-bee-bee").

Babbling is a universal phenomenon, accomplished in the same way throughout all cultures. While they are babbling, infants spontaneously produce all of the sounds found in every language, not just the language they hear people around them speaking.

Babbling typically follows a progression from simple to more complex sounds. Although exposure to the sounds of a particular language does not seem to influence babbling initially, eventually experience does make a difference. By the age of 6 months, babbling reflects the sounds of

language the systematic, meaningful arrangement of symbols, which provides the basis for communication

babbling making speechlike but meaningless sounds

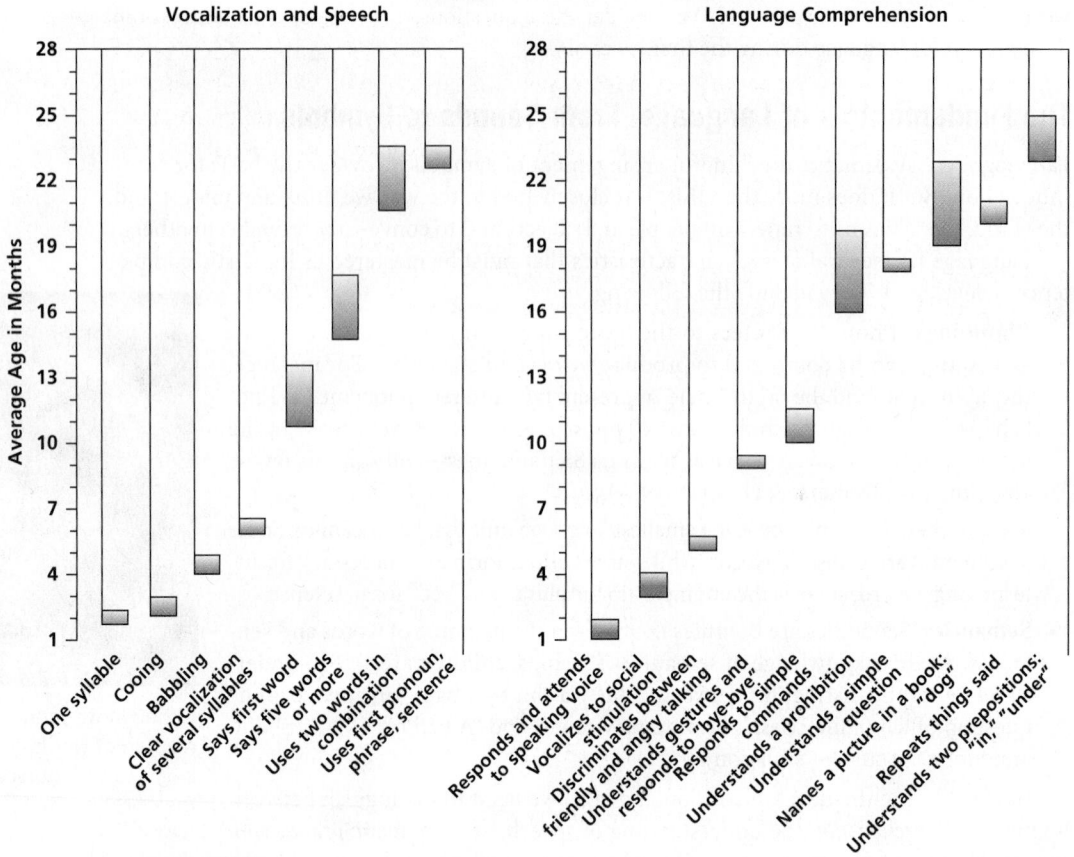

FIGURE 3-14 Comprehension Precedes Production
Throughout infancy, the comprehension of speech precedes the production of speech.
Source: Based on Bornstein & Lamb, 1992.

the language to which infants are exposed. The difference is so noticeable that even untrained listeners can distinguish between babbling infants who have been raised in cultures in which French, Arabic, or Cantonese languages are spoken. Furthermore, the speed at which infants begin homing in on their own language is related to the speed of later language development (Blake & Boysson-Bardies, 1992; Whalen, Levitt, & Goldstein, 2007; Lee, Davis, & MacNeilage, 2010).

First Words. When a mother and father first hear their child say "Mama" or "Dada," or even "baba," as in the case of Maura, the baby described earlier in this section, it is hard to be anything but delighted. But their initial enthusiasm may be dampened a bit when they find that the same sound is used to ask for a cookie, a doll, and a ratty old blanket.

First words generally are spoken somewhere around the age of 10 to 14 months, but may occur as early as 9 months. Once an infant starts to produce words, vocabulary increases at a rapid rate. By the age of 15 months, the average child has a vocabulary of ten words and methodically expands until the one-word stage of language development ends at around 18 months. Once that happens, a sudden spurt in vocabulary occurs. In just a short period—a few weeks somewhere between 16 and 24 months of age—there is an explosion of language, in which a child's vocabulary typically increases from 50 to 400 words (Gleitman & Landau, 1994; Nazzi & Bertoncini, 2003; McMurray, Aslin, & Toscano, 2009).

The first words in children's early vocabularies typically regard objects and things, both animate and inanimate. Most often they refer to people or objects who constantly appear and disappear ("Mama"), to animals ("kitty"), or to temporary states ("wet"). These first words are often **holophrases**, one-word utterances that stand for a whole phrase, whose meaning depends on the particular context in which they are used. For instance, a youngster may use the phrase "ma" to mean, depending on the context, "I want to be picked up by Mom" or "I want something to eat, Mom" or "Where's Mom?" (Dromi, 1987; O'Grady & Aitchison, 2005).

holophrases one-word utterances that stand for a whole phrase, the meaning of which depends on the particular context in which they are used

Culture has an effect on the type of first words spoken. For example, unlike North American English-speaking infants, who are more apt to use nouns initially, Chinese

Mandarin-speaking infants use more verbs than nouns. On the other hand, by the age of 20 months, there are remarkable cross-cultural similarities in the types of words spoken. For example, a comparison of 20-month-olds in Argentina, Belgium, France, Israel, Italy, and the Republic of Korea found that children's vocabularies in every culture contained greater proportions of nouns than other classes of words (Tardif, 1996; Bornstein et al., 2004). **Watch** the **Video** *Language Development Across Cultures* in **MyPsychLab**.

First Sentences. When Aaron was 19 months old, he heard his mother coming up the back steps, as she did every day just before dinner. Aaron turned to his father and distinctly said, "Ma come." In stringing those two words together, Aaron took a giant step in his language development.

The explosive increase in vocabulary that comes at around 18 months is accompanied by another accomplishment: the linking together of individual words into sentences that convey a single thought. Although there is a good deal of variability in the time at which children first create two-word phrases, it is generally around 8 to 12 months after they say their first word.

The linguistic advance represented by two-word combinations is important because the linkage not only provides labels for things in the world but also indicates the relations between them. For instance, the combination may declare something about possession ("Mama key") or recurrent events ("Dog bark"). Interestingly, most early sentences don't represent demands or even necessarily require a response. Instead, they are often merely comments and observations about events occurring in the child's world (Halliday, 1975; O'Grady & Aitchison, 2005; Rossi et al., 2012).

By the age of 2, most children use two-word phrases, such as "ball play."

Two-year-olds using two-word combinations tend to employ particular sequences that are similar to the ways in which adult sentences are constructed. For instance, sentences in English typically follow a pattern in which the subject of the sentence comes first, followed by the verb, and then the object ("Josh threw the ball"). Children's speech most often uses a similar order, although not all the words are initially included. Consequently, a child might say "Josh threw" or "Josh ball" to indicate the same thought. What is significant is that the order is typically not "threw Josh" or "ball Josh," but rather the usual order of English, which makes the utterance much easier for an English speaker to comprehend (Brown, 1973; Hirsh-Pasek & Michnick-Golinkoff, 1995; Masataka, 2003).

Although the creation of two-word sentences represents an advance, the language used by children still is by no means adultlike. As we've just seen, 2-year-olds tend to leave out words that aren't critical to the message, similar to the way we might write a telegram for which we were paying by the word. For that reason, their talk is often called **telegraphic speech**. Rather than saying, "I showed you the book," a child using telegraphic speech might say, "I show book." "I am drawing a dog" might become "Drawing dog" (see Table 3-8 on page 128).

Early language has other characteristics that differentiate it from the language used by adults. For instance, consider Sarah, who refers to the blanket she sleeps with as "blankie." When her Aunt Ethel gives her a new blanket, Sarah refuses to call the new one a "blankie," restricting the word to her original blanket.

Sarah's inability to generalize the label of "blankie" to blankets in general is an example of **underextension**, using words too restrictively, which is common among children just mastering spoken language. Underextension occurs when language novices think that a word refers to a specific instance of a concept, instead of to all examples of the concept (Caplan & Barr, 1989; Masataka, 2003).

As infants like Sarah grow more adept with language, the opposite phenomenon sometimes occurs. In **overextension**, words are used too broadly, overgeneralizing their meaning. For example, when Sarah refers to buses, trucks, and tractors as "cars," she is guilty of overextension, making the assumption that any object with wheels must be a car. Although overextension reflects speech errors, it also shows that advances are occurring in the child's

telegraphic speech speech in which words not critical to the message are left out

underextension the overly restrictive use of words, common among children just mastering spoken language

overextension the overly broad use of words, overgeneralizing their meaning

TABLE 3-8 CHILDREN'S IMITATION OF SENTENCES SHOWING DECLINE OF TELEGRAPHIC SPEECH

Sample Sentences	Speakers	26 months	29 months	32 months	35 months
I put on my shoes	Kim	Shoes	My shoes	I put on shoes	A
	Darden	Shoes on	My shoes on	Put on shoes	Put on my shoes
I will not go to bed	Kim	No bed	Not go bed	I not go bed	I not go to bed
	Darden	Not go bed	I not go bed	I not go to bed	I will not go bed
I want to ride the pony	Kim	Pony, pony	Want ride pony	I want ride pony	I want to ride pony
	Darden	Want pony	I want pony	I want the pony	A

A = accurate imitation.

Source: Based on R. Brown & C. Fraser, 1963.

thought processes: The child is beginning to develop general mental categories and concepts (Johnson & Eilers, 1998; McDonough, 2002).

Infants also show individual differences in the style of language they use. For example, some use a **referential style**, in which language is used primarily to label objects. Others tend to use an **expressive style**, in which language is used primarily to express feelings and needs about oneself and others (Bates et al., 1994; Nelson, 1996). Language styles reflect, in part, cultural factors. For example, mothers in the United States label objects more frequently than do Japanese mothers, encouraging a more referential style of speech. In contrast, mothers in Japan are more apt to speak about social interactions, encouraging a more expressive style of speech (Fernald & Morikawa, 1993).

The Origins of Language Development

referential style a style of language use in which language is used primarily to label objects

expressive style a style of language use in which language is used primarily to express feelings and needs about oneself and others

learning theory approach the theory that language acquisition follows the basic laws of reinforcement and conditioning

The immense strides in language development during the preschool years raise a fundamental question: How does proficiency in language come about? Linguists are deeply divided on how to answer this question.

Learning Theory Approaches: Language as a Learned Skill. One view of language development emphasizes the basic principles of learning. According to the **learning theory approach**, language acquisition follows the basic laws of reinforcement and conditioning discussed in Module 1.2 (Skinner, 1957). For instance, a child who articulates the word "da" may be hugged and praised by her father, who jumps to the conclusion that he or she is referring

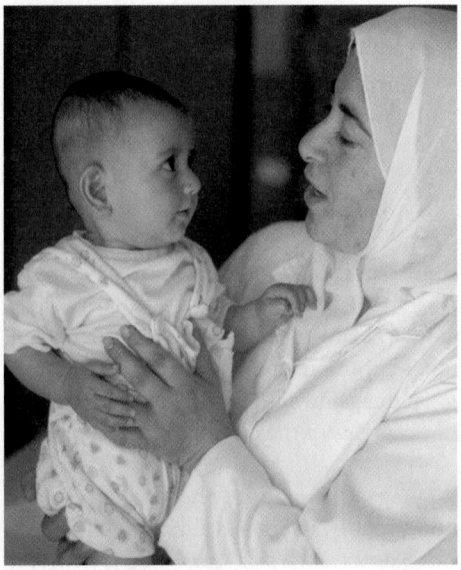

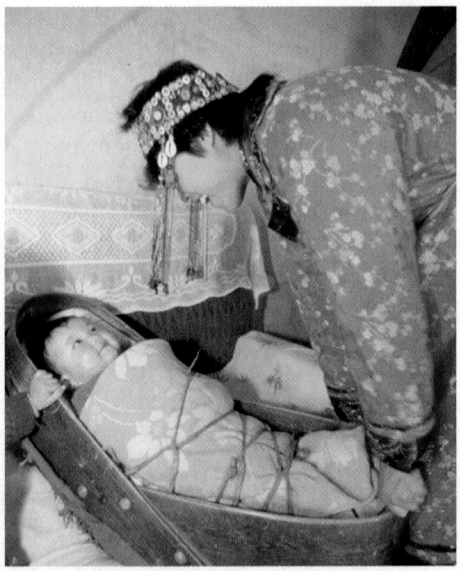

Infant-directed speech, which is common across cultures, includes the use of short, simple sentences and is spoken in a pitch that is higher than that used with older children and adults.

to him. This reaction reinforces the child, who is more likely to repeat the word. In sum, the learning theory perspective on language acquisition suggests that children learn to speak by being rewarded for making sounds that approximate speech. Through the process of *shaping*, language becomes more and more similar to adult speech.

There's a problem, though, with the learning theory approach. It doesn't seem to adequately explain how children acquire the rules of language as readily as they do. For instance, young children are reinforced when they make errors. Parents are apt to be just as responsive if their child says, "Why the dog won't eat?" as they are if the child phrases the question more correctly ("Why won't the dog eat?"). Both forms of the question are understood correctly, and both elicit the same response; reinforcement is provided for both correct and incorrect language usage. Under such circumstances, learning theory is hard put to explain how children learn to speak properly.

Children are also able to move beyond specific utterances they have heard, and produce novel phrases, sentences, and constructions, an ability that also cannot be explained by learning theory. Furthermore, children can apply linguistic rules to nonsense words. In one study, 4-year-old children heard the nonsense verb "to pilk" in the sentence "the bear is pilking the horse." Later, when asked what was happening to the horse, they responded by placing the nonsense verb in the correct tense and voice: "He's getting pilked by the bear."

Nativist Approaches: Language as an Innate Skill. Such conceptual difficulties with the learning theory approach have led to the development of an alternative, championed by the linguist Noam Chomsky and known as the nativist approach (1968, 1978, 1991, 1999, 2005). The **nativist approach** argues that there is a genetically determined, innate mechanism that directs the development of language. According to Chomsky, people are born with an innate capacity to use language, which emerges, more or less automatically, due to maturation.

Chomsky's analysis of different languages suggests that all the world's languages share a similar underlying structure, which he calls **universal grammar**. In this view, the human brain is wired with a neural system called the **language-acquisition device (LAD)**, that both permits the understanding of language structure and provides a set of strategies and techniques for learning the particular characteristics of the language to which a child is exposed. In this view, language is uniquely human, made possible by a genetic predisposition to both comprehend and produce words and sentences (Lidz & Gleitman, 2004; Stromswold, 2006; Boeckx, 2010; Lieven & Stoll, 2010).

Support for Chomsky's nativist approach comes from recent findings identifying a specific gene related to speech production. Further support comes from research showing that language processing in infants involves brain structures similar to those in adult speech processing, suggesting an evolutionary basis to language (Dehaene-Lambertz, Hertz-Pannier, & Dubois, 2006; Clark & Lappin, 2013).

The view that language is an innate ability unique to humans also has its critics. For instance, some researchers argue that certain primates are able to learn at least the basics of language, an ability that calls into question the uniqueness of the human linguistic capacity. Others point out that although humans may be genetically primed to use language, its use still requires significant social experience in order for it to be used effectively (MacWhinney, 1991; Savage-Rumbaugh et al., 1993; Goldberg, 2004).

The Interactionist Approaches. Neither the learning theory nor the nativist perspective fully explains language acquisition. As a result, some theorists have turned to a theory that combines both schools of thought. The *interactionist perspective* suggests that language development is produced through a combination of genetically determined predispositions and environmental circumstances that help teach language.

The interactionist perspective accepts that innate factors shape the broad outlines of language development. However, interactionists also argue that the specific course of language development is determined by the language to which children are exposed and the reinforcement they receive for using language in particular ways. Social factors are considered to be key to development, because the motivation provided by one's membership in a society and culture and one's interactions with others leads to the use of language and the growth of language skills (Dixon, 2004; Yang, 2006).

Just as there is support for some aspects of learning theory and nativist positions, the interactionist perspective has also received some support. We don't know, at the moment, which

nativist approach the theory that a genetically determined, innate mechanism directs language development

universal grammar Noam Chomsky's theory that all the world's languages share a similar underlying structure

language-acquisition device (LAD) a neural system of the brain hypothesized to permit understanding of language of these positions will ultimately provide the best explanation. More likely, different factors play different roles at different times during childhood.

Speaking to Children: The Language of Infant-Directed Speech

Say the following sentence aloud: Do you like the applesauce?

Now pretend that you are going to ask the same question of an infant, and speak it as you would for a young child's ears.

Chances are several things happened when you translated the phrase for the infant. First of all, the wording probably changed, and you may have said something like, "Does baby like the applesauce?" At the same time, the pitch of your voice probably rose, your general intonation most likely had a singsong quality, and you probably separated your words carefully.

Infant-Directed Speech. The shift in your language was due to your use of **infant-directed speech**, a style of speech that characterizes much of the verbal communication directed toward infants. This type of speech pattern used to be called *motherese*, because it was assumed that it applied only to mothers. However, that assumption was wrong, and the gender-neutral term *infant-directed speech* is now used more frequently.

Infant-directed speech is characterized by short, simple sentences. Pitch becomes higher, the range of frequencies increases, and intonation is more varied. There is also repetition of words, and topics are restricted to items that are assumed to be comprehensible to infants, such as concrete objects in the baby's environment (Soderstrom, 2007; Matsuda, 2010).

Sometimes infant-directed speech includes amusing sounds that are not even words, imitating the prelinguistic speech of infants. In other cases, it has little formal structure, but is similar to the kind of telegraphic speech that infants use as they develop their own language skills.

Infant-directed speech changes as children become older. Around the end of the first year, infant-directed speech takes on more adultlike qualities. Sentences become longer and more complex, although individual words are still spoken slowly and deliberately. Pitch is also used to focus attention on particularly important words (Soderstrom et al., 2008; Kitamura & Lam, 2009).

Infant-directed speech plays an important role in infants' acquisition of language. As discussed next, infant-directed speech occurs all over the world, though there are cultural variations. Newborns prefer such speech to regular language, a fact that suggests that they may be particularly receptive to it. Furthermore, some research suggests that babies who are exposed to a great deal of infant-directed speech early in life seem to begin to use words and exhibit other forms of linguistic competence earlier (Werker et al., 2007; Bergelson & Swingley, 2012; Frank, Tenenbaum, & Fernald, 2013).

infant-directed speech a type of speech directed toward infants, characterized by short, simple sentences

Cultural Dimensions

Is Infant-Directed Speech Similar Across All Cultures?

Do mothers in the United States, Sweden, and Russia speak the same way to their infants?

In some respects, they clearly do. Although the words themselves differ across languages, the way the words are spoken to infants is quite similar. According to a growing body of research, there are basic similarities across cultures in the nature of infant-directed speech (Rabain-Jamin & Sabeau-Jouannet, 1997; Werker et al., 2007; Fais et al., 2010).

For example, 6 of the 10 most frequent major characteristics of speech directed at infants used by native speakers of English and Spanish are common to both languages: exaggerated intonation, high pitch, lengthened vowels, repetition, lower volume, and heavy stress on certain key words (such as emphasizing the word "ball" in the sentence, "No, that's a *ball*") (Blount, 1982). Similarly, mothers in the United States, Sweden, and Russia all exaggerate and elongate the pronunciation of the three vowel sounds of "ee," "ah," and "oh" when speaking to infants in similar ways, despite differences in the languages in which the sounds are used (Kuhl et al., 1997).

Even deaf mothers use a form of infant-directed speech: When communicating with their infants, deaf mothers use sign language at a significantly slower tempo than when communicating with adults, and they frequently repeat the signs (Swanson, Leonard, & Gandour, 1992; Masataka, 1996, 1998, 2000).

From an educator's perspective: What are some implications of differences in the ways adults speak to boys and girls? How might such speech differences contribute to later differences not only in speech, but also in attitudes?

Becoming an Informed Consumer of Development

What Can You Do to Promote Infants' Cognitive Development?

All parents want their children to reach their full cognitive potential, but sometimes efforts to reach this goal take a bizarre path. For instance, some parents spend hundreds of dollars enrolling in workshops with titles such as "How to Multiply Your Baby's Intelligence" and buying books with titles such as *How to Teach Your Baby to Read* (Doman & Doman, 2002).

Do such efforts ever succeed? Although some parents swear they do, there is no scientific support for the effectiveness of such programs. For example, despite the many cognitive skills of infants, no infant can actually read. Furthermore, "multiplying" a baby's intelligence is impossible, and such organizations as the American Academy of Pediatrics and the American Academy of Neurology have denounced programs that claim to do so.

On the other hand, certain things can be done to promote cognitive development in infants. The following suggestions, based upon findings of developmental researchers, offer a starting point (Gopnik, Meltzoff, & Kuhl, 2000; Cabrera, Shannon, & Tamis-LeMonda, 2007):

- **Provide infants the opportunity to explore the world.** As Piaget suggests, children learn by doing, and they need the opportunity to explore and probe their environment.
- **Be responsive to infants on both a verbal and a nonverbal level.** Try to speak *with* babies, as opposed to *at* them. Ask questions, listen to their responses, and provide further communication (Merlo, Bowman, & Barnett, 2007).
- **Read to your infants.** Although they may not understand the meaning of your words, they will respond to your tone of voice and the intimacy provided by the activity. Reading together also is associated with later literacy skills and begins to create a lifelong reading habit. In fact, the American Academy of Pediatrics recommends daily reading to children starting at the age of 6 months (American Academy of Pediatrics, 1997; Holland, 2008; Robb, Richert, & Wartella, 2009).
- **Keep in mind that you don't have to be with an infant 24 hours a day.** Just as infants need time to explore their world on their own, parents and other caregivers need time off from child-care activities.
- **Don't push infants and don't expect too much too soon.** Your goal should not be to create a genius; it should be to provide a warm, nurturing environment that will allow an infant to reach his or her potential.

REVIEW, CHECK, AND APPLY

REVIEW

LO13 How do children learn to use language?

- Before they speak, infants understand many adult utterances and engage in several forms of prelinguistic communication.
- Children typically produce their first words between 10 and 14 months and rapidly increase their vocabularies from that point on, especially during a spurt at about 18 months.
- Learning theorists believe that basic learning processes account for language development, whereas nativists like Noam Chomsky and his followers argue that humans have an innate language capacity. The interactionists suggest that language is a consequence of both environmental and innate factors.

LO14 How do infants influence adults' language?

- In using infant-directed speech, adults shift their use of language to a higher pitch and a style of speech using short, simple sentences.

CHECK YOURSELF

1. Like other 2-year-olds, Mason can say "Doggie bye, bye" and "Milk gone." These two-word phrases are examples of _____ speech.
   - a holophrastic
   - b telegraphic
   - c interpretive
   - d active
2. One theory, the _____ approach, suggests that a genetically determined, innate mechanism directs language development.
   - a nativist
   - b universal
   - c learning theory
   - d evolutionary
3. Whenever 9-month-old Ana's mother talks to her, she uses short, simple sentences, repetitive words, and higher pitches. This shift in language is consistent with the use of _____ speech.
   - a infant-directed
   - b telegraphic
   - c nativist
   - d interactionist

APPLYING LIFESPAN DEVELOPMENT

- What are some ways in which children's linguistic development reflects their acquisition of new ways of interpreting and dealing with their world?

✓ **Study** and **Review** on **MyPsychLab.com**

MODULE 3.3

SOCIAL AND PERSONALITY DEVELOPMENT IN INFANCY

The Childproof Bin

Lisa Palermo, 10 years old, had Cheerios on her breath—always, especially in the late morning. At first, Mindy Crowell, Lisa's day care teacher, thought little of it, but when she noticed that the classroom Cheerios stash was slowly dwindling, she began to wonder.

The Cheerios were stored in a plastic bin in the clothes closet. Mindy began to watch the closet out of the corner of her eye. Sure enough, one day she noticed Lisa crawling toward it. What she saw next astonished her. Lisa manipulated the fastener of the bin, reached in, withdrew a hand laden with Cheerios, and let the bin refasten itself, as it was designed to do.

Somehow, Lisa, barely able to hold a colored pencil, had learned how to undo the supposedly childproof fastener—a task that Mindy herself sometimes struggled with. And what was worse, Lisa proved to be an excellent teacher. Soon enough, Rathana, Paul, Olga, and Kelly were crawling to the bin and doing exactly the same thing.

As babies like Lisa show us, children are sociable from a very early age. This anecdote also demonstrates one of the side benefits of infants' participation in child care, and something research has begun to suggest: through their social interactions, babies acquire new skills and abilities from more "expert" peers. Infants, as we will see, have an amazing capacity to learn from other children, and their interactions with others can play a central role in their developing social and emotional worlds.

In this module we consider social and personality development in infancy. We begin by examining the emotional lives of infants, considering which emotions they feel and how well they can read others' emotions. We look at how babies view their own and others' mental lives.

We then turn to infants' social relationships. We look at how they forge bonds of attachment and the ways they interact with family members and peers. Finally, we cover the characteristics that differentiate one infant from another and discuss differences in the way children are treated depending on their gender. We'll consider the nature of family life and look at the advantages and disadvantages of infant child care outside the home, a child-care option that today's families increasingly employ.

DEVELOPING THE ROOTS OF SOCIABILITY

L015 Do infants experience emotions?
L016 What sort of mental lives do infants have?

Germaine smiles when he catches a glimpse of his mother. Tawanda looks angry when her mother takes away the spoon that she is playing with. Sydney scowls when a loud plane flies overhead.

A smile. A look of anger. A scowl. The emotions of infancy are written all over a baby's face. Yet do infants experience emotions in the same way that adults do? When do they become capable of understanding what others are experiencing emotionally? And how do they use others' emotional states to make sense of their environment? We consider some of these questions as we seek to understand how infants develop emotionally and socially.

Emotions in Infancy: Do Infants Experience Emotional Highs and Lows?

Anyone who spends any time at all around infants knows they display facial expressions that seem indicative of their emotional states. In situations in which we expect them to be happy, they seem to smile; when we might assume they are frustrated, they show anger; and when we might expect them to be unhappy, they look sad.

In fact, these basic facial expressions are remarkably similar across the most diverse cultures. Whether we look at babies in India, the United States, or the jungles of New Guinea, the expression of basic emotions is the same (see Figure 3-15). Furthermore, the nonverbal expression of emotion, called *nonverbal encoding*, is fairly consistent among people of all ages. These consistencies have led researchers to conclude that we are born with the capacity to display basic emotions (Sullivan & Lewis, 2003; Ackerman & Izard, 2004).

Infants display a fairly wide range of emotional expressions. Almost all mothers report that by the age of 1 month their babies nonverbally have expressed interest and joy. Careful coding of infants' nonverbal expressions shows that interest, distress, and disgust are present at birth, and that other emotions emerge over the next few months. Such findings are consistent with

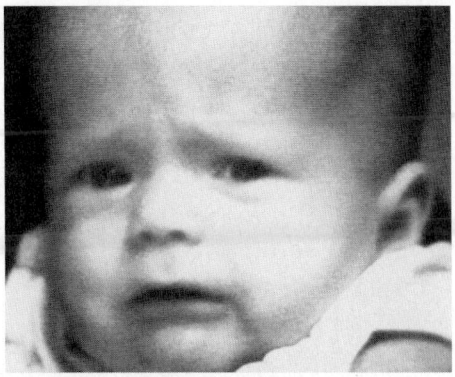

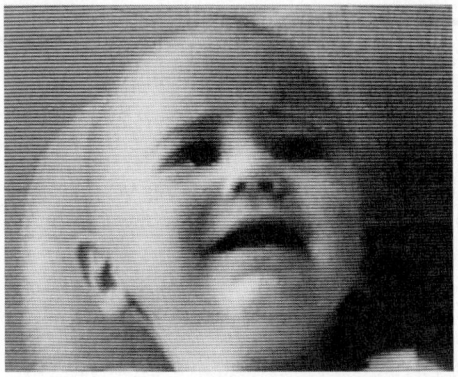

FIGURE 3-15 Universals in Facial Expressions
Across every culture, infants show similar facial expressions relating to basic emotions. Do you think such expressions are similar in nonhuman animals?

stranger anxiety the caution and wariness displayed by infants when encountering an unfamiliar person

the work of the famous naturalist Charles Darwin, whose 1872 book *The Expression of the Emotions in Man and Animals* argued that humans and primates have an inborn, universal set of emotional expressions—a view consistent with today's evolutionary approach to development (Izard, 1982; Sroufe, 1996; Benson, 2003).

Although infants display similar *kinds* of emotions, the *degree* of emotional expressivity varies among infants. Children in different cultures show reliable differences in emotional expressiveness, even during infancy. For example, by the age of 11 months, Chinese infants are generally less expressive than European, American, and Japanese infants (Camras, Meng, & Ujiie, 2002; Camras et al., 2007; Izard, Woodburn, & Finlon, 2010).

Stranger Anxiety and Separation Anxiety. "She used to be such a friendly baby," thought Erika's mother. "No matter whom she encountered, she had a big smile. But almost the day she turned 7 months old, she began to react to strangers as if she were seeing a ghost. Her face crinkles up with a frown, and she either turns away or stares at them with suspicion. It's as if she has undergone a personality transplant."

What happened to Erika is, in fact, quite typical. By the end of the first year, infants often develop both stranger anxiety and separation anxiety. **Stranger anxiety** is the caution and wariness displayed by infants when encountering an unfamiliar person. Such anxiety typically appears in the second half of the first year.

What brings on stranger anxiety? Brain development and the increased cognitive abilities of infants play a role. As infants' memory develops, they are able to separate the people they know from the people they don't. The same cognitive advances that allow them to respond so positively to those people with whom they are familiar also give them the ability to recognize people who are unfamiliar. Furthermore, between 6 and 9 months, infants begin trying to make sense of their world, trying to anticipate and predict events. When something happens that they don't expect—such as

When infants smile at a person, rather than a nonhuman stimulus, they are displaying a social smile.

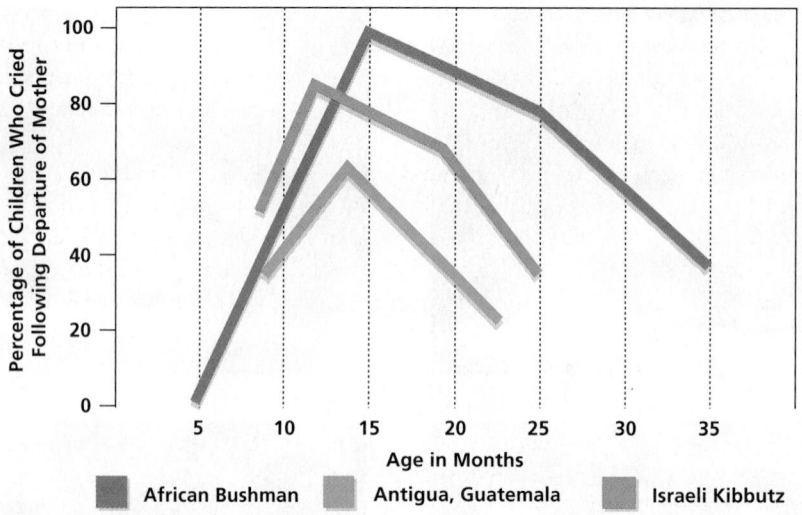

FIGURE 3-16 Separation Anxiety
Separation anxiety, the distress displayed by infants when their usual care provider leaves their presence, is a universal phenomenon beginning at around the age of 7 or 8 months. It peaks at around the age of 14 months and then begins to decline. Does separation anxiety have survival value for humans?
Source: Kagan, Kearsley, & Zelazo, 1978

the appearance of an unknown person—they experience fear. It's as if an infant has a question but is unable to answer it (Volker, 2007).

Separation anxiety is the distress displayed by infants when a customary care provider departs. Separation anxiety, which is also universal across cultures, usually begins at about 7 or 8 months (see Figure 3-16). It peaks around 14 months, and then decreases. Separation anxiety is largely attributable to the same reasons as stranger anxiety. Infants' growing cognitive skills allow them to ask reasonable questions, but they may be questions that they are too young to understand the answer to: "Why is my mother leaving?" "Where is she going?" and "Will she come back?"

Stranger anxiety and separation anxiety represent important social progress. They reflect both cognitive advances and the growing emotional and social bonds between infants and their caregivers—bonds that we'll consider later in the module when we discuss infants' social relationships.

Research suggests that this 18-month-old baby is exhibiting a clearly developing sense of self.

separation anxiety the distress displayed by infants when a customary care provider departs

Smiling. As Luz lay sleeping in her crib, her mother and father caught a glimpse of the most beautiful smile crossing her face. Her parents were sure that Luz was having a pleasant dream. Were they right?

Probably not. The earliest smiles expressed during sleep probably have little meaning, although no one can be absolutely sure. By 6 to 9 weeks babies begin to smile reliably at the sight of stimuli that please them, including toys, mobiles, and—to the delight of parents—people. The first smiles tend to be relatively indiscriminate, as infants first begin to smile at the sight of almost anything they find amusing. However, as they get older, they become more selective in their smiles.

A baby's smile in response to another person, rather than to nonhuman stimuli, is considered a *social smile.* As babies get older, their social smiles become directed toward particular individuals, not just anyone. By the age of 18 months, social smiling, directed more toward mothers and other caregivers, becomes more frequent than smiling directed toward nonhuman objects. Moreover, if an adult is unresponsive to a child, the amount of smiling decreases. In short, by the end of the second year children are quite purposefully using smiling to communicate their positive emotions, and they are sensitive to the emotional expressions of others (Bigelow & Rochat, 2006; Fogel et al., 2006; Gosselin, Perron, & Maassarani, 2010; Reissland & Cohen, 2012).

Decoding Others' Facial Expressions. In Module 2.3, we discussed the possibility that neonates can imitate adults' facial expressions even minutes after birth. Although their imitative abilities certainly do not imply that they can understand the meaning of others' facial

expressions, such imitation does pave the way for *nonverbal decoding* abilities, which begin to emerge fairly soon. Using these abilities, infants can interpret others' facial and vocal expressions that carry emotional meaning. For example, they can tell when a caregiver is happy to see them and pick up on worry or fear in the faces of others (Hernandez-Reif et al., 2006; Striano & Vaish, 2006; Hoehl et al., 2012).

In the first 6 to 8 weeks, infants' visual precision is sufficiently limited that they cannot pay much attention to others' facial expressions. But they soon begin to discriminate among different facial expressions of emotion and even seem to be able to respond to differences in emotional intensity conveyed by facial expressions. By the time they reach the age of 4 months, infants already have begun to understand the emotions that lie behind the facial and vocal expressions of others (Bertin & Striano, 2006; Farroni et al., 2007; Kim & Johnson, 2013).

Social Referencing: Feeling What Others Feel

Twenty-three-month-old Stephania watches as her older brother Eric and his friend Chen argue loudly with each other and begin to wrestle. Uncertain of what is happening, Stephania glances at her mother. Her mother, though, wears a smile, knowing that Eric and Chen are just playing. On seeing her mother's reaction, Stephania smiles too, mimicking her mother's facial expression.

Like Stephania, most of us have been in situations in which we feel uncertain. In such cases, we sometimes turn to others to see how they are reacting. This reliance on others, known as social referencing, helps us decide what an appropriate response ought to be.

Social referencing is the intentional search for information about others' feelings to help explain the meaning of uncertain circumstances and events. Like Stephania, we use social referencing to clarify the meaning of a situation and so to reduce our uncertainty about what is occurring.

Social referencing first occurs around the age of 8 or 9 months. It is a fairly sophisticated social ability: Infants need it not only to understand the significance of others' behavior, by using such cues as their facial expressions, but also understand the meaning of those behaviors within the context of a specific situation (de Rosnay et al., 2006; Carver & Vaccaro, 2007; Stenberg, 2009).

From a social worker's perspective: In what situations do adults rely on social referencing to work out appropriate responses? How might social referencing be used to influence parents' behavior toward their children?

The Development of Self: Do Infants Know Who They Are?

Elysa, 8 months old, crawls past the full-length mirror that hangs on a door in her parents' bedroom. She barely pays any attention to her reflection as she moves by. On the other hand, her cousin Brianna, who is almost 2 years old, stares at herself in the mirror as she passes and laughs as she notices, and then rubs off, a smear of jelly on her forehead.

Perhaps you have had the experience of catching a glimpse of yourself in a mirror and noticing a hair out of place. You probably reacted by attempting to push the unruly hair back into place. Your reaction shows more than that you care about how you look. It implies that you have a sense of yourself, the awareness and knowledge that you are an independent social entity to which others react, and which you attempt to present to the world in ways that reflect favorably upon you.

However, we are not born with the knowledge that we exist independently from others and the larger world. Very young infants do not have a sense of themselves as individuals; they do not recognize themselves in photos or mirrors. However, the roots of **self-awareness**, knowledge of oneself, begin to grow after the age of 12 months.

We know this from a simple but ingenious experimental technique in which an infant's nose is secretly colored with a dab of red powder. Then the infant is seated in front of a mirror. If infants touch their noses or attempt to wipe off the rouge, we have evidence that they have at least some knowledge of their physical characteristics. Although some infants as young as 12 months seem startled on seeing the rouge spot, for most a reaction does not occur until between 17 and 24 months of age. This awareness is one step in infants' understanding of themselves as independent objects (Asendorpf, Warkentin, & Baudonniere, 1996; Rochat, 2004; Brownell et al., 2010; Rochat, Broesch, & Jayne, 2012). **Watch** the **Video** *Self-Awareness Task* in **MyPsychLab**.

social referencing the intentional search for information about others' feelings to help explain the meaning of uncertain circumstances and events

self-awareness knowledge of oneself

Theory of Mind: Infants' Perspectives on the Mental Lives of Others—and Themselves

What are infants' thoughts about thinking? Infants begin to understand certain things about their own and others' mental processes at quite an early age, developing a **theory of mind**, their knowledge and beliefs about how the mind works and how it influences behavior. Theories of mind are the explanations that children use to explain how others think.

For instance, cognitive advances during infancy that we discussed in Module 3.2 permit older infants to see people in a very different way from other objects. They learn to see other people as *compliant agents*, beings similar to themselves who behave under their own power and who have the capacity to respond to infants' requests (Poulin-Dubois, 1999; Rochat, 1999, 2004).

In addition, children's capacity to understand intentionality and causality grows during infancy. For example, 10- and 13-month-olds are able to mentally represent social dominance, believing that larger size is related to the ability to dominate other, smaller sized individuals and objects. Furthermore, infants have a kind of innate morality, in which they show a preference for helpfulness (Hamlin et al., 2011; Hamlin & Wynn, 2011; Thomsen et al., 2011; Sloane, Baillargeon, & Premack, 2012).

Furthermore, as early as 18 months, they begin to understand that others' behaviors have meaning and that the behaviors they see people enacting are designed to accomplish particular goals, in contrast to the "behaviors" of inanimate objects. For example, a child comes to understand that his father has a specific goal when he is in the kitchen making sandwiches. In contrast, his father's car is simply parked in the driveway, having no mental life or goal (Ahn, Gelman, & Amsterlaw, 2000; Wellman et al., 2008; Senju et al., 2011).

Another piece of evidence for infants' growing sense of mental activity is that by the age of 2, infants begin to demonstrate the rudiments of empathy. **Empathy** is an emotional response that corresponds to the feelings of another person. At 24 months of age, infants sometimes comfort others or show concern for them. In order to do this, they need to be aware of the emotional states of others. For example, 1-year-olds are able to pick up emotional cues by observing the behavior of an actress on television (Mumm & Fernald, 2003; Legerstee, Haley, & Bornstein, 2013).

Furthermore, during their second year, infants begin to use deception, both in games of "pretend" and in outright attempts to fool others. A child who plays "pretend" and who uses falsehoods must be aware that others hold beliefs about the world—beliefs that can be manipulated. In short, by the end of infancy children have developed the rudiments of their own personal theory of mind. It helps them understand the actions of others and it affects their own behavior (van der Mark et al., 2002; Caron, 2009).

theory of mind knowledge and beliefs about how the mind works and how it affects behavior

empathy an emotional response that corresponds to the feelings of another person

REVIEW, CHECK, AND APPLY

REVIEW

L015 Do Infants experience emotions?

- Infants appear to express and to experience emotions, and their emotions broaden in range to reflect increasingly complex emotional states.
- The ability to decode the nonverbal facial and vocal expressions of others develops early in infants.

L016 What sort of mental lives do infants have?

- Infants develop self-awareness, the knowledge that they exist separately from the rest of the world, after about 12 months of age, and by the age of 2, children have developed the rudiments of a theory of mind.

CHECK YOURSELF

1. _____ is the caution and wariness expressed by infants when encountering an unfamiliar person.

   a Separation anxiety b Babbling
   c Stretching d Stranger anxiety

2. Marcel has been attending day care without incident since he was 6 weeks old. Now at around 14 months he starts to express difficulty when his mother leaves. He cries, shouts "No!" and then grabs her leg as she attempts to leave for work. Which of the following concepts best explains Marcel's change in behavior?

   a stranger anxiety b intuition
   c egocentrism d separation anxiety

3. When Darius bumped his knee on the table, he gazed at his mother to look at her reaction. When he saw that she was alarmed, he began crying. This is an example of _____.

   a fear
   b anxiety
   c social referencing
   d self-awareness

APPLYING LIFESPAN DEVELOPMENT

- Why would the sad or flat emotional expressiveness of a depressed parent be hard on an infant? How might it be counteracted?

✓ **Study** and **Review** on **MyPsychLab.com**

FORMING RELATIONSHIPS

LO17 What roles do other people play in infants' social development?
LO18 How sociable are infants?

Luis Camacho, now 38, clearly remembers the feelings that haunted him on the way to the hospital to meet his new sister Katy. Though he was only 4 at the time, that day of infamy is still vivid to him today. Luis would no longer be the only kid in the house; he would have to share his life with a baby sister. She would play with his toys, read his books, and be with him in the back seat of the car.

What really bothered him, of course, was that he would have to share his parents' love and attention with a new person. And not just any new person—a girl, who would automatically have a lot of advantages. Katy would be cuter, more needy, more demanding, more interesting—more everything—than he. He would be underfoot at best, neglected at worst.

Luis also knew that he was expected to be cheerful and welcoming. So he put on a brave face at the hospital and walked without hesitation to the room where his mother and Katy were waiting.

The arrival of a newborn brings a dramatic change to a family's dynamics. No matter how welcome a baby's birth, it causes a fundamental shift in the roles that people play within the family. Mothers and fathers must start to build a relationship with their infant, and older children must adjust to the presence of a new member of the family and build their own alliance with their infant brother or sister.

Although the process of social development during infancy is neither simple nor automatic, it is crucial: The bonds that grow between infants and their parents, siblings, family, and others provide the foundation for a lifetime's worth of social relationships.

Attachment: Forming Social Bonds

The most important aspect of social development that takes place during infancy is the formation of attachment. **Attachment** is the positive emotional bond that develops between a child and a particular, special individual. When children experience attachment to a given person, they feel pleasure when they are with them and feel comforted by their presence at times of distress—like the infant Jenna, described in the Chapter 3 opener, who cried in his crib until his mother or father came to comfort him. The nature of our attachment during infancy affects how we relate to others throughout the rest of our lives (Grossmann & Waters, 2005; Hofer, 2006; Johnson et al., 2010).

To understand attachment, the earliest researchers turned to the bonds that form between parents and children in the nonhuman animal kingdom. For instance, ethologist Konrad Lorenz (1965) observed newborn goslings, who have an innate tendency to follow their mother, the first moving object to which they typically are exposed after birth. Lorenz found that goslings hatched from an incubator, who viewed him just after hatching, would follow his every movement, as if he were their mother. As we discussed in Module 1.3, he labeled this process *imprinting*: behavior that takes place during a critical period and involves attachment to the first moving object that is observed.

Lorenz's findings suggested that attachment was based on biologically determined factors, and other theorists agreed. For instance, Freud suggested that attachment grew out of a mother's ability to satisfy a child's oral needs. Similarly, British psychiatrist John Bowlby (1951) argued that attachment is based primarily on infants' needs for safety and security. As they develop, infants come to learn that their safety is best provided by a particular individual, typically the mother, and they develop a relationship with the primary caregiver that is qualitatively different from the bonds formed with others. In his view, attachment provides a type of home base. As children become more independent, they can progressively roam further away from their secure base.

The Ainsworth Strange Situation and Patterns of Attachment. Developmental psychologist Mary Ainsworth built on Bowlby's theorizing to develop a widely used experimental technique to measure attachment (Ainsworth et al., 1978). The **Ainsworth Strange Situation** consists of a sequence of staged episodes that illustrate the strength of attachment

attachment the positive emotional bond that develops between a child and a particular individual

Ainsworth Strange Situation a sequence of staged episodes that illustrate the strength of attachment between a child and (typically) his or her mother

TABLE 3-9 CLASSIFICATIONS OF INFANT ATTACHMENT

Classification Criteria				
Label	**Seeking Proximity with Caregiver**	**Maintaining Contact with Caregiver**	**Avoiding Proximity with Caregiver**	**Resisting Contact with Caregiver**
Avoidant	Low	Low	High	Low
Secure	High	High (if distressed)	Low	Low
Ambivalent	High	High (often preseparation)	Low	High
Disorganized-disoriented	Inconsistent	Inconsistent	Inconsistent	Inconsistent

between a child and (typically) his or her mother. The "strange situation" follows this general eight-step pattern: (1) The mother and baby enter an unfamiliar room; (2) the mother sits down, leaving the baby free to explore; (3) an adult stranger enters the room and converses first with the mother and then with the baby; (4) the mother exits the room, leaving the baby alone with the stranger; (5) the mother returns, greeting and comforting the baby, and the stranger leaves; (6) the mother departs again, leaving the baby alone; (7) the stranger returns; and (8) the mother returns and the stranger leaves (Ainsworth et al., 1978).

Infants' reactions to the various aspects of the Strange Situation vary considerably, depending on the nature of their attachment to their mothers. One-year-olds typically show one of four major patterns—secure, avoidant, ambivalent, and disorganized–disoriented (summarized in Table 3-9). Children who have a **secure attachment pattern** use the mother as the type of home base that Bowlby described. These children seem at ease in the Strange Situation as long as their mothers are present. They explore independently, returning to her occasionally. Although they may or may not appear upset when she leaves, securely attached children immediately go to her when she returns and seek contact. Most North American children—about two-thirds—fall into the securely attached category.

In contrast, children with an **avoidant attachment pattern** do not seek proximity to the mother, and after she has left, they typically do not seem distressed. Furthermore, they seem to avoid her when she returns. It is as if they are indifferent to her behavior. Some 20 percent of 1-year-old children are in the avoidant category.

Children with an **ambivalent attachment pattern** display a combination of positive and negative reactions to their mothers. Initially, ambivalent children are in such close contact with the mother that they hardly explore their environment. They appear anxious even before the mother leaves, and when she does leave, they show great distress. But upon her return, they show ambivalent reactions, seeking to be close to her but also hitting and kicking, apparently in anger. About 10 to 15 percent of 1-year-olds fall into the ambivalent classification (Cassidy & Berlin, 1994).

Although Ainsworth identified only three categories, a more recent expansion of her work finds that there is a fourth category: disorganized–disoriented. Children who have a **disorganized–disoriented attachment pattern** show inconsistent, contradictory, and confused behavior. They may run to the mother when she returns but not look at her, or seem initially calm and then suddenly break into angry weeping. Their confusion suggests that they may be the least securely attached children of all. About 5 to 10 percent of all children fall into this category (Mayseless, 1996; Cole, 2005; Bernier & Meins, 2008).

The quality of attachment between infants and their mothers has significant consequences for relationships at later stages of life. For example, boys who are securely attached at the age of 1 year show fewer psychological difficulties at older ages than do avoidant or ambivalent children. Similarly, children who are securely attached as infants tend to be more socially and emotionally competent later, and others view them more positively (Mikulincer & Shaver, 2005; Simpson et al., 2007; MacDonald et al., 2008; Bergman, Blom, & Polyak, 2012).

In cases in which the development of attachment has been severely disrupted, children may suffer from *reactive attachment disorder*, a psychological problem characterized by

secure attachment pattern a style of attachment in which children use the mother as a kind of home base and are at ease when she is present; when she leaves, they become upset and go to her as soon as she returns

avoidant attachment pattern a style of attachment in which children do not seek proximity to the mother; after the mother has left, they seem to avoid her when she returns as if they are angered by her behavior

ambivalent attachment pattern a style of attachment in which children display a combination of positive and negative reactions to their mothers

disorganized–disoriented attachment pattern a style of attachment in which children show inconsistent, often contradictory behavior, such as approaching the mother when she returns but not looking at her extreme problems in forming attachments to others. In young children, it results in feeding difficulties, unresponsiveness to social overtures from others, and a general failure to thrive. Reactive attachment disorder is rare and typically the result of abuse or neglect (Corbin, 2007; Hardy, 2007; Hornor, 2008; Schechter & Willheim, 2009).

Producing Attachment: The Roles of the Mother and Father

As 5-month-old Annie cries passionately, her mother comes into the room and gently lifts her from her crib. After just a few moments, as her mother rocks Annie and speaks softly, Annie's cries cease, and she cuddles in her mother's arms. But the moment her mother places her back in the crib, Annie begins to wail again, leading her mother to pick her up once again.

The pattern is familiar to most parents. The infant cries, the parent reacts, and the child responds in turn. Such seemingly insignificant sequences as these, repeatedly occurring in the lives of infants and parents, help pave the way for the development of relationships between children, their parents, and the rest of the social world. We'll consider how each of the major caregivers and the infant play a role in the development of attachment.

From a social worker's perspective: What might a social worker seeking to find a good home for a foster child look for when evaluating potential foster parents?

Mothers and Attachment. Sensitivity to their infants' needs and desires is the hallmark of mothers of securely attached infants. Such a mother tends to be aware of her child's moods, and she takes into account her child's feelings as they interact. She is also responsive during face-to-face interactions, provides feeding "on demand," and is warm and affectionate to her infant (Thompson, Easterbrooks, & Padilla-Walker, 2003; McElwain & Booth-LaForce, 2006; Priddis & Howieson, 2009; Evans, Whittingham, & Boyd, 2012).

It is not only a matter of responding in *any* fashion to their infants' signals that separates mothers of securely attached and insecurely attached children. Mothers of secure infants tend to provide the appropriate level of response. In fact, overly responsive mothers are just as likely to have insecurely attached children as underresponsive mothers. In contrast, mothers whose communication involves *interactional synchrony*—in which caregivers respond to infants appropriately and both caregiver and child match emotional states—are more likely to produce secure attachment (Hane, Feldstein, & Dernetz, 2003; Ambrose & Menna, 2013).

Fathers and Attachment. Up to now, we've barely touched upon one of the key players involved in the upbringing of a child: the father. In fact, if you looked at the early theorizing and research on attachment, you'd find little mention of the father and his potential contributions to the life of the infant (Tamis-LeMonda & Cabrera, 1999; Freeman, Newland, & Coyl, 2010).

However, it has become increasingly clear that—despite societal norms that sometimes relegate fathers to secondary childrearing roles—infants can form their primary initial relationship with their fathers. Indeed, much of what we have said about mothers' attachment also applies to fathers. For example, fathers' expressions of nurturance, warmth, affection, support, and concern are extremely important to their children's emotional and social well-being. Furthermore, some psychological disorders, such as substance abuse and depression, have been found to be related more to fathers' than mothers' behavior (Veneziano, 2003; Parke, 2004; Roelofs et al., 2006).

Infants' social bonds extend beyond their parents, especially as they grow older. For example, one study found that although most infants formed their first primary relationship with one person, around one-third had multiple relationships, and it was often difficult to determine which attachment was primary. Furthermore, by the time the infants were 18 months old, most had formed multiple relationships. In sum, infants may develop attachments not only to their mothers, but to a variety of others as well (Silverstein & Auerbach, 1999; Booth, Kelly, & Spieker, 2003; Seibert & Kerns, 2009).

A growing body of research highlights the importance of a father's demonstration of love for his children. In fact, certain disorders such as depression and substance abuse have been found to be more related to fathers' than to mothers' behavior.

Cultural Dimensions

Does Attachment Differ Across Cultures?

John Bowlby's observations of the biologically motivated efforts of the young of other species to seek safety and security were the basis for his views on attachment and his reason for suggesting that seeking attachment was biologically universal, an effort that we should find not only in other species, but among humans of all cultures as well.

Research has shown that human attachment is not as culturally universal as Bowlby predicted. Certain attachment patterns seem more likely among infants of particular cultures. For example, one study of German infants showed that most fell into the avoidant category. Other studies, conducted in Israel and Japan, have found a smaller proportion of infants who were securely attached than in the United States. Finally, comparisons of Chinese and Canadian children show that Chinese children are more inhibited than Canadians in the Strange Situation (Grossmann et al., 1982; Takahashi, 1986; Rothbaum et al., 2000; Tomlinson, Murray, & Cooper, 2010; Kieffer, 2012).

Do such findings suggest that we should abandon the notion that attachment is a universal biological tendency? Not necessarily. Most of the data on attachment have been obtained by using the Ainsworth Strange Situation, which may not be the most appropriate measure in non-Western cultures. For example, Japanese parents seek to avoid separation and stress during infancy, and they don't strive to foster independence to the same degree as parents in many Western societies. Because of their relative lack of prior experience in separation, infants placed in the Strange Situation may experience unusual stress—producing the appearance of less secure attachment in Japanese children. If a different measure of attachment were used, one that might be administered later in infancy, more Japanese infants could likely be classified as secure. In short, attachment is affected by cultural norms and expectations (Nakagawa, Lamb, & Miyaki, 1992; Vereijken et al., 1997; Dennis, Cole, & Zahn-Waxler, 2002).

Infants' Sociability With Their Peers: Infant–Infant Interaction

Although it is clear that they do not form "friendships" in the traditional sense, babies do react positively to the presence of peers from early in life, and they engage in rudimentary forms of social interaction.

Infants' sociability is expressed in several ways. From the earliest months of life, they smile, laugh, and vocalize while looking at their peers. They show more interest in peers than in inanimate objects and pay greater attention to other infants than they do to a mirror image of themselves. They also begin to show preferences for peers with whom they are familiar compared with those they do not know. For example, studies of identical twins show that twins exhibit a higher level of social behavior toward each other than toward an unfamiliar infant (Eid et al., 2003).

Japanese parents seek to avoid separation and stress during infancy and do not foster independence. As a result, Japanese children often have the appearance of being less securely attached according to the Strange Situation, but using other measurement techniques they may well score higher in attachment.

Infants' level of sociability rises with age. Nine- to 12-month-olds mutually present and accept toys, particularly if they know each other. They also play social games, such as peekaboo or crawl-and-chase. Such behavior is important, as it serves as a foundation for future social exchanges in which children will try to elicit responses from others and then offer reactions to those responses. These kinds of exchanges are important to learn, because they continue even into adulthood. For example, someone who says, "Hi, what's up?" may be trying to elicit a response to which he or she can then reply (Endo, 1992; Eckerman & Peterman, 2001).

Finally, as infants age, they begin to imitate each other (Russon & Waite, 1991). For instance, 14-month-old infants who are familiar with one another sometimes reproduce each other's behavior (Mueller & Vandell, 1979). Such imitation serves a social function and can also be a powerful teaching tool (Ray & Heyes, 2011).

To some developmentalists, the capacity of young children to engage in imitation suggests that imitation may be inborn. In support of this view, research has identified a class of neurons in the brain that seems related to an innate ability to imitate. *Mirror neurons* are neurons that fire not only when an individual enacts a particular behavior, but also when the individual simply observes *another* organism carrying out the same behavior (Falck-Ytter, 2006).

For example, research on brain functioning shows activation of the inferior frontal gyrus both when an individual carries out a particular task and when observing another individual carrying out the same task. Mirror neurons may help infants understand others' actions and develop a theory of mind. Dysfunction of mirror neurons may be related to the development of disorders involving children's theory of mind as well as autism spectrum disorder a psychological disorder involving significant emotional and linguistic problems (Kilner, Friston, & Frith, 2007; Martineau et al., 2008; Welsh et al., 2009).

REVIEW, CHECK, AND APPLY

REVIEW

L017 What roles do other people play in infants' social development?

- Attachment, the positive emotional bond between an infant and a significant individual, affects a person's later social competence as an adult.
- Infants and the persons with whom they interact engage in reciprocal socialization as they mutually adjust to one another's interactions.

L018 How sociable are infants?

- Infants react differently to other children than to inanimate objects. Babies react positively to the presence of peers from early in life, and they engage in rudimentary forms of social interactions.

CHECK YOURSELF

1. _____ is the positive emotional bond that develops between a child and a particular individual.
   - a Attachment
   - b Smiling
   - c Playing
   - d Laughing
2. Children who are attached to their primary caregivers feel _____ when they are with them and feel _____ during times of distress.
   - a concern; sad
   - b pleasure; comforted
   - c overwhelmed; distraught
   - d confused; comfort
3. One way mothers can improve the likelihood of secure attachment in their children is to respond to their needs appropriately. Another name for this communication in which mothers and children match emotional states is_____.
   - a emotion matching
   - b goodness of fit
   - c interactional synchrony
   - d environmental assessment

APPLYING LIFESPAN DEVELOPMENT

- In what sort of society might an avoidant attachment style be encouraged by cultural attitudes toward childrearing? In such a society, would characterizing the infant's consistent avoidance of its mother as anger be an accurate interpretation?

✓ **Study** and **Review** on **MyPsychLab.com**

DIFFERENCES AMONG INFANTS

L019 What individual differences distinguish one infant from another?
L020 How does nonparental child care impact infants?

Lincoln was a difficult baby; his parents both agreed. For one thing, it seemed like they could never get him to sleep at night. He cried at the slightest noise—a problem because his crib was near the windows facing a busy street. Worse yet, once he started crying, it seemed to take forever to calm him down again. One day his mother, Aisha, was telling her mother-in-law, Mary, about the challenges of being Lincoln's mom. Mary recalled that her own son, Lincoln's father, Malcom, had been much the same way. "He was my first child, and I thought this was how all babies acted. So, we just kept trying different ways until we found out how he worked. I remember, we put his crib all over the apartment until we finally found out where he could sleep, and it ended up being in the hallway for a long time. Then his sister, Maleah, came along, and she was so quiet and easy, I didn't know what to do with my extra time!"

As the story of Lincoln's family shows, babies are not all alike, and neither are their families. In fact, as we'll see, some of the differences among people seem to be present from the moment we are born. The differences among infants include overall personality and temperament, and differences in the lives they lead—differences based on their gender, the nature of their families, and the ways in which they are cared for.

Personality Development: The Characteristics That Make Infants Unique

The origins of **personality**, the sum total of the enduring characteristics that differentiate one individual from another, stem from infancy. From birth onward, infants begin to show unique, stable traits and behaviors that ultimately lead to their development as distinct, special individuals (Caspi, 2000; Kagan, 2000; Shiner, Masten, & Roberts, 2003).

According to psychologist Erik Erikson, whose approach to personality development we first discussed in Module 1.2, infants' early experiences are responsible for shaping one of the key aspects of their personalities: whether they will be basically trusting or mistrustful.

Erikson's theory of psychosocial development considers how individuals come to understand themselves and the meaning of others'—and their own—behavior (Erikson, 1963). The theory suggests that developmental change occurs throughout people's lives in eight distinct stages, the first of which occurs in infancy.

According to Erikson, during the first 18 months of life, we pass through the **trust-versus-mistrust stage**. During this period, infants develop a sense of trust or mistrust, largely depending on how well their needs are met by their caregivers. Mary's attention to Malcom's needs, in the previous example, probably helped him develop a basic sense of trust in the world. Erikson suggests that if infants are able to develop trust, they experience a sense of hope, which permits them to feel as if they can fulfill their needs successfully. On the other hand, feelings of mistrust lead infants to see the world as harsh and unfriendly, and they may have later difficulties in forming close bonds with others.

During the end of infancy, children enter the **autonomy-versus-shame-and-doubt stage**, which lasts from 18 months to 3 years. During this period, children develop independence and autonomy if parents encourage exploration and freedom within safe boundaries. However, if children are restricted and overly protected, they feel shame, self-doubt, and unhappiness.

Erikson argues that personality is primarily shaped by infants' experiences. However, as we discuss next, other developmentalists concentrate on consistencies of behavior that are present at birth, even before the experiences of infancy. These consistencies are viewed as largely genetically determined and as providing the raw material of personality.

Temperament: Stabilities in Infant Behavior

Sarah's parents thought there must be something wrong. Unlike her older brother Josh, who had been so active as an infant that he seemed never to be still, Sarah was much more placid. She took long naps and was easily soothed on those relatively rare occasions when she became agitated. What could be producing her extreme calmness?

The most likely answer: The difference between Sarah and Josh reflected differences in temperament. As we first discussed in Module 2.1, **temperament** encompasses patterns of arousal and emotionality that are consistent and enduring characteristics of an individual (Kochanska & Aksan, 2004; Rothbart, 2007).

Temperament refers to *how* children behave, as opposed to *what* they do or *why* they do it. Infants show temperamental differences in general disposition from the time of birth, largely due initially to genetic factors, and temperament tends to be fairly stable well into adolescence. On the other hand, temperament is not fixed and unchangeable: Childrearing practices can modify temperament significantly. In fact, some children show little consistency in temperament from one age to another (Rothbart & Derryberry, 2002; Werner et al., 2007; de Lauzon-Guillain et al., 2012).

Temperament is reflected in several dimensions of behavior. One central dimension is *activity level*, which reflects the degree of overall movement. Some babies (like Sarah and Maleah, in the earlier examples) are relatively placid, and their movements are slow and almost leisurely. In contrast, the activity level of other infants (like Josh) is quite high, with strong, restless movements of the arms and legs.

Another important dimension of temperament is the nature and quality of an infant's mood, and in particular a child's *irritability*. Some infants are relatively easygoing, while others are less so. For example, irritable infants fuss a great deal, and they are easily upset. They are also difficult to soothe when they do begin to cry. (Other aspects of temperament are listed in Table 3-10.)

personality the sum total of the enduring characteristics that differentiate one individual from another

Erikson's theory of psychosocial development the theory that considers how individuals come to understand themselves and the meaning of others'—and their own—behavior

trust-versus-mistrust stage according to Erikson, the period during which infants develop a sense of trust or mistrust, largely depending on how well their needs are met by their caregivers

autonomy-versus-shame-and-doubt stage the period during which, according to Erikson, toddlers (aged 18 months to 3 years) develop independence and autonomy if they are allowed the freedom to explore, or shame and self-doubt if they are restricted and overprotected

temperament patterns of arousal and emotionality that are consistent and enduring characteristics of an individual

TABLE 3-10 SOME DIMENSIONS OF TEMPERAMENT IN INFANTS, WITH BEHAVIORAL INDICATORS

Dimension	Behavioral Indicators
Activity level	**High:** wriggles while diaper is changed **Low:** lies still while being dressed
Approach/withdrawal	**Approach orientation:** accepts novel foods and toys easily **Withdrawal orientation:** cries when a stranger comes near
Quality of mood	**Negative:** cries when carriage is rocked **Positive:** smiles or smacks lips when tasting new food
Distractibility	**Low:** continues crying even when diaper is changed **High:** stops fussing when held and rocked
Rhythmicity	**Regular:** has consistent feeding schedule **Irregular:** has varying sleep and waking schedule
Threshold of responsiveness	**High:** not startled by sudden noises or bright lights **Low:** pauses sucking on bottle at approach of parent or slight noise

Categorizing Temperament: Easy, Difficult, and Slow-to-Warm Babies. Because temperament can be viewed along so many dimensions, some researchers have asked whether there are broader categories that can be used to describe children's overall behavior. According to Alexander Thomas and Stella Chess, who carried out a large-scale study of a group of infants that has come to be known as the *New York Longitudinal Study* (Thomas & Chess, 1980), babies can be described according to one of several profiles:

- Easy babies. **Easy babies** have a positive disposition. Their body functions operate regularly, and they are adaptable. They are generally positive, showing curiosity about new situations, and their emotions are moderate or low in intensity. This category applies to about 40 percent (the largest number) of infants.
- Difficult babies. **Difficult babies** have more negative moods and are slow to adapt to new situations. When confronted with a new situation, they tend to withdraw. About 10 percent of infants belong in this category.
- Slow-to-warm babies. **Slow-to-warm babies** are inactive, showing relatively calm reactions to their environment. Their moods are generally negative, and they withdraw from new situations, adapting slowly. Approximately 15 percent of infants are slow-to-warm.

As for the remaining 35 percent, they cannot be consistently categorized. These children show a variety of combinations of characteristics. For instance, one infant may have relatively sunny moods, but react negatively to new situations, or another may show little stability of any sort in terms of general temperament.

The Consequences of Temperament: Does Temperament Matter? One obvious question to emerge from the findings of the relative stability of temperament is whether a particular kind of temperament is beneficial. The answer seems to be that no single type of temperament is invariably good or bad. Instead, children's long-term adjustment depends on the **goodness-of-fit** of their particular temperament to the nature and demands of the environment in which they find themselves. For instance, children with a low activity level and low irritability may do particularly well in an environment in which they are left to explore on their own and are allowed largely to direct their own behavior. In contrast, high-activity-level, highly irritable children may do best with greater direction, which permits them to channel their energy in particular directions (Thomas & Chess, 1980; Strelau, 1998; Schoppe-Sullivan et al., 2007; Yu et al., 2012). Mary, the grandmother in the earlier example, found ways to adjust the environment for her son, Malcom. Malcom and Aisha may need to do the same for their own son, Lincoln.

Some research does suggest that certain temperaments are, in general, more adaptive than others. For instance, difficult children, in general, are more likely to show behavior problems by school age than those classified in infancy as easy children. But not all difficult children experience problems. The key determinant seems to be the way parents react to their infants' difficult behavior. If they react by showing anger and inconsistency—responses that their child's difficult, demanding behavior readily evokes—then the child is ultimately

easy babies babies who have a positive disposition; their body functions operate regularly, and they are adaptable

difficult babies babies who have negative moods and are slow to adapt to new situations; when confronted with a new situation, they tend to withdraw

slow-to-warm babies babies who are inactive, showing relatively calm reactions to their environment; their moods are generally negative, and they withdraw from new situations, adapting slowly

goodness-of-fit the notion that development is dependent on the degree of match between children's temperament and the nature and demands of the environment in which they are being raised more likely to experience behavior problems. On the other hand, parents who display more warmth and consistency in their responses are more likely to have children who avoid later problems (Thomas, Chess, & Birch, 1968; Teerikangas et al., 1998; Pauli-Pott, Mertesacker, & Bade, 2003).

Gender: Boys in Blue, Girls in Pink

"It's a boy." "It's a girl." One of these two statements, or some variant, is probably the first announcement made after the birth of a child. From the moment of birth, girls and boys are treated differently. Their parents send out different kinds of birth announcements. They are dressed in different clothes and wrapped in different-colored blankets. They are given different toys (Bridges, 1993; Coltrane & Adams, 1997; Serbin, Poulin-Dubois, & Colburne, 2001).

Parents play with boy and girl babies differently: From birth on, fathers tend to interact more with sons than daughters, while mothers interact more with daughters. Because, as we noted earlier in the module, mothers and fathers play in different ways (with fathers typically engaging in more physical, rough-and-tumble activities and mothers in traditional games such as peekaboo), male and female infants are clearly exposed to different styles of activity and interaction from their parents (Laflamme, Pomerleau, & Malcuit, 2002; Clearfield & Nelson, 2006; Parke, 2007).

The behavior exhibited by girls and boys is interpreted in very different ways by adults. For instance, when researchers showed adults a video of an infant whose name was given as either "John" or "Mary," adults perceived "John" as adventurous and inquisitive, while "Mary" was fearful and anxious, although it was the same baby performing a single set of behaviors (Condry & Condry, 1976). Clearly, adults view the behavior of children through the lens of gender. **Gender** refers to the sense of being male or female. The term *gender* is often used to mean the same thing as *sex*, but they are not actually the same. *Sex* typically refers to sexual anatomy and sexual behavior, while *gender* refers to the social perceptions of maleness or femaleness.

gender the sense of being male or female

Gender Differences. There is a considerable amount of disagreement over both the extent and causes of such gender differences, even though most agree that boys and girls do experience at least partially different worlds based on gender. Some gender differences are fairly clear from the time of birth. For example, male infants tend to be more active and fussier than female infants. Boys' sleep tends to be more disturbed than that of girls. Boys grimace more, although no gender difference exists in the overall amount of crying. There is also some evidence that male newborns are more irritable than female newborns, although the findings are inconsistent. Differences between male and female infants, however, are generally minor (Crawford & Unger, 2004; Losonczy-Marshall, 2008).

The number of single-parent families has increased dramatically over the past 20 years. If the current trend continues, 60 percent of all children will live at some time with a single parent.

Gender differences emerge more clearly as children age—and become increasingly influenced by the gender roles that society sets out for them. For instance, by the age of 1 year, infants are able to distinguish between males and females. Girls at this age prefer to play with dolls or stuffed animals, while boys seek out blocks and trucks. Often, of course, these are the only options available to them, due to the choices their parents and other adults have made in the toys they provide (Cherney, Kelly-Vance, & Glover, 2003; Alexander, Wilcox, & Woods, 2009).

By the time they reach the age of 2, boys behave more independently and less compliantly than girls. Much of this behavior can be traced to parental reactions to earlier behavior. For instance, when a child takes his or her first steps, parents tend to react differently, depending on the child's gender: Boys are encouraged more to go off and explore the world, while girls are hugged and kept close. It is hardly surprising, then, that by the age of 2, girls tend to show less independence and greater compliance (Kuczynski & Kochanska, 1990; Poulin-Dubois, Serbin, & Eichstedt, 2002).

Societal encouragement and reinforcement do not, however, completely explain differences in behavior between boys and girls. For example, one study examined girls who were exposed before birth to abnormally high levels of *androgen*, a male hormone, because their mothers unwittingly took a drug containing the hormone while pregnant. Later, these girls were more likely to play with toys stereotypically preferred by boys (such as cars) and less likely to play with toys stereotypically associated with girls (such as dolls). Although there are many alternative explanations for these results—you can probably think of several yourself—one possibility is that exposure to male hormones affected the brain development of the girls, leading them to favor toys that involve certain kinds of preferred skills (Levine et al., 1999; Mealey, 2000; Servin et al., 2003; Kahlenberg & Hein, 2010).

In sum, differences in behavior between boys and girls begin in infancy, and—as we will see in future modules—continue throughout childhood (and beyond). Although gender differences have complex causes, representing some combination of innate, biologically related factors and environmental factors, they play a profound role in the social and emotional development of infants.

Family Life in the Twenty-First Century

Family life today is very different from the way it was even a few decades ago. A quick review tells the story:

- The number of single-parent families has increased dramatically in the last 2 decades, as the number of two-parent households has declined. One-third of all families with children are headed by single parents. Nearly a quarter of children live with only their mothers, 4 percent live with only their fathers, and 4 percent live with neither of their parents (U.S. Bureau of the Census, 2000; ChildStats.gov, 2009).
- The average size of families is shrinking. Today, on average, there are 2.6 persons per household, compared to 2.8 in 1980. The number of people living in nonfamily households (without any relatives) is close to 30 million.
- Although the number of adolescents giving birth has declined substantially over the last 5 years, there are still half a million births to teenage women, the vast majority of whom are unmarried.
- More than half of mothers of infants work outside the home.
- One in three children lives in low-income households in the United States. The rates are even higher for African American and Hispanic families, and for single-parent families of young children. More children under 3 live in poverty than do older children, adults, or the elderly. Furthermore, the proportion of children living in low-income families began rising in 2000, reversing a decade of decline (Federal Interagency Forum on Child and Family Statistics, 2003; National Center for Children in Poverty, 2005).

At the very least, these statistics suggest that many infants are being raised in environments in which substantial stressors are present. Such stress makes it an unusually difficult task to raise children—never easy even under the best circumstances.

From a social worker's perspective: Imagine you are a social worker visiting a foster home. It is 11 AM. You find the breakfast dishes in the sink and books and toys all over the floor. The infant you have placed in the home is happily pounding on pots and pans as his foster mother claps time. The kitchen floor is gooey under the baby's high chair. What is your professional assessment?

On the other hand, society is adapting to the new realities of family life in the twenty-first century. Several kinds of social support exist for the parents of infants, and society is evolving new institutions to help in their care. One example is the growing array of child-care arrangements available to help working parents, as we discuss next.

How Does Infant Child Care Affect Later Development?

For most of the years my two kids were in child care, I worried about it. Did that weird day-care home where my daughter stayed briefly as a toddler do irreparable harm? Was my son irretrievably damaged by that child-care center he disliked? (Shellenbarger, 2003, p. D1)

Every day, parents ask themselves questions like these. The issue of how infant child care affects later development is a pressing one for many parents, who, because of economic, family,

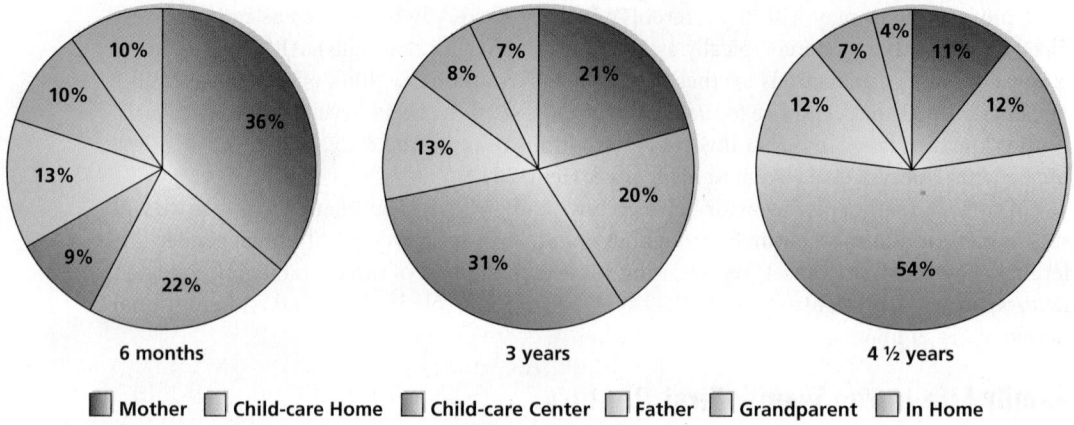

FIGURE 3-17 Where Are Children Cared For?
According to a major study by the National Institute of Child Health and Human Development, children spend more time in some kind of child care outside the home or family as they get older.
Source: NICHD Early Child Care Research Network, 2006.

or career demands, leave their children to the care of others for a portion of the day. In fact, almost two-thirds of all children between 4 months and 3 years of age spend time in nonparental child care. Overall, more than 80 percent of infants are cared for by people other than their mothers at some point during their first year of life. The majority of these infants begin child care outside the home before the age of 4 months and are enrolled for almost 30 hours per week (Federal Interagency Forum on Child and Family Statistics, 2003; NICHD, 2006) (also see Figure 3-17). What effects do such arrangements have on later development?

Although the answer is largely reassuring, the newest research to come from the massive, long-term Study of Early Child Care and Youth Development, the longest-running examination of child care ever conducted, suggests that long-term participation in day care may have unanticipated consequences.

First the good news. According to most of the evidence, high-quality child care outside the home produces only minor differences from home care in most respects, and may even enhance certain aspects of development. For example, research finds little or no difference in the strength or nature of parental attachment bonds of infants who have been in high-quality child care compared with infants raised solely by their parents (NICHD Early Child Care Research Network, 2001; Vandell et al., 2005; Morrissey, 2010).

In addition to the direct benefits from involvement in child care outside the home, there are indirect benefits. For example, children in lower-income households and those whose mothers are single may benefit from the educational and social experiences in child care, as well as from the higher income produced by parental employment (Love et al., 2003; NICHD Early Child Care Research Network, 2003a; Dearing, McCartney, & Taylor, 2009).

High-quality infant child care seems to produce only minor differences from home care in most respects, and some aspects of development may even be enhanced. What aspects of development might be enhanced by participation in infant child care outside the home?

Furthermore, children who participate in Early Head Start—a program that serves at-risk infants and toddlers in high-quality child-care centers—can solve problems better, pay greater attention to others, and use language more effectively than poor children who do not participate in the program. In addition, their parents (who are also involved in the program) benefit from their participation. Participating parents talk and read more to their children, and they are less likely to spank them. Likewise, children who receive good, responsive child care are more likely to play well with other children (NICHD Early Child Care Research Network, 2001a; Maccoby & Lewis, 2003; Loeb et al., 2004).

On the other hand, some of the findings on participation in child care outside the home are less positive. Infants may be somewhat less secure when they are placed in low-quality child care or if they are placed in multiple child-care arrangements. In addition, children who spend long hours in outside-the-home child-care situations have a lower ability to work independently and have less effective time management skills (Vandell et al., 2005).

The newest research, which focuses on preschoolers, finds that children who spend 10 or more hours a week in group child care for a year or more have an increased probability of being disruptive in class, and that the effect continues through the sixth grade. Although the increase in the likelihood of acting disruptive is not substantial—every year spent in a child-care center resulted in a 1 percent higher score on a standardized measure of problem behavior completed by teachers—the results were quite reliable (Belsky et al., 2007).

In sum, the ballooning body of research finds that the effects of participation in group child care are neither unambiguously positive nor unambiguously negative. What is clear, though, is that the *quality* of child care is critical. Ultimately, more research is needed on just who makes use of child care and how it is used by members of different segments of society to fully understand its consequences (Marshall, 2004; NICHD Early Child Care Research Network, 2005; Belsky, 2006, 2009; de Schipper et al., 2006).

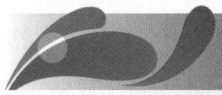

Becoming an Informed Consumer of Development

Choosing the Right Infant Care Provider

One finding that emerges with absolute clarity from research conducted on the consequences of infant child-care programs is that the benefits of child care—peer learning, greater social skills, greater independence—occur only when child care is of high quality. But what distinguishes high-quality child care from low-caliber programs? Parents should consider these questions in choosing a program (Committee on Children, Youth and Families, 1994; Love et al., 2003; de Schipper et al., 2006):

- Are there enough providers? A desirable ratio is one adult for every three infants, although one to four can be adequate.
- Are group sizes manageable? Even with several providers, a group of infants should not be larger than eight.
- Has the center complied with all governmental regulations, and is it licensed?
- Do the people providing the care seem to like what they are doing? What is their motivation? Is child care just a temporary job, or is it a career? Are they experienced? Do they seem happy in the job, or is offering child care just a way to earn money?
- What do the caregivers do during the day? Do they spend their time playing with, listening and talking to, and paying attention to the children? Do they seem genuinely interested in the children? Is there a television constantly on?
- Are the children safe and clean? Does the environment allow infants to move around safely? Is the equipment and furniture in good repair? Do the providers adhere to the highest levels of cleanliness? After changing a baby's diaper, do providers wash their hands?
- What training do the providers have in caring for children? Do they demonstrate a knowledge of the basics of infant development and an understanding of how normal children develop? Do they seem alert to signs that development may depart from normal patterns?
- Finally, is the environment happy and cheerful? Child care is not just a babysitting service: For the time an infant is there, it is the child's whole world. You should feel fully comfortable and confident that the child-care center is a place where your infant will be treated as an individual.

In addition to following these guidelines, contact the National Association for the Education of Young Children (NAEYC), from which you can get the name of a resource and referral agency in your area. Go to the NAEYC website at www.naeyc.org or call (800) 424-2460.

REVIEW, CHECK, AND APPLY

REVIEW

LO19 What individual differences distinguish one infant from another?

- According to Erikson, during infancy individuals move from the trust-versus-mistrust stage of psychosocial development to the autonomy-versus-shame-and-guilt stage.
- Temperament encompasses enduring levels of arousal and emotionality that are characteristic of an individual.
- Gender differences become more pronounced as infants age.

LO20 How does nonparental child care impact infants?

- Child care outside of the home can have neutral, positive, or negative effects on the social development of children, depending largely on its quality.

CHECK YOURSELF

1. Patterns of arousal and emotionality that are consistent and enduring in an individual are known as an individual's _____.
   - a gender
   - b temperament
   - c intelligence
   - d mood
2. _____ are prescribed by societies as activities or positions appropriate for males and females.
   - a Gender expectations
   - b Sex roles
   - c Gender roles
   - d Sex expectations
3. Research finds significant differences in the strength and nature of the parental bond for infants raised in the home compared to infants exposed to high-quality day care.
   - True
   - False

APPLYING LIFESPAN DEVELOPMENT

- If you were introducing a bill in Congress regarding the minimum licensing requirements for child-care centers, what would you emphasize?

✓ **Study** and **Review** on **MyPsychLab.com**

SUMMARY 3

PUTTING IT ALL TOGETHER INFANCY

FOUR-MONTH-OLD JENNA (whom we met in this chapter's opener) was a model infant in almost every respect. However, there was one aspect of her behavior that posed a dilemma: how to respond when she woke up in the middle of the night and cried despondently. It usually was not a matter of being hungry, because typically she had been fed recently. And it was not caused by her diaper being soiled, because usually that had been changed recently. Instead, it seemed that Jenna just wanted to be held and entertained, and when she wasn't, she cried dramatically until someone came to her.

PHYSICAL DEVELOPMENT IN INFANCY

MODULE 3.1

- Jenna's body is developing various rhythms (repetitive, cyclical patterns of behavior) that are responsible for the change from sleep to wakefulness. *(pp. 97–99)*
- Jenna will sleep in spurts of around 2 hours, followed by periods of wakefulness until about 16 weeks, when she will begin to sleep as much as 6 continuous hours. *(p. 98)*
- Because Jenna's sense of touch is one of her most highly developed senses (and one of the earliest developed), she will respond to gentle touches, such as a soothing caress, which can calm a crying, fussy infant. *(p. 110)*

COGNITIVE DEVELOPMENT IN INFANCY

MODULE 3.2

- Jenna has learned that her behavior (crying) can produce a desired effect (someone holding and entertaining her). *(pp. 114–115)*
- As Jenna's brain develops, she is able to separate people she knows from people she doesn't; this is why she responds so positively when someone she knows comes to comfort her during the night. *(pp. 120–121)*

SOCIAL AND PERSONALITY DEVELOPMENT IN INFANCY

MODULE 3.3

- Jenna has developed attachment (the positive emotional bond between her and particular individuals) to those who care for her. *(p. 137)*
- In order to feel secure, Jenna needs to know that her caregivers will provide an appropriate response to the signals she is sending. *(p. 142)*
- Part of Jenna's temperament is that she is irritable. Irritable infants can be fussy and are difficult to soothe when they do begin to cry. *(pp. 142–144)*
- Because irritability is relatively stable, Jenna will continue to display this temperament at age 1 and even age 2. *(pp. 142–144)*

What would a PARENT do?

What strategies would you use in dealing with Jenna? Would you go to her every time she cried? Or, would you try to wait her out, perhaps setting a time limit before going to her?

What would a HEALTH CARE PROVIDER do?

How would you recommend that Jenna's caregivers deal with the situation? Are there any dangers that the caregivers should be aware of?

What would an EDUCATOR do?

Suppose Jenna spends a few hours every weekday afternoon in day care. If you were a child-care provider, how would you deal with Jenna if she wakes up from naps soon after falling asleep?

What would YOU do?

How would you deal with Jenna? What factors would affect your decision? Based on your reading, how do you think Jenna will respond?

Explore on MyPsychLab

To read how real-life parents, health care providers, and educators responded to these questions, log onto MyPsychLab.com.

Do you agree or disagree with their responses? Why? What concepts that you've read about back up their opinion?

4 THE PRESCHOOL YEARS

Chen loved to be outdoors. At the age of 4, he was learning to swim and to ride the new bicycle he'd received on his birthday. He didn't think he'd need the training wheels much longer.

But the real passion of his young life was hiking. Every Sunday his parents went hiking in the Berkshires. Chen had always gone with them, even when he was an infant strapped to his mom. Now he could scamper up and down the rocky slopes with ease. "He's a mountain goat," his mom says. "I try not to worry too much about accidents because he's a born climber, but things can happen so fast out here."

One case in point: Several weeks ago, Chen and his parents were climbing a mountain to view a waterfall. As his parents gazed at this local treasure, Chen scampered away. "Chen, come back here," his dad called. "I just want to see," Chen answered and that was when he disappeared. He'd fallen between two large outcroppings of rock. His parents were terrified the crevice might be filled with water and their son would drown. But seconds later, Chen's head popped up. His cheek was bruised, but otherwise he was fine. "I just wanted to see where the water went after the waterfall ended," he said. "Next time, I'll watch out better."

Four years ago, Chen could not even lift his head. Now he can move with confidence—hiking, swimming, and learning to ride his two-wheeler. These advances in physicality are challenging to parents, who must rise to a whole new level of vigilance to prevent injuries, the greatest threat to preschoolers' physical well-being. (Think what would have happened if Chen had fallen into deep water.)

The preschool period is an exciting time in children's lives. In one sense, the preschool years mark a time of preparation: a period spent anticipating and getting ready for the start of a child's formal education, through which society will begin the process of passing on its intellectual tools to a new generation.

But it is a mistake to take the label "preschool" too literally. The ages between 3 and 6 are hardly a mere way station in life, an interval spent waiting for the next, more important period to start. Instead, the preschool years are a time of tremendous change and growth, where physical, intellectual, and social development proceeds at a rapid pace.

In this chapter, we focus on the physical, cognitive, and social and personality growth that occur during the preschool years. We begin by considering the physical changes children undergo during those years. We discuss weight and height, nutrition, and health and wellness. The brain and its neural pathways change too, and we will touch on some intriguing findings relating to gender differences in the way the brain functions. We also look at how both gross and fine motor skills change over the preschool years.

Intellectual development is the focus of the next section of the chapter. We examine the major approaches to cognitive development, including Piaget's stage theory, information processing approaches, and an emerging view of cognitive development that gives great weight to the influence of culture. We also consider the important advances in language development that occur during the preschool years, and we discuss several factors that influence cognitive development, including exposure to television and participation in child-care and preschool programs.

Finally, we look at social and personality development in these years, focusing first on how children figure out who they are and develop a sense of racial and gender identity. We discuss the nature of their friendships and the significance of the ways they play together. We next look at parents, considering the different styles of parenting that are common today as well as their implications for their children's future development and personalities. We conclude with a look at the ways in which preschool-age children begin to develop a moral sense and learn how to control aggression.

MODULE 4.1

PHYSICAL DEVELOPMENT IN THE PRESCHOOL YEARS

When—and how—should children be toilet trained?

MODULE 4.2

COGNITIVE DEVELOPMENT IN THE PRESCHOOL YEARS

How accurate is a preschooler's memory?

MODULE 4.3

SOCIAL AND PERSONALITY DEVELOPMENT IN THE PRESCHOOL YEARS

Viewing violence on TV: Does it matter?

MyVirtualLife

If you are currently using MyVirtualLife, consider how you will raise your virtual child during the preschool years. What decisions will you make?

Access MyVirtualLife for a chance to help your virtual child navigate the preschool years.

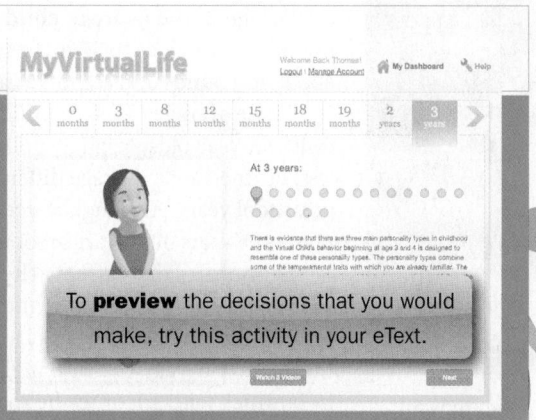

To **preview** the decisions that you would make, try this activity in your eText.

MODULE 4.1

PHYSICAL DEVELOPMENT IN THE PRESCHOOL YEARS

Rosa

Rosa Bello has never stopped moving since the day she was born. In her crib, she batted at mobiles and cycled her legs. Seated on a blanket at 6 months, she struggled to get into a crawling position to retrieve a toy or pat the dog. In the video of her first birthday celebration, Rosa walks among the guests, receiving their hugs. "Actually, Rosa never walked," her father says, laughing. "From the moment she could stand alone, she started running." Now, at age 3, she skips, hops, and leaps to get where she's going. "We should have named her 'Viento,' the Spanish word for 'wind,' " her father says. Rosa's mother agrees it is indeed a race to stay one step ahead of her daughter. She has installed childproof locks on almost every cabinet in the house because Rosa loves to explore. "She climbs up on the counter tops, just like a mountain goat," her mother says.

In just 3 years, Rosa Bello has grown from a nearly immobile newborn to a whirlwind of activity. She moves with confidence—perhaps too much confidence. She runs at breakneck speed, chases her dog everywhere, fearlessly falls to the ground and rolls around, and then jumps up and starts all over again. Indoors she darts from room to room, pulls on handles and knobs, and climbs chairs to reach tables and countertops. These advances in mobility are challenging to her parents, who must rise to a whole new level of vigilance to prevent injuries, the greatest threat to preschoolers' physical well-being. (Think what might happen if someone left a rake or hoe in the yard or if any countertop corner were left unprotected.)

Parents and caregivers also must worry about colds and other illnesses, and, especially in recent years, about making sure their child gets enough of the right kinds of food to eat. As they watch their child grow active, they must insist on quiet time and a bedtime that will afford their child adequate sleep. If this seems like a long list of worries, remember that the list of delights that the preschool years bring is far longer.

THE GROWING BODY

LO1 What is the state of children's bodies and overall health during the preschool years?

During the preschool years, children experience rapid advances in their physical abilities that are nothing short of astounding. Just how far they develop is apparent when we look at the changes they undergo in their size, shape, and physical abilities.

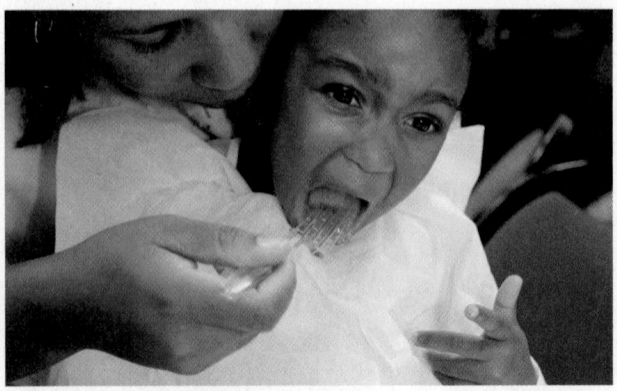

Encouraging children to eat more than they seem to want naturally may lead them to increase their food intake beyond an appropriate level.

By age 2, the average child in the United States weighs around 25 to 30 pounds and is close to 36 inches tall. By the time they are 6 years old, they weigh about 46 pounds and stand 46 inches tall (see Figure 4-1).

These averages mask significant individual differences. For instance, 10 percent of 6-year-olds weigh 55 pounds or more, and 10 percent weigh 36 pounds or less. Furthermore, average differences between boys and girls increase during the preschool years. Although at age 2 the differences are relatively small, during the preschool years boys start becoming taller and heavier, on average, than girls.

Economics also affects these averages. The better nutrition and health care typically received by children in developed countries translates into differences in growth. For instance, the average Swedish 4-year-old is as tall as the average 6-year-old in Bangladesh. Even within the United States, children in families with incomes below the poverty level are more likely to be short than children raised in more affluent homes (United Nations, 1991; Leathers & Foster, 2004; Petrou & Kupek, 2010).

Changes in Body Shape and Structure

The bodies of a 2-year-old and a 6-year-old vary not only in height and weight but also in shape. During the preschool years, boys and girls become less round and more slender. Moreover, their arms and legs lengthen, and the size relationship between the head and the rest of the body becomes more adultlike. In fact, by the time children reach age 6, their proportions are similar to those of adults.

Other physical changes occur internally. Muscle size increases, and children grow stronger. Bones become sturdier, and the sense organs continue to develop. For instance, the *eustachian tube* in the ear changes its orientation so radically that it may cause the earaches that are so typical of the preschool years.

Nutrition: Eating the Right Foods

Because the rate of growth is slower than during infancy, preschoolers need less food, which may cause parents to worry. However, children tend to be adept at eating enough if they are provided with nutritious meals. In fact, anxiously encouraging children to eat more than they want may lead to **obesity**, which is defined as a body weight more than 20 percent higher than the average weight for a person of a given age and height. The prevalence of obesity among older preschoolers has increased significantly over the last 20 years.

obesity body weight more than 20 percent higher than the average weight for a person of a given age and height

The best strategy for parents is to make sure that they make a variety of low-fat, high-nutrition foods available. Foods that have a relatively high iron content are particularly important: Iron-deficiency anemia, which causes constant fatigue, is one of the prevalent nutritional problems in developed countries such as the United States. High-iron foods include dark green vegetables (such as broccoli), whole grains, and some kinds of meat, such as lean hamburger. It is also important to avoid foods with high sodium content and to include foods with low fat content (Brotanek et al., 2007; Grant et al., 2007; Jalonick, 2011).

Within these bounds, children should be given the opportunity to develop their own preferences. Exposing children to new foods by encouraging them to take just one bite is a relatively low-stress way of expanding children's diets (Busick, 2008; Hamel & Robins, 2013).

From a health care worker's perspective: How might biology and environment combine to affect the physical growth of a child adopted as an infant from a developing country and reared in a more industrialized one?

Health and Illness

The average preschooler has 7 to 10 colds and other minor respiratory illnesses in each of the years from age 3 to 5. In the United States, a runny nose due to the common cold is the most frequent—and happily, the least severe—kind of health problem during the preschool years. In fact, the majority of children in the United States are reasonably healthy during this period (Kalb, 1997).

Although the sniffles and coughs that are the symptoms of such illnesses are certainly distressing to children, the unpleasantness is usually not too severe and the illnesses usually last only a few days.

The greatest risk that preschoolers face comes from neither illness nor nutritional problems but from accidents: Before the age of 10, children are twice as likely to die from an injury as from an illness. In fact, U.S. children have a one in three chance every year of receiving an injury that requires medical attention (National Safety Council, 1989; Field & Behrman, 2003; Granié, 2010).

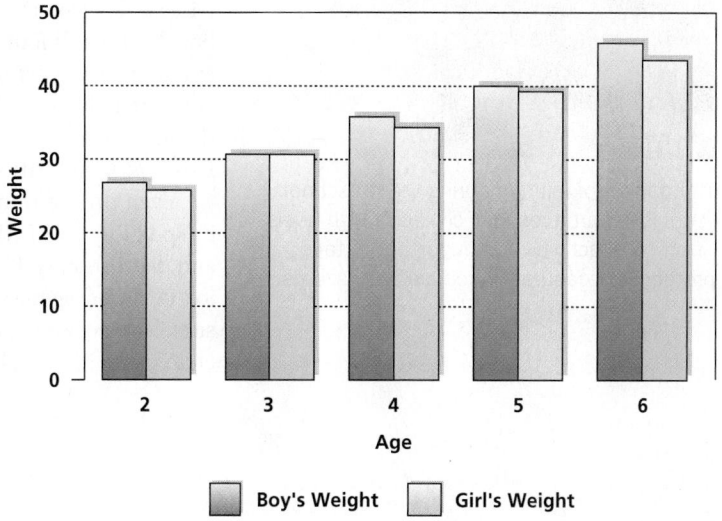

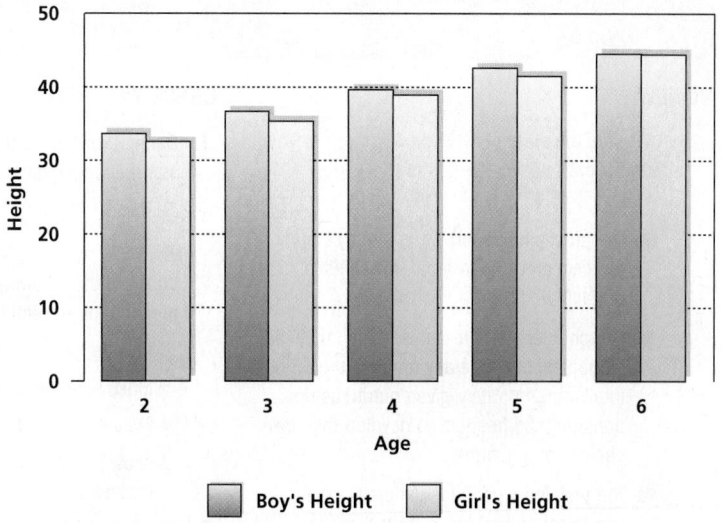

FIGURE 4-1 Gaining Height and Weight
The preschool years are marked by steady increases in height and weight. The figures show the median point for boys and girls at each age, in which 50 percent of children in each category are above this height or weight level and 50 percent are below.
Source: National Center for Health Statistics in collaboration with the National Center for Chronic Disease Prevention and Health Promotion, 2000.

The danger of injuries during the preschool years is in part a result of children's high levels of physical activity. It is important to take protective measures to reduce the hazards.

The danger of injuries during the preschool years is in part a result of high levels of physical activity. Combine the physical activity, curiosity, and lack of judgment that characterize this age group, and it is no wonder that preschoolers are accident prone.

Furthermore, some children are more apt than others to take risks and consequently to be injured. Boys, who typically are more active than girls and tend to take more risks, have a higher rate of injuries. Economic factors also play a role. Children raised under conditions of poverty in urban areas, whose inner-city neighborhoods may contain more hazards than more affluent areas, are two times more likely to die of injuries than children living in affluence (Morrongiello & Hogg, 2004; Morrongiello et al., 2006; Morrongiello, Klemencic, & Corbett, 2008).

Parents and caregivers can take precautions to prevent injuries, starting by "child-proofing" homes and classrooms with electrical outlet covers and child locks on cabinets. Car seats and bike helmets can help prevent injuries from accidents. Parents and teachers also need to be aware of the dangers from long-term hazards (Bull & Durbin, 2008; Morrongiello, Corbett, & Bellissimo, 2008; Morrongiello et al., 2009).

For example, lead poisoning is a significant danger for many children. Some 14 million children are at risk for lead poisoning due to exposure to lead, according to the Centers for Disease Control. Despite stringent legal restrictions on the amount of lead in paint and gasoline, lead is still found on painted walls and window frames—particularly in older homes—and in gasoline, ceramics, lead-soldered pipes, automobile and truck exhaust, and even dust and water. The U.S. Department of Health and Human Services has called lead poisoning the most severe health threat to children under age 6 (Hubbs-Tait et al., 2005; Fiedler, 2012; Dozor & Amler, 2013).

Even tiny amounts of lead can permanently harm children. Exposure to lead has been linked to lower intelligence, problems in verbal and auditory processing, and hyperactivity and distractibility. High lead levels have also been linked to higher levels of antisocial behavior, including aggression and delinquency in school-age children. At yet higher levels of exposure, lead poisoning results in illness and death (Kincl, Dietrich, & Bhattacharya, 2006; Nigg et al., 2008; Marcus, Fulton, & Clarke, 2010).

REVIEW, CHECK, AND APPLY

REVIEW

L01 What is the state of children's bodies and overall health during the preschool years?

- The preschool period is marked by steady physical growth and rapid advances in physical ability.
- Preschoolers tend to eat less than they did as babies, but generally regulate their food intake appropriately, given nutritious options and the freedom to develop their own choices and controls.
- The preschool period is generally the healthiest time of life, with only minor illnesses threatening children. Accidents and environmental hazards are the greatest threats.

CHECK YOURSELF

1. During the preschool years, boys on the average start becoming taller and heavier than girls.
   - True
   - False
2. Which of the following suggestions is NOT recommended for preventing obesity in children?
   - a Provide food that is high in nutritional value.
   - b Make sure meals are low in fat.
   - c Ensure a consistent diet with little variety.
   - d Allow children to develop their own food preferences.
3. Which of the following benefits was NOT included in the discussion of minor illnesses in preschoolers?
   - a Prevents the development of empathy
   - b Builds up immunities
   - c Permits children to understand their bodies
   - d Helps children develop coping skills

APPLYING LIFESPAN DEVELOPMENT

- What are some ways that increased understanding of issues relating to the physical development of preschoolers might help parents and caregivers in their care of children?
- Do you think the fact that preschool boys are more risk-prone than girls is genetic, environmental, or both? Why?

✓ **Study** and **Review** on **MyPsychLab.com**

THE GROWING BRAIN

L02 **How do preschool children's brains and physical skills develop?**

4.1
4.2
4.3

The brain grows at a faster rate than any other part of the body. Two-year-olds have brains that are about three-quarters the size and weight of an adult brain. By age 5, children's brains weigh 90 percent of average adult brain weight. In comparison, the average 5-year-old's total body weight is just 30 percent of average adult body weight (Lowrey, 1986; Nihart, 1993; House, 2007).

Why does the brain grow so rapidly? One reason is an increase in the number of interconnections among cells, which supports more complex communication between neurons and permits the rapid growth of cognitive skills. In addition, the amount of **myelin**—protective insulation that surrounds parts of neurons—increases, which speeds the transmission of electrical impulses along brain cells (Dalton & Bergenn, 2007).

myelin protective insulation that surrounds parts of neurons—which speeds the transmission of electrical impulses along brain cells but also adds to brain weight

lateralization the process in which certain cognitive functions are located more in one hemisphere of the brain than in the other

Brain Lateralization

By the end of the preschool period, the *corpus callosum*, a bundle of nerve fibers that connects the two hemispheres of the brain, becomes considerably thicker, developing as many as 800 million individual fibers that help coordinate brain functioning between the two hemispheres. At the same time, the two halves of the brain become increasingly differentiated and specialized. **Lateralization**, the process in which certain functions are located more in one hemisphere than the other, becomes more pronounced during the preschool years.

For most people, the left hemisphere is primarily involved with tasks that necessitate verbal competence, such as speaking, reading, thinking, and reasoning. The right hemisphere develops its own strengths, especially in nonverbal areas such as comprehension of spatial relationships, recognition of patterns and drawings, music, and emotional expression (Koivisto & Revonsuo, 2003; Pollak, Holt, & Wismer Fries, 2004; Watling & Bourne, 2007) (see Figure 4-2).

Each hemisphere also begins to process information in a slightly different manner. The left hemisphere processes data sequentially, one piece at a time. The right hemisphere processes information in a more global manner, reflecting on it as a whole (Ansaldo, Arguin, & Roch-Locours, 2002; Holowka & Petitto, 2002; Barber et al., 2012).

While there is some specialization, in most respects the two hemispheres act in tandem and are interdependent. In fact, each hemisphere can perform most of the tasks of the other. For example, the right hemisphere does some language processing and plays an important role in language comprehension (Corballis, 2003; Hutchinson, Whitman, & Abeare, 2003; Hall, Neal, & Dean, 2008).

There are also individual differences in lateralization. For example, many of the 10 percent of people who are left-handed or ambidextrous (able to use both hands interchangeably) have language centered in the right hemisphere or have no specific language center (Compton & Weissman, 2002; Isaacs et al., 2006; Szaflarski et al., 2012).

Even more intriguing are differences in lateralization related to gender. For instance, starting during the first year and continuing in the preschool years, boys and girls show some hemispheric differences associated with lower-body reflexes and the processing of auditory information. Boys also clearly tend to show greater lateralization of language in the left hemisphere; among females, language is more evenly divided between the hemispheres. Such differences may help explain why girls' language development proceeds more rapidly during the preschool years than boys' (Bourne & Todd, 2004; Castro-Schilo & Kee, 2010; Filippi et al., 2013).

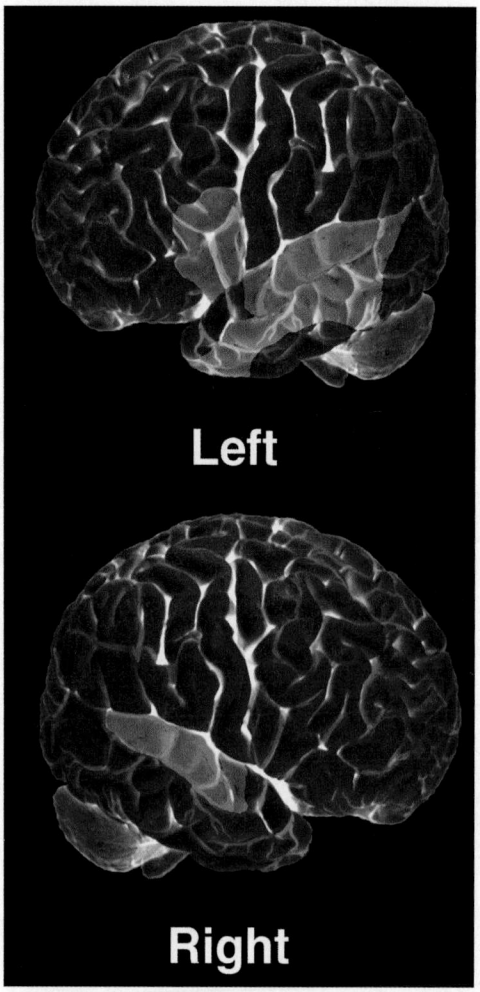

FIGURE 4-2 Looking Into the Brain
This series of PET brain scans illustrates that activity in the right or left hemisphere of the brain differs according to the task in which a person is engaged. How might educators use this finding in their approach to teaching?

The Links Between Brain Growth and Cognitive Development

Neuroscientists are beginning to understand the ways in which brain growth is related to cognitive development. While we do not yet know the direction of causality (Does brain development produce cognitive advances, or vice versa?), we can clearly see the relationship.

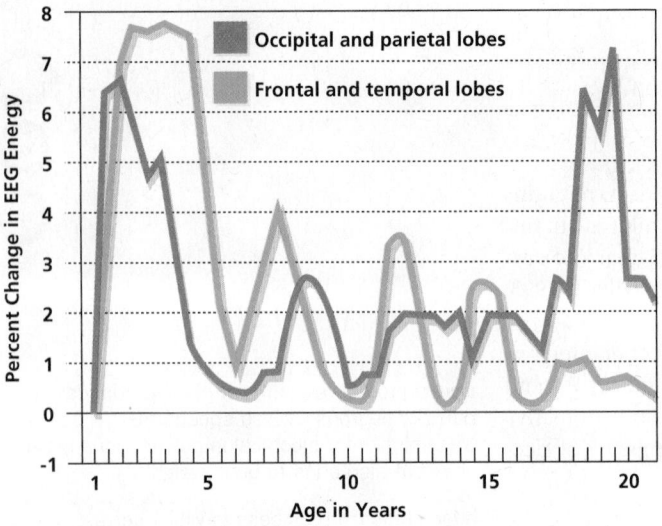

FIGURE 4-3 Brain Growth Spurt
According to one study, electrical activity in the brain has been linked to advances in cognitive abilities at various stages across the life span. In this graph, activity increases dramatically between 1½ and 2 years, a period during which language rapidly develops.
Source: Fischer, K. W., & Rose, S. P. (1995).

For example, there are periods during childhood when the brain shows unusual growth spurts, and these periods are linked to advances in cognitive abilities. One study that measured electrical activity in the brain found unusual spurts at between 1½ and 2 years, a time when language abilities increase rapidly. Other spurts occurred around other ages when cognitive advances are particularly intense (Mabbott et al., 2006; Westermann et al., 2007; Sadeghi et al., 2013) (see Figure 4-3).

Other research has suggested that the increases in myelin in the brain (discussed earlier) may be related to preschoolers' growing cognitive capabilities. For example, myelination of the *reticular formation*, an area of the brain associated with attention and concentration, is completed by the time children are about 5 years old. This may be associated with children's growing attention spans, as they approach school age. The improvement in memory that occurs during the preschool years may also be associated with myelination: During the preschool years, myelination is completed in the hippocampus, an area associated with memory (Rolls, 2000).

In addition, there is significant growth in the nerves connecting the *cerebellum*, a part of the brain that controls balance and movement, to the *cerebral cortex*, the structure responsible for sophisticated information processing. The growth in these nerve fibers is related to the significant advances in motor skills and cognitive processing during the preschool years (Carson, 2006; Gordon, 2007).

REVIEW, CHECK, AND APPLY

REVIEW

L02 How do preschool children's brains and physical skills develop?

- In addition to physical growth, the preschool period is marked by rapid brain growth. The increase in myelin in the brain is particularly important for intellectual development.
- Among other changes, the brain develops lateralization, a tendency of the two hemispheres to adopt specialized tasks.

CHECK YOURSELF

1. During the preschool years, the two halves of the brain become more specialized in a process called _____.
   a homogeneity
   b myelination
   c brain fusion
   d lateralization

2. Language differences between male and female brains may not be just the product of genetics, but also the environment. For example, females may have better language skills because_____.
   a their brains are different in size
   b males are not equipped to learn language at the same pace as are females
   c they listen to language more intently when in the womb
   d they receive more encouragement for verbal skills than do males

APPLYING LIFESPAN DEVELOPMENT

- Does brain growth cause cognitive development, or does cognitive development cause the brain to grow? Pick a side in this endless argument and defend it.
- What do you imagine thinking, planning, and reflection might be like if the two hemispheres of the brain could not communicate with each other (as is the case in some individuals with severe head injuries)?

✓ **Study** and **Review** on **MyPsychLab.com**

MOTOR DEVELOPMENT

L03 How does motor development evolve in preschool children?

Anya sat in the sandbox at the park, chatting with the other parents and playing with her two children, 5-year-old Nicholai and 13-month-old Smetna. While she chatted, she kept a close eye on Smetna, who would still put sand in her mouth sometimes if she wasn't stopped. Today, however, Smetna seemed content to run the sand through her hands and try to put it into a bucket.

Nicholai, meanwhile, was busy with two other boys, rapidly filling and emptying the other sand buckets to build an elaborate sand city, which they would then destroy with toy trucks.

4.1
4.2
4.3

When children of different ages gather at a playground, it's easy to see that preschool children have come a long way in their motor development. Both their gross and fine motor skills have become increasingly fine-tuned. Smetna, for example, is still mastering putting sand into a bucket, while her older brother Nicholai uses that skill easily as part of his larger goal of building a sand city.

Gross Motor Skills

By the time they are 3 years old, children have mastered a variety of skills: jumping, hopping on one foot, skipping, and running. By age 4 and 5, their skills have become more refined as they have gained increasing control over their muscles. For instance, at age 4 they can throw a ball with enough accuracy that a friend can catch it, and by age 5 they can toss a ring and have it land on a peg 5 feet away. Five-year-olds can learn to ride bikes, climb ladders, and ski downhill—activities that all require considerable coordination (Clark & Humphrey, 1985). (Figure 4–4 summarizes major gross motor skills that emerge during the preschool years.)

These achievements may be related to brain development and myelination of neurons in areas of the brain related to balance and coordination. Another likely reason is that children spend a great deal of time practicing these skills. During this period, the general level of activity is extraordinarily high. In fact, the activity level is higher at age 3 than at any other point in the entire life span (Eaton & Yu, 1989; Poest et al., 1990).

Girls and boys differ in certain aspects of gross motor coordination, in part because of differences in muscle strength, which is usually somewhat greater in boys than in girls. For instance, boys can typically throw a ball better and jump higher, and a boy's overall activity level tends to be greater than a girl's (Eaton & Yu, 1989). On the other hand, girls generally surpass boys in tasks that involve limb coordination. For instance, at age 5, girls are better than boys at jumping jacks and balancing on one foot (Cratty, 1979).

Another aspect of muscular skills—one that parents often find most problematic—is bowel and bladder control.

Age 3

Able to walk up stairs, alternating feet

Unable to stop or turn suddenly

Able to jump a length of 15–24 inches

Age 4

Able to walk down a long staircase, alternating feet, with assistance

Have some control in starting, stopping, and turning

Length of jump increases to 24–33 inches

Age 5

Able to walk down a long staircase, alternating feet

Capable of starting, stopping, and turning in games

Able to make a running jump of 28–36 inches

FIGURE 4-4 Significant Gross Motor Skills in Early Childhood

During the preschool years, children grow in both fine and gross motor skills.

The Potty Question: When—and How—Should Children Be Toilet Trained?

Few child-care issues raise so much concern among parents as toilet training. Current guidelines of the American Academy of Pediatrics suggest that there is no single time to begin toilet training and that training should begin only when children are ready (American Academy of Pediatrics, 2009; Lundblad, Hellström, & Berg, 2010).

When are children "ready"? The signs of readiness include staying dry at least 2 hours at a time during the day or waking up dry after naps; regular and predictable bowel movements; an indication, through facial expressions or words, that urination or a bowel movement is about to occur; the ability to follow simple directions; the ability to get to the bathroom and undress alone; discomfort with soiled diapers; asking to use the toilet or potty chair; and the desire to wear underwear.

Furthermore, children must be ready not only physically, but emotionally, and if they show strong signs of resistance to toilet training, toilet training should be put off. Similarly, it may be reasonable to delay toilet training if there is a major change in the home environment, such as the birth of a new baby or a major illness. Although some children show signs of readiness for toilet training between 18 and 24 months, some are not ready until 30 months or older (American Academy of Pediatrics, 2003; Fritz & Rockney, 2004; Connell-Carrick, 2006).

Partially in response to the American Academy of Pediatrics guidelines, toilet training has begun later over the last few decades. For example, in 1957, 92 percent of children were toilet trained by 18 months. In 1999, only 25 percent were toilet trained at that age, and just 60 percent of 36-month-olds were toilet trained. Some 2 percent were still not toilet trained at the age of 4 (Goode, 1999).

Fine Motor Skills

At the same time, children are progressing in their ability to use fine motor skills, which involve more delicate, smaller body movements such as using a fork and spoon, cutting with scissors, tying shoelaces, and playing the piano.

The skills involved in fine motor movements require practice. The emergence of fine motor skills shows clear developmental patterns. At age 3, children can draw a circle and square with a crayon, and they can undo their clothes when they go to the bathroom. They can put a simple jigsaw puzzle together, and they can fit blocks of different shapes into matching holes. However, they do not show much precision and polish in these tasks, often, for example, forcing puzzle pieces into place.

Becoming an Informed Consumer of Development

Keeping Preschoolers Healthy

There is no way around it: Even the healthiest preschooler occasionally gets sick. Social interaction with others ensures that illnesses will be passed from one child to another. However, some diseases are preventable, and others can be minimized if simple precautions are taken:

- Preschoolers should eat a well-balanced diet containing the proper nutrients, particularly foods containing sufficient protein. Keep offering healthy foods; even if children initially reject them, they may grow to like them.
- Encourage preschoolers to exercise.
- Children should get as much sleep as they wish. Being fatigued makes children more susceptible to illness.
- Children should avoid contact with others who are ill. If they play with kids who are sick, parents should make sure they wash their hands thoroughly.
- Be sure that children follow an appropriate schedule of immunizations. Despite the beliefs of some parents, there is no scientific basis for believing that common vaccinations should be avoided because they can increase the risk of autism spectrum disorder. *Children should receive the recommended vaccinations, according to the American Academy of Pediatrics and U.S. Centers of Disease Control and Prevention*, unless otherwise told not to by a reputable medical professional (Daley & Glanz, 2011).
- Finally, if a child does get ill, remember this: Minor illnesses during childhood sometimes provide immunity to more serious illnesses later on.

By age 4, their fine motor skills are better. They can draw a person that looks like a person, and they can fold paper into triangular designs. And by the time they are 5, they can hold and manipulate a thin pencil properly. **Watch** the **Video** *The Growing Child* in **MyPsychLab.**

Handedness. How do preschoolers decide which hand to hold the pencil in as they work on their fine motor skills? For many, their choice was made soon after birth.

Beginning in early infancy, many children show signs of a preference for the use of one hand over the other—the development of **handedness**. By 7 months, some infants seem to favor one hand by grabbing more with it (Segalowitz & Rapin, 2003; Marschik et al., 2008; Morange-Majoux, Lemoine, & Dellatolas, 2013). Most children display a clear tendency by the end of the preschool years. Some 90 percent are right-handed and 10 percent are left-handed, and more boys than girls are left-handed.

handedness the preference of using one hand over another

REVIEW, CHECK, AND APPLY

REVIEW

LO3 How does motor development evolve in preschool children?

- Gross and fine motor developments advance rapidly during the preschool years.
- Boys' and girls' gross motor skills begin to diverge, with boys typically doing better at tasks requiring strength and girls doing better at tasks requiring coordination.
- Also during this period, children develop handedness—a decided preference for one hand over the other.

CHECK YOURSELF

1. During the preschool years, there is significant pruning in the nerves connecting the cerebellum, the part of the brain that controls balance and movement to the cerebral cortex, the structure responsible for sophisticated information processing.
   - True
   - False
2. In addition to changes in myelination, another reason that motor skills develop so rapidly during the preschool years is because children spend a great deal of time_____.
   - a using mental imagery
   - b practicing them
   - c observing adults performing the same behaviors
   - d sleeping

APPLYING LIFESPAN DEVELOPMENT

- To what extent do you think that gender differences in the development of gross motor skills are genetic versus environmental?
- If it could be shown that left-handers had a greater likelihood to be gifted than right-handers, would it make sense to train children to use their left hands for everyday tasks? Why?

Study and **Review** on **MyPsychLab.com**

MODULE 4.2

COGNITIVE DEVELOPMENT IN THE PRESCHOOL YEARS

Jesse and The Three Bears

Three-year-old Jesse is acting out his favorite story—The Three Bears. From the next room, his mother hears him playing each of the characters. "Someone's been eating my porridge," Jesse growls in a deep Papa Bear voice. "Someone's been sitting in my chair," he says moments later in the exact tones of his mother. Jesse then uses his own voice for Baby Bear. "Someone's been sleeping in my bed, and she's still here!" This is followed by the high-pitched squealing his mother knows is Jesse's Goldilocks waking to see the Three Bears.

In some ways, the intellectual sophistication of 3-year-olds is astounding. Their creativity and imagination leap to new heights; their language is increasingly sophisticated; and they reason and think about the world in ways that would have been impossible even a few months earlier. But what underlies the dramatic advances in intellectual development of the preschool years? In this module, we will consider a number of approaches to understanding children's thinking and the development of cognitive abilities in the preschool years.

During the preoperational period children begin to imagine the future.

PIAGET'S APPROACH TO COGNITIVE DEVELOPMENT

LO4 How does Piaget interpret cognitive development during the preschool years?

LO5 How does Piaget's approach stand up to the test of time?

Piaget's Stage of Preoperational Thinking

Jean Piaget, whose stage approach to cognitive development we discussed in Module 3.2, saw the preschool years as a time of both stability and change. He placed the preschool years into a single stage of cognitive development—the preoperational stage—which lasts from age 2 until around age 7.

During the **preoperational stage**, children's use of symbolic thinking grows, mental reasoning emerges, and the use of concepts increases. Seeing Mom's car keys may prompt a question, "Go to store?" as the child comes to see the keys as a symbol of a car ride. In this way, children become better at representing events internally and less dependent on sensorimotor activity to understand the world around them. Yet they are still not capable of **operations**: organized, formal, logical mental processes.

According to Piaget, a key aspect of preoperational thought is *symbolic function*, the ability to use a mental symbol, a word, or an object to stand for or represent something that is not physically present. For example, preschoolers can use a mental symbol for a car (the word *car*), and they understand that a small toy car is representative of the real thing. They have no need to get behind the wheel of an actual car to understand its basic purpose and use.

The Relation Between Language and Thought. Symbolic function is at the heart of one of the major advances of the preoperational period: the increasingly sophisticated use of language. Piaget suggests that the advances in language during the preschool years reflect improvements over the type of thinking that is possible during the earlier sensorimotor period. Instead of slow, sensorimotor-based thinking, symbolic thought, which relies on improved linguistic ability, allows preschoolers to represent actions virtually, at much greater speed.

Even more important, language allows children to think beyond the present to the future. Rather than being grounded in the here-and-now, preschoolers can imagine future possibilities through language in the form of fantasies and daydreams.

Centration: What You See Is What You Think. Place a dog mask on a cat and what do you get? According to 3- and 4-year-old preschoolers, a dog. To them, a cat with a dog mask ought to bark like a dog, wag its tail like a dog, and eat dog food. In every respect, the cat has been transformed into a dog (deVries, 1969).

To Piaget, the root of this belief is centration, a key element, and limitation, of thinking in the preoperational period. **Centration** is the process of concentrating on one limited aspect of a stimulus—typically its superficial elements—and ignoring others. These elements come to dominate preschoolers' thinking, leading to inaccuracy.

Centration is the cause of the error illustrated in Figure 4-5. Asked which row contains more buttons, children who are 4 or 5 usually choose the row that looks longer, rather than the one that actually contains more buttons. This occurs even though children this age know quite well that 10 is more than 8. Rather than taking into account their understanding of quantity, they focus on appearance.

Preschoolers' focus on appearances might be related to another aspect of preoperational thought, the lack of conservation.

Conservation: Learning That Appearances Are Deceiving. Consider the following scenario:

Four-year-old Jaime is shown two drinking glasses. One is short and broad; the other, tall and thin. A teacher half-fills the short, broad glass with apple juice. The teacher then pours the juice

preoperational stage according to Piaget, the stage from approximately age 2 to age 7 in which children's use of symbolic thinking grows, mental reasoning emerges, and the use of concepts increases

operations organized, formal, logical mental processes

centration the process of concentrating on one limited aspect of a stimulus and ignoring other aspects

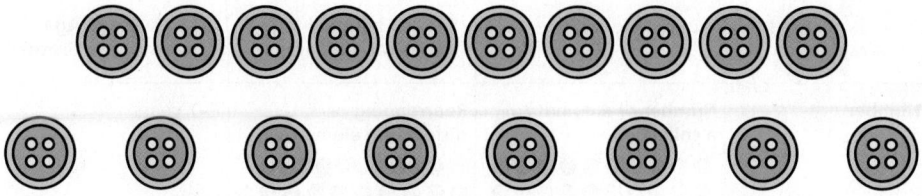

FIGURE 4-5 Which Row Contains More Buttons?
When preschoolers are shown these two rows and asked which row has more buttons, they usually respond that the lower row of buttons contains more, because it looks longer. They answer in this way even though they know quite well that 10 is greater than 8. Do you think preschoolers can be *taught* to answer correctly?

into the tall, thin glass. The juice fills the tall glass almost to the brim. The teacher asks Jaime a question: Is there more juice in the second glass than there was in the first?

If you view this as an easy task, so do children like Jaime. The problem is that they almost always get it wrong.

Most 4-year-olds say that there is more apple juice in the tall, thin glass than there was in the short, broad one. In fact, if the juice is poured back into the shorter glass, they are quick to say that there is now less juice than there was in the taller glass.

The reason is that children of this age have not mastered conservation. **Conservation** is the knowledge that quantity is unrelated to the arrangement and physical appearance of objects. Some other conservation tasks are shown in Figure 4-6 on page 162.

Why do children in the preoperational stage make conservation errors? Piaget suggests that the main reason is that their tendency toward centration prevents them from focusing on the relevant features of the situation. Furthermore, they cannot follow the sequence of transformations that accompanies changes in the appearance of a situation. **Watch** the **Video** *Conservation Tasks* in **MyPsychLab**.

Incomplete Understanding of Transformation. A preoperational, preschool child who sees several worms during a walk in the woods may believe that they are all the same worm. The reason: She views each sighting in isolation, unable to understand that a transformation would be necessary for a worm to move quickly from one location to the next.

As Piaget used the term, **transformation** is the process in which one state is changed into another. For instance, adults know that if a pencil that is held upright is allowed to fall down, it passes through a series of successive stages until it reaches its final, horizontal resting spot. In contrast, children in the preoperational period are unable to envision or recall the successive transformations that the pencil followed in moving from the upright to the horizontal position.

Egocentrism: The Inability to Take Others' Perspectives. Another hallmark of the preoperational period is egocentric thinking. **Egocentric thought** is thinking that does not take into account the viewpoints of others. Preschoolers do not understand that others have different perspectives. Egocentric thought takes two forms: lack of awareness that others see things from a different physical perspective and failure to realize that others may hold thoughts, feelings, and points of view that differ from theirs. (Note that egocentric thought does *not* imply intentional selfishness or a lack of consideration.) **Watch** the **Video** *The Preschool Years: Egocentrism* in **MyPsychLab**.

Egocentric thinking lies behind children's lack of concern over their nonverbal behavior and the impact it has on others. For instance, a 4-year-old who receives a gift of socks may frown as he opens the package, unaware that his face can be seen by others and reveals his true feelings (Feldman, 1992).

Egocentrism largely explains why many preschoolers talk to themselves, even in the presence of others, and often ignore what others are telling them. This behavior illustrates

conservation the knowledge that quantity is unrelated to the arrangement and physical appearance of objects

transformation the process in which one state is changed into another

egocentric thought thinking that does not take into account the viewpoints of others

Type of Conservation	Modality	Change in Physical Appearance	Average Age Invariance Is Grasped
Number	Number of elements in a collection	Rearranging or dislocating elements	6–7 years
Substance (mass)	Amount of a malleable substance (e.g., clay or liquid)	Altering shape	7–8 years
Length	Length of a line or object	Altering shape or configuration	7–8 years
Area	Amount of surface covered by a set of plane figures	Rearranging the figures	8–9 years
Weight	Weight of an object	Altering shape	9–10 years
Volume	Volume of an object (in terms of water displacement)	Altering shape	14–15 years

FIGURE 4-6 Common Tests of Children's Understanding of the Principle of Conservation
Why is a sense of conservation important?

the egocentric nature of preoperational children's thinking: the lack of awareness that their behavior acts as a trigger to others' reactions and responses. Consequently, much of preschoolers' verbal behavior has no social motivation but is meant purely for their own consumption.

Similarly, egocentrism can also be seen in hiding games. In hide-and-seek, 3-year-olds may "hide" by covering their faces with a pillow—even though they remain in plain view. Their reasoning: If they cannot see others, others cannot see them. They assume that everyone else shares their view.

The Emergence of Intuitive Thought. Because Piaget labeled this the "*pre*operational period" and focused on cognitive deficiencies, it is easy to assume that preschoolers are marking time, but the period is far from idle. Cognitive development proceeds steadily, and new abilities emerge, including intuitive thought.

intuitive thought thinking that reflects preschoolers' use of primitive reasoning and their avid acquisition of knowledge about the world

Intuitive thought refers to preschoolers' use of primitive reasoning and their avid acquisition of world knowledge. From about age 4 through 7, curiosity blossoms. Children ask

"Why?" questions about nearly everything. At the same time, they may act as if they are authorities on particular topics, certain that they have the final word on an issue. Their intuitive thought leads them to believe that they know answers to all kinds of questions, with little or no logical basis for this confidence.

In the late stages of the preoperational period, children's intuitive thinking prepares them for more sophisticated reasoning. For instance, preschoolers come to understand that pushing harder on the pedals makes a bicycle move faster, or that pressing a button on a remote control makes the television change channels. By the end of the preoperational stage, preschoolers begin to grasp *functionality*, the idea that actions, events, and outcomes are related to one another in fixed patterns. They also become aware of *identity*, the understanding that certain things stay the same, regardless of changes in shape, size, and appearance—for instance, that a lump of clay contains the same amount of clay whether it is clumped into a ball or stretched out like a snake. Comprehension of identity is necessary for children to develop an understanding of conservation (the understanding, as we discussed earlier, that quantity is not related to physical appearances). Piaget regarded the development of conservation as the transition from the preoperational period to the next stage, concrete operations, which we will discuss in Chapter 5.

Evaluating Piaget's Approach to Cognitive Development. Piaget, a masterly observer of children's behavior, provided a detailed portrait of preschoolers' cognitive abilities. The broad outlines of his approach have given us a useful way of thinking about the progressive advances in cognitive ability during the preschool years (Siegal, 1997).

However, it is important to consider Piaget's approach to cognitive development within the appropriate historical context and in light of more recent research findings. As we discussed earlier, his theory is based on extensive observations of relatively few children. Despite his insightful and groundbreaking observations, recent experimental investigations suggest that in certain regards, Piaget underestimated children's capabilities.

Take, for instance, Piaget's views of how children in the preoperational period understand numbers. He contended that preschoolers' thinking is seriously handicapped, as evidenced by their performance on tasks involving conservation and reversibility, the understanding that a transformation can be reversed to return something to its original state. Yet more recent experimental work suggests otherwise. For instance, children as young as 3 can easily tell the difference between rows of two and three toy animals, regardless of the animals' spacing. Older children are able to note differences in number, performing tasks such as identifying which of two numbers is larger and indicating that they understand some rudiments of addition and subtraction problems (Izard et al., 2009; Brandone et al., 2012; Odic et al., 2013).

Gelman concludes that children have an innate ability to count, akin to the ability to use language that some theorists see as universal and genetically determined. This is clearly at odds with Piagetian notions, which suggest that children's numerical abilities do not blossom until after the preoperational period.

Some developmentalists (particularly those who favor the information processing approach) also believe that cognitive skills develop in a more continuous manner than Piaget's theory implies. They believe that rather than thought changing in quality, as Piaget argues, the changes in thinking ability are more quantitative, improving gradually (Gelman & Baillargeon, 1983; Case, 1991).

There are further difficulties with Piaget's view. His contention that conservation does not emerge until the end of the preoperational period has not stood up to experimental scrutiny. Children can learn to answer correctly on conservation tasks if they are given certain training and experiences. The fact that one can improve children's performance argues against the Piagetian view that children in the preoperational period have not reached a level of cognitive maturity to understand conservation (Ping & Goldin-Meadow, 2008).

In sum, Piaget tended to concentrate on preschoolers' *deficiencies* in logical thought. By focusing more on children's competence, recent theorists have found evidence for a surprising degree of capability in preschoolers.

REVIEW, CHECK, AND APPLY

REVIEW

L04 How does Piaget interpret cognitive development during the preschool years?

- According to Piaget, children in the preoperational stage develop symbolic function, a change in their thinking that is the foundation of further cognitive advances.
- Preoperational children are hampered by a tendency toward egocentric thought.

L05 How does Piaget's approach stand up to the test of time?

- Recent developmentalists, while acknowledging Piaget's gifts and contributions, take issue with his underestimation of preschoolers' capabilities.

CHECK YOURSELF

1. Children in Piaget's preoperational stage begin using symbolic thinking; however, they are not capable of _____, or organized, logical mental processes that characterize schoolchildren.
   - a operations
   - b transcendence
   - c levitation
   - d egocentric thought
2. Egocentric thought can involve (1) the lack of awareness that others see things from a different physical perspective and (2) _____.
   - a the inability to present their own perspectives to others
   - b their unwillingness to consider how their perspectives have been consistent over time
   - c failure to realize that others may hold thoughts, feelings, and points of view that differ from theirs
   - d that preoperational children are intentionally selfish and inconsiderate
3. Piaget's perspective has been criticized by others because he overestimated children's abilities.
   - True
   - False

APPLYING LIFESPAN DEVELOPMENT

- Do you think it is possible to break a preschooler's habit of egocentric thought by directly teaching him to take another person's point of view? Would showing him a picture of himself "hidden" behind a chair change his thinking? Why?

✓ **Study** and **Review** on **MyPsychLab.com**

INFORMATION PROCESSING AND VYGOTSKY'S APPROACH TO COGNITIVE DEVELOPMENT

L06 How do other views of cognitive development differ from Piaget's?
L07 What separates Vygotsky's approach from Piaget's?

Even as an adult, Paco has clear recollections of his first trip to a farm, which he took when he was 3 years old. He was visiting his godfather, who lived in Puerto Rico, and the two of them went to a nearby farm. Paco recounts seeing what seemed like hundreds of chickens, and he clearly recalls his fear of the pigs, who seemed huge, smelly, and frightening. Most of all, he recalls the thrill of riding on a horse with his godfather.

This preschooler may recall this ride in 6 months, but by the time he is 12, it will probably be forgotten. Can you explain why?

The fact that Paco has a clear memory of his farm trip is not surprising: Most people have unambiguous, and seemingly accurate, memories dating as far back as age 3. But are the processes used to form memories at that age similar to those that operate later in life? More broadly, what general changes in the processing of information occur during the preschool years?

Information processing approaches focus on changes in the kinds of "mental programs" that children use when approaching problems. They compare the changes in children's cognitive abilities during the preschool years to the way a computer program becomes more sophisticated as a programmer modifies it based on experience. For many child developmentalists, information processing approaches represent the dominant, most comprehensive, and most accurate explanation of how children develop cognitively (Siegler, 1994; Lacerda, von Hofsten, & Heimann, 2001).

We'll focus on two areas that highlight the approach taken by information processing theorists: understanding of numbers and memory development.

Preschoolers' Understanding of Numbers. As we saw earlier, preschoolers have a greater understanding of numbers than Piaget thought. Researchers using information processing approaches have found increasing evidence for the sophistication of preschoolers' numerical understanding. The average preschooler is not only able to count, but to do so in a fairly systematic, consistent manner (Siegler, 1998).

For instance, developmental psychologist Rochel Gelman suggests that preschoolers follow set principles in their counting. Shown a group of items, they know they should assign just one number to each item and count each item only once. Moreover, even when they get the *names* of numbers wrong, they are consistent in their usage. For instance, a 4-year-old who counts three items as "1, 3, 7" will say "1, 3, 7" when counting another group of different items. And if asked, she will probably say that there are seven items in the group (Gelman, 2006; Gallistel, 2007; Le Corre & Carey, 2007).

By the age of 4, most children are able to carry out simple addition and subtraction problems by counting, and they are able to compare different quantities quite successfully (Donlan, 1998; Gilmore & Spelke, 2008).

Memory: Recalling the Past. Think back to your own earliest memory. If you are like Paco, described earlier, and most other people too, it probably is of an event that occurred after age 3. **Autobiographical memory**, memory of particular events from one's own life, achieves little accuracy until then and increases gradually throughout the preschool years. The accuracy of preschoolers' memories is partly determined by when the memories are assessed. Not all autobiographical memories last into later life. For instance, a child may remember the first day of kindergarten 6 months or a year later, but later in life might not remember it at all. Further, unless an event is particularly vivid or meaningful, it is not likely to be remembered at all (Nelson & Fivush, 2004; Wang, 2008; Morris, Baker-Ward, & Bauer, 2010).

Preschoolers' autobiographical memories not only fade, but may not be wholly accurate. For example, if an event happens often, it may be hard to remember one specific time it happened. Preschoolers' memories of familiar events are often organized into **scripts**, broad representations in memory of events and the order in which they occur. For example, a young preschooler might represent eating in a restaurant in terms of a few steps: talking to a server, getting the food, and eating. With age, the scripts become more elaborate: getting in the car, being seated at the restaurant, choosing food, ordering, waiting for the meal to come, eating, ordering dessert, and paying for the food. Particular instances of such scripted events are recalled with less accuracy than events that are unscripted (Fivush, Kuebli, & Clubb, 1992; Sutherland, Pipe, & Schick, 2003).

Preschoolers' memories are also susceptible to suggestion. This is a special concern when children testify in legal situations, such as when abuse is suspected.

Children's Eyewitness Testimony: Memory on Trial

I saw the crayons. They were all the colors of the rainbow. And gold, too. I was wanting to color with them all day. But then a big man, a giant, came and he stole all the crayons. It happened while we were napping.

Despite the detailed account by this 4-year-old boy of his witnessing the theft of a carton of crayons, there's a problem: The incident didn't happen this way. The memory is entirely false.

The 4-year-old's explicit recounting of a theft that had not actually occurred evolved over a week of questioning about a classroom incident. A sealed carton of crayons disappeared. The children were questioned but none of them knew the carton contained crayons or where it went. The boy quoted above then overheard the teacher tell the principal that the last time she'd seen the crayons was just before nap time. Several days later, she read a fairy tale in class, "Jack and the Beanstalk," which featured a giant. These details became part of his narrative.

This incident has implications for research in a new and rapidly growing field: forensic developmental psychology.

Forensic developmental psychology focuses on the reliability of children's autobiographical memories in the context of the legal system, when they may be witnesses or victims (Bruck & Ceci, 2004; Goodman, 2006).

Children's memories are susceptible to the suggestions of adults asking them questions. This is particularly true of preschoolers, who are considerably more vulnerable to suggestion than either adults or school-age children. The error rate is heightened when the same

Forensic developmental psychologists focus on the reliability of children's memories in a legal context.

autobiographical memory memories about one's own life.

scripts broad representations in memory of events and the order in which they occur question is asked repeatedly. False memories—of the "stolen crayon " type just reported—in fact may be more persistent than actual memories. In addition, when questions are highly suggestive (i.e., when questioners attempt to lead a person to particular conclusions), children are more apt to make mistakes (Goodman & Quas, 2008; Lowenstein, Blank, & Sauer, 2010; Stolzenberg & Pezdek, 2013).

Information Processing in Perspective. According to information processing approaches, cognitive development consists of gradual improvements in the ways people perceive, understand, and remember information. With age and practice, preschoolers process information more efficiently and with greater sophistication, and they are able to handle increasingly complex problems. In this view, it is these quantitative advances in information processing—and not the qualitative changes suggested by Piaget—that constitute cognitive development (Goswami, 1998; Zhe & Siegler, 2000; Rose, Feldman, & Jankowski, 2009).

For supporters of information processing, the reliance on well-defined processes that can be tested by research is one of the perspective's most important features. Rather than relying on somewhat vague concepts, such as Piaget's notions of assimilation and accommodation, information processing approaches provide a comprehensive, logical set of concepts.

For instance, as preschoolers grow older, they have longer attention spans, can monitor and plan what they are attending to more effectively, and become increasingly aware of their cognitive limitations. This places some of Piaget's findings in a different light. For instance, increased attention allows older children—as distinct from preschoolers—to attend to both the height *and* width of tall and short glasses and to understand that the amount of liquid in the glasses stays the same when it is poured back and forth—that is, to grasp conservation (Miller & Seier, 1994; Hudson, Sosa, & Shapiro, 1997).

Yet information processing approaches have their detractors. One important criticism is that information processing approaches "lose the forest for the trees" by paying so much attention to the detailed, individual sequence of mental processes that they never adequately paint a comprehensive picture of cognitive development—which Piaget clearly did quite well.

Information processing approaches have been highly influential over the past several decades. They have inspired a tremendous amount of research that has helped us gain some insights into how children develop cognitively.

Russian developmental psychologist Lev Vygotsky proposed that the focus of cognitive development should be on a child's social and cultural world, as opposed to the Piagetian approach concentrating on individual performance.

Vygotsky's View of Cognitive Development: Taking Culture into Account

As her daughter watches, a member of the Chilcotin Indian tribe prepares a salmon for dinner. When the daughter asks a question about a small detail of the process, the mother takes out another salmon and repeats the entire process. According to the tribal view of learning, understanding and comprehension can come only from grasping the total procedure, and not from learning about the individual subcomponents of the task (Tharp, 1989).

The Chilcotin view of how children learn about the world contrasts with the prevalent view of Western society, which assumes that only by mastering the separate parts of a problem can one fully comprehend it. Do differences in the ways particular cultures and societies approach problems influence cognitive development? According to Russian developmental psychologist Lev Vygotsky, who lived from 1896 to 1934, the answer is a clear yes.

Vygotsky viewed cognitive development as the product of social interactions. Instead of concentrating on individual performance, Vygotsky's increasingly influential view focuses on the social aspects of development and learning.

Vygotsky saw children as apprentices, learning cognitive strategies and other skills from adult and peer mentors who not only present new ways of doing things, but also provide assistance, instruction, and motivation. Consequently, he focused on the child's social and cultural world as the source of cognitive development. According to Vygotsky, children gradually grow intellectually and begin to function on their own because of the assistance that adult and peer partners provide (Vygotsky, 1979, 1926/1997; Tudge & Scrimsher, 2003).

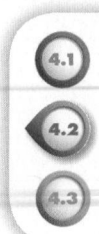

Vygotsky contends that culture and society establish the institutions, such as preschools and play groups, that promote development by providing opportunities for cognitive growth. Furthermore, by emphasizing particular tasks, culture and society shape the nature of specific cognitive advances. Unless we look at what is important and meaningful to members of a given society, we may seriously underestimate the nature and level of cognitive abilities that ultimately will be attained. For example, children's toys reflect what is important and meaningful in a particular society. In Western societies, preschoolers commonly play with toy wagons, automobiles, and other vehicles, in part reflecting the mobile nature of the culture (Tappan, 1997; Schaller & Crandall, 2004; Balakrishnan & Claiborne, 2012).

Vygotsky's approach is therefore quite different from Piaget's. Where Piaget looked at children and saw junior scientists, working by themselves to develop an independent understanding of the world, Vygotsky saw cognitive apprentices, learning from master teachers the skills valued in the child's culture (Fernyhough, 1997; Mahn & John-Steiner, 2013).

The Zone of Proximal Development and Scaffolding: Foundations of Cognitive Development. Vygotsky proposed that children's cognitive abilities increase through exposure to information that is new enough to be intriguing, but not too difficult to contend with. He called this the **zone of proximal development (ZPD)**, the level at which a child can *almost*, but not fully, perform a task independently, but can do so with the assistance of someone more competent. For cognitive development to occur, new information must be presented—by parents, teachers, or more skilled peers—within the zone of proximal development. For example, a preschooler might not be able to figure out by herself how to stick a handle on the clay pot she's making, but she can do it with advice from her child-care teacher (Zuckerman & Shenfield, 2007; Norton & D'Ambrosio, 2008; Zhang, 2010).

The concept of the zone of proximal development suggests that even though two children might be able to achieve the same amount without help, if one child receives aid, he or she may improve substantially more than the other. The greater the improvement that comes with help, the larger the zone of proximal development.

The assistance or structuring provided by others has been termed *scaffolding* after the temporary scaffolds that aid in building construction. **Scaffolding** is the support for learning and problem solving that encourages independence and growth (Puntambekar & Hübscher, 2005; Blewitt et al., 2009). As in construction, the scaffolding that older people provide, which facilitates the completion of identified tasks, is removed once children can solve a problem on their own (Taynieoeaym & Ruffman, 2008; Ankrum, Genest & Belcastro, 2013).

To Vygotsky, scaffolding not only helps children solve specific problems, it also aids in the development of their overall cognitive abilities. In education, scaffolding involves, first of all, helping children think about and frame a task appropriately. In addition, a parent or teacher is likely to provide clues to task completion that fit the child's level of development and to model behavior that can lead to task completion.

From an educator's perspective: If children's cognitive development is dependent on interactions with others, what obligations does society have regarding such social settings as preschools and neighborhoods?

One key aspect of the aid that more accomplished individuals provide to learners comes in the form of cultural tools. *Cultural tools* are actual, physical items (e.g., pencils, paper, calculators, computers, and so forth), as well as an intellectual and conceptual framework for solving problems. The framework includes the language that is used within a culture, its alphabetical and numbering schemes, its mathematical and scientific systems, and even its religious systems. These cultural tools provide a structure that can be used to help children define and solve specific problems, as well as an intellectual point of view that encourages cognitive development.

For example, consider the cultural differences in how people talk about distance. In cities, distance is usually measured in blocks ("the store is about 15 blocks away"). To a child from a rural background, more culturally meaningful terms are needed, such as yards, miles, practical rules of thumb such as "a stone's throw," or references to known distances

zone of proximal development (ZPD) according to Vygotsky, the level at which a child can *almost*, but not fully, perform a task independently, but can do so with the assistance of someone more competent

scaffolding the support for learning and problem solving that encourages independence and growth and landmarks ("about half the distance to town"). To make matters more complicated, "how far" questions are sometimes answered in terms not of distance, but of time ("it's about 15 minutes to the store"), which will be understood variously to refer to walking or riding time, depending on context—and, if riding time, to different forms of riding—by ox cart, bicycle, bus, canoe, or automobile, again depending on cultural context. The nature of the tools available to children to solve problems and perform tasks is highly dependent on the culture in which they live.

Evaluating Vygotsky's Contributions. Vygotsky's view has become increasingly influential, which is surprising given that he died more than 75 years ago at the age of 37 (Winsler, 2003; Gredler & Shields, 2008). His influence has grown because his ideas help explain a growing body of research on the importance of social interaction in promoting cognitive development. The idea that children's comprehension of the world flows from their interactions with their parents, peers, and other members of society is increasingly well supported. It is also consistent with a growing body of multicultural and cross-cultural research, which finds evidence that cognitive development is shaped, in part, by cultural factors (Daniels, 1996; Scrimsher & Tudge, 2003).

Of course, not every aspect of Vygotsky's theorizing has been supported, and he can be criticized for a lack of precision in his conceptualization of cognitive growth. For instance, such broad concepts as the zone of proximal development are not terribly precise, and they do not always lend themselves to experimental tests (Wertsch, 1999).

Furthermore, Vygotsky was largely silent on how basic cognitive processes such as attention and memory develop and how children's natural cognitive capabilities unfold. Because of his emphasis on broad cultural influences, he did not focus on how individual bits of information are processed and synthesized. These processes, essential to a complete understanding of cognitive development, are more directly addressed by information processing theories. Still, Vygotsky's melding of the cognitive and social worlds of children has been an important advance in our understanding of cognitive development.

REVIEW, CHECK, AND APPLY

REVIEW

L06 How do other views of cognitive development differ from Piaget's?

- Proponents of information processing approaches argue that quantitative changes in children's processing skills largely account for their cognitive development.
- Instead of focusing on children's cognitive limitations, developmentalists using an information processing approach focus on the cognitive advances that enable children to develop considerable abilities.

L07 What separates Vygotsky's approach from Piaget's?

- Vygotsky believed that children develop cognitively within a context of culture and society. His theory includes the concepts of the zone of proximal development and scaffolding.
- Piaget viewed children as working by themselves to develop an independent view of the world, whereas Vygotsky proposed that children learned the skills of their culture from master teachers.

CHECK YOURSELF

1. According to the information processing approach of cognitive development, memories of particular events occurring in one's own life are also known as_____.
   - a autobiographical memory
   - b explicit memory
   - c personal memory
   - d cultural memory
2. _____believed that children learn about their world through their interactions with others.
   - a Vygotsky
   - b Piaget
   - c Siegler
   - d Gelman
3. One reason Vygotsky has only begun to have an influence in psychology is because he was largely unknown to developmentalists.
   - True
   - False

APPLYING LIFESPAN DEVELOPMENT

- Do you agree with the view that information processing approaches see too many trees and lose sight of the forest? Or do you think that Piaget saw too much forest without accounting for enough trees? Explain.
- In what ways have educators and others begun to apply Vygotsky's ideas in schools and communities? Should governments take an active role in this?

✓ **Study** and **Review** on **MyPsychLab.com**

THE GROWTH OF LANGUAGE AND LEARNING

LO8 How does language develop in the preschool years?
LO9 What effects does television have on preschoolers?
LO10 What kinds of preschool educational programs are available?

I tried it out and it was very great!
This is a picture of when I was running through the water with Mommy.
Where are you going when I go to the fireworks with Mommy and Daddy?
I didn't know creatures went on floats in pools.
We can always pretend we have another one.
And the teacher put it up on the counter so no one could reach it.
I really want to keep it while we're at the park.
You need to get your own ball if you want to play "hit the tree."
When I grow up and I'm a baseball player, I'll have my baseball hat, and I'll put it on, and I'll play baseball. (Schatz, 1994, p. 179)

Listen to Ricky, at age 3. In addition to recognizing most letters of the alphabet, printing the first letter of his name, and writing the word "HI," he is capable of producing these complex sentences.

During the preschool years, children's language skills reach new heights of sophistication. They begin the period with reasonable linguistic capabilities, but with significant gaps in both comprehension and production. In fact, no one would mistake a 3-year-old's language for an adult's. However, by the end of the preschool years, they can hold their own with adults, comprehending and producing language with many of the qualities of adults' language. How does this transformation occur?

Language Development

Language blooms so rapidly between the late 2s and the mid-3s that researchers have yet to understand the exact pattern. What is clear is that sentence length increases steadily, and the number of ways children combine words and phrases to form sentences—known as **syntax**—doubles each month. By the time a preschooler is 3, the various combinations reach into the thousands.

There are also enormous leaps in the number of words children use. By age 6, the average child has a vocabulary of around 14,000 words—acquired at a rate of nearly one new word every 2 hours, 24 hours a day. They manage this feat through a process known as **fast mapping**, in which new words are associated with their meaning after only a brief encounter (Krcmar, Grela, & Lin, 2007; Kan & Kohnert, 2009; Marinellie & Kneile, 2012).

By the age of 3, preschoolers routinely use plurals and possessive forms of nouns (such as "boys" and "boy's"), the past tense (adding "-ed" at the end of words), and articles ("the" and "a"). They can ask, and answer, complex questions ("Where did you say my book is?" and "Those are trucks, aren't they?").

Preschoolers' skills extend to the appropriate formation of words that they have never before encountered. For example, in one classic experiment (Berko, 1958), the experimenter told the children that a figure was a "wug," and then showed them a card with two of the cartoon figures. "Now there are two of them," the children were told, and they were then asked to supply the missing word in the sentence, "There are two _____" (the answer to which, of course, is "wugs"). (See Figure 4-7.)

Not only did children show that they knew rules about the plural forms of nouns, but they understood possessive forms of nouns and the third-person singular and past-tense forms of verbs—all for words that they had never encountered, because they were nonsense words with no real meaning (O'Grady & Aitchison, 2005).

syntax the way in which an individual combines words and phrases to form sentences

fast mapping instances in which new words are associated with their meaning after only a brief encounter

This is a wug.

Now there is another one.
There are two of them.
There are two _____.

FIGURE 4-7 Appropriate Formation of Words Even though no preschooler—like the rest of us—is likely to have ever before encountered a wug, they are able to produce the appropriate word to fill in the blank (which, for the record, is *wugs*).
Source: WORD, Journal of the International Linguistic Association.

Preschoolers also learn what *cannot* be said as they acquire the principles of grammar. **Grammar** is the system of rules that determine how our thoughts can be expressed. For instance, preschoolers come to learn that "I am sitting" is correct, while the similarly structured "I am knowing [that]" is incorrect. Although they still make frequent mistakes of one sort or another, 3-year-olds follow the principles of grammar most of the time. Some errors are very noticeable—such as the use of "mens" and "catched"—but these errors are actually quite rare. In fact, young preschoolers are correct in their grammatical constructions more than 90 percent of the time (Guasti, 2002; Abbot-Smith & Tomasello, 2010; Normand et al., 2013).

Private Speech and Social Speech. In even a short visit to a preschool, you're likely to notice some children talking to themselves during play periods. A child might be reminding a doll about a trip to the grocery store later, or, while playing with a toy racing car, might speak of an upcoming race. In some cases, the talk is sustained, as when a child, working on a puzzle, says things like, "This piece goes here… . Uh-oh, this one doesn't fit… . Where can I put this piece? … This can't be right."

Some developmentalists suggest that **private speech**, speech by children that is spoken and directed to themselves, performs an important function. For instance, Vygotsky suggested that it is used as a guide to behavior and thought. By communicating with themselves through private speech, children are able to try out ideas, acting as their own sounding boards. In this way, private speech facilitates children's thinking and helps them control their behavior—much as you might say "Take it easy" or "Calm down" when trying to control your anger over some situation. In Vygotsky's view, then, private speech serves as an important social function and is also a forerunner to the internal dialogues that we use when we reason with ourselves during thinking (Winsler, De Leon, & Wallace, 2003; Winsler et al., 2006; Al-Namlah, Meins, & Fernyhough, 2012).

In addition, private speech may be a way for children to practice the practical skills required in conversation, known as *pragmatics*. **Pragmatics** is the aspect of language relating to communicating effectively and appropriately with others. The development of pragmatic abilities permits children to understand the basics of conversations—turn-taking, sticking to a topic, and what should and should not be said, according to the conventions of society. When children are taught that the appropriate response to receiving a gift is "thank you," or that they should use different language in various settings (on the playground versus in the classroom), they are learning the pragmatics of language.

The preschool years also mark the growth of social speech. **Social speech** is speech directed toward another person and meant to be understood by that person. Before age 3, children seem to be speaking only for their own entertainment, apparently uncaring whether anyone else can understand. However, during the preschool years, children begin to direct their speech to others, wanting others to listen and becoming frustrated when they cannot make themselves understood. As a result, they begin to adapt their speech to others through pragmatics, as discussed earlier.

Learning From the Media: Television and the Internet

Ask almost any preschooler, and she or he will be able to identify Snuffleupagus, as well as Big Bird, Bert, Ernie, and a host of other characters: the members of the cast of *Sesame Street*. *Sesame Street* is the most successful television show in history targeted at preschoolers; its audience is in the millions.

But *Sesame Street* is not all that preschoolers are watching or doing, for television, and more recently the Internet and computers, play a central role in many U.S. households. Television is a particularly potent stimulus, with the average preschooler watching more than 21 hours of TV a week. In more than a third of households with children 2 to 7 years of age, the television is on "most of the time," and in one study a fifth of children under the age of 2 had a television in their bedroom. In comparison, preschoolers spend three-quarters of an hour reading on the average day (Roberts et al., 1999; Bryant & Bryant, 2001, 2003; Center for Disease Control and Prevention, 2010).

Computers are also becoming influential in the lives of preschoolers. Seventy percent of preschoolers between the ages of 4 and 6 have used a computer, and a quarter of them use one every day. Those who use a computer spend an average of an hour a day, and the majority use it by themselves. With help from their parents, almost one-fifth have sent an email (Rideout, Vandewater, & Wartella, 2003).

grammar the system of rules that determine how our thoughts can be expressed

private speech speech by children that is spoken and directed to themselves

pragmatics the aspect of language that relates to communicating effectively and appropriately with others

social speech speech directed toward another person and meant to be understood by that person

It's too early to know the effects of computer usage—and of other media such as video games—on preschoolers. However, there is a wealth of research on the consequences of viewing television, as we consider next (Rideout, Vandewater, & Wartella, 2003; Courage & Howe, 2010).

Television: Controlling Exposure. Despite the introduction of a number of high-quality educational programs in recent decades, many children's programs are not of high quality or are not appropriate for a preschool audience. Accordingly, the American Academy of Pediatrics (AAP) recommends that exposure to television should be limited. The AAP suggests that until the age of 2, children watch *no* television, and after that age, no more than 1 to 2 hours of quality programming each day (Schmidt et al., 2009).

In fact, preschoolers are not particularly "television literate." They often do not fully understand the plots of the stories they are viewing, are unable to recall significant story details after viewing a program, and make limited and often erroneous inferences about the motivations of characters. Moreover, preschool children may have difficulty separating fantasy from reality, with some believing, for example, that there is a real Big Bird living on *Sesame Street* (Wright et al., 1994; Kimura & Kato, 2006).

Similarly, preschoolers exposed to TV advertising are not able to critically understand and evaluate the messages they see. Consequently, they are likely to fully accept advertisers' claims about their product. The likelihood of children believing advertising messages is so high that the American Psychological Association has recommended placing restrictions on advertising targeting children under age 8 (Kunkel et al., 2004; Pine, Wilson, & Nash, 2007; Nash, Pine, & Messer, 2009).

As they get older and their information processing capabilities improve, preschoolers' understanding of the material they see on television improves. They remember things more accurately, and they are better able to focus on the central message of a show. This improvement suggests that the powers of the medium of television may be harnessed to bring about cognitive gains—exactly what the producers of *Sesame Street* set out to do (Singer & Singer, 2000; Crawley, Anderson, & Santomero, 2002; Berry, 2003; Uchikoshi, 2006).

Early Childhood Education: Taking the "Pre" Out of the Preschool Period

The term *preschool period* is something of a misnomer: Almost three-quarters of children in the United States are enrolled in some form of care outside the home, much of it designed either explicitly or implicitly to teach skills that will enhance intellectual and social abilities (see Figure 4-8). There are several reasons for this, but one major factor is the rise in the number of families in which both parents work outside the home. For instance, a high proportion of fathers work outside the home, and close to 60 percent of women with children under 6 are employed, most of them full time (Gilbert, 1994; Borden, 1998; Tamis-LeMonda & Cabrera, 2002).

However, there is another reason that preschools are popular: Developmental psychologists have found evidence that children can benefit substantially from involvement in some form of educational activity before they enroll in formal schooling, which typically takes place at age 5 or 6 in the United States. When compared to children who stay at home and have no formal educational involvement, most children enrolled in good preschools experience clear cognitive and social benefits (National Institute of Child Health and Human Development [NICHHD], 1999, 2002; Campbell, Ramey, & Pungello, 2002).

The Varieties of Early Education. The variety of early education alternatives is vast. Some outside-the-home care for children is little more than babysitting, while other options are designed to promote intellectual and social advances. Among the major choices are the following:

- *Child-care centers* typically provide care for children outside the home, while their parents are at work. Although many child-care centers aim to provide some form of intellectual stimulation, their primary purpose tends to be more social and emotional than cognitive.

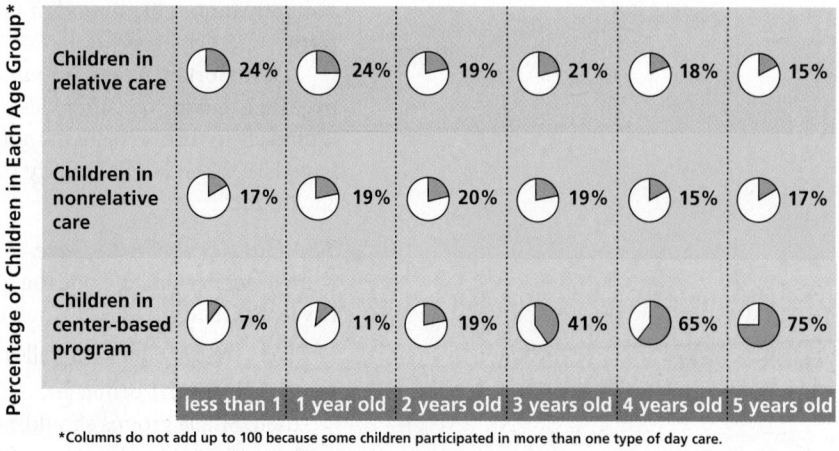

FIGURE 4-8 Care Outside the Home
Approximately 75 percent of children in the United States are enrolled in some form of care outside the home—a trend that is the result of more parents employed full time. Evidence suggests that children can benefit from early childhood education.
Source: U.S. Department of Education, National Center for Child Health, 2003.

- Some child care is provided in *family child-care centers*, small operations run in private homes. Because centers in some areas are unlicensed, the quality of care can be uneven. Because teachers in licensed child-care programs are more often trained professionals than those who provide family child care, the quality of care is often higher.
- *Preschools* are explicitly designed to provide intellectual and social experiences for children. They tend to be more limited in their schedules than family care centers, typically providing care for only 3 to 5 hours per day. Because of this limitation, preschools serve children mainly from middle and higher socioeconomic levels, in cases where parents don't need to work full time. Like child-care centers, preschools vary enormously in the activities they provide. Some emphasize social skills, while others focus on intellectual development. Some do both.

  For instance, Montessori preschools, which use a method developed by Italian educator Maria Montessori, employ a carefully designed set of materials to create an environment that fosters sensory, motor, and language development. Children are provided with a variety of activities to choose from, with the option of moving from one to another (Gutek, 2003).

  Preschool readiness programs also appear to be cost effective. According to a cost-benefit analysis of one readiness program, for every dollar spent on the program, taxpayers saved seven dollars by the time the graduates reached the age of 27 (Schweinhart, Barnes, & Weikart, 1993; Friedman, 2004; Gormley et al., 2005).
- *School child care* is provided by some local school systems in the United States. Almost half the states fund prekindergarten programs for 4-year-olds, often aimed at disadvantaged children. Because they typically are staffed by better-trained teachers than less-regulated child-care centers, school child-care programs are often of higher quality than other early education alternatives.

The Effectiveness of Child Care. How effective are such programs? Most research suggests that preschoolers enrolled in child-care centers show intellectual development that at least matches that of children at home, and often is better. For instance, some studies find that preschoolers in child care are more verbally fluent, show memory and comprehension advantages, and even achieve higher IQ scores than at-home children. Other studies find that early and long-term participation in child care is particularly helpful for children from lower-income homes or those who are at risk. Some research even shows that child-care programs can have positive consequences 25 years later (Vandell, 2004; Mervis, 2011; Reynolds et al., 2011).

Similar advantages are found for social development. Children in high-quality programs tend to be more self-confident, independent, and knowledgeable about the social world in which they live than those who do not participate. On the other hand, not all the outcomes of outside-the-home care are positive: Children in child care have been found to be less polite, less compliant, less respectful of adults, and sometimes more competitive and aggressive than their peers. Furthermore, children who spend more than 10 hours a week in preschools have a slightly higher likelihood of being disruptive in class (NICHD Early Child Care Research Network, 2003; Belsky et al., 2007; Douglass & Klerman, 2012).

It is important to keep in mind that not all early childhood care programs are equally effective. High-quality care provides intellectual and social benefits, while low-quality care not only is unlikely to furnish benefits, but actually may harm children (Votruba-Drzal, Coley, & Chase-Lansdale, 2004; NICHD Early Child Care Research Network, 2006; Dearing, McCartney, & Taylor, 2009).

The Quality of Child Care. How can we define "high quality"? The major characteristics of high-quality care include the following (Love et al., 2003; Vandell, Shumow, & Posner, 2005; Lavzer & Goodson, 2006; Leach et al., 2008; Rudd, Cain, & Saxon, 2008; Lloyd, 2012):

- The care providers are well trained.
- The child-care center has an appropriate overall size and ratio of care providers to children. Single groups should not have many more than 14 to 20 children, and there should be no more than five to ten 3-year-olds per caregiver, or seven to ten 4- or 5-year-olds per caregiver.
- The curriculum of a child-care facility is not left to chance, but is carefully planned out and coordinated among the teachers.

- The language environment is rich, with a great deal of conversation.
- The caregivers are sensitive to children's emotional and social needs, and they know when and when not to intervene.
- Materials and activities are age appropriate.
- Basic health and safety standards are followed.

No one knows how many programs in the United States can be considered "high quality," but there are many fewer than desirable. In fact, the United States lags behind almost every other industrialized country in the quality of its child care as well as in its quantity and affordability (Zigler & Finn-Stevenson, 1995; Scarr, 1998; Muenchow & Marsland, 2007).

From an educator's perspective: What do you think might be some implications for a preschool teacher who has children from China, Japan, and the United States in the classroom?

Cultural Dimensions

Preschools Around the World: Why Does the United States Lag Behind?

In France and Belgium, access to preschool is a legal right. Sweden and Finland provide child care for preschoolers whose parents want it. Russia has an extensive system of state-run *yasli-sads*, nursery schools and kindergartens, attended by 75 percent of children age 3 to 7 in urban areas.

In contrast, the United States has no coordinated national policy on preschool education—or on the care of children in general. There are several reasons for this. For one, decisions about education have traditionally been left to the states and local school districts. For another, the United States, unlike many other countries, has no tradition of teaching preschoolers. Finally, the status of preschools in the United States has been traditionally low. Consider, for instance, that preschool and nursery school teachers are the lowest paid of all teachers. (Teacher salaries increase as the age of students rises. Thus, college and high school teachers are paid most, while preschool and elementary school teachers are paid least.)

Different societies view the purpose of early childhood education differently (Lamb et al., 1992). For instance, in a cross-country comparison of China, Japan, and the United States, researchers found that parents in the three countries view the purpose of preschools very differently. While parents in China tend to see preschools primarily as a way of giving children a good start academically, Japanese parents view them mostly as a way of giving children the opportunity to be members of a group. In the United States, in comparison, parents regard the primary purpose of preschools as making children more independent and self-reliant, although obtaining a good academic start and having group experiences are also important (Tobin, Wu, & Davidson, 1989; Huntsinger et al., 1997; Johnson et al., 2003).

REVIEW, CHECK, AND APPLY

REVIEW

LO8 How does language develop in the preschool years?

- In the preschool years, children rapidly increase in linguistic ability, developing an improved sense of grammar and shifting gradually from private to social speech.

LO9 What effects does television have on preschoolers?

- Preschoolers watch television at high levels, with mixed consequences.

LO10 What kinds of preschool educational programs are available?

- Preschool educational programs are beneficial if they are of high quality, with trained staff, good curriculum, proper group sizes, and small staff-student ratios.

CHECK YOURSELF

1. Being able to combine words and phrases in order to form sentences is also known as _____.
   - a fast mapping
   - b grammar
   - c syntax
   - d social speech
2. Preschoolers are able to learn the meaning of words after only a brief encounter. This is also known as _____.
   - a synaptic explosion
   - b word unification
   - c social speech
   - d fast mapping
3. When it comes to child care and its effectiveness, the key factor is _____.
   - a size
   - b program type (i.e., Montessori)
   - c age of the child
   - d quality

APPLYING LIFESPAN DEVELOPMENT

- Is private speech egocentric or useful? Do adults ever use private speech? What functions does it serve?
- In your view, how do thought and language interact in preschoolers' development? Is it possible to think without language? How do children who have been deaf from birth think?

✓ **Study** and **Review** on **MyPsychLab.com**

MODULE 4.3

SOCIAL AND PERSONALITY DEVELOPMENT IN THE PRESCHOOL YEARS

Lincoln and Beth Avery had expected their son Julian to be just like his older brother Carl. Carl was bold and adventurous, a climber of trees and a leader on the playground. By the age of 4, however, it was clear Julian had his own personality. He liked to sit on the front steps of their brownstone looking at picture books. He liked to draw and make things with clay. He was a calm, thoughtful child who chose to watch others more often than interact with them. The Averys were surprised by the preferences of their younger son and voiced their concerns to his preschool teacher. The teacher confirmed that Julian was indeed a quiet child. No, he was not a leader on the playground, but he did have several friends in the class and he seemed content most of the time, especially when he was creating something out of cardboard or construction paper, or making a story with pictures. The teacher urged the Averys not to worry. "Julian is developing a sense of who he is and what he can do, what he likes to do. He won't be Carl. He can't be. But I think he'll be a marvelous Julian."

Like most preschool-age children, Julian is only just beginning to show the personality that will develop over the rest of his life. Although he is his parents' son, he is not his brother. He may not even share many of his parents' personality traits, but with their love and support, he will, as his teacher put it, become a marvelous Julian.

In this module, we address social and personality development during the preschool period. We begin by examining how children continue to form a sense of self, focusing on how they develop their self-concepts, including their concept of gender. Next we focus on preschoolers' social lives, especially how they play with one another, and we consider how parents and other authority figures use discipline to shape children's behavior.

Finally, we examine two key aspects of social behavior: moral development and aggression. We consider how children develop a notion of right and wrong and we look at factors that lead preschool-age children to behave aggressively.

FORMING A SENSE OF SELF

LO11 How do preschool-age children develop a concept of themselves?
LO12 How do children develop their sense of racial identity and gender?

Although the question "Who am I?" is not explicitly posed by most preschool-age children, it underlies much of their development during the preschool years, and the answer may affect them for the rest of their lives.

Psychosocial development relates to changes in an understanding of oneself and others behavior.

Psychosocial Development: Resolving the Conflicts

Mary-Alice's preschool teacher raised her eyebrows slightly when the 4-year-old took off her coat. Mary-Alice, usually dressed in well-matched play suits, was a medley of prints. She had on a pair of flowered pants, along with a completely clashing plaid top. The outfit was accessorized with a striped headband, socks in an animal print, and Mary-Alice's polka-dotted rain boots. Mary-Alice's mom gave a slightly embarrassed shrug. "Mary-Alice got dressed all by herself this morning," she explained as she handed over a bag containing spare shoes, just in case the rain boots became uncomfortable during the day.

Psychoanalyst Erik Erikson may well have praised Mary-Alice's mother for helping Mary-Alice develop a sense of initiative (if not of fashion), and thereby promoting her psychosocial development. **Psychosocial development** encompasses changes in individuals' understanding of themselves and of others' behavior. According to Erikson, society and culture present a series of challenges, which shift as people age. Erikson believed that people pass through eight distinct stages, each characterized by a crisis or conflict that the person must resolve. Our experiences as we try to resolve these conflicts lead us to develop ideas about ourselves that can last for the rest of our lives.

psychosocial development according to Erikson, development that encompasses changes both in the understandings individuals have of themselves as members of society and in their comprehension of the meaning of others' behavior

In the early part of the preschool period, children are ending the autonomy-versus-shame-and-doubt stage and entering what Erikson called the **initiative-versus-guilt stage**, which lasts from around age 3 to 6. During this period, children face conflicts between the desire to act independently of their parents and the guilt that comes if they don't succeed.

They come to see themselves as persons in their own right, and they begin to make decisions on their own.

Parents (like Mary-Alice's mother) who react positively can help their children resolve these opposing feelings. By providing their children with opportunities to act self-reliantly, while still giving them direction and guidance, parents can support their children's initiative. On the other hand, parents who discourage their children's independence may contribute to a sense of guilt that persists throughout their lives and affects their self-concept, which begins to develop during this period.

Self-Concept in the Preschool Years: Thinking About the Self

If you ask preschool-age children to specify what makes them different from other kids, they readily respond with answers like, "I'm a good runner" or "I'm a big girl." Such answers relate to **self-concept**—their identity, or their set of beliefs about what they are like as individuals (Brown, 1998; Tessor, Felson, & Suls, 2000; Marsh, Ellis, & Craven, 2002).

Children's self-concepts are not necessarily accurate. In fact, preschool children typically overestimate their skills and knowledge across all domains of expertise. Consequently, their view of the future is quite rosy: They expect to win the next game they play, to beat all opponents in an upcoming race, to write great stories when they grow up. Even when they have just experienced failure at a task, they are likely to expect to do well in the future. This optimistic view arises because they do not yet compare themselves and their performance against others, thereby gaining the freedom to take chances and try new activities (Dweck, 2002; Wang, 2004; Verschueren, Doumen, & Buyse, 2012).

Preschool-age children's view of themselves reflects their culture. For example, many Asian societies tend to have a **collectivistic orientation**, in which individuals tend to regard themselves as parts of a larger social network in which they are interconnected with and responsible to others. In contrast, children in Western cultures are more likely to develop an **individualistic orientation** that emphasizes personal identity and the uniqueness of the individual, seeing themselves as self-contained and autonomous, in competition with others for scarce resources (Markus & Kitayama, 1991; Dennis et al., 2002; Lehman, Chiu, & Schaller, 2004; Wang, 2004, 2006).

Preschoolers' developing self-concepts can also be affected by their culture's attitudes toward various racial and ethnic groups. Preschoolers' awareness of their ethnic or racial identity is subtly influenced by the attitudes of the people, schools, and other cultural institutions with which they come into contact.

initiative-versus-guilt stage according to Erikson, the period during which children aged 3 to 6 years experience conflict between independence of action and the sometimes negative results of that action

self-concept a person's identity, or set of beliefs about what one is like as an individual

collectivistic orientation a philosophy that promotes the notion of interdependence

individualistic orientation a philosophy that emphasizes personal identity and the uniqueness of the individual

race dissonance the phenomenon in which minority children indicate preferences for majority values or people

Cultural Dimensions

Developing Racial and Ethnic Awareness

The preschool years mark an important turning point for children. Their answer to the question of who they are begins to take into account their racial and ethnic identity.

For most preschool-age children, racial awareness comes relatively early. Certainly, even infants are able to distinguish different skin colors, but it is only later that children begin to attribute meaning to different racial characteristics.

By the time they are 3 or 4 years of age, preschool-age children notice differences among people based on skin color, and they begin to identify themselves as a member of a particular group, such as "Hispanic" or "black." Although at first they do not realize that ethnicity and race are enduring features of who they are, later they begin to understand the significance that society places on ethnic and racial membership (Cross & Cross, 2008; Quintana & McKown, 2008; Guerrero et al., 2010).

Some preschoolers have mixed feelings about their racial and ethnic identity. Some experience **race dissonance**, the phenomenon in which minority children indicate preferences for majority values or people. For instance, some studies find that as many as 90 percent of African American children, when asked about their reactions to drawings of black and white children, react more negatively to those depicting black children than white children. However, this reaction does not translate into lower self-esteem; rather, the white preference appears to be a result of the powerful influence of the dominant culture, rather than a disparagement of their own race (Holland, 1994; Quintana, 2007).

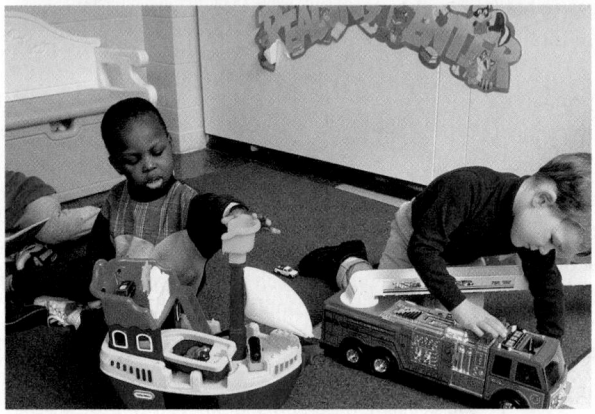

During the preschool period, differences in play according to gender become more pronounced. In addition, boys tend to play with boys, and girls with girls.

Gender Identity: Developing Femaleness and Maleness

Boys' awards: Very Best Thinker, Most Eager Learner, Most Imaginative, Most Enthusiastic, Most Scientific, Best Friend, Mr. Personality, Hardest Worker, Best Sense of Humor.

Girls' awards: All-Around Sweetheart, Sweetest Personality, Cutest Personality, Best Sharer, Best Artist, Biggest Heart, Best Manners, Best Helper, Most Creative.

What's wrong with this picture? Quite a bit to one parent, whose daughter received one of the girls' awards during a kindergarten graduation ceremony. While the girls were getting pats on the back for their pleasing personalities, the boys were receiving awards for their intellectual and analytic skills (Deveny, 1994).

This situation is not rare: Girls and boys often live in very different worlds beginning at birth and continuing into the preschool years and beyond (Bornstein et al., 2008; Conry-Murray, 2013).

Gender, the sense of being male or female, is well established by the time children reach the preschool years. By age 2, children consistently label people as male or female (Raag, 2003; Campbell, Shirley, & Candy, 2004; Fivush, 2010).

One way gender shows up is in play. Preschool boys spend more time than girls in rough-and-tumble play, while preschool girls spend more time in organized games and role-playing. During this time boys begin to play more with boys, and girls with girls, a trend that increases during middle childhood. Girls begin to prefer same-sex playmates a little earlier than boys. They first have a clear preference for interacting with other girls at age 2, while boys don't show much preference for same-sex playmates until age 3 (Boyatzis, Mallis, & Leon, 1999; Martin & Fabes, 2001; Raag, 2003).

Preschool-age children often have very strict ideas about how boys and girls are supposed to act. In fact, their expectations about gender-appropriate behavior are even more gender-stereotyped than those of adults. Beliefs in gender stereotypes become increasingly pronounced up to age 5, and although they become somewhat less rigid by age 7, they do not disappear. In fact, the gender stereotypes held by preschoolers resemble those held by traditional adults in society (Lam & Leman, 2003; Ruble et al., 2007; Martin & Ruble, 2010).

Like adults, preschoolers expect that males are more apt to have traits involving competence, independence, forcefulness, and competitiveness. In contrast, females are viewed as more likely to have traits such as warmth, expressiveness, nurturance, and submissiveness. Although these are *expectations*, and say nothing about the way that men and women actually behave, such expectations provide the lens through which preschool-age children view the world and affect their behavior as well as the way they interact with peers and adults (Blakemore, 2003; Gelman, Taylor, & Nguyen, 2004).

From a child-care provider's perspective: If a girl in a preschool child-care setting loudly tells a boy that he can't play with the dolls in the play area because he's a boy, what is the best way to handle the situation?

Why should gender play such a powerful role during the preschool years (as well as during the rest of the life span)? Developmentalists have proposed several explanations.

Biological Perspectives. It is hardly surprising that the biological characteristics associated with sex lead to gender differences. Hormones, for example, have been found to affect gender-based behaviors. Girls exposed to unusually high levels of *androgens* (male hormones) prenatally are more likely to display "typically male" behaviors than their sisters who were not exposed to androgens (Knickmeyer & Baron-Cohen, 2006; Burton et al., 2009; Mathews et al., 2009).

Androgen-exposed girls preferred boys as playmates and spent more time than other girls playing with toys associated with the male role, such as cars and trucks. Similarly, boys exposed prenatally to atypically high levels of female hormones are apt to display more behaviors that are stereotypically female than is usual (Servin et al., 2003; Knickmeyer & Baron-Cohen, 2006).

Some developmentalists see gender differences as serving the biological goal of survival of the species. Using an evolutionary approach, these theorists suggest that males with stereotypically masculine qualities, such as forcefulness and competitiveness, may have been able to attract females who could give them hardy offspring. Females who excelled at stereotypically feminine tasks, such as nurturing, may have been valued because they could help their children survive the dangers of childhood (Browne, 2006; Ellis, 2006).

Of course, it is difficult to attribute behavioral characteristics unambiguously to biological factors. Because of this, we must consider other explanations for gender differences.

Social Learning Approaches. According to social learning approaches, children learn gender-related behavior and expectations by observing others, including parents, teachers, siblings, and even peers. A boy might admire a major league baseball player and become interested in sports. A girl might watch her babysitter practicing cheerleading moves and begin to try them herself. Observing the praise and honor that gender-appropriate behavior earns leads the child to emulate that behavior (Rust et al., 2000).

Books and the media, and in particular television and video games, also play a role in perpetuating traditional views of gender-related behavior. Analyses of the most popular television shows find that male characters outnumber female characters by two to one. Furthermore, females are more apt to appear with males, whereas female–female relationships are relatively uncommon (Calvert, Kotler, & Zehnder, 2003).

Television also presents men and women in traditional gender roles. Television shows typically define female characters in terms of their relationships with males. Females are more likely to appear as victims than males (Wright et al., 1995; Turner-Bowker, 1996). They are less likely to be presented as productive or as decision makers, and more likely to be portrayed as characters interested in romance, their homes, and their families. Such models, according to social learning theory, have a powerful influence on preschoolers' definitions of appropriate behavior (Scharrer et al., 2006; Hust, Brown, & L'Engle, 2008; Nassif & Gunter, 2008).

In some cases, preschoolers learn social roles directly, not through models. For example, preschool-age children may be told by their parents to act like a "little girl" or "little man." What this generally means is that girls should behave politely and boys should be tough. Such direct training sends a clear message about expected behavior for the different genders (Leaper, 2002).

Cognitive Approaches. In the view of some theorists, one aspect of forming a clear sense of identity is the desire to establish a **gender identity**, a perception of oneself as male or female. To do this, children develop a **gender schema**, a cognitive framework that organizes information relevant to gender (Barbera, 2003; Martin & Ruble, 2004; Signorella & Frieze, 2008).

Gender schemas are developed early in life and serve as a lens through which preschoolers view the world, encompassing "rules" about what is appropriate and inappropriate for males and females. Some girls may decide that wearing pants is what boys do and apply the rule so rigidly that they refuse to wear anything but dresses. Or a preschool boy may reason that it is inappropriate for him to wear makeup for a school play because makeup is worn by girls—even though all the other boys and girls are wearing it (Frawley, 2008).

According to *cognitive-developmental theory*, proposed by Lawrence Kohlberg, this rigidity is in part a reflection of preschoolers' understanding of gender (Kohlberg, 1966). Specifically, young preschoolers erroneously believe that sex differences are based not on biological factors but on differences in appearance or behavior. Employing this view of the world, a boy may think he could turn into a girl if he put on a dress and tied his hair in a ponytail. However, by age 4 or 5, children develop an understanding of **gender constancy**, the awareness that people are permanently males or females, depending on fixed, unchangeable biological factors.

Interestingly, gender schemas appear well before children understand gender constancy. Even young preschool-age children assume that certain behaviors are appropriate—and others are not—on the basis of stereotypic views of gender (Martin & Ruble, 2004; Ruble et al., 2007; Karniol, 2009).

Is it possible to avoid viewing the world in terms of gender schemas? According to Sandra Bem (1987), one way is to encourage children to be **androgynous**, a state in which gender roles encompass characteristics thought typical of both sexes. For instance, parents and caregivers can encourage preschool children to see males as assertive but at the same time warm and tender. Similarly, girls might be encouraged to see the female role as both empathetic and tender and competitive, assertive, and independent.

gender identity the perception of oneself as male or female

gender schema a cognitive framework that organizes information relevant to gender

gender constancy the awareness that people are permanently males or females, depending on fixed, unchangeable biological factors

androgynous a state in which gender roles encompass characteristics thought typical of both sexes

Like the other approaches to gender development, the cognitive perspective does not imply that differences between the two sexes are in any way improper or inappropriate. Instead, it suggests that preschoolers should be taught to treat others as individuals. Furthermore, preschoolers need to learn the importance of fulfilling their own talents, acting as individuals and not as representatives of a gender.

REVIEW, CHECK, AND APPLY

REVIEW

L011 How do preschool-age children develop a concept of themselves?

- According to Erikson's psychosocial development theory, preschool-age children move from the autonomy-versus-shame-and-doubt stage to the initiative-versus-guilt stage.
- During the preschool years, children develop their self-concepts, beliefs about themselves that they derive from their own perceptions, their parents' behaviors, and society.

L012 How do children develop their sense of racial identity and gender?

- Racial, ethnic, and gender awareness begin to form in the preschool years.

CHECK YOURSELF

1. According to Erikson (1963), during the preschool years children face a key conflict relating to psychosocial development that involves the development of _____.

   a repression b identity
   c initiative d trust

2. Five-year-old Kayla has been practicing her jump-roping skills for the past 6 weeks so she can enter a contest at her school. After one afternoon of practice she told her mother, "I am a terrific jump roper." This statement is an example of Kayla's increasing understanding of her identity or _____.

   a self identity b self concept
   c self awareness d self esteem

3. Biological characteristics associated with a person's sex do not appear to be related to gender differences.

   - True
   - False

APPLYING LIFESPAN DEVELOPMENT

- What sorts of activities might you encourage a preschool boy to undertake to help him adopt a less stereotypical gender schema?

✓ **Study** and **Review** on **MyPsychLab.com**

FRIENDS AND FAMILY: PRESCHOOLERS' SOCIAL LIVES

L013 In what sorts of social relationships and play do preschool-age children engage?

L014 What sorts of disciplinary styles do parents employ, and what effects do they have?

L015 What factors contribute to child abuse and neglect?

As preschoolers get older, their conception of friendship evolves and the quality of their interactions changes.

When Juan was 3, he had his first best friend, Emilio. Juan and Emilio, who lived in the same apartment building in San Jose, were inseparable. They played incessantly with toy cars, racing them up and down the apartment hallways until some of the neighbors began to complain about the noise. They pretended to read to one another, and sometimes they slept over at each other's home—a big step for a 3-year-old. Neither boy seemed more joyful than when he was with his "best friend"—the term each used for the other.

An infant's family can provide nearly all the social contact he or she needs. As preschoolers, however, many children, like Juan and Emilio, begin to discover the joys of peer friendships. Let's take a look at both sides of preschoolers' social development, friends, and family.

The Development of Friendships

Before age 3, most social activity involves simply being in the same place at the same time, without real social interaction. However, at around the age of 3, children begin to develop real friendships as peers are seen as individuals who hold special qualities and rewards. While preschoolers' relations with adults reflect children's needs for care, protection, and direction, their relations with peers are based more on the desire for companionship, play, and fun. Gradually, they come to view friendship as a continuing state that offers not just immediate pleasure, but the promise of future activity (Hay, Payne, & Chadwick, 2004; Sebanc et al., 2007; Dwyer et al., 2010).

Interactions with friends change during the preschool period. For 3-year-olds, the focus of friendship is the enjoyment of doing things together and playing jointly. Older preschoolers pay more attention to trust, support, and shared interests (Park, Lay, & Ramsay, 1993). Throughout the entire period, however, play remains an important part of all friendships.

Playing by the Rules: The Work of Play. In Rosie Graiff's class of 3-year-olds, Minnie bounces her doll's feet on the table as she sings softly to herself. Ben pushes his toy car across the floor, making motor noises. Sarah chases Abdul around and around the perimeter of the room.

Play is more than what children of preschool age do to pass the time. Instead, play helps preschoolers develop socially, cognitively, and physically (Whitebread et al., 2009; McGinnis, 2012; Hughett, Kohler, & Raschke, 2013).

According to developmentalist Lev Vygotshy, children are able, through make-believe play, to practice activities that are part of their particular culture and broaden their understanding of the way the world functions.

Categorizing Play. At the beginning of the preschool years, children engage in **functional play**—simple, repetitive activities typical of 3-year-olds, such as pushing cars on the floor, skipping, and jumping. Functional play involves doing something to be active rather than to create something (Bober, Humphry, & Carswell, 2001; Kantrowitz & Evans, 2004).

By age 4, children become involved in a more sophisticated form of play. In **constructive play** children manipulate objects to produce or build something. A child who builds a house out of Legos or puts a puzzle together is involved in constructive play: He or she has an ultimate goal—to produce something. The creation need not be novel, because children may repeatedly build a house of blocks, let it fall, and then rebuild it.

Constructive play gives children a chance to practice their physical and cognitive skills and fine muscle movements. They gain experience in solving problems about the ways and the sequences in which things fit together. They also learn to cooperate with others as the social nature of play becomes more important to them (Edwards, 2000; Shi, 2003; Love & Burns, 2006).

The Social Aspects of Play. If two preschoolers sit side by side at a table, each assembling a different puzzle, are they engaged jointly in play?

According to pioneering work done by Mildred Parten (1932), the answer is yes. She suggests that these preschoolers are engaged in **parallel play**, in which children play with similar toys, in a similar manner, but do not interact with each other. Preschoolers also engage in another form of play, a highly passive one: onlooker play. In **onlooker play**, children simply watch others at play, but do not actually participate themselves.

As they get older, however, preschool-age children engage in more sophisticated forms of social play that involve greater interaction. In **associative play**, two or more children interact with one another by sharing or borrowing toys or materials, although they do not do the same thing. In **cooperative play**, children genuinely play with one another, taking turns, playing games, or devising contests.

Solitary and onlooker play continue in the later stages of the preschool period. There are simply times when children prefer to play by themselves. And when newcomers join a group, one strategy for becoming part of the group—often successful—is to engage in onlooker play, waiting for an opportunity to join the play more actively (Lindsey & Colwell, 2003).

The nature of pretend, or make-believe, play also changes during the period, becoming in some ways more *un*realistic—and imaginative—as preschoolers shift from using only realistic objects to using less concrete ones. Thus, at the start of the preschool period, children may pretend to listen to a radio only if they have a plastic radio on hand. Later, they may use an entirely different object, such as a large cardboard box, as a pretend radio (Bornstein et al., 1996).

functional play play that involves simple, repetitive activities typical of 3-year-olds

constructive play play in which children manipulate objects to produce or build something

parallel play action in which children play with similar toys, in a similar manner, but do not interact with each other

onlooker play action in which children simply watch others at play, but do not actually participate themselves

associative play play in which two or more children actually interact with one another by sharing or borrowing toys or materials, although they do not do the same thing

cooperative play play in which children genuinely interact with one another, taking turns, playing games, or devising contests

Russian developmentalist Lev Vygotsky (1930/1978), discussed in Module 4.2, argued that pretend play, particularly if it involves social play, is an important means for expanding preschool-age children's cognitive skills. Through make-believe play, children are able to "practice" activities (such as pretending to use a computer or read a book) that are a part of their particular culture and broaden their understanding of the way the world functions. **Watch** the **Video** *Play Styles* in **MyPsychLab.**

From an educator's perspective: How might a nursery school teacher encourage a shy child to join a group of preschoolers who are playing?

Preschoolers' Theory of Mind: Understanding What Others Are Thinking

One reason that children's play changes is the continuing development of preschoolers' theory of mind—their knowledge and beliefs about how the mind operates. Using their theory of mind, preschool children increasingly see the world from others' perspectives. Even children as young as 2 are able to understand that others have emotions. By age 3 or 4, preschoolers know that they can imagine something that is not physically present, such as a zebra, and that others can do the same. They can also pretend that something has happened and react as if it really had occurred, a skill that becomes part of their imaginative play (Andrews, Halford, & Bunch, 2003; Wellman, 2012; Lane et al., 2013).

Preschool-age children also become more insightful regarding the motives and reasons behind people's behavior. They begin to understand that their mother is angry because she was late for an appointment, even if they themselves haven't seen her be late. Furthermore, by age 4, children's understanding that people can be fooled by physical reality (such as magic tricks involving sleight-of-hand) becomes surprisingly sophisticated. This increase in understanding helps children become more socially skilled as they gain insight into what others are thinking (Fitzgerald & White, 2002; Eisbach, 2004).

There are limits, however, to 3-year-olds' theory of mind. For instance, their understanding of "belief" is incomplete, as illustrated by their performance on the *false belief* task. In the false belief task, preschoolers are shown a doll named Maxi who places chocolate in a cabinet and then leaves. After Maxi is gone, his mother moves the chocolate somewhere else.

Preschoolers are then asked where Maxi will look for the chocolate when he returns. Three-year-olds answer (erroneously) that Maxi will look for it in the new location. In contrast, 4-year-olds correctly realize that Maxi has the false belief that the chocolate is still in the cabinet, and that's where he will look for it (Flynn, O'Malley, & Wood, 2004; Amsterlaw & Wellman, 2006; Brown & Bull, 2007). By the end of the preschool years, most children easily solve false belief problems. But one group has difficulty with it throughout their lifetimes: children with autsim spectrum disorder. (*Autism spectrum disorder* is the psychological disorder that produces significant language and emotional difficulties.) Children with autism spectrum disorder find it particularly difficult to relate to others, in part because they find it hard to understand what others are thinking.

Bruce Eric Kaplan/The New Yorker Collection/www.cartoonbank.com

"We've done a lot of important playing here today."

Autism spectrum disorder is characterized by a lack of connection to other people, even parents, and an avoidance of interpersonal situations. Individuals with autism spectrum disorder are bewildered by false belief problems no matter how old they are. The disorder is surprisingly common: The Center for Disease Control estimated in 2013 that the incidence is one in fifty, with a higher incidence in males. (Pellicano, 2007; Begeer et al., 2012; Carey, 2012; Miller, 2012.)

Preschoolers' Family Lives

Four-year-old Benjamin was watching TV while his mom cleaned up after dinner. After a while, he wandered in and grabbed a towel, saying, "Mommy, let me help you do the dishes." Surprised by this unprecedented behavior, she asked him, "Where did you learn to do dishes?"

"I saw it on Leave It to Beaver," he replied, "Only it was the dad helping. Since we don't have a dad, I figured I'd do it."

For many preschool-age children, life does not mirror old TV sitcoms. Many face the realities of an increasingly complicated world. For instance, in 1960, less than 10 percent of children under 18 lived with one parent. In 2000, a single parent headed 21 percent of white families, 35 percent of Hispanic families, and 55 percent of African American families.

Still, for most children the preschool years are not a time of turmoil. Instead, the period is characterized by growing interactions with the world at large. Preschoolers form genuine friendships and develop close ties with other children—a circumstance facilitated by a warm, supportive home environment. Research finds that strong, positive relationships between parents and children encourage children's relationships with others (Sroufe, 1994; Howes, Galinsky, & Kontos, 1998).

Effective Parenting: Teaching Desired Behavior

While she thinks no one is looking, Maria goes into her brother Alejandro's bedroom, where he has been saving the last of his Halloween candy. Just as she takes his last Reese's Peanut Butter Cup, the children's mother walks into the room and immediately takes in the situation.

If you were Maria's mother, which of the following reactions seems most reasonable?

1. Tell Maria to go to her room and stay there for the rest of the day, and take away access to her favorite blanket, the one she sleeps with every night and during naps.
2. Mildly tell Maria that what she did was not such a good idea, and she shouldn't do it in the future.
3. Explain why her action would upset her brother, and tell her to go to her room for an hour as punishment.
4. Forget about it, and let the children sort it out themselves.

Each of these responses represents one of the major parenting styles identified by Diana Baumrind (1971, 1980) and updated by Eleanor Maccoby and colleagues (Baumrind, 1971, 1980; Maccoby & Martin, 1983).

Children with authoritarian parents are often uneasy with peers and are not well adjusted. What are the consequences of parents who are too permissive? Too uninvolved?

1. **Authoritarian parents** are controlling, punitive, rigid, and cold. Their word is law, and they value strict, unquestioning obedience. They do not tolerate expressions of disagreement.
2. **Permissive parents** provide lax and inconsistent feedback. They require little of their children and don't see themselves as holding much responsibility for how their children turn out. They place little or no limits or control on their children's behavior.
3. **Authoritative parents** are firm, setting clear and consistent limits. Although they tend to be relatively strict, like authoritarian parents, they are loving and emotionally supportive. They also try to reason with their children, explaining why they should behave in a particular way ("Alejandro is going to be upset"), and communicating the rationale for any punishment they may impose. Authoritative parents encourage their children to be independent.
4. **Uninvolved parents** show virtually no interest in their children, displaying indifferent, rejecting behavior. They are detached emotionally and see their role as no more than feeding, clothing, and providing shelter. In its most extreme form, uninvolved parenting results in *neglect*, a form of child abuse. (The four patterns are summarized in Table 4-1.)

Parents' disciplinary styles usually produce differences in children's behavior—although there are many exceptions (Hoeve et al., 2008; Cheah et al., 2009; Lin, Chiu, & Yeh, 2012):

- Children of authoritarian parents tend to be withdrawn, show little sociability, are not very friendly, and often behave uneasily around their peers. Girls are especially dependent on their parents, whereas boys are unusually hostile.
- Children of permissive parents tend to be dependent and moody, and are low in social skills and self-control. They share many characteristics of children of authoritarian parents.

authoritarian parents parents who are controlling, punitive, rigid, and cold, and whose word is law. They value strict, unquestioning obedience from their children and do not tolerate expressions of disagreement

permissive parents parents who provide lax and inconsistent feedback and require little of their children

authoritative parents parents who are firm, setting clear and consistent limits, but who try to reason with their children, giving explanations for why they should behave in a particular way

uninvolved parents parents who show almost no interest in their children and indifferent, rejecting behavior

TABLE 4-1 PARENTING STYLES

	How Demanding Parents Are of Children	
	Demanding	**Undemanding**
How Responsive Parents Are to a Child	**Authoritative**	**Permissive**
	Characteristics: firm, setting clear and consistent limits	**Characteristics:** lax and inconsistent feedback
Highly Responsive	**Relationship with Children:** Although they tend to be relatively strict, like authoritarian parents they are loving and emotionally supportive and encourage their children to be independent. They also try to reason with their children, giving explanations for why they should behave in a particular way, and communicate the rationale for any punishment they may impose.	**Relationship with Children:** They require little of their children, and they don't see themselves as holding much responsibility for how their children turn out. They place little or no limits or control on their children's behavior.
	Authoritarian	**Uninvolved**
	Characteristics: controlling, punitive, rigid, cold	**Characteristics:** displaying indifferent, rejecting behavior
Low Responsive	**Relationship with Children:** Their word is law, and they value strict, unquestioning obedience from their children. They also do not tolerate expressions of disagreement.	**Relationship with Children:** They are detached emotionally and see their role as only providing food, clothing, and shelter. In its extreme form, this parenting style results in neglect, a form of child abuse.

- Children of authoritative parents fare best. They generally are independent, friendly, self-assertive, and cooperative. They have strong motivation to achieve and are typically successful and likable. They regulate their own behavior effectively, in terms of both their relationships with others and their emotional self-regulation.
- Children of uninvolved parents are the worst off, showing disrupted emotional development. They feel unloved and emotionally detached, and their physical and cognitive development may be impeded as well.

Of course, no classification system is an infallible predictor of how children will fare. In a significant number of cases the children of authoritarian and permissive parents develop successfully.

Furthermore, most parents are inconsistent, switching from their dominant mode to one of the others. For instance, when a child darts into the street, an authoritarian style is generally the most effective (Holden & Miller, 1999; Eisenberg & Valiente, 2002; Gershoff, 2002).

Cultural Differences in Childrearing Practices. It's important to keep in mind that the findings regarding childrearing styles we have been discussing are chiefly applicable to Western societies. The style of parenting that is most successful may depend quite heavily on the norms of a particular culture—and what parents in a particular culture are taught regarding appropriate childrearing practices (Keller et al., 2008; Yagmurlu & Sanson, 2009; Yaman et al., 2010; Calzada et al., 2012).

For example, the Chinese concept of *chiao shun* suggests that parents should learn to be strict, firm, and in tight control of their children's behavior. They accept that they have a duty to train their children to adhere to socially and culturally desirable standards of behavior, particularly in their school performance. Children's acceptance of this style is seen as a sign of parental respect (Chao, 1994; Wu, Robinson, & Yang, 2002; Ng, Pomerantz, & Lam, 2007).

In short, childrearing practices reflect cultural perspectives on the nature of children as well as on the appropriate role of parents. No single parenting pattern or style is universally appropriate (Chang Pettit, & Katsurada, 2006; Wang, Pomerantz, & Chen, 2007; Pomerantz et al., 2011). Similarly, it is important to keep in mind that parents are not the sole influence on children's development. Sibling and peer influences play a significant role, as does the child's unique genetic endowment (Boivin et al., 2005; Loehlin, Neiderhiser, & Reiss, 2005).

Child Abuse and Psychological Maltreatment: The Grim Side of Family Life

The figures are disheartening: At least five children are killed by their parents or caretakers every day, and 140,000 others are physically injured every year. Around 3 million children are abused or neglected in the United States each year. The abuse takes several forms, ranging from actual physical abuse to psychological mistreatment (Briere et al., 1997; Parnell & Day, 1998; National Clearinghouse on Child Abuse and Neglect Information, 2004; U.S. Department of Health and Human Services, 2007) (see Figure 4-9).

Physical Abuse. Child abuse can occur in any household, regardless of economic well-being or social status. It is most prevalent in families living in stressful environments. Poverty, single-parenthood, and higher-than-average levels of marital conflict help create such environments. Stepfathers are more likely to abuse stepchildren than genetic fathers to abuse their own offspring. Child abuse is also more likely when there is a history of violence between spouses (Osofsky, 2003; Evans, 2004; Ezzo & Young, 2012). (Table 4-2 lists some of the warning signs of abuse.)

Abused children are more likely to be fussy, resistant to control, and not readily adaptable to new situations. They have more headaches and stomachaches, experience more bedwetting, are generally more anxious, and may show developmental delays. Children in certain age groups are also more likely to be the targets of abuse: Three- and 4-year-olds and 15- to 17-year-olds are somewhat more likely to be abused than children of other ages (Straus & Gelles, 1990; Ammerman & Patz, 1996; Haugaard, 2000).

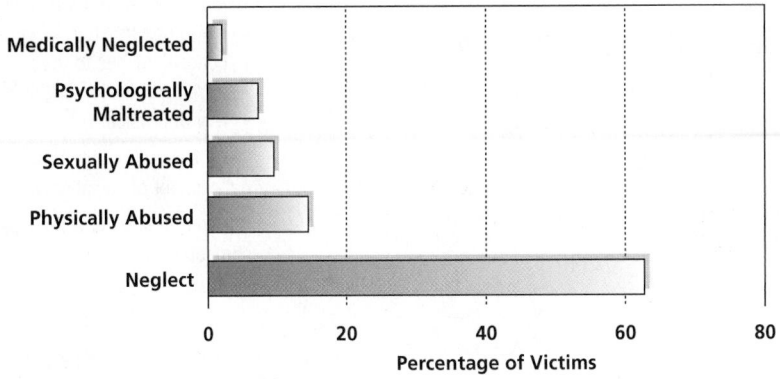

The percentages add up to numbers higher than 100% because some victims were exposed to multiple types of maltreatment. 62.8 percent of victims experienced neglect.

FIGURE 4-9 Types of Child Abuse
Neglect is the most frequent form of abuse. How can educators and health care providers help identify cases of child abuse?
Source: U.S. Department of Health and Human Services, Administration on Children, Youth and Families, 2007.

Reasons for Physical Abuse. Why does physical abuse occur? Most parents do not intend to hurt their children. In fact, most parents who abuse their children later express bewilderment and regret about their behavior.

One reason for child abuse is the vague demarcation between permissible and impermissible forms of physical violence. U.S. folklore says that spanking is not merely acceptable, but often necessary. Almost half of mothers with children under 4 have spanked their child in the previous week, and close to 20 percent believe it is appropriate to spank a child less than 1 year of age. In some other cultures, physical discipline is even more common (Straus, Gelles, & Steinmetz, 2003; Lansford et al., 2005; Deb & Adak, 2006; Shor, 2006).

cycle of violence hypothesis the theory that the abuse and neglect that children suffer predispose them as adults to abuse and neglect their own children

Unfortunately, the line between "spanking" and "beating" is fuzzy, and spankings begun in anger can escalate into abuse. In fact, increasing scientific evidence suggests that spanking should be avoided entirely. Although physical punishment may produce immediate compliance, there are serious long-term side effects. For example, spanking is associated with inferior parent–child relationships, poorer mental health for both child and parent, higher levels of delinquency, and more antisocial behavior. Spanking also teaches children that violence is an acceptable solution to problems. Consequently, the American Academy of Pediatrics strongly recommends *against* the use of physical punishment of any sort (Afifi et al., 2006; Zolotor et al., 2008; Gershoff et al., 2012).

Another factor that leads to high rates of abuse in Western countries is privacy. In most Western cultures children are raised in private, isolated households. In many other cultures, child-rearing is the joint responsibility of several people and even society as a whole, and other people are available to help out when a parent's patience is tested (Chaffin, 2006; Elliott & Urquiza, 2006).

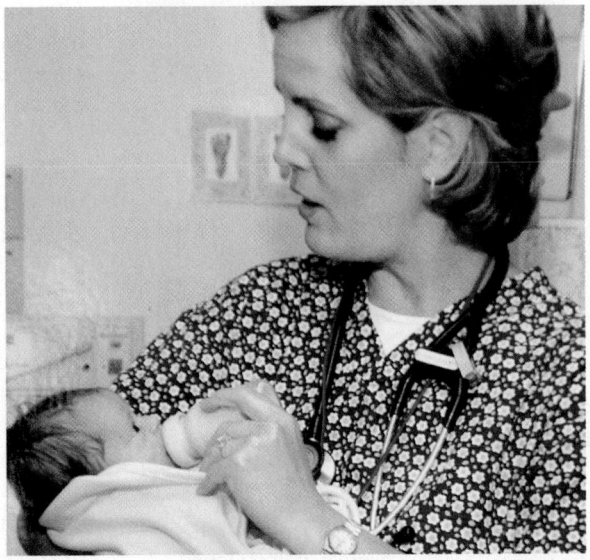

This 9-day-old infant, named Baby Vinnie, was abandoned on the steps behind a church. He was later adopted by a foster family.

The Cycle of Violence Hypothesis. Many people who abuse children were themselves abused as children. According to the **cycle of violence hypothesis**, the abuse and neglect that children suffer predispose them as adults to abuse and neglect their own children (Widom, 2000; Heyman & Slep, 2002; Henschel, Bruin, & Möhler, 2013).

TABLE 4-2 WHAT ARE THE WARNING SIGNS OF CHILD ABUSE?

Because child abuse is typically a secret crime, identifying the victims of abuse is particularly difficult. Still, there are several signs in a child that indicate that he or she is the victim of violence (Robbins, 1990):

- visible, serious injuries that have no reasonable explanation
- bite or choke marks
- burns from cigarettes or immersion in hot water
- feelings of pain for no apparent reason
- fear of adults or care providers
- inappropriate attire in warm weather (long sleeves, long pants, high-necked garments)—possibly to conceal injuries to the neck, arms, and legs
- extreme behavior—highly aggressive, extremely passive, extremely withdrawn
- fear of physical contact

If you suspect a child is a victim of aggression, it is your responsibility to act. Call your local police or the department of social services in your city or state, or call Childhelp U.S.A. at 1-800-422-4453.

Talk to a teacher or a member of the clergy. Remember, by acting decisively you can literally save someone's life.

According to this hypothesis, victims of abuse have learned from their childhood experiences that violence is an appropriate and acceptable form of discipline, and they have failed to learn the skills needed to solve problems and instill discipline without violence (Straus, Sugarman, & Giles-Sims, 1997; Blumenthal, 2000; Ethier, Couture, & Lacharite, 2004).

Of course, being abused as a child does not inevitably lead to abuse of one's own children. In fact, statistics show that only about one-third of people who were abused or neglected as children abuse their own children (Cicchetti, 1996; Straus & McCord, 1998).

Increasingly, spanking and other forms of physical violence are being seen as a human rights violation. The United Nations Committee on the Rights of the Child has called physical punishment "legalized violence against children," and it has called for its elimination. A treaty supporting this view has been ratified by 192 countries, with the exception of the United States and Somalia (Smith, 2012).

psychological maltreatment abuse that occurs when parents or other caregivers harm children's behavioral, cognitive, emotional, or physical functioning

Psychological Maltreatment. Children may also be the victims of more subtle forms of mistreatment. **Psychological maltreatment** occurs when parents or other caregivers harm children's behavioral, cognitive, emotional, or physical functioning. It may be the result of overt behavior or neglect (Hart, Brassard, & Karlson, 1996; Higgins & McCabe, 2003).

For example, abusive parents may frighten, belittle, or humiliate their children, who may be made to feel like disappointments or failures. Parents may say that they wish that their children had never been born. Children may be threatened with abandonment or even death. In other instances, older children may be exploited. They may be forced to seek employment and then to give their earnings to their parents.

In other cases of psychological maltreatment, the abuse takes the form of neglect. Parents may ignore their children or act emotionally unresponsive. The children may be given unrealistic responsibilities or may be left to fend for themselves.

While some children are sufficiently resilient to survive psychological maltreatment, lasting damage often results. Psychological maltreatment has been associated with low self-esteem, lying, misbehavior, and underachievement in school. In extreme cases, it can produce criminal behavior, aggression, and murder. In other instances, children who have been psychologically maltreated become depressed and even commit suicide (Koenig, Cicchetti, & Rogosch, 2004; Allen, 2008; Palusci & Ondersma, 2012).

One reason that psychological maltreatment—as well as physical abuse—produces so many negative consequences is that the brains of victims undergo permanent changes due to the abuse (see Figure 4-10). For example, childhood maltreatment can lead to reductions in the size of the amygdala and hippocampus in adulthood. The stress, fear, and terror accompanying abuse may also produce permanent changes in the brain due to overstimulation of the limbic system. Because the limbic system is involved in the regulation of memory and emotion, the result can be antisocial behavior during adulthood (Watts-English et al., 2006; Rick & Douglas, 2007; Twardosz & Lutzker, 2009).

Two of the children in this large family allegedly were singled out for abuse by their parents and were severely malnourished, while the other children were seemingly well cared for. What might account for this unusual situation?

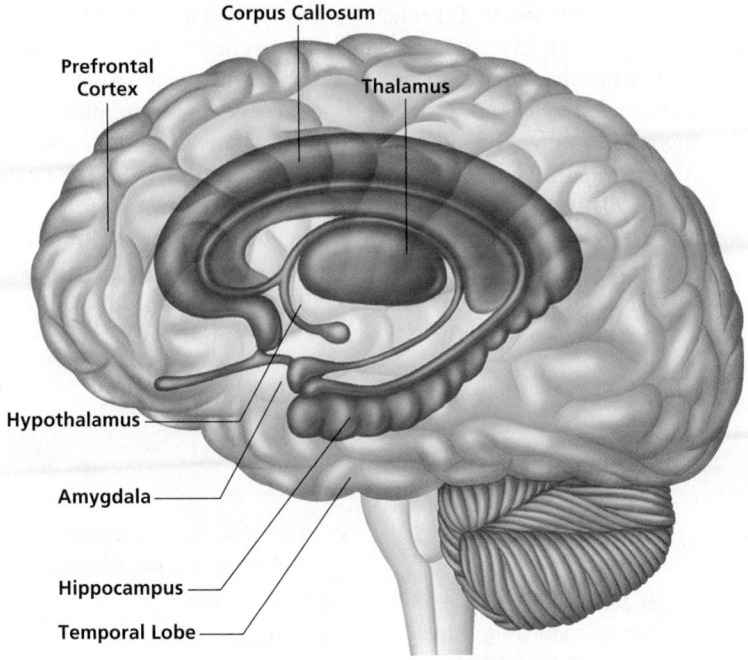

FIGURE 4-10 Abuse Alters the Brain
The limbic system, comprised of the hippocampus and amygdala, can be permanently altered as a result of childhood abuse.
Source: Scientific American, 2002.

Resilience: Overcoming the Odds

Given the seriousness of child abuse and the damage it can cause, it's remarkable that not all children who have been abused are permanently scarred. In fact, some do surprisingly well. What enables some children to overcome stress and trauma that in most cases haunts others for life?

The answer appears to be resilience. **Resilience** is the ability to overcome high-risk circumstances, that place a child at high risk for psychological or physical damage, such as extremes of poverty, prenatal stress, or violence in the home. Several factors seem to reduce and, in certain cases, eliminate some children's reactions to difficult circumstances (Trickett, Kurtz, & Pizzigati, 2004; Collishaw et al., 2007; Monahan, Beeber, & Harden, 2012).

According to developmental psychologist Emmy Werner, resilient children tend to have temperaments that evoke positive responses. They tend to be affectionate, easygoing, and

resilience the ability to overcome circumstances that place a child at high risk for psychological or physical damage

Becoming an Informed Consumer of Development

Disciplining Children

The question of how to discipline children has been raised for generations. Answers from developmentalists today include the following (O'Leary, 1995; Brazelton & Sparrow, 2003; Flouri, 2005):

- **For most children in Western cultures, authoritative parenting works best.** Parents should be firm and consistent, providing clear direction and rules, but explaining why the rules make sense, using language that children can understand.
- **Spanking is never an appropriate discipline technique** according to the American Academy of Pediatrics. Not only is spanking ineffective, but it leads to additional unwanted outcomes, such as the potential for more aggressive behavior (American Academy of Pediatrics, 1998).
- **Use time-out for punishment.** It is best to remove children from a situation in which they have misbehaved and take away enjoyable activities for a set period.
- **Tailor parental discipline to the characteristics of the child and the situation.** Try to keep the child's personality in mind, and adapt discipline to it.
- **Use routines (such as a bath routine or a bedtime routine) to avoid conflict.** To avoid a nightly struggle, make the potential conflict situation predictably enjoyable. For instance, routinely reading a bedtime story or engaging in a nightly "wrestling" match with the child can defuse potential battles.

good-natured. They are easily soothed as infants, and elicit care from the most nurturant people in any given environment. In a sense, resilient children make their own environments by drawing out behavior in others that they need for their own development. As they grow to school age, they are socially pleasant, outgoing, and have good communication skills. They tend to be intelligent and independent, feeling that they can shape their own fate without depending on others or luck (Werner & Smith, 2002; Martinez-Torteya et al., 2009; Naglieri, Goldstein, & LeBuffe, 2010).

These characteristics suggest ways to help children who are at risk. Programs that have been successful in helping especially vulnerable children provide competent and caring adult models who teach the children problem-solving skills and help them to communicate their needs to those who are in a position to help (Davey et al., 2003; Maton, Schellenbach, & Leadbeater, 2004; Condly, 2006).

REVIEW, CHECK, AND APPLY

REVIEW

L013 In what sorts of social relationships and play do preschool-age children engage?

- In the preschool years, children develop friendships on the basis of personal characteristics, trust, and shared interests.
- The character of preschoolers' play changes over time, growing more sophisticated, interactive, and cooperative, and relying increasingly on social skills.

L014 What sorts of disciplinary styles do parents employ, and what effects do they have?

- There are several distinct childrearing styles, including authoritarian, permissive, authoritative, and uninvolved.
- Differences in parenting style are associated with different effects on children. In general, children of authoritative parents fare best, especially when the parents are flexible enough to use elements of different styles when circumstances call for it.

L015 What factors contribute to child abuse and neglect?

- Child abuse can occur in any household regardless of economic well-being or social status. It is most prevalent in families living in stressful environments, created in some cases by poverty, single parenthood, and high levels of marital conflict.

CHECK YOURSELF

1. When it comes to play, younger preschoolers focus on _____ and older preschoolers focus on _____.
   - a sharing activities; trust and shared interests
   - b trust and shared interests; sharing activities
   - c parallel play; solitary play
   - d communicative play; nonverbal play
2. As preschoolers get older, their play shifts from more social to more functional.
   - True
   - False
3. Which of the following characteristics is NOT typical of a child who has authoritative parents?
   - a independent
   - b achievement-oriented
   - c dependent
   - d likeable

APPLYING LIFESPAN DEVELOPMENT

- What cultural and environmental factors in the United States may have contributed to the shift from an authoritarian "spare the rod" parenting style to an authoritative one since World War II? Is another shift under way?

✓ **Study** and **Review** on **MyPsychLab.com**

MORAL DEVELOPMENT AND AGGRESSION

L016 How do children develop a sense of morality?
L017 How does aggression develop in preschool-age children?

Lena and Carrie were part of a group of preschoolers who wanted to act out Cinderella. The teacher began assigning parts. "Lena, you can be Cinderella. And Carrie, you'll be her Fairy Godmother." Tears welled up in Carrie's eyes. "I don't want to be a Fairy Godmother," she sobbed. Lena put her arms around Carrie. "You can be Cinderella, too. We'll be twin Cinderellas." Carrie cheered up at once, grateful that Lena had understood her feelings and responded with kindness.

In this short scenario we see many of the key elements of morality, preschool style. Changes in children's views of the right way to behave are an important element of growth during the preschool years.

At the same time, the kind of aggression displayed by preschoolers is also changing. We can consider the development of morality and aggression as two sides of the coin of human conduct, and both involve a growing awareness of others.

Developing Morality: Following Society's Rights and Wrongs

Moral development refers to changes in people's sense of justice and of what is right and wrong, and in their behavior related to moral issues. Developmentalists have considered moral development in terms of children's reasoning about morality, attitudes toward moral lapses, and behavior when faced with moral issues. In the process of studying moral development, several approaches have evolved.

Piaget's View of Moral Development. Child psychologist Jean Piaget was one of the first to study moral development. He suggested that moral development, like cognitive development, proceeds in stages (Piaget, 1932). He called the earliest stage *heteronomous morality*, in which rules are seen as invariant and unchangeable. During this stage, which lasts from about age 4 through age 7, children play games rigidly, assuming that there is one, and only one, way to play. At the same time, though, they may not even fully grasp game rules. Consequently, a group of children may be playing together, with each child playing according to a slightly different set of rules. Nevertheless, they enjoy playing with each other. Piaget suggests that every child may "win" such a game, because winning means having a good time, as opposed to competing.

Heteronomous morality is ultimately replaced by two later stages of morality: incipient cooperation and autonomous cooperation. In the *incipient cooperation stage*, which lasts from around age 7 to age 10, children's games become more clearly social. Children learn the actual rules and play according to this shared knowledge. Rules are still seen as largely unchangeable, and there is a "right" way to play the game.

It is not until the *autonomous cooperation stage*, which begins at about age 10, that children become fully aware that formal game rules can be modified if the players agree. This is the beginning of the understanding that rules of law are created by people and are subject to change according to the will of people.

Due to their increasing understanding of moral development, children may worry they will be punished even though no one sees them carrying out the misdeed.

Social Learning Approaches to Morality. Whereas Piaget emphasizes how limitations in preschoolers' cognitive development lead to particular forms of moral *reasoning*, social learning approaches focus more on how the environment in which preschoolers operate produces **prosocial behavior**, helping behavior that benefits others (Eisenberg, 2004; Spinrad, Eisenberg & Bernt, 2007; Caputi et al., 2012).

Social learning approaches acknowledge that some instances of children's prosocial behavior stem from situations in which they have received positive reinforcement for acting in a moral way. For instance, when Claire's mother tells her she has been a "good girl" for sharing a box of candy with her brother, Claire's behavior has been reinforced. As a consequence, she is more likely to engage in sharing behavior in the future (Ramaswamy & Bergin, 2009).

However, not all prosocial behavior has to be directly reinforced. According to social learning theorists, children also learn moral behavior indirectly by observing the behavior of others, called *models* (Bandura, 1977). Children imitate models who receive reinforcement for their behavior and ultimately learn to perform the behavior themselves. For example, when Claire's friend Jake watches Claire share her candy with her brother, and Claire is praised for her behavior, Jake is more likely to engage in sharing behavior himself at some later point. Unfortunately, the opposite also holds true: If a model behaves selfishly, children who observe such behavior tend to behave more selfishly themselves (Hastings et al., 2007).

Children do more than simply mimic behavior that they see rewarded in others. When they observe moral conduct, they are reminded of society's norms about the importance of moral behavior as conveyed by parents, teachers, and other authority figures. They notice the connections between particular situations and certain kinds of behavior. This increases the likelihood that similar situations will elicit similar behavior in the observer.

Consequently, modeling paves the way for the development of more general rules and principles in a process called **abstract modeling**. Rather than always modeling the particular behavior of others, older preschoolers begin to develop generalized principles that underlie the behavior they observe. After observing repeated instances in which a model is rewarded

moral development the changes in people's sense of justice and of what is right and wrong, and in their behavior related to moral issues

prosocial behavior helping behavior that benefits others

abstract modeling the process in which modeling paves the way for the development of more general rules and principles for acting in a morally desirable way, children begin the process of inferring and learning the general principles of moral conduct (Bandura, 1991).

Genetic Approaches to Morality. The newest, and highly controversial, approach to morality suggests that particular genes may underlie some aspects of moral behavior. According to this view, preschoolers have a genetic predisposition to behave generously or selfishly.

In one study designed to illustrate this approach, researchers gave preschoolers the opportunity to behave generously by sharing stickers. Those who were more selfish and less generous were more likely to have a variation in a gene called AVPR1A, which regulates a hormone in the brain that is related to social behavior (Avinun et al., 2011).

It is unlikely that the gene mutation fully accounts for the preschoolers' lack of generosity. The environment in which the children were raised also is likely to play a significant, and perhaps predominant, role in determining moral behavior. Still, the findings are provocative in showing that generosity may have genetic roots.

Empathy and Moral Behavior. According to some developmentalists, **empathy**—the understanding of what another individual feels—lies at the heart of some kinds of moral behavior.

The roots of empathy grow early. One-year-old infants cry when they hear other infants crying. By ages 2 and 3, toddlers will offer gifts and spontaneously share toys with other children and adults, even strangers (Zahn-Wexler & Radke-Yarrow, 1990). During the preschool years, empathy continues to grow as children's ability to monitor and regulate their emotional and cognitive responses increases. Some theorists believe that increasing empathy (along with other positive emotions, such as sympathy and admiration) leads children to behave morally. In addition, some negative emotions—such as anger at an unfair situation or shame over previous transgressions—also may promote moral behavior (Decety & Jackson, 2006; Rieffe, Ketelaar, & Wiefferink, 2010; Bischof-Köhler, 2012).

Aggression and Violence in Preschoolers: Sources and Consequences

Four-year-old Duane could not contain his anger and frustration any more. Although he usually was mild-mannered, when Eshu began to tease him about the split in his pants and kept it up for several minutes, Duane finally snapped. Rushing over to Eshu, Duane pushed him to the ground and began to hit him with his small, closed fists. Because he was so distraught, Duane's punches were not terribly effective, but they were severe enough to hurt Eshu and bring him to tears before the preschool teachers could intervene.

empathy the understanding of what another individual feels

aggression intentional injury or harm to another person

Aggression among preschoolers is common, though attacks such as this are not. Verbal hostility, shoving matches, kicking, and other forms of aggression may occur throughout the preschool period, although the degree to which aggression is acted out changes as children become older.

Aggression, both physical and verbal, is present throughout the preschool period.

Eshu's taunting is also a form of aggression. **Aggression** is intentional injury or harm to another person. Infants don't act aggressively; it is hard to contend that their behavior is *intended* to hurt others, even if they inadvertently manage to do so. In contrast, by the time they reach preschool age, children demonstrate true aggression.

During the early preschool years, some of the aggression is addressed at attaining a desired goal, such as getting a toy away from another person or using a particular space occupied by another person. Consequently, in some ways the aggression is inadvertent, and minor scuffles may in fact be a typical part of early preschool life. It is the rare child who does not demonstrate at least an occasional act of aggression.

On the other hand, extreme and sustained aggression is a cause of concern. In most children, the amount of aggression declines as they move through the preschool years, as does the frequency and average length of episodes of aggressive behavior (Persson, 2005).

A child's personality and social development contribute to this decline in aggression. Throughout the preschool years, children become better at controlling the emotions that they are experiencing. **Emotional self-regulation** is the capability to adjust emotions to a desired state and level of intensity. Starting at age 2, children are able to talk about their feelings, and they engage in strategies to regulate them. As they get older, they develop more effective strategies, learning to better cope with negative emotions. In addition to their increasing self-control, children are also developing sophisticated social skills. Most learn to use language to express their wishes and to negotiate with others (Philippot & Feldman, 2005; Cole et al., 2009; Helmsen, Koglin, & Petermann, 2012).

Despite these typical declines in aggression, some children remain aggressive throughout the preschool period. Furthermore, aggression is a relatively stable characteristic: The most aggressive preschoolers tend to be the most aggressive children during the school-age years (Tremblay, 2001; Schaeffer, Petras, & Ialongo, 2003; Davenport & Bourgeois, 2008).

Boys typically show higher levels of physical, instrumental aggression than girls.

Instrumental aggression is aggression motivated by the desire to obtain a concrete goal, such as playing with a desirable toy that another child is playing with.

On the other hand, although girls show lower levels of instrumental aggression, they may be just as aggressive, but in different ways from boys. Girls are more likely to practice **relational aggression**, which is nonphysical aggression that is intended to hurt another person's feelings. Such aggression may manifest as name-calling, withholding friendship, or simply saying mean, hurtful things that make the recipient feel bad (Murray-Close, Ostrov, & Crick, 2007; Valles & Knutson, 2008; Ambrose & Menna, 2013).

The Roots of Aggression. How can we explain the aggression of preschoolers? Some theoreticians suggest that aggression is an instinct, part and parcel of the human condition. For instance, Freud's psychoanalytic theory suggests that we all are motivated by sexual and aggressive instincts (Freud, 1920). And ethologist Konrad Lorenz, an expert in animal behavior, argues that animals—including humans—share a fighting instinct that stems from primitive urges to preserve territory, maintain a steady supply of food, and weed out weaker animals (Lorenz, 1966, 1974).

Similar arguments are made by evolutionary theorists and *sociobiologists*, scientists who consider the biological roots of social behavior. They argue that aggression leads to increased opportunities to mate, improving the likelihood that one's genes will be passed on to future generations. In addition, aggression may help to strengthen the species and its gene pool as a whole, because the strongest survive. Ultimately, then, aggressive instincts promote the survival of one's genes to pass on to future generations (Archer, 2009).

Although instinctual explanations are logical, they have relatively little experimental support. They also fail to take into account the increasingly sophisticated cognitive abilities that humans develop as they get older. Moreover, they provide little guidance in determining when and how children, as well as adults, will behave aggressively, other than noting that aggression is an inevitable part of the human condition. Consequently, developmentalists have turned to other approaches.

Social learning explanations of aggression suggest that children's observation of aggression on television can result in actual aggression.

Social Learning Approaches to Aggression. The day after Duane lashed out at Eshu, Lynn, who had watched the entire scene, got into an argument with Ilya. They verbally bickered for a while, and suddenly Lynn balled her hand into a fist and tried to punch Ilya. The preschool teachers were stunned: It was rare for Lynn to get upset, and she had never displayed aggression before.

Is there a connection between the two events? Social learning theorists would answer yes, because to them aggression is largely a learned behavior based on children's observation and prior learning. To understand the causes of aggressive behavior, then, we should look at the system of rewards and punishments in a child's environment.

Social learning approaches emphasize how social and environmental conditions teach individuals to be aggressive. Using a behavioral perspective, they argue that aggressive behavior is learned through direct reinforcement. For instance, preschool-age children may learn that they can continue to play with the most desirable toys by aggressively refusing their classmates' requests for sharing. In the parlance of traditional learning theory, they have been reinforced for acting aggressively, and they are more likely to behave aggressively in the future.

But as we saw when discussing morality, social learning approaches suggest that reinforcement also comes indirectly. Research suggests that exposure to aggressive models leads to

emotional self-regulation the capability to adjust emotions to a desired state and level of intensity

instrumental aggression aggression motivated by the desire to obtain a concrete goal

relational aggression nonphysical aggression that is intended to hurt another person's psychological well-being

FIGURE 4-11 Modeling Aggression
This series of photos is from Albert Bandura's classic Bobo doll experiment, designed to illustrate social learning of aggression. The photos clearly show how the adult model's aggressive behavior (in the first row) is imitated by children who had viewed the aggressive behavior (second and third rows).

increased aggression, particularly if the observers are themselves angered, insulted, or frustrated. For example, Albert Bandura and his colleagues illustrated the power of models in a classic study of preschool-age children (Bandura, Ross, & Ross, 1963). One group of children watched a film of an adult playing aggressively and violently with a Bobo doll (a large, inflated plastic clown designed as a punching bag for children that always returns to an upright position after being knocked over). In comparison, children in another condition watched a film of an adult playing sedately with a set of Tinkertoys (see Figure 4-11). Later, the preschool-age children were allowed to play with a number of toys, which included both the Bobo doll and the Tinkertoys. But first, the children were led to feel frustration by being refused the opportunity to play with a favorite toy.

As predicted by social learning approaches, the preschool-age children modeled the behavior of the adult. Those who had seen the aggressive model playing with the Bobo doll were considerably more aggressive than those who had watched the calm, unaggressive model playing with the Tinkertoys. **Watch** the **Video** *Classic Footage of Bandura's Bobo Doll Experiment* in **MyPsychLab**.

Viewing Violence on TV: Does It Matter? The majority of preschool-age children are exposed to aggression via television. Children's television programs contain higher levels of violence (69 percent) than other types of programs (57 percent). In an average hour, children's programs contain more than twice as many violent incidents as other types of programs (Wilson, 2002).

This high level of televised violence, viewed in light of research findings on modeling aggression, raises a significant question: Does viewing aggression increase the likelihood that children (and later adults) will perform aggressive acts?

The overwhelming weight of evidence suggests that observation of televised aggression does lead to subsequent aggression. Longitudinal studies have found that children's preferences for violent television shows at age 8 are correlated with the seriousness of criminal convictions by age 30. Other evidence supports the notion that observation of media violence can lead to bullying, a greater readiness to act aggressively, and insensitivity to the suffering of victims of violence (Ostrov, Gentile, & Crick, 2006; Christakis & Zimmerman, 2007; Kirsh, 2012).

From an educator's perspective: How might a preschool teacher or parent help children notice the violence in the programs they watch and protect them from its effects?

Television is not the only source of media violence. Many video games contain highly aggressive behavior, and many children play such games. For example, 14 percent of children age 3 and younger and around 50 percent of those 4 to 6 play video games. Because research conducted with adults shows that playing violent video games is associated with behaving aggressively, children who play video games containing violence may likewise be at risk for behaving aggressively (Polman, de Castro, & van Aken, 2008; Fischer, Kastenmüller, & Greitemeyer, 2010; Hasan, Bègue, & Bushman, 2013).

Fortunately, social learning principles suggest not only the problem but the solution. Children can be explicitly taught to view violence with a critical eye. If they learn that violence is not representative of the real world, that viewing violence can affect them negatively, and that they should avoid imitating the behavior they see on television, they may interpret the programs differently and be less influenced by them (Persson & Musher-Eizenman, 2003; Donnerstein, 2005).

Furthermore, just as exposure to aggressive models leads to aggression, observation of *non-aggressive* models can *reduce* aggression. Preschoolers don't just learn from others how to be aggressive; they can also learn how to avoid confrontation and to control their aggression, as we'll discuss later. (Also see the *From Research to Practice* box.)

From Research to Practice

Do Violent Video Games Make Children Violent?

If you're a traditional-age college student, you probably grew up playing video games—and even if you haven't played them, you've almost certainly seen the dizzying array of violent video games available. These games have been controversial for as long as they've been around. Many parents, educators, and social scientists have voiced concerns that playing violent video games can lead people—especially young children—to become more aggressive. Many fans of these games feel strongly that they are unaffected by them, despite mounting research to the contrary.

But what does the research have to say about the consequences of playing video games? One of the leading researchers in this area is psychologist Craig Anderson. He and his colleagues have conducted a meta-analysis in which he concludes that playing violent video games is a risk factor for increased aggressiveness (Anderson et al., 2010; Bastian, Jetten, & Radke, 2012).

The researchers examined more than 130 published studies on the effects of violent video game play using a total of more than 130,000 participants. The outcome variables they focused on were aggressive thoughts, aggressive behaviors, aggressive feelings, physiological arousal, empathy/desensitization, and helping behavior. Their analysis included longitudinal studies of all of these variables (except arousal, which is a short-term phenomenon) and looked for cross-cultural and gender differences as well.

The results of the meta-analysis were quite clear: increased levels of violent video game play were associated with more aggressive thoughts, feelings, and behaviors, and these findings applied equally well to studies using cross-sectional, longitudinal, or experimental research methods, and they did not differ between Western and Eastern cultures. Violent video game play was also associated with desensitization to violence, lack of empathy, and lack of helping behavior. All of these effects applied to females and to males (Anderson et al., 2010).

Anderson and his team were careful to point out that in addition to being theoretically important, the results they found also have real-world, practical significance. In the case of violent video game play, the effects are cumulative over time, they are being applied to a large percentage of the population (everyone who plays these games), and they can interact with other variables to produce serious consequences.

The researchers note that the contribution of violent video game play to aggressiveness found by this analysis is equivalent to the contributions of other risk factors such as substance abuse, abusive parents, and poverty. They argue that the discussion of violent video games should shift from whether they have harmful effects—clearly they do—to what parents, schools, and society in general can do about it (Anderson et al., 2010).

- *Given that many factors influence any given person's aggressiveness, why would violent video game play be any more important to consider than any of the other factors?*
- *What do you think parents, schools, or society in general might be able to do about the harmful effects of violent video game play?* **Watch** the **Video** *In The Real World: Learning Aggression* in **MyPsychLab**.

Cognitive Approaches to Aggression: The Thoughts Behind Violence. Two children, waiting for their turn in a game of kickball, inadvertently knock into one another. One child's reaction is to apologize; the other's is to shove, saying angrily, "Cut it out."

Despite the fact that each child bears the same responsibility for the minor event, they have different reactions. What the first child sees as an accident, the second child sees as a provocation.

The cognitive approach to aggression suggests that to understand preschoolers' moral development it is necessary to examine their interpretations of others' behavior and of the environmental context of the behavior. According to developmental psychologist Kenneth Dodge and his colleagues, some children are more prone than others to assume that actions are aggressively motivated. They are unable to pay attention to the appropriate cues in a situation and interpret the behaviors in the situation erroneously, assuming that what is happening is hostile. Subsequently, in deciding how to respond, they base their behavior on their inaccurate interpretation, behaving aggressively in response to a situation that never in fact existed (Petit & Dodge, 2003).

Although the cognitive approach describes the process that leads some children to behave aggressively, it fails to explain why they perceive situations inaccurately and why they so readily respond with aggression. On the other hand, the cognitive approach is useful in pointing out a means to reduce aggression: By teaching preschool-age children to interpret situations more accurately, we can induce them to be less prone to view others' behavior as motivated by hostility and less likely to respond with aggression themselves.

Becoming an Informed Consumer of Development

Increasing Moral Behavior and Reducing Aggression in Preschool-Age Children

Here are some practical and readily accomplished strategies for encouraging moral conduct and reducing aggression, based on ideas from the many approaches we have discussed (Bor & Bor, 2004; Eisenberg, 2012):

- *Provide opportunities for preschool-age children to observe others acting in a cooperative, helpful, prosocial manner.* Encourage them to interact with peers in joint activities in which they share a common goal. Such cooperative activities can teach the importance and desirability of working with—and helping—others.
- *Do not ignore aggressive behavior.* Parents and teachers should intervene when they see aggression in preschoolers, sending a clear message that aggression is an unacceptable way to resolve conflicts.
- *Help preschoolers devise alternative explanations for others' behavior.* With children who are prone to aggression and apt to view others' conduct as more hostile than it actually is, parents and teachers should help them see that the behavior of their peers has several possible interpretations.
- *Monitor preschoolers' television viewing, particularly the violence that they view.* Discourage preschoolers from watching shows depicting aggression and encourage them to watch particular shows that are designed, in part, to foster moral conduct, such as *Sesame Street* and *Dora the Explorer*.
- *Help preschoolers understand their feelings.* When children become angry—and all children do—they must learn to deal with their feelings constructively. Tell them *specific* things they can do to improve the situation. ("I see you're really angry with Jake for not giving you a turn. Don't hit him, but tell him you want a chance to play with the game.")
- *Explicitly teach reasoning and self-control.* Preschoolers can understand the rudiments of moral reasoning, and they should be reminded why certain behaviors are desirable. For instance, explicitly saying "If you take all the cookies, others will have no dessert" is preferable to saying, "Good children don't eat all the cookies."

REVIEW, CHECK, AND APPLY

4.1 4.2 4.3

REVIEW

L016 How do children develop a sense of morality?

- Piaget believed that preschoolers are in the heteronomous morality stage of moral development, in which rules are seen as invariant and unchangeable.
- Social learning approaches to moral development emphasize the importance of reinforcement for moral actions and the observation of models of moral conduct.
- Psychoanalytic and other theories focus on children's empathy with others and their wish to help others so they can avoid unpleasant feelings of guilt themselves.

L017 How does aggression develop in preschool-age children?

- Research suggests that exposure to aggressive models leads to increased aggression, particularly if the observers are themselves angered, insulted, or frustrated.
- Aggression typically declines in frequency and duration as children become more able to regulate their emotions and use language to negotiate disputes.

CHECK YOURSELF

1. The term _____ refers to changes in our sense of justice and our understanding of behaviors related to what is right and wrong.
   - a behavioral concern
   - b moral development
   - c perspective taking
   - d self-reflection
2. According to the _____ theory, the factor that increases the likelihood that a preschooler will engage in prosocial behavior is his or her environment.
   - a cognitive-behavioral
   - b social learning
   - c psychoanalytic
   - d humanistic
3. Aggression is an unstable characteristic in that aggressive preschoolers rarely grow up to be aggressive adults.
   - True
   - False

APPLYING LIFESPAN DEVELOPMENT

- If high-prestige models of behavior are particularly effective in influencing moral attitudes and actions, are there implications for individuals in industries such as sports, advertising, and entertainment?

✓ **Study** and **Review** on **MyPsychLab.com**

SUMMARY 4

PUTTING IT ALL TOGETHER THE PRESCHOOL YEARS

CHEN, the enthusiastic 4-year-old hiker we met in the chapter opener was probably born curious and prone to explore. In the comparatively free environment of the outdoors, Chen was testing the limits of his physical abilities and pushing against the barriers that confined him. Chen took advantage of opportunities to explore new places and used his developing skills to help him find answers to the questions that were formulating in his mind as he encountered the world, questions such as where did the water from the waterfall go, and to speculate it might be in the crevice. His adventurous personality seemingly enabled him to explore his environment without a thought for the consequences. But the bruise he received in his fall is a reminder that there are limits to his physical capabilities. As he said, "Next time, I'll watch out better." Chen was putting together all of his emerging developmental tools to exercise control over his world.

PHYSICAL DEVELOPMENT IN THE PRESCHOOL YEARS

MODULE 4.1

- Chen grew physically in the preschool years, learning to exercise with ease abilities such as walking, climbing, and swimming. *(pp. 156–158)*
- Chen also learned to use and control his gross and fine motor skills, showing considerable physical dexterity. *(pp. 156–158)*
- Chen's brain grew, and with it his cognitive abilities, such as the ability to observe phenomena and formulate questions about what he sees. *(pp. 155–156)*

COGNITIVE DEVELOPMENT IN THE PRESCHOOL YEARS

MODULE 4.2

- Chen's memory capacity increased, which will enable him to recall in future the bruise he got on his head from being careless near the crevice. *(pp. 164–166)*
- Chen observed others and learned how to perform challenging tasks, such as climbing mountains and bicycling. *(pp. 166–167)*
- Chen's language skills continued to develop, permitting him to express himself effectively in most situations. *(pp. 168–170)*
- Chen developed the cognitive skills to formulate questions about phenomena he observed and to plan for ways to find the answers to his questions. *(pp. 159–163)*

SOCIAL AND PERSONALITY DEVELOPMENT IN THE PRESCHOOL YEARS

MODULE 4.3

- Chen's self-concept includes seeing himself as a great hiker, a view that he may overestimate putting him at risk for accidents *(pp. 174–175)*
- Chen's gender schema may not include the "rule" that hiking is primarily for boys because both his mother and father take him hiking. *(p. 180)*
- Chen has reached the age where his friendships will likely form around shared interests like hiking and swimming. *(pp. 178–179)*
- Chen's parents appear to have an authoritative parenting style, which supports his sense of independence and self-assertiveness. *(pp. 181–182)*

What would a PARENT do?

How would you help Chen to consider the possible consequences of his adventures? How would you assess his readiness to consider consequences? What would you say to Chen about considering the effects of his actions on his physical safety?

What would a HEALTH CARE WORKER do?

What would you tell Chen's caregivers about risks to which he is especially prone as he develops physically and cognitively? How would you advise Chen's parents to focus their child-proofing efforts in their home as Chen grows?

What would YOU do?

What would you do to promote Chen's development? How would you advise Chen's 's caregivers in helping Chen to channel his adventurous nature and curiosity in appropriate directions? How would you advise Chen's caregivers to deal with Chen's apparent fearlessness? Should it be discouraged?

What would an EDUCATOR do?

What strategies would you use to promote Chen's social development? How would you help Chen to forge relationships with his peers? How would you deal with Chen's potential leadership qualities? What would you do to help him avoid taking foolhardy risks? What would you say to Chen's teachers about steps to take in monitoring the actions of children like Chen?

Explore on MyPsychLab

To read how real parents, health care workers, and educators responded to these questions, log onto MyPsychLab.com.

Do you agree or disagree with their responses? Why? What concepts that you've read about back up their opinion?

5 MIDDLE CHILDHOOD

When Yukio Mara finally graduated from "baby school" to "real school," as he called the transition from kindergarten to first grade, he acted like he'd scaled Mount Everest. He'd watched his four-years-older sister Jackie reading books with no pictures, adding long lines of numbers, writing stories, and doing great projects like her Egyptian mummy diorama, which still stood proudly in the corner of the family room.

Yukio started out well enough. He made friends and became known for telling imaginative stories. But soon he fell behind in reading. According to his school team, he said that he "hated reading," and this was having an effect on everything else. He wasn't keeping up in math or social studies, and his social development was declining. He didn't take part in sports or other activities, preferring to sit alone and draw.

The school prescribed 2 hours per day in the special needs room—"just until we can figure out what to do next." But Yukio's parents, Ted and Rana Mara, feared that their son would be entering the fast track to failure. Oddly, it wasn't anyone from the school who came up with the key suggestion, but one of their friends: She suggested taking Yukio to a vision therapist.

The Maras found a local optometrist who specialized in vision therapy. She soon diagnosed Yukio's problem and prescribed a course of exercises and treatments that Yukio and his parents could pursue at home.

Yukio is now in third grade, having spent much of second grade training his eyes. He has caught up with his peers in reading, math, and writing, and has taken up soccer. He's even catching up academically with his sister, who was his most avid supporter during his home treatments.

In middle childhood, children enter school eager to learn all they can about the world. Often the regular classroom setting serves them well and contributes to their physical, intellectual, and social development; sometimes, however, children display needs or deficits that require special interventions—such as the vision therapist provided for Yukio—to make the most of their abilities and keep their self-esteem intact.

In this chapter, we follow children taking the crucial step into formal schooling. We look at the physical changes that prepare them for new challenges. We discuss the patterns of growth—and excess—that are typical of this period and the new levels of motor skills that enable them to perform actions as diverse as throwing a ball and playing the violin. We also discuss threats to their well-being, and consider the special needs that can impinge on children's school lives.

Next we consider the growing intellectual and conceptual skills and the increasingly sophisticated use of language that are hallmarks of this period. We visit the place where they spend most of their time: school. We consider reading and the policy dispute over the best way to teach it. We also address the surprisingly controversial topic of intelligence.

Finally, we consider school-age children as members of society, including their membership in school and family. We look at the ways school-age children understand themselves and develop self-esteem. We consider how they relate to one another, including members of the opposite sex. We then examine the many shapes and configurations that families take, finishing with a further discussion of schooling.

MODULE 5.1

PHYSICAL DEVELOPMENT IN MIDDLE CHILDHOOD

How do visual, auditory, and speech impairments affect a child's social and personality development?

MODULE 5.2

COGNITIVE DEVELOPMENT IN MIDDLE CHILDHOOD

Schooling around the world and across genders: Who gets educated?

MODULE 5.3

SOCIAL AND PERSONALITY DEVELOPMENT IN MIDDLE CHILDHOOD

How does divorce affect a child's development?

MyVirtualLife

If you are currently using MyVirtualLife, consider how you will raise your virtual child during middle childhood. What decisions will you make?

Access MyVirtualLife for a chance to help your virtual child navigate middle childhood.

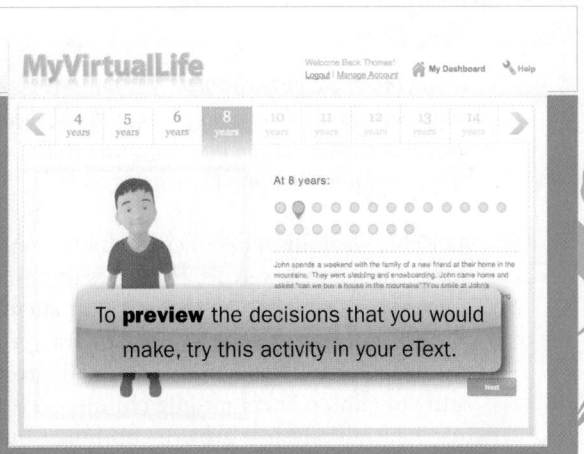

To **preview** the decisions that you would make, try this activity in your eText.

MODULE 5.1

PHYSICAL DEVELOPMENT IN MIDDLE CHILDHOOD

Eleven-year-old Tommy Rinaldo hates gym. Today the game he's being forced to play is basketball. Three times he's dribbled the ball off his foot, and twice other kids have taken it away. Tommy has decided that the best strategy is to avoid the ball entirely.

Now, however, a loose ball has come his way. Instinctively picking it up, he dribbles toward the basket, somehow making it all the way downcourt. With a pretty good motion, he turns and heaves up the ball. It doesn't go in, but after it hits the rim one of his classmates grabs the rebound and makes the shot.

The other kid says "Good assist" to Tommy. Maybe basketball isn't so bad after all.

Tommy Rinaldo has come a long way since the preschool years, when quick, coordinated running, dribbling, and shooting were not possible.

Such moments characterize middle childhood, as children's physical, cognitive, and social skills reach new heights. Beginning at age 6 and continuing to about age 12, this period is often called the "school years." Physical growth is remarkable. Motor skills soar.

We begin by examining physical and motor development in middle childhood. We discuss how children's bodies change, and the twin problems of malnutrition and obesity. We examine the development of gross motor skills—like dribbling a basketball—and fine motor skills—like playing scales on a piano. We discuss the health of children during this period, including their psychological health.

We finish the module by considering the sensory and learning difficulties of children with special needs. We also discuss a disorder that has grown in importance in recent decades, attention deficit hyperactivity disorder.

THE GROWING BODY

L01 In what ways do children grow during the school years, and what factors influence their growth?

Cinderella, dressed in yella,
Went upstairs to kiss her fellah.
But she made a mistake and she kissed a snake.
How many doctors did it take?
One, two, . . .

While the other girls chanted this jump-rope rhyme, Kat proudly displayed her new ability to jump backwards. In second grade, Kat was becoming quite good at jumping rope. In first grade, she simply had not been able to master it. But over the summer, she had spent many hours practicing, and now that practice was paying off.

As Kat is gleefully experiencing, children make great physical strides in middle childhood, mastering many new skills. How does this progress occur? We'll first consider typical physical growth during this period, then turn our attention to exceptional children.

Slow but steady. These words characterize the nature of growth during middle childhood. In contrast to the swift growth from birth to age 5 and the remarkable growth spurt of adolescence, middle childhood is relatively tranquil. The body has not shifted into neutral; physical growth continues, but at a more stately pace than in the preschool years.

Height and Weight Changes

In elementary school, children in the United States grow, on average, 2 to 3 inches a year. By age 11, the average height for girls is 4 feet, 10 inches while boys average 4 feet, 9½ inches. This is the only period in life when girls tend to be taller than boys. This reflects the slightly more rapid physical development of girls, who start their adolescent growth spurt around age 10.

Weight gain in middle childhood follows a similar pattern; boys and girls both gain around 5 to 7 pounds a year. Weight is also redistributed. As "baby fat" disappears, children's bodies become more muscular and their strength increases.

These average height and weight increases disguise significant individual differences. Children of the same age can be 6 or 7 inches apart in height.

Variations of 6 inches in height between children of the same age are not unusual and are well within normal ranges.

Cultural Patterns of Growth

Most children in North America receive sufficient nutrients to grow to their full potential. In other parts of the world, however, inadequate nutrition and disease take their toll, producing children who are shorter and weigh less. The discrepancies can be dramatic: Poor children in cities such as Kolkata, Hong Kong, and Rio de Janeiro are smaller than affluent children in the same cities.

In the United States, most variations in height and weight are the result of people's unique genetic inheritance, including genetic factors relating to racial and ethnic background. Asian and Oceanic Pacific children tend to be shorter than those of northern and central European ancestry. In addition, the rate of growth is generally more rapid for black children than for white (Deurenberg, Deurenberg-Yap, & Guricci, 2002; Deurenberg et al., 2003).

Even within racial and ethnic groups, individuals vary significantly. We cannot attribute racial and ethnic differences solely to genetic factors because dietary customs as well as variations in levels of affluence also may contribute to differences. In addition, severe stress—brought on by factors such as parental conflict or alcoholism—can affect the pituitary gland, thereby affecting growth (Koska et al., 2002).

Inadequate nutrition and disease affect growth significantly. Children in poorer areas of cities such as Kolkata, Hong Kong, and Rio de Janeiro are smaller than their counterparts in affluent areas of the same cities.

Nutrition

There is a relationship between size and nutrition. But size isn't the only area affected by diet. For instance, nutrition is related to social and emotional functioning at school age. Children who receive more nutrients are more involved with their peers, show more positive emotion, and have less anxiety than children with less adequate nutrition. Nutrition is also linked to cognitive performance. For example, in one study, children in Kenya who were well nourished performed better on a test of verbal abilities and on other cognitive measures than those who had mild to moderate undernutrition. Malnutrition may influence cognitive development by dampening children's curiosity, responsiveness, and motivation to learn (Ordovas, 2010; Yousafzai, Yakoob, & Bhutta, 2013).

Although undernutrition and malnutrition clearly lead to physical, social, and cognitive difficulties, in some cases *over*nutrition—the intake of too many calories—leads to problems of its own, in particular childhood obesity.

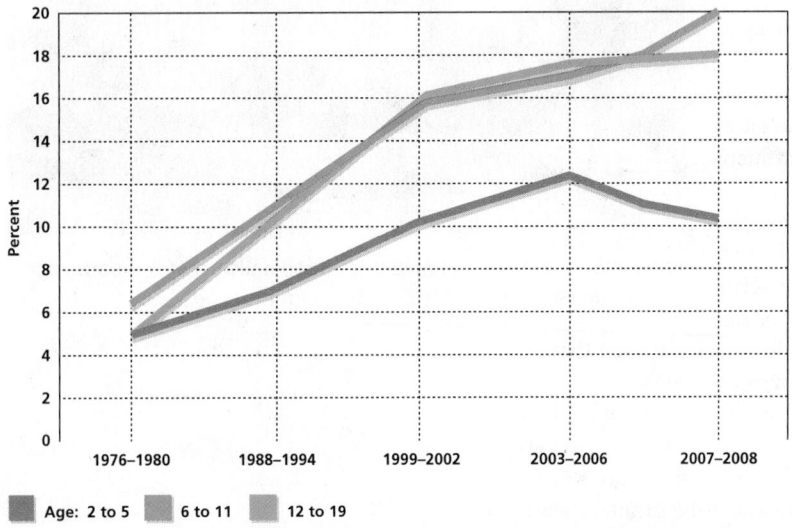

FIGURE 5-1 Fat of the Land
The percentage of children and adolescents who are overweight has increased dramatically in the last 4 decades.
Source: Fryar, C. D., Carroll, M. D., & Ogden, C. L. (2012).

Childhood Obesity

When her mother asks if she would like bread with her meal, Ruthellen replies she better not—she thinks she may be getting fat. Ruthellen, who is of normal weight and height, is 6 years old.

Although height can be of concern to both children and parents, weight is an even greater worry for some. Weight concerns can border on obsession, particularly in girls. Many 6-year-old girls worry about becoming "fat," and some 40 percent of girls ages 9 to 10 are trying to lose weight. Their concern with weight often reflects the U.S. preoccupation with slimness, which permeates the entire society (Schreiber et al., 1996; Greenwood & Pietromonaco, 2004; Liechty, 2010).

Despite the prevalent view that thinness is a virtue, childhood obesity is rising. *Obesity* is defined as body weight that is more than 20 percent above the average for a given age and height. Fifteen percent of U.S. children are obese—a figure that has tripled since the 1960s (Brownlee, 2002; Dietz, 2004; Mann, 2005) (see Figure 5-1).

The costs of childhood obesity last a lifetime. Obese children are more likely to be overweight as adults, and have a greater risk of heart disease, diabetes, and other diseases. Some scientists believe an epidemic of obesity may be leading to a decline in life span in the United States (Krishnamoorthy, Hart, & Jelalian, 2006; Park, 2008; Keel et al., 2010).

Genetic and social characteristics as well as diet influence obesity. Particular inherited genes predispose certain children to be overweight. For example, adopted children's weights tend to reflect those of their birth parents rather than their adoptive parents (Whitaker et al., 1997; Bray, 2008).

Social factors also affect children's weight problems. Children need to control their own eating. Parents who are controlling and directive about their children's eating may produce children who lack internal controls to regulate their own food intake (Johnson & Birch, 1994; Faith, Johnson, & Allison, 1997; Wardle, Guthrie, & Sanderson, 2001).

Poor diets also contribute to obesity. Despite their knowledge that certain foods are necessary for a balanced, nutritious diet, many parents provide their children with too few fruits and vegetables and more fats and sweets than recommended. School lunch programs have sometimes contributed to the problem by failing to provide nutritious options (Story, Nanney, & Schwartz, 2009; Janicke, 2013).

Given how energetic children this age can be, it is surprising that a major factor in childhood obesity is a lack of exercise. School-age children tend to engage in relatively little exercise and are not particularly fit. Around 40 percent of boys aged 6 to 12 are unable to do more than one pull-up, and

Christopher Weyant/The New Yorker Collection/www.cartoonbank.com

"Remember when we used to have to fatten the kids up first?"

a quarter can't do any. Furthermore, children have shown little or no improvement in the amount of exercise they get, despite national efforts to increase the fitness of school-age children, in part because many schools have reduced the time available for recess and gym classes. From ages 6 to 18, boys decrease their physical activity by 24 percent and girls by 36 percent (Moore, Gao, & Bradlee, 2003; Sallis & Glanz, 2006; Weiss & Raz, 2006).

Why is the level of exercise relatively low? One answer is that many kids are watching television and playing computer or video games. Such sedentary activities not only prevent exercise, but children often snack while viewing TV or surfing the Web (Landhuis et al., 2008; Goldfield et al., 2012; Chahal et al., 2013).

REVIEW, CHECK, AND APPLY

REVIEW

L01 In what ways do children grow during the school years, and what factors influence their growth?

- In middle childhood, height and weight increase gradually.
- Differences in height and weight are influenced by both genetic and social factors.
- Adequate nutrition promotes physical, social, and cognitive development, while overnutrition and a sedentary lifestyle may lead to obesity.

CHECK YOURSELF

1. Due to the sudden changes taking place during this stage, it is not uncommon in middle school to see children of the same age who are 6 to 7 inches apart in height.
   - True
   - False
2. Which of the following is NOT a long-term outcome associated with childhood obesity?
   - a cognitive deficits
   - b being overweight as adults
   - c greater risk of heart disease
   - d higher prevalence of diabetes

APPLYING LIFESPAN DEVELOPMENT

- What are some aspects of U.S. culture that may contribute to obesity among school-age children?

✓ **Study** and **Review** on **MyPsychLab.com**

MOTOR DEVELOPMENT AND SAFETY

L02 In what ways do motor skills develop over middle childhood?
L03 What are the main health concerns at this age?

The fact that the fitness level of school-age children is not as high as we would desire does not mean that such children are physically incapable. In fact, even without regular exercise, children's gross and fine motor skills develop substantially over the course of the school years.

Gross Motor Skills

One important improvement in gross motor skills is in muscle coordination. Watching a softball player pitch a ball past a batter to her catcher, or Kat, the jump-roper described earlier in the module, we are struck by the many skills children have mastered since their awkward preschool days. Most can readily learn to ride a bike, ice skate, swim, and skip rope (Cratty, 1986) (see Figure 5-2).

Years ago developmentalists concluded that gender differences in gross motor skills became increasingly pronounced during middle childhood years, with boys outperforming girls (Espenschade, 1960). However, when comparing boys and girls who regularly take part in similar activities—such as softball—gender variations are minimal (Hall & Lee, 1984; Jurimae & Saar, 2003).

Why the change? Expectations probably played a role. Society did not expect girls to be highly active and told girls they would do worse than boys in sports. The girls' performance reflected that message.

Today, society's message has changed, at least officially. For instance, the American Academy of Pediatrics suggests that boys and girls should engage in the same sports and games, and that they can do so in mixed-gender groups. There is no reason to separate the sexes in physical

During middle childhood, children master many types of skills that earlier they could not perform well, such as riding a bike, ice skating, swimming, and skipping rope. Is this the same for children of other cultures?

6 Years	7 Years	8 Years	9 Years	10 Years	11 Years	12 Years
Girls superior in accuracy of movement; boys superior in more forceful, less complex acts. Can throw with the proper weight, shift, and step. Acquire the ability to skip.	Can balance on one foot with eyes closed. Can walk on a 2-inch-wide balance beam without falling off. Can hop and jump accurately into small squares (hopscotch). Can correctly execute a jumping-jack exercise.	Can grip objects with 12 pounds of pressure. Can engage in alternate rhythmical hopping in a 2-2, 2-3, or 3-3 pattern. Girls can throw a small ball 33 feet; boys can throw a small ball 59 feet. The number of games participated in by both sexes is the greatest at this age.	Girls can jump vertically 8.5 inches over their standing height plus reach; boys can jump vertically 10 inches. Boys can run 16.6 feet per second; girls can run 16 feet per second.	Can judge and intercept directions of small balls thrown from a distance. Both girls and boys can run 17 feet per second.	Boys can achieve standing broad jump of 5 feet; girls can achieve standing broad jump of 4.5 feet.	Can achieve high jump of 3 feet.

FIGURE 5-2 Gross Motor Skills Developed from 6 and 12 Years
Source: Adapted from Cratty, B. J., *Perceptual and Motor Development in Infants and Children*, 1986, 3rd ed. Copyright © Pearson Education, Inc. Reprinted with permission from Pearson Education, Inc.

exercise and sports until puberty, when the smaller size of females makes them more susceptible to injury in contact sports (Vilhjalmsson & Kristjansdottir, 2003; American Academy of Pediatrics, 2004; Daniels & Lavoi, 2013).

Fine Motor Skills

Typing at a computer keyboard. Writing in cursive with pen and pencil. Drawing detailed pictures. These are some of the accomplishments that depend on the improved fine motor coordination of early and middle childhood. Six- and 7-year-olds are able to tie their shoes and fasten buttons; by age 8, they can use each hand independently; and by 11 and 12, they can manipulate objects with almost as much capability as they will show in adulthood.

One reason fine motor skills improve is that the amount of myelin in the brain increases significantly between the ages of 6 and 8 (Lecours, 1982), raising the speed at which electrical impulses travel between neurons. Messages reach muscles more rapidly and control them better. Myelin also provides protective insulation that surrounds parts of nerve cells.

Health During Middle Childhood

Imani was miserable. Her nose was running, her lips were chapped, and her throat was sore. Although she had stayed home from school and watched old reruns on TV, she still felt that she was suffering mightily.

Despite her misery, Imani's situation is not so bad. She'll get over the cold in a few days and be none the worse for it. In fact, she may be a little *better* off, for she is now immune to the specific cold germs that made her ill.

Imani's cold may end up being the most serious illness she gets during middle childhood. This is generally a period of robust health, and most ailments children do contract tend to be mild and brief. Routine immunizations have produced a considerably lower incidence of the life-threatening illnesses that 50 years ago claimed a significant number of children. However, illness is not uncommon. More than 90 percent of children are likely to have at least one serious medical condition over the 6-year period of middle childhood, according to one large survey. And though most children have short-term illnesses, about one in nine has a chronic, persistent condition, such as repeated migraine headaches. And some illnesses are actually becoming more prevalent (Dey & Bloom, 2005; Siniatchkin et al., 2010; Celano, Holsey, & Kobrynski, 2012).

Asthma. Asthma is among the diseases that have shown a significant increase in prevalence over the last several decades. *Asthma* is a chronic condition characterized by periodic attacks of wheezing, coughing, and shortness of breath. More than 15 million U.S. children suffer from the disorder, and worldwide the number is more than 150 million. Racial and ethnic minorities are particularly at risk for the disease (Johnson, 2003; Dey & Bloom, 2005; Celano, Holsey, & Kobrynski, 2012).

Asthma attacks occur when the airways leading to the lungs constrict, making breathing more difficult and causing wheezing. Attacks are triggered by a variety of factors. Among the most common are respiratory infections (such as colds or flu), allergic reactions to airborne irritants (such as pollution, cigarette smoke, dust mites, and animal dander and excretions), stress, and exercise (Noonan & Ward, 2007; Marin et al., 2009; Ross et al., 2012).

Accidents. The increasing independence of school-age children leads to new safety issues. Between the ages of 5 and 14, the rate of injury for children increases. Boys are more apt to be injured than girls, probably because their overall level of physical activity is greater. Some ethnic and racial groups are at greater risk than others: Injury death rates are highest for American Indian and Alaska Natives, and lowest for Asian and Pacific Islanders. Whites and African Americans have approximately the same death rates from injuries (Noonan, 2003; Borse et al., 2008).

The increased mobility of this age is a source of several kinds of accidents. Children who regularly walk to school, many traveling such a distance alone for the first time, face being hit by cars and trucks. Due to lack of experience, they may misjudge how far they are from an oncoming vehicle. Bicycle accidents pose an increasing risk, particularly as children venture out onto busier roads (Schnitzer, 2006).

The most frequent injury to children is automobile accidents. Auto crashes annually kill 5 out of every 100,000 children between the ages of 5 and 9. Fires and burns, drowning, and gun-related deaths follow in frequency (Field & Behrman, 2003; Schiller & Bernadel, 2004).

Two ways to reduce auto and bicycle injuries are to use seat belts consistently and to wear appropriate protective cycling gear. Bicycle helmets have significantly reduced head injuries, and in many localities their use is mandatory. Knee and elbow pads have proven to reduce injuries for roller-blading and skateboarding (American Academy of Pediatrics [Committee on Accident and Poison Prevention], 1990; Lee, Schofer, & Koppelman, 2005; Blake et al., 2008).

Safety on the Web. The newest threat to children's safety comes from a source that was unheard of a generation ago: the Internet. Although claims that cyberspace is overrun with pornography and child molesters are exaggerated, it is true that the Web makes available material many parents find objectionable. Furthermore, social-networking sites such as Facebook and video sites allow children to virtually interact with others about whom parents have little or no knowledge. Finally—as we'll consider later in the chapter when we discuss bullying—the Internet provides a place where children can be bullied (Brant, 2003; OSTWG, 2010).

Computer software developers have devised programs that will block particular computer sites, but most experts feel the most reliable safeguard is parental supervision. Parents should warn their children never to provide personal information, such as home addresses or telephone numbers, in chat rooms or on social-network sites such as Facebook. In addition, children should not hold face-to-face meetings with people they meet via computer, at least not without a parent present (National Center for Missing and Exploited Children, 2002; OSTWG, 2010; Livingstone & Helsper, 2013).

From an educator's perspective: Do you think using blocking software or computer chips to screen offensive Internet content is a practical idea? Are such controls the best way to keep children safe in cyberspace?

Children's access to computers and the Internet needs to be monitored.

Psychological Disorders

Ben Cramer, 8, loves baseball and mystery stories. He has a dog, Frankie, and a blue racing bike.

Ben also has bipolar disorder, a serious psychological disorder. Engaged in his schoolwork one minute, he'll refuse to even look at his teacher the next. Often a good friend, he'll suddenly lash out at the other children in the class. Sometimes, he believes he can do anything: touch fire and not get burned or jump off the roof and fly. Other times, he feels so sad and small, and he writes poems about dying.

Bipolar disorder such as Ben's is diagnosed when a person cycles back and forth between two extreme emotional states: unrealistically high spirits and energy, and depression. For years, most people neglected the symptoms of such psychological disorders in children, and even today they may be overlooked. Yet it is a common problem: One in five children and adolescents has a psychological disorder that produces at least some impairment. For example, about 5 percent of preteens suffer from childhood depression, and 13 percent of children between ages 9 and 17 experience an anxiety disorder. The estimated cost of treatment of children's psychological disorders is $250 billion per year (Tolan & Dodge, 2005; Cicchetti & Cohen, 2006; Kluger, 2010).

Advocates for the use of antidepressants such as Prozac, Zoloft, Paxil, and Wellbutrin for children suggest that drug therapies can successfully treat their depression and other psychological disorders. Drugs may provide the only relief in cases where traditional therapies that use verbal methods are ineffective. At least one clinical test shows that the drugs are effective with children (Barton, 2007; Lovrin, 2009; Hirschtritt, 2012).

Critics, however, question the long-term effectiveness of antidepressants for children. No one knows the consequences of their use on the developing brain, nor the overall long-term effects. Little is known about the correct dosage for age or size, and some observers suggest that children's versions of the drugs, in orange- or mint-flavored syrups, might lead to overdoses or eventually encourage the use of illegal drugs (Andersen & Navalta, 2004; Couzin, 2004; Cheung, Emslie, & Mayes, 2006).

Finally, some evidence links antidepressants with an increased risk of suicide. The possible link prompted the U.S. Federal Drug Administration to issue a warning about a class of antidepressants known as selective serotonin reuptake inhibitors (SSRIs) in 2004. Some experts have urged their use with children and adolescents be banned completely (Gören, 2008; Sammons, 2009; Ghaemi, Vohringer, & Whitham, 2013).

Although the use of antidepressants to treat children is controversial, it is clear that childhood depression and other psychological disorders remain a significant problem at other points in the lifespan. Not only are they disruptive during childhood, but they put children at risk for future disorders (Gören, 2008; Franić et al., 2010; Sapyla & March, 2012).

The importance of examining changes in psychological disorders across the lifespan was reflected in the 2013 revision of the *Diagnostic and Statistical Manual of Mental Disorders*, known as *DSM-5*, published by the American Psychiatric Association. DSM-5 provides a standard descriptive system for clinicians and researchers who work with individuals with psychological disabilities. The DSM-5 focuses on reported symptoms to pinpoint and label the specific disorder from which an individual suffers (American Psychiatric Association, 2013).

The revision of DSM made hundreds of changes in the way that disorders are described. For example, we've discussed "autism spectrum disorder" several times in prior chapters. Previously, the disorder was referred to simply as "autism." Similarly, "intellectual disability" was

REVIEW, CHECK, AND APPLY

REVIEW

L02 In what ways do motor skills develop over middle childhood?

- Gross motor skills continue to improve during the school years.
- Muscular coordination and manipulative skills advance to near-adult levels.

L03 What are the main health concerns at this age?

- Threats to safety include accidents, a result of increased independence and mobility, and unsupervised access to cyberspace.

CHECK YOURSELF

1. One explanation for the advances in fine motor skills during middle school involves the increase in the amount of _____ in the brain.

   a myelin b neurons
   c genes d gray matter

2. When it comes to school-age children and injuries associated with accidents, which of the following statements is true?

   a The number of accidents occurring in the school-age years is significantly fewer than in earlier years.
   b Girls are significantly more likely to be injured in accidents than are boys.
   c There is no relationship between gender and the prevalence of injuries associated with accidents.
   d Boys are significantly more likely than girls to be injured.

APPLYING LIFESPAN DEVELOPMENT

- How would you design an experiment to examine the roots of gender differences in gross motor skills? What impediments would you encounter in doing so?

✓ **Study** and **Review** on **MyPsychLab.com**

previously referred to as "mental retardation." The new labels reflect advances in our understanding of psychological disorders and how they are exhibited.

CHILDREN WITH SPECIAL NEEDS

L04 What special needs may become apparent during these years, and how can they be met?

Karen Avery was a happy-go-lucky child. Until she got to first grade. A reading assessment put Karen in the lowest reading group. Despite lots of one-on-one time with her teacher, Karen's reading did not improve. She couldn't recognize words she'd seen the day before, or the day before that. Her retention problems soon became apparent across the curriculum. Karen's parents agreed to let the school give her some diagnostic tests. The results suggested Karen's brain had problems transferring information from her short-term (working) memory to her long-term memory. She was labeled as a child with a learning disability. By law, she could now get the help she really needed.

Karen joined millions of children who are classified as learning disabled, one of several special needs children can have. Although every child has different capabilities, children with *special needs* differ significantly in physical attributes or learning abilities. Their needs present major challenges for care providers and teachers.

We turn now to the most prevalent disorders affecting children of normal intelligence: sensory difficulties, learning disabilities, and attention deficit disorders. (We will consider the special needs of children who are significantly below and above average in intelligence later in the module.)

Sensory Difficulties: Visual, Auditory, and Speech Problems

Anyone who has lost his or her eyeglasses or a contact lens knows how difficult even basic, everyday tasks must be for the sensory impaired. To function without adequate vision, hearing, or speech poses a tremendous challenge.

Visual impairment has both a legal and an educational meaning. Legal impairment is defined precisely: *Blindness* is visual acuity below 20/200 after correction (meaning the inability to see at 20 feet what is typically seen at 200 feet), while *partial sightedness* is visual acuity of less than 20/70 after correction.

Even if a child is not legally blind, visual problems may seriously affect schoolwork. For one thing, the legal criterion pertains solely to distance vision, while most school tasks require close-up vision. The legal definition does not consider abilities in the perception of color, depth, and light, either—all of which might influence a student's success. About one student in a thousand requires special education services due to visual impairment.

Most severe visual problems are identified fairly early, but an impairment can go undetected. Visual problems can also emerge gradually as development brings changes in the apparatus of the eye. Parents and teachers need to look out for frequent eye irritation (redness, sties, or infection), continual blinking and facial contortions when reading, holding reading material unusually close to the face, difficulty in writing, and frequent headaches, dizziness, or burning eyes. All are signs of visual problems.

Auditory impairments can cause social as well as academic problems because much peer interaction involves informal conversation. Hearing loss, affecting 1 to 2 percent of the school-age population, goes beyond not hearing enough, varying on a number of dimensions (Yoshinaga-Itano, 2003; Smith, Bale, & White, 2005).

In some cases, hearing is impaired at only certain frequencies, or pitches. For example, the loss may be great at pitches in the normal speech range, yet minimal in other frequencies, such as those of very high or low sounds. Different levels of amplification at different frequencies may be required; a hearing aid that amplifies all frequencies equally may be ineffective, amplifying sounds the child can hear to an uncomfortable degree.

How a child adapts depends on when the hearing loss begins. The effects will likely be more severe in a child with little or no exposure to the sound of language, producing an inability to understand or produce speech. For a child who has learned language, hearing loss will not seriously affect subsequent linguistic development.

Severe and early loss of hearing can impair abstract thinking. Concrete concepts can be visually illustrated but abstract concepts depend on language for meaning. For example, it is difficult to explain the concept of "freedom" or "soul" without use of language (Butler & Silliman, 2002; Marschark, Spencer, & Newsom, 2003).

Auditory impairments can produce both academic and social difficulties, and they may lead to speech difficulties.

visual impairment a difficulty in seeing that may include blindness or partial sightedness

auditory impairment a special need that involves the loss of hearing or some aspect of hearing

Auditory difficulties may be accompanied by **speech impairments**, one of the most public types of exceptionality: Speech that deviates from the norm is obvious whenever the child speaks. It also interferes with communication, and may produce maladjustment in the speaker. Speech impairments occur in around 3 to 5 percent of the school-age population (Bishop & Leonard, 2001).

Stuttering, the most common speech impairment, produces substantial disruption in the rhythm and fluency of speech. Despite much research, no specific cause has been identified. Occasional stuttering is not unusual in young children—or even normal adults—but chronic stuttering can be a severe problem. Stuttering hinders communication, and can be embarrassing or stressful for children, who may come to fear conversation and speaking aloud in class (Altholz & Golensky, 2004; Choi et al., 2013).

Parents and teachers can help children who stutter by not drawing attention to the issue and giving them sufficient time to finish what they are saying, no matter how protracted the statement becomes. It does not help stutterers to finish their sentences for them or otherwise correct their speech (Ryan, 2001; Howell, Bailey, & Kothari, 2010; Beilby, Byrnes, & Young, 2012).

Learning Disabilities: Discrepancies Between Achievement and Capacity to Learn

Like Karen Avery, described earlier, one in ten children is labeled learning disabled. **Learning disabilities** interfere with children's ability to listen, speak, read, write, reason, or do math. An ill-defined category, learning disabilities are diagnosed when children's academic performance differs from their potential to learn (Lerner, 2002; Bos & Vaughn, 2005).

Such a broad definition includes a wide and varied range of difficulties. For instance, *dyslexia*, a reading disability, can result in the visual misperception of letters, unusual difficulty in spelling or sounding out letters, and left-right confusion. Dyslexia is not fully understood, but the problem may lie in the part of the brain that breaks words into the sound elements that make up language (Paulesu et al., 2001; McGough, 2003; Lachmann et al., 2005).

Although learning disabilities are generally attributed to some form of brain dysfunction, probably due to genetic factors, their causes are not well understood and some experts suggest that environmental causes such as poor early nutrition or allergies are culprits (Shaywitz, 2004).

Attention Deficit Hyperactivity Disorder

Troy Dalton, age 7, exhausted his teacher. Unable to sit still, he roamed the classroom all day, distracting the other children. In reading group, he jumped up and down in his seat, dropping his book and knocking over the whiteboard. During read aloud, he ran around the room, humming noisily and shouting, "I'm a jet plane!" Once, he flung himself through the air, landing on another boy and breaking his arm. "He's the definition of perpetual motion," the teacher told Troy's mother (who looked pretty exhausted herself). The school finally decided to split Troy's day between the three second-grade classrooms. It was not a perfect solution, but it did allow his primary teacher to do some actual teaching.

Seven-year-old Troy Dalton's high energy and low attention span are due to attention deficit hyperactivity disorder, which occurs in 3 to 5 percent of the school-age population. **Attention deficit hyperactivity disorder, or ADHD**, is marked by inattention, impulsiveness, a low tolerance for frustration, and generally a great deal of inappropriate activity. All children show such traits some of the time, but for those diagnosed with ADHD, such behavior is common and interferes with their home and school functioning (Nigg, 2001; Whalen et al., 2002; Sciberras, 2013).

It is often difficult to distinguish between children who are highly active and those with ADHD. Common symptoms of ADHD include:

- persistent difficulty in finishing tasks, following instructions, and organizing work
- fidgeting, squirming, inability to watch an entire television program
- frequent interruption of others or excessive talking
- a tendency to jump into a task before hearing all the instructions
- difficulty in waiting or remaining seated

Lacking a simple test to identify ADHD, it is hard to know for sure how many children have the disorder. The Centers for Disease Control and Prevention put the proportion of children 3 to 17 years of age with ADHD at 9 percent, with boys being twice as likely to be diagnosed with the disorder than girls. Other estimates are lower. Only a trained clinician can

speech impairment speech that deviates so much from the speech of others that it calls attention to itself, interferes with communication, or produces maladjustment in the speaker

stuttering substantial disruption in the rhythm and fluency of speech; the most common speech impairment

learning disabilities difficulties in the acquisition and use of listening, speaking, reading, writing, reasoning, or mathematical abilities

attention deficit hyperactivity disorder (ADHD) a learning disorder marked by inattention, impulsiveness, a low tolerance for frustration, and generally a great deal of inappropriate activity

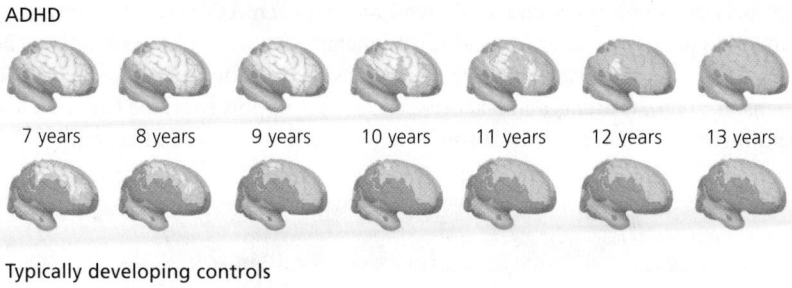

FIGURE 5-3 The Brains of Children with ADHD
The brains of children with ADHD (in the top row) show less thickening of the cortex compared to the brains of typical children at the same age.
Source: Shaw et al., 2007.

make an accurate diagnosis, following an extensive evaluation of the child and interviews with parents and teachers (Sax & Kautz, 2003; CDC, 2010).

The causes of ADHD are not clear, although some research finds that it is related to a delay in neural development. Specifically, it may be that the thickening of the brain's cortex in children with ADHD lags 3 years behind that of children without the disorder (see Figure 5-3).

Considerable controversy surrounds the treatment of ADHD. Because it has been found that doses of Ritalin or Dexedrine (which, paradoxically, are stimulants) reduce activity levels in hyperactive children, many physicians routinely prescribe drug treatment (Schachar et al., 2008; Arnsten, Berridge, & McCracken, 2009; Weissman et al., 2012).

Although in many cases such drugs are effective in increasing attention span and compliance, in some cases the side effects (such as irritability, reduced appetite, and depression) are considerable, and the long-term health consequences of this treatment are unclear. It is also true that though the drugs often help scholastic performance in the short run, the long-term evidence for continuing improvement is mixed. In fact, some studies suggest that after a few years, children treated with drugs do not perform academically any better than untreated children with ADHD. Nonetheless the drugs are being prescribed with increasing frequency (Mayes & Rafalovich, 2007; Rose, 2008; Cortese et al., 2013).

In addition to drugs, behavior therapy is often used to treat ADHD. Parents and teachers learn techniques that primarily use rewards (such as verbal praise) to improve behavior. Teachers can increase the structure of classroom activities, among other management techniques, as ADHD children find unstructured tasks difficult (Chronis, Jones, & Raggi, 2006; DuPaul & Weyandt, 2006). **Watch** the **Video** *Jimmy: ADHD* in **MyPsychLab**.

Becoming an Informed Consumer of Development

Keeping Children Fit

Here is a brief portrait of a contemporary American: Sam works all week at a desk and gets no regular physical exercise. On weekends he spends many hours sitting in front of the TV, often snacking on sodas and sweets. Both at home and at restaurants, his meals feature high-calorie, fat-saturated foods. (Segal & Segal, 1992, p. 235)

Although this sketch fits many adults, Sam is just 6. Many school-age children in the United States, like Sam, get little or no regular exercise and consequently are physically unfit and at risk for obesity and other health problems.

To encourage children to be more physically active (Tyre & Scelfo, 2003; Okie, 2005):

- **Make exercise fun.** Children repeat what they enjoy. Overly competitive activities or those that sideline children with inferior skills, though, may create a lifelong distaste for exercise.
- **Be an exercise role model.** Children who see their parents, teachers, or adult friends exercising regularly may view fitness as a regular part of their lives, too.
- **Gear activities to the child's physical level and motor skills.** Use child-size equipment to make children feel successful.
- **Encourage the child to find a partner.** Roller skating, hiking, and many other activities are more fun when shared with a friend, a sibling, or a parent.
- **Start slowly.** Ease sedentary children into regular physical activity. Try 5 minutes of exercise daily. Over 10 weeks, aim for 30 minutes, three to five times a week.
- **Urge participation in organized sports activities, but do not push too hard.** Not every child is athletically inclined. Make participation and enjoyment—not winning—the goal.
- **Don't use physical activity as a punishment.** Encourage children to join organized activities they enjoy.
- **Provide a healthy diet.** Good nutrition gives children energy. Soda and sugary, fatty snack foods do not.

Finally, because some research has shown links between ADHD and children's diet, particularly in terms of fatty acids or food additives, dietary treatments have sometimes been prescribed. However, dietary treatments are usually insufficient by themselves (Cruz & Bahna, 2006; Stevenson, 2006). (Parents and teachers can receive support from the Children and Adults with Attention-Deficit/Hyperactivity Disorder organization at www.chadd.org.)

REVIEW, CHECK, AND APPLY

REVIEW

L04 What special needs may become apparent during these years, and how can they be met?

- Many children have special needs relating to vision, hearing, and speech that can impact their social relationships and school performance.
- Learning disabilities include difficulties in acquiring and using listening, speaking, reading, writing, reasoning, or mathematical abilities.
- Attention deficit hyperactivity disorder poses attention, organization, and activity problems for 3 to 5 percent of school-age children.

CHECK YOURSELF

1. _____, the most common speech impairment, involves a substantial disruption in the rhythm and fluency of speech.
   - a Telegraphic speech
   - b Stuttering
   - c Private speech
   - d Fast mapping
2. Attention deficit hyperactivity disorder (ADHD), according to the American Academy of Pediatrics, is marked by all of the following symptoms, EXCEPT _____.
   - a a tendency to lie
   - b a low tolerance for frustration
   - c inattention
   - d impulsiveness

APPLYING LIFESPAN DEVELOPMENT

- If hearing is associated with abstract thinking, how do people who were born deaf think?

✓ **Study** and **Review** on **MyPsychLab.com**

MODULE 5.2

COGNITIVE DEVELOPMENT IN MIDDLE CHILDHOOD

Jen Draper stops washing the dishes and comes to the living room. Her 8-year-old daughter Raylene has asked her to listen as she reads from A Single Shard *by Linda Sue Park.*

The book is a novel about a boy in twelfth-century Korea. As Raylene reads, tears come to Jen's eyes, not because of the events in the story, but because her daughter has found a way to grow beyond her small apartment and move confidently into the wider world.

Raylene formed a love of books on her own, taught herself to read them, and takes complete responsibility for finding good books at the local library. Her teachers have told Jen—never much of a reader herself—that her daughter is reading well above her third-grade level.

To support her daughter's habit, Jen has bought Raylene a few books recommended by her teachers. She now looks proudly at the bookcase one of the teachers gave her recently, which is beginning to look occupied.

It was a proud moment for Jen Draper, and a significant accomplishment for her daughter, who has progressed beyond the first-grade books that she had initially chosen to a challenging book written at the fifth-grade level.

Middle childhood is often referred to as the "school years" because it marks the beginning of formal education for most children. Sometimes the physical and cognitive growth that occurs during middle childhood is gradual; other times it is sudden; but always it is remarkable.

During middle childhood, children blossom with ideas and plans—and the language to express them orally and in writing. And it is during this period that much of their future development is charted.

We begin our discussion by examining several approaches to describe and explain cognitive development, including Piagetian and information processing theories and the important ideas of Vygotsky. We look at language development and the questions surrounding bilingualism—an increasingly pressing social policy issue in the United States.

Next we consider several issues involving schooling. After discussing the scope of education throughout the world, we examine the critical skill of reading and the nature of multicultural education. The chapter ends with a discussion of intelligence, a characteristic closely tied to school success. We look at the nature of IQ tests and at the education of children who are either significantly below or above the intellectual norm.

INTELLECTUAL AND LANGUAGE DEVELOPMENT

LO5 In what ways do children develop cognitively during these years, according to major theoretical approaches?
LO6 How do children in middle childhood develop memory?
LO7 How does language develop during the middle childhood period?

Jared's parents were delighted when he came home from kindergarten one day and announced he had learned why the sky was blue. He talked about the earth's atmosphere—although he mispronounced the word—and how tiny bits of moisture in the air reflected the sunlight. His explanation had rough edges (he couldn't quite grasp what "atmosphere" was), but he had the general idea. His parents felt it was quite an achievement for their 5-year-old.

Fast-forward 6 years. Jared, now 11, has already invested an hour in his homework. Having completed a two-page worksheet on multiplying and dividing fractions, he is working on his U.S. Constitution project. He is taking notes for his report, which explains what political factions were involved in creating the document and how the Constitution had been amended over time.

Jared's vast intellectual advances are not uncommon. During middle childhood, cognitive abilities broaden, and children increasingly understand and master complex skills. But their thinking is not yet fully mature.

Several perspectives explain the cognitive advances and limitations of middle childhood.

Piagetian Approaches to Cognitive Development

Let's return to Jean Piaget's view of the preschooler considered in Module 4.2. From Piaget's perspective, preschoolers think *preoperationally*. They are largely egocentric and lack the ability to use *operations*—organized, formal, logical mental processes.

The Rise of Concrete Operational Thought. All this changes during the school years in what Piaget calls the **concrete operational stage**. Occurring between ages 7 and 12, this stage is characterized by the active, and appropriate, use of logic. Concrete operational thought applies *logical operations* to concrete problems. For instance, when children in this stage confront a conservation problem (such as determining whether the amount of liquid poured from one container to another of a different shape stays the same), they use cognitive and logical processes to answer, no longer judging solely by appearance. They are able to reason correctly that because none of the liquid has been lost, the amount stays the same. Being less egocentric, they can consider multiple aspects of a situation, an ability known as **decentering**. Jared, the sixth grader described earlier, used decentering to consider the views of the various factions behind the U.S. Constitution.

The shift from preoperational to concrete operational thought takes time. Children shift between these modes of thought before concrete operations take a firm hold—they are able to answer conservation problems but unable to explain why. When asked for their reasoning, they may simply respond, "Because."

However, once concrete operations take hold, children make several cognitive leaps, such as the concept of *reversibility*—the notion that transformations to a stimulus can be reversed. Grasping this, children realize that a ball of clay squeezed into a long, thin rope can become a ball again. More abstractly, this concept allows children to understand that if 3 + 5 equals 8, then 5 + 3 also equals 8—and, later, that 8 − 3 equals 5.

Concrete operational thinking also permits children to grasp such concepts as the relationship between time and speed. For instance, consider the problem in which two cars traveling different-length routes start and finish at the same points in the same amount of time. Children entering the concrete operational period reason that the cars' speed is the same. However, between ages 8 and 10, children begin to understand that for both cars to arrive simultaneously at the finish point, the car traveling the longer route must be moving faster.

Despite the advances that occur during the concrete operational stage, children still experience one critical limitation in their thinking. They remain tied to concrete, physical reality.

concrete operational stage the period of cognitive development between 7 and 12 years of age, which is characterized by the active, and appropriate, use of logic

decentering the ability to take multiple aspects of a situation into account

Furthermore, they are unable to understand truly abstract or hypothetical questions, or ones that involve formal logic.

Piaget in Perspective: Right and Wrong. As we learned earlier, researchers who followed Piaget have found much to applaud—and much to criticize.

Piaget was a virtuoso observer of children. His many books contain brilliant, careful observations of children at work and play. His theories have had powerful educational implications, and many schools use his principles to guide instruction (Flavell, 1996; Siegler & Ellis, 1996; Brainerd, 2003). **Watch** the **Video** *Conservation Tasks* in **MyPsychLab.**

Cognitive development makes substantial advances in middle childhood

In some ways, Piaget's approach succeeded in describing cognitive development (Lourenco & Machado, 1996). At the same time, critics have raised compelling and reasonable grievances. As noted earlier, many researchers argue that Piaget underestimated children's capabilities, in part due to the limitations of the mini-experiments he conducted. When a broader array of experimental tasks is used, children show less consistency within stages than Piaget predicted (Siegler, 1994; Bjorklund, 1997a). Increasing evidence suggests that children's cognitive abilities emerge earlier than Piaget envisioned. Some children demonstrate concrete operational thinking before age 7, when Piaget suggested these abilities first appear.

Still, we cannot dismiss Piaget. Although some early cross-cultural research implied that children in certain cultures remain preoperational, failing to master conservation and develop concrete operations, more recent research suggests otherwise. For instance, with proper training in conservation, children in non-Western cultures who do not conserve learn to do so. In one study, urban Australian children—who develop concrete operations on Piaget's timetable—were compared to rural Aborigine children, who typically do not conserve at the age of 14 (Dasen, Ngini, & Lavallee, 1979). With training, the rural Aborigine children showed conservation skills similar to those of their urban counterparts, although about 3 years later (see Figure 5-4).

When children are interviewed by researchers from their own culture, who share their language and customs, and whose reasoning tasks relate to important cultural domains, the children are much more likely to display concrete operational thinking (Nyiti, 1982; Jahoda, 1983). Such research suggests that Piaget was right in arguing that concrete operations are universally achieved during middle childhood. Performance differences between Western and some non-Western children on Piagetian measures of conservation and concrete operations probably reflect a difference in experiences. The progress of cognitive development cannot be understood without considering a child's culture (Lau, Lee, & Chiu, 2004; Maynard, 2008; Mishra & Dasen, 2013).

Information Processing in Middle Childhood

It is a significant achievement for first graders to learn basic math tasks, such as single-digit addition and subtraction, as well as the spelling of simple words like *dog*. But by sixth grade, children are able to work with fractions and decimals, completing a worksheet like the one done by Jared, the boy cited earlier. They can spell words like *exhibit* and *residence*.

According to *information processing approaches*, children handle information with increasing sophistication. Like computers, they process more data as the size of their memories increases and the "programs" they use to do this become more complex (Kuhn et al., 1995; Kail, 2003; Zelazo et al., 2003).

Memory. As noted, **memory** in the information processing model is the ability to record, store, and retrieve information. For a child to remember a piece of information, the three processes must all function properly. Through *encoding*, the child records the information in a form usable to memory. Children who never learned that 5 + 6 = 11, or who didn't heed this

memory the process by which information is initially recorded, stored, and retrieved fact when it was taught, will never be able to recall it. They never encoded the information in the first place.

But exposure to a fact is not enough; the information also has to be *stored.* In our example, the information 5 + 6 = 11 must be placed and maintained in the memory system. Finally, proper memory functioning requires that stored material must be *retrieved.* Through retrieval, material in storage is located, made conscious, and used.

During middle childhood, short-term memory (also referred to as *working memory*) capacity greatly improves. Children are increasingly able to hear a string of digits ("1-5-6-3-4") and then repeat them in reverse order ("4-3-6-5-1"). At the start of the preschool period, they can remember and reverse only about two digits; by the beginning of adolescence, they can perform the task with as many as six digits. In addition, they use more sophisticated strategies for recalling information, which can be improved with training (Mayes & Rafalovich, 2007; Rose, 2008; Jack, Simcock, & Hayne, 2012).

Memory capacity may shed light on another issue in cognitive development. Some developmental psychologists suggest that preschool children may have difficulty solving conservation problems due to memory limitations (Siegler & Richards, 1982). They argue that young children simply may not be able to recall all the necessary information to solve such problems.

Metamemory, a grasp of the processes that underlie memory, also emerges and improves during middle childhood. By the start of first grade, when their theory of mind becomes more sophisticated, children have a general notion of what memory is. They understand that some people have better memories than others (Cherney, 2003; Ghetti et al., 2008; Jaswal & Dodson, 2009).

School-age children understand memory in more sophisticated ways as they increasingly engage in *control strategies*—intentionally used tactics to improve cognitive processing. For instance, school-age children know that rehearsal, the repetition of information, improves memory, and they increasingly make use of this strategy. They also progress in organizing material into coherent patterns, a strategy that improves recall. For instance, faced with memorizing a list including cups, knives, forks, and plates, older school-age children are more likely than younger ones to group the items into coherent patterns—cups and plates, forks and knives (Sang, Miao, & Deng, 2002).

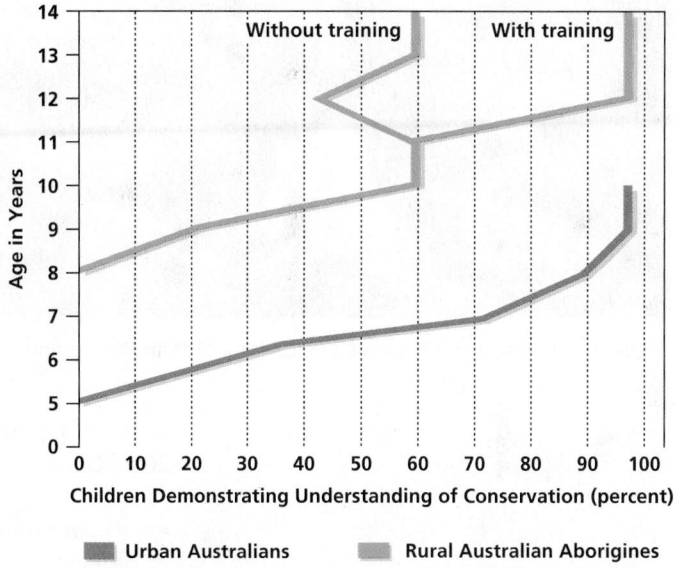

FIGURE 5-4 Conservation Training
Rural Australian Aborigine children trail their urban counterparts in the development of their understanding of conservation; with training, they later catch up. Without training, around half of 14-year-old Aborigines do not have an understanding of conservation. What can be concluded from the fact that training influences the understanding of conservation?
Source: Based on Dasen, Ngini, & Lavallee, 1979.

Improving Memory. Can children be trained to be more effective in the use of control strategies? Definitely. School-age children can be taught to use particular strategies, although such teaching is not a simple matter. For instance, children need to know not only how to use a memory strategy, but also when and where to use it most effectively.

For example, an innovative technique called the *keyword strategy* can help students learn a foreign language, the state capitals, or any information that pairs two sets of words or labels that sound alike (Wyra, Lawson, & Hungi, 2007). For instance, in learning foreign language vocabulary, a foreign word such as the Spanish word for duck (*pato*, pronounced *pot-o*) is paired with a common English word—in this case it might be *pot*. The English word is the keyword. Once the keyword is chosen, children then form a mental image of the two words interacting with one another. For instance, a student might use an image of a duck taking a bath in a pot to remember the word *pato*.

Vygotsky's Approach to Cognitive Development and Classroom Instruction

Learning environments can encourage children to adopt these strategies as well. Recall that Russian developmentalist Lev Vygotsky proposed that cognitive advances occur through exposure to information within a child's *zone of proximal development*, or ZPD. In the ZPD, a child can almost, but not quite, understand or perform a task.

metamemory an understanding about the processes that underlie memory, which emerges and improves during middle childhood

Students working in cooperative groups benefit from the insights of others.

Vygotsky's approach has particularly encouraged the development of classroom practices that promote children's active participation in their learning (e.g., Holzman, 1997). Consequently, classrooms are seen as places where children should experiment and try out new activities (Vygotsky, 1926/1997; Gredler & Shields, 2008).

According to Vygotsky, education should focus on activities that involve interaction with others. Both child–adult and child–child interactions can promote cognitive growth. The interactions must be carefully structured to fall within each child's ZPD.

Vygotsky's work has influenced several current and noteworthy innovations. For example, *cooperative learning*, where children work in groups to achieve a common goal, uses several aspects of Vygotsky's theory. Students working in cooperative groups benefit from the insights of others. A wrong turn by one child may be corrected by others in the group. On the other hand, not every group member is equally helpful: As Vygotsky's approach would imply, individual children benefit most when some of the group members are more competent at the task and can act as experts (DeLisi, 2006; Gillies & Boyle, 2006; Law, 2008).

From an educator's perspective: Suggest how a teacher might use Vygotsky's approach to teach 10-year-olds about colonial America.

Reciprocal teaching is another educational practice that reflects Vygotsky's approach to cognitive development. *Reciprocal teaching* is a technique to teach reading comprehension strategies. Students are taught to skim the content of a passage, raise questions about its central point, summarize the passage, and finally predict what will happen next. A key to this technique is its reciprocal nature, its emphasis on giving students a chance to take on the role of teacher. In the beginning, teachers lead students through the comprehension strategies. Gradually, students progress through their zones of proximal development, taking more and more control over use of the strategies, until the students are able to take on a teaching role. The method has shown impressive success in raising reading comprehension levels, particularly for students experiencing reading difficulties (Takala, 2006; Spörer, Brunstein, & Kieschke, 2009; Lundberg & Reichenberg, 2013).

Language Development: What Words Mean

If you listen to school-age children, their speech sounds similar to that of adults. However, the apparent similarity is deceiving. The linguistic sophistication of children—particularly early in the school-age period—still needs refining to reach adult levels.

Mastering the Mechanics of Language. Vocabulary continues to increase rapidly during the school years. The average 6-year-old has a vocabulary of from 8,000 to 14,000 words, whereas another 5,000 words appear from ages 9 to 11.

Children's mastery of grammar also improves. For instance, the passive voice is seldom used during the early school-age years (as in "The dog was walked by Jon," compared with the active voice, "Jon walked the dog"). Six- and 7-year-olds rarely use conditional sentences, such as "If Sarah will set the table, I will wash the dishes." During middle childhood, however, the use of passive voice and conditional sentences increases. In addition, children's understanding of *syntax*, the rules governing how words and phrases can be combined to form sentences, grows.

By first grade, most children pronounce words quite accurately. However, certain *phonemes*, units of sound, remain troublesome. For instance, the ability to pronounce *j*, *v*, *th*, and *zh* sounds develops later.

School-age children may also have difficulty decoding sentences when the meaning depends on *intonation*, or tone of voice. For example, consider the sentence, "George gave a book to David and he gave one to Bill." If the word "he" is emphasized, the meaning is "George gave a book to David and David gave a different book to Bill." But if the intonation emphasizes the word *and*, then the meaning changes to "George gave a book to David and George also gave a book to Bill." School-age children cannot easily sort out subtleties such as these (Wells, Peppé, & Goulandris, 2004; Thornton, 2010).

Conversational skills also develop as children become more competent in using *pragmatics*, the rules governing the use of language to communicate in social settings.

For example, although children in early childhood are aware of the rules of conversational turn-taking, their use is sometimes primitive. Consider the following conversation between 6-year-olds Yonnie and Max:

Yonnie: My dad drives a FedEx truck.
Max: My sister's name is Molly.
Yonnie: He gets up really early in the morning.
Max: She wet her bed last night.

Later, however, conversations show more give-and-take, with children responding to each other's comments. For instance, this conversation between 11-year-olds Mia and Josh reflects a greater mastery of pragmatics:

Mia: I don't know what to get Claire for her birthday.
Josh: I'm getting her earrings.
Mia: She already has a lot of jewelry.
Josh: I don't think she has that much.

Metalinguistic Awareness. A significant development in middle childhood is children's increasing understanding of their own use of language, or **metalinguistic awareness**. By age 5 or 6, they understand that a set of rules governs language. In the early years they learn and comprehend these rules implicitly, but during middle childhood they understand them more explicitly (Benelli et al., 2006; Saiegh-Haddad, 2007).

Metalinguistic awareness helps children's comprehension when information is fuzzy or incomplete. For instance, when preschoolers receive ambiguous or unclear information, such as directions for a complicated game, they rarely ask for clarification, and tend to blame themselves for any confusion. By the age of 7 or 8, children realize that miscommunication may be due to the person communicating with them as well. Consequently, school-age children are more likely to ask for clarifications (Apperly & Robinson, 2002).

How Language Promotes Self-Control. Their growing sophistication with language helps children control and regulate their behavior. In one experiment, children were told they could have one marshmallow treat if they chose to eat it immediately, but two treats if they waited. Most of the children, who ranged in age from 4 to 8, chose to wait, but the strategies they used differed significantly.

The 4-year-olds often chose to look at the marshmallows while waiting, a strategy that was not terribly effective. In contrast, 6- and 8-year-olds used language to help overcome temptation, although in different ways. The 6-year-olds spoke and sang to themselves, reminding themselves they would get more treats if they waited. The 8-year-olds focused on aspects of the marshmallows unrelated to taste, such as appearance, which helped them to wait.

In short, children used "self-talk" to regulate their behavior. Their self-control grew as their linguistic capabilities increased.

Bilingualism: Speaking in Many Tongues

John Dewey Elementary is a school known for its progressive and democratic attitudes. On the campus of a large university, it boasts a staff of classroom aides who in sum speak 15 different languages, including Hindi and Hausa. The challenge is there are more than 30 languages spoken by the students.

metalinguistic awareness an understanding of one's own use of language

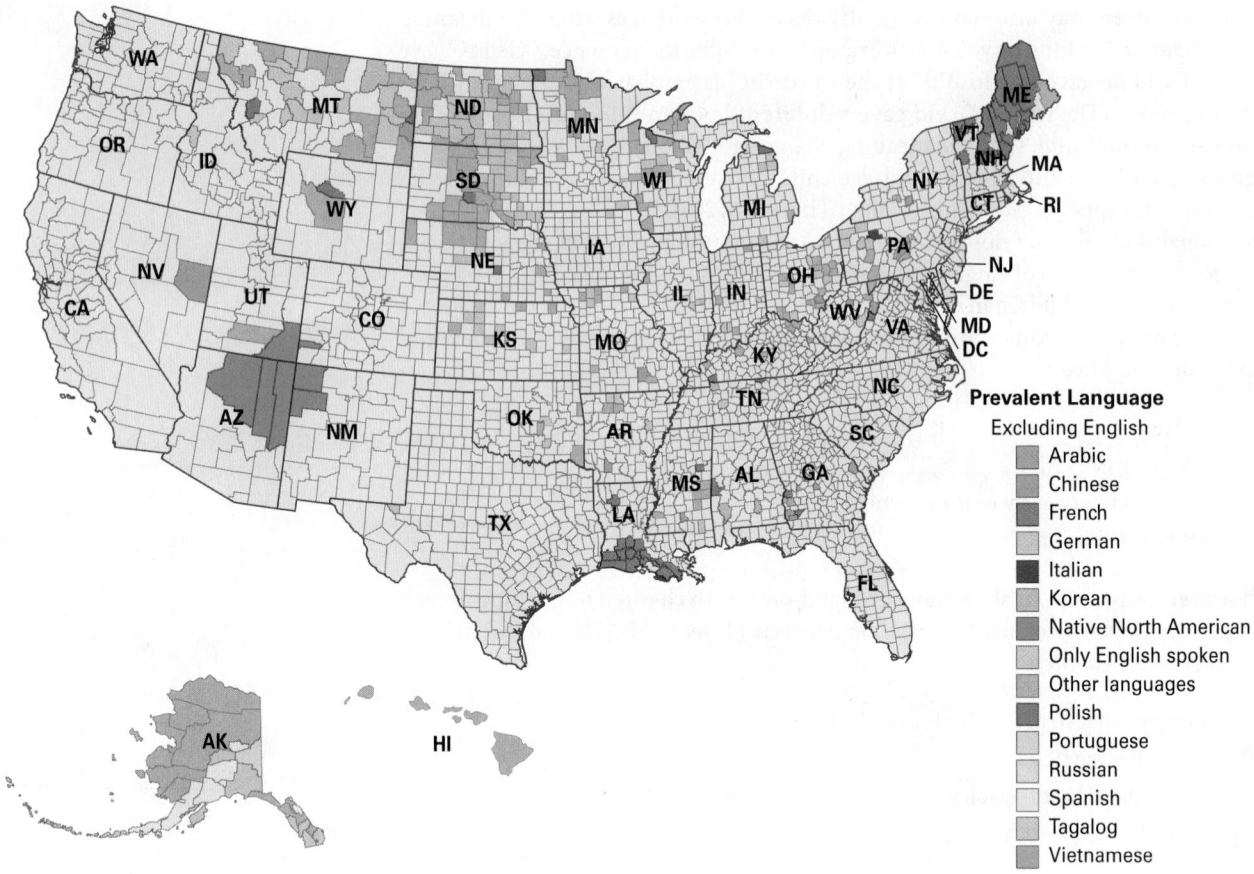

FIGURE 5-5 Prevalent Languages Other than English
This map shows the areas of the United States in which languages other than English are more frequently used.
Source: Modern Language Association, 2013.

Across America, the voices with which children speak are changing. Nearly one in five people in the United States speaks a language other than English at home, a percentage that is growing. **Bilingualism**—the use of more than one language—is increasingly common (Shin & Bruno, 2003; Graddol, 2004) (see Figure 5-5).

Children with little or no English proficiency must learn both the standard school curriculum and the language in which it is taught. One approach to achieving this is *bilingual education*, in which children are initially taught in their native language, while they learn English. This enables students to develop a strong foundation in basic subject areas using their native language. The goal of most bilingual programs is to gradually shift instruction into English.

An alternative approach is to immerse students in English, teaching solely in that language. To proponents of this approach, initially teaching students in another language hinders their efforts to learn English and slows their integration into society. These two quite different, highly politicized approaches have some politicians arguing for "English-only" laws, while others urge schools to respect the challenges nonnative speakers face by offering some instruction in their native language. Still, the psychological research is clear: Being bilingual offers cognitive advantages. With a wider range of linguistic possibilities to choose from in assessing a situation, speakers of two languages show greater cognitive flexibility. They solve problems with greater creativity and versatility. Learning in one's native tongue is also associated with higher self-esteem in minority students (Chen & Bond, 2007; Bialystok & Viswanathan, 2009; Hermanto, Moreno, & Bialystok, 2012).

Bilingual students often have greater metalinguistic awareness, understand the rules of language more explicitly, and show great cognitive sophistication. They may even score higher on tests of intelligence, according to some research. Furthermore, brain scans comparing bilingual individuals with those who speak only one language find differences suggesting different types of brain activation (Kovelman, Baker, & Petitto, 2008; Piller, 2010; Burgaleta et al., 2013).

bilingualism the use of more than one language

Finally, because many linguists contend that universal processes underlie language acquisition, as we noted in Chapter 3, instruction in a native language may enhance instruction in a second language. In fact, as we discuss next, many educators believe that second-language learning should be a regular part of elementary schooling for *all* children (Kecskes & Papp, 2000; McCardle & Hoff, 2006).

REVIEW, CHECK, AND APPLY

REVIEW

L05 In what ways do children develop cognitively during these years, according to major theoretical approaches?

- Piaget believed school-age children are in the concrete operational stage, while information processing approaches focus on quantitative improvements in memory and in the sophistication of the mental programs children use.
- Vygotsky suggests school-age children should have the opportunity to experiment and participate actively with their peers in their learning.

L06 How do children in middle childhood develop memory?

- Children gain increasing control over the memory processes—encoding, storage, and retrieval—and the development of metamemory improves cognitive processing and memorization.

L07 How does language develop during the middle childhood period?

- As language develops, vocabulary, syntax, and pragmatics improve; metalinguistic awareness grows; and language is used as a self-control device.

CHECK YOURSELF

1. Which of the following best describes Piaget's approach to cognitive development in middle childhood?
   - a Piaget overestimated the degree to which young children could problem solve because of the types of tasks he used.
   - b Piaget considered the degree to which culture influences the kind of things we learn.
   - c Piaget's approach provided totally accurate descriptions of young children's cognitive development.
   - d Piaget's theory has had powerful implications for schools and educational materials.
2. Children who have the ability to focus on more than one aspect of a problem at a time are capable of _____.
   - a centering
   - b decentering
   - c irreversibility
   - d mental repression
3. As children reach middle childhood, they get better at understanding the processes that underlie their own memory, including strategies for doing better on tasks requiring memory.
   - True
   - False

APPLYING LIFESPAN DEVELOPMENT

- Do adults use language (and self-talk) as a self-control device? How?

✓ **Study** and **Review** on **MyPsychLab.com**

SCHOOLING: THE THREE Rs (AND MORE) OF MIDDLE CHILDHOOD

L08 What are some trends in schooling today?

As the six other children in his reading group turned to him, Glenn shifted uneasily in his chair. Reading was hard for him, and he always felt anxious when asked to read aloud. But with his teacher's encouraging nod, he plunged in, hesitant at first, then gaining momentum as he read the story of a mother's first day on a new job. He was happy and proud to find that he could read the passage quite nicely. He broke into a broad smile when his teacher said, "Well done, Glenn."

Such moments, repeated over and over, make—or break—a child's educational experience. School is society's formal attempt to transfer its accumulated knowledge, beliefs, values, and wisdom to new generations. The success of this transfer determines, in a very real sense, the future fortunes of the world, as well as the success of each student.

Schooling Around the World and Across Genders: Who Gets Educated?

In the United States, as in most developed countries, a primary school education is both a universal right and a legal requirement. Virtually all children enjoy a free education through the 12th grade.

Children in other parts of the world are not always so fortunate. More than 160 million of the world's children do not even receive a primary education. An additional 100 million children are educated only to a level comparable to our elementary school, and close to a billion individuals (two-thirds of them women) are illiterate throughout their lives.

In almost all developing countries, fewer females than males receive formal education, a discrepancy found at every level of schooling. Even in developed countries, women lag behind men in their exposure to science and technological topics. These differences reflect widespread, deeply held cultural and parental biases that favor males over females. Educational levels in the United States are more nearly equal between men and women. Especially in the early years, boys and girls share equal access to opportunities.

Reading: Learning to Decipher the Meaning Behind Words

The accomplishments of both Glenn (described earlier) and Raylene Draper (described in the prologue) in advancing their reading are significant, for there is no task more fundamental to learning than reading. Reading involves a significant number of skills, from low-level cognitive skills (the identification of single letters and letter–sound association) to higher-level skills (matching written words with meanings stored in memory, and using context and prior knowledge to determine a sentence's meaning).

Reading Stages. Learning to read usually occurs in several broad and frequently overlapping stages (Chall, 1979, 1992). In *Stage 0*, from birth to first grade, children learn the prerequisites for reading, including letter identification, recognition of familiar words (such as their name or *stop* on a stop sign), and perhaps writing their name.

Stage 1 brings the first real type of reading, but it largely involves *phonological recoding* skills. At this stage, which usually encompasses the first and second grade, children can sound out words by blending the letters together. Children also complete the job of learning the names of letters and the sounds that go with them.

In *Stage 2*, typically around second and third grades, children learn to read aloud with fluency. However, they do not attach much meaning to the words, because the effort involved in simply sounding out words is usually so great that relatively few cognitive resources are left over to process the meaning of the words.

The next period, *Stage 3*, extends from fourth to eighth grade. Reading becomes a means to an end—in particular, a way to learn. Whereas earlier reading was an accomplishment in and of itself, by this point children use reading to learn about the world. However, even at this age, understanding gained from reading is not complete. For instance, one limitation children have at this stage is that they are able to comprehend information only when it is presented from a single perspective.

In almost all developing countries, more males than females receive formal education.

In the final period, *Stage 4*, children are able to read and process information that reflects multiple points of view. This ability, which begins during the transition into high school, permits children to develop a far more sophisticated understanding of material. This explains why great works of literature are not read at an earlier stage of education. It is not so much that younger children do not have the vocabulary to understand such works (although this is partially true); it is that they lack the ability to understand the multiple points of view that sophisticated literature invariably presents.

How Should We Teach Reading? Educators have long been engaged in a debate over the most effective means of teaching reading. This debate centers on a disagreement about how information is processed during reading. According to proponents of *code-based approaches to reading*, teachers should focus on the basic skills that underlie reading. Code-based approaches emphasize the components of reading, such as letter sounds and combinations—phonics—and how letters and sounds combine to make words. They suggest that reading consists of processing the components of words, combining them into words, and using these to derive the meaning of sentences and passages (Vellutino, 1991; Jimenez & Guzman, 2003; Gray et al., 2007; Dickinson, Golinkoff, & Hirsh-Pasek, 2010).

In contrast, some educators argue that the most successful approach is *whole language*, which regards reading as a natural process, similar to the acquisition of oral language. According to this view, children learn to read through authentic writing, such as sentences, stories, poems, lists, and charts. Rather than sounding out words, children make guesses about the meaning of words based on the context. Children become proficient readers, learning whole words and phrases through such a trial-and-error approach (Shaw, 2003; Sousa, 2005; Donat, 2006).

A growing body of research suggests the code-based approach is superior to the whole-language approach. One study found that children tutored in phonics for a year improved their reading substantially, compared to a group of good readers, and that the neural pathways involved in reading became closer to those of good readers (Shaywitz et al., 2004; Shapiro & Solity, 2008).

Based on research such as this, the National Reading Panel and National Research Council now support reading instruction using code-based approaches. Their position signals that an end may be near to the debate over which approach to teaching reading is most effective (Rayner et al., 2002; Brady, 2011).

Whatever approach is used to teach reading, reading produces significant changes in the wiring of the brain. It boosts the organization of the visual cortex of the brain and it improves the processing of spoken language (see Figure 5-6) (Dejaeme et al., 2010).

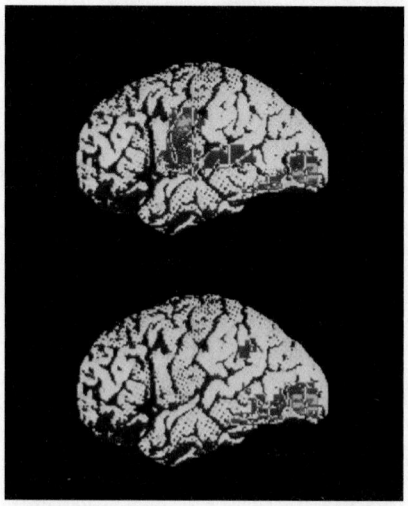

FIGURE 5-6 Reading and the Brain
The act of reading involves activation of significant areas of the brain, as these scans illustrate. In the top scan, an individual is reading aloud; in the bottom scan, the person is reading silently.

Educational Trends: Beyond the Three Rs

Schooling in the twenty-first century has changed significantly in recent years, with U.S. schools returning to the traditional three Rs (reading, writing, and arithmetic). The focus on these fundamentals departs from prior trends that emphasized children's social well-being and allowing students to choose their own study topics instead of following a set curriculum (Schemo, 2003; Yinger, 2004).

Elementary schools today also stress individual accountability. Teachers may be held responsible for their students' learning, and both students and teachers may be required to take state or national tests to assess their competence (McDonnell, 2004).

As the U.S. population becomes more diverse, elementary schools are paying increased attention to student diversity issues and multiculturalism. And with good reason: Cultural, as well as language, differences affect students socially and educationally. The demographic makeup of students in the U.S. is undergoing an extraordinary shift. The proportion of Hispanics is likely to more than double in the next 50 years. By the year 2050, non-Hispanic Caucasians will likely be a minority of the United States' total population (U.S. Bureau of the Census, 2001) (see Figure 5-7). Consequently, educators are increasingly serious about multicultural concerns. The accompanying Cultural Dimensions feature, on multicultural education, discusses how the goals for educating students from different cultures have changed significantly and are still being debated.

Cultural Assimilation or Pluralistic Society? Multicultural education, in part, is a response to a **cultural assimilation model** in which the goal was to assimilate individual cultural identities into a unique, unified American culture. In practice this meant that non-English speakers were discouraged from using their native language and totally immersed in English.

cultural assimilation model the model in which the goal was to assimilate individual cultural identities into a unique, unified American culture

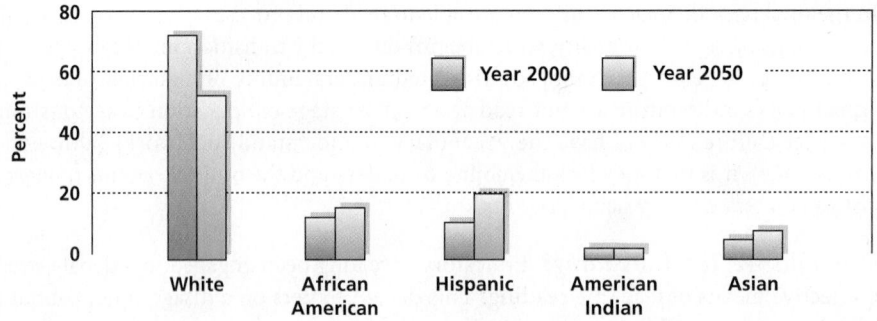

FIGURE 5-7 The Changing Face of America
Current projections of the population makeup of the United States show that by the year 2050, the proportion of non-Hispanic whites will decline as the proportion of minority group members increases. What will be some of the impacts on social workers as the result of changing demographics?
Source: U.S. Bureau of the Census, 2010.

Pupils and teachers exposed to a diverse group could better understand the world and gain a greater sensitivity to the values and needs of others. What are some ways of developing greater sensitivity in the classroom?

From an educator's perspective: Should one goal of society be to foster cultural assimilation in children from other cultures? Why or why not?

In the early 1970s, however, educators and minority groups suggested that cultural assimilation should be replaced by a **pluralistic society model**. In this model, American society is made up of diverse, coequal cultural groups that preserve their unique cultural features.

The pluralistic model grew, in part, from the belief that teachers who emphasized the dominant culture and discouraged nonnative English speakers from using their native tongues in effect devalued subcultural heritages and lowered those students' self-esteem. Instructional materials inevitably feature culture-specific events and understandings. Thus, minority children might never be exposed to important aspects of their culture. For example, English-language texts rarely present the great themes in Spanish literature and history (such as the search for the Fountain of Youth and the Don Juan legend). Hispanic students risked missing important components of their heritage.

Ultimately, educators began to argue that the presence of students representing diverse cultures enriched and broadened the educational experience of all students. Pupils and teachers exposed to people from different backgrounds could better understand the world and gain greater sensitivity to the values and needs of others (Gurin, Nagda, & Lopez, 2004; Zirkel & Cantor, 2004; Levin et al., 2012).

Fostering a Bicultural Identity. Most educators now agree that minority children should develop a **bicultural identity**, where schools support children's original cultural identities while also integrating them into the dominant culture. In this view, an individual lives as a member of two cultures, with two cultural identities, without having to choose one over the other (Oyserman et al., 2003; Vyas, 2004; Collins, 2012).

The best way to achieve this goal is not clear. Consider children who enter school speaking only Spanish. The traditional "melting-pot" technique would immerse them in classes taught in English while providing a crash course in English language (and little else) until the children gain a reasonable proficiency. Unfortunately, this approach has a major drawback: Until they are proficient, students fall further and further behind their peers (First & Cardenas, 1986).

More contemporary bicultural approaches encourage children to maintain membership in more than one culture. For a Spanish-speaking child, instruction would begin in Spanish and shift rapidly to include English. The school would also conduct a multicultural program

pluralistic society model the concept that American society is made up of diverse, coequal cultural groups that should preserve their individual cultural features

bicultural identity Maintaining one's original cultural identity while integrating oneself into the dominant culture for all children, where material on the cultures of all students is presented. Such instruction is meant to enhance the self-image of every student (Bracey, Bamaca, & Umana-Taylor, 2004; Fowers & Davidov, 2006; Mok & Morris, 2012).

Although most educational experts favor bicultural approaches, the general public does not always agree. For instance, the "English-only" movement mentioned earlier seeks to prohibit school instruction in any non-English language. Which view will prevail remains to be seen.

Cultural Dimensions

Multicultural Education

Classrooms in the United States have always been populated by students with diverse backgrounds and experiences. Only recently, though, have variations in student backgrounds been viewed as a major challenge—and opportunity—that educators face.

In fact, this diversity in the classroom relates to a fundamental objective of education, which is to transmit the information a society deems important. As the famous anthropologist Margaret Mead (1942) once said, "In its broadest sense, education is the cultural process, the way in which each newborn human infant, born with a potentiality for learning greater than that of any other mammal, is transformed into a full member of a specific human society, sharing with the other members of a specific human culture" (p. 633).

Culture, then, can be seen as a set of behaviors, beliefs, values, and expectations shared by the members of a society. But culture is not simply "Western culture" or "Asian culture." It is also made up of *subcultural* groups. Membership in a cultural or subcultural group might be of minor concern to educators if it didn't substantially impact the way students experience school. In recent years, considerable thought has gone into providing **multicultural education**, with the goal of helping minority students develop competence in the majority culture while maintaining positive group identities built on their original cultures (Nieto, 2005; Ngo, 2010; Matriano & Swee-Hin, 2013).

REVIEW, CHECK, AND APPLY

REVIEW

L08 What are some trends in schooling today?

- Schooling is considered a legal right in the United States and many other countries, but millions of the world's children do not receive even a primary education.
- Reading skills generally develop in several stages. There is growing evidence that code-based approaches to teaching reading are more successful than the whole language approach.
- U.S. schools have returned in recent decades to a focus on the traditional academic skills.

CHECK YOURSELF

1. According to the _____ approach to reading, reading should be taught by presenting the basic skills underlying reading. Examples include phonics and how letters and words are combined to make words.
   - a whole-language
   - b linguistic
   - c code-based
   - d dynamic
2. The goal of multicultural education is to help minority students develop competence in the culture of the majority group while maintaining positive group identities that build on their original cultures.
   - True
   - False

APPLYING LIFESPAN DEVELOPMENT

- Do you think that the emphasis on the traditional "three Rs" in middle school is appropriate? Do less "academic" subjects have a place in the regular curriculum, or should they be dealt with as "add-ons" and after-school activities. Why?

✓ **Study** and **Review** on **MyPsychLab.com**

INTELLIGENCE: DETERMINING INDIVIDUAL STRENGTHS

L09 How can intelligence be measured?
L010 How are exceptional children educated?

"Why should you tell the truth?" "How far is Los Angeles from New York?" "A table is made of wood; a window of _____."

As 10-year-old Hyacinth sat hunched over her desk, faced with a series of questions like these, she tried to guess the point of the test she was taking. Clearly, the test covered material not discussed by her fifth-grade teacher, Ms. White-Johnston.

multicultural education a form of education in which the goal is to help minority students develop confidence in the culture of the majority group while maintaining positive group identities that build on their original cultures

"What number comes next in this series: 1, 3, 7, 15, 31, _____?"

As she worked through the test, she gave up trying to guess its rationale. She'd leave that to her teacher and simply try to figure out the correct answers.

Hyacinth was taking an intelligence test. It might surprise her to learn that others also questioned the meaning and importance of the test. Intelligence test items are painstakingly prepared, and the tests are designed to predict academic success (for reasons we'll soon discuss). Many developmentalists, however, harbor doubts that such tests are entirely appropriate for assessing intelligence.

Understanding just what intelligence means has proven a major challenge for researchers in defining what separates intelligent from unintelligent behavior. Although nonexperts have their own definitions (one survey found that laypersons view intelligence as three components: problem-solving ability, verbal ability, and social competence), it has been more difficult for experts to concur (Sternberg et al., 1981; Howe, 1997). Still, a general definition of intelligence is possible: **Intelligence** is the capacity to understand the world, think with rationality, and use resources effectively when faced with challenges (Wechsler, 1975).

To understand how researchers have variously approached the task of defining intelligence and devising *intelligence tests*, we need to consider some of the historical milestones in this area.

Intelligence Benchmarks: Differentiating the Intelligent From the Unintelligent

The Paris schools faced a problem as the twentieth century began: Regular instruction was failing many students. These children—many of whom were mentally retarded—were seldom identified early enough to shift them to special classes. The French minister of instruction asked psychologist Alfred Binet to devise a method for identifying students who might benefit from special instruction.

Binet's Test. Binet took a practical approach. Years of observation suggested that prior tests for intelligence—some based on reaction time or eyesight—were ineffectual. Binet, using a trial-and-error approach, administered items and tasks to students identified as either "bright" or "dull." He retained the tasks that the bright students completed correctly and the dull students failed. Tasks that did not discriminate were discarded. The end result was a test that reliably distinguished fast and slow learners.

Binet's pioneering efforts left three important legacies. The first was his pragmatic approach to constructing intelligence tests. Binet did not have theoretical preconceptions about what intelligence was. Instead, he used a trial-and-error approach to psychological measurement that continues to be the predominant approach to test construction. His definition of intelligence as *that which his test measured* has been adopted by many modern researchers, and it is particularly popular among test developers who wish to avoid arguments about the underlying nature of intelligence.

Binet's legacy links intelligence and school success. His approach to constructing a test ensured that intelligence—defined as performance on the test—and school success would be virtually identical. Thus, Binet's intelligence test, and today's tests that use his methods, are reasonable predictors of school performance. They do not, however, provide useful information for other attributes, such as social skills or personality traits, that are largely unrelated to academic proficiency.

intelligence the capacity to understand the world, think with rationality, and use resources effectively when faced with challenges

mental age the typical intelligence level found for people at a given chronological age

chronological (or physical) age the actual age of the child taking the intelligence test

Finally, Binet developed a method to link each intelligence test score with a **mental age**, the age of the children who, on average, achieved that score. If a 6-year-old girl scored 30 on the test, and this was the average score for 10-year-olds, her mental age would be 10. Similarly, a 15-year-old boy who scored a 90—matching the mean score for 15-year-olds—would have a mental age of 15 (Wasserman & Tulsky, 2005).

Although mental age indicates how students are performing relative to their peers, it does not permit adequate comparisons between students of different **chronological (or physical)**

ages. By using mental age alone, for example, it would be assumed that a 15-year-old whose mental age is 17 would be as bright as a 6-year-old whose mental age is 8, when actually the 6-year-old shows a much greater *relative* intelligence.

The **intelligence quotient,** or **IQ**, a score that accounts for a student's mental *and* chronological age, provides a solution. The traditional method of calculating an IQ score uses the following formula, in which MA equals mental age and CA equals chronological age:

$$\text{IQ score} = \frac{\text{MA}}{\text{TA}} \times 100$$

As this formula demonstrates, people whose MA is equal to their CA will always have an IQ of 100. If the CA exceeds the MA—implying below-average intelligence—the score will be below 100; and if the CA is lower than the MA—suggesting above-average intelligence—the score will be above 100.

Using this formula, consider our example of a 15-year-old who scores a MA of 17. This student's IQ is $\frac{17}{15} \times 100$, or 113. In comparison, the IQ of a 6-year-old scoring a mental age of 8 is $\frac{8}{6} \times 100$, or 133—a higher IQ score.

IQ scores today are calculated in a more sophisticated manner and known as *deviation IQ scores*. The average deviation IQ score remains at 100, but now, by the degree of deviation from this score, the proportion of people with similar scores can be calculated. For instance, about two-thirds of all people fall within 15 points of 100, scoring between 85 and 115. Beyond this range, the percentage of people in the same score category drops significantly.

Measuring IQ: Present-Day Approaches to Intelligence. Since Binet, intelligence tests have become increasingly accurate measures of IQ, though most remain rooted in his original work. For example, one of the most widely used tests—the **Stanford-Binet Intelligence Scales, Fifth Edition (SB5)**—began as an American revision of Binet's original test. The test consists of age-appropriate items—for example, young children are asked about everyday activities or given complex figures to copy. Older people are asked to explain proverbs, solve analogies, and describe similarities between word groups. Test-takers are given progressively more difficult problems until they are unable to proceed.

The Wechsler Intelligence Scale for Children, Fourth Edition (WISC-IV) is widely used as an intelligence test that measures verbal and performance (nonverbal) skills.

The **Wechsler Intelligence Scale for Children, Fourth Edition (WISC-IV)** is another widely used test. The test (an offshoot of the Wechsler Adult Intelligence Scale) breaks the total score into measures of verbal and performance (or nonverbal) skills. As you can see from Figure 5-8, word problems are used to test skills such as comprehension, while typical nonverbal tasks are copying a complex design, sequencing pictures, and assembling objects. The test's separate portions make it easier to identify specific problems a test-taker may have. For example, significantly higher scores on the performance part than on the verbal part may indicate linguistic development difficulties (Zhu & Weiss, 2005).

The **Kaufman Assessment Battery for Children, Second Edition (KABC-II)** takes a different approach. It tests children's ability to integrate different kinds of stimuli simultaneously and to use sequential thinking. The KABC-II's special virtue is its flexibility. It allows the test-giver to use alternative wording or gestures, or even to pose questions in a different language, in order to maximize performance. This makes testing more valid and equitable for children to whom English is a second language (Kaufman et al., 2005).

What do the IQ scores mean? For most children, they are reasonable predictors of school performance. That's not surprising, given that intelligence tests were developed to identify students who were having difficulties (Sternberg & Grigorenko, 2002).

But the story differs for performance outside of school; for example, although people with higher scores tend to finish more years of schooling, once this is statistically controlled for, IQ scores do not closely relate to income and later success in life. Two people with different scores may both earn bachelor's degrees at the same college, but the person with a lower IQ might have a higher income and a more successful career. These difficulties with traditional IQ scores have led researchers to consider alternative approaches (McClelland, 1993).

intelligence quotient (or IQ score) a score that accounts for a student's mental *and* chronological age

Stanford-Binet Intelligence Scales, Fifth Edition (SB5) a test that consists of a series of items that vary according to the age of the person being tested

Wechsler Intelligence Scale for Children, Fourth Edition (WISC-IV) a test for children that provides separate measures of verbal and performance (or nonverbal) skills, as well as a total score

Kaufman Assessment Battery for Children, Second Edition (KABC-II) an intelligence test that measures children's ability to integrate different stimuli simultaneously and to use sequential thinking

Name	Goal of Item	Example
Verbal Scale		
Information	Assess general information	How many nickels make a dime?
Comprehension	Assess understanding and evaluation of social norms and past experience	What is the advantage of keeping money in the bank?
Arithmetic	Assess math reasoning through verbal problems	If two buttons cost 15 cents, what will be the cost of a dozen buttons?
Similarities	Test understanding of how objects or concepts are alike, tapping abstract reasoning	In what way are an hour and a week alike?
Performance Scale		
Digit symbol	Assess speed of learning	Match symbols to numbers using key.
Picture completion	Visual memory and attention	Identify what is missing.
Object assembly	Test understanding of relationship of parts to wholes	Put pieces together to form a whole.

FIGURE 5-8 Measuring Intelligence
The Wechsler Intelligence Scale for Children, Fourth Edition (WISC-IV) includes items such as these. What do such items cover? What do they miss?

What IQ Tests Don't Tell: Alternative Conceptions of Intelligence. The intelligence tests schools use most today regard intelligence as a single factor, a unitary mental ability. This attribute is commonly called *g* (Spearman, 1927; Lubinski, 2004). Assumed to underlie performance on every aspect of intelligence, the *g* factor is what IQ tests presumably measure.

However, many theorists disagree that intelligence is unidimensional. Some developmentalists suggest that two kinds of intelligence exist: fluid and crystallized (Catell, 1967, 1987). **Fluid intelligence** reflects information processing capabilities, reasoning, and memory; for

fluid intelligence intelligence that reflects information processing capabilities, reasoning, and memory example, a student asked to group a series of letters according to some criterion or to remember a set of numbers would be using fluid intelligence (Salthouse, Pink, & Tucker-Drob, 2008; Shangguan & Shi, 2009; Ziegler et al., 2012).

In contrast, **crystallized intelligence** is the cumulative information, skills, and strategies people have learned and can apply in solving problems. A student would likely use crystallized intelligence to solve a puzzle or find the solution to a mystery (Alfonso, Flanagan, & Radwan, 2005; MacCann, 2010; Hill et al., 2013).

Other theorists divide intelligence into even more parts. Psychologist Howard Gardner suggests that we have at least eight distinct intelligences, each relatively independent (see Figure 5-9). Gardner suggests that these intelligences operate together, depending on the activity we engage in (Chen & Gardner, 2005; Gardner & Moran, 2006; Roberts & Lipnevich, 2012).

crystallized intelligence the accumulation of information, skills, and strategies that people have learned through experience and that they can apply in problem-solving situations

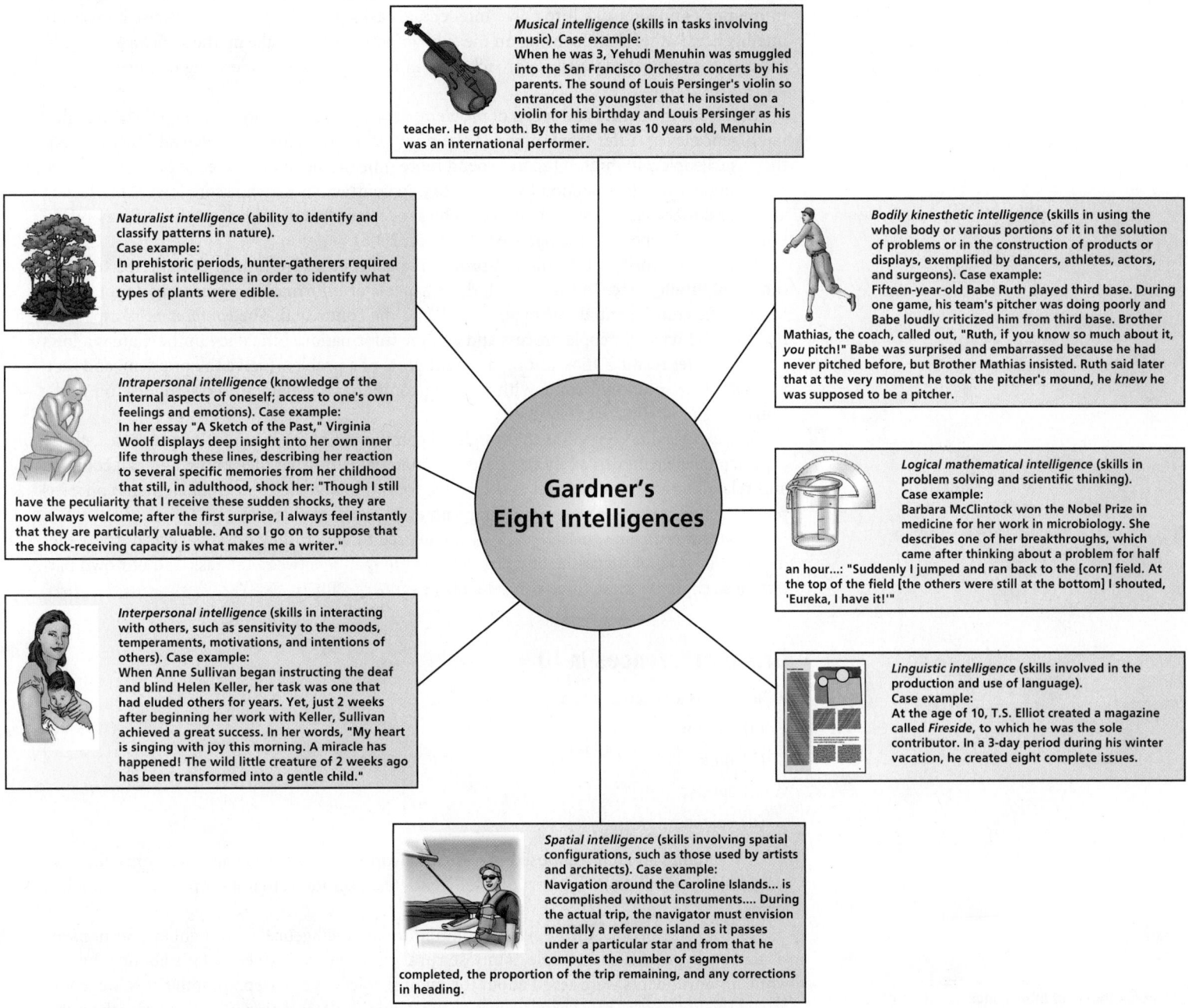

FIGURE 5-9 Gardner's Eight Intelligences
Howard Gardner has theorized that there are eight distinct intelligences, each relatively independent.
Source: Based on Walters & Gardner, 1986.

From an educator's perspective: Does Howard Gardner's theory of multiple intelligences suggest that classroom instruction should be modified from an emphasis on the traditional three Rs of reading, writing, and arithmetic?

Russian psychologist Lev Vygotsky, whose cognitive development approach we discussed earlier, took a very different approach to intelligence. He suggested we assess intelligence by looking not only at fully developed cognitive processes, but also at those in current development as well. To do this, he contended that assessment tasks should involve cooperative interaction between the assessed individual and the assessor—a process called *dynamic assessment*. In short, intelligence is reflected both in how children perform on their own and how they perform when helped by adults (Vygotsky, 1926/1997; Lohman, 2005).

Psychologist Robert Sternberg (1987, 1990, 2003a), taking another approach, suggests intelligence is best viewed as information processing. In this view, how people store material in memory and later use it to solve intellectual tasks provides the most precise concept of intelligence. Rather than focusing on the subcomponents that make up the *structure* of intelligence, information processing approaches examine the *processes* underlying intelligent behavior (Floyd, 2005).

Studies of the nature and speed of problem-solving processes show that people with higher intelligence levels differ from others in the number of problems they solve and the methods they use. People with high IQ scores spend more time on the initial stages of problem solving, retrieving relevant information from memory. In contrast, those who score lower tend to skip ahead and make less informed guesses. The processes used in solving problems may reflect important differences in intelligence (Sternberg, 2005).

Sternberg's work on information processing approaches led him to develop the **triarchic theory of intelligence**. In this model, three aspects of information processing denote intelligence: the componential, the experiential, and the contextual. The *componential* aspect reflects how efficiently people process and analyze information. Efficiency in these areas allows people to infer relationships among different parts of a problem, solve the problem, and then evaluate their solution. People with a strong componential element score highest on traditional tests of intelligence (Sternberg, 2005).

The *experiential* element is the insightful component of intelligence. People with a strong experiential element can easily compare new material with what they know, and can combine and relate known facts in novel and creative ways. Finally, the *contextual* element concerns practical intelligence, or ways of dealing with everyday demands.

In Sternberg's view, people vary in the degree to which they possess each of these elements. Our level of success at any task reflects the match between the task and our own pattern of strength on these three components (Sternberg, 2003b, 2008).

Group Differences in IQ

A "jontry" is an example of a

(a) rulpow

(b) flink

(c) spudge

(d) bakwoe

If you found an item composed of nonsense words such as this on an intelligence test, you would likely complain. What sort of intelligence test uses items that incorporate meaningless terms?

Yet for some people, the items used on traditional intelligence tests might appear nonsensical. As a hypothetical example, suppose rural children were asked details about subways, while urban students were asked about the mating practices of sheep. In both cases, we would expect the test-takers' prior experiences to substantially affect their ability to answer the questions. On an IQ test, such questions could rightly be seen as a measure of prior experience rather than of intelligence.

triarchic theory of intelligence Sternberg's theory that intelligence is made up of three major components: componential, experiential, and contextual

Although traditional IQ tests are not so obviously dependent upon test-takers' prior experiences, cultural background and experience can affect test scores. In fact, many educators feel that traditional measures of intelligence subtly favor white, upper- and middle-class students over other cultural groups (Ortiz & Dynda, 2005).

Explaining Racial Differences in IQ. How cultural background and experience affect IQ test scores has led to much debate among researchers, fueled by the finding that certain racial groups' IQ scores are consistently lower, on average, than those of other groups. For example, the mean score of African Americans tends to be about 15 points below the mean score of whites—although the measured difference varies a great deal depending on the IQ test employed (Fish, 2001; Maller, 2003).

The question that emerges from such differences is whether they reflect differences in intelligence or biases in intelligence tests. For example, if whites outperform African Americans on an IQ test because they are more familiar with the language of the test items, the test can hardly be judged a fair measure of African Americans' intelligence. Similarly, a test that solely used African American vernacular English would not be an impartial measure of intelligence for whites.

How to interpret differences between the IQ test scores of different cultural groups is a major controversy in child development: To what degree is intelligence determined by heredity, and to what degree by environment? The social implications make this issue important. If intelligence is mostly hereditary and therefore largely fixed at birth, attempts to alter cognitive abilities, such as schooling, will have limited success. If intelligence is largely environmentally determined, modifying social and educational conditions is a more promising strategy to increase cognitive functioning (Weiss, 2003; Nisbett et al., 2012).

The Bell Curve Controversy. Although the relative contributions of heredity and environment to intelligence have been investigated for decades, the smoldering debate became a raging fire with the publication of a book by Richard J. Herrnstein and Charles Murray (1994), titled *The Bell Curve*. Herrnstein and Murray argue that the average 15-point IQ difference between whites and African Americans is due primarily to heredity. They also argue that this difference accounts for the higher rates of poverty, lower employment, and higher use of welfare among minority groups.

These conclusions met with outrage, and many researchers who examined the data used in the book came to quite different conclusions. Most developmentalists and psychologists argued that racial differences in measured IQ can be explained by environmental differences. In fact, mean IQ scores of black and white children are quite similar when various economic and social factors are statistically taken into account simultaneously. For instance, children from similar middle-class backgrounds, whether African American or white, tend to have similar IQ scores (Brooks-Gunn, Klebanov, & Duncan, 1996; Alderfer, 2003).

Critics also maintained there is little evidence that IQ causes poverty and other social ills. In fact, some critics suggested, as mentioned earlier, that IQ scores were unrelated to later success in life (e.g., Nisbett, 1994; Reifman, 2000; Sternberg, 2005).

Finally, members of cultural and social minority groups may score lower than those in the majority group due to the biases of the tests. Traditional IQ tests may discriminate against minority groups who lack exposure to the environment majority group members have experienced (Fagan & Holland, 2007; Razani et al., 2007).

Most traditional IQ tests are constructed using white, English-speaking, middle-class populations as their test subjects. Thus, children from different backgrounds may perform poorly on them—not because they are less intelligent, but because the questions are culturally biased in favor of the majority group. A classic study found that in one California school district, Mexican American students were ten times more likely than whites to be placed in special education classes (Mercer, 1973; Hatton, 2002). More recent findings show that nationally, twice as many African American students as white students are classified as mildly retarded, a difference attributed primarily to cultural bias and poverty (Reschly, 1996; Terman et al., 1996). Although certain IQ tests (such as the System of

Performance on traditional IQ tests is dependent in part on test-takers' prior experiences and cultural background.

Multicultural Pluralistic Assessment, or SOMPA) are designed to be valid regardless of cultural background, no test can be completely unbiased (Reschly, 1996; Sandoval et al., 1998; Hatton, 2002).

In short, most experts were not convinced by *The Bell Curve* contention that genetic factors largely determine differences in group IQ scores. Still, we cannot put the issue to rest, because it is impossible to design a definitive experiment to determine the cause of these differences. (One cannot ethically assign children to different living conditions to find the effects of environment, nor genetically control or alter intelligence levels in unborn children.)

Today, IQ is seen as the product of *both* nature and nurture interacting in a complex manner. Genes are seen to affect experiences, and experiences are viewed as influencing the expression of genes. Psychologist Eric Turkheimer found evidence that while environmental factors play a larger role in the IQ of poor children, genes are more influential for affluent children (Turkheimer et al., 2003; Harden, Turkheimer, & Loehlin, 2007).

Ultimately, determining the absolute degree to which intelligence is influenced by genetic and environmental factors may be less important than improving children's living conditions and educational experiences. Enriching the quality of children's environments will better permit all children to reach their full potential and to maximize their contributions to society (Wickelgren, 1999; Posthuma & de Geus, 2006; Nisbett, 2008).

Below and Above Intelligence Norms: Intellectual Disabilities and Intellectual Giftedness

Although Connie kept pace with her peers in kindergarten, by first grade, she was academically the slowest in almost every subject. She tried hard but it took her longer than the others to absorb new material, and she regularly required special attention to keep up with the class.

In some areas, though, she excelled: When asked to draw or produce something with her hands, her performance exceeded her classmates'. She produced beautiful work that was much admired. The other students in the class felt that there was something different about Connie, but they couldn't identify the source of the difference and spent little time pondering the issue.

Connie's parents and teacher, though, knew what made her special. Extensive testing in kindergarten had shown that Connie's intelligence was well below normal, and she was officially classified as a special needs student.

If Connie had been attending school before 1975, she would most likely have been placed in a special needs classroom as soon as her low IQ was identified. Such classes, consisting of students with a range of afflictions, including emotional difficulties, severe reading problems, and physical disabilities such as multiple sclerosis, as well as those with lower IQs, were usually kept separate from the regular educational process.

All that changed in 1975 when Congress passed Public Law 94–142, the Education for All Handicapped Children Act. The intent of the law—an intent largely realized—was to ensure that special needs children were educated in the **least restrictive environment**, that is, the setting most similar to that of children without special needs (Yell, 1995; Rozalski, Stewart, & Miller, 2010).

In practice, the law has integrated children with special needs into regular classrooms and activities to the greatest extent possible, as long as doing so is educationally beneficial. Children are to be removed from the regular classroom only for those subjects specifically affected by their exceptionality; for all other subjects, they are to be taught in regular classrooms. Of course, some children with severe handicaps still need a mostly or entirely separate education. But the law integrates exceptional children and typical children to the fullest extent possible (Yell, 1995).

least restrictive environment the setting that is most similar to that of children without special needs

mainstreaming an educational approach in which exceptional children are integrated to the extent possible into the traditional educational system and are provided with a broad range of educational alternatives

This approach to special education, designed to minimize the segregation of exceptional students, is called mainstreaming. In **mainstreaming**, exceptional children are integrated as much as possible into the regular education system and provided with a broad range of alternatives (Hocutt, 1996; Belkin, 2004; Crosland & Dunlap, 2012).

The benefits of mainstreaming have led some professionals to promote an alternative educational model known as full inclusion. *Full inclusion* is the integration of all students, even those with the most severe disabilities, into regular classes. In such a system, separate special education programs would cease to operate. Full inclusion is controversial, and it remains to be seen how widespread such a practice will become (Begeny & Martens, 2007; Lindsay, 2007; Mangiatordi, 2012).

Regardless of whether they are educated using mainstreaming or full inclusion, children whose intelligence is significantly beyond the typical range represent a challenge for educators. We will consider both those who are below and those who are above the norms.

Below the Norm: Intellectual Disability. Approximately 1 to 3 percent of the school-age population is considered to be intellectually disabled (previously referred to as mental retardation). Estimates vary so widely because the most commonly accepted definition of intellectual disability, which was previously referred to professionally as mental retardation and is still used frequently, is one that leaves a great deal of room for interpretation. According to the American Association on Intellectual and Developmental Disabilities, **intellectual disability** is characterized by significant limitations both in intellectual functioning and in adaptive behavior, which covers many everyday social and practical skills (American Association on Intellectual and Developmental Disabilities, 2012).

This boy with an intellectual disability is mainstreamed into this fifth-grade class.

Most cases of intellectual disability are classified as *familial intellectual disability*, in which no cause is apparent beyond a history of retardation in the family. In other cases, there is a clear biological cause. The most common such causes are *fetal alcohol syndrome*, resulting from the mother's use of alcohol while pregnant, and *Down syndrome*, caused by the presence of an extra chromosome. Birth complications, such as a temporary lack of oxygen, may also produce retardation (Plomin, 2005; West & Blake, 2005; Manning & Hoyme, 2007).

Although limitations in intellectual functioning can be measured in a relatively straightforward manner—using standard IQ tests—it is more difficult to determine how to gauge limitations in other areas. Ultimately, this imprecision leads to a lack of uniformity in the ways experts apply the label of "intellectual disability." Furthermore, it has resulted in significant variation in the abilities of people who are categorized as experiencing intellectual disability. Accordingly, intellectually disabled people range from those who can be taught to work and function with little special attention to those who are virtually untrainable and who never develop speech or such basic motor skills as crawling or walking.

The vast majority of the intellectually disabled—some 90 percent—have relatively low levels of deficits. Classified with **mild intellectual disability**, they score in the range of 50 or 55 to 70 on IQ tests. Typically, their retardation is not even identified before they reach school, although their early development often is slower than average. Once they enter elementary school, their retardation and their need for special attention usually become apparent, as it did with Connie, the first grader profiled at the beginning of this discussion. With appropriate training, these students can reach a third- to sixth-grade educational level, and although they cannot carry out complex intellectual tasks, they are able to hold jobs and function quite independently and successfully.

Intellectual and adaptive limitations become more apparent, however, at higher levels of mental retardation. People whose IQ scores range from 35 or 40 to 50 or 55 are classified with **moderate intellectual disability**. Composing between 5 and 10 percent of those classified as intellectually disabled, those who are moderately intellectually disabled display distinctive behavior early in their lives. They are slow to develop language skills, and their motor development is also affected. Regular schooling is usually not effective in training people with moderate intellectual disability to acquire academic skills, because generally they are unable to progress beyond the second-grade level. Still, they are capable of learning occupational and social skills, and they can

intellectual disability a disability characterized by significant limitations both in intellectual functioning and in adaptive behavior, which covers many everyday social and practical skills

mild intellectual disability intellectual disability in which IQ scores fall in the range of 50 or 55 to 70

moderate intellectual disability intellectual disability in which IQ scores range from 35 or 40 to 50 or 55 learn to travel independently to familiar places. Typically, they require moderate levels of supervision.

At the most significant levels of intellectual disability—those who are classified with **severe intellectual disability** (IQs ranging from 20 or 25 to 35 or 40) and **profound intellectual disability** (IQs below 20 or 25)—the ability to function is severely limited. Usually, such people have little or no speech, have poor motor control, and may need 24-hour nursing care. At the same time, however, some people with severe intellectual disability are capable of learning basic self-care skills, such as dressing and eating, and they may even develop the potential to become partially independent as adults. Still, the need for relatively high levels of care continues throughout the life span, and most severely and profoundly intellectually disabled people are institutionalized for the majority of their lives.

Above the Norm: The Gifted and Talented. *Amy Leibowitz picked up reading at age 3. By 5, she was writing her own books. First grade bored her within a week. As her school had no program for gifted children, it was suggested she skip to second grade. From there, she went to fifth grade. Her parents were proud but concerned. When they asked the fifth-grade teacher where she felt Amy really belonged, the teacher said she was ready, academically, for high school.*

It sometimes surprises people that the gifted and talented are considered to have a form of exceptionality. Yet 3 to 5 percent of such children present special challenges of their own.

There is no formal definition of **gifted and talented** students. However, the federal government considers the term *gifted* to include "children who give evidence of high performance capability in areas such as intellectual, creative, artistic, leadership capacity, or specific academic fields, and who require services or activities not ordinarily provided by the school in order to fully develop such capabilities" (Sec. 582, P.L. 97–35). In addition to intellectual exceptionality, unusual potential in nonacademic areas is also included in the concept. Gifted and talented children, no less than students with low IQs, warrant special concern—although programs for them are often the first to be dropped when schools face budgetary problems (Schemo, 2004; Mendoza, 2006; Olszewski-Kubilius & Thomson, 2013).

Despite the stereotype that the gifted are "unsociable," "poorly adjusted," and "neurotic," research suggests that highly intelligent people tend to be outgoing, well adjusted, and popular (Bracken & Brown, 2006; Shaunessy et al., 2006; Cross et al., 2008).

For instance, one landmark, long-term study of 1,500 gifted students, which began in the 1920s, found that the gifted were healthier, better coordinated, and psychologically better adjusted than their less intelligent classmates. Furthermore, they received more awards and distinctions, earned more money, and made many more contributions in art and literature than the average person. By the time they had reached age 40, they had collectively produced more than 90 books, 375 plays and short stories, and 2,000 articles, and they had registered more than 200 patents. Perhaps not surprisingly, they reported greater satisfaction with their lives than the nongifted (Terman & Oden, 1959; Sears, 1977; Shurkin, 1992; Reis & Renzulli, 2004).

Yet being gifted and talented is no guarantee of school success. The verbal abilities that allow the expression of ideas and feelings can equally voice glib and persuasive statements that happen to be inaccurate. Furthermore, teachers sometimes misinterpret the humor, novelty, and creativity of unusually gifted children and regard their intellectual fervor as disruptive or inappropriate. And peers may be unsympathetic: Some very bright children try to hide their intelligence in an effort to fit in (Swiatek, 2002).

Educating the Gifted and Talented. Educators have devised two approaches to teaching the gifted and talented: acceleration and enrichment. **Acceleration** allows gifted students to move ahead at their own pace, even if this means skipping grade levels. The materials in acceleration programs are not always different; they may simply be provided at a faster pace than for the average student (Wells, Lohman, & Marron, 2009; Wood et al., 2010; Lee, Olszewski-Kubilius, & Thomson, 2012).

severe intellectual disability intellectual disability in which IQ scores range from 20 or 25 to 35 or 40

profound intellectual disability intellectual disability in which IQ scores fall below 20 or 25

gifted and talented children who show evidence of high performance capability in areas such as intellectual, creative, artistic, leadership capacity, or specific academic fields

acceleration special programs that allow gifted students to move ahead at their own pace, even if this means skipping to higher grade levels

enrichment an approach through which students are kept at grade level but are enrolled in special programs and given individual activities to allow greater depth of study on a given topic

An alternative approach is **enrichment**, through which students are kept at grade level but are enrolled in special programs and given individual activities to allow greater depth of study. In enrichment, the material differs not only in the timing of its presentation, but in its sophistication as well. Thus, enrichment materials are designed to provide an intellectual challenge to the gifted student, encouraging higher-order thinking (Worrell, Szarko, & Gabelko, 2001; Rotigel, 2003).

REVIEW, CHECK, AND APPLY

REVIEW

L09 How can intelligence be measured?

- Measuring intelligence has traditionally been a matter of testing skills that promote academic success. Among tests used to measure intelligence are the Wechsler Intelligence Scale for Children, Fourth Edition (WISC-IV), and the Kaufman Assessment Battery for Children, Second Edition (KABC-II).
- Recent theories of intelligence suggest there may be several distinct intelligences or several components of intelligence that reflect different ways of processing information.

L010 How are exceptional children educated?

- U.S. educators are attempting to deal with large numbers of exceptional persons whose intellectual and other skills are significantly lower or higher than normal.
- By law, children with special needs must be educated in the least restrictive environment. This has led to mainstreaming, which integrates such children into the regular education system as much as possible.
- The needs of gifted and talented children are sometimes addressed through acceleration and enrichment programs.

CHECK YOURSELF

1. Intelligence is the capacity to understand the world, think with rationality, and use resources effectively when faced with challenges.
   - True
   - False
2. According to Howard Gardner, we have at least eight distinct intelligences, each relatively independent.
   - True
   - False
3. For children whose intelligence falls below the normal range, the recommendation from the Education for All Handicapped Children Act is that they be educated in the _____ environment.
   - a moderately restrictive
   - b average educational
   - c least restrictive
   - d most restrictive

APPLYING LIFESPAN DEVELOPMENT

- How do fluid and crystallized intelligence interact? Which of the two is likely to be more influenced by genetics and which by environment? Why?

✓ **Study** and **Review** on **MyPsychLab.com**

MODULE 5.3

SOCIAL AND PERSONALITY DEVELOPMENT IN MIDDLE CHILDHOOD

When 9-year-old Matt Donner's family relocated from Topeka, Kansas, to Providence, Rhode Island, so that his father could take a promotion at his employer's corporate headquarters, Matt was both excited and fearful. Moving to a new part of the country was exciting, as was the new standard of living his family would enjoy. But Matt had been a quiet and unassuming fourth grader in his old hometown with a small circle of friends. How well would he make the adjustment to fifth grade in his new home?

Not well, it turns out. His shyness got in the way of making new friends. Instead of sitting with other kids at lunchtime, Matt sat alone with a book. "They all knew each other already. That made it really hard," Matt lamented. "I just didn't fit in."

Matt's midwestern accent and small stature didn't help matters. It wasn't long before classmates were mocking his speech, tripping him in the halls, and throwing rocks at him as he walked home from school. His locker was broken into so many times that Matt gave up using it and just carried his books with him. Teachers either didn't care, or more likely didn't notice—the bullying rarely happened in front of them. Matt's greatest fear was that his parents would find out and be disappointed in him. He didn't want them to know that he had let himself become a victim.

Matt's experience is, sadly, not uncommon. As children grow into middle childhood, the way they relate to others and the way they think of themselves undergo significant transformations. Sometimes, these transformations are fairly smooth. However, as Matt's story shows, they can also present children and parents with new and unexpected challenges.

In this module, we focus on social and personality development during middle childhood. It is a time when children's views of themselves change, they form new bonds with friends and family, and they become increasingly attached to social institutions outside the home.

We start our consideration of personality and social development during middle childhood by examining the changes that occur in the ways children see themselves. We discuss how they view their personal characteristics and examine the complex issue of self-esteem. Next, the module turns to relationships during middle childhood, discussing the stages of friendship and the ways gender and ethnicity affect how and with whom children interact. Finally, we explore the central societal institution in children's lives: the family. We consider the consequences of divorce, self-care children, and the phenomenon of group care.

THE DEVELOPING SELF

LO11 In what ways do children's views of themselves change during middle childhood?
LO12 Why is self-esteem important during middle childhood?
LO13 How does children's sense of right and wrong change as they age?

Nine-year-old Karl Haglund is perched in his eagle's nest, a treehouse built high in the willow that grows in his backyard. Sometimes he sits there alone among the tree's spreading branches, his face turned toward the sky, a boy clearly enjoying his solitude. . . .

This morning Karl is busy sawing and hammering. "It's fun to build," he says. "I started the house when I was 4 years old. Then when I was about 7, my dad built me this platform. 'Cause all my places were falling apart and they were crawling with carpenter ants. So we destroyed them and then built me a deck. And I built on top of it. It's stronger now. You can have privacy here, but it's a bad place to go when it's windy 'cause you almost get blown off." (Kotre & Hall, 1990, p. 116)

Karl's growing sense of competence is reflected in his description of how he and his father built his treehouse. Conveying what psychologist Erik Erikson calls "industriousness," Karl's quiet pride in his accomplishment illustrates one way children's views of themselves evolve.

Psychosocial Development in Middle Childhood: Industry Versus Inferiority

According to Erik Erikson, middle childhood is largely about competence. Lasting roughly from ages 6 to 12, the **industry-versus-inferiority stage** is characterized by efforts to meet the challenges presented by parents, peers, school, and the complex modern world.

During this period, children direct their energies to mastering the enormous body of information presented in school and making a place for themselves in their social worlds. Success in this stage brings feelings of mastery and a growing sense of competence, like those expressed by Karl regarding his building experience. On the other hand, difficulties in this stage lead to feelings of failure and inadequacy. As a result, children may withdraw from academic pursuits, showing less interest and motivation to excel, and from interactions with peers.

The sense of industry that children such as Karl attain at this stage has lasting effects. One study examined how childhood industriousness and hard work were related to adult behavior by following a group of 450 men over a 35-year period, starting in early childhood

industry-versus-inferiority stage according to Erikson the period from age 6 to 12 characterized by a focus on efforts to attain competence in meeting the challenges presented by parents, peers, school, and the other complexities of the modern world

(Vaillant & Vaillant, 1981). The men who were most industrious and hardworking as children were most successful as adults, both professionally and personally. In fact, childhood industriousness was more closely associated with adult success than was intelligence or family background.

Understanding One's Self: A New Response to "Who Am I?"

During middle childhood, children seek to answer the question "Who am I?" Although the question will assume greater urgency in adolescence, elementary-age children still try to find their place in the world.

The Shift in Self-Understanding From the Physical to the Psychological. The cognitive advances discussed in the previous module aid children in their quest for self-understanding. They begin to view themselves less in terms of external, physical attributes and more in terms of psychological traits (Lerner, Theokas, & Jelicic, 2005; Thompson & Virmani, 2010).

For instance, 6-year-old Carey describes herself as "a fast runner and good at drawing"—characteristics dependent on motor skills in external activities. In contrast, 11-year-old Meiping characterizes herself as "pretty smart, friendly, and helpful to my friends." Because of her increasing cognitive skills, Meiping's view of herself is based on psychological characteristics, inner traits that are more abstract.

Children's views of who they are also become more complex. In Erikson's view, children are seeking endeavors where they can be successfully industrious. As they get older, children discover their strengths and weaknesses. Ten-year-old Ginny, for instance, comes to understand she is good at arithmetic but not very good at spelling; 11-year-old Alberto decides he is good at softball but lacks the stamina to play soccer well.

Children's self-concepts become divided into personal and academic spheres. They evaluate themselves in four major areas, each of which can be broken down further; for example, the nonacademic self-concept includes physical appearance, peer relations, and physical ability, while the academic self-concept is similarly divided. Research on students' self-concepts in English, mathematics, and nonacademic realms shows that the separate realms do not always correlate, although overlap exists. For example, a child who sees herself as a star math student will not necessarily feel she is great at English (Burnett & Proctor, 2002; Marsh & Ayotte, 2003; Marsh & Hau, 2004).

As children become older, they begin to characterize themselves in terms of their psychological attributes as well as their physical achievements.

Self-Esteem: Developing a Positive—or Negative—View of Oneself

Children don't dispassionately view themselves as just a list of physical and psychological traits. Instead, they judge themselves as being good or bad in particular ways. **Self-esteem** is an individual's overall and specific self-evaluation. Whereas self-concept reflects beliefs and cognitions about the self (*I am good at trumpet; I am not so good at social studies*), self-esteem is more emotionally oriented (*Everybody thinks I'm a nerd*) (Bracken & Lamprecht, 2003; Mruk, 2013).

Self-esteem develops in important ways during middle childhood. As noted, children increasingly compare themselves to others, assessing how they measure up to society's standards. They also increasingly develop their own internal standards of success, and measure how well they compare to those. One advance that occurs in this period is that, like self-concept, self-esteem becomes increasingly differentiated. At age 7, most children have self-esteem that reflects a global, fairly simple view of themselves. Overall positive self-esteem makes them believe they are relatively good at all things. If their overall self-esteem is negative, they feel inadequate at most things (Harter, 1990b; Lerner, Theokas, & Jelicic, 2005).

As children move into middle childhood, however, their self-esteem is higher for some areas and lower in others; for example, a boy's overall self-esteem may be positive in some areas (such as artistic ability) and negative in others (such as athletic skills).

Change and Stability in Self-Esteem. Overall self-esteem is generally high during middle childhood, but begins to decline around age 12, affected mainly by the change of schools:

self-esteem an individual's overall and specific positive and negative self-evaluation

Students leaving elementary school and entering either middle school or junior high school show a decline in self-esteem, which then gradually rises again (Twenge & Campbell, 2001; Robins & Trzesniewski, 2005).

On the other hand, some children have chronically low self-esteem. Children with low self-esteem face a tough road, in part because their self-esteem becomes enmeshed in a cycle of failure that grows increasingly difficult to break. Assume, for instance, that Harry, a student with chronically low self-esteem, is facing an important test. Because of his low self-esteem, he expects to do poorly. As a consequence, he is quite anxious—so anxious that he is unable to concentrate well and study effectively. Furthermore, he may decide not to study much, because he figures that if he's going to do badly anyway, why bother studying?

Of course, Harry's anxiety and lack of effort bring the result he expected: He does poorly on the test. This failure confirms Harry's expectation, reinforces his low self-esteem, and the cycle of failure continues.

Students with high self-esteem fall into a cycle of success. Higher expectations lead to more effort and less anxiety, increasing the odds of success. In turn, success affirms the high self-esteem that began the cycle.

From an educator's perspective: What can teachers do to help children whose low self-esteem is causing them to fail? How can this cycle of failure be broken?

Parents can help break the cycle of failure by promoting their children's self-esteem. The best way to do this is through the use of the *authoritative* child-rearing style that we discussed in Chapter 4. Authoritative parents are warm and emotionally supportive, while still setting clear limits for their children's behavior. In contrast, other parenting styles have less positive effects on self-esteem. Parents who are highly punitive and controlling send a message to their children that they are untrustworthy and unable to make good decisions—a message that can undermine children's sense of adequacy. Highly indulgent parents, who indiscriminately praise and reinforce their children regardless of their actual performance, can create a false sense of self-esteem in their children, which ultimately may be just as damaging to children (Bender et al., 2007; Milevsky et al., 2007; Taylor et al., 2012).

Race and Self-Esteem. If you were a member of a racial group that routinely experienced prejudice and discrimination, your self-esteem would likely be affected. Early research confirmed that hypothesis and found that African Americans had lower self-esteem than whites. A set of pioneering studies a generation ago found that African American children shown black and white dolls preferred the white dolls over the black ones (Clark & Clark, 1947). The interpretation drawn from the study: The self-esteem of the African American children was low.

In pioneering research conducted several decades ago, African American girls' preference for white dolls was viewed as an indication of low self-esteem. More recent evidence, however, suggests that whites and African American children show little difference in self-esteem.

However, more recent research has shown these assumptions to be overstated. The picture is more complex. For example, although white children initially show higher self-esteem, black children begin to show slightly higher self-esteem than white children around age 11. This shift occurs as African American children become more identified with their racial group, develop more complex views of racial identity, and increasingly view the positive aspects of their group membership (Tatum, 2007; Shaw, Liang, & Krause, 2010; Zeiders, Umaña-Taylor, & Derlan, 2013).

Hispanic children also show an increase in self-esteem toward the end of middle childhood, although even in adolescence their self-esteem still trails that of whites. In contrast, Asian American children show the opposite pattern: their self-esteem in elementary school is higher than that of whites and blacks, but by the end of childhood, it is lower than that of whites (Umana-Taylor, Diveri, & Fine, 2002; Tropp & Wright, 2003; Verkuyten, 2008).

One explanation for the complex relationship between self-esteem and minority group status comes from *social identity theory*. According to the theory, minority group members are likely to accept the majority group's negative views only if they perceive that there is little possibility of changing the power and status differences between the groups. If minority group members feel that prejudice and discrimination can be reduced, and they blame society for the prejudice and not themselves, self-esteem should not differ between majority and minority groups (Tajfel & Turner, 2004; Thompson, Briggs-King, & LaTouche-Howard, 2012).

In fact, as group pride and ethnic awareness on the part of minority group members has grown, differences in self-esteem between members of different ethnic groups have narrowed. This trend has been supported by increased sensitivity to the importance of multiculturalism (Negy, Shreve, & Jensen, 2003; Lee, 2005; Tatum, 2007).

Moral Development

Your wife is near death from an unusual kind of cancer. One drug exists that the physicians think might save her—a form of radium that a scientist in a nearby city has recently developed. The drug, though, is expensive to manufacture, and the scientist is charging ten times what the drug costs him to make. He pays $1,000 for the radium and charges $10,000 for a small dose. You have gone to everyone you know to borrow money, but you can only get $2,500—one-quarter of what you need. You've told the scientist that your wife is dying and asked him to sell it more cheaply or let you pay later. But the scientist has said, "No, I discovered the drug and I'm going to make money from it." In desperation, you consider breaking into the scientist's laboratory to steal the drug for your wife. Should you do it?

According to developmental psychologist Lawrence Kohlberg and his colleagues, the answer that children give to this question reveals central aspects of their sense of morality and justice. He suggests that people's responses to moral dilemmas such as this one reveal their stage of moral development—as well as information about their level of cognitive development (Kohlberg, 1984; Colby & Kohlberg, 1987).

Kohlberg contends that people pass through stages as their sense of justice evolves and the reasoning they use to make moral judgments changes. Younger school-age children tend to think in terms of either concrete, unvarying rules ("It is always wrong to steal" or "I'll be punished if I steal") or the rules of society ("Good people don't steal" or "What if everyone stole?").

Immigrant children tend to fare quite well in the United States, partly because many come from societies that emphasize collectivism, and consequently they may feel more obligation and duty to their family to succeed. What are some other cultural differences that can lead to the success of immigrant children?

Cultural Dimensions

Are Children of Immigrant Families Well Adjusted?

Immigration to the United States has risen significantly in the last 30 years. Children in immigrant families account for almost 25 percent of children in the United States. Children of immigrant families are the fastest-growing segment of children in the country (Hernandez et al., 2008).

In many ways, children of immigrants fare quite well. In fact, in some ways they are better off than their nonimmigrant peers. For example, they tend to have equal or better grades in school than children whose parents were born in the United States. Psychologically, they also do quite well, showing similar levels of self-esteem as nonimmigrant children, although they do report feeling less popular and less in control of their lives (Harris, 2000; Kao, 2000; Driscoll, Russell, & Crockett, 2008).

On the other hand, many children of immigrants face challenges. Their parents often have limited education, and they work at jobs that pay poorly. Unemployment rates are often higher for immigrants than the general population. In addition, parental English proficiency may be lower. Many children of immigrants lack good health insurance (Hernandez et al., 2008; Turney & Kao, 2009).

However, even the immigrant children who are not financially well off are often more highly motivated to succeed and place greater value on education than do children in nonimmigrant families. In addition, many immigrant children come from societies that emphasize collectivism, and consequently they may feel more obligation and duty toward their family to succeed. Finally, their country of origin may give some immigrant children a strong enough cultural identity to prevent them from adopting undesirable "American" behaviors—such as materialism or selfishness (Fuligni & Yoshikawa, 2003; Suárez-Orozco & Suárez-Orozco, 2008).

During the middle childhood years, it thus appears that children in immigrant families often do quite well in the United States. The story is less clear, however, when immigrant children reach adolescence and adulthood. For instance, some research shows higher rates of obesity (a key indicator of physical health) in adolescents. Research is just beginning to clarify how effectively immigrants cope over the course of the life span (Fuligni & Fuligni, 2008; Perreira & Ornelas, 2011; Fuligni, 2012).

By adolescence, however, individuals can reason on a higher plane, typically having reached Piaget's stage of formal operations. They are capable of comprehending abstract, formal principles of morality, and they consider broader issues of morality and of right and wrong in cases like the one just presented. ("Stealing may be acceptable if you are following your own conscience and doing the right thing.")

Kohlberg suggests that moral development emerges in a three-level sequence, further subdivided into six stages (see Table 5-1). At the lowest level, *preconventional morality* (stages

TABLE 5-1 KOHLBERG'S SEQUENCE OF MORAL REASONING

		Sample Moral Reasoning	
Level	**Stage**	**In Favor of Stealing**	**Against Stealing**
LEVEL 1	**STAGE 1**		
Preconventional morality The main considerations are the avoidance of punishment and the desire for rewards.	Obedience and punishment orientation: People obey rules to avoid being punished. Obedience is its own reward.	"You shouldn't just let your wife die. People will blame you for not doing enough, and they'll blame the scientist for not selling you the drug for less money."	"You can't steal the drug because you'll be arrested and go to jail. Even if you aren't caught, you'll feel guilty and you'll always worry that the police may figure out what you did."
	STAGE 2		
	Reward orientation: People obey rules in order to earn rewards for their own benefit.	"Even if you get caught, the jury will understand and give you a short sentence. Meanwhile, your wife is alive. And if you're stopped before you get the drug to your wife, you could probably just return the drug without penalty."	"You shouldn't steal the drug because you're not responsible for your wife's cancer. If you get caught, your wife will still die and you'll be in jail."
LEVEL 2	**STAGE 3**		
Conventional morality Membership in society becomes important. People behave in ways that will win the approval of others.	"Good boy" morality: People want to be respected by others and try to do what they're supposed to do.	"Who will blame you if you steal a life-saving drug? But if you just let your wife die, you won't be able to hold your head up in front of your family or your neighbors."	"If you steal the drug, everyone will treat you like a criminal. They will wonder why you couldn't have found some other way to save your wife."
	STAGE 4		
	Authority and social-order-maintaining morality: People believe that only society, not individuals, can determine what is right. Obeying society's rules is right in itself.	"A husband has certain responsibilities toward his wife. If you want to live an honorable life, you can't let fear of the consequences get in the way of saving her. If you ever want to sleep again, you have to save her."	"You shouldn't let your concern for your wife cloud your judgment. Stealing the drug may feel right at the moment, but you'll live to regret breaking the law."
LEVEL 3	**STAGE 5**		
Postconventional morality People accept that there are certain ideals and principles of morality that must govern our actions. These ideals are more important than any particular society's rules.	Morality of contract, individual rights, and democratically accepted law: People rightly feel obligated to follow the agreed rules of society. But as societies develop over time, rules have to be updated to make societal changes reflect underlying social principles.	"If you simply follow the law, you will violate the underlying principle of saving your wife's life. If you do take the drug, society will understand your actions and respect them. You can't let an outdated law prevent you from doing the right thing."	"Rules represent society's thinking on the morality of actions. You can't let your short-term emotions interfere with the more permanent rules of society. If you do, society will judge you negatively, and in the end you will lose self-respect."
	STAGE 6		
	Morality of individual principles and conscience: People accept that laws are attempts to write down specific applications of universal moral principles. Individuals must test these laws against their consciences, which tend to express an inborn sense of those principles.	"If you allow your wife to die, you will have obeyed the letter of the law, but you will have violated the universal principle of life preservation that resides within your conscience. You will blame yourself forever if your wife dies because you obeyed an imperfect law."	"If you become a thief, your conscience will blame you for putting your own interpretation of moral issues above the legitimate rule of law. You will have betrayed your own standards of morality."

Source: Based on Kohlberg, 1969.

1 and 2), people follow rigid rules based on punishments or rewards (e.g., a student might evaluate the moral dilemma in the story by saying it was not worth stealing the drug because you could go to jail). **Watch** the **Video** *Kohlberg and the Heinz Dilemma* in **MyPsychLab**.

In the next level, *conventional morality* (stages 3 and 4), people approach moral problems as good, responsible members of society. Some would decide *against* stealing the drug because they would feel guilty or dishonest for violating social norms. Others would decide *in favor* of stealing the drug because they would be unable to face others if they did nothing. All of these people would be reasoning at the conventional level of morality.

Finally, individuals using *postconventional morality* (stages 5 and 6) invoke universal moral principles that are considered broader than the rules of their particular society. People who would condemn themselves if they did not steal the drug because they would be violating their own moral principles are reasoning at the postconventional level.

Kohlberg's theory proposes that people move through the stages in a fixed order and are unable to reach the highest stage until adolescence, due to deficits in cognitive development before then (Kurtines & Gewirtz, 1987). However, not everyone is presumed to reach the highest stages: Kohlberg found that postconventional reasoning is relatively rare.

Although Kohlberg's theory provides a good account of the development of moral *judgments*, the links with moral *behavior* are less strong. Still, students at higher stages are less likely to engage in antisocial behavior at school and in the community. One experiment found that 15 percent of students who reasoned at the postconventional level cheated when given the opportunity, compared to more than half of students at lower levels. Though those at higher levels cheated less, they still cheated. Clearly, knowing what is right is not the same as acting that way (Hart, Burock, & London, 2003; Semerci, 2006; Prohaska, 2012).

Kohlberg's theory has also been criticized because it is based solely on observations of Western cultures. In fact, cross-cultural research finds that those in more industrialized, technologically advanced cultures move through the stages more rapidly than members of nonindustrialized countries. One explanation is that Kohlberg's higher stages are based on moral reasoning involving governmental and societal institutions such as the police and court system. In less industrialized areas, morality may be based more on relationships between people. In short, the nature of morality may differ in diverse cultures, and Kohlberg's theory is more suited for Western cultures (Fu et al., 2007).

In addition, developmental psychologist Elliot Turiel has argued that Kohlberg did not sufficiently distinguish moral reasoning from other sorts of reasoning. In Turiel's view, called *moral domain theory*, he argues that children distinguish between the domains of social conventional reasoning and moral reasoning. In social conventional reasoning, the focus is on rules that have been established by society such as eating mashed potatoes with a fork or asking to be excused after eating. Such rules are largely arbitrary (does it really matter if a child uses a spoon to eat mashed potatoes?). In contrast, moral reasoning focuses on issues of fairness, justice, the rights of others, and avoidance of harm to others. In comparison to social conventional rules, whose purpose is to ensure the smooth functioning of society, moral rules are based on more abstract concepts of justice (Turiel, 2006, 2008, 2010).

Finally, an additional problematic aspect of Kohlberg's theory is the difficulty it has explaining *girls'* moral judgments. Because Kohlberg's theory was based largely on data from males, some researchers have argued that it better describes boys' moral development than girls'. This would explain the surprising finding that women typically score at a lower level than men on tests of moral judgments using Kohlberg's stages. This result has led to an alternative account of moral development for girls.

Moral Development in Girls. Psychologist Carol Gilligan (1982, 1987) has suggested that differences in the ways boys and girls are raised in our society lead to basic distinctions in how men and women view moral behavior. According to her, boys view morality primarily in terms of broad principles such as justice or fairness, while girls see it in terms of responsibility toward individuals and willingness to sacrifice themselves to help specific individuals within the context of particular relationships. Compassion for individuals, then, is a greater factor in moral behavior for women than it is for men (Gilligan, Ward, & Taylor, 1988; Gilligan, Lyons, & Hammer, 1990; Gump, Baker, & Roll, 2000; Fumagalli et al., 2010).

Gilligan views morality as developing among females in a three-stage process (summarized in Table 5-2). In the first stage, called "orientation toward individual survival," females first concentrate on what is practical and best for them, gradually making a transition from

TABLE 5-2 GILLIGAN'S THREE STAGES OF MORAL DEVELOPMENT IN WOMEN

Stage	Characteristics	Example
STAGE 1		
Orientation toward individual survival	Initial concentration is on what is practical and best for self. Gradual transition from selfishness to responsibility, which includes thinking about what would be best for others.	A first grader may insist on playing only games of her own choosing when playing with a friend.
STAGE 2		
Goodness as self-sacrifice	Initial view is that a woman must sacrifice her own wishes to what other people want. Gradual transition from "goodness" to "truth," which takes into account needs of both self and others.	Now older, the same girl may believe that to be a good friend, she must play the games her friend chooses, even if she herself doesn't like them.
STAGE 3		
Morality of nonviolence	A moral equivalence is established between self and others. Hurting anyone—including one's self—is seen as immoral. Most sophisticated form of reasoning, according to Gilligan.	The same girl may realize that both friends must enjoy their time together and look for activities that both she and her friend can enjoy.

selfishness to responsibility, that is, thinking about what would be best for others. In the second stage, termed "goodness as self-sacrifice," females begin to think they must sacrifice their own wishes to those of others.

Ideally, women make a transition from "goodness" to "truth," in which they take into account their own needs, too. This transition leads to the third stage, "morality of nonviolence," in which women decide that hurting anyone is immoral—including themselves. This realization establishes a moral equivalence between themselves and others and represents, according to Gilligan, the most sophisticated level of moral reasoning.

It is obvious that Gilligan's sequence of stages is quite different from Kohlberg's, and some developmentalists have suggested that her rejection of Kohlberg's work is too sweeping and that gender differences are not as pronounced as first thought (Colby & Damon, 1987). For instance, some researchers argue that both males and females use similar "justice" and "care" orientations in making moral judgments. Clearly, the question of how boys and girls differ in their moral orientations, as well as the nature of moral development in general, is far from settled (Weisz & Black, 2002; Jorgensen, 2006; Tappan, 2006; Donleavy, 2008).

REVIEW, CHECK, AND APPLY

REVIEW

L011 In what ways do children's views of themselves change during middle childhood?

- According to Erikson, children at this time are in the industry-versus-inferiority stage.
- In middle childhood, children begin to use social comparison, and self-concepts based on psychological rather than physical characteristics.

L012 Why is self-esteem important during middle childhood?

- In middle childhood children increasingly develop their own internal standards of success, and measure how well they compare to those standards.

L013 How does children's sense of right and wrong change as they age?

- According to Kohlberg, moral development proceeds from a concern with rewards and punishments, through a focus on social conventions and rules, toward a sense of universal moral principles. Gilligan has suggested, however, that girls may follow a different progression of moral development.

CHECK YOURSELF

1. According to Erikson, children aged 6 to 12 focus on efforts to meet the challenges presented by parents, peers, and school. This stage is _____.
   - a autonomy versus shame and doubt
   - b trust versus mistrust
   - c self versus others
   - d industry versus inferiority
2. As children develop a better self-understanding in middle childhood, they begin to view themselves less in terms of physical attributes and more in terms of their _____.
   - a familial relationships
   - b psychological traits
   - c environmental characteristics
   - d motor skills
3. According to _____, people pass through a series of six stages as their sense of justice and their level of reasoning evolves with age and cognitive development.
   - a Freud
   - b Piaget
   - c Kohlberg
   - d Skinner

APPLYING LIFESPAN DEVELOPMENT

- Kohlberg and Gilligan each suggest there are three major levels of moral development. Are any of their levels comparable? In which level of either theory do you think that the largest discrepancy between males and females would be observed?

✓ **Study** and **Review** on **MyPsychLab.com**

RELATIONSHIPS: BUILDING FRIENDSHIP IN MIDDLE CHILDHOOD

5.1
5.2
5.3

LO14 What sorts of relationships and friendships are typical of middle childhood?
LO15 How do relationships between boys and girls develop?

In Lunch Room Number Two, Jamillah and her new classmates chew slowly on sandwiches and sip quietly on straws from cartons of milk. . . . Boys and girls look timidly at the strange faces across the table from them, looking for someone who might play with them in the schoolyard, someone who might become a friend.

For these children, what happens in the schoolyard will be just as important as what happens in the school. And when they're out on the playground, there will be no one to protect them. No child will hold back to keep from beating them at a game, humiliating them in a test of skill, or harming them in a fight. No one will run interference or guarantee membership in a group. Out on the playground, it's sink or swim. No one automatically becomes your friend. (Kotre & Hall, 1990, pp. 112–113)

As Jamillah and her classmates demonstrate, friendship plays an increasingly important role in middle childhood. Building and maintaining friendships become a large part of social life.

Friends influence development in several ways. Friendships provide children with information about the world as well as themselves. Friends provide emotional support that allows children to respond more effectively to stress. Having friends makes a child a less likely target of aggression. It can teach them how to manage their emotions and help them interpret their own emotional experiences (Berndt, 2002). Friendships teach children how to communicate and interact with others. They also foster intellectual growth by increasing children's range of experiences (Harris, 1998; Nangle & Erdley, 2001; Gifford-Smith & Brownell, 2003; Majors, 2012).

Friends and other peers become increasingly influential at this stage but parents and other family members remain significant. Most developmentalists believe that children's psychological functioning and their general development are the product of multiple factors, including peers and parents (Vandell, 2000; Parke, Simpkins, & McDowell, 2002). (We'll talk more about the family's influence later in this module.)

Stages of Friendship: Changing Views of Friends

At this stage, a child's concept of friendship passes through three distinct stages, according to developmental psychologist William Damon (Damon & Hart, 1988).

Stage 1: Basing Friendship on Others' Behavior. In this stage, from ages 4 to 7, children see friends as others who like them and with whom they share toys and other activities. They view the children they spend the most time with as their friends. A kindergartner who was asked, "How do you know that someone is your best friend?" responded:

> *I sleep over at his house sometimes. When he's playing ball with his friends he'll let me play. When I slept over, he let me get in front of him in 4-squares. He likes me. (Damon, 1983, p. 140)*

What children in this stage seldom do, however, is consider others' personal qualities as the basis of friendships. Instead, they use a concrete approach, primarily choosing friends for their behavior. They like those who share, shunning those who don't share, who hit, or who don't play with them. In the first stage, friends are viewed largely as presenting opportunities for pleasant interactions.

Mutual trust is considered to be the centerpiece of friendship during middle childhood.

A variety of factors lead some children to be unpopular and socially isolated from their peers.

Stage 2: Basing Friendship on Trust. In the next stage, children's view of friendship becomes complicated. Lasting around ages 8 to 10, this stage involves taking others' personal qualities and traits as well as the rewards they provide into consideration. But the centerpiece of friendship in this second stage is mutual trust. Friends are seen as those one can count on to help out when needed. Violations of trust are taken very seriously, and friends cannot make amends just by engaging in positive play, as they might at earlier ages. Instead, the expectation is that formal explanations and apologies must be provided before a friendship can be reestablished.

Stage 3: Basing Friendship on Psychological Closeness. The third stage of friendship begins toward the end of middle childhood, from ages 11 to 15, when children develop the view of friendship they will hold in adolescence. Although we'll discuss this perspective in detail later, the main criteria for friendship shift toward intimacy and loyalty. Friendship becomes characterized by feelings of closeness, usually brought on by sharing personal thoughts and feelings. They are also somewhat exclusive. By the end of middle childhood, children seek friends who will be loyal, and view friendship less in terms of shared activities than in terms of the psychological benefits it brings.

Children also develop clear ideas about which behaviors they like and dislike in friends, preferring others who invite them to share in activities and who are helpful, both physically and psychologically. They dislike behaviors such as physical or verbal aggression.

Individual Differences in Friendship: What Makes a Child Popular?

Why is it that some children are the schoolyard equivalent of the life of the party, while others are social isolates whose overtures toward peers are dismissed or disdained? Developmentalists have attempted to answer this question by examining individual differences in popularity.

Status Among School-Age Children: Establishing One's Position. Children's friendships exhibit clear status hierarchies. **Status** is the evaluation of a role or person by other relevant members of a group. Children who have high status have greater access to resources such as games, toys, books, and information. Lower-status children are more likely to follow their lead. Status can be measured in several ways. Often, children are asked directly how much they like or dislike particular classmates. They also may be asked whom they would most (and least) like to play or work with.

Status is an important determinant of friendships. High-status children tend to befriend those of a higher status, while lower-status children are likely to have friends of lower status. Status is also related to the number of friends a child has: Higher-status children tend to have more friends than those of lower status.

But it is not only the quantity of social interactions that separates high-status children from low-status children; the nature of their interactions also differs. Higher-status children are more likely to be viewed as friends by other children. They are more likely to form cliques—groups viewed as exclusive and desirable—and to interact with a greater number of children. Lower-status children tend to play with younger or less popular children (Ladd, 1983). Popularity is a reflection of children's status. Mid- to high-status children are more likely to initiate and coordinate social interaction, making their general level of social activity higher than children of low status (Erwin, 1993).

status the evaluation of a role or person by other relevant members of a group

social competence the collection of social skills that permit individuals to perform successfully in social settings

What Personal Characteristics Lead to Popularity? Popular children share several personality traits. They are usually helpful, cooperating with others on joint projects. They also tend to be funny and to appreciate others' attempts at humor. Compared with less popular children, they are better at reading nonverbal behavior and understanding the emotional experiences of others. They also control their nonverbal behavior more effectively, presenting themselves well. In short, popular children are high in **social competence**, the collection of social skills that permits individuals to perform successfully in social settings (Feldman, Tomasian, & Coats, 1999).

Although generally popular children are friendly, open, and cooperative, one subset of popular boys displays an array of negative behaviors, including being aggressive, disruptive, and causing trouble. Despite these behaviors, they are often remarkably popular, being viewed as cool and tough by their peers. This popularity may occur because they are seen as boldly breaking rules that others feel constrained to follow (Meisinger et al., 2007; Woods, 2009; Schonert-Reichl, Smith, & Zaidman-Zait, 2012).

Social Problem-Solving Abilities. Another factor in popularity is children's skill at social problem-solving. **Social problem-solving** is the use of strategies for solving social conflicts in mutually satisfactory ways. Because social conflicts are frequent—even among best friends—successful strategies for dealing with them are an important element of social success (Rose & Asher, 1999; Murphy & Eisenberg, 2002; Siu & Shek, 2010).

According to developmental psychologist Kenneth Dodge, successful social problem-solving proceeds through a series of steps that correspond to children's information processing strategies (see Figure 5-10). Dodge argues that the ways children solve social problems are a result of the decisions they make at each point in the sequence (Dodge & Crick, 1990; Dodge & Price, 1994; Dodge et al., 2003).

By carefully delineating each of the stages, Dodge provides a means to target interventions toward a specific child's deficits. For instance, some children routinely misinterpret the meaning of others' behavior (step 2), and then respond according to their misinterpretation.

Generally, popular children are better at interpreting others' behavior. They also possess a wider inventory of techniques for dealing with social problems. In contrast, less popular children tend to show less understanding of others' behavior, and thus their reactions may be inappropriate. Their strategies for dealing with social problems are more limited; they sometimes simply don't know how to apologize or help someone who is unhappy feel better (Vitaro & Pelletier, 1991; Rose & Asher, 1999; Rinaldi, 2002).

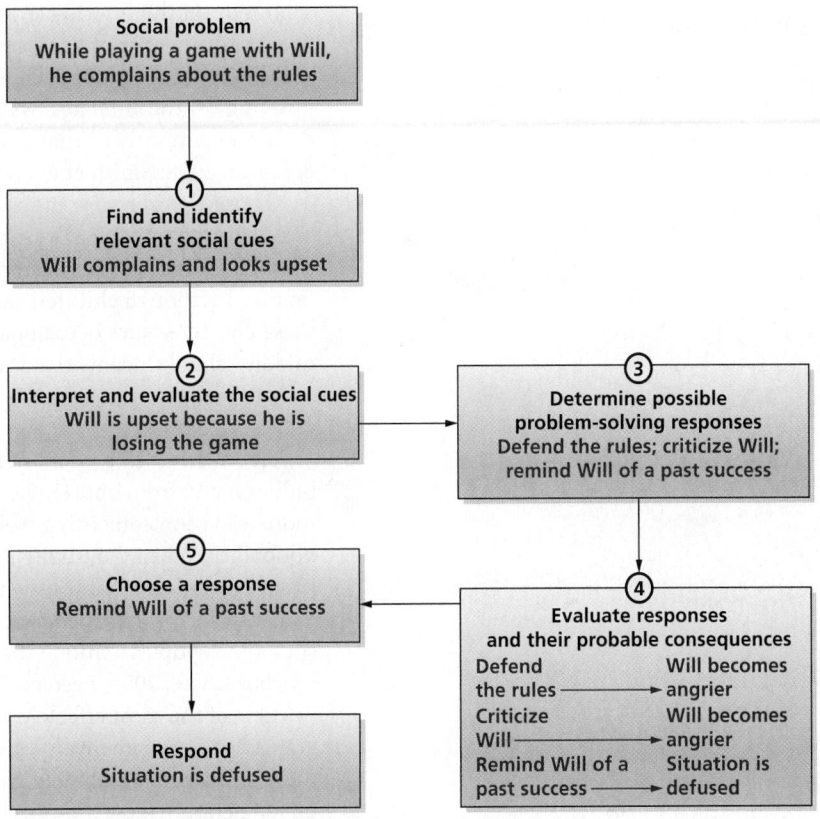

FIGURE 5-10 Problem-Solving Steps
Children's problem-solving proceeds through several steps involving different information processing strategies.
Source: Educational Psychology by K. A. Dodge. Copyright 1985 by Taylor & Francis Informa UK Ltd—Journals. Reproduced with permission of Taylor & Francis Informa UK Ltd—Journals in the format Textbook via Copyright Clearance Center.

Unpopular children may become victims of a phenomenon known as *learned helplessness*. Because they don't understand the root causes of their unpopularity, children may feel that they have little or no ability to improve their situation. As a result, they may simply give up and don't even try to become more involved with their peers. In turn, their learned helplessness becomes a self-fulfilling prophecy, reducing the chances that they will become more popular in the future (Seligman, 2007; Aujoulat, Luminet, & Deccache, 2007).

Teaching Social Competence. Happily, unpopular children can learn social competence. Several programs aim to teach children the skills that seem to underlie general social competence. In one experimental program, a group of unpopular fifth and sixth graders were taught how to converse with friends. They were taught ways to disclose material about themselves, to learn about others by asking questions, and to offer help and suggestions in a nonthreatening way.

Compared with a group who did not receive training, the children in the experiment interacted more with their peers, held more conversations, developed higher self-esteem, and—most critically—were more accepted by their peers than before training (Asher & Rose, 1997; Bierman, 2004).

social problem-solving the use of strategies for solving social conflicts in ways that are satisfactory both to oneself and to others

Bullying: Schoolyard and Online Victimization

Austin Rodriguez, an Ohio teen, attempted suicide after classmates bullied him for being gay. They reportedly hid his gym clothes and tried to prevent him from entering the locker room or the lunchroom. They made nasty remarks on the Internet.

Rachel Ehmke, a Minnesota seventh grader, hung herself when the bullying got too awful to live with. The 13-year-old had been hounded for months by a group of girls who called her "prostitute," scrawled "slut" all over her notebook, and harassed her online.

Austin and Rachel are not alone in facing the torment of bullying, whether it comes at school or on the Internet. Almost 85 percent of girls and 80 percent of boys report experiencing some form of harassment in school at least once, and 160,000 U.S. schoolchildren stay home from school each day because they are afraid of being bullied. Others encounter bullying on the Internet, which may be even more painful because often the bullying is done anonymously or may involve public postings (Dehue, Bolman, & Völlink, 2008; Slonje & Smith, 2008; Smith et al., 2008; Mishna, Saini, & Solomon, 2009; Law et al., 2012).

Those children who experience frequent bullying are most often loners who are fairly passive. They often cry easily, and they tend to lack the social skill that might otherwise defuse a bullying situation. For example, they are unable to think of humorous comebacks to bullies' taunts. But though children such as these are more likely to be bullied, even children without these characteristics occasionally are bullied during their school careers: Some 90 percent of middle-school students report being bullied at some point in their time at school, beginning as early as the preschool years (Ahmed & Braithwaite, 2004; Li, 2006, 2007; Katzer, Fetchenhauer, & Belschak, 2009).

About 10 to 15 percent of students bully others at one time or another. About half of all bullies come from abusive homes—meaning, of course, that half don't. They tend to watch more television containing violence, and they misbehave more at home and at school than do nonbullies. When their bullying gets them into trouble, they may try to lie their way out of the situation, and they show little remorse for their victimization of others. Furthermore, bullies, compared with their peers, are more likely to break the law as adults. Although bullies are sometimes popular among their peers, some ironically become victims of bullies themselves (Barboza et al., 2009; Peeters, Cillessen, & Scholte, 2010; Dupper, 2013).

One of the most effective ways to reduce the incidence of bullying is through school programs that enlist and involve students. For example, schools can train students to intervene when they see an instance of bullying, rather than watching passively. Empowering students to stand up for victims has been shown reduce bullying significantly (Storey et al., 2009; Munsey, 2012).

Gender and Friendships: The Sex Segregation of Middle Childhood

Girls rule; boys drool.

Boys are idiots. Girls have cooties.

Boys go to college to get more knowledge; girls go to Jupiter to get more stupider.

Those are some of the views of elementary school boys and girls regarding members of the other sex. Avoidance of the other sex becomes quite pronounced at this age, with social networks often consisting almost entirely of same-sex groupings (Mehta & Strough, 2009; Rancourt et al., 2012; Rancourt et al., 2013).

Interestingly, this segregation of friendships occurs in almost all societies. In nonindustrialized societies, same-gender segregation may result from the types of activities children engage in. For instance, in many cultures, boys are assigned one type of chore and girls another (Whiting & Edwards, 1988). Participation in different activities may not wholly explain sex segregation, however: Children in more developed countries, who attend the same schools and participate in many of the same activities, still tend to avoid members of the other gender.

When boys and girls make occasional forays into the other gender's territory, the action often has romantic overtones. For instance, girls may threaten to kiss a boy, or boys might try to lure girls into chasing them. Such behavior, termed "border work," emphasizes the clear boundaries between the two sexes. In addition, it may pave the way for adolescent interactions that do involve romantic or sexual interests, when cross-sex interactions become socially endorsed (Thorne, 1986; Beal, 1994).

The lack of cross-gender interaction in middle childhood means that boys' and girls' friendships are restricted to their own sex. The nature of friendships within these two groups is quite different (Lansford & Parker, 1999; Rose, 2002).

Boys typically have larger networks of friends, and they tend to play in groups rather than pairing off. Differences in status within the group are usually pronounced, with an acknowledged leader and a hierarchy of members. Because of the fairly rigid rankings that represent the relative social power of those in the group, known as the **dominance hierarchy**, members of higher status can safely question and oppose those lower in the hierarchy (Beal, 1994; Pedersen et al., 2007).

Boys tend to be concerned with their place in the dominance hierarchy, and they attempt to maintain and improve their status. This makes for a style of play known as *restrictive*. In restrictive play, interactions are interrupted when a boy feels his status is challenged. A boy who feels that he is unjustly challenged by a lower-status peer may attempt to end the interaction by scuffling over a toy or otherwise behaving assertively. Consequently, boys tend to play in bursts, rather than in more extended, tranquil episodes (Benenson & Apostoleris, 1993; Estell et al., 2008).

The language of friendship used among boys reflects their concern over status and challenge. Consider this conversation between two boys who were good friends:

Child 1: Why don't you get out of my yard?

Child 2: Why don't you *make* me get out of the yard?

Child 1: I *know* you don't want that.

Child 2: You're not gonna make me get out of the yard cuz you can't.

Child 1: Don't force me.

Child 2: You can't. Don't force me to hurt you (*snickers*). (Goodwin, 1990, p. 37)

Friendship patterns among girls are quite different. Rather than a wide network of friends, girls focus on one or two "best friends." In contrast to boys, who seek out status differences, girls avoid differences, preferring to maintain equal-status friendships.

Conflicts among girls are usually solved through compromise, by ignoring the situation, or by giving in, rather than by seeking to make one's point of view prevail. The goal is to smooth over disagreements, making social interaction easy and nonconfrontational (Goodwin, 1990; Noakes & Rinaldi, 2006).

According to developmental psychologist Carole Beal, the motivation of girls to solve social conflict indirectly does not stem from a lack of self-confidence or from apprehension over the use of more direct approaches. In fact, when school-age girls interact with other girls who are not friends or with boys, they can be quite confrontational. However, among friends their goal is to maintain equal-status relationships, with no dominance hierarchy (Beal, 1994; Zahn & Wexler, 2008).

The language used by girls tends to reflect their view of relationships. Rather than blatant demands ("Give me the pencil"), girls are more apt to use less confrontational and directive language. Girls tend to use indirect forms of verbs, such as "Let's go to the movies" or "Would you want to trade books with me?" rather than "I want to go to the movies" or "Let me have these books" (Goodwin, 1990; Besage, 2006).

Cross-Race Friendships: Integration In and Out of the Classroom

For the most part, friendships are not color-blind. Children's closest friendships tend to be with others of the same race. In fact, as children age there is a decline in the number and depth of friendships outside their own racial group. By age 11 or 12, it appears that African American children become particularly aware of and sensitive to the prejudice and discrimination directed toward members of their race. At that point, they are likely to make distinctions between members of ingroups (groups to which people feel they belong) and members of outgroups (groups to which they feel they do not belong) (Kao & Vaquera, 2006; Aboud & Sankar, 2007; Rowley et al., 2008).

When third graders from one long-integrated school were asked to name a best friend, around one-quarter of white children and two-thirds of African American children chose a child of the other race. In contrast, by tenth grade, less than 10 percent of whites and 5 percent of African Americans named a different-race best friend (Singleton & Taylor, 1982; McGlothlin & Killen, 2005; Rodkin & Ryan, 2012).

As children age, there is a decline in the number and depth of friendships outside their own racial group. What are some ways in which schools can foster mutual acceptance?

dominance hierarchy rankings that represent the relative social power of those in a group

From a social worker's perspective: How might it be possible to decrease the segregation of friendships along racial lines? What factors would have to change in individuals or in society?

On the other hand, although they may not choose each other as best friends, whites and African Americans—as well as members of other minority groups—can show a high degree of mutual acceptance. This pattern is particularly true in schools with ongoing integration efforts. This makes sense: A good deal of research supports the notion that contact between majority and minority group members can reduce prejudice and discrimination (Hewstone, 2003; Quintana, 2008).

Becoming an Informed Consumer of Development

Increasing Children's Social Competence

It is clear that building and maintaining friendships are critical in children's lives. Fortunately, there are strategies that parents and teachers can use to increase children's social competence.

- **Encourage social interaction.** Teachers can devise ways to get children to take part in group activities, and parents can encourage membership in such groups as Brownies and Cub Scouts or participation in team sports.
- **Teach listening skills to children.** Show them how to listen carefully and respond to the underlying meaning of a communication as well as its overt content.
- **Make children aware that people display emotions and moods nonverbally.** Consequently, they should pay attention to others' nonverbal behavior, not just to what they are saying.
- **Teach conversational skills, including the importance of asking questions and self-disclosure.** Encourage students to use "I" statements in which they clarify their own feelings or opinions, and avoid making generalizations about others.
- **Don't ask children to choose teams or groups publicly.** Instead, assign children randomly: It works just as well in ensuring a distribution of abilities across groups and avoids the public embarrassment of a situation in which some children are chosen last.

REVIEW, CHECK, AND APPLY

REVIEW

L014 What sorts of relationships and friendships are typical of middle childhood?

- Children's understanding of friendship changes from the sharing of enjoyable activities, through the consideration of personal traits that can meet their needs, to a focus on intimacy and loyalty.
- Friendships in childhood display status hierarchies. Improvements in social problem-solving and social information processing can lead to better interpersonal skills and greater popularity.

L015 How do relationships between boys and girls develop?

- Boys and girls engage increasingly in same-sex friendships, with boys' friendships involving group relationships and girls' friendships characterized by pairings of girls with equal status.

CHECK YOURSELF

1. Which of the following statements about friendship in middle childhood are true? Check all that apply.
   - a Friendships provide information about the world.
   - b Friends provide emotional support that is different from the support provided by parents.
   - c Children with friends are less likely to be the target of aggression.
   - d Friendships provide training in communication.
   - e Friendships protect children from interactions with others, which can enhance their intellectual growth.
   - f Children are only able to learn how to manage their emotions within the context of family.
2. _____ is the evaluation of the role or person by other relevant members of the group and is usually discussed in reference to children and their peer groups.
   - a Dominance hierarchy
   - b Social competence
   - c Friendship
   - d Status
3. Which of the following descriptions best characterizes friendships in middle school?
   - a Boys and girls tend to remain in sexsegregated friendship networks.
   - b Boys and girls begin playing in larger groups including males and females.
   - c Boys are much more likely than girls to engage in activities considered more appropriate for the opposite sex.
   - d Girls typically have larger networks of friends than do boys.

APPLYING LIFESPAN DEVELOPMENT

- Do you think the stages of friendship are a childhood phenomenon, or do adults' friendships display similar stages?

Study and **Review** on **MyPsychLab.com**

FAMILY LIFE IN MIDDLE CHILDHOOD

LO16 How do today's diverse family and care arrangements affect children?

Tamara's mother, Brenda, waited outside her daughter's second-grade classroom for the end of the school day. Tamara came over to greet her mother as soon as she spotted her. "Mom, can Anna come over to play today?" Tamara demanded. Brenda had been looking forward to spending some time alone with Tamara, who had spent the last three days at her dad's house. But, Brenda reflected, Tamara hardly ever got to ask kids over after school, so she agreed to the request. Unfortunately, it turned out today wouldn't work for Anna's family, so they tried to find an alternate date. "How about Thursday?" Anna's mother suggested. Before Tamara could reply, her mother reminded her, "You'll have to ask your dad. You're at his house that night." Tamara's face fell. "OK," she mumbled.

How will Tamara's adjustment be affected from dividing her time between the two homes where she lives with her divorced parents? What about the adjustment of her friend, Anna, who lives with both her parents, both of whom work outside the home? These are just a few of the questions we need to consider as we look at the ways that children's schooling and home life affect their lives during middle childhood.

We've noted in earlier chapters how the structure of the family has changed over the last few decades. With an increase in the number of parents who both work outside the home, a soaring divorce rate, and a rise in single-parent families, the environment faced by children passing through middle childhood in the twenty-first century is very different from the one faced by prior generations.

One of the biggest challenges of middle childhood is the increasing independence that characterizes children's behavior. Children move from being controlled to increasingly controlling their own destinies—or at least conduct. Middle childhood, then, is a period of **coregulation** in which children and parents jointly control behavior. Increasingly, parents provide broad guidelines for conduct, while children control their everyday behavior. For instance, parents may urge their daughter to buy a nutritious school lunch, but the daughter's decision to buy pizza and two desserts is her own.

Family Life

During middle childhood, children spend less time with their parents. Still, parents remain their major influence, providing essential assistance, advice, and direction (Parke, 2004).

Siblings also have an important influence, for good and for bad. Although brothers and sisters can provide support, companionship, and security, they can also be a source of strife. *Sibling rivalry* can occur, especially when the siblings are the same sex and similar in age. Parents may intensify sibling rivalry by seeming to favor one child over another—a perception that may or may not be accurate. A decision as straightforward as granting older siblings more freedom may be interpreted as favoritism. In some cases, perceived favoritism may damage the self-esteem of the younger sibling. But sibling rivalry is not inevitable (Branje et al., 2004; McHale, Kim, & Whiteman, 2006; Caspi, 2012).

Cultural differences are linked to sibling experiences. For example, in Mexican American families, which have particularly strong values regarding the importance of family, siblings are less likely to respond negatively when younger siblings receive preferential treatment (McHale et al., 2005; McGuire & Shanahan, 2010).

What about children who have no siblings? Disproving the stereotype that only-children are spoiled and self-centered, they are as well adjusted as children with brothers and sisters. In fact, in some ways, only-children are better adjusted, with higher self-esteem and stronger motivation to achieve. In China, where a strict one-child policy is in effect, studies show that only-children often academically outperform children with siblings (Jiao, Ji, & Jing, 1996; Miao & Wang, 2003; Zheng, 2010).

coregulation a period in which parents and children jointly control children's behavior

Self-care children spend time after school alone while their parents are at work.

Home and Alone: What Do Children Do?

When 10-year-old Johnetta Colvin comes home after a day at Martin Luther King Elementary School, the first thing she does is grab a few cookies and turn on the computer. She takes a quick look at her email, and then typically spends an hour watching television. During commercials, she looks at her homework.

What she doesn't do is chat with her parents. She's home alone.

Johnetta is a **self-care child**, the term for children who let themselves into their homes after school and wait alone until their parents return from work. Some 12 to 14 percent of children in the United States between the ages of 5 and 12 spend some time alone after school, without adult supervision (Lamorey et al., 1998; Berger, 2000).

In the past, such children were called *latchkey children*, a term connoting sadness, loneliness, and neglect. Today a new view is emerging. According to sociologist Sandra Hofferth, given the hectic schedule of many children's lives, a few hours alone may provide a helpful period of decompression. Furthermore, it may give children an opportunity to develop autonomy (Hofferth & Sandberg, 2001).

Research has identified few differences between self-care children and others. Although some children report negative experiences (such as loneliness), they do not seem emotionally damaged by the experience. In addition, if they stay by themselves rather than "hanging out" unsupervised with friends, they may avoid activities that can lead to difficulties (Belle, 1999; Goyette-Ewing, 2000).

The time alone also gives children a chance to focus on homework and school or personal projects. In fact, children with employed parents may have higher self-esteem because they feel they are contributing to the household (Goyette-Ewing, 2000).

Divorce

Having divorced parents is no longer distinctive. Only around half the children in the United States spend their entire childhood in the same household with both parents. The rest will live in single-parent homes or with stepparents, grandparents, or other nonparental relatives; and some end up in foster care (Harvey & Fine, 2004).

How do children react to divorce? The answer is complex. For 6 months to 2 years following a divorce, children and parents may show signs of psychological maladjustment such as anxiety, depression, sleep disturbances, and phobias. Even though most children stay with their mothers, the quality of the mother–child relationship mostly declines, often because children feel caught in the middle between their mothers and fathers (Amato & Afifi, 2006; Juby et al., 2007; Lansford, 2009; Maes, De Mol, & Buysse, 2012).

During the early stage of middle childhood, children often blame themselves for the breakup. By age 10, they feel pressure to choose sides and experience some degree of divided loyalty (Shaw, Winslow, & Flanagan, 1999).

The longer-term consequences of divorce are less clear. Some studies have found that 18 months to 2 years later, most children begin to return to their predivorce state of adjustment. For many children, long-term consequences are minimal (Hetherington & Kelly, 2002; Guttmann & Rosenberg, 2003; Harvey & Fine, 2004).

Other evidence suggests that the fallout from divorce lingers. For example, compared with children from intact families, twice as many children of divorced parents enter psychological counseling (although sometimes counseling is mandated by a judge as part of the divorce). In addition, people who have experienced parental divorce are more at risk for experiencing divorce themselves later in life (Wallerstein & Resnikoff, 2005; Huurre, Junkkari, & Aro, 2006; Uphold-Carrier & Utz, 2012).

How children react to divorce depends on several factors. One is the economic standing of the family the child is living with. In many cases, divorce brings a decline in both parents' standards of living. When this occurs, children may be thrown into poverty (Ozawa & Yoon, 2003; Fischer, 2007).

In other cases, the negative consequences of divorce are less severe because the divorce reduces the hostility and anger in the home. If the household before the divorce was overwhelmed by parental strife—as is the case in around 30 percent of divorces—the greater calm of a postdivorce household may be beneficial to children. This is particularly true for children

self-care children children who let themselves into their homes after school and wait alone until their caretakers return from work; previously known as *latchkey children* who maintain a close, positive relationship with the parent with whom they do not live. Still, in the 70 percent of divorces where the predivorce level of conflict is not high, children may have a more difficult time adjusting (Faber & Wittenborn, 2010; Finley & Schwartz, 2010; Lansford, 2010).

From the perspective of a health care provider: How might the development of self-esteem in middle childhood be affected by a divorce? Can constant hostility and tension between parents lead to a child's health problems?

Single-Parent Families

Almost one-quarter of all children under age 18 in the United States live with only one parent. If present trends continue, almost three-quarters will spend some portion of their lives in a single-parent family before they are 18. For minority children, the numbers are higher: Almost 60 percent of African American children and 35 percent of Hispanic children under 18 live in single-parent homes (U.S. Bureau of the Census, 2000).

In rare cases, death is the reason for single parenthood. More frequently, either no spouse was ever present, the spouses have divorced, or the spouse is absent. In the vast majority of cases, the single parent who is present is the mother.

What consequences are there for children in one-parent homes? Much depends on whether a second parent was present earlier and the nature of the parent's relationship at that time. Furthermore, the economic status of the single-parent family plays a role. Single-parent families are often less well-off financially than two-parent families, and living in relative poverty has a negative impact on children (Davis, 2003; Harvey & Fine, 2004).

Multigenerational Families

In some households children, parents, and grandparents live together. Multigenerational families can make for a rich living experience for children, but there is also the potential for conflict if "layers" of adults act as disciplinarians without coordinating what they do.

The prevalence of three-generation families who live together is greater among African Americans than among Caucasians. In addition, African American families, which are more likely than white families to be headed by single parents, often rely substantially on the help of grandparents in everyday child care, and cultural norms tend to be highly supportive of grandparents taking an active role (Oberlander, Black, & Starr, 2007; Pittman & Boswell, 2007; Kelch-Oliver, 2008).

Blended families occur when previously married husbands and wives with children remarry.

Living in Blended Families

For many children, the aftermath of divorce includes a remarriage. In more than 10 million households in the United States, at least one spouse has remarried. More than 5 million remarried couples have at least one stepchild with them in what have come to be called **blended families**. Overall, 17 percent of all children in the United States live in blended families (U.S. Bureau of the Census, 2001; Bengtson et al., 2004).

Children in a blended family face challenges. They often have to deal with *role ambiguity*, in which roles and expectations are unclear. They may be uncertain about their responsibilities, how to behave toward stepparents and stepsiblings, and how to make a host of tough everyday decisions. For instance, they may have to choose which parent to spend holidays and vacations with, or decide between conflicting advice from biological parent and stepparent. Some find the disruption of routine and of established family relationships difficult. For

blended families remarried couples who have at least one stepchild living with them instance, a child used to her mother's complete attention may find it hard to see her mother showing interest and affection to a stepchild (Cath & Shopper, 2001; Belcher, 2003; Guadalupe & Welkley, 2012).

Still, school-age children in blended families often adjust relatively smoothly—especially compared with adolescents—for several reasons. For one thing, the family's financial situation is often improved after a parent remarries. In addition, there are usually more people to share the burden of household chores. Finally, the higher "population" of the family increases opportunities for social interaction (Greene, Anderson, & Hetherington, 2003; Hetherington & Elmore, 2003).

Families blend most successfully when the parents create an environment that supports self-esteem and a climate of family togetherness. Generally, the younger the children, the easier the transition (Kirby, 2006; Jeynes, 2007).

Families with Gay and Lesbian Parents

An increasing number of children have two mothers or two fathers. Estimates suggest there are between 1 and 5 million families headed by two lesbian or two gay parents in the United States, and some 6 million children have lesbian or gay parents (Patterson & Friel, 2000; Patterson, 2007, 2009).

How do children in lesbian and gay households fare? A growing body of research on the effects of same-sex parenting on children shows that children develop similarly to the children of heterosexual families. Their sexual orientation is unrelated to that of their parents; their behavior is no more or less gender-typed; and they seem equally well adjusted (Parke, 2004; Patterson, 2002, 2003, 2009).

One large-scale analysis that examined 19 studies of children raised by gay and lesbian parents conducted over a 25-year period, encompassing well over a thousand gay, lesbian, and heterosexual families, confirmed these findings. The analysis found no significant differences between children raised by heterosexual parents and children raised by gay or lesbian parents on measures of children's gender role, gender identity, cognitive development, sexual orientation, and social and emotional development. The one significant difference that did emerge was the quality of the relationship between parent and child; interestingly, the gay and lesbian parents reported having *better* relationships with their children than did heterosexual parents (Crowl, Ahn, & Baker, 2008).

Other research shows that children of lesbian and gay parents have similar relationships with their peers as children of heterosexual parents. They also relate to adults—both those who are gay and those who are straight—no differently from children whose parents are heterosexual. And when they reach adolescence, their romantic relationships and sexual behavior are no different from those of adolescents living with opposite-sex parents (Patterson, 2009; Goldberg, 2010a; Farr & Patterson, 2013).

In short, research shows that there is little developmental difference between children whose parents are gay and lesbian and those who have heterosexual parents. What is clearly different for children with same-sex parents is the possibility of discrimination and prejudice due to their parents' sexual orientation. As U.S. citizens engage in an ongoing and highly politicized debate regarding the legality of gay and lesbian marriage, children of such unions may feel singled out and victimized because of societal stereotypes and discrimination (Ryan & Martin, 2000; Davis, Saltzburg, & Locke, 2009).

Race and Family Life

Although there are as many types of families as there are individuals, research finds some consistencies related to race (Parke, 2004). For example, African American families often have a particularly strong sense of family, offering welcome and support to extended family members in their homes. Because there is a relatively high level of female-headed households among African Americans, extended families often lend crucial social and economic support. In addition, there is a relatively high proportion of families headed by older adults, such as grandparents, and some studies find that children in grandmother-headed households are particularly well adjusted (McLoyd et al., 2000; Smith & Drew, 2002; Taylor, 2002).

Hispanic families tend to regard family life and community and religious organizations highly. Children are taught to value their family ties and to see themselves as a central part of an extended family. Ultimately, their sense of self stems from the family. Hispanic families also tend to be larger, with an average size of 3.71, compared to 2.97 for Caucasian families and 3.31 for African American families (Cauce & Domenech-Rodriguez, 2002; U.S. Bureau of the Census, 2003; Halgunseth, Ispa, & Rudy, 2006).

Although relatively little research has been conducted on Asian American families, emerging findings suggest that fathers are apt to be powerful figures who maintain discipline. In keeping with the collectivist orientation of Asian cultures, children tend to believe that family needs have a higher priority than personal needs, and males, in particular, are expected to care for their parents throughout their lifetimes (Ishi-Kuntz, 2000).

Poverty and Family Life

Regardless of race, children in economically disadvantaged families face hardships. Poor families have fewer everyday resources, and there are more disruptions in children's lives. For example, parents may be forced to look for less expensive housing or a different job. As a result, parents may be less responsive to their children's needs and provide less social support (Evans, 2004).

The stress of difficult family environments, along with other stress in the lives of poor children—such as living in unsafe neighborhoods with high rates of violence and attending inferior schools—ultimately takes its toll. Economically disadvantaged children are at risk for poorer academic performance, higher rates of aggression, and conduct problems. In addition, declines in economic well-being are linked to physical and mental health problems. Specifically, the chronic stress associated with poverty makes children more susceptible to cardiovascular disease, depression, and diabetes (also see "From Research to Practice" box; Sapolsky, 2005; Morales & Guerra, 2006; Tracy et al., 2008).

Group Care: Orphanages in the Twenty-first Century

The term *orphanage* evokes stereotypical images of grim institutional life. The reality today is different. *Group homes* or *residential treatment centers* (the word *orphanage* is rarely used) typically house a relatively small number of children whose parents are no longer able to care for them adequately. They are typically funded by a combination of federal, state, and local aid.

Group care has grown significantly. In the period from 1995 to 2000, the number of children in foster care increased by more than 50 percent. Today, more than a half million children in the United States live in foster care (Roche, 2000; Jones-Harden, 2004; Bruskas, 2008).

Although orphanages of the early 1900s were crowded and institutional (top), today the equivalent, called group homes or residential treatment centers (bottom), are much more pleasant.

About three-quarters of children in group care have suffered neglect and abuse. Each year, 300,000 are removed from their homes, most of whom can be returned to their homes after social service agencies intervene with their families. But the remaining one-quarter are so psychologically damaged that they are likely to remain in group care throughout childhood. Adoption (or even temporary foster care) is not an option for most of these children, who have developed severe emotional and behavior problems, such as high levels of aggression or anger (Bass, Shields, & Behrman, 2004; Chamberlain et al., 2006).

Group care is neither inherently good nor bad. The outcome depends on the staff of the group home and whether child- and youth-care workers know how to develop an effective, stable, and strong emotional bond with a child. If a child is unable to form a meaningful relationship with a worker in a group home, the setting may well be harmful (Hawkins-Rodgers, 2007; Knorth et al., 2008).

From Research to Practice

Closing the Digital Divide: Some Unintended Consequences

Back in the 1990s, when home computers and the Internet were first becoming mainstream, many educators expressed concern about the rise of what they called the "digital divide." This term referred to the distinction between the technological "haves"—children whose families could afford home computers, or who at least had reliable public access to computers and the Internet—and the "have nots." The main concern was that this technological disadvantage seemed poised to put the "have nots" at an increasing educational disadvantage.

Those concerns were addressed by widespread efforts to get computers into the homes and hands of all American schoolchildren. Happily, those efforts have been quite successful at reversing the digital divide. But a new problem has emerged, one that educators and social scientists failed to anticipate in their zeal to get all kids connected. It turns out that computers can be used for a lot of noneducational purposes, from Web browsing and social networking to watching movies and playing video games. And that's just what many of these disadvantaged youth are doing.

A recent study by the Kaiser Family Foundation shows that the amount of time children spend using various entertainment media has increased dramatically in recent years, to over 53 hours per week. That's more than 7 hours per day, a figure that rose by 9 hours per week in just 5 years. Time spent on the computer more than doubled over a decade, from less than 1 hour per day to more than 2. However, only about 16 minutes of that time on average is devoted to schoolwork. The rest is for entertainment, with social networking, video gaming, and watching online videos being the top three activities. And much of that media use is unmonitored by parents: only about a third of children reported that they have household rules governing their computer use (Rideout, Foehr, & Roberts, 2010).

Overall media use drops dramatically, by nearly 3 hours per day, when parents set any kind of rule about it. Of course, parental guidance requires parents who are themselves technologically savvy and who have the time and energy to monitor their children's media use. This often isn't the case in the households of disadvantaged children, and indeed, the Kaiser Family Foundation study found that children of non-college-educated parents spent about 90 more minutes per day on entertainment media than did children of college-educated parents (Rideout, Foehr, & Roberts, 2010; Wood & Howley, 2012).

Victoria Rideout, one of the researchers and authors of the study, summarized the issue this way: "Despite the educational potential of computers, the reality is that their use for education or meaningful content creation is minuscule compared to their use for pure entertainment. Instead of closing the achievement gap, they're widening the time-wasting gap" (Richtel, 2012, p. A1).

What can be done to reverse this new "time-wasting divide"? One promising solution is digital literacy training for parents, to help them understand how their children are using computers and what the parents can do to monitor and limit their usage. It's not enough just to put computers into disadvantaged households and just assume that the children will use them to good ends; the parents need to be made sufficiently computer literate to guide their children's efforts.

- *Why do you think parents with good computer literacy are better able to monitor and limit their children's computer usage?*
- *How can children be encouraged to use computers for educational purposes more often?*

REVIEW, CHECK, AND APPLY

REVIEW

LO16 How do today's diverse family and care arrangements affect children?

- Self-care children may develop independence and enhanced self-esteem from their experience.
- How divorce affects children depends on such factors as financial circumstances and the comparative levels of tension in the family before and after the divorce.
- The effects of being raised in a single-parent household depend on financial circumstances, the amount of parent–child interaction, and the level of tension in the family.

CHECK YOURSELF

1. According to sociologist Sandra Hofferth, self-care children may benefit from their situation by having more time to decompress from a hectic schedule and the opportunity to develop greater _____.
   - a fine motor skills
   - b leisure time
   - c autonomy
   - d intelligence
2. Which of the following characteristics have been associated with a child's response to divorce? Check all that apply.
   - a phobiasv
   - b increased anxiety
   - c schizophrenia
   - d sleep disturbances
   - e experiencing depression
2. The impact of living in a single-parent family is less about the number of parents and more about the economic status, stress level, and time spent together in the family.
   - True
   - False

APPLYING LIFESPAN DEVELOPMENT

- Politicians often speak of "family values." How does this term relate to diverse family situations such as divorced parents, single parents, blended families, working parents, self-care children, and group care?

✓ **Study** and **Review** on **MyPsychLab.com**

SUMMARY 5

PUTTING IT ALL TOGETHER MIDDLE CHILDHOOD

YUKIO (the student we met in the chapter prologue) entered first grade with boundless hope and a keen desire to learn. Unfortunately, an undiagnosed vision problem interfered with his reading and writing. In most other ways, Yukio was at least the equal of his peers: physically active, imaginative, and highly intelligent. Socially, however, he was hampered by spending time in special education classes. Because he had been singled out and because he could not do some of the things his classmates could do, he was ignored, even bullied, by some of them. When he finally got the right treatment, though, most of his problems vanished. His physical and social skills advanced to match his cognitive abilities. He became more engaged in his schoolwork and more open to friendships. Yukio's story had a happy ending.

MODULE 5.1 *PHYSICAL DEVELOPMENT* IN MIDDLE CHILDHOOD

- Steady growth and increased abilities—aided by a therapeutic intervention—characterized Yukio's physical development in these years. *(pp. 198–199)*
- Yukio's gross and fine motor skills developed as muscle coordination improved and he practiced new skills. *(pp. 201–202)*
- Yukio's visual problems interfered with his schoolwork. *(pp. 205–206)*

MODULE 5.2 *COGNITIVE DEVELOPMENT* IN MIDDLE CHILDHOOD

- Yukio's intellectual abilities such as language and memory became more skilled in middle childhood. *(pp. 209–210)*
- One of the key academic tasks for Yukio was to read fluently and with appropriate comprehension. *(pp. 216–217)*
- Yukio displayed many components and types of intelligence, and the development of his intellectual skills was aided by his social interactions. *(pp. 219–220)*

MODULE 5.3 *SOCIAL AND PERSONALITY DEVELOPMENT* IN MIDDLE CHILDHOOD

- In this period, Yukio repaired his vision and mastered many of the challenges presented by school and peers, which took on central importance in his life. *(pp. 238–239)*
- The development of Yukio's self-esteem was particularly crucial; when Yukio felt himself inadequate, his self-esteem suffered. *(pp. 231–232)*
- Yukio's friendships helped provide emotional support and fostered intellectual growth. *(pp. 238–239)*

What would a PARENT do?

What strategies would you use to help Yukio stick to his therapeutic exercises in order to overcome his difficulties and function effectively? How would you bolster his self-esteem?

What would a HEALTH CARE WORKER do?

How might you respond to Yukio's vision problems? What if Yukio's parents had refused to believe that there was anything physically wrong with Yukio? How would you convince them to get treatment for Yukio?

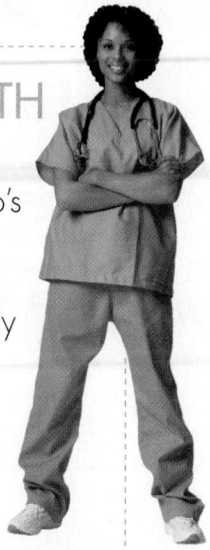

What would YOU do?

How would you deal with a situation in which your child had physical disabilities that would prevent him or her from progressing in school? How would you encourage your child? How would you deal with your child's frustration at falling behind in school?

What would an EDUCATOR do?

How would you deal with Yukio's difficulties in reading and writing? While he was working on his vision therapy, what would you do to help integrate him into his class and help him make friends with his classmates? What would you receommend in terms of educational specialists to deal with his problems?

Explore on MyPsychLab

To read how real parents, health care providers, and educators responded to these questions, log onto MyPsychLab.com.

Do you agree or disagree with their responses? Why? What concepts that you've read about back up their opinion?

6 ADOLESCENCE

In middle school, Julie Jacobs had one goal: to be popular. She ditched her "nerdy" grade school friends, bought a new wardrobe from the trendiest stores at the mall, and started shadowing the kids from the in crowd. She laughed at their jokes and boosted their egos at every opportunity. Soon, she began getting "friended" on Facebook by some of the girls. Then she was invited to a cool party where one of the boys on the football team asked her to dance.

Julie felt she was on her way. But then, she started drinking. It was just something the cool kids did. By ninth grade, she was drinking a lot. "I felt carefree and funny when I was drinking," she recalls. "I felt like nothing really mattered." Her grades began dropping from As to Bs, *then down to* Cs *and worse. She fought with her parents constantly. They grounded her when she came home late. They checked her room for liquor. "The more they pried, the crazier I got," she recalls. It took failing her junior year to wake up. "I realized I wasn't going to graduate with my class, wasn't going to get into college," Julie says. "I'd treated high school like a joke because that was the cool attitude, but I'd always thought of myself as smart. Having to repeat my junior year was devastating."*

Julie signed up with a substance abuse counselor and a therapist. She changed schools, opting for one that specializes in the arts. She'd always been a good writer so she joined a fiction writing club. "I saw kids my age doing amazing work and it made me want to do my best," Julie says. The next summer, she attended a month-long workshop for teen writers. The director was impressed with her work. He introduced her to a New York agent. Julie's first book earned 52 rejections, but her next book scored a contract. It will be out at the end of her second year of college. "I finally figured out that I have to define what's cool for me," she says, "because if I fail, I'm the one who takes the rap."

In this chapter we study adolescence, the transitional stage between childhood and adulthood. Adolescents face many challenges in all aspects of their life. Physically, their bodies are maturing quickly—sometimes distressingly quickly. Adolescents become sexually interested, and many of them face worries about their bodies. We will look at some of the issues that sometimes plague adolescents like Julie, including those relating to obesity and nutrition, harmful substances, and sexually transmitted infections (STIs).

Beyond the physical aspects of development, adolescents grow cognitively as well. The most notable change we will discuss is adolescents' growing awareness of their own thought processes. We also consider how adolescents deal with the institution that occupies a great deal of their waking time—school—and discuss the growing impact of the Internet on adolescents' lives, learning, and relationships.

Finally, we turn to the changes that adolescents undergo in their relationships with others. We begin with a consideration of the ways in which they create their concepts of themselves and how they form and protect their self-esteem and identity. We discuss their relationships with parents as adolescents redefine their place within the family. Finally, we discuss dating and sex, which achieve central importance during this period and which encompass issues of intimacy.

MODULE 6.1

PHYSICAL DEVELOPMENT IN ADOLESCENCE

Teenage boys are affected by early maturation differently than girls. How? What about late maturation?

MODULE 6.2

COGNITIVE DEVELOPMENT IN ADOLESCENCE

How does socioeconomic status affect school performance? What about race and ethnicity?

MODULE 6.3

SOCIAL AND PERSONALITY DEVELOPMENT IN ADOLESCENCE

What determines sexual orientation?

MyVirtualLife

If you are currently using MyVirtualLife, consider how you will raise your virtual child during adolescence. What decisions will you make?

Access MyVirtualLife for a chance to help your virtual child navigate adolescence.

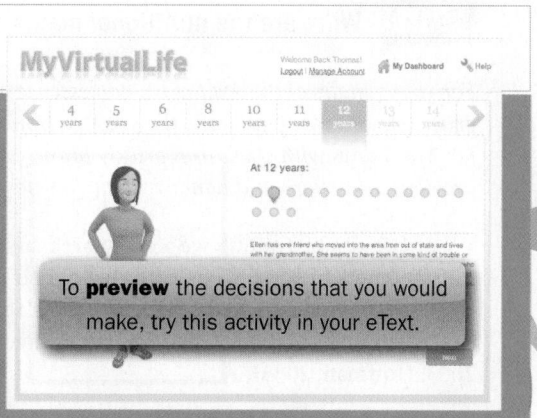

To **preview** the decisions that you would make, try this activity in your eText.

MODULE 6.1

PHYSICAL DEVELOPMENT IN ADOLESCENCE

Changing Circumstances

Ben Kramer had been dreaming of playing varsity basketball ever since he'd gone to a Lakers game at age 6. He played hoops with his friends at recess and eagerly awaited middle school where he was sure he'd shoot up in height to become the perfect center.

But Ben didn't shoot up in middle school, and when he finally experienced puberty at the end of ninth grade, he stopped growing a good deal short of 6 feet. "You've got some skills, son," the coach said, "but we need height." Ben was so depressed, he went home and ate a gallon of ice cream. The next day, he ate another. In 6 months, he'd gained 40 pounds. Some of the kids at school started calling him "Chubs" and the name stuck.

One day, Ben was watching a sports video. A ball player he admired said, "It's not about what you were born with. It's about who you become." Ben started working out, losing weight, and shooting hoops. He focused on learning how to use his height to his advantage. Grab the ball, then duck and dodge the taller guys down the court to the hoop. His strategy worked. He made junior varsity the next year and then varsity the year after that.

Like Ben, many adolescents struggle to accept the changes and challenges of the teenage years. These challenges extend far beyond trying to make the Varsity basketball team. With bodies that are conspicuously changing; temptations of sex, alcohol, and other drugs; cognitive advances that make the world seem increasingly complex; social networks that are in constant flux; and careening emotions, adolescents find themselves in a period of life that evokes excitement, anxiety, glee, and despair, sometimes in equal measure.

Adolescence is the developmental stage between childhood and adulthood. It is generally said to start just before the teenage years, and end just after them. Considered neither children nor adults, adolescents are in a transitional stage marked by considerable growth.

This module focuses on physical growth during adolescence. We first consider the extraordinary physical maturation that occurs during adolescence, triggered by the onset of puberty. We then discuss the consequences of early and late maturation and how they differ for males and females. We also consider nutrition. After examining the causes—and consequences—of obesity, we discuss eating disorders, which are surprisingly common at this stage.

The module concludes with a discussion of several major threats to adolescents' well-being—drugs, alcohol, tobacco, and STIs.

PHYSICAL MATURATION

L01 What physical changes do adolescents experience?
L02 What are the consequences of early and late maturation?
L03 What are the nutritional needs and concerns of adolescents?

For young males of the Awa tribe, adolescence begins with an elaborate and—to Western eyes—gruesome ceremony to mark the passage from childhood to adulthood. The boys are whipped for 2 or 3 days with sticks and prickly branches. Through the whipping, the boys atone for their previous infractions and honor tribesmen who were killed in warfare.

We are no doubt grateful we were spared such physical trials when we entered adolescence. But members of Western cultures have their own rites of passage, admittedly less fearsome, such as bar mitzvahs and bat mitzvahs at age 13 for Jewish boys and girls, and confirmation ceremonies in many Christian denominations (Herdt, 1998; Eccles, Templeton, & Barber, 2003; Hoffman, 2003).

adolescence the developmental stage that lies between childhood and adulthood

From an educator's perspective: Why do you think many cultures regard the passage to adolescence as a significant transition that calls for unique ceremonies?

Regardless of their nature, the underlying purpose of these ceremonies tends to be the same across cultures: symbolically celebrating the physical changes that transform a child's body into an adult body capable of reproduction.

Growth During Adolescence: The Rapid Pace of Physical and Sexual Maturation

In only a few months, adolescents can grow several inches as they are transformed, at least physically, from children to young adults. During such a growth spurt—a period of very rapid growth in height and weight—boys, on average, grow 4.1 inches a year and girls 3.5 inches. Some adolescents grow as much as 5 inches in a single year (Tanner, 1972; Caino et al., 2004).

Boys' and girls' growth spurts begin at different ages. As you can see in Figure 6-1, girls' spurts begin around age 10, while boys start around age 12. During the 2-year period from age 11, girls tend to be taller than boys. But by 13, boys, on average, are taller than girls—a state that persists for the remainder of the life span.

Puberty: The Start of Sexual Maturation

Puberty, the period when the sexual organs mature, begins when the pituitary gland in the brain signals other glands to begin producing the sex hormones, *androgens* (male hormones) or *estrogens* (female hormones), at adult levels. (Males and females produce both types of sex hormones, but males have higher levels of androgens and females, of estrogens.) The pituitary gland also signals the body to produce more growth hormones. These interact with the sex hormones to cause the growth spurt and puberty. The hormone *leptin* also appears to play a role in the onset of puberty.

Like the growth spurt, puberty begins earlier for girls, starting at around age 11 or 12, whereas boys begin at about age 13 or 14. However, this varies widely. Some girls begin puberty as early as 7 or 8 or as late as age 16.

puberty the period during which the sexual organs mature

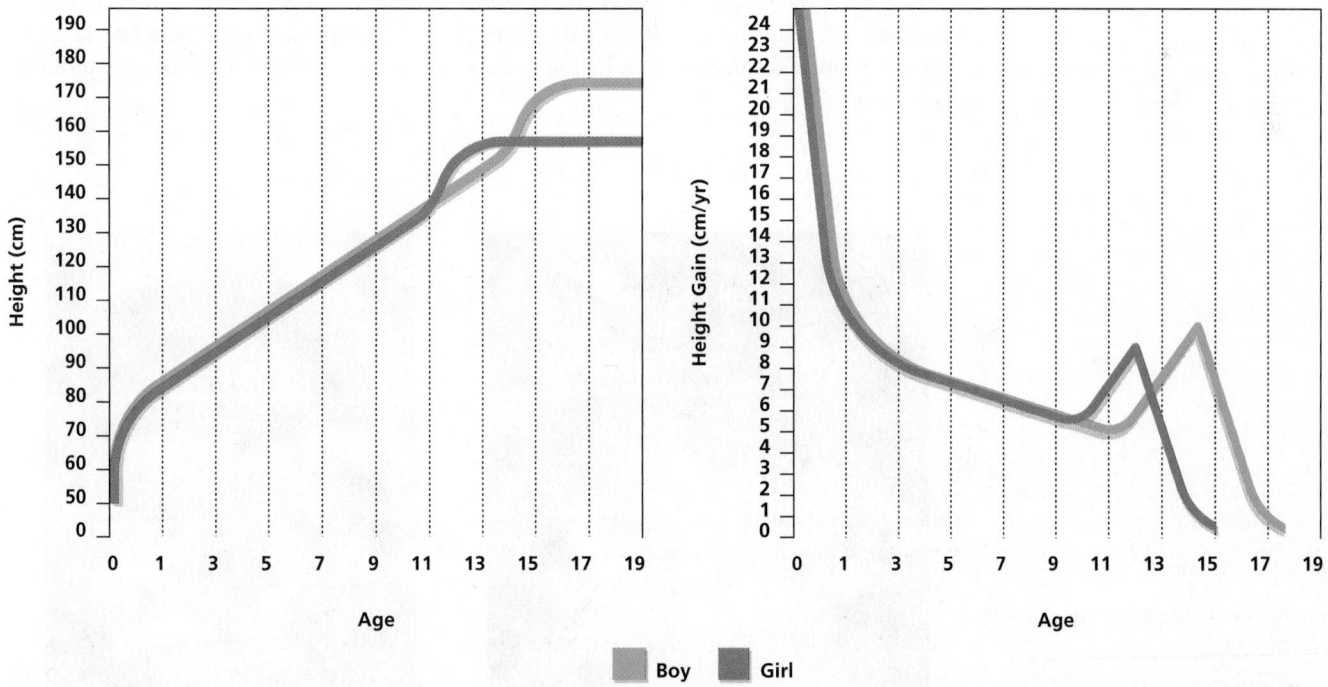

FIGURE 6-1 Growth Patterns
Patterns of growth are depicted in two ways. The first figure shows height at a given age, while the second shows the height increase that occurs from birth through the end of adolescence. Notice that girls begin their growth spurt around age 10, while boys begin their growth spurt at about age 12. However, by the age of 13, boys tend to be taller than girls. What are the social consequences of being taller or shorter than average for boys and girls?
Source: Adapted from Cratty, 1986.

Puberty in Girls. Although it is not clear why puberty begins when it does, environmental and cultural factors play a role. For example **menarche**, the onset of menstruation and probably the most obvious sign of puberty in girls, varies greatly around the world. In poorer, developing countries, menstruation begins later than in more economically advantaged countries. Even within wealthier countries, more affluent girls begin to menstruate earlier than less affluent girls.

It appears that girls who are better nourished and healthier tend to start menstruation earlier than those suffering from malnutrition or chronic disease. Some studies have suggested that weight or the proportion of fat to muscle in the body play a key role in the onset of menarche. For example, in the United States, athletes with a low percentage of body fat may start menstruating later than less active girls. Conversely, obesity—which increases the secretion of leptin, a hormone related to the onset of menstruation—leads to earlier puberty (Richards, 1996; Vizmanos & Marti-Henneberg, 2000; Woelfle, Harz, & Roth, 2007; Oswal & Yeo, 2010).

Other factors can affect the timing of menarche. For example, environmental stress from parental divorce or intense family conflict can effect an early onset (Ellis, 2004; Belsky et al., 2007; Allison & Hyde, 2013).

Over the past century or so, girls in the United States and other cultures have been entering puberty at earlier ages. In the late nineteenth century, menstruation began, on average, around age 14 or 15, compared with today's 11 or 12. The average age for other indicators of puberty, such as the attaining of adult height and sexual maturity, has also dropped, probably due to reduced disease and improved nutrition (McDowell, Brody, & Hughes, 2007; Harris, Prior, & Koehoorn, 2008; James et al., 2012).

The earlier start of puberty is an example of a significant **secular trend**. Secular trends occur when a physical characteristic changes over the course of several generations, such as earlier onset of menstruation or increased height resulting from better nutrition over the centuries.

Menstruation is one of several changes in puberty related to the development of primary and secondary sex characteristics. **Primary sex characteristics** are associated with the development of the organs and body structures related directly to reproduction. **Secondary sex characteristics** are the visible signs of sexual maturity that do not involve the sex organs directly.

In girls, developing primary sex characteristics involves changes in the vagina and uterus. Secondary sex characteristics include the development of breasts and pubic hair. Breasts begin to grow around age 10, and pubic hair appears at about age 11. Underarm hair appears about 2 years later.

menarche the onset of menstruation

secular trend a pattern of change occurring over several generations

primary sex characteristics characteristics associated with the development of the organs and structures of the body that directly relate to reproduction

secondary sex characteristics the visible signs of sexual maturity that do not directly involve the sex organs

Note the changes that have occurred in just a few years in these pre- and post-puberty photos of the same boy.

For some girls, signs of puberty start unusually early. One out of seven Caucasian girls develops breasts or pubic hair by age 8. For African American girls, the figure is one out of two. The reasons for this earlier onset are unclear, and what defines normal and abnormal onset is a controversy among specialists (Lemonick, 2000; The Endocrine Society, 2001; Ritzen, 2003).

Puberty in Boys. Boys' sexual maturation follows a somewhat different course. Growth of the penis and scrotum accelerates around age 12, reaching adult size about 3 or 4 years later. As boys' penises enlarge, other primary sex characteristics develop. The prostate gland and seminal vesicles, which produce semen (the fluid that carries sperm), enlarge. A boy's first ejaculation, known as *spermarche*, usually occurs around age 13, more than a year after the body begins producing sperm. At first, the semen contains relatively few sperm, but the sperm count increases significantly with age. Secondary sex characteristics are also developing. Pubic hair begins to grow around age 12, followed by the growth of underarm and facial hair. Finally, boys' voices deepen as the vocal cords become longer and the larynx larger. (Figure 6-2 summarizes the changes that occur in sexual maturation during early adolescence.)

The surge in hormones that triggers puberty also may lead to rapid mood swings. Boys may have feelings of anger and annoyance associated with higher hormone levels. In girls, higher levels of hormones are associated with depression as well as anger (Buchanan, Eccles, & Becker, 1992; Fujisawa & Shinohara, 2011).

Body Image: Reactions to Physical Changes in Adolescence. Unlike infants, who also undergo rapid growth, adolescents are aware of what is happening to their bodies, and they may react with horror or joy. Few, though, are neutral about the changes they are witnessing.

Some of the changes of adolescence carry psychological weight. In the past, girls tended to view menarche with anxiety because Western society emphasized the negative aspects of menstruation, its cramps and messiness. Today, however, society views menstruation more positively, in part because more open discussion has demystified it; for example, television commercials for tampons are commonplace. As a result, menarche now typically increases self-esteem, enhances status, and provides greater self-awareness, as girls see themselves as young adults (Johnson, Roberts, & Worell, 1999; Matlin, 2003; Yuan, 2012).

A boy's first ejaculation is roughly equivalent to menarche. However, while girls generally tell their mothers about the onset of menstruation, boys rarely mention their first ejaculation to their parents or even their friends (Stein & Reiser, 1994). Why? One reason is that mothers provide the tampons or sanitary napkins girls need. For boys, the first ejaculation may be seen as a sign of their budding sexuality, an area they feel both uncertain about and reluctant to discuss with others.

Menstruation and ejaculations occur privately, but changes in body shape and size are quite public. Teenagers frequently are embarrassed by these changes. Girls, in particular, are often unhappy with their new bodies. Western ideals of beauty call for an extreme thinness at odds with the actual shape of most women. Puberty considerably increases the amount of fatty tissue, and enlarges the hips and buttocks—a far cry from the pencil-thin body society seems to demand (Unger & Crawford, 2004; McCabe & Ricciardelli, 2006; Cotrufo et al., 2007).

How children react to the onset of puberty depends in part on when it happens. Girls and boys who mature either much earlier or later than most of their peers are especially affected. **Watch** the **Video** *Kianna: Body Image* in **MyPsychLab.**

The Timing of Puberty: The Consequences of Early and Late Maturation. There are social consequences for early or late maturation. And these social consequences are very important to adolescents.

Early Maturation. For boys, early maturation is largely a plus. Early-maturing boys tend to be more successful athletes, presumably because of their larger size. They also tend to be more popular and to have a more positive self-concept.

Early maturation in boys, though, does have a downside. Boys who mature early are more apt to have difficulties in school, and to become involved in delinquency and substance abuse. Being larger in size, they are

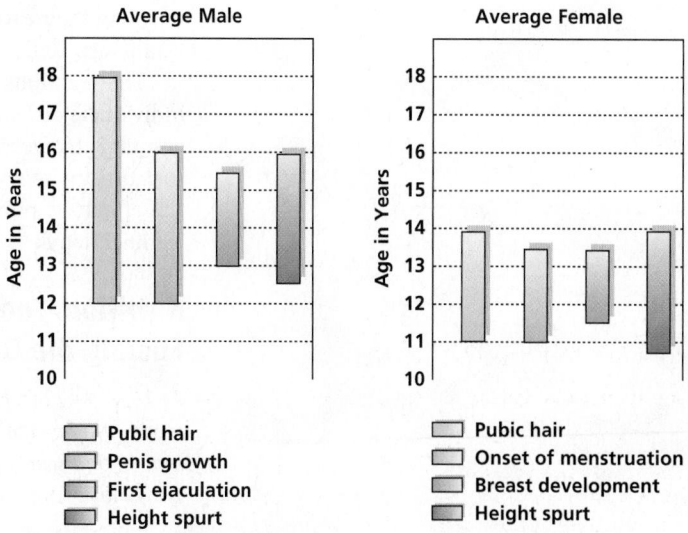

FIGURE 6-2 Sexual Maturation
The changes in sexual maturation that occur for males and females during early adolescence.
Source: Based on Tanner, 1978.

more likely to seek the company of older boys and become involved in age-inappropriate activities. Early-maturers are also more conforming and lacking in humor although they are more responsible and cooperative in adulthood. Overall, though, early maturation is positive for boys (Costello et al., 2007; Lynne et al., 2007; Mensah et al., 2013).

The story is a bit different for early-maturing girls. For them, the obvious changes in their bodies—such as the development of breasts—may lead them to feel uncomfortable and different from their peers. Moreover, because girls, in general, mature earlier than boys, early maturation tends to come at a very young age in the girl's life. Early-maturing girls may have to endure ridicule from their less mature classmates (Olivardia & Pope, 2002; Mendle, Turkheimer, & Emery, 2007; Hubley & Arim, 2012).

Early maturation, though, is not a completely negative experience for girls. Those who mature earlier are more often sought as dates, and their popularity may enhance their self-concept. This can be psychologically challenging, however. Early-maturers may not be socially ready for the kind of one-on-one dating situations that most girls deal with at a later age. Moreover, their obvious deviance from their later-maturing peers may produce anxiety, unhappiness, and depression (Kaltiala-Heino et al., 2003).

Consequently, unless a young girl who has developed secondary sex characteristics early can handle the disapproval she may encounter when she conspicuously displays her growing sexuality, the outcome of early maturation may be negative. In countries in which attitudes about sexuality are more liberal, the results of early maturation may be more positive. For example, in Germany, which has a more open view of sex, early-maturing girls have higher self-esteem than such girls in the United States. Furthermore, the consequences of early maturation vary even within the United States, depending on the views of girls' peer groups and on prevailing community standards regarding sex (Petersen, 2000; Güre, Uçanok, & Sayil, 2006).

Late Maturation. As with early-maturers, the situation for late-maturers is mixed, although here boys fare worse than girls. Boys who are smaller and lighter tend to be considered less attractive. Being small, they are at a disadvantage in sports activities. They may also suffer socially as boys are expected to be taller than their dates. If these difficulties diminish a boy's self-concept, the disadvantages of late maturation could extend well into adulthood. Coping with the challenges of late maturation may actually help males, however. Late-maturing boys grow up to be assertive and insightful, and are more creatively playful than early maturers (Kaltiala-Heino et al., 2003; Skoog, 2013).

The picture for late-maturing girls is quite positive even though they may be overlooked in dating and other mixed-sex activities during junior high and middle school, and may have relatively low social status (Apter et al., 1981; Clarke-Stewart & Friedman, 1987). In fact, late-maturing girls may suffer fewer emotional problems. Before they reach tenth grade and have begun to mature visibly, they are more apt to fit the slender, "leggy" body type society idealizes than their early-maturing peers, who tend to look heavier in comparison (Petersen, 1988; Kaminaga, 2007; Leen-Feldner, Reardon, & Hayward, 2008).

The reactions to early and late maturation paint a complex picture. As we have seen, an individual's development is affected by a constellation of factors. Some developmentalists suggest that changes in peer groups, family dynamics, and particularly schools and other societal institutions may determine an adolescent's behavior more than age of maturation, and the effects of puberty in general (Dorn, Susman, & Ponirakis, 2003; Stice, 2003; Mendle, Turkheimer, & Emery, 2007; Spear, 2010).

Nutrition, Food, and Eating Disorders: Fueling the Growth of Adolescence

At 16, Ariel Porter was pretty, outgoing, and popular. But when a boy she liked kidded her about having thighs like "tree trunks," she took it seriously. She began to obsess about food, using her mom's food scale to weigh everything that went into her mouth. She kept charts to portion sizes and calories, cutting her food into tiny morsels and then leaving most of it on her plate.

In a few months, Ariel went from 110 pounds to 90. Her hips and ribs became clearly visible, and her fingers and knees ached constantly. She stopped menstruating and her fingernails broke easily. Still, Ariel insisted she was overweight. It wasn't until her older sister returned from college that Ariel believed she had a problem. Her sister took one look at her, gasped audibly, and broke down crying.

Ariel's problem was a severe eating disorder, anorexia nervosa. As we have seen, the cultural ideal of slim and fit favors late-developing girls. But when development does occur, how do girls, and increasingly, boys, cope with an image in the mirror that deviates from the popular media ideal?

The rapid physical growth of adolescence is fueled by an increase in food consumption. Particularly during the growth spurt, adolescents eat substantial quantities of food, increasing their intake of calories rather dramatically. During the teenage years, the average girl requires some 2,200 calories a day, and the average boy requires 2,800. Of course, not just any calories nourish this growth. Several nutrients are essential, particularly calcium and iron. Milk and certain vegetables provide calcium for bone growth, and calcium may prevent osteoporosis—the thinning of bones—that affects 25 percent of women in later life. Iron is also necessary, as iron-deficiency anemia is not uncommon among teenagers.

For most adolescents, the major issue is eating a sufficient balance of nutritious foods. Two extremes of nutrition concern a substantial minority and can create real threats to health: obesity and eating disorders like the one afflicting Ariel Porter.

Obesity. The most common nutritional concern in adolescence is obesity. One in 5 adolescents is overweight, and 1 in 20 can be classified as obese (more than 20 percent above average body weight). The proportion of females who are classified as obese increases over the course of adolescence (Brook & Tepper, 1997; Critser, 2003; Kimm et al., 2003).

Adolescents are obese for the same reasons as younger children, but special concerns with body image may have severe psychological consequences at this age. The potential health consequences of obesity during adolescence are also problematic. Obesity taxes the circulatory system, increasing the risk of high blood pressure and diabetes. Obese adolescents also have an 80 percent chance of becoming obese adults (Goble, 2008; Wang et al., 2008; Huang, et al., 2013).

Lack of exercise is a major culprit. One survey found that by the end of the teenage years, few females get much exercise outside of school physical education classes. In fact, the older they get, the less they exercise. This is especially true for older black female adolescents, more than half of whom report *no* physical exercise outside of school, compared with about a third of white adolescents (Reichert et al., 2009; Liou, Liou, & Chang, 2010; Nicholson & Browning, 2012).

Obesity has become the most common nutritional concern during adolescence. In addition to issues of health, what are some psychological concerns about obesity in adolescence?

Additional reasons for the high rate of obesity during adolescence include the easy availability of fast foods, which deliver large portions of high-calorie, high-fat cuisine at prices adolescents can afford. Furthermore, many adolescents spend a significant proportion of their leisure time inside their homes watching television, playing video games, and surfing the Web. Such sedentary activities not only keep adolescents from exercising, but they often are accompanied by snacks of junk foods (Bray, 2008; Thivel et al., 2011; Laska et al., 2012).

Anorexia Nervosa and Bulimia Nervosa. Fear of fat and of growing obese can create its own problems—for example, Ariel Porter suffered from **anorexia nervosa**, a severe eating disorder in which individuals refuse to eat. A troubled body image leads some adolescents to deny that their behavior and appearance, which may become skeletal, are out of the ordinary.

Anorexia is a dangerous psychological disorder; some 15 to 20 percent of its victims starve themselves to death. It primarily afflicts women between the ages of 12 and 40; intelligent, successful, and attractive white adolescent girls from affluent homes are the most susceptible. Anorexia is also becoming a problem for boys; about 10 percent of victims are male. This percentage is rising and is often associated with the use of steroids (Jacobi et al., 2004; Ricciardelli & McCabe, 2004; Crisp et al., 2006; Schecklmann et al., 2012).

Though they eat little, anorexics tend to focus on food. They may shop often, collect cookbooks, talk about food, or cook huge meals for others. They may be incredibly thin but their body images are so distorted that they see themselves as disgustingly fat and try to lose more weight. Even when they grow skeletal, they cannot see what they have become.

Bulimia nervosa, another eating disorder, is characterized by *binge eating*, consuming large amounts of food, followed by *purging* through vomiting or the use of laxatives. Bulimics may eat an entire gallon of ice cream or a whole package of tortilla chips, but then feel such

anorexia nervosa a severe eating disorder in which individuals refuse to eat, while denying that their behavior and appearance, which may become skeletal, are out of the ordinary

bulimia nervosa an eating disorder characterized by binges on large quantities of food, followed by purges of the food through vomiting or the use of laxatives

This young woman suffers from anorexia nervosa, a severe eating disorder in which people refuse to eat, while denying that their behavior and appearance are out of the ordinary.

powerful guilt and depression that they intentionally rid themselves of the food. The disorder poses real risks. Though a bulimia nervosa sufferer's weight remains fairly normal, the constant vomiting and diarrhea of the binge-and-purge cycles may produce a chemical imbalance that triggers heart failure.

Why eating disorders occur is not clear, but several factors may be at work. Dieting often precedes the onset of eating disorders, as society exhorts even normal-weight individuals to be ever thinner. Losing weight may lead to feelings of control and success that encourage more dieting. Girls who mature early and have a higher level of body fat are more susceptible to eating disorders in later adolescence as they try to trim their mature bodies to fit the cultural ideal of a thin, boyish physique. Clinically depressed adolescents are also prone to develop eating disorders later (Courtney, Gamboz, & Johnson, 2008; Rodgers, Paxton, & Chabrol, 2010; Wade & Watson, 2012).

Some experts suggest that a biological cause may underlie both anorexia nervosa and bulimia nervosa. Twin studies suggest genetic components are involved. In addition, hormonal imbalances sometimes occur in sufferers (Wade et al., 2008; Baker et al., 2009; Keski-Rahkonen, et al., 2013).

Other attempts to explain the eating disorders emphasize psychological and social factors. For instance, some experts suggest that the disorders are a result of perfectionistic, overdemanding parents or by-products of other family difficulties. Culture also plays a role. Anorexia nervosa, for instance, is found primarily in cultures that idealize slender female bodies. Because in most places such a standard does not hold, anorexia is not prevalent outside the United States (Harrison & Hefner, 2006; Bennett, 2008; Bodell, Joiner, & Ialongo, 2012).

For example, anorexia is relatively rare in Asia, with the exceptions of areas in which Western influence is greatest. Furthermore, anorexia nervosa is a fairly recent disorder. It was not seen in the seventeenth and eighteenth centuries, when the ideal of the female body was a plump corpulence. The increasing number of boys with anorexia in the United States may be related to a growing emphasis on a muscular male physique that features little body fat (Mangweth, Hausmann, & Walch, 2004; Makino et al., 2006; Greenberg, Cwikel, & Mirsky, 2007; Pearson, Combs, & Smith, 2010).

Because anorexia nervosa and bulimia nervosa have both biological and environmental causes, treatment typically requires a mix of approaches (e.g., both psychological therapy and dietary modifications). In more extreme cases, hospitalization may be necessary (Wilson, Grilo, & Vitousek, 2007; Keel & Haedt, 2008; Stein, Latzer, & Merick, 2009).

Brain Development and Thought: Paving the Way for Cognitive Growth

Teenagers tend to assert themselves more as they gain greater independence. This independence is, in part, the result of changes in the brain that bring significant advances in cognitive abilities. As the number of neurons (the cells of the nervous system) continues to grow, and their interconnections become richer and more complex, adolescent thinking becomes more sophisticated (Toga & Thompson, 2003; Petanjek et al., 2008; Blakemore, 2012).

The brain produces an oversupply of gray matter during adolescence, which is later pruned back by 1 to 2 percent each year (see Figure 6-3). Myelination—the process of insulating nerve cells with fat cells—increases, making the transmission of neural messages more efficient. Both pruning and increased myelination contribute to the growing cognitive abilities of adolescents (Sowell et al., 2001; Sowell et al., 2003).

The prefrontal cortex of the brain, which is not fully developed until the early 20s, undergoes considerable development during adolescence. The *prefrontal cortex* allows people to think, evaluate, and make complex judgments in a uniquely human way. It underlies the increasingly complex intellectual achievements that are possible during adolescence.

At this stage, the prefrontal cortex becomes increasingly efficient in communicating with other parts of the brain, creating a communication system that is more distributed and sophisticated, which permits the different areas of the brain to process information more effectively (Scherf, Sweeney, & Luna, 2006; Hare et al., 2008).

The prefrontal cortex, the area of the brain responsible for impulse control, is biologically immature during adolescence, leading to some of the risky and impulsive behavior associated with the age group.

The prefrontal cortex also provides impulse control. An individual with a fully developed prefrontal cortex is able to inhibit the desire to act on such emotions as anger or rage. In adolescence, however, the prefrontal cortex is biologically immature; the ability to inhibit impulses is not fully developed (Weinberger, 2001; Steinberg & Scott, 2003; Eshel et al., 2007).

Because during adolescence the prefrontal cortex is biologically immature, the ability to inhibit impulses is not fully developed. This brain immaturity may lead to some of the risky and impulsive behaviors that are characteristic of adolescence. Furthermore, some researchers theorize that not only do adolescents underestimate the risks of risky behavior, but they overestimate the rewards that will come from the behavior. Regardless of the causes of risk taking in adolescents, it has led to a heated discussion of whether the death penalty should be applied to adolescents, as we discuss next (Steinberg & Scott, 2003; Casey, Jones, & Somerville, 2011; Gopnik, 2012).

The Immature Brain Argument: Too Young for the Death Penalty?

Just after 2 AM on September 9, 1993, Christopher Simmons, 17, and Charles Benjamin, 15, broke into a trailer south of Fenton, Missouri, just outside of St. Louis. They woke Shirley Ann Crook, a 46-year-old truck driver who was inside, and proceeded to tie her up and cover her eyes and mouth with silver duct tape. They then put her in the back of her minivan, drove her to a railroad bridge and pushed her into the river below, where her body was found the next day. Simmons and Benjamin later confessed to the abduction and murder, which had netted them $6. (Raeburn, 2004, p. 26)

This horrific case sent Benjamin to life in prison, but Simmons was given the death penalty. Simmons's lawyers appealed, and ultimately the U.S. Supreme Court ruled that no one under the age of 18 could be executed, citing their youth. Among the factors affecting the Court's decision was evidence from neuroscientists and child developmentalists that adolescents' brains were still developing in important ways and thus lacked judgment due to brain immaturity. This reasoning says adolescents are not fully capable of making sound decisions because their brains differ from those of adults.

The argument that adolescents may not be as responsible for their crimes stems from research showing continued brain growth and maturation during the teenage

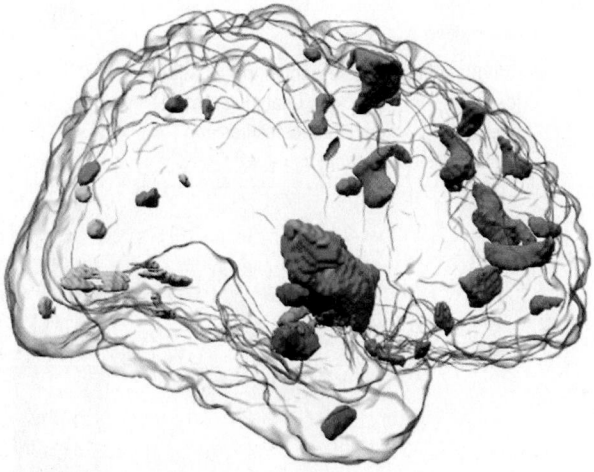

FIGURE 6-3 Pruning Gray Matter
This three-dimensional view of the brain shows areas of gray matter that are pruned from the brain between adolescence and adulthood.
Source: Sowell et al., 1999.

years, and beyond. For example, neurons that make up unnecessary gray matter begin to disappear. The volume of white matter begins to increase. This change permits more sophisticated, thoughtful cognitive processing (Beckman, 2004; Albert, Chein, & Steinberg, 2013).

When the brain's frontal lobes contain more white matter, they are better at restraining impulsivity. Teenagers may act impulsively, responding with emotion rather than reason. Their ability to foresee consequences may also be hindered by their less mature brains.

Are adolescents' brains so immature that offenders should receive a lesser punishment for their crimes than adults? The answer to this difficult question may come from students of ethics rather than science.

Sleep Deprivation. With increasing academic and social demands, adolescents go to bed later and get up earlier, leaving them sleep deprived. This deprivation coincides with a shift in their internal clocks. Older adolescents have a need to go to bed later and to sleep later in the morning, requiring 9 hours of sleep to feel rested. Yet half of adolescents sleep 7 hours or less each night, and almost one in five gets less than 6 hours. Because they typically have early morning classes but don't feel sleepy until late at night, they end up getting far less sleep than their bodies crave (Epstein & Mardon, 2007; Loessl et al., 2008; Wolfson & Richards, 2011; Dagys et al., 2012).

Sleep-deprived teens have lower grades, are more depressed, and have greater difficulty controlling their moods. They are also at great risk for auto accidents (Dahl, 2008; Roberts, Roberts, & Duong, 2009; Luo, Zhang, & Pan, 2013).

REVIEW, CHECK, AND APPLY

REVIEW

L01 What physical changes do adolescents experience?

- Adolescence is a period of rapid physical growth, including the changes puberty brings.

L02 What are the consequences of early and late maturation?

- Adolescents' responses to puberty range widely—from confusion to increased self-esteem. Both boys and girls face positive as well as negative consequences regarding early and late maturation.

L03 What are the nutritional needs and concerns of adolescents?

- Adequate nutrition is essential to fuel adolescents' physical growth. Changing physical needs and environmental pressures can cause obesity or eating disorders.

CHECK YOURSELF

1. The hormone _____ appears to play a role in the start of puberty for males and females.
   - a estrogen
   - b pituitary
   - c serotonin
   - d leptin
2. Which of the following is an example of a primary sex characteristic?
   - a growth of pubic hair
   - b development of breasts
   - c changes in the uterus
   - d sudden increase in height
3. The most common nutritional concern in adolescence is _____.
   - a anorexia
   - b bulimia nervosa
   - c sleep deprivation
   - d obesity

APPLYING LIFESPAN DEVELOPMENT

- How can societal and environmental influences contribute to eating disorders?

✓ **Study** and **Review** on **MyPsychLab.com**

THREATS TO ADOLESCENTS' WELL-BEING

L04 What are the major threats to the well-being of adolescents?
L05 What dangers do adolescent sexual practices present, and how can these dangers be avoided?

It took a car crash to wake Tom Jansen up—literally and figuratively. The police called at 12:30 AM and told him to pick up his 13-year-old daughter at the hospital. The accident wasn't serious, but what Tom learned that night might have saved Roni's life. The police found alcohol on her breath and on that of every other occupant of the car, including the driver.

Tom always knew that someday he'd have to have the "alcohol and drug talk" with Roni, but he had hoped it would be in high school, not middle school. Thinking back, he now saw that he had been wrong to chalk up the classic signs of a drug or alcohol problem—school absences, declining grades, general listlessness—to "adolescent angst." It was time to face facts.

He and Roni met with a counselor weekly for several months. At first Roni was hostile, but one evening she started sobbing while they were doing the dishes. Tom simply held her, never saying word. But from that moment, he knew his Roni was back.

Tom Jansen learned that alcohol was not the only drug Roni was using. As her friends later admitted, Roni had all the signs of becoming what they called a "garbage head"—someone who would try anything. Had the accident never happened, Roni might have gotten into very serious trouble or even lost her life.

Few cases of adolescent alcohol use produce such extreme results, but the use of alcohol, as well as other kinds of substance use and abuse, is one of several health threats in adolescence, usually one of the healthiest periods of life. While the extent of risky behavior is unknown, drugs, alcohol, and tobacco pose serious threats to adolescents' health and well-being.

The use of marijuana among high school students has decreased since the late 1990s.

Illegal Drugs

Illegal drug use in adolescence is very common. A recent survey of nearly 50,000 U.S. students showed that almost 50 percent of high school seniors and almost 20 percent of eighth graders had used marijuana within the past year. Although marijuana usage (and use of other drugs) has declined in recent years, the data on drug use still shows substantial use by adolescents (Tang & Orwin, 2009; Johnston et al., 2012) (see Figure 6-4).

Adolescents use drugs for many reasons. Some seek the pleasure they provide. Others hope to escape the pressures of everyday life, however, temporarily. Some adolescents try drugs simply for the thrill of doing something illegal. The drug use of well-known role models, such as movie stars and athletes, may also be enticing. And peer pressure plays a role: Adolescents are especially influenced by their peer groups (Urberg, Luo, & Pilgrim, 2003; Nation & Heflinger, 2006; Young et al., 2006; Pandina, Johnson, & White, 2010).

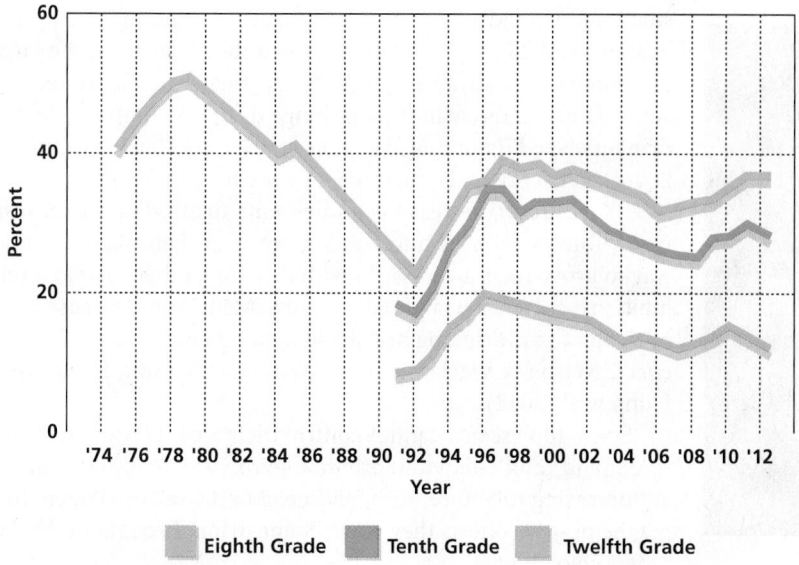

FIGURE 6-4 Downward Trend
According to an annual survey, the proportion of students reporting marijuana use over the past 12 months has decreased since 1999. What might account for the decline in drug use?
Source: Johnston et al., 2012.

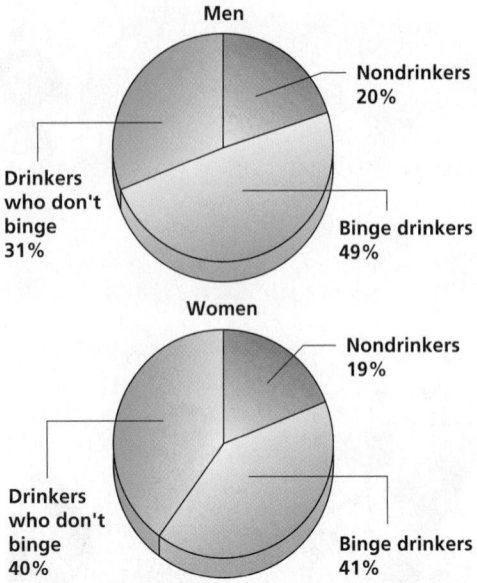

FIGURE 6-5 Binge Drinking Among College Students
For men, binge drinking is defined as consuming five or more drinks in one sitting; for women, the total is four or more. Why is binge drinking popular?
Source: Wechsler et al., 2003.

One of the newest reasons for using drugs is to enhance academic performance. A growing number of high students are using drugs such as Adderall, an amphetamine prescribed for attention deficit hyperactivity disorder. When used illegally, Adderall is assumed to increase focus and is thought to increase the ability to study and allow users to study for long hours (Schwarz, 2012).

The use of illegal drugs poses several dangers. Some drugs are addictive. **Addictive drugs** produce a biological or psychological dependence, leading users to increasingly crave them.

With a biological addiction, the drug's presence becomes so common that the body cannot function in its absence. Addiction causes actual physical—and potentially lingering—changes in the nervous system. The drug may no longer provide a "high," but may be necessary to maintain the perception of normalcy (Cami & Farré, 2003; Munzar, Cami, & Farré, 2003).

Drugs also can produce psychological addiction. People grow to depend on drugs to cope with everyday stress. If used as an escape, drugs may prevent adolescents from confronting—and solving—the problems that led to drug use in the first place. Even casual use of less hazardous drugs can escalate to dangerous forms of substance abuse.

Whatever the reason for using drugs in the first place, drug addiction is among the most difficult of all behaviors to modify. Even with extensive treatment, addictive cravings are hard to suppress (Thobaben, 2010).

Alcohol: Use and Abuse

Three-fourths of college students have something in common: They've consumed at least one alcoholic drink during the last 30 days. More than 40 percent say they've had five or more drinks within the past 2 weeks, and some 16 percent drink 16 or more drinks per week. High school students, too, are drinkers: Nearly three-quarters of high school seniors report having consumed alcohol by the end of high school, and about two-fifths have done so by eighth grade. More than half of twelfth graders and nearly a fifth of eighth graders say that they have been drunk at least once in their lives (Ford, 2007; Johnston et al., 2009).

addictive drugs drugs that produce a biological or psychological dependence in users, leading to increasingly powerful cravings for them

alcoholics persons with alcohol problems who have learned to depend on alcohol and are unable to control their drinking

Binge drinking is a particular problem on college campuses. Binge drinking is defined for men as drinking five or more drinks in one sitting; for women, who tend to weigh less and whose bodies absorb alcohol less efficiently, binge drinking is defined as four drinks in one sitting. Surveys find that almost half of male college students and over 40 percent of female college students say they participated in binge drinking during the previous 2 weeks (see Figure 6-5) (Beets et al., 2009; Griffin, Wardell, & Read, 2013).

Binge drinking affects even those who don't drink or drink very little. Two-thirds of lighter drinkers reported that they have been disturbed by drunken students while sleeping or studying. Around a third have been insulted or humiliated by a drunken student, and 25 percent of women said they have been the target of an unwanted sexual advance by a drunk classmate. Furthermore, brain scans show damaged tissue in teenage binge drinkers compared to non-binge drinkers (see Figure 6-6; Wechsler et al., 2002, 2003; McQueeny, 2009; Squeglia et al., 2012; Herman-Kinney & Kinney, 2013).

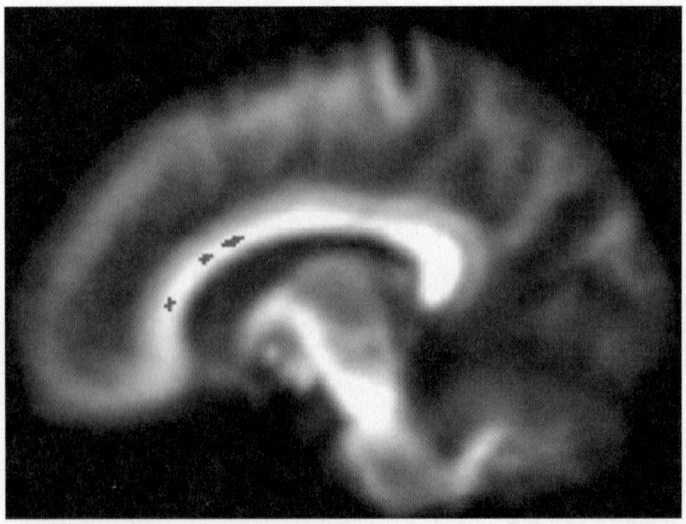

FIGURE 6-6 Binge Drinking Effects on the Brain
Binge Drinking affects certain areas of the white matter of the brain as shown in this scan.
Source: McQueeny et al., 2009, Figure 2.

There are many reasons adolescents drink. For some—especially male athletes, who tend to drink more than their peers—drinking is a way to prove their prowess. As with drug use, others drink to release inhibitions and tension, and reduce stress. Many begin because they believe everyone else is drinking heavily, something known as the *false consensus effect* (Nelson & Wechsler, 2003; Weitzman, Nelson, & Wechsler, 2003; Dunn et al., 2012).

Some adolescents cannot control their alcohol use. **Alcoholics** learn to depend on alcohol and are unable to stop drinking. They develop an increasing tolerance for it, and need to drink ever-larger amounts to get the positive effects they crave. Some drink throughout the day, while others go on binges.

Why some adolescents become alcoholics is not fully understood. Genetics plays a role: Alcoholism runs in families, though not all alcoholics have family members with alcohol problems. For adolescents with an alcoholic parent or family member, alcoholism may be triggered by efforts to deal with the stress (Berenson, 2005; Clarke et al., 2008).

Of course, the origins of an adolescent's alcohol or drug problems matter less than getting help. Parents, teachers, and friends can help a teen—if they realize there is a problem. Some of the telltale signs are described next. **Watch** the **Video** *Chris: Alcoholism* in **MyPsychLab**.

Tobacco: The Dangers of Smoking

Despite an awareness of the dangers of smoking, many adolescents indulge in it. Recent figures show that, overall, smoking is declining among adolescents, but the numbers remain substantial; and within certain groups the numbers are increasing. Smoking is on the rise among girls, and in several countries, including Austria, Norway, and Sweden, the proportion of girls who smoke is higher than for boys. There are racial differences, too: White children and those of lower socioeconomic status are more likely to experiment with cigarettes and to start smoking earlier than African American children and those of higher socioeconomic status. Also, significantly more white males of high school age smoke than do their African American male peers, although the difference is narrowing (Baker, Brandon, & Chassin, 2004; Fergusson et al., 2007; Proctor, Barnett, & Muilenburg, 2012).

Smoking is becoming a habit that is harder to maintain because there are growing social sanctions against it. It's becoming more difficult to find a comfortable place to smoke: More places, including schools and places of business, have become "smoke-free." Even so, a good number of adolescents still smoke, despite knowing the dangers of smoking and of secondhand smoke. Why, then, do adolescents begin to smoke and maintain the habit?

One reason is that for some adolescents, smoking is seen as an adolescent rite of passage, a sign of growing up. In addition, seeing influential models, such as film stars, parents, and peers smoking, increases the chances that an adolescent will take up the habit. Cigarettes are also very addictive. Nicotine, the active chemical ingredient of cigarettes, can produce biological and psychological dependency very quickly. Although one or two cigarettes do not usually produce a lifetime smoker, it takes only a little more to start the habit. In fact, people who smoke as few as 10 cigarettes early in their lives stand an 80 percent chance of becoming habitual smokers (Kodl & Mermelstein, 2004; West, Romero, & Trinidad, 2007; Tucker et al., 2008; Wills et al., 2008).

Becoming an Informed Consumer of Development

Hooked on Drugs or Alcohol?

It is not always easy to know if an adolescent is abusing drugs or alcohol, but there are signals. Among them are the following:

Identification with the drug culture

- Drug-related magazines or slogans on clothing
- Conversation and jokes that involve drugs
- Hostility discussing drugs
- Collection of beer cans

Signs of physical deterioration

- Memory lapses, short attention span, difficulty concentrating
- Poor physical coordination, slurred or incoherent speech
- Unhealthy appearance, indifference to hygiene and grooming
- Bloodshot eyes, dilated pupils

Dramatic changes in school performance

- Marked downturn in grades—not just from C's to F's, but from A's to B's and C's; assignments not completed
- Increased absenteeism or tardiness

Changes in behavior

- Chronic dishonesty (lying, stealing, cheating); trouble with the police
- Changes in friends; evasiveness in talking about new ones
- Possession of large amounts of money
- Increasing and inappropriate anger, hostility, irritability, secretiveness
- Reduced motivation, energy, self-discipline, self-esteem
- Diminished interest in extracurricular activities and hobbies

(Adapted from Franck & Brownstone, 1991; Johnston et al., 2007)

If an adolescent—or anyone else—fits any of these descriptors, help is probably needed. Call the national hotline run by the National Institute on Drug Abuse at (800) 662-4357 or visit its website at www.nida.nih.gov. You can also find a local listing for Alcoholics Anonymous in the telephone book.

Cultural Dimensions

Selling Death: Pushing Smoking to the Less Advantaged

According to a U.S. Cancer Institute report, each major U.S. tobacco company has a leading "youth brand" (Marlboro, Camel, Newport), which it promotes heavily.

New Kool Smooth Fusions cigarettes offer four trendy flavors: Caribbean Chill, Midnight Berry, Mocha Taboo, and Minitrigue, and Skoal chewable tobacco comes in fruity flavors, just like candy.

If you are a cigarette manufacturer and you find that the number of people using your product is declining, what do you do? U.S. companies have sought to carve out new markets by turning to a young and impressionable market, especially among the least advantaged groups of people, both at home and abroad. For instance, in the early 1990s the R.J. Reynolds tobacco company designed a new brand of cigarettes it named "Uptown." The advertising used to herald its arrival made clear who the target was: African Americans living in urban areas. Because of subsequent protests, the tobacco company withdrew "Uptown" from the market (Quinn, 1990; Brown, 2009).

In addition to seeking new converts at home, tobacco companies aggressively recruit adolescent smokers abroad. In many developing countries the number of smokers is still low. Tobacco companies are using marketing strategies such as free samples to increase this number. In countries where American culture and products enjoy high esteem, advertising suggests cigarette smoking is an American—and consequently prestigious—habit (Sesser, 1993).

The strategy is effective. In some Latin American cities as many as 50 percent of teenagers smoke. According to the World Health Organization, smoking will prematurely kill some 200 million of the world's children and adolescents. Overall, 10 percent of the world's population will die from smoking (Ecenbarger, 1993; Picard, 2008).

Sexually Transmitted Infections

One out of four adolescents contracts a **sexually transmitted infection (STI)** before graduating from high school. Overall, around 2.5 million teenagers contract an STI each year (Centers for Disease Control, 2009) (see Figure 6-7).

The most common STI is *human papilloma virus (HPV)*. HPV can be transmitted through genital contact without intercourse. Most infections do not have symptoms, but HPV can produce genital warts and in some cases lead to cervical cancer. A vaccine that protects against some kinds of HPV is now available. The U.S. Centers for Disease Control and Prevention recommends it be routinely administered to girls 11 to 12 years of age—a recommendation that has provoked considerable political reaction (Casper & Carpenter, 2008; Caskey, Lindau, & Caleb, 2009; Schwarz et al., 2012).

Another common STI is *trichomoniasis*, an infection in the vagina or penis, which is caused by a parasite. Initially without symptoms, it can eventually cause a painful discharge. *Chlamydia*, a bacterial infection, starts with few symptoms, but later causes burning urination

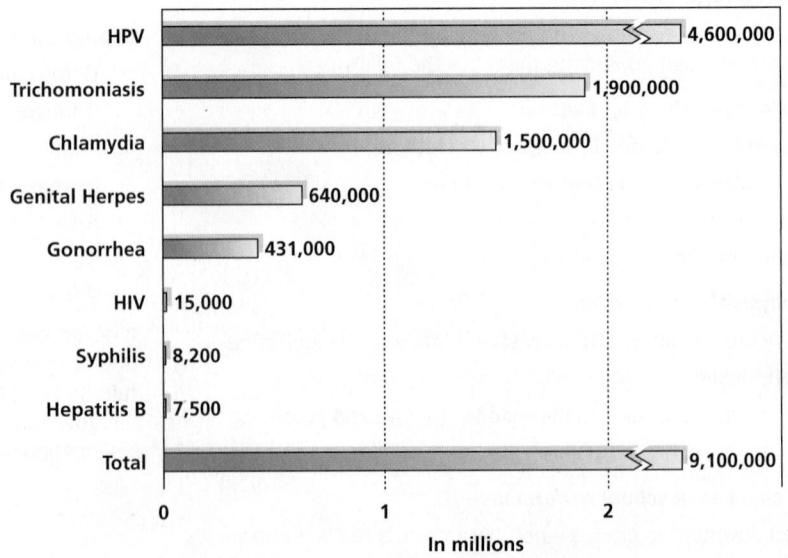

FIGURE 6-7 Sexually Transmitted Infections (STIs) Among Adolescents
Why are adolescents in particular in danger of contracting an STI?
Sources: Alan Guttmacher Institute, 2004; Weinstock, Berman, & Cates, 2006.

sexually transmitted infection (STI) an infection that is spread through sexual contact

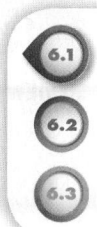

and a discharge from the penis or vagina. It can lead to pelvic inflammation and even to sterility. Chlamydia can be treated with antibiotics (Nockels & Oakshott, 1999; Fayers et al., 2003).

Genital herpes is a virus not unlike the cold sores that appear around the mouth. Its first symptoms are often small blisters or sores around the genitals, which may break open and become quite painful. Although the sores may heal after a few weeks, the infection often recurs and the cycle repeats itself. When the sores reappear, this incurable infection is contagious.

Gonorrhea and *syphilis* are the oldest known STIs, with cases recorded by ancient historians. Both infections were deadly before antibiotics, but can now be treated effectively. *Acquired immunodeficiency syndrome*, or *AIDS*, is the deadliest of sexually transmitted diseases and a leading cause of death among young people. AIDS has no permanent cure, but treatments have improved greatly in recent years and AIDS is no longer the sure death sentence that it used to be. Although it began as a problem that primarily affected homosexuals, it has spread to other populations, including heterosexuals and intravenous drug users. Minorities have been particularly hard hit: African Americans and Hispanics account for 70 percent of new AIDS cases, and African American males have almost eight times the prevalence of AIDS as white males. Already, over 25 million people have died from AIDS worldwide, and people living with the disease number 34 million worldwide.

From a health care provider's perspective: Why do adolescents' increased cognitive abilities, including the ability to reason and to think experimentally, fail to deter them from drug and alcohol abuse, tobacco use, and STIs? How might you use these abilities to design a program to prevent these problems?

Avoiding STIs

Short of abstinence, there is no certain way to avoid STIs. However, there are ways to make sex safer; these are listed in Table 6-1.

Even with substantial sex education, the use of safer sex practices is far from universal. Teenagers believe their chances of contracting STIs are minimal. This is particularly true when they view their partner as "safe"—someone they know well and with whom they have had a relatively long-term relationship (Lefkowitz, Sigman, & Kit-fong Au, 2000; Tinsley, Lees, & Sumartojo, 2004).

Unfortunately, unless one knows a partner's complete sexual history and STI status, unprotected sex remains a risk. And that information is difficult to get. Not only is it embarrassing to ask, partners may not be accurate reporters, whether from ignorance of their own exposure, embarrassment, forgetfulness, or a sense of privacy. As a result, STIs remain a significant problem.

TABLE 6-1 SAFER SEX PRACTICES

The only foolproof method of avoiding a STI is abstinence. However, by following the "safer sex" practices listed here, one can significantly reduce the risk of contracting an STI:

- ***Know your sexual partner—well.*** Before having sex with someone, learn about his or her sexual history.
- ***Use condoms.*** For those in sexual relationships, condoms are the most reliable means of preventing transmission of STIs. In addition, dental dams (also called vaginal dams) can provide a precautionary barrier during oral sex.
- ***Avoid the exchange of bodily fluids, particularly semen.*** In particular, avoid anal intercourse. The AIDS virus in particular can spread through small tears in the rectum, making anal intercourse without condoms particularly dangerous. Oral sex, once thought relatively safe, is now viewed as potentially dangerous for contracting the AIDS virus.
- ***Stay sober.*** Using alcohol and drugs impairs judgment and can lead to poor decisions—and it makes using a condom correctly more difficult.
- ***Consider the benefits of monogamy.*** People in long-term, monogamous relationships with partners who have been faithful are at a lower risk of contracting STIs.

REVIEW, CHECK, AND APPLY

REVIEW

L04 What are the major threats to the well-being of adolescents?

- The use of illegal drugs and alcohol is prevalent among adolescents as a way to find pleasure, avoid pressure, or gain the approval of peers.
- Despite the well-known dangers of smoking, adolescents often smoke to enhance their images or emulate adults.

L05 What dangers do adolescent sexual practices present, and how can these dangers be avoided?

- One out of four adolescents contracts an STI before graduating from high school.
- AIDS is the most serious of the STIs. Safe sex practices or abstinence can prevent AIDS, but adolescents often ignore these strategies.

CHECK YOURSELF

1. Adolescents have a variety of reasons for using drugs. Circle all that apply.
   - a pleasurable feelings
   - b escape from everyday life
   - c thrill of doing something illegal
   - d parental pressure
   - e peer pressure
2. In response to declining markets in the United States, tobacco companies have increased their business by _____.
   - a selling cigarettes in countries where American culture and products are held in high esteem.
   - b diversifying into clothing promoting smoking.
   - c lowering their prices to sell more cigarettes.
   - d increasing their prices so they only have to sell half.
3. _____ is the most common sexually transmitted infection.
   - a Syphilis
   - b Human papilloma virus (HPV)
   - c AIDS
   - d Chlamydia

APPLYING LIFESPAN DEVELOPMENT

- How might adolescents' concerns about self-image contribute to smoking and alcohol use?

✓ **Study** and **Review** on **MyPsychLab.com**

MODULE 6.2

COGNITIVE DEVELOPMENT IN ADOLESCENCE

She grew up to be a lawyer, an advocate for poverty awareness, and the First Lady of the United States, but Michelle Obama did not start life at the top. Descended from slaves, she grew up in a poor but loving home on Chicago's South Side. Her parents taught her the value of work and education. In sixth grade, Michelle was placed in a gifted class at her elementary school. She later applied to and was accepted at Whitney M. Young High School, a magnet school that is consistently one of the top-ranked high schools in Illinois. Every day, Michelle made a 3-hour round trip commute to get the best education she could. She was the salutatorian of her class. After graduation, she came east to attend Princeton and then Harvard Law School. Articulate and eloquent, she has never forgotten where she came from, and how essential a good education is to realizing the potential of every child.

The extraordinary success and perseverance of Michelle Obama is but one example of the impressive intellectual growth that occurs during adolescence. In fact, by the end of this stage, adolescents match adults in cognitive abilities in major respects.

In this module, we examine adolescents' cognitive development. The module begins with a look at several theories. We first consider the Piagetian approach, discussing how adolescents use formal operations to solve problems. We then look at a different viewpoint: the increasingly influential information processing perspectives. We consider the growth of metacognitive abilities, through which adolescents gain awareness of their own thinking processes. We also look at the ways in which metacognition leads to egocentrism and the invention of personal fables.

The module then examines school performance. After discussing the profound impact that socioeconomic status has on school achievement, we consider school performance and ethnicity. We then look at the impact cyberspace has on education, the skills students must learn to use the Internet effectively, and the dangers the Internet poses. We close with a discussion of the role socioeconomic status plays in high school dropout rates.

COGNITIVE DEVELOPMENT

LO6 How does cognitive development proceed during adolescence?
LO7 What aspects of cognitive development cause difficulties for adolescents?

Ms. Mejia smiled as she read a highly creative paper. As part of her eighth-grade American Government class, she asked students to write about what their lives would be like if America had not won its war for independence from Britain. She had tried a similar task with her sixth graders, but many of them were unable to imagine anything other than what they knew. Her eighth graders, however, were inventing some very interesting scenarios. One boy imagined himself as Lord Lucas; a girl imagined that she would serve a rich landowner; another that she would plot to overthrow the government.

What is it that sets adolescents' thinking apart from that of younger children? One of the major changes is the ability to think beyond the concrete, current situation to what *might* or *could* be. Adolescents are able to keep in their heads a variety of abstract possibilities, and they can see issues in relative, as opposed to absolute, terms. Instead of viewing problems as having black-and-white solutions, they are capable of perceiving shades of gray.

Once again we can use several approaches to explain adolescents' cognitive development. We'll begin by returning to Piaget's theory, which has had a significant influence on how developmentalists think about thinking during adolescence.

Piagetian Approaches to Cognitive Development: Using Formal Operations

Leigh, age 14, is asked to solve the problem: What determines the speed at which a pendulum moves back and forth? Leigh is given a weight hanging from a string and told that she can vary several things: the length of the string, the weight of the object, the amount of force used to push the string, and the height to which the weight is raised in an arc before it is released.

Leigh doesn't remember, but she was asked to solve the same problem at age 8 as part of a longitudinal research study. She was then in the concrete operational period, and her efforts were not very successful. Her haphazard approach showed no systematic plan of action. For instance, she simultaneously tried to push the pendulum harder *and* shorten the length of the string *and* increase the weight on the string. Because she varied so many factors at once, when the pendulum's speed changed, she had no way of knowing what had made the difference.

Now, Leigh is more systematic. Rather than immediately pushing and pulling at the pendulum, she stops to think about which factors to consider. She ponders how she might test which factor is important, forming a hypothesis. Then, as a scientist conducts an experiment, she varies only one factor at a time. By examining each variable separately and systematically, she comes to the correct solution: The length of the string determines the speed of the pendulum.

Using Formal Operations to Solve Problems. Leigh's approach to the pendulum question, a problem devised by Piaget, shows she has moved into the formal operational period of cognitive development (Piaget & Inhelder, 1958). In the **formal operational stage** people develop the ability to think abstractly. Piaget suggested that people reach it at the start of adolescence, around age 12.

Adolescents can consider problems in abstract rather than concrete terms by using formal principles of logic. They can test their understanding by systematically conducting rudimentary experiments and observing the results. Thus, the adolescent Leigh could think about the pendulum problem abstractly, and she understood how to test her hypotheses.

Adolescents are able to use formal reasoning, starting with a general theory about what causes a certain outcome and then deducing explanations for the situations in which that outcome occurs. Like the scientists who form hypotheses, discussed in Chapter 1, they can test their theories. What distinguishes this kind of thinking from earlier stages is the ability to

formal operational stage the period at which people develop the ability to think abstractly start with the abstract and move to the concrete; in previous stages, children are tied to the concrete present. At age 8, Leigh just moved things around to see what would happen in the pendulum problem, a concrete approach. At age 12, she began with the abstract idea that each variable should be tested separately.

Adolescents also can use propositional thought during this stage. *Propositional thought* is reasoning that uses abstract logic in the absence of concrete examples. Such thinking allows adolescents to understand that if certain premises are true, then a conclusion must also be true. For example:

All men are mortal.	*[premise]*
Socrates is a man.	*[premise]*
Therefore, Socrates is mortal.	*[conclusion]*

Adolescents understand that if both premises are true, then so is the conclusion. They are capable of using similar reasoning when premises and conclusions are stated more abstractly, as follows:

All A's are B.	*[premise]*
C is an A.	*[premise]*
Therefore, C is a B.	*[conclusion]*

Although Piaget proposed that the formal operational stage begins at the onset of adolescence, he also hypothesized that—as with all the stages—full cognitive capabilities emerge gradually through a combination of physical maturation and environmental experiences. It is not until around age 15, Piaget says, that adolescents fully settle into the formal operational stage.

Like scientists who form hypotheses, adolescents in the formal operational stage use systematic reasoning. They start with a general theory about what produces a particular outcome and then deduce explanations for specific situations in which they see that particular outcome.

In fact, evidence suggests that many people hone these skills at a later age, and some never fully employ them at all. Most studies show that only 40 to 60 percent of college students and adults achieve formal operational thinking completely, with some estimates as low as 25 percent. But many adults who do not use formal operational thought in every domain are fully competent in *some* aspects (Sugarman, 1988; Keating 1990, 2004).

The culture in which they are raised affects how adolescents use formal operations. People with little formal education, who live in isolated, technologically unsophisticated societies are less likely to use formal operations than formally educated persons in more sophisticated societies (Jahoda, 1980; Segall et al., 1990; Commons, Galaz-Fontes, & Morse, 2006).

It is not that adolescents (and adults) from cultures using few formal operations are incapable of attaining them. It is more likely that what characterizes formal operations—scientific reasoning—is not equally valued in all societies. If everyday life does not require or promote a certain type of reasoning, it is not likely that people will use such reasoning when confronting a problem (Gauvain, 1998).

The Consequences of Adolescents' Use of Formal Operations. The ability to reason abstractly, to use formal operations, changes adolescents' everyday behavior. Whereas earlier they may have blindly accepted rules and explanations, their increased abstract reasoning abilities may lead to strenuous questioning of their parents and other authority figures.

In general, adolescents become more argumentative. They enjoy using abstract reasoning to poke holes in others' explanations, and their increased critical thinking abilities zero in on parents' and teachers' perceived shortcomings. For instance, they may see their parents' arguments against using drugs as inconsistent if their parents used drugs in adolescence without consequence. But adolescents can be indecisive, too, as they are able to see the merits of multiple sides to issues (Elkind, 1996; Alberts, Elkind, & Ginsberg, 2007).

Coping with these new critical abilities can be challenging for parents, teachers, and other adults who deal with adolescents. But it makes adolescents more interesting, as they actively seek to understand the values and justifications they encounter.

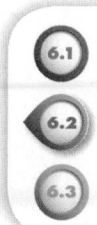

Evaluating Piaget's Approach. Each time we've considered Piaget's theory, several concerns have arisen. Let's summarize some of them here:

- Piaget suggests that cognitive development proceeds in universal, step-like stages. Yet significant differences exist in cognitive abilities from one person to the next, especially when we compare individuals from different cultures. We also find inconsistencies within the same individual. People indicate they have reached a certain level of thinking in some tasks but not others. If Piaget were correct, a person ought to perform uniformly well upon reaching a given stage (Siegler, 2007).
- The Piagetian notion of stages suggests that cognitive growth occurs in relatively rapid shifts from one stage to the next. Many developmentalists, however, argue that cognitive development is more continuous—increasing in quantitative accumulations rather than qualitative leaps forward. They also contend that Piaget's theory better *describes* behavior at a given stage than *explains* why the shift to a new stage occurs (Case, 1999; Birney & Sternberg, 2006).
- Citing the nature of the tasks Piaget used to measure cognitive abilities, critics suggest that he underestimated the age at which certain abilities emerge. It is now widely accepted that infants and children are more sophisticated than Piaget asserted (Siegler, 2007; Siegler & Lin, 2010).
- Some developmentalists argue that formal operations are not the epitome of thinking and that more sophisticated forms do not emerge until early adulthood. Developmental psychologist Giesela Labouvie-Vief (2006) argues that a complex society requires thought not necessarily based on pure logic. Instead, thinking must be flexible, allow for interpretive processes, and reflect the subtlety of cause and effect in real world events—something that Labouvie-Vief calls *postformal thinking* (Labouvie-Vief, 2006).

These criticisms regarding Piaget's approach to cognitive development have genuine merit. Yet, Piaget's theory has inspired countless studies on the development of thinking capacities and processes, and it also has spurred much classroom reform. His bold statements about the nature of cognitive development sparked opposition that brought forth new approaches, such as the information processing perspective we examine next (Taylor & Rosenbach, 2005; Kuhn, 2008).

Information Processing Perspectives: Gradual Transformations in Abilities

From an information processing perspective, adolescents' cognitive abilities grow gradually and continuously. Unlike Piaget's view that increasing cognitive sophistication is a reflection of stage-like spurts, the **information processing perspective** sees changes in adolescents' cognitive abilities as gradual transformations in the capacity to take in, use, and store information. Multiple progressive changes occur in the ways people organize their thinking, develop strategies to deal with new situations, sort facts, and advance in memory capacity and perceptual abilities (Pressley & Schneider, 1997; Wyer, 2004).

Adolescents' general intelligence—as measured by traditional IQ tests—remains stable, but dramatic improvements occur in the specific abilities that underlie intelligence. Verbal, mathematical, and spatial abilities increase. Memory capacity grows, and adolescents become adept at handling more than one stimulus at a time—as when they study for a biology test while listening to a CD.

As Piaget noted, adolescents grow increasingly sophisticated in understanding problems, grasping abstract concepts and hypothetical thinking, and comprehending the possibilities inherent in situations. This permits them, for instance, to endlessly dissect the course their relationships might hypothetically take.

Adolescents know more about the world, too. Their store of knowledge increases as the amount of material they are exposed to grows and their memory capacity enlarges. In sum, mental abilities markedly improve during adolescence (Kail, 2004; Kail & Miller, 2006; Atkins et al., 2012).

According to information processing theories of cognitive development, one of the main reasons for adolescents' advances in mental abilities is the growth of metacognition.

information processing perspective the model that seeks to identify the way that individuals take in, use, and store information

Adolescents' personal fables may lead them to feel invulnerable and to engage in risky behavior, like these Brazilian boys (known as "surfistas") riding on the roof of a high-speed train.

Metacognition is the knowledge of one's own thinking processes, and the ability to monitor one's own cognition. Although younger children can use some metacognitive strategies, adolescents are much more adept at understanding their own mental processes.

For example, as their understanding of their memory capacity improves, adolescents can better gauge how long they need to memorize given material for a test. They also can judge when the material is fully memorized much more accurately than in younger days. Their improved metacognition permits adolescents to comprehend and master school material more effectively (Desoete, Roeyers, & De Clercq, 2003; Schneider, 2010; Dimmitt & McCormick, 2012).

These new abilities also can make adolescents deeply introspective and self-conscious—two characteristics which, as we see next, may produce a high degree of egocentrism.

Egocentrism in Thinking: Adolescents' Self-Absorption

Carlos thinks his parents are "control freaks"; he cannot figure out why they insist he call and let them know where he is when he borrows the car. Jeri views Molly's purchase of earrings just like hers as the ultimate compliment, even though Molly may have been unaware Jeri had a similar pair when she bought them. Lu is upset with his biology teacher for giving a long, difficult midterm exam on which he did poorly.

Adolescents' newly sophisticated metacognitive abilities make them readily imagine that others are focused on them, and they may create elaborate scenarios about others' thoughts. This is the source of the egocentrism that can dominate adolescents' thinking. **Adolescent egocentrism** is a state of self-absorption in which the world is seen as focused on oneself. This egocentrism makes adolescents highly critical of authority figures, hostile to criticism, and quick to find fault with others' behavior (Alberts, Elkind, & Ginsberg, 2007; Schwartz, Maynard, & Uzelac, 2008).

Adolescents may develop an **imaginary audience**, fictitious observers who pay as much attention to their behavior as they do themselves. Unfortunately, these scenarios suffer from the same kind of egocentrism as the rest of their thinking. For instance, a student sitting in a class may be sure a teacher is focusing on her, and a teenager at a basketball game may be convinced that everyone is staring at the pimple on his chin.

metacognition the knowledge that people have about their own thinking processes, and their ability to monitor their cognition

adolescent egocentrism a state of self-absorption in which the world is viewed from one's own point of view

imaginary audience an adolescent's belief that his or her own behavior is a primary focus of others' attention and concerns

Roz Chast/The New Yorker Collection/www.cartoonbank.com

Egocentrism leads to a second distortion in thinking: that one's experiences are unique. Adolescents develop **personal fables**, the view that what happens to them is unique, exceptional, and shared by no other. Teenagers whose romantic relationships have ended may feel that no one has ever hurt the way they do, that no one was ever treated so badly, and that no one can understand their pain (Alberts, Elkind, & Ginsberg, 2007).

From a social worker's perspective: In what ways does egocentrism complicate adolescents' social and family relationships? Do adults entirely outgrow egocentrism and personal fables?

Personal fables may make adolescents feel invulnerable to the risks that threaten others. They may see no need to use condoms during sex because, in the personal fables they construct, pregnancy and STIs only happen to other kinds of people, not to them. They may drink and drive because in their personal fables they are careful drivers, always in control (Greene et al., 2000; Vartanian, 2000; Reyna & Farley, 2006).

personal fables the view held by some adolescents that what happens to them is unique, exceptional, and shared by no one else

REVIEW, CHECK, AND APPLY

REVIEW

L06 How does cognitive development proceed during adolescence?

- Adolescence corresponds to Piaget's formal operations period, a stage characterized by abstract reasoning and an experimental approach to problems.
- According to the information processing perspective, cognitive advances in adolescence are quantitative and gradual, as many aspects of thinking and memory improve. Growth in metacognition enables the monitoring of thought processes and mental capacities.

L07 What aspects of cognitive development cause difficulties for adolescents?

- Adolescents are susceptible to egocentrism and the perception that their behavior is constantly observed by an imaginary audience.
- Adolescents construct personal fables about their uniqueness and immunity to harm.

CHECK YOURSELF

1. Fifteen-year-old Wyatt is able to solve the physics problem from class in abstract rather than in concrete terms. According to Piaget, Wyatt is now capable of _____.
   - a preoperational thought
   - b formal operational thought
   - c egocentrism
   - d sensorimotor thought
2. _____ is the knowledge that people have about their own thinking processes and their ability to monitor their cognition.
   - a Metacognition
   - b Postformal thinking
   - c Egocentrism
   - d Self-absorption
3. Rorie refuses to go to the eighth-grade dance because she is sure that the only thing everyone will see is the pimple on her face. Which of the following limitations in thinking associated with adolescence is at work here?
   - a imaginary audience
   - b personal fable
   - c invincibility fable
   - d hysteria

APPLYING LIFESPAN DEVELOPMENT

- When facing complex problems, do you think most adults spontaneously apply formal operations like those used to solve the pendulum problem? Why or why not?

✓ **Study** and **Review** on **MyPsychLab.com**

SCHOOL PERFORMANCE

L08 What factors affect adolescent school performance?
L09 How much of an influence does the Internet have on adolescent learning?

Jeri Camber is annoyed. His iPod has stopped working and now he has to pull out his earbuds, put his calculus textbook down, and pause the game he's playing on his Playstation 3. He fiddles with the iPod and finally gets it working. As he puts his earbuds back in and returns to his calculus book and video game, he shouts to his father to find out the score of the basketball game he hears playing in the next room. To his surprise, his father answers that he doesn't know because he's been reading a book instead of paying attention. Jeri rolls his eyes and silently judges his dad a bit dim-witted for being unable to do both things at the same time.

Jeri's ability at age 17 to listen to music, do his homework, and play a videogame all at the same time may or may not signal some kind of advance over his father's limited focus on one thing at a time. In part, Jeri's talent for multitasking is surely due to the different eras in which he and his father were raised, but it may also be partly attributable to the cognitive changes that accompanied his advance into adolescence. Think of it this way: It is *possible* that Jeri actually can perform more mental tasks simultaneously than his father, but it is *certain* that he can do more tasks *well* than he could do just a few years earlier.

Do the advances in adolescents' metacognition, reasoning, and other cognitive abilities lead to improved school performance? If we use grades as the measure of performance, the answer is yes. High school students' grades have risen in the last decade. The mean grade point average for college-bound seniors was 3.3 (on a scale of 4), compared with 3.1 a decade ago. More than 40 percent of seniors reported average grades of A+, A, or A– (College Board, 2005).

At the same time, independent measures of achievement, such as SAT scores, have not risen. A more likely explanation for the higher grades is the phenomenon of grade inflation: Students have not changed; instead, instructors are awarding higher grades for the same performance (Cardman, 2004).

Further evidence for grade inflation comes from the relatively poor achievement of students in the United States when compared to students in other countries. For instance, students in the

United States score lower on standardized math and science tests when compared to students in other industrialized countries (National Governors Association, 2008) (see Figure 6-8).

There is no single reason for this achievement gap, but a combination of factors, such as less class time and less intensive instruction, are at work. The broad diversity of the U.S. school population also may affect performance relative to other countries in which the school population is more homogeneous and affluent (Stedman, 1997; Schemo, 2001).

High school graduation rates also reflect the lesser accomplishments of U.S. students. Once first in the number of high school graduates it produces—in terms of total population—the United States is now 24th among industrialized countries. Only 78 percent of U.S. high school students graduate (OECD, 1998; OECD, 2001).

As we discuss next, differences in socioeconomic status are also reflected in school performance within the United States (Stedman, 1997; Schemo, 2001).

Socioeconomic Status and School Performance: Individual Differences in Achievement. All students are entitled to an equal education, but some groups enjoy more advantages than others, as the relationship between educational achievement and socioeconomic status (SES) clearly indicates.

Middle- and high-SES students, on average, earn higher grades, score higher on standardized achievement tests, and complete more years of school than students from lower-SES homes. This disparity does not start in adolescence; the same findings hold for children in lower grades. However, by high school, the effects of socioeconomic status are more pronounced (Frederickson & Petrides, 2008; Shernoff & Schmidt, 2008; Tucker-Drob & Harden, 2012).

Why do children from middle- and high-SES homes show greater academic success? Children living in poverty lack many of the advantages of their more affluent peers. Moreover, their nutrition and health may be poorer. If they live in crowded conditions or attend inadequate schools, they may have few places to study. Their homes may lack the books and computers common in more affluent households (Prater, 2002; Chiu & McBride-Chang, 2006; Wamba, 2010).

For these reasons, impoverished students may be disadvantaged from their first day of school. As they grow up, their school performance may continue to lag and, in fact, the difference may snowball. High school success builds heavily on basic skills presumably learned earlier. Children who experience early problems may find themselves falling ever further behind (Biddle, 2001; Hoff, 2012).

Ethnic and Racial Differences in School Achievement. Significant achievement differences between ethnic and racial groups paint a troubling picture of American education. School achievement data indicate that, on average, African American and Hispanic students perform at lower levels, receive lower grades, and score lower on standardized achievement tests than Caucasian students. In contrast, Asian American students tend to earn higher grades than Caucasian students (Frederickson & Petrides, 2008; Shernoff & Schmidt, 2008; Byun & Park, 2012).

Socioeconomic factors create much of the ethnic and racial differences in academic achievement. More African American and Hispanic families live in poverty, and this fact may affect their children's school performance. In fact, when we compare different ethnic and racial groups at the same socioeconomic level, achievement differences diminish but do not vanish (Meece & Kurtz-Costes, 2001; Cokley, 2003; Guerrero et al., 2006).

Anthropologist John Ogbu (1988, 1992) argues that certain minority groups may perceive school success as relatively unimportant. They may believe societal prejudice in the workplace dictates they will not succeed, no matter how hard they try. They may conclude that effort in school will have no eventual payoff.

Ogbu suggests that minority group members who enter a new culture voluntarily are more likely to succeed in school than those brought into a new culture against their will. He notes that the sons and daughters of voluntary Korean immigrants to the United States tend to be quite successful in school.

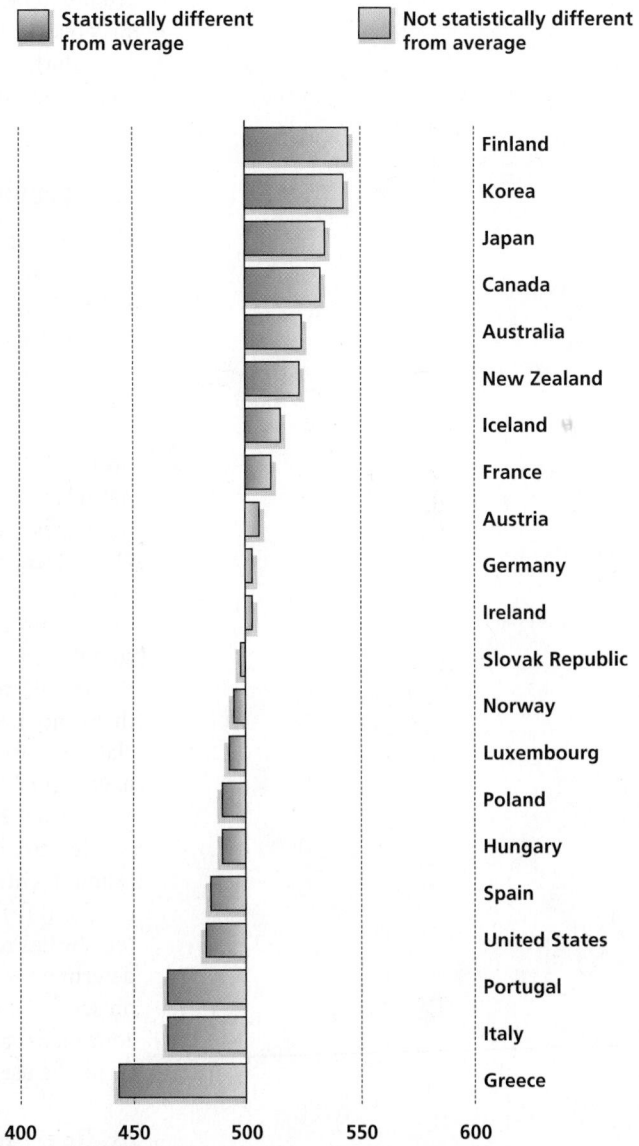

FIGURE 6-8 U.S. 15-Year-Old Performance Compared With Other Countries
When compared to the math performance of students across the world, U.S. students perform at below-average levels.
Source: Based on National Governors Association, 2008.

In contrast, Korean children in Japan, whose parents were forced to immigrate during World War II and work as forced laborers, tend to do poorly in school. Involuntary immigration apparently leaves lasting scars, reducing the motivation to succeed in subsequent generations. Ogbu suggests that in the United States, the involuntary immigration, as slaves, of the ancestors of many African American students might be related to their motivation to succeed (Ogbu, 1992; Toldson & Lemmons, 2013).

From an educator's perspective: Why might descendants of people who were forced to immigrate to a country be less successful academically than those who came voluntarily? What approaches might be used to overcome this obstacle?

Another factor has to do with attributions for academic success. As we discussed previously, students from many Asian cultures tend to relate achievement to situational factors such as their effort. In contrast, African American students are apt to attribute success to external causes beyond their control, such as luck or societal biases. Students who believe effort leads to success, and expend that effort, are likely to do better in school than students who do not believe effort matters (Fuligni, 1997; Saunders, Davis, & Williams, 2004; Hannover et al., 2013).

Adolescents' beliefs about the consequences of poor school performance may also contribute to racial and ethnic differences. Specifically, African American and Hispanic students may believe they can succeed *despite* poor performance. This belief can cause them to expend less effort. In contrast, Asian American students may believe that they must do well in school to get a good job and be successful. Asian Americans, then, are motivated to work hard for fear of the consequences (Steinberg, Dornbusch, & Brown, 1992; Murphy et al., 2010).

Achievement Testing in Schools: Will No Child Be Left Behind?

Concerns about the educational performance of students have led to considerable efforts to improve schooling. No educational reform has had a greater impact than the No Child Left Behind Act.

The No Child Left Behind Act, passed by Congress in 2002, requires that every U.S. state design and administer achievement tests that students must pass in order to graduate from high school. In addition, schools themselves are graded so that the public is aware of which schools have the best (and worst) test results. The basic idea behind the mandatory testing programs like the No Child Left Behind Act is to ensure that students graduate with a minimum level of proficiency. Proponents suggest that students—and teachers—will be motivated by the tests and that overall educational standards will be raised (Jehlen & Winans, 2005; Opfer, Henry, & Mashburn, 2008; Hoy-Watkins, 2008; Cook & Wong, 2012).

Critics of the act (and other forms of mandatory standardized testing) argue that a number of unintended negative consequences will result from implementation of the law. To ensure that the maximum numbers of students pass the tests, they suggest that instructors "teach to the test," meaning that they focus on the content of the tests to the exclusion of material that is not tested. Moreover, because students from lower socioeconomic and ethnic and racial minority backgrounds and those with special needs fail tests disproportionately, critics have argued that mandatory testing programs may be inherently biased (Thurlow, Lazarus, & Thompson, 2005; Linn, 2008; Koretz, 2008).

Because of problems with the law, many states have been exempted from its toughest requirements, and the U.S. Congress is discussing ways of improving the law. Although the *No Child Left Behind Act* has been controversial from the time of its passage, one part of the law has received nearly universal approval. Specifically, the law provides funding to help determine what educational practices and programs have been proven to be effective based on scientific research. Although there is disagreement over what constitutes "proof" of best educational practices, developmental and educational researchers have welcomed the emphasis on the use of objective data (Chatterji, 2004; Sunderman, 2008; Blankinship, 2012).

Adolescents' Media Use

An enormous variety of media and technologies are available to adolescents, ranging from more traditional sorts, such as radio and television, to newer forms, such as instant messaging, cell phones, and MP3 players. And adolescents make use of them—to a staggering degree.

According to a comprehensive survey using a sample of boys and girls 8 to 18 years old conducted by the Kaiser Family Foundation (a well-respected think tank), young people spend an average of 6.5 hours a day with media. Furthermore, because around a quarter of the time they are using more than one form of medium simultaneously, they are actually being exposed to the equivalent of 8.5 hours per day (Boneva et al., 2006; Jordan et al., 2007; Rideout, Foehr & Roberts, 2010).

The amount of media use can be extraordinary. For example, some teenagers send nearly 30,000 texts a month, often carrying on multiple conversations simultaneously. The use of texting often supplants other forms of social interaction, such as telephone calls or even face-to-face interaction (Lenhart, 2010; Richtel, 2010) (see Figure 6-9).

Some forms of online activities can be mean-spirited. For example, some teenagers make use of the web to bully others—a process in which victims are repeatedly texted or emailed with hurtful messages. The source of such *cyberbullying* can remain anonymous, and the messages may be particularly abusive. Although they do not inflict physical harm, they can be psychologically damaging (Zacchilli & Valerio, 2011).

The widespread availability of the Web has produced considerable changes in education, allowing adolescents to tap into a vast array of information. However, it is not yet obvious how Web access will change education or whether the impact will be uniformly positive. For instance, schools must change their curricula to include specific instruction in a key skill for deriving value from the Web: learning to sort through huge bodies of information to identify what is most useful and discard what is not. To obtain the full benefits of the Web, then, students must obtain the ability to search, choose, and integrate information in order to create new knowledge (Oblinger & Rush, 1997; Trotter, 2004).

Despite the substantial benefits of the Web, its use also has a downside. The Web makes material available that many parents and other adults find highly objectionable. In addition, there is a growing problem of Internet gambling. High school and college students can easily bet on sports events and participate in games such as poker on the Web using credit cards (Winters, Stinchfield, & Botzet, 2005; Fleming et al., 2006; Mitchell, Wolak, & Finkelhor, 2007; King, Delfabbro, & Griffiths, 2010; Derevensky, Shek, & Merrick, 2010).

The growing use of computers also presents a challenge involving socioeconomic status, race, and ethnicity. Poorer adolescents and members of minority groups have less access to computers than more affluent adolescents and members of socially advantaged groups—a phenomenon known as the *digital divide* (Fetterman, 2005; Olsen, 2009; Broadbent & Papadopoulos, 2013).

Dropping Out of School. Most students complete high school, but, some half million students each year drop out prior to graduating. The consequences are severe. High school dropouts earn 42 percent less than graduates, and their unemployment rate is 50 percent.

Adolescents leave school for a variety of reasons. Some leave because of pregnancy or problems with the English language. Some must leave for economic reasons, needing to support themselves or their families.

Dropout rates differ according to gender and ethnicity. Males are more likely to drop out than females. Although the dropout rate for all ethnicities has been declining in recent decades, Hispanic and African American students still are less likely to finish

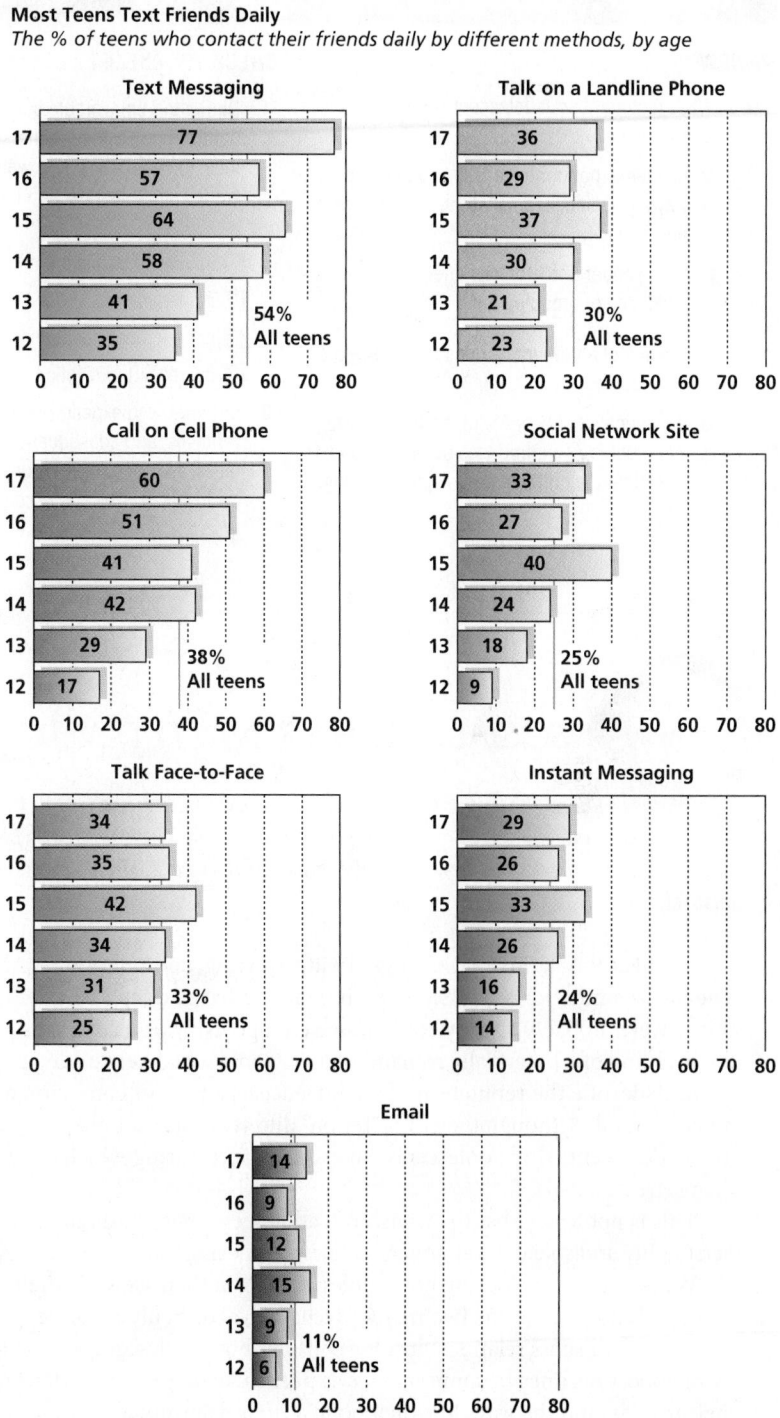

FIGURE 6-9 Teenagers, Cell Phones, and Texting
As they get older, the percentage of teenagers who text their friends daily generally rises.
Source: Pew Research Centre, 2010.

high school than non-Hispanic white students. However, not all minority groups show higher dropout rates; for example, Asians drop out at a lower rate than Caucasians (National Center for Educational Statistics, 2003; Stearns & Glennie, 2006; Bowers, Sprott, & Taff, 2013).

Poverty largely determines whether a student completes high school. Students from lower-income households are three times more likely to drop out than those from middle- and upper-income households. Because economic success is so dependent on education, dropping out often perpetuates a cycle of poverty (National Center for Education Statistics, 2002).

REVIEW, CHECK, AND APPLY

REVIEW

L08 What factors affect adolescent school performance?

- Academic performance is linked in complex ways to socioeconomic status and to race and ethnicity.
- Both gender and ethnicity affect the incidence of dropping out.

L09 How much of an influence does the Internet have on adolescent learning?

- The educational benefits of the Internet are many, but it also introduces adolescents to objectionable material and online gambling.

CHECK YOURSELF

1. Due to the unfavorable comparison of U.S. standardized test scores to the scores of other countries, the gradual shift upward of adolescents' grades in the last decade has been attributed to _____.
   - a increased immigration
   - b grade inflation
   - c achievement deflation
   - d decreased motivation
2. Students who experience socioeconomic disadvantages, and consequently academic disadvantages, as young children usually overcome those disadvantages by adolescence.
   - True
   - False
3. Who is least likely to drop out of high school prior to graduation in the United States?
   - a males
   - b females

APPLYING LIFESPAN DEVELOPMENT

- What sorts of *external* factors (i.e., not attributable to the students) might negatively affect the performance of U.S. students on international achievement tests?

✓ **Study** and **Review** on **MyPsychLab.com**

MODULE 6.3

SOCIAL AND PERSONALITY DEVELOPMENT IN ADOLESCENCE

Throughout the school day, Maya texts her friends. C U in the caf? Did U C Jeff, OMG! After school, she checks in to her page and the pages of her friends on Facebook. Then she reads blogs and leaves comments on them. After dinner, while doing her homework, she checks out new YouTube videos and Tweets. Then she checks for new apps on her smartphone and calls her best friend for a leisurely chat.

Between Facebook, MySpace, blogs, Twitter, texting, and cell phones, the options for digital communication can often seem limitless. The new avenues for expression and interaction have added still another layer of complication at a stage of life—adolescence—when things were probably already complicated enough. Now teenagers must deal with the stigma of being dumped via text message, or parse the meaning of a potentially romantic posting on a social networking page.

Still, despite the reputation of adolescence as a time of confusion and rebellion, most teenagers pass through the period without much turmoil. Although they may "try on" different roles and flirt with activities that adults in their lives find objectionable, the majority of adolescents find adolescence an exciting time during which friendships grow, intimate relationships develop, and their sense of themselves deepens.

This is not to say that the transitions adolescents pass through are unchallenging. As we shall see in this module, where we discuss personality and social development, adolescence brings about major changes in the ways in which individuals must deal with the world.

We begin by considering how adolescents form their views of themselves. We look at self-concept, self-esteem, and identity development. We also examine two major psychological difficulties: depression and suicide.

Next, we discuss relationships. We consider how adolescents reposition themselves within the family and how the influence of family members declines in some spheres as peers take on new importance. We also examine the ways in which adolescents interact with their friends, and the ways in which popularity is determined.

Finally, the module considers dating and sexual behavior. We look at the role of dating and close relationships in adolescents' lives, and we consider sexual behavior and the standards that govern adolescents' sex lives. We conclude by looking at teenage pregnancy and at programs that seek to prevent unwanted pregnancy.

IDENTITY: ASKING "WHO AM I?"

LO10 How does the development of self-concept, self-esteem, and identity proceed during adolescence?
LO11 What role does religion and spirituality play during adolescence?
LO12 What dangers do adolescents face as they deal with the stresses of adolescence?

"You have no idea how much pressure a 13-year-old has to deal with. You've got to look cool, act cool, wear the right clothes, wear your hair a certain way—and your friends have different ideas about all these things than your parents, know what I mean? And you've got to have friends or you're nobody. And then some of your friends say you're not cool if you don't drink or do drugs, but what if you don't want that? —Anton Merced

The thoughts of 13-year-old Anton Merced demonstrate a clear awareness—and self-consciousness—regarding his new place in society. During adolescence, questions like "Who am I?" and "Where do I belong in the world?" begin to take a front seat.

One reason issues of identity become so important is that adolescents' intellectual capacities become more adult-like. They see how they stack up to others and realize they are individuals, separate from everyone else. The dramatic physical changes of puberty make adolescents acutely aware of their own bodies and aware that others are reacting to them in new ways. Whatever the cause, adolescence brings major changes in teenagers' self-concepts and self-esteem—in sum, their views of their own identity.

Self-Concept: What Am I Like?

Valerie describes herself this way: "Others look at me as laid-back, relaxed, and not worrying too much. But really, I'm often nervous and emotional."

The fact that Valerie distinguishes others' views from her own represents a developmental advance. In childhood, she would have characterized herself by traits that would not differentiate her view from others'. However, when adolescents describe who they are, they take into account both their own and others' views (Cole et al., 2001; Updegraff et al., 2004; Chen et al., 2012).

This broader view of themselves is one aspect of adolescents' increasing sense of identity. They can see various aspects of the self simultaneously, and this view becomes more organized and coherent. They look at the self from a psychological perspective, viewing traits not as concrete entities but as abstractions (Adams, Montemayor, & Gullotta, 1996). For example, teenagers are more likely than younger children to define themselves by their ideology (e.g., "I'm an environmentalist") than by physical characteristics (e.g., "I'm the fastest runner in my class").

In some ways, this broader, multifaceted self-concept can be a mixed blessing, especially during early adolescence. At that time, they may be troubled by the complexity of their personalities. Younger adolescents may want to view themselves in a certain way ("I'm a sociable person and love to be with people."), and they may become concerned when their behavior contradicts that view ("Even though I want to be sociable, sometimes I can't stand being around my friends and just want to be alone."). By the end of adolescence, however, teenagers find it easier to accept that behaviors and feelings change with the situation (Trzesniewski, Donnellan, & Robins, 2003; Hitlin, Brown, & Elder, 2006).

Self-Esteem: How Do I Like Myself?

Although adolescents increasingly perceive who they are (their self-concept), this does not mean they like themselves (their self-esteem). Their increasingly accurate self-concept permits them to see themselves fully—warts and all. It's what they do with these perceptions that determines their self-esteem.

The same cognitive sophistication that differentiates various aspects of the self also leads adolescents to evaluate those aspects in different ways (Chan, 1997; Cohen, 1999). An

Alex Gregory/The New Yorker Collection/www.cartoonbank.com

adolescent may have high self-esteem regarding academic performance, but lower self-esteem in relationships. Or the opposite may apply, as this adolescent notes:

> *How much do I like the kind of person I am? Well, I like some things about me, but I don't like others. I'm glad that I'm popular since it's really important to me to have friends. But in school I don't do as well as the really smart kids. That's OK, because if you're too smart you'll lose your friends. So being smart is just not that important. Except to my parents. I feel like I'm letting them down when I don't do as well as they want. (Harter, 1990, p. 364)*

Gender Differences in Self-Esteem. Several factors determine an adolescent's self-esteem, among them gender. Notably in early adolescence, girls' self-esteem tends to be lower and more vulnerable than boys' (Ah-Kion, 2006; Heaven & Ciarrochi, 2008; McLean & Breen, 2009; Mäkinen et al., 2012).

Compared to boys, girls tend to worry more about physical appearance and social success—as well as academic achievement. Although boys care about these things, their attitudes are often more casual. Stereotypical societal messages suggesting brains and popularity do not mix pose a difficult bind for girls: If girls do well academically, they jeopardize their social success. No wonder their self-esteem is more fragile than boys' (Unger, 2001; Ricciardelli & McCabe, 2003; Ata, Ludden, & Lally, 2007; van den Berg et al., 2010).

Although self-esteem tends to be higher in boys, they have their vulnerabilities too. Gender stereotypes may lead boys to believe they should always be confident, tough, and fearless. Boys facing difficulties (e.g., not making a sports team or being rejected for a date) may feel incompetent as males as well as miserable about their defeat (Pollack, 1999; Pollack, Shuster, & Trelease, 2001).

Socioeconomic Status and Race Differences in Self-Esteem. Socioeconomic status (SES) and race also influence self-esteem. Adolescents of higher SES tend to have higher self-esteem than those of lower SES, especially in middle and later adolescence. Social status factors that enhance one's standing and self-esteem, such as having more expensive clothes or a car, may become more conspicuous at this time (Van Tassel-Baska et al., 1994; Dai et al., 2012).

Race and ethnicity also influence self-esteem, but less biased treatment of minorities has eased their impact. Early studies argued that minority status would lead to lower self-esteem, and this was initially supported by research. African Americans and Hispanics, researchers explained, had lower self-esteem than Caucasians because society's prejudice made them feel disliked and rejected, and this was incorporated into their self-concepts. Most recent research, however, suggests that African American adolescents differ little from whites in their levels of self-esteem (Harter, 1990). One explanation is that social movements within the African American community to bolster racial pride have helped. Research finds that a stronger sense of racial identity is related to higher self-esteem in African Americans and Hispanics (Gray-Little & Hafdahl, 2000; Verkuyten, 2003; Phinney, 2008).

Another reason for a similarity in self-esteem between adolescents of different racial groups is that teenagers tend to focus their preferences and priorities on what they excel at. Consequently, African American youths may concentrate on what they most enjoy and gain self-esteem from their successes in that domain (Gray-Little & Hafdahl, 2000; Yang & Blodgett, 2000; Phinney, 2005).

Self-esteem may be influenced not by race alone, but by a complex combination of factors. Some developmentalists have considered race and gender simultaneously, coining the term *ethgender* to refer to their joint influence. One study that took both race and gender into account found that African American and Hispanic males had the highest levels of self-esteem, while Asian and Native American females had the lowest levels (Biro et al., 2006; Adams, 2010; Park et al., 2012).

Identity Formation: Change or Crisis?

According to Erik Erikson, whose theory we discussed earlier, the search for identity inevitably leads some adolescents to an identity crisis involving substantial psychological turmoil (Erikson, 1963). Erikson's theory of this stage, which is summarized with his other stages in Table 6-2, suggests teenagers try to figure out what is unique and distinctive about themselves—a task they manage with increasing sophistication due to the cognitive gains of adolescence.

Erikson argues that adolescents strive to discover their strengths and weaknesses and the roles that best suit their future lives. This often involves "trying on" different roles or choices to see if they fit their capabilities and views about themselves. In this process, adolescents seek to understand who they are by narrowing and making choices about their personal, occupational, sexual, and political commitments. Erikson calls this the **identity-versus-identity-confusion stage**.

identity-versus-identity-confusion stage the period during which teenagers seek to determine what is unique and distinctive about themselves

TABLE 6-2 A SUMMARY OF ERIKSON'S STAGES

Stage	Approximate Age	Positive Outcomes	Negative Outcomes
1. Trust versus mistrust	Birth–1.5 years	Feelings of trust from others' support	Fear and concern regarding others
2. Autonomy versus shame and doubt	1.5–3 years	Self-sufficiency if exploration is encouraged	Doubts about self; lack of independence
3. Initiative versus guilt	3–6 years	Discovery of ways to initiate actions	Guilt from actions and thoughts
4. Industry versus inferiority	6–12 years	Development of sense of competence	Feelings of inferiority; little sense of mastery
5. Identity versus identity confusion	Adolescence	Awareness of uniqueness of self; knowledge of roles	Inability to identify appropriate roles in life
6. Intimacy versus isolation	Early adulthood	Development of loving, sexual relationships and close friendships	Fear of relationships with others
7. Generativity versus stagnation	Middle adulthood	Sense of contribution to continuity of life	Trivialization of one's activities
8. Ego-integrity versus despair	Late adulthood	Sense of unity in life's accomplishments	Regret over lost opportunities of life

Source: Erikson, 1963.

In Erikson's view, adolescents who do not find a suitable identity may go off course in several ways. They may adopt socially unacceptable roles to express what they do *not* want to be. Forming and maintaining lasting, close relationships may elude them. In general, their sense of self becomes "diffuse," failing to organize around a unified core identity.

In contrast, those who forge an appropriate identity set a foundation for future psychosocial development. They learn their unique capabilities and believe in them, and they develop an accurate sense of self. They are prepared to take full advantage of their unique strengths (Archer & Waterman, 1994; Allison & Schultz, 2001).

Societal Pressures and Reliance on Friends and Peers. Societal pressures are also high during the identity-versus-identity-confusion stage. Adolescents feel pressure from parents and friends to decide whether their post-high-school plans include work or college and, if the former, which occupation to follow. Up to this point, their educational lives have followed a universal track, laid out by U.S. society. However, the track ends at high school, leaving adolescents with difficult choices about which path to follow.

During this period, friends and peers are increasingly sought as sources of information. Dependence on adults declines. As we discuss later, this increasing dependence on peers enables adolescents to forge close relationships. Comparing themselves to others helps to clarify their own identities.

This reliance on peers in defining their own identities and learning to form relationships links this stage of psychosocial development and the next stage Erikson proposed, known as intimacy versus isolation. It also relates to gender differences in identity formation. Erikson suggested that males and females move through the identity-versus-identity-confusion period differently. He argued that males are more likely to experience the social development stages in the order shown in Table 6-2, developing a stable identity before committing to an intimate relationship. In contrast, he suggested that females reverse the order, seeking intimate relationships and then defining their identities through these relationships. These ideas largely reflect the social conditions at the time he was writing, when women were less likely to go to college or establish their own careers and instead often married early. Today, the experiences of boys and girls seem relatively similar during the identity-versus-identity-confusion period.

Psychological Moratorium. Because of the pressures of the identity-versus-identity-confusion period, Erikson suggested that many adolescents pursue a *psychological moratorium*, a period during which they take time off from the upcoming responsibilities of adulthood to explore various roles and possibilities. For example, many college students take a semester or year off to travel, work, or find another way to examine their priorities.

Many adolescents, for practical reasons, cannot pursue a psychological moratorium to leisurely explore various identities. For economic reasons, some must work part-time after school and then take jobs immediately after high school, leaving them little time to experiment. Such adolescents need by no means be psychologically damaged. Successfully holding a part-time job while attending school may offer a psychological reward that outweighs the lack of opportunity to try out various roles.

Limitations of Erikson's Theory. Erikson has been criticized for using male identity development as the standard against which to compare female identity. He saw males as developing intimacy only after achieving a stable identity, which is viewed as the norm. To critics, Erikson's view is based on male-oriented concepts of individuality and competitiveness. Alternatively, psychologist Carol Gilligan suggests that women develop identity while establishing relationships. In this view, the building of caring networks between herself and others is key to a woman's identity (Gilligan, Brown & Rogers, 1990; Gilligan, 2004; Kroger, 2006).

Marcia's Approach to Identity Development: Updating Erikson

Using Erikson's theory as a springboard, psychologist James Marcia suggests that identity can be seen in terms of which of two characteristics—crisis or commitment—is present or absent. *Crisis* is a period in which an adolescent consciously chooses between various alternatives and makes decisions. *Commitment* is psychological investment in a course of action or an ideology. One adolescent might careen from one activity to another, with nothing lasting beyond a few

TABLE 6-3 MARCIA'S FOUR CATEGORIES OF ADOLESCENT DEVELOPMENT

CRISIS/EXPLORATION	COMMITMENT: Present	COMMITMENT: Absent
PRESENT	**Identity achievement** "I enjoyed working at an advertising company the last two summers, so I plan to go into advertising."	**Moratorium** "I'm taking a job at my mom's bookstore until I figure out what I really want to do."
ABSENT	**Identity foreclosure** "My dad says I'm good with kids and would be a good teacher, so I guess that's what I'll do."	**Identity diffusion** "Frankly, I have no idea what I'm going to do."

Source: Based on Marcia, 1980.

weeks, while another becomes totally absorbed in volunteering at a homeless shelter (Marcia, 1980; Peterson, Marcia, & Carpendale, 2004).

After conducting lengthy interviews with adolescents, Marcia proposed four categories of identity (see Table 6-3).

1. **Identity achievement**. Teenagers in this category have successfully explored and thought through who they are and what they want to do. Following a period of crisis during which they considered various alternatives, these adolescents have committed to a particular identity. Teens who have reached this identity status tend to be psychologically healthier, higher in achievement motivation and moral reasoning, than adolescents of any other status.
2. **Identity foreclosure**. These are adolescents who have committed to an identity without passing through a period of crisis in which they explored alternatives. Instead, they accepted others' decisions about what was best for them. Typical of this category is a son who enters the family business because it is expected, or a daughter who becomes a physician because her mother is one. Foreclosers are not necessarily unhappy but they tend to have something called "rigid strength": Happy and self-satisfied, they have a high need for social approval and tend to be authoritarian.
3. **Moratorium**. Adolescents in this category have explored some alternatives but made no commitments. As a result, Marcia suggests, they show relatively high anxiety and experience psychological conflict, though they are often lively and appealing, seeking intimacy with others. Such adolescents typically settle on an identity, but only after a struggle.
4. **Identity diffusion**. These adolescents neither explore nor commit to various alternatives. They tend to shift from one thing to the next. While appearing carefree, according to Marcia, their lack of commitment impairs their ability to form close relationships. They are often socially withdrawn.

According to Marcia's approach, psychologically healthy identity development can be seen in adolescents who choose to commit to a course of action or ideology.

Some adolescents shift among the four categories; for example, moving between moratorium and identity achievement in what is called a "MAMA" cycle (moratorium—identity achievement—moratorium—identity achievement). Or, a forecloser who selected a career path without much thought in early adolescence may reassess and make a more active choice later. For some individuals, identity formation takes place beyond adolescence. However, for most people, identity gels in the late teens and early 20s (Kroger, 2007; Al-Owidha, Green, & Kroger, 2009; Duriez et al., 2012).

identity achievement the status of adolescents who commit to a particular identity following a period of crisis during which they consider various alternatives

identity foreclosure the status of adolescents who prematurely commit to an identity without adequately exploring alternatives

moratorium the status of adolescents who may have explored various identity alternatives to some degree, but have not yet committed themselves

identity diffusion the status of adolescents who consider various identity alternatives, but never commit to one or never even consider identity options in any conscious way

From a social worker's perspective: Do you believe that all four of Marcia's identity statuses can lead to reassessment and different choices later in life? Are there stages in Marcia's theory that may be difficult to achieve for adolescents who live in poverty? Why?

Religion and Spirituality

Ever wonder why God made mosquitoes? How about why God gave Adam and Eve the ability to rebel if He knew how much of a mess it would cause? Can someone be saved and later lose their salvation? Do pets go to heaven?

As exemplified in this blog post, questions of religion and spirituality begin to be asked during adolescence. Religion is important to many people because it offers a formal means of satisfying spirituality needs. *Spirituality* is a sense of attachment to some higher power such as God, nature, or something sacred. Although spirituality needs are typically tied to religious beliefs, they may be independent. Many people who consider themselves to be spiritual individuals do not participate in formal religious practices or are not tied to any particular religion. Because their cognitive abilities increase during adolescence, teenagers are able to think more abstractly about religious matters. Furthermore, as they grapple with general questions of identity, religious identity may be questioned. After having accepted their religious identity in an unquestioning manner during childhood, adolescents may view religion more critically and seek to distance themselves from formal religion. In other cases, they may be drawn more closely to their religious affiliation because it offers answers to such abstract questions as "Why am I here on this earth?" and "What is the meaning of life?" Religion provides a way of viewing the world and universe as having intentional design—a place that was created by something or someone (Kiang, Yip, & Fuligni, 2008; Azar, 2010; Yonker, Schnabelrauch, & DeHaan, 2012).

According to James Fowler, our understanding and practice of faith and spirituality proceeds through a series of stages that extend throughout the lifetime. During childhood, individuals hold a fairly literal view of God and Biblical figures. For example, children may think of God as living at the top of the earth and being able to see what everyone is doing (Fowler & Dell, 2006; Boyatzis, 2013).

In adolescence, the view of spirituality becomes more abstract. As they build their identity, adolescents typically develop a core set of beliefs and values. On the other hand, in many cases, adolescents do not consider their views either in depth or systematically, and it is not until later that they become more reflective.

As they leave adolescence, people typically move into the *individuative-reflective stage* of faith in which they reflect on their beliefs and values. They understand that their views are one of many, and that multiple views of God are possible. Ultimately, the final stage of faith development is the *conjunctive stage*, in which individuals develop a broad, inclusive view of religion and all humanity. They see humanity as a whole, and they may work to promote a common good. In this stage, they may move beyond formal religion and hold a unified view of people across the globe.

Identity, Race, and Ethnicity

Forming an identity is often difficult for adolescents, but it is especially challenging for members of racial and ethnic groups that face discrimination. Society's contradictory values tell adolescents that society should be color blind, that race and ethnic background should not affect opportunities and achievement, and that if they do achieve, society will accept them. Based on a traditional *cultural assimilation model*, this view says individual cultural identities should be assimilated into a unified culture in the United States—the melting-pot model.

In contrast, the *pluralistic society model* suggests that U.S. society is made up of diverse, coequal cultural groups that should preserve their individual features. This model grew from the belief that cultural assimilation denigrates the heritage of minorities and lowers their self-esteem.

According to this view, then, racial and ethnic factors become a central part of adolescents' identity and are not submerged in an attempt to assimilate into the majority culture. From this perspective, identity development includes development of *racial and ethnic identity*—the sense of membership in a racial or ethnic group and the feelings that are associated with that membership. It includes a sense of commitment and ties with a particular racial or ethnic group

(Phinney & Alipuria, 2006; Phinney, 2008). The middle ground says minority group members can form a *bicultural identity*, drawing from their own culture while integrating themselves into the dominant culture. This view suggests that an individual can hold two cultural identities, without having to prefer one over the other (LaFromboise, Coleman, & Gerton, 1993; Shi & Lu, 2007). Choosing a bicultural identity is increasingly common. According to the 2000 U.S. census, a considerable number of individuals see themselves as belonging to more than one race (Schmitt, 2001). The choice of a bicultural identity is increasingly common. In fact, the number of people who identify themselves as belonging to more than one race is considerable, and increased 134 percent from 2000 to 2010 (U.S. Bureau of the Census, 2011).

The process of identity formation is always complex and may be doubly so for minority group members. Racial and ethnic identity takes time to form. For some, it may require a prolonged period, but the result can be a rich, multifaceted identity (Quintana, 2007; Jensen, 2008; Klimstra et al., 2012).

Depression and Suicide: Psychological Difficulties in Adolescence

One day in ninth grade it struck Leanne Taunton that she was stuck without hope inside a dreadful world. "It was like the air was a big weight pressing in on me from all sides. I couldn't shake the feeling and I couldn't ignore it. There was nothing I could do."

A friend listened to her sympathetically and invited her to her basement. "We started doing drugs, using whatever was in the medicine cabinet," her friend recalls. "At first it seemed to offer some relief, but in the end we both had to go home again, if you know what I mean."

For Leanne, the relief also proved short. Too short. One day she grabbed her father's razor, filled up the tub, and slashed her wrists. At the ripe age of 15 she had had enough.

Although the vast majority of teenagers weather the search for identity—as well as other challenges of the age—without major psychological difficulties, some find adolescence very stressful and some develop severe psychological problems. Two of the most serious psychological problems are depression and suicide.

Adolescent Depression. No one is immune to sadness and bad moods, including adolescents. The end of a relationship, failure at an important task, the death of a loved one—all may produce profound feelings of sadness, loss, and grief. In such situations, depression is a typical reaction.

More than a quarter of adolescents report feeling so sad or hopeless for 2 or more weeks in a row that they stop doing their normal activities. Almost two-thirds of teenagers say they have experienced such feelings at some point. In contrast, only a small minority of adolescents—some 3 percent—experience *major depression*, a full-blown psychological disorder that is severe and lingers for long periods (Grunbaum, Lowry, & Kahn, 2001; Galambos, Leadbeater, & Barker, 2004).

Gender, ethnic, and racial differences also affect depression rates. As is true for adults, adolescent girls experience depression more often than boys. Some studies show African American adolescents having a higher rate of depression than white adolescents, though not all research support this conclusion. Native Americans, too, have higher rates of depression (Zahn-Waxler, Shirtcliff, & Marceau, 2008; Sanchez, Lambert, & Ialongo, 2012; Verhoeven, Sawyer, & Spence, 2013).

In cases of severe, long-term depression, biological factors are often involved. Some adolescents do seem genetically predisposed to experience depression, but environmental and social factors related to the extraordinary changes in their social lives also have an impact. An adolescent who loses a loved one to death, for example, or who grows up with an alcoholic or depressed parent is at a higher risk of depression. Being unpopular, having few close friends, and rejection are also associated with adolescent depression (Goldsmith et al., 2002; Eley, Liang, & Plomin, 2004; Zalsman et al., 2006).

Between 25 and 40 percent of girls, and 20 to 35 percent of boys, experience occasional episodes of depression during adolescence, although the incidence of major depression is far lower.

Why the depression rate is higher for girls than boys is puzzling. There is little evidence of a link to hormone differences or a particular gene. Some psychologists speculate that stress is greater for girls in adolescence due to the many, often conflicting, demands of the traditional female role. Recall the girl, quoted in our discussion of self-esteem, who feared academic achievement would endanger her popularity. Such conflict may make her feel helpless. Add to this the fact that traditional gender roles still give higher status to men than

The rate of adolescent suicide has tripled in the last 30 years. These students attend a memorial for a classmate who committed suicide.

women (Gilbert, 2004; Hyde, Mezulis, & Abramson, 2008; Chaplin, Gillham, & Seligman, 2009).

Girls' higher levels of depression in adolescence may reflect gender differences in coping with stress, rather than differences in mood. Girls may be more likely to react to stress by turning inward, resulting in a sense of helplessness and hopelessness. In contrast, boys more often externalize the stress and act more impulsively or aggressively, or turn to drugs and alcohol (Wisdom Agnor, 2007; Wu et al., 2007; Brown et al., 2012).

Adolescent Suicide. Adolescent suicide in the United States has tripled in the last 30 years. One teenage suicide occurs every 90 minutes, for an annual rate of 12.2 suicides per 100,000 adolescents. The reported rate may actually understate the true number; parents and medical personnel often prefer to report a death as an accident rather than suicide. Even so, suicide is the third most common cause of death for 15- to 24-year-olds, after accidents and homicide. Despite this rise in suicide—more than for other age groups—the highest rate is still found in late adulthood (Grunbaum et al., 2002; Joe & Marcus, 2003; Conner & Goldston, 2007).

The rate of adolescent suicide is higher for boys, although girls *attempt* suicide more frequently. Attempts among males are more likely to be fatal because boys tend to use more violent means, such as guns, while girls tend to choose less violent means, such as drug overdose. Some estimates suggest there are as many as 200 attempted suicides by both sexes for every successful one (Joseph, Reznik, & Mester, 2003; Dervic et al., 2006; Pompili et al., 2009).

The reasons for the increase in adolescent suicide are unclear. The most obvious explanation is that adolescent stress has increased (Elkind, 1994). But why should stress have increased only for teenagers? The suicide rate for other age groups has remained fairly stable over the same period. Though we are not yet sure why adolescent suicide has increased, certain factors raise the risk. Depression is one. Depressed teenagers who feel profound hopelessness are at greater risk for suicide (although most depressed individuals do not commit suicide). Social inhibition, perfectionism, and high levels of stress and anxiety are also related to an increased risk. The easy availability of guns—more prevalent in the United States than in other industrialized nations—contributes to the suicide rate as well (Wright, Wintemute, & Claire, 2008; Arnautovska & Grad, 2010; Hetrick et al., 2012).

Some suicide cases are associated with family conflicts and relationship or school difficulties. Some stem from a history of abuse and neglect. The rate of suicide among drug and alcohol abusers is also relatively high. As shown in Figure 6-10, teens who called a hotline because they were considering suicide mentioned other factors as well (Lyon et al., 2000; Bergen, Martin, & Richardson, 2003; Wilcox, Conner, & Caine, 2004; Xing et al., 2010).

Some suicides appear to be caused by exposure to the suicide of others. In *cluster suicide*, one suicide leads to attempts by others to kill themselves. For instance, some high schools have experienced a series of suicides following a well-publicized case. As a result, many schools have established crisis intervention teams to counsel students when one student commits suicide (Arenson, 2004; Insel & Gould, 2008; Daniel & Goldston, 2009). There are several warning signs of potential suicide. Among them are the following:

- Direct or indirect talk about suicide, such as "I wish I were dead" or "You won't have me to worry about any longer"
- School difficulties, such as missed classes or a decline in grades
- Making arrangements as if preparing for a long trip, such as giving away prized possessions or arranging for the care of a pet
- Writing a will
- Loss of appetite or excessive eating
- General depression, including a change in sleeping patterns, slowness and lethargy, and uncommunicativeness
- Dramatic changes in behavior, such as a shy person suddenly acting outgoing
- Preoccupation with death in music, art, or literature.

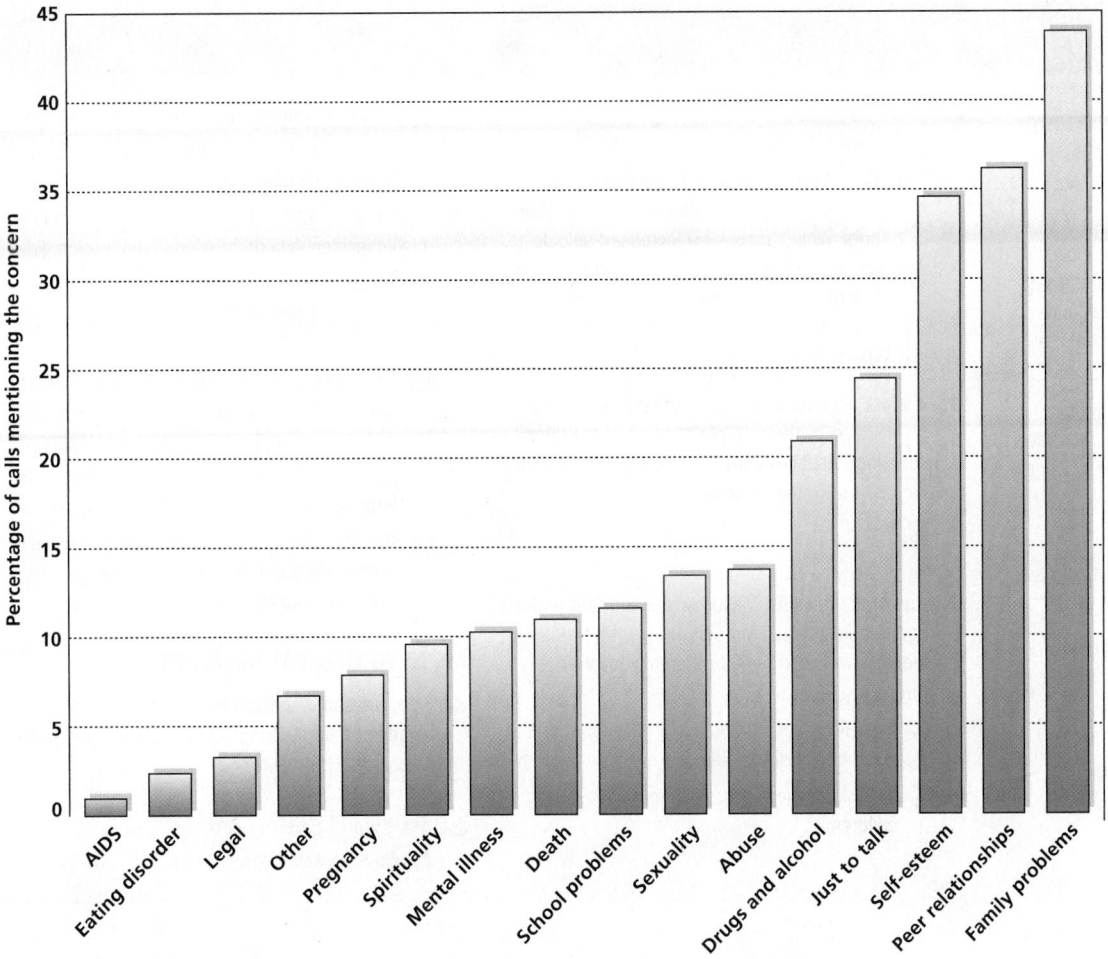

FIGURE 6-10 Adolescent Difficulties
Family, peer relationships, and self-esteem problems were most often mentioned by adolescents contemplating suicide, according to a review of phone calls to a telephone help line.
Source: Based on Boehm & Campbell, 1995.

Becoming an Informed Consumer of Development

Preventing Adolescent Suicide

If you suspect an adolescent, or anyone else, is contemplating suicide, act! Here are several suggestions:

- Talk to the person. Listen with understanding and without judging.
- Talk specifically about suicidal thoughts; ask questions such as: Do you have a plan? Have you bought a gun? Where is it? Have you stockpiled pills? Where are they? The Public Health Service notes that, "contrary to popular belief, such candor will not give a person dangerous ideas or encourage a suicidal act."
- Try to distinguish between general upset and more serious danger, as when suicide plans *have* been made. If the crisis is acute, *do not leave the person alone*.
- Be supportive, let the person know you care, and try to break down his or her feelings of isolation.
- Take charge of finding help. Do not fear invading the person's privacy. Do not try to handle the problem alone. Get professional help immediately.
- Make the environment safe, removing (not just hiding) weapons such as guns, razors, scissors, medication, and other potentially dangerous items.
- Do not keep suicide talk or threats secret; these are calls for help and call for immediate action.
- Do not challenge, dare, or use verbal shock treatment on the person to correct his or her thinking.
- Make a contract with the person, getting a promise or commitment, preferably in writing, not to attempt suicide until you have talked further.
- Don't be overly reassured by a sudden improvement of mood. Such quick "recoveries" may be merely the relief of deciding to commit suicide or the temporary release of talking to someone; most likely, the underlying problems have not been resolved.

For immediate help with a suicide-related problem, call (800) 784-2433 or (800) 621-4000, national hotlines staffed with trained counselors.

REVIEW, CHECK, AND APPLY

REVIEW

L010 How does the development of self-concept, self-esteem, and identity proceed during adolescence?

- Self-concept during adolescence grows more differentiated as the view of the self becomes more organized, broader, and more abstract, and takes account of the views of others.
- Both Erikson's identity-versus-identity-confusion stage and Marcia's four identity statuses focus on the adolescent's struggle to determine an identity and a role in society.

L011 What role does religion and spirituality play during adolescence?

- Spirituality is a sense of attachment to some higher power such as God, nature, or something sacred.
- Because of an increase in their cognitive abilities, adolescents think more abstractly about religion and their religious identity.

L012 What dangers do adolescents face as they deal with the stresses of adolescence?

- One of the dangers that adolescents face is depression, which affects girls more than boys. While reasons for increased suicide among adolescents are unclear, depression has been found to be one risk factor.

CHECK YOURSELF

1. It is not uncommon for younger adolescents to be troubled by the multiple aspects of their personalities, especially when these aspects appear inconsistent with one another.
   - True
   - False
2. One of the reasons Erikson suggested that males and females moved through the identity-versus-identity-confusion period differently involved the _____.
   - a inherent genetic differences between men and women related to goals and needs.
   - b lack of apparent interest men had in raising children.
   - c social conditions at the time he was writing.
   - d lack of effort expended by women in reaching goals as compared to men.
3. Which of the following hypotheses may explain the higher incidence of depression in adolescent girls?
   - a Stress is more pronounced for girls due to the conflicting demands of the traditional female role.
   - b Females traditionally are less able to deal with stress than are males.
   - c Females are more likely to turn to drugs and alcohol than are males; therefore, their problems are more apparent.
   - d Parents are more concerned and protective of their daughters than their sons; therefore, they notice depression in girls earlier.

APPLYING LIFESPAN DEVELOPMENT

- What are some consequences of the shift from reliance on adults to reliance on peers? Are there advantages? Dangers?

✓ **Study** and **Review** on **MyPsychLab.com**

RELATIONSHIPS: FAMILY AND FRIENDS

L013 How do relationships between adolescents and their parents change?
L014 What does it mean to be popular and unpopular in adolescence, and how do adolescents respond to peer pressure?
L015 How do race and gender figure into adolescent relationships?

When Paco Lizzagara entered junior high school, his good relationship with his parents changed drastically. Paco felt his parents were always "on his case." Instead of giving him the freedom he felt he deserved at age 13, they seemed to be more restrictive. Paco's parents saw things differently. They felt that they were not the source of tension in the house—he was. In their eyes, Paco, with whom they'd always enjoyed a stable, loving relationship, suddenly seemed transformed. They saw him shutting them out, and when he did speak with them, he criticized their politics, their dress, and their preferences in TV shows. To his parents, Paco's behavior was upsetting and bewildering.

Family Ties: Changing Relations With Relations

The social world of adolescents is far wider than that of younger children. As relationships outside the home grow in significance, interactions with family evolve, taking on a new, and sometimes difficult, character (Collins & Andrew, 2004).

The Quest for Autonomy. Parents are sometimes angered, and more frequently puzzled, by adolescents' conduct. Children who previously accepted their parents' judgments, declarations, and guidelines begin to question—and sometimes rebel against—their parents' views.

One cause of these clashes is the shifting roles children and parents confront during adolescence. Adolescents seek **autonomy**, independence and a sense of control over their lives. Most parents intellectually view this shift as a normal part of adolescence—a primary

autonomy having independence and a sense of control over one's life developmental task of the period—and in many ways they welcome it as a sign of growth. However, the day-to-day realities of adolescents' increasing autonomy may prove difficult for them to deal with (Smetana, 1995). Intellectually appreciating this growing independence and allowing a teen to attend an unsupervised party are two different things. To the adolescent, her parents' refusal indicates a lack of trust or confidence. To the parents, it's simply good sense: "I trust you," they may say. "It's the others who will be there that I worry about."

In most families, teenagers' autonomy grows gradually over the adolescent years. One study of adolescents' changing views of their parents found that as autonomy increases, parents are seen more realistically as persons in their own right. For example, rather than seeing their parents as authoritarian disciplinarians mindlessly reminding them to do their homework, they may come to see their parents' emphasis on excelling in school as evidence of parental regrets about their own lack of education and a wish to see their children have more options in life. At the same time, adolescents come to depend more on themselves and to feel more like separate individuals.

The increase in adolescent autonomy changes the parent–child relationship, which tends to be asymmetrical in early adolescence, when parents hold most of the power and influence. By the end of adolescence, power and influence are more balanced; the relationship is more egalitarian, although parents typically retain the upper hand (Goede, Branje, & Meeus, 2009).

Culture and Autonomy. The degree of autonomy achieved varies from one family to the next. Cultural factors play a role. In Western societies, which value individualism, adolescents seek autonomy at a relatively early stage. In contrast, Asian societies are more collectivistic, believing the welfare of the group is above that of the individual. In such societies, adolescents' aspirations to autonomy are less pronounced (Raeff, 2004; Supple et al., 2009; Perez-Brena, Updegraff, & Umaña-Taylor, 2012).

From a social worker's perspective: In what ways do you think parents with different styles—authoritarian, authoritative, permissive, and uninvolved—react to attempts to establish autonomy during adolescence? Are the styles of parenting different for a single parent? Are there cultural differences?

Compared with adolescents from more individualistic societies, adolescents from more collectivistic cultures tend to feel greater obligation to their families.

A sense of obligation to family also varies among cultures. In collectivistic cultures, adolescents tend to feel a greater obligation to fulfill their family's expectations—to provide assistance, show respect, and offer financial support. In such societies, the push for autonomy is weaker and its development is slower (Chao, 2001; Fuligni & Zhang, 2004; Leung, Pe-Pua, & Karnilowicz, 2006).

The extended timetable for autonomy in collectivistic cultures appears to have no negative consequences for adolescents. What matters is the match between cultural expectations and developmental patterns, not the specific timetable (Rothbaum et al., 2000; Zimmer-Gembeck & Collins, 2003; Updegraff et al., 2006).

Gender also plays a role. In general, male adolescents are permitted more autonomy at an earlier age than females. This is consistent with traditional gender stereotypes, in which males are seen as more independent and females as more dependent on others. In fact, parents who hold traditional views on gender are less likely to encourage their daughters' autonomy (Bumpus, Crouter, & McHale, 2001).

The Myth of the Generation Gap. Teen movies often depict adolescents and their parents in total opposition, victims of a **generation gap**, a deep divide in attitudes, values, aspirations, and world views. For example, the parent of an environmentalist might turn out to own a polluting factory. These exaggerations are funny because they contain a truth—parents and teenagers often see things differently.

generation gap a divide between parents and adolescents in attitudes, values, aspirations, and world views

The reality, however, is another matter. The generation gap, when it exists, is really quite narrow. Adolescents and their parents tend to agree on many things. Republican parents

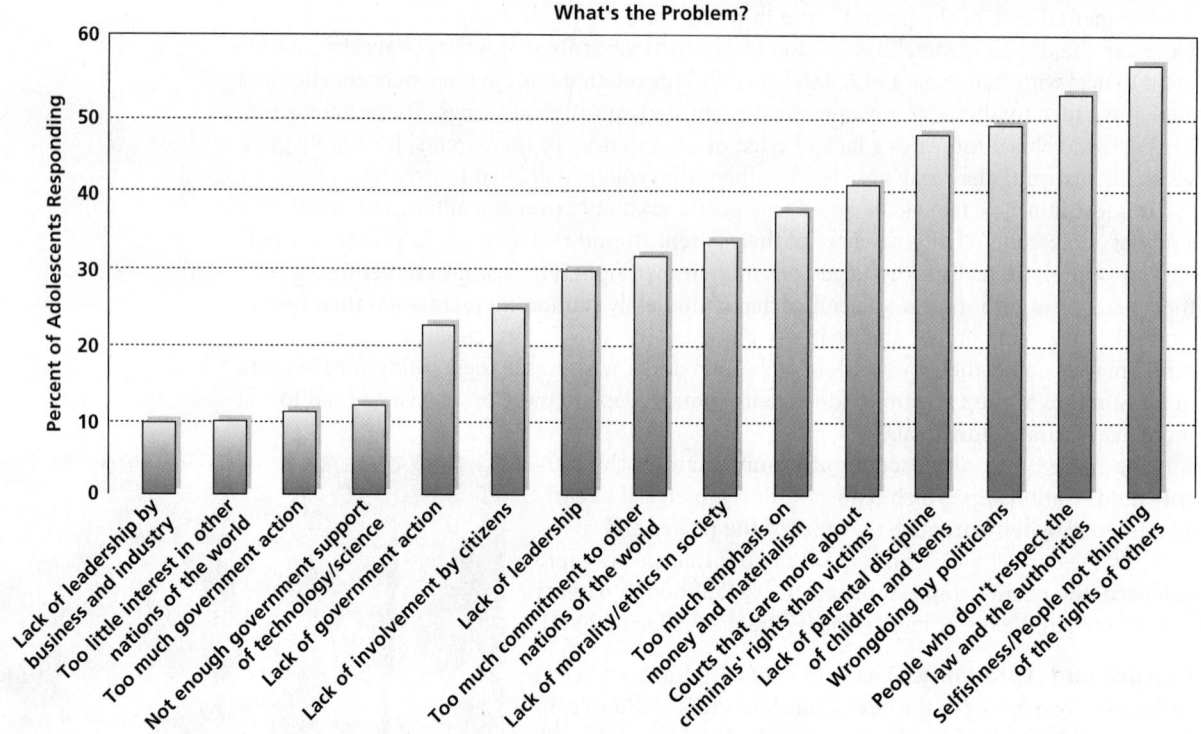

FIGURE 6-11 What's the Problem?
Adolescents' views of society's ills are ones with which their parents would be likely to agree.
Source: Based on PRIMEDIA/Roper National Youth Survey, 1999.

generally have Republican children; members of the Christian right have children with similar views; parents who advocate for abortion rights have children who are pro-choice. On social, political, and religious issues, parents and adolescents tend to be in synch, and children's worries mirror those of their parents. Adolescents' concerns about society's problems (see Figure 6-11) reflect those of many adults (Knafo & Schwartz, 2003; Smetana, 2005; Grønhøj & Thøgersen, 2012).

Most adolescents and their parents get along quite well. Despite their quest for autonomy and independence, most teenagers have deep love, affection, and respect for their parents—as their parents do for them. Although some parent–adolescent relationships are seriously troubled, the majority are positive and help adolescents avoid the kind of peer pressure discussed later in the module (Gavin & Furman, 1996; Resnick et al., 1997; Black, 2002; Riesch et al., 2010).

Even though teenagers spend less time with their families in general, the amount of time they spend alone with each parent remains remarkably stable across adolescence (see Figure 6-12).

There is no evidence that suggests family problems are worse in adolescence than at other stages of development (Steinberg, 1993; Larson et al., 1996; Granic, Hollenstein, & Dishion, 2003).

Conflicts With Parents. Of course, if most adolescents get along with their parents most of the time, that means sometimes they don't. No relationship is always smooth. Parents and teens may agree about social and political issues, but they often differ on matters of personal taste, such as music and clothing. Also, parents and children may disagree when children act on their autonomy and independence sooner than parents feel is right. Consequently, parent–child conflicts are more likely to occur during adolescence, particularly in the early stages, although not every family is affected to the same degree (Arnett, 2000; Smetana, Daddis, & Chuang, 2003).

According to developmental psychologist Judith Smetana, conflict is greater in early adolescence because of differing definitions of, and rationales for, appropriate and inappropriate conduct. Parents may frown on multiple ear piercings because society traditionally deems it inappropriate, while adolescents may view the issue as one of personal choice (Smetana, 2005, 2006; Rote et al., 2012).

The newly sophisticated reasoning of adolescents (discussed in the previous module) leads them to regard parental rules in more complex ways. Arguments that might convince a school-age child ("Do it because I tell you to do it.") are less compelling to an adolescent.

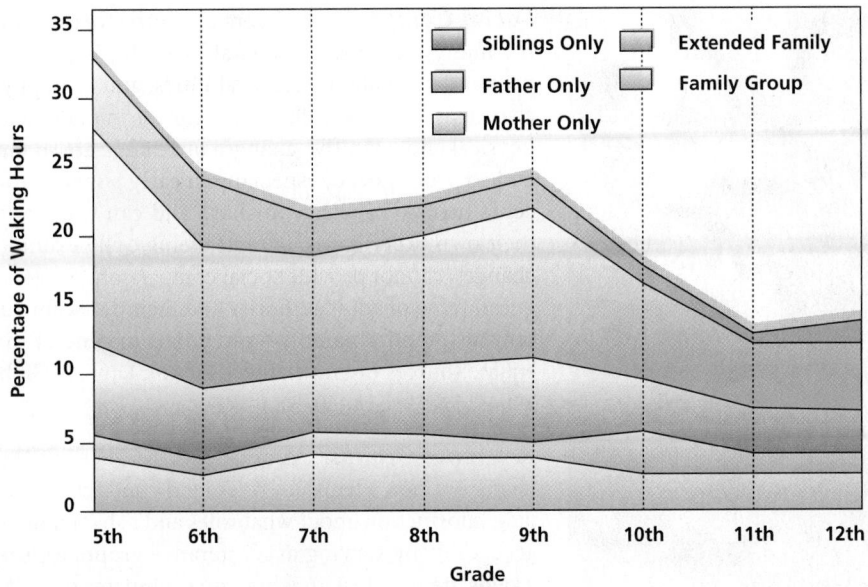

FIGURE 6-12 Time Spent by Adolescents With Parents
Despite their quest for autonomy and independence, most adolescents have deep love, affection, and respect for their parents, and the amount of time they spend alone with each parent (the lower two segments) remains remarkably stable across adolescence.
Source: From Reed Larson et al., Developmental Psychology. Copyright © 1996 by the American Psychological Association. Reproduced with permission.

The argumentativeness and assertiveness of early adolescence may at first increase conflict, but they play a key role in the evolution of parent–child relationships. While parents may initially react defensively to their children's challenges and grow inflexible and rigid, in most cases they come to realize their children *are* growing up and they want to support them in that process.

As parents realize that their children's arguments are often compelling and fairly reasonable, and that they can be trusted with more freedom, they become more yielding, allowing and perhaps even encouraging independence. As this process occurs in mid-adolescence, the conflict of the early years declines.

This does not hold true for all adolescents. The majority of teenagers maintain stable relations with their parents, but as many as 20 percent pass through a fairly rough time (Dryfoos, 1990; Dmitrieva et al., 2004).

Cultural Differences in Parent–Child Conflicts During Adolescence. Parent–child conflicts are found in every culture, but there does seem to be less conflict between parents and teenagers in "traditional," preindustrial cultures. Teens in such cultures experience fewer mood swings and instances of risky behavior than teens in industrialized countries (Arnett, 2000; Nelson, Badger, & Wu, 2004; Kapadia, 2008; Eichelsheim et al., 2010).

The reason may be the degree of independence that adolescents expect and adults permit. In more industrialized societies, with an emphasis on individualism, independence is expected of adolescents. Consequently, adolescents and their parents must negotiate the amount and timing of that independence—a process that often leads to strife. In more traditional societies, individualism is less valued; therefore, adolescents are less inclined to seek independence. The result is less parent–child conflict (Dasen, 2000, 2002) **Watch** the **Video** *Adolescent Conflict with Parents Across Cultures* in **MyPsychLab**.

Relationships With Peers: The Importance of Belonging

For many parents, the key symbols of adolescence are the cell phone and the computer. For their children, communicating with friends is an indispensable lifeline, a compulsive need that underscores their significance at this stage. Continuing the trend from middle childhood, adolescents spend increasing hours with their peers as these relationships grow in importance. In fact, there is probably no period of life in which peer relationships matter as much as in adolescence (Youniss & Haynie, 1992).

The sex segregation of childhood continues during the early stages of adolescence. However, by the time of middle adolescence, this segregation decreases, and boys' and girls' cliques begin to converge.

Social Comparison. Peers become more important for many reasons. They enable adolescents to compare and evaluate opinions, abilities, and even physical changes—a process called *social comparison*. Because the physical and cognitive changes of this age are so unique and so pronounced, especially in early puberty, adolescents turn to others who share and can shed light on their own experiences. Parents, being well beyond these changes, cannot provide social comparison. Adolescents' questioning of adult authority and their desire for autonomy also render parents—and adults in general—inadequate sources of knowledge (Rankin, Lane, & Gibbons, 2004; Li & Wright, 2013).

Reference Groups. As noted, adolescence is a time of trying out new identities, roles, and conduct. Peers provide information about what roles and behavior are most acceptable by serving as a reference group. **Reference groups** are people with whom one compares oneself. Just as a professional ballplayer compares his performance to that of other pro players, so do teenagers compare themselves to peers similar to them.

Reference groups offer a set of *norms*, or standards, by which abilities and social success can be judged. A teenager need not belong to a group for it to serve as a reference. Unpopular adolescents, belittled and rejected by members of a popular group, may yet use it as a reference group (Berndt, 1999).

Cliques and Crowds: Belonging to a Group. Increased cognitive sophistication allows adolescents to group others in more discriminating ways. Even if they do not belong to their reference group, they typically are part of some identifiable group. Rather than defining people in concrete terms by what they do ("football players" or "musicians") as a younger child might, adolescents use more abstract terms ("jocks" or "skaters" or "stoners") (Brown, 2004).

Adolescents form two types of groups: cliques and crowds. **Cliques** are groups of from 2 to 12 people whose members have frequent social interactions with one another. **Crowds** are larger, comprising individuals who share certain characteristics but do not necessarily interact. "Jocks" and "nerds" represent crowds found in many high schools.

Membership in a clique or a crowd is determined by the degree of similarity with other members. One key similarity is substance use; adolescents tend to choose friends whose alcohol and drug use matches their own. Their friends often mirror their academic success and general behavior patterns, although this is not always true. For instance, in early adolescence, peers who are aggressive may be more attractive than those who are well behaved (Kupersmidt & Dodge, 2004; Hutchinson & Rapee, 2007; Kiuru et al., 2009).

The emergence of distinct cliques and crowds at this stage reflects adolescents' increased cognitive capabilities. Group labels are abstractions, requiring teens to judge people they may seldom interact with and have little direct knowledge about. It is not until mid-adolescence that teenagers are cognitively able to make the subtle judgments that distinguish between different cliques and crowds (Burgess & Rubin, 2000; Brown & Klute, 2003; Witvliet et al., 2010).

reference groups groups of people with whom one compares oneself

cliques groups of from 2 to 12 people whose members have frequent social interactions with one another

crowds larger groups than cliques, composed of individuals who share particular characteristics but who may not interact with one another

sex cleavage sex segregation in which boys interact primarily with boys and girls primarily with girls

Gender Relations. As children enter adolescence, their social groups are composed almost universally of same-sex friends. Boys hang out with boys; girls hang out with girls. This sex segregation is called the **sex cleavage**.

The situation changes with the onset of puberty. Boys and girls experience the hormonal surge that causes the sex organs to mature. At the same time, society suggests it is time for romantic involvement. These developments change the ways the opposite sex is viewed. Where a 10-year-old is likely to see every member of the other sex as "annoying" and "a pain," heterosexual teenage boys and girls regard each other's personality and sexuality with greater interest. (For gays and lesbians, pairing off holds other complexities, as we will see when we discuss adolescent dating.)

In early puberty, boys' and girls' cliques, previously on parallel but separate tracks, begin to converge. Adolescents attend boy–girl dances or parties, although the boys still tend to socialize with boys, and the girls with girls (Richards et al., 1998). Soon, adolescents spend more time with the other sex. New cliques emerge, composed of both genders. Not everyone participates initially: Early on, the leaders of the same-sex cliques and those with the highest status lead the way. Eventually, however, most teenagers belong to mixed-gender cliques. At the end of adolescence, cliques and crowds become less influential. Many dissolve as pairing off occurs.

Popularity and Rejection

Most adolescents are highly tuned in to who is popular and who is not. In fact, for some, popularity—or lack of it—is the central focus of their lives.

The social world of adolescents is more complex than who is popular or unpopular. Some adolescents are controversial. In contrast to *popular* adolescents, who are mostly liked, **controversial adolescents** are liked by some and disliked by others. A controversial adolescent may be highly popular within a particular group, such as the string orchestra, but less so among other classmates. There are also **rejected adolescents**,

controversial adolescents children who are liked by some peers and disliked by others.

rejected adolescents children who are actively disliked, and whose peers may react to them in an obviously negative manner

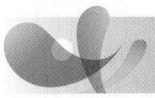

Cultural Dimensions

Race Segregation: The Great Divide of Adolescence

When Robert Corker, *a student at Tufts University, first stepped into the gym, he was immediately pulled into a pick-up basketball game. "The guys thought I'd be good at basketball just because I'm tall and black. Actually, I stink at sports and quickly changed their minds. Fortunately we all laughed about it later," Robert says.*

***

When *Sandra Cantú*, a Puerto Rican nursing student at the University of Alabama, entered the cafeteria wearing her hospital whites, two female students assumed she was a cafeteria worker and asked her to clear off their table.

***

Race relations are no easier for white students to manage. Ted Connors, a white senior at Southern Methodist, recalls the day he asked a student in his dorm for help with his Spanish homework. "He laughed in my face," Ted recalls, "I assumed he spoke Spanish just because his name was Gonzalez. Actually, he had grown up in Michigan and spoke only English. It took quite a while to live that one down."

The pattern of racial misunderstanding experienced by these students is repeated over and over in schools and colleges throughout the United States. Even when they attend desegregated schools with significant diversity, people of different ethnicities and races interact very little. Moreover, even if they have a friend of a different ethnicity within the confines of a school, most adolescents don't interact with that friend outside of school (DuBois & Hirsch, 1990).

***

It doesn't start out this way. During elementary school and early adolescence, integration is common among students of differing ethnicities. However, by middle and late adolescence, students segregate (Spencer & Dornbusch, 1990; Ennett & Bauman, 1996).

Why is racial and ethnic segregation the rule, even in schools that have long been desegregated? One reason is that minority students may seek support from others who share their status (where "minority," used in its sociological sense, indicates a subordinate group lacking power compared to a dominant group). By associating with others of their own group, members of minority groups are able to affirm their own identity.

Members of different racial and ethnic groups may be segregated in the classroom as well. As discussed earlier, members of groups that have experienced discrimination tend to be less successful in school. Thus, ethnic and racial segregation in high school may be based on academic achievement rather than ethnicity.

Lower academic performance may place minority students in classes with fewer majority students, and vice versa. Such class assignment practices may maintain and promote racial and ethnic segregation, especially in schools where rigid academic tracking assigns students to "low," "medium," and "high" tracks depending on their prior achievement (Lucas & Berends, 2002).

Segregation in school may also reflect prejudice, both perceived and real, toward members of other groups. Students of color may feel that the white majority is discriminatory and hostile, and thus prefer to stick to same-race groups. White students may assume that minority students are antagonistic and unfriendly. Such mutually destructive attitudes make meaningful interaction difficult (Phinney, Ferguson, & Tate, 1997; Tropp, 2003).

Is this voluntary racial and ethnic segregation inevitable? No. Adolescents who have interacted regularly and extensively with other races in childhood are more likely to have friends of different races. Schools that actively promote integration in classes create an environment that fosters cross-race friendships (Hewstone, 2003).

Still, many societal pressures prevent social integration. Peer pressure, too, may discourage clique members from crossing racial and ethnic lines to form new friendships.

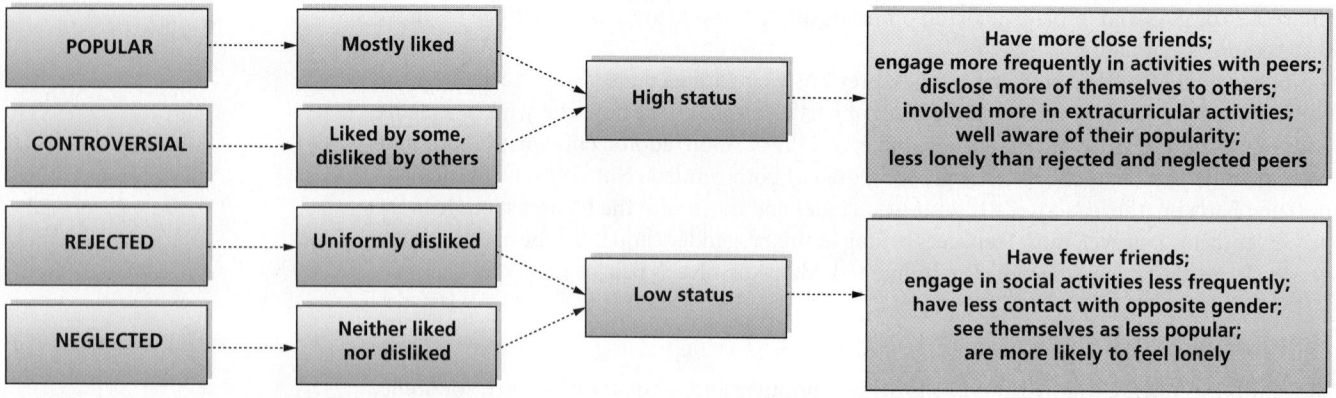

FIGURE 6-13 The Social World of Adolescence
An adolescent's popularity can fall into one of four categories, depending on the opinions of his or her peers. Popularity is related to differences in status, behavior, and adjustment.

Unpopular adolescents fall into several categories. Controversial adolescents are liked by some and disliked by others; rejected adolescents are uniformly disliked; and neglected adolescents are neither liked nor disliked.

neglected adolescents children who receive relatively little attention from their peers in the form of either positive or negative interactions

who are uniformly disliked, and **neglected adolescents**, who are neither liked nor disliked (see Figure 6-13)—whose status is so low everyone overlooks them.

In most cases, popular and controversial adolescents tend to enjoy a higher status, while rejected and neglected teenagers share a lower status. Popular and controversial adolescents have more close friends, engage in more activities with their peers, and disclose more about themselves than less popular students. They participate in more extracurricular school activities. Well aware of their own popularity, they are less lonely than their less popular classmates (Farmer et al., 2003; Zettergren, 2004; Becker & Luthar, 2007; Closson, 2009).

The social world of rejected and neglected adolescents is far less pleasant. They have fewer friends, engage in fewer social activities, and have less contact with the opposite sex. They see themselves—accurately—as less popular, and they are more likely to feel lonely (McElhaney, Antonishak, & Allen, 2008; Woodhouse, Dykas, & Cassidy, 2012).

As illustrated in Table 6-4, men and women differ in their ideas of what determines status in high school. College men suggest that appearance is what most determines a girl's status, while college women believe it is her grades and intelligence (Suitor et al., 2001).

TABLE 6-4 HIGH SCHOOL STATUS

According to College Men		According to College Women	
High-status high-school girls:	**High-status high-school boys:**	**High-status high-school girls:**	**High-status high-school boys:**
1. Are good-looking	1. Take part in sports	1. Have high grades and are intelligent	1. Take part in sports
2. Have high grades and are intelligent	2. Have high grades and are intelligent	2. Participate in sports	2. Have high grades and are intelligent
3. Take part in sports	3. Are popular with girls	3. Are sociable	3. Are sociable
4. Are sociable	4. Are sociable	4. Are good-looking	4. Are good-looking
5. Are popular with boys	5. Have nice cars	5. Have nice clothes	5. Participate in school clubs or government

Note: Results are based on responses from students at Louisiana State University, Southeastern Louisiana University, State University of New York at Albany, State University of New York at Stony Brook, University of Georgia, and the University of New Hampshire.

Source: Based on Suitor et al., 2001.

Conformity: Peer Pressure in Adolescence

Whenever Aldos Henry said he wanted a particular brand of sneakers or a certain style of shirt, his parents blamed it on peer pressure and told him to think for himself.

In arguing with Aldos, his parents were taking a view prevalent in U.S. society: that teenagers are highly susceptible to **peer pressure**, the pressure to conform to the behavior and attitudes of one's peers. Were his parents correct?

Adolescents *are* highly susceptible to the influence of their peers when considering what to wear, whom to date, and what movies to see. Wearing the right clothes, down to the right brand, can be a ticket to popularity. It shows you know what's what. But when it comes to nonsocial matters, such as choosing a career path or trying to solve a problem, they are more likely to consult an adult (Phelan, Yu, & Davidson, 1994).

Especially in middle and late adolescence, teenagers look to those they see as experts. For social concerns, they turn to the experts—their peers. For arenas where adults hold the knowledge, teenagers tend to ask their advice and accept their opinions (Perrine & Aloise-Young, 2004; Choo & Shek, 2013).

Overall, susceptibility to peer pressure does not suddenly soar in adolescence. Instead, adolescence changes the source of influence. Whereas children conform fairly consistently to their parents, pressures to conform to peers increase in adolescence as teens establish an identity apart from their parents.

Ultimately, adolescents conform less to both peers *and* adults as their autonomy increases. As their confidence grows and they are able to make their own decisions, adolescents are apt to act independently and to reject pressures from others. Before they learn to resist peer pressure, however, teenagers may get into trouble, often along with their friends (See also "From Research to Practice" box; Steinberg & Monahan, 2007; Cook, Buehler, & Henson, 2009; Monahan, Steinberg, & Cauffman, 2009).

peer pressure the influence of one's peers to conform to their behavior and attitudes

From Research to Practice

R U Friends 4 Real?: Are Digital Communications Changing Teenagers' Friendships?

"Ugh, Eddie Kane is such a jerk!" Marissa exclaimed. "I know," her best friend Camille chimed in. "But he's cute!" They both laughed. "Should I tell him you said that?" joked Marissa. "What? No!" Camille responded emphatically. "You're such a jerk!" They both laughed again.

It as a typical conversation for two 15-year-old girls riding the bus to school. But Marissa and Camille weren't sitting next to each other. They weren't even on the same bus. They were conversing on Facebook. Marissa opened with a status update; Camille commented on it. Their shared laughter was typed "lol"s and "ha ha"s. "Know" became "no," "what" became "wut," and "you're" became "ur."

Adolescents' mode of communication is rapidly changing. Communication is less personal, and emotion and other nuances of conversations are more difficult to convey. Recently collected data from the Pew Research Center show that text messaging has overtaken every other form of interaction between teenagers. Two-thirds of teens would rather use their cell phone to text their friends than to call them. And social networking has gotten big, too, rivaling face-to-face conversations in popularity (Lenhart, 2010; Novotney, 2012).

One issue that has grabbed a lot of attention is the rise of sexting, in which teens share nude or sexually suggestive photos of themselves via text messages. But the sensationalism of sexting masks a more basic issue—that these new communication channels are leading adolescents to communicate in fundamentally different ways. More nuanced, protracted give and take conversations that take place in face-to-face get-togethers are being replaced with context-free snippets of abbreviated textual phrases. The result may be that adolescents are missing out on the kinds of connections that help them to learn social cues, nuanced emotional expressions, and nonverbal communication such as body language and facial expressions (Small & Vorgan, 2008; Stout, 2010; Ling, Bertel, & Sundsoy, 2012).

On the other hand, some researchers focus on possible benefits of these new ways of communicating. They make staying in touch a lot easier, which may mean young people are actually sharing more of themselves more often. And digital communication can be used as a tool to facilitate real-world social interaction, as when word spreads of social events. Finally, communication channels that are a bit less direct and personal are often attractive to shy people—texting and social networking may be a less threatening way for shy teens to expand their social circles. But until more research is done, we won't know for sure how technology is changing the nature of adolescents' friendships (Richtel, 2010; Stout, 2010; Drouin & Landgraff, 2012).

- *New communication technologies have emerged continually over the last hundred-plus years—what reason is there to be particularly concerned about texting?*
- *If the way in which adolescents relate to each other is better suited to the latest technology than to older ways of communicating, why is that a bad thing?*

Undersocialized delinquents are raised with little discipline or by harsh, uncaring parents, and they begin antisocial activities at a relatively early age. In contrast, socialized delinquents know and usually follow the norms of society, and they are highly influenced by their peers.

undersocialized delinquents adolescent delinquents who are raised with little discipline or with harsh, uncaring parental supervision

socialized delinquents adolescent delinquents who know and subscribe to the norms of society and who are fairly normal psychologically

Juvenile Delinquency: The Crimes of Adolescence

Adolescents, along with young adults, commit more crimes than any other age group. This is a somewhat misleading statistic: Because certain behaviors (such as drinking) are illegal for adolescents, it is easy for them to break the law. But even disregarding such crimes, adolescents are disproportionately responsible for violent crimes, such as murder, assaults, and rape, and property crimes involving theft, robbery, and arson.

What steers adolescents toward criminal activity? Some offenders, known as **undersocialized delinquents**, were raised with little discipline or by harsh, uncaring parents. Although they are influenced by peers, their parents did not teach them appropriate social behavior or how to regulate their own conduct. Undersocialized delinquents typically begin criminal activities well before the onset of adolescence (Hoeve et al., 2008; Thomas, 2010).

Undersocialized delinquents share several characteristics. They tend to be aggressive and violent early in life, leading to peer rejection and academic failure. They are more likely to have been diagnosed with attention deficit hyperactivity disorder as children, and they tend to be less intelligent than average (Silverthorn & Frick, 1999; Rutter, 2003).

Undersocialized delinquents often suffer from psychological problems, and as adults fit a pattern called antisocial personality disorder. They are unlikely to be successfully rehabilitated, and many undersocialized delinquents live on the margins of society their entire lives (Frick et al., 2003; Peach & Gaultney, 2013).

A larger group of adolescent offenders are socialized delinquents. **Socialized delinquents** know and subscribe to the norms of society; they are fairly normal psychologically. For them, offenses committed in adolescence do not lead to a life of crime. Instead, most socialized delinquents engage in some petty crimes (such as shoplifting) during adolescence, but do not continue into adulthood.

Socialized delinquents are typically highly peer influenced, their delinquency often occurring in groups. Some research also suggests that their parents supervise their behavior less than other parents. But these minor delinquencies are often a result of giving in to group pressure or seeking to establish one's identity as an adult (Fletcher et al., 1995; Thornberry & Krohn, 1997).

REVIEW, CHECK, AND APPLY

REVIEW

L013 How do relationships between adolescents and their parents change?

- The search for autonomy may change relations between teenagers and their parents, temporarily creating conflict in some cases, but the generation gap is narrower than is generally thought.

L014 What does it mean to be popular and unpopular in adolescence, and how do adolescents respond to peer pressure?

- Cliques and crowds serve as reference groups in adolescence, offering a means of social comparison. Sex cleavage gradually diminishes, until boys and girls begin to pair off.
- In early adolescence, adolescents may be highly susceptible to peer pressure, especially regarding what clothes to wear or movies to see, but as they mature and their confidence grows, adolescents look less to others and more to themselves in making decisions.

L015 How do race and gender figure into adolescent relationships?

- Racial separation increases in adolescence, bolstered by socioeconomic status differences, different academic experiences, and mutually distrustful attitudes. Sex cleavage eventually dissolves as most teenagers join mixed gender cliques.

CHECK YOURSELF

1. Depending on one's cultural framework, some adolescents may expect less autonomy from their parents than will others.
   - True
   - False
2. _____ are people with whom one compares oneself. For example, teens would compare themselves to other teens.
   - a Cliques
   - b Crowds
   - c In-groups
   - d Reference groups
3. Cross-sex cliques begin forming _____.
   - a once parents and teachers begin rewarding students for cross-sex interactions.
   - b once the leaders in the same-sex cliques begin dating.
   - c after sixth grade.
   - d when same-sex peers become bored with one another.

APPLYING LIFESPAN DEVELOPMENT

- Thinking back to your own high school days, what was the dominant clique in your school, and what factors were related to group membership?

✓ **Study** and **Review** on **MyPsychLab.com**

DATING, SEXUAL BEHAVIOR, AND TEENAGE PREGNANCY

LO16 What are the functions and characteristics of dating during adolescence?
LO17 How does sexuality develop in the adolescent years?

It took him almost a month, but Sylvester Chiu finally got up the courage to ask Jackie Durbin to the movies. It was hardly a surprise to Jackie, though. Sylvester had first told his friend Erik about his plans, and Erik had told Jackie's friend Cynthia, who had in turn told Jackie, who was primed to say "yes" when Sylvester finally called.

Welcome to the complex world of adolescent dating, an important ritual in the liturgy of adolescent relationships.

Dating: Close Relationships in the Twenty-First Century

Changing cultural factors largely determine when and how adolescents begin to date. Until recently, exclusive dating was a cultural ideal, viewed in the context of romance. Society encouraged dating as a way for adolescents to explore relationships that might lead to marriage. Today, some adolescents believe that dating is outmoded and limiting, and in some places *hooking up*—a vague term that covers everything from kissing to sexual intercourse—is regarded as more appropriate. Still, despite changing cultural norms, dating remains the dominant form of social interaction that leads to intimacy among adolescents (Denizet-Lewis, 2004; Manning, Giordano, & Longmore, 2006; Bogle, 2008).

The Functions of Dating. Dating is a way to learn how to establish intimacy with another individual. It can provide entertainment and, depending on the status of the person one is dating, prestige. It even can be used to develop a sense of one's own identity (Zimmer-Gembeck & Gallaty, 2006; Friedlander et al., 2007; Paludi, 2012).

Unfortunately, dating, at least in early and middle adolescence, does not serve the function of developing intimacy very well. On the contrary, it is often a superficial activity in which the participants rarely let down their guards and never expose themselves emotionally. Psychological intimacy may be lacking even when sex is part of the relationship (Savin-Williams & Berndt, 1990; Collins, 2003; Furman & Shaffer, 2003).

True intimacy becomes more common during later adolescence. At that point, both participants may take dating more seriously as a way to select a possible mate for marriage.

For homosexual adolescents, dating presents special challenges. In some cases, blatant homophobic prejudice expressed by classmates may lead gays and lesbians to date members of the other sex in an effort to fit in. If they do seek relationships with other gays and lesbians, they may find it difficult to find partners, who may not openly express their sexual orientation. Homosexual couples who do openly date face possible harassment, making the development of a relationship all the more difficult (Savin-Williams, 2003, 2006).

Dating, Race, and Ethnicity. Culture influences dating patterns among adolescents of different racial and ethnic groups, particularly those whose parents have immigrated from other countries. Foreign-born parents may try to control dating behavior to preserve traditional values or confine dating to their own racial or ethnic group.

Asian parents may hold especially conservative attitudes because they themselves may be living in an arranged marriage and may never have experienced dating. They may insist that there will be no dating without chaperones, a position that will inevitably lead to conflict with their children (Hamon & Ingoldsby, 2003; Hoelter, Axinn, & Ghimire, 2004; Lau et al., 2009).

Sexual Relationships

The hormonal changes of puberty trigger not only the maturation of the sexual organs, but also a new range of feelings. Sexual behavior and thoughts are among the central concerns of adolescents, occupying the minds of almost all adolescents a good deal of the time (Kelly, 2001; Ponton, 2001).

Masturbation. Often the first sex act in which adolescents engage is solitary sexual self-stimulation, or masturbation. By age 15, 80 percent of teenage boys and 20 percent of teenage girls report that they have masturbated. In males, frequency is high in the early teens and then begins to decline, while in females, frequency is lower initially and increases throughout adolescence. There are also racial differences. For example, African American men and women masturbate less than whites (Schwartz, 1999; Hyde & DeLamater, 2004).

Although masturbation is widespread, it still may produce feelings of shame and guilt, a legacy from years of misguided views. In the nineteenth century, people were warned about the horrible effects of masturbation, including "dyspepsia, spinal disease, headache, epilepsy, various kinds of fits,... impaired eyesight, palpitation of the heart, pain in the side and bleeding at the lungs, spasm of the heart, and sometimes sudden death" (Gregory, 1856). Suggested remedies included bandaging the genitals, covering them with a cage, tying the hands, male circumcision without anesthesia (so that it might better be remembered), and for girls, the administration of carbolic acid to the clitoris. One physician, J. W. Kellogg, believed that certain grains would be less likely to provoke sexual excitation—leading to his invention of corn flakes (Hunt, 1974; Michael et al., 1994).

Today, experts on sexual behavior view masturbation as a normal, healthy, and harmless activity. In fact, some suggest that it provides a useful way to learn about one's own sexuality (Hyde & DeLamater, 2003; Levin, 2007).

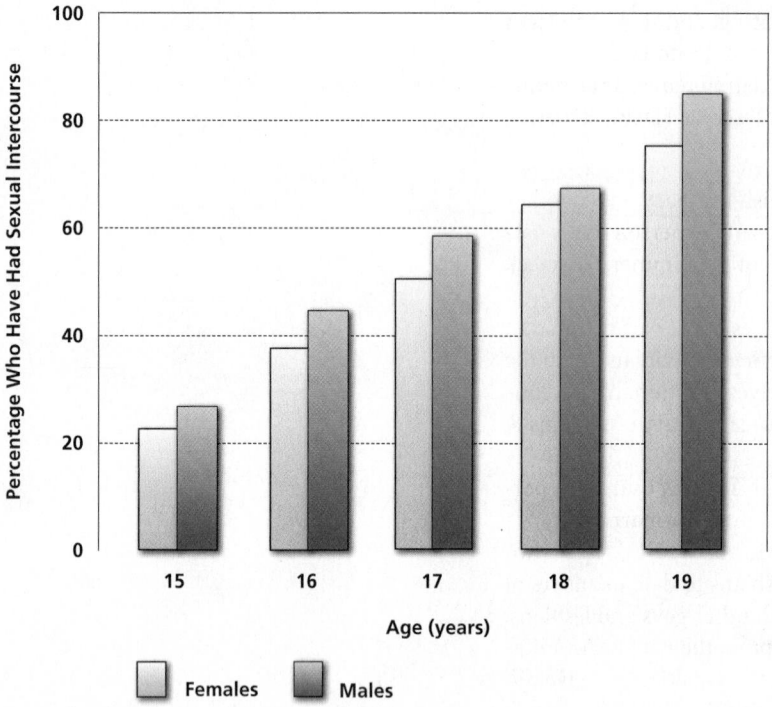

FIGURE 6-14 Adolescents and Sexual Activity
The age at which adolescents have sexual intercourse for the first time is declining, and about three-quarters have had sex before the age of 20.
Source: Morbidity and Mortality Weekly Report, 2008.

Sexual Intercourse. Although it may be preceded by many different types of sexual intimacy, including deep kissing, massaging, petting, and oral sex, sexual intercourse remains a major milestone in the perceptions of most adolescents. Consequently, the main focus of researchers investigating sexual behavior has been on the act of heterosexual intercourse.

The average age at which adolescents first have sexual intercourse has been steadily declining over the last 50 years, and about one in five adolescents have had sex before the age of 15. Overall, the average age of first sexual intercourse is 17, and around three-quarters of adolescents have had sex before the age of 20 (see Figure 6-14). At the same time, though, many teenagers are postponing sex, and the number of adolescents who say they have never had sexual intercourse increased by 13 percent from 1991 to 2007 (MMWR, 2008; Guttmacher Institute, 2012).

There also are racial and ethnic differences in timing of initial sexual intercourse: African Americans generally have sex for the first time earlier than do Puerto Ricans, who have sex earlier than whites do. These racial and ethnic differences likely reflect differences in socioeconomic conditions, cultural values, and family structure (Singh & Darroch, 2000; Hyde & DeLamater, 2008).

Strong societal norms govern sexual conduct. A few decades ago the prevailing norm was the *double standard*: Premarital sex was permissible for males but not females, but men should be sure to marry virgins. Today the double standard has begun to give way to *permissiveness with affection*. Under this standard, premarital intercourse is permissible for both men and women in the context of a long-term, committed, or loving relationship (Hyde & Delamater, 2004; Earle et al., 2007).

From the perspective of a health care provider: A parent asks you how to prevent her 14-year-old son from engaging in sexual activity until he is older. What would you tell her?

The demise of the double standard is far from complete. Attitudes toward sexual conduct are still typically more lenient for males than for females, even in socially liberal cultures. And in some cultures, the standards for men and women are quite distinct. For example, in North Africa, the Middle East, and the majority of Asian countries, women are expected to abstain from sexual intercourse until they are married. In Mexico, males are considerably more likely than females to have premarital sex. In contrast, in sub-Saharan Africa, women are more likely to have sexual intercourse before marriage, and intercourse is common among unmarried teenage women (Johnson et al., 1992; Peltzer & Pengpid, 2006; Wellings et al., 2006; Ghule, Balaiah, & Joshi, 2007).

Sexual Orientation: Heterosexuality, Homosexuality, and Bisexuality

When we consider adolescents' sexual development, the most frequent pattern is *heterosexuality*, sexual attraction and behavior directed to the other sex. Yet some teenagers are *homosexual*, in which their sexual attraction and behavior is oriented to members of their own sex. (Many male homosexuals prefer the term *gay* and female homosexuals the label *lesbian*, because they refer to a broader array of attitudes and lifestyle than the term *homosexual*, which focuses on the sexual act.) Other people find they are *bisexual*, sexually attracted to people of both sexes.

Many teens experiment with homosexuality. Around 20 to 25 percent of adolescent boys and 10 percent of adolescent girls have at least one same-sex sexual encounter. In fact, homosexuality and heterosexuality are not completely distinct sexual orientations. Alfred Kinsey, a pioneer sex researcher, argued that sexual orientation should be viewed as a continuum in which "exclusively homosexual" is at one end and "exclusively heterosexual" is at the other. In between are people who show both homosexual and heterosexual behavior. Although accurate figures are difficult to obtain, most experts believe that between 4 percent and 10 percent of both men and women are exclusively homosexual during extended periods of their lives (Kinsey, Pomeroy, & Martin, 1948; McWhirter, Sanders, & Reinisch, 1990; Michael et al., 1994; Diamond, 2003a, 2003b; Russell & Consolacion, 2003).

Sexuality is further complicated by the distinction between sexual orientation, which refers to a person's sexual interests, and gender identity—the gender a person believes he or she is psychologically. Sexual orientation and gender identity are not necessarily related to one another: A man with a strong masculine gender identity may be attracted to other men, and traditional "masculine" or "feminine" behavior is not necessarily related to a person's sexual orientation or gender identity (Hunter & Mallon, 2000).

Some people feel they have been born the wrong physical sex (e.g., believing that they are a woman trapped in a man's body). These *transgendered* individuals may pursue sexual reassignment surgery, a prolonged course of treatment in which they receive hormones and reconstructive surgery to enable them to take on the physical characteristics of the other sex. **Watch** the **Video** *Thinking Like a Psychologist: Sexual Orientation* in **MyPsychLab**.

What Determines Sexual Orientation? The factors that induce people to develop as heterosexual, homosexual, or bisexual are not well understood. Evidence suggests that genetic and biological factors play a central role. Identical twins are more likely to both be homosexual than pairs of siblings who don't share their genetic makeup. Other research finds that various structures of the brain are different in homosexuals and heterosexuals, and hormone production also seems to be linked to sexual orientation (Ellis et al., 2008; Fitzgerald, 2008).

In the past, some theoreticians suggested that family or peer environmental factors play a role. For example, Freud argued that homosexuality was the result of inappropriate identification with the opposite-sex parent (Freud, 1922/1959). The difficulty with Freud's theoretical perspective and other, similar perspectives that followed is that there simply is no research evidence to suggest that any particular family dynamic or childrearing practice is consistently related to sexual orientation. Similarly, explanations based on learning theory, which suggest that homosexuality arises because of rewarding, pleasant homosexual experiences and unsatisfying heterosexual ones, are not supported by research (Bell & Weinberg, 1978; Isay, 1990; Golombok & Tasker, 1996).

In short, there is no accepted explanation of why some adolescents develop a heterosexual orientation and others a homosexual orientation. Most experts believe that sexual orientation develops out of a complex interplay of genetic, physiological, and environmental factors (LeVay & Valente, 2003).

Challenges Facing Gay and Lesbian Adolescents. Adolescents who are attracted to members of the same sex face a more difficult time than other teens. U.S. society still

This 16-year-old mother and her child are representative of a major social problem: teenage pregnancy. Why is teenage pregnancy a greater problem in the United States than in other countries?

harbors ignorance and prejudice about homosexuality, insisting that people have a choice in the matter—which they do not. Gay and lesbian teens may be rejected by their family or peers and harassed or even assaulted by others. As a result, adolescents who are homosexual are at greater risk for depression, with suicide rates significantly higher than for heterosexual adolescents. Gays and lesbians who do not conform to gender stereotypes are particularly susceptible to victimization, and they have lower rates of adjustment (Silenzio et al., 2007; Bos et al., 2008; Toomey et al., 2010; Madsen & Green, 2012).

Ultimately, though, most people become comfortable with their sexual orientation. And while lesbian, gay, and bisexual adolescents may experience mental health difficulties, homosexuality is not considered a psychological disorder by any of the major psychological or medical associations. All of them endorse efforts to reduce discrimination against homosexuals. Furthermore, society's attitudes toward homosexuality are changing, particularly among younger individuals. For example, a majority of U.S. citizens now favor the legalization of gay marriage (Davison, 2005; Russell & McGuire, 2006; Baker & Sussman, 2012).

Teenage Pregnancies

Feedings at 3:00 AM, diaper changes, and visits to the pediatrician are not part of most people's vision of adolescence. Yet, every year, tens of thousands of adolescents in the United States give birth. The good news, though, is that the number of teenage pregnancies has decreased significantly in the last 2 decades. In fact, in 2012, the birth rate for U.S. teenagers was the lowest level ever reported in the seven decades that the government has been tracking pregnancies (see Figure 6-15). Birth rates declined to historic lows in all racial and ethnic groups, but disparities remain, with the rate of teenage births higher for non-Hispanic blacks and Hispanics than for whites. Overall, the pregnancy rate of teenagers is 34.3 births per 1,000 (Colen, Geronimus, & Phipps, 2006; Hamilton et al., 2009; Hamilton & Ventura, 2012).

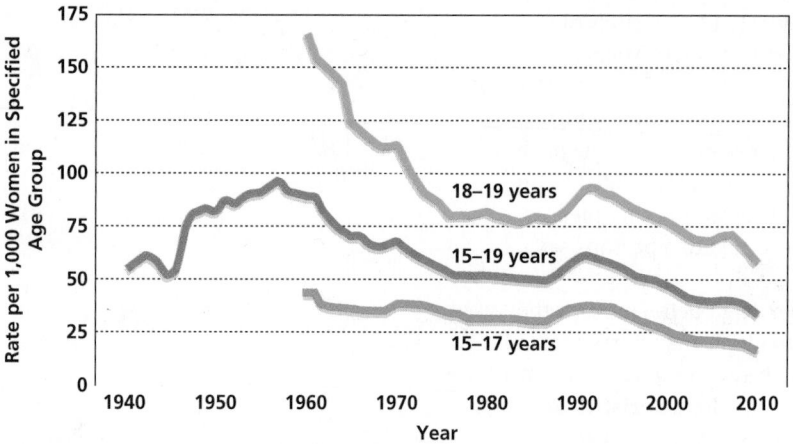

FIGURE 6-15 Teenage Pregnancy Rates
Although there has been a small increase in recent years, the rate of teenage pregnancies has dropped dramatically among all ethnic groups since 1991.
Source: Hamilton & Ventura, 2012.

Several factors explain the drop in teenage pregnancies:

- New initiatives have raised awareness of the risks of unprotected sex. For example, about two-thirds of U.S. high schools have comprehensive sex education programs (Villarosa, 2003; Corcoran & Pillai, 2007).
- The rates of sexual intercourse among teenagers have declined. The percent of teenage girls who have ever had sexual intercourse dropped from 51 percent in 1988 to 43 percent in 2006–2010 (Martinez, Copen, & Abma, 2011).
- The use of condoms and other forms of contraception has increased. For example, virtually all sexually experienced girls aged 15–19 have used some method of contraception (Martinez, Copen, & Abma, 2011).
- Substitutes for sexual intercourse may be more prevalent. For example, data from the 1995 National Survey of Adolescent Males found that about half of 15- to 19-year-old boys reported having received oral sex, an increase of 44 percent since the late 1980s. It is possible that oral sex, which many teenagers do not even consider "sex," may increasingly be viewed as an alternative to sexual intercourse (Bernstein, 2004).

One thing that apparently hasn't led to a reduction in teenage pregnancies is asking adolescents to take a virginity pledge. These public pledges—a centerpiece of some forms of sex education—apparently are ineffective. In one study of 12,000 teenagers who had taken the pledge, 88 percent reported eventually having sexual intercourse. However, pledges did delay the start of sex an average of 18 months (Bearman & Bruckner, 2004).

An unintended pregnancy can be devastating to mother and child. Teenage mothers today are much less likely than in earlier years to be married. In many cases, mothers care for their children without the help of the father. Lacking financial and emotional support, the mother may have to abandon her own education and be relegated to unskilled, poorly paying jobs for the rest of her life. In some cases, she may develop long-term dependency on welfare. Furthermore, her physical and mental health may suffer as she faces unrelenting stress from the continual demands on her time (Manlove et al., 2004; Gillmore et al., 2006; Oxford et al., 2006).

REVIEW, CHECK, AND APPLY

REVIEW

LO16 What are the functions and characteristics of dating during adolescence?

- Dating in adolescence serves a number of functions, including intimacy, entertainment, and prestige.
- Sexual intercourse is a major milestone that most people reach during adolescence. The age of first intercourse reflects cultural differences and has been declining over the last 50 years.

LO17 How does sexuality develop in the adolescent years?

- Sexual orientation, which is most accurately viewed as a continuum rather than categorically, develops as the result of a complex combination of factors.

CHECK YOURSELF

1. Dating has several functions in adolescence. Check all that apply.
   - a It usually leads to marriage.
   - b It provides entertainment.
   - c It can provide prestige depending on the status of the person one is dating.
   - d It assists in developing identity.
   - e It is a way to learn how to establish intimacy.
2. Overall, _____ of adolescents begin having intercourse between the ages of 15 and 18.
   - a 20 percent
   - b 10 percent
   - c 70 percent
   - d 50 percent
3. Which of the following factors are considered influential in reducing the teenage birth rate? Check all that apply.
   - a Awareness in teens has increased concerning the risks of unprotected sex.
   - b Teens are more likely to take the virginity pledge.
   - c Teens are using condoms and other forms of contraceptives at higher rates.
   - d Teens are so involved in school and sports activities that there is less time for sexual intercourse.
   - e Adolescents are engaging in sexual behaviors other than sexual intercourse.
   - f The rates of sexual intercourse among teens have declined.

APPLYING LIFESPAN DEVELOPMENT

- What aspects of the social world of adolescents work against the achievement of true intimacy in dating?

✓ **Study** and **Review** on **MyPsychLab.com**

SUMMARY

PUTTING IT ALL TOGETHER ADOLESCENCE

FROM AGE 13 TO AGE 18, Julie, the young woman we met in the chapter opener, evolved from a young adolescent consumed with her social status to a mature teenager capable of defining her own "cool." In mid-adolescence, she abused alcohol and let her grades go to be popular, but she got a wake-up call when she failed her junior year. She knew she was smart so she began making smart choices. She left her old school for one that specialized in the arts and joined a club dedicated to something she was good at—fiction writing. She enrolled in a summer workshop for teen writers where she connected with adults who could help her. She completed a novel. When it was rejected, she wrote another and started college. Her second book won a contract. Julie had weathered adolescence successfully.

PHYSICAL DEVELOPMENT IN ADOLESCENCE

MODULE 6.1

- Adolescents have many physical issues to deal with. *(pp. 254–258)*
- Julie's concern about her appearance is typical in adolescence, especially for girls, when the body changes and normal weight gain puberty brings can cause anxiety. *(p. 256)*
- Adolescent brain development, including the growth of the prefrontal cortex of the brain, permitted Julie to think about and evaluate the behavior of her old friends in comparison to the new identity she wished to have. Such complex thinking, emerging in adolescence, can sometimes lead to confusion. *(p. 260)*
- The pressure to be popular led Julie to abuse alcohol—a major threat to the well-being of adolescents. *(pp. 263–265)*

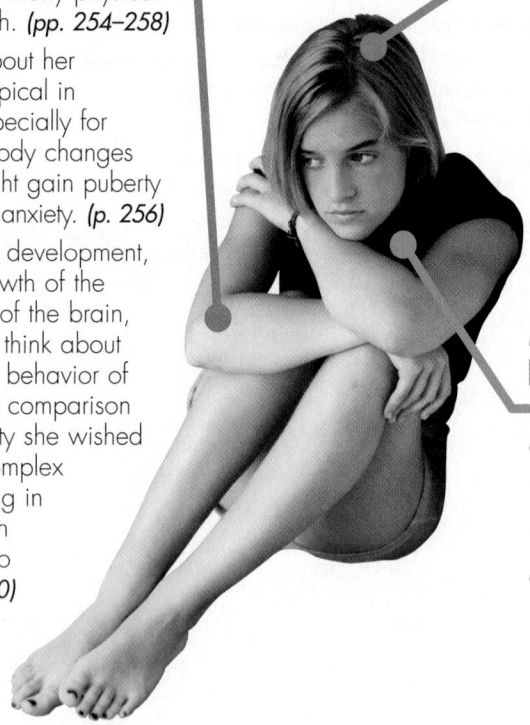

COGNITIVE DEVELOPMENT IN ADOLESCENCE

MODULE 6.2

- Adolescents' personal fables can make them feel invulnerable to risk, as Julie felt when she started drinking to be cool. *(pp. 272–273)*
- Julie's awareness of what she values in herself and her ability to reflect on what gives her the most joy exemplify adolescents' advanced mental abilities. *(pp. 269–271)*

SOCIAL AND PERSONALITY DEVELOPMENT IN ADOLESCENCE

MODULE 6.3

- Julie's devotion to connecting with the in crowd typifies the great importance of peer relationships in adolescence. *(pp. 291–294)*
- Though Julie knows her parents love her, she was annoyed when they checked her room for alcohol and fought with her about her dropping grades in school. Such conflicts often occur in early adolescence when teens are struggling for autonomy and independence. *(pp. 290–291)*
- For Julie, being smart and making independent choices became positive, key aspects of her identity, answering the question, "Who am I?" *(pp. 279–283)*
- Julie thinks she has to be part of the in crowd to have high self-esteem, but her social status is not the only factor that affects her feelings about herself. *(pp. 280–282)*
- Julie's enrollment in a fiction writing workshop and her subsequent decision to publish a novel is an example of Marcia's *identity achievement*. *(pp. 282–283)*

What would a PARENT do?

Was Julie's parents' anger at their daughter's late hours and drinking the best response to the problem? In what ways did they show their love for Julie? In what ways might they have been more supportive?

What would a HEALTH CARE WORKER do?

Julie's concern with popularity drove her to make poor decisions about using alcohol. How could a health care provider help Julie to understand the risks she was taking? Should suggestions include advice about how to socialize without drinking when alcohol is readily available?

What would YOU do?

If you were Julie's friend, how would you offer encouragement and support for the independent decisions she's making? Do you think your friendship would survive her choosing path different from yours?

What would an EDUCATOR do?

If you were Julie's writing instructor, how would you help her prepare for a career in fiction writing ? Would you advise her to develop other interests and experiment more before choosing a career path?

Explore on MyPsychLab

To read how real parents, health care workers, and educators responded to these questions, log onto MyPsychLab.com.

Do you agree or disagree with their responses? Why? What concepts that you've read about back up their opinion?

7 EARLY ADULTHOOD

Petra Tarkif, 26, and Mo Wright, 27, work as sales clerks for an office supply chain. They've been living together for 4 years. Both of them are college graduates with degrees that, as Mo says, "have no visible relationship with what we're doing."

"We need to take stock" says Petra. "We're nearly 30 with nothing to show for it but a couple of low-level jobs. We should be doing something better with our lives."

"Right," Mo chimes in. "We've been talking about getting married and having kids, but to do that we'd really like to buy a house, which we can't afford on our salaries. One idea we've talked about is to move to a bigger city and look for better jobs, but houses are even more expensive in big cities."

"Meanwhile the clock is ticking," says Petra. "We want to be young parents, healthy and active enough to keep up with our kids." She looks at Mo. "You've talked about business school, and I'd like to become a computer technician, but going back to school would take more time and money than we can afford."

Mo pulls out some papers. "Maybe there's a way. I talked to Doug, our manager. He says the company offers career training for management and technical jobs. He thinks we're good candidates for the program and he'll recommend both of us, if we want. Maybe we should see if they'll put their money where their mouth is. At least we'll feel we're doing something."

Early adulthood, the period from approximately age 20 to 40, is a time of continued development. In fact, young adults like Petra and Mo face some of the most pressing questions they will ever face and experience considerable stress as they answer them.

At their physical peak in their 20s, they are on the threshold of the worrisome 30s, when the body begins to send messages of decline and to exact a price for excess and inattention. Cognitively, most have stopped their formal learning, but some want to take it up again either in college or in some other setting. Socially, young adults are often settling into a career, and sometimes they have to consider whether the path they are on is right for them after all. And they still have to answer the really big questions about marriage and children. Staring so many weighty decisions in the face can cause a great deal of stress in young adults.

In fact, some psychologists believe that the beginning of early adulthood can be characterized as a special stage of development known as emerging adulthood. *Emerging adulthood* is the period beginning in the late teenage years and extending into the mid-20s. Although they are no longer adolescents, people in their early 20s are not fully adults because they haven't fully taken on the responsibilities of adulthood. Instead, they are still seeking to identify who they are and what course their life will follow (Arnett, 2007; Tanner, Arnett, & Leis, 2009).

In this chapter, we'll look at the physical, cognitive, and social and personality changes that accompany young adulthood. This period of life, in which people are too often considered "developed" rather than "developing," in fact harbors many changes. Like Petra and Mo, young adults continue to develop throughout the period.

MODULE 7.1

PHYSICAL DEVELOPMENT IN EARLY ADULTHOOD

How does stress affect the body? What are some strategies for coping with stress?

MODULE 7.2

COGNITIVE DEVELOPMENT IN EARLY ADULTHOOD

What does gender bias in the classroom look like?

MODULE 7.3

SOCIAL AND PERSONALITY DEVELOPMENT IN EARLY ADULTHOOD

Is love the only thing that matters in seeking a spouse?

MyVirtualLife

If you are currently using MyVirtualLife, consider how you will navigate early adulthood. What decisions will you make?

Access MyVirtualLife for a chance to live your own virtual life.

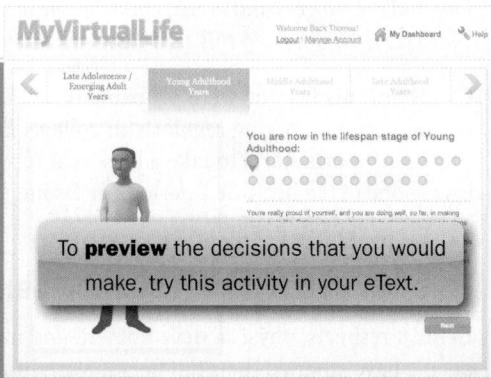

To **preview** the decisions that you would make, try this activity in your eText.

MODULE 7.1

PHYSICAL DEVELOPMENT IN EARLY ADULTHOOD

I first met Marcus Robinson as he was lazily taking shots on the basketball court at the local playground. I must have been staring at his prosthetic leg, because he opened with, "Afghanistan, four years ago. Want to shoot hoops?"

I could hardly say no. "Fine," I said.

He flipped me the ball, saying "Your shot." I drove for the basket and he stepped in front of me to block me. I avoided contact to spare his leg and took an awkward shot, which missed badly. When he took the ball, he drove for the basket and I set up to block him. He came hard and ran right into me, knocking me flat.

As he helped me up he said quietly, "When we play, we play. Don't patronize me by backing off, okay?"

"Right," I said, laughing. After that we played like two regular guys, and he won as often as I did. I found out the hard way that he was missing a leg, not a heart.

As the speaker learned, many people have disabilities, and focusing on what they lack instead of what they have is itself a kind of disability. Regarding such people as disadvantaged may diminish them and cause the observer to miss their complexity and individuality.

Most people in early adulthood are at their physical peak. For them, the body acts as if it's on automatic pilot: Physical health and fitness are never better. Still, there are others who have mild or severe disabilities, and they too are developing during this period. And often, aside from the area of their disability, they too are at their peak.

Physical development proceeds throughout early adulthood, which starts at the end of adolescence (around age 20) and continues until roughly the start of middle age (around age 40). As we see throughout this chapter, significant changes occur as new opportunities arise and people choose to take on (or forgo) new roles in society.

This module focuses on physical development during this period. It begins with a look at the physical changes that extend into early adulthood. Though more subtle than the physical changes of adolescence, growth continues and various motor skills change as well. We look at diet and weight, examining the prevalence of obesity in this age group. We also consider what other health risks young adults face. Next, we look at physical disabilities and the ways that people deal with them. Finally, we discuss stress and coping during the early years of adulthood.

PHYSICAL DEVELOPMENT

LO1 How does the body develop during early adulthood?
LO2 What risks do young adults face?

Grady McKinnon grinned as his mountain bike left the ground briefly. The 27-year-old financial auditor was delighted to be out for a camping and biking weekend with four of his college buddies. Grady had been worried that an upcoming deadline at work would make him miss this trip. When they were still in school, Grady and his friends used to go biking nearly every weekend. But jobs and marriage—and even a child for one of the guys—started taking up a lot of their attention. This was their only trip this summer. He was sure glad he hadn't missed it.

Grady and his friends were probably in the best physical condition of their lives when they began mountain biking regularly in college. Even now, as Grady's life becomes more complicated and sports starts to take a back seat to work and other personal demands, he is still enjoying one of the healthiest periods of his life. Still, Grady has to cope with the stress produced by the challenges of adult life.

Physical Development and the Senses

In most respects, physical development and maturation are complete at early adulthood. Most people have attained their full height, with limbs proportional to their size, rendering the gangliness of adolescence a memory. People in their early 20s tend to be healthy, vigorous, and energetic. Although **senescence**, the natural physical decline brought about by increasing age, has begun, age-related changes are not usually obvious until later in life. At the same time,

senescence the natural physical decline brought about by aging some growth continues; for example, some people, particularly late maturers, continue to gain height in their early 20s.

Other parts of the body also reach full maturity. The brain grows in both size and weight, reaching its maximum during early adulthood (and then contracting later in life). The gray matter continues to be pruned back, and myelination (the process in which nerve cells are insulated by a covering of fat cells) continues to increase. These brain changes help support the cognitive advances of early adulthood (Sowell et al., 2001; Toga, Thompson, & Sowell, 2006; Li, 2012).

The senses are as sharp as they will ever be. Although there are changes in the elasticity of the eye—a process that may begin as early as age 10—they are so minor that they produce no deterioration in vision. Hearing, too, is at its peak, although women can detect higher tones more readily than men (McGuinness, 1972). Under quiet conditions, the average young adult can hear the ticking of a watch 20 feet away. The other senses, including taste, smell, and sensitivity to touch and pain, are good and remain so throughout early adulthood.

Motor Functioning, Fitness, and Health: Staying Well

If you are a professional athlete, you are generally considered over the hill by the end of your 20s. Although there are notable exceptions, even athletes who train constantly tend to lose their physical edge once they reach their 30s. In some sports, the peak passes even sooner. Swimmers are at their best in their late teens and gymnasts even younger (Schultz & Curnow, 1988).

Our psychomotor abilities also peak during early adulthood. Reaction time is quicker, muscle strength greater, and eye–hand coordination better than at any other period (Salthouse, 1993; Sliwinski et al., 1994).

Physical Fitness. The fitness of early adulthood doesn't come naturally or to everyone. To reach their physical potential, people must exercise and maintain a proper diet.

Only a small time commitment is needed to yield significant health benefits. According to the American College of Sports Medicine and the Centers for Disease Control and Prevention, people should engage in at least 30 minutes of moderate physical activity at least 5 days a week. Exercise time can be continuous or in bouts of at least 10 minutes, as long as the daily total reaches 30 minutes. Moderate activity includes walking briskly at 3 to 4 mph, biking at speeds up to 10 mph, golfing while carrying or pulling clubs, fishing by casting from shore, playing ping-pong, or canoeing at 2 to 4 mph. Even common household chores, such as weeding, vacuuming, and mowing with a power mower, provide moderate exercise (American College of Sports Medicine, 1997).

From an educator's perspective: Can people be taught the lifelong advantages of regular exercise? Should school-based physical education programs be changed to foster a lifelong commitment to exercise?

People in their early 20s tend to be healthy, vigorous, and energetic, but they often experience quite a lot of stress.

The advantages are many. Exercise increases cardiovascular fitness, meaning that the heart and circulatory system operate more efficiently. Furthermore, lung capacity increases, raising endurance. Muscles become stronger, and the body is more flexible. The range of movement is greater, and the muscles, tendons, and ligaments are more elastic. Moreover, exercise during this period helps reduce *osteoporosis*, the thinning of the bones, in later life.

Exercise also may optimize the immune response of the body, helping it fight off disease. It may even decrease stress and anxiety and reduce depression. It can provide a sense of control over the body and a feeling of accomplishment. Regular exercise offers the possibility of another, ultimately more important, reward: It is associated with increased longevity (Stevens et al., 2002; Rethorst, Wipfli, & Landers, 2009; Jung & Brawley, 2010) (see Figure 7-1).

People in their early 20s tend to be healthy, vigorous, and energetic, but they often experience quite a lot of stress.

Health. Health risks in general are slight during early adulthood. People are less susceptible to colds and other minor illnesses than they were as children, and they recover quickly from those that they do catch.

Adults in their 20s and 30s stand a higher risk of dying from accidents, primarily car accidents, than from most other causes. But there are other killers: Among the leading sources of death for people 25 to 34 are AIDS, cancer, heart disease, and

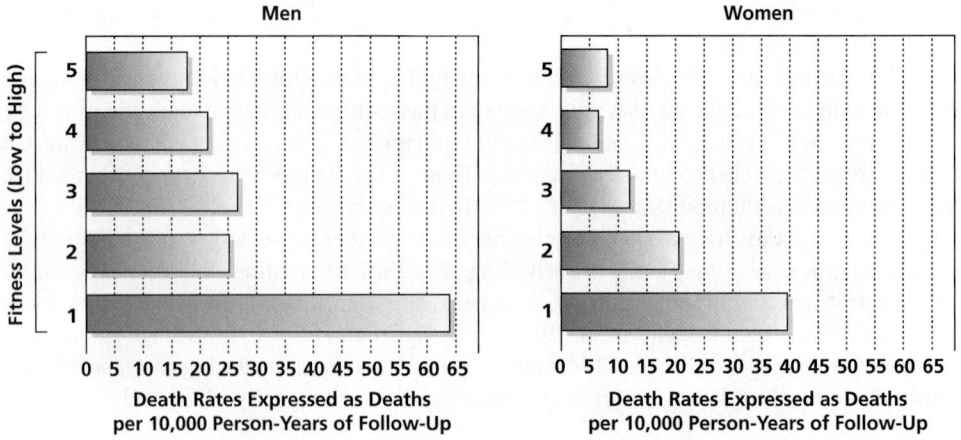

FIGURE 7-1 The Result of Fitness: Longevity
The greater the fitness level, the lower the death rate tends to be for both men and women.
Source: Based on Blair et al., 1989.

suicide. Amid the grim statistics of mortality, the age 35 represents a significant milestone. It is at that point that illness and disease overtake accidents as the leading cause of death—the first time this is true since infancy.

Not all people fare equally well during early adulthood. Lifestyle decisions, such as the use—or abuse—of alcohol, tobacco, or drugs, or engaging in unprotected sex, can hasten *secondary aging*, physical declines brought about by environmental factors or behavioral choices. These substances can also increase the mortality risk from the causes just mentioned.

Cultural factors, including gender and race, are related to the risk of dying. For instance, men are more apt to die than women, primarily in automobile accidents. Furthermore, African Americans have twice the death rate of Caucasians, and minorities in general have a higher likelihood of dying than their Caucasian peers.

Another major cause of death for men in this age group is violence. The murder rate is significantly higher in the United States than in any other developed country (see Figure 7-2). Racial factors are also related to the homicide rate in the United States. Although homicide is the third most frequent cause of death for white males between the ages of 20 to 34, it is *the* most frequent cause of death for black males and the second most frequent cause of death for Hispanic males in the same age range.

Cultural factors also influence young adults' lifestyles and health-related behavior, as discussed in the "Cultural Dimensions" feature.

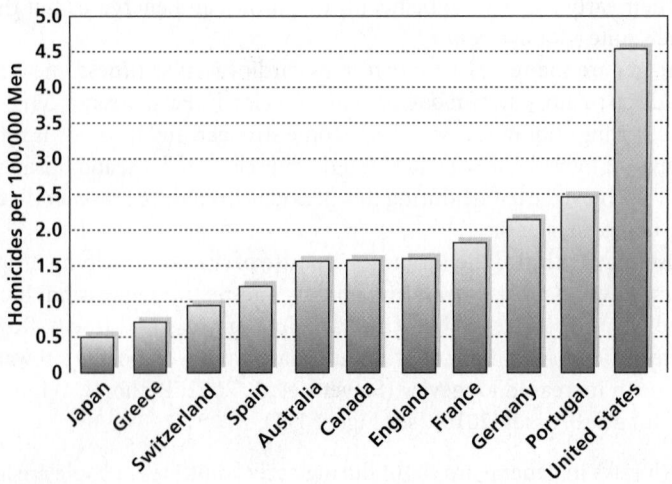

FIGURE 7-2 Tracking Murder
The murder rate (per 100,000 men) is far higher in the United States than in any other developed country. What features of U.S. society contribute to this higher rate?
Source: Based on United Nations Survey on Crime Trends, 2000.

Violence represents a serious issue in the United States.

Cultural Dimensions

How Cultural Beliefs Influence Health and Health Care

Manolita recently suffered a heart attack. She was advised by her doctor to change her eating and activity habits or face the risk of another life-threatening heart attack. During the period that followed, Manolita dramatically changed her eating and activity habits. She also began going to church and praying extensively. After a recent checkup, Manolita is in the best shape of her life. What are some of the reasons for Manolita's amazing recovery? (Murguia, Peterson, & Zea, 1997, p. 16)

After reading the previous passage, would you conclude that Manolita recovered her health because (1) she changed her eating and activity habits; (2) she became a better person; (3) God was testing her faith; or (4) her doctor prescribed the correct changes?

When asked this question in a survey, more than two-thirds of Latino immigrants from Central America, South America, or the Caribbean believed that "God was testing her faith" had a moderate or great effect on her recovery, although most also agreed that a change in eating and activity habits was important (Murguia, Peterson, & Zea, 1997; Gurung, 2010).

According to psychologists Alejandro Murguia, Rolf Peterson, and Maria Zea (1997), cultural health beliefs, along with demographic characteristics and psychological barriers, can affect the use of physicians and medical care. They suggest that Latinos are more likely than non-Hispanic whites to believe in supernatural causes of illness, which may explain why Latinos are the least likely of any Western ethnic group to seek the help of a physician when they are ill.

Health care providers need to take cultural beliefs into account when treating members of different cultural groups. For example, if a patient believes that the source of his or her illness is a spell cast by a jealous romantic rival, the patient may not comply with medical regimens that ignore that perceived source. To provide effective health care, then, health care providers must be sensitive to such cultural health beliefs.

REVIEW, CHECK, AND APPLY

REVIEW

LO1 How does the body develop during early adulthood?

- By young adulthood, the body and the senses are at their peak, but growth still proceeds, particularly in the brain.

LO2 What risks do young adults face?

- Young adults are generally as fit and healthy as they will ever be. Accidents present the greatest risk of death.
- In the United States, violence is also a significant risk during young adulthood, particularly for non-white males.

CHECK YOURSELF

1. _____ is the natural physical decline brought about by aging.
   - a Maturation
   - b Plasticity
   - c Senescence
   - d Lateralization
2. At the age of _____, illness and disease overtake accidents as the leading cause of death.
   - a 25
   - b 35
   - c 40
   - d 50
3. Compared to all other developed countries, one of the greatest risks for death in young adult men in the United States is murder.
   - True
   - False

APPLYING LIFESPAN DEVELOPMENT

- What factors do you think contribute to the comparatively high risk of automobile accidents during young adulthood? How can this be changed?

✓ **Study** and **Review** on **MyPsychLab.com**

PHYSICAL LIMITATIONS AND CHALLENGES

L03 What is the key to good health and proper weight?
L04 What types of challenges do people with disabilities face?

Aidan Tindell, accustomed to the shaving mirror in his own apartment, got a shock when he glimpsed his image in a friend's full-length mirror. It was not a pretty sight. Aidan had somehow developed a belly—and a pretty good-sized one. As if in a vision, he conjured up the long evenings he spent in a local sports bar with his friends. He saw the beers he downed without a second thought, the bar snacks he ate incessantly, and the burgers and fries and pizzas that were his basic food groups. Aidan knew something had to give, and he was afraid it was going to be his lifestyle.

For many young adults, this period is the first time that they have to deal seriously with the negative consequences of developmental change. As they leave adolescence, they gradually learn that they can't simply extend their living habits indefinitely. One particularly painful area of change is diet.

Good Nutrition: No Such Thing as a Free Lunch?

According to guidelines provided by the U.S. Department of Agriculture, people can achieve good nutrition by eating foods that are low in fat, including vegetables, fruits, whole-grain foods, fish, poultry, lean meats, and low-fat dairy products. In addition, whole-grain foods and cereal products, vegetables (including dried beans and peas), and fruits are beneficial in another way: They help people raise the amount of complex carbohydrates and fiber they ingest. Milk and other sources of calcium are also needed to prevent osteoporosis. Finally, people should reduce salt intake (USDA, 2006; Jones et al., 2012).

Adolescents don't suffer too much from a diet high in junk foods and fat because they are undergoing tremendous growth. The body is less forgiving to young adults, who must reduce their caloric intake to maintain their health (Insel & Roth, 1991). **Watch** the **Video** *Young Adulthood: Health, Mak* in **MyPsychLab**.

Tribune Media Services TMS Reprints

Obesity: A Weighty Concern

The adult population of the United States is growing—in more ways than one. Obesity, defined as body weight that is 20 percent or more above the average weight for a person of a given height, is on the rise in the United States. A third of adults are obese, a percentage that has nearly tripled since the 1960s. Furthermore, as age increases, more and more people are classified as obese (Centers for Disease Control and Prevention, 2010) (see Figure 7-3).

Weight control is a difficult, and often losing, battle for many young adults. Most diets fail, producing nothing more than a seesaw cycle of gain and loss. Some obesity experts argue that the rate of dieting failure is so great that people should avoid dieting altogether. Instead, if people eat the foods they really want in moderation, they may be able to avoid the binge eating that often occurs when diets fail. Even though obese people may never reach their desired weight, they may, according to this reasoning, ultimately control their weight more effectively (Roehrig et al., 2009; Tremblay & Chaput, 2012; Quick et al., 2013).

Obesity is particularly prevalent in the United States. The world average weight for adults is 137 pounds; in the United States, the average is 180 (Walpole, 2012) (see Figure 7-4).

Physical Disabilities: Coping With Physical Challenge

Over 50 million people in the United States are physically or mentally challenged, according to the official definition of *disability*—a condition that substantially limits a major life activity such as walking or vision. People with disabilities are in large part an undereducated and underemployed minority group. Fewer than 10 percent of people with major handicaps have finished high school, fewer than 25 percent of disabled men and 15 percent of disabled women work full time, and unemployment rates are high. In addition, the jobs that people with disabilities find are often routine and low-paying positions (Albrecht, 2005; Power & Green, 2010; Foote, 2013).

Some barriers to a full life are physical. Despite passage in 1990 of the landmark ADA, which mandates full access to public establishments such as stores, office buildings, hotels, and theaters, people in wheelchairs still cannot gain access to many older buildings.

Despite the passage of the Americans with Disabilities Act (ADA), people with physical disabilities still cannot gain access to many older buildings.

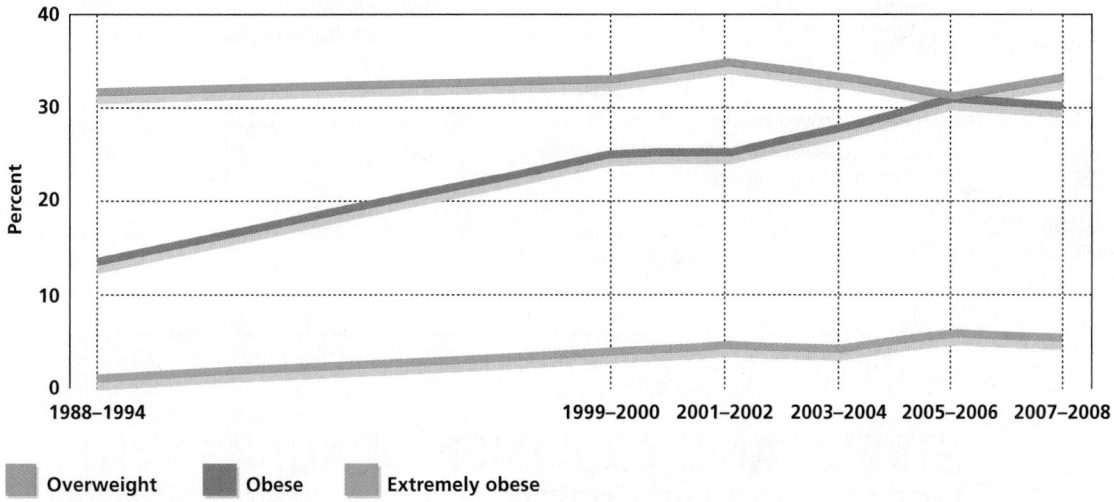

Overweight is defined as a body mass index (BMI) of 25 or greater but less than 30; obesity is a BMI greater than or equal to 30; extreme obesity is a BMI greater than or equal to 40. Source: CDC/NCHS, National Health and Nutrition Examination Survey III 1988–1994, 1999–2000, 2001–2002, 2003–2004, 2005–2006, and 2007–2008.

FIGURE 7-3 Obesity on the Rise
In spite of greater awareness of the importance of good nutrition, the percentage of adults with weight problems in the United States has risen dramatically over the past few decades. Why do you think this rise has occurred?
Source: Centers for Disease Control and Prevention, 2010.

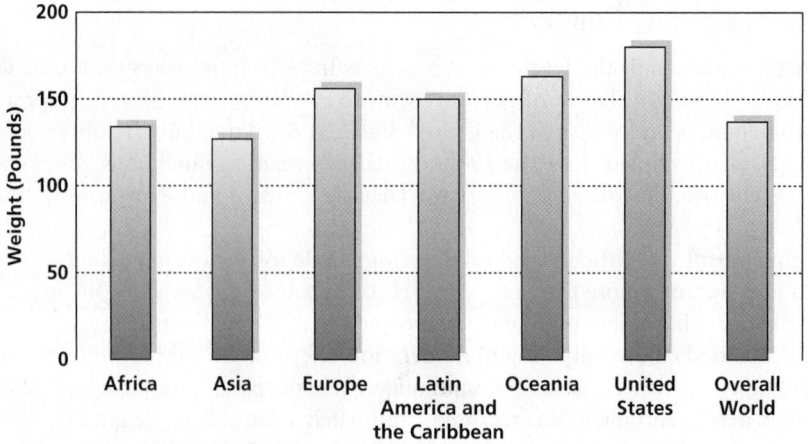

FIGURE 7-4 First in Obesity
Obesity is particularly prevalent in the United States. The world average weight for adults is 137 pounds; in the United States, the average is 180.
Source: Walpole, 2012.

From a social worker's perspective: What sorts of interpersonal barriers do people with disabilities face? How can those barriers be removed?

Another barrier is prejudice. People with disabilities sometimes face pity or avoidance as nondisabled people focus so much on the disability that they overlook other characteristics. Others treat people with disabilities as if they were children. This can take its toll on the way people with disabilities think about themselves (French & Swain, 1997).

REVIEW, CHECK, AND APPLY

REVIEW

L03 What is the key to good health and proper weight?

- Even in young adulthood, health must be maintained by proper diet and exercise. Obesity is increasingly a problem for young adults.

L04 What types of challenges do people with disabilities face?

- People with physical disabilities face not only physical barriers but also psychological barriers caused by prejudice.

CHECK YOURSELF

1. As age increases, fewer individuals are classified as obese.
   - True
   - False
2. Obesity is defined as body weight that is _____ percent or more above the average weight for a person of a given height.
   - a 10
   - b 20
   - c 25
   - d 30

APPLYING LIFESPAN DEVELOPMENT

- What developmental factors make it hard for young adults to understand that they may have to change their eating habits and personal choices?

Study and **Review** on **MyPsychLab.com**

STRESS AND COPING: DEALING WITH LIFE'S CHALLENGES

L05 What are the consequences of long-term stress?
L06 What are strategies for preventing or reducing stress?

It's 5:00 PM Rosa Convoy, a 25-year-old single mother, has just finished her work as a receptionist at a dentist's office and is on her way home. She has exactly 2 hours to pick up her daughter Zoe from child care, get home, make and eat dinner, pick up and return with a babysitter from down the street, say goodbye to Zoe, and get to her 7 o'clock programming class at a local community college. It's a marathon she runs every Tuesday and Thursday night, and she knows she doesn't have a second to spare if she wants to reach the class on time.

Rosa Convoy is experiencing **stress**, the physical and emotional response to events that threaten or challenge us. Our lives are crowded with events and circumstances, known as stressors, that threaten our equilibrium. Stressors need not be unpleasant events: Even the happiest events—starting a long-sought job or planning a wedding—can produce stress (Shimizu & Pelham, 2004; Aschbacher et al., 2013).

Researchers in the new field of **psychoneuroimmunology (PNI)**—the study of the relationship among the brain, the immune system, and psychological factors—have examined the outcomes of stress. The most immediate is a biological reaction, as hormones secreted by the adrenal glands cause a rise in heart rate, blood pressure, respiration rate, and sweating. In some situations, these immediate effects are beneficial because the "emergency reaction" they produce in the sympathetic nervous system enables people to defend themselves from a sudden, threatening situation (Kiecolt-Glaser, 2009; Janusek, Cooper, & Mathews, 2012).

On the other hand, long-term, continuous exposure to stressors may result in a reduction of the body's ability to deal with stress. As stress-related hormones are constantly secreted, the heart, blood vessels, and other body tissues may deteriorate. As a consequence, people become more susceptible to diseases as their ability to fight off germs declines. In short, both *acute stressors* (sudden, one-time events) and *chronic stressors* (long-term, continuing events) have the potential to produce significant physiological consequences (Graham, Christian, & Kiecolt-Glaser, 2006; Wheaton & Montazer, 2010; Rohleder, 2012).

The Origins of Stress

Experienced job interviewers, college counselors, and owners of bridal shops all know that not everyone reacts the same way to a potentially stressful event. What makes the difference? According to psychologists Arnold Lazarus and Susan Folkman, people move through a series of stages that determine whether they will experience stress (Lazarus & Folkman, 1984; Lazarus, 1968, 1991).

Primary appraisal is the first step—the individual's assessment of an event to determine whether its implications are positive, negative, or neutral. If a person sees the event as primarily negative, he or she appraises it in terms of the harm that it has caused in the past, how threatening it is likely to be, and how likely it is that the challenge can be resisted successfully. For example, you are likely to feel differently about an upcoming French test if you passed the last one with flying colors than you would if you did poorly.

Secondary appraisal follows. **Secondary appraisal** is the person's answer to the question, "Can I handle it?," an assessment of whether the coping abilities and resources on hand are adequate. If resources are lacking and the threat is great, the person will feel stress. A traffic ticket is always upsetting, but if you can't afford the fine, the stress is greater.

Stress varies with the person's appraisal, and that appraisal varies with the person's temperament and circumstances. There are some general principles that help predict when an event will be appraised as stressful. Psychologist Shelley Taylor (1991) suggests the following characteristics of events that have a high likelihood of producing stress:

- Events and circumstances that produce negative emotions—for example, dealing with the illness of a loved one produces more stress than planning for the adoption of a new baby.
- Situations that are uncontrollable or unpredictable—for example, professors who give surprise quizzes produce more stress than those who schedule them in advance.
- Events and circumstances that are ambiguous and confusing—for example, a new job that does not have a clear job description is likely to produce more stress than a well-defined position.
- Having to simultaneously accomplish many tasks that strain a person's capabilities—for example, a graduate student who is expecting her first child the same month she is scheduled to submit her dissertation is likely to be feeling more stress than a student with less on her agenda.

stress the physical and emotional response to events that threaten or challenge us

psychoneuroimmunology (PNI) the study of the relationship among the brain, the immune system, and psychological factors

primary appraisal the assessment of an event to determine whether its implications are positive, negative, or neutral

secondary appraisal the assessment of whether one's coping abilities and resources are adequate to overcome the harm, threat, or challenge posed by the potential stressor

Although we commonly think of negative events, such as auto mishaps, as leading to stress, even welcome events, like getting married, can be stressful.

From the perspective of a health care provider: Are there periods of life that are relatively stress free, or do people of all ages experience stress? Do stressors differ from age to age?

The Consequences of Stress

Over the long run, the constant wear and tear of fighting off stress can have formidable costs. Headaches, backaches, skin rashes, indigestion, chronic fatigue, and even the common cold are stress-related illnesses (Cohen, Tyrell, & Smith, 1997; Suinn, 2001; Kalynchuk, 2010).

In addition, *the immune system*—the organs, glands, and cells that are the body's line of defense against disease—may be damaged by stress. Stress can interfere with the immune system's ability to stop germs from reproducing or cancer cells from spreading. In addition, stress may overstimulate the immune system into attacking the body itself and damaging healthy tissue (Cohen et al., 2002; Caserta et al., 2008; Liu, et al., 2012).

Stress may also lead to **somatic symptom disorders**, medical problems caused by the interaction of psychological, emotional, and physical difficulties. For instance, ulcers, asthma, arthritis, and high blood pressure may sometimes be produced by stress (Marin et al., 2009; Kradin, 2013).

To get a sense of how much stress you have in your own life, complete the questionnaire in Table 7-1. **Watch** the **Video** *Stress and Your Health* in **MyPsychLab**.

Coping With Stress

Stress is a normal part of every life. But some young adults are better than others at **coping**, the effort to control, reduce, or learn to tolerate the threats that lead to stress (Taylor & Stanton, 2007). What's the secret to coping? It turns out that people use a variety of strategies.

Some people use *problem-focused coping*—managing a threatening situation by directly changing it to make it less stressful. For example, a man having difficulties on the job may ask his boss to change his responsibilities, or he may look for another job.

Other people employ *emotion-focused coping*—the conscious regulation of emotion. For instance, a mother having trouble finding appropriate care for her child while she is at work may tell herself that she should look at the bright side: At least she has a job in a difficult economy (Master et al., 2009; Gruszczyńska, 2013).

Sometimes, people acknowledge that they are in a stressful situation that cannot be changed, but they cope by managing their reactions. For example, they may take up meditation or exercise to reduce their physical reactions.

somatic symptom disorders medical problems caused by the interaction of psychological, emotional, and physical difficulties

coping the effort to control, reduce, or learn to tolerate the threats that lead to stress

TABLE 7-1 HOW STRESSED ARE YOU?

The statements below will help you determine your level of stress. Mark the appropriate number in each box, then add up those numbers to find your score. Your answers should reflect your experiences in the last month only. To help you rate the extent of your stress, use the key at the bottom.

1. I become upset when something happens unexpectedly.
   ☐ 0 = never, 1 = almost never, 2 = sometimes, 3 = fairly often, 4 = very often
2. I feel I'm unable to control the things that are most important in my life.
   ☐ 0 = never, 1 = almost never, 2 = sometimes, 3 = fairly often, 4 = very often
3. I feel nervous and "stressed."
   ☐ 0 = never, 1 = almost never, 2 = sometimes, 3 = fairly often, 4 = very often
4. I feel confident about my ability to handle my personal problems.
   ☐ 4 = never, 3 = almost never, 2 = sometimes, 1 = fairly often, 0 = very often
5. In general, I feel things are going my way.
   ☐ 4 = never, 3 = almost never, 2 = sometimes, 1 = fairly often, 0 = very often
6. I'm able to control irritations in my life.
   ☐ 4 = never, 3 = almost never, 2 = sometimes, 1 = fairly often, 0 = very often
7. I feel I cannot cope with all the things I need to do.
   ☐ 0 = never, 1 = almost never, 2 = sometimes, 3 = fairly often, 4 = very often
8. Generally, I feel on top of things.
   ☐ 4 = never, 3 = almost never, 2 = sometimes, 1 = fairly often, 0 = very often
9. I get angry at things that are beyond my control.
   ☐ 0 = never, 1 = almost never, 2 = sometimes, 3 = fairly often, 4 = very often
10. I feel problems pile up to such an extent that I cannot overcome them.
    ☐ 0 = never, 1 = almost never, 2 = sometimes, 3 = fairly often, 4 = very often

How Do you Measure up?

Stress levels vary from person to person, but you can compare your total score to the averages below:

Age		Gender		Marital Status	
18–29	14.2	Men	12.1	Widowed	12.6
30–44	13.0	Women	13.7	Married or living with	12.4
45–54	2.6			Single or never wed	14.1
55–64	11.9			Divorced	14.7
65 & over	12.0			Separated	16.6

Source: Based on Sheldon Cohen, Dept. of Psychology, Carnegie Mellon University.

Coping is also aided by the presence of *social support*, assistance and comfort supplied by others. Turning to others can provide both emotional support (in the form of a shoulder to cry on) and practical, tangible support (such as a temporary loan). In addition, others can provide information, offering specific advice on how to deal with stressful situations. The ability to learn from others' experiences is one of the reasons that people use the Web to connect with people who have similar experiences (Kim, Sherman, & Taylor, 2008; Green, DeCourville, & Sadava, 2012; Seçkin, 2013).

Finally, even if people do not consciously cope with stress, some psychologists suggest that they may unconsciously use defensive coping mechanisms. **Defensive coping** involves unconscious strategies that distort or deny the true nature of a situation. For instance, people may trivialize a life-threatening illness or tell themselves that failing a major test is unimportant.

Another type of defensive coping is *emotional insulation*, through which people unconsciously try to block emotions and thereby avoid pain. But if defensive coping becomes a habitual response to stress, its reliance on avoidance can stand in the way of dealing with the reality of the situation (Ormont, 2001).

In some cases, people use drugs or alcohol to escape from stressful situations. Like defensive coping, drinking and drug use do not help address the situation causing the stress, and they can increase a person's difficulties. For example, people may become addicted to the substances that initially provided them with a pleasurable sense of escape.

Hardiness, Resilience, and Coping. The success with which young adults deal with stress depends in part on their *coping style*, their general tendency to deal with stress in a particular way. For example, people with a "hardy" coping style are especially successful. **Hardiness** is a personality characteristic associated with a lower rate of stress-related illness.

defensive coping coping that involves unconscious strategies that distort or deny the true nature of a situation

hardiness a personality characteristic associated with a lower rate of stress-related illness

Becoming an Informed Consumer of Development

Coping With Stress

Some general guidelines can help people cope with stress, including the following (Sacks, 1993; Bionna, 2006):

- Seek control over the situation. Taking charge of a situation that is producing stress can take you a long way toward coping with it. For example, if you are feeling stress about a test, do something about it—such as starting to study.
- Redefine "threat" as "challenge." Changing the definition can make a situation seem less threatening. "Look for the silver lining" is not bad advice. For example, if you're fired, look at it as an opportunity to get a new and better job.
- Find social support. Almost any difficulty can be faced more easily with the help of others. Friends, family members, and even telephone hotlines staffed by trained counselors can provide significant support.
- Use relaxation techniques. Reducing the physiological arousal brought about by stress can be effective in coping with stress. Techniques that produce relaxation, such as transcendental meditation, Zen and yoga, progressive muscle relaxation, and even hypnosis, have been shown to be effective. One that works particularly well was devised by physician Herbert Benson and is illustrated in Table 7-2 (Benson, 1993).
- Maintain a healthy lifestyle that will reinforce your body's natural coping mechanisms. Exercise, eat nutritiously, get enough sleep, and avoid or reduce use of alcohol, tobacco, or other drugs.
- If all else fails, keep in mind that a life without stress would be dull. Stress is natural, and successfully coping with it can be gratifying.

Hardy individuals are take-charge people who revel in life's challenges. People who are high in hardiness are more resistant to stress-related illness than those with less hardiness. Hardy people react to stressors with optimism, convinced that they can respond effectively. By turning threats into challenges, they are less apt to experience high levels of stress (Maddi et al., 2006; Andrew et al., 2008; Delahaij, Gaillard, & van Dam, 2010).

TABLE 7-2 HOW TO ELICIT THE RELAXATION RESPONSE

Some general advice on regular practice of the relaxation response:

- Try to find 10 to 20 minutes in your daily routine; before breakfast is a good time.
- Sit comfortably.
- For the period you will practice, try to arrange your life so you won't have distractions. Put on the answering machine, and ask someone else to watch the kids.
- Time yourself by glancing periodically at a clock or watch (but don't set an alarm). Commit yourself to a specific length of practice, and try to stick to it.

There are several approaches to eliciting the relaxation response. Here is one standard set of instructions:

Step 1. Pick a focus word or short phrase that's firmly rooted in your personal belief system. For example, a nonreligious individual might choose a neutral word like *one* or *peace* or *love*. A Christian person desiring to use a prayer could pick the opening words of Psalm 23, *The Lord is my shepherd;* a Jewish person could choose *Shalom*.

Step 2. Sit quietly in a comfortable position.

Step 3. Close your eyes.

Step 4. Relax your muscles.

Step 5. Breathe slowly and naturally, repeating your focus word or phrase silently as you exhale.

Step 6. Throughout, assume a passive attitude. Don't worry about how well you're doing. When other thoughts come to mind, simply say to yourself, "Oh, well," and gently return to the repetition.

Step 7. Continue for 10 to 20 minutes. You may open your eyes to check the time, but do not use an alarm. When you finish, sit quietly for a minute or so, at first with your eyes closed and later with your eyes open. Then do not stand for 1 or 2 minutes.

Step 8. Practice the technique once or twice a day.

Source: Benson, 1993.

For people who face the most profound difficulties—such as the unexpected death of a loved one—a key factor in their reactions is their level of resilience. As we discussed earlier, *resilience* is the ability to withstand, overcome, and even thrive after profound adversity (Werner, 2005; Kim-Cohen, 2007; Lipsitt & Demick, 2012).

Resilient young adults tend to be easygoing and good-natured, with good social and communication skills. They are independent, feeling that they can shape their own fate and are not dependent on others or luck. They work with what they have and make the best of any situation (Friborg et al., 2005; Clauss-Ehlers, 2008; Saklofske et al., 2013).

REVIEW, CHECK, AND APPLY

REVIEW

L05 What are the consequences of long-term stress?

- Stress, which is healthy in small doses, can be harmful to body and mind if it is frequent or long lasting.
- Long-term exposure to stressors may cause deterioration in the heart, blood vessels, and other body tissues. Stress is linked to many common ailments.

L06 What are strategies for preventing or reducing stress?

- Strategies for coping with stress include problem-focused coping, emotion-focused coping, and the use of social support. Utilizing the relaxation technique can also be helpful. Another strategy, defensive coping, which relies on avoidance, can prevent a person from dealing with the reality of the situation.

CHECK YOURSELF

1. Stressful events are limited to the negative events in our lives.
   - True
   - False
2. Researchers in the field of _____ study the relationship among the brain, the immune system, and psychological factors, and have found that stress can produce several outcomes.
   - a psychoanalysis
   - b disease management
   - c pilates
   - d psychoneuroimmunology
3. Avoiding thinking about a stressful situation by drinking, doing drugs, or just denying the true nature of a situation are all examples of _____ coping.
   - a defensive
   - b emotion-focused
   - c social support
   - d hardiness

APPLYING LIFESPAN DEVELOPMENT

- In what circumstances can stress be an adaptive, helpful response? In what circumstances is it maladaptive?

✓ **Study** and **Review** on **MyPsychLab.com**

MODULE 7.2

COGNITIVE DEVELOPMENT IN EARLY ADULTHOOD

Paul Galesko was an "A-list" student in high school—popular, a member of the drama society and the marching band, and at the top of his class. Paul had been a driven student since his first year, challenging himself each semester with a strict diet of advanced and honors classes. Paul's parents had instilled in him the value of education as a way to a better life; their lives had been difficult because they lacked a college education and had decided to have children while they were still young and not yet financially established.

Paul was excited when he got into his first-choice college, but things didn't go as he expected that first year. Actually, he hadn't known what to expect at all. Because no one in his family had gone to college, he was exploring new territory. He tried to do it all—tough classes, weekend parties, a job at the student union, writing for the campus newspaper, and more. Finally, the pressure wore him down and he showed up at the campus infirmary with signs of exhaustion. A mental health counselor helped him prioritize his schedule and take control of his life and health.

Although Paul was, in his own words, "exploring new territory" by going to college, he and his parents shared a belief in the value of higher education. The different paths taken by Paul and his parents represent the increasing diversity in family background, socioeconomic status, race, and ethnicity that characterizes college populations today.

This module focuses on cognitive development during early adulthood. Although traditional approaches to cognitive development regarded adulthood as an inconsequential plateau, we will examine some new theories that suggest that significant cognitive growth occurs during the period. We also consider the nature of adult intelligence and the impact of life events on cognitive development.

The last part of the module considers college, an institution that shapes intellectual growth. We examine who goes to college, and how gender and race can influence achievement. We end by looking at the troubling issue of gambling among students and examining some of the adjustment problems that college students face.

COGNITIVE DEVELOPMENT

LO7 Does cognitive development continue in young adulthood?
LO8 How does postformal thinking develop in early adulthood?

Ben is known to be a heavy drinker, especially when he goes to parties. Tyra, Ben's wife, warns him that if he comes home drunk one more time, she will leave him and take the children. Tonight Ben is out late at an office party. He comes home drunk. Does Tyra leave Ben?

To the typical adolescent this case (drawn from research by Adams and Labouvie-Vief, 1986) is open-and-shut: Tyra leaves Ben. But in early adulthood, the answer is less clear. People become less concerned with sheer logic and instead take into account real-life concerns that may influence and temper behavior.

Intellectual Growth in Early Adulthood

If we subscribed to the traditional view of cognitive development, we would expect to find little intellectual growth in early adulthood. Piaget argued that by the time people left adolescence, their thinking, at least qualitatively, had largely become what it would be for the rest of their lives. They might gather more information, but the ways in which they thought about it would not change.

Was Piaget's view correct? Increasing evidence suggests that he was mistaken.

Postformal Thought

The nature of thought changes qualitatively during early adulthood.

Developmental psychologist Giesela Labouvie-Vief suggests that the nature of thinking changes during early adulthood. She asserts that thinking based solely on formal operations (Piaget's final stage, reached during adolescence) is insufficient to meet the demands placed on young adults. The complexity of society, which requires specialization, and the challenge of finding one's way through that complexity require thought that transcends logic to include practical experience, moral judgments, and values (Labouvie-Vief, 1990, 2006).

For example, imagine a young, single woman in her first job. Her boss, a married man she respects greatly and who is in a position to help her career, invites her to go with him to make an important presentation to a client. When the presentation, which has gone very well, is over, he suggests they go out to dinner and celebrate. Later that evening, after sharing a bottle of wine, he attempts to accompany her to her hotel room. What should she do?

Logic alone doesn't answer such questions. Labouvie-Vief suggests that young adults' thinking must develop to handle ambiguous situations like these. She suggests that young adults learn to use analogies and metaphors to make comparisons, confront society's paradoxes, and become comfortable with a more subjective understanding. This requires weighing all aspects of a situation according to one's values and beliefs. It allows for interpretive processes and reflects the fact that reasons behind events in the real world are painted in shades of gray rather than black and white (Labouvie-Vief, 1990; Sinnott, 1998; Thornton, 2004).

To demonstrate how this sort of thinking develops, Labouvie-Vief presented experimental subjects, ranging in age from 10 to 40, with scenarios similar to the Ben and Tyra scenario presented earlier. Each story had a clear, logical conclusion, but it could be interpreted differently if real-world demands and pressures were taken into account.

In responding to the scenarios, adolescents relied heavily on the logic of formal operations. They tended to predict that Tyra would immediately pack up her bags and leave with the children when Ben came home drunk. After all, that's what she said she would do. In contrast, young adults were more apt to consider various real-life possibilities: Would Ben be apologetic and beg Tyra not to leave? Did Tyra really mean it when she said she would leave? Does Tyra have someplace to go?

Young adults exhibited what Labouvie-Vief calls postformal thinking. **Postformal thought** is thinking that goes beyond Piaget's formal operations. Rather than being based on purely logical processes, with absolutely right and wrong answers to problems, postformal thought acknowledges that adult predicaments must sometimes be solved in relativistic terms.

Postformal thought also encompasses *dialectical thinking*, an interest in and appreciation for argument, counterargument, and debate (Basseches, 1984). Dialectical thinking accepts that issues are not always clear-cut and that answers to questions must sometimes be negotiated. According to psychologist Jan Sinnott (1998), postformal thinkers shift back and forth between an abstract, ideal solution and real-world constraints that might prevent implementation of that solution. Postformal thinkers understand that just as there can be multiple causes of a situation, there can be multiple solutions.

Perry's Approach to Postformal Thinking

To psychologist William Perry (1970, 1981), the developmental growth of early adulthood involves mastering new ways of understanding the world. To examine intellectual and moral growth during college, Perry interviewed students at Harvard University. He found that students entering college tended to use *dualistic thinking* in their views of the world: Something was either right or wrong; people were either good or bad; others were either for them or against them.

However, as these students encountered new ideas and points of view from other students and their professors, their dualistic thinking declined. Consistent with postformal thinking, students began to accept that issues can have more than one plausible side. Furthermore, they understood that it is possible to hold multiple perspectives on an issue. Their attitude toward authorities also changed: Instead of assuming that experts had all the answers, they began to realize that their own thinking had validity if their position was well thought out and rational.

In fact, according to Perry, they had reached a stage in which knowledge and values were regarded as relativistic. Rather than seeing the world as having absolute standards and values, they argued that different societies, cultures, and individuals could have different standards and values, and all of them could be equally valid.

It's important to keep in mind that Perry's theory is based on a sample of interviews conducted with well-educated students attending an elite college. His findings may not apply as well to people who have never learned how to examine multiple points of view.

From an educator's perspective: Do you think it is possible for adolescent students to learn postformal thinking (e.g., by direct instruction on breaking the habit of dualistic thinking)? Why or why not?

Schaie's Stages of Development

Developmental psychologist K. Warner Schaie offers another perspective on postformal thought. Taking up where Piaget left off, Schaie suggests that adults' thinking follows a set pattern of stages (illustrated in Figure 7-5). But Schaie focuses on the ways in which information is *used* during adulthood, rather than on changes in the acquisition and understanding of new information, as in Piaget's approach (Schaie & Willis, 1993; Schaie & Zanjani, 2006).

Schaie suggests that before adulthood, the main cognitive developmental task is acquisition of information. Consequently, he labels the first stage of cognitive development, which encompasses all of childhood and adolescence, the **acquisitive stage**. Information gathered before we grow up is largely squirreled away for future use. In fact, much of the rationale for education during childhood and adolescence is to prepare people for future activities.

The situation changes considerably in early adulthood when the focus shifts from the future to the here and now. According to Schaie, young adults are in the achieving stage, applying their intelligence to attain long-term goals regarding their careers, family, and contributions to society. During the **achieving stage**, young adults must confront and resolve several major issues, and the decisions they make—such as what job to take and whom to marry—have implications for the rest of their lives.

postformal thought thinking that acknowledges that adult predicaments must sometimes be solved in relativistic terms

acquisitive stage according to Schaie, the first stage of cognitive development, encompassing all of childhood and adolescence

achieving stage the point reached by young adults in which intelligence is applied to specific situations involving the attainment of long-term goals regarding careers, family, and societal contributions

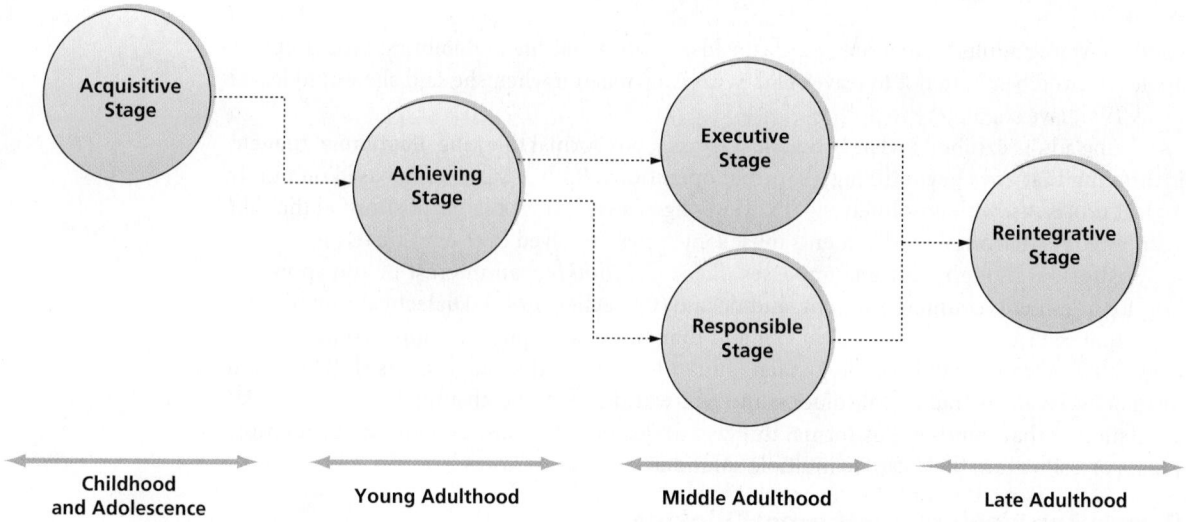

FIGURE 7-5 Schaie's Stages of Adult Development
Source: Based on Schaie, 1977–1978.

During the late stages of early adulthood and in middle adulthood, people move into the responsible and executive stages. In the **responsible stage**, middle-aged adults are mainly concerned with protecting and nourishing their spouses, families, and careers.

Sometime later, further into middle adulthood, many people (but not all) enter the **executive stage** in which they take a broader perspective, becoming more concerned about the larger world (Sinnott, 1997). People in the executive stage put energy into nourishing and sustaining societal institutions. They may become involved in town government, religious congregations, service clubs, charitable groups, and factory unions—organizations that have a larger purpose in society.

Finally, the **reintegrative stage** is the period of late adulthood during which people focus on tasks that have personal meaning. They no longer focus on acquiring knowledge to solve potential problems that they may encounter. Instead, they acquire information about issues that specifically interest them. Furthermore, they have less interest in—and patience for—things that they do not see as having some immediate application to their lives.

responsible stage the stage where the major concerns of middle-aged adults relate to their personal situations, including protecting and nourishing their spouses, families, and careers

executive stage the period in middle adulthood when people take a broader perspective than earlier, including concerns about the world

reintegrative stage the period of late adulthood during which the focus is on tasks that have personal meaning

REVIEW, CHECK, AND APPLY

REVIEW

L07 Does cognitive development continue in young adulthood?

- Cognitive development continues in young adulthood with the emergence of postformal thought, which goes beyond logic to encompass interpretive and subjective thinking.

L08 How does postformal thinking develop in early adulthood?

- Postformal thought acknowledges that adult predicaments must sometimes be solved in relativistic terms, rather than being based on purely logical processes with absolute right or wrong answers.
- Perry suggests that people move from dualistic thinking to relativistic thought during early adulthood.
- According to Schaie, people pass through five stages in the way they use information: acquisitive, achieving, responsible, executive, and reintegrative.

CHECK YOURSELF

1. The idea that problem solving in adulthood has to consider previous experiences, logical thinking, and the relative benefits and costs to a decision is also known as _____.
   - a formal operational thought
   - b concrete operational thought
   - c postformal thought
   - d dualistic thinking
2. Postformal thought and dialectical thinking acknowledge that the world sometimes lacks clearly right and wrong solutions to problems.
   - True
   - False

APPLYING LIFESPAN DEVELOPMENT

- Can you think of situations that you would deal with differently as an adult than as an adolescent? Do the differences reflect postformal thinking?

✓ **Study** and **Review** on **MyPsychLab.com**

INTELLIGENCE: WHAT MATTERS IN EARLY ADULTHOOD?

LO9 What are the major contemporary approaches to intelligence?
LO10 What causes cognitive growth in young adults?

Your year on the job has been generally favorable. Performance ratings for your department are at least as good as they were before you took over, and perhaps even a little better. You have two assistants. One is quite capable. The other just seems to go through the motions and is of little real help. Even though you are well liked, you believe that there is little that would distinguish you in the eyes of your superiors from the nine other managers at a comparable level in the company. Your goal is rapid promotion to an executive position. (Based on Wagner & Sternberg, 1985, p. 447)

How do you meet your goal?

The way adults answer this question may affect their future success. The question is one of a series designed to assess a particular type of intelligence that may have more of an impact on future success than the IQ measured by traditional tests.

Smart Thinking: Alternative Views of Intelligence

Many researchers argue that the kind of intelligence measured by IQ tests is not the only valid kind. Depending on what one wants to know about individuals, other theories of intelligence—and other measures of it—may be more appropriate.

In his **triarchic theory of intelligence**, psychologist Robert Sternberg, who is responsible for the executive question just posed, suggests that intelligence is made up of three major components: componential, experiential, and contextual. The *componential* aspect involves the mental components used to solve problems (e.g., selecting and using formulas, choosing problem-solving strategies, and in general making use of what has been learned in the past). The *experiential* component refers to the relationship between intelligence, prior experience, and the ability to cope with new situations. This is the insightful aspect of intelligence, which allows people to relate what they already know to a new situation and facts never before encountered. Finally, the *contextual* component of intelligence takes account of the demands of everyday, real-world environments. For instance, the contextual component is involved in adapting to on-the-job professional demands (Sternberg, 2005).

Traditional IQ tests tend to focus on the componential aspect. Yet increasing evidence suggests that a more useful measure, particularly when comparing and predicting adult success, is the contextual component—the aspect of intelligence that has come to be called practical intelligence.

Practical and Emotional Intelligence. According to Sternberg, traditional IQ scores relate quite well to academic success but not to other types of achievement, such as career success. Although it is clear that success in business requires some level of the IQ sort of intelligence, the rate of career advancement and the ultimate success of business executives is only marginally related to IQ scores (Cianciolo et al., 2006; Sternberg, 2006; Grigorenko et al., 2009).

Sternberg contends that success in a career necessitates practical intelligence (Sternberg et al., 1997). While academic success is based on knowledge obtained largely from reading and listening, **practical intelligence** is learned primarily by observing others and modeling their behavior. People with practical intelligence have good "social radar." They understand and handle even new situations effectively, reading people and circumstances insightfully based on their previous experiences..

There is another, related type of intelligence. **Emotional intelligence** is the set of skills that underlies the accurate assessment, evaluation, expression, and regulation of emotions. Emotional intelligence is what enables people to get along well with others, to understand what they are feeling and experiencing, and to respond appropriately to their needs. Emotional intelligence is of obvious value to career and personal success as a young adult (Ferguson & Austin, 2010; Kross & Grossmann, 2012; Crowne, 2013).

triarchic theory of intelligence Sternberg's theory that intelligence is made up of three major components: componential, experiential, and contextual

practical intelligence according to Sternberg, intelligence that is learned primarily by observing others and modeling their behavior

emotional intelligence the set of skills that underlie the accurate assessment, evaluation, expression, and regulation of emotions

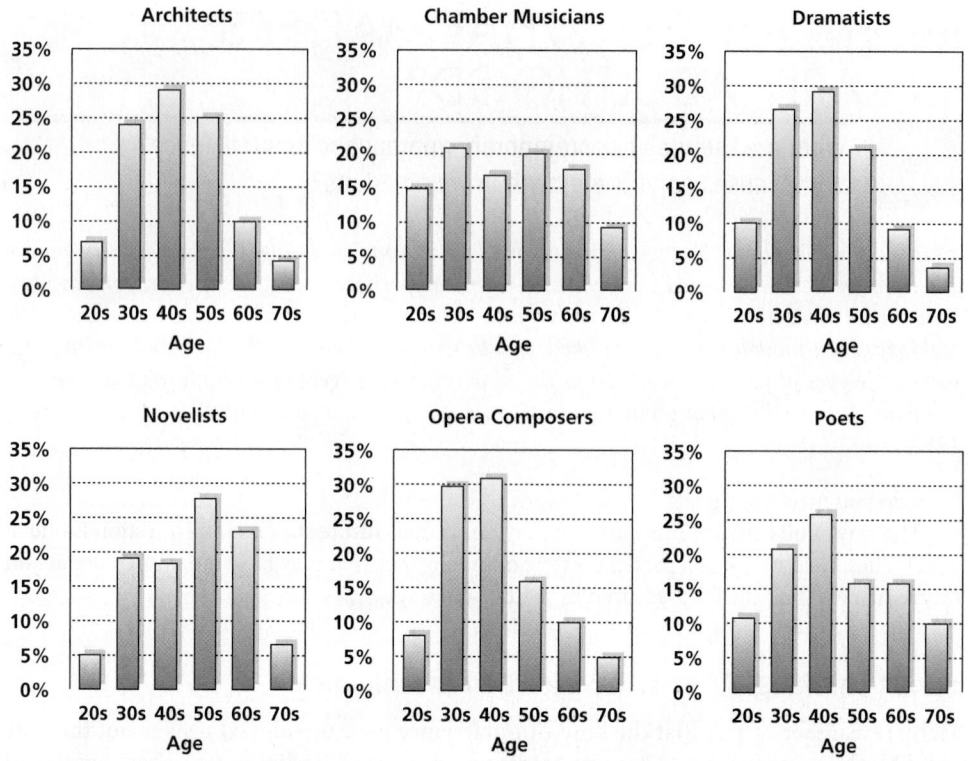

FIGURE 7-6 Creativity and Age
The period of maximum creativity differs depending on the particular field. The percentages refer to the percent of total lifetime major works produced during the particular age period. Why do poets peak earlier than novelists?
Source: Based on Dennis, 1966.

From an educator's perspective: Do you think educators can teach people to be more intelligent? Are there components or varieties of intelligence that might be more "teachable" than others? If so, which: componential, experiential, contextual, practical, or emotional?

Creativity: Novel Thought

The hundreds of musical compositions of Wolfgang Amadeus Mozart, who died at the age of 35, were largely written during early adulthood. This pattern—major works produced during early adulthood—is true of many other creative individuals (Dennis, 1966a) (see Figure 7-6).

One reason for the productivity of early adulthood may be that after this period creativity can be stifled by a phenomenon that psychologist Sarnoff Mednick (1963) called "familiarity breeds rigidity." By this he meant that the more people know about a subject, the less likely they are to be creative. Early adulthood may be the peak of creativity because many problems encountered professionally are novel.

On the other hand, many people do not reach their pinnacle of creativity until much later in life. For instance, Buckminster Fuller did not devise the geodesic dome until he was in his 50s. Frank Lloyd Wright designed the Guggenheim Museum in New York at age 70. Charles Darwin and Jean Piaget were still writing influential works well into their 70s, and Picasso was painting in his 90s. Furthermore, overall productivity, as opposed to the period of a person's most important output, remains fairly steady throughout adulthood, particularly in the humanities (Simonton, 2009).

Overall, the study of creativity reveals few consistent developmental patterns. One reason is the difficulty of determining just what constitutes **creativity**, which is defined as combining responses or ideas in novel ways. Because definitions of what is "novel" may vary from one person to the next, it is hard to identify a particular behavior unambiguously as creative.

creativity the combination of responses or ideas in novel ways

This hasn't stopped psychologists from trying. One suggested component of creativity is a person's willingness to take risks that may yield high payoffs. Creative people are like successful stock market investors who follow the "buy low, sell high" rule. Creative people develop and endorse ideas that are unfashionable or regarded as wrong ("buying low"), assuming that eventually others will see their value and embrace them ("selling high"). According to this theory, creative adults take a fresh look at ideas that were initially discarded, particularly if the problem is a familiar one. They are flexible enough to move away from tried-and-true ways of doing things and to consider new approaches (Sternberg, Kaufman, & Pretz, 2002; Sternberg, 2009; Sawyer, 2012).

Profound events such as the birth of a child or the death of a loved one can stimulate cognitive development by offering an opportunity to reevaluate our place in the world. What are some other profound events that might stimulate cognitive development?

Life Events and Cognitive Development

Marriage. The death of a parent. Starting a first job. The birth of a child. Buying a house.

Milestones such as these, whether welcome or unwanted, can cause stress. But do they also cause cognitive growth?

Some research evidence—spotty and largely based on case studies—suggests that the answer may be yes. For instance, the birth of a child may trigger fresh insights into the nature of relationships—one's place in the world and one's role in perpetuating humanity. Similarly, the death of a loved one may cause a reevaluation of what is important and a new look at the way life should be led (Kandler et al., 2012; Andersson & Conley, 2013).

Experiencing the ups and downs of life may lead young adults to think about the world in novel, more complex and sophisticated, less rigid ways. They are now capable of using postformal thought to see and grasp trends and patterns, personalities, and choices. This allows them to deal effectively with the complex social worlds of which they are a part.

REVIEW, CHECK, AND APPLY

REVIEW

L09 What are the major contemporary approaches to intelligence?

- New views of intelligence encompass the triarchic theory, practical intelligence, and emotional intelligence.
- Creativity seems to peak during early adulthood, with young adults viewing even long-standing problems as novel situations.

L010 What causes cognitive growth in young adults?

- Major life events contribute to cognitive growth by providing opportunities and incentives to rethink one's self and one's world.

CHECK YOURSELF

1. Sternberg's _____ theory of intelligence suggests that intelligence is made up of three major components.
2. According to psychologist Sarnoff Mednick (1963), creativity is at its highest in young adulthood because as we get older and more familiar with our areas of study (or occupations), creativity may be stunted.
   - True
   - False
3. Major life events can influence our cognitive development because positive and negative life circumstances lead us to think differently about our relationships with others, what's important to us, or our place in the world.
   - True
   - False

APPLYING LIFESPAN DEVELOPMENT

- What does "familiarity breeds rigidity" mean? Can you think of examples of this phenomenon from your own experience?

Study and **Review** on **MyPsychLab.com**

COLLEGE: PURSUING HIGHER EDUCATION

L011 Who attends college today, and how is the college population changing?
L012 What difficulties do students face in college?

As soon as the class ends at 3:30, Laura Twombly, restarting college at age 30, packs her books and rushes to her car. She speeds to reach her job by 4 PM, anxious to avoid another warning from her supervisor. After her shift, she picks up her son, Derek, from her mother's house and hurries home.

From 8:30 to 9:30 Laura spends time with Derek before putting him to bed. At 10, she starts studying for her business ethics test. She gives up at 11, setting the alarm for 5 AM so she can finish studying before Derek wakes around 7. Then she dresses and feeds him and herself and hurries to drop Derek off at her mother's house and start another round of classes, work, study, and mothering.

Laura Twombly, one of the one-third of college students who are above the age of 24, faces unusual challenges as she pursues her college degree. Older students like her are just one aspect of the increasing diversity—in family background, socioeconomic status, race, and ethnicity—that characterizes college campuses today.

For any student, though, attending college is a significant accomplishment. College attendance is not commonplace: Nationwide, high school graduates who enter college are in the minority.

The Demographics of Higher Education

What types of students enter college? Mirroring the U.S. population, U.S. college students are primarily white and middle class. Nearly 69 percent of white high school graduates enter college, compared with 61 percent of African American graduates and 47 percent of Hispanic graduates. Even more striking, although the absolute number of minority students in college has increased, the overall *proportion* of the minority population that enters college has *decreased* over the past decade—probably because of the diminished availability of financial aid (U.S. Bureau of the Census, 1998, 2000).

Furthermore, only around 40 percent of those who start college finish 4 years later with a degree. Although about half of those who drop out eventually finish college, the other half never obtain a college degree. For minorities, the picture is even worse: The national dropout rate for African American college students stands at 70 percent (American College Testing Program, 2001).

College attendance makes a difference in many aspects of life, including economic well-being. Just 3 percent of adults who have a college education live below the poverty line; high school dropouts, on the other hand, are 10 times more likely to be living in poverty (U.S. Bureau of the Census, 2003) (see Figure 7-7).

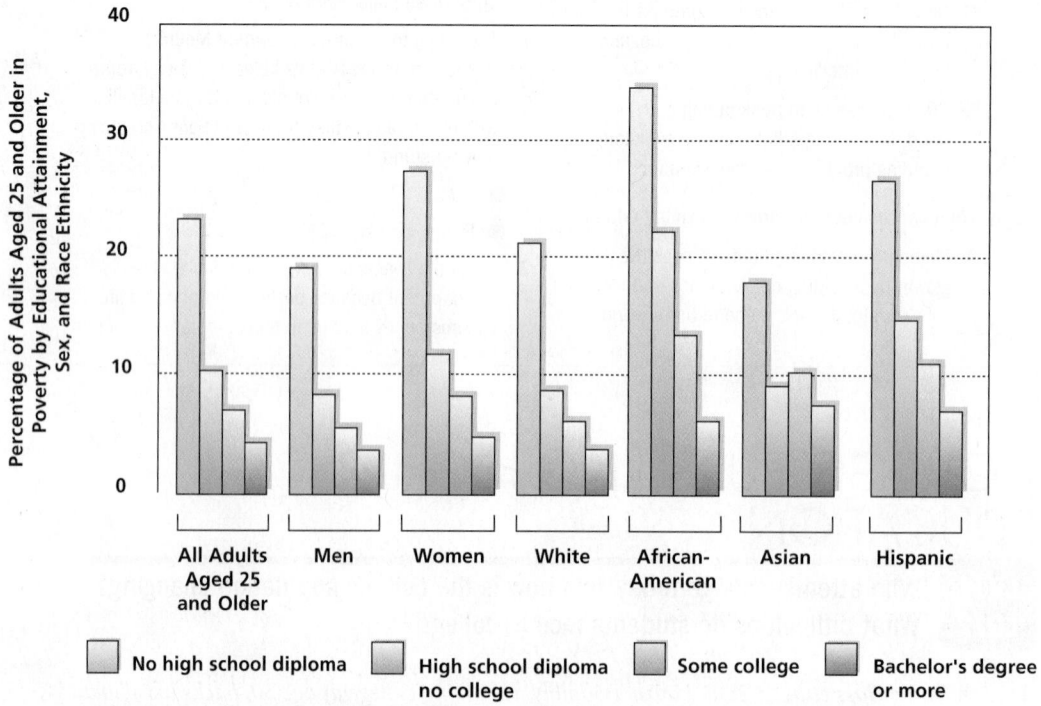

FIGURE 7-7 College Enrollment by Racial Group
The proportion of non-whites who attend college has increased in the last few decades.
Source: The Condition of Education 2004; National Center for Education Statistics, 2004.

The Gender Gap in College Attendance

More women than men attend college and the proportion of women, relative to men, is increasing. Women receive 133 bachelor's degrees for every 100 men receive. The gender gap is even more evident for minority students, with 166 African American women attending college for every 100 African American men (Adebayo, 2008; Conger & Long, 2010; Flashman, 2013).

Why the gender gap? It may be that men have more job opportunities when they graduate from high school. For instance, the military, trade unions, and jobs that require physical strength may be both more available and more attractive to men. Furthermore, women often have better high school academic records than men, and they may be admitted to college at greater rates (Dortch, 1997; Buchmann & DiPrete, 2006; England & Li, 2006).

The Changing College Student: Never Too Late to Go to College?

If you picture the "average college student" as an 18- or 19-year-old, it's time to rethink. In fact, 26 percent of students taking college courses for credit in the United States are between 25 and 35, like Laura Twombly, the 30-year-old student profiled earlier. Over a third of community college students are over 30 (Dortch, 1997; U.S. Department of Education, 2005).

Why are so many older, nontraditional students taking college courses? One reason is economic. A college degree is becoming increasingly important for obtaining a job. Many employers encourage or require workers to undergo college-based training to learn new skills or update old ones.

In addition, as young adults age, they begin to feel the need to settle down with a family. This change in attitude can reduce their risk-taking behavior and make them focus more on acquiring the ability to support their family—a phenomenon that has been labeled *maturation reform*.

According to developmental psychologist Sherry Willis (1985), several broad goals underlie adults' participation in learning. First, adults sometimes seek to understand their own aging, trying to figure out what is happening to them and what to expect in the future. Second, some adults seek to understand more fully the rapid technological and cultural changes of modern life.

Third, some adult learners may be seeking a practical edge in combating obsolescence on the job by acquiring new vocational skills. Finally, education may be seen as helpful in preparing for future retirement. Concerned about shifting from a work orientation to a leisure orientation, they may see education as a means of broadening their possibilities.

The number of older students, starting or returning to college, continues to grow. More than a third of college students are 24 years old or older. Why are so many older, nontraditional students taking college courses?

From an educator's perspective: How is the presence of older students likely to affect the college classroom, given what you know about human development? Why?

College Adjustment: Reacting to the Demands of College Life

When you began college, did you feel depressed, lonely, anxious, withdrawn? If so, you weren't alone. Many students, particularly recent high school graduates living away from home for the first time, have problems adjusting during their first year in college. The **first-year adjustment reaction** is a cluster of psychological symptoms, including loneliness, anxiety, and depression, relating to the college experience. Although any first-year student may experience this reaction, it is particularly prevalent among students who were unusually successful, either academically or socially, in high school. When they begin college, their sudden change in status may cause distress.

first-year adjustment reaction a cluster of psychological symptoms, including loneliness, anxiety, withdrawal, and depression, relating to the college experience suffered by first-year college students

Students who have been successful and popular in high school are particularly vulnerable to first-year adjustment reaction in college. Counseling, as well as increasing familiarity with campus life, can help a student adjust.

First-generation college students, who are the first in their families to attend college, are particularly susceptible to difficulties during their first year of college. They may arrive at college without a clear understanding of how the demands of college differ from high school, and the social support they have from their families may be inadequate. In addition, they may be less well-prepared for college work (Barry et al., 2009; Credé & Niehorster, 2012).

Most often, first-year adjustment reaction passes as students make friends, experience academic success, and integrate themselves into campus life. In other cases, though, the problems remain and may fester, leading to more serious psychological difficulties.

Both male and female college professors may unintentionally favor their male students over their female students, calling on their male students more and making more eye contact with them than with the female students. Why do you think unconscious sexism like this persists?

Gender and College Performance

I registered for a calculus course my first year at DePauw. Even twenty years ago I was not timid, so on the very first day I raised my hand and asked a question. I still have a vivid memory of the professor rolling his eyes, hitting his head with his hand in frustration, and announcing to everyone, "Why do they expect me to teach calculus to girls?" I never asked another question. Several weeks later I went to a football game, but I had forgotten to bring my ID. My calculus professor was at the gate checking IDs, so I went up to him and said, "I forgot my ID but you know me, I'm in your class." He looked right at me and said, "I don't remember you in my class." I couldn't believe that someone who changed my life and whom I remember to this day didn't even recognize me. (Sadker & Sadker, 1994, p. 162)

Although such blatant sexism is less likely today, prejudice and discrimination directed at women is still a fact of college life. For instance, the next time you are in class, consider the gender of your classmates—and the subject matter of the class. Although men and women attend college in roughly equal proportions, they tend to take different courses. Classes in education and the social sciences, for instance, typically have a larger proportion of women than men; and classes in engineering, the physical sciences, and mathematics tend to have more men than women.

Even women who start out in mathematics, engineering, and the physical sciences are more than twice as likely as men to drop out. And although the number of women seeking graduate degrees in science and engineering has been increasing, women still lag behind men (National Science Foundation, 2002; York, 2008).

Becoming an Informed Consumer of Development

When Do College Students Need Professional Help With Their Problems?

How can you tell if a student who is feeling depressed and unhappy may need professional help? Although there are no hard-and-fast rules, there are signals that indicate that professional help is warranted (Engler & Goleman, 1992). Among them:

- psychological distress that lingers and interferes with a person's sense of well-being and ability to function
- feelings that one is unable to cope effectively with the stress
- hopeless or depressed feelings, with no apparent reason
- the inability to build close relationships
- physical symptoms—such as headaches, stomach cramps, or skin rashes—that have no apparent underlying cause

If some of these signals are present, it would be helpful to discuss them with a help-provider, such as a counseling psychologist, clinical psychologist, or other mental health worker. The best place to start is the campus medical center. A personal physician, neighborhood clinic, or local board of health can also provide a referral.

How prevalent are psychological problems? Surveys find that almost half of college students report having at least one significant psychological issue. Other research finds that more than 40 percent of students who visited a college counseling center reported being depressed (see Figure 7-8). Remember, though, that these figures include only the students who sought help. Consequently, they may not be representative of the entire college population (Benton et al., 2003).

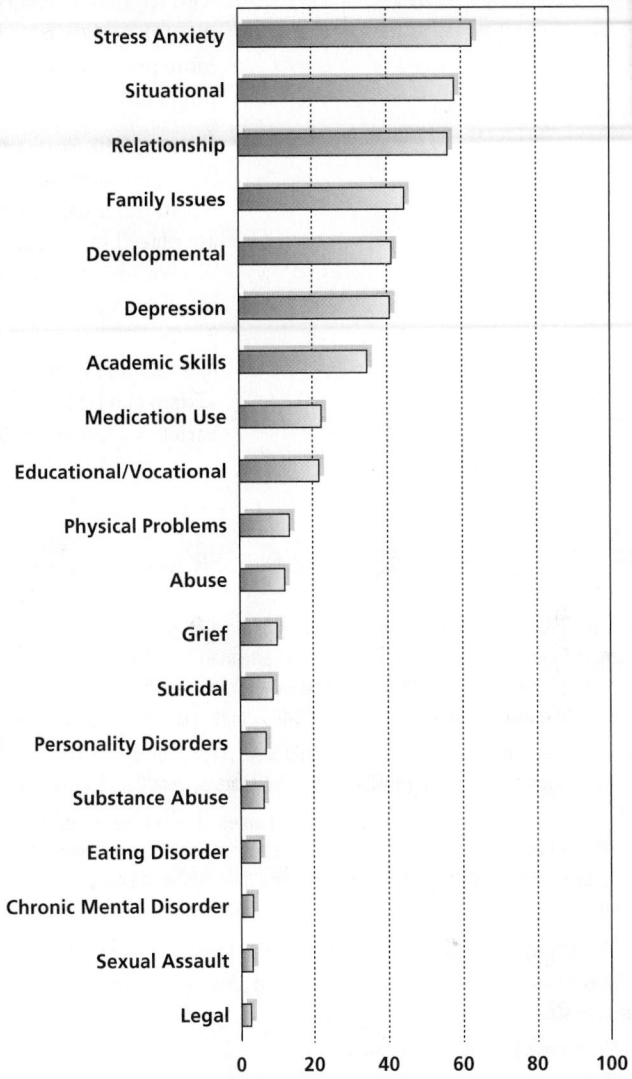

FIGURE 7-8 College Problems
The difficulties most frequently reported by college students visiting a campus counseling center.
Source: Benton et al., 2003.

The differences in gender distribution and attrition rates across subject areas are no accident. They reflect the powerful influence of gender stereotypes that operate throughout the world of education—and beyond. For instance, when women in their first year of college are asked to name a likely career choice, they are much less apt to choose careers that have traditionally been dominated by men, such as engineering or computer programming, and more likely to choose professions that have traditionally been populated by women, such as nursing and social work. Furthermore, even when they do choose to enter math- and science-related fields, they may face sex discrimination (Ceci & Williams, 2010; Lane, Goh, & Driver-Linn, 2012; Heilbronner, 2013).

Male and female college students also have different expectations regarding their areas of competence. For instance, one survey asked first-year college students whether they were above or below average on a variety of traits and abilities. As shown in Figure 7-9, men were more likely than women to think of themselves as above average in overall academic and mathematical ability and emotional health.

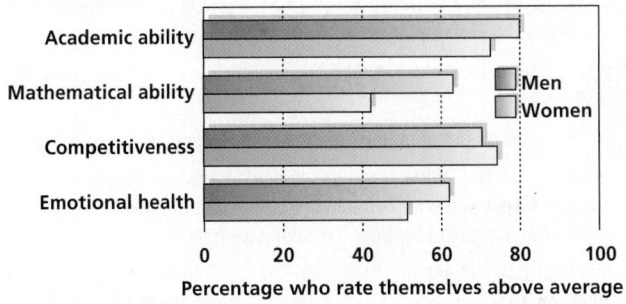

FIGURE 7-9 The Great Gender Divide
During their first year of college, men, compared to women, are more apt to view themselves as above average on several spheres relevant to academic success. What is the root of this difference?
Source: The American Freshman: National Norms for Fall, 1990; Astin, Korn, & Berz, 1989. Higher Education Research Institute, UCLA.

Both male and female college professors treat men and women differently, even though the different treatment is largely unintentional and the professors are unaware of their actions. Professors call on men more frequently than women and make more eye contact with men than with women. Furthermore, male students are more likely to receive extra help. Finally, the quality of the responses received by male and female students differs, with male students receiving more positive reinforcement for their comments than female students—exemplified by the startling illustration in Table 7-3 (Epperson, 1988; AAUW, 1992; Sadker & Sadker, 1994).

Benevolent Sexism: When Being Nice Is Not So Nice. Although some cases of unequal treatment represent *hostile sexism* in which people treat women in a way that is overtly harmful, in other cases women are the victims of benevolent sexism. In *benevolent sexism*, women are placed in stereotyped and restrictive roles that appear, on the surface, to be positive.

For instance, a male college professor may compliment a female student on her good looks or offer to give her an easier research project so she won't have to work so hard. While the professor may feel that he is merely being thoughtful, in fact he may be making the woman feel that she is not taken seriously and undermining her view of her competence. Benevolent sexism can be just as harmful as hostile sexism (Dardenne, Dumont, & Bollier, 2007; Dumont, Sarlet, & Dardenne, 2010; Glick & Fiske, 2012).

TABLE 7-3 GENDER BIAS IN THE CLASSROOM

The course on American Political History is one of four required university courses for freshmen. The last class before the final exam is attended by 70 students, divided almost equally between males and females. The professor begins by asking if there are questions about the final. Several people raise their hands.

JAMES: Do we have to memorize specific bills that were passed or the amendments to the Constitution? Or will the test be more general?

PROFESSOR: You will need to know the content and dates of major legislation, including constitutional amendments. You don't have to memorize every word, but know what they mean, when they happened, and why they matter. If I were you, James, I would go over my notes with a fine-toothed comb.

CAITLIN: Will there be any multiple choice questions?

PROFESSOR: Seven essay questions. You'll select five. I'd advise bringing two or three blue books.

CAITLIN: Will we have the whole two hours?

PROFESSOR: Yes. Anyone else?

DAVE (calling out): Will we be allowed to bring one page of notes, like on the midterm?

PROFESSOR: I haven't yet decided. Do you think the notes really help you?

DAVE: Yeah. I think they take some of the pressure off. And preparing them gets people to study for the test.

PROFESSOR: You make a good point about getting people to study. I'll consider it. Brian?

BRIAN: If we do better on the final than the midterm, will it raise our final grade?

PROFESSOR: The midterm and the research paper are 30 percent each. The final exam is 40 percent. But I look for improvement, so an excellent grade on the final will tip the scales in your favor. Why don't we begin?

The professor lectures on *Citizens United* for 20 minutes before he asks a question about campaign funding. Interest in campaign funding runs a distant second to what's on the final exam, so only a few hands are raised. The professor calls on Dave.

DAVE: Citizens United doesn't allow corporations or unions to contribute directly to a candidate's campaign fund, but it does allow them to pay for ads asking people to vote for a particular candidate.

PROFESSOR: Good point, Dave. You've zeroed in on what was an important distinction in the mind of the court. (He smiles at Dave, and Dave smiles back.) Do you think, in actual practice, the distinction holds up? (Five hands go up, five out of seventy.) Eleanor?

ELEANOR: I think—well, I don't know if this is right—but I think maybe the Supreme Court justices who voted in favor of *CU*, they tend to be conservative and I think they wanted—"

DAVE (calling out): Oh yeah, blame it on the conservatives. You guys on the left are just sore because no one with bucks to spend wants to do ads for any of your loser candidates. (Eleanor looks upset but says nothing. Several students laugh, and the professor smiles. He calls on Jessica.)

JESSICA: I think the recent election shows you can't just buy—

NICK (interrupting Jessica, calls out): The distinction holds up because in the corporate ads, the candidate can't come out and say 'I'm so-and-so and I approve this ad.' People can tell the difference."

PROFESSOR: Good point, Nick. But doesn't the potential volume of advertising possible under *CU* have to be considered? Jacob?

JACOB: I guess so. If one candidate gets all the big corporate advertising, it could maybe wipe out the other candidate.

PROFESSOR: Do you think people are ultimately swayed by campaign ads? If they see a hundred ads saying don't vote for Candidate X and only ten ads saying vote for Candidate X, do they make up their minds by the numbers?

JACOB: They probably just tune out after a while. Maybe the candidate who says don't vote for the other person, they're a loser, maybe people get tired of hearing those attacks.

PROFESSOR: There's some real evidence for that, Jacob. Good. Melissa, do you want to say something? (Melissa's hand is at "half-mast," raised but just barely. When the professor calls her name, she looks a bit startled.)

MELISSA (speaking very softly): Maybe we need to rethink this whole thing about a corporation being an association of persons and having first amendment rights. A lot of people don't like it. (As Melissa speaks, students begin to close their laptops and gather their books. Conversations begin and the professor dismisses the class.)

Source: Based on Sadker & Sadker, 1994.

Stereotype Threat and Disidentification With School

African Americans don't do well in academic pursuits. Women lack ability in math and science. So say erroneous, damaging, and yet persistent stereotypes about African Americans and women. And in the real world these stereotypes play out in vicious ways. For instance, when African Americans start elementary school, their standardized test scores are only slightly lower than those of Caucasian students, and yet a 2-year gap emerges by the sixth grade. And even though more African American high-school graduates are enrolling in college, the eventual graduation rate for blacks is far lower at 43 percent than for whites at 81 percent (National Center for Education Statistics, 2011).

Analogously, even though boys and girls perform virtually identically on standardized math tests in elementary and middle school, this changes when they reach high school. At that level, and even more so in college, males tend to do better in math than females. In fact, when women take college math, science, and engineering courses, they are more likely to do poorly than men who enter college with the same level of preparation and identical SAT scores. Strangely, though, this phenomenon does not hold true for other areas of the curriculum, where men and women perform at similar levels (Hyde, Fennema, & Lamon, 1990).

According to psychologist Claude Steele, the reason behind the declining levels of performance for both women and African Americans is the same: *academic disidentification*, a lack of personal identification with an academic domain. For women, disidentification is specific to math and science; for African Americans, it is more generalized across academic domains. In both cases, negative societal stereotypes produce a state of **stereotype threat,** which are obstacles to performance that come from awareness of the stereotypes held by society about academic abilities (Steele, 1997; Carr & Steele, 2009; Ganley et al., 2013).

For instance, women seeking to achieve in fields that rely on math and science may worry about the failure that society predicts for them. They may decide, paradoxically, that failure in a male-dominated field, because it would confirm societal stereotypes, presents such great risks that the struggle to succeed is not worth the effort, and they may not try very hard (Inzlicht & Ben-Zeev, 2000; Johnson et al., 2012).

Similarly, African Americans may work under the pressure of feeling that they must disconfirm the negative stereotype regarding their academic performance. The pressure can be anxiety provoking and threatening, and can reduce their performance below their true ability level. Ironically, stereotype threat may be most severe for better, more confident students, who have not internalized the negative stereotype to the extent of questioning their own abilities (Carr & Steele, 2009; Steele, 2012).

Rather than ignoring negative stereotypes, women and African Americans may perform less well and, ultimately, disidentify with schooling and academic pursuits relevant to the stereotype. This is exactly what a recent longitudinal study of African Americans found. The study recruited participants when they were in fifth grade and periodically reassessed them until shortly after high school. Even in the fifth grade, nearly 90 percent of the children had already experienced at least minimal discrimination, and more than one in five had experienced a moderate level of discrimination. Nearly all the students expected to finish high school, and in tenth grade more than 70 percent expected to attend college. By age 18 or 19, only a little over 30 percent were enrolled in college.

What happened? Early experience of discrimination was in fact negatively associated with later college enrollment. The researchers noted that the experience of discrimination in fifth grade predicted a change in the teenagers' academic orientation in seventh and tenth grades. Specifically, students who experienced more discrimination in fifth grade were later more likely to be tolerant of deviant behavior, such as drug-using peers, and to have lowered expectations of attending college (O'Hara et al., 2012).

Interestingly, a personality variable known as "future orientation" played a pivotal role in how students' expectations of attending college were affected by their earlier discriminatory experiences. Future orientation is the tendency to think about and prepare for the future. Students with a low future orientation were discouraged from attending college by earlier discrimination, but students with a high future orientation actually increased their determination to attend college in response to discriminatory experiences. This finding suggests a helpful intervention for keeping African American students on course to attend college: Teach them stay focused on the future, so that they view college as a means of transcending the harmful effects of discrimination rather than feeling helpless (O'Hara et al., 2012).

stereotype threat obstacles to performance that come from awareness of the stereotypes held by society about academic abilities

REVIEW, CHECK, AND APPLY

REVIEW

L011 Who attends college today, and how is the college population changing?

- Rates of college enrollment differ across gender, racial, and ethnic lines.
- The average age of college students is steadily increasing as more adults return to college.

L012 What difficulties do students face in college?

- The phenomena of academic disidentification and stereotype threat help explain the lower performance of women and African Americans in certain academic domains.
- First-year students may experience first-year adjustment reaction, characterized by a cluster of psychological symptoms, including loneliness, anxiety, and depression.
- First-generation college students may lack a clear understanding of the demands of college and may be less well-prepared for the work.
- In addition to drinking and drug use, gambling—another addictive behavior—has become a threat to students' well-being.

CHECK YOURSELF

1. Although attending college is an important event in one's life, the number of individuals who begin college _____.
   - a are in the majority
   - b has been decreasing
   - c are in the minority
   - d is the same as the number of people not entering college
2. More women than men attend and graduate from college, and the proportion of women, relative to men, is increasing.
   - True
   - False
3. Jared is having difficulty in his first year of college. Psychological symptoms include loneliness, anxiety, withdrawal, and depression. It appears that Jared is suffering from a cluster of symptoms called _____.
   - a first-year adjustment reaction
   - b classical conditioning
   - c high anxiety
   - d social referencing
4. Failing to identify oneself as successful in a certain academic domain such as math and science for women and academics in general for African Americans is known as _____.
   - a stereotype threat
   - b academic disidentification
   - c inadequate self-concept
   - d somatic symptom illness

APPLYING LIFESPAN DEVELOPMENT

- How would you educate college professors who behave differently toward male and female students? What factors contribute to this phenomenon? Can this situation be changed?

✓ **Study** and **Review** on **MyPsychLab.com**

MODULE 7.3

SOCIAL AND PERSONALITY DEVELOPMENT IN EARLY ADULTHOOD

Paul Gerard and Mario Deluca are recalling how they first met 5 years ago in freshman biology lab in college. "Our usual lab partners were out that day, so we kind of got stuck together," remembers Mario. "We were just making small talk at first, but then it kept going. I think we ended up closing down the dining hall that night."

Paul chimes in, laughing, "Yeah, if we sat there any longer I think they would have charged us rent!" The couple smile and exchange glances.

"It was so amazing," Paul continues. "That day started just like any other, but by the time I went to bed that night I knew I had met my soulmate. We just had so much in common! But it was more than that—it was the way I felt while we were together. It was like a drug. I can't even explain it." He pauses thoughtfully, then answers with conviction, "In that moment, nothing else mattered. Not the exam I had the next day, not the people who were starting at us—it was me and Mario. We felt connected. It felt… it felt right."

In early adulthood we face many developmental tasks (see Table 7-4). We come to grips with the notion that we are no longer other people's children, and we begin to perceive ourselves as adults, full members of society with significant responsibilities (Tanner, Arnett, & Leis, 2009; Arnett, 2010).

This module examines those challenges, concentrating on relationships with others. First, we consider the question of love in its many varieties, including gay and lesbian relationships. We look at how people choose partners, influenced by societal and cultural factors.

Then we examine marriage, including the choice of whether to marry and the factors that influence the success of marriage. We consider how children affect marital happiness and we look at the roles children play in a marriage for heterosexual, gay, and lesbian couples. Also, we discuss the factors that influence family size today, which reflect the complexity of issues young adults face in relationships.

Finally, we move to careers, another major preoccupation of young adults. We see how identity during early adulthood is often tied to one's job and how people decide on the kind of work they do. The module ends with a discussion of the reasons people work and ways to choose a career.

FORGING RELATIONSHIPS: INTIMACY, LIKING, AND LOVING DURING EARLY ADULTHOOD

7.1
7.2
7.3

L05 How do young adults form loving relationships?
L06 How do people choose spouses?
L07 Are there differences between gay and lesbian relationships and heterosexual relationships?

Dianne Maher swept Thad Ramon off his feet—literally. "I was setting up the cafeteria for a dance and she was sweeping the floor. Next thing I knew a push broom was under my heels and down I went. I didn't hurt myself or anything, and my pride wasn't injured, but you could say my heart took a beating. There she was, sly grin on her face, and all I could do was stare and laugh. We started talking and laughing some more and soon we discovered we had a lot more than silliness in common. We've been together ever since."

Thad followed his heart and in senior year publicly proposed to Dianne in that same cafeteria during lunch hour. They plan to get married beside the college duck pond and at the end of the ceremony march beneath crossed push brooms held by their ushers and bridesmaids.

The road to love is not as smooth for everyone as it was for Thad. For some, it is tortuous, meandering through soured relationships and fallen dreams; for others, it is a road never taken. For some, love leads to marriage and the storybook picture of home, children, and long years together. For many, it leads to a less happy ending, to divorce and custody battles.

Intimacy and relationships are major considerations during early adulthood. Relationships are the core of young adults' happiness, and many worry whether they are developing serious relationships "on time." Even those who are not interested in forming long-term relationships typically are focused, to some extent, on connecting with others.

TABLE 7-4 THE DEVELOPMENTAL TASKS OF ADULTHOOD

Adulthood (Ages 20–40)	Middle Adulthood (Ages 40–60)	Late Adulthood (Ages 60+)
• Taking responsibility for yourself	• Understanding that time is passing and accepting it	• Spending time well
• Understanding that you have a unique history and that it is not permanent	• Accepting that you are aging	• Remaining social rather than isolated
• Managing the separation from your parents	• Accepting changes in your body, including appearance and health	• Making friends and new connections
• Redefining the relationship with your parents	• Developing an acceptable work identity	• Adjusting to changing sexuality
• Gaining and interpreting your sexual experiences	• Becoming a member of society	• Staying healthy
• Becoming capable of intimacy with another (non-family) person	• Understanding that society is constantly changing	• Managing physical pain, ailments, and limitations
• Managing money	• Keeping old friends and making new ones	• Making life without work a comfortable lifestyle
• Developing skills that can lead to a career	• Coping with changes in your sexuality	• Using time wisely for engaging work and recreation
• Considering career possibilities	• Continuously reworking your spousal or partner relationship	• Managing finances effectively for yourself and your dependents
• Considering parenthood and possibly becoming a parent	• Altering your relationship with your children as they age	• Focusing on the present and future, not dwelling on the past
• Defining your values	• Passing on knowledge, skills, and values to the next generation	• Adjusting to ongoing losses of close connections
• Finding a place in society	• Managing money effectively for short- and long-term goals	• Accepting care from children and grandchildren
	• Experiencing the illness and death of persons close to you, especially parents	
	• Finding a place in society	

Source: Based on Colarusso & Nemiroff, 1981.

Seeking Intimacy: Erikson's View of Young Adulthood

Erik Erikson regarded young adulthood as the time of the **intimacy-versus-isolation stage**, which spans the period of postadolescence into the early 30s. During this period, the focus is on developing close, intimate relationships with others.

Erikson's idea of intimacy comprises several aspects. One is selflessness, the sacrifice of one's own needs to those of another. Another is sexuality, the experience of joint pleasure from focusing not just on one's own gratification but also on that of one's partner. Finally, there is deep devotion, marked by efforts to fuse one's identity with the identity of a partner.

According to Erikson, those who experience difficulties during this stage are often lonely, isolated, and fearful of relationships. Their difficulties may stem from an earlier failure to develop a strong identity. In contrast, young adults who are able to form intimate relationships on a physical, intellectual, and emotional level successfully resolve the crisis of this stage of development.

Although Erikson's approach has been influential, it's troubling today because he limited healthy intimacy to heterosexuality. Same-sex partnerships, couples childless by choice, and other relationships different from Erikson's ideal were regarded as less than satisfactory. Furthermore, Erikson focused more on men than women and did not consider racial and ethnic identity, greatly limiting the applicability of his theory (Yip, Sellers, & Seaton, 2006).

intimacy-versus-isolation stage according to Erikson, the period of postadolescence into the early 30s that focuses on developing close, intimate relationships with others

emerging adulthood according to Arnett the period from the end of teenage years through early 20's in which people are still sorting out their options for the future

Still, Erikson's work has been influential historically because of its emphasis on examining the continued growth and development of personality throughout the life span. Furthermore, it inspired other developmentalists to consider psychosocial growth during young adulthood and the range of intimate relationships we develop, from friendship to mates for life (Whitbourne, Sneed, & Sayer, 2009). For example, as we discuss in the accompanying "From Research to Practice" box, some developmentalists believe there is a unique developmental stage that begins at the end of the teenage years and extends through the early twenties.

From Research to Practice

Emerging Adulthood: A New Stage of Life?

Boomerang children. Failures to launch. Whatever you call the phenomenon, young adults are increasingly likely to get a later start in life than older generations did. When once certain milestones were expected to be achieved before age 30—completing school, leaving home, attaining financial independence, getting married, and having a child—20-somethings today are often delaying or even rejecting that traditional sequence of events. Remaining single, travelling, taking internships, and returning to school for more education are alternative options that are gaining popularity. Rather than rushing to settle down, many young adults are keeping their options open—living together without being married, switching jobs, moving from residence to residence, and often returning home with their parents for periods of time.

In short, young adults are taking longer to start acting like adults. Are they being lazy? Are they just spoiled and self-indulgent? Perhaps, but some researchers think that what we're seeing is the emergence of an entirely new stage of life they call "emerging adulthood." **Emerging adulthood** encompasses the period between 18 and the late 20s and may be a response to shifting cultural forces, including an increasing amount of education needed for a good career and fewer employment opportunities overall—meaning that financial security is harder to come by. Combine that with the frequency of couples living together without being fully committed, and it's not hard to see why young people put off marriage and child raising (Arnett, 2011).

It's not clear whether changing cultural expectations and opportunities have created the delayed onset of full adulthood or if it's more the case that the emerging adulthood stage was always there but hidden by societal pressure to fall in line with adult obligations. Researchers studying brain development have noted that young people's brains continue to grow and change into their mid-20s—most significantly in the prefrontal cortex, which is involved in emotional regulation and planning, as we noted when we discussed adolescence (Giedd et al., 2011).

Emerging adulthood as a life stage is marked by continuing the identity exploration that started in adolescence. It includes a sense of not knowing one's place in life yet and of not quite fitting into the adult role. There is instability, insecurity, great self-focus, and a "sense of possibilities." This last characteristic encompasses an idealistic optimism about the future—an exciting sense that many possible pathways to success and fulfillment exist—but with a sense of uncertainty and frustration (Arnett, 2011).

The notion of emerging adulthood as a new stage of life has its detractors. One criticism is that the ability to spend several years dabbling and exploring before taking on serious responsibilities is a luxury that some can afford, but many cannot. True developmental stages aren't "optional"—they can't be skipped or dismissed by those who find them inconvenient. Perhaps emerging adulthood is just a way that some people respond when coming of age in a time of great economic uncertainty or social change (Diamond, Fagundes, & Butterworth, 2010; Smith, 2012; Padilla-Walker, Nelson, & Carroll, 2012).

- *Do you think that emerging adulthood is a real stage of life or just a transitory consequence of particular social and economic times? Why do you think so?*
- *If emerging adulthood is a real stage of life, how might social institutions such as education and social services be adjusted to better serve young adults' needs?*

Friendship

Most of our relationships are friendships and maintaining them is an important part of adult life. Why? One reason is that people have a basic *need for belongingness* that leads them in early adulthood to establish and maintain at least a minimum number of relationships that foster a sense of belonging with others (Manstead, 1997; Rice, 1999).

But how do particular people end up becoming our friends? One of the most important factors is proximity—people form friendships with others who live nearby and with whom they have frequent contact. People who are nearby can obtain the rewards of friendship, such as companionship, social approval, and the occasional helping hand, at relatively little cost.

Similarity also plays an important role in friendship formation. Birds of a feather *do* flock together: People are more attracted to others who hold attitudes and values similar to their own (Simpkins et al., 2006; Morry, 2007; Selfhout et al., 2009; Preciado et al., 2012).

The importance of similarity becomes evident when we consider cross-race friendships. As we noted in our discussion of adolescence, the number of cross-race close friendships dwindles throughout the life span. In fact, although most adults claim to have a close friend of a different race, when they are queried regarding the names of close friends, few include a person of a different race (see Figure 7-10).

We also choose friends for their personal qualities. What's most important? According to results of surveys, people are most attracted to others who keep confidences and are loyal, warm, and affectionate. In addition, people like those who are supportive, frank, and have a good sense of humor (Parlee, 1979; Hartup & Stevens, 1999; You & Bellmore, 2012).

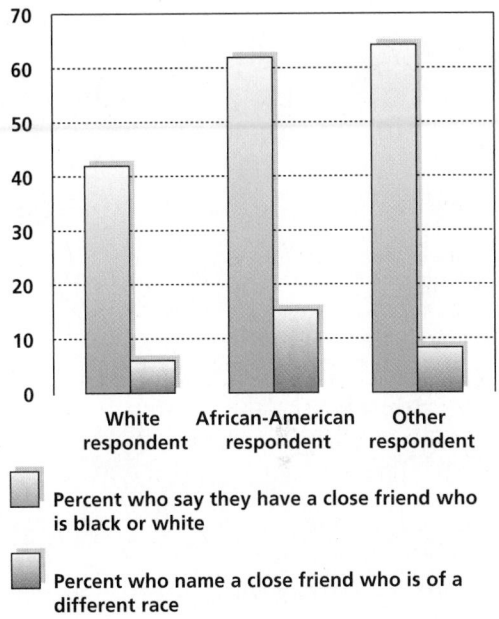

FIGURE 7-10 Rephrasing the Question
Although a relatively high percentage of whites and blacks claim to have a close friend who is a member of a different race, only a small majority actually name a person of another race or ethnicity when asked to list the names of their close friends.
Source: General Social Survey, 1998.

Falling in Love: When Liking Turns to Loving

After a few chance encounters at the laundromat where they wash their clothes each week, Rebecca and Jerry begin talking. They find they have a lot in common and they begin to look forward to what are now semiplanned meetings. After several weeks, they go out on their first official date and discover that they are well suited to each other.

If such a pattern seems predictable, it is: Most relationships develop by following a surprisingly regular progression (Burgess & Huston, 1979; Berscheid, 1985):

- Two people interact more often and for longer periods, and the range of settings increases.
- They increasingly seek each other's company.
- They open up more and more, disclosing more intimate information. They begin to share physical intimacies.
- They are more willing to share both positive and negative feelings, and they may offer criticism in addition to praise.
- They begin to agree on their goals for the relationship.
- Their reactions to situations become more similar.
- They begin to feel that their own psychological well-being is tied to the success of the relationship, viewing it as unique, irreplaceable, and cherished.
- Finally, their definition of themselves and their behavior changes: They begin to see themselves and act as a couple, rather than as two separate individuals.

Another view of the evolution of a relationship was put forward by psychologist Bernard Murstein (1976, 1986, 1987). According to **stimulus-value-role (SVR) theory**, relationships proceed in three stages.

In the first stage, the *stimulus stage*, relationships are built on surface, physical characteristics such as the way a person looks. Usually, this represents just the initial encounter. The second stage, the *value stage*, usually occurs between the second and the seventh encounter. In the value stage, the relationship is characterized by increasing similarity of values and beliefs. Finally, in the third stage, the *role stage*, the relationship is built on specific roles played by the participants. For instance, the couple may define themselves as boyfriend–girlfriend or husband–wife.

SVR theory has come under criticism because not every relationship follows a similar pattern (Gupta & Singh, 1982; Sternberg, 1986). For instance, there is no logical reason why value factors, rather than stimulus factors, could not predominate early in a relationship. Two people who meet at a political meeting could be attracted to each other's views of current issues.

stimulus-value-role (SVR) theory the theory that relationships proceed in a fixed order of three stages: stimulus, value, and role

Passionate and Companionate Love: The Two Faces of Love

Is "love" just a lot of "liking"? Most developmental psychologists would say no; love not only differs quantitatively from liking, it represents a qualitatively different state. For example, love, at least in its early stages, involves relatively intense physiological arousal, all-encompassing interest, recurrent fantasies, and rapid swings of emotion. Furthermore, compared to liking, love includes closeness, passion, and exclusivity (Lamm & Wiesmann, 1997; Hendrick & Hendrick, 2003; Ramsay, 2010).

Not all love is the same. We don't love our mothers the same way we love girlfriends or boyfriends, brothers or sisters, or lifelong friends. What distinguishes these different types of love? Some psychologists suggest that our love relationships can fall into two different categories: passionate or companionate.

Passionate (or romantic) love is a state of powerful absorption in someone. It includes intense physiological interest and arousal, and caring for another's needs. In comparison, **companionate love** is the strong affection that we have for those with whom our lives are deeply involved (Lamm & Wiesmann, 1997; Hendrick & Hendrick, 2003).

What is it that fuels the fires of passionate love? According to one theory, strong emotions—even negative ones such as jealousy, anger, or fear of rejection—may be the source of deepening passionate love.

In psychologists Elaine Hatfield and Ellen Berscheid's **labeling theory of passionate love**, individuals experience romantic love when two events occur together: intense physiological arousal and situational cues that indicate that "love" is the appropriate label for the feelings being experienced (Berscheid & Walster, 1974). The physiological arousal can be produced by sexual arousal, excitement, or even negative emotions such as jealousy. If that arousal is subsequently labeled as "I must be falling in love" or "he really turns me on," the experience is attributed to passionate love.

The theory helps to explain why people may feel deepened love even in the face of rejection or hurt. If negative emotions produce strong physiological arousal and this arousal is interpreted as "love," then people may decide that they are even more in love than they were before they experienced the negative emotions.

But why should people label an emotional experience "love" when there are so many alternative explanations? One answer is that in Western cultures, romantic love is seen as possible, acceptable, and desirable. The virtues of passion are extolled in songs, commercials, TV shows, and films. Young adults are primed and ready to experience love in their lives (Dion & Dion, 1988; Hatfield & Rapson, 1993; Florsheim, 2003).

This is not universal across cultures; in many cultures, passionate, romantic love is a foreign concept. Marriages are arranged on the basis of economic and status considerations. Even in Western cultures, the concept of romantic love was not "invented" until the Middle Ages, when social philosophers first suggested that love ought to be a requirement for marriage. Their goal was to provide an alternative to the raw sexual desire that had served as the primary basis for marriage before (Xiaohe & Whyte, 1990; Haslett, 2004; Moore & Wei, 2012).

passionate (or romantic) love a state of powerful absorption in someone

companionate love the strong affection for those with whom our lives are deeply involved

labeling theory of passionate love the theory that individuals experience romantic love when two events occur together: intense physiological arousal and situational cues suggesting that the arousal is due to love

Sternberg's Triangular Theory: The Three Faces of Love

Psychologist Robert Sternberg suggests that love is made up of three components: intimacy, passion, and decision/commitment. The **intimacy component** encompasses feelings of closeness, affection, and connectedness. The **passion component** comprises the motivational drives relating to sex, physical closeness, and romance. The **decision/commitment component** embodies both the initial cognition that one loves another person and the longer-term determination to maintain that love (Sternberg, 2006).

These components can be combined to form eight different types of love depending on which of the three components is either present or missing from a relationship (see Table 7-5). For instance, *nonlove* refers to people who have only the most casual of relationships; it consists of the absence of the three components of intimacy, passion, and decision/commitment. *Liking* develops when only intimacy is present; *infatuated love* exists when only passion is felt; and *empty love* exists when only decision/commitment is present.

Other types of love involve a mix of two or more components. For instance, *romantic love* occurs when intimacy and passion are present, and *companionate love* when intimacy and

intimacy component according to Sternberg the component of love that encompasses feelings of closeness, affection, and connectedness

passion component according to Sternberg the component of love that comprises the motivational drives relating to sex, physical closeness, and romance

decision/commitment component according to Sternberg the third aspect of love that embodies both the initial cognition that one loves another person and the longer-term determination to maintain that love decision/commitment occur jointly. When two people experience romantic love, they are drawn together physically and emotionally, but they do not necessarily view the relationship as lasting. Companionate love, on the other hand, may occur in long-lasting relationships in which physical passion has taken a backseat.

Fatuous love exists when passion and decision/commitment, without intimacy, are present. Fatuous love is a kind of mindless loving in which there is no emotional bond between the partners.

Finally, the eighth kind of love is *consummate love*. In consummate love, all three components of love are present. But don't assume that consummate love is the "ideal" love. Many long-lasting and entirely satisfactory relationships are based on other types of love. Furthermore, the type of love that predominates in a relationship varies over time. In strong, loving relationships the level of decision/commitment peaks and remains fairly stable. By contrast, passion tends to peak early in a relationship, but then declines and levels off. Intimacy also increases fairly rapidly, but can continue to grow over time.

Sternberg's triangular theory of love emphasizes both the complexity of love and its dynamic, evolving quality. As people and relationships develop, so does their love.

Choosing a Partner: Recognizing Mr. or Ms. Right

For many young adults, the search for a partner is a major pursuit during early adulthood. Society offers a wealth of advice, as a glance at the magazines at supermarket check-out counters confirms. Still, the road to identifying a life partner is not always easy.

Seeking a Spouse: Is Love the Only Thing That Matters? Most people have no hesitation in declaring that the major factor in choosing a spouse is love. Most people in the United States, that is: If we ask people in other societies, love becomes a secondary consideration. For instance, college students were asked in a survey if they would marry someone they did not love. Hardly anyone in the United States, Japan, or Brazil would consider it. On the other hand, a high proportion of college students in Pakistan and India would find it acceptable to marry without love (Levine, 1993). **Watch** the **Video** *Marriage and Love Relationships Across Cultures* in **MyPsychLab**.

What else matters? The characteristics differ considerably from one culture to another. For instance, a survey of nearly 10,000 people from around the world found that in China men ranked good health most important and women rated emotional stability and maturity most critical. In South Africa men from a Zulu background rated emotional stability first, and Zulu women rated dependable character the greatest concern (Buss et al., 1990; Buss, 2003).

Yet, there are commonalities across cultures. For instance, love and mutual attraction, even if not at the top of a specific culture's list, were relatively highly desired across all cultures. Furthermore, traits such as dependability, emotional stability, pleasing disposition, and intelligence were highly valued almost universally.

TABLE 7-5 THE COMBINATIONS OF LOVE

	Component			
Type of Love	**Intimacy**	**Passion**	**Decision/Commitment**	**Example**
Nonlove	Absent	Absent	Absent	The way you might feel about the person who takes your ticket at the movies.
Liking	Present	Absent	Absent	Good friends who have lunch together at least once or twice a week.
Infatuated love	Absent	Present	Absent	A "fling" or short-term relationship based only on sexual attraction.
Empty love	Absent	Absent	Present	An arranged marriage or a couple who have decided to stay married "for the sake of the children."
Romantic love	Present	Present	Absent	A couple who have been happily dating a few months, but have not made any plans for a future together.
Companionate love	Present	Absent	Present	A couple who enjoy each other's company and their relationship, although they no longer feel much sexual interest in each other.
Fatuous love	Absent	Present	Present	A couple who decides to move in together after knowing each other for only 2 weeks.
Consummate love	Present	Present	Present	A loving, sexually vibrant, long-term relationship.

Certain gender differences were similar across cultures—as confirmed by other surveys (e.g., Sprecher, Sullivan, & Hatfield, 1994). Men, more than women, prefer a potential marriage partner who is physically attractive. In contrast, women, more than men, prefer a potential spouse who is ambitious and industrious.

One explanation for cross-cultural similarities in gender differences rests on evolutionary theory. According to psychologist David Buss and colleagues (Buss, 2004), human beings, as a species, seek out certain characteristics in their mates that are likely to maximize the availability of beneficial genes. He argues that males in particular are genetically programmed to seek out mates with traits that indicate they have high reproductive capacity. Consequently, physically attractive, younger women might be more desirable because they are more capable of having children over a longer time period.

In contrast, women are genetically programmed to seek out men who have the potential to provide scarce resources in order to increase the likelihood that their offspring will survive. Consequently, they are attracted to mates who offer the highest potential of providing economic well-being (Li et al., 2002).

The evolutionary explanation for gender differences has come under heavy fire. Not only is the explanation untestable, but the similarities across cultures relating to different gender preferences may simply reflect similar patterns of gender stereotyping that have nothing to do with evolution. In addition, although some of the gender differences in what men and women prefer are consistent across cultures, there are numerous inconsistencies as well.

Finally, some critics of the evolutionary approach suggest that the finding that women prefer a partner who has good earning potential may have nothing to do with evolution and everything to do with the fact that men generally hold more power, status, and other resources fairly consistently across different cultures. Consequently, it is a rational choice for women to prefer a high-earning-potential spouse. On the other hand, because men don't need to take economic considerations into account, they can use more inconsequential criteria—like physical attractiveness—in choosing a spouse. In short, the consistencies that are found across cultures may be due to the realities of economic life that are similar throughout different cultures (Eagly & Wood, 2003; Wood & Eagly, 2010).

Filtering Models: Sifting Out a Spouse. While surveys help to identify valued characteristics, they are less helpful in illuminating how individual partners are chosen. According to the *filter explanation*, people seeking a mate screen potential candidates through successively finer-grained filters. The explanation assumes that people first filter for factors relating to broad determinants of attractiveness. Once these early screens have done their work, more sophisticated types of screening are used (see Figure 7-11). The end result is a choice based on compatibility between the two individuals (Janda & Klenke-Hamel, 1980).

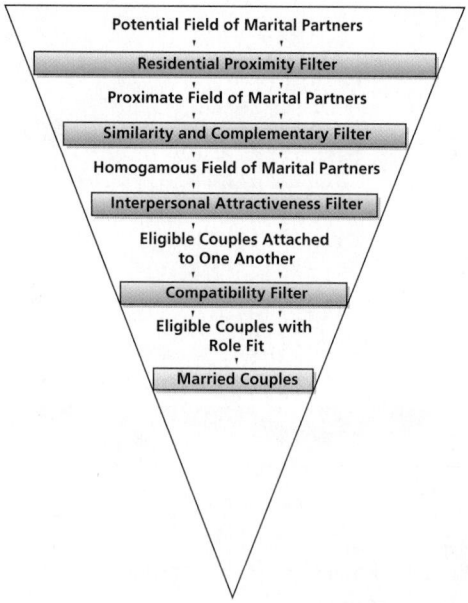

FIGURE 7-11 Filtering Potential Marriage Partners
According to one approach, we screen potential mates through successively finer-grained filters in order to settle on an appropriate spouse.
Source: Based on Janda & Klenke-Hamel, 1980.

What determines compatibility? People often marry according to the principle of homogamy. **Homogamy** is the tendency to marry someone who is similar in age, race, education, religion, and other basic demographic characteristics. Homogamy, long the dominant standard for U.S. marriages, has been declining recently, particularly among certain ethnic groups. For example, the rate of marriage between African American men and women of other races increased by three-quarters in the 1990s. Still, for other groups—such as Hispanic and Asian immigrants—the principle of homogamy still has considerable influence (Suro, 1999; Qian & Lichter, 2007; Fu & Heaton, 2008).

Another important societal standard is the *marriage gradient*, the tendency for men to marry women who are slightly younger, smaller, and lower in status, and women to marry men who are slightly older, larger, and higher in status (Bernard, 1982; Pyke & Adams, 2010).

From a social worker's perspective: How do the principles of homogamy and the marriage gradient work to limit options for high-status women? How do they affect men's options?

homogamy the tendency to marry someone who is similar in age, race, education, religion, and other basic demographic characteristics

The marriage gradient has important, and unfortunate, effects on partner choice. For one thing, it limits the number of potential mates for women, especially as they age, while allowing men a wider choice of partners throughout life. But it is unfortunate for low-status men, who do not marry because they cannot find women of low enough status or cannot find women of the same or higher status who are willing to accept them as mates. Consequently, they are, in the words of sociologist Jessie Bernard (1982), "bottom of the barrel" men. On the other hand, some women will be unable to marry because they are higher in status or seek someone of higher status than anyone in the available pool of men—"cream of the crop" women, in Bernard's words.

The marriage gradient makes finding a spouse particularly difficult for well-educated African American women who would prefer to marry an African American man. Fewer African American men attend college than African American women, making the potential pool of men who are suitable—as defined by society and the marriage gradient—relatively small. The pool of men is further limited because of the relatively higher rate of incarceration of black males (which is six times greater than that of whites). Consequently, relative to women of other races, African American women are more apt to marry men who are less educated than they are—or not marry at all (Kiecolt & Fossett, 1997; Willie & Reddick, 2003; Johnson, 2010).

Attachment Styles and Romantic Relationships: Do Adult Loving Styles Reflect Attachment in Infancy?

"I want a girl just like the girl that married dear old Dad." So go the lyrics of an old song, suggesting that the songwriter would like to find someone who loves him as much as his mother did. Is this just a corny tune, or is there a kernel of truth in this sentiment? Put more broadly, is the kind of attachment that people experience during infancy reflected in their adult romantic relationships?

Increasing evidence suggests that it very well may be. As we discussed earlier, attachment refers to the positive emotional bond that develops between a child and a particular individual. Most infants fall into one of three attachment categories: securely attached infants, who have healthy, positive, trusting relationships with their caregivers; avoidant infants, who are relatively indifferent to caregivers and avoid interactions with them; and ambivalent infants, who show great distress when separated from a caregiver but appear angry upon the caregiver's return.

Some psychologists believe that our attachment style as infants is repeated in the quality of our intimate relationships as adults.

According to psychologist Phillip Shaver and his colleagues, attachment styles continue into adulthood and affect the nature of romantic relationships (Davis et al., 2006; Mikulincer & Shaver, 2007; Dinero et al., 2008). For instance, consider the following statements:

1. I find it relatively easy to get close to others and am comfortable depending on them and having them depend on me. I don't often worry about being abandoned or about someone getting too close to me.
2. I am somewhat uncomfortable being close to others; I find it difficult to trust them completely, difficult to allow myself to depend on them. I am nervous when anyone gets too close, and often love partners want me to be more intimate than I feel comfortable being.
3. I find that others are reluctant to get as close as I would like. I often worry that my partner doesn't really love me or won't want to stay with me. I want to merge completely with another person, and this desire sometimes scares people away (Shaver, Hazan, & Bradshaw, 1988).

According to Shaver, agreement with the first statement reflects a secure attachment style. Adults who agree with this statement readily enter into relationships and feel happy and confident about the future success of their relationships. Most young adults—just over half—display the secure style of attachment (Hazan & Shaver, 1987; Luke, Sedikides, & Carnelley, 2012).

In contrast, adults who agree with the second statement typically display the avoidant attachment style. These individuals, who make up about a quarter of the population, tend to be less invested in relationships, have higher break-up rates, and often feel lonely.

Finally, agreement with the third category is reflective of an ambivalent style. Adults with an ambivalent style have a tendency to become overly invested in relationships, have repeated break ups with the same partner, and have relatively low self-esteem. Around 20 percent of adults, gay and straight, fall into this category (Simpson, 1990; Li & Chan, 2012).

Research finds that the quality of lesbian and gay relationships differs little from that of heterosexual relationships.

Attachment style is also related to the care that adults give their romantic partners when they need assistance. Secure adults tend to provide more sensitive and supportive care, responding to their partner's psychological needs. In contrast, anxious adults are more likely to provide compulsive, intrusive (and ultimately less helpful) assistance (Feeney & Collins, 2003; Gleason, Iida, & Bolger, 2003; Mikulincer & Shaver, 2009).

In short, there are similarities between infants' attachment styles and their behavior as adults. People who are having difficulty in relationships might look back to their infancy as a root of their problems (Simpson et al., 2007; Berlin, Cassidy, & Appleyard, 2008; Draper et al., 2008).

Cultural Dimensions

Gay and Lesbian Relationships: Men With Men and Women With Women

Most developmental research has examined heterosexual relationships, but an increasing number of studies have looked at gay and lesbian relationships. The findings suggest that gay relationships are similar to straight relationships.

For example, gay men describe successful relationships in much the same way heterosexual couples do. They believe that successful relationships involve greater appreciation for the partner and the couple as a whole, less conflict, and more positive feelings toward the partner. Similarly, lesbian women in a relationship show high levels of attachment, caring, intimacy, affection, and respect (Brehm, 1992; Beals, Impett, & Peplau, 2002; Kurdek, 2006).

Furthermore, the age preferences expressed in the marriage gradient for heterosexuals also extend to homosexual men, who also prefer partners who are the same age or younger. On the other hand, lesbians' age preferences fall somewhere between those of heterosexual women and heterosexual men (Kenrick et al., 1995).

Finally, despite the stereotype that gay males, in particular, find it difficult to form relationships and are interested in only sexual alliances, the reality is different. Most gays and lesbians seek loving, long-term, and meaningful relationships that differ little qualitatively from those desired by heterosexuals. Although some research suggests that homosexual relationships are less long-lasting that heterosexual relationships, the factors that lead to relationship stability—partners' personality traits, support for the relationship from others, and dependence on the relationship—are similar for homosexual and heterosexual couples (Diamond, 2003b; Diamond & Savin-Williams, 2003; Kurdek, 2005, 2008). There are virtually no scientific data regarding gay and lesbian marriage, which became a major social issue when the first legal homosexual marriages occurred in the United States in 2004. It is clear that the question produces strong reactions, but more so among older adults than younger ones. Although only 18 percent of those older than 65 support the legalization of gay marriage, a clear majority—61 percent—of people younger than 30 support the practice (Deakin, 2004).

REVIEW, CHECK, AND APPLY

7.1 7.2 7.3

REVIEW

L013 How do young adults form loving relationships?

- According to Erikson, young adults are in the intimacy-versus-isolation stage that focuses on developing close, intimate relationships with others.

L014 How do people choose spouses?

- Many factors go into choosing a spouse, including love and mutual attraction, which in some cultures are rated behind good health and maturity.
- Types of love include passionate and companionate love. Sternberg's triangular theory identifies three basic components (intimacy, passion, and decision/commitment).

L015 Are there differences between gay and lesbian relationships and heterosexual relationships?

- In general, the values applied to relationships by heterosexual, gay, and lesbian couples are more similar than different.

CHECK YOURSELF

1. According to Erikson, adults spend their early adult years _____.
   - a consolidating careers
   - b developing their identities
   - c being industrious
   - d focusing on developing relationships with others
2. _____ love is the strong affection we have for those individuals with whom our lives are deeply involved.
   - a Passionate
   - b Puppy
   - c Intimate
   - d Companionate
3. According to Sternberg, to determine the type of love that best describes a relationship, one must look at the presence or absence of intimacy, passion, and commitment.
   - True
   - False

APPLYING LIFESPAN DEVELOPMENT

- Consider a long-term marriage with which you are familiar. Do you think the relationship involves passionate love or companionate love (or both)? What changes when a relationship moves from passionate to companionate love? From companionate to passionate love? In which direction is it more difficult for a relationship to move? Why?

✓ **Study** and **Review** on **MyPsychLab.com**

THE COURSE OF RELATIONSHIPS

L016 What makes a successful marriage?
L017 Why do couples decide to have children?

He wasn't being a chauvinist or anything, expecting me to do everything and him nothing. He just didn't volunteer to do things that obviously needed doing, so I had to put down some ground rules. Like if I'm in a bad mood, I may just yell: "I work eight hours just like you. This is half your house and half your child, too. You've got to do your share!" Jackson never changed the kitty litter box once in four years, but he changes it now, so we've made great progress. I just didn't expect it to take so much work. We planned this child together and we went through Lamaze together, and Jackson stayed home for the first two weeks. But then—wham—the partnership was over. (Cowan & Cowan, 1992, p. 63)

Relationships are especially challenging in early adulthood. One of the primary questions young adults face is whether and when to marry.

Couples living together without being married now make up about 10 percent of all couples in the United States—almost 7.5 million people.

Marriage, Cohabitation, and Other Relationship Choices: Sorting Out the Options of Early Adulthood

For some people, the primary issue is not *whom* to marry, but *whether* to marry. Although surveys show that most heterosexuals (and a growing number of homosexuals) say they want to get married, a significant number choose some other route. For instance, the past 3 decades have seen both a decline in the number of married couples and a significant rise in couples living together without being married, a status known

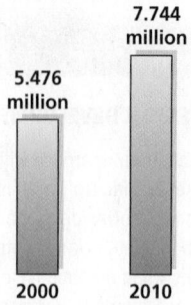

FIGURE 7-12 Cohabitation
The number of couples living together prior to marriage increased by 41 percent from the year 2000 to 2010.
Source: U.S. Bureau of the Census, 2010.

as **cohabitation** (see Figure 7-12). In fact, today, some 7.5 million people are cohabiting in the United States. In fact, married couples now make up a minority of households: as of 2011, 48 percent of all U.S. households contained a married couple, a historically low figure. In comparison, in 1950, 78 percent of households were occupied by a married couple (Doyle, 2004b; Roberts, 2006; Jay, 2012).

Most young adults will live with a romantic partner for at least one period of time during their 20s. Furthermore, most marriages today occur after a period in which the couple has cohabited. Why do so many couples choose to cohabit rather than to marry? Some feel they are not ready to make a lifelong commitment. Others feel that cohabitation provides "practice" for marriage. (This is more likely for women than men. Women tend to see cohabitation as a step toward marriage; men are more likely to view it as a way to test a relationship; Jay, 2012).

Why cohabit? Some couples feel they are not ready for a lifelong commitment. Others feel that cohabitation provides "practice" for marriage. Some reject marriage altogether, maintaining that marriage is outmoded and that it is unrealistic to expect a couple to spend a lifetime together (Martin, Martin, & Martin, 2001; Miller, Sassler, & Kus-Appough, 2011; Pope & Cashwell, 2013).

Those who feel that cohabiting increases their chances of a happy marriage are incorrect. In fact, the chances of divorce are higher for those who have previously cohabited, according to data collected in both the United States and Western Europe (Hohmann-Marriott, 2006; Rhoades, Stanley, & Markman, 2006, 2009).

Despite the prevalence of cohabitation, marriage remains the preferred alternative for most people during early adulthood. Many see marriage as the appropriate culmination of a loving relationship, while others feel it is the "right" thing to do after reaching a particular age. Others seek marriage because spouses fill many roles, including economic, sexual, therapeutic, and recreational. Marriage is also the only fully accepted way to have children. Finally, marriage offers legal benefits and protections (Furstenberg, 1996).

Marriage is not a static institution. Fewer U.S. citizens are now married than at any time since the late 1890s. In part this is attributable to higher divorce rates, but the tendency of people to marry later in life is also a contributing factor. The median age of first marriage in the United States is now 27 for men and 25 for women—the oldest age for women since national statistics were first collected in the 1880s (Furstenberg, 1996; U.S. Bureau of the Census, 2001) (see Figure 7-13).

Many European countries offer legal alternatives to marriage. For instance, France offers "Civil Solidarity Pacts," in which couples receive many of the same legal rights as married couples. What differs is the lack of a legal lifetime commitment; Civil Solidarity Pacts can be dissolved more easily than marriages (Lyall, 2004).

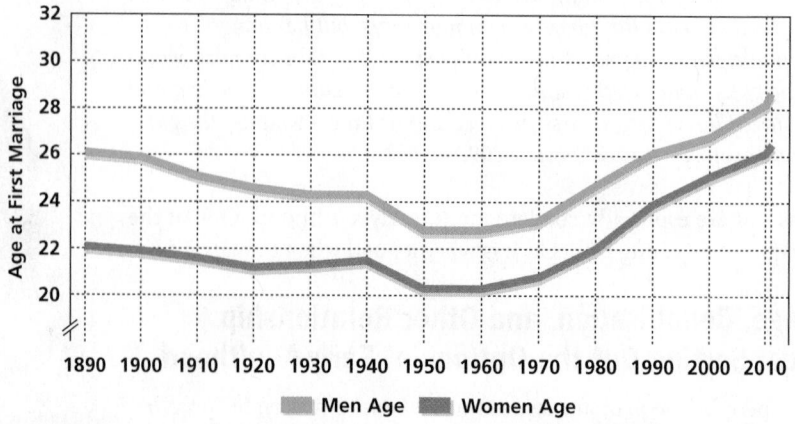

FIGURE 7-13 Postponing Marriage
The age at which women and men first marry is the highest since national statistics were first collected in the late 1800s. What factors account for this?
Source: U.S. Bureau of the Census, 2011.

cohabitation couples living together without being married

Does this mean that marriage is losing its viability as a social institution? Probably not. Some 90 percent of people eventually marry, and on national polls almost everyone agrees that a good family life is important. In fact, almost nine out of ten 18- to 29-year-olds believe that a happy marriage is an ingredient of a good life (Roper Starch Worldwide, 1997).

Why are people getting married later in life? The delay reflects economic and career concerns. Choosing and starting a career presents a series of increasingly difficult decisions, and some young adults decide to put marriage on hold until they get a foothold on a career path and an adequate salary (Dreman, 1997).

From a social worker's perspective: Why do you think society has established such a powerful norm in favor of marriage? What effects might such a norm have on a person who prefers to remain single?

What Makes Marriage Work?

Successful marriages share several characteristics. The partners visibly show affection and communicate relatively little negativity. They tend to perceive themselves as an interdependent couple rather than two independent individuals. They experience social homogamy, having similar interests and agreeing on role distribution—such as who takes out the garbage and who takes care of the children (Gottman, Fainsilber-Katz, & Hooven, 1996; Carrere et al., 2000; Huston et al., 2001; Stutzer & Frey, 2006).

The increasing understanding of the components of successful marriages has not prevented an epidemic of divorce. The statistics are grim: Only about half of U.S. marriages remain intact, and countries around the world have shown increases in divorce during the last several decades (see Figure 7-14). Over a million U.S. marriages end in divorce each year, and there are 5 divorces for every 1,000 individuals. This is a decline from the mid-1970s peak of 5.3 divorces per 1,000 people, and most experts think that the rate is leveling off (National Center for Health Statistics, 2001).

Robert Weber/The New Yorker Collection/www.cartoonbank.com

Early Marital Conflict. Conflict in marriage is not unusual. According to some statistics, nearly half of newly married couples experience a significant degree of conflict. One of the major reasons is that partners may initially idealize one another, but as reality sets in they become more aware of flaws. In fact, spousal perceptions of marital quality over the first 10 years of marriage decline in the early years, followed by a period of stabilization, and then additional decline (Kurdek, 2003; Karney & Bradbury, 2005; Kilmann & Vendemia, 2013).

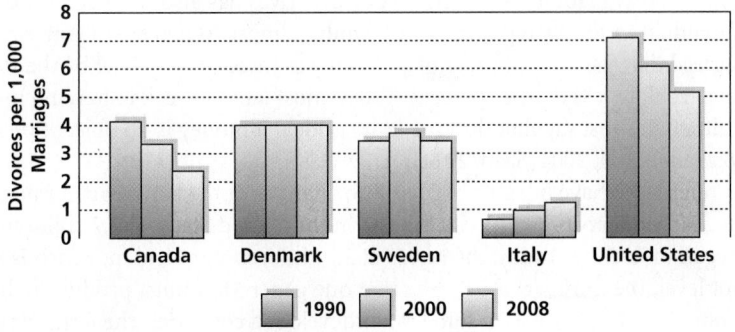

FIGURE 7-14 Divorce Around the World
Increases in divorce rates are not just a U.S. phenomenon: Data from other countries also show significant increases.
Source: Adapted from Population Council Report, 2009.

Common sources of marital conflict include difficulty making the transition from adolescence to adulthood; trouble developing a separate identity; and the challenge of allocating time across spouse, friends, and family members (Caughlin, 2002; Crawford, Houts, & Huston, 2002; Murray, Bellavia, & Rose, 2003).

Still, most married couples view the early years of marriage as deeply satisfying. In negotiating changes in their relationship and learning more about each other, many couples find themselves more deeply in love than before. In fact, the newlywed period is for many couples one of the happiest of their married lives (Bird & Melville, 1994; Orbuch et al., 1996; McNulty & Karney, 2004).

Parenthood: Choosing to Have Children

What makes a couple decide to have children? Certainly not economics: According to the U.S. government, a middle-class family with two children spends around $235,000 for each child by the time the child reaches the age of 18. Add in the costs of college and the figure comes to over $300,000 per child. And if you take into account the cost of care provided by families for their children, the total costs of caring for children are at least twice as high as the government estimates (Lino & Carlson, 2009; Folbre, 2012).

The most commonly cited reasons are psychological. Parents expect to derive pleasure from helping their children grow, fulfillment from their children's accomplishments, satisfaction from seeing them become successful, and enjoyment from forging a close bond with them. For some there may also be a self-serving element in the decision, focusing on the hope that their children will provide for them in their old age, maintain a family business or farm, or offer companionship. Others have children because of a strong societal norm: More than 90 percent of married couples have at least one child.

In some cases children are unplanned, the result of the failure or absence of birth control. If the couple had planned to have children in the future, the pregnancy may be welcome. But in families that had actively not wanted children, or already had "enough" children, the pregnancy can be problematic (Clinton & Kelber, 1993; Leathers & Kelley, 2000; Pajulo, Helenius, & MaYes, 2006).

The couples most likely to have unwanted pregnancies are often the most vulnerable—younger, poorer, and less educated couples. Fortunately, there has been a dramatic rise in the use and effectiveness of contraceptives, and the incidence of undesired pregnancies has declined in recent decades (Centers for Disease Control, 2003; Villarosa, 2003).

For many young adults, the decision to have children is independent of marriage. Although overall most women (59 percent) are married when they have children, more than half of births to women in the United States under the age of 30 now occur outside of marriage. The only demographic group for which this is not true is young adult women with a college education; they overwhelmingly still choose to be married before having children (DeParle & Tavernise, 2012).

As increasing numbers of women have joined the workforce, more are choosing to have fewer children and have them later.

Family Size. The availability of effective contraceptives has also dramatically decreased the number of children in the average American family. Almost 70 percent of Americans polled in the 1930s agreed that the ideal number of children was three or more, but by the 1990s the percentage had shrunk to less than 40 percent. Today, most families seek to have no more than two children—although most say that three or more is ideal if money is no object (see Figure 7-15) (Kate, 1998; Gallup Poll, 2004; Saad, 2011).

These preferences have been translated into changes in the actual birth rate. In 1957, the fertility rate reached a post–World War II peak in the United States of 3.7 children per woman and then began to decline. Today, the rate is at 2.1 children per woman, which is less than the replacement level, the number of children that one generation must produce to be able to replenish its numbers. In contrast, in some underdeveloped countries, the fertility rate is as high as 6.3 in Afghanistan and Zambia (World Bank, 2012).

What has produced this decline in the fertility rate? In addition to the availability of birth control, increasing numbers of women have joined the workforce. The pressures of simultaneously holding a job and raising a child have convinced many women to have fewer children.

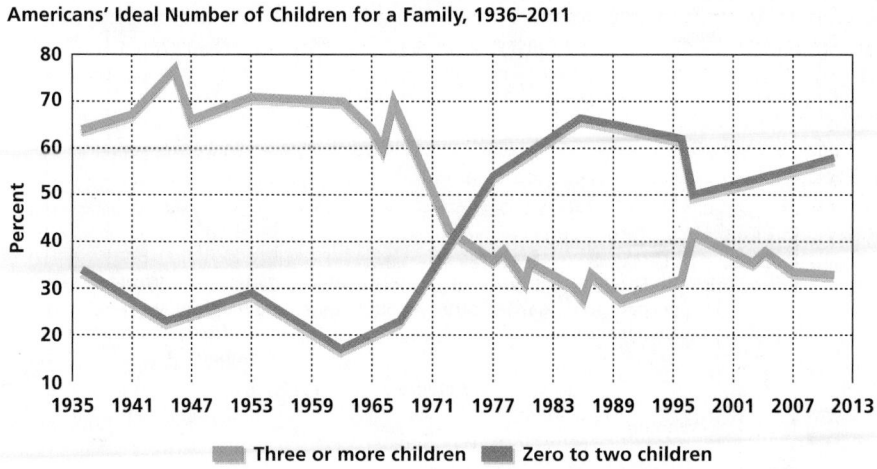

FIGURE 7-15 Smaller Is Better
Continuing trends over the last 75 years, U.S. parents continue to prefer families with fewer children. What do you think is the ideal number of children for a family to have?
Source: Saad, 2011.

Furthermore, many women who are developing their careers choose to have children later. In fact, women between 30 and 34 are the only ones whose rate of births has actually increased over earlier decades. Still, women who have their first child in their 30s do not have as many children as women who begin earlier. Also, research suggesting that there are health benefits for mothers who space their children apart may lead families to have fewer children (Marcus, 2004).

Financial considerations, particularly the increasing cost of college, may also act as a disincentive for bearing larger numbers of children. Finally, some couples doubt they will be good parents or simply don't want the work and responsibility involved in childrearing.

Dual-Earner Couples. One of the major historical shifts affecting young adults began in the last half of the twentieth century: a marked increase in the number of families in which both parents work. Close to three-quarters of married women with school-aged children are employed outside the home, and more than half of mothers with children under age 6 are working. In the mid-1960s, only 17 percent of mothers of 1-year-olds worked full time; now, more than 50 percent do. In the majority of families, both husband and wife work (Darnton, 1990; Carnegie Task Force, 1994; Barnett & Hyde, 2001).

For married couples who both work and have no children, the combined total of paid (in the office) and unpaid work (the chores at home) is nearly identical, at 8 hours 11 minutes for men, and 8 hours 3 minutes for women. And even for those families who have children under the age of 18, women who are employed full time do only 20 minutes more of combined paid and unpaid work (Konigsberg, 2010).

On the other hand, the nature of husbands' contributions to the household often differs from that of wives. For instance, husbands tend to carry out chores such as mowing the lawn or house repairs that are more easily scheduled in advance (or sometimes postponed), while women's household chores tend to be devoted to things that need immediate attention, such as child care and meal preparation. As a result, wives experience greater levels of anxiety and stress (Haddock & Rattenborg, 2003; Lee, Vernon-Feagans, & Vazquez, 2003; Coltrane & Shih, 2010; Bureau of Labor Statistics, 2012) (see Figure 7-16).

The Transition to Parenthood: Two's a Couple, Three's a Crowd? Consider this quote from a spouse who just became a parent:

> *We had no idea what we were getting into when our first child was born. We certainly prepared for the event, reading magazine articles and books and even attending a class on child care. But when Sheanna was actually born, the sheer enormity of the task of*

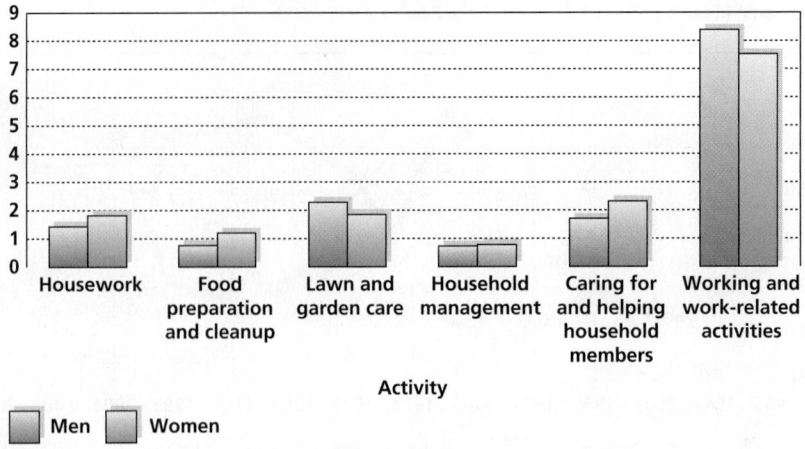

Note: Figures refer to average hours per day for persons who engaged in the activity.

FIGURE 7-16 Division of Labor
Although husbands and wives generally work at their paying jobs a similar number of hours each week, wives are apt to spend more time than their husbands doing home chores and in child-care activities. Why do you think this pattern exists?
Source: Bureau of Labor Statistics, 2012.

> *taking care of her, her presence at every moment of the day, and the awesome responsibility of raising another human being weighed on us like nothing we'd ever faced. Not that it was a burden. But it did make us look at the world with an entirely different perspective.*

The arrival of a child alters virtually every aspect of family life. Spouses are suddenly placed in new roles—"mother" and "father"—which may overwhelm their older, continuing roles of "wife" and "husband." In addition, new parents face significant physical and psychological demands, including near-constant fatigue, new financial responsibilities, and an increase in household chores (Meijer & van den Wittenboer, 2007).

Furthermore, in contrast with cultures in which childrearing is regarded as a communal task, Western culture's emphasis on individualism leaves parents to forge their own paths after the birth of a child, often without community support (Rubin & Chung, 2006; Lamm & Keller, 2007).

The consequence is that many couples experience the lowest level of marital satisfaction of any point in their marriage. This is particularly true for women, who tend to be more dissatisfied than men with their marriages after the arrival of children. The most likely reason is that women often bear the brunt of childrearing, even if both parents seek to share these responsibilities (Levy-Shiff, 1994; Laflamme, Pomerleau, & Malcuit, 2002; Lu, 2006).

Marital satisfaction does not decrease for all couples upon the birth of a child. According to work by John Gottman and colleagues (Shapiro, Gottman, & Carrère, 2000), satisfaction can stay steady or even rise. Three factors permit couples to successfully weather the stress that follows the birth of a child:

- Working to build fondness and affection toward each other
- Remaining aware of events in each other's life, and responding to those events
- Considering problems as controllable and solvable

In addition, couples who are well satisfied with their marriages as newlyweds are more likely to be satisfied as they raise their children. Couples who harbor realistic expectations regarding the effort involved in childrearing also tend to be more satisfied after they become parents. Furthermore, parents who work together as a *coparenting team*, thoughtfully adopting common childrearing goals and strategies, are more apt to be satisfied with their parenting roles (Schoppe-Sullivan et al., 2006; McHale & Rotman, 2007).

In short, having children can lead to greater marital satisfaction for couples already satisfied with their marriage. For dissatisfied couples, having children may make a bad situation worse (Driver, Tabares, & Shapiro, 2003; Lawrence et al., 2008; Holland & McElwain, 2013).

"If Heather has two mommies, and each of them has two brothers, and one of those brothers has another man for a 'roommate,' how many uncles does Heather have?"

William Haefeli/The New Yorker Collection/www.cartoonbank.com

Gay and Lesbian Parents

In increasing numbers, children are being raised in families with two moms or two dads. Some 20 percent of gay men and lesbian women are parents.

How do lesbian and gay households compare to heterosexual households? Studies of couples before children arrive show that, compared to heterosexual households, homosexual partners tend to divide labor more evenly and the ideal of an egalitarian allocation of household work is more strongly held (Patterson, 1994; Parks, 1998; Kurdek, 1993, 2003).

However, the arrival of a child (usually through adoption or artificial insemination) changes the dynamics of household life considerably. As in heterosexual unions, role specialization develops. For instance, childrearing tends to fall more to one member of the couple, while the other spends more time in paid employment. Although both partners usually say they share household tasks and decision making equally, biological mothers are often more involved in child care (Patterson, 1995; Fulcher et al., 2006; Goldberg, 2010c).

The evolution of homosexual couples when children arrive appears to be more similar to that of heterosexual couples than dissimilar, particularly in the increased role specialization occasioned by the requirements of child care. The experience for children of being in a household with two parents of the same sex is also similar. Most research suggests that children raised in households in which the parents are homosexual show no differences in terms of eventual adjustment from those raised in heterosexual households. Although they may face greater challenges from a society in which the roots of prejudice against homosexuality are deep, children who have two moms or two dads ultimately seem to fare well (Crowl, Ahn, & Baker, 2008; Patterson, 2009; Goldberg, 2010c).

Staying Single: I Want to Be Alone

For some people, living alone is the right path, consciously chosen, through life. In fact, *singlehood*, living alone without an intimate partner, has increased significantly in the last several decades, encompassing around 20 percent of women and 30 percent of men. Almost 10 percent will probably spend their entire lives in singlehood (Gerber, 2002; U.S. Bureau of the Census, 2002; DePaulo & Morris, 2006).

People who choose singlehood give several reasons for their decision. One is that they view marriage negatively. Rather than seeing marriage in idealized terms, they focus more on high divorce rates and marital strife. Ultimately, they conclude that the risks of forming a lifetime union are too high.

Others view marriage as too restrictive, valuing their personal change and growth, and reasoning that growth would be impeded by the stable, long-term commitment of marriage. Finally, some people simply do not meet anyone with whom they wish to spend their lives. Instead, they value their independence and autonomy (DePaulo & Morris, 2006). Despite the advantages of singlehood, there are also drawbacks. Society often stigmatizes single individuals, particularly women, holding up marriage as the idealized norm. Furthermore, there can be a lack of companionship and sexual outlets, and singles may feel that their futures are less secure financially (Byrne, 2000; Schachner, Shaver, & Gillath, 2008).

REVIEW, CHECK, AND APPLY

REVIEW

L016 What makes a successful marriage?

- Success in marriage includes partners who visibly show affection and communicate relatively little negativity, perceive themselves as an interdependent couple instead of two independent individuals, share similar interests, and agree on role distribution.

L017 Why do couples decide to have children?

- The most common reasons for having children are psychological. Parents derive pleasure from helping their children grow, fulfillment from their accomplishments, and enjoyment from forging a close bond with them.

CHECK YOURSELF

1. During the past three decades there has been a decline in both the number of married couples and the number of individuals living together without being married.
   - True
   - False
2. Divorce is more likely to occur when couples marry without first cohabiting.
   - True
   - False
3. When asked why they want to have children, most young adults cite _____ reasons.
   - a personal
   - b physical
   - c psychological
   - d societal

APPLYING LIFESPAN DEVELOPMENT

- In what ways do you think cognitive changes in early adulthood (e.g., the emergence of postformal thought and practical intelligence) affect how young adults deal with questions of marriage, divorce, and childrearing?

✓ **Study** and **Review** on **MyPsychLab.com**

WORK: CHOOSING AND EMBARKING ON A CAREER

L018 What factors influence the choice of a career?
L019 How have women who pursue careers advanced in the workplace?
L020 Why do people work, and what elements of a job bring satisfaction?

Why did I decide that I wanted to be a lawyer? The answer is embarrassing. When I got to my senior year of college, I began to worry about what I was going to do when I graduated. My parents kept asking what kind of work I was thinking about, and I felt the pressure rising with each call from home. At the time, the O. J. Simpson trial was in the news, and it got me thinking about what it might be like to be an attorney. I had always been fascinated by L.A. Law when it had been on television, and I could envision myself in one of those big corner offices with a view of the city. For these reasons, and just about none other, I decided to take the law boards and apply to law school.

Early adulthood is a period of decisions with lifelong implications. One of the most critical is the choice of a career path. This decision influences financial prosperity, of course, but also status, the sense of self-worth, and the contribution that a person will make in life. Decisions about work go to the core of a young adult's identity.

Identity During Young Adulthood: The Role of Work

According to psychiatrist George Vaillant, the stage of development that young adults reach is called career consolidation. During **career consolidation**, which begins between the ages of 20 and 40, young adults become centered on their careers. Vaillant based his conclusion on a comprehensive longitudinal study of male graduates of Harvard, begun when they were freshmen in the 1930s (Vaillant, 1977; Vaillant & Vaillant, 1990).

In their early 20s, the men tended to be influenced by their parents' authority. But in their late 20s and early 30s, they started to act with greater autonomy. They married, had children, and began to focus on their careers—the period of career consolidation.

Vaillant draws a relatively uninspiring portrait of people in this stage. His participants worked very hard as they climbed the corporate ladder. They tended to be rule followers

career consolidation according to Vaillant a stage that is entered between the ages of 20 and 40, when young adults become centered on their careers conforming to the norms of their professions. Rather than showing the independence and questioning that they had displayed in college, they threw themselves unquestioningly into their work.

Vaillant argues that work plays such an important role that the career consolidation stage should be seen as an addition to Erikson's intimacy-versus-isolation stage of psychosocial identity. In Vaillant's view, career concerns supplant the focus on intimacy, and the career consolidation stage marks a bridge between intimacy-versus-isolation and generativity-versus-stagnation. (Generativity refers to an individual's contribution to society, as we discuss later.)

The reaction to Vaillant's viewpoint has been mixed. Critics point out that Vaillant's sample, although relatively large, comprised a highly restricted, unusually bright group of men. Furthermore, societal norms have changed considerably since the 1930s, and people's views of the importance of work may have shifted. Finally, the lack of women in the sample and the fact that there have been major changes in the role of work in *women's* lives make Vaillant's conclusions even less generalizable.

Still, it is hard to dispute the importance of work in most people's lives, and research suggests that it makes up a significant part of both men's and women's identity—if for no other reason than that it occupies so much of their time (Deaux et al., 1995).

According to one theory, people move through a series of life stages in choosing a career. The first stage is the fantasy period, which lasts until a person is around 11 years old.

Picking an Occupation: Choosing Life's Work

Some people know from childhood what they want to do for a living; for others, the choice of a career is a matter of chance. Many of us fall somewhere in the middle.

Ginzberg's Career Choice Theory. According to Eli Ginzberg (1972), people typically move through stages in choosing a career. The first stage is the **fantasy period**, which lasts until around age 11. During the fantasy period, people make and discard career choices without regard to skills, abilities, or available job opportunities. A child may decide she wants to be a rock star—despite being unable to carry a tune.

During the **tentative period**, which spans adolescence, people begin to think more practically about the requirements of various jobs and their own abilities and interests. They also consider how well a particular occupation might satisfy their personal values and goals.

Finally, in early adulthood, people enter the **realistic period**, in which they explore specific career options either through actual experience on the job or through training for a profession. After initially exploring what they might do, people begin to narrow their choices and eventually commit to a particular career.

Critics have charged that Ginzberg's theory oversimplifies the process of choosing a career. Because it was based on subjects from middle socioeconomic levels, his theory may overstate the choices available to people in lower socioeconomic levels. Furthermore, the ages associated with the various stages may be too rigid. For instance, a person who begins to work immediately after high school most likely makes serious career decisions earlier than a person who attends college. In addition, economic factors cause many people to change careers at different points in their adult lives.

Holland's Personality Type Theory. Other theories of career choice emphasize how personality affects career decisions. According to John Holland, certain personality types match particularly well with certain careers. If the correspondence between personality and career is good, people will enjoy their careers more and be more likely to stay in them; but if the match is poor, they will be unhappy and more likely to shift to other careers (Holland, 1997).

According to Holland, six personality types are important in career choice:

- **Realistic.** These are down-to-earth, practical problem solvers, physically strong but with mediocre social skills. They make good farmers, laborers, and truck drivers.
- **Intellectual.** Intellectual types are oriented toward the theoretical and abstract. Although not particularly good with people, they are well suited to careers in math and science.
- **Social.** People with this personality type have strong verbal skills and are good with people. They make good salespersons, teachers, and counselors.
- **Conventional.** Conventional types prefer highly structured tasks. They make good clerks, secretaries, and bank tellers.

fantasy period according to Ginzberg, the period, lasting until about age 11, when career choices are made, and discarded, without regard to skills, abilities, or available job opportunities

tentative period the second stage of Ginzberg's theory, which spans adolescence, when people begin to think more practically about the requirements of various jobs and how their own abilities might fit with them

realistic period the third stage of Ginzberg's theory, which occurs in early adulthood, when people begin to explore specific career options, either through actual experience on the job or through training for a profession, and then narrow their choices and make a commitment

- **Enterprising.** These are risk-takers and take-charge types. They are good leaders and may be particularly effective as managers or politicians.
- **Artistic.** These individuals use art to express themselves and often prefer the world of art to interactions with people. They are best suited to occupations involving the arts.

Holland's theory suffers from a central flaw: Not everyone fits neatly into personality types. Furthermore, there are clear exceptions, with people holding jobs that are "wrong" for their personality type. Still, the basics of the theory have been validated, and they form the foundation of several of the "job quizzes" that people take to see what occupations they might be right for (Deng, Armstrong, & Rounds, 2007; Armstrong, Rounds, & Hubert, 2008).

Gender and Career Choices: Women's Work

WANTED: Full-time employee for small family firm. DUTIES: Including but not limited to general cleaning, cooking, gardening, laundry, ironing and mending, purchasing, bookkeeping and money management. Child care may also be required. HOURS: Avg. 55/wk but standby duty required 24 hours/day, 7 days/wk. Extra workload on holidays. SALARY AND BENEFITS: No salary, but food, clothing, and shelter provided at employer's discretion; job security and benefits depend on continued goodwill of employer. No vacation. No retirement plan. No opportunities for advancement. REQUIREMENTS: No previous experience necessary, can learn on the job. Only women need apply. (Unger & Crawford, 1992, p. 446)

Always culturally determined, women's social clocks have changed over the years

A generation ago, many women entering early adulthood assumed that this admittedly exaggerated job description matched the position that they would occupy: housewife. Even women who sought work outside the home were relegated to certain professions. Until the 1960s, employment ads in U.S. newspapers were almost always divided into two sections: "Help Wanted: Male" and "Help Wanted: Female." The men's ads included professions such as police officer, construction worker, and legal counsel; the women's ads were for secretaries, teachers, cashiers, and librarians.

The breakdown of jobs reflected society's view of what the two genders were best suited for. Traditionally, women were considered most appropriate for **communal professions**, occupations associated with relationships, such as nursing. In contrast, men were perceived as best suited for agentic professions. **Agentic professions** are associated with getting things accomplished, such as carpentry. It is probably no coincidence that communal professions typically have lower status and pay than agentic professions (Eagly & Steffen, 1986; Hattery, 2000; Trapnell & Paulhus, 2012).

From a social worker's perspective: How does the division of jobs into communal and agentic relate to traditional views of male–female differences?

Although discrimination based on gender is far less blatant today than it was several decades ago—it is now illegal, for instance, to advertise a position specifically for one gender—remnants of gender prejudice persist. Women are less likely to be found in traditionally male-dominated professions such as engineering and computer programming. As shown in Figure 7-17, despite significant progress in the last 40 years, women's earnings still lag behind those of men. In fact, women in many professions earn significantly less than men in identical jobs (Frome et al., 2006; U.S. Bureau of the Census, 2012).

More women are working outside the home than ever. Between 1950 and 2003, the percentage of the female population (aged 16 and over) in the U.S. labor force increased from around 35 percent to over 60 percent, and women today make up around 55 percent of the labor force, a figure comparable to their presence in the general population. Almost all women expect to earn a living, and almost all do at some point in their lives. Furthermore, in about one-half of U.S. households, women earn about as much as their husbands (U.S. Bureau of Labor Statistics, 2003).

communal professions occupations that are associated with relationships, such as nursing

agentic professions occupations that are associated with getting things accomplished, such as carpentry

Opportunities for women have improved considerably. Women are more likely to be physicians, lawyers, insurance agents, and bus drivers than in the past. However, within job categories gender differences persist. For example, female bus drivers are more apt to have part-time school bus routes, while men hold better-paying, full-time routes in cities. Female pharmacists

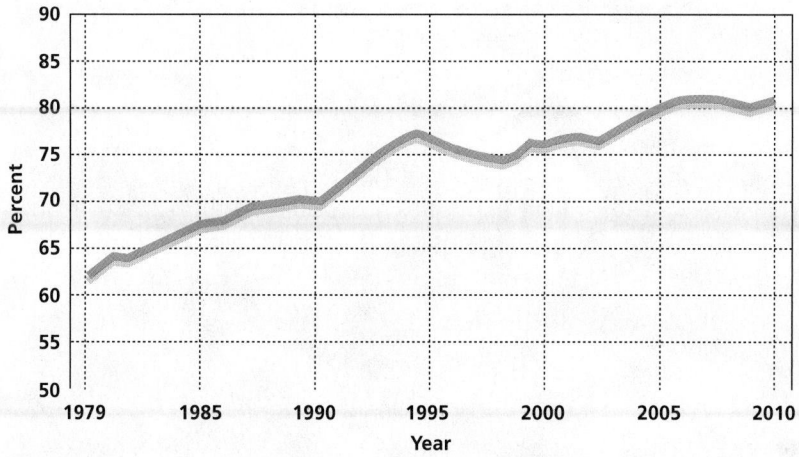

FIGURE 7-17 The Gender–Wage Gap
In spite of men's wages remaining stable, women continue to earn an average of 80 cents for every dollar men earn. Minority women face an even greater discrepancy in wages.
Source: U.S. Bureau of the Census, 2011.

are more likely to work in hospitals, while men work in higher-paying jobs in retail stores (Crawford & Unger, 2004).

Women and minorities in high-status, visible professional roles often hit what has come to be called the *glass ceiling*. The glass ceiling is an invisible barrier in an organization that prevents individuals from being promoted beyond a certain level. It operates subtly, and often the people responsible for it are unaware of how their actions perpetuate discrimination (Goodman, Fields, & Blum, 2003; Stockdale & Crosby, 2004).

Why Do People Work? More Than Earning a Living

Young adults express many reasons—well beyond earning money—for seeking a job.

Intrinsic and Extrinsic Motivation. Certainly, people work to obtain concrete rewards, or out of extrinsic motivation. **Extrinsic motivation** drives people to obtain tangible rewards, such as money and prestige (Singer, Stacey, & Lange, 1993).

But people also work for their own enjoyment, for personal rewards. This is known as **intrinsic motivation**. People in many Western societies tend to subscribe to the Puritan work ethic, the notion that work is important in and of itself. According to this view, working is a meaningful act that brings psychological well-being and satisfaction.

Work also contributes to personal identity. Consider what people say about themselves when they first meet someone. After their name and where they live, they typically tell what they do for a living. What they do is a large part of who they are.

Work may also be central to people's social lives as a source of friends and activities. Work relationships can easily become personal friendships. In addition, work brings social obligations, such as dinner with the boss or the annual year-end party.

Finally, the kind of work people do helps to determine **status**, the evaluation by society of the role a person plays. Many jobs are associated with a particular status. For instance, physicians and college teachers are near the top of the status hierarchy, while ushers and shoe shiners occupy the bottom.

Satisfaction on the Job. Status affects job satisfaction: The higher the status of the job, the more satisfied people tend to be. Furthermore, the status of the job of the major wage-earner can affect the status of the other members of the family (Green, 1995; Schieman, McBrier, & van Gundy, 2003).

Of course, status isn't everything: Worker satisfaction depends on a number of factors, not the least of which is the nature of the job itself. For example, some people who work at computers are monitored on a minute-by-minute basis; supervisors can consistently see how many keystrokes they are entering. In some firms in which workers use the telephone for sales

extrinsic motivation motivation that drives people to obtain tangible rewards, such as money and prestige

intrinsic motivation motivation that causes people to work for their own enjoyment, for personal rewards

status the evaluation of a role or person by other relevant members of a group or society

Extrinsic motivation drives people as a way of obtaining tangible rewards, such as money, prestige, or an expensive automobile. How might extrinsic motivation be illustrated in a less developed, non-Western culture?

or to take customer orders, conversations are monitored by supervisors. Workers' Web use and email are also monitored or restricted by a large number of employers. Not surprisingly, such forms of job stress produce worker dissatisfaction (MacDonald, 2003).

Job satisfaction is higher when workers have input into the nature of their jobs and feel their ideas and opinions are valued. They also prefer jobs that offer variety over those that require only a few repeated skills. Finally, the more influence employees have over others, either directly as supervisors or more informally, the greater their job satisfaction (Peterson & Wilson, 2004; Thompson & Prottas, 2006; Carton & Aiello, 2009). **Watch** the **Video** *Young Adulthood: Work, Jessica* in **MyPsychLab**.

Becoming an Informed Consumer of Development

Choosing a Career

One of the greatest challenges of early adulthood is making a decision that will have lifelong implications: the choice of a career. Although most people can be happy in a variety of jobs, choosing among the options can be daunting. Here are some guidelines for facing the career question.

- Systematically evaluate your choices. Libraries contain a wealth of career information and most colleges and universities have helpful career centers.
- Know yourself. Evaluate your strengths and weaknesses, perhaps by completing a questionnaire on your interests, skills, and values at a college career center.
- Create a "balance sheet" listing the gains and losses from a particular profession. First list gains and losses for yourself and then for others, such as family members. Next, write down your projected self-approval or self-disapproval from the potential career—and the projected social approval or disapproval you are likely to receive from others.
- "Try out" different careers through paid or unpaid internships. By seeing a job first-hand, interns get a sense of what an occupation is truly like.
- Remember that there are no permanent mistakes. People today increasingly change careers in early adulthood and even beyond. No one should feel locked into a decision made earlier in life. As we have seen throughout this book, people develop substantially over the course of their lives.
- It is reasonable to expect that shifting values, interests, abilities, and life circumstances might make a different career more appropriate later in life than the one chosen during early adulthood.

REVIEW, CHECK, AND APPLY

7.1 7.2 7.3

REVIEW

LO18 What factors influence the choice of a career?

- Choosing a career is an important step in early adulthood.
- According to Vaillant, young adults reach the stage of career consolidation where they focus on their careers.
- Ginzberg offers a three-stage period of career development.
- Holland describes how personality affects career decisions.

LO19 How have women who pursue careers advanced in the workplace?

- Gender stereotypes are changing, but women still experience subtle prejudice in career choices, roles, and wages.

LO20 Why do people work, and what elements of a job bring satisfaction?

- People work because of both extrinsic and intrinsic motivation factors.
- The nature of a job, the degree of status it confers, and the variety it offers all contribute to job satisfaction. It's also important to workers to feel their ideas and opinions are valued.

CHECK YOURSELF

1. According to Vaillant, during young adulthood, individuals become centered on their careers. This stage is known as _____.
   - a career consolidation
   - b life comprehension
   - c personal attainment
   - d realism
2. Which of the following is NOT one of the six personality types Holland indicates is important when it comes to career choice?
   - a social
   - b realistic
   - c intellectual
   - d enterprising
3. Even though there are more job opportunities for women in many fields than there used to be, women are often not afforded the same opportunities as men for advancement within those fields. Specifically, many women are not promoted because they have hit what is known as the _____, or an invisible barrier to advancement.
   - a concrete wall
   - b final resting place
   - c glass ceiling
   - d transparent dome

APPLYING LIFESPAN DEVELOPMENT

- If Vaillant's study were performed today on women, in what ways do you think the results would be similar to or different from those of the original study?

✓ **Study** and **Review** on **MyPsychLab.com**

SUMMARY 7

PUTTING IT ALL TOGETHER EARLY ADULTHOOD

PETRA TARKIF AND MO WRIGHT face many developmental issues typical of young adults. They have to consider the questions of health and aging, and the uncomfortable admission that they do not have all the time in the world. They have to look at their relationship and decide whether to take what society and many of their friends consider the next logical step: marriage. They have to face the questions they have about children and career, and the possibility of moving and giving up their jobs . They have to reevaluate their wish to continue their education. Fortunately they have each other to help deal with the stress of this weighty combination of questions and decisions, a supportive company—and a considerable developmental arsenal of useful skills and abilities.

MODULE 7.1 *PHYSICAL DEVELOPMENT* IN EARLY ADULTHOOD

- Petra and Mo's bodies and senses are at their peak, with their physical development nearly complete. *(p. 306)*
- During this period, the couple will increasingly need to pay attention to diet and exercise. *(pp. 310–311)*
- Because they face so many important decisions, Petra and Mo are prime candidates for stress. *(pp. 313–316)*

MODULE 7.2 *COGNITIVE DEVELOPMENT* IN EARLY ADULTHOOD

- Petra and Mo are in Schaie's achieving stage, confronting major life issues, including career and marriage. *(p. 319)*
- They are able to apply postformal thought to the complex issues they face. *(pp. 324–325)*
- Dealing with major life events, while causing stress, may also foster cognitive growth in both of them. *(p. 323)*
- Petra and Mo's idea about returning to college is not unusual today, when colleges are serving a diversity of students, including many older students. *(pp. 323–325)*

MODULE 7.3 *SOCIAL AND PERSONALITY DEVELOPMENT* IN EARLY ADULTHOOD

- Petra and Mo are at a time when love relationships and friendship are of major importance. *(p. 339)*
- The couple are likely to be experiencing a combination of intimacy, passion, and decision/commitment. *(pp. 334–335)*
- Petra and Mo have been cohabiting and are now exploring marriage as a relationship option. *(p. 339)*
- Petra and Mo are not unusual in deciding about marriage and children—decisions with major implications for the relationship. *(pp. 341–344)*
- The couple must also decide how to handle the possible shift from two jobs to one, at least temporarily—a decision that is far more than financial. *(p. 343)*

What would a HEALTH CARE PROVIDER do?

Given that Petra and Mo are young, in good health, and physically fit, what strategies would you advise them to pursue to stay that way?

What would a CAREER COUNSELOR do?

Assuming Petra and Mo decide to have children, what advice would you give them about handling the major expenses they face and the impact of children on their careers? Would you advise one of them to put his or her career on hold and pursue childrearing full-time? If so, how would you counsel them to decide which career should be put on hold?

What would YOU do?

If you were a friend of Petra and Mo, what factors would you advise them to consider as they contemplate moving from cohabitation to marriage? Would your advice be the same if only Petra or Mo asked you?

What would an EDUCATOR do?

A friend of Mo's has told him that he might "feel like an old man" if he pursues management training or business school such a long time after getting his undergraduate degree. Do you agree? Would you advise Mo to pursue his studies right away, before he gets too old, or to wait until his life settles down?

Explore on MyPsychLab

To read how a real health care provider, career counselor, and educator responded to these questions, log onto MyPsychLab.com

Do you agree or disagree with their response? Why? What concepts that you've read about back up their opinion?

8 MIDDLE ADULTHOOD

Terri Donovan, 50, raised five kids while working full time as an urban planner for the city of New York. "It was not a cushy job," Terri says. "I raced about the city all day, and there were meetings almost every night. Zoning Board. Planning Board. I was lucky my husband Brian likes to cook." Terri did her share of parenting, too. "I never missed a school play or band concert. I read the bedtime stories most nights. And we did everything together on the weekends, even the laundry." Sometimes she felt she would "go nuts." Yet, when her youngest child left home last year, she wandered around for 3 months, thinking "What next?"

It was Brian who helped her figure out the answer. He booked a trip to Italy, their first real vacation in over a decade. "We went sightseeing and ate fabulous leisurely meals, but most of all we focused on being together." Back home, she and Brian scheduled a weekly date night. "We finally have time for sex and long walks and Sunday brunch with the New York Times," she says. Terri also started helping out one night a week at the local soup kitchen. "The people we serve have some interesting stories, and another way of looking at things. They've enriched my outlook." The biggest change came when Terri decided to quit her job. "I wanted to help the people in my community," she says. Now, she's running for a seat in the state legislature. And her oldest daughter is pregnant. "When my kids left home, I realized they hadn't been in the way of my life. They'd been the center of it," Terri says. "So I'm looking forward to my grandchild—as long as my daughter and her family don't move in."

Middle adulthood is a time of significant transitions. Grown children leave home. People change the way they view their career. Sometimes, they change careers entirely as Terri did. Marriages undergo reevaluation. Often, couples find this a period of strengthened ties, as the "empty nest" leaves them free for uninterrupted intimacy. But sometimes they divorce. Middle age is also a period of deepening roots. Family and friends ascend in importance as career ambitions begin to take a backseat. And there is more time for leisure activities.

In this chapter, we first look at the physical changes of middle adulthood and how people cope with them. Then, we consider sexuality and menopause and debate the use of hormone replacement drugs for women. We also look at health issues that become of increasing concern in midlife.

Next, we consider the changing intellectual abilities of middle-aged adults, and ask the question: Does intelligence decline over time? We investigate various types of intelligence and look at how each is affected by the aging process. We also look at memory. Finally, we look at social development and examine what changes and what remains stable over time in an adult's personality. We consider the evidence for the so-called midlife crisis and discuss how family relationships change. We end by examining how people are spending their increased leisure time in middle age.

MODULE 8.1

PHYSICAL DEVELOPMENT IN MIDDLE ADULTHOOD

Do men experience the equivalent of menopause?

MODULE 8.2

COGNITIVE DEVELOPMENT IN MIDDLE ADULTHOOD

Does intelligence decline in adulthood?

MODULE 8.3

SOCIAL AND PERSONALITY DEVELOPMENT IN MIDDLE ADULTHOOD

The midlife crisis: reality or myth?

MyVirtualLife

If you are currently using MyVirtualLife, consider how you will navigate middle adulthood. What decisions will you make?

Access MyVirtualLife for a chance to live your own virtual life.

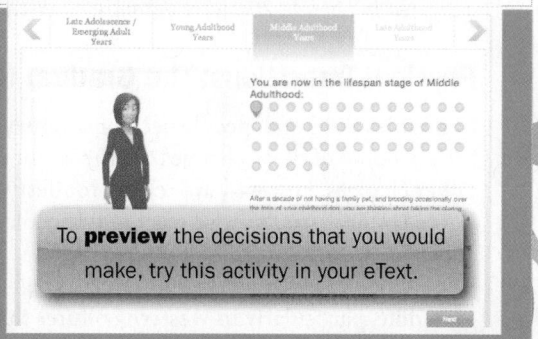

To **preview** the decisions that you would make, try this activity in your eText.

MODULE 8.1

PHYSICAL DEVELOPMENT IN MIDDLE ADULTHOOD

Improving What Is

Derek Reed has been building houses since he was 19 years old. "I was just a hired hand then," Derek, now 48, says, "It was a lot of up and down ladders. A lot of monkey work."

Those days are long gone—Derek's owned his construction firm for over 20 years—but it's still a lot of work. He builds five houses a year and he's up and down ladders on every one, scrambling over roof beams, and lugging heavy weights. Last spring, he had trouble with his knees, then his neck. "Not as young as I used to be," he admits with a smile. Derek asked his doctor what he could do to keep going. He was surprised by the answer: Yoga. But he gave it a try and now he wouldn't think of skipping a day. "I also meditate," he says. "The meditation relaxes me and the yoga strengthens me without strain. I'll be building houses when I'm 70."

Derek Reed's expectation that he will still be building houses at age 70 is indicative of a revolution that is occurring in terms of the physical activity of people in middle adulthood. People reaching the midcentury mark are joining health clubs in record numbers, seeking to remain healthy and agile as they age.

It is in middle adulthood, roughly the period from age 40 to 65, that people often first notice and feel the effects of aging. Their bodies and, to some extent, their cognitive abilities begin to change in unwelcome ways. Looking at the physical, cognitive, and social changes of midlife, however, we see this is also a time when many people reach the height of their capabilities, when they are engaged in shaping their lives as never before.

We begin the module by considering physical development. We consider changes in height, weight, and strength, and discuss the subtle declines in various senses.

We also look at sexuality in middle adulthood. We examine the effects of change in hormone production for both men and women—particularly, menopause—and the various therapies available to ease this transition. We consider, too, the role attitude plays.

We then examine both health and illness in midlife. We consider the impact of stress and pay special attention to two major health problems—heart disease and cancer.

PHYSICAL DEVELOPMENT

L01 What physical changes affect people in middle adulthood?

Soon after turning 40, Sharon Boker-Tov noticed that it took longer to bounce back from minor illnesses such as colds and the flu. Then she noticed changes in her eyesight: She needed more light to read fine print, and she had to adjust how far she held newspapers from her face in order to read them easily. Finally, she couldn't deny that the gray strands in her hair, which had first appeared in her late 20s, were becoming a virtual forest.

Physical Transitions: The Gradual Change in the Body's Capabilities

In middle adulthood, people become aware of the gradual changes in their bodies that aging brings. Some of these changes are the result of senescence, or naturally occurring declines. Other changes, however, are related to lifestyle choices, such as diet, exercise, smoking, and alcohol or drug use. As we'll see, lifestyle choices can have a major impact on people's physical, and even cognitive, fitness in midlife.

Although physical changes occur throughout life, these changes take on new significance in midlife, particularly in Western cultures that highly value a youthful appearance. The psychological significance of aging may far exceed the relatively minor and gradual changes a person experiences. Sharon Boker-Tov had gray hairs in her 20s, but in her 40s they multiplied to an extent she could not ignore. She was no longer young.

People's emotional reactions to midlife's physical changes depend in part on their self-concepts. When self-image is tied closely to one's physical attributes—as it often is for those who are very athletic or are physically quite attractive—middle adulthood can be particularly difficult. The changes the mirror reveals signal aging and mortality as well as a loss of physical attractiveness.

Physical appearance often plays an especially significant role in how women see themselves. This is particularly true in Western cultures, where women face strong societal pressures to retain a youthful look. Society applies a double standard to men and women regarding appearance: Older women tend to be viewed in unflattering terms, while older men are frequently seen as attractively "mature" (Andreoni & Petrie, 2008; Pruis & Janowsky, 2010).

Height, Weight, and Strength: The Benchmarks of Change

Most people reach their maximum height in their 20s and remain close to that height until around age 55. People then begin a "settling" process in which the bones attached to the spinal column become less dense. Although the loss of height is very slow, women average a 2-inch decline and men a 1-inch decline over the rest of the life span (Rossman, 1977; Bennani et al., 2009).

Women are more prone to this decline because they are at greater risk of osteoporosis. **Osteoporosis**, a condition in which the bones become brittle, fragile, and thin, is often caused by a lack of calcium in the diet. Although it has a genetic component, osteoporosis is one aspect of aging that can be affected by lifestyle choices. Women—and men—can reduce the risk of osteoporosis by eating a calcium-rich diet (calcium is found in milk, yogurt, cheese, and other dairy products) and by exercising regularly (Prentice et al., 2006; Swaim, Barner, & Brown, 2008; Wang, L. et al., 2013).

Body fat tends to increase in middle adulthood. Even those who have always been slim may begin to gain weight. Because height is not increasing, and actually may be declining, these gains increase the incidence of obesity. This weight gain can often be avoided. Lifestyle choices play a major role. People who exercise regularly tend to avoid obesity, as do those who live in cultures where life is more active than it is in many Western cultures.

Declines in strength accompany height and weight changes. Strength gradually decreases, particularly in the back and leg muscles. By age 60, people average a 10 percent loss of their maximum strength. Still, such a loss is relatively minor, and most people are easily able to compensate for it (Spence, 1989). Again, lifestyle choices matter. Regular exercise tends to make people feel stronger and more able to compensate for any losses.

The Senses: The Sights and Sounds of Middle Age

The vision changes Sharon Boker-Tov experienced are so common that reading glasses and bifocals have become a stereotypical emblem of middle age. Like Sharon, most people notice changes in the sensitivity, not only of their eyes, but also of other sense organs. All the organs seem to shift at about the same rate, but the changes are particularly marked in vision and hearing.

Vision. Starting at around age 40, *visual acuity*—the ability to discern fine spatial detail in both close and distant objects—begins to decline. The shape of the eye's lens changes and its elasticity deteriorates, which makes it harder to focus images sharply onto the retina. The lens becomes less transparent, so less light passes through the eye (DiGiovanna, 1994; Yan, Li, & Liao, 2010).

A nearly universal change in midlife is the loss of near vision, called **presbyopia**. Even people who have never needed glasses or contact lenses find themselves holding print at an increasing distance in order to bring it into focus. Eventually, they need reading glasses. For those who were already nearsighted, presbyopia may require bifocals or two sets of glasses (Koopmans & Kooijman, 2006; Kemper, 2012).

Midlife brings other vision changes. Depth perception, distance perception, and the ability to see in three dimensions all decline. The loss of rods (a kind of receptor cell in the eye) and a decrease in lens transparency also impairs people's ability to adapt to darkness, making it more difficult to navigate a dark room (Spear, 1993).

Although normal aging brings changes in vision, in some cases disease is involved. One of the most frequent eye problems is glaucoma, which may, if left untreated, lead to blindness. **Glaucoma** occurs when pressure in the fluid of the eye increases, either because the fluid cannot drain properly or because too much is produced. Around 1 to 2 percent of people over age 40 are afflicted, and African Americans are particularly susceptible (Wilson, 1989).

Beginning at or around the age of 40, visual acuity, the ability to discern fine spatial detail, begins to drop. Most people begin to suffer from presbyopia, a decline in near vision.

osteoporosis a condition in which the bones become brittle, fragile, and thin, often brought about by a lack of calcium in the diet

presbyopia a nearly universal change in eyesight during middle adulthood that results in some loss of near vision

glaucoma a condition in which pressure in the fluid of the eye increases, either because the fluid cannot drain properly or because too much fluid is produced

Initially, the increased pressure may constrict the neurons involved in peripheral vision and lead to tunnel vision. Ultimately, the pressure can become so high that all nerve cells are constricted, which causes complete blindness. Fortunately, with early detection, glaucoma can be treated. Medication can reduce the pressure, as can surgery to restore normal drainage of eye fluid (Lambiase et al., 2009; Jindal, 2013).

Hearing. Hearing declines in acuity in midlife, though the changes tend to be less evident than those affecting vision.

Environmental factors cause some of the hearing losses. People who work near loud noises—such as airplane mechanics and construction workers—are more apt to suffer debilitating and permanent hearing loss.

Many changes are simply related to aging. Age brings a loss of *cilia*, or *hair cells*, in the inner ear, which transmit neural messages to the brain when vibrations bend them. Like the lens of the eye, the eardrum becomes less elastic with age, reducing sensitivity to sound (Wiley et al., 2005).

The ability to hear high-pitched, high-frequency sounds usually degrades first, a problem called **presbycusis**. About 12 percent of people between 45 and 65 suffer from presbycusis. Men are more prone to hearing loss than women, starting at around age 55. People with hearing problems may also have trouble identifying the direction and origin of a sound, a process called *sound localization* (Veras & Mattos, 2007; Gopinath et al., 2012).

Declines in hearing do not markedly affect most people in middle age. Many compensate for any losses relatively easily—by asking people to speak up, turning up the volume of a television set, or paying closer attention to what others are saying.

Reaction Time: Not-So-Slowing Down

One common concern is that people slow down once they reach middle adulthood. Such a worry is not valid in most cases. Reaction time does increase (i.e., it takes longer to react to a stimulus), but usually the increase is mild and hardly noticeable. For instance, reaction time in responding to a loud noise increases by about 20 percent from age 20 to 60. Tasks requiring the coordination of various skills—such as driving a car—show less of an increase. Still, it takes more time to move the foot from the gas pedal to the brake when a driver faces an emergency situation. Changes in the speed at which the nervous system processes nerve impulses increases reaction time (Nobuyuki, 1997; Roggeveen, Prime, & Ward, 2007; Godefroy et al., 2010).

Despite increased reaction time, middle-aged drivers have fewer accidents than younger ones, partly because they tend to be more careful and take fewer risks. Moreover, older drivers' greater experience benefits them. The minor slowing of reaction time is compensated by their expertise (Makishita & Matsunaga, 2008; Cantin et al., 2009; Endrass Schreiber & Kathmann, 2012).

Lifestyle choices can retard the slowing down process. An active exercise program counteracts the effects of aging, improving health, muscle strength, and endurance (see Figure 8-1). Developmentalists would agree: "Use it or lose it" (Conn et al., 2003; Guiney & Machado, 2013).

presbycusis loss of the ability to hear sounds of high frequency

REVIEW, CHECK, AND APPLY

REVIEW

L01 What physical changes affect people in middle adulthood?

- People in middle adulthood experience gradual changes in physical characteristics and appearance.
- The acuity of the senses, particularly vision and hearing, and speed of reaction declines slightly during middle age.
- Weight gain—commonly referred to as "middle-age spread"—can be controlled through regular exercise and a healthy diet.

CHECK YOURSELF

1. Starting around age 40, visual acuity or the ability to discern fine spatial detail in both close and distant objects begins to decline.
   - True
   - False
2. _____ occurs when pressure of the fluid in the eye increases, either because the fluid cannot drain properly or because too much is produced.
   - a presbyopia
   - b glaucoma
   - c presbycusis
   - d visual acuity
3. Although general reaction time increases in middle age, reaction time involving complex tasks such as driving a car shows less of an increase.
   - True
   - False

APPLYING LIFESPAN DEVELOPMENT

- Would you rather fly on an airplane with a middle-aged pilot or a young one? Why?

✓ **Study** and **Review** on **MyPsychLab.com**

The advantages of exercise include

Muscle System

Slower decline in energy molecules, muscle cell thickness, number of muscle cells, muscle thickness, muscle mass, muscle strength, blood supply, speed of movement, stamina

Slower increase in fat and fibers, reaction time, recovery time, development of muscle soreness

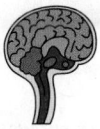

Nervous System

Slower decline in processing impulses by the central nervous system

Slower increase in variations in speed of motor neuron impulses

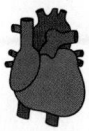

Circulatory System

Maintenance of lower levels of LDLs and higher HDL/cholesterol and HDL/LDL ratios

Decreased risk of high blood pressure, atherosclerosis, heart attack, stroke

Skeletal System

Slower decline in bone minerals

Decreased risk of fractures and osteoporosis

Psychological Benefits

Enhanced mood

Feelings of well-being

Reduces stress

FIGURE 8-1 The Benefits of Exercise
There are many benefits from maintaining a high level of physical activity throughout life.
Source: DiGiovanna, 1994.

SEXUALITY IN MIDDLE ADULTHOOD

LO2 What changes occur in sexuality for midlife men and women?
LO3 Why is there controversy over hormone therapy (HT) for women?

At age 51, Elaine was really looking forward to her postmenopausal life. Her youngest child had just left home to study art, and she had recently reduced her work schedule to a comfortable 30 hours a week. She envisioned the year to come as an opportunity for a "second honeymoon" with her husband, Greg, with no need for contraceptives or fears of becoming pregnant.

Her imagined honeymoon quickly evaporated in a heat wave of hot flashes and night sweats. Though Elaine recognized these as normal symptoms of menopause, she was having to change her clothing three or more times a day. And she was having more headaches. Her doctor prescribed HT to replace the estrogen she was losing through menopause. As she was not a likely candidate for any of the drug's negative side effects, she took her doctor's recommendation. The HT eased her symptoms and revitalized her spirits. Four months later, she and Greg booked a month's romantic getaway in Greece.

Although interest in sex remains fairly high for many people in middle adulthood, as Elaine's story illustrates, the physical changes associated with aging, such as menopause for women, can throw a curve ball at romance. We will look at some of the factors that affect men's and women's sexuality in midlife and the roles both attitude and prescription drugs can play in alleviating some of the problems commonly associated with this life stage.

Sexuality continues to be a vital part of most couples' lives in middle adulthood.

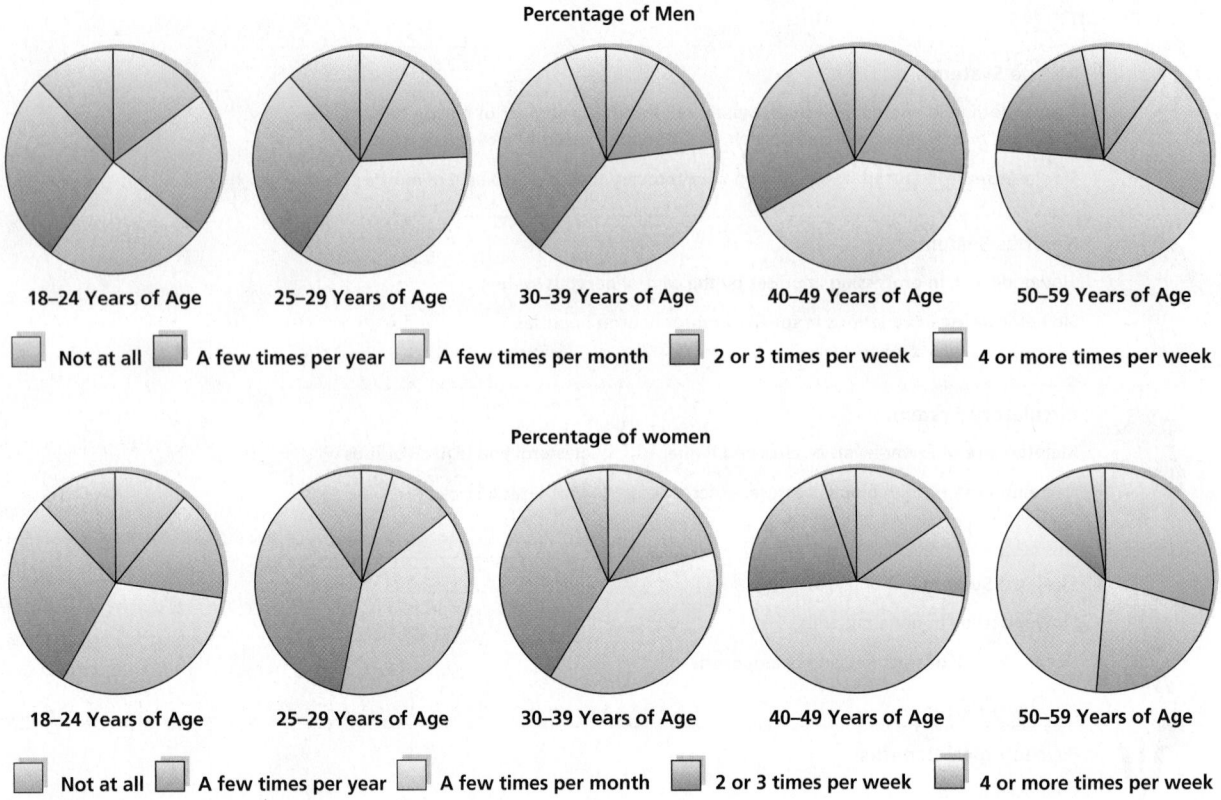

FIGURE 8-2 Frequency of Sexual Intercourse
As people age, the frequency of sexual intercourse declines.
Source: Based on Michael et al., 1994.

The Ongoing Sexuality of Middle Age

The frequency of sexual intercourse declines with age (see Figure 8-2), but sexual pleasure remains a vital part of most middle-aged adults' lives. About half of men and women age 45 to 59 report having sexual intercourse once a week or more. Close to three-quarters of men and more than half of women age 50 to 59 report masturbating. Half of men age 50 to 59 and a third of women in that age group have received oral sex from a different-sex partner in the last year. Similarly, sex remains an important activity for gay and lesbian couples during middle adulthood (Herbenick et al., 2010).

For many, midlife brings a sexual enjoyment and freedom that was missing earlier. With their children grown and away from home, married couples have more time for uninterrupted sex. Women who have gone through menopause no longer fear pregnancy or need to use birth control (Lamont, 1997; DeLamater, 2012).

Both men and women may face challenges to their sexuality in midlife. A man often needs more time to achieve an erection, and it takes longer after an orgasm to have another. The volume of fluid that is ejaculated declines, as does the production of *testosterone*, the male sex hormone (Hyde & Delameter, 2003).

For women, the vaginal walls thin and grow less elastic. The vagina begins to shrink and its entrance becomes compressed, which can make intercourse painful. For most women, though, the changes do not reduce sexual pleasure. Those women who do find intercourse less enjoyable can seek help from an increasing array of drugs, such as topical creams and testosterone patches, designed to increase sexual pleasure (Laumann, Paik, & Rosen, 1999; Freedman & Ellison, 2004; Nappi & Polatti, 2009).

female climacteric the period that marks the transition from being able to bear children to being unable to do so

The Female Climacteric and Menopause. Women enter a period, around age 45, known as the climacteric that lasts for 15 to 20 years. The **female climacteric** marks the transition that ends the childbearing years.

The most notable sign of this transition is menopause. **Menopause** is the cessation of menstruation. Menstrual periods begin to occur irregularly and less frequently during a 2-year period starting at around age 47 or 48, although this may begin as early as age 40 or as late as age 60. Menopause is completed when a woman passes a year without a menstrual period.

Menopause is important because it marks the end of a woman's natural fertility (although eggs implanted in a postmenopausal woman can produce a pregnancy). In addition, estrogen and progesterone levels—the female sex hormones—begin to drop (Schwenkhagen, 2007).

These changes in hormone production may produce a variety of symptoms, although this varies significantly for individuals. One of the most prevalent symptoms is "hot flashes," in which women experience a surge of heat above the waist. A woman may get red and begin to sweat when a hot flash occurs. Afterward, she may feel chilled. Some women have hot flashes several times a day; others, not at all.

During menopause, headaches, feelings of dizziness, heart palpitations, and aching joints are relatively common, though not universal. In one survey, only half of the women reported having hot flashes, and only about one-tenth of all women experience severe distress during menopause. Many women—perhaps as many as half—have no significant symptoms at all (Grady, 2006; Ishizuka, Kudo, & Tango, 2008; Strauss, 2013).

For many women, menopause symptoms may begin a decade before menopause actually occurs. *Perimenopause* describes this period prior to menopause when hormone production begins to change. It is marked by sometimes radical fluctuations in hormone levels, resulting in some of the same symptoms found in menopause (Winterich, 2003; Shea, 2006; Shuster et al., 2010).

For some women, the symptoms of perimenopause and menopause are considerable. Treating these problems, though, can be challenging, as we consider next.

The Dilemma of Hormone Therapy: No Easy Answer

Sandra Kendrick was certain she was having a heart attack. She had been weeding her garden when suddenly she couldn't get enough air into her lungs. She felt as if she were on fire, becoming lightheaded and dizzy. A feeling of nausea came over her. She made it to the kitchen to call 911 and then fell to the floor. When the emergency team examined her, she was both relieved and embarrassed to learn that her symptoms indicated not a heart attack but her first hot flash.

A decade ago, physicians would have had a straightforward remedy for hot flashes and other uncomfortable symptoms caused by the onset of menopause: They would have prescribed regular doses of a hormone replacement drug.

For millions of women who experienced similar difficulties, it was a solution that worked. In *HT*, estrogen and progesterone are administered to alleviate the worst of the symptoms experienced by menopausal women. HT clearly reduces a variety of problems, such as hot flashes and loss of skin elasticity. In addition, HT may reduce coronary heart disease by changing the ratio of "good" cholesterol to "bad" cholesterol. HT also decreases the thinning of the bones related to osteoporosis, which, as we discussed, becomes a problem for many people in late adulthood (McCauley, 2007; Alexandersen, Karsdal, & Christiansen, 2009; Lisabeth & Bushnell, 2012).

Furthermore, some studies show that HT is associated with reduced risks of stroke and colon cancer. Estrogen may improve memory and cognitive performance in healthy women and reduce depression. Finally, increased estrogen may lead to a greater sex drive (Cumming et al., 2009; Garcia-Portilla, 2009; Lambrinoudaki & Pérez-López, 2013).

Although HT may sound like a cure-all, in fact since it became popular in the early 1990s, it has been well understood that there were risks involved. For instance, it seemed to increase the risk of breast cancer and blood clots. The thinking was, though, that the benefits of HT outweighed the risks. All that changed after 2002, when a large study conducted by the Women's Health Initiative determined that the long-term risks of HT outweighed the benefits. Women taking a combination of estrogen and progesterone were found to be at higher risk for breast cancer, stroke, pulmonary embolism, and heart disease. Increased risk of stroke and pulmonary embolism were later found to be associated with estrogen-alone therapy (Lobo, 2009).

menopause the cessation of menstruation

The results of the Women's Health Initiative study led to a profound rethinking of the benefits of HT, calling into question the wisdom that HT could protect postmenopausal women against chronic disease. Many women stopped taking hormone replacement drugs. Statistics tell the story: Forty percent of postmenopausal women in the U.S. were using HT in 2002; it was down to 20 percent a decade later (Newton et al., 2006; Chelebowski et al., 2009; Beck, 2012).

The sharp decline among menopausal women using HT is probably an overreaction, however. The most recent thinking among medical experts is that it's not a simple all-or-nothing proposition; some women are simply better candidates for HT than others. While HT seems to be less appropriate for older, postmenopausal women (such as those who participated in the Women's Health Initiative study) because of the increased risk of coronary heart disease and other health complications, younger women at the onset of menopause and who are experiencing severe symptoms might still benefit from the therapy, at least on a short-term basis (Rossouw et al., 2007; Lewis, 2009; Beck, 2012).

Ultimately, HT presents a risk, although one that most physicians believe is worth taking. Women nearing menopause need to read literature on the topic, consult their physicians, and ultimately come to an informed decision about how to proceed.

The Psychological Consequences of Menopause. Traditionally, many people, including experts, believed that menopause was linked directly to depression, anxiety, crying spells, lack of concentration, and irritability. Some researchers estimated that as many as 10 percent of menopausal women suffered severe depression. It was assumed that the physiological changes of menopause caused such problems (Schmidt & Rubinow, 1991; Soares & Frey, 2010).

Today, most researchers take a different view, regarding menopause as a normal part of aging that does not, by itself, produce psychological symptoms. Some women do experience psychological difficulties, but they do so at other times in life as well (Freeman, Sammel, & Liu, 2004; Somerset et al., 2006; Wroolie & Holcomb, 2010).

Research shows that a woman's expectations can significantly affect her experience of menopause. Women who expect to have difficulties are more likely to attribute every physical symptom and emotional swing to menopause, while those with more positive attitudes are less apt to do so. A woman's attribution of physical symptoms, then, may affect her perception of menopause—and thus her actual experience of the period (Breheny & Stephens, 2003; Bauld & Brown, 2009; Strauss, 2011).

From the perspective of a health care provider: What cultural factors in the United States might contribute to a woman's negative experience of menopause? How?

The Male Climacteric. Do men experience the equivalent of menopause? Not really. Lacking anything akin to menstruation, they cannot experience its discontinuation. But men do experience changes in midlife that are referred to as the male climacteric. The **male climacteric** is the period of physical changes in the reproductive system (which may be accompanied by psychological changes) that occurs late in midlife, typically in a man's 50s.

Because the changes are gradual, it is hard to pinpoint the exact period of the male climacteric. For instance, despite declines in testosterone levels and sperm count, men are able to father children throughout middle age. And it is no easier in men than in women to attribute psychological symptoms to subtle physiological changes.

One physical change that occurs frequently is enlargement of the *prostate gland*. By age 40, about 10 percent of men have enlarged prostates, and the percentage increases to half of all men by the age of 80. Enlargement of the prostate produces problems with urination, including difficulty starting urination or a need to urinate frequently at night.

Sexual problems also increase as men age. In particular, *erectile dysfunction*, in which men are unable to achieve or maintain an erection, becomes more common. Drugs such as Viagra, Levitra, and Cialis, as well as patches that deliver doses of testosterone, often prove an effective treatment (Abdo et al., 2008; Shamloul & Ghanem, 2013).

male climacteric the period of physical and psychological change relating to the male reproductive system that occurs during late middle age

Men, like women, undergo psychological development in middle adulthood, but the extent to which psychological changes—discussed in the next module—are related to reproductive or other physical changes remains an open question.

REVIEW, CHECK, AND APPLY

8.1 8.2 8.3

REVIEW

LO2 What changes occur in sexuality for midlife men and women?

- Sexuality in middle adulthood changes slightly, but couples, freed from childbearing and parenting, can enjoy a new level of intimacy and pleasure.
- Physical changes affecting sexuality occur in both genders. Both the female climacteric, which includes menopause, and the male climacteric seem to have physical and perhaps psychological symptoms.

LO3 Why is there controversy over HT for women?

- While some research have found that long-term risks of HT, including breast cancer, stroke, and heart disease, outweigh the benefits, current thinking among medical experts is that some women are better candidates for HT than others.

CHECK YOURSELF

1. The period of time that marks a woman's transition from being able to bear children to not being able to do so is also known as the _____.
   - a midlife transition
   - b female climacteric
   - c perimenopause stage
   - d secular trend
2. In HT, _____ and progesterone are administered to alleviate the worst of the symptoms experienced by menopausal women.
   - a estrogen
   - b testosterone
   - c antibiotics
   - d placebos
3. Roger is a middle-aged man who has started having difficulty with urinating. Sometimes he has difficulty starting to urinate. Other times he needs to urinate frequently at night. One of the first things his doctor will check is the functioning of his _____.
   - a liver
   - b gall bladder
   - c testicles
   - d prostate

APPLYING LIFESPAN DEVELOPMENT

- How do you think society's view of women as losing their sexual allure in middle age affects women's physical and psychological experience of menopause?

✓ **Study** and **Review** on **MyPsychLab.com**

HEALTH

LO4 Is midlife a time of health or disease for men and women?
LO5 Who is likely to get coronary disease?
LO6 What causes cancer, and what tools are available to diagnose and treat it?

It was a normal exercise session for Jerome Yanger. Up at 5:30 AM, he climbed onto his exercise bike and began vigorously peddling, hoping to meet, and exceed, his average speed of 14 miles per hour. Stationed in front of the television, he used the remote control to tune to the morning business news. Occasionally glancing up at the television, he began reading a report he had begun the night before, silently cursing at some of the poor sales figures he was seeing. By the time his half-hour of exercise was over, he had finished the report, signed a few letters his administrative assistant had typed for him, and left two voice-mail messages for some colleagues.

Most of us would be ready for a nap after such a packed half hour. For Jerome Yanger, however, it was routine: He always tried to multitask, thinking it more efficient. Developmentalists might see it as symptomatic of a behavior style that puts Jerome at risk for coronary heart disease.

Although most people are healthy in middle adulthood, they also grow increasingly susceptible to many health problems. We will look at some typical midlife health issues, focusing on coronary heart disease and cancer.

Wellness and Illness: The Ups and Downs of Middle Adulthood

Health concerns become increasingly important to people in middle age. Surveys asking what worries adults show health—as well as safety and money—to be an issue of concern. More than half of adults say they are either "afraid" or "very afraid" of having cancer (see Figure 8-3).

For most people, however, midlife is a period of health. According to census figures, the vast majority of middle-aged adults report no chronic health difficulties and face no limitations on their activities.

In fact, in some ways health is better in middle adulthood than in earlier periods of life. People ages 45 to 65 are less likely than younger adults to experience infections, allergies, respiratory diseases, and digestive problems. They may contract fewer of these diseases now because they have already experienced them and built up immunities (Sterns, Barrett, & Alexander, 1985).

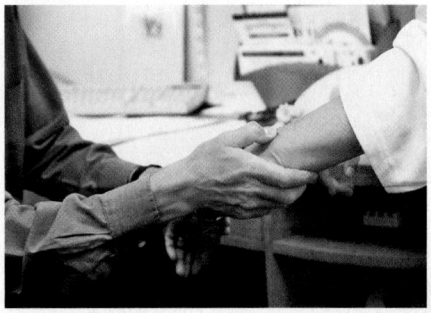

Health becomes increasingly of concern during middle adulthood.

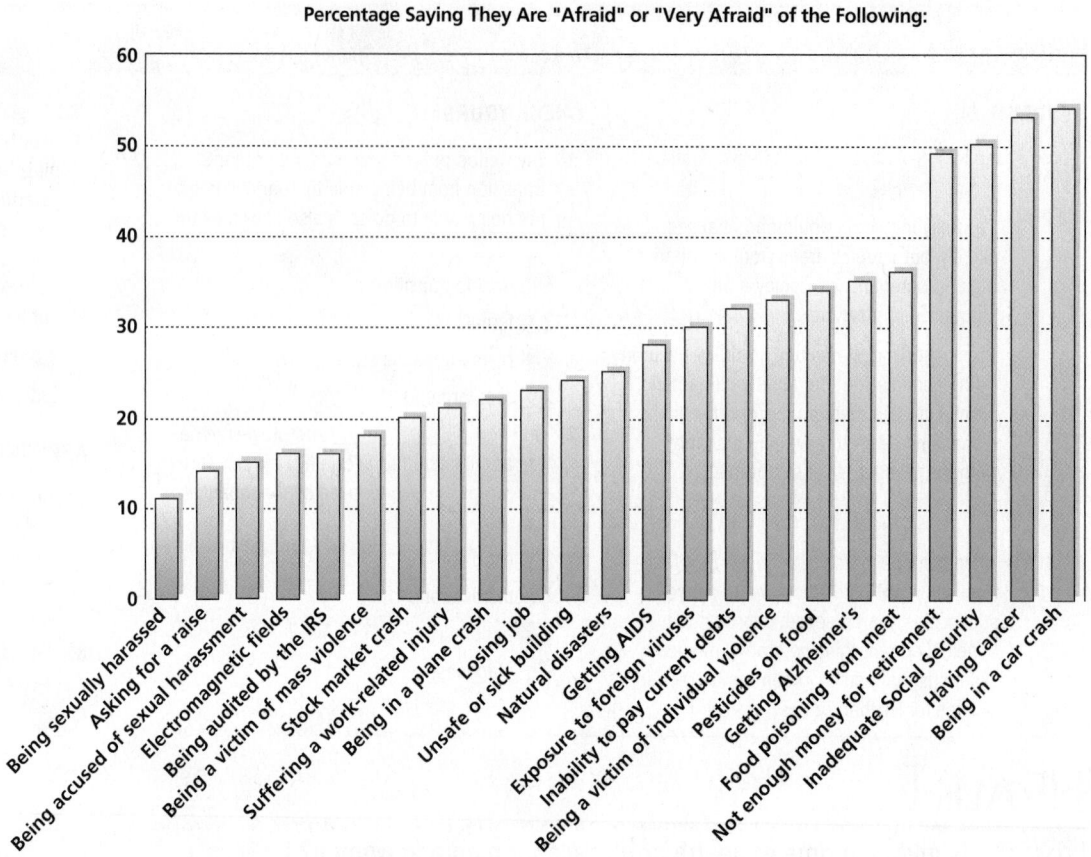

FIGURE 8-3 Worries of Adulthood
As people enter middle adulthood, health and safety concerns become increasingly important, followed by financial worries.
(*Source: USA Weekend*, 1997.)

Certain chronic diseases do begin to appear in middle adulthood. Arthritis typically begins after age 40, and diabetes is most likely to occur between ages 50 and 60, particularly in those who are overweight. Hypertension (high blood pressure) is one of the most frequent chronic disorders. Often called the "silent killer" because it is symptomless, hypertension, if left untreated, greatly increases the risk of strokes and heart disease. For such reasons, a variety of preventive and diagnostic medical tests are routinely recommended for adults during middle adulthood (Walters & Rye, 2009) (see Table 8-1).

The onset of chronic diseases in middle age boosts the death rate above that of earlier periods. Still, death remains rare: Only three out of every hundred 40-year-olds are expected to die before age 50, and eight out of every hundred 50-year-olds are expected to die before age 60. And the death rate for people between 40 and 60 has declined dramatically over the past 50 years. It now stands at just half of what it was in the 1940s. There also are cultural variations in health, as we consider next (Smedley & Syme, 2000). **Watch** the **Video** *Middle Adulthood: Physical Health, Jeff* in **MyPsychLab**.

Stress in Middle Adulthood

Stress continues to have a significant impact on health, as it did in young adulthood, although the stressors may have changed. For example, parents may worry about their adolescent child's potential drug use rather than whether their toddler is ready to give up his pacifier.

No matter what events trigger stress, the results are similar. *Psychoneuroimmunologists*, who study the relationship between the brain, the immune system, and psychological factors, report that stress has three main consequences, summarized in Figure 8-4. First, stress has direct physiological effects, ranging from increased blood pressure and hormonal activity to decreased immune system response. Second, stress leads people to engage in unhealthy behaviors, such as cutting back on sleep, smoking, drinking, or taking other drugs. Finally,

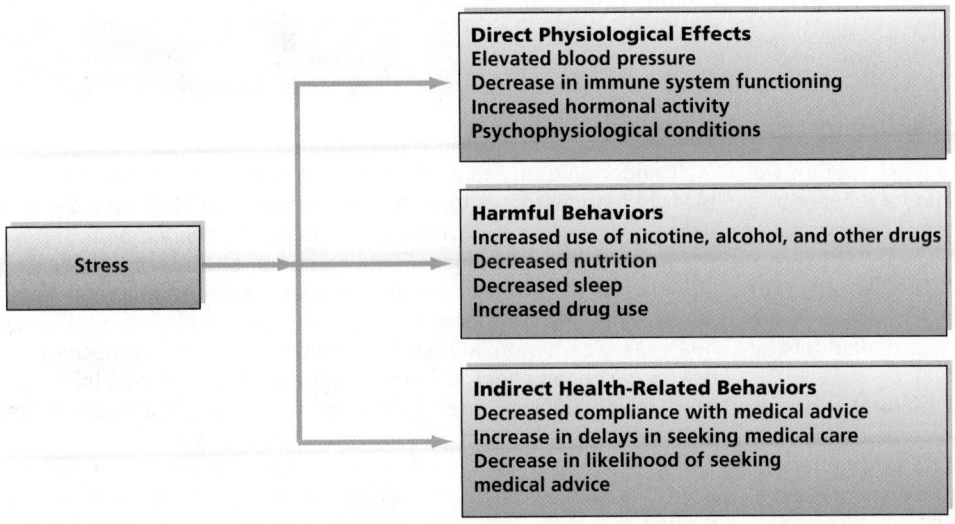

FIGURE 8-4 The Consequences of Stress
Stress produces three major consequences: direct physiological effects, harmful behaviors, and indirect health-related behaviors.
Source: Adapted from Baum, 1994.

TABLE 8-1 ADULT PREVENTIVE HEALTH CARE SCREENING RECOMMENDATIONS

These are general guidelines for healthy adults who have no symptoms of disease.

Screening	Description	Ages 40–49	Ages 50–59	Age 60+
Blood Pressure	Used to detect hypertension, which can lead to heart attack, stroke, or kidney disease.	Every 2 years.	Every 2 years.	Every 2 years, every year if family history of hypertension.
Cholesterol—Total/HDL	Used to detect high cholesterol levels, which increase risk of heart disease.	All adults should receive total cholesterol screening, HDL cholesterol, LDL cholesterol, and triglycerides AT LEAST ONCE. Cardiac risk factors and lipoprotein results will determine frequency of follow-up by your health care provider.		
Eye Examination	Used to determine if glasses are required and to check for eye disease.	Every 2–4 years. Diabetics—Every year.	Every 2–4 years. Diabetics—Every year.	Every 2–4 years. At age 65 and over, every 1–2 years. Diabetics—Every year.
Flexible Sigmoidoscopy or Double Contrast Barium Enema or Colonoscopy	A procedure using a scope or x-ray to detect cancer of the colon and rectum.	–	Baseline at age 50. Every 3–5 years after initial test.	Every 3–5 years. Age to stop depends on health. Follow-up normal colonoscopy in 8–10 yrs.
Fecal Occult Blood Screening	Detects unseen blood in stool, which is early warning sign for colon cancer.	–	Every year.	Every year.
Rectal Exam (Digital)	Examination of prostate or ovaries to detect cancer.	–	Every year.	Every year.
Urinalysis Screening	Examination to detect presence of excess protein in urine.	Every 5 years.	Every 5 years.	Every 3–5 years.
Immunizations (Shots) Tetanus	Protection against infection after injury.	Every 10 years.	Every 10 years.	Every 10 years.
Influenza (Flu)	Protection against the influenza virus.	Any person with chronic medical conditions such as heart, lung, kidney disease, diabetes.	Annually, age 50 and over.	Annually, age 65 and over.
Pneumococcal	Protection against pneumonia.			At age 65, then every 6 years.

Note: Additional guidelines specific to women include breast exams, mammograms, pap smears, and pelvic exams; additional guidelines for men include prostate specific antigen tests and testicular self-exams.

ural Dimensions

ealth: Ethnic and Gender Differences

he health of middle-aged adults mask vast individ-
es. While most people are healthy, some are beset by a
of ailments. Genetics play a role. For instance, hypertension
ten runs in families.

Social and environmental factors also affect health. For instance, the death rate for middle-aged African Americans in the United States is twice the rate for Caucasians. Why should this be true?

Socioeconomic status (SES) is a significant factor. For whites and African Americans of the same SES level, the death rate for African Americans is actually lower than for whites. Members of lower-income families, however, are more likely to experience a disabling illness. There are many reasons for this. People in lower-SES households are more apt to work in dangerous occupations, such as mining or construction work. Lower-income people also often have inferior health care coverage. The crime rates and environmental pollutants are generally higher in lower-income neighborhoods. A higher incidence of accidents and health hazards, and thus a higher death rate, are linked to lower levels of income (Fingerhut & Makuc, 1992; Dahl & Birkelund, 1997; Hendren, Humiston, & Fiscella, 2012).

Gender also makes a difference. Women's overall mortality rate is lower than men's—a trend that holds true from birth—but the incidence of illness among midlife women is higher than for men.

Women are more susceptible to minor, short-term illness and chronic, but non-life-threatening diseases such as migraine headaches, while men are more susceptible to serious illnesses such as heart disease. Fewer women smoke than men, which reduces their risk for cancer and heart disease; women drink less alcohol than men, which lowers the incidence of cirrhosis of the liver and auto accidents; and they work at less dangerous jobs (McDonald, 1999).

Another reason for the higher rate of illness in women may be that more medical research targets men and the disorders they suffer. The vast majority of medical research money goes to preventing life-threatening diseases faced mostly by men, rather than to chronic conditions such as heart disease that may cause disability and suffering, but not necessarily death. Typically, research on diseases that strike both men and women focuses on men as subjects rather than women. This bias is now being addressed in initiatives by the U.S. National Institutes of Health, but the historical pattern has been one of gender discrimination by a male-dominated research community (Vidaver et al., 2000). **Watch** the **Video** *Special Topics: Health Disparities* in **MyPsychLab**.

---

stress has indirect effects on health-related behavior. People under a lot of stress may be less likely to seek out good medical care, exercise, or to comply with medical advice. All of these can lead to or affect serious health conditions, including heart disease (Dagher et al., 2009; Ihle et al., 2012; Emery, Anderson, & Goodwin, 2013). **Watch** the **Video** *Thinking Like a Psychologist: Personality and Health* in **MyPsychLab**.

The A's and B's of Coronary Heart Disease: Linking Health and Personality

More men die in middle age from diseases relating to the heart and circulatory system than from any other cause. Women are less vulnerable, as we'll see, but they are not immune. Each year such diseases kill around 151,000 people under the age of 65, and they are responsible for more loss of work and disability days due to hospitalization than any other cause (American Heart Association, 2010).

Risk Factors for Heart Disease. Although heart and circulatory diseases are a major problem, some people have a much lower risk than others. The death rate in some countries, such as Japan, is only a quarter of the rate in the United States. A few other countries have a considerably higher death rate. Why?

The answer is both genetics and environment. Some people seem genetically predisposed to heart disease. If a person's parents suffered from it, the likelihood is greater that she or he will too. Similarly, sex and age are risk factors: Men are more likely to suffer from heart disease, and the risk rises as people age.

Environment and lifestyle choices are also important. Cigarette smoking, a diet high in fats and cholesterol, and a lack of physical exercise all increase the risk of heart disease. Such factors may explain country-to-country variations in the rate of heart disease. For example, the death rate from heart disease in Japan is relatively low and may be due to differences in diet: The typical Japanese diet is much lower in fat than it is in the United States (Wilcox, Castro, & King 2006; De Meersman & Stein, 2007; Scarbourough et al., 2012).

Diet is not the only factor. Psychological factors—particularly how stress is perceived and experienced—appear to be related to heart disease. For instance, a set of personality characteristics, known as Type A behavior, appears to be a factor in the development of coronary heart disease.

The *Type A behavior pattern* is characterized by competitiveness, impatience, and a tendency toward frustration and hostility. Type A people are extremely ambitious and they engage in *polyphasic activities*—multiple activities carried out simultaneously. They are the true multitaskers whom you see talking on their phones while working on their laptop computers while riding the commuter train—and eating breakfast. Easily angered, they become both verbally and nonverbally hostile if prevented from reaching their goals.

In contrast, many people have virtually the opposite characteristics in what is known as the Type B behavior pattern. The *Type B behavior pattern* is characterized by noncompetitiveness, patience, and a lack of aggression. In contrast to Type A's, Type B's experience little sense of time urgency, and they are rarely hostile.

In addition to being characterized as competitive, people with Type A personalities also tend to engage in polyphasic activities, or doing a number of things at once. Does a Type A personality deal with stress differently from a Type B personality?

Type A and Type B behavior is significant because the distinction is related to the risk of coronary heart disease. Type A men have twice the rate of coronary heart disease, a greater number of fatal heart attacks, and five times as many heart problems as Type B men (Strube, 1990; Wielgosz & Nolan, 2000).

It's important to note that some critics believe that the evidence for the existence of Type A and Type B behavior patterns is questionable. Moreover, some evidence suggests that only certain components of Type A behavior are most involved in producing disease, and not the entire constellation of behaviors associated with the pattern. Specifically, it seems as if the hostility and anger components of Type A behavior are the central link to coronary heart disease (Demaree & Everhart, 2004; Eaker et al., 2004; Kahn, 2004; Myrtek, 2007).

Although the relationship between at least some Type A behaviors and heart disease is relatively clear, this does not mean that all middle-aged adults who can be characterized as Type A's are destined to suffer from coronary heart disease. Other types of negative emotions besides the hostility found in Type A behavior have been linked to heart disease. For example, psychologist Johan Denollet has identified behavior he calls *Type D*—for "distressed"—that is linked to coronary heart disease. He believes that insecurity, anxiety, and having a negative outlook put people at risk for heart attacks (Pedersen et al., 2009; Mols & Denollet, 2010; Kupper et al., 2013).

The Threat of Cancer

Few diseases are as frightening as cancer, and many middle-aged adults view a cancer diagnosis as a death sentence. Although the reality is different—many forms of cancer respond well to medical treatment, and 40 percent of those diagnosed are still alive 5 years later—the disease raises many fears. And there is no denying that cancer is the second-leading cause of death in the United States (Smedley & Syme, 2000).

The precise trigger for cancer is still not known, but the process by which it spreads is clear. Certain cells in the body begin to multiply rapidly and uncontrollably. As they increase in number, these cells form tumors. Unimpeded, they draw nutrients from healthy cells and body tissue. Eventually, they destroy the body's ability to function.

Like heart disease, cancer is associated with a variety of genetic and environmental risk factors. Some cancers have clear genetic components. For example, a family history of breast cancer—the most common cause of cancer death among women—raises the risk for a woman.

Several environmental and behavioral factors are also related to the risk of cancer. Poor nutrition, smoking, alcohol use, exposure to sunlight, exposure to radiation, and particular occupational hazards (such as exposure to certain chemicals or asbestos) are all known to increase the chances of developing cancer.

After a diagnosis, several forms of treatment are possible, depending on the type of cancer. One treatment is *radiation therapy*, in which radiation targets the tumor in an attempt to destroy it. Patients undergoing *chemotherapy* ingest controlled doses of toxic substances meant to poison the tumor. Finally, surgery is used to remove the tumor (and often the surrounding tissue). The form of treatment is determined by how far the cancer has spread when it is first identified.

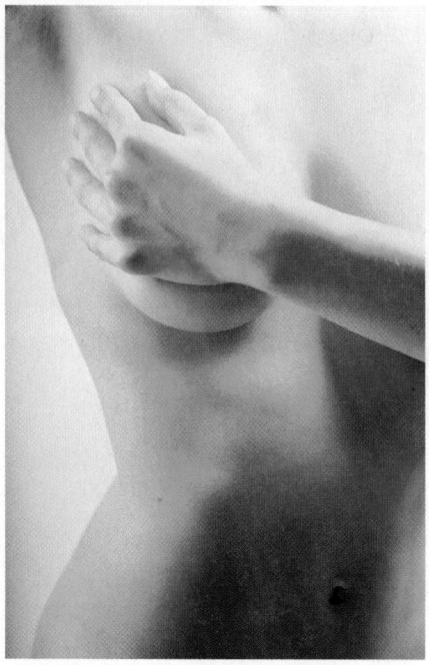

Women should routinely examine their breasts for signs of breast cancer.

Because early detection improves a patient's chances, diagnostic techniques that help identify the first signs of cancer are of great importance. This is especially true in middle adulthood, when the risk of certain cancers increases.

Physicians urge that women do routine breast exams and men regularly check their testicles for signs of cancer. Cancer of the prostate gland, the most common type of cancer in men, can be detected by routine rectal exams and by a blood test that identifies prostate-specific antigen (PSA).

Mammograms provide internal scans of women's breasts to help identify early-stage cancer. However, at what age women should begin to routinely have the procedure has been controversial.

Routine Mammograms: At What Age Should Women Start?

Life had been totally on track for Kristy Cajulo. She ate well, exercised routinely, and her most serious illness had been the flu a year back. So when she carried out a routine breast examination on the day of her 36th birthday and found a small lump, she was surprised, but assumed it was nothing. But the bigger shock was to come after her physician had the lump biopsied and learned she had early-stage breast cancer.

In many ways, Linda was lucky: She found her cancer early. Statistically, the earlier breast cancer is diagnosed, the better a woman's chances of survival. But just how to accomplish early identification has produced some degree of contention in the medical field. In particular, controversy surrounds the age at which *mammograms*, a kind of weak x-ray used to examine breast tissue, should be routinely administered to women.

Mammograms are among the best means of detecting breast cancer in its earliest stages. The technique allows physicians to identify tumors while they are still very small. Patients have time for treatment before the tumor grows and spreads to other parts of the body. Mammograms have the potential for saving many lives, and nearly all medical professionals suggest that at some point during middle adulthood women should routinely obtain them.

But at what age should women start having annual mammograms? The risk of breast cancer begins to grow at around the age of 30 and then becomes increasingly more likely. Ninety-five percent of new cases occur in women aged 40 and above (SEER, 2005).

Determining the age to begin routine screening mammograms is complicated by two considerations. First, there is the problem of *false positives*, instances in which the test suggests something is wrong when in fact there is no problem. Because the breast tissue of younger women is denser than that of older women, younger women are more likely to have false positives. In fact, some estimates suggest that as many as a third of all younger women who have repeated mammograms are likely to have a false positive that necessitates further testing or a biopsy. Furthermore, the opposite problem also may occur: *false negatives*, in which a mammogram does not detect indications of cancer (Destounis et al., 2009; Elmore et al., 2009; Armstrong et al., 2013).

In what proved to be a controversial proposal, the U.S. Preventive Services Task Force, a panel appointed by the government, recommended in 2009 that women in their 40s should *not* routinely have mammograms, and that women between the ages of 50 and 74 should have mammograms every 2 years, rather than annually. Their recommendation was based on a cost-benefit analysis showing that the risks of mammograms could be cut in half while still offering 80 percent of the benefits of annual mammograms (Nelson et al., 2009).

Their recommendation was immediately criticized by several major women's groups, along with the American Cancer Society and American College of Radiology. They argued that women aged 40 and above should receive annual screenings (Grady, 2009).

Ultimately, the determination of the timing of screenings is a highly personal one. Women should consult their health care providers and discuss the latest research regarding the frequency of mammograms. And for certain women, who have a history of breast cancer in their families or a mutation in a gene called BRCA, the evidence is clear that mammograms starting at age 40 are beneficial (Grady, 2009; Alonso et al., 2012; Smith, Duffy, & Tabar, 2012).

REVIEW, CHECK, AND APPLY

8.1 8.2 8.3

REVIEW

L04 Is midlife a time of health or disease for men and women?

- In general, middle adulthood is a period of good health, although susceptibility to chronic diseases, such as arthritis, diabetes, and hypertension, increases.

L05 Who is likely to get coronary disease?

- Heart disease is a risk for middle-aged adults. Both genetic and environmental factors contribute to heart disease, including the Type A behavior pattern.

L06 What causes cancer, and what tools are available to diagnose and treat it?

- The precise causes of cancer are still unknown, but the process by which it spreads is clear.
- Therapies such as radiation therapy, chemotherapy, and surgery can successfully treat cancer.

CHECK YOURSELF

1. Insecurity, anxiety, and having a negative outlook put people at risk for heart attacks. This behavior is referred to as _____.
   - a Type D
   - b Type B
   - c Disassociative Identity Disorder
   - d Type A
2. Cancer is the _____ leading cause of death in the United States.
   - a fifth
   - b first
   - c third
   - d second

APPLYING LIFESPAN DEVELOPMENT

- What social policies might be developed to lower the incidence of disabling illness among members of lower-socioeconomic groups?

✓ **Study** and **Review** on **MyPsychLab.com**

MODULE 8.2

COGNITIVE DEVELOPMENT IN MIDDLE ADULTHOOD

Taking the Challenge

Gina Madison has always loved a challenge. That's why she applied to be a contestant on the game show Jeopardy! "Why should young people have all the fun?" she asks, laughing. I figure at age 46, I know a thing or two." Jeopardy! requires quick thinking and quick response time. Was Gina worried that despite her world experience and accumulated knowledge, she would be bested by contestants half her age? "Not really," she says. "My husband and I do cryptic puzzles every morning at breakfast." Gina also reads a great deal. "I make notes while I read and review them at the end of a book," she explains. "That way I remember a lot more than just a few main characters and how the plot came out." She also loves nonfiction—books about science, history, and world events. "Books about brain research are my favorites," she says. "They're discovering that you really can teach an 'old dog' new tricks."

Gina, like many people in midlife, enjoys challenging her mind and keeping it sharp. She feels confident to take on people half her age in a contest of wits and quick response time. She knows she has something that younger contestants do not: decades of life experience and knowledge.

The second module of the chapter focuses on cognitive development in middle age. We look at the tricky question of whether intelligence declines during the period, and we consider the difficulty of answering the question fully. We also examine memory and how its capabilities change in middle adulthood.

COGNITIVE DEVELOPMENT

L07 What happens to a person's intelligence in middle adulthood?
L08 How does one attain expertise?

It began innocently enough. Forty-five-year-old Bina Clingman couldn't remember whether she had mailed the letter that her husband had given her, and she wondered, briefly, whether this was a sign of aging. The next day, the question recurred when she spent 20 minutes looking for a phone number she knew she had written down on a piece of paper—somewhere. By the time she found it, she was surprised and even a little anxious. "Am I losing my memory?" she asked herself, feeling both annoyance and a degree of concern.

Many people in their 40s feel more absentminded than they did 20 years earlier, and they have some concern about becoming less mentally able as they age. Common wisdom suggests that people lose some mental sharpness in midlife. But how accurate is this notion?

Does Intelligence Decline in Adulthood?

For years, experts provided an unwavering response when asked whether intelligence declined in adulthood: Intelligence peaks at age 18, stays fairly steady until the mid-20s, and then gradually declines until the end of life.

Today, developmentalists view questions about changes in intelligence across the life span as more complicated—and they have come to different, and more complex, conclusions.

The Difficulties in Answering the Question. The conclusion that intelligence starts to diminish in the mid-20s was based on extensive research. *Cross-sectional studies*—which test people of different ages at the same point in time—clearly showed that older subjects were less likely to score well than younger subjects on traditional intelligence tests of the sort we discussed earlier.

But consider the drawbacks of cross-sectional research—in particular, the possibility that it may suffer from *cohort effects*. Recall that cohort effects are influences associated with growing up at a particular historical time that affect persons of a particular age. For instance, suppose that compared to younger subjects, the older people in a cross-sectional study had had less adequate educations, less stimulating jobs, or were less healthy. In that case, the lower IQ scores of the older group could not be attributed solely, or perhaps even partially, to differences in intelligence based on age. Because they do not control for cohort effects, cross-sectional studies may well *underestimate* intelligence in older subjects.

fluid intelligence reflects information processing capabilities, reasoning, and memory

crystallized intelligence the accumulation of information, skills, and strategies that people have learned through experience and that they can apply in problem-solving situations

To overcome the cohort problems of cross-sectional studies, developmentalists began to use *longitudinal studies*, in which the same people are studied periodically over a span of time. These studies revealed a different developmental pattern for intelligence: Adults tended to show stable and even increasing intelligence test scores until their mid-30s, and in some cases up to their 50s. Then the scores began to decline (Bayley & Oden, 1955).

But let's consider the drawbacks of longitudinal studies, too. People taking an intelligence test repeatedly may perform better because they become familiar—and comfortable—with the testing situation. Similarly, through repeated exposure to the same test, they may begin to remember some of the test items. Consequently, practice effects may account for the superior performance of people on longitudinal measures of intelligence as opposed to cross-sectional measures (Salthouse, 2009).

It is also difficult for researchers using longitudinal studies to keep their samples intact. Participants may move away, decide they no longer want to participate, or become ill and die. Over time, the participants who remain may represent a healthier, more stable, and more psychologically positive group of people than those who are no longer part of the sample. If this is the case, longitudinal studies may *overestimate* intelligence in older subjects.

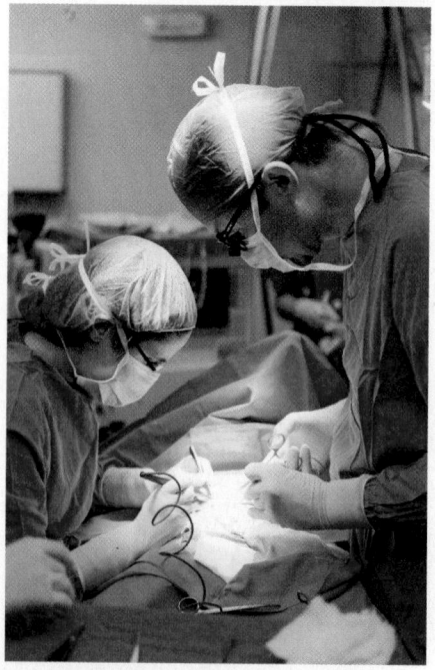

It is difficult to evaluate cognitive abilities in middle adulthood. While some types of mental abilities may begin to decline, crystallized intelligence holds steady and actually may increase.

Crystallized and Fluid Intelligence. Drawing conclusions about age-related changes in intelligence is challenging. For instance, many IQ tests include sections based on physical performance, such as arranging a group of blocks. These sections are timed and scored on the basis of how quickly an item is completed. If older people take longer on physical tasks—recall that reaction time slows with age—then their poorer performance on IQ tests may result from physical rather than cognitive changes.

To complicate the issue further, many researchers believe there are two kinds of intelligence: fluid intelligence and crystallized intelligence. As we noted earlier, **fluid intelligence** reflects information processing capabilities, reasoning, and memory. To arrange a series of letters according to some rule or to memorize a set of numbers uses fluid intelligence. **Crystallized intelligence** is the information, skills, and strategies that people have accumulated through experience and that they can apply to solve problems. Someone who is solving a crossword puzzle or attempting to identify the murderer in a mystery story is using crystallized intelligence, relying on past experience as a resource.

Researchers once believed that fluid intelligence was largely determined by genetic factors, and crystallized intelligence by experiential, environmental factors. They later abandoned this distinction when they found that crystallized intelligence is determined in part by fluid intelligence. For instance, a person's ability to solve a crossword puzzle (which involves crystallized intelligence) relies on that person's proficiency with letters and patterns (a manifestation of fluid intelligence).

When developmentalists examined the two kinds of intelligence separately, they discovered there are two answers to the question of whether intelligence declines with age: yes and no. Yes, because fluid intelligence does decline with age; no, because crystallized intelligence holds steady and can actually improve (Salthouse, Pink, & Tucker-Drob, 2008; Deary, 2010; Ghisletta et al., 2012) (see Figure 8-5).

If we look at more specific types of intelligence, true age-related differences and developments begin to show up. According to developmental psychologist K. Warner Schaie, who has conducted extensive longitudinal research on adult intellectual development, we should consider many types of ability, such as spatial orientation, numeric ability, verbal ability, and so on, rather than the broad divisions of crystallized and fluid intelligence (Schaie, Willis, & Pennak, 2005).

Examined this way, the question of how intelligence changes in adulthood yields yet another, more specific, answer. Schaie has found that certain abilities, such as inductive reasoning, spatial orientation, perceptual speed, and verbal memory, begin to decline very gradually at around age 25 and continue to do so through old age. Numeric and verbal abilities show a different pattern. Numeric ability tends to increase until the mid-40s, is lower at age 60, and then remains steady. Verbal ability rises until the start of middle adulthood, around age 40, then stays fairly steady (Schaie et al., 2005).

Why do these changes occur? One reason is that brain functioning begins to change in middle adulthood. For example, researchers have found that 20 genes that are vital to learning, memory, and mental flexibility begin to function less efficiently as early as age 40. Furthermore, as people age, the specific areas of their brains used to accomplish particular tasks changes. For instance, older adults use both brain hemispheres for tasks that in younger people involve just one hemisphere (Fling et al., 2011; Phillips, 2011; Bielak et al., 2013).

Reframing the Issue: What Is the Source of Competence During Middle Adulthood?
It is during midlife that people come to hold some of the most important and powerful positions in society, despite gradual declines in certain cognitive abilities. How do we explain such continuing, even growing, competence?

Psychologist Timothy Salthouse (1990, 1994a, 2010) suggests there are four reasons why this discrepancy exists. First, it is possible that typical measures of cognitive skills tap a different type of cognition than what is required to be successful in certain occupations. Recall the earlier discussion of practical intelligence, in which we found that traditional IQ tests fail

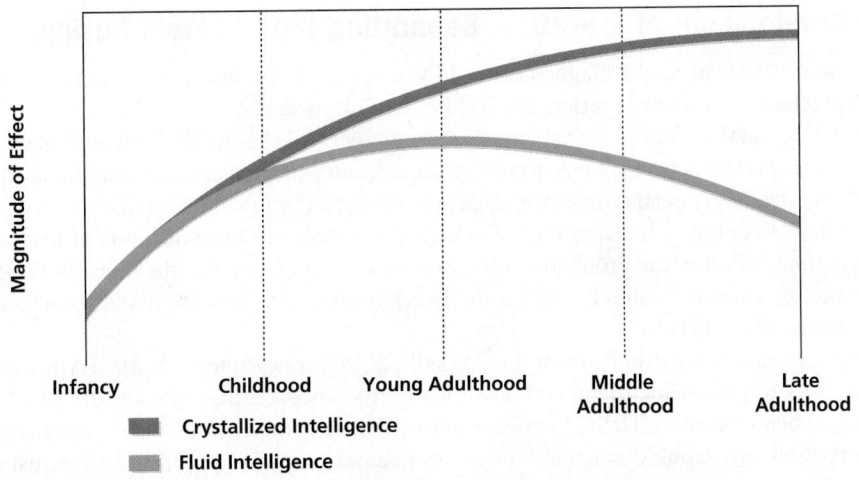

FIGURE 8-5 Changes in Crystallized and Fluid Intelligence
Although crystallized intelligence increases with age, fluid intelligence begins to decline in middle age. What are the implications for general competence in middle adulthood?
Source: Schaie, 1985.

to measure cognitive abilities that are related to occupational success. Perhaps we would find no discrepancy between intelligence and cognitive abilities in midlife if we used measures of practical intelligence rather than traditional IQ tests to assess intelligence.

A second factor also relates to the measurement of IQ and occupational success. It is possible that the most successful middle-aged adults are not representative of midlife adults in general. It may be that only a small proportion of people are highly successful, and the rest, who experience only moderate or little success, have changed occupations, retired, or become sick and died. Highly successful people, then, may be an unrepresentative sample.

Also, the degree of cognitive ability required for professional success may simply not be that high. According to this argument, people can succeed professionally and still be on the decline in certain cognitive abilities. In other words, they have brains to spare.

Finally, it may be that older people are successful because they have developed specific kinds of expertise and particular competencies. Whereas IQ tests measure reactions to novel situations, occupational success may be influenced by very specific, well-practiced abilities. Consequently, middle-aged individuals may maintain and even expand the distinctive talents they need for professional accomplishment, despite a decline in overall intellectual skills. This explanation has generated research on expertise.

Expertise develops as people become more experienced in a particular domain and are able to be flexible with procedures and rules.

From the perspective of an educator: How do you think the apparent discrepancy between declining IQ scores and continuing cognitive competence in middle adulthood would affect the learning ability of middle adults who return to school?

For example, developmental psychologists Paul Baltes and Margaret Baltes have studied a strategy called selective optimization with compensation. **Selective optimization with compensation** is the process people use in concentrating on particular skill areas to compensate for losses in other areas. Baltes suggests that cognitive development during middle and later adulthood is a mixture of growth and decline. As people begin to lose certain abilities, they advance in other areas by strengthening their skills. In so doing, they avoid showing any practical deterioration. Overall cognitive competence, then, remains stable and may even improve (Ebner, Freund, & Baltes, 2006; Erber, 2010; Deary, 2012).

For instance, recall that reaction time lengthens as people age. Because reaction time is a component of typing skill, we would expect that typists would slow as they age. This is not the case. Though their reaction time is increasing, older typists compensate by looking further ahead in the material as they type. Similarly, a business executive may be slower to recall names, but he may have a mental file of deals he has completed and be able to forge new agreements easily because of it.

Selective optimization with compensation is one of several strategies adults use to maintain high performance.

The Development of Expertise: Separating Experts From Novices

If you were ill and needed a diagnosis, would you rather visit a young physician fresh out of medical school, or a more experienced, middle-aged physician?

If you chose the older physician, you probably assumed that he or she would have more expertise. **Expertise** is the skill or knowledge acquired in a particular area. More focused than broad intelligence, expertise develops as people devote attention and practice to a subject or skill and, in so doing, gain experience. For example, physicians become better at diagnosing the symptoms of a medical problem as they gain experience. A person who does a lot of cooking comes to know how a recipe will taste if certain modifications are made (Morita et al., 2008; Reuter et al., 2012).

What separates the experts from the less skilled? While beginners use formal procedures and rules, often following them very strictly, experts rely on experience and intuition, and they often bend the rules. Their experience allows them to process information automatically. Experts often have trouble articulating how they draw conclusions; their solutions just seem right to them—and *are* likely to be right. Brain imaging studies show that experts use different neural pathways than novices to solve problems (Grabner, Neubauer, & Stern, 2006).

Finally, experts develop better problem-solving strategies than nonexperts, and they're more flexible in their approach. Experience provides them with alternative solutions to the same

selective optimization with compensation the process by which people concentrate on particular skill areas to compensate for losses in other areas

expertise the acquisition of skill or knowledge in a particular area

From Research to Practice

What Is Multitasking Doing to Our Brains?

Victor Norris's home office looks like a lot like his teenage son's room. He has three computer monitors on his desk—one for email and instant messaging, one for news and video streaming, and one for productivity software. Then there's the television, the smart phone, and a video game console for relaxing. Victor switches from task to task all day long, often letting simple tasks such as writing an email drag on for hours because they keep getting interrupted. He's so used to working this way that he doesn't even realize he's doing it.

Victor Norris isn't alone. The digital age has brought a wealth of gadgets providing instant access to information and is changing the way people work and socialize. Obsessive checking of email, text messages, and social networking sites is the new norm. But might all this frantic multitasking be changing the way people think? Research suggests that it does, and not necessarily in a good way.

One researcher compared the performance of heavy multitaskers to non-multitaskers on a perceptual task. While seated at a computer, participants were flashed an image of red rectangles and then were shown the image again and asked whether any of the rectangles had changed position from the previous image. Then the task was complicated by addition of blue triangles, which the participants were instructed to ignore and continue performing the task exactly as before. But the heavy multitaskers just couldn't ignore them, and their performance on the task worsened. Multitaksers also had significantly more difficulty switching from task to task when performing tasks in a series, and were less likely to use old but useful information to solve a new problem. The conclusion: Multitaskers may be oversensitive to incoming information (Ophir, Nass, & Wagner, 2009).

But it's far from conclusive that multitasking technology usage is harmful. Other research shows that middle-aged adults who have previous Internet searching experience show higher levels of brain activation while engaging in that task compared to merely reading pages of text, suggesting that new neural pathways are developed that are involved in decision making and reasoning. Furthermore, other studies show that people with considerable experience playing video games actually become better at reacting to stimuli, singling out important information, and switching between tasks (Small et al., 2009; Green et al., 2012).

In short, we don't know for sure whether multitasking is helpful or a hindrance in terms of quality of thinking. What is clear is that certain kinds of tasks are inherently difficult to carry out, such as driving and texting simultaneously: A considerable body of research shows that it can't be done safely (Cook & Jones, 2011; Long, Gillespie, & Tanaka, 2012).

Watch the **Video** *The Myth of Multitasking* in **MyPsychLab.**

- *Could it be the case that people who are prone to distraction are more likely to become multitaskers in the first place? Explain.*
- *Are there any possible benefits to having difficulty tuning out irrelevant information?*

problem, increasing the probability of success (Willis, 1996; Clark, 1998; Arts, Gijselaers, & Boshuizen, 2006; McGugin & Tanaka, 2010).

Not everyone develops an area of expertise in middle adulthood. Professional responsibilities, amount of leisure time, educational level, income, and marital status all affect the development of expertise.

REVIEW, CHECK, AND APPLY

REVIEW

L07 What happens to a person's intelligence in middle adulthood?

- The question of whether intelligence declines in middle adulthood is complicated by limitations in cross-sectional studies and longitudinal studies.
- Intelligence appears to be divided into components, some of which decline while others hold steady or even improve.
- In general, cognitive competence in middle adulthood holds fairly steady despite declines in some areas of intellectual functioning.

L08 How does one attain expertise?

- The skill or knowledge acquired in a particular area, expertise develops as people devote attention and practice to a subject or skill and, in so doing, gain experience.

CHECK YOURSELF

1. According to _____ studies that test people of different ages at the same time, older subjects scored lower than younger subjects on traditional intelligence tests.
   - a longitudinal
   - b objective
   - c cross-sectional
   - d observational
2. Because cross-sectional studies do not control for cohort effects, these research designs may underestimate intelligence in older subjects.
   - True
   - False
3. Over the years, one of the types of intelligence that increases with age is _____ intelligence, or the accumulation of information, skills, and strategies that people have learned through experience.
   - a emotional
   - b crystallized
   - c intrapersonal
   - d naturalist

APPLYING LIFESPAN DEVELOPMENT

- How might crystallized and fluid intelligence work together to help middle-aged people deal with novel situations and problems?

Study and **Review** on **MyPsychLab.com**

MEMORY

LO9 How does aging affect memory?
LO10 How can memory be improved?

Mary Donovan races around the kitchen and makes one last frantic search through her purse. "I must be losing my memory," she mutters. "I always leave my keys on the counter next to the toaster." It's not until her son David comes downstairs ready for hockey practice that Mary remembers she loaned him her car the day before. Sure enough, David produces the keys from the pocket of his varsity jacket. Relieved to have her keys in hand once more, Mary sighs. After all, she is 47. Such episodes are to be expected, she supposes.

Like Bina Clingman, who was worried about forgetting letters and phone numbers, Mary probably believes that memory loss is common in middle age. However, if she is a typical midlife adult, her assessment may not be accurate. Research shows that most people exhibit minimal or no memory loss. Because of societal stereotypes, however, people may attribute their absentmindedness to aging, even though they have been that way all their lives. It is the *meaning* they give to their forgetfulness that changes, rather than their actual ability to remember (Chasteen et al., 2005; Hoessler & Chasteen, 2008; Hess, Hinson, & Hodges, 2009).

Types of Memory

To understand the nature of memory changes, we must consider that memory is traditionally viewed as three sequential components: sensory memory, short-term memory (also called working memory), and long-term memory. *Sensory memory* is an initial, momentary storage of information. Information is recorded by the sensory system as a raw, meaningless stimulus. Next, information moves into *short-term memory*, which holds it for 15 to 25 seconds. If the information is rehearsed, it then moves into *long-term memory*, where it is stored on a relatively permanent basis.

Both sensory memory and short-term memory show virtually no weakening in middle age. Long-term memory, however, declines for some people. It appears this decline is not a fading or a complete loss of memory, but rather a less efficient registering and storing of information. Age also makes people less efficient at retrieving information. Even if the information was adequately stored in long-term memory, it may become more difficult to locate or isolate it (Salthouse, 2007, 2010).

Memory declines in middle age are relatively minor, and most can be compensated for by various cognitive strategies. Paying greater attention to material when it is first encountered can aid in its later recall. Your lost car keys may have more to do with your inattentiveness when you put them down than with a decline in memory.

Many middle adults find it hard to pay attention to certain things for some of the same reasons expertise develops. They are used to using memory shortcuts, *schemas*, to ease the burden of remembering the many things they experience each day.

Memory Schemas. To recall information, people often use **schemas**, organized bodies of information stored in memory. Schemas represent the way the world is organized, allowing people to categorize and interpret new information. For example, if we have a schema for eating in a restaurant, we don't regard a meal in a new restaurant as a completely new experience. We know we will be seated at a table or counter and offered a menu from which to select food. Our schema for eating out tells us how to treat the server, what sorts of food to eat first, and that we should leave a tip.

People hold schemas for individuals (such as the particular behavior patterns of one's mother, wife, or child) as well as for categories of people (mail carriers, lawyers, or professors) and behaviors or events (dining in a restaurant or visiting the dentist). People's schemas organize their behavior and help them to interpret social events. A person who knows the schema for visiting the doctor will not be surprised when he is asked to undress.

schemas organized bodies of information stored in memory

Schemas also convey cultural information. Psychologists Susan Fiske and Shelley Taylor (1991) use an example of an old Native American folktale in which the hero participates with

Becoming an Informed Consumer of Development

8.1 8.2 8.3

Effective Strategies for Remembering

We are all forgetful at times. However, there are techniques for more effective recall. **Mnemonics** *(pronounced "nee-MON-iks") are formal strategies for organizing material in ways that make it easier to remember. Among the mnemonics that work are the following (Bloom & Lamkin, 2006; Morris & Fritz, 2006; Collins, 2007):*

- **Get organized.** For people who have trouble recalling where they left their keys or remembering appointments, the simplest approach is to become more organized. Using a date book, hanging keys on a hook, or using Post-It notes can aid recall.
- **Pay attention.** You can improve your recall by paying close attention to new information, and purposefully thinking that you will need to recall it. For example, when you park your car at the mall, pay attention at the moment you park, and remind yourself that you really want to remember the location.
- **Use the encoding specificity phenomenon.** According to the encoding specificity phenomenon, people are most likely to recall information in environments that are similar to those in which they initially learned ("encoded") it (Tulving & Thompson, 1973). For instance, people are best able to recall information on a test if the test is held in the room in which they studied.
- **Visualize.** Making mental images of ideas can help you recall them later. For example, if you want to remember that global warming may lead to rising oceans, think of yourself on a beach on a hot day, with the waves coming closer and closer to where you're sitting.
- **Rehearse.** Practice makes memory perfect, or if not perfect, at least better. By practicing or rehearsing what you wish to recall, you can substantially improve your memory. **Watch** the **Video** *Making it Stick* in **MyPsychLab**.

several companions in a battle and is shot by an arrow. He feels no pain. When he returns home and tells the story, something black emerges from his mouth, and he dies the next morning.

This tale puzzles most Westerners. They are unschooled in the particular Native American culture the story comes from. However, to someone familiar with that culture, the story makes perfect sense: The hero feels no pain because his companions are ghosts, and the "black thing" coming from his mouth is his departing soul.

For a Native American, it may be easy to recall the story, because it makes sense in a way that it doesn't to members of other cultures. Material that fits into existing schemas is easier to recall than material that doesn't fit. For example, a person who usually puts her keys in her purse may lose them because she doesn't recall putting them on the counter. It's not the "usual place" (Tse et al., 2007).

mnemonics formal strategies for organizing material in ways that make it more likely to be remembered

REVIEW, CHECK, AND APPLY

REVIEW

L09 How does aging affect memory?

- Memory may appear to decline in middle age, but, in fact, long-term memory deficits are probably due to ineffective strategies of storage and retrieval.

L010 How can memory be improved?

- People categorize and interpret new information according to the schemas they have developed about how the world is organized and operates.
- Mnemonics help people organize material in ways that improve recall. These formal strategies include getting organized, visualizing, rehearsing, paying attention, and using the encoding specificity phenomenon.

CHECK YOURSELF

1. Both sensory memory and short-term memory show virtually no weakening during middle adulthood.
   - True
   - False
2. Middle-aged individuals find it hard to pay attention to everything that is going on around them and often rely on _____, or mental shortcuts, to reduce the stress of remembering so many things.
   - a schemas
   - b theory of mind
   - c naturalistic observation
   - d memory
3. _____ are formal strategies for organizing material in ways that make it more likely to be remembered.
   - a Mnemonics
   - b Schemas
   - c Perceptions
   - d Heuristics

APPLYING LIFESPAN DEVELOPMENT

- In what ways do schemas give midlife adults an edge over younger adults?

Study and **Review** on **MyPsychLab.com**

MODULE 8.3

SOCIAL AND PERSONALITY DEVELOPMENT IN MIDDLE ADULTHOOD

From Wall Street to Sesame Street

You wouldn't expect to find a 20-year veteran of Wall Street reading Winnie-the-Pooh to a circle of 4-year-olds. Yet, that's exactly what Ted Lewis, age 53, does most days in his new career as a Head Start teacher. "I made a good living on the Street," Lewis says of his days as a stockbroker. "But I missed a lot, too. I never read to my own kids. Never was able to attend teacher-parent conferences or go to school plays."

Some Wall Street types, Lewis explains, go sort of crazy. They get caught up in insider trading or cocaine or some Cayman Islands scam. Lewis didn't go that route. "I just watched as my life slowly unraveled," he says. "My wife left. My kids grew up, moved away, and stopped returning my calls. Then, I turned 50 and I thought, 'Life doesn't get any emptier than this.'"

Lewis decided to go back to school in a field so foreign to his experience, he told none of his former co-workers: early childhood education. "I guess I was hoping to atone for being such an absent dad. I know I wanted to do something worthwhile," he says. Lewis loves his work. "I finally discovered what giving is all about," he explains. "And it's not about money." A few months ago, his daughter called and asked if he was really working with little kids. They've since had a few lunches together and now she's invited him to spend a week at the summer cottage she and her husband rent on Nantucket. His son, Lewis says, is taking longer to thaw. "But last week, he asked if I'd like to see a Yankees game. He said it was the thing he most wanted to do with me when he was a kid," Lewis says. "I cried when we hung up. And you can bet I'm going. Maybe it's never to late to say 'sorry' while you're still alive."

The one-eighty Ted Lewis took when he reached 50 is not unusual: Few lives follow a set, predictable pattern through middle adulthood. In fact, one of the remarkable characteristics of middle age is its variety, as the paths that different people travel continue to diverge. In this module we focus on the personality and social development that occurs in midlife. We begin by examining the changes that typify this period. We also explore some of the controversies in developmental psychologists' understandings of midlife, including whether the midlife crisis, a phenomenon popularized in the media, is fact or fiction.

Next we consider the various familial ties that bind people together (or come unglued) in middle adulthood, including marriage, divorce, the empty nest, and grandparenting. We also look at a bleak, but prevalent, side of family relations: family violence.

Finally, the module examines work and leisure in midlife. We consider the changing role of work in people's lives and look at work-related problems, such as burnout and unemployment. The module concludes with a discussion of leisure time, which becomes more important during middle age.

PERSONALITY DEVELOPMENT

LO11 In what ways does personality develop during middle adulthood?
LO12 Is there continuity in personality development during adulthood?

My 40th birthday was not an easy one. I did not wake up feeling different—that's never been the case. But during my 40th year, I did come to realize the finiteness of life. The die was cast. I understood that I probably wasn't going to be president of the United States—a secret ambition—or CEO of a major corporation. Time had become more of an adversary than an ally. But it was curious: My usual pattern of focusing on the future, planning each step, began to shift. I started appreciating what I had. I looked at my life and was pretty satisfied with some of my accomplishments. I began focusing on what was going right, not on what I was lacking. This didn't happen in a day; it took several years after turning 40 before I felt this way. Even now, it is hard to fully accept that I am middle-aged.

As this 47-year-old man suggests, realizing that one has reached midlife can be difficult. In many Western societies, age 40 undeniably marks one as middle-aged—at least in the public eye—and suggests that one is on the threshold of a "midlife crisis." How true this view is, as we'll see, depends on your perspective.

Perspectives on Adult Personality Development: Normative-Crisis Versus Life Events

Traditional views of adult personality development have suggested that people move through a fixed series of stages, each tied closely to age. These stages are related to specific crises in which an individual undergoes an intense period of questioning and psychological turmoil. This perspective is a feature of the normative-crisis models of personality development. **Normative-crisis models** see personality development as universal stages of sequential, age-related crises. For example, Erik Erikson's psychosocial theory predicts that people move through a series of stages and crises throughout their life span.

Some critics suggest that normative-crisis approaches may be outmoded. They arose at a time when society had fairly rigid and uniform roles for people. Traditionally, men were expected to work and support a family; women were expected to stay at home and take care of the children. These roles played out at relatively uniform ages.

Today, there is considerable variety in both the roles and the timing. Some people marry and have children at 40. Others have children and marry later. Others never marry and live with a partner of the same or opposite sex and perhaps adopt a child or forgo children altogether. In sum, social changes have called into question the normative-crisis models closely tied to age (Fugate & Mitchell, 1997; Barnett & Hyde, 2001; Fraenkel, 2003).

From a social worker's perspective: In what ways might normative-crisis models of personality development be specific to Western culture?

Because of this variation, some theorists, such as Ravenna Helson, focus on **life events models**, which suggest that particular events, rather than age per se, determine how personality develops. For instance, a woman who has her first child at age 21 may experience similar psychological forces as a woman who has her first child at age 39. These two women, despite their very different ages, share certain commonalities of personality development (Helson & Srivastava, 2001; Roberts, Helson, & Klohnen, 2002; Luhmann et al., 2013).

It is not clear whether the normative-crisis view or the life events perspective more accurately depicts personality development and change in adulthood. What is clear is that developmental theorists all agree that midlife is a time of continuing, significant psychological growth.

Erikson's Stage of Generativity Versus Stagnation

As we discussed earlier, psychoanalyst Erik Erikson characterized midlife as a period of **generativity-versus-stagnation**. One's middle adulthood, according to Erikson, is either spent in generativity—making a contribution to family, community, work, and society—or in stagnation. Generative people strive to guide and encourage future generations. Often, people find generativity through parenting, but other roles can fill this need, such as working directly with young people, acting as mentors. Or the need for generativity may be satisfied through creative and artistic output, seeking to leave a lasting contribution. The focus of generativity, then, is beyond the self, as one looks toward the continuation of one's own life through others (Clark & Arnold, 2008; Penningroth & Scott, 2012; Schoklitsch & Baumann, 2012).

A lack of psychological growth in this period results in stagnation. Focusing on their own trivial activities, people may feel they have contributed little to the world, that their presence has counted for little. Some people find themselves floundering, still seeking new, potentially more fulfilling careers. Others become frustrated and bored.

Erikson provides a broad overview, but some psychologists suggest that we need a more precise look at midlife changes in personality. We'll consider three alternative approaches.

Building on Erikson's Views: Vaillant, Gould, and Levinson. Developmentalist George Vaillant (1977) argues that an important period between ages 45 and 55 centers on "keeping

normative-crisis models the approach to personality development that is based on fairly universal stages tied to a sequence of age-related crises

life events models the approach to personality development that is based on the timing of particular events in an adult's life rather than on age per se

generativity-versus-stagnation according to Erikson, the stage during middle adulthood in which people consider their contributions to family and society the meaning" versus rigidity. Seeking to extract meaning from their lives, adults also seek to "keep the meaning" by accepting the strengths and weaknesses of others. Although they realize it is not perfect, they strive to safeguard their world, and they are relatively content. The man quoted at the beginning of this section, for example, appears content with the meaning he has found in his life. People who are unable to achieve this risk becoming rigid and increasingly isolated from others.

Psychiatrist Roger Gould (1978) offers an alternative to Erikson's and Vaillant's views. He agrees that people move through a series of stages and potential crises, but he suggests that adults pass through seven stages associated with specific age periods (see Table 8-2). According to Gould, people in their late 30s and early 40s begin to feel a sense of urgency about attaining life's goals as they realize that their life is finite. Coming to grips with this reality can propel people toward maturity.

Gould based his model of development on a small sample and relied heavily on his own clinical judgments. Little research has supported his description of the various stages, which was heavily influenced by the psychoanalytic perspective.

Another alternative to Erikson's work is psychologist Daniel Levinson's *seasons of life* theory. According to Levinson (1986, 1992), who intensively interviewed men, the early 40s are a period of transition and crisis. He suggests that adult men pass through a series of stages beginning with early adulthood, around age 20, and continuing into midlife. The beginning stages center on leaving one's family and entering the adult world.

However, at around age 40 or 45, people move to what Levinson calls the midlife transition. The *midlife transition* is a time of questioning, a focus on the finite nature of life. People begin to question some of their fundamental assumptions. They experience the first signs of aging, and they confront the fact that they will not accomplish all their aims before they die.

In Levinson's view, this assessment may lead to a **midlife crisis**, a stage of uncertainty and indecision. Facing signs of physical aging, men may also discover that even the accomplishments of which they are proudest have brought them less satisfaction than they expected. They may try to define what went wrong and seek ways to correct past mistakes. The midlife crisis is a painful and tumultuous period of questioning.

Levinson's view is that most people are susceptible to a fairly profound midlife crisis. Before accepting his perspective, we need to consider some critical drawbacks in his research. First, his initial theory was based on 40 men, and his work with women was conducted years later and, again, on a small sample. Levinson also overstated the consistency and generality of the patterns he found. In fact, the notion of a universal midlife crisis has come under considerable criticism (McFadden & Swan, 2012; Cousins, 2013).

midlife crisis a stage of uncertainty and indecision brought about by the realization that life is finite

TABLE 8-2 SUMMARY OF GOULD'S TRANSFORMATIONS IN ADULT DEVELOPMENT

Stage	Approximate Age	Development(s)
1	16 to 18	Plan to leave home and terminate parental control
2	18 to 22	Leave the family and begin to reorient toward peers
3	22 to 28	Become independent and commit to career and (often) spouse and children
4	29 to 34	Question themselves and experience confusion; they may become dissatisfied with marriage and career
5	35 to 43	Feel an urgent need to achieve life goals, becoming increasingly aware of the passage and limits of time; they often realign life goals
6	43 to 53	Settle down at last, with acceptance of their lives
7	53 to 60	Grow more tolerant, accepting their past; they become less negative and generally more mellow

Source: Based on *Transformations*, by R. L. Gould & M. D. Gould, 1978, New York: Simon & Schuster.

In spite of there being no strong evidence that people universally experience "midlife crisis," the belief that it is commonplace remains. Why is this belief so prevalent?

The Midlife Crisis: Reality or Myth? Central to Levinson's model is the concept of midlife crisis, a period in the early 40s presumed to be marked by intense psychological turmoil. The notion has taken on a life of its own: There is a general expectation in U.S. society that age 40 is an important psychological juncture.

Such a view is problematic: The evidence is simply lacking. In fact, most research suggests that most people pass into middle age with relative ease. The majority regard midlife as a particularly rewarding time. If they are parents, the physically demanding period of childrearing is usually over, and in some cases children have left the home, allowing parents the opportunity to rekindle their intimacy. Many people find that their careers have blossomed, and they feel quite content with their lives. Focusing on the present, they seek to maximize their involvement with family, friends, and other social groups. Those who regret the course of their lives may be motivated to change directions, and those who do change end up better off psychologically. Furthermore, most people feel younger entering midlife than they actually are (Wethington, Cooper, & Holmes, 1997; Stewart & Vandewater, 1999; Willis, Martin, & Rocke, 2010).

The evidence for the inevitability of midlife crisis is no more compelling than was the evidence for a stormy adolescence, discussed earlier. Yet, the notion of a universal midlife crisis seems well entrenched in "common wisdom." Why?

One reason may be that turmoil in middle age is both obvious and easily remembered by observers. A 40-year-old man who divorces his wife, trades his Ford Taurus station wagon for a red Saab convertible and marries a much younger woman makes a greater impression than a happily married man who remains with his spouse (and Taurus) through middle adulthood. We are more likely to notice and recall marital difficulties than the lack of them. In this way the myth of a blustery and universal midlife crisis is perpetuated. For most people, though, a midlife crisis is more the stuff of fiction than of reality. In fact, for some people midlife brings few, if any, changes. As we consider in the "Cultural Dimensions" segment, in some cultures, middle age is not even considered a separate period of life.

Stability Versus Change in Personality

Harry Hennesey, age 53 and a vice president of an investment banking firm, says he still feels like a kid. Many middle-aged adults would agree. Although most people say they have changed a good deal since adolescence—and mostly for the better—many also perceive important similarities in basic personality traits between their present and younger selves.

The degree to which personality is stable across the life span or changes as we age is a major issue of personality development in middle adulthood. Theorists such as Erikson and Levinson clearly suggest that substantial change occurs over time. Erikson's stages and Levinson's seasons describe set patterns of change. The change may be predictable and age related, but it is substantial.

Cultural Dimensions

Middle Age: In Some Cultures It Doesn't Exist

There's no such thing as middle age.

One could draw that conclusion by looking at the women living in the Oriya culture in Orissa, India. According to research by developmental anthropologist Richard Shweder, who studied how high-caste Hindu women view aging, a distinct period of middle age does not exist. These women view their life course not by chronological age, but by the nature of one's social responsibility, family management issues, and moral sense at a given time (Shweder, 1998, 2003).

The model of aging of the Oriyan women encompasses two phases of life: life in her father's house (*bapa gharo*), followed by life in her husband's mother's house (*sasu gharo*). These two segments fit the context of Oriyan family life, which consists of multigenerational households in which marriages are arranged. After they are married, husbands remain with their parents and wives are expected to move in with their in-laws. Upon marriage, a wife changes social status from a child (someone's daughter) to a sexually active female (a daughter-in-law).

The shift from child to daughter-in-law typically occurs around the ages of 18 or 20. However, chronological age, per se, does not mark significant boundaries in life for Oriyan women, nor do physical changes, such as the onset of menstruation nor its cessation at menopause. It is the change from daughter to daughter-in-law that significantly alters social responsibility. Women must shift their focus from their own parents to the parents of their husband, and they must become sexually active in order to perpetuate the husband's family line.

To a Western eye, the life course of these women might seem restricted, because they rarely have careers outside the home, but Oriyan women do not see themselves in this light. In fact, in the Oriya culture, domestic work is highly respected and valued. Oriyan women also view themselves as more cultured and civilized than men, who must work outside the home.

The notion of a separate middle age is clearly a cultural construction. The significance of a particular age range differs widely, depending on the culture in which one lives.

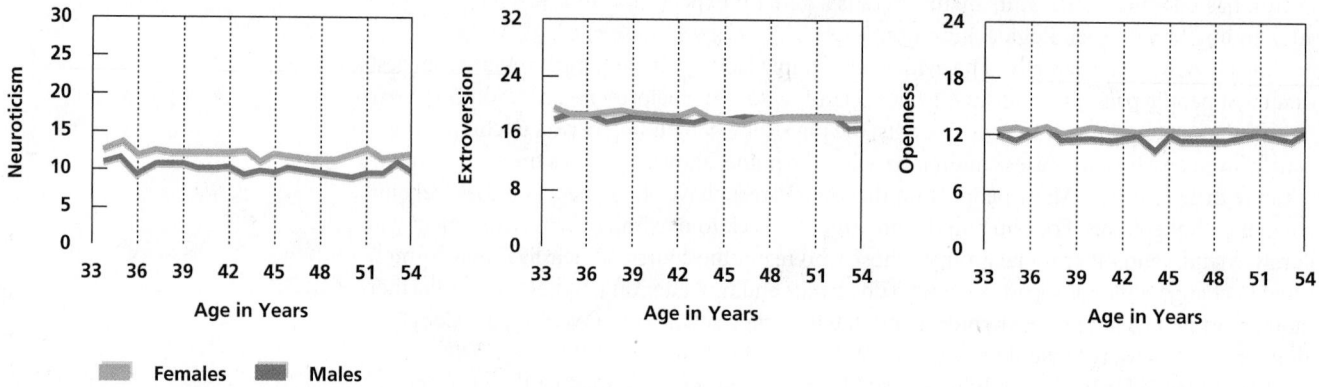

FIGURE 8-6 The Stability of Personality
According to Paul Costa and Robert McCrae, basic personality traits such as neuroticism, extroversion, and openness are stable and consistent throughout adulthood.
Source: Based on Costa et al., 1989, p. 148.

An impressive body of research, however, suggests that for individual traits, personality is quite stable and continuous over the life span. Developmental psychologists Paul Costa and Robert McCrae find remarkable stability in particular traits. Even-tempered 20-year-olds are even-tempered at age 75; affectionate 25-year-olds become affectionate 50-year-olds; and disorganized 26-year-olds are still disorganized at age 60. Similarly, self-concept at age 30 is a good indication of self-concept at age 80. In fact, traits may become more ingrained as people age (Terracciano, Costa, & McCrae, 2006; Terracciano, McCrae, & Costa, 2009; Mõttus, Johnson, & Deary, 2012) (also see Figure 8-6).

Stability and Change in the "Big Five" Personality Traits. Quite a bit of research has centered on the personality traits known as the "Big Five"—because they represent the five major clusters of personality characteristics. These are:

- Neuroticism, the degree to which a person is moody, anxious, and self-critical
- Extraversion, how outgoing or shy a person is
- Openness, a person's level of curiosity and interest in new experiences
- Agreeableness, how easygoing and helpful a person tends to be
- Conscientiousness, a person's tendencies to be organized and responsible

While Erikson and Levinson suggest there is substantial personality change over time, other research has shown that personality in terms of individual traits remains stable over the life span. How many of these high school swimmers do you think are still physically active after 40 years? Why?

The majority of studies find that the Big Five traits are relatively stable past the age of 30, although variations exist for specific traits. In particular, neuroticism, extraversion, and openness to experience decline somewhat from early adulthood, while agreeableness and conscientiousness tend to increase—findings that are consistent across cultures. The basic pattern, however, is one of stability through adulthood (McCrae & Costa, 2003; Srivastava et al., 2003; Renner, 2010; Hahn, Gottschling, & Spinath, 2012).

Does evidence for the stability of traits contradict the theories of personality change championed by Erikson, Gould, and Levinson? Not necessarily, for the contradictions may be more apparent than real.

People's basic traits do show continuity over the course of their adult lives. But, people are also susceptible to changes, and adulthood is packed with major changes in family status, career, and even the economy. The physical changes of aging, illness, the death of a loved one, and an increased awareness of life's finite span also can spur changes in how people view themselves and the world at large (Krueger & Heckhausen, 1993; Roberts, Walton, & Viechtbauer, 2006).

In support of this view, new research on a group of baby boomers that stretches back to their college years traces changes in their personality that extend over the course of their adult lives.

Happiness Across the Life Span. Suppose you hit it big winning the Powerball lottery. Would you be a happier person? For most people, the answer would be no. A growing body of research shows that adults' *subjective well-being* or general happiness remains stable over their lives. Even winning the lottery increases subjective well-being only temporarily; one year later, people's happiness tends to return to pre-lottery levels (Diener, 2000; Stone et al., 2010).

The steadiness of subjective well-being suggests that most people have a general "set point" for happiness, a level of happiness that is relatively consistent despite the day-to-day ups and downs of life. Although specific events may temporarily elevate or depress a person's mood (e.g., a surprisingly high job evaluation or being laid off from work), people eventually return to their general level of happiness.

On the other hand, happiness set points are not completely fixed. Under some conditions, set points can change as a result of particular life events, such as divorce, death of a spouse, unemployment, and disability. Furthermore, people differ in the extent to which they can adapt to events (Lucas, 2007; Diener, Lucas, & Scollon, 2009).

Most people's happiness set points seem to be fairly high. Some 30 percent of people in the United States rate themselves as "very happy," while only 10 percent rate themselves as "not too happy." Most people say they are "pretty happy." These findings are similar across different social groups. Men and women rate themselves as equally happy, and African Americans rate themselves as "very happy" at only slightly lower rates than whites. Regardless of their economic situation, residents of countries across the world have similar levels of happiness (Diener, 2000; Diener, Oishi, & Lucas, 2003; Kahneman et al., 2006; Delle Fave et al., 2013). The conclusion: Money doesn't buy happiness. **Watch** the **Video** *Middle Adulthood: Happiness, Mary* in **MyPsychLab.**

REVIEW, CHECK, AND APPLY

REVIEW

L011 In what ways does personality develop during middle adulthood?

- In normative-crisis models, people pass through age-related stages of development; life events models focus on how people change in response to various life events.
- Levinson argues that the transition to middle age can lead to a midlife crisis, but there is little evidence for this in the majority of people.

L012 Is there continuity in personality development during adulthood?

- Broad, basic personality characteristics are relatively stable. Specific aspects of personality do seem to change in response to life events.

CHECK YOURSELF

1. According to _____ models, researchers understand personality development as the product of universal stages tied to age-related crises.
   - a goodness of fit
   - b normative-crisis
   - c life events
   - d subjective well-being
2. According to the _____ model, individuals at different ages can experience the same emotional and personality changes because they have shared common occurrences in their lives.
   - a normative-crisis
   - b psychosexual
   - c life events
   - d self-understanding
3. According to Roger Gould (1978, 1980) people in their late 30s and early 40s feel a sense of urgency in terms of reaching their life goals because they realize their lives are limited.
   - True
   - False

APPLYING LIFESPAN DEVELOPMENT

- How do you think the midlife transition is different for a middle-aged person whose child has just entered adolescence versus a middle-aged person who has just become a parent for the first time?

Study and **Review** on **MyPsychLab.com**

RELATIONSHIPS: FAMILY IN MIDDLE AGE

L013 What are the typical patterns of marriage and divorce in middle adulthood?
L014 What changing family situations do middle-aged adults face?
L015 What are the causes and characteristics of family violence in the United States?

For Kathy and Bob, going to their son Jon's college orientation was a shockingly new experience in the life of their family. It hadn't really registered that he would be leaving home when he was accepted at a college on the other side of the country. It didn't hit them just how much this would change their family until they said good-bye and left him on his new campus. It was a wrenching experience. Kathy and Bob worried about their son in the ways that parents always do, but they also felt a profound loss—their job of raising their son, basically, was done. Now he was largely on his own. This thought filled them with pride and anticipation for his future, but with great sadness, too. They would miss him.

For members of many non-Western cultures who live in extended families in which multiple generations spend their lives in the same household or village, middle adulthood is nothing special. But in Western cultures, family dynamics change significantly in midlife. For most parents, there are major shifts in their relationships with their children, and with other family members as well. It is a period of changing roles that, in twenty-first-century Western cultures, encompasses an increasing number of combinations and permutations. We'll start by looking at how marriage develops and changes over this period, and then consider some of the many alternative forms of family life today (Kaslow, 2001).

Marriage

Fifty years ago, midlife was similar for most people. Men and women, married since early adulthood, were still married to each other. One hundred years ago, when life expectancy was much shorter, people in their 40s were usually married—but not necessarily to the persons they had first married. Spouses often died; people might be well into their second marriage by middle age.

Today, the story is different and more varied. More people are single at midlife, having never married. Single people may live alone or with a partner. Gay and lesbian adults may have committed relationships even though marriage is often not an option for them. Among heterosexuals, some have divorced, lived alone, and then remarried. Many people's marriages end in divorce, and many families "blend" together into new households, containing children and stepchildren from previous marriages. Some couples still spend 40 to 50 years together, the bulk of those years during middle adulthood. Many experience the peak of marital satisfaction during middle age.

The Ups and Downs of Marriage. Even happily married couples have their ups and downs, with satisfaction rising and falling over the course of the marriage. In the past, most research has suggested that marital satisfaction follows the U-shaped configuration shown in Figure 8-7 (Figley, 1973). Specifically, marital satisfaction begins to decline just after the marriage, falling until it reaches its lowest point following the births of the couple's children. At that point, satisfaction begins to grow, eventually returning to the same level as before the marriage (Harvey & Weber, 2002; Gorchoff, John, & Helson, 2008; Medina, Lederhos, & Lillis, 2009).

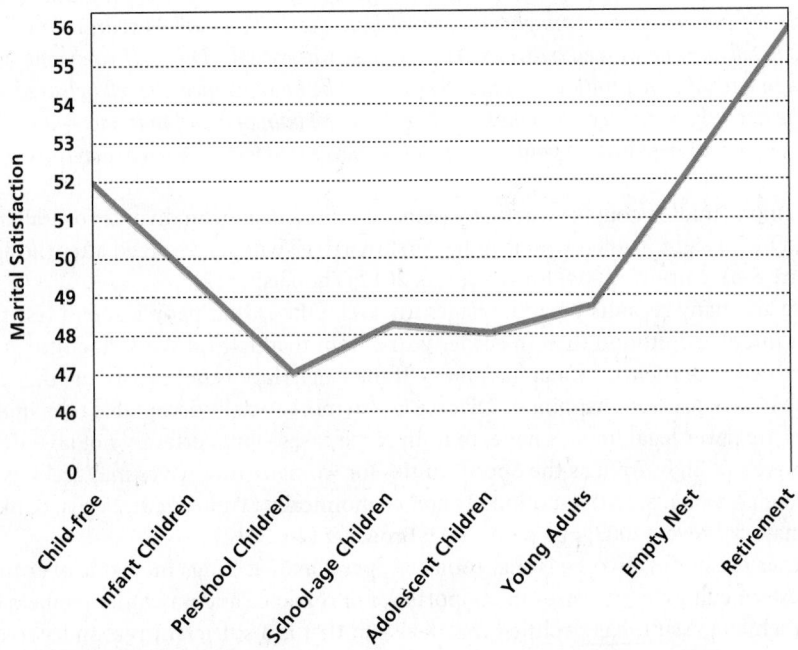

FIGURE 8-7 The Phases of Marital Satisfaction
For many couples, marital satisfaction falls and rises in a U-shaped configuration. It begins to decline after the birth of children but increases when the youngest child leaves home and eventually returns to a level of satisfaction similar to that at the start of marriage. Why do you think this pattern of satisfaction occurs?
Source: Based on Rollins & Cannon, 1974.

On the other hand, newer research has called the U-shaped pattern into question. This research suggests that marital satisfaction actually continues to decline across the life span (Umberson et al., 2006; Liu, Elliott, & Umberson, 2010).

We don't know enough to reject the U-shaped view of marital satisfaction, and it may be that personality differences account for the discrepancy in findings. What is clear is that middle-aged couples cite several sources of marital satisfaction. For instance, both men and women typically state that their spouse is "their best friend" and that they like their spouses as people. They also view marriage as a long-term commitment and agree on their aims and goals. Finally, most also feel that their spouses have grown more interesting over the course of the marriage (Schmitt, Kliegel, & Shapiro, 2007; Landis et al., 2013).

Sexual satisfaction is related to general marital satisfaction. What matters is not how often couples have sex. Instead, satisfaction is related to *agreeing* about their sex lives (Spence 1997; Litzinger & Gordon, 2005; Butzer & Campbell, 2008).

Are there "secrets" to successful marriages? Not really. However, there are proven coping mechanisms that allow couples to remain together happily. Among them (Orbuch, 2009; Bernstein, 2010):

- **Holding realistic expectations.** Successful couples understand that there are some things about your partner that you may not like all that much. They accept that their partner will do things that they don't like some of the time.
- **Focusing on the positive.** Thinking about the things that they like about their partner helps them to accept the things that bother them.
- **Compromising.** Partners in successful marriages understand that they are not going to win every argument, and they don't keep score.
- **Avoiding suffering in silence.** If something does bother them, they let their partner know about it. But they don't bring it up in an accusatory way. Instead, they talk about it at a time when they are both calm.

Divorce

Louise knew after a year that the marriage was doomed. Tom never listened to a word she said, never asked her how her day had been, and never lifted a hand to help around the house. He was completely self-centered and seemingly unaware of existence. Still, it took 23 years before she got up the nerve to tell him she wanted a divorce. His response was casual: "Do what you want. Makes no difference to me." After her initial relief that there would be no resistance, she felt betrayed and foolish. All the anguish, all the trying to make a go of it, all the pain of a bad marriage—and they both knew all along that there was no point. "Why did we never face facts?" she wondered.

Divorce among midlife couples is actually rising, despite a decline in divorces overall in recent decades. One in eight women who is in her first marriage will get divorced after the age of 40 (see Figure 8-8) (Enright, 2004; Brown & Lin, 2012; Thomas, 2012).

There are many reasons why marriages unravel. One is that people spend less time together in middle adulthood than in earlier years. In individualistic Western cultures, people are concerned with their personal happiness. If their marriage is not satisfying, they feel that divorce may increase their happiness. Divorce is also more socially acceptable than in the past, and there are fewer legal impediments to it. In some cases—but certainly not all—the financial costs are not high. And, as the opportunities for women grow, wives may feel less dependent on their husbands, both emotionally and economically (Wallerstein, Lewis, & Blakeslee, 2000; Amato & Previti, 2003; Fincham, 2003; Brown & Lin, 2012).

Another reason for divorce is that romantic, passionate feelings may fade over time. Because Western culture emphasizes the importance of romance and passion, members of marriages in which passion has declined may feel that that is a sufficient reason to divorce. In some marriages, it is a lack of excitement and boredom that leads to marital dissatisfaction. Finally, there is a great deal of stress in households in which both parents work, and this stress puts a strain on marriages. Much of the energy directed toward families and maintaining relationships in the past is now directed toward work and other institutions outside the home (Macionis, 2001; Tsapelas, Aron, & Orbuch, 2009).

Finally, some marriages end because of *infidelity*, in which a spouse engages in sexual activity with a person outside of the marriage. Although statistics are highly suspect—if you lie

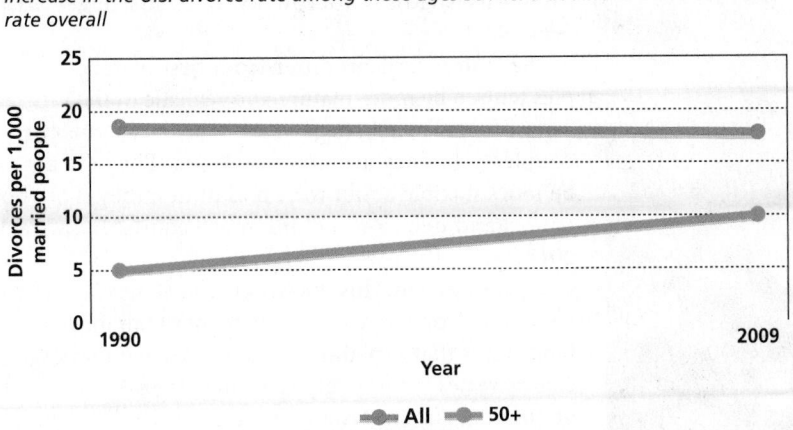

Source: The Gray Revolution; Susan Brown and I-Fen Lin, Bowling Green State University.

FIGURE 8-8 Rising Divorces in Middle Adulthood
Both the divorce rate and the number of people that experience divorce in those 50 years and above have risen significantly, and the increases are projected to continue in the future.
Source: Brown & Lin, 2012, Figure 1.

to your spouse, why would you be honest to a pollster?—one survey found that 20 percent of men and 15 percent of women under the age of 35 say they have been unfaithful. In a given year, about 12 percent of men and 7 percent of women say they have had sex outside their marriage (Atkins & Furrow, 2008).

Whatever the causes, divorce can be especially difficult in midlife. It can be particularly hard for women who have played the traditional role of mother and never performed substantial work outside the home. They may face age discrimination, finding younger people are preferred, even in jobs with minimal requirements. Without a good deal of training and support, these divorced women, lacking recognized job skills, may remain virtually unemployable (McDaniel & Coleman, 2003; Williams & Dunne-Bryant, 2006; Hilton & Anderson, 2009).

Many people who divorce in midlife, though, end up happy. Women, in particular, are apt to find that developing a new, independent self-identity is a positive outcome. Both men and women who divorce in midlife are also likely to form new relationships, and they typically remarry (Enright, 2004).

Remarriage. Many people who divorce—some 75 to 80 percent—end up marrying again, usually within 2 to 5 years. They are likely to marry people who are also divorced, partly because they tend to be available, but also because divorced people share a similar experience (McCarthy & Ginsberg, 2007).

Although the rate of remarriage is high, it is far higher in some groups than in others. For instance, it is harder for women to remarry than men, particularly older women. Whereas 90 percent of women under age 25 remarry after divorce, less than one-third of women over age 40 remarry (Bumpass, Sweet, & Martin, 1990; Besharov & West, 2002).

This age difference stems from the *marriage gradient* we discussed earlier: Societal norms push men to marry women who are younger, smaller, and lower in status than themselves. The older a woman is, the fewer socially acceptable men she has available to her because those men her age are likely to be looking for younger women. As we discussed earlier, women are also disadvantaged by double standards regarding physical attractiveness. Older women may be perceived as unattractive, while older men may be seen as "distinguished" and "mature" (Bernard, 1982; Buss, 2003; Doyle, 2004b).

There are several reasons marrying again may be more appealing than remaining single. A person who remarries avoids the social consequences of divorce. Even in the twenty-first century, when divorce is common, it carries with it a certain stigma. In addition, divorced people overall report less satisfaction with life than married people (Lucas, 2005).

Divorced people miss the companionship that marriage provides. Men in particular report feeling lonely and experience more physical and mental health problems following divorce. Marriage also provides clear economic benefits, such as

Around three-quarters of people who divorce remarry again, usually within two to five years.

sharing the cost of a house and medical benefits reserved for spouses (Ross, Microwsky, & Goldsteen, 1991; Stewart et al., 1997).

Second marriages differ from first marriages. Older couples tend to be more mature and realistic in their expectations. They often view marriage in less romantic terms than younger couples, and they are more cautious. They are also likely to be more flexible about roles and duties; they share household chores and decision making more equitably (Mirecki et al., 2013).

Unfortunately, this doesn't guarantee second marriages will last. The divorce rate is slightly higher than for first marriages. One factor that explains this is that second marriages may include stresses not present in first marriages, such as the blending of different families. Another reason is that having experienced and survived one divorce, partners may be less committed and more ready to walk away from an unhappy second marriage. Finally, they may have personality and emotional characteristics that don't make them easy to live with (Cherlin, 1993; Warshak, 2000; Coleman, Ganong, & Weaver, 2001).

Despite the high divorce rate for second marriages, many people remarry quite successfully. In such cases, couples report as great a degree of satisfaction as those who are in successful first marriages (Bird & Melville, 1994; Michaels, 2006).

Family Evolutions: From Full House to Empty Nest

For many parents, a major midlife transition is the departure of children who are going to college, getting married, joining the military, or taking a job far from home. Even people who become parents at relatively late ages are likely to face this transition, because the middle adulthood spans nearly a quarter century. As we saw in Kathy and Bob's story, a child's departure can be wrenching—so much so, in fact, that it has been labeled the "empty nest syndrome." The **empty nest syndrome** refers to the unhappiness, worry, loneliness, and depression some parents feel when their children leave home (Lauer & Lauer, 1999; Erickson, Martinengo, & Hill, 2010).

Many parents report that major adjustments are required. For women who were stay-at-home mothers, the loss can be very difficult. Traditional homemakers, who focus significant time and energy on their children, face a challenging time.

While the loss can be difficult, parents also find that some aspects of this transition are quite positive. Even mothers who have stayed at home find they have time for other interests, such as community or recreational activities, when the children leave. They may also enjoy the opportunity to get a job or return to school. Finally, many women find that motherhood is not easy; surveys show that most people regard motherhood as harder than it used to be. Such women may now feel liberated from a difficult set of responsibilities (Heubusch, 1997; Morfei et al., 2004; Chen, Yang, & Aagard, 2012).

Though feelings of loss are common for most people, there is little, if any, evidence that the departure of children produces anything more than temporary feelings of sadness and distress. This is especially true for women who have worked outside the home (Antonucci, 2001; Crowley, Hayslip, & Hobdy, 2003).

In fact, there are discernible benefits when children leave home. Spouses have more time for one another. Married or unmarried people can attend to their own work without having to worry about helping the kids with homework, carpools, and the like. The house stays neater, and the telephone rings less often (Gorchoff, John, & Helson, 2008).

Most research on the so-called empty nest syndrome has focused on women. Men, traditionally not as involved in childrearing, were assumed to weather the transition more smoothly. However, some research suggest that men also experience feelings of loss when their children depart, although these feelings may differ from those felt by women.

empty nest syndrome the experience that relates to parents' feelings of unhappiness, worry, loneliness, and depression resulting from their children's departure from home

One survey found that although most fathers felt either happy or neutral about the departure of their children, almost a quarter felt unhappy (Lewis, Freneau, & Roberts, 1979). Those fathers tended to mention lost opportunities, regretting things they had not done with their children. Some felt they had been too busy for their children or hadn't been sufficiently nurturing or caring.

Some parents react to the departure of their children by becoming what have become known as *helicopter parents*, parents who intrusively intervene in their children's lives. Helicopter parenting first became apparent when parents micro-managed their children's college careers, complaining to instructors and administrators about poor grades that their children received or seeking to get them into certain classes. In some cases, the phenomenon extends to the workplace; some employers complain that parents call human relations departments to extoll the virtues of their children as potential employees.

Although statistics about the prevalence of helicopter parenting are hard to come by, it is clear that the phenomenon is real. One survey of 799 employers found that nearly one-third said that parents had submitted resumes for their child, sometimes not even informing their son or daughter. One-quarter said that parents had contacted them, urging them to hire their son or daughter. And 4 percent said that a parent had accompanied the child on a job interview. Some parents even help their children complete work assignments once they get a job (Gardner, 2007; Ludden, 2012)

In most cases, though, parents permit their children to develop independently once they leave home. On the other hand, children may not always leave home for good, and the empty nest sometimes becomes replenished with what have been called "boomerang children," as we discuss next.

Boomerang Children: Refilling the Empty Nest

Carole Olis doesn't know what to make of her 23-year-old son, Rob. He has been living at home since his graduation from college more than 2 years ago. Her six older children returned to the nest for just a few months and then bolted.

"I ask him, 'Why don't you move out with your friends?' " says Mrs. Olis. Rob has a ready answer: "They all live at home, too."

Carole Olis is not alone in being surprised by the return of her son. In the United States, a significant number of young adults are coming back to live with their middle-aged parents.

Known as **boomerang children**, these returning offspring typically cite economic issues as the main reason for coming back home. Because of a difficult economy, many young adults cannot find jobs after college, or the positions they do find pay so little that they have difficulty making ends meet. Others return home after the breakup of a marriage. Overall, close to one-third of young adults ages 25 to 34 are living with their parents. In some European countries, the proportion is even higher (Roberts, 2009; Parker, 2012).

Because about half of boomerang children pay rent to their parents, parental finances may benefit. The arrangement doesn't seem to effect social relationships within the family: half say it makes no difference or is a plus. Only a quarter of boomerang children find the arrangement has been bad for their relationship with their parents (Parker, 2012) (see Figure 8-9).

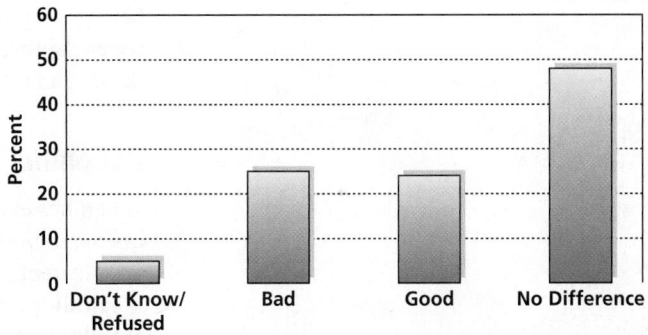

FIGURE 8-9 More Boomerang Children, Enjoying it Less
The percentage of those saying that living with their parents at this stage of life has been bad, good, or no different in terms of their relationship.
Source: Pew Research Center, 2012.

The Sandwich Generation: Between Children and Parents. At the same time children are leaving the nest, or returning as boomerang children, many middle-aged adults face another challenge: the care of their own aging parents. The term **sandwich generation** refers to these middle adults who are squeezed between the needs of their children and their parents (Riley & Bowen, 2005; Grundy & Henretta, 2006; Chassin et al., 2009).

The sandwich generation is a relatively new phenomenon, produced by several converging trends. First, people are marrying later and having children at an older age. At the same time, people are living longer. Thus, it is not unlikely that midlife adults will have parents who are alive and require care while they still have children who need a significant amount of nurturing.

The care of aging parents can be psychologically tricky. There is a degree of role reversal, with children becoming more parental and parents becoming more dependent. As we'll discuss later, elderly people, used to being independent, may resent and resist their children's help. They do not want to be burdens. Almost all elderly people who live alone say they do not wish to live with their children (CFCEPLA, 1986; Merrill, 1997).

boomerang children young adults who return, after leaving home for some period, to live in the homes of their middle-aged parents

sandwich generation couples who in middle adulthood must fulfill the needs of both their children and their aging parents

"I'm in the sandwich generation—my parents don't approve of me and my kids hate me."

Barbara Smaller/The New Yorker Collection/www.cartoonbank.com

Middle-aged adults provide a range of care for their parents. They may provide financial support to supplement a parent's meager pension. They might also help manage a household, doing tasks such as removing storm windows in the spring or shoveling snow in the winter.

In some cases, elderly parents may be invited to live in their child's home. Census data reveal that multigenerational households—three or more generations—are the fastest growing of all household arrangements. Increasing by more than a third between 1990 and 2000, they represent 4 percent of all households (Navarro, 2006).

Multigenerational families present a tricky situation, as roles are renegotiated. Typically, the adult children—who are no longer children—are in charge of the household. Both they and their parents must make adjustments and find some common ground in making decisions. Elderly parents may find their new dependence difficult, and this can be wrenching for their adult child as well. The youngest generation may resist, including the oldest generation.

In many cases, the burden of care is not shared equally, with the larger share most often assumed by women. Even when both husband and wife are in the labor force, women tend to be more involved in the day-to-day care, even when the parent or parents are their in-laws (Soldo, 1996; Putney & Bengtson, 2001).

Culture also influences how caregivers view their roles. Members of Asian cultures, which are more collectivistic, are more likely to view caregiving as a traditional and ordinary duty. In contrast, members of more individualistic cultures may feel familial ties are less central, and caring for the older generation may be seen as a burden (Ho et al., 2003; Kim & Lee, 2003).

Despite the burden of being sandwiched in between two generations, which can stretch the caregiving child's resources, there are significant rewards. The psychological attachment between middle-aged children and their elderly parents can continue to grow. Both sides can see each other more realistically. They may grow closer, more accepting of each other's weaknesses and more appreciative of each other's strengths (Vincent, Phillipson, & Downs, 2006).

Becoming a Grandparent: Who, Me?

When her eldest son and daughter-in-law had their first child, Leah couldn't believe it. At age 54, she was a grandmother! She kept telling herself she felt far too young to be anybody's grandparent.

Middle adulthood often brings one of the unmistakable symbols of aging: becoming a grandparent. For some people, the new role has been eagerly awaited. They may miss the energy and excitement and even demands of young children, and they may see grandparenthood as the next stage in the natural progression of life. Others are less pleased with the prospect, seeing it as a clear signpost of aging.

Grandparenting tends to fall into different styles. *Involved* grandparents are actively engaged in and have influence over their grandchildren's lives. They hold clear expectations about the ways their grandchildren should behave. A retired grandparent who takes care of a grandchild while his or her parents work is an example of an involved grandparent (Mueller, Wilhelm, & Elder, 2002; Fergusson, Maughan, & Golding, 2008; Mansson, 2013).

In contrast, *companionate* grandparents are more relaxed. Rather than taking responsibility for their grandchildren, they act as supporters and buddies to them. Grandparents who visit and call frequently, and perhaps occasionally take their grandchildren on vacations or invite them to visit without their parents, are companionate grandparents.

Finally, the most aloof type of grandparents are *remote*. They are detached and distant, showing little interest in their grandchildren. Remote grandparents, for example, would rarely make visits to see their grandchildren and might complain about their childish behavior when they did see them.

There are marked gender differences in the extent to which people enjoy grandparenthood. Generally, grandmothers are more interested and experience greater satisfaction than grandfathers, particularly when they have a high level of interaction with younger grandchildren (Smith, 1995; Smith & Drew, 2002).

African American grandparents are more apt to be involved than white grandparents. The most reasonable explanation for this is the greater prevalence of multigenerational households among African Americans than among Caucasians. In addition, African American families are more likely to be headed by single parents. Thus, they often rely substantially on the help of grandparents in everyday child care, and cultural norms tend to be highly supportive of grandparents taking an active role (Stevenson, Henderson, & Baugh, 2007; Keene, Prokos, & Held, 2012; Bertera & Crewe, 2013).

Family Violence: The Hidden Epidemic

Domestic violence is epidemic in the United States, occurring in one-fourth of all marriages. More than half the women who were murdered in one recent 10-year period were murdered by a partner. Between 21 percent and 34 percent of women will be slapped, kicked, beaten, choked, or threatened or attacked with a weapon at least once by an intimate partner. In fact, continuing, severe violence characterizes close to 15 percent of all marriages in the United States. In addition, many women are victims of psychological abuse, such as verbal or emotional abuse. Domestic violence is also a worldwide problem. Estimates suggest that one in three women around the globe experience violent victimization during their lives (Walker, 1999; Garcia-Moreno et al., 2005).

Parents who abuse their own spouses and children were often victims of abuse themselves as children, reflecting a cycle of violence.

In the United States, no segment of society is immune from spousal abuse. Violence occurs across social strata, races, ethnic groups, and religions. Both gay and straight partnerships can be abusive. It also occurs across genders: Although in most instances, the husband is the abuser, in about 8 percent of the cases wives physically abuse their husbands (Harway, 2000; Cameron, 2003; Dixon & Browne, 2003).

Certain factors increase the likelihood of abuse. Spousal abuse is more apt to occur in large families for whom both financial strain and verbal aggression are common. Those husbands and wives who grew up in families where violence was present are also more likely to be violent themselves (Straus & Yodanis, 1996; Ehrensaft, Cohen, & Brown, 2003; Lackey, 2003).

The factors that put a family at risk are similar to those associated with child abuse, another form of family violence. Child abuse occurs most frequently in stressful environments, at lower socioeconomic levels, in single-parent families, and in situations of intense marital conflict. Families with four or more children have higher abuse rates, and those with incomes under $15,000 a year have seven times the rate of families with higher incomes. But not all types of abuse are higher in poorer families: Incest is more likely to occur in affluent families (APA, 1996; Cox, Kotch, & Everson, 2003).

Marital aggression by a husband typically occurs in three stages (Walker, 1999) (see Figure 8-10). In the initial *tension-building* stage, a batterer becomes upset and shows dissatisfaction through verbal abuse. He may also use some physical aggression, such as shoving or grabbing. The wife may desperately try to avoid the impending violence, attempting to calm her spouse or withdraw from the situation. Such behavior may only enrage the husband, who senses his wife's vulnerability. Her efforts to escape may escalate his anger.

In the next stage—an *acute battering incident*—the physical abuse actually occurs, lasting from several minutes to hours. Wives may be shoved against walls, choked, slapped, punched, kicked, and stepped on. Their arms may be twisted or broken, they may be shaken severely, thrown down a flight of stairs, or burned with cigarettes or scalding liquids. About a quarter of wives are forced to engage in sexual activity, which takes the form of aggressive sexual acts and rape.

Finally, in some—but not all—cases, the episode ends with the *loving contrition* stage. At this point, the husband feels remorse and apologizes for his actions. He may provide first aid and sympathy, assuring his wife that he will never act violently again. Because wives may feel they were somehow partly at fault, they may accept the apology and forgive their husbands. They want to believe that the aggression will never occur again.

The loving contrition stage helps explain why many wives remain with abusive husbands and continue to be victims. Wishing desperately to keep their marriages intact, and believing that they

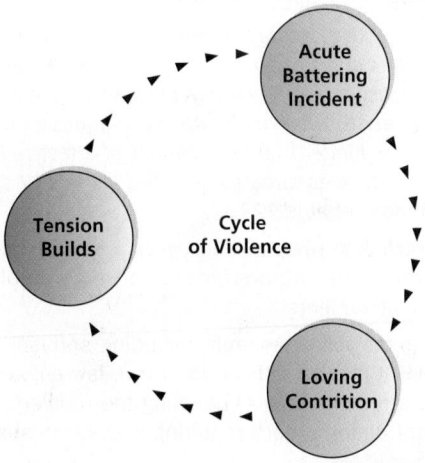

FIGURE 8-10 The Stages of Violence
(*Source:* Adapted from Walker, 1979, 1984; Gondolf, 1985.)

have no good alternatives, some wives remain out of a vague sense that they are responsible for the abuse. In other cases, wives fear their husbands may come after them if they leave.

The Cycle of Violence. Still other wives stay with batterers because they, like their husbands, learned in childhood that violence is an acceptable means of settling disputes.

Individuals who abuse their spouses and children were often the victims of abuse themselves. According to the **cycle of violence hypothesis**, abuse and neglect of children predisposes them to abusiveness as adults. In line with social learning theory, the cycle of violence hypothesis suggests that family aggression is perpetuated from one generation to another. It is a fact that individuals who abuse their wives often witnessed spousal abuse at home as children, just as parents who abuse their children frequently were the victims of abuse as children (Serbin & Karp, 2004; Renner & Slack, 2006; Whiting et al., 2009).

From the perspective of a health care provider: What can be done to end the cycle of violence, in which people who were abused as children grow up to be abusers of others?

Growing up in an abusive home does not invariably lead to abusiveness as an adult. Only about one-third of people who were abused or neglected as children abuse their own children as adults, and two-thirds of abusers were not themselves abused as children. The cycle of violence, then, does not tell the full story of abuse (Jacobson & Gottman, 1998).

Whatever the causes of abuse, there are ways to deal with it, as we consider next.

Spousal Abuse and Society: The Cultural Roots of Violence. *After Dong Lu Chen beat his wife to death, he was sentenced to 5 years' probation. He had confessed to the act but claimed that his wife had been unfaithful to him. His lawyer (and an anthropologist) had argued in court that traditional Chinese values might have led to his violent reaction to his wife's purported infidelity.*

After Lee Fong, a Laotian immigrant, had abducted a 16-year-old girl, he was acquitted of kidnapping, sexual assault, and menacing. During his trial, his lawyer argued that "bride stealing" is a traditional custom among the Hmong people of Laos.

Both cases were decided in courts in the United States. In both cases, lawyers based their arguments on the claim that in the Asian countries from which the defendants had emigrated, the use of violence against women was common and may even have received social approval. The juries obviously agreed with this "cultural defense" justification. (Findlen, 1990)

cycle of violence hypothesis the theory that the abuse and neglect that children suffer predispose them as adults to abuse and neglect their own children

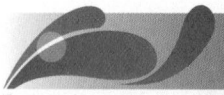

Becoming an Informed Consumer of Development

Dealing With Spousal Abuse

Spousal abuse occurs in some 25 percent of all marriages, but efforts to deal with victims of abuse are underfunded and inadequate to meet current needs. In fact, some psychologists argue that the same factors that led society to underestimate the magnitude of the problem for many years now hinder the development of effective interventions. Still, there are several measures to help the victims of spousal abuse (Browne, 1993; Koss et al., 1993):

- **Teach both wives and husbands a basic premise:** Violence is *never*, under *any* circumstances, an acceptable means of resolving disagreements.
- **Call the police.** Assault, including spousal assault, is against the law. It may be difficult to involve law enforcement officers, but this is a realistic way of handling the problem. Judges can also issue restraining orders requiring abusive husbands to stay away from their wives.
- **Understand that the remorse shown by a spouse, no matter how heartfelt, may have no bearing on possible future violence.** Even if a husband shows loving regret and vows that he will never be violent again, such a promise is no guarantee against future abuse.
- **If you are the victim of abuse, seek a safe haven.** Many communities have shelters for the victims of domestic violence that can house women and their children. Because addresses of shelters are kept confidential, an abusive spouse will not be able to find you. Telephone numbers are listed in the yellow or blue pages of phone books, and local police should also have the numbers.
- **If you feel in danger from an abusive partner, seek a restraining order** from a judge in court. A restraining order forbids a spouse to come near you, under penalty of law.
- **Call the National Domestic Violence Hotline at 1-800-799-7233** for immediate advice.

Although marital violence and aggression is often seen as a particularly North American phenomenon, other cultures have traditions that regard violence as acceptable (Rao, 1997). Wife battering is especially prevalent in cultures that view women as inferior to men and treat them as property.

In Western societies, too, wife beating was once acceptable. According to English common law—the foundation of the legal system in the United States—husbands could beat their wives. In the 1800s, this law was modified to permit only certain kinds of beating. Specifically, a husband could not beat his wife with a stick or rod that was thicker than his thumb—the origin of the phrase "rule of thumb." It was not until the late nineteenth century that this law was removed from the books in the United States (Davidson, 1977).

Some experts on abuse suggest that its root cause is the traditional power structure in which women and men function. They argue that the more a society differentiates between men's and women's status, the more likely it is that abuse will occur.

They cite research examining the legal, political, educational, and economic roles of women and men. For example, some research has compared battering statistics across the various states in the United States. Abuse is more likely to occur in states where women are of particularly low or high status compared with women in other states. Apparently, relatively low status makes women easy targets of violence, while unusually high status may make husbands feel threatened and thus more likely to behave abusively (Dutton, 1994; Vandello & Cohen, 2003).

REVIEW, CHECK, AND APPLY

REVIEW

L013 What are the typical patterns of marriage and divorce in middle adulthood?

- Marital satisfaction rises and falls over the course of marriage, generally following a U-shaped configuration over the years.
- Marital satisfaction tends to be highest when both partners feel that their spouse is "their best friend," when they like their spouses as people, when they agree on aims and goals, and when they view marriage as a long-term commitment. In happy marriages, most people also feel that their spouses have grown more interesting over the years.
- There are many reasons why marriages end in divorce, including lack of satisfaction, less time spent together, and infidelity. Divorce may increase happiness, and the process of divorce is more socially acceptable.

L014 What changing family situations do middle-aged adults face?

- Family changes in middle adulthood include the departure of children. In recent years, the phenomenon of "boomerang children" has emerged.
- Middle-aged adults often have increasing responsibilities for their aging parents.

L015 What are the causes and characteristics of family violence in the United States?

- Abuse is more likely to occur in large families who are experiencing financial strain and for whom verbal aggression is common. Adults who experienced family violence as children are also more likely to be violent themselves.
- Marital violence tends to pass through three stages: tension building, an acute battering incident, and loving contrition.

CHECK YOURSELF

1. According to the U-shaped curve illustrating the changes in marital satisfaction, typically marriage satisfaction tends to decrease after marriage, reach its lowest point after the birth of children, and then:
   - a take a sharper dip that relates to more marriages ending in divorce.
   - b slowly begin to increase again, eventually returning to the same level it was before marriage.
   - c begin a drastic increase to levels surpassing premarriage levels of satisfaction.
   - d steadily decrease until children leave the house.
2. Both men and women who divorce during midlife are likely to enter new relationships, but typically do not remarry.
   - True
   - False
3. Couples who in middle adulthood need to take care of their aging parents and their children are often referred to by psychologists as the _____.
   - a boomer generation
   - b pizza generation
   - c sandwich generation
   - d hot-dog generation
4. Match each of the following descriptions of spousal violence to its appropriate stage.

a Batterer expresses remorse and apologizes for actions.	1. Tension-building stage
b Batterer becomes upset and shows dissatisfaction through verbal abuse.	2. Acute battering incident
c Physical abuse actually occurs.	3. Loving contrition stage

APPLYING LIFESPAN DEVELOPMENT

- Are the phenomena of the empty nest, boomerang children, the sandwich generation, and grandparenting culturally dependent? Why might such phenomena be different in societies where multigenerational families are the norm?

✓ **Study** and **Review** on **MyPsychLab.com**

WORK AND LEISURE

LO16 What are the characteristics of work in middle adulthood?
LO17 How is leisure time different in middle adulthood?

Enjoying a weekly game of golf . . . starting a neighborhood watch program . . . coaching a Little League baseball team . . . joining an investment club . . . traveling . . . taking a cooking class . . . attending a theater series . . . running for the local town council . . . going to the movies with friends . . . hearing lectures on Buddhism . . . fixing up a porch in the back of the house . . . chaperoning a high school class on an out-of-state trip . . . lying on a beach, reading a book during an annual vacation . . .

Adults in their middle years actually enjoy a rich variety of activities. Although middle adulthood often represents the peak of career success and earning power, it is also a time when people throw themselves into leisure and recreational activities. In fact, midlife may be the period when work and leisure activities are balanced most easily. No longer feeling a need to prove themselves on the job, and increasingly valuing their contributions to family, community, and—more broadly—society, middle-aged adults may find that work and leisure complement one another in ways that enhance overall happiness.

Work and Careers: Jobs at Midlife

For many, productivity, success, and earning power are greatest in middle age, but occupational success may become far less alluring than it once was. This is particularly true for those who have not achieved the career success they had hoped for. In such cases, family and other off-the-job interests become more important than work (Howard, 1992; Simonton, 1997).

The factors that make a job satisfying change during middle age. Younger adults focus on abstract and future-oriented concerns, such as the opportunity for advancement or the possibility of recognition and approval. Middle-aged employees care more about the here-and-now qualities of work. They are more concerned with pay, working conditions, and specific policies, such as how vacation time is calculated. As at earlier stages of life, changes in overall job quality are associated with changes in stress levels for both men and women (Peterson & Wilson, 2004; Cohrs, Abele, & Dette, 2006; Rantanen et al., 2012).

burnout a situation that occurs when workers experience dissatisfaction, disillusionment, frustration, and weariness from their jobs

In general, though, the relationship between age and work is positive: The older workers are, the more overall job satisfaction they experience. This is not altogether surprising, because younger adults who are dissatisfied with their jobs will quit them and find new positions that they like better. Also, because older workers have fewer opportunities to change jobs, they may learn to live with what they have and accept that it is the best they are likely to get. Such acceptance may ultimately translate into satisfaction (Tangri, Thomas, & Mednick, 2003).

Burnout occurs when a worker experiences dissatisfaction, disillusionment, frustration, or weariness from his or her job.

Challenges of Work: On-the-Job Dissatisfaction

Job satisfaction is not universal in middle adulthood. For some people, dissatisfaction with working conditions or with the nature of the job increases their stress. Conditions may become so bad that the result is burnout or a decision to change jobs.

Burnout. For 44-year-old Peggy Augarten, her early-morning shifts in the intensive care unit of a suburban hospital were becoming increasingly difficult. It had always been hard to lose a patient, but recently she found herself crying over patients at the strangest moments: while she was doing the laundry, washing the dishes, or watching TV. When she began to dread going to work, she knew that her feelings about her job were undergoing a fundamental change.

Augarten's response probably reflects the phenomenon of burnout. **Burnout** occurs when workers experience dissatisfaction, disillusionment, frustration, and weariness from their jobs. It occurs most often in jobs that involve helping others, and it often strikes those who once were the most idealistic and driven. In some ways, such workers may be overcommitted to their jobs. Realizing that they can make only minor dents in huge social problems such as poverty and medical care can be disappointing and demoralizing (Taris, van Horn, & Schaufeli, 2004; Bakker & Heuven, 2006; Dunford et al., 2012).

A growing cynicism about one's work characterizes burnout. An employee might say to himself, "What am I working so hard for? No one is going to notice that I've come in on budget for the last two years." Workers also may feel indifferent about their job performance. The idealism a worker felt entering a profession may give way to pessimism and the attitude that no meaningful solution to a problem exists (Lock, 1992).

People can combat burnout, even those in professions with high demands and seemingly insurmountable burdens. For example, the nurse who despairs of not having enough time for every patient can be helped to realize that a more feasible goal—such as giving patients a quick backrub—can be equally important. Jobs can also be structured so that workers (and their supervisors) pay attention to small victories in their daily work, such as the pleasure of a client's gratitude, even though the "big picture" of disease, poverty, racism, and an inadequate educational system may look gloomy. In addition, it is important to mentally disengage from work during leisure time (deJonge et al., 2012; Sonnentag, 2012; Bährer-Kohler, 2013).

Unemployment: The Dashing of the Dream

For many workers, unemployment is a hard reality, affecting them psychologically and economically. For those who have been fired, laid-off by corporate downsizing, or forced out of jobs by technological advances, being out of work can be psychologically and even physically devastating (Sharf, 1992).

Unemployment can leave people feeling anxious, depressed, and irritable. Their self-confidence may plummet, and they may be unable to concentrate. According to one analysis, every time the unemployment rate goes up 1 percent, there is a 4 percent rise in suicide, and admissions to psychiatric facilities go up by some 4 percent for men and 2 percent for women (Connor, 1992; Inoue et al., 2006; Paul & Moser, 2009).

Even seemingly positive aspects of unemployment, such as having more time, can affect people negatively. Unemployed people may feel depressed and at loose ends, making them less apt to take part in community activities, use libraries, and read than employed people. They are more likely to be late for appointments and even for meals (Ball & Orford, 2002; Tyre & McGinn, 2003).

And these problems may linger. Middle-aged adults tend to stay unemployed longer than younger workers, and have fewer opportunities for gratifying work as they age. Employers may discriminate against older applicants, making it more difficult to find a new job. Such discrimination is both illegal and based on misguided assumptions: Research finds that older workers miss fewer work days, hold their jobs longer, are more reliable, and are more willing to learn new skills (Connor, 1992).

Midlife unemployment is a shattering experience. For some people, especially those who never find meaningful work again, it taints their view of life. Such involuntary—and premature—retirement can lead to pessimism, cynicism, and despondency. Accepting the new situation takes time and a good deal of psychological adjustment. And there are challenges for those who *do* find a new career, too (Waters & Moore, 2002).

Becoming unemployed in midlife can be a shattering experience that may taint your view of the world.

Switching—and Starting—Careers at Midlife

For some people, midlife brings a hunger for change. For those who are dissatisfied with their jobs, who switch careers after a period of unemployment, or who return to a job market they left years ago, development leads to new careers.

People change careers in middle adulthood for several reasons. Their job may offer little challenge, or they have achieved mastery, making the once difficult, routine. Other people switch because their jobs have changed in ways they do not like, or they may have lost their job. They may be asked to accomplish more with fewer resources, or technology may have drastically changed their daily activities and they no longer enjoy what they do.

Still others are unhappy with their status and wish to make a fresh start. Some are burned out or feel that they are on a treadmill. And some people simply want something new. They view middle age as the last chance to make a meaningful occupational change.

Finally, a significant number of people, most of them women, return to the job market after raising children. Some need to find paying work after a divorce. Since the mid-1980s, the number of women in the workforce who are in their 50s has grown significantly. Around half of women between the ages of 55 and 64—and an even larger percentage of those who graduated from college—are now in the workforce.

People may enter new professions with unrealistically high expectations and then be disappointed by the realities. Middle-aged people, starting new careers, may also be placed in entry-level positions. Thus, their peers on the job may be considerably younger than they are (Sharf, 1992; Barnett & Hyde, 2001).

But in the long run, starting a new career in midlife can be invigorating. Those who switch or begin new careers may be especially valued employees (Bromberger & Matthews, 1994; Otto, Dette-Hagenmeyer, & Dalbert, 2010; Feldman & Ng, 2013).

Some forecasters suggest that career changes will become the rule, not the exception. According to this view, technological advances will occur so rapidly that people will be forced periodically to change their profession, often dramatically. People will have not one, but several, careers during their lifetimes. As the "Cultural Dimensions" segment shows, this is especially true for those who make the major life and career change: immigrating to another country as adults.

From the perspective of a social worker: Why do you think immigrants' ambition and achievements are widely underestimated? Do conspicuous negative examples play a role (as they do in perceptions of the midlife crisis and stormy adolescence)?

Leisure Time: Life Beyond Work

With the typical work week hovering between 35 and 40 hours—and becoming shorter for most people—most middle-aged adults have some 70 waking hours per week of leisure time (Kacapyr, 1997). What do they do with it?

For one thing, they watch television. Middle-aged people average around 15 hours of television each week. But adults do much more with their leisure time. For many people, midlife offers a renewed opportunity to take up activities outside the home. As children leave, parents have substantial time to participate in leisure activities like sports or participate in town committees. Middle-aged adults in the United States spend about 6 hours each week socializing (Robinson & Godbey, 1997; Lindstrom et al., 2005).

A significant number of people find leisure so alluring that they take early retirement. For early retirees who have adequate financial resources to last the remainder of their years, life can be quite gratifying. Early retirees tend to be in good health, and they may take up a variety of new activities (Cliff, 1991; Jopp & Hertzog, 2010).

Although midlife offers the opportunity for more leisure, most people report that the pace of their lives does not seem slower. Much of their free time is scattered throughout the week in 15- and 30-minute chunks as they pursue a variety of activities. Thus, despite a documented increase of 5 hours of weekly leisure time since 1965, many people feel they have no more free time than they did earlier (Robinson & Godbey, 1997).

One reason why extra leisure time seems to evaporate is that the pace of life in the United States is considerably faster than in many countries. By measuring the length of time average pedestrians cover 60 feet, the time it takes to purchase a stamp, and the accuracy of public clocks, research has compared the tempo of living in a variety of countries. According to a composite of these measures, the United States has a quicker tempo than many other countries, particularly Latin American, Asian, Middle Eastern, and African countries. But, many countries outpace the United States. Western European countries and Japan move more quickly than the United States, with Switzerland ranking first (Levine, 1997a, 1997b).

Cultural Dimensions

Immigrants on the Job: Making It in America

Seventeen years ago, Mankekolo Mahlangu-Ngcobo was placed in solitary confinement for 21 days in South Africa's Moletsane police station, falsely accused of terrorism. In 1980, once again in danger of imprisonment for her anti-apartheid protests, she fled to Botswana, leaving her 12-year-old son Ratijawe with her mother. She came to the U.S. in 1981, won political asylum in 1984 and now lives with her 13-year-old daughter Ntokozo in a $60,000 Baltimore row house. Her experiences left her with a deep appreciation of her adopted land. "If you have never lived somewhere else," she says, "you cannot know how much freedom you have here."

Ngcobo also found prosperity here. As with many of her fellow immigrants, the key was education. Since her arrival, she has earned a bachelor's degree, two master's, and a doctorate in theology—which she paid for largely with scholarships or with her own money. Her academic credentials and dedication to helping others have won her two soul-satisfying careers, as a lecturer in public health at Baltimore's Morgan State University and as assistant minister at the Metropolitan African Methodist Episcopal Church in Washington, D.C. (Kim, 1995, p. 133)

Public opinion often portrays immigrants to the United States as straining the educational, health care, welfare, and prison systems while contributing little to society. But—as Mankekolo Mahlangu-Ngcobo's story shows—these assumptions are quite wrong.

With around 1.2 million immigrants entering the United States each year, foreign-born residents now represent 10 percent of the population, more than twice the percentage in 1970. First- and second-generation immigrants comprise almost a quarter of the population of the United States (Deaux, 2006).

Today's immigrants are somewhat different from those of the earlier waves at the beginning of the twentieth century. Only a third are white, compared with almost 90 percent of immigrants who arrived before 1960.

Critics argue that many new immigrants lack the skills that will allow them to make a contribution to the high-tech economy of the twenty-first century. However, the critics are wrong in many fundamental respects. For instance, consider the following data (Camarota, 2001; Flanigan, 2005; Gorman, 2010):

- **Most legal and illegal immigrants ultimately succeed financially.** Although they initially experienced higher rates of poverty, immigrants who arrived in the United States prior to 1980 and established themselves have a higher family income than native-born Americans. Immigrants match nonimmigrants in entrepreneurship, with one in nine owning their own business.
- **Only a few immigrants come to the United States to get on welfare.** Instead, most say they come for the opportunities to work and prosper. Nonrefugee immigrants of working age are less likely to be on welfare than native-born U.S. citizens.
- **Given time, immigrants contribute more to the economy than they take away.** Although initially costly to the government, often because they hold low-paying jobs and therefore pay no income taxes, immigrants become more productive as they get older.

Why are immigrants often ultimately financially successful? One explanation is that immigrants who voluntarily choose to leave their native countries are particularly motivated and driven to be successful.

REVIEW, CHECK, AND APPLY

REVIEW

L016 What are the characteristics of work in middle adulthood?

- People in middle age view their jobs differently than before, placing more emphasis on specific job factors such as pay and working conditions, and less on career striving and ambition.
- Midlife career changes are becoming more prevalent, motivated usually by dissatisfaction, the need for more challenge or status, or the desire to return to the workforce after childrearing.

L017 How is leisure time different in middle adulthood?

- People in midlife usually have increased leisure time. Often they use it to become more involved outside the home in recreational and community activities.

CHECK YOURSELF

1. Burnout is more likely to strike individuals who are in helping professions.
   - True
   - False
2. Compared to younger adults, middle-aged adults who lose their jobs _____.
   - a tend to stay unemployed longer and have fewer opportunities for gratifying work as they age.
   - b tend to find jobs quickly because of their skills but find it difficult to stay employed.
   - c find it difficult to get new jobs, but once employed have a stable work history.
   - d are less likely to become depressed, which makes it easier for them to obtain employment.

APPLYING LIFESPAN DEVELOPMENT

- Why might striving for occupational success be less appealing in middle age than before? What cognitive and personality changes might contribute to this phenomenon?

✓ **Study** and **Review** on **MyPsychLab.com**

SUMMARY

8

PUTTING IT ALL TOGETHER MIDDLE ADULTHOOD

TERRI DONOVAN, at 50, found the free time that had eluded her for several decades as she raised her family while working full time. Chronologically and developmentally right in the middle of middle adulthood, she sent her youngest child to college, reignited her romance with her husband, took up volunteer work at a soup kitchen, and quit her job as an urban planner to run for the state legislature. Though Terri was certainly in a midlife transition, she did not experience a "midlife crisis." She realized she still had half a life ahead of her if all went well, and she was determined to forge strong connections with her husband, her grandchild, the people she met at the soup kitchen, and, through her bid for the legislature, with her entire community.

PHYSICAL DEVELOPMENT IN MIDDLE ADULTHOOD

MODULE 8.1

- Although certain chronic diseases, like arthritis and hypertension, do begin to appear in midlife, like most middle-aged adults, Terri is in good health. *(p. 363)*
- Walking helps Terri stay healthy and agile as she ages, a goal shared by many of her same-age peers. *(p. 358)*
- If Terri makes walking a regular exercise, it will compensate for the gradual loss of strength that occurs in middle adulthood. *(p. 358)*
- With an easing of obligations to her children, Terri has more time and energy to enjoy sex with her husband. However, if she hasn't gone through menopause, she will still need to use contraception. *(pp. 360–362)*

COGNITIVE DEVELOPMENT IN MIDDLE ADULTHOOD

MODULE 8.2

- Terri has developed expertise and a high competency in her work as an urban planner, which brings her continued success even though midlife brings an overall decline in intellectual skills. *(pp. 372–373)*
- Her understanding of what is involved in urban planning allows Terri to quickly evaluate a potential project, see what's involved, and decide if it interests her. *(p. 374)*
- It is likely that Terri has a great deal of practical intelligence in addition to the more traditional kind. *(pp. 369–372)*

SOCIAL AND PERSONALITY DEVELOPMENT IN MIDDLE ADULTHOOD

MODULE 8.3

- Though Terri is in midlife transition, the actions she takes to find more connected relationships, and to change her career in a way that's truly satisfying to her, result in growth rather than stagnation. *(pp. 378–379)*
- Terri's openness to new experiences, her extraversion, and her talent for organization are personality traits that have remained stable throughout her life. *(pp. 379–380)*
- Volunteering in her local soup kitchen, running for state legislature, and rekindling her romance with her husband eased any sadness Terri might have experienced when her youngest child left for college. *(p. 386)*

What would YOU do?

Would you advise Terri to slow up on the transitions in her life, to consolidate her changes? Why or why not?

What would a MARRIAGE COUNSELOR do?

Would you advise Terri to focus on rekindling her romance with Brian and put off running for the legislature for a year or two? If Terri wins the election, what suggestions would you give her to keep her marriage in focus as she starts a challenging new career?

What would a HEALTH CARE PROVIDER do?

Considering her age and the physical changes her body is going through, what dietary and exercise guidelines would you recommend Terri observe to prevent fatigue and combat stress in a demanding public service job?

What would a CAREER COUNSELOR do?

Would you advise Terri to set aside her political aspirations and take up work as a consultant in urban planning for New York City, a position for which she is exceptionally qualified and which would allow her to control her own schedule?

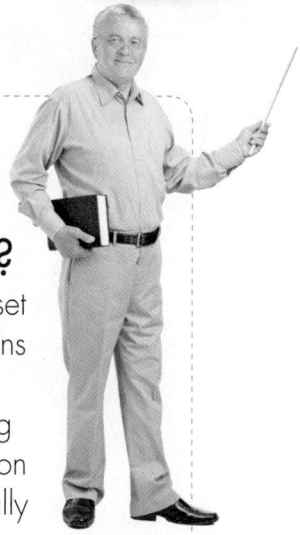

Explore on MyPsychLab

To read how real-life marriage counselors, health care providers, and career counselors responded to these questions, log onto MyPsychLab.com.

Do you agree or disagree with their responses? Why? What concepts that you've read about back up their opinion?

9 LATE ADULTHOOD

Peter Sarnov, 79, and his sister Ella Malone, 73, live together in a house they purchased 5 years ago after both their spouses died in the same year. "We lived together as kids back in Newark," says Peter, "and we always got along well despite the 6-year age difference. When we were suddenly alone, we talked to each other at my wife's wake and basically said, 'Why not?' And it's been working out great, so far. At least I think so."

At this, Ella takes up the thread. "Great is right. We fit like a couple of matched spoons. No conflict, no hassle, and exactly as much togetherness as we want. And you know what? That 6-year age difference doesn't seem so big anymore."

Asked if their compatibility stems from their sibling similarity, they both laugh out loud. "What similarity?" asks Peter. "It would be hard to find two people more different. Look, I'm a homebody. I like sitting around the house and reading. I'm a movie buff with millions of movies on DVD. I'm a gardener and I love cooking. My greatest pleasure is to have a couple of old friends over for dinner and a movie. I even like keeping the house reasonably clean and doing the laundry."

"And I'm always on the go," adds Ella. "I'm in a sewing circle and two book clubs, I play golf as often as I can, and I work in the hospital gift shop. I'm taking Spanish at the community college, I'm learning to play chess, and I often take trips out west or abroad with or without Peter.

"Basically we're two sides of a coin," says Peter. "I'm neat, she's not. She goes out, I stay home. She's competitive, I'm laid back. I cook, she eats. But neither of us is ever bored."

"And though we're both a little forgetful," Ella says with a smile, "we seem to forget different things. If I forget an appointment, Peter reminds me, and if he's trying to recall a name, I always know it. The absolute best thing is that we never get on each other's nerves. I know we couldn't say that about our marriages," she laughs.

And Peter laughs with her.

The period of late adulthood, which starts around age 65, is characterized by great changes—and ongoing personal development. Older adults face profound physical, cognitive, and social changes, and by and large they figure out strategies for adjusting to them. No two strategies are exactly alike, as illustrated by the quite different paths chosen by Peter Sarnov and Ella Malone, but most older adults manage this stage successfully.

In late adulthood, people begin the decline that will be part of their lives until death. But we will see that all aspects of this period—physical, cognitive, and social—are largely misrepresented in popular stereotypes. Older people can maintain physical and mental strength virtually until the day they die, and their social worlds can also remain as vital and active as they want.

Physically, people over 65 certainly begin a gradual transition from full strength and health to an increasing concern about illness, pain, and disease. But this is not the only thing going on in their lives. They can stay healthy for quite a long time and can continue most if not all of the activities that they enjoyed when younger. Cognitively, we find that older people adjust quite well to the changes that seem designed to impede them by adopting new strategies for solving problems and compensating for lost abilities. And socially, many of them become adept at coping with the changes in their lives, such as the death of a spouse and retirement from work.

Peter and Ella are typical only in being atypical. Through their unique approaches to aging, they make the point that old age can be what people want it to be—not what society thinks it ought to be.

MODULE 9.1

PHYSICAL DEVELOPMENT IN LATE ADULTHOOD

Life expectancy: How long have I got?

MODULE 9.2

COGNITIVE DEVELOPMENT IN LATE ADULTHOOD

How can you exercise your brain to stay sharp?

MODULE 9.3

SOCIAL AND PERSONALITY DEVELOPMENT IN LATE ADULTHOOD

How does culture affect how we treat people in late adulthood?

MyVirtualLife

If you are currently using MyVirtualLife, consider how you will navigate late adulthood. What decisions will you make?

Access MyVirtualLife for a chance to live your own virtual life.

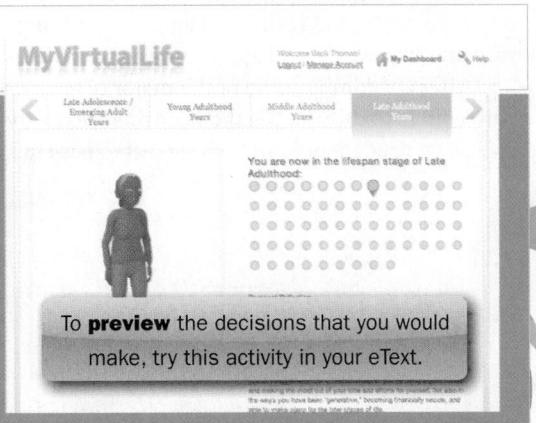

To **preview** the decisions that you would make, try this activity in your eText.

MODULE 9.1

PHYSICAL DEVELOPMENT IN LATE ADULTHOOD

Rust and Relaxation

Amy Wenham, a second grade teacher for 35 years, took advantage of an attractive early retirement package from her school district and left the classroom. Then, after only 2 years of what she calls "rust and relaxation," she needed a change.

"I was 65 and I was bored. I wanted to do something more, something else, with my life," she says. "So I made an inventory of things I liked, things I was good at, and things that might make some money. My best idea was to use my lifelong hobby—traveling—as the basis for a business."

With a small investment in advertising, business cards, posters, a website, and a brochure, and after gathering her notes, pictures, and recollections from more than 4 decades of traveling, Amy announced a new service, called Tailored Europe, Inc.

"Basically, clients tell me where they plan to go and how long they want to spend there, and then we have a discussion about the sorts of things they like to do. Using this information, I custom-design a varied and unusual itinerary of lesser-known places to visit, stay, shop, and eat. I'm not a travel agent, but I've been around. I provide good information for a reasonable fee, and they make their own arrangements."

To Amy's delight—and surprise—she has found an eager market among current and former educators and small business owners. And the feedback has been tremendous. "Thanks to word of mouth, Tailored Europe has taken off," she says. "I can't believe it, but I'm so busy I'm going to have to hire an assistant."

Amy Wenham is not alone when it comes to showing extraordinary restlessness and vitality in late adulthood. Increasingly, older people are pioneering new fields, achieving new endeavors, and generally reshaping how we perceive the later stages of life. For a growing number of people in late adulthood, vigorous mental and physical activity remains an important part of daily life.

Old age used to be equated with loss: loss of brain cells, intellectual capabilities, energy, and sex drive. That view is being displaced as **gerontologists**, specialists who study aging, paint a very different picture. Rather than a period of decline, late adulthood is seen as a stage in which people continue to change—to grow in some areas and, yes, to decline in others.

Even the definition of "old" is changing. Many people in late adulthood, which begins around age 65 and continues to death, are as vigorous and involved with life as people several decades younger. We can no longer define old age by chronological years alone; we must also take into account people's physical and psychological well-being, their *functional ages*. Some researchers divide people into three groups according to functional ages: the *young old* are healthy and active; the *old old* have some health problems and difficulties with daily activities; and the *oldest old* are frail and need care. According to functional age, an active, healthy 100-year-old would be considered young old, while a 65-year-old in the late stages of emphysema would be among the oldest old.

We begin this module with a discussion of the myths and realities of aging, examining some stereotypes that color our understanding of late adulthood. We look at the outward and inward signs of aging and the ways the nervous system and senses change with age.

Next, we consider health and well-being. After examining some of the major disorders that affect older people, we look at what determines wellness and why old people are susceptible to disease. We then consider sexuality in late adulthood. We also focus on theories that seek to explain the aging process, as well as on gender, race, and ethnic differences in life expectancy.

gerontologists specialists who study aging

PHYSICAL DEVELOPMENT IN LATE ADULTHOOD

LO1 What sorts of physical changes occur in old age?
LO2 How are the senses affected by aging?

The astronaut-turned-senator, John Glenn, was 77 years old when he returned to space on a 10-day mission to help NASA study how the elderly adjust to space travel. Although sheer altitude sets Glenn apart from others, many people lead active, vigorous lives during late adulthood, fully engaged with life.

Aging: Myth and Reality

Late adulthood holds a unique distinction among life's stages: Because people are living longer, late adulthood is getting longer. Whether we start counting at 65 or 70, there is today a greater proportion of people alive in late adulthood than at any time in world history. In fact, demographers have divided the period using the same terms—but with different meanings—as researchers of functional aging. For demographers, the terms are purely chronological. The *young old* are 65 to 74 years old. The *old old* are between 75 and 84, and the *oldest old* are 85 and older.

The Demographics of Late Adulthood. One out of every eight Americans is 65 or older, and projections suggest that by 2050 nearly one-quarter of the population will be 65 and above. The number of people over 85 is projected to increase from 4 to 18 million by 2050 (Schneider, 1999; Administration on Aging, 2003) (see Figure 9-1).

The fastest growing segment of the population is the oldest old—people 85 or older. In the last 2 decades, the size of this group has nearly doubled. The population explosion among older people is not limited to the United States. As can be seen in Figure 9-2, the number of elderly is increasing substantially in countries around the globe. By 2050, the number of adults worldwide over 60 will exceed the number of people under 15 for the first time in history (Sandis, 2000; United Nations Population Division, 2002).

ageism prejudice and discrimination directed at older people

Ageism: Confronting the Stereotypes of Late Adulthood. Crotchety. Old codger. Old coot. Senile. Geezer. Old hag.

Such are the labels of late adulthood. They don't draw a pretty picture: These words are demeaning and biased, representing both overt and subtle ageism. **Ageism** is prejudice and discrimination directed at older people.

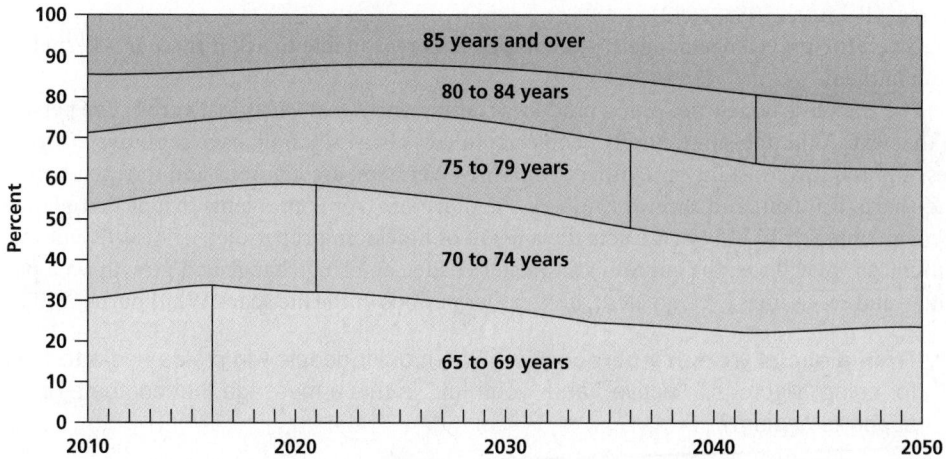

Note: Line indicates the year that each age group is the largest proportion of the older population.

FIGURE 9-1 The Flourishing Elderly
The percentage of people over the age of 65 is projected to rise to almost 25 percent of the population by the year 2050. Can you name two factors that contribute to this?
Source: Adapted from U.S. Bureau of the Census, 2008.

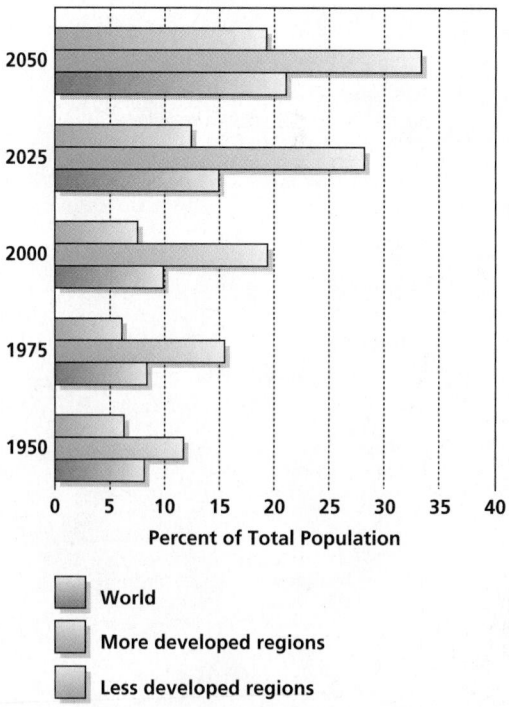

FIGURE 9-2 The Elderly Population Worldwide
Longer life is transforming population profiles worldwide, with the proportion of those over the age of 60 predicted to increase substantially by the year 2050.
Source: Based on United Nations Population Division, 2002.

What do you see when you look at this woman? Ageism is found in widespread negative attitudes toward older people, suggesting that they are in less than full command of their faculties.

Ageism suggests that older people are in less than full command of their mental faculties. Many attitude studies find that older adults are viewed more negatively than younger ones on a variety of traits, particularly those relating to general competence and attractiveness (Iverson, Larsen, & Solem, 2009; Helmes & Campbell, 2010; Woodspring, 2012).

Even when older and younger people perform exactly the same behavior, it is likely to be interpreted differently. Imagine you hear someone describing his search for his house keys. Would your perception of the person change if he was 80 rather than 20? Research says yes. Older adults are more likely to be viewed as chronically forgetful and perhaps suffering from some mental disorder. Young adults are judged more charitably, perhaps as temporarily forgetful because they have too much on their minds (Nelson, 2004; Lassonde et al., 2012; North & Fiske, 2013).

Many Western societies revere youth and admire a youthful appearance. It is the rare advertisement that includes an elderly person, unless it is for a product specifically designed for older adults. And in television programs, older persons are often presented as someone's parents or grandparents rather than as individuals in their own right (Vernon, 1990; McVittie, McKinlay, & Widdicombe, 2003; Ferguson & Brohaugh, 2010).

The ageism that produces such negative views of older people is reflected in the way they are treated. For instance, elderly individuals seeking jobs may face open prejudice, being told in job interviews that they lack the stamina for particular jobs. Or they sometimes are relegated to jobs for which they are overqualified. In addition, such stereotypes are accepted by people in late adulthood, becoming self-fulfilling prophecies that hinder performance (Rupp, Vodanovich, & Credé, 2006; Levy, 2009).

Today's ageism is, in some ways, a peculiarly modern and Western cultural phenomenon. In the American colonial period, a long life was an indication of a virtuous life, and older people were held in high esteem. Similarly, elders are venerated in most Asian societies because they have attained special wisdom by living so long, and many Native American societies have traditionally viewed older people as storehouses of information about the past (Bodner, Bergman, & Cohen-Fridel, 2012 ; Maxmen, 2012).

Today, however, negative views of older people prevail in U.S. society, and they are based on misinformation. Test your knowledge about aging by answering the questions in Table 9-1. Most people score no higher than chance on the items, getting about 50 percent correct (Palmore, 1988, 1992).

Given the prevalence of ageist stereotypes, it is reasonable to ask if there is a kernel of truth in them.

The answer is largely no. Aging produces consequences that vary greatly from one person to the next. Although some elderly people are in fact physically frail, have cognitive difficulties, and require constant care, others, like Amy Wenham, are vigorous and independent—and sharp, brilliant, and shrewd thinkers. Furthermore, some problems that at first glance seem attributable to old age are actually a result of illness, improper diet, or insufficient nutrition. As we will see, the autumn and winter of life can bring change and growth on a par with—and sometimes even greater than—earlier periods of the life span (Whitbourne, 2007).

From a social worker's perspective: When older people win praise and attention for being "vigorous," "active," and "youthful," is this a message that combats or supports ageism?

Physical Transitions in Older People

"Feel the burn." That's what the exercise tape says, and many of the 14 women in the group are doing just that. As the tape continues through its drills, some of the women stretch and reach vigorously, while others mostly just sway to the music. It's not much different from thousands of

TABLE 9-1 THE MYTHS OF AGING

1. The majority of old people (age 65 and older) have defective memory, are disoriented, or are demented. T or F?
2. The five senses (sight, hearing, taste, touch, and smell) all tend to weaken in old age. T or F?
3. The majority of old people have no interest in, nor capacity for, sexual relations. T or F?
4. Lung capacity tends to decline in old age. T or F?
5. The majority of old people are sick most of the time. T or F?
6. Physical strength tends to decline in old age. T or F?
7. At least one-tenth of the aged are living in long-stay institutions (such as nursing homes, mental hospitals, and homes for the aged). T or F?
8. Many older adults maintain large social networks of friends. T or F?
9. Older workers usually cannot work as effectively as younger workers. T or F?
10. Over three-fourths of the aged are healthy enough to carry out their normal activities. T or F?
11. The majority of old people are unable to adapt to change. T or F?
12. Old people usually take longer to learn something new. T or F?
13. It is almost impossible for the average old person to learn something new. T or F?
14. Older people tend to react slower than do younger people. T or F?
15. In general, old people tend to be pretty much alike. T or F?
16. The majority of old people say they are seldom bored. T or F?
17. The majority of old people are socially isolated. T or F?
18. Older workers have fewer accidents than do younger workers. T or F?

Scoring

All odd-numbered statements are false; all even-numbered statements are true. Most college students miss about six, and high school students miss about nine. Even college instructors miss an average of about three.

Source: Adapted from Palmore, 1988; Rowe & Kahn, 1999.

exercise classes across the United States, and yet there is one surprise: The youngest woman in the group is 66 years old, and the oldest, dressed in a sleek Spandex leotard, is 81.

The surprise registered by this observer reflects the stereotype that people over 65 are sedentary, incapable of vigorous exercise. The reality is different. Although their physical capabilities are likely to have changed, many older persons remain agile and fit long into old age. Still, the outer and inner changes that began subtly during middle adulthood become unmistakable during old age (Sargent-Cox, Anstey, & Luszcz, 2012; Fontes & Oliveira, 2013).

As we discuss aging, we should take note of the distinction between primary and secondary aging. **Primary aging**, or *senescence*, involves universal and irreversible changes due to genetic programming. In contrast, **secondary aging** encompasses changes that are due to illness, health habits, and other individual factors, which are not inevitable. Although the physical and cognitive changes of secondary aging are common, they are potentially avoidable and can sometimes be reversed.

Outward Signs of Aging. One of the most obvious indicators of aging is the hair, which usually becomes distinctly gray and eventually white, and may thin out. The face and other parts of the body become wrinkled as the skin loses elasticity and *collagen*, the protein that forms the basic fibers of body tissue (Bowers & Thomas, 1995; Medina, 1996).

People may become shorter by as much as 4 inches, partially due to changes in posture, but mostly because the cartilage in the disks of the backbone becomes thinner. This is particularly true for women, who are more susceptible than men to **osteoporosis**, or thinning of the bones, largely a result of reduced estrogen production.

Osteoporosis, which affects 25 percent of women over 60, is a primary cause of broken bones among older people. It is largely preventable if exercise is adequate and calcium and

primary aging aging that involves universal and irreversible changes that, due to genetic programming, occur as people get older

secondary aging changes in physical and cognitive functioning that are due to illness, health habits, and other individual differences, but are not due to increased age itself and are not inevitable

osteoporosis a condition in which the bones become brittle, fragile, and thin, often brought about by a lack of calcium in the diet

Although gray hair is often characterized as "distinguished" in men, the same trait in women is viewed more often as a sign of being "over the hill"—a clear double standard.

protein intake are sufficient earlier in life. Osteoporosis can be treated and even prevented with drugs such as Fosamax (alendronate) (Picavet & Hoeymans, 2004; Swaim, Barner, & Brown, 2008; Wang et al., 2013).

Although negative stereotypes against appearing old affect both genders, they are particularly potent for women. In fact, in Western cultures there is a *double standard* for appearance, by which women are judged more harshly than men. For instance, gray hair in men is often viewed as "distinguished"; in women it is a sign of being "over the hill" (Sontag, 1979; Bell, 1989).

As a consequence, women feel considerably more pressure than men to hide the signs of aging by dyeing their hair, undergoing cosmetic surgery, and using age-concealing cosmetics (Unger & Crawford, 1992). The double standard is diminishing, however, as more men grow interested in looking younger and fall prey to a new wave of male-oriented cosmetic products, such as wrinkle creams. Ironically, as the double standard eases, ageism is becoming more of a concern for both sexes.

Internal Aging. As the outward signs become more apparent, there are also changes in the internal functioning of the organ systems (Whitbourne, 2001; Aldwin & Gilmer, 2004).

The brain becomes smaller and lighter. As it shrinks, it pulls away from the skull; the space between the brain and skull doubles from age 20 to age 70. The brain uses less oxygen and glucose, and blood flow is reduced. The number of neurons, or brain cells, declines in some parts of the brain, although not as much as was once thought. Research suggests that the number of cells in the cortex may drop only minimally or not at all. In fact, some evidence suggests that certain types of neuronal growth may continue throughout the life span (Raz et al., 2007; Ziegler et al., 2010; Gattringer et al., 2012).

The reduced flow of blood in the brain is due in part to the heart's reduced ability to pump blood through hardening and shrinking blood vessels. A 75-year-old man pumps less than three-quarters of the blood that he could pump during early adulthood (Kart, 1990; Yildiz, 2007).

Other bodily systems also work at lower capacity. The respiratory system is less efficient, and the digestive system produces less digestive juice and is less efficient in pushing food through the system—thereby increasing the incidence of constipation. Some hormones are produced at lower levels. Muscle fibers decrease both in size and in amount, and they become less efficient at using oxygen from the bloodstream and storing nutrients (Deruelle et al., 2008; Suetta & Kjaer, 2010; Morley, 2012).

Although these changes are normal, they often occur earlier in people who have less healthy lifestyles. For example, smoking accelerates declines in cardiovascular capacity at any age.

Lifestyle factors can also slow the changes associated with aging. For instance, people whose exercise program includes weightlifting may lose muscle fiber at a slower rate than those who are sedentary. Similarly, physical fitness is related to better performance on mental tests, may prevent a loss of brain tissue, and may even aid in the development of new neurons. In fact, studies suggest that sedentary older adults who begin aerobic fitness training ultimately show cognitive benefits (Kramer, Erickson, & Colcombe, 2006; Pereira et al., 2007; Solberg et al., 2013).

Slowing Reaction Time

Karl winced as the "game over" message came up on his grandsons' video game system. He enjoyed trying out their games, but he just couldn't shoot down those bad guys as quickly as his grandkids could.

As people get older, they take longer: longer to put on a tie, reach a ringing phone, press the buttons in a video game. One reason is a lengthening of reaction time, which begins to increase in middle age and by late adulthood may rise significantly (Fozard et al., 1994; Benjuya, Melzer, & Kaplanski, 2004; Der & Deary, 2006).

It is not clear why people slow down. One explanation, known as the **peripheral slowing hypothesis**, suggests that the peripheral nervous system, which encompasses the nerves that branch from the spinal cord and brain to the extremities of the body, becomes less efficient with age. Because of this, it takes longer for information from the environment to reach the brain and for commands from the brain to be transmitted to the muscles (Salthouse, 2006; Kimura, Yasunaga, & Wang, 2013).

According to the **generalized slowing hypothesis**, on the other hand, processing in all parts of the nervous system, including the brain, is less efficient. As a consequence, slowing occurs throughout the body, including the processing of both simple and complex stimuli, and the transmission of commands to the muscles (Cerella, 1990).

Although we don't know which explanation is more accurate, it is clear that the slowing of reaction time and general processing results in a higher incidence of accidents for elderly persons. Slowed reaction and processing time means they can't efficiently receive information from the environment that may indicate a dangerous situation. Slowed decision-making processes impair their ability to remove themselves from harm's way. Drivers over 70 have as many fatal accidents per mile driven as teenagers (Whitbourne, Jacobo, & Munoz-Ruiz, 1996; Leversen, Hopkins, & Sigmundsson, 2013) (see Figure 9-3).

Although response time slows, the *perception* of time actually seems to speed up with age. The days and weeks seem to go by more quickly and time seems to rush by faster for older adults, perhaps because of changes in the way the brain coordinates its internal time clock (Mangan, 1997).

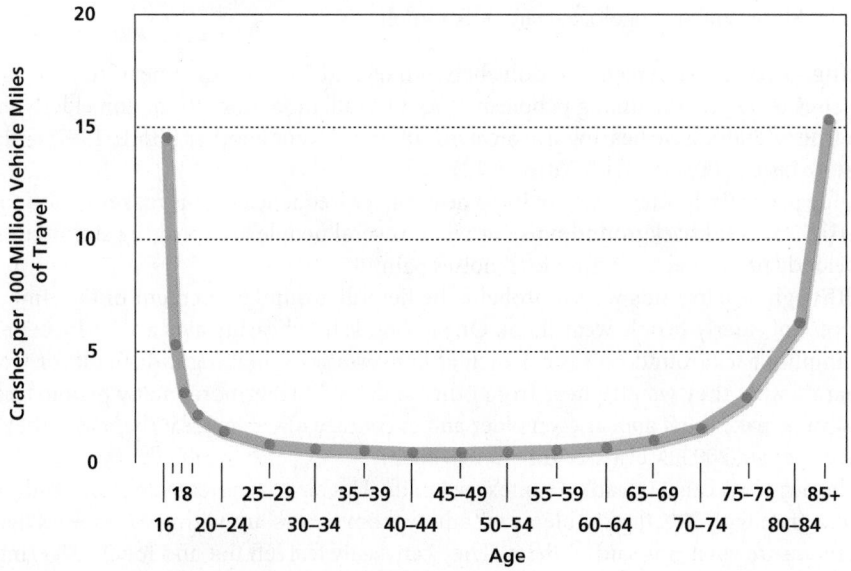

FIGURE 9-3 Vehicle Fatalities Across the Life Span
Drivers over age 70 have a fatal accident record comparable to that of teenagers when crashes are calculated per mile of driving. Why is this the case?
Source: National Highway Traffic Safety Administration, 1994.

peripheral slowing hypothesis the theory that suggests that overall processing speed declines in the peripheral nervous system with increasing age

generalized slowing hypothesis the theory that processing in all parts of the nervous system, including the brain, is less efficient as we age

FIGURE 9-4 The World Through Macular Degeneration
Macular degeneration leads to a gradual deterioration of the center of the retina, leaving only peripheral vision. This is an example of what a person with macular degeneration might see.
Source: AARP, 2005, p. 34.

The Senses: Sight, Sound, Taste, and Smell

Old age brings declines in the sense organs, which has major psychological consequences because the senses are people's link with the world.

Vision. Changes in the physical apparatus of the eye—the cornea, lens, retina, and optic nerve—diminish visual abilities. The lens becomes less transparent, allowing only a third as much light to reach the retina at 60 as at 20. The optic nerve also becomes less efficient in transmitting nerve impulses (Gawande, 2007). As a result, vision declines along several dimensions. We see distant objects less well, need more light to see clearly, and take longer to adjust from dark to light and vice versa.

These changes cause everyday problems. Driving, particularly at night, becomes more challenging. Reading requires more light, and eye strain comes more easily. Of course, eyeglasses and contact lenses can correct many of these problems, and the majority of older people see reasonably well (Ball & Rebok, 1994; Horowitz, 1994; Owsley, Stalvey, & Phillips, 2003; Boerner et al., 2010).

Several eye diseases become more common during late adulthood. For instance, *cataracts*—cloudy or opaque areas on the lens of the eye that interfere with the passage of light—frequently develop. Cataracts bring blurred vision and glare in bright light. If cataracts are left untreated, the lens becomes milky white and blindness results. However, cataracts can be surgically removed, and eyesight can be restored with eyeglasses, contact lenses, or *intraocular lens implants*, in which a plastic lens is permanently placed in the eye (Walker, Anstey, & Lord, 2006).

Another serious problem among elderly individuals is glaucoma. As we noted earlier, *glaucoma* occurs when pressure in the fluid of the eye increases, either because the fluid cannot drain properly or because too much fluid is produced. Glaucoma can be treated by drugs or surgery if it is detected early enough.

The most common cause of blindness in people over 60 is *age-related macular degeneration* (AMD), which affects the *macula*, a yellowish area near the retina at which visual perception is most acute. When a portion of the macula thins and degenerates, the eyesight gradually deteriorates (see Figure 9-4). If diagnosed early, macular degeneration can sometimes be treated with medication or lasers. There is also some evidence that a diet rich in antioxidant vitamins (C, E, and A) can reduce the risk of AMD (Coleman et al., 2008; Jager, Mieler, & Miller, 2008; Vingolo, Salvatore, & Limoli, 2013).

Hearing. Around 30 percent of adults between 65 and 74 have some hearing loss, and the figure rises to 50 percent among people over 75. Overall, more than 10 million elderly people in the United States have hearing impairments of one kind or another (HHL, 1997; Chisolm, Willott, & Lister, 2003; Pacala & Yueh, 2012).

Aging particularly affects the ability to hear higher frequencies. This makes it hard to hear conversations amid background noise or when several people are speaking simultaneously. Some elderly persons actually find loud noises painful.

Although hearing aids would probably be helpful around 75 percent of the time, only 20 percent of elderly people wear them. One reason is that hearing aids are far from perfect. They amplify background noises as much as conversations, making it difficult for wearers to separate what they want to hear from other sounds. Furthermore, many people feel that hearing aids make them appear even older and encourage others to treat them as if they were disabled (Lesner, 2003; Meister & von Wedel, 2003).

A hearing loss can be deadly to one's social life. Unable to hear conversations fully, some elderly people with hearing problems withdraw from others, unwilling to respond because they are unsure what was said to them. They can easily feel left out and lonely. Hearing loss can also lead to feelings of paranoia as conversational blanks are filled according to fear rather than reality. If someone hears "I hate going to Maude's" instead of "I hate going to the mall," a bland opinion about shopping can be interpreted as an expression of personal animosity (Myers, 2000; Goorabi, Hoseinabadi, & Share, 2008).

Hearing loss may hasten cognitive decline. The struggle to understand what is being said can shunt mental resources away from processing information, causing difficulties in remembering and understanding information (Wingfield, Tun, & McCoy, 2005).

Taste and Smell. Elderly people who have always enjoyed eating may experience a real decline in the quality of life because of changes in sensitivity to taste and smell. Both senses become less discriminating, causing food to be less appetizing than it was earlier (Kaneda et al., 2000; Nordin, Razani, & Markison, 2003; Murphy, 2008). The decrease in taste and smell sensitivity has a physical cause. The tongue loses taste buds over time, making food less tasty. The problem is compounded as the olfactory bulbs in the brain begin to shrivel. Because taste depends on smell, this makes food taste even blander.

The loss of taste and smell sensitivity has an unfortunate side effect: Because food does not taste as good, people eat less and open the door to malnutrition. They may also oversalt their food, thereby increasing their risk of *hypertension*, or high blood pressure, one of the most common health problems of old age (Smith et al., 2006).

REVIEW, CHECK, AND APPLY

REVIEW

L01 What sorts of physical changes occur in old age?

- Older people are often subject to ageism—prejudice and discrimination against people based on their age.
- Old age brings many physical transitions, internal changes, and changes in sensory perception.
- Many of the physical changes associated with aging can cause social and psychological difficulties for older people.

L02 How are the senses affected by aging?

- Old age brings declines in vision, hearing, taste, and smell.
- The declines in the senses can have major psychological consequences.

CHECK YOURSELF

1. The fastest growing segment of the elderly population is the oldest old, or people who are 85 and older.
   - True
   - False
2. _____ aging involves universal and irreversible changes that, due to genetic programming, occur as people get older.
   - a Secondary
   - b Internal
   - c Inactive
   - d Primary
3. According to the _____ slowing hypothesis, for elderly individuals processing in all parts of the nervous system, including the brain, is less efficient.
   - a automated
   - b global
   - c generalized
   - d peripheral

APPLYING LIFESPAN DEVELOPMENT

- Should older people be subject to strict examinations to renew their drivers' licenses? Should such tests cover more than eyesight (e.g., response time, mental abilities)? What issues should be taken into consideration?

✓ **Study** and **Review** on **MyPsychLab.com**

HEALTH AND WELLNESS IN LATE ADULTHOOD

L03 What is the general state of health of older people, and to what disorders are they susceptible?

L04 Can wellness and sexuality be maintained in late adulthood?

L05 How long can people expect to live, and what are the major causes of death?

Sandra Frye passes around a photo of her father. "He was 75 when this was taken. He looks great and he could still sail back then, but he was already forgetting things like what he'd done yesterday or what he'd eaten for breakfast."

Frye takes part in a support group for family members of Alzheimer's patients. The second picture she shares shows her father 10 years later. "It was sad. He'd start talking to me and his words would jumble. Then he'd forget who I was. He forgot he had a younger brother or that he'd been a pilot in World War II. A year after this photo, he was bedridden. Six months later, he died."

Before his death, at the age of 93, former President Ronald Reagan suffered from Alzheimer's disease for a decade.

When Sandra Frye's father was diagnosed with Alzheimer's, he joined the 4.5 million Americans with Alzheimer's disease, a debilitating condition that saps both physical and mental powers. In some ways, Alzheimer's feeds the stereotypical view of elderly people as more apt to be ill than healthy.

However, the reality is different: Most elderly people are in relatively good health for most of old age.

According to surveys conducted in the United States, almost three-quarters of people 65 years old and above rate their health as good, very good, or excellent (USDHHS, 1990; Kahn & Rowe, 1999).

On the other hand, to be old is in fact to be susceptible to diseases. We now consider some of the major physical and psychological disorders of older people.

Health Problems in Older People: Physical and Psychological Disorders

Most of the illnesses and diseases of late adulthood are not peculiar to old age; people of all ages suffer from cancer and heart disease, for instance. However, the incidence of these diseases rises with age, raising the odds that a person will be ill during old age. Moreover, older persons bounce back more slowly from illnesses than younger people, and a full recovery may be impossible.

Common Physical Disorders. The leading causes of death in elderly people are heart disease, cancer, and stroke, which claim close to three-quarters of people in late adulthood. Because aging weakens the immune system, older adults are also more susceptible to infectious diseases (Feinberg, 2000). In addition, most older people have at least one chronic, long-term condition (AARP, 1990). For instance, *arthritis*, an inflammation of one or more joints, afflicts roughly half of older people. Arthritis can cause painful swelling, and it can be disabling, preventing people from performing the simplest of everyday tasks, such as unscrewing a jar of food or turning a key in a lock. Although aspirin and other drugs can relieve some of the swelling and reduce the pain, arthritis cannot be cured (Burt & Harris, 1994; Leverone & Epstein, 2010).

Around one-third of older people have *hypertension*, or high blood pressure. Many people who have high blood pressure are unaware of their condition because it has no symptoms, which makes it more dangerous. Left untreated, hypertension can weaken and damage blood vessels and the heart and may raise the risk of strokes (Wiggins & Uwaydat, 2006; Hermida et al., 2013). **Watch** the **Video** *Late Adulthood, Physical Health: Sandra* in **MyPsychLab.**

Psychological and Mental Disorders. Some 15 to 25 percent of people over 65 are thought to show some symptoms of psychological disorder, a lower percentage than in younger adults. The behavioral symptoms related to these disorders are sometimes different in older and younger adults (Whitbourne, 2001).

One of the more prevalent problems is major depression, which is characterized by feelings of intense sadness, pessimism, and hopelessness. Among the reasons cited for depression are the experience of cumulative losses of their spouses and friends, and their own declining health and physical capabilities (Penninx et al., 1998; Kahn, Hessling, & Russell, 2003; Menzel, 2008; Vink et al., 2009).

Some elderly people suffer from psychological disorders induced by the combinations of drugs they may be taking for various medical conditions. They may also be taking inappropriate doses of some medications because the metabolism of a 75-year-old and that of a 25-year-old differ, and the doses appropriate for them may differ too. Because of these possibilities, older people who take medications must be careful to inform their physicians and pharmacists of every drug—with dosage information—that they take. They should also avoid medicating themselves with over-the-counter drugs, because a combination of nonprescription and prescription drugs may be dangerous.

The most common mental disorder of elderly people is **major neurocognitive disorder**, previously referred to as dementia a broad category of diseases encompassing serious memory loss accompanied by declines in other mental functioning. Although major neurocognitive disorder has many causes, the symptoms are similar: declining memory, lessened intellectual abilities, and impaired judgment. The chances of experiencing major neurocognitive disorder increase with age. Less than 2 percent of people between 60 and 65 are diagnosed with the

major neurocognitive disorder the most common mental disorder of the elderly, it covers several diseases, each of which includes serious memory loss accompanied by declines in other mental functioning disorder, but the percentages double for every 5-year period past 65. Consequently, almost one-third of people over 85 suffer from some sort of major neurocognitive disorder. There are some ethnic differences, too, with African Americans and Hispanics showing higher levels of major neurocognitive disorder than Caucasians (National Research Council, 1997; Weissberger et al., 2013).

Alzheimer's Disease. **Alzheimer's disease**, a progressive brain disorder that produces loss of memory and confusion, leads to the deaths of 100,000 people in the United States each year. Nineteen percent of people age 75 to 84 have Alzheimer's, and nearly half of people over the age of 85 are affected by the disease. In fact, unless a cure is found, some 14 million people will be victims of Alzheimer's by 2050—more than triple the current number (Cowley, 2000).

The first sign of Alzheimer's is usually forgetfulness. A person may have trouble recalling words during a conversation or may return to the grocery store several times after having already done the shopping. At first, recent memories are affected, and then older ones. Eventually, people with the disease are totally confused, unable to speak intelligibly or to recognize even their closest family and friends. In the final stages, they lose voluntary control of their muscles and are bedridden. Because victims of the disorder are initially aware of the future course of the disease, they may understandably suffer from anxiety, fear, and depression.

Biologically, Alzheimer's occurs when production of the protein *beta amyloid precursor protein*—which normally promotes the production and growth of neurons—goes awry, creating large clumps of cells that trigger inflammation and deterioration of nerve cells. The brain shrinks, and several areas of the hippocampus and frontal and temporal lobes show deterioration. Furthermore, certain neurons die, which leads to a shortage of various neurotransmitters, such as acetylcholine (Medeiros et al., 2007; Bredesen, 2009; Callahan et al., 2013).

Although the physical changes that produce Alzheimer's are clear, what is not known is the trigger. Genetics clearly plays a role, with some families showing a much higher incidence of Alzheimer's than others. In fact, in certain families half the children appear to inherit the disease from their parents. Furthermore, years before Alzheimer's symptoms emerge, people who are genetically at high risk for the disease show differences in brain functioning when they are trying to recall information, as illustrated in the brain scans in Figure 9-5 (Thomas & Fenech, 2007; Baulac et al., 2009; Désiréa et al., 2013) (also see the "From Research to Practice" box).

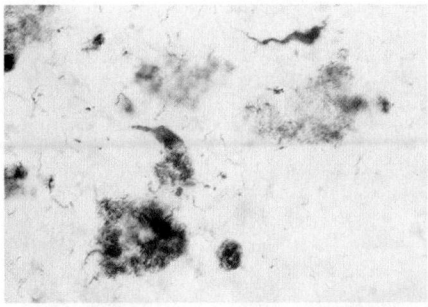

Brain scans of a patient with Alzheimer's disease show twisted clumps of nerve cells that are characteristic of the disease.

Alzheimer's disease a progressive brain disorder that produces loss of memory and confusion

From Research to Practice

Alzheimer's Disease: A Step Toward Prevention?

More than 5 million Americans currently have symptoms of Alzheimer's disease, a number that will more than double in coming years as the population ages. Many more have the disease but don't know it yet, as the cognitive symptoms start showing up only after significant brain damage has already been done (Marcus et al., 2010; Stix, 2010; Carter et al., 2012).

There are treatments available for Alzheimer's disease, but so far they only reduce the severity of the symptoms but do nothing to slow the progress of the disease. Attempts to find a cure have focused on the amyloid plaques in the brain that are the hallmark of the disease. Treatments have been devised that inhibit the process that produces the amyloid, that clear the amyloid from the brain, or that prevent the amyloid from doing damage to neurons, but they have all been frustratingly ineffective at stopping the disease (De Meyer et al., 2010; Khachaturian, Khachaturian, & Thies, 2012).

However, a new discovery provides hope for a cure. Scientists have idenitfied a rare gene mutation that keeps plaque from forming in the brain, preventing the symptoms of the disease. If a drug can be found to mimic the effects of the mutation, a cure for Alzheimer's may be at hand—a major breakthrough in dealing with the disease (Jonsson et al., 2012).

For now, what can be done for people who test positive for Alzheimer's disease but don't yet show symptoms? Until an effective treatment is developed, not much. But one new approach, called Cognitive Fitness and Innovative Therapies, doesn't rely upon curing the disease. It's an intervention that makes modifications in lifestyle factors thought to prevent the disease from getting a toehold in the first place, or at least slowing it down. Participants in the program are evaluated for their current level of cognitive fitness, and then they are given a tailored regimen of exercise, diet, social interaction, and intellectual stimulation. The program does seem to help participants maintain or improve their level of cognitive fitness, although it is not clear it actually staves off Alzheimer's disease (Marcus et al., 2010).

- *Given that Alzheimer's disease is currently incurable, would you want to know the results of a test for it? Why or why not?*
- *Why might intellectual stimulation help slow the progress of Alzheimer's disease in people who are not yet symptomatic, but not help much once the symptoms show?*

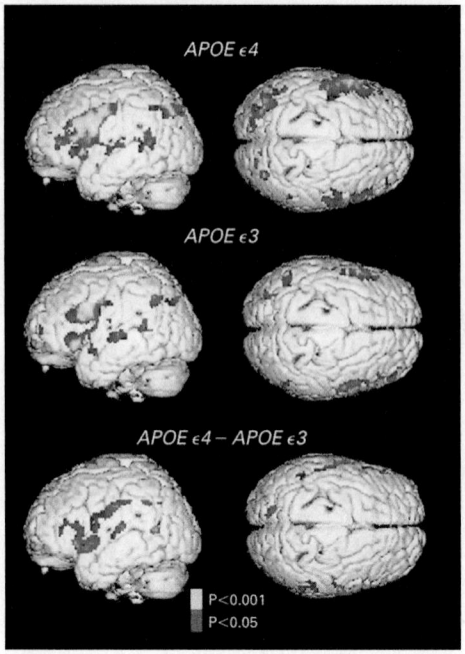

FIGURE 9-5 A Different Brain?
Brain scans during memory recall tasks show differences between the brains of people who have an inherited tendency toward Alzheimer's disease and those who do not. The brains at the top are a composite of those at risk; the brains in the middle are a composite of normal brains. The bottom row indicates areas of difference between the first two.
Source: Bookheimer et al., 2000.

Most evidence suggests that Alzheimer's is an inherited disorder, but nongenetic factors such as high blood pressure or diet may increase susceptibility. In one cross-cultural study, poor black residents in a Nigerian town were less likely to develop Alzheimer's than a comparable sample of African Americans living in the United States. The researchers speculate that variations in diet between the two groups—the residents of Nigeria ate mainly vegetables—might account for the differences in the Alzheimer's rates (Hendrie et al., 2001; Lahiri et al., 2007; Chen et al., 2010; Fuso et al., 2012).

Scientists are also studying certain viruses, dysfunctions of the immune system, and hormone imbalances that may produce the disease. Other studies have found that lower levels of linguistic ability in the early 20s are associated with declines in cognitive capabilities due to Alzheimer's much later in life (Snowdon et al., 1996; Alisky, 2007).

At present, there is no cure for Alzheimer's, only treatments for the symptoms. The most promising drugs are related to the loss of the neurotransmitter acetylcholine (Ach) that occurs in some forms of the disease. Donepezil (Aricept), galantamine (Razadyne), rivastigmine (Exelon), and tacrine (Cognex) are among the most common drugs prescribed, but they are effective in only half of Alzheimer's patients, and only temporarily (de Jesus Moreno, 2003; Gauthier & Scheltens, 2009).

Other drugs being studied include anti-inflammatory drugs, which may reduce the brain inflammation that occurs in Alzheimer's. In addition, the chemicals in vitamins C and E are being tested, because some evidence suggests that people who take such vitamins are at lower risk for developing the disorder (Alzheimer's Association, 2004; Mohajeri & Leuba, 2009; Sabbagh, 2009).

As victims lose the ability to feed and clothe themselves, or even to control bladder and bowel functions, they must be cared for 24 hours a day. Because of this, most people with Alzheimer's live out their lives in nursing homes, accounting for some two-thirds of the residents of nursing homes (Prigerson, 2003; Sparks, 2008).

Caregivers often become secondary victims of the disease. It is easy to become frustrated, angry, and exhausted by the demands of Alzheimer's patients, whose needs may be overpowering. In addition to the physical chore of providing total care, caregivers face the loss of a loved one, who not only is visibly deteriorating but can act emotionally unstable and even fly into rages (Thomas et al., 2006; Ott, Sanders, & Kelber, 2007; Sanders et al., 2008). **Watch** the **Video** *Alzheimer's* in **MyPsychLab**.

Wellness in Late Adulthood: The Relationship Between Aging and Illness

Sickness is not inevitable in old age. Whether an older person is ill or well depends less on age than on a variety of factors, including genetic predisposition, past and present environmental factors, and psychological factors.

Becoming an Informed Consumer of Development

Caring for People With Alzheimer's Disease

Alzheimer's disease is one of the most difficult illnesses to deal with, but several steps can be taken to help both patient and caregiver deal with Alzheimer's.

- Make patients feel secure in their home environments by keeping them occupied in everyday tasks of living as long as possible.
- Label everyday objects, furnish calendars and detailed but simple lists, and give oral reminders of time and place.
- Keep clothing simple: Provide clothes with few zippers and buttons, and lay them out in the order in which they should be put on.
- Put bathing on a schedule. People with Alzheimer's may be afraid of falling and of hot water, and may therefore avoid needed bathing.
- Prevent driving. Although patients often want to continue driving, their accident rate is high—some 20 times higher than average.
- Monitor telephone use. Alzheimer's patients who answer the phone may agree to offers from telephone salespeople and investment counselors.
- Provide opportunities for exercise, such as a daily walk. This prevents muscle deterioration and stiffness.
- Caregivers should remember to take time off and lead their own lives. Seek out support from community service organizations.
- Call or write to the Alzheimer's Association, which can provide support and information. The Association can be reached at 225 N. Michigan Ave. Fl. 17, Chicago, IL 60601-7633; Tel. 1-800-272-3900; http://www.alz.org.

Certain diseases, such as cancer and heart disease, have a clear genetic component, but a genetic predisposition does not automatically mean that a person will get a particular illness. People's lifestyles—smoking, diet, and exposure to cancer-causing agents such as sunlight or asbestos—may raise or lower their chances of coming down with such a disease.

Economic well-being also plays a role. Older individuals are less likely to have regular checkups, and when they finally go for treatment, their illnesses may be more advanced. Furthermore, poor people and even relatively well-off people may have difficulties finding affordable health care, the costs of which have increased significantly. For example, after adjusting for inflation, health care costs increased from $9,224 in 1992 to $15,081 in 2006 for older Americans. Out-of-pocket spending for health care services rose among those living in poverty from 12 percent to 28 percent for people age 65 and older (Federal Interagency Forum on Aging-Related Statistics, 2010).

Finally, psychological factors play an important role in determining susceptibility to illness. For example, a sense of control over one's environment, such as making choices involving everyday matters, leads to a better psychological state and superior health outcomes (Taylor et al., 1991; Levy et al., 2002).

Economic well-being is an important factor in the relationship between aging and illness, in part because poverty restricts access to medical care.

Promoting Good Health. People can enhance their physical well-being—and longevity—simply by doing what people of all ages should do: Eat wisely, exercise, and avoid obvious threats to health, such as smoking. The goal of medical and social service professionals is now to extend people's *active life spans*, the amount of time they remain healthy and able to enjoy their lives (Burns, 2000; Resnick, 2000; Sawatzky & Naimark, 2002; Gavin & Myers, 2003; Katz & Marshall, 2003).

Sometimes, older people have trouble following even these simple guidelines. For instance, estimates suggest that between 15 percent and 50 percent of elderly people do not have adequate nutrition, and several million experience hunger every day (de-Castro, 2002; Donini, Savina, & Cannella, 2003; Strohl, Bednar, & Longley, 2012).

The reasons are varied. Some elderly people have too little money to purchase adequate food, and some are too frail to shop or cook for themselves. Others feel little motivation to prepare and eat proper meals, particularly if they live alone or are depressed. For those with decreased taste and smell sensitivity, eating may no longer be enjoyable. And some older people may never have eaten well-balanced meals in earlier periods of their lives (Wolfe, Olson, & Kendall, 1998).

Obtaining sufficient exercise may also prove problematic for older persons. Illness may interfere with exercise, and inclement weather may confine an older person to the house. Furthermore, problems can combine: A poor person with insufficient money to eat properly may have little energy to put into physical activity (Kamijo et al., 2009; Kelley et al., 2009; Logsdon et al., 2009).

Sexuality in Old Age: Use It or Lose It

Do your grandparents have sex?

Quite possibly, yes. Increasing evidence suggests that people are sexually active well into their 80s and 90s, despite societal stereotypes prevalent in the United States, suggesting that it is somehow improper for two 75-year-olds to have sexual intercourse, and even worse for a 75-year-old to masturbate. In many other cultures, elderly people are expected to remain sexually active, and in some societies, people are expected to become less inhibited as they age (Hyde, 1994; Hillman, 2000; Lindau et al., 2007).

Two major factors determine whether an elderly person will engage in sexual activity. One is good physical and mental health. The other is previous regular sexual activity. "Use it or lose it" seems an accurate description of sexual functioning in older people. Sexual activity can and often does continue throughout the life span. Furthermore, there's some intriguing evidence that having sex may have some unexpected side benefits: One study found that having sex regularly is associated with an increased life span (Masters, Johnson, & Kolodny, 1982; Huang et al., 2009; Hillman, 2012)!

One survey found that 43 percent of men and 33 percent of women over the age of 70 masturbated. The average frequency for those who masturbated was once a week. Around two-thirds of married men and women had sex with their spouses, again averaging around once a week. In addition, the percentage of people who view their sexual partners as physically attractive actually increases with age (Budd, 1999; Araujo, Mohr, & McKinlay, 2004; Ravanipour, Gharibi, & Gharibi, 2013).

Of course, there are some changes in sexual functioning. Testosterone declines during adulthood by approximately 30 to 40 percent from the late 40s to the early 70s. It takes a longer time, and more stimulation, for men to get a full erection. The refractory period—the time following an orgasm before a man can become aroused again—may last one or more days. Women's vaginas become thin and inelastic, and they produce less natural lubrication, making intercourse more difficult. It is important to realize that older adults—like younger ones—are susceptible to sexually transmitted diseases. In fact, 10 percent of people diagnosed with AIDS are over 50, and the rate of new cases of other sexually transmitted infections is among the highest for any age group (Seidman, 2003; National Institute of Aging, 2004).

Approaches to Aging: Why Is Death Inevitable?

Hovering over late adulthood is the specter of death. At some point, no matter how healthy we have been throughout life, we know that we will experience physical declines and that life will end. But why?

There are two major approaches to explaining why we undergo physical deterioration and death: genetic programming theories and wear-and-tear theories.

Genetic programming theories of aging suggest that our body's DNA contains a built-in time limit for the reproduction of human cells. After a genetically determined period, the cells can no longer divide and the individual begins to deteriorate (Finch & Tanzi, 1997; Rattan, Kristensen, & Clark, 2006).

The theory comes in several variants. One is that the genetic material contains a "death gene" programmed to tell the body to deteriorate and die. Researchers who take an evolutionary viewpoint suggest that a long life span after the reproductive years is unnecessary for the survival of the species. According to this view, genetic diseases that strike later in life continue to exist because they allow people time to have children, thus passing along genes that are "programmed" to cause diseases and death.

Another variant is that the cells can duplicate only a certain number of times. Throughout our lives, new cells are produced through cell duplication to repair and replenish our various tissues and organs. According to this view, the genetic instructions for running the body can be read only a certain number of times before they become illegible and cells stop reproducing. Because the body is not being renewed at the same rate, bodily deterioration and death ensue (Hayflick, 1974; Thoms, Kuschal, & Emmert, 2007).

Evidence for the genetic programming theory comes from research, showing that human cells permitted to divide in the laboratory can do so successfully only around 50 times. Each time they divide, *telomeres*, which are tiny, protective areas of DNA at the tip of chromosomes, grow shorter. When a cell's telomere has just about disappeared, the cell stops replicating, making it susceptible to damage and producing signs of aging (Chung et al., 2007; Epel, 2009).

On the other hand, **wear-and-tear theories of aging** argue that the mechanical functions of the body simply wear out—the way cars and washing machines do. In addition, some wear-and-tear theorists suggest that the body's constant manufacture of energy to fuel its activities creates by-products. These by-products, combined with the toxins and threats of everyday life (such as radiation, chemical exposure, accidents, and disease), eventually reach such high levels that they impair the body's normal functioning. The ultimate result is deterioration and death.

One specific category of by-products that has been related to aging includes free radicals, electrically charged molecules or atoms that are produced by the cells of the body. Because

genetic programming theories of aging theories that suggest that our body's DNA genetic code contains a built-in time limit for the reproduction of human cells

wear-and-tear theories of aging the theory that the mechanical functions of the body simply wear out with age of their electrical charge, free radicals may cause negative effects on other cells of the body. A great deal of research suggests that oxygen-free radicals may be implicated in a number of age-related problems, including cancer, heart disease, and diabetes (Sierra, 2006; Hayflick, 2007; Sonnen et al., 2009).

Reconciling the Theories of Aging. Genetic programming theories and wear-and-tear theories make different suggestions about the inevitability of death. Genetic programming theories suggest that there is a built-in time limit to life—it's programmed in the genes, after all. On the other hand, wear-and-tear theories, particularly those that focus on the toxins that are built up during the course of life, paint a somewhat more optimistic view. They suggest that if a means can be found to eliminate the toxins produced by the body and by exposure to the environment, aging might well be slowed. For example, certain genes seem to slow aging and increase their ability to withstand age-related diseases (Ghazi, Henis-Korenblit, & Kenyon, 2009). We don't know which class of theories provides the more accurate account. Each is supported by some research, and each seems to explain certain aspects of aging. Ultimately, though, the mystery remains (Horiuchi, Finch, & Mesle, 2003; Friedman & Janssen, 2010).

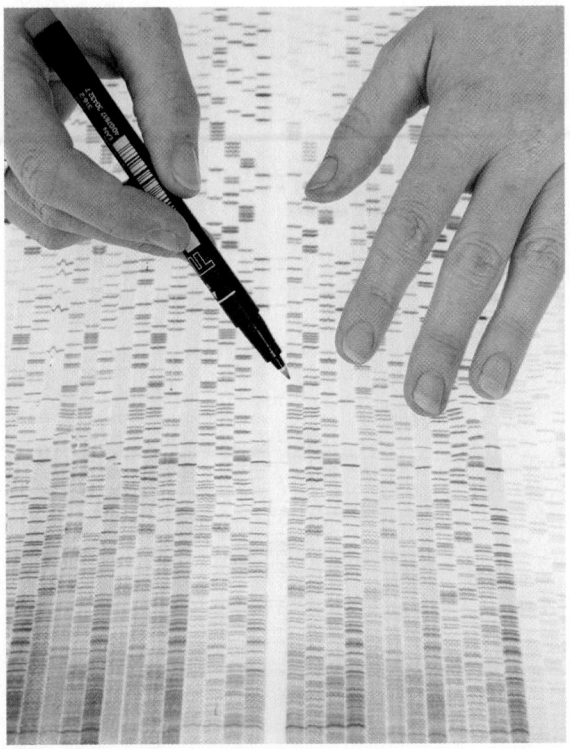

According to genetic preprogramming theories of aging, our DNA genetic code contains a built-in limit on the length of life.

Life Expectancy: How Long Have I Got? Although why we die is not fully understood, we do know how to calculate our average life expectancy: Most of us can expect to live into old age. The **life expectancy**—the average age of death for members of a population—of a person born in 2012, for instance, is 79 years of age.

Average life expectancy is on the rise. In 1776, average U.S. life expectancy was 35. By the early 1900s, it had risen to 47. And in only 4 decades, from 1950 to 1990, it increased from 68 to over 75. Predictions are that it will continue to rise steadily, possibly reaching 80 by the year 2050 (see Figure 9-6).

There are several reasons for this. Health and sanitation are generally better, with many diseases, such as smallpox, wiped out entirely. There are now vaccines and preventive measures for many diseases that used to kill young people, such as measles and mumps. Working conditions are better and products are safer. Many people are making healthful lifestyle choices such as keeping their weight down, eating fresh fruit and vegetables, and exercising—all of which can extend their active life spans, the years they spend in health and enjoyment of life.

Just how much can the life span be increased? The most common answer is around 120 years, the age reached by Jeanne Calment, the oldest person in the world until she died in 1997 at 122. Living longer would probably require major

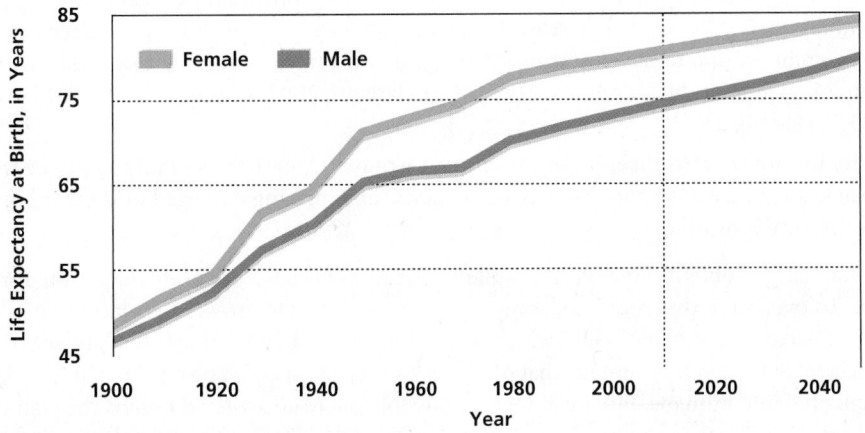

FIGURE 9-6 Living to Age 100
If increases in life expectancy continue, it may be a common occurrence for people to live to be 100 by the end of this century. What implications does this have for society?
Source: U.S. Bureau of the Census, 1997.

life expectancy the average age of death for members of a population genetic alterations that are both technically and ethically improbable. Still, recent scientific and technological advances suggest that significantly extending the life span is not an impossibility.

Postponing Aging: Can Scientists Find the Fountain of Youth?

Are researchers close to finding the scientific equivalent of the fountain of youth?

Not yet, but they're getting closer, at least in nonhuman species. For instance, researchers have extended the lives of nematodes (microscopic, transparent worms that typically live for just 9 days) to 50 days—the equivalent of extending human life to 420 years. Researchers have also doubled fruit flies' lives (Whitbourne, 2001; Libert et al., 2007; Ocorr et al., 2007).

The most promising avenues for increasing the length of life are these:

- **Telomere therapy.** Telomeres are the tiny areas at the tip of chromosomes that grow shorter each time a cell divides and eventually disappear, ending cell replication. Some scientists believe that if telomeres could be lengthened, aging could be slowed. Researchers are now looking for genes that control the production of telomerase, an enzyme that seems to regulate the length of telomeres (Urquidi, Tarin, & Goodison, 2000; Chung et al., 2007; Shalev et al., 2013).
- **Drug therapy.** Scientists in 2009 discovered that the drug *rapamycin* could extend life in mice by 14 percent by interfering with the activity of a protein *mTOR* (Blagosklonny et al., 2010; Stipp, 2012).
- **Unlocking longevity genes.** Certain genes control the body's ability to cope with environmental challenges and physical adversity. If harnessed, those genes may provide a way to increase the life span. One particularly promising family of genes are *sirtuins*, which may regulate and promote longer life (Guarente, 2006; Sinclair & Guarente, 2006; Glatt et al., 2007).
- **Reducing free radicals through antioxidant drugs.** Free radicals—unstable molecules that drift through the body—damage other cells and lead to aging. Antioxidant drugs that can reduce the number of free radicals may eventually be perfected. Furthermore, it may be possible to insert in human cells genes that produce enzymes that act as antioxidants. In the meantime, nutritionists urge a diet rich in antioxidant vitamins, which are found in fruits and vegetables (Birlouez-Aragon & Tessier, 2003; Kedziora-Kornatowska et al., 2007; Haleem et al., 2008).
- **Restricting calories.** For at least the last decade, researchers have known that laboratory rats who are fed an extremely low-calorie diet, providing 30 to 50 percent of their normal intake, often live 30 percent longer than better-fed rats, provided they get all the vitamins and minerals they need. The reason appears to be that they produce fewer free radicals. Researchers hope to develop drugs that mimic the effects of calorie restriction without forcing people to feel hungry all the time (Mattson, 2003; Ingram, Young, & Mattison, 2007; Cuervo, 2008).
- **The bionic solution: replacing worn-out organs.** Heart transplants . . . liver transplants . . . lung transplants. We live in an age when replacing damaged or diseased organs seems nearly routine.

One major problem remains: Transplants often fail because the body rejects the foreign tissue. To overcome this problem, some researchers advocate growing replacement organs from the person's own cloned cells, which will not be rejected. Even more radically, genetically engineered cells from nonhumans that do not evoke rejection could be cloned, harvested, and transplanted into humans. Finally, it may be possible to create artificial organs that can completely replace diseased or damaged ones (Cascalho, Ogle, & Platt, 2006; Kwant et al., 2007; Li & Zhu, 2007).

Sci-fi ideas for extending human life are exciting, but society must work to solve a more immediate problem: the significant disparity in life expectancies between members of different racial and ethnic groups. We discuss this important issue in the accompanying "Cultural Dimensions" segment.

From the perspective of a health care professional: Given what you've learned about explanations of life expectancy, how might you try to extend your own life?

Cultural Dimensions

Gender, Race, and Ethnic Differences in Average Life Expectancy: Separate Lives, Separate Deaths

- The average white child born in the United States is likely to live 78 years. The average African American child is likely to live 5.5 years less.
- A child born in Japan has a life expectancy of more than 83 years; for a child born in Mozambique, life expectancy is less than 40 years.
- A male born in the United States today is most likely to live to the age of 76; a female will probably live some 5 years longer.

There are several reasons for these discrepancies. Consider, for example, the gender gap in life expectancy, which is particularly pronounced. Across the industrialized world, women live longer than men by some 4 to 10 years. This female advantage begins just after conception: Although slightly more males are conceived, males are more likely to die during the prenatal period, infancy, and childhood. Consequently, by the age of 30 there are roughly equal numbers of men and women. But by the age of 65, 84 percent of females and only 70 percent of males are still alive. For those over 85, the gender gap widens: For every male, 2.57 women are still alive (United Nations World Population Prospects, 2006; World Factbook, 2009).

There are several explanations for the gender gap. One is that the naturally higher levels of the hormones estrogen and progesterone in women provide some protection from diseases such as heart attacks. It is also possible that women engage in healthier behavior during their lives, such as eating well. However, no conclusive evidence supports any of these explanations fully (DiGiovanna, 1994; Emslie & Hunt, 2008).

Whatever its cause, the gender gap has continued to increase. During the early part of the twentieth century, there was only a 2-year difference in favor of women, but in the 1980s this gap grew to 7 years. The size of the gap now seems to have leveled off, largely because men are more likely than previously to engage in positive health behaviors (such as smoking less, eating better, and exercising more).

Racial and ethnic differences are more troubling because they underline socioeconomic disparities in the United States. Life expectancy is almost 10 percent greater for Caucasians than for African Americans (see Figure 9-7). Furthermore, in contrast to Caucasians, whose life expectancy keeps edging up, African Americans have actually experienced slight declines in life expectancy in recent years.

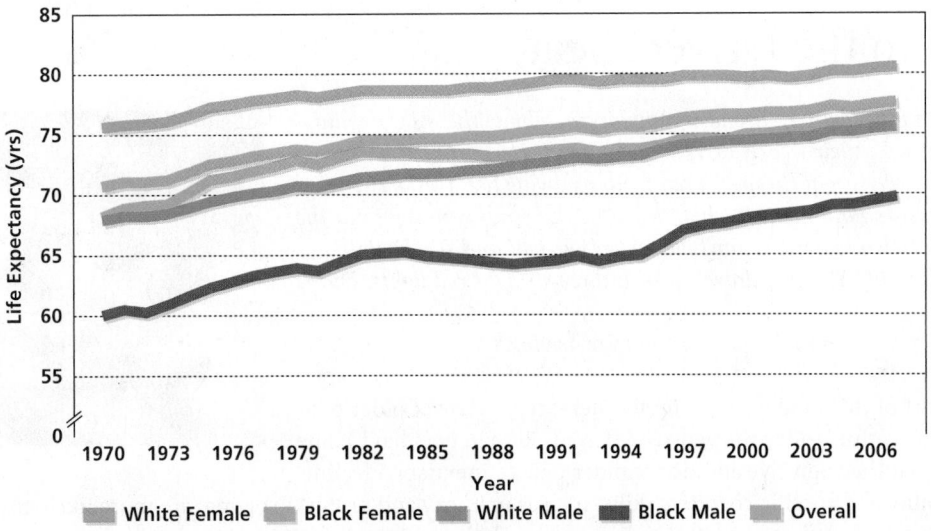

FIGURE 9-7 Life Expectancy of African Americans and Whites
Male African Americans have a shorter life expectancy than other demographic groups. Are the reasons for this genetic, cultural, or both?
Source: Xu, Kochanek & Murphy, 2010.

REVIEW, CHECK, AND APPLY

REVIEW

L03 What is the general state of health of older people, and to what disorders are they susceptible?

- Most illnesses and diseases of late adulthood are not peculiar to old age; however, incidents of cancer and heart disease rise with age. People in late adulthood are also more prone to develop arthritis, hypertension, major neurocognitive disorder, and Alzheimer's disease.

L04 Can wellness and sexuality be maintained in late adulthood?

- Proper diet, exercise, and avoidance of health risks can lead to prolonged wellness during old age, and sexuality can continue throughout the life span in healthy adults.

L05 How long can people expect to live, and what are the major causes of death?

- Whether death is caused by genetic programming or by general physical wear and tear is an unresolved question. Life expectancy, which has risen for centuries, varies with gender, race, and ethnicity.
- New approaches to increasing life expectancy include telomere therapy, reducing free radicals through antioxidant drugs, restricting caloric intake, and replacing worn-out organs.

CHECK YOURSELF

1. Although we may expect the elderly to be in poor health or sickly, approximately _____ of people 65 and older rate their health as good, very good, or excellent.
   - a one-half
   - b three-fourths
   - c two-thirds
   - d one-fourth
2. Which of the following is NOT a physical change in the brain associated with Alzheimer's?
   - a The hippocampus shows deterioration.
   - b The frontal and temporal lobes show deterioration.
   - c Specific neurons die, leading to a shortage of transmitters such as acetylcholine.
   - d The brain enlarges.
3. A strong relationship exists between economic well-being and illness in that those individuals who can afford to maintain good health care in their later years remain in better health.
   - True
   - False

APPLYING LIFESPAN DEVELOPMENT

- In what ways is socioeconomic status related to wellness in old age and to life expectancy?

✓ **Study** and **Review** on **MyPsychLab.com**

MODULE 9.2

COGNITIVE DEVELOPMENT IN LATE ADULTHOOD

Not in the Driver's Seat

Grace and Helen, both 80 years old, are idly complaining about the minor annoyances of old age as they take their weekly drive to the market. Helen, in the passenger seat, watches as Grace drives right through a red light. Knowing her eyes aren't what they used to be, Helen says nothing. But when the same thing happens again at the next two intersections, Helen knows she can't blame her eyesight and speaks up.

"Grace, are you all right? You just drove through three straight red lights. Didn't you see them?"

"Good heavens!" Grace exclaims. "I thought you were driving."

The old joke at the start of this module sums up the stereotypic view of older people as befuddled and forgetful. Today the view is different. Researchers have come to discount the view that the cognitive abilities of older people inevitably decline. Overall intellectual ability and specific cognitive skills, such as memory and problem solving, are more likely to remain strong. In fact, with appropriate practice and environmental stimuli, cognitive skills can actually improve.

This module discusses intellectual development during late adulthood. We look at the nature of intelligence in older people and the various ways cognitive abilities change. We also assess how different types of memory fare during late adulthood, and we consider ways to reverse intellectual declines in older people.

INTELLIGENCE

LO6 How well do people in late adulthood function intellectually?
LO7 What is the nature of intellectual change during late adulthood?

When CNN didn't renew Daniel Schorr's reporting contract in 1985, he was 69 and no one was surprised to see him retiring.

Except Daniel Schorr.

Instead of hanging up his typewriter, Schorr quickly found work at National Public Radio (NPR). Until 2 weeks before his death at the age of 93, he continued to deliver regular analysis and commentary on NPR's Weekend Edition, All Things Considered, and other news programs.

Daniel Schorr's story of durable intellectual activity is unusual but not unique. A growing number of people who depend on their wits for a livelihood, or just to keep going, have reached ages that would have been considered unthinkable when they started out—and have remained intellectually active. In the world of entertainment alone, comedians Bob Hope and George Burns and composer Irving Berlin all lived to see their hundredth birthdays.

Intelligence in Older People

The notion that older people become less cognitively adept initially arose from misinterpretations of research evidence comparing younger and older people's performance on the same IQ test, using traditional cross-sectional experimental methods. For example, a group of 30-year-olds and 70-year-olds might have taken the same test and had their performance compared.

However, cross-sectional methods do not take into account *cohort effects*—influences attributable to growing up in a particular era. If the younger group—because of when they grew up—has more education, on average, they will probably do better on the test for that reason alone. Furthermore, older people might do worse on any intelligence test with a timed portion simply because of their slower reaction time.

Longitudinal studies, which follow the same individuals for many years, are not much better. As we discussed earlier, repeated exposure to the same test may cause overfamiliarity, and participants may become unavailable over time, leaving a smaller and possibly more cognitively skilled group of subjects.

Recent Conclusions About the Nature of Intelligence in Late Adulthood

More recent research has attempted to address these drawbacks. In an ambitious—and ongoing—study of intelligence in older people, developmental psychologist K. Warner Schaie uses sequential methods, which combine cross-sectional and longitudinal methods by examining several different age groups at a number of points in time.

In Schaie's massive study, carried out in Seattle, Washington, 500 randomly chosen individuals took a battery of tests of cognitive ability. The people belonged to different age groups, starting at age 20 and extending at 5-year intervals to age 70. The participants were tested, and continue to be tested, every 7 years, and more people are recruited every year. At this point, more than 5,000 participants have been tested (Schaie, Willis, & Pennak, 2005).

The study, along with other research, supports several generalizations (Craik & Salthouse, 1999, 2008):

- Some abilities gradually decline starting at around age 25, while others stay relatively steady (see Figure 9-8). There is no uniform pattern of age-related intellectual changes. For example, fluid intelligence (the ability to deal with new problems and situations) declines with age, while crystallized intelligence (the store of information, skills, and strategies that people have acquired) remains steady and in some cases improves (Schaie, 1993).
- On average, some cognitive declines are found in all abilities by age 67, but they are minimal until the 80s. Even at age 81, less than half of the people tested showed consistent declines over the previous 7 years.

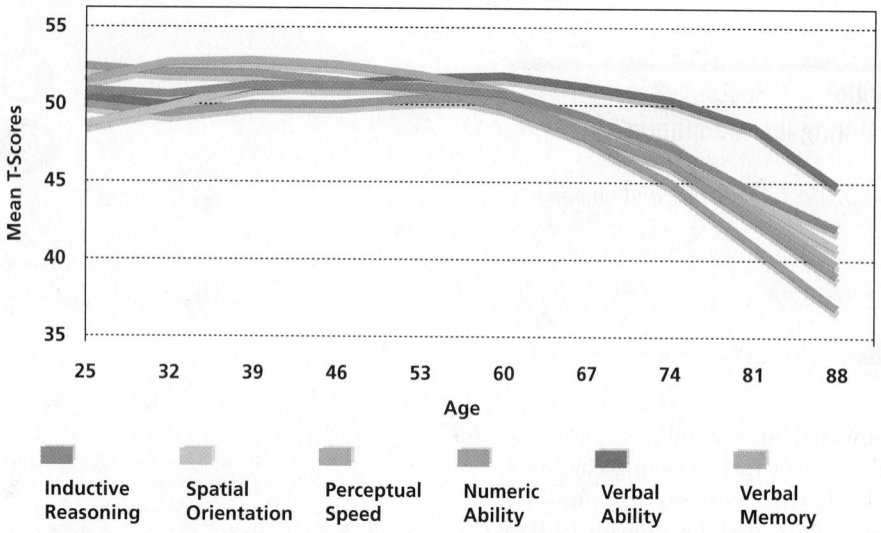

FIGURE 9-8 Changes in Intellectual Functioning
Although some intellectual abilities decline across adulthood, others stay relatively steady.
Source: Changes in Intellectual Functioning from Schaie, K. W. (1994). "The course of adult intellectual development." p. 307. American Psychologist, 49, 304–313. Copyright © 1994 by the American Psychological Association. Reproduced with permission.

- There are also significant individual differences. Some people begin to show declines in their 30s, while others show no declines until their 70s. In fact, around a third of people in their 70s score higher than the average young adult.
- Environmental and cultural factors play a role. People with no chronic disease, higher socioeconomic status (SES), involvement in an intellectually stimulating environment, a flexible personality style, a bright spouse, good perceptual processing speed, and satisfaction with one's accomplishments in midlife or early old age showed less decline.

The relationship between environmental factors and intellectual skills suggests that with stimulation, practice, and motivation, older people can maintain their mental abilities. Such *plasticity* illustrates that the changes that occur in intellectual abilities during late adulthood are not fixed. In mental life, as in so many other areas of human development, the motto "use it or lose it" fits. This suggests that there may be interventions to help older adults maintain their information processing skills.

However, not all developmentalists accept the "use it or lose it" hypothesis. Developmental psychologist Timothy Salthouse suggests that the rate of true, underlying cognitive decline in late adulthood is unaffected by mental exercise. Instead, he argues that some people—the kind who have consistently engaged in high levels of mental activity such as completing crossword puzzles—enter late adulthood with a "cognitive reserve." This allows them to continue to perform at relatively high mental levels, despite underlying declines. Still, most developmentalists accept the hypothesis that mental exercise is beneficial (Basak et al., 2008; Hertzog et al., 2008; Salthouse, 2006, 2012a, 2012b).

REVIEW, CHECK, AND APPLY

REVIEW

L06 How well do people in late adulthood function intellectually?

- Although some intellectual abilities gradually decline throughout adulthood, starting at around age 25, others stay relatively steady. For example, research shows that while fluid intelligence declines with age, crystallized intelligence remains steady, and may even improve, in late adulthood.

L07 What is the nature of intellectual change during late adulthood?

- The intellect retains considerable plasticity and can be maintained with stimulation, practice, and motivation.

CHECK YOURSELF

1. One problem with conducting cross-sectional research on aging and cognition is that this method does not take into consideration _____, the influences attributable to growing up in a particular era.
   - a genetic effects
   - b environmental effects
   - c cohort effects
   - d religious effects
2. Based on the sequential study of aging and cognition conducted by Schaie (1994), there is no uniform pattern in adulthood of age-related change across all intellectual abilities.
   - True
   - False
3. Not all developmentalists believe in the "use it or lose it" hypothesis. For example, Salthouse suggests that the rate of true, underlying cognitive decline in late adulthood is unaffected by mental exercise, and the lack of decline is a function of a larger cognitive reserve.
   - True
   - False

APPLYING LIFESPAN DEVELOPMENT

- Do you think steady or increasing crystallized intelligence can partially or fully compensate for declines in fluid intelligence? Why or why not?

✓ **Study** and **Review** on **MyPsychLab.com**

MEMORY

L08 How does memory capability change in late adulthood?

I have no trouble remembering everything that happened 40 or 50 years ago—dates, places, faces, music. But I'm going to be 90 my next birthday, November 14th, and I find I can't remember what happened yesterday. (Time, 1980, p. 57)

This is the way composer Aaron Copland described his memory in old age. Our confidence in the accuracy of Copland's analysis is strengthened by an error in his statement: On his next birthday, he would be only 80 years old!

Is memory loss inevitable? Not necessarily. Cross-cultural research reveals that in societies that hold older people in relatively high esteem, such as in China, people are less likely to show memory losses. In such cultures, positive expectations may lead people to think more positively about their own capabilities (Levy & Langer, 1994; Hess, Auman, & Colcombe, 2003).

Even those memory declines that do occur are limited primarily to *episodic memories*, which relate to specific life experiences, such as when you first visited New York City. Other types of memory, such as *semantic memories* (general knowledge and facts, such as the capital of North Dakota) and *implicit memories* (memories about which people are not consciously aware, such as how to ride a bike), are largely unaffected by age (Nilsson et al., 1997; Dixon, 2003; Nilsson, 2003).

Memory loss is not as common among Chinese elderly as it is in the West. What are some factors that contribute to cultural differences in memory loss of the elderly?

Memory capacity changes during old age. For instance, *short-term memory* slips gradually until age 70, when the decline becomes more pronounced. The largest drop is for information that is presented quickly and orally, such as when someone at a computer helpline rattles off a series of complicated steps for fixing a computer problem. In addition, older people find it harder to recall information about unfamiliar things, such as prose passages, names and faces of people, and the directions on a medicine label, possibly because new information is not registered and processed effectively when initially encountered. Still, these changes are minor and most elderly people automatically learn to compensate for them (Light, 2000; Rentz, 2010; Carmichael et al., 2012).

autobiographical memory memories about one's own life

Autobiographical Memory: Recalling the Days of Our Lives. When it comes to **autobiographical memory**, memories about one's own life, older people are as subject to lapses as younger individuals. For instance, recall frequently follows the *Pollyanna principle*, in which pleasant memories are more likely to be recalled than unpleasant memories. Similarly, people tend to forget information that is not congruent with the way they currently see themselves. Thus a strict parent who forgets that she got drunk at her high school prom is making her memories "fit" her current conception of herself (Loftus, 2004; Rubin & Greenberg, 2003; Skowronski, Walker, & Betz, 2003; Martinelli et al., 2013).

Everyone tends to recall particular periods of life better than others. As can be seen in Figure 9-9, 70-year-olds tend to recall autobiographical details from their 20s and 30s best, while 50-year-olds are likely to have more memories of their teenage years and their 20s. In both cases, recall is better for earlier years than for more recent decades, but not as complete as for very recent events (Fromholt & Larsen, 1991; Rubin, 2000).

People in late adulthood also use information that they recall in different ways from younger individuals when they make decisions. For example, they process information more slowly and may make poorer judgments when complex rules are involved, and they focus more on emotional content than younger people. On the other hand, the accumulated knowledge and experience of people in late adulthood can compensate for their deficits, particularly if they are highly motivated to make good decisions (Peters et al., 2007).

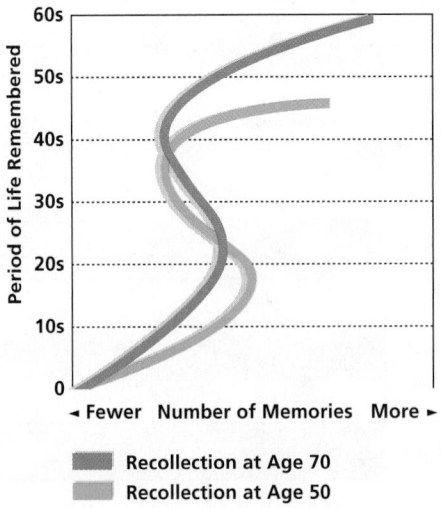

FIGURE 9-9 Remembrances of Things Past
Recall of autobiographical memories varies with age, with 70-year-olds recalling details from their 20s and 30s best, and 50-year-olds recalling memories from their teenage years and 20s. People of both ages also recall more recent memories best of all.
Source: Rubin, 1986.

Explaining Memory Changes in Old Age. Explanations for memory changes in older people focus on three main categories: environmental factors, information processing deficits, and biological factors.

- **Environmental factors.** Certain environmental factors common to many older people may cause declines in memory. For example, older people often take prescription drugs that hinder memory, and this, rather than age *per se*, may account for their lower performance on memory tasks.

An increasing number of people in late adulthood are using technology.

In addition, retirees, no longer facing job challenges, may use memory less. Further, their motivation to recall information may be lower than before, and they may be less motivated than younger people to do their best in experimental testing situations.

- **Information processing deficits.** Memory declines may also be linked to changes in information processing capabilities. The ability to inhibit irrelevant information and thoughts that interfere with problem solving may decrease, and the speed of information processing may decline (Palfai, Halperin, & Hoyer, 2003; Salthouse, Atkinson, & Berish, 2003).

  Another information processing view suggests that older adults lose the ability to concentrate on new material and have difficulty paying attention to appropriate stimuli and organizing material in memory. According to this information-processing-deficit approach, which has substantial research support, older people use less efficient processes to retrieve information from memory. This leads to declines in recall abilities (Castel & Craik, 2003; Luo & Craik, 2008, 2009).
- **Biological factors.** The last of the major approaches concentrates on biological factors. According to this view, memory changes are a result of brain and body deterioration. For instance, declines in episodic memory may be related to the deterioration of the frontal lobes of the brain or a reduction in estrogen. Some studies also show a loss of cells in the hippocampus, which is critical to memory. However, some memory deficits occur without any evidence of underlying biological deterioration (Eberling et al., 2004; Lye et al., 2004; Bird & Burgess, 2008; Stevens et al., 2008).

Never Too Late to Learn

Martha Tilden and Jim Hertz, both 71, loved the Metropolitan Opera House tour, the talk by the famous tenor, the ballet, and the lectures they attended during the "Lincoln Center Festival" trip they are just finishing.

Martha and Jim are veterans of Road Scholar (formerly Elderhostel), which has updated itself by scrapping any suggestion of "elderness" or cheap student housing. All the educational programs that Martha and Jim have taken have featured comfortable hotel or dorm rooms and mixed-age events. Now Martha and Jim are discussing their next program, trying to decide between a wildlife trip to Ontario and a "Building Bridges to Islam" program in Virginia.

Road Scholar is one of the largest educational program for people in late adulthood, offering travel and learning classes worldwide. Represented on campuses across the world, Road Scholar is further evidence that intellectual growth and change continue throughout people's lives. As we saw earlier, exercising cognitive skills may help older adults maintain their intellectual functioning (Simson, Wilson, & Harlow-Rosentraub, 2006).

In addition, many public colleges encourage senior citizens to enroll in classes by offering free tuition. In addition, some retirement communities are located at or near college campuses (Powell, 2004).

Although some elderly people are doubtful about their intellectual capabilities and consequently hesitate to compete with younger students in regular classes, their concern is largely misplaced. Older adults often have no trouble maintaining their standing in rigorous college classes. Furthermore, professors and other students generally find the presence of older people, with their varied and substantial life experiences, a real educational benefit (Simson et al., 2006).

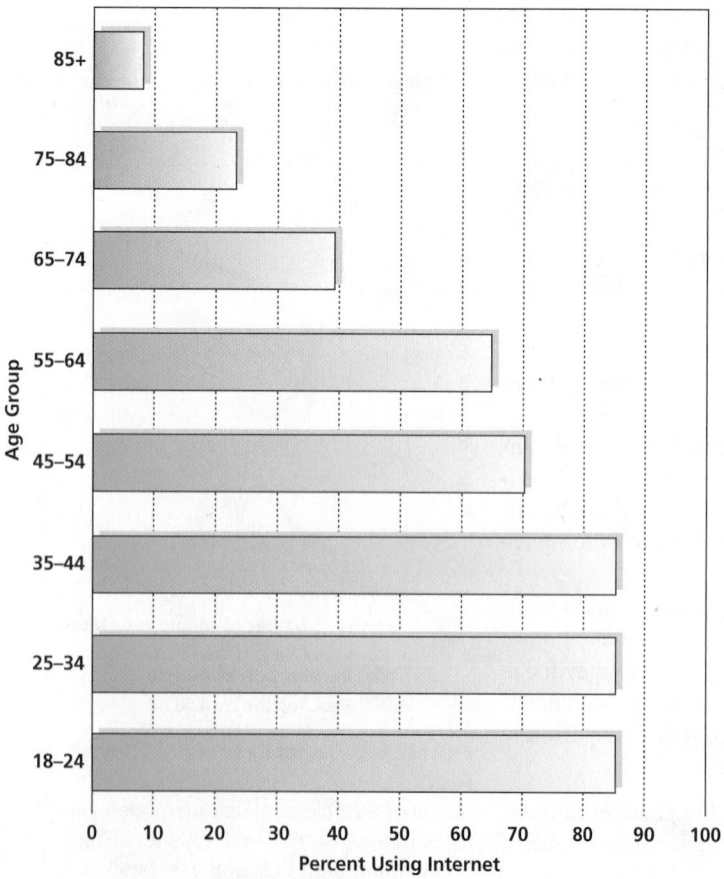

FIGURE 9-10 Technology Use and Age
Older individuals in the United States are far less likely to use the Internet than those who are younger.
Source: Charness & Boot, 2009, Figure 1A.

Technology and Learning in Late Adulthood

One of the biggest generational divides involves the use of technology. People 65 and older are far less likely to use technology than younger individuals (see Figure 9-10).

Why are older people less likely to use technology? One reason is that they are less interested and motivated, in part because they are less likely to be working and therefore less in need of learning new technology skills. But another barrier is cognitive. For example, because fluid intelligence (the ability to deal with new problems and situations) shows some declines with age, this may impact on the ability to learn technology (Ownby et al., 2008; Charness & Boot, 2009).

This hardly means that people in late adulthood are unable to learn to use technology. In fact, an increasing number of individuals are using email and social networking sites such as Facebook. It is likely that the lag in the adoption of technology between younger and older adults will decrease as technology use becomes even more widespread in the general society (Lee Czaja, & Sharit, 2009).

REVIEW, CHECK, AND APPLY

REVIEW

L08 How does memory capability change in late adulthood?

- Declines in memory affect mainly episodic memories and short-term memory.
- Explanations of memory changes in old age have focused on environmental factors, information processing declines, and biological factors.

CHECK YOURSELF

1. When it comes to autobiographical memories, older individuals, like younger individuals, follow the _____, in that they are more likely to remember pleasant memories.
   - a saliency effect
   - b environmental effect
   - c Pollyanna principle
   - d positive effect
2. Explanations for changes in memory tend to focus on three main categories: environmental factors, biological factors, and _____.
   - a social support
   - b life changes
   - c information processing deficits
   - d personal influences
3. Despite concerns about memory and intellectual capabilities, older adults have no trouble maintaining their standing in rigorous college classes.
   - True
   - False

APPLYING LIFESPAN DEVELOPMENT

- How might cultural factors, such as the esteem in which a society holds its older members, work to affect an older person's memory performance?

✓ **Study** and **Review** on **MyPsychLab.com**

MODULE 9.3

SOCIAL AND PERSONALITY DEVELOPMENT IN LATE ADULTHOOD

Reaching Out, Not Fading Out

Following a successful liver transplant in his late 60s, Edward Murphy decided not to retire but to continue his freelance editing business. "Not to retire was an easy choice," he says. "When you're freelance, the boundary between working and retirement is more like a dotted line between semi-working and semi-retirement."

At the same time, Edward, already in possession of advanced degrees, began taking courses at nearby Greenfield Community College. "I have to keep learning no matter how old I get, and I love meeting new people. I took a couple of French courses last year, and this year I'm starting Spanish. To me it makes sense. I love to travel, and I love to talk to people. And I firmly believe you should be able to speak at least a little of the local language when you travel, instead of only what I call LGE—Loud, Gesticulated English."

Edward's latest venture is a blog. "I noticed in Spanish class that my learning was aided by a lucky break: I went to elementary school in the 1950s, when grammar was actually taught. As a way to help my classmates, I started a blog on grammar, with a focus on diagramming sentences. I can't say there's been a gold rush to my site, but blogging keeps me engaged with a topic I love and a growing community of fellow grammar geeks."

The desire to connect and interact with others is not exclusive to any age group. For older people such as Edward Murphy, the Internet offers an opportunity to establish relationships at a time of life when connections with family members and friends are often broken by central as in earlier stages of the life span. We begin by considering how personality continues to develop, and we examine various ways people can age successfully. We also look at how culture governs the way we treat older people.

We then consider how various societal factors affect older adults. We discuss living arrangements and economic and financial issues. Next, we examine the influence of work and retirement on elderly individuals.

Finally, we consider relationships in late adulthood among married couples, relatives, and friends. We will see how social networks play an important—and sustaining—role in people's lives. We end with a discussion of elder abuse.

PERSONALITY DEVELOPMENT AND SUCCESSFUL AGING

LO9 In what ways does personality develop during late adulthood?
LO10 How do people deal with aging?

Greta Roach has a puckish manner, a habit of nudging you when she is about to say something funny. This happens often, because that is how she views the world. Even last year's knee injury, which forced her to drop out of her bowling league and halted the march of blue-and-chrome trophies across her living-room table, is not—in her mind—a frailty of age.

Roach, 93, takes the same spirited approach to life in her 90s as she did in her 20s, something not all elders can do.... "I enjoy life. I belong to all the clubs. I love to talk on the telephone. I write to my old friends." She pauses. "Those that are still alive." (Pappano, 1994, pp. 19, 30)

In many ways, Roach, with her wit, high spirits, and enormous activity level, is the same person she was in earlier years. Yet for other older adults, time and circumstances bring changes in their outlook on life, their views of themselves, and perhaps even their basic personalities. In fact, one of the fundamental questions asked by lifespan developmentalists concerns the degree to which personality remains stable or changes in later adulthood.

Continuity and Change in Personality During Late Adulthood

Is personality relatively stable throughout adulthood, or does it vary significantly? The answer depends on which facets of personality we consider. According to developmental psychologists Paul Costa and Robert McCrae, whose work we discussed earlier, the "Big Five" basic personality traits (neuroticism, extraversion, openness, agreeableness, and conscientiousness) are remarkably stable across adulthood. For instance, even-tempered people at 20 are still even-tempered at 75, and people who hold positive self-concepts early in adulthood still view themselves positively in late adulthood (Costa & McCrae, 1988, 1989, 1997; McCrae & Costa, 1990, 2003; Terracciano, McCrae, & Costa, 2010).

For example, at 93, Greta Roach is active and humorous, as she was in her 20s. There seems to be a fundamental continuity to personality (Field & Millsap, 1991).

Despite this continuity, change is still possible. Profound changes in people's social environments may produce personality changes. What is important to a person at 80 is not necessarily the same as what was important at 40.

To account for these changes, some theorists have focused on the discontinuities of development. As we'll see next, Erik Erikson, Robert Peck, Daniel Levinson, and Bernice Neugarten have examined personality changes that accompany new challenges in later adulthood.

Ego Integrity Versus Despair: Erikson's Final Stage. Psychoanalyst Erik Erikson characterizes late adulthood as the time when people move into the last of life's eight stages of psychosocial development. Labeled the **ego-integrity-versus-despair stage**, this period is characterized by a process of looking back over one's life, evaluating it, and coming to terms with it.

ego-integrity-versus-despair stage Erikson's final stage of life, characterized by a process of looking back over one's life, evaluating it, and coming to terms with it

People who are successful in this stage of development experience satisfaction and accomplishment, which Erikson terms "integrity." When people achieve integrity, they feel they have fulfilled the possibilities that have come their way in life, and they have few regrets. Other people look back on their lives with dissatisfaction. They may feel that they have missed important opportunities and have not accomplished what they wished. Such individuals may be unhappy, depressed, angry, or despondent over what they have done, or failed to do, with their lives—in short, they despair.

Peck's Developmental Tasks. Although Erikson's approach provides a picture of the broad possibilities of later adulthood, other theorists offer a more differentiated view of the final stage of life. Psychologist Robert Peck (1968) suggests that personality development in elderly people is occupied by three major developmental tasks or challenges.

In Peck's view—part of a comprehensive description of change across adulthood—the first task in old age is to redefine oneself in ways that do not relate to work roles or occupations. He labels this stage **redefinition of self versus preoccupation with work role**. As we will see, the changes that occur when people stop working can trigger a difficult adjustment in the way people view themselves. Peck suggests that people must adjust their values to place less emphasis on themselves as workers or professionals and more on attributes that don't involve work, such as being a grandparent or a gardener.

The second major developmental task in late adulthood, according to Peck, is **body transcendence versus body preoccupation**. Elderly individuals can undergo significant changes in their physical abilities as a result of aging. In the body-transcendence-versus-body-preoccupation stage, people must learn to cope with and move beyond those physical changes (transcendence). If they don't, they become preoccupied with their physical deterioration, to the detriment of their personality development. Greta Roach, who gave up bowling only in her 90s, is an example of coping well with the physical changes of aging.

The third developmental task in old age is **ego transcendence versus ego preoccupation**, in which elderly people must come to grips with their coming death. They need to understand that although death is inevitable, and probably not too far off, they have made contributions to society. If they see these contributions, which can take the form of children or work and civic activities, as lasting beyond their own lives, they will experience ego transcendence. If not, they may become preoccupied with asking whether their lives had value and worth to society.

Levinson's Final Season: The Winter of Life. Daniel Levinson's theory of adult development does not focus as much on the challenges that aging adults must overcome. Instead, he looks at the processes that can lead to personality change as we grow old. According to Levinson, people enter late adulthood by passing through a transition stage that typically

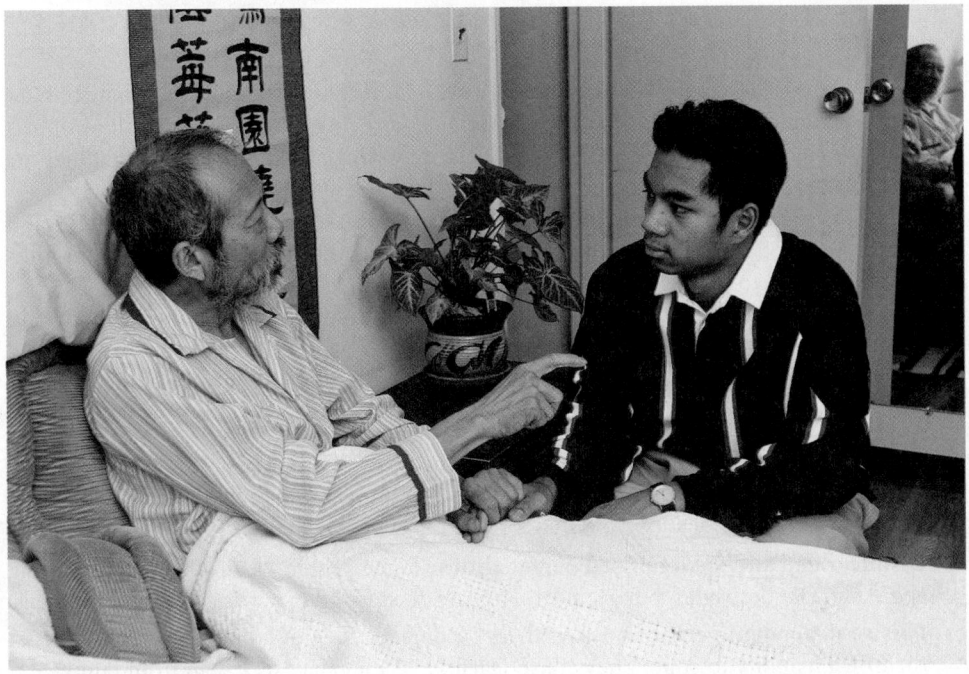

Older adults may become "venerated elders," whose advice is sought and relied upon.

redefinition of self versus preoccupation with work role the theory that those in old age must redefine themselves in ways that do not relate to their work roles or occupations

body transcendence versus body preoccupation a period in which people must learn to cope with and move beyond changes in physical capabilities as a result of aging

ego transcendence versus ego preoccupation the period in which elderly people must come to grips with their coming death

Roz Chast

occurs around ages 60 to 65 (Levinson, 1986, 1992). During this stage, people come to view themselves as entering late adulthood—or, ultimately, as being "old." Knowing full well society's negative stereotypes about elderly individuals, they struggle with the notion that they are now in this category.

According to Levinson, people come to realize that they are no longer on the center stage, but are playing bit parts. This loss of power, respect, and authority may be difficult for individuals accustomed to having control in their lives.

On the other hand, people in late adulthood can serve as resources to younger individuals, and they may find that they are viewed as "venerated elders" whose advice is sought and relied upon. Furthermore, old age can bring a new freedom to do things simply for enjoyment and pleasure, rather than as obligations.

Coping With Aging: Neugarten's Study. Bernice Neugarten (1972, 1977)—in what became a classic study—examined the different ways that people cope with aging. Neugarten found four different personality types in her research on people in their 70s:

- **Disintegrated and disorganized personalities.** Some people are unable to accept aging and experience despair as they get older. They are often found in nursing homes or hospitals.
- **Passive-dependent personalities.** Others become fearful—of falling ill, of the future, of their own inability to cope. They are so fearful that they may seek help from family and care providers, even when they don't need it.

- **Defended personalities.** Others respond to the fear of aging quite differently—by trying to stop it in its tracks. They may attempt to act young, exercising vigorously and engaging in youthful activities. Unfortunately, they may set unrealistic expectations and run the risk of disappointment as a result.
- **Integrated personalities.** The most successful individuals cope comfortably with aging. They accept it with a sense of self-dignity.

Neugarten found that the majority of the people she studied fell into the final category. They acknowledged aging, and could look back at their lives and gaze into the future with acceptance.

Life Review and Reminiscence: The Common Theme of Personality Development. **Life review**, in which people examine and evaluate their lives, is a major thread running through the work of Erikson, Peck, Neugarten, and Levinson, and a common theme among personality theorists who focus on late adulthood.

According to gerontologist Robert Butler (2002), life review is triggered by the increasingly obvious prospect of death. People look back on their lives, remembering and reconsidering what has happened to them. Far from being a harmful process of reliving the past, wallowing in past problems, and reviving old wounds, life review usually leads to a better understanding of the past. People may resolve lingering problems and conflicts with others, such as an estrangement from a child, and they may feel they can face their current lives with greater serenity (Bohlmeijer et al., 2007; Bohlmeijer, Westerhof, & de Jong, 2008; Korte, Westerhof, & Bohlmeijer, 2012).

Life review offers other benefits, including a sense of mutuality, a feeling of interconnectedness with others. Moreover, it can be a source of social interaction, as older adults share their experiences with others (Sherman, 1991; Parks, Sanna, & Posey, 2003).

Reminiscence may even have cognitive benefits, improving memory. By reflecting on the past, people activate a variety of memories, which may trigger other memories and bring back sights, sounds, and even smells of the past (Kartman, 1991; Brinker, 2013).

On the other hand, life review can sometimes produce declines in psychological functioning. If people become obsessive about the past, reliving old insults and mistakes that cannot be rectified, they may end up feeling guilt, depression, and anger against acquaintances who may not even still be alive (DeGenova, 1993; Cappeliez, Guindon, & Robitaille, 2008).

Overall, though, the process of life review and reminiscence can play an important role by providing continuity between past and present, and increasing awareness of the contemporary world. It can also provide new insights into the past and into others, allowing people to continue personality growth and to function more effectively in the present (Coleman, 2005; Haber, 2006; Alwin, 2012).

Age Stratification Approaches to Late Adulthood

Age, like race and gender, provides a way of ranking people within a society. **Age stratification theories** suggest that economic resources, power, and privilege are distributed unequally among people at different stages of life. Such inequality is particularly pronounced during late adulthood.

Even as medical advances have lengthened the life span, power and prestige for the elderly have eroded, at least in highly industrialized societies. The peak earning years are the 50s; later, earnings tend to decline. Further, younger people are often physically removed from their elders, and their increased independence may make older adults feel less important. In addition, rapidly changing technology makes older adults seem out of date and lacking in important skills. Ultimately, they are seen as not particularly productive members of society and, in some cases, simply irrelevant (Cohn, 1982; Macionis, 2001). According to Levinson's theory, older people are keenly aware of their decline in status, and adjusting to it is the major transition of late adulthood.

Age stratification theories help explain why aging is viewed more positively in less industrialized societies. In predominantly agricultural societies, older people accumulate control over important resources such as animals and land. In such societies, the concept of retirement is unknown. Older individuals (especially males) are highly respected because they continue to be involved in daily activities central to the society. Furthermore, because the pace of

life review the point in life in which people examine and evaluate their lives

age stratification theories the view that an unequal distribution of economic resources, power, and privilege exists among people at different stages of life

Cultural Dimensions

How Culture Shapes the Way We Treat People in Late Adulthood

Views of late adulthood are colored by culture. For example, compared to Western cultures, Asian societies generally hold elderly people, particularly family members, in higher esteem. Although this is changing in rapidly industrializing areas of Asia, the view of aging and the treatment of people in late adulthood still tend to be more positive than in Western cultures (Cobbe, 2003; Degnen, 2007; Smith & Hung, 2012).

What is it about Asian cultures that leads to esteem for old age? In general, cultures that value the elderly are relatively homogeneous in socioeconomic terms. In addition, the roles that people play in those societies entail greater responsibility with increasing age, and elderly people control resources to a relatively large extent.

Moreover, the roles of people in Asian societies display more continuity throughout the life span than in Western cultures, and older adults continue to engage in activities that are valued by society. Finally, Asian cultures are more organized around extended families in which the older generations are well integrated into the family structure (Fry, 1985; Sangree, 1989). In such an arrangement, younger family members tend to rely on older members to share their considerable accumulated wisdom.

What aspects of Asian cultures lead them to hold higher levels of esteem for old age?

On the other hand, even societies that articulate strong ideals regarding older adults do not always live up to those standards. For instance, the attitudes of Chinese people, typified by admiration, respect, and even worship for individuals in late adulthood, are more positive than their actual behavior in all but the most elite segment of the society. Furthermore, sons and their wives—but not daughters—are typically expected to care for elderly parents; parents with only daughters may find themselves with no one to care for them. In short, broad, global statements about how older adults are treated in a given society almost always mask exceptions (Comunian & Gielen, 2000; Browne, 2010).

Asian cultures are not alone in esteeming the elderly. In many Latino cultures, the elderly are thought to have a special inner strength, and in many African cultures, reaching an old age is seen as a sign of divine intervention (Diop, 1989; Holmes & Holmes, 1995; Lehr, Seiler, & Thomae, 2000).

change in agricultural societies is slower than in more technological societies, people in late adulthood have considerable relevant wisdom. Nor is respect for elders limited to agricultural countries; it is a characteristic of a variety of cultures. **Watch** the **Video** *Work and Retirement Across Cultures* in **MyPsychLab.**

Does Age Bring Wisdom?

One of the benefits of age is supposed to be wisdom. But do people gain wisdom as they become older?

In fact we don't know for sure, because the concept of **wisdom**—expert knowledge in the practical aspects of life—is only recently receiving attention from gerontologists and other researchers. This is partly due to the difficulty of defining and measuring the concept (Helmuth, 2003; Brugman, 2006). Wisdom can be seen as reflecting an accumulation of knowledge, experience, and contemplation, and by this definition, aging contributes to wisdom (Kunzmann & Baltes, 2005; Staudinger, 2008; Randall, 2012).

wisdom expert knowledge in the practical aspects of life

Distinguishing wisdom from intelligence is tricky. Some researchers have made suggestions: While knowledge derived from intelligence is related to the here and now, wisdom is more timeless. While intelligence permits a person to think logically and systematically, wisdom provides an understanding of human behavior. According to psychologist Robert

Sternberg, intelligence permits humans to invent the atom bomb, while wisdom prevents them from using it (Seppa, 1997).

Measuring wisdom is difficult. Ursula Staudinger and Paul Baltes (2000) designed a study showing that it is possible to assess people reliably on the concept. Pairs of people ranging in age from 20 to 70 discussed difficulties relating to life events. One problem involved someone who gets a phone call from a friend who is planning to commit suicide. Another involved a 14-year-old girl who wanted to move out of her family home immediately. Participants were asked what they should do and consider.

Although there were no absolute right or wrong answers, the responses were evaluated against several criteria, including how much factual knowledge they brought to bear; their knowledge of decision-making strategies; how well the participants considered the context of the central character's life span and values; and their recognition that there might not be a single, absolute solution. Using these criteria, the older participants' responses were wiser than those of younger participants.

The study also found that the older participants benefited more from an experimental condition designed to promote wise thinking, and other research suggests that the very wisest individuals may be older adults.

Other research has looked at wisdom in terms of the development of theory of mind—the ability to make inferences about others' thoughts, feelings, and intentions, their mental states. Although the research findings are mixed, some research finds that older adults, with their added years of experience to draw upon, utilize a more sophisticated theory of mind (Karelitz, Jarvin, & Sternberg, 2010; Rakoczy, Harder-Kasten, & Sturm, 2012).

Successful Aging: What Is the Secret?

At age 77, Elinor Reynolds spends most of her time at home, leading a quiet, routine existence. Never married, Elinor receives visits from her two sisters every few weeks, and some of her nieces and nephews stop by on occasion. But for the most part, she keeps to herself. When asked, she says she is quite happy.

In contrast, Carrie Masterson, also 77, is involved in something different almost every day. If she is not visiting the senior center and participating in some activity, she is out shopping. Her daughter complains that Carrie is "never home" when she tries to reach her by phone, and Carrie replies that she has never been busier—or happier.

Clearly, there is no single way to age successfully. How people age depends on personality factors and people's circumstances. Some people become progressively less involved with day-to-day activities, while others maintain active ties to people and their personal interests. Three major approaches provide explanations: disengagement theory, activity theory, and continuity theory.

Disengagement Theory: Gradual Retreat. According to **disengagement theory**, late adulthood often involves a gradual withdrawal from the world on physical, psychological, and social levels (Cummings & Henry, 1961). On a physical level, elderly people have lower energy levels and slow down progressively. Psychologically, they begin to withdraw, showing less interest in the world around them and spending more time looking inward. Finally, on a social level, they engage in fewer interactions—both day-to-day, face-to-face encounters and participation in society as a whole. Older adults also become less involved and invested in the lives of others (Quinnan, 1997; Cashdollar et al., 2013).

Disengagement theory suggests that withdrawal is a mutual process. Because of norms and expectations about aging, society begins to disengage from those in late adulthood. For example, mandatory retirement ages compel elderly people to withdraw from work, which accelerates disengagement.

While there is logic to disengagement theory, research support is limited. Furthermore, the theory has been criticized because it takes the failure of society to provide sufficient opportunities for meaningful engagement during late adulthood and then, in a sense, blames people in this age group for not being engaged.

Of course, some degree of disengagement is not necessarily all negative. For example, a gradual withdrawal in late adulthood may permit people to become more reflective about their own lives and less constrained by social roles. In addition, people can become more discerning in their social relationships, focusing on those who best meet their needs (Settersten, 2002; Wrosch, Bauer, & Scheier, 2005; Liang & Luo, 2012).

disengagement theory the period in late adulthood that marks a gradual withdrawal from the world on physical, psychological, and social levels

Today, most gerontologists reject disengagement theory, pointing out that disengagement is relatively uncommon. In most cases, people remain engaged, active, and busy throughout old age, and (especially in non-Western cultures) the expectation is that people will remain actively involved in everyday life. Clearly, disengagement is not an automatic, universal process (Bergstrom & Holmes, 2000; Crosnoe & Elder, 2002).

Activity Theory: Continued Involvement. Although early findings were consistent with disengagement theory, later research was not so supportive. For example, a follow-up study found that although some of the subjects were happily disengaged, others, who had remained involved and active, were as happy as—and sometimes happier than—those who disengaged. Furthermore, people in many non-Western cultures remain engaged, active, and busy throughout old age, and are expected to do so. Clearly, disengagement is not a universal process (Havighurst, 1973; Bergstrom & Holmes, 2000; Crosnoe & Elder, 2002).

The lack of support for disengagement theory led to an alternative. **Activity theory** suggests that successful aging occurs when people maintain the interests and activities of middle age and the amount and type of their social interactions. According to this perspective, happiness and satisfaction with life spring from involvement with the world (Charles, Reynolds, & Gatz, 2001; Consedine, Magai, & King, 2004; Hutchinson & Wexler, 2007).

Activity theory suggests that continuation of activities is important. Even when continuation is no longer possible—such as continuing work after retirement—activity theory argues that successful aging occurs when replacement activities are found.

But activity theory, like disengagement theory, is not the full story. For one thing, activity theory makes little distinction among activities. Not every activity will have an equal impact on a person's satisfaction with life; in fact, the nature and quality of the activities are likely to be more critical than mere quantity or frequency (Burrus-Bammel & Bammel, 1985; Adams, 2004).

A more significant concern is that for some people in late adulthood, the principle of "less is more" clearly holds: less activity brings greater enjoyment because they can slow down and do only the things that bring them the greatest satisfaction. In fact, some people view the ability to moderate their pace as one of the bounties of late adulthood. For them, a relatively inactive, and perhaps even solitary, existence is welcome (Ward, 1984; Hansson & Carpenter, 1994).

From a social worker's perspective: How might cultural factors affect an older person's likelihood of pursuing either the disengagement theory or the activity theory?

Continuity Theory: A Compromise Position. Neither disengagement theory nor activity theory provides a complete picture of successful aging (Johnson & Barer, 1992; Rapkin & Fischer, 1992; Ouwehand, de Ridder, & Bensing, 2007). A compromise view is needed. **Continuity theory** suggests that people simply need to maintain their desired level of involvement in society in order to maximize their sense of well-being and self-esteem (Whitbourne, 2001; Atchley, 2003; Pushkar et al., 2010).

According to continuity theory, those who were highly active and social will be happiest if they largely remain so. Those who enjoy solitude and solitary interests, such as reading or walks in the woods, will be happiest pursuing that level of sociability (Holahan & Chapman, 2002).

It is also clear that most older adults experience positive emotions as frequently as younger individuals. Furthermore, they become more skilled at regulating their emotions.

Other factors enhance happiness during late adulthood. The importance of physical and mental health cannot be overestimated, and having enough financial security to provide for basic needs is critical. In addition, a sense of autonomy, independence, and personal control over one's life is a significant advantage (Charles, Mather, & Carstensen, 2003; Charles & Carstensen, 2010; Vacha-Haase, Hil, & Bermingham, 2012).

Finally, as we discussed earlier, people's perceptions can influence their happiness and satisfaction. Those who view late adulthood favorably are apt to perceive themselves more positively than those who view old age in a more pessimistic way (Levy, Slade, & Kasl, 2002; Levy, 2003).

activity theory the theory suggesting that successful aging occurs when people maintain the interests, activities, and social interactions with which they were involved during middle age

continuity theory the theory suggesting that people need to maintain their desired level of involvement in society in order to maximize their sense of well-being and self-esteem

Ultimately, surveys find that as a group, people in late adulthood report being happier than younger people. And it's not that those over 65 have always been happier. Instead, being older seems to bring a degree of contentment in the majority of people (Yang, 2008). **Watch** the **Video** *Late Adulthood, Happiness and Attitude Toward Aging: Chris* in **MyPsychLab**.

Selective Optimization With Compensation: A General Model of Successful Aging. In considering the factors that lead to successful aging, developmental psychologists Paul Baltes and Margret Baltes focus on the "selective optimization with compensation" model. As we noted earlier, the assumption underlying the model is that late adulthood brings with it changes and losses in underlying capabilities, which vary from one person to another. However, it is possible to overcome such shifts in capabilities through selective optimization.

Selective optimization is the process by which people concentrate on particular skill areas to compensate for losses in other areas. They do this to fortify their general motivational, cognitive, and physical resources. A person who has run marathons all her life may have to cut back or give up other activities entirely in order to increase her training. By giving up other activities, she may be able to maintain her running skills through concentration on them (Baltes & Freund, 2003; Rapp, Krampe, & Baltes, 2006; Burnett-Wolle & Godbey, 2007; Scheibner & Leathem, 2012).

Similarly, elderly individuals engage in compensation for age-related losses. For instance, a person may compensate for a hearing loss by using a hearing aid. Piano virtuoso Arthur Rubinstein provides another example of selective optimization with compensation. In his later years, he maintained his concert career by reducing the number of pieces he played at concerts—an example of being selective—and by practicing those pieces more often—optimization. Finally, in an example of compensation, he slowed down the tempo of musical passages immediately preceding faster passages, thereby fostering the illusion that he was playing as fast as ever (Baltes & Baltes, 1990).

In short, the model of selective optimization with compensation illustrates the fundamentals of successful aging. Although late adulthood may bring changes in capabilities, people who focus on making the most of particular areas may be able to compensate for limitations and losses. The outcome is a life that is reduced in some areas, but transformed and modified and, ultimately, successful.

selective optimization the process by which people concentrate on selected skill areas to compensate for losses in other areas

REVIEW, CHECK, AND APPLY

REVIEW

L09 In what ways does personality develop during late adulthood?

- Erikson calls older adulthood the ego-integrity-versus-despair stage, Peck focuses on three tasks that define the period, Levinson suggests that older people can experience liberation and self-regard, and Neugarten focuses on the ways people cope with aging.

L010 How do people deal with aging?

- Societies in which elderly people are respected are generally characterized by social homogeneity, extended families, responsible roles for older people, and control of significant resources by older people.
- Disengagement theory suggests that older people gradually withdraw from the world, while activity theory suggests that the happiest people continue to be engaged with the world. A compromise theory—continuity theory—may be the most useful approach to successful aging, and the most successful model for aging may be selective optimization with compensation.

CHECK YOURSELF

1. According to Erikson, individuals in late adulthood engage in looking back over their lives, evaluating their experiences and coming to terms with decisions. This is also known as _____.
   - a ego transcendence versus ego preoccupation
   - b acceptance of growing old
   - c generativity versus stagnation
   - d ego integrity versus despair
2. According to Peck, the first major developmental task is to decide on your identity even though you are no longer employed. This is also known as _____.
   - a redefinition of self versus preoccupation with work role
   - b ego integrity versus despair
   - c body transcendence versus body preoccupation
   - d ego transcendence versus ego preoccupation
3. According to Levinson, as individuals enter late adulthood one of the hardest struggles they experience is the acceptance that they are "old."
   - True
   - False

APPLYING LIFESPAN DEVELOPMENT

- How might personality traits account for success or failure in achieving satisfaction through the life review process?

Study and **Review** on **MyPsychLab.com**

THE DAILY LIFE OF LATE ADULTHOOD

LO11 What is the quality of life in late adulthood?
LO12 What is the nature of retirement?

Before I retired 10 years ago, everyone told me I'd miss work, get lonely, and feel flat without the challenges of business. Baloney! This is the best time of my life! Miss work? No way. What's to miss? Meetings? Training sessions? Evaluations? Sure, there's less money and people, but I have all I need with my savings, my hobbies, and my traveling.

This positive view of life in late adulthood was expressed by a 75-year-old retired insurance worker. Although the story is certainly not the same for all retirees, many, if not most, find their post-work lives happy and involving. We will consider some of the ways in which people lead their lives in late adulthood, beginning with where they live.

Living in a multigenerational setting with children and their families can be rewarding and helpful for those in late adulthood. Are there any disadvantages to this type of situation? What are some solutions?

Living Arrangements: The Places and Spaces of Their Lives

Think "old age," and your thoughts are likely to turn to nursing homes. But the reality is different. Only 5 percent of people finish their lives in nursing homes; most live out their entire lives in home environments, typically with at least one family member.

Living at Home. Many older adults live alone. People over 65 represent a quarter of America's 9.6 million single-person households. Roughly two-thirds of people over 65 live with other members of the family, mostly spouses. Some older adults live with their siblings, and others live in multigenerational settings with their children, grandchildren, and even great-grandchildren.

The setting in which an older adult lives has varied effects. For married couples, living with a spouse represents continuity. On the other hand, moving in with children represents an adjustment to a multigenerational setting that can be jarring. Not only is there a potential loss of independence and privacy, but older adults may feel uncomfortable with the way their children are raising their grandchildren. Unless there are household ground rules about people's roles, conflicts can arise (Navarro, 2006).

For some groups, living in extended families is more typical than for other groups. For instance, African Americans are more likely than whites to live in multigenerational families. Furthermore, the amount of influence that family members have over one another and the interdependence of extended families are generally greater in African American, Asian American, and Hispanic families than in Caucasian families (Becker, Beyene, & Newsom, 2003).

Specialized Living Environments. For some 10 percent of those in late adulthood, home is an institution. In fact, there are many types of specialized environments in which elderly people live.

One of the more recent innovations is the **continuing-care community**, typically an environment in which all the residents are of retirement age or older. The community provides various levels of care, and residents sign contracts for the level they need. In many such communities, people start out in separate houses or apartments, living either independently or with occasional home care. As they age, they may move into *assisted living*, which involves independent housing supported by medical providers to the extent required. Continuing care ultimately extends all the way to full-time nursing care, which is often provided at an on-site nursing home.

Continuing-care communities tend to be fairly homogeneous in terms of religious, racial, and ethnic backgrounds, and they are often organized by private or religious organizations. Because joining may involve a substantial initial payment, members tend to be relatively well-off. Increasingly, though, continuing-care communities are making efforts to increase diversity and also to enhance intergenerational interaction by establishing day-care centers on the premises and developing programs that involve younger populations (Barton, 1997; Chaker, 2003; Berkman, 2006).

Several types of nursing institutions exist, ranging from those that provide part-time day care to homes that offer 24-hour-a-day, live-in care. In **adult day-care facilities**, elderly individuals

continuing-care community a community that offers an environment in which all the residents are of retirement age or older

adult day-care facilities a facility in which elderly individuals receive care only during the day, but spend nights and weekends in their own homes receive care only during the day, but spend nights and weekends in their own homes. During the time that they are at the facility, people receive nursing care, take their meals, and participate in scheduled activities. Sometimes adult facilities are combined with infant and child day-care programs, an arrangement that allows for interaction between the old and the young (Ritchie, 2003; Tse & Howie, 2005; Gitlin et al., 2006; Dabelko & Zimmerman, 2008).

Other institutional settings offer more extensive care. The most intensive are **skilled-nursing facilities**, which provide full-time nursing care for people who have chronic illnesses or are recovering from a temporary medical condition. The number of people living in nursing homes increases dramatically with age. Specifically, 1.3 percent of 65- to 74-years-old, 4.4 percent of those 75 to 84, and 15.4 percent of persons 85 and older live in nursing homes and other institutions (Administration on Aging, 2010).

The more intensive the care, the greater the adjustment required of residents. Although some newcomers adjust relatively rapidly, the loss of independence may lead to difficulties. In addition, elderly people are as susceptible as other people to society's stereotypes about nursing homes, and their expectations may be negative. They may see themselves as just marking time until they die, forgotten and discarded by a society that venerates youth (Baltes, 1996; Natan, 2008; Kostka & Jachimowicz, 2010).

Institutionalism and Learned Helplessness. Although the fears of those in nursing homes may be exaggerated, they can lead to **institutionalism**, a psychological state in which people develop apathy, indifference, and a lack of caring about themselves. Institutionalism is brought about, in part, by *learned helplessness*, a belief that one has no control over one's environment (Butler & Lewis, 1981; Peterson & Park, 2007).

The sense of helplessness brought about by institutionalism can be literally deadly. When people enter nursing homes in late adulthood, they lose control over their most basic activities. They may be told when and what to eat, when to sleep, and even when to go to the bathroom (Wolinsky, Wyrwich, & Babu, 2003; Iecovich & Biderman, 2012).

A classic experiment showed the consequences of such a loss of control. Psychologists Ellen Langer and Irving Janis (1979) divided elderly residents of a nursing home into two groups. One group was encouraged to make choices about their day-to-day activities. The other group was given no choices and was encouraged to let the nursing home staff care for them. The results were clear. The participants who had choices were not only happier, they were also healthier. In fact, 18 months after the experiment began, only 15 percent of the choice group had died—compared to 30 percent of the comparison group.

skilled-nursing facilities a facility that provides full-time nursing care for people who have chronic illnesses or are recovering from a temporary medical condition

institutionalism a psychological state in which people in nursing homes develop apathy, indifference, and a lack of caring about themselves

During late adulthood, the range of socioeconomic well-being mirrors that of earlier years.

In short, loss of control can have a profound effect on well-being. The best nursing homes go out of their way to permit residents to make basic life decisions and maintain a sense of control over their lives.

From the perspective of a health care provider: What policies might a nursing home institute to minimize the chances that its residents will develop "institutionalism"? Why are such policies relatively uncommon?

Financial Issues: The Economics of Late Adulthood

Like everyone, people in late adulthood range from one end of the socioeconomic spectrum to the other.

However, social inequities affecting various groups earlier in life are magnified with increasing age. Even so, everyone who reaches late adulthood today may experience growing economic pressure because the increasing human life span means it is more likely that they will run through their savings.

Overall, 10 percent of people age 65 and older live in poverty, a proportion about equal to that for people under 65, and around 6 percent of the elderly live in near poverty. However, there are significant gender and racial differences. Women are almost twice as likely as men to be living in poverty. About a quarter of elderly women living alone live on incomes below the poverty line. A married woman may also slip into poverty if she becomes widowed, for she may have used up savings to pay for her husband's final illness, and the husband's pension may cease with his death (Spraggins, 2003; Administration on Aging, 2010) (see Figure 9-11).

As for racial differences, 8 percent of whites in late adulthood live below the poverty line, contrasted with 19 percent of Hispanics and 24 percent of African Americans. Minority women fare the worst of any category. For example, 47 percent of divorced black women aged 65 to 74 were below the poverty level (Rank & Hirschl, 1999; Federal Interagency Forum on Age-Related Statistics, 2000; U.S. Bureau of the Census, 2005).

One source of financial vulnerability is the reliance on a fixed income. The income of an elderly person, which typically comes from a combination of Social Security, pensions, and savings, rarely keeps up with inflation. What may have been a reasonable income at age 65 is worth much less 20 years later, as the elderly person gradually slips into poverty.

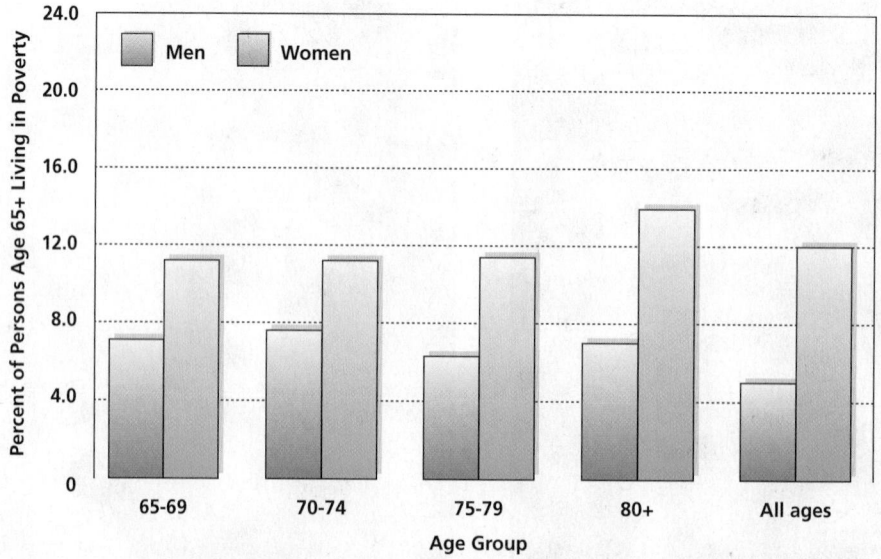

FIGURE 9-11 Poverty and Elderly
While 10 percent of those 65 years of age and older live in poverty, women are almost twice as likely as men to be living in poverty.
Source: U.S. Bureau of the Census, 2005.

The rising cost of health care is another source of financial vulnerability in older adults. The average older person spends close to 20 percent of his or her income for health care costs. For those who require care in nursing home facilities, the financial costs can be staggering, running an average of close to $80,000 a year (MetLife Mature Market Institute, 2009).

Unless major changes are made in the way that Social Security and Medicare are financed, a larger proportion of younger people's pay will have to be taxed to fund benefits for the elderly. This is apt to lead to increasing friction and segregation between younger and older generations. Indeed, as we'll see, Social Security payments are one key factor in many people's decisions about how long to work.

Work and Retirement in Late Adulthood

"Don't forget your change, Mrs. Brody," Jim Hardy reminds his customer. "And enjoy your grandkids' visit." Hardy waves goodbye and the woman smiles as she waves back.

Jim Hardy turned 84 last month and he works 24 hours a week at the local supermarket. "I wasn't always a cashier," Hardy says. "I've done lots of work in my time. Started out on a logging operation, first in Vancouver, then up in Maine. But I got married and the missus wanted me to do something steady, so I got a job doing repairs for the telephone company. Worked that job for more than 40 years."

When Hardy's wife died 5 years ago, he thought about retiring and moving to Hawaii. "Beautiful country out there and the people are friendly." But Hardy didn't retire. He took the supermarket job instead.

"I like it here," he says. "I see folks. Talk to 'em. I'm not sure I'd know what to do if I wasn't working."

Retirement is a different journey for each individual. Some are content with a more sedate lifestyle, while others continue to remain active and in some cases pursue new activities. Can you explain why many non-Western cultures do not follow the disengagement theory of retirement?

Deciding when to retire is a major decision faced by the majority of individuals in late adulthood. Some wish to work as long as they can. Others retire the moment their financial circumstances permit it.

When they do retire, many people have some difficulty with the identity shift from "worker" to "retiree." They lack a professional title, they may no longer have people asking them for advice, and they can't say "I work for the Diamond Company."

For others, though, retirement offers the chance to lead, perhaps for the first time in adulthood, a life of leisure. Because a significant number of people retire as early as age 55 or 60, and because life spans are expanding, many people spend far more time in retirement than in previous generations. Moreover, because the number of people in late adulthood continues to increase, retirees are an increasingly significant and influential segment of the U.S. population.

Older Workers: Combating Age Discrimination. Many people continue to work, either full- or part-time, for some part of late adulthood. That they can do so is largely because of age discrimination legislation that was passed in the late 1970s, in which mandatory retirement ages were made illegal in almost every profession (Lindemann & Kadue, 2003; Lain, 2012).

Whether older adults continue to work for intellectual and social reasons or financial reasons, many encounter age discrimination, which is a reality despite laws against it. Some employers encourage older workers to leave their jobs so they can replace them with younger employees with lower salaries. And some employers believe that older workers are not up to the demands of the job or are less willing to adapt to a changing workplace—enduring stereotypes that laws can't change (Moss, 1997).

There is little evidence to support the idea that older workers lose their ability to perform their jobs. In many fields, such as art, literature, science, politics, and entertainment, it is easy to find examples of people who have made some of their greatest contributions during late adulthood. Even in those few professions that were specifically exempted from laws prohibiting mandatory retirement ages—those involving public safety—the evidence does not support the notion that workers should be retired early.

For instance, one large-scale, careful study of older police officers, firefighters, and prison guards concluded that age was not a good predictor of whether a worker was likely to be incapacitated on the job, or the level of his or her general work performance. Accurate prediction required a case-by-case analysis of the performance of individuals (Landy & Conte, 2004).

Although age discrimination remains a problem, market forces may help reduce its severity. As baby boomers retire and the workforce drastically shrinks, companies may begin to offer incentives to older adults to either remain in or return to the workforce. Still, for most older adults, retirement is the norm.

Retirement: Filling a Life of Leisure. Why do people retire? Although the basic reason seems apparent—to stop working—there are actually many factors. For instance, sometimes workers burn out after a lifetime of work and seek to ease the tension and frustration of their jobs and the sense that they have not accomplished as much as they wished. Others retire because their health has declined, and still others because they receive incentives from their employers. Finally, some people have planned for years to retire and intend to use their increased leisure to travel, study, or spend more time with their children and grandchildren (Sener, Terzioglu, & Karabulut, 2007; Nordenmark & Stattin, 2009; Petkoska & Earl, 2009).

Whatever the reason they retire, people often pass through a series of retirement stages. Retirement may begin with a *honeymoon* period, in which people engage in a variety of activities, such as travel, that were previously hindered by work. The next phase may be *disenchantment*, in which they conclude that retirement is not all they thought it would be because they miss the stimulation and companionship of work or find it hard to keep busy (Atchley & Barusch, 2005; Osborne, 2012; Schlosser, Zinni, & Armstrong-Stassen, 2012).

The next phase is *reorientation*, in which retirees reconsider their options and become engaged in new, more fulfilling activities. If successful, this leads to the *retirement routine* stage, in which they come to grips with the realities of retirement and feel fulfilled. Not all people reach this stage; some may feel disenchanted for years.

The last phase is *termination*. Although for some people this occurs when they go back to work, for most it follows major physical deterioration. In this case, health becomes so bad that the person can no longer function independently.

Obviously, not everyone passes through all stages, and the sequence is not universal. In large measure, a person's reactions to retirement stem from the reasons he or she retired in the first place. For example, a person forced to retire for health reasons will have a different experience from a person who eagerly chose to retire at a particular age. Similarly, the retirement of people who loved their jobs may differ from that of people who despised their work.

In short, the psychological consequences of retirement vary from one individual to the next. For many people, retirement is a continuation of a life well-lived. Moreover, as we see next, there are ways to plan a good retirement.

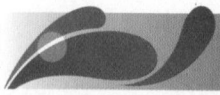

Becoming an Informed Consumer of Development

Planning for—and Living—a Good Retirement

What makes for a good retirement? Gerontologists suggest several factors (Kreitlow & Kreitlow, 1997; Rowe & Kahn, 1998; Borchard, 2008; Noone, Stephens, & Alpass, 2009):

- **Plan ahead financially.** Because Social Security pensions are likely to be inadequate in the future, personal savings are critical, as is adequate health insurance.
- **Consider tapering off from work gradually.** Sometimes it is helpful to prepare for retirement by shifting from full-time to part-time work.
- **Explore your interests before you retire.** Assess what you like about your current job and think about how to translate those things into leisure activities.
- **If you are married or in a long-term partnership, spend some time discussing your views of the ideal retirement with your partner.** You may find that you need to negotiate a vision that will suit you both.
- **Consider where you want to live.** Try out, temporarily, a community to which you are thinking of moving.
- **Determine the advantages and disadvantages of downsizing your current home.**
- **Plan to volunteer your time.** People who retire have a wealth of skills that are often needed by nonprofit organizations and small businesses. Organizations such as the Retired Senior Volunteer Program or the Foster Grandparent Program can help match your skills with people who need them.

REVIEW, CHECK, AND APPLY

REVIEW

LO11 What is the quality of life in late adulthood?

- Elderly people live in a variety of settings, although most live at home with a family member. For others there are specialized living environments that range from continuing-care communities to skilled-nursing facilities.
- Financial issues can trouble older people, largely because their incomes are fixed, health care costs are increasing, and the life span is lengthening.

LO12 What is the nature of retirement?

- After retirement, many people pass through stages, including a honeymoon period, disenchantment, reorientation, retirement routine, and termination.
- There are ways to plan a good retirement including tapering off from work gradually, exploring interests before retiring, and trying to plan ahead financially.

CHECK YOURSELF

1. Older adults living in communities that offer an environment in which all the residents are of retirement age or older and need various levels of care reside in a _____ home.
   - a retirement
   - b single-family
   - c continuing-care
   - d multifamily
2. After age 65, women are twice as likely as men to be living in poverty.
   - True
   - False
3. Which of the following is NOT cited in your text as a reason older adults decide to retire?
   - a declining health
   - b job burnout
   - c incentives from their employers
   - d spouses have retired

APPLYING LIFESPAN DEVELOPMENT

- Based on the research on successful aging, what advice would you give someone who is nearing retirement?

✓ **Study** and **Review** on **MyPsychLab.com**

RELATIONSHIPS: OLD AND NEW

LO13 How do marriages fare in late adulthood?
LO14 What sorts of relationships are important to older adults?

Leonard Timbola, 94, describes how he met his wife, Ellen, 90.

"I was 23 when Pearl Harbor happened and I enlisted right away. I was sent to Fort Bragg and I was lonely. I'd often go into Fayetteville and just poke around. One day I was in a bookstore reaching for a book. You remember what it was?"

"Out of the Silent Planet," Ellen says. "I happened to be reaching for it at the same time. Our hands met, and then our eyes."

"And that was the end of my bachelorhood," says Leonard. "Fate sent me to that bookstore."

Ellen continues. "We shared that book and everything else from then on. We were married 4 months later."

"Just before I shipped out," says Leonard.

This is the way they are: He starts a thought, she finishes it. Unless it's the other way around.

"She wrote every day. I got her letters in bunches, and that was the best reading I ever did." He places his hand on Ellen's knee. Her hand joins his there.

"You weren't nearly as frequent a writer," she reminds him gently. "But when I did get one from you, I read it every day."

"Well that's the same thing," he laughs.

The warmth and affection between Leonard and Ellen are unmistakable. Their relationship, spanning 8 decades, continues to bring them quiet joy, and their life is the sort to which many couples aspire. Yet it is also rare for the last stage of life. For every older person who is part of a couple, many more are alone.

What is the social world of late adulthood? To answer the question, we will first consider marriage.

Marriage in the Later Years: Together, Then Alone

It's a man's world—at least when it comes to marriage after 65. The proportion of men who are married is far greater than that of women (see Figure 9-12). One reason is that

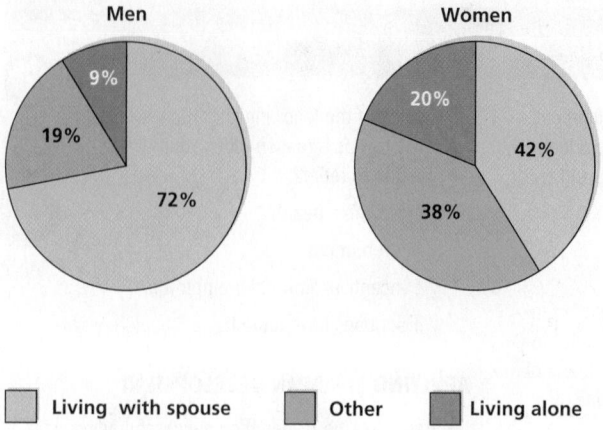

FIGURE 9-12 Living Patterns of Older Americans
What, if anything, do these patterns suggest about the relative health and adjustment of men and women?
Source: Administration on Aging, 2006.

70 percent of women outlive their husbands by at least a few years. Because there are fewer men available (many have died), these women are unlikely to remarry (Barer, 1994).

Furthermore, the marriage gradient that we discussed earlier is still a powerful influence. Reflecting societal norms that women should marry older men, the marriage gradient keeps women single even in the later years of life. At the same time, it makes remarriage for men much easier, because the pool of eligible partners is much larger (AARP, 1990).

The vast majority of people who are still married in later life report that they are satisfied with their marriages. Their partners provide substantial companionship and emotional support. Because at this period in life they have typically been together for a long time, they have great insight into their partners (Brubaker, 1991; Levenson, Cerstensen, & Gottman, 1993; Jose & Alfons, 2007).

Still, not every aspect of marriage is satisfying, and marriages may undergo stress as spouses experience changes in their lives. For instance, the retirement of one or both spouses can shift the nature of a couple's relationship (Askham, 1994; Henry, Miller, & Giarrusso, 2005).

For some couples, the stress is so great that one spouse or the other seeks a divorce. Although the exact numbers are hard to come by, at least 2 percent of divorces in the United States involve women over 60 (Uhlenberg, Cooney, & Boyd, 1990).

The reasons for divorce so late in life are varied. Often, women divorce because their husbands are abusive or alcoholic. But in the more frequent case of a husband divorcing from his wife, the reason is often that he has found a younger woman. Often the divorce occurs soon after retirement, when men who have been highly involved in their careers are in psychological turmoil (Cain, 1982; Solomon et al., 1998).

Divorce so late in life is particularly difficult for women. Between the marriage gradient and the limited pool of eligible men, it is unlikely that an older divorced woman will remarry. For many women, marriage has been their primary role and the center of their identities, and they may view divorce as a major failure. As a consequence, happiness and the quality of life for divorced women often plummet (Goldscheider, 1994; Davies & Denton, 2002; Connidis, 2010).

Seeking a new relationship becomes a priority for many men and women who are divorced or whose spouses have died. People seeking to develop relationships use the same strategies to meet potential partners as younger people, such as joining singles organizations or even using the Internet to seek out companionship (Durbin, 2003).

Of course, some people enter late adulthood having never married. For this group—about 5 percent of the population—late adulthood may bring fewer transitions, because living status does not change. In fact, never-married individuals report feeling less lonely than do most people their age, and they have a greater sense of independence (Essex & Nam, 1987; Newston & Keith, 1997).

Dealing With Retirement: Too Much Togetherness? When Morris Abercrombie finally stopped working full time, his wife, Roxanne, found some aspects of his increased presence at home troubling. Although their marriage was strong, his intrusion into her daily routine and his constant questioning about whom she was on the phone with and where she was going were irksome. Finally, she began to wish he would spend less time around the house. This was ironic: She had passed much of Morris's preretirement years wishing that he would spend more time at home.

The situation in which Morris and Roxanne found themselves is not unique. For many couples, relationships need to be renegotiated because the couple will probably spend more time together than at any other point in their marriage. For others, retirement alters the longstanding distribution of household chores, with men taking on more responsibility than before for the everyday functioning of the household.

In fact, research suggests that an interesting role reversal often takes place. In contrast to the early years of marriage, in late adulthood husbands' companionship needs tend to be greater than their wives'. The power structure of marriage also changes: Men become more affiliative and less competitive following retirement. At the same time, women become more assertive and autonomous (Blumstein & Schwartz, 1989; Bird & Melville, 1994).

Caring for an Aging Spouse. The shifts in health that accompany late adulthood sometimes require women and men to care for their spouses in ways that they never envisioned. Consider, for example, one woman's comments of frustration:

> *I cry a lot because I never thought it would be this way. I didn't expect to be mopping up the bathroom, changing him, doing laundry all the time. I was taking care of babies at twenty; now I'm taking care of my husband. (Doress et al., 1987, pp. 199–200)*

At the same time, some people view caring for an ailing and dying spouse as a final opportunity to demonstrate love and devotion. In fact, some caregivers report feeling satisfied at fulfilling what they see as their responsibility to their spouse. And some of those who experience emotional distress initially find that the distress declines as they successfully adapt (Zarit & Reid, 1994).

Yet there is no getting around the fact that giving care is arduous, made more difficult by the fact that the spouses providing the care are probably not in the peak of health themselves. In fact, caregiving may be detrimental to the provider's own physical and psychological health. For instance, caregivers report lower levels of satisfaction with life than do noncaregivers (Choi & Marks, 2006; Percy, 2010; Mausbach, 2012).

In almost three-quarters of the cases, it should be noted, the spouse who provides the care is the wife. Part of the reason is demographic: Men tend to die earlier than women, and consequently to contract the diseases leading to death earlier than women. A second reason, though, relates to society's traditional gender roles, which view women as "natural" caregivers. As a consequence, health care providers may be more likely to suggest that a wife care for her husband than that a husband care for his wife (Unger & Crawford, 1992).

The Death of a Spouse: Becoming Widowed. Hardly any event is more painful and stressful than the death of one's spouse. Especially for those who married young, the death leads to profound feelings of loss and often brings drastic changes in economic and social circumstances. If the marriage was a good one, the death means the loss of a companion, a lover, a confidante, a helper.

Upon a partner's death, spouses suddenly assume a new and unfamiliar societal role: widowhood. At the same time, they lose the role with which they were most familiar: spouse. Suddenly, they are no longer part of a couple; instead, they are viewed by society, and themselves, as individuals. All this occurs as they are dealing with profound and sometimes overwhelming grief (which we discuss more in the next chapter).

Widowhood brings new demands and concerns. There is no longer a companion to share the day's events. If the deceased spouse primarily did the household chores, the surviving spouse must learn how to do these tasks every day. Although initially family and friends provide a great deal of support, this assistance quickly fades and newly widowed people are left to make the adjustment on their own (Wortman & Silver, 1990; Hanson & Hayslip, 2000; Smith, J. M., 2012).

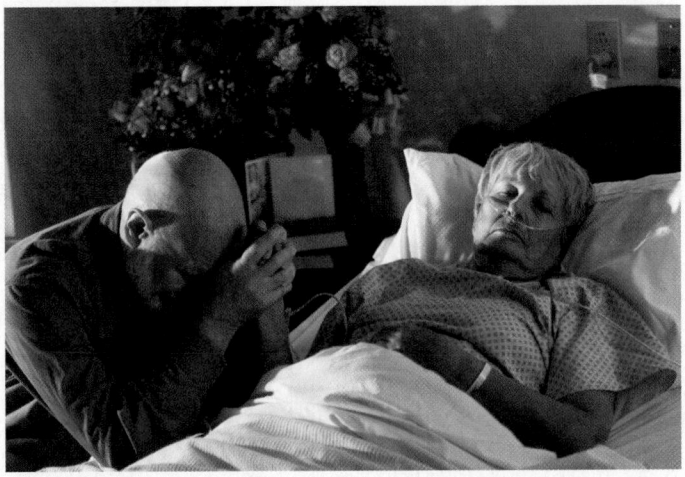

One of the most difficult responsibilities of later adulthood can be caring for one's ill spouse.

People's social lives often change drastically. Married couples tend to socialize with other married couples; widowed people may feel like "fifth wheels" as they seek to maintain the friendships they enjoyed as part of a couple. Eventually, such friendships may cease, although they may be replaced by friendships with other single people (van den Hoonaard, 1994).

Economic issues are of major concern to many widowed people. Although many have insurance, savings, and pensions to provide economic security, some persons, most often women, experience a decline in their economic well-being as the result of a spouse's death. This can force wrenching decisions, such as selling the house in which the couple spent their married lives (Meyer, Wolf, & Himes, 2006).

The process of adjusting to widowhood encompasses three stages. In the first stage, *preparation*, spouses prepare, in some cases years and even decades ahead of time, for the eventual death of the partner. Consider, for instance, the purchase of life insurance, the preparation of a will, and the decision to have children who may eventually provide care in one's old age. Each of these actions helps prepare for the eventuality that one will be widowed and will require some degree of assistance (Heinemann & Evans, 1990; Roecke & Cherry, 2002).

The second stage of adjustment to widowhood, *grief and mourning*, is an immediate reaction to the death of a spouse. It starts with the shock and pain of loss, and continues as the survivor works through the emotions the loss brings up. The time a person spends in this period depends on the support received from others, as well as on personality factors. In some cases, grief and mourning may last for years, while in others it lasts a few months.

The last stage of adjustment to the death of a spouse is *adaptation*. In adaptation, the widowed individual starts a new life. The period begins with the acceptance of loss and continues with the reorganization of roles and the formation of new friendships. The adaptation stage also encompasses a period of reintegration in which a new identity—as an unmarried person—is developed.

It is important to keep in mind that this three-stage model of loss and change does not apply to everyone, and the timing of the stages varies considerably. Moreover, some people experience *complicated grief*, a form of unrelenting mourning that continues sometimes for months and even years. In complicated grief, people find it difficult to let go of a loved one, and they have intrusive memories of the deceased that impede normal functioning (Holland et al., 2009; Piper et al., 2009; Zisook & Shear, 2009).

For most people, though, life returns to normal and becomes enjoyable once again after the death of a spouse. Still, the death of a spouse is a profound event in any period of life. During late adulthood, its implications are particularly powerful, because it can be seen as a forewarning of one's own mortality.

From a social worker's perspective: What are some factors that can combine to make older adulthood a more difficult time for women than for men?

The Social Networks of Late Adulthood

Elderly people enjoy friends as much as younger people do, and friendships play an important role in their lives. In fact, time spent with friends is often valued more highly during late adulthood than time spent with family, with friends often seen as more important providers of support. Furthermore, around one-third of older persons report that they made a new friend within the past year, and many older adults engage in significant interaction (Hansson & Carpenter, 1994; Hartshorne, 1994; Ansberry, 1997) (see Figure 9-13).

Friendship: Why Friends Matter in Late Adulthood. Friendships are characterized by a sense of control: In friendship relationships, unlike family relationships, we choose whom we like and whom we dislike. Because late adulthood often causes a gradual loss of control in other areas, such as in health, the ability to maintain friendships may take on more importance than in other stages of life (Stevens, Martina, & Westerhof, 2006; Demir, Orthel, & Andelin, 2013).

In addition, friendships—especially recent ones—may be more flexible than family relationships, because they lack the long history of obligations and conflicts that often typify family ties and that can reduce the emotional sustenance they provide (Magai & McFadden, 1996; McLaughlin, 2010; Lester et al., 2012).

Friendships in late adulthood are also important because of the increasing likelihood, over time, that one will be without a marital partner. When a spouse dies, people typically seek out friends to help deal with their loss and for some of the companionship that was provided by the deceased spouse.

Of course, it isn't only spouses who die during old age; friends die, too. The way adults view friendship in late adulthood determines how vulnerable they are to the death of a friend. If they have defined the friendship as irreplaceable, the loss of the friend may be quite difficult. On the other hand, if the friendship is defined as one of many, the death of a friend may be less traumatic (Hartshorne, 1994).

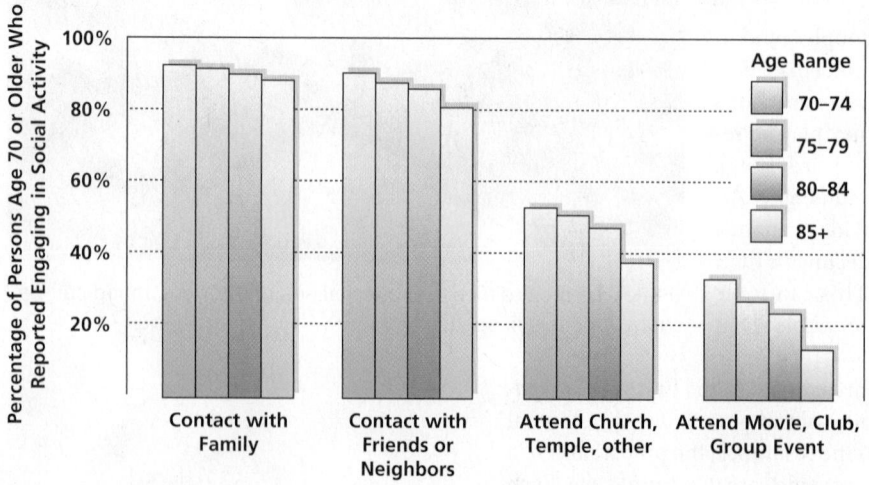

FIGURE 9-13 Social Activity in Late Adulthood
Friends and family play an important role in the social activity of the elderly.
Source: Federal Interagency Forum on Age Related Statistics, 2000.

Social Support: The Significance of Others. Friendships also provide one of the basic social needs: social support. **Social support** is assistance and comfort supplied by a network of caring, interested people. Such support plays a critical role in successful aging (Avlund, Lund, & Holstein, 2004; Gow et al., 2007; Evans, 2009).

Social support brings considerable benefits. A social support network can offer emotional support by lending a sympathetic ear and providing a sounding board for concerns. Furthermore, people who are experiencing similar problems—such as the loss of a spouse—can provide an unmatched degree of understanding and a pool of helpful suggestions for coping strategies that would be less credible coming from others.

Finally, people can furnish material support, such as helping with rides or picking up groceries. They can provide help in solving problems, such as dealing with a difficult landlord or fixing a broken appliance.

The benefits of social support extend to the provider as well as the recipient. People who offer support experience feelings of usefulness and heightened self-esteem, knowing that they are making a contribution to someone else's welfare.

What kinds of social support are most effective and appropriate? Certainly preparing food, accompanying someone to a movie, or inviting someone to dinner is helpful. But the opportunity for reciprocity is important, too. Reciprocity is the expectation that if someone provides something positive to another person, eventually, the favor will be returned. In Western societies, older adults—like younger people—value relationships in which reciprocity is possible (Clark & Mills, 1993; Becker, Beyene, & Newsom, 2003).

With increasing age, it may be progressively more difficult to reciprocate the social support that one receives. As a consequence, relationships may become more asymmetrical, placing the recipient in a difficult psychological position (Selig, Tomlinson, & Hickey, 1991).

Watch the **Video** *Late Adulthood, Relationships: Molly* in **MyPsychLab.**

Family Relationships: The Ties That Bind

Even after the death of a spouse, most older adults are part of a larger family unit. Connections with siblings, children, grandchildren, and even great-grandchildren continue and may be an important source of comfort to adults in the last years of their lives.

Siblings can provide unusually strong emotional support because they often share old, pleasant memories of childhood, and because they usually represent a person's oldest existing relationships. While not every memory of childhood may be pleasant, continuing interaction with brothers and sisters can enhance late adulthood (Moyer, 1992).

Children. Even more important than siblings are children and grandchildren. Even in an age in which geographic mobility is high, most parents and children remain fairly close, both geographically and psychologically. Some 75 percent of children live within a 30-minute drive of their parents, and parents and children visit and talk with one another frequently. Daughters tend to be in more frequent contact with their parents than sons, and mothers tend to be the recipients of communication more often than fathers (Ji-liang, Li-qing, & Yan, 2003; Diamond, Fagundes, & Butterworth, 2010; Byrd-Craven et al., 2012).

Because the great majority of older adults have at least one child who lives fairly close, family members still provide significant aid to one another. Moreover, parents and children tend to share similar views of how adult children should behave toward their parents (see Table 9-2). In particular, they expect that children should help their parents understand their resources, provide emotional support, and talk over such important matters as medical issues. Furthermore, it is most often children who end up caring for their aging parents when they require assistance (Dellmann-Jenkins & Brittain, 2003; Ron, 2006; Funk, 2010).

The bonds between parents and children are sometimes asymmetrical, with parents seeking a closer relationship and children a more distant one. Parents have a greater *developmental stake* in close ties, because they see their children as perpetuating their beliefs, values, and standards. On the other hand, children are motivated to maintain their autonomy and live independently from their parents. These divergent perspectives make parents more likely to minimize conflicts they experience with their children, and children more likely to maximize them (O'Connor, 1994).

For parents, their children remain a source of great interest and concern. Some surveys show, for instance, that even in late adulthood parents talk about their children nearly every day, particularly if the children are having some sort of problem. At the same time, children may turn to their elderly parents for advice, information, and sometimes tangible help, such as money (Greenberg & Becker, 1988).

social support assistance and comfort supplied by another person or a network of caring, interested people

TABLE 9-2 VIEWS OF PARENTS AND CHILDREN REGARDING BEHAVIOR OF ADULT CHILDREN TOWARD PARENTS

Rank	Children's Ranking	Parents' Ranking
1	Help understand resources	Discuss matters of importance
2	Give emotional support	Help understand resources
3	Discuss matters of importance	Give emotional support
4	Make room in home in emergency	Give parents advice
5	Sacrifice personal freedom	Be together on special occasions
6	Care when sick	Sacrifice personal freedom
7	Be together on special occasions	Make room in home in emergency
8	Provide financial help	Feel responsible for parent
9	Give parents advice	Care when sick
10	Adjust family schedule to help	Adjust family schedule to help
11	Feel responsible for parent	Visit once a week
12	Adjust work schedule to help	Adjust work schedule to help
13	Believe that parent should live with child	Provide financial help
14	Visit once a week	Write once a week
15	Live close to parent	Believe that parent should live with child
16	Write once a week	Live close to parent

Source: Based on Hamon & Blieszner, 1990.

Grandchildren and Great-Grandchildren. As we discussed earlier, not all grandparents are equally involved with their grandchildren. Even those grandparents who take great pride in their grandchildren may be relatively detached from them, avoiding any direct care role. On the other hand, many grandparents include their grandchildren as an integral part of their social networks. (Coall & Hertwig, 2010, 2011; Geurts, van Tilburg, & Poortman, 2012).

As we saw, grandmothers tend to be more involved than grandfathers, and most young adult grandchildren feel closer to their grandmothers. In addition, most express a preference for their maternal grandmothers over their paternal grandmothers (Hayslip, Shore, & Henderson, 2000; Lavers-Preston & Sonuga-Barke, 2003; Bishop et al., 2009).

African American grandparents tend to be more involved with their grandchildren than white grandparents, and African American grandchildren often feel closer to their grandparents. Moreover, grandfathers seem to play a more central role in the lives of African American children than in the lives of white children. These racial differences probably stem in large measure from the higher proportion of multigenerational families among African Americans than among whites. In such families, grandparents usually play a central role in childrearing (Crowther & Rodriguez, 2003; Stevenson, Henderson, & Baugh, 2007).

Great-grandchildren play less of a role in the lives of both white and African American great-grandparents. Most great-grandparents do not have close relationships with their great-grandchildren. Close relationships tend to occur only when the great-grandparents and great-grandchildren live relatively near one another (Roberto & Skoglund, 1996; McConnell, 2012).

There are several explanations for this relative lack of involvement. One is that by the time they reach great-grandparenthood, people are so old that they do not have much physical or psychological energy to expend on relationships with their great-grandchildren. Another is that there may be so many great-grandchildren that great-grandparents do not feel strong emotional ties to them and may not even be able to keep track of them. When President John Kennedy's mother, Rose Kennedy (who had given birth to a total of nine children), died at the age of 104, she had 30 grandchildren and 41 great-grandchildren!

Still, great-grandparents profit emotionally from the mere fact that they have great-grandchildren. They may see their great-grandchildren as representing both their own and their family's continuation, as well as providing a concrete sign of their longevity.

Furthermore, as health advances in late adulthood continue to increase, great-grandparents are physically able to contribute more to the lives of their great-grandchildren (McConnell, 2012).

Elder Abuse: Relationships Gone Wrong

When Lorene Templeton was 74, her son Aaron moved in with her. "I was lonely and welcomed the company. When Aaron offered to take care of my finances, I gave him my power of attorney."

For the next 3 years, Aaron cashed Lorene's checks, withdrew her money, and used her credit card. "When I found out, Aaron apologized. He said he needed the money to get out of trouble. He promised to stop."

But he didn't. Aaron emptied Lorene's accounts and then demanded the key to her safe deposit box. When she refused, he beat her until she lost consciousness.

"His problem was drugs," Lorene says. "Finally, I called the police and they arrested him. Now I feel free for the first time in years."

It would be easy to assume that such cases are rare. The truth of the matter, however, is that they are considerably more common than we would like to believe. According to some estimates, **elder abuse**, the physical or psychological mistreatment or neglect of elderly individuals, may affect as many as 11 percent of the elderly had experienced some form of abuse or potential neglect during the previous year. Even these estimates may be too low, because people who are abused are often too embarrassed or humiliated to report their plight. And as the number of elderly people increases, experts believe that the number of cases of elder abuse will also rise (Acierno et al., 2010; Starr, 2010; Dow & Joosten, 2012).

Elder abuse is most frequently directed at family members and particularly at parents. Those most at risk are likely to be less healthy and more isolated than average, and they are more likely to be living in a caregiver's home. Although there is no single cause for elder abuse, it often stems from economic, psychological, and social pressures on caregivers who must provide high levels of care 24 hours a day. Thus, people with Alzheimer's disease or other sorts of major neurocognitive disorder are particularly likely to be targets of abuse (Baker, 2007; Lee, 2008; Castle & Beach, 2013).

The best way to deal with elder abuse is to prevent it. Family members caring for an older adult should take breaks and should contact social support agencies for advice and concrete support. For instance, the National Family Caregivers Association (800-896-3650) maintains a caregivers' network and publishes a newsletter.

Anyone suspecting that an elderly person is being abused should contact local authorities, such as their state's Adult Protective Services or Elder Protective Services.

elder abuse the physical or psychological mistreatment or neglect of elderly individuals

REVIEW, CHECK, AND APPLY

REVIEW

L013 How do marriages fare in late adulthood?

- While marriages in older adulthood are generally happy, the many changes of the period cause stresses that can bring divorce.
- The death of a spouse has major psychological, social, and material effects on the survivor and makes the formation and continuation of friendships highly important.

L014 What sorts of relationships are important to older adults?

- Family relationships are a continuing part of most older people's lives, especially relationships with siblings and children.
- Friendships are highly valued in late adulthood and an important source of social support.

CHECK YOURSELF

1. Individuals still married in later life report being significantly less satisfied with their marriages than they were in earlier years.
   - True
   - False
2. The first stage of adjustment to the death of a spouse is _____.
   - a adaptation
   - b preparation
   - c anger
   - d bargaining
3. Which of the following characteristics is associated with elder abuse?
   - a being healthy
   - b being a victim of Alzheimer's
   - c being less isolated
   - d having a caregiver who lives outside of the home

APPLYING LIFESPAN DEVELOPMENT

- What are some ways the retirement of a spouse can bring stress to a marriage? Is retirement likely to be less stressful in households where both spouses work, or twice as stressful?

✓ **Study** and **Review** on **MyPsychLab.com**

SUMMARY

9 PUTTING IT ALL TOGETHER LATE ADULTHOOD

PETER SARNOV AND ELLA MALONE may live together, but they have chosen two different ways to live out their late adulthood. While Peter loves staying home and taking care of domestic things, Ella enjoys a hectic retirement filled with activities, company, social engagements, and even work. What the two retirees have in common is their commitment to maintaining their physical health, intellectual activity, and key relationships—even if they have chosen radically different ways to do these things. By paying attention to their needs in all three spheres, Peter and Ella have remained optimistic and cheerful. Clearly, they both look forward to every day they spend in the world.

MODULE 9.1 *PHYSICAL DEVELOPMENT* IN LATE ADULTHOOD

- Though both are chronologically among the "oldest old," Peter and Ella are "young old" in their functional ages. *(p. 401)*
- Both defy ageist stereotypes in their health and attitudes. *(pp. 401–402)*
- Both appear to have avoided Alzheimer's and most of the other physical and psychological disorders associated with old age. *(pp. 407–410)*
- Peter and Ella have made healthy lifestyle choices—exercising, eating right, and avoiding bad habits. *(p. 414)*

MODULE 9.2 *COGNITIVE DEVELOPMENT* IN LATE ADULTHOOD

- Both Peter and Ella are apparently rich in crystallized intelligence—their store of information, skills, and strategies. *(p. 417)*
- They demonstrate plasticity by using stimulation, practice, and motivation to maintain their mental abilities. *(pp. 417–418)*
- Both may have slight memory problems, such as a decline in episodic or autobiographical memory. *(p. 419)*

MODULE 9.3 *SOCIAL AND PERSONALITY DEVELOPMENT* IN LATE ADULTHOOD

- Peter and Ella are navigating Erikson's ego-integrity-versus-despair stage, but they seem to have chosen different answers to Peck's developmental task of redefinition of self versus preoccupation with work role. *(pp. 422–424)*
- The two appear to be coping with aging differently, according to Neugarten's personality categories. *(p. 424)*
- Both seem to have acquired wisdom with age, knowing who they are and how to deal with others. *(pp. 426–428)*
- In avoiding competitive games and book discussion groups, Peter might be engaging in compensation for slowed reaction time or less-than-perfect recall. *(p. 429)*
- Both siblings have chosen to establish themselves together in a new home. *(p. 430)*
- Neither Peter nor Ella seems to have gone through the classic retirement stages. *(p. 434)*

What would a RETIREMENT COUNSELOR do?

What advice would you give a person who wants to keep working forever, the way Ella seems to want to do? What advice would you give someone like Peter, who seems content with a relaxed retirement? What characteristics would you look for in these individuals that would help you give the right advice?

What would a HEALTH CARE PROVIDER do?

Why do you think Peter and Ella continue to be in good physical health? What strategies has Ella used that Peter may not have? What strategies has Peter used that Ella may not have? What strategies do they share?

What would YOU do?

If you were asked to do an oral history project involving Peter and Ella, how complete and accurate would you expect their recollections to be? Would they be more reliable about the 1960s or the 1990s? Which sibling do you think you would enjoy talking to more?

What would an EDUCATOR do?

Would you recommend cognitive training for either Peter or Ella? What about college courses via Road Scholar (formerly Elderhostel) or online? Why or why not?

Explore on MyPsychLab

To read how a real retirement counselor, health care provider, and educator responded to these questions, log onto MyPsychLab.com.

Do you agree or disagree with their responses? Why? What concepts that you've read about back up their opinions?

10 DEATH AND DYING

Alice Cahill, 68, had prepared well ahead for this day—the day she would die. Diagnosed 6 months earlier with an inoperable brain tumor, she had used her good days to plan the kind of send-off she wanted, a good Irish Wake that would bring family and friends together to celebrate her life rather than mourn her death. She would die at home, not in a hospital, and be laid out in her coffin in the living room as tradition dictated. Three of her friends had a small chamber music group. She asked them to perform at the wake and she gave them a list of her favorite songs. She made copies of her favorite poems and asked her daughter to read them. Last of all, she drew up a menu and ordered food for 200 from a local caterer. It was going to be grand party.

Appropriately enough, in this last chapter we discuss the final chapter of life. We begin by considering how the moment of death is defined, and we examine how people view and react to death at different points in the life span. Then we look at how people confront their own deaths, covering a theory that people pass through stages as they come to grips with their approaching death. We also look at how people endeavor to exert control over the circumstances that surround death, using living wills and assisted suicide. Finally, we consider bereavement and grief. We distinguish normal from unhealthy grief, and we discuss the consequences of a loss. Finally, we look at mourning and funerals, discussing how people acknowledge the passing of a loved one.

MODULE 10.1

DEATH AND DYING ACROSS THE LIFE SPAN

What are the moral and ethical issues surrounding defining death?

MODULE 10.2

CONFRONTING DEATH

DNR, assisted suicide, euthanasia . . . Where do you stand?

MODULE 10.3

GRIEF AND BEREAVEMENT

What's the difference between bereavement and grief?

MyVirtualLife

If you are currently using MyVirtualLife, consider how you will navigate the end-of-life experience. What decisions will you make?

Access MyVirtualLife for a chance to live your own virtual life.

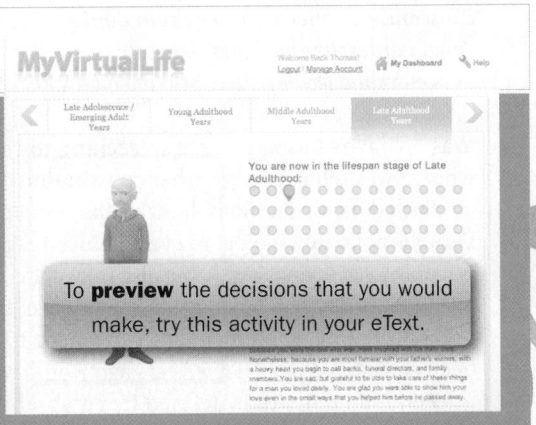

To **preview** the decisions that you would make, try this activity in your eText.

MODULE 10.1

DYING AND DEATH ACROSS THE LIFE SPAN

Choosing Death

At 88, Adrian Carsini had had enough. The lung cancer he was diagnosed with 3 months ago was not responding well to chemotherapy. His doctors had told him it wouldn't and they'd recommended against it, but as there wasn't anything else they could do for him and Adrian was shocked and frightened by the prospect of dying, he had wanted to try it anyway. But now he realized that there just wasn't much point to it—why prolong the inevitable? The end of life was drawing near. Why spend his last few months bedridden and feeling weak and sick from the cancer drugs?

After the chemotherapy was terminated, Adrian used drugs to manage his pain while he lived at home with his wife of 37 years, Karen. Some days were better than others—on the good days, Adrian visited with his family, which now included three great-grandchildren, or with old friends. Once the bad days started outnumbering the good, the end came quickly. Adrian spent his last days at home in bed, surrounded by the people who loved him.

If ever death can be said to be good, this was a good death. After 88 years, Adrian Carsini slipped away in the company of those he loved.

Death is an experience that will happen to all of us, as universal to the human condition as birth. As such, it is central to an understanding of the life span.

Only recently have lifespan developmentalists given serious study to the developmental implications of dying. In this module we will discuss death and dying from several perspectives. We begin by considering how we define death—a determination that is more complex than it seems. We then examine how people view and react to death at different points in the life span. And we consider the very different views of death held by various societies.

DEFINING DEATH: DETERMINING THE POINT AT WHICH LIFE ENDS

L01 **What defines the moment of death?**

It took a major legal and political battle, but eventually Terri Schiavo's husband won the right to remove a feeding tube that had kept her alive for 15 years. Lying in a hospital bed all those years in what physicians called a "persistent vegetative state," Schiavo was never expected to regain consciousness after suffering brain damage due to respiratory and cardiac arrest. After a series of court battles, her husband—despite the wishes of her parents—was allowed to direct caretakers to remove the feeding tube; Schiavo died soon afterward.

Was Schiavo's husband right in seeking to remove her feeding tube? Was she already dead when it was removed? Were her constitutional rights ignored by her husband's action?

Such difficult questions illustrate the complexity of what are, literally, matters of life and death. Death is not only a biological event; it involves psychological aspects as well. We need to consider not only what defines death, but also how our conception of death changes across the life span.

What is death? The question seems clear, but defining the point at which life ceases is surprisingly complex. Medicine has advanced to the point where some people who would have been considered dead a few years ago would now be considered alive.

Functional death is defined by an absence of heartbeat and breathing. This definition, however, is more ambiguous than it seems. For example, a person whose heartbeat and breathing have ceased for as long as 5 minutes may be resuscitated and suffer little damage

functional death the absence of a heartbeat and breathing

from the experience. Was the person who is now alive previously dead, as the functional definition would have it?

Because of this imprecision, brain functioning is now used to determine the moment of death rather than heartbeat or respiration. In **brain death**, all signs of brain activity, as measured by electrical brain waves, have ceased. When brain death occurs, it is impossible to restore functioning.

Some medical experts suggest that defining death only as a lack of brain waves is too restrictive. They argue that losing the ability to think, reason, feel, and experience the world may define death, as well. In this view, which considers the psychological ramifications, a person who suffers irreversible brain damage, who is in a coma, and who will never experience anything approaching a human life can be considered dead, even if some sort of primitive brain activity continues (Ressner, 2001; Young & Teitelbaum, 2010).

This argument, which moves us from strictly medical criteria to moral and philosophical considerations, is controversial. As a result, death is legally defined in most localities in the United States as the absence of brain functioning, although some laws still include the absence of respiration and heartbeat in their definition. In reality, no matter where a death occurs, brain waves are seldom measured. Usually, they are closely monitored only in special circumstances—when the time of death is significant, when organs may be transplanted, or when criminal or legal issues are involved.

The difficulty in establishing legal and medical definitions of death may reflect changes in understanding and attitudes that occur over the course of people's lives.

brain death a diagnosis of death based on the cessation of all signs of brain activity, as measured by electrical brain waves

REVIEW, CHECK, AND APPLY

REVIEW

LO1 What defines the moment of death?

- Functional death is defined as the cessation of heartbeat and respiration; brain death is defined by the absence of electrical brain waves.
- The definition of death has changed as medical advances allow us to resuscitate people who would once have been considered dead. Some medical experts believe that death occurs when a person can no longer think, reason, or feel, and can never again live anything resembling a human life.

CHECK YOURSELF

1. Once an individual no longer has a heartbeat or breathing, he or she is said to have experienced a _____.
   - a functional death
   - b system shutdown
   - c brain death
   - d legal death
2. It is impossible to restore functioning or resuscitate a person after brain death occurs.
   - True
   - False

APPLYING LIFESPAN DEVELOPMENT

- Do you think people who have lost the ability to think, feel, and experience the world, but still have detectable brain waves, should be declared dead? Why or why not? What criteria would you apply to the definition of death?

✓ **Study** and **Review** on **MyPsychLab.com**

DEATH ACROSS THE LIFE SPAN: CAUSES AND REACTIONS

LO2 How is death perceived at different stages of the life span?

Cheryl played flute in the school band. She had shoulder-length brown hair, brown eyes, and a smile that often gave way to a lopsided grin when her friends or older brother said something funny.

Cheryl's family owned a small farm, and it was her job to feed the chickens and gather any eggs every morning before the school bus arrived. After she completed her chores, she gathered up whatever sewing project she was working on in Family and Consumer Sciences—Cheryl loved designing and creating her own clothing—and waved good-bye to her parents. "Don't take any wooden nickels," her dad always called after her. Cheryl thought it was a really dumb joke, but she loved that her dad never forgot to say it.

One Friday night, Cheryl's dad suggested they hop in the truck and go get pizza. There were only two seat belts in the narrow cab, but Cheryl felt safe wedged in between her dad and her brother. They were riding down a two-lane highway, singing along with some silly song on the radio, when a car in the lane opposite lost control and crossed the center line, slamming into the truck. Without a seat belt, Cheryl's body flew through the windshield. Her father and brother survived, but for Cheryl, 13, life was over.

Death is something we associate with old age, but for many individuals, death comes earlier. Because it seems "unnatural" for a young person like Cheryl to die, the reactions to such a death are particularly extreme. In the United States, in fact, some people believe that children should be sheltered from the reality of death. Yet people of every age can experience the death of friends and family members, as well as their own death. How do our reactions to death evolve as we age? We will consider several age groups.

Death in Infancy and Childhood. Despite its economic wealth, the United States has a relatively high infant mortality rate. Although the rate has declined since the mid-1960s, the United States ranks behind 48 other countries in the proportion of infants who die during the first year of life (World Fact Book, 2012).

As these statistics indicate, the number of parents who lose an infant is substantial. The death of a child arouses all the typical reactions one would have to a more timely death, but family members may suffer severe effects as they struggle to deal with death at such an early age. One common reaction is extreme depression (Murphy, Johnson, & Wu, 2003; Cacciatore, 2010).

One exceptionally difficult death to confront is prenatal death, or *miscarriage*. Parents often form psychological bonds with their unborn child and may feel profound grief if it dies before birth. Moreover, friends and relatives often fail to understand the emotional impact of miscarriage, making parents feel their loss all the more keenly (Wheeler & Austin, 2001).

Another form of death that produces extreme stress, in part because it is so unanticipated, is sudden infant death syndrome. With **sudden infant death syndrome**, or **SIDS**, which usually occurs between the ages of 2 and 4 months, a seemingly healthy baby stops breathing and dies inexplicably.

In cases of SIDS, parents often feel intense guilt, and acquaintances may be suspicious of the "true" cause of death. However, there is no known cause for SIDS, which seems to strike randomly, and parents' guilt is unwarranted (Paterson et al., 2006; Kinney & Thach, 2009; Mitchell, 2009).

For children, accidents are the most frequent cause of death—motor vehicle crashes, fires, and drowning. However, a substantial number of children in the United States are homicide victims. By the early 1990s, homicides had nearly tripled since 1960 to become the fourth leading cause of death for children ages 1 to 9 (Finkelhor, 1997; Centers for Disease Control, 2004).

For parents, the death of a child produces a profound sense of loss and grief. There is no worse death for most parents, including the loss of a spouse or of one's own parents. They may feel their trust in the natural order of the world—where children "should" outlive their parents—has been violated. Believing it is their primary responsibility to protect their children from harm, they may feel they have failed when a child dies (Strength, 1999).

Parents are almost never prepared to deal with the death of a child, and they may obsessively ask themselves why the death occurred. Because the bond between children and parents is so strong, parents sometimes feel that a part of themselves has died as well. The stress is so profound that it significantly increases the risk of hospitalization for a mental disorder (Feigelman, Jordan, & Gorman, 2009; Nikkola, Kaunonen, & Aho, 2013).

Childhood Conceptions of Death. Children do not really begin to develop a concept of death until around age 5. Although they are already well aware of death, they tend to view it as a temporary, reduced state of living, rather than a cessation. A preschool-age child might say, "Dead people don't get hungry—well, maybe a little" (Kastenbaum, 1985, p. 629).

sudden infant death syndrome (SIDS) the unexplained death of a seemingly healthy baby

Some preschool children think of death as a sleep people may wake from, just as Sleeping Beauty awoke in the fairy tale (Lonetto, 1980). For these children, death is not particularly fearsome; rather, it is a curiosity. If people merely tried hard enough—by administering medicine, providing food, or using magic—dead people might "return."

Children's misunderstanding of death can have devastating emotional consequences. Children may believe they are somehow responsible for a person's death. They may assume their bad behavior caused the death. They may also think that if the dead person really wanted to, she or he could return.

From an educator's perspective: Given their developmental level and understanding of death, how do you think preschool children react to the death of a parent?

Around age 5, children better grasp the finality and irreversibility of death. They may personify death as a ghostlike or devilish figure. They do not regard death as universal, but as something that happens only to certain people. It is not until about age 9 that they accept the universality and finality of death (Nagy, 1948). By middle childhood, there is an awareness of the customs around death, such as funerals, cremation, and cemeteries (Hunter & Smith, 2008; Corr, 2010).

Death in Adolescence. We might expect the significant cognitive development that occurs in adolescence to bring about a sophisticated, thoughtful, and reasoned view of death. However, in many ways, adolescents' views of death are as unrealistic as those of younger children, although along different lines.

Adolescents understand the finality and irreversibility of death, yet they tend to think it can't happen to them, which can lead to risky behavior. As we discussed earlier, adolescents develop a *personal fable*, a set of beliefs that makes them feel unique and special. Thus, they may believe they are invulnerable and that the bad things that happen to other people won't happen to them (Elkind, 1985).

This risky behavior causes many deaths in adolescence. For instance, accidents, often involving motor vehicles, are the most frequent cause of death at this age. Other frequent causes include homicide, suicide, cancer, and heart disease (*ChildHealth*, 2009).

When adolescent feelings of invulnerability confront a fatal illness, the results can be shattering. Adolescents who learn they are terminally ill often feel angry and cheated—that life has been unjust to them. Because they feel—and act—so negatively, it may be difficult for medical personnel to treat them effectively.

In contrast, some adolescents who are terminally ill react with total denial. Feeling indestructible, they may not accept the seriousness of their illness. If it does not cause them to reject medical treatment, some degree of denial may be useful, as it allows an adolescent to continue living a normal life as long as possible (Beale, Baile, & Aaron, 2003; Barrera et al., 2013).

Adolescents' views of death may be highly romanticized and dramatic.

Death in Young Adulthood. Young adults feel primed to begin their lives. Past the preparatory time of childhood and adolescence, they are ready to make their mark on the world. Because death at such a point seems close to un3thinkable, its occurrence is particularly difficult. In active pursuit of life goals, they are angry and impatient with any illness that threatens their future.

For young adults, the leading cause of death continues to be accidents, followed by suicide, homicide, and cancer. By the end of early adulthood, however, death from disease becomes more prevalent.

For young adults facing death, several concerns are acutely important. One is the desire to develop intimate relationships and express sexuality, each of which is inhibited, or completely prevented, by a terminal illness. For instance, people who test positive for the AIDS virus may find it quite difficult to start new relationships. Within evolving relationships, sexual activities present even more challenging issues (Rabkin, Remien, & Wilson, 1994).

Future planning is another concern of young adults. At a time when most people are mapping out careers and deciding when to start a family, young adults who are terminally ill face additional burdens. Should they marry, even though they may soon leave a partner widowed? Should a couple seek to conceive a child if it is likely to be raised by only one parent? How soon should one's employer be told about a terminal illness, when the revelation may cost the young adult his or her job? None of these questions is easily answered.

Death in Middle Adulthood. For middle-aged people, the shock of a life-threatening disease—the most common cause of death in this period—is not so great. By this point, people are well aware that they will die someday, and they may be able to accept this possibility in a realistic manner.

Their sense of realism, though, doesn't make the possibility of dying any easier. Fears about death are often greater in midlife than at any time previously—or even in later life. These fears may lead people to switch their focus to the number of years they have remaining rather than the number of years they have already lived (Levinson, 1992; Akhtar, 2010).

The most frequent cause of death in midlife is heart attack or stroke. Dying so unexpectedly does not allow for preparation, but it may be easier than a slow and painful death from a disease such as cancer. It is the kind of death most people prefer: When asked, they say they would like an instant and painless death that does not involve loss of any body part (Taylor, 1991).

Death in Late Adulthood. By late adulthood, people know that the end is approaching. They face an increasing number of deaths in their environment. Spouses, siblings, and friends may have already died, a constant reminder of their own mortality.

At this age, the most likely causes of death are cancer, stroke, and heart disease. What would happen if these were eliminated? According to demographers' estimates, the average 70-year-old's life expectancy would increase by around 7 years (Hayward, Crimmins, & Saito, 1997).

The prevalence of death in the lives of the elderly makes them less anxious about dying. However, this does not mean that people in late adulthood welcome death. Rather, they are more realistic and reflective about it. They think about death, and they may begin to prepare for it. Some begin to pull away from the world as physical and psychological energy diminishes (Turner & Helms, 1994).

Impending death is sometimes accompanied by rapid declines in cognitive functioning. In what is known as the *terminal decline*, a significant drop in memory and reading ability may foreshadow death within the next few years (Gerstorf et al., 2008; Thorvaldsson et al., 2008; Hülür et al., 2013).

Some elderly people actively seek out death, turning to suicide. In fact, the suicide rate for men climbs steadily during late adulthood, and no age group has a higher suicide rate than white men over age 85. (Adolescents and young adults commit suicide in greater numbers, but their *rate* of suicide—the number of suicides as a proportion of the general adolescent population—is actually lower.) Suicide is often a consequence of severe depression or some form of dementia, or it may arise from the loss of a spouse (Mezuk et al., 2008; Kjølseth, Ekeberg, & Steihaug, 2010; Dombrovski et al., 2012).

A critical issue for older adults who are terminally ill is whether their lives still have value. More than younger adults, elderly people who are dying worry that they are burdens to their family or to society. They may even be given the message, sometimes inadvertently, that society no longer values them and that they are viewed as "dying" rather than being "very sick" (Kastenbaum, 2000).

In most cases, older people want to know if death is impending. Like younger patients, who usually prefer to know the truth about an illness, older people want the details. Ironically, caregivers usually wish to avoid telling patients that they are dying (Goold, Williams, & Arnold, 2000; Hagerty et al., 2004).

Not all people, however, wish to know about their condition or that they are dying. Individuals react to death in substantially different ways, in part due to personality factors. For example, people who are generally anxious worry more about death. There are also significant cultural differences in how people view and react to death, as we consider in the "Cultural Dimensions" box.

Cultural Dimensions

Differing Conceptions of Death

In the midst of a tribal celebration, an older man waits for his oldest son to place a cord around his neck. The older man has been sick, and he is ready to relinquish his ties to this earthly world. He asks that his son lift him to his death, and the son complies.

To Hindus in India, death is not an ending, but rather part of a continual cycle. Because they believe in reincarnation, death is thought to be followed by rebirth into a new life. Death, then, is seen as a companion to life.

Differing conceptions of death lead to different rituals, as this ceremony in India illustrates.

People's responses to death take many forms, particularly in different cultures. But even in Western societies, reactions to death and dying are quite diverse. For instance, is it better for a man to die after a full life in which he has raised a family and been successful in his job, or for a courageous and valiant young soldier to die defending his country in wartime? Has one person died a better death than the other?

The answer depends on one's values, which reflect cultural and subcultural teachings, often shared through religious beliefs. Some societies view death as a punishment or as a judgment about one's contributions to the world. Others see death as redemption from an earthly life of travail. Some view death as the start of an eternal life, while others believe that an earthly life is all there is (Bryant, 2003).

For members of Native American tribes, death is seen as a continuation of life. Members of the Lakota tribe believe that in death, people move to a spirit land called "Wanagi Makoce," inhabited by all people and animals. Death, then, is not viewed with anger or seen as unfair. Similarly, some religions, such as Buddhism and Hinduism, believe in *reincarnation*, the conviction that the soul or spirit comes back to life in a newborn body, continuing the cycle of life (Huang, 2004).

The age at which people learn about death varies among cultures. In cultures with high levels of violence and death, an awareness of death may come earlier in life. Research shows that children in Northern Ireland and Israel understand the finality, irreversibility, and inevitability of death at an earlier age than children in the United States and Britain (Atchley, 2000; Braun, Pietsch, & Blanchette, 2000).

REVIEW, CHECK, AND APPLY

REVIEW

L02 How is death perceived at different stages of the life span?

- The death of an infant or young child can be particularly difficult for parents, and for an adolescent death appears to be unthinkable.
- Cultural differences in attitudes and beliefs about death strongly influence people's reactions to it.

CHECK YOURSELF

1. In spite of its economic wealth, the United States has a relatively high infant mortality rate.
   - True
   - False
2. Parents' extreme reaction to their child's death is partly based on the sense that the natural order of the world in which children "should" outlive their parents has now been violated.
   - True
   - False

APPLYING LIFESPAN DEVELOPMENT

- Do you think people who are going to die should be told? Does your response depend on the person's age?

Study and **Review** on **MyPsychLab.com**

DEATH EDUCATION: PREPARING FOR THE INEVITABLE?

L03 **Why is it helpful to educate people about death and dying?**

"When will Mom come back from being dead?"
"Why did Barry have to die?"
"Did Grandpa die because I was bad?"

Children's questions such as these illustrate why many developmentalists, as well as **thanatologists**, people who study death and dying, have suggested that death education should be a component of everyone's schooling. Recently, such instruction has emerged. *Death education* encompasses programs designed to help people of all ages deal better with death, dying, and grief—both others' deaths and their own.

Death education arose as a response to the way we hide death, at least in most Western societies. We typically let hospitals deal with the dying, and we do not talk to children about death or allow them to go to funerals for fear of disturbing them. Even emergency workers and medical specialists are uncomfortable talking about it. Because it is seldom discussed and is so removed from everyday life, people may have little opportunity to confront their feelings about death or to gain a realistic sense of it (Wass, 2004; Kim & Lee, 2009; Waldrop & Kirkendall, 2009).

Several types of death education programs exist. Among them:

- **Crisis intervention education.** When the World Trade Center was attacked, children in the area were the subjects of several kinds of crisis intervention designed to deal with their anxieties. Younger children, whose conceptions of death were shaky at best, needed explanations of the loss of life that day geared to their levels of cognitive development. Crisis intervention education is used in less extreme times as well. For example, it is common for schools to make emergency counseling available if a student is killed or commits suicide (Sandoval, Scott, & Padilla, 2009; Markell, 2010).
- **Routine death education.** Although relatively little curricular material on death exists for elementary students, coursework in high schools is increasingly common. Colleges and universities increasingly include courses about death in such departments as psychology, human development, sociology, and education (Eckerd, 2009; Bonoti, Leondari, & Mastora, 2013).
- **Death education for members of the helping professions.** Professionals who will deal with death, dying, and grief in their careers have a special need for death education. Almost all medical and nursing schools now offer some form of death education. The most successful programs not only offer providers ways to help patients deal with their own impending deaths or those of family members, but also allow students to explore their feelings about the topic (Haas-Thompson, Alston, & Holbert, 2008; Kehl & McCarty, 2012).

Although death education will not completely demystify death, the programs just described may help people come to grips with what is, along with birth, the most universal—and certain—of all human experiences.

thanatologists people who study death and dying

REVIEW, CHECK, AND APPLY

REVIEW

L03 Why is it helpful to educate people about death and dying?

- Thanatologists recommend that death education become a normal part of learning to help people understand one of the most universal, and certain, of all human experiences.

CHECK YOURSELF

1. _____ are people who study death and dying.

a Cytologists
b Neuropathologists
c Thanatologists
d Teratologists

2. Emergency counseling provided within schools to help students deal with sudden events such as the 2001 attacks on the World Trade Center and the Pentagon is known as: _____.

a routine death education
b thanatology training
c crisis intervention education
d demystification training

APPLYING LIFESPAN DEVELOPMENT

- Do you think schools should teach preteens and adolescents about suicide? Are there disadvantages to teaching this age group about suicide, or is it best to deal with the topic early?

✓ **Study** and **Review** on **MyPsychLab.com**

MODULE 10.2

CONFRONTING DEATH DECIDING TO SAY GOOD-BYE

Carol Reyes had been active all her life. When she broke her pelvis at 89, she was determined to walk again. With 6 months of intensive physical therapy, she did. At 93, she came down with pneumonia. After a month in the hospital, she returned home to the things she loved—her cats, her books, and taking an active part in local politics—a little weaker, but basically sound.

Three years later, Carol's doctor told her she had ALS, a disease in which the motor neurons in the brain and spinal cord slowly die. She could take a drug called Rilutek to slow its progress, but eventually her muscles would atrophy, making it hard to use her hands or walk. She'd have trouble speaking and swallowing. In the end, her lungs would be paralyzed.

Carol agreed to try the drug, but told her doctor she wanted a DNR—Do Not Resuscitate Order—for when her lungs began seizing up and breathing became difficult. "That's not a life I'd like to be living," she said.

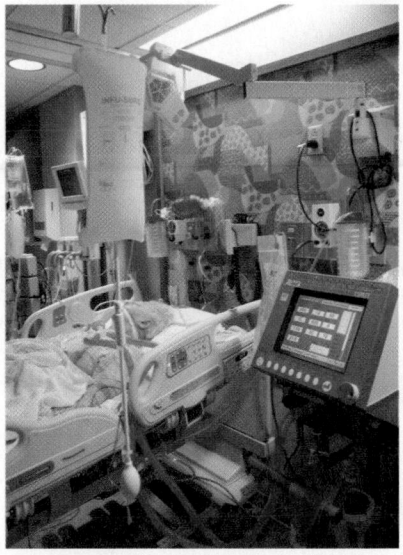

Four months later, Carol Reyes found herself gasping for breath. She refused oxygen. She refused to go to the hospital. She died quickly, in her own bed. Like other deaths, Reyes's raises a myriad of difficult questions. Was her refusal to take oxygen equivalent to suicide? Should the ambulance medic have complied with the request? Was she coping with her impending death effectively? How do people come to terms with death, and how do they react and adapt to it? Lifespan developmentalists and other specialists in death and dying have struggled to find answers.

In this module, we look at how people confront their own death. We discuss the theory that people move through stages as they come to grips with their approaching death. We also look at how people use living wills and assisted suicide.

UNDERSTANDING THE PROCESS OF DYING: TAKING STEPS TOWARD DEATH

L04 **In what ways do people face the prospect of their own death?**

No individual has influenced our understanding of the way people confront death more than Elisabeth Kübler-Ross. A psychiatrist, Kübler-Ross developed a theory of death and dying based on interviews with dying people and those caring for them (Kübler-Ross, 1969, 1982).

Kübler-Ross initially suggested that people pass through five basic steps as they move toward death (summarized in Figure 10-1).

Denial. "No, I can't be dying. There must be some mistake." It is typical for people to protest on learning that they have a terminal disease. This is the first stage of dying, *denial*. In denial, people resist the idea that they are going to die. They may argue that their test results have been mixed up, an x-ray has been misread, or their physician is just wrong. They may flatly reject the diagnosis, simply refusing to believe the news. In extreme cases, memories of weeks in the hospital are forgotten. In other forms of denial, patients fluctuate between refusing to accept the news and confiding that they know they are going to die (Teutsch, 2003).

Far from a sign of a lost sense of reality and deteriorating mental health, denial is a defense mechanism that helps people absorb the news on their own terms and pace. Then they can move on and come to grips with the reality of their death.

Anger. After denial, people may express *anger*. They may be angry at everyone: people in good health, spouses and family members, caregivers, children. They may lash out and wonder—sometimes aloud—why *they* are dying and not someone else. They may be furious at God, reasoning that they have led good lives and far worse people in the world should be dying.

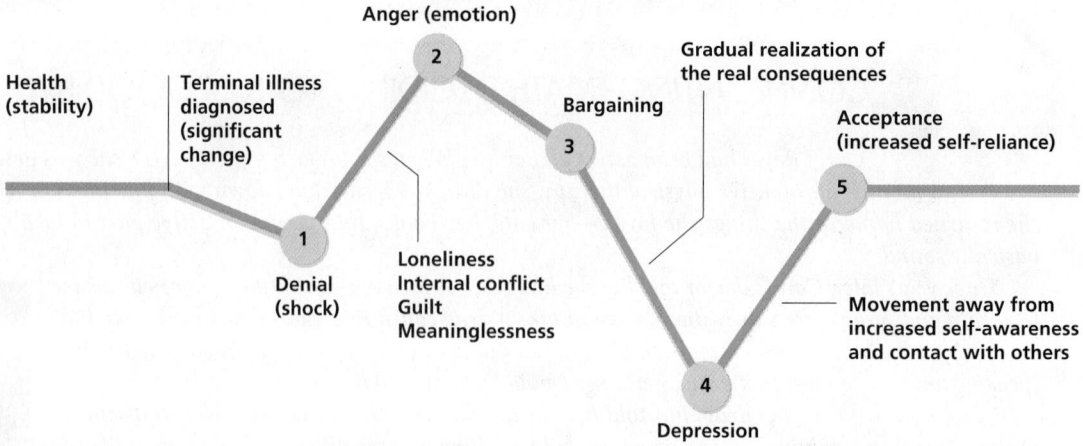

FIGURE 10-1 Moving Toward the End of Life
The steps toward death, according to Kübler-Ross (1975). Do you think there are cultural differences in the steps?

It is not easy to be around people in the anger stage. They may say and do things that are painful and sometimes unfathomable. Eventually, though, most move beyond anger to another development—bargaining.

Bargaining. "If you're good, you'll be rewarded." Many people try to apply this pearl of childhood wisdom to their impending death, promising to be better people if they are rewarded by staying alive.

In *bargaining*, dying people try to negotiate their way out of death. They may swear to dedicate their lives to the poor if God saves them. They may promise that if they can just live long enough to see a son married, they will willingly accept death later.

However, these promises are rarely kept. If one request appears to be granted, people typically seek another, and yet another. Furthermore, they may be unable to fulfill their promises because their illnesses keep progressing and prevent them from achieving what they said they would do.

In some ways, bargaining may have positive consequences. Although death cannot be postponed indefinitely, having a goal of attending a particular event or living until a certain time may in fact delay death until then. For instance, death rates of Jewish people fall just before the Passover and rise just after. Similarly, the death rate among older Chinese women falls before and during important holidays and rises after (Phillips, 1992).

In the end, of course, no one can bargain away death. When people eventually realize this, they often move into the depression stage.

Depression. Many dying people experience *depression*. Realizing that the issue is settled and can't be bargained away, they are overwhelmed with a deep sense of loss. They know that they are losing their loved ones and reaching the end of their lives.

Their depression may be reactive or preparatory. In *reactive depression*, the sadness is based on events that have already occurred: the loss of dignity with many medical procedures, the end of a job, or the knowledge that they will never return home. In *preparatory depression*, people feel sadness over future losses. They know that death will end their relationships and that they will never see future generations. The reality of death is inescapable in this stage, and it brings profound sadness over the unalterable conclusion of one's life.

Acceptance. Kübler-Ross suggested that the final step of dying is *acceptance*. People who have developed acceptance are fully aware that death is impending. Unemotional and uncommunicative, they have virtually no feelings—positive or negative—about the present or future. They have made peace with themselves, and they may wish to be left alone. For them, death holds no sting.

From an educator's perspective: Do you think Kübler-Ross's five steps of dying might be subject to cultural influences? Age differences? Why or why not?

Evaluating Kübler-Ross's Theory. Kübler-Ross has had an enormous impact on the way we look at death. She is recognized as a pioneer in observing systematically how people approach their own deaths. She was almost single-handedly responsible for bringing death as a phenomenon into public awareness. Her contributions have been particularly influential among those who provide direct care to the dying.

On the other hand, there are some obvious limitations to her conception of dying. It is largely limited to those who are aware that they are dying and who die relatively slowly. It does not apply to people who suffer from diseases where the outcome and timing are uncertain.

The most important criticisms, however, concern the stage-like nature of Kübler-Ross's theory. Not every person passes through every step on the way to death, and some people move through the steps in a different sequence. Some people even go through the same steps several times. Depressed patients may show bursts of anger, and an angry patient may bargain for more time (Kastenbaum, 1992).

Not everyone, then, proceeds through the stages in the same way. For example, a study of more than 200 recently bereaved people were interviewed immediately and then several months later. If Kübler-Ross's theory was correct, the final stage of acceptance comes at the end of a lengthy grieving process. But most of the participants expressed acceptance of the passing of their loved one right from the beginning. Moreover, rather than feeling anger or depression, two of the other putative stages of grief, participants reported mostly feeling a yearning for the deceased person. Rather than a series of fixed stages, grief looks more like an assortment of symptoms that rise and fall and eventually dissipate (Maciejewski, Zhang, Block, & Prigerso, 2007; Genevro & Miller, 2010; Gamino & Ritter, 2012).

The finding that people often follow their own, unique personal trajectories of grief has been especially important for medical and other caregivers who work with dying people. Because Kübler-Ross's stages have become so well known, well-meaning caregivers have sometimes tried to encourage patients to work through the steps in a prescribed order, without enough consideration for their individual needs.

Finally, people's reactions to impending death differ. The cause of death; the duration of the dying process; the person's age, sex, and personality; and the social support available from family and friends all influence the course of dying and one's responses to it (Carver & Scheier, 2002; Roos, 2013).

In response to concerns about Kübler-Ross's account, other theorists have developed alternative ideas. Psychologist Edwin Shneidman, for example, suggests that "themes" in people's reactions to dying can occur—and recur—in any order. These include incredulity, a sense of unfairness, fear of pain or even general terror, and fantasies of being rescued (Leenaars & Shneidman, 1999).

Another theorist, Charles Corr, suggests that, as in other periods of life, people who are dying face a set of psychological tasks. These include minimizing physical stress, maintaining the richness of life, continuing or deepening their relationships with other people, and fostering hope, often through spiritual searching (Corr & Doka, 2001; Corr, Nabe, & Corr, 2006, 2010).

REVIEW, CHECK, AND APPLY

REVIEW

L04 In what ways do people face the prospect of their own death?

- Elisabeth Kübler-Ross identified five steps toward dying: denial, anger, bargaining, depression, and acceptance.
- While Kübler-Ross has added to our understanding of the process of dying, the steps she identified are not universal. Recently, other theorists have developed alternative ideas.

CHECK YOURSELF

1. Kübler-Ross initially suggested that individuals pass through basic steps or stages as they approach death. The first stage is _____.

   a grief
   b acceptance
   c anger
   d denial

APPLYING LIFESPAN DEVELOPMENT

- What response, if any, should a family member offer to a terminally ill relative in each of the stages that Kübler-Ross identified?

✓ **Study** and **Review** on **MyPsychLab.com**

CHOOSING THE NATURE OF DEATH: IS DNR THE WAY TO GO?

L05 How do people exercise some control over the place and the manner in which they die?

When Colin Rapasand was a first-year resident years ago, one of his first assignments was the geriatric ward. Cheerful and outgoing, Colin invariably addressed the patients as "Uncle" and "Auntie," reflecting his deep-South roots.

He recalls one patient in particular. "When my crazy schedule allowed, I loved spending time with Auntie Jessica. Auntie J was 93 years old, rapidly failing, but with the sharpest mind. When I had late rounds, I would sometimes sit on the foot of her bed and chat with her. Great stories, huge spirit, lively intelligence.

"Auntie J's chart had her listed as a DNR, and I knew that she didn't want 'any of that mechanical nonsense' done to her, as she put it. But one night I was all alone on rounds and stopped in to see her. Her respiration was just about zero and her heart was beating fitfully. I watched as her numbers got worse. Instead of 'letting nature take its course,' I went to her side and leaned over her, calling her name. At the same time I compressed her chest rapidly, 100 times a minute, performing CPR on her slight body. I got the respiration going fairly well, but her heart was still weak and fluttering.

"I grabbed the paddles and jolted her once, twice, then third time lucky. Her breathing became audible and her heartbeat returned to its usual level. Auntie J lived another four months.

"I claimed to the administrators that in the heat of the moment I had forgotten about the DNR. But I knew I hadn't. I had simply 'let nature take its course'—my nature, my human nature."

The letters "DNR" on a patient's medical chart have a simple and clear meaning: "Do Not Resuscitate." DNR means that no extraordinary means are to be taken to keep a patient alive. For terminally ill patients, "DNR" may mean the difference between dying immediately or living additional days, months, or even years, kept alive only by the most extreme, invasive, and even painful medical procedures.

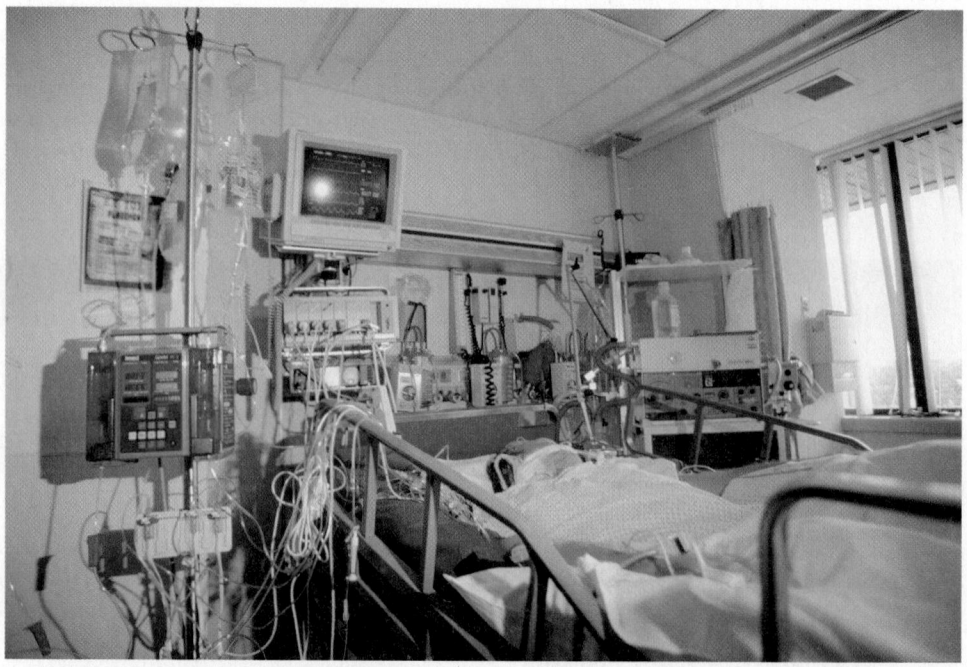

Many terminally ill patients choose "DNR," or "Do Not Resuscitate," as a way to avoid extraordinary medical interventions.

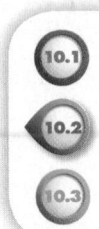

The DNR decision entails several issues. One is differentiating "extreme" and "extraordinary" measures from routine ones. There are no hard-and-fast rules; people making the decision must consider the needs of the patient, his or her prior medical history, and factors such as age and even religion. For instance, different standards might apply to a 12-year-old and an 85-year-old with the same medical condition. Other questions concern quality of life. How can we determine an individual's current quality of life and whether it will be improved or diminished by a medical intervention? Who makes these decisions—the patient, a family member, or medical personnel?

One thing is clear: Like Colin Rapasand, medical personnel are reluctant to carry out the wishes of the terminally ill and their families to suspend aggressive treatment. Even when it is certain that a patient is going to die, and the patient does not wish further treatment, physicians often claim to be unaware of their patients' wishes. Although one-third of patients ask not to be resuscitated, less than half of these people's physicians say they know their patients' preferences. In addition, only 49 percent of patients have their wishes entered on their medical charts. Physicians and other providers may be reluctant to act on DNR requests in part because they are trained to save patients, not permit them to die, and in part to avoid legal liability (Goold, Williams, & Arnold, 2000; McArdle, 2002; Goldman et al., 2013).

Living Wills. To gain more control over death decisions, people are increasingly signing living wills. A **living will** is a legal document that designates the medical treatments a person does or does not want if the person cannot express his or her wishes (see Figure 10-2 on page 458).

Some people designate a specific person, called a *health care proxy*, to act as their representative for health care decisions. Health care proxies are authorized either in living wills or in a legal document known as a *durable power of attorney*. Health care proxies may be authorized to deal with all medical care problems (such as a coma) or only terminal illnesses.

As with DNR orders, living wills are ineffective unless people make sure their health care proxies and doctors know their wishes. Although they may be reluctant to do this, people should have frank conversations with their health care proxies.

Euthanasia and Assisted Suicide. Dr. Jack Kevorkian became well known in the 1990s for his invention and promotion of a "suicide machine," which allowed patients to push a button and release anesthesia and a drug that stops the heart. By supplying the machine and the drugs, which patients administered themselves, Kevorkian was participating in *assisted suicide*, providing the means for a terminally ill person to commit suicide. Kevorkian spent 8 years in prison for second-degree murder for his participation in an assisted suicide shown on the television show *60 Minutes*.

Assisted suicide is bitterly controversial in the United States and illegal in most states. The exception is Oregon, which passed a "right to die law" in 1998. Far from releasing a flood of assisted suicides, in its first decade fewer than 300 people took medication to end their lives (Ganzini, Beer, & Brouns, 2006; Davey, 2007).

In many countries, assisted suicide is accepted. For instance, in the Netherlands medical personnel may help end their patients' lives if they meet several conditions: At least two physicians must determine that the patient is terminally ill, there must be unbearable physical or mental suffering, the patient must give informed consent in writing, and relatives must be informed beforehand (Battin et al., 2007; Onwuteaka-Philipsen et al., 2010; Augestad et al., 2013).

Assisted suicide is one form of **euthanasia**, the practice of assisting terminally ill people to die more quickly. Popularly known as "mercy killing," euthanasia has several forms. *Passive euthanasia* involves removing respirators or other medical equipment that may be sustaining a patient's life, to allow him or her to die naturally—such as when medical staff follow a DNR order. In *voluntary active euthanasia* caregivers or medical staff act to end a person's life before death would normally occur, perhaps by administering a lethal dose of pain medication. Assisted suicide, as we have seen, lies between passive and voluntary active euthanasia. For all the controversy surrounding the practice, euthanasia is surprisingly widespread. One survey of nurses in intensive care units found that 20 percent had deliberately hastened a patient's death at least once, and other experts assert that euthanasia is far from rare (Asch, 1996).

The controversy arises from the question of who should control life. Does the right to one's life belong to the individual, the person's physicians, his or her dependents, the government, or some deity? Because we claim to have the absolute right to create lives in the form of

living wills legal documents designating what medical treatments people want or do not want if they cannot express their wishes

euthanasia the practice of assisting people who are terminally ill to die more quickly

I,_____,
being of sound mind, make this statement as a directive to be followed if I become permanently unable to participate in decisions regarding my medical care. These instructions reflect my firm and settled commitment to decline medical treatment under the circumstances indicated below:

I direct my attending physician to withhold or withdraw treatment that merely prolongs my dying, if I should be in **an incurable or irreversible mental or physical condition** with no reasonable expectation of recovery, including but not limited to: (a) a **terminal condition**; (b) a **permanently unconscious condition**; or (c) a **minimally conscious condition in which I am permanently unable to make decisions or express my wishes**.

I direct that treatment be limited to measures to keep me comfortable and to relieve pain, including any pain that might occur by withholding or withdrawing treatment.
While I understand that I am not legally required to be specific about future treatments, **if I am in the condition(s) described above I feel especially strongly about the following treatments**:

I do not want cardiac resuscitation.
I do not want mechanical respiration.
I do not want tube feeding.
I do not want antibiotics.

However, I **do want** maximum pain relief, even if it may hasten my death.

Other directions (insert personal instructions):

These directions express my legal right to refuse treatment under federal and state law. I intend my instructions to be carried out, unless I have revoked them in a new writing or by clearly indicating that I have changed my mind.

Signed:_____ Date:_____

Address:_____

- -

Statement by Witnesses
I declare that the person who signed this document appears to be at least eighteen (18) years of age, of sound mind, and under no constraint or undue influence. The person who signed this document appeared to do so willingly and free from duress. He or she signed (or asked another to sign for him or her) this document in my presence.

Witness:_____

Address:_____

- -

Witness:_____

Address:_____

- -

FIGURE 10-2 An Example of a Living Will
What steps can people take to make sure the wishes they write into their living wills are carried out?

babies, some people argue that we should also have the absolute right to end our lives (Allen et al., 2006; Goldney, 2012).

Many opponents argue that the practice is morally wrong. In their view, prematurely ending the life of a person, no matter how willing, is murder. Others point out that physicians are often inaccurate in predicting how long a person will live. For example, a large-scale study known as SUPPORT—the Study to Understand Prognoses and Preferences for Outcomes and Risks of Treatment—found that patients often outlive physicians' predictions of when they will die—in some cases living years after being given no more than a 50 percent chance of living 6 more months (Bishop, 2006).

Another argument against euthanasia focuses on the emotional state of the patient. Even if patients beg health care providers to help them die, they may be suffering from a form of depression that may be treated with antidepressant drugs. Once the depression lifts, patients may change their minds about wanting to die (Gostin, 2006; McLachlan, 2008; Schildmann & Schildmann, 2013).

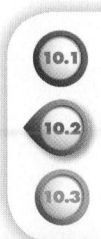

REVIEW, CHECK, AND APPLY

REVIEW

L05 How do people exercise some control over the place and the manner in which they die?

- Issues surrounding dying are highly controversial, including the measures that physicians should apply to keep dying patients alive and who should make the decisions about those measures.
- Assisted suicide and, more generally, euthanasia are highly controversial and are illegal in most of the United States, although many people believe they should be legalized if they are regulated.

CHECK YOURSELF

1. In the medical community, DNR stands for _____.
   - a Do Not Renew
   - b Daily Notice of Revision
   - c Do Not Revive
   - d Do Not Resuscitate
2. Some people designate a specific person, called a _____ to act as their representative for health care decisions.
   - a health associate
   - b health care proxy
   - c legal aide
   - d personal care attendant

APPLYING LIFESPAN DEVELOPMENT

- Do you think assisted suicide should be permissible? Other forms of euthanasia? Why or why not?

✓ **Study** and **Review** on **MyPsychLab.com**

CARING FOR THE TERMINALLY ILL: THE PLACE OF DEATH

L06 What are some alternatives for providing end-of-life care for the terminally ill?

Dina Bianga loves her work. Dina is a registered nurse with the Hospice of Michigan; her job is to meet the physical and psychological needs of the terminally ill.

"You need compassion and a good clinical background," she says. "You also have to be flexible. You go into the home, hospital, nursing home, adult foster care—wherever the patient is."

Dina likes the interdisciplinary approach that hospice work requires. "You form a team with others who provide social work, spiritual care, home health aid, grief support, and administrative support."

Surprisingly, the patients are not the most challenging part of the job. Families and friends are.

"Families are frightened, and everything seems out of control. They're not always ready to accept that death is coming soon, so you have to be careful and sensitive how you word things. If they are well informed on what to expect, the transition is smoother and a more comfortable atmosphere is created for the patient."

About half the people in the United States who die do so in hospitals. Yet, hospitals are among the least desirable places in which to face death. They are typically impersonal, with staff rotating through the day. Because visiting hours are limited, people frequently die alone, without the comfort of loved ones.

Hospitals are designed to make people better, not provide custodial care for the dying, which is extraordinarily expensive. Consequently, hospitals typically don't have the resources to deal adequately with the emotional requirements of terminally ill patients and their families.

Because of this, several alternatives to hospitalization have arisen. In **home care**, dying people stay in their homes and receive treatment from their families and visiting medical staff. Many dying patients prefer home care, because they can spend their final days in a familiar environment, with people they love and a lifetime accumulation of treasures around them.

But home care can be quite difficult for family members. True, giving something precious to people they love offers family members substantial emotional solace, but being on call 24 hours a day is extraordinarily draining, both physically and emotionally. Furthermore, because most relatives are not trained in nursing, they may provide less than optimal medical care (Perreault, Fothergill-Bourbonnais, & Fiset, 2004).

Another alternative to hospitalization that is becoming increasingly prevalent is hospice care. **Hospice care** is care for the dying provided in institutions devoted to the terminally ill. They are designed to provide a warm, supportive environment for the dying. They do not focus on extending people's lives, but on making their final days pleasant and meaningful. Typically, people who go to hospices no longer face painful treatments or extraordinary or invasive means to extend their lives. The emphasis is on making patients' lives as full as possible, not on squeezing out every possible moment of life at any cost (Johnson, Kassner, & Kutner, 2004; Hanson et al., 2010; York et al., 2012).

Although the research is far from conclusive, hospice patients appear to be more satisfied with the care they receive than those who receive treatment in more traditional settings. Hospice care, then, provides a clear alternative to traditional hospitalization for the terminally ill (Tang, Aaronson, & Forbes, 2004; Seymour et al., 2007; Rhodes et al., 2008). **Watch** the **Video** *Hospice Care* in **MyPsychLab.**

home care an alternative to hospitalization in which dying people stay in their homes and receive treatment from their families and visiting medical staff

hospice care care provided for the dying in institutions devoted to those who are terminally ill

REVIEW, CHECK, AND APPLY

REVIEW

L06 What are some alternatives for providing end-of-life care for the terminally ill?

- Although most people in the United States die in hospitals, increasing numbers are choosing home care or hospice care for their final days.

CHECK YOURSELF

1. Some people designate a specific person called a_____ to act as their representative for health care decisions.
   - a health associate
   - b health care proxy
   - c legal aide
   - d personal care attendant
2. The focus in hospice care is on extending the last stage of life as long as possible.
   - True
   - False

APPLYING LIFESPAN DEVELOPMENT

- Do you think it would be wise to suggest hospice care to a terminally ill family member who is in the bargaining stage of dying? Which of the stages identified by Kübler-Ross would be the most appropriate for making such a suggestion?

Study and **Review** on **MyPsychLab.com**

MODULE 10.3

GRIEF AND BEREAVEMENT FACING THE VOID

When they told me my husband Jim had died during surgery, I went mute. All I wanted was to go into a dark room, curl up in a ball, and sleep. Spooky, isn't it, because what I wanted to do was a lot like dying. But I couldn't stand words and I couldn't stand feeling—I didn't want to feel anything. Because, of course, the pain was so huge, I was afraid it would break me. I went home 2 days after he died and everything hurt. The sight of his clothing, his guitar, and all the photographs. It's been 2 months and I'm better now, but it still hurts: Kate S., 78, widow.

It is a universal experience, but most of us are surprisingly ill-prepared for the grief that follows the death of a loved one. Particularly in Western societies, where life expectancy is long and mortality rates are low, people view death as atypical rather than expected. This attitude makes grief all the more difficult to bear.

In this module, we consider bereavement and grief. We examine the difficulties in distinguishing normal from unhealthy grief and the consequences of loss. The module also looks at mourning and funerals, discussing how people can prepare themselves for the inevitability of death.

MOURNING AND FUNERALS: FINAL RITES

10.1
10.2
10.3

L07 What are the basic components of a Western funeral rite, and how are other cultures' rites similar and different?

In our culture, only babies are buried; just about everyone else is cremated. When my father died, my elder brother took the lead and, with the other men observing, approached the pyre and lit it.

My father's body burned well. After the fire died down, my brother oversaw the gathering of the ashes and bone fragments, and we all took a bath to purify us. Despite this and subsequent baths, we in the close family were considered polluted for 13 days.

Finally, after the 13 days, we gathered for a big meal. The centerpiece was the preparation of rice balls (pinda), which we offered to the spirit of my father. At the end of the meal we dedicated gifts for distribution to the poor.

In Hindu culture, the idea behind these ceremonies is to honor the dead person's memory. More traditional people believe that it helps the soul pass to the realm of Yama, the god of death, rather than hanging on in this world as a ghost.

Every society has its own ways of mourning.

This ritual is specifically Hindu, and yet, in its carefully prescribed roles for survivors and its focus on honoring the dead, it shares key elements with Western rituals. The first step in grieving, for most survivors in Western countries, is some sort of funeral. Death is a big business in the United States. The average funeral and burial costs $7,000, including an ornate, polished coffin, limousine transportation, and preservation and viewing of the body (Bryant, 2003; AARP, 2004).

Funerals are grandiose in part because of the vulnerability of the survivors who typically make the arrangements. Wishing to demonstrate love and affection, the survivors are susceptible to suggestions that they should "provide the best" for the deceased (Culver, 2003).

But in large measure, social norms and customs determine the nature of funerals just as they do for weddings. In a sense a funeral is not only a public acknowledgment that an individual has died, but recognition of everyone's mortality and an acceptance of the cycle of life.

In Western societies, funeral rituals follow a typical pattern. The body is prepared in some way and dressed in special clothing. There is usually a religious rite, a eulogy, a procession of some sort, and some formal period, such as the wake for Irish Catholics and shivah for Jews, in which relatives and friends visit the family and pay their respects. Military funerals typically include the firing of weapons and a flag draped over the coffin.

Cultural Differences in Grieving. As we saw in the prologue, non-Western funerals are different. In some societies mourners shave their heads as a sign of grief, while in others they allow the hair to grow and stop shaving for a time. In other cultures, mourners may be hired to wail and grieve. Sometimes noisy celebrations take place, while in other cultures silence is the norm. Culture determines even the nature of emotional displays, such as the amount and timing of crying (Peters, 2010; Hoy, 2013).

Mourners in Balinese funerals in Indonesia show little emotion, because they believe the gods will hear their prayers only if they are calm. In contrast, mourners at African American funerals show their grief, and funeral rituals allow attendees to display their feelings (Rosenblatt & Wallace, 2005; Collins & Doolittle, 2006; Walter, 2012).

Historically, some cultures developed rather extreme funeral rites. For example, in *suttee*, a traditional Hindu practice in India that is now illegal, a widow was expected to throw herself into the fire that consumed her husband's body. In ancient China, servants were sometimes buried (alive) with their masters' bodies.

Ultimately, no matter the ritual, all funerals basically serve the same function: They mark the endpoint of the life of the person who has died—and provide a formal forum for the feelings of the survivors, a place where they can come together, share their grief, and comfort one another. **Watch** the **Video** *Remembering and Honoring the Dead Across Cultures* in **MyPsychLab**.

Because an individual's death represents an important transition, not only for loved ones but for an entire community, the rites associated with death take on an added importance. The emotional significance of death, combined with the pressure of enterprising salespersons, lead many to overspend on funerals.

REVIEW, CHECK, AND APPLY

REVIEW

L07 What are the basic components of a Western funeral rite, and how are other cultures' rites similar and different?

- After a death, most cultures prescribe some sort of funeral ritual to honor the passing of a community member.
- Funeral rites play a significant role in helping people acknowledge the death of a loved one, recognize their own mortality, and proceed with their lives.

CHECK YOURSELF

1. Funeral rituals in modern times follow a universal pattern across cultures and societies.
   - True
   - False
2. Modern American funerals are grandiose and expensive largely because: _____.
   - a American social norms essentially mandate that a funeral be complex and costly
   - b the survivors are motivated to provide the best for their loved ones
   - c the typical American funeral rite involves large numbers of mourners
   - d the survivors wish to display their wealth and social standing

APPLYING LIFESPAN DEVELOPMENT

- What role do funeral planners play in tilting family members toward ostentatious funerals? How do they do this?

✓ **Study** and **Review** on **MyPsychLab.com**

BEREAVEMENT AND GRIEF: ADJUSTING TO THE DEATH OF A LOVED ONE

L08 How do survivors react to and cope with death?

The news on June 25, 2009, hit the world like a tidal wave: Michael Jackson was dead at age 50. Jackson, a pop phenomenon who had earned hundreds of millions of dollars from his recordings and performances, seemed too young to die.

Jackson's death set off an explosion of public grief. The streets around the hospital where Jackson had died were blocked off. Offices around the world were shut down as workers left to watch the ceremony on television. Memorial services were conducted in many countries, and tributes poured in from politicians and celebrities. Musical tributes were held in many locales and sales of Michael Jackson and Jackson 5 records reached unprecedented levels. Amazon sold out its Michael Jackson CDs mere minutes after news of his death got out, and his songs topped the charts of the major online music retailers.

After the death of a loved one, a painful period of adjustment follows, involving bereavement and grief. **Bereavement** is acknowledgment of the objective fact that one has experienced a death, while **grief** is the emotional response to one's loss.

The first stage of grief typically entails shock, numbness, disbelief, or outright denial. People try to avoid the reality of the situation and pursue their usual routines, although the pain may break through, causing anguish, fear, and deep sorrow and distress. In some ways, numbness may be beneficial, because it permits the survivor to make funeral arrangements and carry out other psychologically difficult tasks. Typically, people pass through this stage in a few days or weeks.

In the next phase, people begin to confront the death and realize the extent of their loss. They fully experience their grief and begin to acknowledge that the separation from the dead person will be permanent. They may suffer deep unhappiness or even depression, a normal feeling in this situation. They may yearn for the dead individual. Emotions can range from impatient to lethargic. However, they also begin to view their past relationship with the deceased realistically, good and bad. In so doing, they begin to free themselves from some of the bonds that tied them to the loved one (de Vries et al., 1997; Norton & Gino, 2013).

Finally, they reach the accommodation stage. They begin to pick up the pieces of their lives and to construct new identities. For instance, rather than seeing herself as a widowed spouse, a woman whose husband has died may come to regard herself as a single person. Still, there are moments when intense feelings of grief occur.

bereavement acknowledgment of the objective fact that one has experienced a death

grief the emotional response to one's loss

Ultimately, most people emerge from grieving and live new, independent lives. They form new relationships, and some even find that coping with the death has helped them to grow as individuals. They become more self-reliant and more appreciative of life.

It is important to keep in mind that not everyone passes through the stages of grief in the same manner and in the same order. People display vast individual differences, partly due to their personalities, the nature of the relationship with the deceased, and the opportunities that are available to them for continuing their lives after the loss. In fact, most bereaved people are quite resilient, experiencing strong positive emotions such as joy even soon after the death of a loved one. According to psychologist George Bonanno, who has studied bereavement extensively, humans are prepared in an evolutionary sense to move on after the death of someone close. He rejects the notion that there are fixed stages of mourning and argues that most people move on with their lives quite effectively (Bonanno, 2009; Mancini & Bonanno, 2012).

Watch the **Video** *Grieving a Loss* in **MyPsychLab**.

After a death, people move through a painful period of bereavement and grief. These mourners in Bosnia grieve the loss of a friend who was killed by enemy bombardment.

Differentiating Unhealthy Grief From Normal Grief

Although ideas abound about what separates normal grief from unhealthy grief, careful research has shown that many of the assumptions that both laypersons and clinicians hold are wrong. There is no particular timetable for grieving, particularly the common notion that grieving should be complete a year after a spouse has died. For some people (but not all), grieving may take considerably longer than a year. And some individuals experience *complicated grief* (or sometimes *prolonged grief disorder*), a type of mourning that continues unceasingly for months and years (as we discussed in the previous chapter). An estimated 15 percent of those who are bereaved suffer from complicated grief (Piper et al., 2009; Schumer, 2009; Zisook & Shear, 2009).

Research also contradicts the assumption that depression inevitably follows a death; only 15 to 30 percent of people show relatively deep depression following the loss of a loved one (Prigerson et al., 1995; Bonanno et al., 2002; Hensley, 2006).

Similarly, it is often assumed that people who show little initial distress are not facing up to reality, and that they are likely to have problems later. In fact, those who show the most intense distress immediately after a death are the most apt to have adjustment difficulties and health problems later (Boerner, Wortman, & Bonanno, 2005) (also see the "From Research to Practice" box).

The Consequences of Grief and Bereavement. In a sense, death is catching. Evidence suggests that widowed people are particularly at risk of death. Some studies find that the risk of death can be seven times higher than normal in the first year after the death of a spouse, particularly for men and younger women. Remarriage seems to lower the risk of death, especially for widowed men, although the reasons are not clear (Gluhoski et al., 1994; Martikainen & Valkonen, 1996; Aiken, 2000).

Bereavement is more likely to produce depression or other negative consequences if the person is already insecure, anxious, or fearful and therefore less able to cope effectively. Relationships marked by ambivalence before death are more apt to cause poor post-death outcomes than secure relationships. Highly dependent people are apt to suffer more after the death, as are those who spend a lot of time reflecting on the death and their own grief.

Bereaved people who lack social support from family, friends, or a connection to some other group, religious or otherwise, are more likely to experience feelings of loneliness, and therefore are more at risk. Finally, people who are unable to make sense of the death or find meaning in it (such as a new appreciation of life) show less overall adjustment (Nolen-Hoeksema, 2001; Nolen-Hoeksema & Davis, 2002; Torges, Stewart, & Nolen-Hoeksema, 2008).

The suddenness of the death also affects the course of grieving. People who unexpectedly lose their loved ones are less able to cope than those who could anticipate the death. In one study, people who experienced a sudden death had not fully recovered 4 years later.

From Research to Practice

How Helpful Is Grief Counseling?

The bereaved don't have to look very far to find grief counseling services. Often a grief counselor is on the scene soon after a sudden or tragic death occurs, or at hospitals and hospices. Colleges routinely offer grief counseling after the death of a student, hoping to support classmates who are grieving.

But the effectiveness, and certainly the necessity, of such services has recently been called into question. A meta-analysis of more than 60 studies of therapeutic interventions for bereaved people concluded that grief counseling didn't help significantly more than the mere passage of time. That's not to say that grief counseling is never helpful; people who were having an unusual time dealing with their grief were helped by interventions. But most people experiencing typical grief felt better in time whether they got the counseling or not (Currier, Neimeyer, & Berman, 2008; Currier, Holland, & Neimeyer, 2010).

This doesn't mean that counseling is not helpful to some people. In fact, certain kinds of therapy have been shown to be helpful for at least some individuals. But it does appear that most people are able to cope with death without requiring counseling (Currier, Holland, & Neimeyer, 2010; Bonanno & Mancini, 2012).

Similarly, despite common wisdom that people need to work through their grief by expressing it, rather than bottling it up, research suggests that this is not the case. For example, in one study on grief, people who had lost a spouse or a child and were encouraged to express their negative emotions 6 months after the loss were actually more depressed and anxious and had more health problems at follow ups approximately 1 year and 2 years after the loss, compared to people who hadn't expressed negative emotions at the 6-month mark. Other research shows that bereaved people who "work through" their grief by talking or writing about it do not show any better adjustment than do people who do not work through their grief in this manner (Bonanno, Boerner, & Wortman, 2008; Stroebe et al., 2008).

In short, there are many variations on how people react to the death of a loved one, friend, or acquaintance. We need to be careful about applying preconceptions about the course of grief as we help others (and ourselves) cope with death.

- *Why do you think people believe there is a "correct" way to deal with grief?*
- *How might a well-meaning person do more harm than good by applying preconceptions about grief when trying to assist a bereaved friend?*

In part, this may be because sudden deaths are often the result of violence, which occurs more frequently among younger individuals (Rando, 1993; Burton, Haley, & Small, 2006).

From a social worker's perspective: Why do you think the risk of death is so high for people who have recently lost a spouse? Why might remarriage lower the risk?

As we noted earlier, children may need special help understanding and mourning the death of someone they love.

Social networking sites like Facebook provide a means for public grieving.

Becoming an Informed Consumer of Development

Helping a Child Cope With Grief

Because of their limited understanding of death, younger children need special help in coping with grief. Among the strategies that can help are the following:

- **Be honest.** Don't say that the person is "sleeping" or "on a long trip." Use age-appropriate language to tell the truth. Gently but clearly point out that death is final and universal.
- **Encourage expressions of grief.** Don't tell children not to cry or show their feelings. Instead, tell them that it is understandable to feel terrible, and that they may always miss the deceased. Encourage them to draw a picture, write a letter, or express their feelings some other way.
- **Reassure children that they are not to blame.** Children sometimes attribute a loved one's death to their own behavior—if they had not misbehaved, they mistakenly reason, the person would not have died.
- **Understand that children's grief may surface in unanticipated ways.** Children may show little initial grief but later may become upset for no apparent reason or revert to behaviors like thumbsucking or wanting to sleep with their parents.
- **Children may respond to books for young persons about death.** One especially effective book is *When Dinosaurs Die*, by Laurie Krasny Brown and Marc Brown.

REVIEW, CHECK, AND APPLY

REVIEW

LO8 How do survivors react to and cope with death?

- Bereavement refers to the loss of a loved one; grief refers to the emotional response to that loss.
- For many people, grief passes through denial, sorrow, and accommodation stages.

CHECK YOURSELF

1. The nature of emotional displays, such as the amount and timing of crying in response to someone's death, are determined culturally.
   - True
   - False
2. Bereaved people who lack _____ are more likely to experience feelings of loneliness and are therefore at greater risk for more negative post-death outcomes.
   - a ambivalence
   - b rituals
   - c independence
   - d social support
3. In the final stage of grief, people tend to: _____.
   - a reach the accommodation stage, where they pick up the pieces of their lives and construct new identities
   - b cycle back to numbness if the pain is too severe
   - c avoid the reality of the situation through denial
   - d suffer deep unhappiness and even depression

APPLYING LIFESPAN DEVELOPMENT

- Why do so many people in the United States feel reluctant to think and talk about death? Why do people in other cultures feel less reluctant?

✓ **Study** and **Review** on **MyPsychLab.com**

SUMMARY 10

PUTTING IT ALL TOGETHER DEATH AND DYING

ALICE CAHILL, the 68-year-old woman we met in the chapter opener, resigned to her impending death, decided not to die in a hospital or to have the usual formal funeral. She was determined to go out the way she wanted—dying at home among family and friends, and holding a traditional Irish Wake to celebrate her life rather than mourn her death. She planned every detail of her wake—the music, the readings, the food—relieving her family of that burden, and took the time to say proper good-byes to her loved ones. It was Alice's last party, and it was a grand one!

MODULE 10.1 DYING AND DEATH ACROSS THE LIFE SPAN

- Alice has confronted the question of when life ends and prepared for it. *(pp. 446–447)*
- Alice, at age 68, clearly feels that she has had a life worth celebrating. *(pp. 450–451)*
- She has tried to anticipate and deal with in advance the feelings of her family members. *(p. 452)*

MODULE 10.2 CONFRONTING DEATH

- Alice appears to have passed successfully through the steps of dying. *(pp. 453–454)*
- She has decided to make her own life-or-death (e.g., DNR) decisions. *(pp. 456–457)*
- She does not seem to have even considered the idea of assisted suicide, preferring to die naturally at home with her family and friends at her side. *(p. 460)*
- Alice has clearly considered, and rejected, the hospital as a place to die. *(p. 460)*

MODULE 10.3 GRIEF AND BEREAVEMENT

- Alice understands the importance of funeral ceremonies and has undertaken the planning of her own Irish Wake. *(pp. 461–462)*
- She has evidently anticipated the grief that her family and friends will experience and has planned an event that emphasizes celebration of a life rather than mourning of a death. *(pp. 462–465)*
- Alice has clearly taken on the difficult task of speaking frankly to her daughter and friends about her own death. *(p. 463)*

What would YOU do?

Given what you know about possible places to die, what would you recommend for your closest loved one, in the event it was needed: hospitalization, home care, or hospice care? Why? Would other choices be more appropriate for other loved ones you know?

What would a POLICYMAKER do?

Should the government get involved in determining whether to permit individuals to make decisions about continuing their own lives in times of critical illness or extreme pain? Should this be a matter of law or of personal conscience?

What would a HEALTH CARE PROVIDER do?

Which criteria are most important in deciding whether or not to discontinue life-support systems? Do you think the criteria differ in different cultures?

What would an EDUCATOR do?

What sorts of topics should be covered in depth in death education courses for health providers? For laypeople?

Explore on MyPsychLab

To read how a real policymaker, health care provider, and educator responded to these questions, log onto MyPsychLab.com.

Do you agree or disagree with their responses? Why? What concepts that you've read about back up their opinion?

References

AARP (American Association of Retired Persons). (1990). *A profile of older Americans*. Washington, DC: Author.

AARP (American Association of Retired Persons). (2004, May 25). *Funeral arrangements and memorial service*. Available online at http://www.aarp.org/griefandloss/articles/73_a.html

AARP (American Association of Retired Persons). (2005). *A profile of older Americans*. Washington, DC: Author.

Abbot-Smith, K., & Tomasello, M. (2010). The influence of frequency and semantic similarity on how children learn grammar. *First Language, 30,* 79–101.

Abdo, C., Afif-Abdo, J., Otani, F., & Machado, A. (2008). Sexual satisfaction among patients with erectile dysfunction treated with counseling, sildenafil, or both. *Journal of Sexual Medicine, 5,* 1720–1726.

Aber, J. L., Bishop-Josef, S. J., Jones, S. M., McLearn, K. T., & Phillips, D. A. (Eds.). (2007). *Child development and social policy: Knowledge for action*. Washington, DC: American Psychological Association.

Aboud, F. E., & Sankar, J. (2007). Friendship and identity in a language-integrated school. *International Journal of Behavioral Development, 31,* 445–453.

Acierno, R., Hernandez, M. A., Amstadter, A. B., Resnick, H. S., Steve, K., Muzzy, W., et al. (2010). Prevalence and correlates of emotional, physical, sexual, and financial abuse and potential neglect in the United States: The National Elder Mistreatment Study. *American Journal of Public Health, 100,* 292–297.

Ackerman, B. P., & Izard, C. E. (2004). Emotion cognition in children and adolescents: Introduction to the special issue. [Special issue: Emotional cognition in children] *Journal of Experimental Child Psychology, 89,* 271–275.

Acocella, J. (2003, August 18 & 25). Little people. *The New Yorker*, pp. 138–143.

ACOG (American Congress of Obstetricians and Gynecologists). (2002). *Guidelines for perinatal care*. Elk Grove, IN: Author.

Adair, L. (2008). Child and adolescent obesity: Epidemiology and developmental perspectives. *Physiology & Behavior, 94,* 8–16.

Adams, C., & Labouvie-Vief, G. (1986, November 20). *Modes of knowing and language processing. Symposium on developmental dimensions of adult adaptations. Perspectives in mind, self, and emotion*. Paper presented at the meeting of the Gerontological Association of America. Chicago.

Adams, G. R., Montemayor, R., & Gullotta, T. P. (Eds.). (1996). *Psychosocial development during adolescence*. Thousand Oaks, CA: Sage Publications.

Adams, K. B. (2004). Changing investment in activities and interests in elders' lives: Theory and measurement. *International Journal of Aging and Human Development, 58,* 87–108.

Adams, P. (2010). Understanding the different realities, experience, and use of self-esteem between Black and White adolescent girls. *Journal of Black Psychology, 36,* 255–276.

Adams Hillard, P. J. (2001). Gynecologic disorders and surgery. In N. L. Stotland & D. E. Stewart (Eds.), *Psychological aspects of women's health care: The interface between psychiatry and obstetrics and gynecology* (2nd ed.). Washington, DC: American Psychiatric Publishing, Inc.

Adebayo, B. (2008). Gender gaps in college enrollment and degree attainment: An exploratory analysis. *College Student Journal, 42,* 232–237.

Administration on Aging. (2003). *A profile of older Americans: 2003*. Washington, DC: U.S. Department of Health and Human Services.

Administration on Aging. (2006). *Profiles of older Americans 2005: Research report*. Washington, DC: U.S. Department of Health and Human Resources.

Administration on Aging. (2010). *A statistical profile of older Americans aged 65+*. Washington, DC: Administration on Aging, U.S. Department of Health and Human Services.

Afifi, T., Brownridge, D., Cox, B., & Sareen, J. (2006, October). Physical punishment, childhood abuse and psychiatric disorders. *Child Abuse & Neglect, 30,* 1093–1103.

Agrawal, A., & Lynskey, M. (2008). Are there genetic influences on addiction: Evidence from family, adoption and twin studies. *Addiction, 103,* 1069–1081. Available online at http://search.ebscohost.com

Ah-Kion, J. (2006, June). Body image and self-esteem: A study of gender differences among mid-adolescents. *Gender & Behaviour, 4,* 534–549.

Ahmed, E., & Braithwaite, V. (2004). Bullying and victimization: Cause for concern for both families and schools. *Social Psychology of Education, 7,* 35–54.

Ahn, W., Gelman, S., & Amsterlaw, J. (2000). Causal status effect in children's categorization. *Cognition, 76,* B35–B43.

Aiken, L. R. (2000). *Dying, death, and bereavement* (4th ed.). Mahwah, NJ: Lawrence Erlbaum.

Ainsworth, M. D. S., Blehar, M. C., Waters, E., & Wall, S. (1978). *Patterns of attachment: A psychological study of the strange situation*. Hillsdale, NJ: Lawrence Erlbaum.

Aitken, R. J. (1995, July 7). The complexities of conception. *Science, 269,* 39–40.

Akhtar, S. (2010). *The wound of mortality: Fear, denial, and acceptance of death*. Lanham, MD: Jason Aronson.

Akmajian, A., Demers, R. A., & Harnish, R. M. (1984). *Linguistics*. Cambridge, MA: MIT Press.

Akshoomoff, N. (2006). Autism spectrum disorders: Introduction. *Child Neuropsychology, 12,* 245–246.

Alan Guttmacher Institute. (2004). *Report on viral sexual diseases*. Chicago: Author.

Albers, L. L., & Krulewitch, C. J. (1993). Electronic fetal monitoring in the United States in the 1980s. *Obstetrics & Gynecology, 82,* 8–10.

Albert, D., Chein, J., & Steinberg, L. (2013). The teenage brain: Peer influences on adolescent decision making. *Current Directions in Psychological Science, 22,* 114–120.

Alberts, A., Elkind, D., & Ginsberg, S. (2007). The personal fable and risk-taking in early adolescence. *Journal of Youth and Adolescence, 36,* 71–76.

Albrecht, G. L. (2005). *Encyclopedia of disability* (General ed.). Thousand Oaks, CA: Sage Publications.

Alderfer, C. (2003). The science and nonscience of psychologists' responses to *The Bell Curve*. *Professional Psychology: Research & Practice, 34,* 287–293.

Aldwin, C., & Gilmer, D. (2004). *Health, illness, and optimal aging: Biological and psychosocial perspectives*. Thousand Oaks, CA: Sage Publications.

Ales, K. L., Druzin, M. L., & Santini, D. L. (1990). Impact of advanced maternal age on the outcome of pregnancy. *Surgery, Gynecology & Obstetrics, 171,* 209–216.

Alexander, B., Turnbull, D., & Cyna, A. (2009). The effect of pregnancy on hypnotizability. *American Journal of Clinical Hypnosis, 52,* 13–22.

Alexander, G. M., & Hines, M. (2002). Sex differences in response to children's toys in nonhuman primates. *Evolution and Human Behavior, 23,* 467–479.

Alexander, G. M., Wilcox, T., & Woods, R. (2009). Sex differences in infants' visual interest in toys. *Archives of Sexual Behavior, 38,* 427–433.

Alexandersen, P., Karsdal, M. A., & Christiansen, C. (2009). Long-term prevention with hormone-replacement therapy after the menopause: Which women should be targeted? *Womens Health (London, England), 5,* 637–647.

Alfonso, V. C., Flanagan, D. P., & Radwan, S. (2005). The impact of the Cattell-Horn-Carroll theory on test development and interpretation of cognitive and academic abilities. In D. P. Flanagan & P. L. Harrison (Eds.), *Contemporary intellectual assessment: Theories, tests, and issues*. New York: Guilford Press.

Alfred, M., & Chlup, D. (2010). Making the invisible, visible: Race matters in human resource development. *Advances in Developing Human Resources, 12,* 332–351.

Alisky, J. M. (2007). The coming problem of HIV-associated Alzheimer's disease. *Medical Hypotheses, 12,* 47–55.

Allam, M. D., Marlier, L., & Schall, B. (2006). Learning at the breast: Preference formation for an artificial scent and its attraction against the odor of maternal milk. *Infant Behavior & Development, 29,* 308–321.

Allen, B. (2008). An analysis of the impact of diverse forms of childhood psychological maltreatment on emotional adjustment in early adulthood. *Child Maltreatment, 13,* 307–312.

Allen, J., Chavez, S., DeSimone, S., Howard, D., Johnson, K., LaPierre, L., et al. (2006, June). Americans' attitudes toward euthanasia and physician-assisted suicide, 1936-2002. *Journal of Sociology & Social Welfare, 33,* 5–23.

Allison, B., & Schultz, J. (2001). Interpersonal identity formation during early adolescence. *Adolescence, 36,* 509–523.

Allison, C. M., & Hyde, J. (2013). Early menarche: Confluence of biological and contextual factors. *Sex Roles, 68,* 55–64.

Al-Namlah, A. S., Meins, E., & Fernyhough, C. (2012). Self-regulatory private speech relates to children's recall and organization of autobiographical memories. *Early Childhood Research Quarterly*. Accessed online, July 18, 2012, http://www.sciencedirect.com/science/article/pii/S0885200612000300

Alonso, R. S., Jimenez, A. S., Delgado, L. A. B., Quintana, C. V., & Grifol, C. E. (2012). Breast cancer screening in high risk populations. *Radiologia*. Accessed online, December 7, 2012, http://www.ncbi.nlm.nih.gov/pubmed/22579381

Al-Owidha, A., Green, K., & Kroger, J. (2009). On the question of an identity status category order: Rasch model step and scale statistics used to identify category order. *International Journal of Behavioral Development, 33,* 88–96.

Altholz, S., & Golensky, M. (2004). Counseling, support, and advocacy for clients who stutter. *Health & Social Work, 29,* 197–205.

Alwin, D. F. (2012). Integrating varieties of life course concepts. *The Journals of Gerontology: Series B: Psychological Sciences and Social Sciences, 67B,* 206–220.

Alzheimer's Association. (2004, May 28). *Standard prescriptions for Alzheimer's*. Available online at http://www.alz.org/AboutAD/Treatment/Standard.asp

Amato, P., & Afifi, T. (2006, February). Feeling caught between parents: Adult children's relations with parents and subjective well-being. *Journal of Marriage and Family, 68,* 222–235.

Amato, P., & Previti, D. (2003). People's reasons for divorcing: Gender, social class, the life course, and adjustment. *Journal of Family Issues, 24,* 602–626.

Ambrose, H. N., & Menna, R. (2013). Physical and relational aggression in young children: The role of mother-child interactional synchrony. *Early Child Development and Care, 183,* 207–222.

American Academy of Pediatrics (Committee on Accident and Poison Prevention). (1990). Trampolines at home, school, and recreational centers. *Pediatrics, 103,* 1053–1056.

American Academy of Pediatrics (Committee on Psychosocial Aspects of Child and Family Health). (1998, April). Guidance for effective discipline. *Pediatrics, 101,* 723–728.

American Academy of Pediatrics. (1997, April 16). Press release.

American Academy of Pediatrics. (1999, August). Media education. *Pediatrics, 104,* 341–343.

American Academy of Pediatrics. (2003). *Guide to toilet training*. Washington, DC: Author.

American Academy of Pediatrics. (2004, June 3). *Sports programs*. Available online at http://www.medem.com/medlb/article_detaillb_for_printer.cfm?article_

American Academy of Pediatrics. (2005). Breastfeeding and the use of human milk: Policy statement. *Pediatrics, 115,* 496–506.

American Academy of Pediatrics. (2009). *Toilet training.* Elk Grove Village, IL: Author.

American Academy of Pediatrics, Dietz, W. H. (Ed.), & Stern, L. (Ed.). (1999). *American Academy of Pediatrics guide to your child's nutrition: Making peace at the table and building healthy eating habits for life.* New York: Villard.

American Association of Neurological Surgeons. (2012). *Shaken baby syndrome.* Accessed online, April 7, 2012, http://www.aans.org/Patient%20Information/Conditions%20and%20Treatments/Shaken%20Baby%20Syndrome.aspx

American Association of University Women. (1992). *How schools shortchange women: The AAUW report.* Washington, DC: Author.

American Association on Intellectual and Developmental Disabilities. (2012). *Definition of intellectual disability.* Accessed online, July 23, 2012, www.aamr.org

American College of Medical Genetics. (2006). *Genetics in Medicine, 8*(5, Suppl.).

American College of Sports Medicine. (1997, November 3). *Consensus development conference statement on physical activity and cardiovascular health.* Available online at http://www.acsm.org/nhlbi.htm

American College Testing Program. (2001). *National dropout rates.* Iowa City, IA: Author.

American Heart Association. (2010). *Heart facts.* Dallas, TX: Author.

American SIDS Institute (Center for Disease Control). (2004). *SIDS death rate: 1980-2000.* Washington, DC: National Center for Health Statistics.

Amitai, Y., Haringman, M., Meiraz, H., Baram, N., & Leventhal, A. (2004). Increased awareness, knowledge and utilization of preconceptional folic acid in Israel following a national campaign. *Preventive Medicine: An International Journal Devoted to Practice and Theory, 39,* 731–737.

Ammerman, R. T., & Patz, R. J. (1996). Determinants of child abuse potential: Contribution of parent and child factors. *Journal of Clinical Child Psychology, 25,* 300–307.

Amsterlaw, J., & Wellman, H. (2006). Theories of mind in transition: A microgenetic study of the development of false belief understanding. *Journal of Cognition and Development, 7,* 139–172.

Anand, K. J. S., & Hickey, P. R. (1992). Halothane-morphine compared with high-dose sufentanil for anesthesia and post-operative analgesia in neonatal cardiac surgery. *New England Journal of Medicine, 326*(1), 1–9.

Anders, T. F., & Taylor, T. (1994). Babies and their sleep environment. *Children's Environments, 11,* 123–134.

Andersen, S. L., & Navalta, C. P. (2004). Altering the course of neurodevelopment: A framework for understanding the enduring effects of psychotropic drugs. *International Journal of Developmental Neuroscience, 22,* 423–440.

Anderson, C. A., Shibuya, A., Ihori, N., Swing, E. L., Bushman, B. J., Sakamoto, A., et al. (2010). Violent video game effects on aggression, empathy, and prosocial behavior in Eastern and Western countries: A meta-analytic review. *Psychological Bulletin, 136,* 151–173.

Anderson, G., & Maes, M. (2013). Postpartum depression: Psychoneuroimmunological underpinnings and treatment. *Neuropsychiatric Disease and Treatment, 9,* 88–97.

Anderson, R. N. (2001). United States life tables, 1998. *National vital statistics reports* (Vol., 48, No. (18). Hyattsville, MD: National Center for Health Statistics.

Andersson, M. A., & Conley, C. S. (2013). Optimizing the perceived benefits and health outcomes of writing about traumatic life events. *Stress and Health: Journal of the International Society for the Investigation of Stress, 29,* 40–49.

Andreoni, J., & Petrie, R. (2008). Beauty, gender and stereotypes: Evidence from laboratory experiments. *Journal of Economic Psychology, 29,* 73–93.

Andrew, M., McCanlies, E., Burchfiel, C., Charles, L., Hartley, T., Fekedulegn, D., et al. (2008). Hardiness and psychological distress in a cohort of police officers. *International Journal of Emergency Mental Health, 10,* 137–148.

Andrews, G., Halford, G., & Bunch, K. (2003). Theory of mind and relational complexity. *Child Development, 74,* 1476–1499.

Ankrum, J. W., Genest, M. T., & Belcastro, E. G. (2013). The power of verbal scaffolding: "Showing" beginning readers how to use reading strategies. *Early Childhood Education Journal.* Accessed online, June 5, 2013, http://link.springer.com/article/10.1007%2Fs10643-013-0586-5#page-1

Ansaldo, A. I., Arguin, M., & RochLocours, L. A. (2002). The contribution of the right cerebral hemisphere to the recovery from aphasia: A single longitudinal case study. *Brain Languages, 82,* 206–222.

Ansberry, C. (1997, November 14). Women of Troy: For ladies on a hill, friendships are a balm in the passages of life. *Wall Street Journal,* pp. A1, A6.

Antonucci, T. C. (2001). Social relations: An examination of social networks, social support, and sense of control. In J. E. Birren & K. W. Schaie (Eds.), *Handbook of the psychology of aging* (5th ed., pp. 427–453). San Diego: Academic Press.

APA (American Psychological Association). (1996). *Violence and the family.* Washington, DC: Author.

(APA) American Psychological Association. (2002). *Ethical principles of psychologists and code of conduct. Updated.* Washington, DC: Author.

APA Reproductive Choice Working Group. (2000). *Reproductive choice and abortion: A resource packet.* Washington, DC: American Psychological Association.

Apperly, I., & Robinson, E. (2002). Five-year-olds' handling of reference and description in the domains of language and mental representation. *Journal of Experimental Child Psychology, 83,* 53–75.

Apter, A., Galatzer, A., Beth-Halachmi, N., & Laron, Z. (1981). Self-image in adolescents with delayed puberty and growth retardation. *Journal of Youth and Adolescence, 10,* 501–505.

Arai, J., Li, S., Hartley, D., & Feig, L. (2009). Transgenerational rescue of a genetic defect in long-term potentiation and memory formation by juvenile enrichment. *Journal of Neuroscience, 29,* 1496–1502.

Araujo, M. A., Mohr, B. A., & McKinlay, J. B. (2004). Changes in sexual function in middle-aged and older men: Longitudinal data from the Massachusetts male aging study. *Journal of the American Geriatrics Society, 52,* 1502–1509.

Archer, J. (2009). The nature of human aggression. *International Journal of Law and Psychiatry, 32,* 202–208.

Archer, S. L., & Waterman, A. S. (1994). Adolescent identity development: Contextual perspectives. In C. B. Fisher & R. M. Lerner (Eds.), *Applied developmental psychology.* New York: McGraw-Hill.

Arenson, K. W. (2004, December 3). Worried colleges step up efforts over suicide. *The New York Times,* p. A1.

Ariès, P. (1962). *Centuries of childhood.* New York: Knopf.

Armstrong, J., Hutchinson, I., Laing, D., & Jinks, A. (2006). Facial electromyography: Responses of children to odor and taste stimuli. *Chemical Senses, 32,* 611–621.

Armstrong, K., Handorf, E. A., Chen, J., & Demeter, M. (2013). Breast cancer risk prediction and mammography biopsy decisions: A model-based study. *American Journal of Preventive Medicine, 44,* 15–22.

Armstrong, P., Rounds, J., & Hubert, L. (2008). Reconceptualizing the past: Historical data in vocational interest research. *Journal of Vocational Behavior, 72,* 284–297.

Arnautovska, U., & Grad, O. (2010). Attitudes toward suicide in the adolescent population. *Crisis: The Journal of Crisis Intervention and Suicide Prevention, 31,* 22–29.

Arnett, J. J. (2000). Emerging adulthood: A theory of development from the late teens through the twenties. *American Psychologist, 55,* 469–480.

Arnett, J. (2007). Emerging adulthood: What is it, and what is it good for? *Child Development Perspectives, 1,* 68–73.

Arnett, J. (2010). Oh, grow up! Generational grumbling and the new life stage of emerging adulthood—Commentary on Trzesniewski & Donnellan (2010). *Perspectives on Psychological Science, 5,* 89–92.

Arnett, J. (2011). Emerging adulthood(s): The cultural psychology of a new life stage. In L. Jensen (Ed.), *Bridging cultural and developmental approaches to psychology: New syntheses in theory, research, and policy.* New York: Oxford University Press.

Arnsten, A., Berridge, C., & McCracken, J. (2009). The neurobiological basis of attention-deficit/hyperactivity disorder. *Primary Psychiatry, 16,* 47–54.

Arseneault, L., Moffitt, T. E., & Caspi, A. (2003). Strong genetic effects on cross-situational antisocial behavior among 5-year-old children according to mothers, teachers, examiner-observers, and twins' self-reports. *Journal of Child Psychology and Psychiatry and Allied Disciplines, 44,* 832–848.

Arsenault, L., Moffitt, T. E., Caspi, A., Taylor, A., Rijsdijk, F. V., Jaffee, S. R., Ablow, J. C, & Measelle, J. R. (2003). Strong genetic effects on cross-situational antisocial behaviour among 5-year-old children according to mothers, teachers, examiner-observers, and twins' self-reports. *Journal of Child Psychology and Psychiatry, 44,* 832–848.

Arts, J. A. R., Gijselaers, W. H., & Boshuizen, H. P. A. (2006). Understanding managerial problem-solving, knowledge use and information processing: Investigating stages from school to the workplace. *Contemporary Educational Psychology, 31,* 387–410.

Asch, D. A. (1996, May 23). The role of critical care nurses in euthanasia and assisted suicide. *New England Journal of Medicine, 334,* 1374–1379.

Aschbacher, K., O'Donovan, A., Wolkowitz, O. M., Dhabhar, F. S., Su, Y., & Epel, E. (2013). Good stress, bad stress and oxidative stress: Insights from anticipatory cortisol reactivity. *Psychoneuroendocrinology.* Accessed online, June 7, 2013, http://www.sciencedirect.com/science/article/pii/S0306453013000425

Asendorpf, J. B., Warkentin, V., & Baudonniere, P. (1996). Self-awareness and other-awareness II: Mirror self-recognition, social contingency awareness, and synchronic imitation. *Developmental Psychology, 32,* 313–321.

Asher, S. R., & Rose, A. J. (1997). Promoting chidren's social-emotional adjustment with peers. In P. Salovey & D. Sluyter (Eds.), *Emotional development and emotional intelligence: Educational implications* (pp. 196–230). New York: Basic Books.

Askham, J. (1994). Marriage relationships of older people. *Reviews in Clinical Gerontology, 4,* 261–268.

Astin, A., Korn, W., & Berg, E. (1989). *The American freshman: National norms for Fall, 1989.* Los Angeles: University of California, Los Angeles, American Council on Education.

Ata, R. N., Ludden, A. B., & Lally, M. M. (2007). The effects of gender and family, friend, and media influences on eating behaviors and body image during adolescence. *Journal of Youth and Adolescence, 36,* 1024–1037.

Atchley, R. C. (2000). *Social forces and aging* (9th ed.). Belmont, CA: Wadsworth Thomson Learning.

Atchley, R. C. (2003). Why most people cope well with retirement. In J. Ronch & J. Goldfield (Eds.), *Mental wellness in aging: Strengths-based approaches* (pp. 123–138). Baltimore, MD: Health Professions Press.

Atchley, R. C., & Barusch, A. (2005). *Social forces and aging* (10th ed.). Belmont, CA: Wadsworth.

Atkins, D. C., & Furrow, J. (2008, November). *Infidelity is on the rise: But for whom and why?* Paper presented at the annual meeting of the Association for Behavioral and Cognitive Therapies, Orlando, FL.

Atkins, S. M., Bunting, M. F., Bolger, D. J., & Dougherty, M. R. (2012). Training the adolescent brain: Neural plasticity and the acquisition of cognitive abilities. In V. F. Reyna, S. B. Chapman, M. R. Dougherty, & J. Confrey (Eds.), *The adolescent brain: Learning, reasoning, and decision making* (pp. 211–241). Washington, DC: American Psychological Association.

Augestad, K. M., Norum, J., Dehof, S., Aspevik, R., Ringber, U., Nestvold, T., et al. (2013). Cost-effectiveness and quality of life in surgeon versus general practitioner-organised colon cancer surveillance: A randomised controlled trial. *British Medical Journal, 3,* 88–96.

Aujoulat, I., Luminet, O., & Deccache, A. (2007). The perspective of patients on their experience of powerlessness. *Qualitative Health Research, 17,* 772–785.

Avinun, R., Israel, S., Shalev, I., Grtsenko, I., Bornstein, G., Ebstein, R. P., et al. (2011). AVPRIA variant associated with preschoolers' lower altruistic behavior. *PLoS One, 6.* Accessed online, July 5, 2012, http://www.sproutonline.com/kindnesscounts/dr-nancy-eisenberg/eight-tips-for-developing-caring-kids

Avlund, K., Lund, R., & Holstein, B. (2004). Social relations as determinant of onset of disability in aging. *Archives of Gerontology & Geriatrics, 38,* 85–99.

Axia, G., Bonichini, S., & Benini, F. (1995). Pain in infancy: Individual differences. *Perceptual and Motor Skills, 81,* 142.

Aydiner, F., Yetkin, C. E., & Seli, E. (2010). Perspectives on emerging biomarkers for non-invasive assessment of embryo viability in assisted reproduction. *Current Molecular Medicine, 10,* 206–215.

Aylward, G. P., & Verhulst, S. J. (2000). Predictive utility of the Bayley Infant Neurodevelopmental Screener (BINS) risk status classifications: Clinical interpretation and application. *Developmental Medicine & Child Neurology, 42,* 25–31.

Ayoola, A., Nettleman, M., Stommel, M., & Canady, R. (2010). Time of pregnancy recognition and prenatal care use: A population-based study in the United States. *Birth: Issues in Perinatal Care, 37,* 37–43.

Ayoub, N. C. (2005, February 25). A pleasing birth: Midwives and maternity care in the Netherlands. *The Chronicle of Higher Education*, p. 9.

Azar, B. (2010, December). A reason to believe. *Monitor on Psychology*, pp. 53–56.

Bacchus, L., Mezey, G., & Bewley, S. (2006). A qualitative exploration of the nature of domestic violence in pregnancy. *Violence against Women, 12,* 588–604.

Badenhorst, W., Riches, S., Turton, P., & Hughes, P. (2006). The psychological effects of stillbirth and neonatal death on fathers: Systematic review. *Journal of Psychosomatic Obstetrics & Gynecology, 27,* 245–256.

Bader, A. P. (1995). Engrossment revisited: Fathers are still falling in love with their newborn babies. In J. L. Shapiro, M. J. Diamond, & M. Greenberg (Eds.), *Becoming a father* (pp. 224–233). New York: Springer.

Baer, J. S., Sampson, P. D., & Barr, H. M. (2003). A 21-year longitudinal analysis of the effects of prenatal alcohol exposure on young adult drinking. *Archives of General Psychiatry, 60,* 377–385.

Bährer-Kohler, S. (2013). *Burnout for experts: Prevention in the context of living and working.* New York: Springer Science + Business Media.

Baillargeon, R. (2004). Infants' physical world. *Current Directions in Psychological Science, 13,* 89–94.

Baillargeon, R. (2008). Innate ideas revisited: For a principle of persistence in infants' physical reasoning. *Perspectives on Psychological Science, 3,* 2–13.

Baker, J., Maes, H., Lissner, L., Aggen, S., Lichtenstein, P., & Kendler, K. (2009). Genetic risk factors for disordered eating in adolescent males and females. *Journal of Abnormal Psychology, 118,* 576–586.

Baker, J., Mazzeo, S., & Kendler, K. (2007). Association between broadly defined bulimia nervosa and drug use disorders: Common genetic and environmental influences. *International Journal of Eating Disorders, 40,* 673–678.

Baker, P., & Sussman, D. (2012, May 15). Obama's switch on same-sex marriage stirs skepticism. *The New York Times*, p. A17.

Baker, T., Brandon, T., & Chassin, L. (2004). Motivational influences on cigarette smoking. *Annual Review of Psychology, 55,* 463–491.

Bakker, A., & Heuven, E. (2006, November). Emotional dissonance, burnout, and in-role performance among nurses and police officers. *International Journal of Stress Management, 13,* 423–440.

Bal, E., Harden, E., Lamb, D., Van Hecke, A., Denver, J., & Porges, S. (2010). Emotion recognition in children with autism spectrum disorders: Relations to eye gaze and autonomic state. *Journal of Autism and Developmental Disorders, 40,* 358–370.

Balakrishnan, V., & Claiborne, L. (2012). Vygotsky from ZPD to ZCD in moral education: Reshaping Western theory and practices in local context. *Journal of Moral Education, 41,* 225–243.

Ball, K., & Rebok, G. W. (1994). Evaluating the driving ability of older adults [Special issue: Research translation in gerontology: A behavioral and social perspective]. *Journal of Applied Gerontology, 13,* 20–38.

Ball, M., & Orford, J. (2002). Meaningful patterns of activity amongst the long-term inner city unemployed: A qualitative study. *Journal of Community & Applied Social Psychology, 12,* 377–396.

Ballas, S. (2010). Neurocognitive complications of sickle cell anemia in adults. *JAMA: Journal of the American Medical Association, 303,* 1862–1863.

Balsam, R. H. (2013). Appreciating difference: Roy Schafer on psychoanalysis and women. *The Psychoanalytic Quarterly, 82,* 23–38.

Baltes, M. M. (1996). *The many faces of dependency in old age.* New York: Cambridge University Press.

Baltes, M. M., & Carstensen, L. (2003). The process of successful aging: Selection, optimization and compensation. In U. Staudinger & U. Lindenberger (Eds.), *Understanding human development: Dialogues with lifespan psychology* (pp. 81–104). Netherlands: Kluwer Academic Publishers.

Baltes, P. B. (2003). On the incomplete architecture of human ontogeny: Selection, optimization and compensation as foundation of developmental theory. In U. M. Staudinger & U. Lindenberger (Eds.), *Understanding human development: Dialogues with lifespan psychology* (pp. 17–43). Dordrecht, Netherlands: Kluwer Academic Publishers.

Baltes, P. B., & Baltes, M. M. (1990). Psychological perspectives on successful aging: The model of selective optimization with compensation. In P. B. Baltes & M. M. Baltes (Eds.), *Successful aging: Perspectives from the behavioral sciences.* Cambridge, England: Cambridge University Press.

Baltes, P. B., & Freund, A. M. (2003a). Human strengths as the orchestration of wisdom and selective optimization with compensation. In L. G. Aspinwall & U. M. Staudinger (Eds.), *A psychology of human strengths: Perspectives on an emerging field.* Washington, DC: American Psychological Association.

Baltes, P. B., Staudinger, U. M., & Lindenberger, U. (1999). Lifespan psychology: Theory and application to intellectual functioning. *Annual Review of Psychology, 50,* 471–507.

Bandura, A. (1977). *Social learning theory.* Englewood Cliffs, NJ: Prentice-Hall.

Bandura, A. (1991). Social cognitive theory of self-regulation [Special issue: Theories of cognitive self-regulation]. *Organizational Behavior and Human Decision Processes, 50,* 248–287.

Bandura, A. (1994). Social cognitive theory of mass communication. In J. Bryant & D. Zillmann (Eds.), *Media effects: Advances in theory and research. LEA's communication series* (pp. 61–90). Hillsdale, NJ: Lawrence Erlbaum.

Bandura, A. (2002). Social cognitive theory in cultural context [Special Issue]. *Applied Psychology: An International Review, 51,* 269–290.

Bandura, A., Grusec, J. E., & Menlove, F. L. (1967). Vicarious extinction of avoidance behavior. *Journal of Personality and Social Psychology, 5,* 16–23.

Bandura, A., Ross, D., & Ross, S. (1963). Vicarious extinction of avoidance behavior. *Journal of Personality and Social Psychology, 67,* 601–607.

Baptista, T., Aldana, E., Angeles, F., & Beaulieu, S. (2008). Evolution theory: An overview of its applications in psychiatry. *Psychopathology, 41,* 17–27.

Barber, A. D., Srinivasan, P., Joel, S. E., Caffo, B. S., Pekar, J. J., & Mostofsky, S. H. (2012). Motor 'dexterity'? Evidence that left hemisphere lateralization of motor circuit connectivity is associated with better motor performance in children. *Cerebral Cortex, 22,* 51–59.

Barber, S., & Gertler, P. (2009). Empowering women to obtain high quality care: Evidence from an evaluation of Mexico's conditional cash transfer programme. *Health Policy and Planning, 24,* 18–25.

Barberá, E. (2003). Gender schemas: Configuration and activation processes. *Canadian Journal of Behavioural Science, 35,* 176–180.

Barboza, G., Schiamberg, L., Oehmke, J., Korzeniewski, S., Post, L., & Heraux, C. (2009). Individual characteristics and the multiple contexts of adolescent bullying: An ecological perspective. *Journal of Youth and Adolescence, 38,* 101–121.

Barer, B. M. (1994). Men and women aging differently. *International Journal of Aging and Human Development, 38,* 29–40.

Barnes, J. C., & Boutwell, B. B. (2013). A demonstration of the generalizability of twin-based research on antisocial behavior. *Behavior Genetics, 43,* 120–131.

Barnes, J. C., & Jacobs, B. A. (2013). Genetic risk for violent behavior and environmental exposure to disadvantage and violent crime: The case for gene-environment interaction. *Journal of Interpersonal Violence, 28,* 92–120.

Barnett, R. C., & Hyde, J. S. (2001). Women, men, work, and family. *American Psychologist, 56,* 781–796.

Barrera, M., Alam, R., D'Agostino, N., Nicholas, D. B., & Schneiderman, G. (2013). Parental perceptions of siblings' grieving after a childhood cancer death: A longitudinal study. *Death Studies, 37,* 25–46.

Barrett, T., & Needham, A. (2008). Developmental differences in infants' use of an object's shape to grasp it securely. *Developmental Psychobiology, 50,* 97–106.

Barry, L. M., Hudley, C., Kelly, M., & Cho, S. (2009). Differences in self-reported disclosure of college experiences by first-generation college student status. *Adolescence, 44,* 55–68.

Barton, J. (2007). The autobiographical self: Who we know and who we are. *Psychiatric Annals, 37,* 276–284.

Barton, L. J. (1997, July). A shoulder to lean on: Assisted living in the U.S. *American Demographics,* 45–51.

Basak, C., Boot, W., Voss, M., & Kramer, A. (2008). Can training in a real-time strategy video game attenuate cognitive decline in older adults? *Psychology and Aging, 23,* 765–777.

Bass, S., Shields, M. K., & Behrman, R. E. (2004). Children, families, and foster care: Analysis and recommendations. *The Future of Children, 14,* 5–30.

Basseches, M. (1984). *Dialectical thinking and adult development.* Norwood, NJ: Ablex.

Bastian, B., Jetten, J., & Radke, H. M. (2012). Cyber-dehumanization: Violent video game play diminishes our humanity. *Journal of Experimental Social Psychology, 48,* 486–491.

Bates, J. E., Marvinney, D., Kelly, T., Dodge, K. A., Bennett, D. S., & Pettit, G. S. (1994). Child-care history and kindergarten adjustment. *Developmental Psychology, 30,* 690–700.

Battin, M., van der Heide, A., Ganzini, L., van der Wal, G., & Onwuteaka-Philipsen, B. (2007). Legal physician-assisted dying in Oregon and the Netherlands: Evidence concerning the impact on patients in "vulnerable" groups. *Journal of Medical Ethics, 33,* 591–597.

Bauer, P. J. (2007). Recall in infancy: A neurodevelopmental account. *Current Directions in Psychological Science, 16,* 142–146.

Baulac, S., Lu, H., Strahle, J., Yang, T., Goldberg, M., Shen, J., et al. (2009). Increased DJ-1 expression under oxidative stress and in Alzheimer's disease brains. *Molecular Neurodegeneration, 4,* 27–37.

Bauld, R., & Brown, R. (2009). Stress, psychological distress, psychosocial factors, menopause symptoms and physical health in women. *Maturitas, 62,* 160–165.

Baum, A. (1994). Behavioral, biological, and environmental interactions in disease processes. In S. Blumenthal, K. Matthews, & S. Weiss (Eds.), *New research frontiers in behavioral medicine: Proceedings of the National Conference* (pp. 61–70). Washington, DC: NIH Publications.

Baumrind, D. (1971). Current patterns of parental authority. *Developmental Psychology Monographs, 4*(1), 1–103.

Baumrind, D. (1980). New directions in socialization research. *Psychological Bulletin, 35,* 639–652.

Bayley, N. (1969). *Manual for the Bayley scales of infant development*. New York: Psychological Corporation.

Bayley, N., & Oden, M. (1955). The maintenance of intellectual ability in gifted adults. *Journal of Gerontology, 10,* 91–107.

Beal, C. R. (1994). *Boys and girls: The development of gender roles*. New York: McGraw-Hill.

Beals, K., Impett, E., & Peplau, L. (2002). Lesbians in love: Why some relationships endure and others end. *Journal of Lesbian Studies, 6,* 53–63.

Bearce, K., & Rovee-Collier, C. (2006). Repeated priming increases memory accessibility in infants. *Journal of Experimental Child Psychology, 93,* 357–376.

Bearman, P., & Bruckner, H. (2004). *Study on teenage virginity pledge*. Paper presented at meeting of the National STD Prevention Conference, Phildadelphia, PA.

Beck, M. (2012, June 5). Hormone use benefits may trump risks; age matters. *Wall Street Journal*, pp. D1, D2.

Becker, B., & Luthar, S. (2007, March). Peer-perceived admiration and social preference: Contextual correlates of positive peer regard among suburban and urban adolescents. *Journal of Research on Adolescence, 17,* 117–144.

Becker, G., Beyene, Y., & Newsom, E. (2003). Creating continuity through mutual assistance: Intergenerational reciprocity in four ethnic groups. *Journals of Gerontology: Series B: Psychological Sciences & Social Sciences, 58B,* S151–S159.

Beckman, M. (2004, July 30). Neuroscience: Crime, culpability, and the adolescent brain. *Science, 305,* 596–599.

Beets, M., Flay, B., Vuchinich, S., Li, K., Acock, A., & Snyder, F. (2009). Longitudinal patterns of binge drinking among first year college students with a history of tobacco use. *Drug and Alcohol Dependence, 103,* 1–8.

Begeer, S., Bernstein, D. M., van Wijhe, J., Schleeren, A. M., & Koot, H. (2012). A continuous false belief task reveals egocentric biases in children and adolescents with autism spectrum disorders. *Autism, 16,* 357–366.

Begeny, J., & Martens, B. (2007). Inclusionary education in Italy: A literature review and call for more empirical research. *Remedial and Special Education, 28,* 80–94.

Begley, S. (1995, July 10). Deliver, then depart. *Newsweek*, p. 62.

Begley, S. (2010, November 8). Sins of the grandfathers. *Newsweek*, p. 48.

Beilby, J. M., Byrnes, M. L., & Young, K. N. (2012). The experiences of living with a sibling who stutters: A preliminary study. *Journal of Fluency Disorders, 37,* 135–148.

Beisert, M., Zmyj, N., Liepelt, R., Jung, F., Prinz, W., & Daum, M. M. (2012). Rethinking 'rational imitation' in 14-month-old infants: A perceptual distraction approach. *PLoS One, 7*(3). Accessed online, July 9, 2012, http://www.plosone.org/article/info%3Adoi%2F10.1371%2Fjournal.pone.0032563

Belcher, J. R. (2003). Stepparenting: Creating and recreating families in America today. *Journal of Nervous & Mental Disease, 191,* 837–838.

Belkin, L. (1999, July 25). Getting the girl. *The New York Times Magazine*, pp. 26–35.

Belkin, L. (2004, September 12). The lessons of Classroom 506: What happens when a boy with cerebral palsy goes to kindergarten like all the other kids. *The New York Times Magazine*, pp. 41–49.

Bell, A., & Weinberg, M. S. (1978). *Homosexuality: A study of diversities among men and women*. New York: Simon & Schuster.

Bell, I. P. (1989). The double standard: Age. In J. Freeman (Ed.), *Women: A feminist perspective* (4th ed., pp. 236–244). Mountain View, CA: Mayfield.

Belle, D. (1999). *The after-school lives of children: Alone and with others while parents work*. Mahwah, NJ: Lawrence Erlbaum.

Belsky, J. (2006). Early child care and early child development: Major findings from the NICHD Study of Early Child Care. *European Journal of Developmental Psychology, 3,* 95–110.

Belsky, J. (2009). Classroom composition, childcare history and social development: Are childcare effects disappearing or spreading? *Social Development, 18,* 230–238.

Belsky, J., Vandell, D. L., Burchinal, M., Clarke-Stewart, A. K., McCartney, K., & Owen, M. T. (2007). Are there long-term effects of early child care? *Child Development, 78,* 188–193.

Bender, H., Allen, J., McElhaney, K., Antonishak, J., Moore, C., Kelly, H., et al. (2007, December). Use of harsh physical discipline and developmental outcomes in adolescence. *Development and Psychopathology, 19,* 227–242.

Benelli, B., Belacchi, C., Gini, G., & Lucangeli, D. (2006, February). "To define means to say what you know about things": The development of definitional skills as metalinguistic acquisition. *Journal of Child Language, 33,* 71–97.

Benenson, J. F., & Apostoleris, N. H. (1993, March). *Gender differences in group interaction in early childhood*. Paper presented at the biennial meeting of the Society for Research in Child Development, New Orleans, LA.

Bengtson, V. L., Acock, A. C., Allen, K. R., & Dilworth-Anderson, P. (Eds.). (2004). *Sourcebook of family theory and research*. Thousand Oaks, CA: Sage Publications.

Benjuya, N., Melzer, I., & Kaplanski, J. (2004). Aging-induced shifts from a reliance on sensory input to muscle cocontraction during balanced standing. *Journal of Gerontology: Series A: Biological Sciences and Medical Sciences, 59,* 166–171.

Bennani, L., Allali, F., Rostom, S., Hmamouchi, I., Khazzani, H., El Mansouri, L., et al. (2009). Relationship between historical height loss and vertebral fractures in postmenopausal women. *Clinical Rheumatology, 28,* 1283–1289.

Bennett, J. (2008, September 15). It's not just white girls. *Newsweek*, p. 96.

Benson, E. (2003, March). Goo, gaa, grr? *Monitor on Psychology*, pp. 50–51.

Benson, H. (1993). The relaxation response. In D. Goleman & J. Guerin (Eds.), *Mind-body medicine: How to use your mind for better health* (pp. 233–257). Yonkers, NY: Consumer Reports Publications.

Benton, S. A., Robertson, J. M., Tseng, W.-C., Newton, F. B., & Benton, S. L. (2003). Changes in counseling center client problems across 13 years. *Professional Psychology: Research and Practice, 34,* 66–72.

Berenson, P. (2005). *Understand and treat alcoholism*. New York: Basic Books.

Bergelson, E., & Swingley, D. (2012). At 6-9 months, human infants know the meanings of many common nouns. *PNAS Proceedings of the National Academy of Sciences of the United States of America, 109,* 3253–3258.

Bergen, H., Martin, G., & Richardson, A. (2003). Sexual abuse and suicidal behavior: A model constructed from a large community sample of adolescents. *Journal of the American Academy of Child & Adolescent Psychiatry, 42,* 1301–1309.

Berger, L. (2000, April 11). What children do when home and alone. *The New York Times*, p. F8.

Bergman, A., Blom, I., & Polyak, D. (2012). Attachment and separation-individuation: Two ways of looking at the mother/infant relationship. In S. Akhtar (Ed.), *The mother and her child: Clinical aspects of attachment, separation, and loss* (pp. 55–68). Lanham, MD: Jason Aronson.

Bergmann, R. L., Bergman, K. E., & Dudenhausen, J. W. (2008). Undernutrition and growth restriction in pregnancy. *Nestle Nutritional Workshop Series; Pediatrics Program, 61,* 103–121.

Bergstrom, M. J., & Holmes, M. E. (2000). Lay theories of successful aging after the death of a spouse: A network text analysis of bereavement advice. *Health Communication, 12,* 377–406.

Berkman, R. (Ed.). (2006). *Handbook of social work in health and aging*. New York: Oxford University Press.

Berko, J. (1958). The child's learning of English morphology. *Word, 14,* 150–177.

Berlin, L., Cassidy, J., & Appleyard, K. (2008). The influence of early attachments on other relationships. In J. Cassidy & P. R. Shaver (Eds.), *Handbook of attachment: Theory, research, and clinical applications* (2nd ed. pp. 295–316). New York: Guilford Press.

Bernard, J. (1982). *The future of marriage*. New Haven, CT: Yale University Press.

Berndt, T. J. (1999). Friends' influence on students' adjustment to school. *Educational Psychologist, 34,* 15–28.

Berndt, T. J. (2002). Friendship quality and social development. *Current Directions in Psychological Science, 11,* 7–10.

Bernier, A., & Meins, E. (2008). A threshold approach to understanding the origins of attachment disorganization. *Developmental Psychology, 44,* 969–982.

Bernstein, E. (2010, April 20). Honey, do you have to… *Wall Street Journal*, pp. D1, D3.

Bernstein, N. (2004, March 7). Behind fall in pregnancy, a new teenage culture of restraint. *The New York Times*, pp. 1, 20.

Berry, G. L. (2003). Developing children and multicultural attitudes: The systemic psychosocial influences of television portrayals in a multimedia society. *Cultural Diversity and Ethnic Minority Psychology, 9,* 360–366.

Berscheid, E. (1985). Interpersonal attraction. In G. Lindzey & E. Aronson (Eds.), *Handbook of social psychology* (3rd ed., pp. 413–484). New York: Random House.

Berscheid, E., & Walster, E. (1974). Physical attractiveness. In G. Lindzey & E. Aronson (Eds.), *Handbook of social psychology* (3rd ed.). New York: Random House.

Bertera, E. M., & Crewe, S. (2013). Parenthood in the twenty-first century: African American grandparents as surrogate parents. *Journal of Human Behavior in the Social Environment, 23,* 178–192.

Bertin, E., & Striano, T. (2006, April). The still-face response in newborn, 1.5-, and 3-month-old infants. *Infant Behavior & Development, 29,* 294–297.

Besage, V. E. (2006). *Understanding girls' friendships, fights and feuds: A practical approach to girls' bullying*. Maidenhead, Berkshire: Open University Press/McGraw-Hill Education.

Besharov, D. J., & West, A. (2002). African American marriage patterns. In A. Thernstrom & S. Thernstrom (Eds.), *Beyond the color line: New perspectives on race and ethnicity in America* (pp. 95–114). Stanford, CA: Hoover Institution Press.

Bialystok, E., & Viswanathan, M. (2009). Components of executive control with advantages for bilingual children in two cultures. *Cognition, 112,* 494–500.

Biddle, B. J. (2001). *Social class, poverty, and education*. London: Falmer Press.

Bielak, A. M., Cherbuin, N., Bunce, D., & Anstey, K. J. (2013). Intraindividual variability is a fundamental phenomenon of aging: Evidence from an 8-year Longitudinal Study Across Young, Middle, and Older Adulthood. *Developmental Psychology*. Accessed online, June 11, 2012, http://www.ncbi.nlm.nih.gov/pubmed/23586940

Bierman, K. L. (2004). *Peer rejection: Developmental processes and intervention strategies*. New York: Guilford Press.

Bigelow, A. E., & Power, M. (2012). The effect of mother-infant skin-to-skin contact on infants' response to the Still Face Task from newborn to three months of age. *Infant Behavior & Development, 35,* 240–251.

Bigelow, A. E., & Rochat, P. (2006). Two-month-old infants' sensitivity to social contingency in mother-infant and stranger-infant interaction. *Infancy, 9,* 313–325.

Bionna, R. (2006). *Coping with stress in a changing world.* New York: McGraw-Hill.

Bird, C. M., & Burgess, N. (2008). The hippocampus and memory: Insights from spatial processing. *Nature Reviews Neuroscience, 9,* 182–194.

Bird, G., & Melville, K. (1994). *Families and intimate relationships.* New York: McGraw-Hill.

Birlouez-Aragon, I., & Tessier, F. (2003). Antioxidant vitamins and degenerative pathologies: A review of vitamin C. *Journal of Nutrition, Health & Aging, 7,* 103–109.

Biro, F., Striegel-Moore, R., Franko, D., Padgett, J., & Bean, J. (2006, October). Self-esteem in adolescent females. *Journal of Adolescent Health, 39,* 501–507.

Bischoföhler, D. (2012). Empathy and self-recognition in phylogenetic and ontogenetic perspective. *Emotion Review, 4,* 40–48.

Bishop, D. I., Meyer, B., Schmidt, T., & Gray, B. (2009). Differential investment behavior between grandparents and grandchildren: The role of paternity uncertainty. *Evolutionary Psychology, 7,* 66–77.

Bishop, D. V. M., & Leonard, L. B. (Eds.). (2001). *Speech and language impairments in children: Causes, characteristics, intervention and outcome.* Philadelphia: Psychology Press.

Bishop, J. (2006, April). Euthanasia, efficiency, and the historical distinction between killing a patient and allowing a patient to die. *Journal of Medical Ethics, 32,* 220–224.

Bjorklund, D. (2006). Mother knows best: Epigenetic inheritance, maternal effects, and the evolution of human intelligence. *Developmental Review, 26,* 213– 242.

Bjorklund, D. F., & Ellis, B. (2005). Evolutionary psychology and child development: An emerging synthesis. In B. J. Ellis (Ed.), *Origins of the social mind: Evolutionary psychology and child development* (pp. 3–18). New York: Guilford Press.

Black, K. (2002). Associations between adolescent—mother and adolescent-best friend interactions. *Adolescence, 37,* 235–253.

Black, M. M., & Matula, K. (1999). *Essentials of Bayley scales of infant development II assessment.* New York: Wiley.

Blagosklonny, M. V., Campisi, J., Sinclair, D. A., Bartke, A., Blasco, M. A., Bonner, W. M., et al. (2010). Impact papers on aging in 2009. *Aging, 2,* 111–121.

Blair, P., Sidebotham, P., Berry, P., Evans, M., & Fleming, P. (2006). Major epidemiological changes in sudden infant death syndrome: A 20-year population-based study in the UK. *Lancet, 367,* 314–319.

Blair, S. N., Kohl, H. W., Paffenberger, R. S., Clark, D. G., Cooper, K. H., & Gibbons, L. W. (1989). Physical fitness and all-cause mortality: A prospective study of healthy men and women. *JAMA: The Journal of the American Medical Association, 262,* 2395–2401.

Blake, G., Velikonja, D., Pepper, V., Jilderda, I., & Georgiou, G. (2008). Evaluating an in-school injury prevention programme's effect on children's helmet wearing habits. *Brain Injury, 22,* 501–507.

Blake, J., & de Boysson-Bardies, B. (1992). Patterns in babbling: A cross-linguistic study. *Journal of Child Language, 19,* 51–74.

Blakemore, J. (2003). Children's beliefs about violating gender norms: Boys shouldn't look like girls, and girls shouldn't act like boys. *Sex Roles, 48,* 411–419.

Blakemore, S. (2012). Imaging brain development: The adolescent brain. *Neuroimage, 61,* 397–406.

Blankinship, D. G. (2012, July 7). Two more states are granted 'No Child Left Behind' waivers. *The Virginian Pilot,* p. 5.

Blass, E. M., Ganchrow, J. R., & Steiner, J. E. (1984). Classical conditioning in newborn humans 2-48 hours of age. *Infant Behavior and Development, 7,* 223–235.

Blewitt, P., Rump, K., Shealy, S., & Cook, S. (2009). Shared book reading: When and how questions affect young children's word learning. *Journal of Educational Psychology, 101.*

Bloom, C., & Lamkin, D. (2006). The Olympian struggle to remember the cranial nerves: Mnemonics and student success. *Teaching of Psychology, 33,* 128–129.

Blount, B. G. (1982). Culture and the language of socialization: Parental speech. In D. A. Wagner & H. W. Stevenson (Eds.), *Cultural perspectives on child development* (pp. 54–76). San Francisco: Freeman.

Blumenthal, S. (2000). Developmental aspects of violence and the institutional response. *Criminal Behaviour & Mental Health, 10,* 185–198.

Blumstein, P., & Schwartz, P. (1989). *American couples: Money, work, sex.* New York: Morrow.

Bober, S., Humphry, R., & Carswell, H. (2001). Toddlers' persistence in the emerging occupations of functional play and self-feeding. *American Journal of Occupational Therapy, 55,* 369–376.

Bodell, L. P., Joiner, T. E., & Ialongo, N. S. (2012). Longitudinal association between childhood impulsivity and bulimic symptoms in African American adolescent girls. *Journal of Consulting and Clinical Psychology, 80,* 313–316.

Bodner, E., Bergman, Y. S., & Cohen-Fridel, S. (2012). Different dimensions of ageist attitudes among men and women: A multigenerational perspective. *International Psychogeriatrics, 24*(6), 895–901. doi:10.1017/S1041610211002936

Boeckx, C. (2010). *Language in cognition: Uncovering mental structures and the rules behind them.* New York: Wiley-Blackwell.

Boehm, K. E., & Campbell, N. B. (1995). Suicide: A review of calls to an adolescent peer listening phone service. *Child Psychiatry & Human Development, 26,* 61–66.

Boerner, K., Brennan, M., Horowitz, A., & Reinhardt, J. (2010). Tackling vision-related disability in old age: An application of the life-span theory of control to narrative data. *Journals of Gerontology: Series B: Psychological Sciences and Social Sciences, 65B,* 22–31.

Boerner, K., Wortman, C. B., & Bonanno, G. A. (2005). Resilient or at risk? A 4-year study of older adults who initially showed high or low distress following conjugal loss. *Journals of Gerontology: Series B, Psychological Sciences and Social Sciences, 60,* P67–P73.

Bogle, K. A. (2008). 'Hooking up': What educators need to know. *Chronicle of Higher Education,* p. A32.

Bohlmeijer, E., Roemer, M., Cuijpers, P., & Smit, F. (2007). The effects of reminiscence on psychological well-being in order adults: A meta-analysis. *Aging & Mental Health, 11.*

Bohlmeijer, E., Westerhof, G., & de Jong, M. (2008). The effects of integrative reminiscence on meaning in life: Results of a quasi-experimental study. *Aging & Mental Health, 12,* 639–646.

Boivin, M., Perusse, D., Dionne, G., Saysset, V., Zoccolilo, M., Tarabulsy, G. M., et al. (2005). The genetic-environmental etiology of parents' perceptions and self-assessed behaviours toward their 5-month-old infants in a large twin and singleton sample. *Journal of Child Psychology and Psychiatry, 46,* 612–630.

Boles, T., Le, H., & Nguyen, H. (2010). Persons, organizations, and societies: The effects of collectivism and individualism on cooperation. In R. Kramer, A. Tenbrunsel, & M. H. Bazerman (Eds.), *Social decision making: Social dilemmas, social values, and ethical judgments* (pp. 171–200). New York: Routledge / Taylor & Francis Group.

Bonanno, G. A. (2009). *The other side of sadness.* New York: Basic Books.

Bonanno, G. A., Boerner, K., & Wortman, C. B. (2008). Trajectories of grieving. In M. S. Stroebe, R. O. Hansson, H. Schut, & W. Stroebe (Eds.), *Handbook of bereavement research and practice: Advances in theory and intervention* (pp. 287–308). Washington, DC: American Psychological Association.

Bonanno, G. A., Galea, S., Bucciarelli, A., & Vlahov, D. (2006). Psychological resilience after disaster: New York City in the aftermath of the September 11th terrorist attack. *Psychological Science, 17,* 181–186.

Bonanno, G. A., & Mancini, A. D. (2012). Beyond resilience and PTSD: Mapping the heterogeneity of responses to potential trauma. *Psychological Trauma: Theory, Research, Practice, and Policy, 4,* 15–24.

Bonanno, G. A., Wortman, C. B., Lehman, D. R., Tweed, R. G., Haring, M., Sonnega, J., et al. (2002). Resilience to loss and chronic grief: A prospective study from preloss to 18-months postloss. *Journal of Personality and Social Psychology, 83,* 1150–1164.

Boneva, B., Quinn, A., Kraut, R., Kiesler, S., & Shklovski, I. (2006). Teenage communication in the instant messaging era. In R. Kraut & M. Brynin (Eds.), *Computers, phones, and the Internet: Domesticating information technology.* New York: Oxford University Press.

Bonke, B., Tibben, A., Lindhout, D., Clarke, A. J., & Stijnen, T. (2005). Genetic risk estimation by healthcare professionals. *Medical Journal of Autism, 182,* 116–118.

Bonoti, F., Leondari, A., & Mastora, A. (2013). Exploring children's understanding of death: Through drawings and the Death Concept Questionnaire. *Death Studies, 37,* 47–60.

Bookstein, F. L., Sampson, P. D., Streissguth, A. P., & Barr, H. M. (1996). Exploiting redundant measurement of dose and developmental outcome: New methods from the behavioral teratology of alcohol. *Developmental Psychology, 32,* 404–415.

Booth, C., Kelly, J., & Spieker, S. (2003). Toddlers' attachment security to child-care providers: The Safe and Secure Scale. *Early Education & Development, 14,* 83–100.

Borden, M. E. (1998). *Smart start: The parents' complete guide to preschool education.* New York: Facts on File.

Bornstein, M. H., Cote, L., & Maital, S. (2004). Cross-linguistic analysis of vocabulary in young children: Spanish, Dutch, French, Hebrew, Italian, Korean, and American English. *Child Development, 75,* 1115–1139.

Bornstein, M. H., Haynes, O. M., O'Reilly, A. W., & Painter, K. M. (1996). Solitary and collaborative pretense play in early childhood: Sources of individual variation in the development of representational competence. *Child Development, 67,* 2910–2929.

Bornstein, M. H., & Lamb, M. E. (1992). *Development in infancy: An introduction.* New York: McGraw-Hill.

Bornstein, M. H., Putnick, D. L., Suwalsky, T. D., & Gini, M. (2006). Maternal chronological age, prenatal and perinatal history, social support, and parenting of infants. *Child Development, 77,* 875–892.

Bornstein, M. H., Tamis-LeMonda, C. S., Hahn, C., & Haynes, O. M. (2008). Maternal responsiveness to young children at three ages: Longitudinal analysis of a multidimensional, modular, and specific parenting construct. *Developmental Psychology, 44,* 867–874.

Borse, N. N., Gilchrist, J., Dellinger, A. M., Rudd, R. A., Ballesteros, M. F., & Sleet, D. A. (2008). *CDC childhood injury report: Patterns of unintentional injuries among 0–19 year olds in the United States, 2000-2006.* Atlanta, GA: Centers for Disease Control and Prevention, National Center for Injury Prevention and Control.

Bos, C. S., & Vaughn, S. S. (2005). *Strategies for teaching students with learning and behavior problems* (6th ed.). Boston: Allyn & Bacon.

Bos, H., Sandfort, T., de Bruyn, E., & Hakvoort, E. (2008). Same-sex attraction, social relationships, psychosocial functioning, and school performance in early adolescence. *Developmental Psychology, 44,* 59–68.

Bouchard, T. J., Jr. (1997, September/October). Whenever the twain shall meet. *The Sciences,* 52–57.

Bouchard, T. J., Jr. (2004). Genetic influence on human psychological traits: A survey. *Current Directions in Psychological Science, 13,* 148–153.

Bouchard, T. J., Jr., Lykken, D. T., McGue, M., Segal, N. L., & Tellegen, A. (1990, October 12). Sources of human psychological differences: The Minnesota study of twins reared apart. *Science, 250,* 223–228.

Bouchard, T. J., Jr., & McGue, M. (1981). Familial studies of intelligence: A review. *Science, 212,* 1055–1059.

Bourne, V., & Todd, B. (2004). When left means right: An explanation of the left cradling bias in terms of right hemisphere specializations. *Developmental Science, 7,* 19–24.

Bower, T. G. R. (1977). *A primer of infant development.* San Francisco: Freeman.

Bowers, A. J., Sprott, R., & Taff, S. A. (2013). Do we know who will drop out? A review of the predictors of dropping out of high school: Precision, sensitivity, and specificity. *The High School Journal, 96,* 77–100.

Bowers, K. E., & Thomas, P. (1995, August). Handle with care. *Harvard Health Letter,* pp. 6–7.

Boyatzis, C. J. (2013). The nature and functions of religion and spirituality in children. In K. I. Pargament, J. J. Exline, & J. W. Jones (Eds.), *APA handbook of psychology, religion, and spirituality (Vol 1): Context, theory, and research.* Washington, DC: American Psychological Association.

Boyatzis, C. J., Mallis, M., & Leon, I. (1999). Effects of game type of children's gender-based peer preferences: A naturalistic observational study. *Sex Roles, 40,* 93–105.

Bracey, J., Bamaca, M., & Umana-Taylor, A. (2004). Examining ethnic identity and self-esteem among biracial and monoracial adolescents. *Journal of Youth & Adolescence, 33,* 123–132.

Bracken, B., & Brown, E. (2006, June). Behavioral identification and assessment of gifted and talented students. *Journal of Psychoeducational Assessment, 24,* 112–122.

Bracken, B., & Lamprecht, M. (2003). Positive self-concept: An equal opportunity construct. *School Psychology Quarterly, 18,* 103–121.

Bradshaw, M., & Ellison, C. (2008). Do genetic factors influence religious life? Findings from a behavior genetic analysis of twin siblings. *Journal for the Scientific Study of Religion, 47,* 529–544. Available online at http://search.ebscohost.com

Brady, S. A. (2011). Efficacy of phonics teaching for reading outcomes: Indications from post-NRP research. In S. A. Brady, D. Braze, & C. A. Fowler (Eds.), *Explaining individual differences in reading: Theory and evidence* (pp. 69–96). New York: Psychology Press.

Brainerd, C. (2003). Jean Piaget, learning research, and American education. In B. Zimmerman (Ed.), *Educational psychology: A century of contributions* (pp. 251–287). Mahwah, NJ: Lawrence Erlbaum.

Brandone, A. C., Cimpian, A., Leslie, S., & Gelman, S. A. (2012). Do lions have manes? For children, generics are about kinds rather than quantities. *Child Development, 83,* 423–433.

Branje, S. J. T., van Lieshout, C. F. M., van Aken, M. A. G., & Haselager, G. J. T. (2004). Perceived support in sibling relationships and adolescent adjustment. *Journal of Child Psychology and Psychiatry, 45,* 1385–1396.

Brant, M. (2003, September 8). Log on and learn. *Newsweek,* p. E14.

Branum, A. (2006). Teen maternal age and very preterm birth of twins. *Maternal & Child Health Journal, 10,* 229–233.

Braun, K. L., Pietsch, J. H., & Blanchette, P. L. (Eds.). (2000). *Cultural issues in end-of-life decision making.* Thousand Oaks, CA: Sage Publications.

Bray, G. A. (2008). Is new hope on the horizon for obesity? *The Lancet, 372,* 1859–1860.

Brazelton, T. B. (1990). Saving the bathwater. *Child Development, 61,* 1661–1671.

Brazelton, T. B., & Sparrow, J. D. (2003). *Discipline: The Brazelton way.* New York: Perseus.

Bredesen, D. (2009). Neurodegeneration in Alzheimer's disease: Caspases and synaptic element interdependence. *Molecular Neurodegeneration, 4,* 52–59.

Breheny, M., & Stephens, C. (2003). Healthy living and keeping busy: A discourse analysis of mid-aged women's attributions for menopausal experience. *Journal of Language & Social Psychology, 22,* 169–189.

Brehm, S. S. (1992). *Intimate relationships* (2nd ed.). New York: McGraw-Hill.

Bremner, G., & Fogel, A. (Eds.). (2004). *Blackwell handbook of infant development.* Malden, MA: Blackwell Publishers.

Breslau, N., Bohnert, K., & Koenen, K. (2010). The 9/11 terrorist attack and posttraumatic stress disorder revisited. *Journal of Nervous and Mental Disease, 198,* 539–543.

Bridges, J. S. (1993). Pink or blue: Gender-stereotypic perceptions of infants as conveyed by birth congratulations cards. *Psychology of Women Quarterly, 17,* 193–205.

Bridgett, D., Gartstein, M., Putnam, S., McKay, T., Iddins, E., Robertson, C., et al. (2009). Maternal and contextual influences and the effect of temperament development during infancy on parenting in toddlerhood. *Infant Behavior & Development, 32,* 103–116.

Briere, J. N., Berliner, L., Bulkley, J., Jenny, C., & Reid, T. (Eds.). (1997). *The APSAC handbook on child maltreatment.* Thousand Oaks, CA: Sage Publications.

Brinker, J. K. (2013). Rumination and reminiscence in older adults: Implications for clinical practice. *European Journal of Ageing.* Accessed online, June 13, 2013, http://link.springer.com/article/10.1007/s10433-013-0271-y#page-1

Broadbent, R., & Papadopoulos, T. (2013). Bridging the digital divide—An Australian story. *Behaviour & Information Technology, 32,* 4–13.

Brody, N. (1993). Intelligence and the behavioral genetics of personality. In R. Plomin & G. E. McClearn (Eds.), *Nature, nurture, and psychology* (pp. 161–178). Washington, DC: American Psychological Association.

Bromberger, J. T., & Matthews, K. A. (1994). Employment status and depressive symptoms in middle-aged women: A longitudinal investigation. *American Journal of Public Health, 84,* 202–206.

Bronfenbrenner, U. (1989). Ecological systems theory. In R. Vasta (Ed.), *Six theories of child development* (pp. 187–250). Greenwich, CT: JAI Press.

Bronfenbrenner, U. (2000). Ecological theory. In A. Kazdin (Ed.), *Encyclopedia of psychology* (pp. 129–133). Washington, DC: American Psychological Association/Oxford University Press.

Bronfenbrenner, U. (2002). Preparing a world for the infant in the twenty-first century: The research challenge. In J. Gomes-Pedro, J. Nugent, J. Young, & T. Brazelton (Eds.), *The infant and family in the twenty-first century* (pp. 45–52). New York: Brunner-Routledge.

Brook, U., & Tepper, I. (1997). High school students' attitudes and knowledge of food consumption and body image: Implications for school-based education. *Patient Education & Counseling, 30,* 282–288.

Brooks-Gunn, J. (2003). Do you believe in magic? What we can expect from early childhood intervention programs. *Social Policy Report, 17,* 1–16.

Brooks-Gunn, J., Klebanov, P. K., & Duncan, G. J. (1996). Ethnic differences in children's intelligence test scores: Role of economic deprivation, home environment, and maternal characteristics. *Child Development, 67,* 396–408.

Brotanek, J., Gosz, J., Weitzman, M., & Flores, G. (2007). Iron deficiency in early childhood in the United States: Risk factors and racial/ethnic disparities. *Pediatrics, 120,* 568–575.

Brown, B. B., & Klute, C. (2003). Friendships, cliques, and crowds. In G. R. Adams & M. D. Berzonsky (Eds.), *Blackwell handbook of adolescence* (pp. 330–348). Malden, MA: Blackwell Publishing.

Brown, C. P. (2009). Pivoting a prekindergarten program off the child or the standard? A case study of integrating the practices of early childhood education into elementary school. *The Elementary School Journal, 110,* 202–227.

Brown, D. L., Jewell, J. D., Stevens, A. L., Crawford, J. D., & Thompson, R. (2012). Suicidal risk in adolescent residential treatment: Being female is more important than a depression diagnosis. *Journal of Child and Family Studies, 21,* 359–367.

Brown, E. L., & Bull, R. (2007). Can task modifications influence children's performance on false belief tasks? *European Journal of Developmental Psychology, 4,* 273–292.

Brown, J. D. (1998). *The self.* New York: McGraw-Hill.

Brown, J. V., Bakeman, R., Coles, C. D., Platzman, K. A., & Lynch, M. E. (2004). Prenatal cocaine exposure: A comparison of 2-year-old children in prenatal and non-parental care. *Child Development, 75,* 1282–1295.

Brown, R. (1973). *A first language.* Cambridge, MA: Harvard University Press.

Brown, R., & Fraser, C. (1963). The acquisition syntax. In C. N. Cofer & B. Musgrave (Eds.), *Verbal behavior and learning: Problems and processes* (pp. 158–201). New York: McGraw-Hill.

Brown, S., & Lin, I-Fen. (2012, March). *The gray divorce revolution: Rising divorce among middle-aged and older adults, 1990-2009* (Working Paper Series WP-12-04). Bowling Green, OH: National Center for Family & Marriage Research, Bowling Green State University.

Brown, S. A. (2004). Measuring youth outcomes from alcohol and drug treatment. *Addiction, 99,* 38–46.

Brown, W. M., Hines, M., & Fane, B. A. (2002). Masculinized finger length patterns in human males and females with congenital adrenal hyperplasia. *Hormones and Behavior, 42,* 380–386.

Browne, A. (1993). Violence against women by male partners: Prevalence, outcomes, and policy implications. *American Psychologist, 48,* 1077–1087.

Browne, C. (2010). Review of 'Asian American elders in the twenty-first century: Key indicators of well-being'. *Journal of Women & Aging, 22,* 151–153.

Browne, K. (2006, March). Evolved sex differences and occupational segregation. *Journal of Organizational Behavior, 27,* 143–162.

Brownell, C., Nichols, S., Svetlova, M., Zerwas, S., & Ramani, G. (2010). The head bone's connected to the neck bone: When do toddlers represent their own body topography? *Child Development, 81,* 797–810.

Brownlee, S. (2002, January 21). Too heavy, too young. *Time,* pp. 21–23.

Brubaker, T. (1991). Families in later life: A burgeoning research area. In A. Booth (Ed.), *Contemporary families* (pp. 226–248). Minneapolis, MN: National Council on Family Relations.

Bruck, M., & Ceci, S. (2004). Forensic developmental psychology: Unveiling four common misconceptions. *Current Directions in Psychological Science, 13,* 229–232.

Brugman, G. (2006). *Wisdom and aging.* Amsterdam, Netherlands: Elsevier.

Bruskas, D. (2008). Children in foster care: A vulnerable population at risk. *Journal of Child and Adolescent Psychiatric Nursing, 21,* 70–77.

Bryant, C. D. (Ed.). (2003). *Handbook of death and dying.* Thousand Oaks, CA: Sage Publications.

Bryant, J., & Bryant, J. A. (Eds.). (2001). *Television and the American family* (2nd ed.). Mahwah, NJ: Lawrence Erlbaum.

Bryant, J., & Bryant, J. A. (2003). Effects of entertainment televisual media on children. In E. Palmer & B. Young (Eds.), *The faces of televisual media: Teaching, violence, selling to children* (pp. 195–217). Mahwah, NJ: Lawrence Erlbaum.

Buchanan, C. M., Eccles, J. S., & Becker, J. B. (1992). Are adolescents the victims of raging hormones? Evidence for activational effects of hormones on moods and behavior at adolescence. *Psychological Bulletin, 111,* 62–107.

Buchmann, C., & DiPrete, T. (2006, August). The growing female advantage in college completion: The role of family background and academic achievement. *American Sociological Review, 7,* 515–541.

Budd, K. (1999). The facts of life: Everything you wanted to know about sex (after 50). *Modern Maturity, 42,* 78.

Bull, M., & Durbin, D. (2008). Rear-facing car safety seats: Getting the message right. *Pediatrics, 121,* 619–620.

Bullinger, A. (1997). Sensorimotor function and its evolution. In J. Guimon (Ed.), *The body in psychotherapy* (pp. 25–29). Basil, Switzerland: Karger.

Bumpass, L., Sweet, J., & Martin, T. (1990). Changing patterns of remarriage. *Journal of Marriage and the Family, 52,* 747–756.

Bumpus, M. F., Crouter, A. C., & McHale, S. M. (2001). Parental autonomy granting during adolescence: Exploring gender differences in context. *Developmental Psychology, 37,* 163–173.

Burbach, J., & van der Zwaag, B. (2009). Contact in the genetics of autism and schizophrenia. *Trends in Neurosciences, 32,* 69–72. Available online at http://search.ebscohost.com

Burd, L., Cotsonas-Hassler, T. M., Martsolf, J. T., & Kerbeshian, J. (2003). Recognition and management of fetal alcohol syndrome. *Neurotoxicological Teratology, 25,* 681–688.

Bureau of Labor Statistics. (2012, March 1). *Labor force statistics from the Current Population Survey.* Downloaded July 10, 2012, from http://www.bls.gov/cps/cpsaat37.htm

Burgaleta, M., Baus, C., Díaz, B., & Sebastián-Gallés, N. (2013). Brain structure is related to speech perception abilities in bilinguals. *Brain Structure & Function.* Accessed online, June 6, 2013, http://www.ncbi.nlm.nih.gov/pubmed/23686398

Burgess, K. B., & Rubin, K. H. (2000). Middle childhood: Social and emotional development. In A. E. Kazdin (Ed.), *Encyclopedia of psychology,* (Vol. 5, pp. 234–239). Washington, DC: American Psychological Association.

Burgess, R. L., & Huston, T. L. (Eds.). (1979). *Social exchanges in developing relationships.* New York: Academic Press.

Burnett, P., & Proctor, R. (2002). Elementary school students' learner self-concept, academic self-concepts and approaches to learning. *Educational Psychology in Practice, 18,* 325–333.

Burnett-Wolle, S., & Godbey, G. (2007). Refining research on older adults' leisure: Implications of selection, optimization, and compensation and socioemotional selectivity theories. *Journal of Leisure Research, 39,* 498–513.

Burnham, M., Goodlin-Jones, B., & Gaylor, E. (2002). Nighttime sleep-wake patterns and self-soothing from birth to one year of age: A longitudinal intervention study. *Journal of Child Psychology & Psychiatry & Allied Disciplines, 43,* 713–725.

Burns, D. M. (2000). Cigarette smoking among the elderly: Disease consequences and the benefits of cessation. *American Journal of Health Promotion, 14,* 357–361.

Burrus-Bammel, L. L., & Bammel, G. (1985). Leisure and recreation. In J. E. Birren & K. W. Schaie (Eds.), *Handbook of the psychology of aging* (pp. 848–863). New York: Van Nostrand Reinhold.

Burt, V. L., & Harris, T. (1994). The third National Health and Nutrition Examination Survey: Contributing data on aging and health. *Gerontologist, 34,* 486–490.

Burton, A., Haley, W., & Small, B. (2006, May). Bereavement after caregiving or unexpected death: Effects on elderly spouses. *Aging & Mental Health, 10,* 319–326.

Burton, L., Henninger, D., Hafetz, J., & Cofer, J. (2009). Aggression, gender-typical childhood play, and a prenatal hormonal index. *Social Behavior and Personality, 37,* 105–116.

Busick, D., Brooks, J., Pernecky, S., Dawson, R., & Petzoldt, J. (2008). Parent food purchases as a measure of exposure and preschool-aged children's willingness to identify and taste fruit and vegetables. *Appetite, 51,* 468–473.

Buss, A. H. (2012). *Pathways to individuality: Evolution and development of personality traits.* Washington, DC: American Psychological Association.

Buss, D. M. (2003). *The evolution of desire: Strategies of human mating* (Rev. ed.). New York: Basic Books.

Buss, D. M. (2004). *Evolutionary psychology: The new science of the mind* (2nd ed.). Boston: Allyn & Bacon.

Buss, D. M., Abbott, M., Angleitner, A., Asherian, A., Biaggio, A., Blanco-Villasenor, A., et al. (1990). International preferences in selecting mates: A study of 37 cultures. *Journal of Cross-Cultural Psychology, 21,* 5–47.

Buss, D. M., & Reeve, H. K. (2003). Evolutionary psychology and developmental dynamics: Comment on Lickliter and Honeycutt. *Psychological Bulletin, 129,* 848–853.

Butler, K. G., & Silliman, E. R. (2002). *Speaking, reading, and writing in children with language learning disabilities: New paradigms in research and practice.* Mahwah, NJ: Lawrence Erlbaum.

Butler, R. J., Wilson, B. L., & Johnson, W. G. (2012). A modified measure of health care disparities applied to birth weight disparities and subsequent mortality. *Health Economics, 21,* 113–126.

Butler, R. N. (2002). The life review. *Journal of Geriatric Psychiatry, 35,* 7–10.

Butler, R. N., & Lewis, M. I. (1981). *Aging and mental health.* St. Louis: Mosby.

Butterworth, G. (1994). Infant intelligence. In J. Khalfa (Ed.), *What is intelligence? The Darwin College lecture series* (pp. 49–71). Cambridge, England: Cambridge University Press.

Butzer, B., & Campbell, L. (2008). Adult attachment, sexual satisfaction, and relationship satisfaction: A study of married couples. *Personal Relationships, 15,* 141–154.

Buysse, D. J. (2005). Diagnosis and assessment of sleep and circadian rhythm disorders. *Journal of Psychiatric Practice, 11,* 102–115.

Byrd-Craven, J., Auer, B. J., Granger, D. A., & Massey, A. R. (2012). The father-daughter dance: The relationship between father-daughter relationship quality and daughters' stress response. *Journal of Family Psychology, 26,* 87–94.

Byrne, A. (2000). Singular identities: Managing stigma, resisting voices. *Women's Studies Review, 7,* 13–24.

Byun, S., & Park, H. (2012). The academic success of East Asian American youth: The role of shadow education. *Sociology of Education, 85,* 40–60.

Cabrera, N., Shannon, J., & Tamis-LeMonda, C. (2007). Fathers' influence on their children's cognitive and emotional development: From toddlers to pre-K. *Applied Developmental Science, 11,* 208–213.

Cacciatore, J. (2010). The unique experiences of women and their families after the death of a baby. *Social Work in Health Care, 49,* 134–148.

Cacciatore, J., & Bushfield, S. (2007). Stillbirth: The mother's experience and implications for improving care. *Journal of Social Work in End-of-Life & Palliative Care, 3,* 59–79.

Cain, B. S. (1982, December 19). Plight of the gray divorcee. *The New York Times Magazine,* pp. 89–93.

Caino, S., Kelmansky, D., Lejarraga, H., & Adamo, P. (2004). Short-term growth at adolescence in healthy girls. *Annals of Human Biology, 31,* 182–195.

Calhoun, F., & Warren, K. (2007). Fetal alcohol syndrome: Historical perspectives. *Neuroscience & Biobehavioral Reviews, 31,* 168–171.

Callahan, P. M., Hutchings, E. J., Kille, N. J., Chapman, J. M., & Terry, A. R. (2013). Positive allosteric modulator of alpha 7 nicotinic-acetylcholine receptors, PNU-120596 augments the effects of donepezil on learning and memory in aged rodents and non-human primates. *Neuropharmacology, 67,* 201–212.

Callister, L. C., Khalaf, I., Semenic, S., Kartchner, R., & Vehvilainen-Julkunen, K. (2003). The pain of childbirth: Perceptions of culturally diverse women. *Pain Management Nursing, 4,* 145–154.

Calvert, S. L., Kotler, J. A., Zehnder, S., & Shockey, E. (2003). Gender stereotyping in children's reports about educational and informational television programs. *Media Psychology, 5,* 139–162.

Calzada, E. J., Huang, K., Anicama, C., Fernandez, Y., & Brotman, L. (2012). Test of a cultural framework of parenting with Latino families of young children. *Cultural Diversity and Ethnic Minority Psychology, 18,* 285–296.

Camarota, S. A. (2001). *Immigrants in the United States—2000: A snapshot of America's foreign-born population.* Washington, DC: Center for Immigration Studies.

Cameron, P. (2003). Domestic violence among homosexual partners. *Psychological Reports, 93,* 410–416.

Cami, J., & Farré, M. (2003). Drug addiction. *New England Journal of Medicine, 349,* 975–986.

Campbell, A., Shirley, L., & Candy, J. (2004). A longitudinal study of gender-related cognition and behaviour. *Developmental Science, 7,* 1–9.

Campbell, D., Scott, K., Klaus, M., & Falk, M. (2007). Female relatives or friends trained as labor doulas: Outcomes at 6 to 8 weeks postpartum. *Birth: Issues in Perinatal Care, 34,* 220–227.

Campbell, F., Ramey, C., & Pungello, E. (2002). Early childhood education: Young adult outcomes from the Abecedarian Project. *Applied Developmental Science, 6,* 42–57.

Campos, J. J., Langer, A., & Krowitz, A. (1970). Cardiac responses on the visual cliff in prelocomotor human infants. *Science, 170,* 196–197.

Camras, L., Meng, Z., & Ujiie, T. (2002). Observing emotion in infants: Facial expression, body behavior, and rater judgments of responses to an expectancy-violating event. *Emotion, 2,* 179–193.

Camras, L., Oster, H., Bakeman, R., Meng, Z., Ujiie, T., & Campos, J. (2007). Do infants show distinct negative facial expressions for fear and anger? Emotional expression in 11-month-old European American, Chinese, and Japanese Infants. *Infancy, 11,* 131–155.

Canals, J., Fernandez-Ballart, J., & Esparo, G. (2003). Evolution of Neonatal Behavior Assessment Scale scores in the first month of life. *Infant Behavior & Development, 26,* 227–237.

Cantin, V., Lavallière, M., Simoneau, M., & Teasdale, N. (2009). Mental workload when driving in a simulator: Effects of age and driving complexity. *Accident Analysis and Prevention, 41,* 763–771.

Caplan, L. J., & Barr, R. A. (1989). On the relationship between category intensions and extensions in children. *Journal of Experimental Child Psychology, 47,* 413–429.

Cappeliez, P., Guindon, M., & Robitaille, A. (2008). Functions of reminiscence and emotional regulation among older adults. *Journal of Aging Studies, 22,* 266–272.

Caputi, M., Lecce, S., Pagnin, A., & Banerjee, R. (2012). Longitudinal effects of theory of mind on later peer relations: The role of prosocial behavior. *Developmental Psychology, 48,* 257–270.

Cardman, M. (2004). Rising GPAs, course loads a mystery to researchers. *Education Daily, 37,* 1–3.

Carey, B. (2012, March 29). Diagnoses of autism on the rise, report says. *The New York Times,* p. A20.

Carnegie Task Force on Meeting the Needs of Young Children. (1994). *Starting points: Meeting the needs of our youngest children.* New York: Carnegie Corporation.

Carnell, S., Benson, L., Pryor, K., & Driggin, E. (2013). Appetitive traits from infancy to adolescence: Using behavioral and neural measures to investigate obesity risk. *Physiology & Behavior.* Accessed online, June 4, 2013, http://www.ncbi.nlm.nih.gov/pubmed/23458627

Caron, A. (2009). Comprehension of the representational mind in infancy. *Developmental Review, 29,* 69–95.

Carr, P. B., & Steele, C. M. (2009). Stereotype threat and inflexible perseverance in problem solving. *Journal of Experimental Social Psychology, 45,* 853–859.

Carrère, S., Buehlman, K. T., Gottman, J. M., Coan, J. A., & Ruckstuhl, L. (2000). Predicting marital stability and divorce in newlywed couples. *Journal of Family Psychology, 14,* 42–58.

Carson, R. G. (2006). Neural pathways mediating bilateral interactions between the upper limbs. *Brain Research Review, 49,* 641–662.

Carter, S. F., Caine, D. B., Burns, D., Herholz, K., & Lambon, M. (2012). Staging of the cognitive decline in Alzheimer's disease: Insights from a detailed neuropsychological investigation of mild cognitive impairment and mild Alzheimer's disease. *International Journal of Geriatric Psychiatry, 27,* 423–432.

Carton, A., & Aiello, J. (2009). Control and anticipation of social interruptions: Reduced stress and improved task performance. *Journal of Applied Social Psychology, 39,* 169–185.

Carver, C., & Scheier, M. (2002). Coping processes and adjustment to chronic illness. In A. Christensen & M. Antoni (Eds.), *Chronic physical disorders: Behavioral medicine's perspective* (pp. 47–68). Malden, MA: Blackwell Publishers.

Carver, L., & Vaccaro, B. (2007, January). 12-month-old infants allocate increased neural resources to stimuli associated with negative adult emotion. *Developmental Psychology, 43,* 54–69.

Casalin, S., Luyten, P., Vliegen, N., & Meurs, P. (2012). The structure and stability of temperament from infancy to toddlerhood: A one-year prospective study. *Infant Behavior & Development, 35,* 94–108.

Cascalho, M., Ogle, B. M., & Platt, J. L. (2006). The future of organ transplantation. *Annals of Transplantation, 11,* 44–47.

Case, R. (1991). Stages in the development of the young child's first sense of self. *Developmental Review, 11,* 210–230.

Case, R. (1999). Conceptual development. In M. Bennett (Ed.), *Developmental psychology: Achievements and prospects* (pp. 36–54). Philadelphia: Psychology Press.

Case, R., Demetriou, A., & Platsidou, M. (2001). Integrating concepts and tests of intelligence from the differential and developmental traditions. *Intelligence, 29,* 307–336.

Caserta, M., O'Connor, T., Wyman, P., Wang, H., Moynihan, J., Cross, W., et al. (2008). The associations between psychosocial stress and the frequency of illness, and innate and adaptive immune function in children. *Brain, Behavior, and Immunity, 22,* 933–940.

Casey, B. J., Jones, R. M., & Somerville, L. H. (2011). Braking and accelerating of the adolescent brain. *Journal of Research on Adolescence, 21,* 21–33.

Cashdollar, N., Fukuda, K., Bocklage, A., Aurtenetxe, S., Vogel, E. K., & Gazzaley, A. (2013). Prolonged disengagement from attentional capture in normal aging. *Psychology and Aging, 28,* 77–86.

Caskey, R., Lindau, S., & Caleb Alexander, G. (2009). Knowledge and early adoption of the HPV vaccine among girls and young women: Results of a national survey. *Journal of Adolescent Health, 45,* 453–462.

Casper, M., & Carpenter, L. (2008). Sex, drugs, and politics: The HPV vaccine for cervical cancer. *Sociology of Health & Illness, 30,* 886–899.

Caspi, A. (2000). The child is father of the man: Personality continuities from childhood to adulthood. *Journal of Personality and Social Psychology, 78,* 158–172.

Caspi, J. (2012). *Sibling aggression: Assessment and treatment.* New York: Springer Publishing Co.

Caspi, A., & Moffitt, T. E. (1993). *Continuity amidst change: A paradoxical theory of personality coherence.* Manuscript submitted for publication.

Cassidy, J., & Berlin, L. J. (1994). The insecure/ambivalent pattern of attachment: Theory and research. *Child Development, 65,* 971–991.

Castel, A., & Craik, F. (2003). The effects of aging and divided attention on memory for item and associative information. *Psychology & Aging, 18,* 873–885.

Castle, N., & Beach, S. (2013). Elder abuse in assisted living. *Journal of Applied Gerontology, 32,* 248–267.

Castro, J., Jones, D., Lopez, M., Barradas, I., & Weiss, S. (2010). Making the case for circumcision as a public health strategy: Opening the dialogue. *AIDS Patient Care and STDs, 24,* 367–372.

Castro-Schilo, L., & Kee, D. (2010). Gender differences in the relationship between emotional intelligence and right hemisphere lateralization for facial processing. *Brain and Cognition, 73,* 62–67.

Catell, R. B. (1987). *Intelligence: Its structure, growth, and action.* Amsterdam: North-Holland.

Cath, S., & Shopper, M. (2001). *Stepparenting: Creating and recreating families in America today.* Hillsdale, NJ: Analytic Press.

Cattani, A., Bonifacio, S., Fertz, M., Iverson, J., Zocconi, E., & Caselli, M. (2010). Communicative and linguistic development in preterm children: A longitudinal study from 12 to 24 months. *International Journal of Language & Communication Disorders, 45,* 162–173.

Cauce, A. (2008). Parenting, culture, and context: Reflections on excavating culture. *Applied Developmental Science, 12,* 227–229.

Cauce, A., & Domenech-Rodriguez, M. (2002). Latino families: Myths and realities. In J. M. Contreras, J. K. A. Kerns, & A. M. Neal-Barnett (Eds.), *Latino children and families in the United States* (pp. 3–26). Westport, CT: Praeger.

Caughlin, J. (2002). The demand/withdraw pattern of communication as a predictor of marital satisfaction over time. *Human Communication Research, 28,* 49–85.

Cavallini, A., Fazzi, E., & Viviani, V. (2002). Visual acuity in the first two years of life in healthy term newborns: An experience with the Teller Acuity Cards. *Functional Neurology: New Trends in Adaptive & Behavioral Disorders, 17,* 87–92.

Ceci, S. J., & Williams, W. M. (2010). *The mathematics of sex: How biology and society conspire to limit talented women and girls.* New York: Oxford University Press.

Celano, M. P., Holsey, C., & Kobrynski, L. J. (2012). Home-based family intervention for low-income children with asthma: A randomized controlled pilot study. *Journal of Family Psychology, 26,* 171–178.

Center for Communication and Social Policy, University of California. (1998). *National television violence study, Vol. 2.* Thousand Oaks, CA: Sage Publications.

Centers for Disease Control. (2003). *Incidence-surveillance, epidemiology, and end results program, 1973-2000.* Atlanta, GA: Author.

Centers for Disease Control. (2004). Health behaviors of adults: United States, 1999–2001. *Vital and Health Statistics, Series 10* (219). Washington, DC: U.S. Department of Health and Human Services.

Centers for Disease Control. (2009). Births: Preliminary data for 2007. *National Vital Statistics Reports.* Statistics available online at www.cdc.gov/nchs/data/nvsr/nvsr57/nvsr57_12.pdf

Centers for Disease Control and Prevention. (2010). *Sexually Transmitted Disease Surveillance, 2008.* Atlanta, GA: U.S. Department of Health and Human Services.

Cerella, J. (1990). Aging and information-processing rate. In J. E. Birren & K. W. Schaie (Eds.), *Handbook of the psychology of aging* (3rd ed., pp. 201–221). San Diego: Academic Press.

CFCEPLA (Commonwealth Fund Commission on Elderly People Living Alone). (1986). *Problems facing elderly Americans living alone. New.* York: Louis Harris & Associates.

Chaffin, M. (2006). The changing focus of child maltreatment research and practice within psychology. *Journal of Social Issues, 62,* 663–684.

Chahal, H. H., Fung, C. C., Kuhle, S. S., & Veugelers, P. J. (2013). Availability and night-time use of electronic entertainment and communication devices are associated with short sleep duration and obesity among Canadian children. *Pediatric Obesity, 8,* 42–51.

Chaker, A. M. (2003, September 23). Putting toddlers in a nursing home. *Wall Street Journal,* p. D1.

Chall, J. S. (1979). The great debate: Ten years later, with a modest proposal for reading stages. In L. B. Resnick & P. A. Weaver (Eds.), *Theory and practice of early reading.* Hillsdale, NJ: Lawrence Erlbaum.

Chall, J. S. (1992). The new reading debates: Evidence from science, art, and ideology. *Teachers College Record, 94,* 315–328.

Chamberlain, P., Price, J., Reid, J., Landsverk, J., Fisher, P., & Stoolmiller, M. (2006, April). Who disrupts from placement in foster and kinship care? *Child Abuse & Neglect, 30,* 409–424.

Chamorro-Premuzic, T., Harlaar, N., Greven, C., & Plomin, R. (2010). More than just IQ: A longitudinal examination of self-perceived abilities as predictors of academic performance in a large sample of UK twins. *Intelligence, 38,* 385–392.

Chan, D. W. (1997). Self-concept and global self-worth among Chinese adolescents in Hong Kong. *Personality & Individual Differences, 22,* 511–520.

Chang, I. J., Pettit, R. W., & Katsurada, E. (2006). Where and when to spank: A comparison between U.S. and Japanese college students. *Journal of Family Violence, 21,* 281–286.

Chao, R. K. (1994). Beyond parental control and authoritarian parenting style: Understanding Chinese parenting through the cultural notion of training. *Child Development, 65,* 1111–1119.

Chao, R. K. (2001). Extending research on the consequences of parenting style for Chinese Americans and European Americans. *Child Development, 72,* 1832–1843.

Chaplin, T., Gillham, J., & Seligman, M. (2009). Gender, anxiety, and depressive symptoms: A longitudinal study of early adolescents. *Journal of Early Adolescence, 29,* 307–327.

Charles, S., & Carstensen, L. (2010). Social and emotional aging. *Annual Review of Psychology, 61,* 383–409.

Charles, S. T., Mather, M., & Carstensen, L. L. (2003). Aging and emotional memory: The forgettable nature of negative images for older adults. *Journal of Experimental Psychology: General, 132,* 237–244.

Charles, S. T., Reynolds, C. A., & Gatz, M. (2001). Age-related differences and change in positive and negative affect over 23 years. *Journal of Personality and Social Psychology, 80,* 136–151.

Charness, N., & Boot, W. R. (2009). Aging and information technology use: Potential and barriers. *Current Directions in Psychological Science, 18,* 253–258.

Chassin, L., Macy, J., Seo, D., Presson, C., & Sherman, S. (2009). The association between membership in the sandwich generation and health behaviors: A longitudinal study. *Journal of Applied Developmental Psychology,* 31, 38–46.

Chasteen, A. L., Bhattacharyya, S., Horhota, M., Tam, R., & Hasher, L. (2005). How feelings of stereotype threat influence older adults' memory performance. *Experimental Aging Research, 31,* 235–260.

Chatterji, M. (2004). Evidence on "What works": An argument for extended-term mixed-method (ETMM) evaluation designs. *Educational Researcher, 33,* 3–14.

Chaudhary, N., & Sharma, N. (2012). India. In J. Arnett (Ed.), *Adolescent psychology around the world* (pp. 103–120). New York: Psychology Press.

Cheah, C., Leung, C., Tahseen, M., & Schultz, D. (2009). Authoritative parenting among immigrant Chinese mothers of preschoolers. *Journal of Family Psychology, 23,* 311–320.

Chelebowski, R. T., Schwartz, A. G., Wakelee, H., Anderson, G. L., Stefanick, M. L., Manson, J. E., et al. (2009). Oestrogen plus progestin and lung cancer in postmenopausal women (Women's Health Initiative trial): A post-hoc analysis of a randomised controlled trial. *Lancet, 374,* 1243–1251.

Chen, C., Mizuno, T., Elston, R., Kariuki, M., Hall, K., Unverzagt, F., et al. (2010). A comparative study to screen dementia and APOE genotypes in an ageing East African population. *Neurobiology of Aging, 31,* 732–740.

Chen, D., Yang, X., & Dale Aagard, S. (2012). The empty nest syndrome: Ways to enhance quality of life. *Educational Gerontology, 38,* 520–529.

Chen, J., Chen, T., & Zheng, X. (2012). Parenting styles and practices among Chinese immigrant mothers with young children. *Early Child Development and Care, 182,* 1–21.

Chen, J., & Gardner, H. (2005). Assessment based on multiple-intelligences theory. In D. P. Flanagan & P. L. Harrison (Eds.), *Contemporary intellectual assessment: Theories, tests, and issues* (pp. 77–102). New York: Guilford Press.

Chen, S., Hwang, F., Yeh, Y., & Lin, S. J. (2012). Cognitive ability, academic achievement and academic self-concept: Extending the internal/external frame of reference model. *British Journal of Educational Psychology, 82,* 308–326.

Chen, S. X., & Bond, M. H. (2007). Explaining language priming effects: Further evidence for ethnic affirmation among Chinese-English bilinguals. *Journal of Language and Social Psychology, 26,* 398–406.

Cherlin, A. (1993). *Marriage, divorce, remarriage.* Cambridge, MA: Harvard University Press.

Cherney, I. (2003). Young children's spontaneous utterances of mental terms and the accuracy of their memory behaviors: A different methodological approach. *Infant & Child Development, 12,* 89–105.

Cherney, I., Kelly-Vance, L., & Glover, K. (2003). The effects of stereotyped toys and gender on play assessment in children aged 18 to 47 months. *Educational Psychology, 23,* 95–105.

Cheung, A. H., Emslie, G. J., & Mayes, T. L. (2006). The use of antidepressants to treat depression in children and adolescents. *Canadian Medical Association Journal, 174,* 193–200.

Chien, S., Bronson-Castain, K., Palmer, J., & Teller, D. (2006). Lightness constancy in 4-month-old infants. *Vision Research, 46,* 2139–2148.

Childers, J. (2009). Early verb learners: Creative or not? *Monographs of the Society for Research in Child Development, 74,* 133–139. Available online at http://search.ebscohost.com

ChildStats.gov. (2009). *America's children 2009.* Washington, DC: National Maternal and Child Health Clearinghouse.

Chiodo, L. M., Bailey, B. A., Sokol, R. J., Janisse, J., Delaney-Black, V., & Hannigan, J. H. (2012). Recognized spontaneous abortion in mid-pregnancy and patterns of pregnancy alcohol use. *Alcohol, 46,* 261–267.

Chisolm, T., Willott, J., & Lister, J. (2003). The aging auditory system: Anatomic and physiologic changes and implications for rehabilitation. *International Journal of Audiology, 42,* 2S3–2S10.

Chiu, M. M., & McBride-Chang, C. (2006). Gender, context, and reading: A comparison of students in 43 countries. *Scientific Studies of Reading, 10,* 331–362.

Choi, Y. (2013). The influence of conflict management culture on job satisfaction. *Social Behavior and Personality, 41(4),* 687–692.

Choi, H., & Marks, N. (2006, December). Transition to caregiving, marital disagreement, and psychological well-being: A prospective U.S. National Study. *Journal of Family Issues, 27,* 1701–1722.

Chomsky, N. (1968). *Language and mind.* New York: Harcourt Brace Jovanovich.

Chomsky, N. (1978). On the biological basis of language capacities. In G. A. Miller & E. Lennenberg (Eds.), *Psychology and biology of language and thought* (pp. 199–220). New York: Academic Press.

Chomsky, N. (1991). Linguistics and cognitive science: Problems and mysteries. In A. Kasher (Ed.), *The Chomskyan turn* (pp. 26–53). Cambridge, MA: Blackwell.

Chomsky, N. (1999). On the nature, use, and acquisition of language. In W. C. Ritchie & T. J. Bhatia (Eds.), *Handbook of child language acquisition* (pp. 33–54). San Diego: Academic Press.

Chomsky, N. (2005). Editorial: Universals of human nature [serial online]. *Psychotherapy and Psychosomatics, 74,* 263–268.

Choo, H., & Shek, D. (2013). Quality of parent-child relationship, family conflict, peer pressure, and drinking behaviors of adolescents in an Asian context: The case of Singapore. *Social Indicators Research, 110,* 1141–1157.

Choy, C. M., Yeung, Q. S., Briton-Jones, C. M., Cheung, C. K., Lam, C. W., & Haines, C. J. (2002). Relationship between semen parameters and mercury concentrations in blood and in seminal fluid from subfertile males in Hong Kong. *Fertility and Sterility, 78,* 426–428.

Christakis, D., & Zimmerman, F. (2007). Violent television viewing during preschool is associated with antisocial behavior during school age. *Pediatrics, 120,* 993–999.

Chronis, A., Jones, H., & Raggi, V. (2006, June). Evidence-based psychosocial treatments for children and adolescents with attention-deficit/hyperactivity disorder. *Clinical Psychology Review, 26,* 486–502.

Chung, S. A., Wei, A. Q., Connor, D. E., Webb, G. C., Molloy, T., Pajic, M., et al. (2007). Nucleus pulposus cellular longevity by telomerase gene therapy. *Spine, 15,* 1188–1196.

Cianciolo, A. T., Matthew, C., & Sternberg, R. J. (2006). Tacit knowledge, practical intelligence, and expertise. In K. A. Ericsson, N. Charness, P. J. Feltovich, & R. R. Hoffman (Eds.), *The Cambridge handbook of expertise and expert performance* (pp. 613–632). New York: Cambridge University Press.

Cicchetti, D. (1996). Child maltreatment: Implications for developmental theory and research. *Human Development, 39,* 18–39.

Cicchetti, D., & Cohen, D. J. (2006). *Developmental psychopathology, Vol. 1: Theory and method* (2nd ed.). Hoboken, NJ: Wiley.

CIRE (Cooperative Institutional Research Program of the American Council on Education). (1990). *The American freshman: National norms for fall 1990.* Los Angeles: American Council on Education.

Cirulli, F., Berry, A., & Alleva, E. (2003). Early disruption of the mother-infant relationship: Effects on brain plasticity and implications for psychopathology. *Neuroscience & Biobehavioral Reviews, 27,* 73–82.

Clark, A., & Lappin, S. (2013). Complexity in language acquisition. *Topics in Cognitive Science, 5,* 89–110.

Clark, J. E., & Humphrey, J. H. (Eds.). (1985). *Motor development: Current selected research.* Princeton, NJ: Princeton Book Company.

Clark, K. B., & Clark, M. P. (1947). Racial identification and preference in Negro children. In T. M. Newcomb & E. L. Hartley (Eds.), *Readings in social psychology* (pp. 169–178). New York: Holt, Rinehart & Winston.

Clark, M., & Arnold, J. (2008). The nature, prevalence and correlates of generativity among men in middle career. *Journal of Vocational Behavior,* 73, 473–484.

Clark, M. S., & Mills, J. (1993). The difference between communal and exchange relationships: What it is and is not. *Personality and Social Psychology Bulletin,* 19, 684–691.

Clark, R. (1998). *Expertise.* Silver Spring, MD: International Society for Performance Improvement.

Clark, R., Hyde, J. S., Essex, M. J., & Klein, M. H. (1997). Length of maternity leave and quality of mother-infant interactions. *Child Development, 68,* 364–383.

Clarke, A. R., Barry, R. J., McCarthy, R., Selikowitz, M., & Johnstone, S. J. (2008). Effects of imipramine hydrochloride on the EEG of children with Attention-Deficit/Hyperactivity Disorder who are non-responsive to stimulants. *International Journal of Psychophysiology, 68,* 186–192.

Clarke-Stewart, A., & Friedman, S. (1987). *Child development: Infancy through adolescence.* New York: Wiley.

Clauss-Ehlers, C. (2008). Sociocultural factors, resilience, and coping: Support for a culturally sensitive measure of resilience. *Journal of Applied Developmental Psychology, 29,* 197–212.

Claxton, L., McCarty, M., & Keen, R. (2009). Self-directed action affects planning in tool-use tasks with toddlers. *Infant Behavior & Development, 32,* 230–233.

Clearfield, M., & Nelson, N. (2006, January). Sex differences in mothers' speech and play behavior with 6-, 9-, and 14-month-old infants. *Sex Roles, 54,* 127–137.

Cliff, D. (1991). Negotiating a livable retirement: Further paid work and the quality of life in early retirement. *Aging and Society, 11,* 319–340.

Clinton, J. F., & Kelber, S. T. (1993). Stress and coping in fathers of newborns: Comparisons of planned versus unplanned pregnancy. *International Journal of Nursing Studies, 30,* 437–443.

Closson, L. (2009). Status and gender differences in early adolescents' descriptions of popularity. *Social Development, 18,* 412–426.

Cnattingius, S., Berendes, H., & Forman, M. (1993). Do delayed childbearers face increased risks of adverse pregnancy outcomes after the first birth? *Obstetrics and Gynecology, 81,* 512–516.

Coall, D. A., & Hertwig, R. (2010). Grandparental investment: Past, present, and future. *Behavioral and Brain Sciences, 33,* 1–19.

Coall, D. A., & Hertwig, R. (2011). Grandparental investment: A relic of the past or a resource for the future? *Current Directions in Psychological Science, 20,* 93–98.

Cobbe, E. (2003, September 25). France ups heat toll. *CBS Evening News.*

Cockrill, K., & Gould, H. (2012). Letter to the editor: Response to "What women want from abortion counseling in the United States: A qualitative study of abortion patients in 2008". *Social Work in Health Care, 51,* 191–194.

Cogan, L. W., Josberger, R. E., Gesten, F. C., & Roohan, P. J. (2012). Can prenatal care impact future well-child visits? The experience of a low income population in New York State Medicaid managed care. *Maternal and Child Health Journal, 16,* 92–99.

Cohen, J. (1999, March 19). Nurture helps mold able minds. *Science, 283,* 1832–1833.

Cohen, L. B., & Cashon, C. H. (2003). Infant perception and cognition. In R. M. Lerner & M. A. Easterbrooks (Eds.), *Handbook of psychology: Developmental psychology, Vol. 6.* New York: Wiley.

Cohen, S., Hamrick, N., Rodriguez, M. S., Feldman, P. J., Rabin, B. S., & Manuck, S. B. (2002). Reactivity and vulnerability to stress-associated risk for upper respiratory illness. *Psychosomatic Medicine, 64,* 302–310.

Cohen, S., Kamarck, T., & Mermelstein, R. (1983). A global measure of perceived stress. *Journal of Health and Social Behavior, 24,* 385–396.

Cohn, R. M. (1982). Economic development and status change of the aged. *American Journal of Sociology, 87,* 1150–1161.

Cohrs, J., Abele, A., & Dette, D. (2006, July). Integrating situational and dispositional determinants of job satisfaction: Findings from three samples of professionals. *Journal of Psychology: Interdisciplinary and Applied, 140,* 363–395.

Cokley, K. (2003). What do we know about the motivation of African American students? Challenging the "anti-intellectual" myth. *Harvard Educational Review, 73,* 524–558.

Colarusso, C. A., & Nemiroff, R. A. (1981). *Adult development: A new dimension in psychodynamic theory and practice.* New York: Plenum.

Colby, A., & Damon, W. (1987). Listening to a different voice: A review of Gilligan's in a different voice. In M. R. Walsh (Ed.), *The psychology of women.* New Haven, CT: Yale University Press.

Colby, A., & Kohlberg, L. (1987). *The measurement of moral adjudgment* (Vols. 1–2). New York: Cambridge University Press.

Cole, D. A., Maxwell, S. E., Martin, J. M., Peeke, L. G., Seroczynski, A. D., Tram, J. M., et al. (2001). The development of multiple domains of child and adolescent self-concept: A cohort sequential longitudinal design. *Child Development, 72,* 1723–1746.

Cole, M. (1992). Culture in development. In M. H. Bornstein & M. E. Lamb (Eds.), *Developmental psychology: An advanced textbook* (3rd ed.). Hillsdale, NJ: Lawrence Erlbaum.

Cole, P., Dennis, T., Smith-Simon, K., & Cohen, L. (2009). Preschoolers' emotion regulation strategy understanding: Relations with emotion socialization and child self-regulation. *Social Development, 18,* 324–352.

Cole, S. A. (2005). Infants in foster care: Relational and environmental factors affecting attachment. *Journal of Reproductive & Infant Psychology, 23,* 43–61.

Coleman, H., Chan, C., Ferris, F., & Chew, E. (2008). Age-related macular degeneration. *The Lancet, 372,* 1835–1845.

Coleman, M., Ganong, L., & Weaver, S. (2001). Relationship maintenance and enhancement in remarried families. In J. Harvey & A. Wenzel (Eds.), *Close romantic relationships: Maintenance and enhancement.* Mahwah, NJ: Lawrence Erlbaum.

Coleman, P. (2005, July). Editorial: Uses of reminiscence: Functions and benefits. *Aging & Mental Health, 9,* 291–294.

Colen, C., Geronimus, A., & Phipps, M. (2006, September). Getting a piece of the pie? The economic boom of the 1990s and declining teen birth rates in the United States. *Social Science & Medicine, 63,* 1531–1545.

College Board. (2005). *2001 college bound seniors are the largest, most diverse group in history.* New York: College Board.

Collins, J. (2012). Growing up bicultural in the United States: The case of Japanese-Americans. In R. Josselson & M. Harway (Eds.), *Navigating multiple identities: Race, gender, culture, nationality, and roles.* New York: Oxford University Press.

Collins, W. (2003). More than myth: The developmental significance of romantic relationships during adolescence. *Journal of Research on Adolescence, 13,* 1–24.

Collins, W., & Andrew, L. (2004). Changing relationships, changing youth: Interpersonal contexts of adolescent development. *Journal of Early Adolescence, 24,* 55–62.

Collins, W., & Doolittle, A. (2006, December). Personal reflections of funeral rituals and spirituality in a Kentucky African American family. *Death Studies, 30,* 957–969.

Collishaw, S., Pickles, A., Messer, J., Rutter, M., Shearer, C., & Maughan, B. (2007). Resilience to adult psychopathology following childhood maltreatment: Evidence from a community sample. *Child Abuse & Neglect, 31,* 211–229.

Colom, R., Lluis-Font, J. M., & André-Pueyo, A. (2005). The generational intelligence gains are caused by decreasing variance in the lower half of the distribution: Supporting evidence for the nutrition hypothesis. *Intelligence, 33,* 83–91.

Colombo, J., & Mitchell, D. (2009). Infant visual habituation. *Neurobiology of Learning and Memory, 92,* 225–234.

Colpin, H., & Soenen, S. (2004). Bonding through an adoptive mother's eyes. *Midwifery Today: International Midwife, 70,* 30–31.

Coltrane, S., & Adams, M. (1997). Children and gender. In T. Arendell (Ed.), *Contemporary parenting: Challenges and issues. Understanding families* (Vol. 9, pp. 219–253). Thousand Oaks, CA: Sage Publications.

Coltrane, S., & Shih, K. (2010). Gender and the division of labor. In J. C. Chrisler & D. R. McCreary (Eds.), *Handbook of gender research in psychology, Vol. 2: Gender research in social and applied psychology* (pp. 401–422). New York: Springer Publishing Co.

Committee on Children, Youth and Families. (1994). *When you need child day care.* Washington, DC: American Psychological Association.

Commons, M. L., Galaz-Fontes, J. F., & Morse, S. J. (2006). Leadership, cross-cultural contact, socio-economic status, and formal operational reasoning about moral dilemmas among Mexican non-literate adults and high school students. *Journal of Moral Education, 35,* 247–267.

Compton, R., & Weissman, D. (2002). Hemispheric asymmetries in global-local perception: Effects of individual differences in neuroticism. *Laterality, 7,* 333–350.

Comunian, A. L., & Gielen, U. P. (2000). Sociomoral reflection and prosocial and antisocial behavior: Two Italian studies. *Psychological Reports, 87,* 161–175.

Condly, S. (2006, May). Resilience in children: A review of literature with implications for education. *Urban Education, 41,* 211–236.

Condry, J., & Condry, S. (1976). Sex differences: A study of the eye of the beholder. *Child Development, 47,* 812–819.

Conel, J. L. (1939, 1975). *The postnatal development of the human cerebral cortex* (Vols. I–VIII). Cambridge, MA: Harvard University Press.

Conger, D., & Long, M. (2010). Why are men falling behind? Gender gaps in college performance and persistence. *Annals of the American Academy of Political and Social Science, 627,* 184–214.

Conn, V. S. (2003). Integrative review of physical activity intervention research with aging adults. *Journal of the American Geriatrics Society, 51,* 1159–1168.

Connell-Carrick, K. (2006). Early child care and early child development: Major findings of the NICHD study of early child care. *Child Welfare Journal, 85,* 819–836.

Conner, K., & Goldston, D. (2007, March). Rates of suicide among males increase steadily from age 11 to 21: Developmental framework and outline for prevention. *Aggression and Violent Behavior, 12*(2), 193–207.

Connidis, I. (2010). *Family ties and aging* (2nd ed.). Thousand Oaks, CA: Pine Forge Press/Sage Publications.

Connor, R. (1992). *Cracking the over-50 job market.* New York: Penguin Books.

Conry-Murray, C. (2013). Children's reasoning about gender-atypical preferences in different settings. *Journal of Experimental Child Psychology, 115,* 210–217.

Consedine, N., Magai, C., & King, A. (2004). Deconstructing positive affect in later life: A differential functionalist analysis of joy and interest. *International Journal of Aging & Human Development, 58,* 49–68.

Cook, E., Buehler, C., & Henson, R. (2009). Parents and peers as social influences to deter antisocial behavior. *Journal of Youth and Adolescence, 38,* 1240–1252.

Cook, J. L., & Jones, R. M. (2011). Texting and accessing the web while driving: Traffic citations and crashes among young adult drivers. *Traffic Injury Prevention, 12,* 545–549.

Cook, T. D., Wong, M., & Steiner, P. (2012). Evaluating national programs: A case study of the No Child Left Behind program in the United States. In T. Bliesener, A. Beelmann, & M. Stemmler (Eds.), *Antisocial behavior and crime: Contributions of developmental and evaluation research to prevention and intervention* (pp. 333–356). Cambridge, MA: Hogrefe Publishing.

Corballis, P. (2003). Visuospatial processing and the right-hemisphere interpreter. *Brain & Cognition, 53,* 171–176.

Corbin, C. B. (1973). *A textbook of motor development.* Boston, MA: McGraw-Hill.

Corbin, J. (2007). Reactive attachment disorder: A biopsychosocial disturbance of attachment. *Child & Adolescent Social Work Journal, 24,* 539–552.

Corcoran, J., & Pillai, V. (2007, January). Effectiveness of secondary pregnancy prevention programs: A meta-analysis. *Research on Social Work Practice, 17,* 5–18.

Cornforth, S. (2010). Bridging the gap: Weaving humanism and poststructuralism. *British Journal of Guidance & Counselling, 38,* 167–178.

Cornish, K., Turk, J., & Hagerman, R. (2008). The fragile X continuum: New advances and perspectives. *Journal of Intellectual Disability Research, 52,* 469–482.

Corr, C. (2010a). Children, development, and encounters with death, bereavement, and coping. In C. A. Corr & D. E. Balk (Eds.), *Children's encounters with death, bereavement, and coping* (pp. 3–20). New York: Springer Publishing Co.

Corr, C. (2010b). Children's emerging awareness and understandings of loss and death. In C. A. Corr & D. E. Balk (Eds.), *Children's encounters with death, bereavement, and coping* (pp. 21–38). New York: Springer Publishing Co.

Corr, C., & Doka, K. (2001). Master concepts in the field of death, dying, and bereavement: Coping versus adaptive strategies. *Omega: Journal of Death & Dying, 43,* 183–199.

Corr, C., Nabe, C., & Corr, D. (2006). *Death & dying, life & living* (6th ed.). Belmont, CA: Thomson Wadsworth.

Corr, C., Nabe, C., & Corr, D. (2010). *Death & dying, life & living* (8th ed.). Belmont, CA: Thomson Wadsworth.

Corrow, S., Granrud, C. E., Mathison, J., & Yonas, A. (2012). Infants and adults use line junction information to perceive 3D shape. *Journal of Vision, 12,* 8.

Cortese, S., Holtmann, M., Banaschewski, T., Buitelaar, J., Coghill, D., Danckaerts, M., et al. (2013). Practitioner review: Current best practice in the management of adverse events during treatment with ADHD medications in children and adolescents. *Journal of Child Psychology and Psychiatry, 54,* 227–246.

Costa, P. T., Jr., & McCrae, R. R. (1988). Personality in adulthood: A six-year longitudinal study of self-report and spouse ratings on the NEO Personality Inventory. *Journal of Personality and Social Psychology, 54,* 853–863.

Costa, P. T., Jr., & McCrae, R. R. (1989). Personality continuity and the changes of adult life. In M. Storandt & G. R. VandenBos (Eds.), *The adult years: Continuity and change* (pp. 45–77). Washington, DC: American Psychological Association.

Costa, P. T., & McCrae, R. R. (1997). Longitudinal stability of adult personality. In R. Hogan, J. A. Johnson, & S. R. Briggs (Eds.), *Handbook of personality psychology* (pp. 269–290). San Diego, CA: Academic Press.

Costello, E., Compton, S., & Keeler, G. (2003). Relationships between poverty and psychopathology: A natural experiment. *JAMA: The Journal of the American Medical Association, 290,* 2023–2029.

Costello, E., Sung, M., Worthman, C., & Angold, A. (2007, April). Pubertal maturation and the development of alcohol use and abuse. *Drug and Alcohol Dependence, 88,* S50–S59.

Cotrufo, P., Monteleone, P., d'Istria, M., Fuschino, A., Serino, I., & Maj, M. (2007). Aggressive behavioral characteristics and endogenous hormones in women with bulimia nervosa. *Neuropsychobiology, 42,* 58–61.

Couperus, J., & Nelson, C. (2006). Early brain development and plasticity. In *Blackwell handbook of early childhood development* (pp. 85–105). New York: Blackwell Publishing.

Courage, M., & Howe, M. (2010). To watch or not to watch: Infants and toddlers in a brave new electronic world. *Developmental Review, 30,* 101–115.

Courtney, E., Gamboz, J., & Johnson, J. (2008). Problematic eating behaviors in adolescents with low self-esteem and elevated depressive symptoms. *Eating Behaviors, 9,* 408–414.

Cousins, W. (2013). Maps for the midway journey. *PsycCRITIQUES, 58*(8), 88–94.

Couzin, J. (2002, June 21). Quirks of fetal environment felt decades later. *Science, 296,* 2167–2169.

Couzin, J. (2004, July 23). Volatile chemistry: Children and antidepressants. *Science, 305,* 468–470.

Cowan, C. P., & Cowan, P. A. (1992). *When partners become parents.* New York: Wiley.

Cowley, G. (2000, January 31). Alzheimer's: Unlocking the mystery. *Newsweek,* pp. 46–51.

Cox, C., Kotch, J., & Everson, M. (2003). A longitudinal study of modifying influences in the relationship between domestic violence and child maltreatment. *Journal of Family Violence, 18,* 5–17.

Coyne, J., Thombs, B., Stefanek, M., & Palmer, S. (2009). Time to let go of the illusion that psychotherapy extends the survival of cancer patients: Reply to Kraemer, Kuchler, and Spiegel (2009). *Psychological Bulletin, 135,* 179–182.

Craik, F., & Salthouse, T. A. (Eds.). (1999). *The handbook of aging and cognition* (2nd ed.). Mahwah, NJ: Erlbaum.

Craik, F., & Salthouse, T. A. (Eds.). (2008). *The handbook of aging and cognition* (3rd ed.). New York: Psychology Press.

Cramer, M., Chen, L., Roberts, S., & Clute, D. (2007). Evaluating the social and economic impact of community-based prenatal care. *Public Health Nursing, 24,* 329–336.

Crane, E., & Morris, J. (2006). Changes in maternal age in England and Wales—Implications for Down syndrome. *Down Syndrome: Research & Practice, 10,* 41–43.

Cratty, B. (1979). *Perceptual and motor development in infants and children* (2nd ed.). Englewood Cliffs, NJ: Prentice-Hall.

Cratty, B. (1986). *Perceptual and motor development in infants and children* (3rd ed.). Englewood Cliffs, NJ: Prentice-Hall.

Crawford, D., Houts, R., & Huston, T. (2002). Compatibility, leisure, and satisfaction in marital relationships. *Journal of Marriage & Family, 64,* 433–449.

Crawford, M., & Unger, R. (2004). *Women and gender: A feminist psychology* (4th ed.). New York: McGraw-Hill.

Crawley, A., Anderson, D., & Santomero, A. (2002). Do children learn how to watch television? The impact of extensive experience with Blue's Clues on preschool children's television viewing behavior. *Journal of Communication, 52,* 264–280.

Credé, M., & Niehorster, S. (2012). Adjustment to college as measured by the Student Adaptation to College Questionnaire: A quantitative review of its structure and relationships with correlates and consequences. *Educational Psychology Review, 24,* 133–165.

Crisp, A., Gowers, S., Joughin, N., McClelland, L., Rooney, B., Nielsen, S., et al. (2006, May). Anorexia nervosa in males: Similarities and differences to anorexia nervosa in females. *European Eating Disorders Review, 14,* 163–167.

Critser, G. (2003). *Fat land: How Americans became the fattest people in the world.* Boston: Houghton Mifflin.

Crosland, K., & Dunlap, G. (2012). Effective strategies for the inclusion of children with autism in general education classrooms. *Behavior Modification, 36,* 251–269.

Crosnoe, R., & Elder, G. H., Jr. (2002). Successful adaptation in the later years: A life course approach to aging. *Social Psychology Quarterly, 65,* 309–328.

Cross, T., Cassady, J., Dixon, F., & Adams, C. (2008). The psychology of gifted adolescents as measured by the MMPI-A. *Gifted Child Quarterly, 52,* 326–339.

Cross, W. E., & Cross, T. B. (2008). The big picture: Theorizing self-concept structure and construal. In P. B. Pedersen et al. (Eds.), *Counseling across cultures* (6th ed.). Thousand Oaks, CA: Sage Publications.

Crowl, A., Ahn, S., & Baker, J. (2008). A meta-analysis of developmental outcomes for children of same-sex and heterosexual parents. *Journal of GLBT Family Studies, 4,* 385–407.

Crowley, B., Hayslip, B., & Hobdy, J. (2003). Psychological hardiness and adjustment to life events in adulthood. *Journal of Adult Development, 10,* 237–248.

Crowne, K. (2013). An empirical analysis of three intelligences. *Canadian Journal of Behavioural Science/Revue Canadienne Des Sciences Du Comportement, 45,* 105–114.

Crowther, M., & Rodriguez, R. (2003). A stress and coping model of custodial grandparenting among African Americans. In B. Hayslip & J. Patrick (Eds.), *Working with custodial grandparents* (pp. 145–162). New York: Springer Publishing Co.

Cruz, N., & Bahna, S. (2006, October). Do foods or additives cause behavior disorders? *Psychiatric Annals, 36,* 724–732.

Cuervo, A. (2008). Calorie restriction and aging: The ultimate "cleansing diet." *Journals of Gerontology: Series A: Biological Sciences and Medical Sciences, 63A,* 547–549.

Culver, V. (2003, August 26). Funeral expenses overwhelm survivors: $10,000-plus tab often requires aid. *Denver Post,* p. B2.

Cumming, G. P., Currie, H. D., Moncur, R., & Lee, A. J. (2009). Web-based survey on the effect of menopause on women's libido in a computer-literate population. *Menopause International, 15,* 8–12.

Cummings, E., & Henry, W. E. (1961). *Growing old.* New York: Basic Books.

Curlette, W., & Kern, R. (2010). Ethics, research, and applications. *The Journal of Individual Psychology, 66,* 133–134.

Currier, J. M., Holland, J. M., & Neimeyer, R. A. (2010). Do CBT-based interventions alleviate distress following bereavement? A review of the current evidence. *International Journal of Cognitive Therapy, 3,* 112–121.

Currier, J. M., Neimeyer, R. A., & Berman, J. S. (2008). The effectiveness of psychotherapeutic interventions for bereaved persons: A comprehensive quantitative review. *Psychological Bulletin, 134,* 648–661.

Dabelko, H., & Zimmerman, J. (2008). Outcomes of adult day services for participants: A conceptual model. *Journal of Applied Gerontology, 27,* 78–92.

Dagher, A., Tannenbaum, B., Hayashi, T., Pruessner, J., & McBride, D. (2009). An acute psychosocial stress enhances the neural response to smoking cues. *Brain Research, 129,* 340–348.

Dagys, N., McGlinchey, E. L., Talbot, L. S., Kaplan, K. A., Dahl, R. E., & Harvey, A. G. (2012). Double trouble? The effects of sleep deprivation and chronotype on adolescent affect. *Journal of Child Psychology and Psychiatry, 53,* 660–667.

Dahl, E., & Birkelund, E. (1997). Health inequalities in later life in a social democratic welfare state. *Social Science & Medicine, 44,* 871–881.

Dahl, R. (2008). Biological, developmental, and neurobehavioral factors relevant to adolescent driving risks. *American Journal of Preventive Medicine, 35,* S278–SS284.

Dai, D., Tan, X., Marathe, D., Valtcheva, A., Pruzek, R. M., & Shen, J. (2012). Influences of social and educational environments on creativity during adolescence: Does SES matter? *Creativity Research Journal, 24,* 191–199.

Daley, K. C. (2004). Update on sudden infant death syndrome. *Current Opinion in Pediatrics, 16,* 227–232.

Daley, M. F., & Glanz, J. M. (2011). Straight talk about vaccination. *Scientific American, 305, 32,* 34.

Dalton, T. C., & Bergenn, V. W. (2007). *Early experience, the brain, and consciousness: An historical and interdisciplinary synthesis.* Mahwah, NJ: Lawrence Erlbaum.

Damon, W. (1983). *Social and personality development.* New York: Norton.

Damon, W., & Hart, D. (1988). *Self-understanding in childhood and adolescence.* New York: Cambridge University Press.

Daniel, S., & Goldston, D. (2009). Interventions for suicidal youth: A review of the literature and developmental considerations. *Suicide and Life-Threatening Behavior, 39,* 252–268.

Daniels, H. (Ed.). (1996). *An introduction to Vygotsky.* New York: Routledge.

Daniels, E. A., & Lavoi, N. M. (2013). Athletics as solution and problem: Sport participation for girls and the sexualization of female athletes. In E. L. Zurbriggen & T. Roberts (Eds.), *The sexualization of girls and girlhood: Causes, consequences, and resistance* (pp. 63–83). New York: Oxford University Press.

Dardenne, B., Dumont, M., & Bollier, T. (2007). Insidious dangers of benevolent sexism: Consequences for women's performance. *Journal of Personality and Social Psychology, 93,* 764–779.

Dare, W. N., Noronha, C. C., Kusemiju, O. T., & Okanlawon, O. A. (2002). The effect of ethanol on spermatogenesis and fertility in male Sprague-Dawley rats pretreated with acetylsalicylic acid. *Nigeria Postgraduate Medical Journal, 9,* 194–198.

Darnton, N. (1990, June 4). Mommy vs. Mommy. *Newsweek,* pp. 64–67.

Dasen, P. R. (2000). Rapid social change and the turmoil of adolescence: A cross-cultural perspective. *International Journal of Group Tensions, 29,* 17–49.

Dasen, P. R., Inhelder, B., Lavallee, M., & Retschitzki, J. (1978). *Naissance de l'intelligence chez l'enfant Baoule de Cote d'Ivoire.* Berne: Hans Huber.

Dasen, P. R., & Mishra, R. C. (2002). Cross-cultural views on human development in the third millennium. In W. W. Hartup & R. K. Silbereisen (Eds.), *Growing points in developmental science: An introduction* (pp. 266–286). Philadelphia, PA: Psychology Press.

Dasen, P. R., Ngini, L., & Lavallee, M. (1979). Cross-cultural training studies of concrete operations. In L. H. Eckenberger, W. J. Lonner, & Y. H. Poortinga (Eds.), *Cross-cultural contributions to psychology.* Amsterdam: Swets & Zeilinger.

Davenport, B., & Bourgeois, N. (2008). Play, aggression, the preschool child, and the family: A review of literature to guide empirically informed play therapy with aggressive preschool children. *International Journal of Play Therapy, 17,* 2–23.

Davey, M. (2007, June 2). Kevorkian freed after years in prison for aiding suicide. *The New York Times,* p. A1.

Davey, M., Eaker, D. G., & Walters, L. H. (2003). Resilience processes in adolescents: Personality profiles, self-worth, and coping. *Journal of Adolescent Research, 18,* 347–362.

Davidson, T. (1977). Wife beating: A recurring phenomenon throughout history. In M. Roy (Ed.), *Battered women: A psychosociological study of domestic violence* (pp. 1–23). New York: Van Nostrand Reinhold.

Davies, S., & Denton, M. (2002). The economic well-being of older women who become divorced or separated in mid- or later life. *Canadian Journal on Aging, 21,* 477–493.

Davis, A. (2003). *Your divorce, your dollars: Financial planning before, during, and after divorce.* Bellingham, WA: Self-Counsel Press.

Davis, A. (2008). Children with Down syndrome: Implications for assessment and intervention in the school. *School Psychology Quarterly, 23,* 271–281. Available online at http://search.ebscohost.com

Davis, R. R., & Hofferth, S. L. (2012). The association between inadequate gestational weight gain and infant mortality among U.S. infants born in 2002. *Maternal and Child Health Journal, 16,* 119–124.

Davis, T. S., Saltzburg, S., & Locke, C. R. (2009). Supporting the emotional and psychological well being of sexual minority youth: Youth ideas for action. *Children and Youth Services Review, 31,* 1030–1041.

Davis, D., Shaver, P., Widaman, K., Vernon, M., Follette, W., & Beitz, K. (2006, December). "I can't get no satisfaction": Insecure attachment, inhibited sexual communication, and sexual dissatisfaction. *Personal Relationships, 13,* 465–483.

Davison, G. C. (2005). Issues and nonissues in the gay-affirmative treatment of patients who are gay, lesbian, or bisexual. *Clinical Psychology: Science & Practice, 12,* 25–28.

Daxinger, L., & Whitelaw, E. (2012). Understanding transgenerational epigenetic inheritance via the gametes in mammals. *National Review of Genetics, 13,* 153–162.

de Dios, A. (2012). United States of America. In J. Arnett (Ed.), *Adolescent psychology around the world.* New York: Psychology Press.

de Graag, J. A., Cox, R. A., Hasselman, F., Jansen, J., & de Weerth, C. (2012). Functioning within a relationship: Mother-infant synchrony and infant sleep. *Infant Behavior & Development, 35,* 252–263.

De Jesus-Zayas, S. R., Buigas, R., & Denney, R. L. (2012). Evaluation of culturally diverse populations. In D. Faust (Ed.), *Coping with psychiatric and psychological testimony: Based on the original work by Jay Ziskin* (6th ed., pp. 248–265). New York: Oxford University Press.

de Lauzon-Guillain, B., Wijndaele, K., Clark, M., Acerini, C. L., Hughes, I. A., Dunger, D. B., et al. (2012). Breastfeeding and infant temperament at age three months. *PLoS One, 7,* 182–190.

De Meersman, R., & Stein, P. (2007, February). Vagal modulation and aging. *Biological Psychology, 74,* 165–173.

De Meyer, G., Shapiro, F., Vanderstichele, H., Vanmechelen, E., Engelborghs, S., De Deyn, P., et al. (2010). Diagnosis-independent Alzheimer disease biomarker signature in cognitively normal elderly people. *Archives of Neurology, 67,* 949–956.

de Onis, M., Garza, C., Onyango, A. W., & Borghi, E. (2007). Comparison of the WHO child growth standards and the CDC 2000 growth charts. *Journal of Nutrition, 137,* 144–148.

de Rosnay, M., Cooper, P., Tsigaras, N., & Murray, L. (2006, August). Transmission of social anxiety from mother to infant: An experimental study using a social referencing paradigm. *Behaviour Research and Therapy, 44,* 1165–1175.

de Schipper, E. J., Riksen-Walraven, J. M., & Geurts, S. A. E. (2006). Effects of child-caregiver ratio on the interactions between caregivers and children in child-care centers: An experimental study. *Child Development, 77,* 861–874.

de St. Aubin, E., & McAdams, D. P. (Eds.). (2004). *The generative society: Caring for future generations.* Washington, DC: American Psychological Association.

de St. Aubin, E., McAdams, D. P., & Kim, T. C. (Eds.). (2004). *The generative society: Caring for future generations.* Washington, DC: American Psychological Association.

de Vries, B., Davis, C. G., Wortman, C. B., & Lehman, D. R. (1997). Long-term psychological and somatic consequences of later life parental bereavement. *Omega—Journal of Death & Dying, 35,* 97–117.

Deakin, M. B. (2004, May 9). The (new) parent trap. *Boston Globe Magazine,* pp. 18–21, 28–33.

Dearing, E., McCartney, K., & Taylor, B. (2009). Does higher quality early child care promote low-income children's math and reading achievement in middle childhood? *Child Development, 80,* 1329–1349.

Deary, I. (2010). Cognitive epidemiology: Its rise, its current issues, and its challenges. *Personality and Individual Differences, 49,* 337–343.

Deary, I. J. (2012). Intelligence. *Annual Review of Psychology, 63,* 453–482.

Deater-Deckard, K., & Cahill, K. (2006). Nature and nurture in early childhood. In K. McCartney & D. Phillips (Eds.), *Blackwell handbook of early childhood development* (pp. 3–21). New York: Blackwell Publishing.

Deaux, K. (2006). A nation of immigrants: Living our legacy. *Journal of Social Issues, 62,* 633–651.

Deaux, K., Reind, A., Mizrahi, K., & Ethier, K. A. (1995). Parameters of social identity. *Journal of Personality and Social Psychology, 68,* 280–291.

Deb, S., & Adak, M. (2006, July). Corporal punishment of children: Attitude, practice and perception of parents. *Social Science International, 22,* 3–13.

Decarrie, T. G. (1969). A study of the mental and emotional development of the thalidomide child. In B. M. Foss (Ed.), *Determinants of infant behavior* (Vol. 4). London: Methuen.

DeCasper, A. J., & Fifer, W. P. (1980). Of human bonding: Newborns prefer their mothers' voices. *Science, 208,* 1174–1176.

deCastro, J. (2002). Age-related changes in the social, psychological, and temporal influences on food intake in free-living, healthy, adult humans. *Journals of Gerontology: Series A: Biological Sciences & Medical Sciences, 57A,* M368–M377.

Decety, J., & Jackson, P. L. (2006). A social-neuroscience perspective on empathy. *Current Directions in Psychological Science, 15,* 54–61.

DeFrancisco, B., & Rovee-Collier, C. (2008). The specificity of priming effects over the first year of life. *Developmental Psychobiology, 50,* 486–501.

DeGenova, M. K. (1993). Reflections of the past: New variables affecting life satisfaction in later life. *Educational Gerontology, 19,* 191–201.

Degnen, C. (2007). Minding the gap: The construction of old age and oldness amongst peers. *Journal of Aging Studies, 21,* 69–80.

Dehaene-Lambertz, G., Hertz-Pannier, L., & Dubois, J. (2006). Nature and nurture in language acquisition: Anatomical and functional brain-imaging studies in infants [Special issue: Nature and nurture in brain development and neurological disorders]. *Neurosciences, 29,* 367–373.

Dehue, F., Bolman, C., & Vollnik, T. (2008). Cyberbullying: Youngsters' experiences and parental perception. *CyberPsychology & Behavior, 11,* 217–223.

de Jonge, J., Spoor, E., Sonnentag, S., Dormann, C., & van den Tooren, M. (2012). 'Take a break?' off-job recovery, job demands, and job resources as predictors of health, active learning, and creativity. *European Journal of Work and Organizational Psychology, 21,* 321–348.

Delahaij, R., Gaillard, A., & van Dam, K. (2010). Hardiness and the response to stressful situations: Investigating mediating processes. *Personality and Individual Differences, 49,* 386–390.

Delamater, J. (2012). Sexual expression in later life: A review and synthesis. *The Journal of Sex Research, 49,* 125–141.

DeLisi, L., & Fleischhaker, W. (2007). Schizophrenia research in the era of the genome, 2007. *Current Opinion in Psychiatry, 20,* 109–110.

DeLisi, M. (2006). Zeroing in on early arrest onset: Results from a population of extreme career criminals. *Journal of Criminal Justice, 34,* 17–26.

Delle Fave, A., Wissing, M., Brdar, I., Vella-Brodrick, D., & Freire, T. (2013). Cross-cultural perceptions of meaning and goals in adulthood: Their roots and relations with happiness. In A. S. Waterman (Ed.), *The best within us: Positive psychology perspectives on eudaimonia.* Washington, DC: American Psychological Association.

DeLoache, J. S., Chiong, C., Sherman, K., Islam, N., Vanderborght, M., Troseth, G. L., et al. (2010). Do babies learn from baby media? *Psychological Science, 21,* 1570–1574.

Demaree, H. A., & Everhart, D. E. (2004). Healthy high-hostiles: Reduced parasympathetic activity and decreased sympathovagal flexibility during negative emotional processing. *Personality and Individual Differences, 36,* 457–469.

Demir, M., Orthel, H., & Andelin, A. (2013). Friendship and happiness. In S. A. David, I. Boniwell, & A. Conley Ayers (Eds.), *The oxford handbook of happiness.* New York: Oxford University Press.

Deng, C., Armstrong, P., & Rounds, J. (2007). The fit of Holland's RIASEC model to US occupations. *Journal of Vocational Behavior, 71,* 1–22.

Denizet-Lewis, B. (2004, May 30). Friends, friends with benefits and the benefits of the local mall. *The New York Times Magazine,* pp. 30–35, 54–58.

Dennis, T. A., Cole, P. M., Zahn-Wexler, C., & Mizuta, I. (2002). Self in context: Autonomy and relatedness in Japanese and U.S. mother-preschooler dyads. *Child Development, 73,* 1803–1817.

Dennis, W. (1966). Age and creative productivity. *Journal of Gerontology, 21,* 1–8.

DeParle, J., & Tavernise, S. (2012, February 17). Unwed mothers now a majority before age of 30. *The New York Times,* p. A1.

DePaulo, B. M., & Morris, W. L. (2006). The unrecognized stereotyping and discrimination against singles. *Current Directions in Psychological Science, 15,* 251–254.

Der, G., & Deary, I. (2006, March). Age sex differences in reaction time in adulthood: Results from the United Kingdom health and lifestyle survey. *Psychology and Aging, 21*(1), 62–73.

Derevensky, J., Shek, D., & Merrick, J. (2010). Adolescent gambling. *International Journal of Adolescent Medicine and Health, 22,* 1–2.

Deruelle, F., Nourry, C., Mucci, P., Bart, F., Grosbois, J. M., Lensel, G. H., et al. (2008). Difference in breathing strategies during exercise between trained elderly men and women. *Scandinavian Journal of Medical Science in Sports, 18,* 213–220.

Dervic, K., Friedrich, E., Oquendo, M., Voracek, M., Friedrich, M., & Sonneck, G. (2006, October). Suicide in Austrian children and young adolescents aged 14 and younger. *European Child & Adolescent Psychiatry, 15,* 427–434.

Désiréa, L., Blondiaux, E., Carrière, J., Haddad, R., Sol, O., Fehlbaum-Beurdeley, P., et al. (2013). Blood transcriptomic biomarkers of Alzheimer's disease patients treated with EHT 0202. *Journal of Alzheimer's Disease, 34,* 469–483.

Desoete, A., Roeyers, H., & De Clercq, A. (2003). Can offline metacognition enhance mathematical problem solving? *Journal of Educational Psychology, 95,* 188–200.

Destounis, S., Hanson, S., Morgan, R., Murphy, P., Somerville, P., Seifert, P., et al. (2009). Computer-aided detection of breast carcinoma in standard mammographic projections with digital mammography. *International Journal of Computer Assisted Radiological Surgery, 4,* 331–336.

Deurenberg, P., Deurenberg-Yap, M., Foo, L. F., Schmidt, G., & Wang, J. (2003). Differences in body composition between Singapore Chinese, Beijing Chinese and Dutch children. *European Journal of Clinical Nutrition, 57,* 405–409.

Deurenberg, P., Deurenberg-Yap, M., & Guricci, S. (2002). Asians are different from Caucasians and from each other in their body mass index/body fat percent relationship. *Obesity Review, 3,* 141–146.

DeVader, S. R., Neeley, N. L., Myles, T. D., & Leet, T. L. (2007). Evaluation of gestational weight gain guidelines for women with normal prepregnancy body mass index. *Obstetrics and Gynecology, 110,* 745–751.

Deveny, K. (1994, December 5). Chart of kindergarten awards. *Wall Street Journal,* p. B1.

Devlin, B., Daniels, M., & Roeder, K. (1997). The heritability of IQ. *Nature, 388,* 468–471.

deVries, R. (1969). Constancy of generic identity in the years 3 to 6. *Monographs of the Society for Research in Child Development, 34*(3, Serial No. 127).

Dey, A. N., & Bloom, B. (2005). Summary health statistics for U.S. Children: National Health Interview Survey, 2003. *Vital Health Statistics, 10*(223), 1–78.

DeYoung, C., Quilty, L., & Peterson, J. (2007). Between facets and domains: 10 aspects of the Big Five. *Journal of Personality and Social Psychology, 93,* 880–896.

Diambra, L., & Menna-Barreto, L. (2004). Infradian rhythmicity in sleep/wake ratio in developing infants. *Chronobiology International, 21,* 217–227.

Diamond, L. (2003a). Love matters: Romantic relationships among sexual-minority adolescents. In P. Florsheim (Ed.), *Adolescent romantic relations and sexual behavior: Theory, research, and practical implications.* Mahwah, NJ: Lawrence Erlbaum.

Diamond, L. (2003b). Was it a phase? Young women's relinquishment of lesbian/bisexual identities over a 5-year period. *Journal of Personality & Social Psychology, 84,* 352–364.

Diamond, L, Fagundes, C. P., & Butterworth, M. R. (2010). Intimate relationships across the life span. In M. E. Lamb & A. M. Freund (Eds.), *The handbook of life-span development* (pp. 379–433). New York: Wiley.

Diamond, L. M., & Savin-Williams, R. (2003). The intimate relationships of sexual-minority youths. In G. Adams & M. Berzonsky (Eds.), *Blackwell handbook of adolescence* (pp. 393–412). Malden, MA: Blackwell Publishers.

Dick, D., Rose, R., & Kaprio, J. (2006). The next challenge for psychiatric genetics: Characterizing the risk associated with identified genes. *Annals of Clinical Psychiatry, 18,* 223–231.

Dickinson, D., Golinkoff, R., & Hirsh-Pasek, K. (2010). Speaking out for language: Why language is central to reading development. *Educational Researcher, 39,* 305–310.

Diego, M., Field, T., & Hernandez-Reif, M. (2008). Temperature increases in preterm infants during massage therapy. *Infant Behavior & Development, 31,* 149–152.

Diego, M., Field, T., & Hernandez-Reif, M. (2009). Procedural pain heart rate responses in massaged preterm infants. *Infant Behavior & Development, 32,* 226–229.

Diego, M., Field, T., Hernandez-Reif, M., Vera, Y., Gil, K., & Gonzalez-Garcia, A. (2007). Caffeine use affects pregnancy outcome. *Journal of Child & Adolescent Substance Abuse, 17,* 41–49.

Diener, E. (2000). Subjective well-being: The science of happiness and a proposal for a national index. *American Psychologist, 55,* 34–43.

Diener, E., Lucas, R. E., & Scollon, C. N. (2009). Beyond the hedonic treadmill: Revising the adaptation theory of well-being. In E. Diener (Ed.), *The science of well-being: The collected works of Ed Diener.* New York: Springer Science + Business Media.

Diener, E., Oishi, S., & Lucas, R. (2003). Personality, culture, and subjective well-being: Emotional and cognitive evaluations of life. *Annual Review of Psychology, 54,* 403–425.

Dietz, W. (2004). Overweight in childhood and adolescence. *New England Journal of Medicine, 350,* 855–857.

Dietz, W. H., & Stern, L. (Eds.). (1999). *American Academy of Pediatrics guide to your child's nutrition: Making peace at the table and building healthy eating habits for life.* New York: Villard.

DiGiovanna, A. G. (1994). *Human aging: Biological perspectives.* New York: McGraw-Hill.

Dildy, G. A., Jackson, G. M., Fowers, G. K., Oshiro, B. T., Varner, M. W., & Clark, S. L. (1996). Very advanced maternal age: Pregnancy after 45. *American Journal of Obstetrics and Gynecology, 175,* 668–674.

Dimmitt, C., & McCormick, C. B. (2012). Metacognition in education. In K. R. Harris, S. Graham, T. Urdan, C. B. McCormick, G. M. Sinatra, & J. Sweller (Eds.), *APA educational psychology handbook, Vol 1: Theories, constructs, and critical issues.* Washington, DC: American Psychological Association.

DiNallo, J. M., Downs, D., & Le Masurier, G. (2012). Objectively assessing treadmill walking during the second and third pregnancy trimesters. *Journal of Physical Activity & Health, 9,* 21–28.

Dinero, R., Conger, R., Shaver, P., Widaman, K., & Larsen-Rife, D. (2008). Influence of family of origin and adult romantic partners on romantic attachment security. *Journal of Family Psychology, 22,* 622–632.

Dion, K. L., & Dion, K. K. (1988). Romantic love: Individual and cultural perspectives. In R. J. Sternberg & M. L. Barnes (Eds.), *The psychology of love.* New Haven, CT: Yale University Press.

Diop, A. M. (1989). The place of the elderly in African society. *Impact of Science on Society, 153,* 93–98.

DiPietro, J. A., Costigan, K. A., & Gurewitsch, E. D. (2005). Maternal psychophysiological change during the second half of gestation. *Biological Psychology, 69,* 23–39.

Dittman, M. (2005). Generational differences at work. *Monitor on Psychology, 36,* 54–55.

Dixon, L., & Browne, K. (2003). The heterogeneity of spouse abuse: A review. *Aggression & Violent Behavior, 8,* 107–130.

Dixon, W. E., Jr. (2004). There's a long, long way to go. *PsycCRITIQUES.*

Dmitrieva, J., Chen, C., & Greenberg, E. (2004). Family relationships and adolescent psychosocial outcomes: Converging findings from Eastern and Western cultures. *Journal of Research on Adolescence, 14,* 425–447.

Dobson, V. (2000). The developing visual brain. *Perception, 29,* 1501–1503.

Dodge, K. A., Lansford, J. E., & Burks, V. S. (2003). Peer rejection and social information-processing factors in the development of aggressive behavior problems in children. *Child Development, 74,* 374–393.

Doman, G., & Doman, J. (2002). *How to teach your baby to read.* Wyndmoor, PA: Gentle Revolution Press.

Dombrovski, A. Y., Siegle, G. J., Szanto, K. K., Clark, L. L., Reynolds, C., & Aizenstein, H. H. (2012). The temptation of suicide: Striatal gray matter, discounting of delayed rewards, and suicide attempts in late-life depression. *Psychological Medicine, 42,* 1203–1215.

Dombrowski, S., Noonan, K., & Martin, R. (2007). Low birth weight and cognitive outcomes: Evidence for a gradient relationship in an urban, poor, African American birth cohort. *School Psychology Quarterly, 22,* 26–43.

Dominguez, H. D., Lopez, M. F., & Molina, J. C. (1999). Interactions between perinatal and neonatal associative learning defined by contiguous olfactory and tactile stimulation. *Neurobiology of Learning and Memory, 71,* 272–288.

Domsch, H., Lohaus, A., & Thomas, H. (2009). Prediction of childhood cognitive abilities from a set of early indicators of information processing capabilities. *Infant Behavior & Development, 32,* 91–102.

Domsch, H., Thomas, H., & Lohaus, A. (2010). Infant attention, heart rate, and looking time during habituation/dishabituation. *Infant Behavior & Development, 33,* 321–329.

Donat, D. (2006, October). Reading their way: A balanced approach that increases achievement. *Reading & Writing Quarterly: Overcoming Learning Difficulties, 22,* 305–323.

Dondi, M., Simion, F., & Caltran, G. (1999). Can newborns discriminate between their own cry and the cry of another newborn infant? *Developmental Psychology, 35,* 418–426.

Donini, L., Savina, C., & Cannella, C. (2003). Eating habits and appetite control in the elderly: The anorexia of aging. *International Psychogeriatrics, 15,* 73–87.

Donlan, C. (1998). *The development of mathematical skills.* Philadelphia: Psychology Press.

Donleavy, G. (2008). No man's land: Exploring the space between Gilligan and Kohlberg. *Journal of Business Ethics, 80,* 807–822.

Donnerstein, E. (2005, January). *Media violence and children: What do we know, what do we do?.* Paper presented at the annual National Teaching of Psychology meeting, St. Petersburg.

Doress, P. B., Siegal, D. L., & The Midlife and Old Women Book Project. (1987). *Ourselves, growing older.* New York: Simon & Schuster.

Dorn, L., Susman, E., & Ponirakis, A. (2003). Pubertal timing and adolescent adjustment and behavior: Conclusions vary by rater. *Journal of Youth & Adolescence, 32,* 157–167.

Dortch, S. (1997, September). Hey guys: Hit the books. *American Demographics,* pp. 4–12.

Douglass, A., & Klerman, L. (2012). The strengthening families initiative and child care quality improvement: How strengthening families influenced change in child care programs in one state. *Early Education and Development, 23,* 373–392.

Douglass, R., & McGadney-Douglass, B. (2008). The role of grandmothers and older women in the survival of children with Kwashiorkor in urban Accra, Ghana. *Research in Human Development, 5,* 26–43.

Doussard-Roosevelt, J. A., Porges, S. W., Scanlon, J. W., Alemi, B., & Scanlon, K. B. (1997). Vagal regulation of heart rate in the prediction of developmental outcome for very low birth weight preterm infants. *Child Development, 68,* 173–186.

Dow, B., & Joosten, M. (2012). Understanding elder abuse: A social rights perspective. *International Psychogeriatrics, 24,* 853–855.

Doyle, R. (2004, April). By the numbers: A surplus of women. *Scientific American, 290,* 33.

Dozor, A. J., & Amler, R. W. (2013). Children's environmental health. *The Journal of Pediatrics, 162,* 6–7.

Draper, T., Holman, T., Grandy, S., & Blake, W. (2008). Individual, demographic, and family correlates of romantic attachments in a group of American young adults. *Psychological Reports, 103,* 857–872.

Dreman, S. (Ed.). (1997). *The family on the threshold of the 21st century.* Mahwah, NJ: Lawrence Erlbaum.

Driscoll, A. K., Russell, S. T., & Crockett, L. J. (2008). Parenting styles and youth well-being across immigrant generations. *Journal of Family Issues, 29,* 185–209.

Driver, J., Tabares, A., & Shapiro, A. (2003). Interactional patterns in marital success and failure: Gottman laboratory studies. In F. Walsh (Ed.), *Normal family processes: Growing diversity and complexity* (3rd ed.). New York: Guilford Press.

Dromi, E. (1987). *Early lexical development.* Cambridge, England: Cambridge University Press.

Drouin, M., & Landgraff, C. (2012). Texting, sexting, and attachment in college students' romantic relationships. *Computers in Human Behavior, 28,* 88–100.

Dryfoos, J. G. (1990). *Adolescents at risk: Prevalence and prevention.* New York: Oxford University Press.

DuBois, D. L., & Hirsch, B. J. (1990). School and neighborhood friendship patterns of blacks and whites in early adolescence. *Child Development, 61,* 524–536.

Dudding, T. C., Vaizey, C. J., & Kamm, M. A. (2008). Obstetric anal sphincter injury: Incidence, risk factors, and management. *Annals of Surgery, 247,* 224–237.

Duenwald, M. (2003, July 15). After 25 years, new ideas in the prenatal test tube. *The New York Times,* p. D5.

Duenwald, M. (2004, May 11). For couples, stress without a promise of success. *The New York Times,* p. D3.

Duijts, L., Jaddoe, V. W. V., Hofman, A., & Moll, H. A. (2010, June 21). Prolonged and exclusive breastfeeding reduces the risk of infectious diseases in infancy. *Pediatrics.* doi:10.1542/peds.2008-3256

Dumont, M., Sarlet, M., & Dardenne, B. (2010). Be too kind to a woman, she'll feel incompetent: Benevolent sexism shifts self-construal and autobiographical memories toward incompetence. *Sex Roles, 62*(7–8), 545–553.

Duncan, G. J., & Brooks-Gunn, J. (2000). Family poverty, welfare reform, and child development. *Child Development, 71,* 188–196.

Duncan, J. R., Paterson, D. S., Hoffman, J. M., Mokler, D. J., Borenstein, N. S., Belliveau, R. A., et al. (2010). Brainstem serotonergic deficiency in sudden infant death syndrome. *Journal of the American Medical Association, 303,* 430–437.

Dunford, B. B., Shipp, A. J., Boss, R., Angermeier, I., & Boss, A. D. (2012). Is burnout static or dynamic? A career transition perspective of employee burnout trajectories. *Journal of Applied Psychology, 97,* 637–650.

Dunkel, C. S., Kim, J. K., & Papini, D. R. (2012). The general factor of psychosocial development and its relation to the general factor of personality and life history strategy. *Personality and Individual Differences, 52,* 202–206.

Dunn, M., Thomas, J. O., Swift, W., & Burns, L. (2012). Elite athletes' estimates of the prevalence of illicit drug use: Evidence for the false consensus effect. *Drug and Alcohol Review, 31,* 27–32.

DuPaul, G., & Weyandt, L. (2006, June). School-based intervention for children with attention deficit hyperactivity disorder: Effects on academic, social, and behavioural functioning. *International Journal of Disability, Development and Education, 53,* 161–176.

Dupper, D. R. (2013). *School bullying: New perspectives on a growing problem.* New York: Oxford University Press.

Durbin, J. (2003, October 6). Internet sex unzipped. *McCleans,* p. 18.

Duriez, B., Luyckx, K., Soenens, B., & Berzonsky, M. (2012). A process-content approach to adolescent identity formation: Examining longitudinal associations between identity styles and goal pursuits. *Journal of Personality, 80,* 135–161.

Dutton, D. G. (1994). *The domestic assault of women: Psychological and criminal justice perspectives* (2nd ed.). Vancouver, BC, Canada: University of British Columbia Press.

Dweck, C. (2002). The development of ability conceptions. In A. Wigfield & J. Eccles (Eds.), *Development of achievement motivation* (pp. 57–88). San Diego: Academic Press.

Dwyer, K., Fredstrom, B., Rubin, K., Booth-LaForce, C., Rose-Krasnor, L., & Burgess, K. (2010). Attachment, social information processing, and friendship quality of early adolescent girls and boys. *Journal of Social and Personal Relationships, 27,* 91–116.

Dyson, A. H. (2003). "Welcome to the jam": Popular culture, school literacy and making of childhoods. *Harvard Educational Review, 73,* 328–361.

Eagly, A. H., & Steffen, V. J. (1986). Gender and aggressive behavior: A meta-analytic review of the social psychological literature. *Psychological Bulletin, 100,* 309–330.

Eagly, A. H., & Wood, W. (2003). In C. B. Travis (Ed.), *Evolution, gender, and rape.* Cambridge, MA: MIT Press.

Eaker, E. D., Sullivan, L. M., Kelly-Hayes, M., D'Agostino, R. B., Sr., & Benjamin, E. J. (2004). Anger and hostility predict the development of atrial fibrillation in men in the Framingham Offspring Study. *Circulation, 109,* 1267–1271.

Easton, J., Schipper, L., & Shackelford, T. (2007). Morbid jealousy from an evolutionary psychological perspective. *Evolution and Human Behavior, 28,* 399–402.

Eaton, W. O., & Yu, A. P. (1989). Are sex differences in child motor activity level a function of sex differences in maturational status? *Child Development, 60,* 1005–1011.

Eberling, J. L., Wu, C., Tong-Turnbeaugh, R., & Jagust, W. J. (2004). Estrogen- and tamoxifen-associated effects on brain structure and function. *NeuroImage, 21,* 364–371.

Ebner, N., Freund, A., & Baltes, P. (2006, December). Developmental changes in personal goal orientation from young to late adulthood: From striving for gains to maintenance and prevention of losses. *Psychology and Aging, 21,* 664–678.

Eccles, J., Templeton, J., & Barber, B. (2003). Adolescence and emerging adulthood: The critical passage ways to adulthood. In M. Bornstein & L. Davidson (Eds.), *Well-being: Positive development across the life course* (pp. 383–406). Mahwah, NJ: Lawrence Erlbaum.

Ecenbarger, W. (1993, April 1). America's new merchants of death. *The Reader's Digest,* 50.

Eckerd, L. (2009). Death and dying course offerings in psychology: A survey of nine Midwestern states. *Death Studies, 33,* 762–770.

Eckerman, C. O., & Oehler, J. M. (1992). Very-low-birthweight newborns and parents as early social partners. In S. L. Friedman & M. D. Sigman (Eds.), *The psychological development of low-birthweight children* (pp. 91–124). Norwood, NJ: Ablex.

Eckerman, C. O., & Peterman, K. (2001). Peers and infant social/communicative development. In G. Bremner & A. Fogel (Eds.), *Blackwell handbook of infant development.* Malden, MA: Blackwell Publishers.

Edgerley, L., El-Sayed, Y., Druzin, M., Kiernan, M., & Daniels, K. (2007). Use of a community mobile health van to increase early access to prenatal care. *Maternal & Child Health Journal, 11,* 235–239.

Edwards, C. P. (2000). Children's play in cross-cultural perspective: A new look at the six cultures study. *Cross-Cultural Research: The Journal of Comparative Social Science, 34,* 318–338.

Edwards, S. (2005). Constructivism does not only happen in the individual: Sociocultural theory and early childhood education. *Early Child Development & Care, 175,* 37–47.

Ehrensaft, M., Cohen, P., & Brown, J. (2003). Intergenerational transmission of partner violence: A 20-year prospective study. *Journal of Consulting & Clinical Psychology, 71,* 741–753.

Eichelsheim, V., Buist, K., Dekovic, M., Wissink, I., Frijns, T., van Lier, P., et al. (2010). Associations among the parent-adolescent relationship, aggression and delinquency in different ethnic groups: A replication across two Dutch samples. *Social Psychiatry and Psychiatric Epidemiology, 45,* 293–300.

Eid, M., Riemann, R., Angleitner, A., & Borkenau, P. (2003). Sociability and positive emotionality: Genetic and environmental contributions to the covariation between different facets of extraversion. *Journal of Personality, 71,* 319–346.

Eiden, R., Foote, A., & Schuetze, P. (2007). Maternal cocaine use and caregiving status: Group differences in caregiver and infant risk variables. *Addictive Behaviors, 32,* 465–476.

Eisenberg, N. (2004). Another slant on moral judgment. *PsycCRITQUES,* 12–15.

Eisenberg, N. (2012). *Eight tips to developing caring kids.* Accessed online, July 15, 2012, http://www.csee.org/products/87

Eisenberg, N., & Valiente, C. (2002). Parenting and children's prosocial and moral development. In M. Bornstein (Ed.), *Handbook of parenting: Vol. 5: Practical issues in parenting* (pp. 111–142). Mahwah, NJ: Lawrence Erlbaum.

Eley, T., Liang, H., & Plomin, R. (2004). Parental familial vulnerability, family environment, and their interactions as predictors of depressive symptoms in adolescents. *Child & Adolescent Social Work Journal, 21,* 298–306.

Elkind, D. (1985). Egocentrism redux. *Developmental Review, 5,* 218–226.

Elkind, D. (1994). *Ties that stress: The new family imbalance.* Cambridge, MA: Harvard University Press.

Elkind, D. (1996). Inhelder and Piaget on adolescence and adulthood: A postmodern appraisal. *Psychological Science, 7,* 216–220.

Elkins, D. (2009). Why humanistic psychology lost its power and influence in American psychology: Implications for advancing humanistic psychology. *Journal of Humanistic Psychology, 49,* 267–291. Available online at http://search.ebscohost.com

Elliott, K., & Urquiza, A. (2006). Ethnicity, culture, and child maltreatment. *Journal of Social Issues, 62,* 787–809.

Ellis, B. H., MacDonald, H. Z., Lincoln, A. K., & Cabral, H. J. (2008). Mental health of Somali adolescent refugees: The role of trauma, stress, and perceived discrimination. *Journal of Consulting and Clinical Psychology, 76,* 184–193.

Ellis, B. J. (2004). Timing of pubertal maturation in girls: An integrated life history approach. *Psychological Bulletin, 130,* 920–958.

Ellis, L. (2006, July). Gender differences in smiling: An evolutionary neuroandrogenic theory. *Physiology & Behavior, 88,* 303–308.

Elmore, J. G., Jackson, S. L., Abraham, L., Miglioretti, D. L., Carney, P. A., Geller, B. M., et al. (2009). Variability in interpretive performance at screening mammography and radiologists' characteristics associated with accuracy. *Radiology, 253,* 641–651.

Emery, C. F., Anderson, D. R., & Goodwin, C. L. (2013). Coronary heart disease and hypertension. In A. M. Nezu, C. Nezu, P. A. Geller, & I. B. Weiner (Eds.), *Handbook of psychology, Vol. 9: Health psychology* (2nd ed.). Hoboken, NJ: John Wiley & Sons Inc.

Emslie, C., & Hunt, K. (2008). The weaker sex? Exploring lay understandings of gender differences in life expectancy: A qualitative study. *Social Science & Medicine, 67,* 808–816.

Endo, S. (1992). Infant-infant play from 7 to 12 months of age: An analysis of games in infant-peer triads. *Japanese Journal of Child and Adolescent Psychiatry, 33,* 145–162.

Endrass, T., Schreiber, M., & Kathmann, N. (2012). Speeding up older adults: Age-effects on error processing in speed and accuracy conditions. *Biological Psychology, 89,* 426–432.

England, P., & Li, S. (2006, October). Desegregation stalled: The changing gender composition of college majors, 1971-2002. *Gender & Society, 20,* 657–677.

Engler, J., & Goleman, D. (1992). *The consumer's guide to psychotherapy.* New York: Simon & Schuster.

Ennett, S. T., & Bauman, K. E. (1996). Adolescent social networks: School, demographic, and longitudinal considerations. *Journal of Adolescent Research, 11,* 194–215.

Enright, E. (2004, July/August). A house divided. *AARP Magazine,* pp. 54, 57.

Ensenauer, R. E., Michels, V. V., & Reinke, S. S. (2005). Genetic testing: Practical, ethical, and counseling considerations. *Mayo Clinic Proceedings, 80,* 63–73.

Epel, E. (2009). Telomeres in a life-span perspective: A new "psychobiomarker"? *Current Directions in Psychological Science, 18,* 6–10.

Epperson, S. E. (1988, September 16). Studies link subtle sex bias in schools with women's behavior in the workplace. *Wall Street Journal,* p. 19.

Epstein, L., & Mardon, S. (2007, September 17). Homeroom zombies. *Newsweek,* pp. 64–65.

Erber, J. (2010). *Aging and older adulthood* (2nd ed.). New York: Wiley-Blackwell.

Erikson, E. H. (1963). *Childhood and society.* New York: Norton.

Erlandsson, K., Dsilna, A., Fagerberg, I., & Christensson, K. (2007). Skin-to-skin care with the father after cesarean birth and its effect on newborn crying and prefeeding behavior. *Birth: Issues in Perinatal Care, 34,* 105–114.

Erwin, P. (1993). *Friendship and peer relations in children.* Chichester, England: Wiley.

Eshel, N., Nelson, E. E., Blair, R. J., Pine, D. S., & Ernst, M. (2007). Neural substrates of choice selection in adults and adolescents: Development of the ventrolateral prefrontal and anterior cingulated cortices. *Neuropsychologia, 45,* 1270–1279.

Espenschade, A. (1960). Motor development. In W. R. Johnson (Ed.), *Science and medicine of exercise and sports* (pp. 419–439). New York: Harper & Row.

Essex, M. J., & Nam, S. (1987). Marital status and loneliness among older women: The differential importance of close family and friends. *Journal of Marriage and the Family, 49,* 92–106.

Estell, D. B., Jones, M. H., Pearl, R., Van Acker, R., Farmer, T. W., & Rodkin, P. C. (2008). Peer groups, popularity, and social preference: Trajectories of social functioning among students with and without learning disabilities. *Journal of Learning Disabilities, 41,* 5–14.

Ethier, L., Couture, G., & Lacharite, C. (2004). Risk factors associated with the chronicity of high potential for child abuse and neglect. *Journal of Family Violence, 19,* 13–24.

Evans, G. W. (2004). The environment of childhood poverty. *American Psychologist, 59,* 77–92.

Evans, R. (2009). A comparison of rural and urban older adults in Iowa on specific markers of successful aging. *Journal of Gerontological Social Work, 52,* 423–438.

Evans, T., Whittingham, K., & Boyd, R. (2012). What helps the mother of a preterm infant become securely attached, responsive and well-adjusted? *Infant Behavior & Development, 35,* 1–11.

Ezzo, F., & Young, K. (2012). Child maltreatment risk inventory: Pilot data for the Cleveland child abuse potential scale. *Journal of Family Violence, 27,* 145–155.

Faber, A., & Wittenborn, A. (2010). The role of attachment in children's adjustment to divorce and remarriage. *Journal of Family Psychotherapy, 21,* 89–104.

Fagan, J., Holland, C., & Wheeler, K. (2007). The prediction, from infancy, of adult IQ and achievement. *Intelligence, 35,* 225–231.

Fagan, J., & Holland, C. (2007). Racial equality in intelligence: Predictions from a theory of intelligence as processing. *Intelligence, 35,* 319–334.

Fagan, M. (2009). Mean length of utterance before words and grammar: Longitudinal trends and developmental implications of infant vocalizations. *Journal of Child Language, 36,* 495–527. Available online at http://search.ebscohost.com

Fais, L., Kajikawa, S., Amano, S., & Werker, J. (2010). Now you hear it, now you don't: Vowel devoicing in Japanese infant-directed speech. *Journal of Child Language, 37,* 319–340.

Faith, M. S., Johnson, S. L., & Allison, D. B. (1997). Putting the behavior into the behavior genetics of obesity. *Behavior Genetics, 27,* 423–439.

Falck-Ytter, T., Gredeback, G., & von Hofsten, C. (2006). Infants predict other people's action goals. *Nature Neuroscience, 9,* 878–879.

Falco, M. (2012, July 3). Since IVF began, 5 million babies born. *CNN News.* Accessed online, July 3, 2012, http://www.10news.com/health/31243126/detail.html

Fanger, S., Frankel, L., & Hazen, N. (2012). Peer exclusion in preschool children's play: Naturalistic observations in a playground setting. *Merrill-Palmer Quarterly, 58,* 224–254.

Fantz, R. L. (1961). The origin of form perception. *Scientific American, 204,* 66–72.

Fantz, R. L. (1963). Pattern vision in newborn infants. *Science, 140,* 296–297.

Farmer, T. W., Estell, D. B., Bishop, J. L., O'Neal, K. K., & Cairns, B. D. (2003). Rejected bullies or popular leaders? The social relations of aggressive subtypes of rural African American early adolescents. *Developmental Psychology, 39,* 992–1004.

Farr, R. H., & Patterson, C. J. (2013). Lesbian and gay adoptive parents and their children. In A. E. Goldberg & K. R. Allen (Eds.), *LGBT-parent families: Innovations in research and implications for practice* (pp. 39–55). New York: Springer Science + Business Media.

Farroni, T., Menon, E., Rigato, S., & Johnson, M. (2007). The perception of facial expressions in newborns. *European Journal of Developmental Psychology, 4,* 2–13.

Farzin, F., Charles, E., & Rivera, S. (2009). Development of multimodal processing in infancy. *Infancy, 14,* 563–578.

Fayers, T., Crowley, T., Jenkins, J. M., & Cahill, D. J. (2003). Medical student awareness of sexual health is poor. *International Journal STD/AIDS, 14,* 386–389.

Federal Interagency Forum on Aging-Related Statistics. (2000). *Older Americans 2000: Key indicators of well-being.* Hyattsville, MD: Author.

Federal Interagency Forum on Aging-Related Statistics. (2010). *Older Americans 2010: Key indicators of well-being.* Washington, DC: Author.

Federal Interagency Forum on Child and Family Statistics. (2003). *America's children: Key national indicators of well-being, 2003.* Federal Interagency Forum on Child and Family Statistics. Washington, DC: U.S. Government Printing Office.

Feeney, B. C., & Collins, N. L. (2003). Motivations for caregiving in adult intimate relationships: Influences on caregiving behavior and relationship functioning. *Personality and Social Psychology Bulletin, 29,* 950–968.

Feigelman, W., Jordan, J., & Gorman, B. (2009). How they died, time since loss, and bereavement outcomes. *Omega: Journal of Death and Dying, 58,* 251–273.

Feinberg, T. E. (2000). The nested hierarchy of consciousness: A neurobiological solution to the problem of mental unity. *Neurocase, 6,* 75–81.

Feldhusen, J. (2003). Precocity and acceleration. *Gifted Education International, 17,* 55–58.

Feldman, D. (2013). Cognitive development in childhood: A contemporary perspective. In R. M. Lerner, M. Easterbrooks, J. Mistry, & I. B. Weiner (Eds.), *Handbook of psychology, Vol. 6: Developmental psychology* (2nd ed.). Hoboken, NJ: John Wiley & Sons Inc.

Feldman, D. C., & Ng, T. H. (2013). Theoretical approaches to the study of job transitions. In N. W. Schmitt, S. Highhouse, & I. B. Weiner (Eds.), *Handbook of psychology, Vol. 12: Industrial and organizational psychology* (2nd ed.). Hoboken, NJ: John Wiley & Sons Inc.

Feldman, R., & Masalha, S. (2007). The role of culture in moderating the links between early ecological risk and young children's adaptation. *Development and Psychopathology, 19,* 1–21.

Feldman, R. S. (Eds.). (1992). *Applications of nonverbal behavioral theories and research.* Hillsdale, NJ: Lawrence Erlbaum.

Feldman, R. S., Tomasian, J., & Coats, E. J. (1999). Adolescents' social competence and nonverbal deception abilities: Adolescents with higher social skills are better liars. *Journal of Nonverbal Behavior, 23,* 237–249.

Fell, J., & Williams, A. (2008). The effect of aging on skeletal-muscle recovery from exercise: Possible implications for aging athletes. *Journal of Aging and Physical Activity, 16,* 97–115. Available online at http://search.ebscohost.com

Fenwick, K., & Morrongiello, B. (1991). Development of frequency perception in infants and children. *Journal of Speech, Language Pathology, and Audiology, 15,* 7–22.

Fenwick, K. D., & Morrongiello, B. A. (1998). Spatial co-location and infants' learning of auditory-visual associations. *Behavior & Development, 21,* 745–759.

Ferguson, F., & Austin, E. (2010). Associations of trait and ability emotional intelligence with performance on Theory of Mind tasks in an adult sample. *Personality and Individual Differences, 49,* 414–418.

Ferguson, R., & Brohaugh, B. (2010). The aging of Aquarius. *Journal of Consumer Marketing, 27,* 76–81.

Fergusson, D., Horwood, L., Boden, J., & Jenkin, G. (2007, March). Childhood social disadvantage and smoking in adulthood: Results of a 25-year longitudinal study. *Addiction, 102,* 475–482.

Fergusson, D. M., Horwood, L. J., & Ridder, E. M. (2006). Abortion in young women and subsequent mental health. *Journal of Child Psychology and Psychiatry, 47,* 16–24.

Fergusson, E., Maughan, B., & Golding, J. (2008). Which children receive grandparental care and what effect does it have? *Journal of Child Psychology and Psychiatry, 49,* 161–169.

Ferholt, B., & Lecusay, R. (2010). Adult and child development in the zone of proximal development: Socratic dialogue in a playworld. *Mind, Culture, and Activity, 17,* 59–83.

Fernald, A. (2001). Hearing, listening, and understanding: Auditory development in infancy. In G. Bremner & A. Fogel (Eds.), *Blackwell handbook of infant development* (pp. 35–70). Malden, MA: Blackwell Publishers.

Fernald, A., & Morikawa, H. (1993). Common themes and cultural variations in Japanese and American mothers' speech to infants. *Child Development, 64,* 637–656.

Fernyhough, C. (1997). Vygotsky's sociocultural approach: Theoretical issues and implications for current research. In S. Hala (Ed.), *The development of social cognition.* Hove, England: Psychology Press/Lawrence Erlbaum, Taylor & Francis.

Feshbach, S., & Tangney, J. (2008). Television viewing and aggression: Some alternative perspectives. *Perspectives on Psychological Science, 3,* 387–389. Available online at http://search.ebscohost.com

Fetterman, D. M. (2005). Empowerment evaluation: From the digital divide to academic distress. In D. Fetterman & A. Wandersman (Eds.), *Empowerment evaluation principles in practice* (pp. 107–122). New York: Guilford Press.

Fiedler, N. L. (2012). Gender (sex) differences in response to prenatal lead exposure. In M. Lewis & L. Kestler (Eds.), *Gender differences in prenatal substance exposure.* Washington, DC: American Psychological Association.

Field, D., & Millsap, R. E. (1991). Personality in advanced old age: Continuity or change? *Journals of Gerontology: Series B: Psychological Sciences and Social Sciences, 46,* pp. 299–308.

Field, M. J., & Behrman, R. E. (Eds.). (2003). *When children die.* Washington, DC: National Academies Press.

Field, T., Diego, M., & Hernandez-Reif, M. (2006). Prenatal depression effects on the fetus and newborn: A review. *Infant Behavior & Development, 29,* 445–455.

Field, T., Diego, M., & Hernandez-Reif, M. (2008). Prematurity and potential predictors. *International Journal of Neuroscience, 118,* 277–289.

Field, T., Diego, M., & Hernandez-Reif, M. (2009). Depressed mothers' infants are less responsive to faces and voices. *Infant Behavior & Development, 32,* 239–244.

Field, T., Diego, M., & Hernandez-Reif, M. (2010). Preterm infant massage therapy research: A review. *Infant Behavior & Development, 33,* 115–124.

Field, T., Hernandez-Reif, M., & Diego, M. (2006). Newborns of depressed mothers who received moderate versus light pressure massage during pregnancy. *Infant Behavior & Development, 29(1),* 54–58.

Field, T., & Walden, T. (1982). Perception and production of facial expression in infancy and early childhood. In H. Reese & L. Lipsitt (Eds.), *Advances in child development and behavior* (Vol. 16, pp. 169–211). New York: Academic Press.

Figley, C. R. (1973). Child density and the marital relationship. *Journal of Marriage and the Family, 35,* 272–282.

Filippi, M., Valsasina, P., Misci, P., Falini, A., Comi, G., & Rocca, M. A. (2013). The organization of intrinsic brain activity differs between genders: A resting-state FMRI study in a large cohort of young healthy subjects. *Human Brain Mapping, 34,* 1330–1343.

Finch, C. E., & Tanzi, R. E. (1997, October 17). Genetics of aging. *Science, 278,* 407–410.

Fincham, F. D. (2003). Marital conflict: Correlates, structure, and context. *Current Directions in Psychological Science, 12,* 23–27.

Findlen, B. (1990). Culture: A refuge for murder. *Ms.,* pp. 1, 47.

Fingerhut, L. A., & MaKuc, D. M. (1992). Mortality among minority populations in the United States. *American Journal of Public Health, 82,* 1168–1170.

Finkelhor, D. (1997). The homicides of children and youth: A developmental perspective. In G. K. Kantor & J. L. Janinski (Eds.), *Out of the darkness: Contemporary perspectives on family violence* (pp. 17–34). Thousand Oaks, CA: Sage Publications.

Finkelstein, D. L., Harper, D. A., & Rosenthal, G. E. (1998). Does length of hospital stay during labor and delivery influence patient satisfaction? Results from a regional study. *American Journal of Managed Care, 4,* 1701–1708.

Finley, G., & Schwartz, S. (2010). The divided world of the child: Divorce and long-term psychosocial adjustment. *Family Court Review, 48,* 516–527.

First, J. M., & Cardenas, J. (1986). A minority view on testing. *Educational Measurement Issues and Practice, 5,* 6–11.

Fischer, T. (2007). Parental divorce and children's socioeconomic success: Conditional effects of parental resources prior to divorce, and gender of the child. *Sociology, 41,* 475–495.

Fischer, K. W., & Hencke, R. W. (1996). Infants' construction of actions in context: Piaget's contributions to research on early development. *Psychological Science, 7,* 204–210.

Fischer, K. W., & Rose, S. P. (1995). Concurrent cycles in the dynamic development of brain and behavior. *Newsletter of the Society for Research in Child Development,* p. 16.

Fish, J. M. (Ed.). (2001). *Race and intelligence: Separating science from myth.* Mahwah, NJ: Lawrence Erlbaum.

Fisher, C., Hauck, Y., & Fenwick, J. (2006). How social context impacts on women's fears of childbirth: A Western Australian example. *Social Science & Medicine, 63,* 64–75.

Fisher, C. B. (2003). *Decoding the ethics code: A practical guide for psychologists.* Thousand Oaks, CA: Sage Publications.

Fisher, C. B. (2004). Informed consent and clinical research involving children and adolescents: Implications of the revised APA Ethics Code and HIPAA. *Journal of Clinical Child & Adolescent Psychology, 33,* 832–839.

Fisher, C. B. (2005). Deception research involving children: Ethical practices and paradoxes. *Ethics & Behavior, 15,* 271–287.

Fiske, S. T., & Taylor, S. E. (1991). *Social cognition* (2nd ed.). New York: McGraw-Hill.

Fitzgerald, D., & White, K. (2002). Linking children's social worlds: Perspective-taking in parent-child and peer contexts. *Social Behavior & Personality, 31,* 509–522.

Fitzgerald, P. (2008). A neurotransmitter system theory of sexual orientation. *Journal of Sexual Medicine, 5,* 746–748.

Fivush, R. (2010). Developing gender in a changing world. *Journal of Applied Developmental Psychology, 31,* 348–349.

Fivush, R., Kuebli, J., & Clubb, P. A. (1992). The structure of events and event representations: A developmental analysis. *Child Development, 63,* 188–201.

Flanigan, J. (2005, July 3). Immigrants benefit U.S. economy now as ever. *Los Angeles Times.*

Flashman, J. (2013). A cohort perspective on gender gaps in college attendance and completion. *Research in Higher Education.* Accessed online, June 7, 2013, http://link.springer.com/article/10.1007/s11162-013-9285-8#page-1

Flavell, J. H. (1994). Cognitive development: Past, present, and future. In R. D. Parke, P. A. Ornstein, J. J. Rieser, & C. Zahn-Waxler (Eds.), *A century of developmental psychology* (pp. 569–588). Washington, DC: American Psychological Association.

Flavell, J. H. (1996). Piaget's legacy. *Psychological Science, 7,* 200–203.

Fleming, M., Greentree, S., Cocotti-Muller, D., Elias, K., & Morrison, S. (2006, December). Safety in cyberspace: Adolescents' safety and exposure online. *Youth & Society, 38,* 135–154.

Fletcher, A. C., Darling, N. E., Steinberg, L., & Dornbusch, S. M. (1995). The company they keep: Relation of adolescents' adjustment and behavior to their friends' perceptions of authoritative parenting in the social network. *Developmental Psychology, 31,* 300–310.

Fling, B. W., Walsh, C. M., Bangert, A. S., Reuter-Lorenz, P. A., Welsh, R. C., & Seidler, R. D. (2011). Differential callosal contributions to bimanual control in young and older adults. *Journal of Cognitive Neuroscience, 23,* 2171–2185.

Flom, R., & Bahrick, L. (2007). The development of infant discrimination of affect in multimodal and unimodal stimulation: The role of intersensory redundancy. *Developmental Psychology, 43,* 238–252.

Florsheim, P. (2003). Adolescent romantic and sexual behavior: What we know and where we go from here. In P. Florsheim (Ed.), *Adolescent romantic relations and sexual behavior: Theory, research, and practical implications* (pp. 371–385). Mahwah, NJ: Lawrence Erlbaum.

Flouri, E. (2005). *Fathering and child outcomes.* New York: Wiley.

Floyd, R. G. (2005). Information-processing approaches to interpretation of contemporary intellectual assessment instruments. In D. P. Flanagan & P. L. Harrison (Eds.), *Contemporary intellectual assessment: Theories, tests, and issues* (pp. 203–233). New York: Guilford Press.

Flynn, E., O'Malley, C., & Wood, D. (2004). A longitudinal, microgenetic study of the emergence of false belief understanding and inhibition skills. *Developmental Science, 7,* 103–115.

Fogel, A., Hsu, H., Shapiro, A., Nelson-Goens, G., & Secrist, C. (2006, May). Effects of normal and perturbed social play on the duration and amplitude of different types of infant smiles. *Developmental Psychology, 42,* 459–473.

Fok, M. S. M., & Tsang, W. Y. W. (2006). 'Development of an instrument measuring Chinese adolescent beliefs and attitudes towards substance use': Response to commentary. *Journal of Clinical Nursing, 15,* 1062–1063.

Folbre, N. (2012, July 2). Price tags for parents. *Economix-The New York Times.* Accessed online, July 7, 2012, http://economix.blogs.nytimes.com/2012//07/02/price-tags-for-parents

Fontes, S., & Oliveira, A. (2013). Senescence with more time and better. *Arquivos De Neuro-Psiquiatria, 71*(2), 72–73.

Foote, W. E. (2013). Forensic evaluation in Americans with Disabilities Act cases. In R. K. Otto & I. B. Weiner (Eds.), *Handbook of psychology, Vol. 11: Forensic psychology* (2nd ed.). Hoboken, NJ: John Wiley & Sons Inc.

Ford, J. A. (2007). Alcohol use among college students: A comparison of athletes and nonathletes. *Substance Use & Misuse, 42,* 1367–1377.

Foroud, A., & Whishaw, I. Q. (2012). The consummatory origins of visually guided reaching in human infants: A dynamic integration of whole-body and upper-limb movements. *Behavioural Brain Research, 231,* 343–355.

Fowers, B. J., & Davidov, B. J. (2006). The virtue of multiculturalism: Personal transformation, character, and openness to the other. *American Psychologist, 61,* 581–594.

Fowler, J. W., & Dell, M. L. (2006). Stages of faith from infancy through adolescence: Reflections on three decades of faith development theory. In E. C. Roehlkepartain, P. E. King, L. Wagener, & P. L. Benson (Eds.), *The handbook of spiritual development in childhood and adolescence.* Thousand Oaks, CA: Sage Publications.

Fozard, J. L., Vercruyssen, M., Reynolds, S. L., Hancock, P. A., & Quilter, R. E. (1994). Age differences and changes in reaction time: The Baltimore Longitudinal Study of Aging. *Journal of Gerontology, 49,* 179–189.

Fraenkel, P. (2003). Contemporary two-parent families: Navigating work and family challenges. In F. Walsh (Ed.), *Normal family processes: Growing diversity and complexity* (3rd ed.). New York: Guilford Press.

Francis, A. N., Bhojraj, T. S., Prasad, K. M., Montrose, D., Eack, S. M., Rajarethinam, R., et al. (2013). Alterations in the cerebral white matter of genetic high risk offspring of patients with schizophrenia spectrum disorder. *Progress in Neuro-Psychopharmacology & Biological Psychiatry, 40,* 187–192.

Franck, I., & Brownstone, D. (1991). *The parent's desk reference.* New York: Prentice-Hall.

Franic, S., Middeldorp, C., Dolan, C., Ligthart, L., & Boomsma, D. (2010). Childhood and adolescent anxiety and depression: Beyond heritability. *Journal of the American Academy of Child & Adolescent Psychiatry, 49,* 820–829.

Frank, M. C., Tenenbaum, J. B., & Fernald, A. (2013). Social and discourse contributions to the determination of reference in cross-situational word learning. *Language Learning and Development, 9,* 1–24.

Frankenburg, W. K., Dodds, J., Archer, P., Shapiro, H., & Bresnick, B. (1992). The Denver II: A major revision and restandardization of the Denver Developmental Screening Test. *Pediatrics, 89,* 91–97.

Frawley, T. (2008). Gender schema and prejudicial recall: How children misremember, fabricate, and distort gendered picture book information. *Journal of Research in Childhood Education, 22,* 291–303.

Frazier, L. M., Grainger, D. A., Schieve, L. A., & Toner, J. P. (2004). Follicle-stimulating hormone and estradiol levels independently predict the success of assisted reproductive technology treatment. *Fertility and Sterility, 82,* 834–840.

Frederickson, N., & Petrides, K. (2008). Ethnic, gender, and socio-economic group differences in academic performance and secondary school selection: A longitudinal analysis. *Learning and Individual Differences, 18,* 144–151.

Freedman, A. M., & Ellison, S. (2004, May 6). Testosterone patch for women shows promise. *Wall Street Journal,* pp. A1, B2.

Freedman, D. G. (1979, January). Ethnic differences in babies. *Human Nature,* 15–20.

Freeman, E., Sammel, M., & Liu, L. (2004). Hormones and menopausal status as predictors of depression in women in transition to menopause. *Archives of General Psychiatry, 61,* 62–70.

Freeman, H., Newland, L. A., & Coyl, D. D. (2010). New directions in father attachment. *Early Child Development and Care, 180,* 1–8.

Freeman, J. M. (2007). Beware: The misuse of technology and the law of unintended consequences. *Neurotherapeutics, 4,* 549–554.

French, S., & Swain, J. (1997). Young disabled people. In J. Roche & S. Tucker (Eds.), *Youth in society: Contemporary theory, policy and practice.* London, England: Sage Publications.

Freud, S. (1920). *A general introduction to psychoanalysis.* New York: Boni & Liveright.

Freud, S. (1922/1959). *Group psychology and the analysis of the ego.* London: Hogarth.

Friborg, O., Barlaug, D., Martinussen, M., Rosenvinge, J. H., & Hjemdal, O. (2005). Resilience in relation to personality and intelligence. *International Journal of Methods in Psychiatric Research, 14,* 29–42.

Frick, P. J., Cornell, A. H., Bodin, S. D., Dane, H. A., Barry, C. T., & Loney, B. R. (2003). Callous-unemotional traits and developmental pathways to severe conduct problems. *Developmental Psychology, 39,* 246–260.

Fridlund, A. J., Beck, H. P., Goldie, W. D., & Irons, G. (2012, July 9). Little Albert: A neurologically impaired child. *History of Psychology.* Accessed online July 9, 2012, http://psycnet.apa.org/psycinfo/2012-01974-001/

Friedlander, L. J., Connolly, J. A., Pepler, D. J., & Craig, W. M. (2007). Biological, familial, and peer influences on dating in early adolescence. *Archives of Sexual Behavior, 36,* 821–830.

Friedman, D. E. (2004). *The new economics of preschool.* Washington, DC: Early Childhood Funders' Collaborative/NAEYC.

Friedman, W., & Janssen, S. (2010). Aging and the speed of time. *Acta Psychologica, 134,* 130–141.

Frisch, M., Friis, S., Kjear, S. K., & Melbye, M. (1995). Falling incidence of penis cancer in an uncircumcised population (Denmark 1943–90). *British Medical Journal, 311,* 1471.

Fritz, G., & Rockney, R. (2004). Summary of the practice parameter for the assessment and treatment of children and adolescents with enuresis. *Work Group on Quality Issues; Journal of the American Academy of Child & Adolescent Psychiatry, 43,* 123–125.

Frome, P., Alfeld, C., Eccles, J., & Barber, B. (2006, August). Why don't they want a male-dominated job? An investigation of young women who changed their occupational aspirations. *Educational Research and Evaluation, 12,* 359–372.

Fromholt, P., & Larsen, S. F. (1991). Autobiographical memory in normal, aging and primary degenerative dementia (dementia of the Alzheimer type). *Journal of Gerontology, 46,* 85–91.

Fry, C. L. (1985). Culture, behavior, and aging in the comparative perspective. In J. E. Birren & K. W. Schaie (Eds.), *Handbook of the psychology of aging.* New York: Van Nostrand Reinhold.

Fryar, C. D., Carroll, M. D., & Ogden, C. L. (2012). *Prevalence of obesity among children and adolescents: United States, trends 1963–1965 through 2009–2010.* Hyattsville, MD: National Center for Health Statistics, Health E-Stat.

Fu, G., Xu, F., Cameron, C., Heyman, G., & Lee, K. (2007, March). Cross-cultural differences in children's choices, categorizations, and evaluations of truths and lies. *Developmental Psychology, 43*(2), 278–293.

Fu, X., & Heaton, T. (2008). Racial and educational homogamy: 1980 to 2000. *Sociological Perspectives, 51,* 735–758.

Fugate, W. N., & Mitchell, E. S. (1997). Women's images of midlife: Observations from the Seattle Midlife Women's Health Study. *Health Care for Women International, 18,* 439–453.

Fulcher, M., Sutfin, E., Chan, R., Scheib, J., & Patterson, C. (2006). Lesbian mothers and their children: Findings from the Contemporary Families Study. In A. M. Omoto & H. S. Kurtzman (Eds.), *Sexual orientation and mental health: Examining identity and development in lesbian, gay, and bisexual people.* Washington, DC: American Psychological Association.

Fuligni, A. J. (1997). The academic achievement of adolescents from immigrant families: The roles of family background, attitudes, and behavior. *Child Development, 68,* 351–368.

Fuligni, A. J. (2012). The intersection of aspirations and resources in the development of children from immigrant families. In C. Coll & A. Marks (Eds.), *The immigrant paradox in children and adolescents: Is becoming American a developmental risk?.* Washington, DC: American Psychological Association.

Fuligni, A. J., & Fuligni, A. S. (2008). Immigrant families and the educational development of their children. In J. E. Lansford et al. (Eds.), *Immigrant families in contemporary society.* New York: Guilford Press.

Fuligni, A. J., & Yoshikawa, H. (2003). Socioeconomic resources, parenting, and child development among immigrant families. In M. Bornstein & R. Bradley (Eds.), *Socioeconomic status, parenting, and child development* (pp. 107–124). Mahwah, NJ: Lawrence Erlbaum.

Fuligni, A. J., & Zhang, W. (2004). Attitudes toward family obligation among adolescents in contemporary urban and rural China. *Child Development, 75,* 180–192.

Funk, L. (2010). Prioritizing parental autonomy: Adult children's accounts of feeling responsible and supporting aging parents. *Journal of Aging Studies, 24,* 57–64.

Furman, W., & Shaffer, L. (2003). The role of romantic relationships in adolescent development. In P. Florsheim (Ed.), *Adolescent romantic relations and sexual behavior: Theory, research, and practical implications.* Mahwah, NJ: Lawrence Erlbaum.

Furstenberg, F. F., Jr. (1996, June). The future of marriage. *American Demographics,* 34–40.

Fuso, A., Nicolia, V., Ricceri, L., Cavallaro, R. A., Isopi, E., Mangia, F., et al. (2012). S-adenosylmethionine reduces the progress of the Alzheimer-like features induced by B-vitamin deficiency in mice. *Neurobiology of Aging, 33,* e1–e16.

Gagnon, S. G., & Nagle, R. J. (2000). Comparison of the revised and original versions of the Bayley Scales of Infant Development. *School Psychology International, 21,* 293–305.

Galambos, N., Leadbeater, B., & Barker, E. (2004). Gender differences in and risk factors for depression in adolescence: A 4-year longitudinal study. *International Journal of Behavioral Development, 28,* 16–25.

Galler, J., Bryce, C., Waber, D., Hock, R., Exner, N., Eaglesfield, D., et al. (2010). Early childhood malnutrition predicts depressive symptoms at ages 11–17. *Journal of Child Psychology and Psychiatry, 51,* 789–798.

Gallistel, C. (2007). Commentary on Le Corre & Carey. *Cognition, 105,* 439–445.

Gallup Poll. (2004). How many children? *The Gallup Poll Monthly.*

Gamino, L. A., & Ritter, R. R. (2012). Death competence: An ethical imperative. *Death Studies, 36,* 23–40.

Gangestad, S. (2010). Evolutionary biology looks at behavior genetics. *Personality and Individual Differences, 49,* 289–295.

Ganley, C. M., Mingle, L. A., Ryan, A. M., Ryan, K., Vasilyeva, M., & Perry, M. (2013). An examination of stereotype threat effects on girls' mathematics performance. *Developmental Psychology.* Accessed online, June 7, 2013, http://psycnet.apa.org/index.cfm?a=buy.optionToBuy&am p;id=2013-02693-001

Ganzini, L., Beer, T., & Brouns, M. (2006, September). Views on physician-assisted suicide among family members of Oregon cancer patients. *Journal of Pain and Symptom Management, 32,* 230–236.

Garcia, C., & Saewyc, E. (2007). Perceptions of mental health among recently immigrated Mexican adolescents. *Issues in Mental Health Nursing, 28,* 37–54.

Garcia-Moreno, C., Heise, L., Jansen, H. A. F. M., Ellsberg, M., & Watts, C. (2005, November 25). Violence against women. *Science, 310,* 1282–1283.

Garcia-Portilla, M. (2009). Depression and perimenopause: A review. *Actas Esp Psiquiatr, 37,* 231–321.

Gardner, P. (2007). *Parent involvement in the college recruiting process: To what extent?* (Research Brief 2-2007). Collegiate Employment Research Institute, Michigan State University.

Gardner, H., & Moran, S. (2006). The science of multiple intelligences theory: A response to Lynn Waterhouse. *Educational Psychologist, 41,* 227–232.

Garlick, D. (2003). Integrating brain science research with intelligence research. *Current Directions in Psychological Science, 12,* 185–189.

Gartrell, N., & Bos, H. (2010). US National Longitudinal Lesbian Family Study: Psychological adjustment of 17-year-old adolescents. *Pediatrics, 126,* 28–36.

Gartstein, M., Slobodskaya, H., & Kinsht, I. (2003). Cross-cultural differences in temperament in the first year of life: United States of America (US) and Russia. *International Journal of Behavioral Development, 27,* 316–328.

Gattringer, T., Enzinger, C., Ropele, S., Gorani, F., Petrovic, K., Schmidt, R., et al. (2012). Vascular risk factors, white matter hyperintensities and hippocampal volume in normal elderly individuals. *Dementia and Geriatric Cognitive Disorders, 33*(1), 29–34.

Gaulden, M. E. (1992). Maternal age effect: The enigma of Down syndrome and other trisomic conditions. *Mutation Research, 296,* 69–88.

Gauthier, S., & Scheltens, P. (2009). Can we do better in developing new drugs for Alzheimer's disease? *Alzheimer's & Dementia, 5,* 489–491.

Gauvain, M. (1998). Cognitive development in social and cultural context. *Current Directions in Psychological Science, 7,* 188–194.

Gavin, L. A., & Furman, W. (1996). Adolescent girls' relationships with mothers and best friends. *Child Development, 67,* 375–386.

Gavin, T., & Myers, A. (2003). Characteristics, enrollment, attendance, and dropout patterns of older adults in beginner Tai-Chi and line-dancing programs. *Journal of Aging & Physical Activity, 11,* 123–141.

Gawande, A. (2007, April 30). The way we age now. *The New Yorker*, pp. 49–59.

Gazmararian, J. A., Petersen, R., Spitz, A. M., Goodwin, M. M., Saltzman, L. E., & Marks, J. S. (2000). Violence and reproductive health: Current knowledge and future research directions. *Mat Child Health, 4,* 79–84.

Geller, P. A., Nelson, A. R., & Bonacquisti, A. (2013). Women's health psychology. In A. M. Nezu, C. Nezu, P. A. Geller, & I. B. Weiner (Eds.), *Handbook of psychology, Vol. 9: Health psychology* (2nd ed.). Hoboken, NJ: John Wiley & Sons Inc.

Gelman, R. (2006, August). Young natural-number arithmeticians. *Current Directions in Psychological Science, 15,* 193–197.

Gelman, R., & Baillargeon, R. (1983). A review of some Piagetian concepts. In P. H. Mussen (Ed.), *Handbook of child psychology: Vol 3. Cognitive development* (4th ed.). New York: Wiley.

Gelman, R., & Gallistel, C. R. (2004, October 15). Language and the origin of numerical concepts. *Science, 306,* 441–443.

Gelman, S. A., Taylor, M. G., & Nguyen, S. (2004). Mother–child conversations about gender. *Monographs of the Society for Research in Child Development, 69.*

General Social Survey. (1998). *National opinion research center*. Chicago: University of Chicago.

Genevro, J. L., & Miller, T. L. (2010). The emotional and economic costs of bereavement in health care settings. *Psychologica Belgica, 50,* 69–88.

Gerard, C. M., Harris, K. A., & Thach, B. T. (2002). Spontaneous arousals in supine infants while swaddled and unswaddled during rapid eye movement and quiet sleep. *Pediatrics, 110,* 70.

Gerber, M. S. (2002, October 9). Eighty million strong—the singles lobby. *The Hill*, p. 45.

Gershkoff-Stowe, L., & Hahn, E. (2007). Fast mapping skills in the developing lexicon. *Journal of Speech, Language, and Hearing Research, 50,* 682–696.

Gershoff, E. T. (2002). Parental corporal punishment and associated child behaviors and experiences: A meta-analytic and theoretical review. *Pychological Bulletin, 128,* 539–579.

Gershoff, E. T., Lansford, J. E., Sexton, H. R., Davis-Kean, P., & Sameroff, A. J. (2012). Longitudinal links between spanking and children's externalizing behaviors in a national sample of White, Black, Hispanic, and Asian American families. *Clinical Psychology Review, 23,* 197–224.

Gerstorf, D., Ram, N., Estabrook, R., Schupp, J., Wagner, G., & Lindenberger, U. (2008). Life satisfaction shows terminal decline in old age: Longitudinal evidence from the German Socio-Economic Panel Study (SOEP). *Developmental Psychology, 44,* 1148–1159.

Gesell, A. L. (1946). The ontogenesis of infant behavior. In L. Carmichael (Ed.), *Manual of child psychology*. New York: Harper.

Geurts, T., van Tilburg, T. G., & Poortman, A. (2012). The grandparent-grandchild relationship in childhood and adulthood: A matter of continuation? *Personal Relationships, 19,* 267–278.

Ghaemi, S., Vohringer, P. A., & Whitham, E. A. (2013). Antidepressants from a public health perspective: Re-examining effectiveness, suicide, and carcinogenicity. *Acta Psychiatrica Scandinavica, 127,* 89–93.

Ghazi, A., Henis-Korenblit, S., & Kenyon, C. (2009). A transcription elongation factor that links signals from the reproductive system to lifespan extension in Caenorhabditis elegans. *PLoS Genetics, 5,* 71–77.

Ghisletta, P., Kennedy, K., Rodrigue, K., Lindenberger, U., & Raz, N. (2010). Adult age differences and the role of cognitive resources in perceptual-motor skill acquisition: Application of a multilevel negative exponential model. *The Journals of Gerontology: Series B: Psychological Sciences and Social Sciences, 65B,* 163–173.

Ghisletta, P., Rabbitt, P., Lunn, M., & Lindenberger, U. (2012). Two thirds of the age-based changes in fluid and crystallized intelligence, perceptual speed, and memory in adulthood are shared. *Intelligence, 40,* 260–268.

Ghule, M., Balaiah, D., & Joshi, B. (2007). Attitude towards premarital sex among rural college youth in Maharashtra, India. *Sexuality & Culture, 11,* 1–17.

Gibbs, N. (2002, April 15). Making time for a baby. *Time*, pp. 48–54.

Giedd, J. N., Raznahan, A., Lee, N. R., Weddle, C., Liverpool, M., Stockman, M., et al. (2011). Structural brain magnetic resonance imaging of typically developing children and adolescents. In E. Amsel & J. G. Smetana (Eds.), *Adolescent vulnerabilities and opportunities: Developmental and constructivist perspectives*. New York: Cambridge University Press.

Gifford-Smith, M., & Brownell, C. (2003). Childhood peer relationships: Social acceptance, friendships, and peer networks. *Journal of School Psychology, 41,* 235–284.

Gilbert, L. A. (1994). Current perspectives on dual-career families. *Current Directions in Psychological Science, 3,* 101–105.

Gilbert, S. (2004, March 16). New clues to women veiled in black. *The New York Times*, p. D1.

Gillespie, N. A., Cloninger, C. R., & Heath, A. C. (2003). The genetic and environmental relationship between Cloninger's dimensions of temperament and character. *Personality and Individual Differences, 35,* 1931–1946.

Gillham, A., Law, A., & Hickey, L. (2010). A psychodynamic perspective. In C. Cupitt (Eds.), *Reaching out: The psychology of assertive outreach*. New York: Routledge/Taylor & Francis Group.

Gillies, R., & Boyle, M. (2006, May). Ten Australian elementary teachers' discourse and reported pedagogical practices during cooperative learning. *The Elementary School Journal, 106,* 429–451.

Gilligan, C. (1982). *In a different voice: Psychological theory and women's development*. Cambridge, MA: Harvard University Press.

Gilligan, C. (1987). Adolescent development reconsidered. In C. E. Irwin (Ed.), *Adolescent social behavior and health*. San Francisco: Jossey-Bass.

Gilligan, C. (2004). Recovering psyche: Reflections on life-history and history. *Annual of Psychoanalysis, 32,* 131–147.

Gilligan, C., Brown, L. M., & Rogers, A. G. (1990). Psyche embedded: A place for body, relationships, and culture in personality theory. In A. I. Rabin & R. A. Zucker (Eds.), *Studying persons and lives*. New York: Springer.

Gilligan, C., Lyons, N. P., & Hammer, T. J. (Eds.). (1990). *Making connections*. Cambridge, MA: Harvard University Press.

Gilligan, C., Ward, J. V., & Taylor, J. M. (Eds.). (1988). *Mapping the moral domain: A contribution of women's thinking to psychological theory and education*. Cambridge, MA: Harvard University Press.

Gilliland, A. L., & Verny, T. R. (1999). The effects of domestic abuse on the unborn child [Special issue]. *Journal of Prenatal and Perinatal Psychology and Health, 13,* 235–246.

Gillmore, M., Gilchrist, L., Lee, J., & Oxford, M. (2006, August). Women who gave birth as unmarried adolescents: Trends in substance use from adolescence to adulthood. *Journal of Adolescent Health, 39,* 237–243.

Gilmore, C. K., & Spelke, E. S. (2008). Children's understanding of the relationship between addition and subtraction. *Cognition, 107,* 932–945.

Ginzberg, E. (1972). Toward a theory of occupational choice: A restatement. *Vocational Guidance Quarterly, 12,* 10–14.

Gitlin, L., Reever, K., Dennis, M., Mathieu, E., & Hauck, W. (2006, October). Enhancing quality of life of families who use adult day services: Short- and long-term effects of the Adult Day Services Plus Program. *The Gerontologist, 46,* 630–639.

Glaser, D. (2012). Effects of child maltreatment on the developing brain. In M. Garralda & J. Raynaud (Eds.), *Brain, mind, and developmental psychopathology in childhood*. Lanham, MD: Jason Aronson.

Glatt, S., Chayavichitsilp, P., Depp, C., Schork, N., & Jeste, D. (2007). Successful aging: From phenotype to genotype. *Biological Psychiatry, 62,* 282–293.

Gleason, M., Iida, M., & Bolger, N. (2003). Daily supportive equity in close relationships. *Personality & Social Psychology Bulletin, 29,* 1036–1045.

Gleitman, L., & Landau, B. (1994). *The acquisition of the lexicon*. Cambridge, MA: Bradford.

Glick, P., & Fiske, S. T. (2012). An ambivalent alliance: Hostile and benevolent sexism as complementary justifications for gender inequality. In J. Dixon & M. Levine (Eds.), *Beyond prejudice: Extending the social psychology of conflict, inequality and social change*. New York: Cambridge University Press.

Gliga, T., Elsabbagh, M., Andravizou, A., & Johnson, M. (2009). Faces attract infants' attention in complex displays. *Infancy, 14,* 550–562.

Gluhoski, V., Leader, J., & Wortman, C. B. (1994). Grief and bereavement. In V. S. Ramachandran (Ed.), *Encyclopedia of human behavior*. San Diego: Academic Press.

Goble, M. M. (2008). Medical and psychological complications of obesity. In H. D. Davies et al. (Eds.), *Obesity in childhood and adolescence, Vol. 1: Medical, biological, and social issues*. Westport, CT: Praeger Publishers / Greenwood Publishing.

Godefroy, O., Roussel, M., Despretz, P., Quaglino, V., & Boucart, M. (2010). Age-related slowing: Perceptuomotor, decision, or attention decline? *Experimental Aging Research, 36,* 169–189.

Goede, I., Branje, S., & Meeus, W. (2009). Developmental changes in adolescents' perceptions of relationships with their parents. *Journal of Youth and Adolescence, 38,* 75–88.

Goetz, A., & Shackelford, T. (2006). Modern application of evolutionary theory to psychology: Key concepts and clarifications. *American Journal of Psychology, 119,* 567–584.

Goldberg, A. E. (2004). But do we need universal grammar? Comment on Lidz et al. *Cognition, 94,* 77–84.

Goldberg, A. E. (2010a). Children of lesbian and gay parents: Adjustment and experiences. In *Lesbian and gay parents and their children: Research on the family life cycle*. Washington, DC: American Psychological Association.

Goldberg, A. (2010b). *Lesbian and gay parents and their children: Research on the family life cycle*. Washington, DC: American Psychological Association.

Goldberg, J., Pereira, L., & Berghella, V. (2002). Pregnancy after uterine artery emobilization. *Obstetrics and Gynecology, 100,* 869–872.

Goldfarb, Z. (2005, July 12). Newborn medical screening expands. *Wall Street Journal*, p. D6.

Goldfield, G. S., Harvey, A., Grattan, K., & Adamo, K. B. (2012). Physical activity promotion in the preschool years: A critical period to intervene. *International Journal of Environmental research and Public Health, 9,* 1326–1342.

Goldman, L., Chu, P. W., Osmond, D., & Bindman, A. (2013). Accuracy of do not resuscitate (DNR) in administrative data. *Medical Care Research and Review, 70,* 98–112.

Goldman, R. (2004). Circumcision policy: A psychosocial perspective. *Pediatrics and Child Health, 9,* 630–633.

Goldney, R. D. (2012). Neither euthanasia nor suicide, but rather assisted death. *Australian and New Zealand Journal of Psychiatry, 46,* 185–187.

Goldscheider, F. K. (1994). Divorce and remarriage: Effects on the elderly population. *Reviews in Clinical Gerontology, 4,* 253–259.

Goldschmidt, L., Richardson, G., Willford, J., & Day, N. (2008). Prenatal marijuana exposure and intelligence test performance at age 6. *Journal of the American Academy of Child & Adolescent Psychiatry, 47,* 254–263.

Goldsmith, S. K., Pellmar, T. C., Kleinman, A. M., & Bunney, W. E. (2002). *Reducing suicide: A national imperative.* Washington, DC: National Academies Press.

Goldstein, M. H., Schwade, J., Briesch, J., & Syal, S. (2010). Learning while babbling: Prelinguistic object-directed vocalizations indicate a readiness to learn. *Infancy, 15,* 362–391.

Golombok, S., & Tasker, F. (1996). Do parents influence the sexual orientation of their children? Findings from a longitudinal study of lesbian families. *Developmental Psychology, 32,* 3–11.

Göncü, A., & Gauvain, M. (2012). Sociocultural approaches to educational psychology: Theory, research, and application. In K. R. Harris, S. Graham, T. Urdan, C. B. McCormick, G. M. Sinatra, & J. Sweller (Eds.), *APA educational psychology handbook, Vol 1: Theories, constructs, and critical issues.* Washington, DC: American Psychological Association.

Goode, E. (1999, January 12). Clash over when, and how, to toilet-train. *The New York Times*, pp. A1, A17.

Goode, E. (2004, February 3). Stronger warning is urged on antidepressants for teenagers. *The New York Times*, p. A12.

Goodman, G., & Quas, J. (2008). Repeated interviews and children's memory: It's more than just how many. *Current Directions in Psychological Science, 17,* 386–390.

Goodman, G. S. (2006). Children's eyewitness memory: A modern history and contemporary commentary. *Journal of Social Issues, 62,* 811–832.

Goodman, J. S., Fields, D. L., & Blum, T. C. (2003). Cracks in the glass ceiling: In what kinds of organizations do women make it to the top? *Group & Organization Management, 28,* 475–501.

Goodwin, M. H. (1990). Tactical uses of stories: Participation frameworks within girls' and boys' disputes. *Discourse Processes, 13,* 33–71.

Goold, S. D., Williams, B., & Arnold, R. M. (2000). Conflicts regarding decisions to limit treatment: A differential diagnosis. *JAMA: The Journal of the American Medical Association, 283,* 909–914.

Goorabi, K., Hoseinabadi, R., & Share, H. (2008). Hearing aid effect on elderly depression in nursing home patients. *Asia Pacific Journal of Speech, Language, and Hearing, 11,* 119–124.

Gopinath, B., Schneider, J., Hickson, L., McMahon, C. M., Burlutsky, G., Leeder, S. R., et al. (2012). Hearing handicap, rather than measured hearing impairment, predicts poorer quality of life over 10 years in older adults. *Maturitas, 72,* 146–151.

Gopnik, A. (2010, July). How babies think. *Scientific American*, pp. 76–81.

Gopnik, A. (2012, January 28). What's wrong with the teenage mind? *Wall Street Journal*, pp. C1–C2.

Gopnik, A., Meltzoff, A. N., & Kuhl, P. K. (2000). *The scientist in the crib: What early learning tells us about the mind.* New York: HarperCollins.

Gorchoff, S., John, O., & Helson, R. (2008). Contextualizing change in marital satisfaction during middle age: An 18-year longitudinal study. *Psychological Science, 19,* 1194–1200.

Gordon, N. (2007). The cerebellum and cognition. *European Journal of Paediatric Neurology, 30,* 214–220.

Gorman, A. (2010, January 7). UCLA study says legalizing undocumented immigrants would help the economy. *Los Angeles Times.*

Gormley, W. T., Jr., Gayer, T., Phillips, D., & Dawson, B. (2005). The effects of universal pre-K on cognitive development. *Developmental Psychology, 41,* 872–884.

Gosselin, P., Perron, M., & Maassarani, R. (2010). Children's ability to distinguish between enjoyment and non-enjoyment smiles. *Infant and Child Development, 19,* 297–312.

Gostin, L. (2006, April). Physician-assisted suicide a legitimate medical practice? *JAMA: The Journal of the American Medical Association, 295,* 1941–1943.

Goswami, U. (1998). *Cognition in children.* Philadelphia: Psychology Press.

Gottesman, I. I. (1991). *Schizophrenia genesis: The origins of madness.* New York: Freeman.

Gottman, J. M., Fainsilber-Katz, L., & Hooven, C. (1996). *Meta-emotion: How families communicate emotionally.* Mahwah, NJ: Lawrence Erlbaum.

Gould, S. J. (1977). *Ontogeny and phylogeny.* Cambridge, MA: Harvard University Press.

Gould, R. L. (1978). *Transformations: Growth and change in adult life.* New York: Simon & Schuster.

Gould, S. (1980). Need for achievement, career mobility, and the Mexican-American college graduate. *Journal of Vocational Behavior, 16,* 73–82.

Gow, A., Pattie, A., Whiteman, M., Whalley, L., & Deary, I. (2007). Social support and successful aging: Investigating the relationships between lifetime cognitive change and life satisfaction. *Journal of Individual Differences, 28,* 103–115.

Goyette-Ewing, M. (2000). Children's after-school arrangements: A study of self-care and developmental outcomes. *Journal of Prevention & Intervention in the Community, 20,* 55–67.

Grabner, R. H., Neubauer, A. C., & Stern, E. (2006). Superior performance and neural efficiency: The impact of intelligence and expertise. *Brain Research Bulletin, 69,* 422–439.

Graddol, D. (2004, February 27). The future of language. *Science, 303,* 1329–1331.

Grady, D. (2006, November). Management of menopausal symptoms. *New England Journal of Medicine, 355,* 2338–2347.

Grady, D. (2009, November 3). Quandary with mammograms: Get a screening or just skip it? *The New York Times*, p. D2.

Graham, I., Carroli, G., Davies, C., & Medves, J. (2005). Episiotomy rates around the world: An update. *Birth: Issues in Perinatal Care, 32,* 219–223.

Graham, J. E., Christian, L. M., & Kiecolt-Glaser, J. K. (2006). Stress, age, and immune function: Toward a lifespan approach. *Journal of Behavioral Medicine, 29,* 389–400.

Granic, I., Hollenstein, T., & Dishion, T. (2003). Longitudinal analysis of flexibility and reorganization in early adolescence: A dynamic systems study of family interactions. *Developmental Psychology, 39,* 606–617.

Granié, M. (2010). Gender stereotype conformity and age as determinants of preschoolers' injury-risk behaviors. *Accident Analysis and Prevention, 42,* 726–733.

Grant, C., Wall, C., Brewster, D., Nicholson, R., Whitehall, J., Super, L., et al. (2007). Policy statement on iron deficiency in pre-school-aged children. *Journal of Paediatrics and Child Health, 43,* 513–521.

Grantham-McGregor, S., Ani, C., & Fernald, L. (2001). The role of nutrition in intellectual development. In R. J. Sternberg & E. L. Grigorenko (Eds.), *Environmental effects on cognitive abilities.* Mahwah, NJ: Lawrence Erlbaum.

Grantham-McGregor, S., Powell, C., Walker, S., Chang, S., & Fletcher, P. (1994). The long-term follow-up of severely malnourished children who participated in an intervention program. *Child Development, 65,* 428–439.

Gray, C., Ferguson, J., Behan, S., Dunbar, C., Dunn, J., & Mitchell, D. (2007, March). Developing young readers through the linguistic phonics approach. *International Journal of Early Years Education, 15,* 15–33.

Gray-Little, B., & Hafdahl, A. R. (2000). Factors influencing racial comparisons of self-esteem: A quantitative review. *Psychological Bulletin, 126,* 26–54.

Gredler, M. E., & Shields, C. C. (2008). *Vygotsky's legacy: A foundation for research and practice.* New York: Guilford Press.

Green, C., Sugarman, M. A., Medford, K., Klobusicky, E., & Bavelier, D. (2012). The effect of action video game experience on task-switching. *Computers in Human Behavior, 28,* 984–994.

Green, M., DeCourville, N., & Sadava, S. (2012). Positive affect, negative affect, stress, and social support as mediators of the forgiveness-health relationship. *The Journal of Social Psychology, 152,* 288–307.

Green, M. H. (1995). Influences of job type, job status, and gender on achievement motivation. *Current Psychology: Developmental, Learning, Personality, Social, 14,* 159–165.

Greenberg, J. (2012). Psychoanalysis in North America after Freud. In G. O. Gabbard, B. E. Litowitz, & P. Williams (Eds.), *Textbook of psychoanalysis* (2nd ed.). Arlington, VA: American Psychiatric Publishing, Inc.

Greenberg, J., & Becker, M. (1988). Aging parents as family resources. *Gerontologist, 28,* 786–790.

Greenberg, L., Cwikel, J., & Mirsky, J. (2007, January). Cultural correlates of eating attitudes: A comparison between native-born and immigrant university students in Israel. *International Journal of Eating Disorders, 40,* 51–58.

Greene, K., Krcmar, M., Walters, L. H., Rubin, D. L., & Hale, J. L. (2000). Targeting adolescent risk-taking behaviors: The contribution of egocentrism and sensation-seeking. *Journal of Adolescence, 23,* 439–461.

Greene, S., Anderson, E., & Hetherington, E. (2003). Risk and resilience after divorce. In F. Walsh (Ed.), *Normal family processes: Growing diversity and complexity.* New York: Guilford Press.

Greenwood, D. N., & Pietromonaco, P. R. (2004). The interplay among attachment orientation, idealized media images of women, and body dissatisfaction: A social psychological analysis. In L. J. Shrum (Ed.), *Psychology of entertainment media: Blurring the lines between entertainment and persuasion.* Mahwah, NJ: Lawrence Erlbaum.

Gregory, K. (2005). Update on nutrition for preterm and full-term infants. *Journal of Obstetrics and Gynecological Neonatal Nursing, 34,* 98–108.

Gregory, S. (1856). *Facts for young women.* Boston: Stearns & Co.

Griffin, M. J., Wardell, J. D., & Read, J. P. (2013). Recent sexual victimization and drinking behavior in newly matriculated college students: A latent growth analysis. *Psychology of Addictive Behaviors.* Accessed online, June 6, 2013, http://psycnet.apa.org/psycinfo/2013-10252-001/

Griffith, D. R., Azuma, S. D., & Chasnoff, I. J. (1994). Three-year outcome of children exposed prenatally to drugs. *Journal of the American Academy of Child and Adolescent Psychiatry, 33,* 20–27.

Grigorenko, E., Jarvin, L., Diffley, R., Goodyear, J., Shanahan, E., & Sternberg, R. (2009). Are SSATS and GPA enough? A theory-based approach to predicting academic success in secondary school. *Journal of Educational Psychology, 101,* 964–981.

Grissmer, D., Grimm, K., Aiyer, S., Murrah, W., & Steele, J. (2010). Fine motor skills and early comprehension of the world: Two new school readiness indicators. *Developmental Psychology, 46,* 1008–1017.

Grønhøj, A., & Thøgersen, J. (2012). Action speaks louder than words: The effect of personal attitudes and family norms on adolescents' pro-environmental behaviour. *Journal of Economic Psychology, 33,* 292–302.

Groome, L. J., Swiber, M. J., Atterbury, J. L., Bentz, L. S., & Holland, S. B. (1997). Similarities and differences in behavioral state organization during sleep periods in the perinatal infant before and after birth. *Child Development, 68,* 1–11.

Groome, L. J., Swiber, M. J., Bentz, L. S., Holland, S. B., & Atterbury, J. L. (1995). Maternal anxiety during pregnancy: Effect on fetal behavior at 38 to 40 weeks of gestation. *Developmental and Behavioral Pediatrics, 16,* 391–396.

Gross, R. T., Spiker, D., & Haynes, C. W. (Eds.). (1997). *Helping low-birthweight, premature babies: The Infant Health and Development Program.* Stanford, CA: Stanford University Press.

Grossmann, K. E., Grossmann, K., & Waters, E. (Eds.). (2005). *Attachment from infancy to adulthood: The major longitudinal studies.* New York: Guilford Press.

Grossmann, K. E., Grossmann, K., Huber, F., & Wartner, U. (1982). German children's behavior towards their mothers at 12 months and their fathers at 18 months in Ainsworth's Strange Situation. *International Journal of Behavioral Development, 4,* 157–181.

Grunbaum, J. A., Kann, L., Kinchen, S. A., Williams, B., Ross, J. G., Lowry, R., et al. (2002). *Youth risk behavior surveillance—United States, 2001.* Atlanta, GA: Centers for Disease Control.

Grunbaum, J. A., Lowry, R., & Kann, L. (2001). Prevalence of health-related behaviors among alternative high school students as compared with students attending regular high schools. *Journal of Adolescent Health, 29,* 337–343.

Grundy, E., & Henretta, J. (2006, September). Between elderly parents and adult children: A new look at the intergenerational care provided by the "sandwich generation." *Ageing & Society, 26,* 707–722.

Gruszczynska, E. (2013). State affect and emotion-focused coping: Examining correlated change and causality. *Anxiety, Stress & Coping: An International Journal, 26,* 103–119.

Guadalupe, K. L., & Welkley, D. L. (2012). *Diversity in family constellations: Implications for practice.* Chicago: Lyceum Books.

Guarente, L. (2006, December 14). Sirtuins as potential targets for metabolic syndrome. *Nature, 14,* 868–874.

Guasti, M. T. (2002). *Language acquisition: The growth of grammar.* Cambridge, MA: MIT Press.

Guerrero, A., Hishinuma, E., Andrade, N., Nishimura, S., & Cunanan, V. (2006, July). Correlations among socioeconomic and family factors and academic, behavioral, and emotional difficulties in Filipino adolescents in Hawaii. *International Journal of Social Psychiatry, 52,* 343–359.

Guerrero, S., Enesco, I., Lago, O., & Rodríguez, P. (2010). Preschool children's understanding of racial cues in drawings and photographs. *Cognitive Development, 25,* 79–89.

Guerrini, I., Thomson, A., & Gurling, H. (2007). The importance of alcohol misuse, malnutrition and genetic susceptibility on brain growth and plasticity. *Neuroscience & Biobehavioral Reviews, 31,* 212–220.

Guiney, H., & Machado, L. (2013). Benefits of regular aerobic exercise for executive functioning in healthy populations. *Psychonomic Bulletin & Review, 20,* 73–86.

Gump, L. S., Baker, R. C., & Roll, S. (2000). Cultural and gender differences in moral judgment: A study of Mexican Americans and Anglo-Americans. *Hispanic Journal of Behavioral Sciences, 22,* 78–93.

Gumz, A., Kästner, D., Geyer, M., Wutzler, U., Villmann, T., & Brähler, E. (2010). Instability and discontinuous change in the experience of therapeutic interaction: An extended single-case study of psychodynamic therapy processes. *Psychotherapy Research, 20,* 398–412.

Gupta, A., & State, M. (2007). Recent advances in the genetics of autism. *Biological Psychiatry, 61,* 429–437.

Gupta, U., & Singh, P. (1982). An exploratory study of love and liking and type of marriages. *Indian Journal of Applied Psychology, 19,* 92–97.

Gure, A., Ucanok, Z., & Sayil, M. (2006). The associations among perceived pubertal timing, parental relations and self-perception in Turkish adolescents. *Journal of Youth and Adolescence, 35,* 541–550.

Gurin, P., Nagda, B. R. A., & Lopez, G. E. (2004). The benefits of diversity in education for democratic citizenship. *Journal of Social Issues, 60,* 17–34.

Gurung, R. (2010). *Health psychology: A cultural approach* (2nd ed.). Belmont, CA: Wadsworth/Cengage Learning.

Gutek, G. L. (2003). Maria Montessori: Contributions to educational psychology. In B. J. Zimmerman (Ed.), *Educational psychology: A century of contributions.* Mahwah, NJ: Lawrence Erlbaum.

Guttmacher Institute. (2012, February). *Facts on American teens' sexual and reproductive health.* New York: Guttmacher Institute.

Guttmann, J., & Rosenberg, M. (2003). Emotional intimacy and children's adjustment: A comparison between single-parent divorced and intact families. *Educational Psychology, 23,* 457–472.

Haas-Thompson, T., Alston, P., & Holbert, D. (2008). The impact of education and death-related experiences on rehabilitation counselor attitudes toward death and dying. *Journal of Applied Rehabilitation Counseling, 39,* 20–27.

Haber, D. (2006). Life review: Implementation, theory, research, and therapy. *International Journal of Aging & Human Development, 63,* 153–171.

Hack, M., Flannery, D. J., Schluchter, M., Cartar, L., Borawski, E., & Klein, N. (2002). Outcomes in young adulthood for very low birth weight infants. *New England Journal of Medicine, 346,* 149–157.

Haddock, S., & Rattenborg, K. (2003). Benefits and challenges of dual-earning: Perspectives of successful couples. *American Journal of Family Therapy, 31,* 325–344.

Haeffel, G., Getchell, M., Koposov, R., Yrigollen, C., DeYoung, C., Klinteberg, B., et al. (2008). Association between polymorphisms in the dopamine transporter gene and depression: Evidence for a gene-environment interaction in a sample of juvenile detainees. *Psychological Science, 19,* 62–69.

Hagerty, R. G., Butow, P. N., Ellis, P. A., Lobb, E. A., Pendlebury, S., Leighl, N., et al. (2004). Cancer patient preferences for communication of prognosis in the metastatic setting. *Journal of Clinical Oncology, 22,* 1721–1730.

Hahn, E., Gottschling, J., & Spinath, F. M. (2012). Short measurements of personality—Validity and reliability of the GSOEP Big Five Inventory (BFI-S). *Journal of Research in Personality, 46,* 355–359.

Haith, M. H. (1986). Sensory and perceptual processes in early infancy. *Journal of Pediatrics, 109*(1), 158–171.

Haith, M. H. (1991, April). *Setting a path for the 90s: Some goals and challenges in infant sensory and perceptual development.* Paper presented at the biennial meeting of the Society for Research in Child Development, Seattle, WA.

Haleem, M., Barton, K., Borges, G., Crozier, A., & Anderson, A. (2008). Increasing antioxidant intake from fruits and vegetables: Practical strategies for the Scottish population. *Journal of Human Nutrition and Dietetics, 21,* 539–546.

Haley, D., Grunau, R., Weinberg, J., Keidar, A., & Oberlander, T. (2010). Physiological correlates of memory recall in infancy: Vagal tone, cortisol, and imitation in preterm and full-term infants at 6 months. *Infant Behavior & Development, 33,* 219–234.

Halgunseth, L. C., Ispa, J. M., & Rudy, D. (2006). Parental control in Latino families: An integrated review of the literature. *Child Development, 77,* 1282–1297.

Halkier, B. (2013). Review of the case study as research method: A practical handbook and how to do your case study: A guide for students & researchers. *Qualitative Research, 13*(1), 107–110.

Hall, E. G., & Lee, A. M. (1984). Sex differences in motor performance of young children: Fact or fiction? *Sex Roles, 10,* 217–230.

Hall, J. J., Neal, T., & Dean, R. S. (2008). Lateralization of cerebral functions. In A. M. McNeil & D. Wedding (Eds.), *The neuropsychology handbook* (3rd ed.). New York: Springer Publishing.

Halliday, M. A. K. (1975). *Learning how to mean—Explorations in the development of language.* London: Edward Arnold.

Hamel, L. M., & Robbins, L. B. (2013). Computer- and web-based interventions to promote healthy eating among children and adolescents: A systematic review. *Journal of Advanced Nursing, 69,* 16–30.

Hamilton, B. E., Martin, J. A., & Ventura, S. J. (2009). *National vital statistics reports.* Washington, DC.

Hamilton, B. S., & Ventura, J. A. (2012, April) *Birth rates for U.S. teenagers reach historic lows for all age and ethnic groups* (NCHS Data Brief, No. 89). Washington, DC: National Center for Health Statistics.

Hamilton, G. (1998). Positively testing. *Families in Society, 79,* 570–576.

Hamlin, J. K., & Wynn, K. (2011). Young infants prefer prosocial to antisocial others. *Cognitive Development, 26,* 30–39.

Hamlin, J. K., Wynn, K., Bloom, P., & Mahajan, N. (2011). How infants and toddlers react to antisocial others. *Proceedings of the National Academy of Sciences, 108,* 19931–19936.

Hamon, R. R., & Blieszner, R. (1990). Filial responsibility expectations among adult child-older parent pairs. *Journal of Gerontology, 45,* 110–112.

Hamon, R. R., & Ingoldsby, B. B. (Eds.). (2003). *Mate selection across cultures.* Thousand Oaks, CA: Sage Publications.

Hane, A., Feldstein, S., & Dernetz, V. (2003). The relation between coordinated interpersonal timing and maternal sensitivity in four-month-old infants. *Journal of Psycholinguistic Research, 32,* 525–539.

Hannover, B., Morf, C. C., Neuhaus, J., Rau, M., Wolfgramm, C., & Zander-Music, L. (2013). How immigrant adolescents' self-views in school and family context relate to academic success in Germany. *Journal of Applied Social Psychology, 43,* 175–189.

Hanson, D. R., & Gottesman, I. I. (2005). Theories of schizophrenia: A genetic-inflammatory-vascular synthesis. *BMC Medical Genetics, 6,* 7.

Hanson, J. D. (2012). Understanding prenatal health care for American Indian women in a Northern Plains Tribe. *Journal of Transcultural Nursing, 23,* 29–37.

Hanson, L., Schenck, A., Rokoske, F., Abernethy, A., Kutner, J., Spence, C., et al. (2010). Hospices' preparation and practices for quality measurement. *Journal of Pain and Symptom Management, 39,* 1–8.

Hanson, R., & Hayslip, B. (2000). Widowhood in later life. In J. Harvey & E. Miller (Eds.), *Loss and trauma: General and close relationship perspectives.* New York: Brunner-Routledge.

Hansson, R. O., & Carpenter, B. N. (1994). *Relationship in old age: Coping with the challenge of transition.* New York: Guilford Press.

Harden, K., Turkheimer, E., & Loehlin, J. (2007). Genotype by environment interaction in adolescents' cognitive aptitude. *Behavior Genetics, 37,* 273–283.

Hardy, L. T. (2007). Attachment theory and reactive attachment disorder: Theoretical perspectives and treatment implications. *Journal of Child and Adolescent Psychiatric Nursing, 20,* 27–39.

Hardy, S., & Grogan, S. (2009). Preventing disability through exercise: Investigating older adults' influences and motivations to engage in physical activity. *Journal of Health Psychology, 14,* 1036–1046.

Hare, T. A., Tottenham, N., Galvan, A., & Voss, H. U. (2008). Biological substrates of emotional reactivity and regulation in adolescence during an emotional go-nogo task. *Biological Psychiatry, 63,* 927–934.

Harris, J., Vernon, P., & Jang, K. (2007). Rated personality and measured intelligence in young twin children. *Personality and Individual Differences, 42,* 75–86.

Harris, J. R. (1998). *The nurture assumption: Why children turn out the way they do.* New York: Free Press.

Harris, J. R. (2000). Socialization, personality development, and the child's environments: Comment on Vandell. *Developmental Psychology, 36,* 711–723.

Harris, M., Prior, J., & Koehoorn, M. (2008). Age at menarche in the Canadian population: Secular trends and relationship to adulthood BMI. *Journal of Adolescent Health, 43,* 548–554.

Harris, P. L. (1987). The development of search. In P. Sallapatek & L. Cohen (Eds.), *Handbook of infant perception: From perception to cognition* (Vol. 2, pp. 155–207). Orlando, FL: Academic Press.

Harrison, K., & Hefner, V. (2006, April). Media exposure, current and future body ideals, and disordered eating among preadolescent girls: A longitudinal panel study. *Journal of Youth and Adolescence, 35,* 153–163.

Hart, B. (2004). What toddlers talk about. *First Language, 24,* 91–106.

Hart, D., Burock, D., & London, B. (2003). Prosocial tendencies, antisocial behavior, and moral development. In A. Slater & G. Bremner (Eds.), *An introduction to developmental psychology.* Malden, MA: Blackwell Publishers.

Hart, S. N., Brassard, M. R., & Karlson, H. (1996). Psychological maltreatment. In J. N. Briere, L. Berliner, J. Bulkley, C. Jenny, & T. Reid (Eds.), *The APSAC handbook on child maltreatment.* Thousand Oaks, CA: Sage Publications.

Harter, S. (1990). Issues in the assessment of self-concept of children and adolescents. In A. LaGreca (Ed.), *Through the eyes of a child.* Boston: Allyn & Bacon.

Hartshorne, T. S. (1994). Friendship. In V. S. Ramachandran (Ed.), *Encyclopedia of human behavior.* San Diego: Academic Press.

Hartup, W. W., & Stevens, N. (1999). Friendships and adaptation across the life span. *Current Directions in Psychological Science, 8,* 76–79.

Harvey, J., & Weber, A. (2002). *Odyssey of the heart: Close relationships in the 21st century* (2nd ed.). Mahwah, NJ: Lawrence Erlbaum.

Harvey, J. H., & Fine, M. A. (2004). *Children of divorce: Stories of loss and growth.* Mahwah, NJ: Lawrence Erlbaum.

Harway, M. (2000). Families experiencing violence. In W. C. Nichols, M. A. Pace-Nichols, et al. (Eds.), *Handbook of family development and intervention. Wiley series in couples and family dynamics and treatment.* New York: Wiley.

Haslett, A. (2004, May 31). Love supreme. *The New Yorker,* pp. 76–80.

Hastings, P. D., McShane, K. E., Parker, R., & Ladha, F. (2007). Ready to make nice: Parental socialization of young sons' and daughters' prosocial behaviors with peers. *Journal of Genetic Psychology, 168,* 177–200.

Hatfield, E., & Rapson, R. L. (1993). Historical and cross-cultural perspectives on passionate love and sexual desire. *Annual Review of Sex Research, 4,* 67–97.

Hatton, C. (2002). People with intellectual disabilities from ethnic minority communities in the United States and the United Kingdom. In L. M. Glidden (Ed.), *International review of research in mental retardation, vol. 25.* San Diego: Academic Press.

Haugaard, J. J. (2000). The challenge of defining child sexual abuse. *American Psychologist, 55,* 1036–1039.

Havighurst, R. J. (1973). Social roles, work, leisure, and education. In C. Eisdorfer & M. P. Lawton (Eds.), *The psychology of adult development and aging.* Washington, DC: American Psychological Association.

Hawkins-Rodgers, Y. (2007). Adolescents adjusting to a group home environment: A residential care model of reorganizing attachment behavior and building resiliency. *Children and Youth Services Review, 29,* 1131–1141.

Hay, D., Payne, A., & Chadwick, A. (2004). Peer relations in childhood. *Journal of Child Psychology & Psychiatry & Allied Disciplines, 45,* 84–108.

Hayden, T. (1998, September 21). The brave new world of sex selection. *Newsweek,* p. 93.

Hayflick, L. (1974). The strategy of senescence. *The Journal of Gerontology, 14,* 37–45.

Hayflick, L. (2007). Biological aging is no longer an unsolved problem. *Annals of the New York Academy of Sciences,* pp. 1–13.

Hayslip, B., Jr., Shore, R. J., & Henderson, C. E. (2000). Perceptions of grandparents' influence in the lives of their grandchildren. In B. Hayslip, Jr., & R. S. Goldberg-Glen (Eds.), *Grandparents raising grandchildren: Theoretical, empirical, and clinical perspectives.* New York: Springer.

Hayward, M., Crimmins, E., & Saito, Y. (1997). Cause of death and active life expectancy in the older population of the United States. *Journal of Aging and Health,* 122–131.

Hazan, C., & Shaver, P. (1987). Romantic love conceptualized as an attachment process. *Journal of Personality and Social Psychology, 52,* 511–524.

Heaven, P., & Ciarrochi, J. (2008). Parental styles, gender and the development of hope and self-esteem. *European Journal of Personality, 22,* 707–724.

Heilbronner, N. N. (2013). The STEM pathway for women: What has changed? *Gifted Child Quarterly, 57,* 39–55.

Heimann, M. (2001). Neonatal imitation—a "fuzzy" phenomenon? In F. Lacerda & C. von Hofsten (Eds.), *Emerging cognitive abilities in early infancy.* Mahwah, NJ: Lawrence Erlbaum.

Heimann, M. (Ed.). (2003). *Regression periods in human infancy.* Mahwah, NJ: Lawrence Erlbaum.

Heinemann, G. D., & Evans, P. L. (1990). Widowhood: Loss, change, and adaptation. In T. H. Brubaker (Ed.), *Family relationships in later life.* Newbury Park, CA: Sage Publications.

Helmes, E., & Campbell, A. (2010). Differential sensitivity to administration format of measures of attitudes toward older adults. *The Gerontologist, 50,* 60–65.

Helms, J. E., Jernigan, M., & Mascher, J. (2005). The meaning of race in psychology and how to change it: A methodological perspective. *American Psychologist, 60,* 27–36.

Helmsen, J., Koglin, U., & Petermann, F. (2012). Emotion regulation and aggressive behavior in preschoolers: The mediating role of social information processing. *Child Psychiatry and Human Development, 43,* 87–101.

Helmuth, L. (2003, February 28). The wisdom of the wizened. *Science, 299,* 1300–1302.

Helson, R., & Srivastava, S. (2001). Three paths of adult development: Conservers, seekers, and achievers. *Journal of Personality and Social Psychology, 80,* 995–1010.

Hendren, S., Humiston, S., & Fiscella, K. (2012). Partnering with safety-net primary care clinics: A model to enhance screening in low-income populations—Principles, challenges, and key lessons. In R. Elk & H. Landrine (Eds.), *Cancer disparities: Causes and evidence-based solutions.* New York: Springer Publishing Co.

Hendrick, C., & Hendrick, S. (2003). Romantic love: Measuring cupid's arrow. In S. Lopez & C. Snyder (Eds.), *Positive psychological assessment: A handbook of models and measures.* Washington, DC: American Psychological Association.

Hendrie, H. C., Ogunniyi, A., Hall, K. S., Baiyewu, O., Unverzagt, F. W., Gureje, O., et al. (2001). Incidence of dementia and Alzheimer disease in 2 communities: Yoruba residing in Ibadan, Nigeria, and African Americans residing in Indianapolis, Indiana. *JAMA: The Journal of the American Medical Association, 285,* 739–747.

Henry, R., Miller, R., & Giarrusso, R. (2005). Difficulties, disagreements, and disappointments in late-life marriages. *International Journal of Aging & Human Development, 61,* 243–264.

Henschel, S., Bruin, M., & Möhler, E. (2013). Self-control and child abuse potential in mothers with an abuse history and their preschool children. *Journal of Child and Family Studies.* Accessed online, June 5, 2013, http://link.springer.com/article/10.1007%2Fs10826-013-9735-0#page-1

Hensley, P. (2006, July). Treatment of bereavement-related depression and traumatic grief. *Journal of Affective Disorders, 92,* 117–124.

Herbenick, D., Reece, M., Schick, V., Sanders, S., Dodge, B., & Fortenberry, J. D. (2010). Sexual behavior in the United States: Results from a national probability sample of men and women ages 14 to 94. *Journal of Sexual Medicine, 7*(Suppl. 5), 255–265.

Herdt, G. H. (Ed.). (1998). *Rituals of manhood: Male initiation in Papua New Guinea.* Somerset, NJ: Transaction Books.

Herman-Kinney, N. J., & Kinney, D. A. (2013). Sober as deviant: The stigma of sobriety and how some college students 'stay dry' on a 'wet' campus. *Journal of Contemporary Ethnography, 42,* 64–103.

Hermida, R. C., Ayala, D. E., Crespo, J. J., Mojón, A., Chayán, L., Fontao, M. J., et al. (2013). Influence of age and hypertension treatment-time on ambulatory blood pressure in hypertensive patients. *Chronobiology International, 30,* 176–191.

Hernandez, D. J., Denton, N. A., & McCartney, S. E. (2008). Children in immigrant families: Looking to America's Future. *Social Policy Report, 22,* 3–24.

Hernandez-Reif, M., Field, T., Diego, M., Vera, Y., & Pickens, J. (2006, January). Brief report: Happy faces are habituated more slowly by infants of depressed mothers. *Infant Behavior & Development, 29,* 131–135.

Herrnstein, R. J., & Murray, C. (1994). *The bell curve: Intelligence and class structure in American life.* New York: Free Press.

Hertelendy, F., & Zakar, T. (2004). Prostaglandins and the myometrium and cervix. *Prostaglandins, Leukotrienes and Essential Fatty Acids, 70,* 207–222.

Hertzberg, V. S., Hinton, C. F., Therrell, B. L., & Shapira, S. K. (2011). Birth prevalence rates of newborn screening disorders in relation to screening practices in the United States. *The Journal of Pediatrics, 159,* 555–560.

Hertzog, C., Kramer, A., Wilson, R., & Lindenberger, U. (2008). Enrichment effects on adult cognitive development: Can the functional capacity of older adults be preserved and enhanced? *Psychological Science in the Public Interest, 9,* 1–65.

Hespos, S. J., & vanMarle, K. (2012). *Everyday physics: How infants learn about objects and entities in their environment.* Invited manuscript for Wiley Interdisciplinary Reviews, Cognitive Science.

Hess, T., Auman, C., & Colcombe, S. (2003). The impact of stereotype threat on age differences in memory performance. *Journals of Gerontology: Series B: Psychological Sciences & Social Sciences, 58B,* P3–P11.

Hess, T. M., Hinson, J. T., & Hodges, E. A. (2009). Moderators of and mechanisms underlying stereotype threat effects on older adults' memory performance. *Experimental Aging Research, 31,* 153–177.

Heston, C. (2002, August 9). *Quoted in Charlton Heston has Alzheimer's symptoms.* Accessed online, May 13, 2004, http://www.cnn.com/2002/US/08/09/heston.illness

Hetherington, E., & Elmore, A. (2003). Risk and resilience in children coping with their parents' divorce and remarriage. In S. Luthar (Ed.), *Resilience and vulnerability: Adaptation in the context of childhood adversities.* New York: Cambridge University Press.

Hetherington, E. M., & Kelly, J. (2002). *For better or worse: Divorce reconsidered.* New York: Norton.

Hetrick, S. E., Parker, A. G., Robinson, J., Hall, N., & Vance, A. (2012). Predicting suicidal risk in a cohort of depressed children and adolescents. *Crisis: The Journal of Crisis Intervention and Suicide Prevention, 33,* 13–20.

Heubusch, K. (1997, September). A tough job gets tougher. *American Demographics, 39.*

Hewstone, M. (2003). Intergroup contact: Panacea for prejudice? *Psychologist, 16,* 352–355.

Heyman, R., & Slep, A. M. (2002). Do child abuse and interparental violence lead to adulthood family violence? *Journal of Marriage & Family, 64,* 864–870.

HHL (Harvard Health Letter). (1997, May). Turning up the volume. *Harvard Mental Health Letter,* p. 4.

Hietala, J., Cannon, T. D., & van Erp, T. G. M. (2003). Regional brain morphology and duration of illness in never-medicated first-episode patients with schizophrenia. *Schizophrenia, 64,* 79–81.

Higgins, D., & McCabe, M. (2003). Maltreatment and family dysfunction in childhood and the subsequent adjustment of children and adults. *Journal of Family Violence, 18,* 107–120.

Hill, B. D., Foster, J. D., Elliott, E. M., Shelton, J., McCain, J., & Gouvier, W. (2013). Need for cognition is related to higher general intelligence, fluid intelligence, and crystallized intelligence, but not working memory. *Journal of Research in Personality, 47,* 22–25.

Hillman, J. (2000). *Clinical perspectives on elderly sexuality.* Dordrecht, Netherlands: Kluwer Academic Publishers.

Hillman, J. (2012). *Sexuality and aging: Clinical perspectives.* New York: Springer Science + Business Media.

Hilton, J., & Anderson, T. (2009). Characteristics of women with children who divorce in midlife compared to those who remain married. *Journal of Divorce & Remarriage, 50,* 309–329.

Hirschtritt, M. E., Pagano, M. E., Christian, K. M., McNamara, N. K., Stansbrey, R. J., Lingler, J., et al. (2012). Moderators of fluoxetine treatment response for children and adolescents with comorbid depression and substance use disorders. *Journal of Substance Abuse Treatment, 42,* 366–372.

Hirsh-Pasek, K., & Michnick-Golinkoff, R. (1995). *The origins of grammar: Evidence from early language comprehension.* Cambridge, MA: MIT Press.

Hitchcock, J. (2012). The debate over shaken baby syndrome. *Journal of Neonatal Nursing, 18,* 20–21.

Hitlin, S., Brown, J. S., & Elder, G. H., Jr. (2006). Racial self-categorization in adolescence: Multiracial development and social pathways. *Child Development, 77,* 1298–1308.

Hjelmstedt, A., Widström, A., & Collins, A. (2006). Psychological correlates of prenatal attachment in women who conceived after in vitro fertilization and women who conceived naturally. *Birth: Issues in Perinatal Care, 33,* 303–310.

Ho, B., Friedland, J., Rappolt, S., & Noh, S. (2003). Caregiving for relatives with Alzheimer's disease: Feelings of Chinese-Canadian women. *Journal of Aging Studies, 17,* 301–321.

Hocking, D. R., Kogan, C. S., & Cornish, K. M. (2012). Selective spatial processing deficits in an at-risk subgroup of the fragile X premutation. *Brain and Cognition, 79,* 39–44.

Hocutt, A. M. (1996). Effectiveness of special education: Is placement the critical factor? *The Future of Children, 6,* 77–102.

Hoehl, S., Wahl, S., Michel, C., & Striano, T. (2012). Effects of eye gaze cues provided by the caregiver compared to a stranger on infants' object processing. *Developmental Cognitive Neuroscience, 2,* 81–89.

Hoelter, L. F., Axinn, W. G., & Ghimire, D. J. (2004). Social change, premarital nonfamily experiences, and marital dynamics. *Journal of Marriage & Family, 66,* 1131–1151.

Hoessler, C., & Chasteen, A. L. (2008). Does aging affect the use of shifting standards? *Experimental Aging Research, 34,* 1–12.

Hoeve, M., Blokland, A., Dubas, J., Loeber, R., Gerris, J., & van der Laan, P. (2008). Trajectories of delinquency and parenting styles. *Journal of Abnormal Child Psychology: An Official Publication of the International Society for Research in Child and Adolescent Psychopathology, 36,* 223–235.

Hofer, M. A. (2006). Psychobiological roots of early attachment. *Current Directions in Psychological Science, 15,* 84–88.

Hoff, E. (2012). Interpreting the early language trajectories of children from low-SES and language minority homes: Implications for closing achievement gaps. *Developmental Psychology.* Accessed online, July 22, 2012, http://www.ncbi.nlm.nih.gov/pubmed/22329382

Hofferth, S., & Sandberg, J. F. (2001). How American children spend their time. *Journal of Marriage and the Family, 63,* 295–308.

Hoffman, L. (2003). Why high schools don't change: What students and their yearbooks tell us. *High School Journal, 86,* 22–37.

Hohmann-Marriott, B. (2006, November). Shared beliefs and the union stability of married and cohabiting couples. *Journal of Marriage and Family, 68,* 1015–1028.

Holahan, C., & Chapman, J. (2002). Longitudinal predictors of proactive goals and activity participation at age 80. *Journals of Gerontology: Series B: Psychological Sciences & Social Sciences, 57B,* P418–P425.

Holden, G. W., & Miller, P. C. (1999). Enduring and different: A meta-analysis of the similarity in parents' child rearing. *Psychological Bulletin, 125,* 223–254.

Holland, N. (1994, August). *Race dissonance—Implications for African American children.* Paper presented at the annual meeting of the American Psychological Association, Los Angeles, CA.

Holland, A. S., & McElwain, N. L. (2013). Maternal and paternal perceptions of coparenting as a link between marital quality and the parent-toddler relationship. *Journal of Family Psychology, 27,* 117–126.

Holland, J. L. (1997). *Making vocational choices: A theory of vocational personalities and environments* (3rd ed.). Odessa, FL: Psychological Assessment Resources.

Holland, J. M., Neimeyer, R. A., Boelen, P. A., & Prigerson, H. G. (2009). The underlying structure of grief: A taxometric investigation of prolonged and normal reactions to loss. *Journal of Psychopathology and Behavioral Assessment, 31,* 190–201.

Holland, J. W. (2008). Reading aloud with infants: The controversy, the myth, and a case study. *Early Childhood Education Journal, 35,* 383–385.

Holmes, E. R., & Holmes, L. D. (1995). *Other cultures, elder years.* Thousand Oaks, CA: Sage Publications.

Holowaka, S., & Petitto, L. A. (2002). Left hemisphere cerebral specialization for babies while babbling. *Science, 287,* 1515.

Holzman, L. (1997). *Schools for growth: Radical alternatives to current educational models.* Mahwah, NJ: Lawrence Erlbaum.

Homae, F., Watanabe, H., Nakano, T., & Taga, G. (2012). Functional development in the infant brain for auditory pitch processing. *Human Brain Mapping, 33,* 596–608.

Hooks, B., & Chen, C. (2008). Vision triggers an experience-dependent sensitive period at the retinogeniculate synapse. *The Journal of Neuroscience, 28,* 4807–4817. Available online at http://search.ebscohost.com

Hopkins, B., & Westra, T. (1989). Maternal expectations of their infants' development: Some cultural differences. *Developmental Medicine and Child Neurology, 31,* 384–390.

Hopkins, B., & Westra, T. (1990). Motor development, maternal expectation, and the role of handling. *Infant Behavior and Development, 13,* 117–122.

Hopkins-Golightly, T., Raz, S., & Sander, C. (2003). Influence of slight to moderate risk for birth hypoxia on acquisition of cognitive and language function in the preterm infant: A cross-sectional comparison with preterm-birth controls. *Neuropsychology, 17,* 3–13.

Horiuchi, S., Finch, C., & Mesle, F. (2003). Differential patterns of age-related mortality increase in middle age and old age. *Journals of Gerontology: Series A: Biological Sciences & Medical Sciences, 58A,* 495–507.

Hornor, G. (2008). Reactive attachment disorder. *Journal of Pediatric Health Care, 22,* 234–239.

Horowitz, A. (1994). Vision impairment and functional disability among nursing home residents. *Gerontologist, 34,* 316–323.

Horwitz, B. N., Luong, G., & Charles, G. T. (2008). Neuroticism and extraversion share genetic and environmental effects with negative and positive mood spillover in a nationally representative sample. *Personality and Individual Differences, 45,* 636–642.

House, S. H. (2007). Nurturing the brain nutritionally and emotionally from before conception to late adolescence. *Nutritional Health, 19,* 143–161.

Howard, A. (1992). Work and family crossroads spanning the career. In S. Zedeck (Ed.), *Work, families and organizations.* San Francisco: Jossey-Bass.

Howe, M. J. (1997). *IQ in question: The truth about intelligence.* London, England: Sage Publications.

Howe, M. L. (2003). Memories from the cradle. *Current Directions in Psychological Science, 12,* 62–65.

Howe, M. L., Courage, M. L., & Edison, S. C. (2004). When autobiographical memory begins. In S. Algarabel, A. Pitarque, T. Bajo, S. E. Gathercole, & M. A. Conway (Eds.), *Theories of memory: Vol. 3.* New York: Psychology Press.

Howell, E., Mora, P., Chassin, M., & Leventhal, H. (2010). Lack of preparation, physical health after childbirth, and early postpartum depressive symptoms. *Journal of Women's Health, 19,* 703–708.

Howell, P., Bailey, E., & Kothari, N. (2010). Changes in the pattern of stuttering over development for children who recover or persist. *Clinical Linguistics & Phonetics, 24,* 556–575.

Howes, C., Galinsky, E., & Kontos, S. (1998). Child care caregiver sensitivity and attachment. *Social Development, 7,* 25–36.

Howes, O., & Kapur, S. (2009). The dopamine hypothesis of schizophrenia: Version III—The final common pathway. *Schizophrenia Bulletin, 35,* 549–562.

Hoy, W. G. (2013). *Do funerals matter? The purposes and practices of death rituals in global perspective.* New York: Routledge/Taylor & Francis Group.

Hoy-Watkins, M. (2008). Manual for the contemporized-themes concerning blacks test (C-TCB). In S. Jenkins (Ed.), *A handbook of clinical scoring systems for thematic apperceptive techniques.* Mahwah, NJ: Lawrence Erlbaum Associates Publishers.

Huang, A., Subak, L., Thom, D., Van Den Eeden, S., Ragins, A., Kuppermann, M., et al. (2009). Sexual function and aging in racially and ethnically diverse women. *Journal of the American Geriatrics Society, 57,* 1362–1368.

Huang, C. T. (2012). Outcome-based observational learning in human infants. *Journal of Comparative Psychology, 126,* 139–149.

Huang, D. C., Lanza, H., Wright-Volel, K., & Anglin, M. (2013). Developmental trajectories of childhood obesity and risk behaviors in adolescence. *Journal of Adolescence, 36,* 139–148.

Huang, J. (2004). Death: Cultural traditions. *From On Our Own Terms: Moyers on Dying.* Available online, www.pbs.org

Hubbs-Tait, L., Nation, J. R., Krebs, N. F., & Bellinger, D. C. (2005). Neurotoxicants, micronutrients, and social environments: Individual and combined effects on children's development. *Journal of the American Psychological Society, 6,* 57–101.

Hubel, D. H., & Wiesel, T. N. (1979). Brain mechanisms of vision. *Scientific American, 241,* 150–162.

Hubel, D. H., & Wiesel, T. N. (2004). *Brain and visual perception: The story of a 25-year collaboration.* New York: Oxford University Press.

Hubley, A. M., & Arim, R. G. (2012). Subjective age in early adolescence: Relationships with chronological age, pubertal timing, desired age, and problem behaviors. *Journal of Adolescence, 35,* 357–366.

Hudson, J. A., Sosa, B. B., & Shapiro, L. R. (1997). Scripts and plans: The development of preschool children's event knowledge and event planning. In S. L. Friedman & E. K. Scholnick (Eds.), *The developmental psychology of planning: Why, how and when do we plan.* Mahwah, NJ: Lawrence Erlbaum.

Hueston, W., Geesey, M., & Diaz, V. (2008). Prenatal care initiation among pregnant teens in the United States: An analysis over 25 years. *Journal of Adolescent Health, 42,* 243–248.

Hugdahl, K., & Westerhausen, R. (2010). *The two halves of the brain: Information processing in the cerebral hemispheres.* Cambridge, MA: MIT Press.

Hughett, K., Kohler, F. W., & Raschke, D. (2013). The effects of a buddy skills package on preschool children's social interactions and play. *Topics in Early Childhood Special Education, 32,* 246–254.

Huh, S. Y., Rifas-Shiman, S. L., Zera, C. A., Rich Edwards, J. W., Oken, E., Weiss, S. T., et al. (2011). Delivery by caesarean section and risk of obesity in preschool age children: A prospective cohort study. *Archives of Disable Children, 34,* 66–79.

Huijbregts, S., Tavecchio, L., Leseman, P., & Hoffenaar, P. (2009). Child rearing in a group setting: Beliefs of Dutch,

Caribbean Dutch, and Mediterranean Dutch caregivers in center-based child care. *Journal of Cross-Cultural Psychology, 40,* 797–815. Available online at http://search.ebscohost.com

Huizink, A., Mulder, E., & Buitelaar, J. (2004). Prenatal stress and risk for psychopathology: Specific effects or induction of general susceptibility? *Psychological Bulletin, 130,* 115–142.

Hülür, G., Infurna, F. J., Ram, N., & Gerstorf, D. (2013). Cohorts based on decade of death: No evidence for secular trends favoring later cohorts in cognitive aging and terminal decline in the AHEAD study. *Psychology and Aging, 28,* 115–127.

Human Genome Project. (2006). Available online at http://www.ornl.gov/sci/techresources/Human_Genome/medicine/genetest.shtml

Humphries, M. L., & Korfmacher, J. (2012). The good, the bad, and the ambivalent: Quality of alliance in a support program for young mothers. *Infant Mental Health Journal, 33,* 22–33.

Hunt, M. (1974). *Sexual behaviors in the 1970s.* New York: Dell.

Hunt, M. (1993). *The story of psychology.* New York: Doubleday.

Hunter, J., & Mallon, G. P. (2000). Lesbian, gay, and bisexual adolescent development: Dancing with your feet tied together. In B. Greene & G. L. Croom (Eds.), *Education, research, and practice in lesbian, gay, bisexual, and transgendered psychology: A resource manual, Vol. 5.* Thousand Oaks, CA: Sage Publications.

Hunter, S., & Smith, D. (2008). Predictors of children's understandings of death: Age, cognitive ability, death experience and maternal communicative competence. *Omega: Journal of Death and Dying, 57,* 143–162.

Huntsinger, C. S., Jose, P. E., Liaw, F., & Ching, W.-D. (1997). Cultural differences in early mathematics learning: A comparison of Euro-American, Chinese-American, and Taiwan-Chinese families. *International Journal of Behavioral Development, 21,* 371–388.

Hust, S., & Brown, J. (2008). Gender, media use, and effects. In S. L. Calvert & B. J. Wilson (Eds.), *The handbook of children, media, and development.* Malden, MA: Blackwell Publishing.

Huston, T. L., Caughlin, J. P., Houts, R. M., & Smith, S. E. (2001). The connubial crucible: Newlywed years as predictors of marital delight, distress, and divorce. *Journal of Personality and Social Psychology, 80,* 237–252.

Hutchinson, D., & Rapee, R. (2007). Do friends share similar body image and eating problems? The role of social networks and peer influences in early adolescence. *Behaviour Research and Therapy, 45,* 1557–1577.

Hutton, P. H. (2004). *Phillippe Arièe and the politics of French cultural history.* Amherst: University of Massachusetts Press.

Huurre, T., Junkkari, H., & Aro, H. (2006, June). Long-term psychosocial effects of parental divorce: A follow-up study from adolescence to adulthood. *European Archives of Psychiatry and Clinical Neuroscience, 256,* 256–263.

Hyde, J. S. (1994). *Understanding human sexuality* (5th ed.). New York: McGraw-Hill.

Hyde, J. S., & DeLamater, J. D. (2003). *Understanding human sexuality* (8th ed.). New York: McGraw-Hill.

Hyde, J. S., & DeLamater, J. D. (2004). *Understanding human sexuality* (9th ed.). Boston: McGraw-Hill.

Hyde, J. S., & DeLamater, J. D. (2008). *Understanding human sexuality* (10th ed.). New York: McGraw-Hill.

Hyde, J. S., Fennema, E., & Lamon, S. J. (1990). Gender differences in mathematics performance: A meta-analysis. *Psychological Bulletin, 107,* 139–155.

Hyde, J. S., Mezulis, A., & Abramson, L. (2008). The ABCs of depression: Integrating affective, biological, and cognitive models to explain the emergence of the gender difference in depression. *Psychological Review, 115,* 291–313.

Hyssaelae, L., Rautava, P., & Helenius, H. (1995). Fathers' smoking and use of alcohol: The viewpoint of maternity health care clinics and well-baby clinics. *Family Practice, 12,* 22–27.

Iecovich, E., & Biderman, A. (2012). Attendance in adult day care centers and its relation to loneliness among frail older adults. *International Psychogeriatrics, 24,* 439–448.

Iglesias, J., Eriksson, J., Grize, F., Tomassini, M., & Villa, A. E. (2005). Dynamics of pruning in simulated large-scale spiking neural networks. *Biosystems, 79,* 11–20.

Ihle, A., Schnitzspahn, K., Rendell, P. G., Luong, C., & Kliegel, M. (2012). Age benefits in everyday prospective memory: The influence of personal task importance, use of reminders and everyday stress. *Aging, Neuropsychology, and Cognition, 19,* 84–101.

Ingersoll, E. W., & Thoman, E. B. (1999). Sleep/wake states of preterm infants: Stability, developmental change, diurnal variation, and relation with caregiving activity. *Child Development, 70,* 1–10.

Ingram, D. K., Young, J., & Mattison, J. A. (2007). Calorie restriction in nonhuman primates: Assessing effects on brain and behavioral aging. *Neuroscience, 14,* 1359–1364.

Inoue, K., Tanii, H., Abe, S., Kaiya, H., Nata, M., & Fukunaga, T. (2006, December). The correlation between rates of unemployment and suicide rates in Japan between 1985 and 2002. *International Medical Journal, 13,* 261–263.

Insel, B. J., & Gould, M. S. (2008). Impact of modeling on adolescent suicidal behavior. *Psychiatric Clinics of North America, 31,* 293–316.

Insel, P. M., & Roth, W. T. (1991). *Core concepts in health* (6th ed.). Mountain View, CA: Mayfield.

Interlandi, J. (2007). Chemo control. *Scientific American, 296,* 30–38.

International Cesarean Awareness Network. (2004). Available online at http://www.ican-online.org

International Cesarean Awareness Network. (2007, April 10). Available online at http://www.birthchoiceuk.com

International Human Genome Sequencing Consortium. (2001). Initial sequencing and analysis of the human genome. *Nature, 409,* 860–921.

Inzlicht, M., & Ben-Zeev, T. (2000). A threatening intellectual environment: Why females are susceptible to experiencing problem-solving deficits in the presence of males. *Psychological Science, 11,* 365–371.

Irland, J. M. (2010). Childbirth. In F. A. Barabasz & K. Olness (Eds.), *Medical hypnosis primer: Clinical and research evidence.* New York: Routledge/Taylor & Francis Group.

Isaacs, K. L., Barr, W. B., Nelson, P. K., & Devinsky, O. (2006). Degree of handedness and cerebral dominance. *Neurology, 66,* 1855–1858.

Isay, R. A. (1990). *Being homosexual: Gay men and their development.* New York: Avon.

Ishi-Kuntz, M. (2000). Diversity within Asian-American families. In D. H. Demo, K. R. Allen, & M. A. Fine (Eds.), *Handbook of family diversity.* New York: Oxford.

Ishizuka, B., Kudo, Y., & Tango, T. (2008). Cross-sectional community survey of menopause symptoms among Japanese women. *Maturitas, 61,* 260–267.

Iverson, T., Larsen, L., & Solem, P. (2009). A conceptual analysis of ageism. *Nordic Psychology, 61,* 4–22.

Izard, C. E. (1982). The psychology of emotion comes of age on the coattails of darwin. *PsycCRITIQUES, 27,* 426–429.

Izard, C. E., Woodburn, E., & Finlon, K. (2010). Extending emotion science to the study of discrete emotions in infants. *Emotion Review, 2,* 134–136.

Izard, V., Sann, C., Spelke, E., & Streri, A. (2009). Newborn infants perceive abstract numbers. *Proceedings of the National Academy of Sciences of the United States of America, 106,* 10382–10385.

Jack, F., Simcock, G., & Hayne, H. (2012). Magic memories: Young children's verbal recall after a 6-year delay. *Child Development, 83,* 159–172.

Jacobi, C., Hayward, C., de Zwaan, M., Kraemer, H. C., & Agras, W. S. (2004). Coming to terms with risk factors for eating disorders: Application of risk terminology and suggestions for a general taxonomy. *Psychological Bulletin, 130,* 19–65.

Jacobson, N., & Gottman, J. (1998). *When men batter women.* New York: Simon & Schuster.

Jager, R., Mieler, W., & Miller, J. (2008). Age-related macular degeneration. *The New England Journal of Medicine, 358,* 2606–2617.

Jahoda, G. (1980). Theoretical and systematic approaches in mass-cultural psychology. In H. C. Triandis & W. W. Lambert (Eds.), *Handbook of cross-cultural psychology* (Vol. 1). Boston: Allyn & Bacon.

Jahoda, G. (1983). European "lag" in the development of an economic concept: A study in Zimbabwe. *British Journal of Developmental Psychology, 1,* 113–120.

Jalonick, M. C. (2011, January 13). New guidelines would make school lunches healthier. *The Washington Post.*

James, W. (1890/1950). *The principles of psychology.* New York: Holt.

James, J., Ellis, B. J., Schlomer, G. L., & Garber, J. (2012). Sex-specific pathways to early puberty, sexual debut, and sexual risk taking: Tests of an integrated evolutionary-developmental model. *Developmental Psychology, 48,* 687–702.

Janda, L. H., & Klenke-Hamel, K. E. (1980). *Human sexuality.* New York: Van Nostrand.

Janevic, T. T., Loftfield, E. E., Savitz, D. A., Bradley, E. E., Illuzzi, J. J., & Lipkind, H. H. (2013). Disparities in cesarean delivery by ethnicity and nativity in New York City. *Maternal and Child Health Journal.* Accessed online, June 4, 2013, http://www.ncbi.nlm.nih.gov/pubmed/23504133

Janicke, D. M. (2013). Treatment of pediatric obesity using a parent-only approach: A case example. *Health Psychology, 32,* 345–350.

Janusek, L., Cooper, D., & Mathews, H. L. (2012). Stress, immunity, and health outcomes. In V. Rice (Ed.), *Handbook of stress, coping, and health: Implications for nursing research, theory, and practice* (2nd ed.). Thousand Oaks, CA: Sage Publications, Inc.

Jaswal, V., & Dodson, C. (2009). Metamemory development: Understanding the role of similarity in false memories. *Child Development, 80,* 629–635.

Jaworski, M., & Accardo, P. (2010). Behavioral phenotypes: Nature versus nurture revisited. In B. K. Shapiro & P. J. Accardo (Eds.), *Neurogenetic syndromes: Behavioral issues and their treatment.* Baltimore, MD: Paul H. Brookes Publishing.

Jay, M. (2012, April 14). The downside of cohabiting before marriage. *The New York Times,* p. SR4.

Jehlen, A., & Winans, D. (2005). No Child Left Behind—myth or truth? *NEA Today, 23,* 32–34.

Jensen, L. A. (2008). Coming of age in a multicultural world: Globalization and adolescent cultural identity formation. In D. L. Browning (Ed.), *Adolescent identities: A collection of readings.* New York: Analytic Press/Taylor & Francis Group.

Jeynes, W. (2007). The impact of parental remarriage on children: A meta-analysis. *Marriage & Family Review, 40,* 75–102.

Jiao, S., Ji, G., & Jing, Q. (1996). Cognitive development of Chinese urban only children and children with siblings. *Child Development, 67,* 387–395.

Ji-liang, S., Li-qing, Z., & Yan, T. (2003). The impact of intergenerational social support and filial expectation on the loneliness of elder parents. *Chinese Journal of Clinical Psychology, 11,* 167–169.

Jimenez, J., & Guzman, R. (2003). The influence of code-oriented versus meaning-oriented approaches to reading instruction on word recognition in the Spanish language. *International Journal of Psychology, 38,* 65–78.

Jindal, V. (2013). Glaucoma: An extension of various chronic neurodegenerative disorders. *Molecular Neurobiology.* Accessed online, June 11, 2013, http://link.springer.com/article/10.1007/s12035-013-8416-8#page-1

Joe, S., & Marcus, S. (2003). Datapoints: Trends by race and gender in suicide attempts among U.S. adolescents, 1991-2001. *Psychiatric Services, 54,* 454.

Johnson, A. M., Wadsworth, J., Wellings, K., & Bradshaw, S. (1992). Sexual lifestyles and HIV risk. *Nature, 360,* 410–412.

Johnson, D. C., Kassner, C. T., & Kutner, J. S. (2004). Current use of guidelines, protocols, and care pathways for symptom management in hospice. *American Journal of Hospital Palliative Care, 21,* 51–57.

Johnson, D. J., Jaeger, E., Randolph, S. M., Cauce, A. M., Ward, J., & National Institute of Child Health and Human Development: Early Child Care Research Network. (2003). Studying the effects of early child care experiences on the development of children of color in the United States: Toward a more inclusive research agenda. *Child Development, 74,* 1227–1244.

Johnson, H. J., Barnard-Brak, L. S., Terrill, F., & Johnson, M. K. (2012). An experimental study of the effects of stereotype threat and stereotype lift on men and women's performance in mathematics. *Journal of Experimental Education, 80,* 137–149.

Johnson, K., & Eilers, A. (1998). Effects of knowledge and development on subordinate level categorization. *Cognitive Development, 13,* 515–545.

Johnson, N. (2003). Psychology and health: Research, practice, and policy. *American Psychologist, 58,* 670–677.

Johnson, N. G., Roberts, M. C., & Worell, J. (Eds.). (1999). *Beyond appearance: A new look at adolescent girls.* Washington, DC: American Psychological Association.

Johnson, S. L., & Birch, L. L. (1994). Parents' and children's adiposity and eating style. *Pediatrics, 94,* 653–661.

Johnson, S., Dweck, C., Chen, F., Stern, H., Ok, S., & Barth, M. (2010). At the intersection of social and cognitive development: Internal working models of attachment in infancy. *Cognitive Science: A Multidisciplinary Journal, 34,* 807–825.

Johnston, L. D., Bachman, J. G., & O'Malley, P. M. (2009). *Monitoring the future study.* Lansing: University of Michigan.

Johnston, L. D., Bachman, J. G., & O'Malley, P. M. (2012). *Monitoring the future study.* Lansing, MI: University of Michigan.

Johnston, L. D., O'Malley, P. M., Bachman, J. G., & Schulenberg, J. E. (2007). *Monitoring the future national results on adolescent drug use: Overview of key findings, 2006* (NIH Publication No. 07-6202). Bethesda, MD: National Institute on Drug Abuse.

Jones, A., & Crandall, R. (Eds.). (1991). Handbook of self-actualization. *Journal of Social Behavior and Personality, 6,* 1–362.

Jones, D. E., Carson, K. A., Bleich, S. N., & Cooper, L. A. (2012). Patient trust in physicians and adoption of lifestyle behaviors to control high blood pressure. *Patient Education and Counseling.* Accessed online, July 22, 2012, http://www.ncbi.nlm.nih.gov/pubmed/22770676

Jones, H. (2006). Drug addiction during pregnancy: Advances in maternal treatment and understanding child outcomes. *Current Directions in Psychological Science, 15,* 126–130.

Jones-Harden, B. (2004). Safety and stability for foster children: A developmental perspective. *The Future of Children, 14,* 31–48.

Jonsson, T., Atwal, J. K., Steinberg, S., Snaedal, J., Jonsson, P. V., Bjornsson, S., et al. (2012). A mutation in APP protects against Alzheimer's disease and age-related cognitive decline. *Nature, 488,* 96–99.

Jopp, D. S., & Hertzog, C. (2010). Assessing adult leisure activities: An extension of a self-report activity questionnaire. *Psychological Assessment, 22,* 108–120.

Jordan, A., Trentacoste, N., Henderson, V., Manganello, J., & Fishbein, M. (2007). Measuring the time teens spend with media: Challenges and opportunities. *Media Psychology, 9,* 19–41.

Jordan-Young, R. M. (2012). Hormones, context, and "brain gender": A review of evidence from congenital adrenal hyperplasia. *Social Science & Medicine, 74,* 1738–1744.

Jorgensen, G. (2006, June). Kohlberg and Gilligan: Duet or duel? *Journal of Moral Education, 35,* 179–196.

Jose, O., & Alfons, V. (2007). Do demographics affect marital satisfaction? *Journal of Sex and Marital Therapy, 33,* 73–85.

Joseph, H., Reznik, I., & Mester, R. (2003). Suicidal behavior of adolescent girls: Profile and meaning. *Israel Journal of Psychiatry & Related Sciences, 40,* 209–219.

Juby, H., Billette, J., Laplante, B., & Le Bourdais, C. (2007). Nonresident fathers and children: Parents' new unions and frequency of contact. *Journal of Family Issues, 28,* 1220–1245.

Judge, T. A., Ilies, R., & Zhang, Z. (2012). Genetic influences on core self-evaluations, job satisfaction, and work stress: A behavioral genetics mediated model. *Organizational Behavior and Human Decision Processes, 117,* 208–220.

Jung, M., & Brawley, L. (2010). Concurrent management of exercise with other valued life goals: Comparison of frequent and less frequent exercisers. *Psychology of Sport and Exercise, 11,* 372–377.

Jurimae, T., & Saar, M. (2003). Self-perceived and actual indicators of motor abilities in children and adolescents. *Perception and Motor Skills, 97,* 862–866.

Kacapyr, E. (1997, October). Are we having fun yet? *American Demographics,* 28–30.

Kagan, J. (2000, October). Adult personality and early experience. *Harvard Mental Health Letter,* pp. 4–5.

Kagan, J. (2003). An unwilling rebel. In R. J. Sternberg (Ed.), *Psychologists defying the crowd: Stories of those who battled the establishment and won.* Washington, DC: American Psychological Association.

Kagan, J. (2008). In defense of qualitative changes in development. *Child Development, 79,* 1606–1624.

Kagan, J. (2010). *The temperamental thread: How genes, culture, time, and luck make us who we are.* Washington, DC: Dana Press.

Kagan, J., Arcus, D., & Snidman, N. (1993). The idea of temperament: Where do we go from here? In R. Plomin & G. E. McClearn (Eds.), *Nature, nurture, and psychology.* Washington, DC: American Psychological Association.

Kagan, J., Arcus, D., Snidman, N., Feng, W. Y., Hendler, J., & Greene, S. (1994). Reactivity in infants: A cross-national comparison. *Developmental Psychology, 30,* 342–345.

Kagan, J., Kearsley, R., & Zelazo, P. R. (1978). *Infancy: Its place in human development.* Cambridge, MA: Harvard University Press.

Kagan, J., & Snidman, N. (1991). Infant predictors of inhibited and uninhibited profiles. *Psychological Science, 2,* 40–44.

Kahn, J. H., Hessling, R., & Russell, D. (2003). Social support, health, and well-being among the elderly: What is the role of negative affectivity? *Personality & Individual Differences, 35,* 5–17.

Kahn, J. P. (2004). Hostility, coronary risk, and alpha-adrenergic to beta-adrenergic receptor density ratio. *Psychosomatic Medicine, 66,* 289–297.

Kahn, R. L., & Rowe, J. W. (1999). *Successful aging.* New York: Dell.

Kahneman, D., Krueger, A., Schkade, D., Schwarz, N., & Stone, A. (2006, June). Would you be happier if you were richer? A focusing illusion. *Science, 312,* 1908–1910.

Kail, R. (2003). Information processing and memory. In M. Bornstein & L. Davidson (Eds.), *Well-being: Positive development across the life course.* Mahwah, NJ: Lawrence Erlbaum Associates.

Kail, R. V. (2004). Cognitive development includes global and domain-specific processes [Special issue: 50th anniversary issue: Part II, the maturing of the human development sciences: Appraising past, present, and prospective agendas]. *Merrill-Palmer Quarterly, 50,* 445–455.

Kail, R. V., & Miller, C. A. (2006). Developmental change in processing speed: Domain specificity and stability during childhood and adolescence. *Journal of Cognition and Development, 7,* 119–137.

Kaiser, L. L., Allen, L., & American Dietetic Association. (2002). Position of the American dietetic association: Nutrition and lifestyle for a healthy pregnancy outcome. *Journal of the American Dietetic Association, 102,* 1479–1490.

Kalb, C. (1997, Spring/Summer). The top 10 health worries. *Newsweek Special Issue,* pp. 42–43.

Kalb, C. (2003, March 10). Preemies grow up. *Newsweek,* pp. 50–51.

Kalb, C. (2004, January 26). Brave new babies. *Newsweek,* pp. 45–53.

Kalb, C. (2012, February). Fetal armor. *Scientific American,* p. 73.

Kaltiala-Heino, R., Kosunen, E., & Rimpela, M. (2003). Pubertal timing, sexual behaviour and self-reported depression in middle adolescence. *Journal of Adolescence, 26,* 531–545.

Kalynchuk, L. (2010). Behavioral and neurobiological consequences of stress. *Progress in Neuro-Psychopharmacology & Biological Psychiatry, 34,* 731–732.

Kamijo, K., Hayashi, Y., Sakai, T., Yahiro, T., Tanaka, K., & Nishihira, Y. (2009). Acute effects of aerobic exercise on cognitive function in older adults. *Journals of Gerontology: Series B: Psychological Sciences and Social Sciences, 64B,* 356–363.

Kaminaga, M. (2007). Pubertal development and depression in adolescent boys and girls. *Japanese Journal of Educational Psychology, 55,* 21–33.

Kan, P., & Kohnert, K. (2009). Fast mapping by bilingual preschool children. *Journal of Child Language, 35,* 495–514.

Kandler, C., Bleidorn, W., Riemann, R., Angleitner, A., & Spinath, F. M. (2012). Life events as environmental states and genetic traits and the role of personality: A longitudinal twin study. *Behavior Genetics, 42,* 57–72.

Kaneda, H., Maeshima, K., Goto, N., Kobayakawa, T., Ayabe-Kanamura, S., & Saito, S. (2000). Decline in taste and odor discrimination abilities with age, and relationship between gustation and olfaction. *Chemical Senses, 25,* 331–337.

Kantrowitz, E. J., & Evans, G. W. (2004). The relation between the ratio of children per activity area and off-task behavior and type of play in day care centers. *Environment & Behavior, 36,* 541–557.

Kao, G. (2000). Psychological well-being and educational achievement among immigrant youth. In D. J. Hernandez (Ed.), *Children of immigrants: Health, adjustment, and public assistance.* Washington, DC: National Academy Press.

Kao, G., & Vaquera, E. (2006, February). The salience of racial and ethnic identification in friendship choices among Hispanic adolescents. *Hispanic Journal of Behavioral Sciences, 28,* 23–47.

Kapadia, S. (2008). Adolescent-parent relationships in Indian and Indian immigrant families in the US: Intersections and disparities. *Psychology and Developing Societies, 20,* 257–275.

Kaplan, H., & Dove, H. (1987). Infant development among the Ache of Eastern Paraguay. *Developmental Psychology, 23,* 190–198.

Kaplan, R. M., Sallis, J. F., Jr., & Patterson, T. L. (1993). *Health and human behavior: Age specific breast cancer annual incidence.* New York: McGraw-Hill.

Karagianni, P., Kyriakidou, M., Mitsiakos, G., Chatzioanidis, H., Koumbaras, E., Evangeliou, A., et al. (2010). Neurological outcome in preterm small for gestational age infants compared to appropriate for gestational age preterm at the age of 18 months: A prospective study. *Journal of Child Neurology, 25,* 165–170.

Karelitz, T. M., Jarvin, L., & Sternberg, R. J. (2010). The meaning of wisdom and its development throughout life. In W. F. Overton & R. M. Lerner (Eds.), *The handbook of lifespan development, Vol. 1: Cognition, biology, and methods.* Hoboken, NJ: John Wiley & Sons.

Karmiloff-Smith, A., Aschersleben, G., de Schonen, S., Elsabbagh, M., Hohenberger, A., & Serres, J. (2010). Constraints on the timing of infant cognitive change: Domain-specific or domain-general? *European Journal of Developmental Science, 4,* 31–45.

Karney, B. R., & Bradbury, T. N. (2005). Contextual influences on marriage. *Current Directions in Psychological Science, 14,* 171–174.

Karniol, R. (2009). Israeli kindergarten children's gender constancy for others' counter-stereotypic toy play and appearance: The role of sibling gender and relative age. *Infant and Child Development, 18,* 73–94.

Kart, C. S. (1990). *The realities of aging* (3rd ed.). Boston: Allyn & Bacon.

Kartman, L. L. (1991). Life review: One aspect of making meaningful music for the elderly. *Activities, Adaptations, and Aging, 15,* 42–45.

Kaslow, F. W. (2001). Families and family psychology at the millennium: Intersecting crossroads. *American Psychologist, 56,* 37–44.

Kastenbaum, R. (1985). Dying and death: A life-span approach. In J. E. Birren & K. W. Schaie (Eds.), *Handbook of the psychology of aging.* New York: Van Nostrand Reinhold.

Kastenbaum, R. (2000). *The psychology of death* (3rd ed.). New York: Springer.

Kastenbaum, R. J. (1992). *The psychology of death.* New York: Springer-Verlag.

Kate, N. T. (1998, March). How many children? *American Demographics,* 35.

Kato, K., & Pedersen, N. L. (2005). Personality and coping: A study of twins reared apart and twins reared together. *Behavior Genetics, 35,* 147–158.

Katz, S., & Marshall, B. (2003). New sex for old: Lifestyle, consumerism, and the ethics of aging well. *Journal of Aging Studies, 17,* 3–16.

Katzer, C., Fetchenhauer, D., & Belschak, F. (2009). Cyberbullying: Who are the victims? A comparison of victimization in Internet chatrooms and victimization in school. *Journal of Media Psychology: Theories, Methods, and Applications, 21,* 25–36.

Kaufman, J. C., Kaufman, A. S., Kaufman-Singer, J., & Kaufman, N. L. (2005). The Kaufman assessment battery for children—second edition and the Kaufman adolescent and adult intelligence test. In D. P. Flanagan & P. L. Harrison (Eds.), *Contemporary intellectual assessment: Theories, tests, and issues.* New York: Guilford Press.

Kayton, A. (2007). Newborn screening: A literature review. *Neonatal Network, 26,* 85–95.

Keating, D. (1990). Adolescent thinking. In S. S. Feldman & G. R. Elliott (Eds.), *At the threshold.* Cambridge, MA: Harvard University Press.

Kecskes, I., & Papp, T. (2000). *Foreign language and mother tongue.* Mahwah, NJ: Lawrence Erlbaum.

Kedziora-Kornatowski, K., Szewczyk-Golec, K., Czuczejko, J., van Marke de Lumen, K., Pawluk, H., Motyl, J., et al. (2007). Effect of melatonin on the oxidative stress in erythrocytes of healthy young and elderly subjects. *Journal of Pineal Research, 42,* 153–158.

Keefer, B. L., Kraus, R. F., Parker, B. L., Elliott, R., & Patton, G. (1991). A state university collaboration program: Residents' perspectives [Annual meeting of the American Psychiatric Association (1990, New York, NY)]. *Hospital and Community Psychiatry, 42,* 62–66.

Keel, P., & Haedt, A. (2008). Evidence-based psychosocial treatments for eating problems and eating disorders. *Journal of Clinical Child and Adolescent Psychology, 37,* 39–61.

Keel, P. K., Gravener, J. A., Joiner, T. E., Jr., & Haedt, A. (2010). Twenty-year follow-up of bulimia nervosa and related eating disorders not otherwise specified. *International Journal of Eating Disorders, 43,* 492–497.

Keene, J. R., Prokos, A. H., & Held, B. (2012). Grandfather caregivers: Race and ethnic differences in poverty. *Sociological Inquiry, 82,* 49–77.

Kehl, K. A., & McCarty, K. N. (2012). Readability of hospice materials to prepare families for caregiving at the time of death. *Research in Nursing & Health, 35,* 242–249.

Kelch-Oliver, K. (2008). African American grandparent caregivers: Stresses and implications for counselors. *The Family Journal, 16,* 43–50.

Keller, H., Otto, H., Lamm, B., Yovsi, R. D., & Kartner, J. (2008). The timing of verbal/vocal communications between mothers and their infants: A longitudinal cross-cultural comparison. *Infant Behavior & Development, 31,* 217–226.

Kelley, G., Kelley, K., Hootman, J., & Jones, D. (2009). Exercise and health-related quality of life in older community-dwelling adults: A meta-analysis of randomized controlled trials. *Journal of Applied Gerontology, 28,* 369–394.

Kelly, G. (2001). *Sexuality today: A human perspective* (7th ed.). New York: McGraw-Hill.

Kelly-Weeder, S., & Cox, C. (2007). The impact of lifestyle risk factors on female infertility. *Women & Health, 44,* 1–23.

Kemper, S. (2012). The interaction of linguistic constraints, working memory, and aging on language production and comprehension. In M. Naveh-Benjamin & N. Ohta (Eds.), *Memory and aging: Current issues and future directions.* New York: Psychology Press.

Kennell, J. H. (2002). On becoming a family: Bonding and the changing patterns in baby and family behavior. In J. Gomes-Pedro & J. K. Nugent (Eds.), *The infant and family in the twenty-first century.* New York: Brunner-Routledge.

Kenrick, D. T., Keefe, R. C., Bryna, A., Barr, A., & Brown, S. (1995). Age preferences and mate choice among homosexuals and heterosexuals: A case for modular psychological mechanisms. *Journal of Personality and Social Psychology, 69,* 1166–1172.

Keski-Rahkonen, A., Raevuori, A., Bulik, C. M., Hoek, H. W., Sihvola, E., Kaprio, J., et al. (2013). Depression and drive for thinness are associated with persistent bulimia nervosa in the community. *European Eating Disorders Review, 21,* 121–129.

Kesselring, T., & Müller, U. (2010). The concept of egocentrism in the context of Piaget's theory. *New Ideas in Psychology, 10,* 56–63.

Khachaturian, Z. S., Khachaturian, A. S., & Thies, W. (2012). The draft "National Plan" to address Alzheimer's disease—National Alzheimer's Project Act (NAPA). *Alzheimer's & Dementia, 8,* 234–236.

Kiang, L., Yip, T., & Fuligni, A. J. (2008). Multiple social identities and adjustment in young adults from ethnically diverse backgrounds. *Journal of Research on Adolescence, 18,* 643–670.

Kiecolt, K. J., & Fossett, M. A. (1997). The effects of mate availability on marriage among black Americans: A contextual analysis. In R. J. Taylor, J. S. Jackson, & L. M. Chatters (Eds.), *Family life in black America.* Thousand Oaks, CA: Sage Publications.

Kiecolt-Glaser, J. K. (2009). Psychoneuroimmunology: Psychology's gateway to biomedical future [Special issue: Next big questions in psychology]. *Perspectives on Psychological Science, 4,* 367–369.

Kieffer, C. C. (2012). Secure connections, the extended family system, and the socio-cultural construction of attachment theory. In S. Akhtar (Ed.), *The mother and her child: Clinical aspects of attachment, separation, and loss.* Lanham, MD: Jason Aronson.

Kilmann, P., & Vendemia, J. C. (2013). Partner discrepancies in distressed marriages. *The Journal of Social Psychology, 153,* 196–211.

Kilner, J. M., Friston, J. J., & Frith, C. D. (2007). Predictive coding: An account of the mirror neuron system. *Cognitive Processes, 33,* 88–997.

Kim, E. H., & Lee, E. (2009). Effects of a death education program on life satisfaction and attitude toward death in college students. *Journal of Korean Academic Nursing, 39,* 1–9.

Kim, H. I., & Johnson, S. P. (2013). Do young infants prefer an infant-directed face or a happy face? *International Journal of Behavioral Development, 37,* 125–130.

Kim, H. S., Sherman, D., & Taylor, S. (2008). Culture and social support. *American Psychologist, 63,* 518–526.

Kim, J. (1995, January). You cannot know how much freedom you have here. *Money,* p. 133.

Kim, J.-S., & Lee, E.-H. (2003). Cultural and noncultural predictors of health outcomes in Korean daughter and daughter in-law caregivers. *Public Health Nursing, 20,* 111–119.

Kim-Cohen, J. (2007). Resilience and developmental psychopathology. *Child and Adolescent Psychiatric Clinics of North America, 16,* 271–283.

Kimm, S., Glynn, N. W., Kriska, A., Barton, B. A., Kronsberg, S. S., Daniels, S. R., et al. (2003). Decline in physical activity in Black girls and White girls during adolescence. *New England Journal of Medicine, 347,* 709–715.

Kimura, K., Yasunaga, A., & Wang, L. (2013). Correlation between moderate daily physical activity and neurocognitive variability in healthy elderly people. *Archives of Gerontology and Geriatrics, 56,* 109–117.

Kincl, L., Dietrich, K., & Bhattacharya, A. (2006, October). Injury trends for adolescents with early childhood lead exposure. *Journal of Adolescent Health, 39,* 604–606.

King, D., Delfabbro, P., & Griffiths, M. (2010). The convergence of gambling and digital media: Implications for gambling in young people. *Journal of Gambling Studies, 26,* 175–187.

Kinney, H. C., Randall, L. L., Sleeper, L. A., Willinger, M., Beliveau, R. A., Zec, N., et al. (2003). Serotonergic brainstem abnormalities in Northern Plains Indians with the sudden infant death syndrome. *Journal of Neuropathology and Experimental Neurology, 62,* 1178–1191.

Kinney, H. C., & Thach, B. (2009). Medical progress: The sudden infant death syndrome. *New England Journal of Medicine, 361,* 795–805.

Kinsey, A. C., Pomeroy, W. B., & Martin, C. E. (1948). *Sexual behavior in the human male.* Philadelphia: Saunders.

Kirby, J. (2006, May). From single-parent families to stepfamilies: Is the transition associated with adolescent alcohol initiation? *Journal of Family Issues, 27,* 685–711.

Kirchengast, S., & Hartmann, B. (2003). Impact of maternal age and maternal-somatic characteristics on newborn size. *American Journal of Human Biology, 15,* 220–228.

Kisilevsky, B. S., Hains, S. M. J., Xing Xie, K. L., Huang, H., Ye, H. H., Zhang, Z., et al. (2003). Effects of experience on fetal voice recognition. *Psychological Science, 14,* 220–224.

Kitamura, C., & Lam, C. (2009). Age-specific preferences for infant-directed affective intent. *Infancy, 14,* 77–100.

Kiuru, N., Nurmi, J., Aunola, K., & Salmela-Aro, K. (2009). Peer group homogeneity in adolescents' school adjustment varies according to peer group type and gender. *International Journal of Behavioral Development, 33,* 65–76.

Kjølseth, I., Ekeberg, Ø., & Steihaug, S. (2010). Why suicide? Elderly people who committed suicide and their experience of life in the period before their death. *International Psychogeriatrics, 22,* 209–218.

Klass, P. (2010, October 11). Understanding 'bababa' as a key to development. *The New York Times,* p. D5.

Klein, M. C. (2012). The tyranny of meta-analysis and the misuse of randomized controlled trials in maternity care. *Birth: Issues in Perinatal Care, 39,* 80–82.

Klier, C. M., Muzik, M., Dervic, K., Mossaheb, N., Benesch, T., Ulm, B., et al. (2007). The role of estrogen and progesterone in depression after birth. *Journal of Psychiatric Research, 41,* 273–279.

Klimstra, T. A., Luyckx, K., Germeijs, V., Meeus, W. J., & Goossens, L. (2012). Personality traits and educational identity formation in late adolescents: Longitudinal associations and academic progress. *Journal of Youth and Adolescence, 41,* 346–361.

Klitzman, R. L. (2012). *Am I my genes? Confronting fate and family secrets in the age of genetic testing.* New York: Oxford University Press.

Kloep, M., Güney, N., Çok, F., & Simsek, Ö. (2009). Motives for risk-taking in adolescence: A cross-cultural study. *Journal of Adolescence, 32,* 135–151.

Kluger, J. (2010, November 1). Keeping young minds healthy. *Time,* pp. 40–50.

Knafo, A., & Schwartz, S. H. (2003). Parenting and accuracy of perception of parental values by adolescents. *Child Development, 73,* 595–611.

Knickmeyer, R., & Baron-Cohen, S. (2006, December). Fetal testosterone and sex differences. *Early Human Development, 82,* 755–760.

Knorth, E. J., Harder, A. T., Zandberg, T., & Kendrick, A. J. (2008). Under one roof: A review and selective meta-analysis on the outcomes of residential child and youth care. *Children and Youth Services Review, 30,* 123–140.

Kochanska, G., & Aksan, N. (2004). Development of mutual responsiveness between parents and their young children. *Child Development, 75,* 1657–1676.

Kodl, M., & Mermelstein, R. (2004). Beyond modeling: Parenting practices, parental smoking history, and adolescent cigarette smoking. *Addictive Behaviors, 29,* 17–32.

Koenig, A., Cicchetti, D., & Rogosch, F. (2004). Moral development: The association between maltreatment and young children's prosocial behaviors and moral transgressions. *Social Development, 13,* 97–106.

Koenig, L. B., McGue, M., Krueger, R. F., & Bouchard, T. J., Jr. (2005). Genetic and environmental influences on religiousness: Findings for retrospective and current religiousness ratings. *Journal of Personality, 73,* 471–488.

Kohlberg, L. (1966). A cognitive-developmental anaylsis of children's sex-role concepts and attitudes. In E. E. Maccoby (Ed.), *The development of sex differences.* Stanford, CA: Stanford University Press.

Kohlberg, L. (1984). *The psychology of moral development: Essays on moral development* (Vol. 2). San Francisco: Harper & Row.

Kohut, S. A., & Riddell, R. P. (2009). Does the Neonatal Facial Coding System differentiate between infants experiencing pain-related and non-pain-related distress? *The Journal of Pain, 10,* 214–220.

Koivisto, M., & Revonsuo, A. (2003). Object recognition in the cerebral hemispheres as revealed by visual field experiments. *Laterality: Asymmetries of Body, Brain & Cognition, 8,* 135–153.

Kolata, G. (2004, May 11). The heart's desire. *The New York Times,* p. D1.

Koopmans, S., & Kooijman, A. (2006, November). Presbyopia correction and accommodative intraocular lenses. *Gerontechnology, 5,* 222–230.

Koretz, D. (2008). The pending reauthorization of NCLB: An opportunity to rethink the basic strategy. In G. L. Sunderman (Ed.), *Holding NCLB accountable: Achieving, accountability, equity, & school reform.* Thousand Oaks, CA: Corwin Press.

Koroukian, S. M., Trisel, B., & Rimm, A. A. (1998). Estimating the proportion of unnecessary cesarean sections in Ohio using birth certificate data. *Journal of Clinical Epidemiology, 51,* 1327–1334.

Korte, J., Westerhof, G. J., & Bohlmeijer, E. T. (2012). Mediating processes in an effective life-review intervention. *Psychology and Aging.* Accessed online, July 24, 2012, http://psycnet.apa.org/psycinfo/2012-17923-001/

Koshmanova, T. (2007). Vygotskian scholars: Visions and implementation of cultural-historical theory. *Journal of Russian & East European Psychology, 45,* 61–95.

Koska, J., Ksinantova, L., Sebokova, E., Kvetnansky, R., Klimes, I., Chrousos, G., et al. (2002). Endocrine regulation of subcutaneous fat metabolism during cold exposure in humans. *Annals of the New York Academy of Science, 967,* 500–505.

Koss, M. P., Goodman, L. A., Browne, A., Fitzgerald, L. F., Keita, G. P., & Russo, N. F. (1993). *No safe haven: Violence against women, at home, at work, and in the community.* Final report of the American Psychological Association Women's Programs Office Task Force on Violence Against Women. Washington, DC: American Psychological Association.

Kostka, T., & Jachimowicz, V. (2010). Relationship of quality of life to dispositional optimism, health locus of control and self-efficacy in older subjects living in different environments. *Quality of Life Research, 19,* 351–361.

Kotre, J., & Hall, E. (1990). *Seasons of life.* Boston: Little, Brown.

Kovelman, I., Baker, S. A., & Petitto, L. A. (2008). Bilingual and monolingual brains compared: A functional magnetic resonance imaging investigation of syntactic processing and a possible 'neural signature' of bilingualism. *Journal of Cognitive Neuroscience, 20,* 153–169.

Kradin, R. L. (2013). *Pathologies of the mind/body interface: Exploring the curious domain of the psychosomatic disorders.* New York: Routledge/Taylor & Francis Group.

Kramer, A. F., Erickson, K. I., & Colcombe, S. J. (2006). Exercise, cognition, and the aging brain. *Journal of Applied Physiology, 101,* 1237–1242.

Krcmar, M., Grela, B., & Lin, K. (2007). Can toddlers learn vocabulary from television? An experimental approach. *Media Psychology, 10,* 41–63.

Kretch, K. S., & Adolph, K. E. (2013). Cliff or step? Posture-specific learning at the edge of a drop-off. *Child Development, 84,* 226–240.

Krishnamoorthy, J. S., Hart, C., & Jelalian, E. (2006). The epidemic of childhood obesity: Review of research and implications for public policy. *Social Policy Report, 19,* 3–19.

Kroger, J. (2006). *Identity development: Adolescence through adulthood.* Thousand Oaks, CA: Sage Publications.

Kroger, J. (2007). Why is identity achievement so elusive? *Identity: An International Journal of Theory and Research, 7,* 331–348.

Krojgaard, P. (2005). Infants' search for hidden persons. *International Journal of Behavioral Development, 29,* 70–79.

Kross, E., & Grossmann, I. (2012). Boosting wisdom: Distance from the self enhances wise reasoning, attitudes, and behavior. *Journal of Experimental Psychology: General, 141,* 43–48.

Krueger, J., & Heckhausen, J. (1993). Personality development across the adult life span: Subjective conceptions vs. cross-sectional contrasts. *Journals of Gerontology, 48,* 100–108.

Kübler-Ross, E. (1969). *On death and dying.* New York: Macmillan.

Kübler-Ross, E. (Ed.). (1975). *Death: The final stage of growth.* Englewood Cliffs, NJ: Prentice-Hall.

Kuczynski, L., & Kochanska, G. (1990). Development of children's noncompliance strategies from toddlerhood to age 5. *Developmental Psychology, 26,* 398–408.

Kuczmarski, R. J., Ogden, C. J., Guo, S. S., Grummer-Strawn, L. M., Flegal, K. M., Mei, Z., et al. (2002). *2000 CDC growth charts for the United States: Methods and development.* Washington, DC: National Center for Health Statistics.

Kuhl, P. K., Andruski, J. E., Chistovich, I. A., Chistovich, L. A., Kozhevnikova, E. V., Ryskina, V. L., et al. (1997, August 1). Cross-language analysis of phonetic units in language addressed to infants. *Science, 277,* 684–686.

Kuhn, D. (2008). Formal operations from a twenty-first century perspective. *Human Development, 51,* 48–55.

Kuhn, D., Garcia-Mila, M., Zohar, A., & Andersen, C. (1995). Strategies of knowledge acquisition. With commentary by S. H. White, D. Klahr, & S. M. Carver, and a reply by D. Kuhn. *Monographs of the Society for Research in Child Development, 60,* 122–137.

Kunkel, D., Wilcox, B. L., Cantor, J., Palmer, E., Linn, S., & Dowrick, P. (2004, February 20). *Report of the APA task force on advertising and children.* Washington, DC: American Psychological Association.

Kunzmann, U., & Baltes, P. (2005). *The psychology of wisdom: Theoretical and empirical challenges.* New York: Cambridge University Press.

Kupersmidt, J. B., & Dodge, K. A. (Eds.). (2004). *Children's peer relations: From development to intervention.* Washington, DC: American Psychological Association.

Kupper, N., Denollet, J., Widdershoven, J., & Kop, W. J. (2013). Type D personality is associated with low cardiovascular reactivity to acute mental stress in heart failure patients. *International Journal of Psychophysiology.* Accessed online, June 11, 2013, http://www.ncbi.nlm.nih.gov/pubmed/23361112

Kurdek, L. A. (1993). The allocation of household labor in gay, lesbian, and heterosexual married children. *Journal of Social Issues, 49,* 127–139.

Kurdek, L. A. (2003). Negative representations of the self/spouse and marital distress. *Personal Relationships, 10,* 511–534.

Kurdek, L. A. (2006, May). Differences between partners from heterosexual, gay, and lesbian cohabiting couples. *Journal of Marriage and Family, 68,* 509–528.

Kurdek, L. A. (2008). Change in relationship quality for partners from lesbian, gay male, and heterosexual couples. *Journal of Family Psychology, 22,* 701–711.

Kurtines, W. M., & Gewirtz, J. L. (1987). *Moral development through social interaction.* New York: Wiley.

Kwant, P. B., Finocchiaro, T., Forster, F., Reul, H., Rau, G., Morshuis, M., et al. (2007). The MiniACcor: Constructive redesign of an implantable total artificial heart, initial laboratory testing and further steps. *International Journal of Artificial Organs, 30,* 345–351.

Laas, I. (2006). Self-actualization and society: A new application for an old theory. *Journal of Humanistic Psychology, 46,* 77–91.

Labouvie-Vief, G. (1990). Modes of knowledge and the organization of development. In M. L. Commons, C. Armon, L. Kohlberg, F. A. Richards, T. A. Grotzer, & J. Sinnott (Eds.), *Adult development (Vol. 2). Models and methods in the study of adolescent thought.* New York: Praeger.

Labouvie-Vief, G. (2006). Emerging structures of adult thought. In J. J. Arnett & J. L. Tanner (Eds.), *Emerging adults in America: Coming of age in the 21st century.* Washington, DC: American Psychological Association.

Lacerda, F., von Hofsten, C., & Heimann, M. (2001). *Emerging cognitive abilities in early infancy.* Mahwah, NJ: Lawrence Erlbaum.

Lachmann, T., Berti, S., Kujala, T., & Schroger, E. (2005). Diagnostic subgroups of developmental dyslexia have different deficits in neural processing of tones and phonemes. *International Journal of Psychophysiology, 56,* 105–120.

Lackey, C. (2003). Violent family heritage, the transition to adulthood, and later partner violence. *Journal of Family Issues, 24,* 74–98.

LaCoursiere, D., Hirst, K. P., & Barrett-Connor, E. (2012). Depression and pregnancy stressors affect the association between abuse and postpartum depression. *Maternal and Child Health Journal, 16,* 929–935.

Ladd, G. W. (1983). Social networks of popular, average and rejected children in social settings. *Merrill-Palmer Quarterly, 29,* 282–307.

Laflamme, D., Pomerleau, A., & Malcuit, G. (2002). A comparison of fathers' and mothers' involvement in childcare and stimulation behaviors during free-play with their infants at 9 and 15 months. *Sex Roles, 47,* 507–518.

LaFromboise, T., Coleman, H. L., & Gerton, J. (1993). Psychological impact of biculturalism: Evidence and theory. *Psychological Bulletin, 114,* 395–412.

Lafuente, M. J., Grifol, R., Segarra, J., & Soriano, J. (1997). Effects of the Firstart method of prenatal stimulation on psychomotor development: The first six months. *Pre- & PeriNatal Psychology, 11,* 151–162.

Lahiri, D. K., Maloney, B., Basha, M. R., Ge, Y. W., & Zawia, N. H. (2007). How and when environmental agents and dietary factors affect the course of Alzheimer's disease: The "LEARn" model (latent early-life associated regulation) may explain the triggering of AD. *Current Alzheimer Research, 4,* 219–228.

Lain, D. (2012). Working past 65 in the UK and the USA: Segregation into 'Lopaq' occupations? *Work, Employment and Society, 26,* 78–94.

Lam, V., & Leman, P. (2003). The influence of gender and ethnicity on children's inferences about toy choice. *Social Development, 12,* 269–287.

Lamaze, F. (1970). *Painless childbirth: The Lamaze method.* Chicago: Regnery.

Lamb, M. E., Sternberg, K. J., Hwang, C. P., & Broberg, A. G. (Eds.). (1992). *Child care in context: Cross-cultural perspectives.* Hillsdale, NJ: Erlbaum.

Lambiase, A., Aloe, L., Centofanti, M., Parisi, V., Mantelli, F., Colafrancesco, V., et al. (2009). Experimental and clinical evidence of neuroprotection by nerve growth factor eye drops: Implications for glaucoma. *Proceedings of the National Academy of Sciences of the United States of America, 106,* 13469–13474.

Lambrinoudaki, I., & Pérez-Ló, F. R. (2013). Hormone therapy and the prevention of cardiovascular disease and cognitive decline: Where do we stand? *Maturitas, 74,* 107–108.

Lamm, B., & Keller, H. (2007). Understanding cultural models of parenting: The role of intracultural variation and response style. *Journal of Cross-Cultural Psychology, 38,* 50–57.

Lamm, H., & Wiesmann, U. (1997). Subjective attributes of attraction: How people characterize their liking, their love, and their being in love. *Personal Relationships, 4,* 271–284.

Lamont, J. A. (1997). Sexuality. In D. E. Stewart & G. E. Robinson (Eds.), *A clinician's guide to menopause. Clinical practice.* Washington, DC: Health Press International.

Lamorey, S., Robinson, B. E., & Rowland, B. H. (1998). *Latchkey kids: Unlocking doors for children and their families.* Newbury Park, CA: Sage Publications.

Landhuis, C., Poulton, R., Welch, D., & Hancox, R. (2008). Programming obesity and poor fitness: The long-term impact of childhood television. *Obesity, 16,* 1457–1459.

Landis, M., Peter-Wight, M., Martin, M., & Bodenmann, G. (2013). Dyadic coping and marital satisfaction of older spouses in long-term marriage. *Geropsych: The Journal of Gerontopsychology and Geriatric Psychiatry, 26,* 39–47.

Landy, F., & Conte, J. M. (2004). *Work in the 21st century.* New York: McGraw-Hill.

Lane, J. D., Wellman, H. M., Olson, S. L., Miller, A. L., Wang, L., & Tardif, T. (2013). Relations between temperament and theory of mind development in the United States and China: Biological and behavioral correlates of preschoolers' false-belief understanding. *Developmental Psychology, 49,* 825–836.

Lane, K. A., Goh, J. X., & Driver-Linn, E. (2012). Implicit science stereotypes mediate the relationship between gender and academic participation. *Sex Roles, 66,* 220–234.

Langille, D. (2007). Teenage pregnancy: Trends, contributing factors and the physician's role. *Canadian Medical Association Journal, 176,* 1601–1602.

Lansford, J. (2009). Parental divorce and children's adjustment. *Perspectives on Psychological Science, 4,* 140–152.

Lansford, J. E., Chang, L., Dodge, K. A., Malone, P. S., Oburu, P., Palmérus, K., et al. (2005). Physical discipline and children's adjustment: Cultural normativeness as a moderator. *Child Development, 76,* 1234–1246.

Lansford, J. E., & Parker, J. G. (1999). Children's interactions in triads: Behavioral profiles and effects of gender and patterns of friendships among members. *Developmental Psychology, 35,* 80–93.

Larsen, K. E., O'Hara, M. W., & Brewer, K. K. (2001). A prospective study of self-efficacy expectancies and labor pain. *Journal of Reproductive and Infant Psychology, 19,* 203–214.

Larson, R. W., Richards, M. H., Moneta, G., Holmbeck, G., & Duckett, E. (1996). Changes in adolescents' daily interactions with their families from ages 10 to 18: Disengagement and transformation. *Developmental Psychology, 32,* 744–754.

Laska, M. N., Murray, D. M., Lytle, L. A., & Harnack, L. J. (2012). Longitudinal associations between key dietary behaviors and weight gain over time: Transitions through the adolescent years. *Obesity, 20,* 118–125.

Lassonde, K. A., Surla, C., Buchanan, J. A., & O'Brien, E. J. (2012). Using the contradiction paradigm to assess ageism. *Journal of Aging Studies, 26*(2), 174–181. doi:10.1016/j.jaging.2011.12.002

Lau, I., Lee, S., & Chiu, C. (2004). Language, cognition, and reality: Constructing shared meanings through communication. In M. Schaller & C. Crandall (Eds.), *The psychological foundations of culture.* Mahwah, NJ: Lawrence Erlbaum.

Lau, M., Markham, C., Lin, H., Flores, G., & Chacko, M. (2009). Dating and sexual attitudes in Asian-American adolescents. *Journal of Adolescent Research, 24,* 91–113.

Lauer, J. C., & Lauer, R. H. (1999). *How to survive and thrive in an empty nest.* Oakland, CA: New Harbinger Publications.

Laumann, E. O., Paik, A., & Rosen, R. C. (1999). Sexual dysfunction in the United States: Prevalence and predictors. *JAMA: The Journal of the American Medical Association, 281,* 537–544.

Lauter, J. L. (1998). Neuroimaging and the trimodal brain: Applications for developmental communication neuroscience. *Phoniatrica et Logopaedica, 50,* 118–145.

Lavers-Preston, C., & Sonuga-Barke, E. (2003). An intergenerational perspective on parent-child relationships: The reciprocal effects of tri-generational grandparent–parent–child relationships. In R. Gupta & D. Parry-Gupta (Eds.), *Children and parents: Clinical issues for psychologists and psychiatrists.* London: Whurr Publishers, Ltd.

Lavezzi, A. M., Corna, M. F., & Matturri, L. (2013). Neuronal nuclear antigen (NeuN): A useful marker of neuronal immaturity in sudden unexplained perinatal death. *Journal of the Neurological Sciences, 329,* 45–50.

Law, D. M., Shapka, J. D., Hymel, S., Olson, B. F., & Waterhouse, T. (2012). The changing face of bullying: An empirical comparison between traditional and internet bullying and victimization. *Computers in Human Behavior, 28,* 226–232.

Lawrence, E., Rothman, A., Cobb, R., Rothman, M., & Bradbury, T. (2008). Marital satisfaction across the transition to parenthood. *Journal of Family Psychology, 22,* 41–50.

Lazarus, R. S. (1968). Emotions and adaptations: Conceptual and empirical relations. In W. Arnold (Ed.), *Nebraska symposium on motivation.* Lincoln: University of Nebraska.

Lazarus, R. S. (1991). *Emotion and adaptation.* New York: Oxford University Press.

Lazarus, R. S., & Folkman, S. (1984). *Stress, appraisal, and coping.* New York: Springer.

Le, H., Oh, I., Shaffer, J., & Schmidt, F. (2010). Implications of methodological advances for the practice of personnel selection: How practitioners benefit from meta-analysis. In *Readings in organizational behavior.* New York: Routledge/Taylor & Francis.

Leach, P., Barnes, J., Malmberg, L., Sylva, K., & Stein, A. (2008). The quality of different types of child care at 10 and 18 months: A comparison between types and factors related to quality. *Early Child Development and Care, 178,* 177–209.

Leaper, C. (2002). Parenting girls and boys. In M. Bornstein (Ed.), *Handbook of parenting: Vol. 1: Children and parenting.* Mahwah, NJ: Lawrence Erlbaum.

Leathers, H. D., & Foster, P. (2004). *The world food problem: Tackling causes of undernutrition in the third world.* Boulder, CO: Lynne Rienner Publishers.

Leathers, S., & Kelley, M. (2000). Unintended pregnancy and depressive symptoms among first-time mothers and fathers. *American Journal of Orthopsychiatry, 70,* 523–531.

Leavitt, L. A., & Goldson, E. (1996). Introduction to special section: Biomedicine and developmental psychology: New areas of common ground. *Developmental Psychology, 32,* 387–389.

Le Corre, M., & Carey, S. (2007). One, two, three, four, nothing more: An investigation of the conceptual sources of the verbal counting principles. *Cognition, 105,* 395–438.

Lecours, A. R. (1982). Correlates of developmental behavior in brain maturation. In T. Bever (Ed.), *Regressions in mental development.* Hillsdale, NJ: Lawrence Erlbaum.

Lee, B. H., Schofer, J. L., & Koppelman, F. S. (2005). Bicycle safety helmet legislation and bicycle-related non-fatal injuries in California. *Accidental Analysis and Prevention, 37,* 93–102.

Lee, C. (2010). Gender, health, and health behaviors. In *Handbook of gender research in psychology, Vol. 2: Gender research in social and applied psychology.* New York: Springer Publishing Co.

Lee, C. C., Czaja, S. J., & Sharit, J. (2009). Training older workers for technology-based employment. *Educational Gerontology, 35,* 15–31.

Lee, M. (2008). Caregiver stress and elder abuse among Korean family caregivers of older adults with disabilities. *Journal of Family Violence, 23,* 707–712.

Lee, M., Vernon-Feagans, L., & Vazquez, A. (2003). The influence of family environment and child temperament on work/family role strain for mothers and fathers. *Infant & Child Development, 12,* 421–439.

Lee, R. M. (2005). Resilience against discrimination: Ethnic identity and other-group orientation as protective factors for Korean Americans. *Journal of Counseling Psychology, 52,* 36–44.

Lee, S., Olszewski-Kubilius, P., & Thomson, D. (2012). Academically gifted students' perceived interpersonal competence and peer relationships. *Gifted Child Quarterly, 56,* 90–104.

Leenaars, A. A., & Shneidman, E. S. (Eds.). (1999). *Lives and deaths: Selections from the works of Edwin S. Shneidman.* New York: Bruuner-Routledge.

Leen-Feldmer, E. W., Reardon, L. E., Hayward, C., & Smith, R. C. (2008). The relation between puberty and adolescent anxiety: Theory and evidence. In M. J. Zvolensky & J. A. Smits (Eds.), *Anxiety in health behaviors and physical illness.* New York: Springer Science + Business Media.

Lefkowitz, E. S., Sigman, M., & Kit-fong Au, T. (2000). Helping mothers discuss sexuality and AIDS with adolescents. *Child Development, 71,* 1383–1394.

Legerstee, M., & Markova, G. (2008). Variations in 10-month-old infant imitation of people and things. *Infant Behavior & Development, 31,* 81–91.

Lehman, D., Chiu, C., & Schaller, M. (2004). Psychology and culture. *Annual Review of Psychology, 55,* 689–714.

Lehr, U., Seiler, E., & Thomae, H. (2000). Aging in a cross-cultural perspective. In A. L. Comunian & U. P. Gielen (Eds.), *International perspectives on human development.* Lengerich, Germany: Pabst Science Publishers.

Leis-Newman, E. (2012, June). Miscarriage and loss. *Monitor on Psychology,* pp. 57–59.

Lemery-Chalfant, K., Kao, K., Swann, G., & Goldsmith, H. (2013). Childhood temperament: Passive gene-environment correlation, gene-environment interaction, and the hidden importance of the family environment. *Development and Psychopathology, 25,* 51–63.

Lemonick, M. D. (2000, October 30). Teens before their time. *Time,* pp. 68–74.

Lenhart, A. (2010, April 20). *Teens, cell phones, and texting.* Washington, DC: Pew Research Center.

Lerner, J. W. (2002). *Learning disabilities: Theories, diagnosis, and teaching strategies.* Boston: Houghton Mifflin.

Lerner, R. M., Fisher, C. B., & Weinberg, R. A. (2000). Toward a science for and of the people: Promoting civil society through the application of developmental science. *Child Development, 71,* 11–20.

Lerner, R. M., Theokas, C., & Jelicic, H. (2005). Youth as active agents in their own positive development: A developmental systems perspective. In W. Greve, K. Rothermund, & D. Wentura (Eds.), *Adaptive self: Personal continuity and intentional self-development.* Ashland, OH: Hogrefe & Huber.

Lesner, S. (2003). Candidacy and management of assistive listening devices: Special needs of the elderly. *International Journal of Audiology, 42,* 2S68–2S76.

Leung, C., Pe-Pua, R., & Karnilowicz, W. (2006, January). Psychological adaptation and autonomy among adolescents in Australia: A comparison of Anglo-Celtic and three Asian groups. *International Journal of Intercultural Relations, 30,* 99–118.

LeVay, S., & Valente, S. M. (2003). *Human sexuality.* Sunderland, MA: Sinauer Associates.

Levenson, R. W., Carstensen, L. L., & Gottman, J. M. (1993). Long-term marriage: Age, gender, and satisfaction. *Psychology and Aging, 8,* 301–313.

Leverone, D., & Epstein, B. (2010). Nonpharmacological interventions for the treatment of rheumatoid arthritis: A focus on mind-body medicine. *Journal of Pharmacy Practice, 23,* 101–109.

Leversen, J. R., Hopkins, B., & Sigmundsson, H. (2013). Ageing and driving: Examining the effects of visual processing demands. *Transportation Research Part F: Traffic Psychology and Behaviour, 17,* 1–4.

Levin, R. J. (2007). Sexual activity, health and well-being—the beneficial roles of coitus and masturbation. *Sexual and Relationship Therapy, 22,* 135–148.

Levin, S., Matthews, M., Guimond, S., Sidanius, J., Pratto, F., Kteily, N., et al. (2012). Assimilation, multiculturalism, and colorblindness: Mediated and moderated relationships between social dominance orientation and prejudice. *Journal of Experimental Social Psychology, 48,* 207–212.

Levine, R. (1997a). *A geography of time: The temporal misadventures of a social psychologist, or how every culture keeps time just a little bit differently.* New York: HarperCollins.

Levine, R. (1997b, November). The pace of life in 31 countries. *American Demographics,* pp. 20–29.

Levine, R. V. (1993, February). Is love a luxury? *American Demographics,* 29–37.

Levine, S. C., Huttenlocher, J., Taylor, A., & Langrock, A. (1999). Early sex differences in spatial skill. *Developmental Psychology, 35,* 940–949.

Levinson, D. (1992). *The seasons of a woman's life.* New York: Knopf.

Levinson, D. J. (1986). A conception of adult development. *American Psychologist, 41,* 3–13.

Levy, B. (2009). Stereotype embodiment: A psychosocial approach to aging. *Current Directions in Psychological Science, 18,* 332–336.

Levy, B. L., & Langer, E. (1994). Aging free from negative stereotypes: Successful memory in China and among the American deaf. *Journal of Personality and Social Psychology, 66,* 989–997.

Levy, B. R. (2003). Mind matters: Cognitive and physical effects of aging self-stereotypes. *Journal of Gerontology: Series B: Psychological Sciences and Social Sciences, 58B,* P203–P211.

Levy, B. R., Slade, M. D., & Kasl, S. V. (2002). Longitudinal benefit of positive self-perceptions of aging on functioning health. *Journal of Gerontology: Psychological Sciences, 57,* 166–195.

Levy-Shiff, R. (1994). Individual and contextual correlates of marital change across the transition to parenthood. *Developmental Psychology, 30,* 591–601.

Lewis, B., Legato, M., & Fisch, H. (2006). Medical implications of the male biological clock. *JAMA: The Journal of the American Medical Association, 296,* 2369–2371.

Lewis, J., & Elman, J. (2008). Growth-related neural reorganization and the autism phenotype: A test of the hypothesis that altered brain growth leads to altered connectivity. *Developmental Science, 11,* 135–155.

Lewis, R., Freneau, P., & Roberts, C. (1979). Fathers and the postparental transition. *Family Coordinator, 28,* 514–520.

Lewis, V. (2009). Undertreatment of menopausal symptoms and novel options for comprehensive management. *Current Medical Research Opinion, 25,* 2689–2698.

Lewkowicz, D. (2002). Heterogeneity and heterochrony in the development of intersensory perception. *Cognitive Brain Research, 14,* 41–63.

Leyens, J. P., Camino, L., Parke, R. D., & Berkowitz, L. (1975). Effects of movie violence on aggression in a field setting as a function of group dominance and cohesion. *Journal of Personality and Social Psychology, 32,* 346–360.

Li, Q. (2006). Cyberbullying in schools: A research of gender differences. *School Psychology International, 27,* 157–170.

Li, Q. (2007). New bottle but old wine: A research of cyberbullying in schools. *Computers in Human Behavior, 23,* 1777–1791.

Li, S. (2003). Biocultural orchestration of developmental plasticity across levels: The interplay of biology and culture in shaping the mind and behavior across the life span. *Psychological Bulletin, 129,* 171–194.

Li, S. (2012). Neuromodulation of behavioral and cognitive development across the life span. *Developmental Psychology, 48,* 810–814.

Li, G. R., & Zhu, X. D. (2007). Development of the functionally total artificial heart using an artery pump. *ASAIO Journal, 53,* 288–291.

Li, N. P., Bailey, J. M., Kenrick, D. T., & Linsenmeier, J. A. W. (2002). The necessities and luxuries of mate preferences: Testing the tradeoffs. *Journal of Personality and Social Psychology, 82,* 947–955.

Li, Y., & Wright, M. F. (2013). *Adolescents' social status goals: Relationships to social status insecurity, aggression, and prosocial behavior.* Accessed online, June 6, 2013, http://link.springer.com/article/10.1007/s10964-013-9939-z#page-1

Liang, J., & Luo, B. (2012). Toward a discourse shift in social gerontology: From successful aging to harmonious aging. *Journal of Aging Studies, 26,* 327–334.

Libert, S., Zwiener, J., Chu, X., Vanvoorhies, W., Roman, G., & Pletcher, S. D. (2007, February 23). Regulation of Drosophila life span by olfaction and food-derived odors. *Science, 315,* 1133–1137.

Lickliter, R., & Bahrick, L. E. (2000). The development of infant intersensory perception: Advantages of a comparative convergent-operations approach. *Psychological Bulletin, 126,* 260–280.

Lidz, J., & Gleitman, L. R. (2004). Yes, we still need Universal Grammar: Reply. *Cognition, 94,* 85–93.

Liechty, J. (2010). Body image distortion and three types of weight loss behaviors among nonoverweight girls in the United States. *Journal of Adolescent Health, 47,* 176–182.

Lieven, E., & Stoll, S. (2010). Language. In M. H. Bornstein (Ed.), *Handbook of cultural developmental science.* New York: Psychology Press.

Light, L. L. (2000). Memory changes in adulthood. In S. H. Qualls & N. Abeles et al. (Eds.), *Psychology and the aging revolution: How we adapt to longer life.* Washington, DC: American Psychological Association.

Lin, C., Chiu, H., & Yeh, C. (2012). Impact of socioeconomic backgrounds, experiences of being disciplined in early childhood, and parenting value on parenting styles of preschool children's parents. *Chinese Journal of Guidance and Counseling, 32,* 123–149.

Lindau, S., Schumm, L., Laumann, E., Levinson, W., O'Muircheartaigh, C., & Waite, L. (2007). A study of sexuality and health among older adults in the United States. *The New England Journal of Medicine, 357,* 762–775.

Lindemann, B. T., & Kadue, D. D. (2003). *Age discrimination in employment law.* Washington, DC: BNA Books.

Lindsay, G. (2007). Educational psychology and the effectiveness of inclusive education/mainstreaming. *British Journal of Educational Psychology, 77,* 1–24.

Lindsey, E., & Colwell, M. (2003). Preschoolers' emotional competence: Links to pretend and physical play. *Child Study Journal, 33,* 39–52.

Lindstrom, H., Fritsch, T., Petot, G., Smyth, K., Chen, C., Debanne, S., et al. (2005, July). The relationships between television viewing in midlife and the development of Alzheimer's disease in a case-control study. *Brain and Cognition, 58,* 157–165.

Ling, R., Bertel, T., & Sundsoy, P. (2012). The socio-demographics of texting: An analysis of traffic data. *New Media & Society, 14,* 281–298.

Linn, R. L. (2008). Toward a more effective definition of Adequate Yearly Progress. In G. L. Sunderman (Ed.), *Holding NCLB accountable: Achieving accountability, equity, and school reform.* Thousand Oaks, CA: Corwin.

Lino, M., & Carlson, A. (Eds.). (2009). *Expenditures on Children by Families, 2008* (Miscellaneous Publication No. 1528-2008). Washington, DC: U.S. Department of Agriculture.

Liou, Y., Liou, T., & Chang, L. (2010). Obesity among adolescents: Sedentary leisure time and sleeping as determinants. *Journal of Advanced Nursing, 66,* 1246–1256.

Lipsitt, L. P. (1986). Toward understanding the hedonic nature of infancy. In L. P. Lipsitt & J. H. Cantor (Eds.), *Experimental child psychologist: Essays and experiments in honor of Charles C. Spiker.* Hillsdale, NJ: Lawrence Erlbaum.

Lipsitt, L. (2003). Crib death: A biobehavioral phenomenon? *Current Directions in Psychological Science, 12,* 164–170.

Lipsitt, L. P., & Rovee-Collier, C. (2012). The psychophysics of olfaction in the human newborn: Habituation and cross-adaptation. In G. M. Zucco, R. S. Herz, & B. Schaal (Eds.), *Olfactory cognition: From perception and memory to environmental odours and neuroscience.* Amsterdam, Netherlands: John Benjamins Publishing Company.

Lipsitt, L. R., & Demick, J. (2012). Theory and measurement of resilience: Views from development. In M. Ungar (Ed.), *The social ecology of resilience: A handbook of theory and practice.* New York: Springer Science + Business Media.

Lisabeth, L., & Bushnell, C. (2012). Stroke risk in women: The role of menopause and hormone therapy. *The Lancet Neurology, 11,* 82–91.

Litzinger, S., & Gordon, K. (2005, October). Exploring relationships among communication, sexual satisfaction, and marital satisfaction. *Journal of Sex & Marital Therapy, 31,* 409–424.

Liu, H., Elliott, S., & Umberson, D. J. (2010). Marriage in young adulthood. In Jon E. Grant & Marc N. Potenza (Eds.), *Young adult mental heath.* New York: Oxford University Press.

Liu, N., Liang, Z., Li, Z., Yan, J., & Guo, W. (2012). Chronic stress on IL-2, IL-4, IL-18 content in SD rats. *Chinese Journal of Clinical Psychology, 20,* 35–36.

Livingstone, S., & Helsper, E. J. (2013). Children, internet and risk in comparative perspective. *Journal of Children and Media, 7,* 1–8.

Lloyd, K. K. (2012). Health-related quality of life and children's happiness with their childcare. *Child: Care, Health and Development, 38,* 244–250.

Lobo, R. A. (2009). The risk of stroke in postmenopausal women receiving hormonal therapy. *Climacteric, 12*(Suppl. 1), 81–85

Lock, R. D. (1992). *Taking charge of your career direction* (2nd ed.). Pacific Grove, CA: Brooks/Cole.

Loeb, S., Fuller, B., Kagan, S. L., & Carrol, B. (2004). Child care in poor communities: Early learning effects of type, quality and stability. *Child Development, 75,* 47–65.

Loehlin, J. C., Neiderhiser, J. M., & Reiss, D. (2005). Genetic and environmental components of adolescent adjustment and parental behavior: A multivariate analysis. *Child Development, 76,* 1104–1115.

Loessl, B., Valerius, G., Kopasz, M., Hornyak, M., Riemann, D., & Voderholzer, U. (2008). Are adolescents chronically sleep-deprived? An investigation of sleep habits of adolescents in the southwest of Germany. *Child: Care, Health and Development, 34,* 549–556.

Loewen, S. (2006). Exceptional intellectual performance: A neo-Piagetian perspective. *High Ability Studies, 17,* 159–181.

Logsdon, R., McCurry, S., Pike, K., & Teri, L. (2009). Making physical activity accessible to older adults with memory loss: A feasibility study. *The Gerontologist, 49*(Suppl. 1), S94–S99.

Lohman, D. (2005). Reasoning abilities. In R. J. Sternberg & J. E. Pretz (Eds.), *Cognition and intelligence: Identifying the mechanisms of the mind.* New York: Cambridge University Press.

Lonetto, R. (1980). *Children's conception of death.* New York: Springer.

Long, B. L., Gillespie, A. I., & Tanaka, M. L. (2012). Mathematical model to predict drivers' reaction speeds. *Journal of Applied Biomechanics, 28,* 48–56.

Lorenz, K. (1966). *On aggression.* New York: Harcourt Brace Jovanovich.

Lorenz, K. (1974). *Civilized man's eight deadly sins*. New York: Harcourt Brace Jovanovich.

Losonczy-Marshall, M. (2008). Gender differences in latency and duration of emotional expression in 7- through 13-month-old infants. *Social Behavior and Personality, 36,* 267–274.

Lourenco, F., & Casey, B. J. (2013). Adjusting behavior to changing environmental demands with development. *Neuroscience and Biobehavioral Reviews*. Accessed online, June 4, 2013, http://www.ncbi.nlm.nih.gov/pubmed/23518271

Lourenco, O., & Machado, A. (1996). In defense of Piaget's theory: A reply to 10 common criticisms. *Psychological Review, 103,* 143–164.

Love, A., & Burns, M. S. (2006). 'It's a hurricane! it's a hurricane!': Can music facilitate social constructive and sociodramatic play in a preschool classroom? *Journal of Genetic Psychology, 167,* 383–391.

Love, J. M., Harrison, L., Sagi-Schwartz, A., van Ijzendoorn, M. H., Ross, C., Ungerer, J. A., et al. (2003). Child care quality matters: How conclusions may vary with context. *Child Development, 74,* 1021–1033.

Lovrin, M. (2009). Treatment of major depression in adolescents: Weighing the evidence of risk and benefit in light of black box warnings. *Journal of Child and Adolescent Psychiatric Nursing, 22,* 63–68.

Low, J., & Perner, J. (2012). Implicit and explicit theory of mind: State of the art. *British Journal of Developmental Psychology, 30,* 1–13.

Lowenstein, J., Blank, H., & Sauer, J. (2010). Uniforms affect the accuracy of children's eyewitness identification decisions. *Journal of Investigative Psychology and Offender Profiling, 7,* 59–73.

Lowrey, G. H. (1986). *Growth and development of children* (8th ed.). Chicago: Year Book Medical Publishers.

Lu, L. (2006). The transition to parenthood: Stress, resources, and gender differences in a Chinese society. *Journal of Community Psychology, 34,* 471–488.

Lubinski, D. (2004). Introduction to the special section on cognitive abilities: 100 years after Spearman's (1904) "'General intelligence,' objectively determined and measured." *Journal of Personality and Social Psychology, 86,* 96–111.

Lucas, R. E. (2005). Time does not heal all wounds: A longitudinal study of reaction and adaptation to divorce. *Psychological Science, 16,* 945–951.

Lucas, S. R., & Berends, M. (2002). Sociodemographic diversity, correlated achievement, and de facto tracking. *Sociology of Education, 75,* 328–349.

Lucassen, A. (2012). Ethical implications of new genetic technologies. *Developmental Medicine & Child Neurology, 54,* 124–130.

Ludden, J. (2012, February 6). Helicopter parents hover in the workplace. *All things considered. National Public Radio.*

Ludlow, V., Newhook, L., Newhook, J., Bonia, K., Goodridge, J., & Twells, L. (2012). How formula feeding mothers balance risks and define themselves as 'good mothers'. *Health, Risk & Society, 14,* 291–306.

Luhmann, M., Lucas, R. E., Eid, M., & Diener, E. (2013). The prospective effect of life satisfaction on life events. *Social Psychological and Personality Science, 4,* 39–45.

Luke, B., & Brown, M. B. (2008). Maternal morbidity and infant death in twin vs triplet and quadruplet pregnancies. *American Journal of Obstetrics and Gynecology, 198,* 1–10.

Luke, M. A., Sedikides, C., & Carmelley, K. (2012). Your love lifts me higher! the energizing quality of secure relationships. *Personality and Social Psychology Bulletin, 38,* 721–735.

Lundberg, I., & Reichenberg, M. (2013). Developing reading comprehension among students with mild intellectual disabilities: An intervention study. *Scandinavian Journal of Educational Research, 57,* 89–100.

Lundblad, B., Hellström, A., & Berg, M. (2010). Children's experiences of attitudes and rules for going to the toilet in school. *Scandinavian Journal of Caring Sciences, 24,* 219–223.

Luo, L., & Craik, F. (2008). Aging and memory: A cognitive approach. *The Canadian Journal of Psychiatry/La Revue canadienne de psychiatrie, 53,* 346–353.

Luo, L., & Craik, F. (2009). Age differences in recollection: Specificity effects at retrieval. *Journal of Memory and Language, 60,* 421–436.

Luo, C., Zhang, J., & Pan, J. (2013). One-year course and effects of insomnia in rural Chinese adolescents. *Sleep: Journal of Sleep and Sleep Disorders Research, 36,* 377–384.

Lyall, S. (2004, February 15). In Europe, lovers now propose: Marry me, a little. *The New York Times*, p. D2.

Lye, T. C., Piguet, O., Grayson, D. A., Creasey, H., Ridley, L. J., Bennett, H. P., et al. (2004). Hippocampal size and memory function in the ninth and tenth decades of life: The Sydney Older Persons Study. *Journal of Neurology, Neurosurgery, and Psychiatry, 75,* 548–554.

Lynch, M. E., Coles, C. D., & Corely, T. (2003). Examining delinquency in adolescents: Risk factors. *Journal of Studies on Alcohol, 64,* 678–686.

Lynn, R. (2009). What has caused the Flynn effect? Secular increases in the Development Quotients of infants. *Intelligence, 37,* 16–24.

Lynne, S., Graber, J., Nichols, T., Brooks-Gunn, J., & Botvin, G. (2007, February). Links between pubertal timing, peer influences, and externalizing behaviors among urban students followed through middle school. *Journal of Adolescent Health, 40,* 35–44.

Lyon, G. J. (2012). Bring clinical standards to human-genetics research. *Nature, 482,* 300–301.

Lyon, M. E., Benoit, M., O'Donnell, R. M., Getson, P. R., Silber, T., & Walsh, T. (2000). Assessing African American adolescents' risk for suicide attempts: Attachment theory. *Adolescence, 35,* 121–134.

Mabbott, D. J., Noseworthy, M., Bouffet, E., Laughlin, S., & Rockel, C. (2006). White matter growth as a mechanism of cognitive development in children. *Neuroimaging, 15,* 936–946.

MacCann, C. (2010). Further examination of emotional intelligence as a standard intelligence: A latent variable analysis of fluid intelligence, crystallized intelligence, and emotional intelligence. *Personality and Individual Differences, 49,* 490–496.

Macchi Cassia, V., Picozzi, M., Girelli, L., & de Hevia, M. (2012). Increasing magnitude counts more: Asymmetrical processing of ordinality in 4-month-old infants. *Cognition, 124,* 183–193.

Maccoby, E. E., & Lewis, C. C. (2003). Less day care or different day care? *Child Development, 74,* 1069–1075.

Maccoby, E. E., & Martin, J. A. (1983). Socialization in the context of the family: Parent-child interaction. In P. H. Mussen (Ed.) & E. M. Hetherington (Vol. Ed.), *Handbook of child psychology: Vol. 4. Socialization, personality, and social development* (4th ed.). New York: Wiley.

MacDonald, W. (2003). The impact of job demands and workload stress and fatigue. *Australian Psychologist, 38,* 102–117.

MacDorman, M. F., Declercq, E., Menacker, F., & Malloy, M. (2008). Neonatal mortality for primary cesarean and vaginal births to low-risk women: Application of an 'intention-to-treat' model. *Birth: Issues in Perinatal Care, 35,* 3–8.

MacDorman, M. F., Martin, J. A., Mathews, T. J., Hoyert, D. L., & Ventura, S. J. (2005). Explaining the 2001-02 infant mortality increase: Data from the linked birth/infant death data set. *National Vital Statistics Report, 53,* 1–22.

Maciejewski, P. K., Zhang, B., Block, S. D., & Prigerson, H. G. (2007). An empirical examination of the stage theory of grief. *JAMA: Journal of the American Medical Association, 297,* 716–723.

Macionis, J. J. (2001). *Sociology*. Upper Saddle River, NJ: Prentice Hall.

MacWhinney, B. (1991). Connectionism as a framework for language acquisition. In J. Miller (Ed.), *Research on child language disorders*. Austin, TX: Pro-ed.

Maddi, S. R., Harvey, R. H., Khoshaba, D. M., Lu, J. L., Persico, M., & Brow, M. (2006). The personality construct of hardiness, III: Relationships with repression, innovativeness, authoritarianism, and performance. *Journal of Personality, 74,* 575–598.

Madsen, P. B., & Green, R. (2012). Gay adolescent males' effective coping with discrimination: A qualitative study. *Journal of LGBT Issues in Counseling, 6,* 139–155.

Maes, S. J., De Mol, J., & Buysse, A. (2012). Children's experiences and meaning construction on parental divorce: A focus group study. *Childhood: A Global Journal of Child Research, 19,* 266–279.

Magai, C., & McFadden, S. H. (Eds.). (1996). *Handbook of emotion, adult development, and aging*. New York: Academic Press.

Mahn, H., & John-Steiner, V. (2013). Vygotsky and sociocultural approaches to teaching and learning. In W. M. Reynolds, G. E. Miller, & I. B. Weiner (Eds.), *Handbook of psychology, Vol. 7: Educational psychology* (2nd ed.). Hoboken, NJ: John Wiley & Sons Inc.

Mäkinen, M., Puukko-Viertomies, L., Lindberg, N., Siimes, M. A., & Aalberg, V. (2012). Body dissatisfaction and body mass in girls and boys transitioning from early to mid-adolescence: Additional role of self-esteem and eating habits. *BMC Psychiatry, 12,* 123–131.

Makino, M., Hashizume, M., Tsuboi, K., Yasushi, M., & Dennerstein, L. (2006, September). Comparative study of attitudes to eating between male and female students in the people's Republic of China. *Eating and Weight Disorders, 11,* 111–117.

Makishita, H., & Matsunaga, K. (2008). Differences of drivers' reaction times according to age and mental workload. *Accident Analysis & Prevention, 40,* 567–575.

Malchiodi, C. A. (2012). Humanistic approaches. In C. A. Malchiodi (Ed.), *Handbook of art therapy* (2nd ed.). New York: Guilford Press.

Maller, S. (2003). Best practices in detecting bias in nonverbal tests. In R. McCallum (Ed.), *Handbook of nonverbal assessment*. New York: Kluwer Academic/Plenum Publishers.

Mancini, A. D., & Bonanno, G. A. (2012). Differential pathways to resilience after loss and trauma. In R. A. McMackin, E. Newman, J. M. Fogler, & T. M. Keane (Eds.), *Trauma therapy in context: The science and craft of evidence-based practice*. Washington, DC: American Psychological Association.

Mangan, P. A. (1997, November). *Time perception*. Paper presented at the annual meeting of the Society for Neuroscience, New Orleans.

Mangiatordi, A. (2012). Inclusion of mobility-impaired children in the one-to-one computing era: A case study. *Mind, Brain, and Education, 6,* 54–62.

Mangweth, B., Hausmann, A., & Walch, T. (2004). Body fat perception in eating-disordered men. *International Journal of Eating Disorders, 35,* 102–108.

Manlove, J., Franzetta, K., McKinney, K., Romano-Papillo, A., & Terry-Humen, E. (2004). *No time to waste: Programs to reduce teen pregnancy among middle school-aged youth*. Washington, DC: National Campaign to Prevent Teen Pregnancy.

Mann, C. C. (2005, March 18). Provocative study says obesity may reduce U.S. life expectancy. *Science, 307,* 1716–1717.

Manning, M., & Hoyme, H. (2007). Fetal alcohol spectrum disorders: A practical clinical approach to diagnosis. *Neuroscience & Biobehavioral Reviews, 31,* 230–238.

Manning, W., Giordano, P., & Longmore, M. (2006, September). Hooking up: The relationship contexts of "nonrelationship" sex. *Journal of Adolescent Research, 21,* 459–483.

Mansson, D. (2013). The grandchildren received affection scale: Examining affectual solidarity factors. *Southern Communication Journal, 78,* 70–90.

Manstead, A. S. R. (1997). Situations, belongingness, attitudes, and culture: Four lessons learned from social psychology. In C. McGarty & S. A. Haslam et al. (Eds.), *The message of social psychology: Perspectives on mind in society*. Oxford, England: Blackwell Publishers, Inc.

Mao, A., Burnham, M. M., Goodlin-Jones, B. L., Gaylor, E. E., & Anders, T. F. (2004). A comparison of the sleep-wake patterns of cosleeping and solitary-sleeping infants. *Child Psychiatry and Human Development, 35,* 95–105.

Marcia, J. E. (1980). Identity in adolescence. In J. Adelson (Ed.), *Handbook of adolescent psychology*. New York: Wiley.

Marcovitch, S., Zelazo, P., & Schmuckler, M. (2003). The effect of the number of A trials on performance on the A-not-B task. *Infancy, 3,* 519–529.

Marcus, A. D. (2004, February 3). The new math on when to have kids. *Wall Street Journal,* pp. D1, D4.

Marcus, D., Fulton, J., & Clarke, E. (2010). Lead and conduct problems: A meta-analysis. *Journal of Clinical Child and Adolescent Psychology, 39,* 234–241.

Marin, T., Chen, E., Munch, J., & Miller, G. (2009). Double-exposure to acute stress and chronic family stress is associated with immune changes in children with asthma. *Psychosomatic Medicine, 71,* 378–384.

Marinellie, S. A., & Kneile, L. A. (2012). Acquiring knowledge of derived nominals and derived adjectives in context. *Language, Speech, and Hearing Services in Schools, 43,* 53–65.

Markell, K. (2010). Educating children about death-related issues. In C. A. Corr & D. E. Balk (Eds.), *Children's encounters with death, bereavement, and coping*. New York: Springer Publishing.

Markus, H. R., & Kitayama, S. (1991). Culture and the self: Implications for cognition, emotion, and motivation. *Psychological Review, 98,* 224–253.

Marschark, M., Spencer, P. E., & Newsom, C. A. (Eds.). (2003). *Oxford handbook of deaf students, language, and education*. London: Oxford University Press.

Marschik, P., Einspieler, C., Strohmeier, A., Plienegger, J., Garzarolli, B., & Prechtl, H. (2008). From the reaching behavior at 5 months of age to hand preference at preschool age. *Developmental Psychobiology, 50,* 512–518.

Marsh, H. W., Ellis, L., & Craven, R. (2002). How do preschool children feel about themselves? Unraveling measurement and multidimensional self-concept structure. *Developmental Psychology, 38,* 376–393.

Marsh, H. W., & Hau, K. T. (2003). Big-fish-little-pond effect on academic self-concept. *American Psychologist, 58,* 364–376.

Marshall, N. L. (2004). The quality of early child care and children's development. *Current Directions in Psychological Science, 13,* 165–168.

Martikainen, P., & Valkonen, T. (1996). Mortality after the death of a spouse: Rates and causes of death in a large Finnish cohort. *American Journal of Public Health, 86,* 1087–1093.

Martin, A., Onishi, K. H., & Vouloumanos, A. (2012). Understanding the abstract role of speech in communication at 12 months. *Cognition, 123,* 50–60.

Martin, C. L., & Fabes, R. (2001). The stability and consequences of young children's same-sex peer interactions. *Developmental Psychology, 37,* 431–446.

Martin, C. L., & Ruble, D. (2004). Children's search for gender cues: Cognitive perspectives on gender development. *Current Directions in Psychological Science, 13,* 67–70.

Martin, C. L., & Ruble, D. (2010). Patterns of gender development. *Annual Review of Psychology, 61,* 353–381.

Martin, D., Greenwood, H., & Nisker, J. (2010). Public perceptions of ethical issues regarding adult predictive genetic testing. *Health Care Analysis, 18,* 103–112.

Martin, J. A., Hamilton, B. E., Sutton, P. D., Ventura, S. J., Menacker, F., & Munson, M. L. (2005). Births: Final data for 2003. *National Vital Statistics Reports, 54,* Table J, 21.

Martin, P., Martin, D., & Martin, M. (2001). Adolescent premarital sexual activity, cohabitation, and attitudes toward marriage. *Adolescence, 36,* 601–609.

Martin, S., Li, Y., Casanueva, C., Harris-Britt, A., Kupper, L., & Cloutier, S. (2006). Intimate partner violence and women's depression before and during pregnancy. *Violence Against Women, 12,* 221–239.

Martineau, J., Cochin, S., Magne, R., & Barthelemy, C. (2008). Impaired cortical activation in autistic children: Is the mirror neuron system involved? *International Journal of Psychophysiology, 68,* 35–40.

Martinelli, P., Anssens, A., Sperduti, M., & Piolino, P. (2013). The influence of normal aging and Alzheimer's disease in autobiographical memory highly related to the self. *Neuropsychology, 27,* 69–78.

Martinez, G., Copen, C. E., & Abma, J. C. (2011). Teenagers in the United States: Sexual activity, contraceptive use, and childbearing, 2006-2010 National Survey of Family Growth. *National Center for Health Statistics. Vital Health Stat, 23*(31).

Martinez-Torteya, C., Bogat, G., von Eye, A., & Levendosky, A. (2009). Resilience among children exposed to domestic violence: The role of risk and protective factors. *Child Development, 80,* 562–577.

Masataka, N. (1996). Perception of motherese in a signed language by 6-month-old deaf infants. *Developmental Psychology, 32,* 874–879.

Masataka, N. (1998). Perception of motherese in Japanese sign language by 6-month-old hearing infants. *Developmental Psychology, 34,* 241–246.

Masataka, N. (2000). The role of modality and input in the earliest stage of language acquisition: Studies of Japanese sign language. In C. Chamerlain & J. P. Morford (Eds.), *Language acquisition by eye*. Mahwah, NJ: Lawrence Erlbaum.

Masataka, N. (2003). *The onset of language*. Cambridge, England: Cambridge University Press.

Masling, J. M., & Bornstein, R. F. (Eds.). (1996). *Psychoanalytic perspectives on developmental psychology*. Washington, DC: American Psychological Association.

Maslow, A. H. (1970). *Motivation and personality* (2nd ed.). New York: Harper & Row.

Massaro, A., Rothbaum, R., & Aly, H. (2006). Fetal brain development: The role of maternal nutrition, exposures and behaviors. *Journal of Pediatric Neurology, 4,* 1–9.

Master, S., Amodio, D., Stanton, A., Yee, C., Hilmert, C., & Taylor, S. (2009). Neurobiological correlates of coping through emotional approach. *Brain, Behavior, and Immunity, 23,* 27–35.

Masters, W. H., Johnson, V., & Kolodny, R. C. (1982). *Human sexuality*. Boston: Little, Brown.

Mathews, G., Fane, B., Conway, G., Brook, C., & Hines, M. (2009). Personality and congenital adrenal hyperplasia: Possible effects of prenatal androgen exposure. *Hormones and Behavior, 55,* 285–291.

Matlin, M. (2003). From menarche to menopause: Misconceptions about women's reproductive lives. *Psychology Science, 45,* 106–122.

Maton, K. I., Schellenbach, C. J., Leadbeater, B. J., & Solarz, A. L. (Eds.). (2004). *Investing in children, youth, families and communities*. Washington, DC: American Psychological Association.

Matriano, E., & Swee-Hin, T. (2013). Multicultural education, global education: Synergies for a peaceful world. In R. L. Lowman (Ed.), *Internationalizing multiculturalism: Expanding professional competencies in a globalized world*. Washington, DC: American Psychological Association.

Matson, J., & LoVullo, S. (2008). A review of behavioral treatments for self-injurious behaviors of persons with autism spectrum disorders. *Behavior Modification, 32,* 61–76.

Matsuda, Y., Ueno, K., Waggoner, R., Erickson, D., Shimura, Y., Tanaka, K., et al. (2010). Processing of infant-directed speech by adults. *NeuroImage, 54,* 122–131.

Matsumoto, D., & Yoo, S. H. (2006). Toward a new generation of cross-cultural research. *Perspectives on Psychological Science, 1,* 234–250.

Mattson, M. (2003). Will caloric restriction and folate protect against AD and PD? *Neurology, 60,* 690–695.

Mattson, S., Calarco, K., & Lang, A. (2006). Focused and shifting attention in children with heavy prenatal alcohol exposure. *Neuropsychology, 20,* 361–369.

Mausbach, B. T., Roepke, S. K., Chattillion, E. A., Harmell, A. L., Moore, R., Romero-Moreno, R., et al. (2012). Multiple mediators of the relations between caregiving stress and depressive symptoms. *Aging & Mental Health, 16,* 27–38.

Maxmen, A. (2012, February). Harnessing the wisdom of the ages. *Monitor on Psychology,* pp. 50–53.

Maxson, S. C. (2013). Behavioral genetics. In R. J. Nelson, S. Y. Mizumori, & I. B. Weiner (Eds.), *Handbook of psychology, Vol. 3: Behavioral neuroscience (2nd ed.)*. New York: John Wiley & Sons Ltd.

Mayes, L., Snyder, P., Langlois, E., & Hunter, N. (2007). Visuospatial working memory in school-aged children exposed in utero to cocaine. *Child Neuropsychology, 13,* 205–218.

Mayes, R., & Rafalovich, A. (2007). Suffer the restless children: The evolution of ADHD and paediatric stimulant use, 1900-80. *History of Psychiatry, 18,* 435–457.

Maynard, A. (2008). What we thought we knew and how we came to know it: Four decades of cross-cultural research from a Piagetian point of view. *Human Development, 51,* 56–65.

Mayseless, O. (1996). Attachment patterns and their outcomes. *Human Development, 39,* 206–223.

Mazoyer, B., Houdé, O., Joliot, M., Mellet, E., & Tzourio-Mazoyer, N. (2009). Regional cerebral blood flow increases during wakeful rest following cognitive training. *Brain Research Bulletin, 80,* 133–138. Available online at http://search.ebscohost.com

McArdle, E. F. (2002). New York's Do-Not-Resuscitate law: Groundbreaking protection of patient autonomy or a physician's right to make medical futility determinations? *DePaul Journal of Health Care Law, 8,* 55–82.

McCabe, M. P., & Ricciardelli, L. A. (2006). A prospective study of extreme weight change behaviors among adolescent boys and girls. *Journal of Youth and Adolescence, 35,* 425–434.

McCabe, P., & Shaw, S. (2010). *Genetic and acquired disorders*. Thousand Oaks, CA: Corwin Press.

McCall, R. B. (1979). *Infants*. Cambridge, MA: Harvard University Press.

McCardle, P., & Hoff, E. (Eds.). (2006). *Childhood bilingualism: Research on infancy through school age*. Clevedon, Avon, UK: Multilingual Matters.

McCarthy, B., & Ginsberg, R. (2007). Second marriages: Challenges and risks. *The Family Journal, 15,* 119–123.

McCauley, K. M. (2007). Modifying women's risk for cardiovascular disease. *Journal of Obstetric and Gynecological Neonatal Nursing, 36,* 116–124.

McClelland, D. C. (1993). Intelligence is not the best predictor of job performance. *Current Directions in Psychological Research, 2,* 5–8.

McConnell, V. (2012, February 16). Great granny to the rescue! *Mail Online*. Downloaded July 13, 2012, from http://www.dailymail.co.uk/femail/article-2101720/As-live-work-longer-great-grandparents-filling-childcare-gap.html

McCrae, R. R., & Costa, P. T., Jr. (1990). *Personality in adulthood*. New York: Guilford Press.

McCrae, R. R., & Costa, P. T., Jr. (2003). *Personality in adulthood: A five-factor theory perspective* (2nd ed.). New York: Guilford Press.

McCrae, R. R., Costa, P. T., Jr., Ostendorf, F., Angleitner, A., Hebíková, M., Avia, M. D., et al. (2000). Nature over nurture: Temperament, personality, and life span development. *Journal of Personality and Social Psychology, 78,* 173–186.

McCrink, K., & Wynn, K. (2004). Large-number addition and subtraction by 9-month-old infants. *Psychological Science, 15,* 776–782.

McCrink, K., & Wynn, K. (2007). Ratio abstraction by 6-month-old infants. *Psychological Science, 18,* 74–745.

McCrink, K., & Wynn, K. (2009). Operational momentum in large-number addition and subtraction by 9-month-olds. *Journal of Experimental Child Psychology, 103,* 400–408.

McCullough, M. E., Tsang, J., & Brion, S. (2003). Personality traits in adolescence as predictors of religiousness in early maturity: Findings from the Terman longitudinal study. *Personality & Social Psychology Bulletin, 29,* 980–991.

McCutcheon-Rosegg, S., Ingraham, E., & Bradley, R. A. (1996). *Natural childbirth the Bradley way: Revised edition.* New York: Plume Books.

McDaniel, A., & Coleman, M. (2003). Women's experiences of midlife divorce following long-term marriage. *Journal of Divorce & Remarriage, 38,* 103–128.

McDonald, K. A. (1999, June 25). Studies of women's health produce a wealth of knowledge on the biology of gender differences. *Chronicle of Higher Education,* pp. A19, A22.

McDonnell, L. M. (2004). *Politics, persuasion, and educational testing.* Cambridge, MA: Harvard University Press.

McDonough, L. (2002). Basic-level nouns: First learned but misunderstood. *Journal of Child Language, 29,* 357–377.

McDowell, M., Brody, D., & Hughes, J. (2007). Has age at menarche changed? Results from the National Health and Nutrition Examination Survey (NHANES) 1999-2004. *Journal of Adolescent Health, 40,* 227–231.

McElhaney, K., Antonishak, J., & Allen, J. (2008). "They like me, they like me not": Popularity and adolescents' perceptions of acceptance predicting social functioning over time. *Child Development, 79,* 720–731.

McElwain, N., & Booth-LaForce, C. (2006, June). Maternal sensitivity to infant distress and nondistress as predictors of infant-mother attachment security. *Journal of Family Psychology, 20,* 247–255.

McFadden, J. R., & Rawson Swan, K. T. (2012). Women during midlife: Is it transition or crisis? *Family and Consumer Sciences Research Journal, 40,* 313–325.

McGinnis, E. (2012). *Skillstreaming in early childhood: A guide for teaching prosocial skills* (3rd ed.). Champaign, IL: Research Press.

McGlothlin, H., & Killen, M. (2005). Children's perceptions of intergroup and intragroup similarity and the role of social experience. *Journal of Applied Developmental Psychology, 26,* 680–698.

McGough, R. (2003, May 20). MRIs take a look at reading minds. *Wall Street Journal,* p. D8.

McGue, M. (2010). The end of behavioral genetics? *Behavior Genetics, 40,* 284–296.

McGuffin, P., Riley, B., & Plomin, R. (2001, February 16). Toward behavioral genomics. *Science, 291,* 1232–1233.

McGugin, R., & Tanaka, J. (2010). Transfer and interference in perceptual expertise: When expertise helps and when it hurts. In M. T. Banich & D. Caccamise (Eds.), *Generalization of knowledge: Multidisciplinary perspectives.* New York: Psychology Press.

McGuinness, D. (1972). Hearing: Individual differences in perceiving. *Perception, 1,* 465–473.

McGuire, S., & Shanahan, L. (2010). Sibling experiences in diverse family contexts. *Child Development Perspectives, 4,* 72–79.

McHale, J. P., & Rotman, T. (2007). Is seeing believing? Expectant parents' outlooks on coparenting and later coparenting solidarity. *Infant Behavior & Development, 30,* 63–81.

McHale, S. M., Kim, J.-Y., & Whiteman, S. D. (2006). Sibling relationships in childhood and adolescence. In P. Noller & J. A. Feeney (Eds.), *Close relationships: Functions, forms and processes.* Hove, England: Psychology Press/ Taylor & Francis.

McHale, S. M., Updegraff, K. A., Shanahna, L., Crouter, A. C., & Killoren, S. E. (2005). Gender, culture, and family dynamics: Diffferential treatment of siblings in Mexican American families. *Journal of Marriage and the Family, 67,* 1259–1274.

McKee, K., Wilson, F., Chung, M., Hinchliff, S., Goudie, F., Elford, H., et al. (2005, November). Reminiscence, regrets and activity in older people in residential care: Associations with psychological health. *British Journal of Clinical Psychology, 44,* 543–561.

McLachlan, H. (2008). The ethics of killing and letting die: Active and passive euthanasia. *Journal of Medical Ethics, 34,* 636–638.

McLaughlin, D., Vagenas, D., Pachana, N., Begum, N., & Dobson, A. (2010). Gender differences in social network size and satisfaction in adults in their 70s. *Journal of Health Psychology, 15,* 671–679.

McLean, K., & Breen, A. (2009). Processes and content of narrative identity development in adolescence: Gender and well-being. *Developmental Psychology, 45,* 702–710.

McLoyd, V. C., Cauce, A. M., Takeuchi, D., & Wilson, L. (2000). Marital processes and parental socialization in families of color: A decade review of research. *Journal of Marriage and Family, 62,* 1070–1093.

McMurray, B., Aslin, R. N., & Toscano, J. C. (2009). Statistical learning of phonetic categories: Insights from a computational approach. *Developmental Science, 12,* 369–378.

McNulty, J. K., & Karney, B. R. (2004). Positive expectations in the early years of marriage: Should couples expect the best or brace for the worst? *Journal of Personality and Social Psychology, 86,* 729–743.

McQueeny, T., Schweinsburg, B. C., Schweinsburg, A. D., Jacobus, J., Bava, S., Frank, L. R., et al. (2009). Altered white matter integrity in adolescent binge drinkers. *Alcoholism: Clinical and Experimental Research, 33,* 1278–1285.

McVittie, C., McKinlay, A., & Widdicombe, S. (2003). Committed to (un)equal opportunities? "New ageism" and the older worker. *British Journal of Social Psychology, 42,* 595–612.

McWhirter, D. P., Sanders, S., & Reinisch, J. M. (1990). *Homosexuality, heterosexuality: Concepts of sexual orientation.* New York: Oxford University Press.

Mead, M. (1942). *Environment and education, a symposium held in connection with the fiftieth anniversary celebration of the University of Chicago.* Chicago: University of Chicago.

Meade, C., Kershaw, T., & Ickovics, J. (2008). The intergenerational cycle of teenage motherhood: An ecological approach. *Health Psychology, 27,* 419–429.

Mealey, L. (2000). *Sex differences: Developmental and evolutionary strategies.* Orlando, FL: Academic Press.

Medeiros, R., Prediger, R. D., Passos, G. F., Pandolfo, P., Duarte, F. S., Franco, J. L., et al. (2007). Connecting TNF-alpha signaling pathways to iNOS expression in a mouse model of Alzheimer's disease: Relevance for the behavioral and synaptic deficits induced by amyloid beta protein. *Journal of Neuroscience, 16,* 5394–5404.

Medina, A., Lederhos, C., & Lillis, T. (2009). Sleep disruption and decline in marital satisfaction across the transition to parenthood. *Families, Systems, & Health, 27,* 153–160.

Medina, J. J. (1996). *The clock of ages: Why we age—How we age—Winding back the clock.* New York: Cambridge University Press.

Mednick, S. A. (1963). Research creativity in psychology graduate students. *Journal of Consulting Psychology, 27,* 265–266.

Meece, J. L., & Kurtz-Costes, B. (2001). Introduction: The schooling of ethnic minority children and youth. *Educational Psychologist, 36,* 1–7.

Mehta, C. M., & Strough, J. (2009). Sex segregation in friendships and normative contexts across the life span. *Developmental Review, 29,* 201–220.

Meijer, A. M., & van den Wittenboer, G. L. H. (2007). Contribution of infants' sleep and crying to marital relationship of first-time parent couples in the first year after childbirth. *Journal of Family Psychology, 21,* 49–57.

Meisinger, E., Blake, J., Lease, A., Palardy, G., & Olejnik, S. (2007). Variant and invariant predictors of perceived popularity across majority-Black and majority-White classrooms. *Journal of School Psychology, 45,* 21–44.

Meister, H., & von Wedel, H. (2003). Demands on hearing aid features—special signal processing for elderly users? *International Journal of Audiology, 42,* 2S58–2S62.

Meltzoff, A. N. (1981). Imitation, intermodal coordination and representation in early infancy. In G. Butterworth (Ed.), *Infancy and epistemology.* Brighton, UK: Harvester Press.

Meltzoff, A. N. (2002). Elements of a developmental theory of imitation. In A. Meltzoff & W. Prinz (Eds.), *The imitative mind: Development, evolution, and brain bases.* New York: Cambridge University Press.

Meltzoff, A. N., & Moore, M. (2002). Imitation, memory, and the representation of persons. *Infant Behavior & Development, 25,* 39–61.

Melzer, D., Hurst, A., & Frayling, T. (2007). Genetic variation and human aging: Progress and prospects. *Journals of Gerontology: Series A: Biological Sciences and Medical Sciences, 62,* 301–307. Available online at http://search.ebscohost.com

Mendle, J., Turkheimer, E., & Emery, R. E. (2007). Detrimental psychological outcomes associated with early pubertal timing in adolescent girls. *Developmental Review, 27,* 151–171.

Mendoza, C. (2006, September). Inside today's classrooms: Teacher voices on No Child Left Behind and the education of gifted children. *Roeper Review, 29,* 28–31.

Mensah, F. K., Bayer, J. K., Wake, M., Carlin, J. B., Allen, N. B., & Patton, G. C. (2013). Early puberty and childhood social and behavioral adjustment. *Journal of Adolescent Health.* Accessed online, June 6, 2013, http://www.sciencedirect.com/science/article/pii/S1054139X13000487

Menzel, J. (2008). Depression in the elderly after traumatic brain injury: A systematic review. *Brain Injury, 22,* 375–380.

Mercado, E. (2009). Cognitive plasticity and cortical modules. *Current Directions in Psychological Science, 18,* 153–158.

Mercer, J. R. (1973). *Labeling the mentally retarded.* Berkeley: University of California Press.

Merlo, L., Bowman, M., & Barnett, D. (2007). Parental nurturance promotes reading acquisition in low socioeconomic status children. *Early Education and Development, 18,* 51–69.

Merrill, D. M. (1997). *Caring for elderly parents: Juggling work, family, and caregiving in middle and working class families.* Westport, CT: Auburn House/Greenwood Publishing Group.

Mervis, J. (2004, June 11). Meager evaluations make it hard to find out what works. *Science, 304,* 1583.

Mervis, J. (2011, August 19). Past successes shape effort to expand early intervention. *Science, 333,* 952–956.

Messer, S. B., & McWilliams, N. (2003). The impact of Sigmund Freud and the interpretation of dreams. In R. J. Sternberg (Ed.), *The anatomy of impact: What makes the great works of psychology great.* Washington, DC: American Psychological Association.

MetLife Mature Market Institute. (2009). *The Metlife Market Survey of Nursing Home & Home Care Costs 2008.* Westport, CT: MetLife Mature Market Institute.

Meyer, M., Wolf, D., & Himes, C. (2006, March). Declining eligibility for social security spouse and widow benefits in the United States? *Research on Aging, 28,* 240–260.

Mezuk, B., Prescott, M., Tardiff, K., Vlahov, D., & Galea, S. (2008). Suicide in older adults in long-term care: 1990 to 2005. *Journal of the American Geriatrics Society, 56,* 2107–2111.

Miao, X., & Wang, W. (2003). A century of Chinese developmental psychology. *International Journal of Psychology, 38,* 258–273.

Michael, R. T., Gagnon, J. H., Laumann, E. O., & Kolata, G. (1994). *Sex in America: A definitive survey.* Boston: Little, Brown.

Michaels, M. (2006). Factors that contribute to stepfamily success: A qualitative analysis. *Journal of Divorce & Remarriage, 44,* 53–66.

Miesnik, S., & Reale, B. (2007). A review of issues surrounding medically elective cesarean delivery. *Journal of Obstetric, Gynecologic, & Neonatal Nursing: Clinical Scholarship for the Care of Women, Childbearing Families, & Newborns, 36,* 605–615.

Mikulincer, M., & Shaver, P. R. (2005). Attachment security, compassion, and altruism. *Current Directions in Psychological Science, 14,* 34–38.

Mikulincer, M., & Shaver, P. R. (2007). *Attachment in adulthood: Structure, dynamics, and change.* New York: Guilford Press.

Mikulincer, M., & Shaver, P. R. (2009). An attachment and behavioral systems perspective on social support. *Journal of Social and Personal Relationships, 26,* 7–19.

Miles, L., Keitel, M., Jackson, M., Harris, A., & Licciardi, F. (2009). Predictors of distress in women being treated for infertility. *Journal of Reproductive and Infant Psychology, 27,* 238–257.

Miles, R., Cowan, F., Glover, V., Stevenson, J., & Modi, N. (2006). A controlled trial of skin-to-skin contact in extremely preterm infants. *Early Human Development, 2*(7), 447–455.

Milevsky, A., Schlechter, M., Netter, S., & Keehn, D. (2007). Maternal and paternal parenting styles in adolescents: Associations with self-esteem, depression and life-satisfaction. *Journal of Child and Family Studies, 16,* 39–47.

Miller, A. J., Sassler, S., & Kus-Appough. (2011). The specter of divorce: Views from work- and middle-class cohabitors. *Family Relations, 60,* 602–616.

Miller, E. M. (1998). Evidence from opposite-sex twins for the effects of prenatal sex hormones. In L. Ellis & L. Ebertz (Eds.), *Males, females, and behavior: Toward biological understanding.* Westport, CT: Praeger Publishers / Greenwood Publishing Group.

Miller, L. J. (2007). The use of cognitive enhancers in behavioral disturbances of Alzheimer's disease. *Consultant Pharmacist, 9,* 754–762.

Miller, P. H., & Seier, W. L. (1994). *Strategy utilization deficiencies in children: When, where, and why.* San Diego: Academic Press.

Miller, S. A. (2012). *Theory of mind: Beyond the preschool years.* New York: Psychology Press.

Mills, E., & Siegfried, N. (2006). Cautious optimism for new HIV/AIDS prevention strategies. *The Lancet, 368,* 1236.

Mimura, K., Kimoto, T., & Okada, M. (2003). Synapse efficiency diverges due to synaptic pruning following overgrowth. *Physical Review E: Statistical, Nonlinear, and Soft Matter Physics, 68,* 124–131.

Mirecki, R. M., Chou, J. L., Elliott, M., & Schneider, C. M. (2013). What factors influence marital satisfaction? Differences between first and second marriages. *Journal of Divorce & Remarriage, 54,* 78–93.

Mishna, F., Saini, M., & Solomon, S. (2009). Ongoing and online: Children and youth's perceptions of cyber bullying. *Children and Youth Services Review, 31,* 1222–1228.

Mishra, R. C. (1997). Cognition and cognitive development. In J. W. Berry, P. R. Dasen, & T. S. Saraswathi (Eds.), *Handbook of cross-cultural psychology, Vol. 2: Basic processes and human development* (2nd ed.). Boston, MA: Allyn & Bacon.

Mishra, R. C., & Dasen, P. R. (2013). Culture and cognitive development: The development of geocentric language and cognition. In B. Kar (Ed.), *Cognition and brain development: Converging evidence from various methodologies.* Washington, DC: American Psychological Association.

Misri, S. (2007). Suffering in silence: The burden of perinatal depression. *The Canadian Journal of Psychiatry / La Revue canadienne de psychiatrie, 52,* 477–478.

Mistry, J., & Saraswathi, T. (2003). The cultural context of child development. In R. Lerner & M. Easterbrooks (Eds.), *Handbook of psychology: Developmental psychology* (Vol. 6). New York: Wiley.

Mitchell, E. (2009). What is the mechanism of SIDS? Clues from epidemiology. *Developmental Psychobiology, 51,* 215–222.

Mitchell, K., Wolak, J., & Finkelhor, D. (2007, February). Trends in youth reports of sexual solicitations, harassment and unwanted exposure to pornography on the Internet. *Journal of Adolescent Health, 40,* 116–126.

Mitchell, S. (2002). *American generations: Who they are, how they live, what they think.* Ithaca, NY: New Strategists Publications.

Mittal, V., Ellman, L., & Cannon, T. (2008). Gene-environment interaction and covariation in schizophrenia: The role of obstetric complications. *Schizophrenia Bulletin, 34,* 1083–1094. Available online at http://search.ebscohost.com

Mittendorf, R., Williams, M. A., Berkey, C. S., & Cotter, R. F. (1990). The length of uncomplicated human gestation. *Obstetrics and Gynecology, 75,* 73–78.

Mohajeri, M., & Leuba, G. (2009). Prevention of age-associated dementia. *Brain Research Bulletin, 80,* 315–325.

Moher, M., Tuerk, A. S., & Feigenson, L. (2012). Seven-month-old infants chunk items in memory. *Journal of Experimental Child Psychology.* Accessed online, July 17, 2012, http://www.ncbi.nlm.nih.gov/pubmed/22575845

Mok, A., & Morris, M. W. (2012). Managing two cultural identities: The malleability of bicultural identity integration as a function of induced global or local processing. *Personality and Social Psychology Bulletin, 38,* 233–246.

Molina, J. C., Spear, N. E., Spear, L. P., Mennella, J. A., & Lewis, M. J. (2007). The International Society for Developmental Psychobiology 39th annual meeting symposium: Alcohol and development: Beyond fetal alcohol syndrome. *Developmental Psychobiology, 49,* 227–242.

Mols, F., & Denollet, J. (2010). Type D personality among noncardiovascular patient populations: A systematic review. *General Hospital Psychiatry, 32,* 66–72.

Monahan, C. I., Beeber, L. S., & Harden, B. (2012). Finding family strengths in the midst of adversity: Using risk and resilience models to promote mental health. In S. Summers & R. Chazan-Cohen (Eds.), *Understanding early childhood mental health: A practical guide for professionals.* Baltimore: Paul H Brookes Publishing.

Monahan, K., Steinberg, L., & Cauffman, E. (2009). Affiliation with antisocial peers, susceptibility to peer influence, and antisocial behavior during the transition to adulthood. *Developmental Psychology, 45,* 1520–1530.

Monastra, V. (2008). The etiology of ADHD: A neurological perspective. In V. J. Monastra (Eds.), *Unlocking the potential of patients with ADHD: A model for clinical practice.* Washington, DC: American Psychological Association.

Monk, C., Georgieff, M. K., & Osterholm, E. A. (2013). Research review: Maternal prenatal distress and poor nutrition—mutually influencing risk factors affecting infant neurocognitive development. *Journal of Child Psychology and Psychiatry, 54,* 115–130.

Montgomery-Downs, H., & Thomas, E. B. (1998). Biological and behavioral correlates of quiet sleep respiration rates in infants. *Physiology and Behavior, 64,* 637–643.

Moon, C. (2002). Learning in early infancy. *Advances in Neonatal Care, 2,* 81–83.

Moore, K. L. (1974). *Before we are born: Basic embryology and birth defects.* Philadelphia: Saunders.

Moore, K. L., Gao, D., & Bradlee, M. (2003). Does early physical activity predict body fat change throughout childhood? *Preventive Medicine: An International Journal Devoted to Practice & Theory, 37,* 10–17.

Moore, K. L., & Persaud, T. V. N. (2003). *Before we were born* (6th ed.). Philadelphia: Saunders.

Moore, R. L., & Wei, L. (2012). Modern love in China. In M. A. Paludi (Ed.), *The psychology of love* (Vols. 1–4). Santa Barbara, CA: Praeger/ABC-CLIO.

Morales, J. R., & Guerra, N. F. (2006). Effects of multiple context and cumulative stress on urban children's adjustment in elementary school. *Child Development, 77,* 907–923.

Morange-Majoux, F. F., Lemoine, C. C., & Dellatolas, G. G. (2013). Early manifestations of manual specialisation in infants: A longitudinal study from 20 to 30 weeks. *Laterality: Asymmetries of Body, Brain and Cognition, 18,* 231–250.

Morelli, G. A., Rogoff, B., Oppenheim, D., & Goldsmith, D. (1992). Cultural variation in infants' sleeping arrangements: Questions of independence [Special section: Cross-cultural studies of development]. *Developmental Psychology, 28,* 604–613.

Moreton, C. (2007). World's first test-tube baby Louise Brown has a child of her own. *The Independent (London).*

Morfei, M. Z., Hooker, K., Carpenter, J., Blakeley, E., & Mix, C. (2004). Agentic and communal generative behavior in four areas of adult life: Implications for psychological well-being. *Journal of Adult Development, 11,* 55–58.

Morice, A. (1998, February 27–28). Future moms, please note: Benefits vary. *Wall Street Journal,* p. 15.

Morita, J., Miwa, K., Kitasaka, T., Mori, K., Suenaga, Y., Iwano, S., et al. (2008). Interactions of perceptual and conceptual processing: Expertise in medical image diagnosis. *International Journal of Human-Computer Studies, 66,* 370–390.

Morley, J. E. (2012). Sarcopenia in the elderly. *Family Practice, 29*(Suppl. 1), I44–I48

Morris, G., Baker-Ward, L., & Bauer, P. (2010). What remains of that day: The survival of children's autobiographical memories across time. *Applied Cognitive Psychology, 24,* 527–544.

Morris, P., & Fritz, C. (2006, October). How to improve your memory. *The Psychologist, 19,* 608–611.

Morrissey, T. (2010). Sequence of child care type and child development: What role does peer exposure play? *Early Childhood Research Quarterly, 25,* 33–50.

Morrongiello, B., Corbett, M., & Bellissimo, A. (2008). 'Do as I say, not as I do': Family influences on children's safety and risk behaviors. *Health Psychology, 27,* 498–503.

Morrongiello, B., Corbett, M., McCourt, M., & Johnston, N. (2006, July). Understanding unintentional injury-risk in young children I. The nature and scope of caregiver supervision of children at home. *Journal of Pediatric Psychology, 31,* 529–539.

Morrongiello, B., & Hogg, K. (2004). Mothers' reactions to children misbehaving in ways that can lead to injury: Implications for gender differences in children's risk taking and injuries. *Sex Roles, 50,* 103–118.

Morrongiello, B., Klemencic, N., & Corbett, M. (2008). Interactions between child behavior patterns and parent supervision: Implications for children's risk of unintentional injury. *Child Development, 79,* 627–638.

Morrongiello, B., Zdzieborski, D., Sandomierski, M., & Lasenby-Lessard, J. (2009). Video messaging: What works to persuade mothers to supervise young children more closely in order to reduce injury risk? *Social Science & Medicine, 68,* 1030–1037.

Morry, M. (2007, February). The attraction-similarity hypothesis among cross-sex friends: Relationship satisfaction, perceived similarities, and self-serving perceptions. *Journal of Social and Personal Relationships, 24,* 117–138.

Mortensen, C., & Cialdini, R. (2010). Full-cycle social psychology for theory and application. *Social and Personality Psychology Compass, 4,* 53–63.

Moss, M. (1997, March 31). Golden years? For one 73-year-old, punching time clock isn't a labor of love. *The Wall Street Journal,* pp. A1, A8.

Motschnig, R., & Nykl, L. (2003). Toward a cognitive-emotional model of Rogers's person-centered approach. *Journal of Humanistic Psychology, 43,* 8–45.

Mottl-Santiago, J., Walker, C., Ewan, J., Vragovic, O., Winder, S., & Stubblefield, P. (2008). A hospital-based doula program and childbirth outcomes in an urban, multicultural setting. *Maternal and Child Health Journal, 12,* 372–377.

Mõttus, R., Johnson, W., & Deary, I. J. (2012). Personality traits in old age: Measurement and rank-order stability and some mean-level change. *Psychology and Aging, 27,* 243–249.

Moyer, M. S. (1992). Sibling relationships among older adults. *Generations, 16,* 55–58.

Mruk, C. J. (2013). *Self-esteem and positive psychology: Research, theory, and practice* (4th ed.). New York: Springer Publishing Co.

Mueller, E., & Vandell, D. (1979). Infant-infant interactions. In J. Osofsky (Ed.), *Handbook of infant development.* New York: Wiley.

Mueller, M., Wilhelm, B., & Elder, G. (2002). Variations in grandparenting. *Research on Aging,24,* 360–388.

Muenchow, S., & Marsland, K. W. (2007). Beyond baby steps: Promoting the growth and development of U.S. child-care policy. In L. J. Aber, et al. (Eds.), *Child development and social policy: Knowledge for action.* Washington, DC: American Psychological Association.

Müller, U., Burman, J., & Hutchison, S. (2013). The developmental psychology of jean piaget: A quinquagenary retrospective. *Journal of Applied Developmental Psychology, 34,* 52–55.

Mumme, D., & Fernald, A. (2003). The infant as onlooker: Learning from emotional reactions observed in a television scenario. *Child Development, 74,* 221–237.

Munsey, C. (2012, February). Anti-bullying efforts ramp up. *Monitor on Psychology*, pp. 54–57.

Munzar, P., Cami, J., & Farré, M. (2003). Mechanisms of drug addiction. *New England Journal of Medicine, 349,* 2365–2365.

Murguia, A., Peterson, R. A., & Zea, M. C. (1997, August). *Cultural health beliefs.* Paper presented at the annual meeting of the American Psychological Association, Toronto, Canada.

Murphy, B., & Eisenberg, N. (2002). An integrative examination of peer conflict: Children's reported goals, emotions, and behaviors. *Social Development, 11,* 534–557.

Murphy, C. (2008). The chemical senses and nutrition in older adults. *Journal of Nutrition for the Elderly, 27,* 247–265.

Murphy, F. A., Lipp, A., & Powles, D. L. (2012, March 14). Follow-up for improving psychological well being for women after a miscarriage. *Cochrane Database System Reviews.*

Murphy, M. (2009). Language and literacy in individuals with Turner syndrome. *Topics in Language Disorders, 29,* 187–194. Available online at http://search.ebscohost.com

Murphy, P., Buehl, M., Zeruth, J., Edwards, M., Long, J., & Monoi, S. (2010). Examining the influence of epistemic beliefs and goal orientations on the academic performance of adolescent students enrolled in high-poverty, high-minority schools. In L. D. Bendixen & F. C. Feucht (Eds.), *Personal epistemology in the classroom: Theory, research, and implications for practice.* New York: Cambridge University Press.

Murphy, S., Johnson, L., & Wu, L. (2003). Bereaved parents' outcomes 4 to 60 months after their children's death by accident, suicide, or homicide: A comparative study demonstrating differences. *Death Studies, 27,* 39–61.

Murray, L., Cooper, P., Creswell, C., Schofield, E., & Sack, C. (2007, January). The effects of maternal social phobia on mother-infant interactions and infant social responsiveness. *Journal of Child Psychology and Psychiatry, 48,* 45–52.

Murray, S., Bellavia, G., & Rose, P. (2003). Once hurt, twice hurtful: How perceived regard regulates daily marital interactions. *Journal of Personality & Social Psychology, 84,* 126–147.

Murray-Close, D., Ostrov, J., & Crick, N. (2007, December). A short-term longitudinal study of growth of relational aggression during middle childhood: Associations with gender, friendship intimacy, and internalizing problems. *Development and Psychopathology, 19,* 187–203.

Murstein, B. I. (1976). *Who will marry whom? Theories and research in marital choice.* New York: Springer.

Murstein, B. I. (1986). *Paths to marriage.* Beverly Hills, CA: Sage Publications.

Murstein, B. I. (1987). A clarification and extension of the SVR theory of dyadic pairing. *Journal of Marriage and the Family, 49,* 929–933.

Myers, D. (2000). *A quiet world: Living with hearing loss.* New Haven, CT: Yale University Press.

Myers, R. H. (2004). Huntington's disease genetics. *NeuroRx, 1,* 255–262.

Myklebust, B. M., & Gottlieb, G. L. (1993). Development of the stretch reflex in the newborn: Reciprocal excitation and reflex irradation. *Child Development, 64,* 1036–1045.

Myrtek, M. (2007). *Type A behavior and hostility as independent risk factors for coronary heart disease.* Washington, DC: American Psychological Association.

Nadel, S., & Poss, J. E. (2007). Early detection of autism spectrum disorders: Screening between 12 and 24 months of age. *Journal of the American Academy of Nurse Practitioners, 19,* 408–417.

Naglieri, J., Goldstein, S., & LeBuffe, P. (2010). Resilience and impairment: An exploratory study of resilience factors and situational impairment. *Journal of Psychoeducational Assessment, 28,* 349–356.

Nagy, E. (2006). From imitation to conversation: The first dialogues with human neonates. *Infant and Child Development, 15,* 223–232.

Nagy, M. (1948). The child's theories concerning death. *Journal of Genetic Psychology, 73,* 3–27.

Nakagawa, M., Lamb, M. E., & Miyaki, K. (1992). Antecedents and correlates of the Strange Situation behavior of Japanese infants. *Journal of Cross-Cultural Psychology, 23,* 300–310.

Nangle, D. W., & Erdley, C. A. (Eds.). (2001). *The role of friendship in psychological adjustment.* San Francisco: Jossey-Bass.

Nappi, R., & Polatti, F. (2009). The use of estrogen therapy in women's sexual functioning. *Journal of Sexual Medicine, 6,* 603–616.

Nash, A., Pine, K., & Messer, D. (2009). Television alcohol advertising: Do children really mean what they say? *British Journal of Developmental Psychology, 27,* 85–104.

Nassif, A., & Gunter, B. (2008). Gender representation in television advertisements in Britain and Saudi Arabia. *Sex Roles, 58,* 752–760.

Natan, B. M. (2008). Perceptions of nurses, families, and residents in nursing homes concerning residents' needs. *International Journal of Nursing Practice, 14,* 195–199.

Nation, M., & Heflinger, C. (2006). Risk factors for serious alcohol and drug use: The role of psychosocial variables in predicting the frequency of substance use among adolescents. *American Journal of Drug and Alcohol Abuse, 32,* 415–433.

National Center for Children in Poverty. (2005). *Basic facts about low-income children in the United States.* New York: National Center for Children in Poverty.

National Center for Education Statistics. (2002). *Dropout rates in the United States: 2000.* Washington, DC: Author.

National Center for Educational Statistics. (2003). *Public high school dropouts and completers from the common core of data: School year 2000-01 statistical analysis report.* Washington, DC: Author.

National Center for Education Statistics. (2004). *The condition of education, 2004.* Washington, DC: Author.

National Center for Education Statistics. (2011). *The Condition of Education 2011* (NCES 2011-033), Indicator 23. Washington, DC: Author.

National Center for Health Statistics. (1997). *Division of vital statistics.* Washington, DC: Public Health Service.

National Center for Health Statistics. (2001). *Division of vital statistics.* Washington, DC: Public Health Service.

National Center for Health Statistics. (2006). *Division of vital statistics.* Washington, DC: Public Health Service.

National Clearinghouse on Child Abuse and Neglect Information. (2004). *Child maltreatment 2002: Summary of key findings/National Clearinghouse on Child Abuse and Neglect Information.* Washington, DC: Author.

National Highway Traffic Safety Administration. (1994). *Age-related incidence of traffic accidents.* Washington, DC: National Highway Traffic Safety Administration.

National Institute of Aging. (2004, May 31). *Sexuality in later life.* Available online at http://www.niapublications.org/engagepages/sexuality.asp

National Institute of Child Health and Human Development (NICHD). (1999). Child-care and mother-child interaction in the first 3 years of life. *Developmental Psychology, 35,* 1399–1413.

National Institute of Child Health and Human Development (NICHD). (2002). Child-care structure—process—outcome: Direct and indirect effects of child-care quality on young children's development. *Psychological Science, 13,* 199–206.

National Institutes of Health. (2006, December 13). *Adult male circumcision significantly reduces risk of acquiring HIV.* NIH news release. Accessed online, January 7, 2006, http://www.nih.gov/news/pr/dec2006/niaid-13.htm

National Research Council. (1997). *Racial and ethnic differences in the health of older Americans.* New York: Author.

National Safety Council. (1989). *Accident facts: 1989 edition.* Chicago: National Safety Council.

National Science Foundation (NSF), Division of Science Resources Statistics. (2002). *Women, minorities, and persons with disabilities in science and engineering: 2002.* Arlington, VA: Author.

Navarro, M. (2006, May 25). Families add 3rd generation to households. *The New York Times*, pp. A1, A22.

Nazzi, T., & Bertoncini, J. (2003). Before and after the vocabulary spurt: Two modes of word acquisition? *Developmental Science, 6,* 136–142.

Needleman, H. L., & Bellinger, D. (Eds.). (1994). *Prenatal exposure to toxicants: Developmental consequences.* Baltimore: Johns Hopkins University Press.

Negy, C., Shreve, T., & Jensen, B. (2003). Ethnic identity, self-esteem, and ethnocentrism: A study of social identity versus multicultural theory of development. *Cultural Diversity & Ethnic Minority Psychology, 9,* 333–344.

Neisser, U. (2004). Memory development: New questions and old. *Developmental Review, 24,* 154–158.

Nelson, H. D., Tyne, K., Naik, A., Bougatsos, C., Chan, B. K., & Humphrey, L. (2009). Screening for breast cancer: An update for the U.S. Preventive Services Task Force. *Annals of Internal Medicine, 151,* 727–737.

Nelson, K. (1996). *Language in cognitive development: Emergence of the mediated mind.* New York: Cambridge University Press.

Nelson, L., Badger, S., & Wu, B. (2004). The influence of culture in emerging adulthood: Perspectives of Chinese college students. *International Journal of Behavioral Development, 28,* 26–36.

Nelson, K., & Fivush, R. (2004). The emergence of autobiographical memory: A social cultural developmental theory. *Psychological Review, 111,* 486–511.

Nelson, T. (2004). *Ageism: Stereotyping and prejudice against older persons.* Cambridge, MA: MIT Press.

Nelson, T., & Wechsler, H. (2003). School spirits: Alcohol and collegiate sports fans. *Addictive Behaviors, 28,* 1–11.

Nesheim, S., Henderson, S., Lindsay, M., Zuberi, J., Grimes, V., Buehler, J., et al. (2004). *Prenatal HIV testing and antiretroviral prophylaxis at an urban hospital—Atlanta, Georgia, 1997-2000.* Atlanta, GA: Centers for Disease Control.

Nestler, E. J. (2011, December). Hidden switches in the mind. *Scientific American*, pp. 77–83.

Neugarten, B. L. (1972). Personality and the aging process. *The Gerontologist, 12,* 9–15.

Neugarten, B. L. (1977). Personality and aging. In J. E. Birren & K. W. Schaie (Eds.), *Handbook for the psychology of aging.* New York: Van Nostrand Reinhold.

Newman, R., & Hussain, I. (2006). Changes in preference for infant-directed speech in low and moderate noise by 4.5- to 13-month-olds. *Infancy, 10,* 61–76.

Newston, R. L., & Keith, P. M. (1997). Single women later in life. In J. M. Coyle (Ed.), *Handbook on women and aging.* Westport, CT: Greenwood Press.

Newton, K., Reed, S., LaCroix, A., Grothaus, L., Ehrlich, K., & Guiltinan, J. (2006). Treatment of vasomotor symptoms of menopause with black cohosh, multibotanicals, soy, hormone therapy, or placebo. *Annals of Internal Medicine, 145,* 869–879.

Ng, F. F., Pomerantz, E. M., & Lam, S. (2007). European American and Chinese parents' responses to children's success and failure: Implications for children's responses. *Developmental Psychology, 43,* 1239–1255.

Ng, W., & Nicholas, H. (2010). A progressive pedagogy for online learning with high-ability secondary school students: A case study. *Gifted Child Quarterly, 54,* 239–251.

Ngo, B. (2010). Doing "diversity" at dynamic high: Problems and possibilities of multicultural education in practice. *Education and Urban Society, 42,* 473–495.

NICHD Early Child Care Research Network. (2001). Child care and children's peer interaction at 24 and 36 months: The NICHD study of early child care. *Child Development, 72,* 1478–1500.

NICHD Early Child Care Research Network. (2003a). Does quality of child care affect child outcomes at age 4 1/2? *Developmental Psychology, 39,* 451–469.

NICHD Early Child Care Research Network. (2003b). Families matter—even for kids in child care. *Journal of Developmental and Behavioral Pediatrics, 24,* 58–62.

NICHD Early Child Care Research Network. (2005). *Child care and child development: Results from the NICHD study of early child care and youth development.* New York: Guilford Press.

NICHD Early Child Care Research Network. (2006). *The NICHD study of early child care and youth development: Findings for children up to age 4 1/2 years* (Figure 5, p. 20). Washington, DC: Author.

Nicholson, L. M., & Browning, C. R. (2012). Racial and ethnic disparities in obesity during the transition to adulthood: The contingent and nonlinear impact of neighborhood disadvantage. *Journal of Youth and Adolescence, 41,* 53–66.

Niederhofer, H. (2004). A longitudinal study: Some preliminary results of association of prenatal maternal stress and fetal movements, temperament factors in early childhood and behavior at age 2 years. *Psychological Reports, 95,* 767–770.

Nieto, S. (2005). Public education in the twentieth century and beyond: High hopes, broken promises, and an uncertain future. *Harvard Educational Review, 75,* 43–65.

Nigg, J. T. (2001). Is ADHD a disinhibatory disorder? *Psychological Bulletin, 127,* 571–598.

Nigg, J. T., Knottnerus, G., Martel, M., Nikolas, M., Cavanagh, K., Karmaus, W., et al. (2008). Low blood lead levels associated with clinically diagnosed attention-deficit/hyperactivity disorder and mediated by weak cognitive control. *Biological Psychiatry, 63,* 325–331.

Nihart, M. A. (1993). Growth and development of the brain. *Journal of Child and Adolescent Psychiatric and Mental Health Nursing, 6,* 39–40.

Nikkola, I., Kaunonen, M., & Aho, A. (2013). Mother's experience of the support from a bereavement follow-up intervention after the death of a child. *Journal of Clinical Nursing, 22,* 1151–1162.

Nikolas, M., Klump, K. L., & Burt, S. (2012). Youth appraisals of inter-parental conflict and genetic and environmental contributions to attention-deficit hyperactivity disorder: Examination of GxE effects in a twin sample. *Journal of Abnormal Child Psychology, 40,* 543–554.

Nilsson, L. (2003). Memory function in normal aging. *Acta Neurologica Scandinavica, 107,* 7–13.

Nilsson, L. G., Bäckman, L., Erngrund, K., Nyberg, L., Adolfsson, R., Bucht, G., et al. (1997). The Betula prospective cohort study: Memory, health, and aging. *Aging Neuropsychology & Cognition, 4,* 1–32.

Nisbett, R. (1994, October 31). Blue genes. *New Republic, 211,* 15.

Nisbett, R. E., Aronson, J., Blair, C., Dickens, W., Flynn, J., Halpern, D. F., et al. (2012). Intelligence: New findings and theoretical developments. *American Psychologist, 67,* 130–159.

Noakes, M. A., & Rinaldi, C. M. (2006). Age and gender differences in peer conflict. *Journal of Youth and Adolescence, 35,* 881–891.

Nobuyuki, I. (1997). Simple reaction times and timing of serial reactions of middle-aged and old men. *Perceptual & Motor Skills, 84,* 219–225.

Nockels, R., & Oakeshott, P. (1999). Awareness among young women of sexually transmitted chlamydia infection. *Family Practice, 16,* 94.

Nolen-Hoeksema, S. (2001). Ruminative coping and adjustment to bereavement. In M. Stroebe & R. Hansson (Eds.), *Handbook of bereavement research: Consequences, coping, and care.* Washington, DC: American Psychological Association.

Nolen-Hoeksema, S., & Davis, C. (2002). Positive responses to loss: Perceiving benefits and growth. In C. Snyder & S. Lopez (Eds.), *Handbook of positive psychology.* London: Oxford University Press.

Noonan, D. (2003, September 22). When safety is the name of the game. *Newsweek,* pp. 64–66.

Noonan, C. W., & Ward, T. J. (2007). Environmental tobacco smoke, woodstove heating and risk of asthma symptoms. *Journal of Asthma, 44,* 735–738.

Noone, J., Stephens, C., & Alpass, F. (2009). Preretirement planning and well-being in later life: A prospective study. *Research on Aging, 31,* 295–317.

Nordenmark, M., & Stattin, M. (2009). Psychosocial well-being and reasons for retirement in Sweden. *Ageing & Society, 29,* 413–430.

Nordin, S., Razani, L., & Markison, S. (2003). Age-associated increases in intensity discrimination for taste. *Experimental Aging Research, 29,* 371–381.

Normand, M. T., Moreno-Torres, I. I., Parisse, C. C., & Dellatolas, G. G. (2013). How do children acquire early grammar and build multiword utterances? A corpus study of French children aged 2 to 4. *Child Development, 84,* 647–661.

North, M. S., & Fiske, S. T. (2013). A Prescriptive Intergenerational-Tension Ageism Scale: Succession, Identity, and Consumption (SIC). *Psychological Assessment.* Accessed online, June 13, 2013, http://www.ncbi.nlm.nih.gov/pubmed/23544391

Norton, A., & D'Ambrosio, B. (2008). ZPC and ZPD: Zones of teaching and learning. *Journal for Research in Mathematics Education, 39,* 220–246.

Norton, M. I., & Gino, F. (2013). Rituals alleviate grieving for loved ones, lovers, and lotteries. *Journal of Experimental Psychology: General.* Accessed online, June 13, 2013, http://www.ncbi.nlm.nih.gov/pubmed/23398180

Nosarti, C., Reichenberg, A., Murray, R. M., Cnattingius, S., Lambe, M. P., Yin, L., et al. (2012). Preterm birth and psychiatric disorders in young adult life preterm birth and psychiatric disorders. *Archives of General Psychiatry, 155,* 610–617.

Novotney, A. (2012, February). R u friends 4 real? *Monitor on Psychology,* pp. 62–65.

Nugent, J. K., Lester, B. M., & Brazelton, T. B. (Eds.). (1989). *The cultural context of infancy, Vol. 1: Biology, culture, and infant development.* Norwood, NJ: Ablex.

Nyiti, R. M. (1982). The validity of "culture differences explanations" for cross-cultural variation in the rate of Piagetian cognitive development. In D. Wagner & H. Stevenson (Eds.), *Cultural perspectives on child development.* New York: Freeman.

Nylen, K., Moran, T., Franklin, C., & O'Hara, M. (2006). Maternal depression: A review of relevant treatment approaches for mothers and infants. *Infant Mental Health Journal, 27,* 327–343.

Oberlander, S. E., Black, M., & Starr, R. H. (2007). African American adolescent mothers and grandmothers: A multigenerational approach to parenting. *American Journal of Community Psychology, 39,* 37–46.

Oblinger, D. G., & Rush, S. C. (1997). *The learning revolution: The challenge of information technology in the academy.* Bolton, MA: Anker Publishing Co.

Ochsner Clinic Foundation. (2003). *Adult preventive health care screening recommendations.* New Orleans, LA: Ochsner Clinic Foundation.

O'Connor, P. (1994). Very close parent/child relationships: The perspective of the elderly person. *Journal of Cross-Cultural Gerontology, 9,* 53–76.

O'Connor, M., & Whaley, S. (2006). Health care provider advice and risk factors associated with alcohol consumption following pregnancy recognition. *Journal of Studies on Alcohol, 67,* 22–31.

Ocorr, K., Reeves, N. L., Wessells, R. J., Fink, M., Chen, H. S., Akasaka, T., et al. (2007). KCNQ potassium channel mutations cause cardiac arrhythmias in Drosophila that mimic the effects of aging. *Proceedings of the National Academy of Sciences of the United States of America, 104,* 3943–3948.

Odic, D., Pietroski, P., Hunter, T., Lidz, J., & Halberda, J. (2013). Young children's understanding of "more" and discrimination of number and surface area. *Journal of Experimental Psychology: Learning, Memory, and Cognition, 39,* 451–461.

OECD (Organization for Economic Cooperation and Development). (1998). *Education at a glance: OECD indicators, 1998.* Paris: Author.

OECD (Organization for Economic Cooperation and Development). (2001). *Education at a glance: OECD indicators, 2001.* Paris: Author.

Ogbu, J. U. (1988). Black education: A cultural-ecological perspective. In H. P. McAdoo (Ed.), *Black families.* Beverly Hills, CA: Sage Publications.

Ogbu, J. U. (1992). Understanding cultural diversity and learning. *Educational Researcher, 21,* 5–14.

O'Grady, W., & Aitchison, J. (2005). *How children learn language.* New York: Cambridge University Press.

O'Hara, R., Gibbons, F., Weng, C., Gerrard, M., & Simons, R. (2012). Perceived racial discrimination as a barrier to college enrollment for African Americans. *Personality and Social Psychology Bulletin, 38,* 77–89.

Ohta, H., & Ohgi, S. (2013). Review of 'The Neonatal Behavioral Assessment Scale'. *Brain & Development, 35,* 79–80.

Okie, S. (2005). *Winning the war against childhood obesity.* Washington, DC: Joseph Henry Publications.

Oksenberg, J., & Hauser, S. (2010). Mapping the human genome with newfound precision. *Annals of Neurology, 67,* A8–A10.

O'Leary, S. G. (1995). Parental discipline mistakes. *Current Directions in Psychological Science, 4,* 11–13.

Olivardia, R., & Pope, H. (2002). Body image disturbance in childhood and adolescence. In D. Castle & K. Phillips (Eds.), *Disorders of body image.* Petersfield, England: Wrightson Biomedical Publishing.

Oliver, B., & Plomin, R. (2007). Twins' Early Development Study (TEDS): A multivariate, longitudinal genetic investigation of language, cognition and behavior problems from childhood through adolescence. *Twin Research and Human Genetics, 10,* 96–105.

Olness, K. (2003). Effects on brain development leading to cognitive impairment: A worldwide epidemic. *Journal of Developmental & Behavioral Pediatrics, 24,* 120–130.

Olsen, S. (2009, October 30). Will the digital divide close by itself? *The New York Times.* Available online at http://bits.blogs.nytimes.com/2009/10/30/will-the-digital-divide-close-by-itself

Olson, E. (2006, April 27). You're in labor, and getting sleeeepy. The *New York Times,* p. C2.

Olszewski-Kubilius, P., & Thomson, D. (2013). Gifted education programs and procedures. In W. M. Reynolds, G. E. Miller, & I. B. Weiner (Eds.), *Handbook of psychology, Vol. 7: Educational psychology* (2nd ed.). Hoboken, NJ: John Wiley & Sons Inc.

Onwuteaka-Philipsen, B., Rurup, M., Pasman, H., & van der Heide, A. (2010). The last phase of life: Who requests and who receives euthanasia or physician-assisted suicide? *Medical Care, 48,* 596–603.

Opfer, V. D., Henry, G. T., & Mashburn, A. J. (2008). The district effect: Systemic responses to high stakes accountability policies in six southern states. *American Journal of Education, 114,* 299–332.

Ophir, E., Nass, C., & Wagner, A. D. (2009). Cognitive control in media multitaskers. *PNAS Proceedings of the National Academy of Sciences of the United States of America, 106,* 15583–15587.

Orbuch, T. (2009). *Five simple steps to take your marriage from good to great.* Oakland, CA: The Oakland Press.

Orbuch, T. L., House, J. S., Mero, R. P., & Webster, P. S. (1996). Marital quality over the life course. *Social Psychology Quarterly, 59,* 162–171.

Ordovas, J. (2010). Nutrition and cognitive health. In M.Dan (Eds.), *Mental capital and wellbeing.* Wiley-Blackwell.

Oretti, R. G., Harris, B., & Lazarus, J. H. (2003). Is there an association between life events, postnatal depression and thyroid dysfunction in thyroid antibody positive women? *International Journal of Social Psychiatry, 49,* 70–76.

Ormont, L. R. (2001). Developing emotional insulation (1994). In L. B. Fugeri (Ed.), *The technique of group treatment: The collected papers of Louis R. Ormont.* Madison, CT: Psychosocial Press.

Ortiz, S. O., & Dynda, A. M. (2005). Use of intelligence tests with culturally and linguistically diverse populations. In D. P. Flanagan & P. L. Harrison (Eds.), *Contemporary intellectual assessment: Theories, tests, and issues.* New York: Guilford Press.

Osborne, J. W. (2012). Psychological effects of the transition to retirement. *Canadian Journal of Counselling and Psychotherapy, 46,* 45–58.

Osofsky, J. (2003). Prevalence of children's exposure to domestic violence and child maltreatment: Implications for prevention and intervention. *Clinical Child & Family Psychology Review, 6,* 161–170.

Ostrov, J., Gentile, D., & Crick, N. (2006, November). Media exposure, aggression and prosocial behavior during early childhood: A longitudinal study. *Social Development, 15,* 612–627.

OSTWG (Online Safety and Technology Working Group). (2010). *Youth safety on a living Internet: Report of the Online Safety and Technology Working Group.*

Oswal, A., & Yeo, G. (2010). Leptin and the control of body weight: A review of its diverse central targets, signaling mechanisms, and role in the pathogenesis of obesity. *Obesity, 18,* 221–229.

O'Toole, M. L., Sawicki, M. A., & Artal, R. (2003). Structured diet and physical activity prevent postpartum weight retention. *Journal of Women's Health, 12,* 991–998.

Otsuka, Y., Hill, H. H., Kanazawa, S., Yamaguchi, M. K., & Spehar, B. (2012). Perception of Mooney faces by young infants: The role of local feature visibility, contrast polarity, and motion. *Journal of Experimental Child Psychology, 111,* 164–179.

Ott, C., Sanders, S., & Kelber, S. (2007). Grief and personal growth experience of spouses and adult-child caregivers of individuals with Alzheimer's disease and related dementias. *The Gerontologist, 47,* 798–809.

Otto, K., Dette-Hagenmeyer, D. E., & Dalbert, C. (2010). Occupational mobility in members of the labor force: Explaining the willingness to change occupations. *Journal of Career Development, 36,* 262–288.

Ownby, R. L., Czaja, S. J., Loewenstein, D., & Rubert, M. (2008). Cognitive abilities that predict success in a computer-based training program. *The Gerontologist, 48,* 170–180.

Owsley, C., Stalvey, B., & Phillips, J. (2003). The efficacy of an educational intervention in promoting self-regulation among high-risk older drivers. *Accident Analysis & Prevention, 35,* 393–400.

Oxford, M., Gilchrist, L., Gillmore, M., & Lohr, M. (2006, July). Predicting variation in the life course of adolescent mothers as they enter adulthood. *Journal of Adolescent Health, 39,* 20–26.

Oyserman, D., Kemmelmeier, M., Fryberg, S., Brosh, H., & Hart-Johnson, T. (2003). Racial ethnic self-schemas. *Social Psychology Quarterly, 66,* 333–347.

Ozawa, M., & Yoon, H. (2003). Economic impact of marital disruption on children. *Children & Youth Services Review, 25,* 611–632.

Pacala, J. T., & Yueh, B. (2012). Hearing deficits in the older patient: 'I didn't notice anything.' *JAMA: Journal of the American Medical Association, 307*(11), 1185–1194.

Padilla-Walker, L. M., Nelson, L. J., & Carroll, J. S. (2012). Affording emerging adulthood: Parental financial assistance of their college-aged children. *Journal of Adult Development, 19,* 50–58.

Paisley, T. S., Joy, E. A., & Price, R. J., Jr. (2003). Exercise during pregnancy: A practical approach. *Current Sports Medicine Reports, 2,* 325–330.

Pajkrt, E., Weisz, B., Firth, H. V., & Chitty, L. S. (2004). Fetal cardiac anomalies and genetic syndromes. *Prenatal Diagnosis, 24,* 1104–1115.

Pajulo, M., Helenius, H., & MaYes, L. (2006, May). Prenatal views of baby and parenthood: Association with sociodemographic and pregnancy factors. *Infant Mental Health Journal, 27,* 229–250.

Palfai, T., Halperin, S., & Hoyer, W. (2003). Age inequalities in recognition memory: Effects of stimulus presentation time and list repetitions. *Aging, Neuropsychology, & Cognition, 10,* 134–140.

Palmore, E. B. (1988). *The facts on aging quiz.* New York: Springer Publishing Co.

Palmore, E. B. (1992). Knowledge about aging: What we know and need to know. *Gerontologist, 32,* 149–150.

Paludi, M. A. (2012). *The psychology of love* (Vols. 1–4). Santa Barbara, CA: Praeger/ABC-CLIO.

Palusci, V. J., & Ondersma, S. J. (2012). Services and recurrence after psychological maltreatment confirmed by child protective services. *Child Maltreatment, 17,* 153–163.

Pandina, R., Johnson, V., & White, H. (2010). Peer influences on substance use during adolescence and emerging adulthood. In L. M. Scheier (Ed.), *Handbook of drug use etiology: Theory, methods, and empirical findings.* Washington, DC: American Psychological Association.

Pappano, L. (1994, November 27). The new old generation. *Boston Globe Magazine,* 18–38.

Park, A. (2008, June 23). Living large. *Time,* pp. 90–92.

Park, C. L., Riley, K. E., & Snyder, L. B. (2012). Meaning making coping, making sense, and post-traumatic growth following the 9/11 terrorist attacks. *The Journal of Positive Psychology, 7,* 198–207.

Park, K. A., Lay, K., & Ramsay, L. (1993). Individual differences and developmental changes in preschoolers' friendships. *Developmental Psychology, 29,* 264–270.

Park, S., Holloway, S. D., Arendtsz, A., Bempechat, J., & Li, J. (2012). What makes students engaged in learning? A time-use study of within- and between-individual predictors of emotional engagement in low-performing high schools. *Journal of Youth and Adolescence, 41,* 390–401.

Parke, R., Simpkins, S., & McDowell, D. (2002). Relative contributions of families and peers to children's social development. In P. Smith & C. Hart (Eds.), *Blackwell handbook of childhood social development.* Malden, MA: Blackwell Publishers.

Parke, R. D. (2004). Development in the family. *Annual Review of Psychology, 55,* 365–399.

Parker, K. (2012). *The Boomerang generation.* Washington, DC: Pew Research Center.

Parker, S. T. (2005). Piaget's legacy in cognitive constructivism, niche construction, and phenotype development and evolution. In S. T. Parker & J. Langer (Eds.), *Biology and knowledge revisited: From neurogenesis to psychogenesis.* Mahwah, NJ: Lawrence Erlbaum.

Parks, C. A. (1998). Lesbian parenthood: A review of the literature. *American Journal of Orthopsychiatry, 68,* 376–389.

Parks, C. D., Sanna, L., & Posey, D. (2003). Retrospection in social dilemmas: How thinking about the past affects future cooperation. *Journal of Personality & Social Psychology, 84,* 988–996.

Parlee, M. B. (1979, October). The friendship bond. *Psychology Today, 13,* 43–45.

Parmalee, A. H., Jr., & Sigman, M. D. (1983). Prenatal brain development and behavior. In P. H. Mussen (Ed.), *Handbook of child psychology* (4th ed., Vol. 2). New York: Wiley.

Parnell, T. F., & Day, D. O. (Eds.). (1998). *Munchausen by proxy syndrome: Misunderstood child abuse.* Thousand Oaks, CA: Sage Publications.

Paterson, D. S., Trachtenberg, F. L., Thompson, E. G., Belliveau, R. A., Beggs, A. H., Darnall, R., et al. (2006). Multiple serotonergic brainstem abnormalities in sudden infant death syndrome. *JAMA: The Journal of the American Medical Association, 296,* 2124–2132.

Patterson, C. J. (1994). Lesbian and gay families. *Current Directions in Psychological Science, 3,* 62–64.

Patterson, C. J. (1995). Families of the baby boom: Parents' division of labor and children's adjustment [Special issue: Sexual orientation and human development]. *Developmental Psychology, 31,* 115–123.

Patterson, C. J. (2002). Lesbian and gay parenthood. In M. Bornstein (Ed.), *Handbook of parenting.* Mahwah, NJ: Lawrence Erlbaum.

Patterson, C. J. (2003). Children of lesbian and gay parents. In L. Garnets & D. Kimmel (Eds.), *Psychological perspectives on lesbian, gay, and bisexual experiences* (2nd ed.). New York: Columbia University Press.

Patterson, C. J. (2007). Lesbian and gay family issues in the context of changing legal and social policy environments. In K. J. Bieschke, R. M. Perez, & K. A. DeBord (Eds.), *Handbook of counseling and psychotherapy with lesbian, gay, bisexual, and transgender clients* (2nd ed.). Washington, DC: American Psychological Association.

Patterson, C. J. (2009). Children of lesbian and gay parents: Psychology, law, and policy. *American Psychologist, 64,* 727–736.

Patterson, C. J., & Friel, L. V. (2000). Sexual orientation and fertility. In G. R. Bentley & N. Mascie-Taylor (Eds.), *Infertility in the modern world: Biosocial perspectives.* Cambridge, UK: Cambridge University Press.

Paul, K., & Moser, K. (2009). Unemployment impairs mental health: Meta-analyses. *Journal of Vocational Behavior, 74,* 264–282.

Paulesu, E., Démonet, J. F., Fazio, F., McCrory, E., Chanoine, V., Brunswick, N., et al. (2001, March 16). Dyslexia: Cultural diversity and biological unity. *Science, 291,* 2165–2167.

Pauli-Pott, U., Mertesacker, B., & Bade, U. (2003). Parental perceptions and infant temperament development. *Infant Behavior & Development, 26,* 27–48.

Pavlov, I. P. (1927). *Conditioned reflexes.* London: Oxford University Press.

Peach, H. D., & Gaultney, J. F. (2013). Sleep, impulse control, and sensation-seeking predict delinquent behavior in adolescents, emerging adults, and adults. *Journal of Adolescent Health.* Accessed online, June 6, 2013, http://www.ncbi.nlm.nih.gov/pubmed/23672770

Pearson, C., Combs, J., & Smith, G. (2010). A risk model for disordered eating in late elementary school boys. *Psychology of Addictive Behaviors, 22,* 88–97.

Peck, R. C. (1968). Psychological developments in the second half of life. In B. L. Neugarten (Ed.), *Middle age and aging.* Chicago: University of Chicago Press.

Pedersen, S., Vitaro, F., Barker, E. D., & Borge, A. I. H. (2007). The timing of middle-childhood peer rejection and friendship: Linking early behavior to early-adolescent adjustment. *Child Development, 78,* 1037–1051.

Pedersen, S., Yagensky, A., Smith, O., Yagenska, O., Shpak, V., & Denollet, J. (2009). Preliminary evidence for the cross-cultural utility of the type D personality construct in the Ukraine. *International Journal of Behavioral Medicine, 16,* 108–115.

Peeters, M., Cillessen, A., & Scholte, R. (2010). Clueless or powerful? Identifying subtypes of bullies in adolescence. *Journal of Youth and Adolescence, 39,* 1041–1052.

Pellicano, E. (2007). Links between theory of mind and executive function in young children with autism: Clues to developmental primacy. *Developmental Psychology, 43,* 974–990.

Peltzer, K., & Pengpid, S. (2006). Sexuality of 16- to 17-year-old South Africans in the context of HIV/AIDS. *Social Behavior and Personality, 34,* 239–256.

Penido, A., de Souza Rezende, G., Abreu, R., de Oliveira, A., Guidine, P., Pereira, G., et al. (2012). Malnutrition during central nervous system growth and development impairs permanently the subcortical auditory pathway. *Nutritional Neuroscience, 15,* 31–36.

Penningroth, S., & Scott, W. D. (2012). Age-related differences in goals: Testing predictions form selection, optimization, and compensation theory and socioemotional selectivity theory. *The International Journal of Aging & Human Development, 74,* 87–111.

Penninx, B., Guralnik, J. M., Ferrucci, L., Simonsick, E. M., Deeg, D., & Wallace, R. B. (1998). Depressive symptoms and physical decline in community-dwelling older persons. *JAMA: The Journal of the American Medical Association, 279,* 1720–1726.

Pennisi, E. (2000, May 19). And the gene number is ...? *Science, 288,* 1146–1147.

Percy, K. (2010). *Working with aging families: Therapeutic solutions for caregivers, spouses, & adult children.* New York: Norton.

Pereira, A. C., Huddleston, D. E., Brickman, A. M., Sosunov, A. A., Hen, R., McKhann, G. M., et al. (2007). An in vivo correlate of exercise-induced neurogenesis in the adult dentate gyrus. *Proceedings of the National Academy of Sciences of the United States of America, 104,* 5638–5643.

Perez-Brena, N. J., Updegraff, K. A., & Umañ-Taylor, A. J. (2012). Father- and mother-adolescent decision-making in Mexican-origin families. *Journal of Youth and Adolescence, 41,* 460–473.

Perreault, A., Fothergill-Bourbonnais, F., & Fiset, V. (2004). The experience of family members caring for a dying loved one. *International Journal of Palliative Nursing, 10,* 133–143.

Perreira, K. M., & Ornelas, I. J. (2011, Spring). The physical and psychological well-being of immigrant children. *The Future of Children, 21,* 195–218.

Perrine, N. E., & Aloise-Young, P. A. (2004). The role of self-monitoring in adolescents' susceptibility to passive peer pressure. *Personality & Individual Differences, 37,* 1701–1716.

Perry, W. G. (1981). Cognitive and ethical growth: The making of meaning. In A. W. Chickering & Associates (Eds.), *The modern American college.* San Francisco: Jossey-Bass.

Persson, G. E. B. (2005). Developmental perspectives on prosocial and aggressive motives in preschoolers' peer interactions. *International Journal of Behavioral Development, 29,* 80–91.

Petanjek, Z., Judas, M., Kostovic, I., & Uylings, H. B. M. (2008). Lifespan alterations of basal dendritic trees of pyramidal neurons in the human prefrontal cortex: A layer-specific pattern. *Cerebral Cortex, 18,* 915–929.

Peters, B. (2010). Under threat from HIV/AIDS: Burial societies in Limpopo Province, South Africa. In A. Kalayjian & D. Eugene (Eds.), *Mass trauma and emotional healing around the world: Rituals and practices for resilience and meaning-making, Vol. 2: Human-made disasters.* Santa Barbara, CA: Praeger/ABC-CLIO.

Peters, E., Hess, T. M., Vastfjall, D., & Auman, C. (2007). Adult age differences in dual information processes: Implications for the role of affective and deliberative processes in older adults' decision making. *Perspectives on Psychological Science, 2,* 1–23.

Petersen, A. (2000). A longitudinal investigation of adolescents' changing perceptions of pubertal timing. *Developmental Psychology, 36,* 37–43.

Peterson, A. C. (1988, September). Those gangly years. *Psychology Today,* pp. 28–34.

Peterson, C., & Park, N. (2007). Explanatory style and emotion regulation. In J. J. Gross (Ed.), *Handbook of emotion regulation.* New York: Guilford Press.

Peterson, D. M., Marcia, J. E., & Carpendale, J. I. (2004). Identity: Does thinking make it so? In C. Lightfood, C. Lalonde, & M. Chandler (Eds.), *Changing conceptions of psychological life.* Mahwah, NJ: Lawrence Erlbaum.

Peterson, M., & Wilson, J. F. (2004). Work stress in America. *International Journal of Stress Management, 11,* 91–113.

Peterson, R. A., & Brown, S. P. (2005). On the use of beta coefficients in meta-analysis. *Journal of Applied Psychology, 90,* 175–181.

Petkoska, J., & Earl, J. (2009). Understanding the influence of demographic and psychological variables on retirement planning. *Psychology and Aging, 24,* 245–251.

Petrou, S. (2006). Preterm birth—What are the relevant economic issues? *Early Human Development, 82*(2), 75–76.

Petrou, S., & Kupek, E. (2010). Poverty and childhood undernutrition in developing countries: A multi-national cohort study. *Social Science & Medicine, 71,* 1366–1373.

Phelan, P., Yu, H. C., & Davidson, A. L. (1994). Navigating the psychosocial pressures of adolescence: The voices and experiences of high school youth. *American Educational Research Journal, 31,* 415–447.

Philippot, P., & Feldman, R. S. (Eds.). (2005). *The regulation of emotion.* Mahwah, NJ: Lawrence Erlbaum.

Phillips, D. (1992, September). Death postponement and birthday celebrations. *Psychosomatic Medicine, 26,* 12–18.

Phillips, M. L. (2011, April). The mind at midlife. *Monitor on Psychology,* pp. 39–41.

Phinney, J. S. (2005). Ethnic identity in late modern times: A response to Rattansi and Phoenix. *Identity, 5,* 187–194.

Phinney, J. S. (2008). Ethnic identity exploration in emerging adulthood. In D. L. Browning (Ed.), *Adolescent identities: A collection of readings.* New York: Analytic Press/Taylor & Francis Group.

Phinney, J. S., & Alipuria, L. L. (2006). Multiple social categorization and identity among multiracial, multiethnic, and multicultural individuals: Processes and implications. In R. J. Crips & M. Hewstone (Eds.), *Multiple social categorization: Processes, models and applications.* New York: Psychology Press.

Phinney, J. S., Ferguson, D. L., & Tate, J. D. (1997). Intergroup attitudes among ethnic minority adolescents: A causal model. *Child Development, 68,* 955–969.

Piaget, J. (1932). *The moral judgment of the child.* New York: Harcourt, Brace & World.

Piaget, J. (1952). *The origins of intelligence in children.* New York: International Universities Press.

Piaget, J. (1962). *Play, dreams and imitation in childhood.* New York: Norton.

Piaget, J. (1983). Piaget's theory. In W. Kessen (Ed.), & P. H. Mussen (Series Ed.), *Handbook of child psychology: Vol. 1. History, theory, and methods.* New York: Wiley.

Piaget, J., & Inhelder, B. (1958). *The growth of logical thinking from childhood to adolescence* (A. Parsons & S. Seagrin, Trans.). New York: Basic Books.

Picard, A. (2008, February 14). Health study: Tobacco will soon claim one million lives a year. *The Globe and Mail,* p. A15.

Picavet, H. S., & Hoeymans, N. (2004). Health related quality of life in multiple musculoskeletal diseases: SF-36 and EQ-5D in the DMC3 study. *Annals of the Rheumatic Diseases, 63,* 723–729.

Piller, I. (2010). Review of 'The bilingual edge: Why, when, and how to teach your child a second language.' *International Journal of Bilingual Education and Bilingualism, 13,* 115–118.

Pine, K. J., Wilson, P., & Nash, A. S. (2007). The relationship between television advertising, children's viewing and their requests to Father Christmas. *Journal of Developmental & Behavioral Pediatrics, 28,* 456–461.

Ping, R., & Goldin-Meadow, S. (2008). Hands in the air: Using ungrounded iconic gestures to teach children conservation of quantity. *Developmental Psychology, 44,* 1277–1287.

Pinker, S. (1994). *The language instinct.* New York: William Morrow.

Pinker, S. (2005). So how does the mind work? *Mind & Language, 20,* 1–24.

Piper, W. E., Ogrodniczuk, J. S., Joyce, A. S., & Weidman, R. (2009). Follow-up outcome in short-term group therapy for complicated grief. *Group Dynamics: Theory, Research, and Practice, 13,* 46–58.

Pittman, L. D., & Boswell, M. K. (2007). The role of grandmothers in the lives of preschoolers growing up in urban poverty. *Applied Developmental Science, 11,* 20–42.

Plomin, R. (1994). *Genetics and experience: The interplay between nature and nurture.* Newbury Park, CA: Sage Publications.

Plomin, R. (2005). Finding genes in child psychology and psychiatry: When are we going to be there? *Journal of Child Psychology and Psychiatry, 46,* 1030–1038.

Poest, C. A., Williams, J. R., Witt, D. D., & Atwood, M. E. (1990). Challenge me to move: Large muscle development in young children. *Young Children, 45,* 4–10.

Polkinghorne, D. E. (2005). Language and meaning: Data collection in qualitative research [Special issue: Knowledge in context: Qualitative methods in counseling psychology research]. *Journal of Counseling Psychology, 52,* 137–145.

Pollack, W. (1999). *Real boys: Rescuing our sons from the myths of boyhood.* New York: Owl Books.

Pollack, W., Shuster, T., & Trelease, J. (2001). *Real boys' voices.* New York: Penguin.

Pollak, S., Holt, L., & Wismer Fries, A. (2004). Hemispheric asymmetries in children's perception of nonlinguistic human affective sounds. *Developmental Science, 7,* 10–18.

Polman, H., de Castro, B.O. & van Aken, M. A. (2008). Experimental study of differential effects of playing versus watching violent video games on children's aggressive behavior. *Aggressive Behavior,* 34, 256–264.

Pomares, C. G., Schirrer, J., & Abadie, V. (2002). Analysis of the olfactory capacity of healthy children before language acquisition. *Journal of Developmental Behavior and Pediatrics, 23,* 203–207.

Pompili, M., Masocco, M., Vichi, M., Lester, D., Innamorati, M., Tatarelli, R., et al. (2009). Suicide among Italian adolescents: 1970-2002. *European Child & Adolescent Psychiatry, 18,* 525–533.

Ponton, L. E. (2001). *The sex lives of teenagers: Revealing the secret world of adolescent boys and girls.* New York: Penguin Putnam.

Pope, A. L., & Cashwell, C. S. (2013). Moral commitment in intimate committed relationships: A conceptualization from cohabiting same-sex and opposite-sex partners. *The Family Journal, 21,* 5–14.

Population Council Report. (2009). *Divorce rates around the world.* New York: Population Council.

Porges, S. W., & Lipsitt, L. P. (1993). Neonatal responsivity to gustatory stimulation: The gustatory-vagal hypothesis. *Infant Behavior & Development, 16,* 487–494.

Porter, M., van Teijlingen, E., Yip, L., & Bhattacharya, S. (2007). Satisfaction with cesarean section: Qualitative analysis of open-ended questions in a large postal survey. *Birth: Issues in Perinatal Care, 34,* 148–154.

Posthuma, D., & de Geus, E. (2006, August). Progress in the molecular-genetic study of intelligence. *Current Directions in Psychological Science, 15,* 151–155.

Poulin-Dubois, D. (1999). Infants' distinction between animate and inanimate objects: The origins of naive psychology. In P. Rochat (Ed.), *Early social cognition.* Hillsdale, NJ: Lawrence Erlbaum.

Poulin-Dubois, D., Serbin, L., & Eichstedt, J. (2002). Men don't put on make-up: Toddlers' knowledge of the gender stereotyping of household activities. *Social Development, 11,* 166–181.

Poulton, R., & Caspi, A. (2005). Commentary: How does socioeconomic disadvantage during childhood damage health in adulthood? Testing psychosocial pathways. *International Journal of Epidemiology, 23,* 51–55.

Powell, R. (2004, June 19). Colleges construct housing for elderly: Retiree students move to campus. *Washington Post,* p. F13.

Power, M., & Green, A. (2010). The Attitudes to Disability Scale (ADS): Development and psychometric properties. *Journal of Intellectual Disability Research, 54,* 860–874.

Prater, L. (2002). African American families: Equal partners in general and special education. In F. Obiakor & A. Ford (Eds.), *Creating successful learning environments for African American learners with exceptionalities.* Thousand Oaks, CA: Corwin Press.

Prechtl, H. F. R. (1982). Regressions and transformations during neurological development. In T. G. Bever (Ed.), *Regressions in mental development.* Hillsdale, NJ: Lawrence Erlbaum.

Preciado, P., Snijders, T. B., Burk, W. J., Stattin, H., & Kerr, M. (2012). Does proximity matter? Distance dependence of adolescent friendships. *Social Networks, 34,* 18–31.

Prentice, A., Schoenmakers, I., Laskey, M. A., de Bono, S., Ginty, F., & Goldberg, G. R. (2006). Nutrition and bone growth and development. *Proceedings of the Nutritional Society, 65,* 348–360.

Prescott, C., & Gottesman, I. (1993). Genetically mediated vulnerability to schizophrenia. *Psychiatric Clinics of North America, 16,* 245–267.

Pressley, M., & Schneider, W. (1997). *Introduction to memory development during childhood and adolescence.* Mahwah, NJ: Lawrence Erlbaum.

Prezbindowski, A. K., & Lederberg, A. R. (2003). Vocabulary assessment of deaf and hard-of-hearing children from infancy through the preschool years. *Journal of Deaf Studies and Deaf Education, 8,* 383–400.

Price, C. S., Thompson, W. W., Goodson, B., Weintraub, E. S., Croen, L. A., Hinrichsen, V. L., et al. (2010). Prenatal and infant exposure to thimerosal from vaccines and immunoglobulins and risk of autism. *Pediatrics, 126,* 656–664.

Price, R., & Gottesman, I. (1991). Body fat in identical twins reared apart: Roles for genes and environment. *Behavior Genetics, 21,* 1–7.

Priddis, L., & Howieson, N. (2009). The vicissitudes of mother-infant relationships between birth and six years. *Early Child Development and Care, 179,* 43–53.

Prigerson, H. (2003). Costs to society of family caregiving for patients with end-stage Alzheimer's disease. *New England Journal of Medicine, 349,* 1891–1892.

Prigerson, H. G., Frank, E., Kasl, S. V., Reynolds, C. F., III, Anderson, B., Zubenko, G. S., et al. (1995). Complicated grief and bereavement-related depression as distinct disorders: Preliminary empirical validation in elderly bereaved spouses. *American Journal of Psychiatry, 152,* 22–30.

PRIMEDIA/Roper. (1999). *Roper National Youth Survey.* Storrs, CT: Roper Center for Public Opinion Research.

Prince, M. (2000, November 13). How technology has changed the way we have babies. *Wall Street Journal,* pp. R4, R13.

Proctor, C., Barnett, J., & Muilenburg, J. (2012). Investigating race, gender, and access to cigarettes in an adolescent population. *American Journal of Health Behavior, 36,* 513–521.

Prohaska, V. (2012). Strategies for encouraging ethical student behavior. In R. Landrum & M. A. McCarthy (Eds.), *Teaching ethically: Challenges and opportunities.* Washington, DC: American Psychological Association.

Propper, C., & Moore, G. (2006, December). The influence of parenting on infant emotionality: A multi-level psychobiological perspective. *Developmental Review, 26,* 427–460.

Pruis, T., & Janowsky, J. (2010). Assessment of body image in younger and older women. *Journal of General Psychology, 137,* 225–238.

Puchalski, M., & Hummel, P. (2002). The reality of neonatal pain. *Advances in Neonatal Care, 2,* 245–247.

Puntambekar, S., & Hübscher, R. (2005). Tools for scaffolding students in a complex learning environment: What have we gained and what have we missed? *Educational Psychologist, 40,* 1–12.

Purdy, S. C., Sharma, M. M., Munro, K. J., & Morgan, C. A. (2013). Stimulus level effects on speech-evoked obligatory cortical auditory evoked potentials in infants with normal hearing. *Clinical Neurophysiology, 124,* 474–480.

Pushkar, D., Chaikelson, J., Conway, M., Etezadi, J., Giannopoulus, C., Li, K., et al. (2010). Testing continuity and activity variables as predictors of positive and negative affect in retirement. *Journals of Gerontology: Series B: Psychological Sciences and Social Sciences, 65B,* 42–49.

Putney, N. M., & Bengtson, V. L. (2001). Families, intergenerational relationships and kinkeeping in midlife. In M. E. Lachman (Ed.), *Handbook of midlife development.* Hoboken, NJ: Wiley.

Pyke, K., & Adams, M. (2010). What's age got to do with it? A case study analysis of power and gender in husband-older marriages. *Journal of Family Issues, 31,* 748–777.

Qian, Z.-C., & Lichter, D. T. (2007). Social boundary and marital assimilation: Evaluating trends in racial and ethnic intermarriage. *American Sociological Review, 72,* 68–94.

Quick, V., Wall, M., Larson, N., Haines, J., & Neumark-Sztainer, D. (2013). Personal, behavioral and socio-environmental predictors of overweight incidence in young adults: 10-yr longitudinal findings. *The International Journal of Behavioral Nutrition and Physical Activity, 10.* Accessed online, June 7, 2013, http://www.ijbnpa.org/content/10/1/37

Quinn, M. (1990, January 29). Don't aim that pack at us. *Time,* p. 60.

Quinn, P. (2008). In defense of core competencies, quantitative change, and continuity. *Child Development, 79,* 1633–1638.

Quinn, P., Uttley, L., Lee, K., Gibson, A., Smith, M., Slater, A., et al. (2008). Infant preference for female faces occurs for same- but not other-race faces. *Journal of Neuropsychology, 2,* 15–26.

Quinnan, E. J. (1997). Connection and autonomy in the lives of elderly male celibates: Degrees of disengagement. *Journal of Aging Studies, 11,* 115–130.

Quintana, S. M. (2007). Racial and ethnic identity: Developmental perspectives and research. *Journal of Counseling Psychology, 54,* 259–270.

Quintana, S. M., McKown, C., Cross, W. E., & Cross, T. B. (2008). In S. M. Quintana & C. McKown (Eds.), *Handbook of race, racism, and the developing child.* Hoboken, NJ: John Wiley.

Raag, T. (2003). Racism, gender identities and young children: Social relations in a multi-ethnic, inner-city primary school. *Archives of Sexual Behavior, 32,* 392–393.

Rabain-Jamin, J., & Sabeau-Jouannet, E. (1997). Maternal speech to 4-month-old infants in two cultures: Wolof and French. *International Journal of Behavioral Development, 20,* 425–451.

Rabin, R. (2006, June 13). Breast-feed or else. *The New York Times,* p. D1.

Rabkin, J., Remien, R., & Wilson, C. (1994). *Good doctors, good patients: Partners in HIV treatment.* New York: NCM Publishers.

Raeburn, P. (2004, October 1). Too immature for the death penalty? *The New York Times Magazine,* 26–29.

Raeff, C. (2004). Within-culture complexities: Multifaceted and interrelated autonomy and connectedness characteristics in late adolescent selves. In M. E. Mascolo & J. Li (Eds.), *Culture and developing selves: Beyond dichotomization.* San Francisco, CA: Jossey-Bass.

Rakison, D. H., & Krogh, L. (2012). Does causal action facilitate causal perception in infants younger than 6 months of age? *Developmental Science, 15,* 43–53.

Rakison, D. H., & Oakes, L. (2003). *Early category and concept development: Making sense of the blooming, buzzing confusion.* London: Oxford University Press.

Rakoczy, H., Harder-Kasten, A., & Sturm, L. (2012). The decline of theory of mind in old age is (partly) mediated by developmental changes in domain-general abilities. *British Journal of Psychology, 103,* 58–72.

Ramaswamy, V., & Bergin, C. (2009). Do reinforcement and induction increase prosocial behavior? Results of a teacher-based intervention in preschools. *Journal of Research in Childhood Education, 23,* 527–538.

Ramsay, J. R. (2010). Relationships and social functioning. In J. R. Ramsay (Ed.), *Nonmedication treatments for adult ADHD: Evaluating impact on daily functioning and well-being.* Washington, DC: American Psychological Association.

Rancourt, D., Conway, C. C., Burk, W. J., & Prinstein, M. J. (2012). Gender composition of preadolescents' friendship groups moderates peer socialization of body change behaviors. *Health Psychology.* Accessed online, July 21, 2012, http://www.ncbi.nlm.nih.gov/pubmed/22545975

Randall, W. L. (2012). Positive aging through reading our lives: On the poetics of growing old. *Psychological Studies, 57,* 172–178.

Rando, T. A. (1993). *Treatment of complicated mourning.* Champaign, IL: Research Press.

Ranganath, C., Minzenberg, M., & Ragland, J. (2008). The cognitive neuroscience of memory function and dysfunction in schizophrenia. *Biological Psychiatry, 64,* 18–25. Available online at http://search.ebscohost.com

Rank, M. R., & Hirschl, T. A. (1999). Estimating the proportion of Americans ever experiencing poverty during their elderly years. *Journals of Gerontology: Series B: Psychological Science and Social Sciences, 54,* S184–S193.

Rankin, J., Lane, D., & Gibbons, F. (2004). Adolescent self-consciousness: Longitudinal age changes and gender differences in two cohorts. *Journal of Research on Adolescence, 14,* 1–21.

Ransjö-Arvidson, A. B., Matthiesen, A. S., Lilja, G., Nissen, E., Widström, A. M., & Unvä-Moberg, K. (2001). Maternal analgesia during labor disturbs newborn behavior: Effects on breastfeeding, temperature, and crying. *Birth, 28,* 5–12.

Rantanen, J., Kinnunen, U., Pulkkinen, L., & Kokko, K. (2012). Developmental trajectories of work-family conflict for Finnish workers in midlife. *Journal of Occupational Health Psychology, 17,* 290–303.

Rao, V. (1997). Wife-beating in rural South India: A qualitative and econometric analysis. *Social Science & Medicine, 44,* 1169–1180.

Rapkin, B. D., & Fischer, K. (1992). Personal goals of older adults: Issues in assessment and prediction. *Psychology and Aging, 7,* 127–137.

Rapp, M., Krampe, R., & Baltes, P. (2006, January). Adaptive task prioritization in aging: Selective resource allocation to postural control is preserved in Alzheimer disease. *American Journal of Geriatric Psychiatry, 14,* 52–61.

Ratanachu-Ek, S. (2003). Effects of multivitamin and folic acid supplementation in malnourished children. *Journal of the Medical Association of Thailand, 4,* 86–91.

Rattan, S. I. S., Kristensen, P., & Clark, B. F. C. (Eds.). (2006). *Understanding and modulating aging.* Malden, MA: Blackwell Publishing on behalf of the New York Academy of Sciences, 2006.

Ravanipour, M., Gharibi, T., & Gharibi, T. (2013). Elderly women's views about sexual desire during old age: A qualitative study. *Sexuality and Disability.* Accessed online, June 13, 2013, http://link.springer.com/article/10.1007%2Fs11195-013-9295-7#page-1

Ray, E., & Heyes, C. (2011). Imitation in infancy: The wealth of the stimulus. *Developmental Science, 14,* 92–105.

Ray, L., Bryan, A., MacKillop, J., McGeary, J., Hesterberg, K., & Hutchison, K. (2009). The dopamine D receptor (DRD4) gene exon III polymorphism, problematic alcohol use and novelty seeking: Direct and mediated genetic effects. *Addiction Biology, 14,* 238–244. Available online at http://search.ebscohost.com

Rayner, K., Foorman, B. R., Perfetti, C. A., Pesetsky, D., & Seidenberg, M. S. (2002, March). How should reading be taught? *Scientific American,* 85–91.

Raz, N., Rodrigue, K., Kennedy, K., & Acker, J. (2007, March). Vascular health and longitudinal changes in brain and cognition in middle-aged and older adults. *Neuropsychology, 21,* 149–157.

Razani, J., Murcia, G., Tabares, J., & Wong, J. (2007). The effects of culture on WASI test performance in ethnically diverse individuals. *The Clinical Neuropsy-chologist, 21,* 776–788.

Reddy, V. (1999). Prelinguistic communication. In M. Barrett (Ed.), *The development of language.* Philadelphia: Psychology Press.

Reed, R. K. (2005). *Birthing fathers: The transformation of men in American rites of birth.* New Brunswick, NJ: Rutgers University Press.

Reichert, F., Menezes, A., Wells, J., Dumith, C., & Hallal, P. (2009). Physical activity as a predictor of adolescent body fatness: A systematic review. *Sports Medicine, 39,* 279–294.

Reifman, A. (2000). Revisiting *The Bell Curve. Psycoloquy, 11.*

Reis, S., & Renzulli, J. (2004). Current research on the social and emotional development of gifted and talented students: Good news and future possibilities. *Psychology in the Schools, 41,* 119–130.

Reissland, N., & Cohen, D. (2012). *The development of emotional intelligence: A case study.* New York: Routledge/Taylor & Francis Group.

Rembis, M. (2009). (Re)defining disability in the 'genetic age': Behavioral genetics, 'new' eugenics and the future of impairment. *Disability & Society, 24,* 585–597. Available online at http://search.ebscohost.com

Renner, L., & Slack, K. (2006, June). Intimate partner violence and child maltreatment: Understanding intra- and intergenerational connections. *Child Abuse & Neglect, 30,* 599–617.

Rentz, D., Locascio, J., Becker, J., Moran, E., Eng, E., Buckner, R., et al. (2010). Cognition, reserve, and amyloid deposition in normal aging. *Annals of Neurology, 67,* 353–364. Available online at PsycINFO database

Reschly, D. J. (1996). Identification and assessment of students with disabilities. *The Future of Children, 6,* 40–53.

Rescorla, L., Alley, A., & Christine, J. (2001). Word frequencies in toddlers' lexicons. *Journal of Speech, Language, & Hearing Research, 44,* 598–609.

Resnick, B. (2000). A seven step approach to starting an exercise program for older adults. *Patient Education & Counseling, 39,* 243–252.

Resnick, M. D., Bearman, P. S., Blum, R. W., Bauman, K. E., Harris, M. R., Jones, L., et al. (1997). Protecting adolescents from harm: Findings from the National Longitudinal Study on Adolescent Health. *JAMA: The Journal of the American Medical Association, 278,* 823–832.

Ressner, J. (2001, March 6). When a coma isn't one. *Time Magazine,* p. 62.

Resta, R., Biesecker, B. B., Bennett, R. L., Blum, S., Estabrooks, H. S., Strecker, M. N., et al. (2006). A new definition of genetic counseling: National Society of Genetic Counselors' Task Force Report. *Journal of Genetic Counseling, 15,* 77–83.

Rethorst, C., Wipfli, B., & Landers, D. (2009). The antidepressive effects of exercise: A meta-analysis of randomized trials. *Sports Medicine, 39,* 491–511.

Reuter, E., Voelcker-Rehage, C., Vieluf, S., & Godde, B. (2012). Touch perception throughout working life: Effects of age and expertise. *Experimental Brain Research, 216,* 287–297.

Reuters Health eLine. (2002, June 26). Baby's injuring points to danger of kids imitating television. *Reuters Health eline.*

Reyna, V. F., & Farley, F. (2006). Risk and rationality in adolescent decision making. *Psychological Science in the Public Interest, 7,* 1–44.

Reynolds, A. J., Temple, J. A., Ou, S. R., Arteaga, I. A., & White, B. A. (2011). School based early childhood education and age 28 well-being: Effects by timing, dosage, and subgroups. *Science, 333,* 360–364.

Rhoades, G., Stanley, S., & Markman, H. (2006, December). Pre-engagement cohabitation and gender asymmetry in marital commitment. *Journal of Family Psychology, 20,* 553–560.

Rhoades, G., Stanley, S., & Markman, H. (2009). The pre-engagement cohabitation effect: A replication and extension of previous findings. *Journal of Family Psychology, 23,* 107–111.

Rhodes, R., Mitchell, S., Miller, S., Connor, S., & Teno, J. (2008). Bereaved family members' evaluation of hospice care: What factors influence overall satisfaction with services? *Journal of Pain and Symptom Management, 35,* 365–371.

Rhule, D. (2005). Take care to do no harm: Harmful interventions for youth problem behavior. *Professional Psychology: Research and Practice, 36,* 618–625.

Ribordy, F., Jabès, A., Banta Lavenex, P., & Lavenex, P. (2013). Development of allocentric spatial memory abilities in children from 18 months to 5 years of age. *Cognitive Psychology, 66,* 1–29.

Ricciardelli, L. A., & McCabe, M. (2003). Sociocultural and individual influences on muscle gain and weight loss strategies among adolescent boys and girls. *Psychology in the Schools, 40,* 209–224.

Ricciardelli, L. A., & McCabe, M. P. (2004). A biopsychosocial model of disordered eating and the pursuit of muscularity in adolescent boys. *Psychological Bulletin, 130,* 179–205.

Rice, F. P. (1999). *Intimate relationships, marriages, & families* (4th ed.). Mountain View, CA: Mayfield.

Richards, M. H., Crowe, P. A., Larson, R., & Swarr, A. (1998). Developmental patterns and gender differences in the experience of peer companionship during adolescence. *Child Development, 69,* 154–163.

Richards, M. P. M. (1996). The childhood environment and the development of sexuality. In C. J. K. Henry & S. J. Ulijaszek (Eds.), *Long-term consequences of early environment: Growth, development and the lifespan developmental perspective.* Cambridge, England: Cambridge University Press.

Richardson, G., Goldschmidt, L., & Willford, J. (2009). Continued effects of prenatal cocaine use: Preschool development. *Neurotoxicology and Teratology, 31,* 325–333.

Richardson, G. A., Larkby, C., Goldschmidt, L., & Day, N. L. (2013). Adolescent initiation of drug use: Effects of prenatal cocaine exposure. *Journal of the American Academy of Child & Adolescent Psychiatry, 52,* 37–46.

Richardson, K. (2013). The eclipse of heritability and the foundations of intelligence. *New Ideas in Psychology, 31,* 122–129.

Richardson, K., & Norgate, S. (2007). A critical analysis of IQ studies of adopted children. *Human Development, 49,* 319–335.

Richmond-Rakerd, L. S. (2013). Modern advances in genetic testing: Ethical challenges and training implications for current and future psychologists. *Ethics & Behavior, 23,* 31–43.

Richtel, M. (2010, November 21). Growing up digital, wired for distraction. *The New York Times,* pp. A1, A20.

Richtel, M. (2012, May 30). Wasting time is new divide in digital era. *The New York Times,* p. A1.

Rick, S., & Douglas, D. (2007). Neurobiological effects of childhood abuse. *Journal of Psychosocial Nursing & Mental Health Services, 45,* 47–54.

Rideout, V., Foehr, U., & Roberts, D. (2010). *Generation M2: Media in the lives of 8-to-18-year-olds.* Menlo Park, CA: The Henry J. Kaiser Family Foundation.

Rideout, V., Vandewater, E., & Wartella, E. (2003). *Zero to Six: Electronic media in the lives of infants, toddlers, and preschoolers.* Menlo Park, CA: Kaiser Family Foundation.

Rieffe, C., Ketelaar, L., & Wiefferink, C. (2010). Assessing empathy in young children: Construction and validation of an Empathy Questionnaire (EmQue). *Personality and Individual Differences, 49,* 362–367.

Riesch, S., Anderson, L., Pridham, K., Lutz, K., & Becker, P. (2010). Furthering the understanding of parent-child relationships: A nursing scholarship review series. Part 5: Parent-adolescent and teen parent-child relationships. *Journal for Specialists in Pediatric Nursing, 15,* 182–201.

Riley, L., & Bowen, C. (2005, January). The sandwich generation: Challenges and coping strategies of multigenerational families. *The Family Journal, 13,* 52–58.

Rinaldi, C. (2002). Social conflict abilities of children identified as sociable, aggressive, and isolated: Developmental implications for children at-risk for impaired peer relations. *Developmental Disabilities Bulletin, 30,* 77–94.

Ritchie, L. (2003). Adult day care: Northern perspectives. *Public Health Nursing, 20,* 120–131.

Ritzen, E. M. (2003). Early puberty: What is normal and when is treatment indicated? *Hormone Research, 60*(Suppl. 3), 31–34

Robb, M., Richert, R., & Wartella, E. (2009). Just a talking book? Word learning from watching baby videos. *British Journal of Developmental Psychology, 27,* 27–45. Available online at http://search.ebscohost.com

Robbins, M. W. (1990, December 10). Sparing the child: How to intervene when you suspect abuse. *The New York Times Magazine,* pp. 42–53.

Roberto, K. A., & Skoglund, R. R. (1996). Interactions with grandparents and great-grandparents: A comparison of activities, influences, and relationships. *The International Journal of Aging & Human Development, 43,* 107–118.

Roberts, S. (2006, October 15). It's official: To be married means to be outnumbered. *The New York Times,* p. 22.

Roberts, S. (2009, November 24). Economy is forcing young adults back home in big numbers, survey finds. *The New York Times,* p. A16.

Roberts, B., Helson, R., & Klohnen, E. (2002). Personality development and growth in women across 30 years: Three perspectives. *Journal of Personality, 70,* 79–102.

Roberts, B. W., Walton, K. E., & Viechtbauer, W. (2006). Patterns of mean-level change in personality traits across the life course: A meta-analysis of longitudinal studies. *Psychological Bulletin, 132,* 1–25.

Roberts, R. D., & Lipnevich, A. A. (2012). From general intelligence to multiple intelligences: Meanings, models, and measures. In K. R. Harris, S. Graham, T. Urdan, S. Graham, J. M. Royer, & M. Zeidner (Eds.), *APA educational psychology handbook, Vol. 2: Individual differences and cultural and contextual factors.* Washington, DC: American Psychological Association.

Roberts, R. E., Phinney, J. S., Masse, L. C., Chen, Y. R., Roberts, C. R., & Romero, A. (1999). The structure of ethnic identity of young adolescents from diverse ethnocultural groups. *Journal of Early Adolescence, 19,* 301–322.

Roberts, R. E., Roberts, C., & Duong, H. (2009). Sleepless in adolescence: Prospective data on sleep deprivation, health and functioning. *Journal of Adolescence, 32,* 1045–1057.

Robins, R. W., & Trzesniewski, K. H. (2005). Self-esteem development across the lifespan. *Current Directions in Psychological Science, 14,* 158–162.

Robinson, A. J., & Pascalis, O. (2005). Development of flexible visual recognition memory in human infants. *Developmental Science, 7,* 527–533.

Robinson, G. E. (2004, April 16). Beyond nature and nurture. *Science, 304,* 397–399.

Robinson, J. P., & Godbey, G. (1997). *Time for life: The surprising ways Americans use their time.* College Park: Pennsylvania State University Press.

Rochat, P. (Ed.). (1999). *Early social cognition: Understanding others in the first months of life.* Mahwah, NJ: Erlbaum.

Rochat, P. (2004). Emerging co-awareness. In G. Bremner & A. Slater (Eds.), *Theories of infant development.* Malden, MA: Blackwell Publishers.

Rochat, P., Broesch, T., & Jayne, K. (2012). Social awareness and early self-recognition. *Consciousness and Cognition: An International Journal.* Accessed online, July 18, 2012, http://www.sciencedirect.com/science/article/pii/S1053810012001225

Roche, T. (2000, November 13). The crisis of foster care. *Time,* pp. 74–82.

Rodgers, R., Paxton, S., & Chabrol, H. (2010). Depression as a moderator of sociocultural influences on eating disorder symptoms in adolescent females and males. *Journal of Youth and Adolescence, 39,* 393–402.

Rodkin, P. C., & Ryan, A. M. (2012). Child and adolescent peer relations in educational context. In K. R. Harris, S. Graham, T. Urdan, S. Graham, J. M. Royer, & M. Zeidner (Eds.), *APA educational psychology handbook, Vol. 2: Individual differences and cultural and contextual factors.* Washington, DC: American Psychological Association.

Rodnitzky, R. L. (2012). Upcoming treatments in Parkinson's disease, including gene therapy. *Parkinsonism & Related Disorders, 18*(Suppl. 1), S37–S40.

Roecke, C., & Cherry, K. (2002). Death at the end of the 20th century: Individual processes and developmental tasks in old age. *International Journal of Aging & Human Development, 54,* 315–333.

Roehrig, M., Masheb, R., White, M., & Grilo, C. (2009). Dieting frequency in obese patients with binge eating disorder: Behavioral and metabolic correlates. *Obesity, 17,* 689–697.

Roelofs, J., Meesters, C., Ter Huurne, M., Bamelis, L., & Muris, P. (2006, June). On the links between attachment style, parental rearing behaviors, and internalizing and externalizing problems in non-clinical children. *Journal of Child and Family Studies, 15,* 331–344.

Roffwarg, H. P., Muzio, J. N., & Dement, W. C. (1966). Ontogenic development of the human sleep-dream cycle. *Science, 152,* 604–619.

Rogan, J. (2007). How much curriculum change is appropriate? Defining a zone of feasible innovation. *Science Education, 91,* 439–460.

Rogers, C. R. (1971). A theory of personality. In S. Maddi (Ed.), *Perspectives on personality.* Boston: Little, Brown.

Rogers, S., & Willams, J. (2006). *Imitation and the social mind: Autism and typical development.* New York: Guilford Press.

Roggeveen, A. B., Prime, D. J., & Ward, L. M. (2007). Lateralized readiness potentials reveal motor slowing in the aging brain. *Journals of Gerontology: Series B: Psychological Science and Social Science, 62,* P78–P84.

Rohleder, N. (2012). Acute and chronic stress induced changes in sensitivity of peripheral inflammatory pathways to the signals of multiple stress systems-2011 Curt Richter Award Winner. *Psychoneuroendocrinology, 37,* 307–316.

Rolls, E. (2000). Memory systems in the brain. *Annual Review of Psychology, 51,* 599–630.

Romero, S. T., Coulson, C. C., & Galvin, S. L. (2012). Cesarean delivery on maternal request: A western North Carolina perspective. *Maternal and Child Health Journal, 16,* 725–734.

Ron, P. (2006). Care giving offspring to aging parents: How it affects their marital relations, parenthood, and mental health. *Illness, Crisis, & Loss, 14,* 1–21.

Roos, S. (2013). The Kubler-Ross Model: An esteemed relic. *Gestalt Review, 17*(3), 312–315.

Roper Starch Worldwide. (1997, August). Romantic resurgence. *American Demographics,* p. 35.

Rose, A. J. (2002). Co-rumination in the friendships of girls and boys. *Child Development, 73,* 1830–1843.

Rose, A. J., & Asher, S. R. (1999). Children's goals and strategies in response to conflicts within a friendship. *Developmental Psychology, 35,* 69–79.

Rose, R. J., Viken, R. J., Dick, D. M., Bates, J. E., Pulkkinen, L., & Kaprio, J. (2003). It does take a village: Nonfamilial environments and children's behavior. *Psychological Science, 14,* 273–278.

Rose, S. (2008, January 21). Drugging unruly children is a method of social control. *Nature, 451,* 521.

Rose, S. A., & Feldman, J. F. (1997). Memory and speed: Their role in the relation of infant information processing to later IQ. *Child Development, 68,* 630–641.

Rose, S. A., Feldman, J. F., & Jankowski, J. J. (2004). Dimensions of cognition in infancy. *Intelligence, 32,* 245–262.

Rose, S. A., Feldman, J. F., & Jankowski, J. J. (2009). Information processing in toddlers: Continuity from infancy and persistence of preterm deficits. *Intelligence, 37,* 311–320.

Rosenblatt, P. C. (1988). Grief: The social context of private feelings. *Journal of Social Issues, 44,* 67–78.

Rosenblatt, P. C. (2001). A social constructionist perspective on cultural differences in grief. In M. S. Stroebe, R. O. Hansson, W. Stroebe, & H. Schut (Eds.), *Handbook of bereavement research: Consequences, coping, and care.* Washington, DC: American Psychological Association Press.

Ross, C. E., Microwsky, J., & Goldsteen, K. (1991). The impact of the family on health. In A. Booth (Ed.), *Contemporary families.* Minneapolis, MN: National Council on Family Relations.

Ross, J., Stefanatos, G., & Roeltgen, D. (2007). Klinefelter syndrome. In *Neurogenetic developmental disorders: Variation of manifestation in childhood.* Cambridge, MA: MIT Press.

Rossetti, A. O., Carrera, E., & Oddo, M. (2012). Early EEG correlates of neuronal injury after brain anoxia. *Neurology, 78,* 796–802.

Rossi, S., Telkemeyer, S., Wartenburger, I., & Obrig, H. (2012). Shedding light on words and sentences: Near-infrared spectroscopy in language research. *Brain and Language, 121,* 152–163.

Rossman, I. (1977). Anatomic and body composition changes with aging. In C. E. Finch & L. Hayflick (Eds.), *Handbook of the biology of aging.* New York: Van Nostrand Reinhold.

Rossouw, J. E., Prentice, R. L., Manson, J. E., Wu, L., Barad, D., Barnabei, V. M., et al. (2007). Postmenopausal hormone therapy and risk of cardiovascular disease by age and years since menopause. *JAMA: The Journal of the American Medical Association, 297,* 1465–1477.

Rote, W. M., Smetana, J. G., Campione-Barr, N., Villalobos, M., & Tasopoulos-Chan, M. (2012). Associations between observed mother-adolescent interactions and adolescent information management. *Journal of Research on Adolescence, 22,* 206–214.

Roth, D., Slone, M., & Dar, R. (2000). Which way cognitive development? An evaluation of the Piagetian and the domain-specific research programs. *Theory & Psychology, 10,* 353–373.

Rothbart, M., & Derryberry, D. (2002). Temperament in children. In C. von Hofsten & L. Backman (Eds.), *Psychology at the turn of the millennium, Vol. 2: Social, developmental, and clinical perspectives.* Florence, KY: Taylor & Frances/Routledge.

Rothbaum, F., Weisz, J., Pott, M., Miyake, K., & Morelli, G. (2000). Attachment and culture: Security in the United States and Japan. *American Psychologist, 55,* 1093–1104.

Rotigel, J. V. (2003). Understanding the young gifted child: Guidelines for parents, families, and educators. *Early Childhood Education Journal, 30,* 209–214.

Rovee-Collier, C. (1993). The capacity for long-term memory in infancy. *Current Directions in Psychological Science, 2,* 130–135.

Rovee-Collier, C. (1999). The development of infant memory. *Current Directions in Psychological Science, 8,* 80–85.

Rowe, J. W., & Kahn, R. L. (1998). *Successful aging.* New York: Pantheon.

Rowley, S., Burchinal, M., Roberts, J., & Zeisel, S. (2008). Racial identity, social context, and race-related social cognition in African Americans during middle childhood. *Developmental Psychology, 44,* 1537–1546.

Rozalski, M., Stewart, A., & Miller, J. (2010). How to determine the least restrictive environment for students with disabilities. *Exceptionality, 18,* 151–163.

Rubin, D. C. (1986). *Autobiographical memory.* Cambridge, England: Cambridge University Press.

Rubin, D. C. (2000). Autobiographical memory and aging. In C. D. Park & N. Schwarz et al. (Eds.), *Cognitive aging: A primer.* Philadelphia: Psychology Press/Taylor & Francis.

Rubin, D. C., & Greenberg, D. (2003). The role of narrative in recollection: A view from cognitive psychology and neuropsychology. In G. Fireman & T. McVay (Eds.), *Narrative and consciousness: Literature, psychology, and the brain.* London: Oxford University Press.

Rubin, K. H., & Chung, O. B. (Eds.). (2006). *Parenting beliefs, behaviors, and parent-child relations: A cross-cultural perspective.* New York: Psychology Press.

Ruble, D. N., Taylor, L. J., Cyphers, L., Greulich, F. K., Lurye, L. E., & Shrout, P. E. (2007). The role of gender constancy in early gender development. *Child Development, 78,* 1121–1136.

Rudd, L. C., Cain, D. W., & Saxon, T. F. (2008). Does improving joint attention in low-quality child-care enhance language development? *Early Child Development and Care, 178,* 315–338.

Ruff, H. A. (1989). The infant's use of visual and haptic information in the perception and recognition of objects. *Canadian Journal of Psychology, 43,* 302–319.

Ruffman, T., Slade, L., & Redman, J. (2006). Young infants' expectations about hidden objects [serial online]. *Cognition, 97,* B35–B43.

Runyan, D. (2008). The challenges of assessing the incidence of inflicted traumatic brain injury: A world perspective. *American Journal of Preventive Medicine, 34,* S112–SS115.

Rupp, D., Vodanovich, S., & Credé, M. (2006, June). Age bias in the workplace: The impact of ageism and causal attributions. *Journal of Applied Social Psychology, 36,* 1337–1364.

Russell, S. T., & Consolacion, T. (2003). Adolescent romance and emotional health in the United States: Beyond binaries. *Journal of Clinical Child & Adolescent Psychology, 32,* 499–508.

Russell, S. T., & McGuire, J. K. (2006). Critical mental health issues for sexual minority adolescents. Citation. In F. A. Villarruel & T. Luster (Eds.), *The crisis in youth mental health: Critical issues and effective programs, Vol. 2: Disorders in adolescence.* Westport, CT: Praeger Publishers / Greenwood Publishing Group.

Rust, J., Golombok, S., Hines, M., Johnston, K., & Golding, J., & ALSPAC Study Team. (2000). The role of brothers and sisters in the gender development of preschool children. *Journal of Experimental Child Psychology, 77,* 292–303.

Rutter, M. (2003). Commentary: Causal processes leading to antisocial behavior. *Developmental Psychology, 39,* 372–378.

Rutter, M. (2006). *Genes and behavior: Nature-nurture interplay explained.* New York: Blackwell Publishing.

Ryan, B. P. (2001). *Programmed therapy for stuttering in children and adults* (2nd ed.). Springfield, IL: Charles C. Thomas.

Ryan, D., & Martin, A. (2000). Lesbian, gay, bisexual, and transgender parents in the school systems. *The School Psychology Review, 29,* 207–216.

Saad, L. (2011, June 30). *Americans' preference for smaller families edges higher.* Princeton, NJ: Gallup Poll.

Sabbagh, M. (2009). Drug development for Alzheimer's disease: Where are we now and where are we headed? *American Journal of Geriatric Pharmacotherapy (AJGP), 7,* 167–185.

Sacks, M. H. (1993). Exercise for stress control. In D. Goleman & J. Gurin (Eds.), *Mind-body medicine.* Yonkers, NY: Consumer Reports Books.

Sadeghi, N., Prastawa, M., Fletcher, P., Wolff, J., Gilmore, J. H., & Gerig, G. (2013). Regional characterization of longitudinal DT-MRI to study white matter maturation of the early developing brain. *NeuroImage, 68,* 236–247.

Sadker, M., & Sadker, D. (1994). *Failing at fairness: How America's schools cheat girls.* New York: Scribner's.

Saiegh-Haddad, E. (2007). Linguistic constraints on children's ability to isolate phonemes in Arabic. *Applied Psycholinguistics, 28,* 607–625.

Saklofske, D. H., Nordstokke, D. W., Prince-Embury, S., Crumpler, T., Nugent, S., Vesely, A., et al. (2013). Assessing personal resiliency in young adults: The Resiliency Scale for children and adolescents. In S. Prince-Embury & D. H. Saklofske (Eds.), *Resilience in children, adolescents, and adults: Translating research into practice.* New York: Springer Science + Business Media.

Sales, B. D., & Folkman, S. (Eds.). (2000). *Ethics in research with human participants.* Washington, DC: American Psychological Association.

Sallis, J., & Glanz, K. (2006, March). The role of built environments in physical activity, eating, and obesity in childhood. *The Future of Children, 16,* 89–108.

Salthouse, T. A. (1990). Cognitive competence and expertise in aging. In J. E. Birren & W. K. Schaie et al. (Eds.), *Handbook of the psychology of aging* (3rd ed.). San Diego: Academic Press.

Salthouse, T. A. (1993). Speed mediation of adult age differences in cognition. *Developmental Psychology, 29,* 722–738.

Salthouse, T. A. (1994). The aging of working memory. *Neuropsychology, 8,* 535–543.

Salthouse, T. A. (2006). Mental exercise and mental aging: Evaluating the validity of the "Use it or lose it" hypothesis. *Perspectives on Psychological Science, 1,* 68–87.

Salthouse, T. A. (2009). When does age-related cognitive decline begin? *Neurobiology of Aging, 30,* 507–514.

Salthouse, T. A. (2010). *Major issues in cognitive aging.* New York: Oxford University Press.

Salthouse, T. A. (2012a). Consequences of age-related cognitive declines. *Annual Review of Psychology, 63,* 201–226.

Salthouse, T. A. (2012b). Does the level at which cognitive change occurs change with age? *Psychological Science, 23,* 18–23.

Salthouse, T. A., Atkinson, T. M., & Berish, D. E. (2003). Executive functioning as a potential mediator of age-related cognitive decline in normal adults. *Journal of Experimental Psychology: General, 132,* 566–594.

Salthouse, T. A., Pink, J., & Tucker-Drob, E. (2008). Contextual analysis of fluid intelligence. *Intelligence, 36,* 464–486.

Samet, J. H., De Marini, D. M., & Malling, H. V. (2004, May 14). Do airborne particles induce heritable mutations? *Science, 304,* 971.

Sammons, M. (2009). Writing a wrong: Factors influencing the overprescription of antidepressants to youth. *Professional Psychology: Research and Practice, 40,* 327–329.

Sanchez, Y. M., Lambert, S. F., & Ialongo, N. S. (2012). Life events and depressive symptoms in African American adolescents: Do ecological domains and timing of life events matter? *Journal of Youth and Adolescence, 41,* 438–448.

Sanders, S., Ott, C., Kelber, S., & Noonan, P. (2008). The experience of high levels of grief in caregivers of persons with Alzheimer's disease and related dementia. *Death Studies, 32,* 495–523.

Sandis, E. (2000). The aging and their families: A cross-national review. In A. L. Comunian & U. P. Gielen (Eds.), *International perspectives on human development.* Lengerich, Germany: Pabst Science Publishers.

Sandoval, J., Frisby, C. L., Geisinger, K. F., Scheuneman, J. D., & Grenier, J. R. (Eds.). (1998). *Test interpretation and diversity: Achieving equity in assessment.* Washington, DC: APA Books.

Sandoval, J., Scott, A., & Padilla, I. (2009). Crisis counseling: An overview. *Psychology in the Schools, 46,* 246–256.

Sang, B., Miao, X., & Deng, C. (2002). The development of gifted and nongifted young children in metamemory knowledge. *Psychological Science (China), 25,* 406–409, 424.

Sangree, W. H. (1989). Age and power: Life-course trajectories and age structuring of power relations in East and West Africa. In D. I. Kertzer & K. W. Schaie (Eds.), *Age structuring in comparative perspective.* Hillsdale, NJ: Lawrence Erlbaum.

Santesso, D., Schmidt, L., & Trainor, L. (2007). Frontal brain electrical activity (EEG) and heart rate in response to affective infant-directed (ID) speech in 9-month-old infants. *Brain and Cognition, 65,* 14–21. Available online at http://search.ebscohost.com

Sapolsky, R. (2005, December). Sick of poverty. *Scientific American,* 93–99.

Sapyla, J. J., & March, J. S. (2012). Integrating medical and psychological therapies in child mental health: An evidence-based medicine approach. In M. Garralda & J. Raynaud (Eds.), *Brain, mind, and developmental psychopathology in childhood.* Lanham, MD: Jason Aronson.

Sargent-Cox, K. A., Anstey, K. J., & Luszcz, M. A. (2012). The relationship between change in self-perceptions of aging and physical functioning in older adults. *Psychology and Aging.* doi:10.1037/a0027578

Saul, S. (2009). The gift of life, and its price. *The New York Times,* pp. A1, A26–27.

Saunders, J., Davis, L., & Williams, T. (2004). Gender differences in self-perceptions and academic outcomes: A study of African American high school students. *Journal of Youth & Adolescence, 33,* 81–90.

Savage-Rumbaugh, E. S., Murphy, J., Sevcik, R. A., Brakke, K. E., Williams, S. L., & Rumbaugh, D. M. (1993). Language and comprehension in ape and child. *Monographs of the Society for Research in Child Development, 58*(3–4, Serial No. 233).

Savin-Williams, R. C. (2003). Lesbian, gay, and bisexual youths' relationships with their parents. In L. Garnets & D. Kimmel (Eds.), *Psychological perspectives on lesbian, gay, and bisexual experiences* (2nd ed.). New York: Columbia University Press.

Savin-Williams, R. C. (2006). *The new gay teenager.* Cambridge, MA: Harvard University Press.

Savin-Williams, R. C., & Berndt, T. J. (1990). Friendship and peer relations. In S. Feldman & G. Elliott (Eds.), *At the threshold: The developing adolescent.* Cambridge, MA: Harvard University Press.

Sawatzky, J., & Naimark, B. (2002). Physical activity and cardiovascular health in aging women: A health-promotion perspective. *Journal of Aging & Physical Activity, 10,* 396–412.

Sawyer, R. (2012). *Explaining creativity: The science of human innovation* (2nd ed.). New York: Oxford University Press.

Sax, L. J., Hurtado, S., Lindholm, J. A., Korn, W. S., & Mahoney, K. M. (2005). *The American freshman: National norms for fall 2004.* Los Angeles: Higher Education Research Institute, UCLA.

Scarr, S. (1998). American child care today. *American Psychologist, 53,* 95–108.

Scarr, S., & Carter-Saltzman, L. (1982). Genetics and intelligence. In R. J. Sternberg (Ed.), *Handbook of human intelligence.* Cambridge, England: Cambridge University Press.

Schachar, R., Ickowicz, A., Crosbie, J., Donnelly, G. A. E., Reiz, J. L., Miceli, P. C., et al. (2008). Cognitive and behavioral effects of multilayer-release methylphenidate in the treatment of children with attention-deficit/hyperactivity disorder. *Journal of Child and Adolescent Psychopharmacology, 18,* 11–24.

Schachner, D., Shaver, P., & Gillath, O. (2008). Attachment style and long-term singlehood. *Personal Relationships, 15,* 479–491.

Schachter, E. P. (2005). Erikson meets the postmodern: Can classic identity theory rise to the challenge? *Identity, 5,* 137–160.

Schaeffer, C., Petras, H., & Ialongo, N. (2003). Modeling growth in boys' aggressive behavior across elementary school: Links to later criminal involvement, conduct disorder, and antisocial personality disorder. *Developmental Psychology, 39,* 1020–1035.

Schaie, K. W. (1977–1978). Toward a stage of adult theory of adult cognitive development. *Journal of Aging and Human Development, 8,* 129–138.

Schaie, K. W. (1985). *Longitudinal studies of adult psychological development.* New York: Guilford Press.

Schaie, K. W. (1993). The Seattle longitudinal studies of adult intelligence. *Current Directions in Psychological Science, 2,* 171–175.

Schaie, K. W. (1994). The course of adult intellectual development. *American Psychologist, 49,* 304–313.

Schaie, K. W., & Willis, S. L. (1993). Age difference patterns of psychometric intelligence in adulthood: Generalizability within and across ability domains. *Psychology and Aging, 8,* 44–55.

Schaie, W. K., Willis, S. L., & Pennak, S. (2005). An historical framework for cohort differences in intelligence. *Research in Human Development, 2,* 43–67.

Schaie, K. W., & Zanjani, F. A. K. (2006). Intellectual development across adulthood. In C. Hoare (Ed.), *Handbook of adult development and learning.* New York: Oxford University Press.

Schaller, M., & Crandall, C. S. (Eds.). (2004). *The psychological foundations of culture.* Mahwah, NJ: Lawrence Erlbaum.

Scharrer, E., Kim, D., Lin, K., & Liu, Z. (2006). Working hard or hardly working? Gender, humor, and the performance of domestic chores in television commercials. *Mass Communication and Society, 9,* 215–238.

Schatz, M. (1994). *A toddler's life.* New York: Oxford University Press.

Schechter, D., & Willheim, E. (2009). Disturbances of attachment and parental psychopathology in early childhood. *Child and Adolescent Psychiatric Clinics of North America, 18,* 665–686.

Schecklmann, M., Pfannstiel, C., Fallgatter, A. J., Warnke, A., Gerlach, M., & Romanos, M. (2012). Olfaction in child and adolescent anorexia nervosa. *Journal of Neural Transmission, 119,* 721–728.

Schecter, T., Finkelstein, Y., & Koren, G. (2005). Pregnant "DES daughters" and their offspring. *Canadian Family Physician, 51,* 493–494.

Scheibner, G., & Leathem, J. (2012). Memory control beliefs and everyday forgetfulness in adulthood: The effects of selection, optimization, and compensation strategies. *Aging, Neuropsychology, and Cognition, 19,* 362–379.

Schemo, D. J. (2001, December 5). U.S. students prove middling on 32-nation test. *The New York Times,* p. A21.

Schemo, D. J. (2003, November 13). Students' scores rise in math, not in reading. *The New York Times,* p. A2.

Schemo, D. J. (2004, March 2). Schools, facing tight budgets, leave gifted programs behind. *The New York Times,* pp. A1, A18.

Scherf, K. S., Sweeney, J. A., & Luna, B. (2006). Brain basis of developmental change in visuospatial working memory. *Journal of Cognitive Neuroscience, 18,* 1045–1058.

Schieman, S., McBrier, D. B., & van Gundy, K. (2003). Home-to-work conflict, work qualities, and emotional distress. *Sociological Forum, 18,* 137–164.

Schildmann, J., & Schildmann, E. (2013). There is more to end-life practices than euthanasia. *The Lancet, 381,* 202.

Schiller, J. S., & Bernadel, L. (2004). Summary health statistics for the U.S. population: National Health Interview Survey, 2002. *Vital Health Statistics, 10,* 1–110.

Schlosser, F., Zinni, D., & Armstrong-Stassen, M. (2012). Intention to unretire: HR and the boomerang effect. *The Career Development International, 17,* 149–167.

Schlottmann, A., & Wilkening, F. (2012). Judgment and decision making in young children. In M. K. Dhami, A. Schlottmann, & M. R. Waldmann (Eds.), *Judgment and decision making as a skill: Learning, development and evolution.* New York: Cambridge University Press.

Schmidt, M., Pekow, P., Freedson, P., Markenson, G., & Chasan-Taber, L. (2006). Physical activity patterns during pregnancy in a diverse population of women. *Journal of Women's Health, 15,* 909–918.

Schmidt, M. E., Rich, M., Rifas-Shiman, S. L., Oken, E., & Taveras, E. M. (2009). Television viewing in infancy and child cognition at 3 years of age in a U.S. cohort. *Pediatrics, 123,* 370–375.

Schmidt, P. J., & Rubinow, D. R. (1991). Menopause-related affective disorders: A justification for further study. *American Journal of Psychiatry, 148,* 844–852.

Schmitt, E. (2001, March 13). For 7 million people in census, one race category isn't enough. *The New York Times,* pp. A1, A14.

Schmitt, M., Kliegel, M., & Shapiro, A. (2007). Marital interaction in middle and old age: A predictor of marital satisfaction? *International Journal of Aging & Human Development, 65,* 283–300.

Schneider, E. L. (1999, February 5). Aging in the third millennium. *Science, 283,* 796–797.

Schneider, W. (2010). Metacognition and memory development in childhood and adolescence. In H. S. Waters, W. Schneider, & J. G. Borkowski (Eds.), *Metacognition, strategy use, and instruction.* New York: Guilford Press.

Schoklitsch, A., & Baumann, U. (2012). Generativity and aging: A promising future research topic? *Journal of Aging Studies, 26,* 262–272.

Schonert-Reichl, K. A., Smith, V., Zaidman-Zait, A., & Hertzman, C. (2012). Promoting children's prosocial behaviors in school: Impact of the 'Roots of Empathy' program on the social and emotional competence of school-aged children. *School Mental Health, 4,* 1–21.

Schoppe-Sullivan, S., Diener, M., Mangelsdorf, S., Brown, G., McHale, J., & Frosch, C. (2006, July). Attachment and sensitivity in family context: The roles of parent and infant gender. *Infant and Child Development, 15,* 367–385.

Schoppe-Sullivan, S., Mangelsdorf, S., Brown, G., & Sokolowski, M. (2007, February). Goodness-of-fit in family context: Infant temperament, marital quality, and early coparenting behavior. *Infant Behavior & Development, 30,* 82–96.

Schreiber, G. B., Robins, M., Striegel-Moore, R., Obarzanek, M., Morrison, J. A., & Wright, D. J. (1996). Weight modification efforts reported by black and white preadolescent girls: National Heart, Lung, and Blood Institute Growth and Health Study. *Pediatrics, 98,* 63–70.

Schuetze, P., Eiden, R., & Coles, C. (2007). Prenatal cocaine and other substance exposure: Effects on infant autonomic regulation at 7 months of age. *Developmental Psychobiology, 49,* 276–289.

Schultz, A. H. (1969). *The life of primates.* New York: Universe.

Schultz, N. (2009, August 22). Do expanding waistlines cause shrinking brains? *New Scientist,* p. 9.

Schultz, R., & Curnow, C. (1988). Peak performance and age among superathletes: Track and field, swimming, baseball, tennis, and golf. *Journal of Gerontology, 43,* P113–P120.

Schumer, F. (2009, September 29). After a death, the pain that doesn't go away. *The New York Times,* p. D1.

Schutt, R. K. (2001). *Investigating the social world: The process and practice of research.* Thousand Oaks, CA: Sage Publications.

Schwartz, I. M. (1999). Sexual activity prior to coital interaction: A comparison between males and females. *Archives of Sexual Behavior, 28,* 63–69.

Schwartz, P., Maynard, A., & Uzelac, S. (2008). Adolescent egocentrism: A contemporary view. *Adolescence, 43,* 441–448.

Schwarz, T. F., Huang, L., Medina, D., Valencia, A., Lin, T., Behre, U., et al. (2012). Four-year follow-up of the immunogenicity and safety of the HPV-16/18 AS04-adjuvanted vaccine when administered to adolescent girls aged 10-14 years. *Journal of Adolescent Health, 50,* 187–194.

Schweinhart, L. J., Barnes, H. V., & Weikart, D. P. (1993). *Significant benefits: The High/Scope Perry Preschool Study through age 27* (Monographs of the High/Scope Educational Research Foundation, No. 10). Ypsilanti, MI: High/Scope Press.

Schwenkhagen, A. (2007). Hormonal changes in menopause and implications on sexual health. *The Journal of Sexual Medicine, 4*(Suppl. 3), 220–226.

Sciberras, E., Efron, D., Schilpzand, E. J., Anderson, V., Jongeling, B., Hazell, P., et al. (2013). The Children's Attention Project: A community-based longitudinal study of children with ADHD and non-ADHD controls. *BMC Psychiatry, 13,* 13–18.

Scrimsher, S., & Tudge, J. (2003). The teaching/learning relationship in the first years of school: Some revolutionary implications of Vygotsky's theory. *Early Education and Development, 14*(Special issue), 293–312.

Sears, R. R. (1977). Sources of life satisfaction of the Terman gifted men. *American Psychologist, 32,* 119–129.

Seaton, S. E., King, S., Manktelow, B. N., Draper, E. S., & Field, D. J. (2012). Babies born at the threshold of viability: Changes in survival and workload over 20 years. *Archives of Disable Children and Neonatal Education, 9,* 22–35.

Sebanc, A., Kearns, K., Hernandez, M., & Galvin, K. (2007). Predicting having a best friend in young children: Individual characteristics and friendship features. *Journal of Genetic Psychology, 168,* 81–95.

Seçkin, G. (2013). Satisfaction with health status among cyber patients: Testing a mediation model of electronic coping support. *Behaviour & Information Technology, 32,* 91–101.

Sedgh, G., Singh, S., Shah, I. H., Ahman, E., Henshaw, S. K., & Kankole, A. (2012). Induced abortion: Incidence and trends worldwide from 1995 to 2008. *The Lancet, 379,* 625–632.

SEER. (2005). *Surveillance, epidemiology, and end results (SEER) program (www.seer.cancer.gov). SEER*Stat Database: Incidence—SEER 9 Regs Public-Use, Nov 2004 Sub (1973–2002).* National Cancer Institute, DCCPS, Surveillance Research Program, Cancer Statistics Branch, released April 2005, based on the November 2004 submission.

Segal, J., & Segal, Z. (1992, September). No more couch potatoes. *Parents,* p. 235.

Segal, N. L. (1993). Twin, sibling, and adoption methods: Tests of evolutionary hypotheses. *American Psychologist, 48,* 943–956.

Segal, N. L. (2000). Virtual twins: New findings on within-family environmental influences on intelligence. *Journal of Educational Psychology, 92,* 188–194.

Segall, M. H., Dasen, P. R., Berry, J. W., & Poortinga, Y. H. (1990). *Human behavior in global perspective.* Boston: Allyn & Bacon.

Segalowitz, S. J., & Rapin, I. (Eds.). (2003). *Child neuropsychology, Part I.* Amsterdam, The Netherlands: Elsevier Science.

Seibert, A., & Kerns, K. (2009). Attachment figures in middle childhood. *International Journal of Behavioral Development, 33,* 347–355.

Seidman, S. (2003). The aging male: Androgens, erectile dysfunction, and depression. *Journal of Clinical Psychiatry, 64,* 31–37.

Selfhout, M., Denissen, J., Branje, S., & Meeus, W. (2009). In the eye of the beholder: Perceived, actual, and peer-rated similarity in personality, communication, and friendship intensity during the acquaintanceship process. *Journal of Personality and Social Psychology, 96,* 1152–1165.

Selig, S., Tomlinson, T., & Hickey, T. (1991). Ethical dimensions of intergenerational reciprocity: Implications for practice. *Gerontologist, 31,* 624–630.

Seligman, M. E. P. (2007). Coaching and positive psychology. *Australian Psychologist, 42,* 266–267.

Semerci, Ç. (2006). The opinions of medicine faculty students regarding cheating in relation to Kohlberg's moral development concept. *Social Behavior and Personality, 34,* 41–50.

Sener, A., Terzioglu, R., & Karabulut, E. (2007, January). Life satisfaction and leisure activities during men's retirement: A Turkish sample. *Aging & Mental Health, 11,* 30–36.

Senju, A., Southgate, V., Snape, C., Leonard, M., & Csibra, G. (2011). Do 18 month olds really attribute mental states to others? A critical test. *Science, 331,* 477–480.

Seppa, N. (1997, February). Wisdom: A quality that may defy age. *APA Monitor,* pp. 1, 9.

Serbin, L., & Karp, J. (2004). The intergenerational transfer of psychosocial risk: Mediators of vulnerability and resilience. *Annual Review of Psychology, 55,* 333–363.

Serbin, L., Poulin-Dubois, D., & Colburne, K. (2001). Gender stereotyping in infancy: Visual preferences for and knowledge of gender-stereotyped toys in the second year. *International Journal of Behavioral Development, 25,* 7–15.

Serretti, A., Calati, R., Ferrari, B., & De Ronchi, D. (2007). Personality and genetics. *Current Psychiatry Reviews, 3,* 147–159.

Serretti, A., & Fabbri, C. (2013). Shared genetics among major psychiatric disorders. *The Lancet, 381,* 1339–1341.

Servin, A., Nordenström, A., Larsson, A., & Bohlin, G. (2003). Prenatal adrogens and gender-typed behavior: A study of girls with mild and severe forms of congenital adrenal hyperplasia. *Developmental Psychology, 39,* 440–450.

Sesser, S. (1993, September 13). Opium war redux. *The New Yorker,* pp. 78–89.

Settersten, R. (2002). Social sources of meaning in later life. In R. Weiss & S. Bass (Eds.), *Challenges of the third age: Meaning and purpose in later life.* London: Oxford University Press.

Sexton, M., Byrd, M., & von Kluge, S. (2010). Measuring resilience in women experiencing infertility using the CD-RISC: Examining infertility-related stress, general distress, and coping styles. *Journal of Psychiatric Research, 44,* 236–241.

Seymour, J., Payne, S., Chapman, A., & Holloway, M. (2007). Hospice or home? Expectations of end-of-life care among white and Chinese older people in the UK. *Sociology of Health & Illness, 29,* 872–890.

Shafto, C. L., Conway, C. M., Field, S. L., & Houston, D. M. (2012). Visual sequence learning in infancy: Domain-general and domain-specific associations with language. *Infancy, 17,* 247–271.

Shalev, I., Entringer, S., Wadhwa, P. D., Wolkowitz, O. M., Puterman, E., Lin, J., et al. (2013). Stress and telomere biology: A lifespan perspective. *Psychoneuroendocrinology.* Accessed online, June 13, 2013, http://www.sciencedirect.com/science/article/pii/S0306453013001054

Shamloul, R., & Ghanem, H. (2013). Erectile dysfunction. *The Lancet, 381,* 153–165.

Shangguan, F., & Shi, J. (2009). Puberty timing and fluid intelligence: A study of correlations between testosterone and intelligence in 8- to 12-year-old Chinese boys. *Psychoneuroendocrinology, 34,* 983–988.

Shapiro, A. F., Gottman, J. M., & Carrè, S. (2000). The baby and the marriage: Identifying factors that buffer against decline in marital satisfaction after the first baby arrives. *Journal of Family Psychology, 14,* 124–130.

Shapiro, L., & Solity, J. (2008). Delivering phonological and phonics training within whole-class teaching. *British Journal of Educational Psychology, 78,* 597–620.

Sharf, R. S. (1992). *Applying career development theory to counseling.* Pacific Grove, CA: Brooks/Cole.

Shaunessy, E., Suldo, S., Hardesty, R., & Shaffer, E. (2006, December). School functioning and psychological well-being of international baccalaureate and general education students: A preliminary examination. *Journal of Secondary Gifted Education, 17,* 76–89.

Shaver, P. R., Hazan, C., & Bradshaw, D. (1988). Love as attachment: The integration of three behavioral systems. In R. J. Sternberg & M. L. Barnes (Eds.), *The psychology of love.* New Haven, CT: Yale University Press.

Shaw, B., Liang, J., & Krause, N. (2010). Age and race differences in the trajectories of self-esteem. *Psychology and Aging, 25,* 84–94.

Shaw, D. S., Winslow, E. B., & Flanagan, C. (1999). A prospective study of the effects of marital status and family relations on young children's adjustment among African American and European American families. *Child Development, 70,* 742–755.

Shaw, M. L. (2003). Creativity and whole language. In J. Houtz (Ed.), *The educational psychology of creativity.* Cresskill, NJ: Hampton Press.

Shaw, P., Eckstrand, K., Sharp, W., Blumenthal, J., Lerch, J. P., Greenstein, D., et al. (2007). Attention-deficit/hyperactivity disorder is characterized by a delay in cortical maturation. *Proceedings of the National Academy of Sciences of the United States of America, 104,* 19649–19654.

Shaywitz, B. A., Shaywitz, S. E., Blachman, B. A., Pugh, K. R., Fulbright, R. K., Skudlarski, P., et al. (2004). Development of left occipitotemporal systems for skilled reading in children after a phonologically-based intervention. *Biological Psychiatry, 55,* 926–933.

Shea, J. (2006, September). Cross-cultural comparison of women's midlife symptom-reporting: A China study. *Culture, Medicine and Psychiatry, 30,* 331–362.

Shea, K. M., Wilcox, A. J., & Little, R. E. (1998). Postterm delivery: A challenge for epidemiologic research. *Epidemiology, 9,* 199–204.

Sheldon, K. M., Joiner, T. E., Jr., & Pettit, J. W. (2003). Reconciling humanistic ideals and scientific clinical practice. *Clinical Psychology, 10,* 302–315.

Shellenbarger, S. (2003, January 9). Yes, that weird day-care center could scar your child, researchers say. *Wall Street Journal,* p. D1.

Sherman, E. (1991). *Reminiscence and the self in old age.* New York: Springer.

Sherman, S., Allen, E., Bean, L., & Freeman, S. (2007). Epidemiology of Down syndrome. *Mental Retardation and Developmental Disabilities Research Reviews, 13,* 221–227. Available online at http://search.ebscohost.com

Shernoff, D., & Schmidt, J. (2008). Further evidence of an engagement-achievement paradox among U.S. high school students. *Journal of Youth and Adolescence, 37,* 564–580.

Shi, L. (2003). Facilitating constructive parent-child play: Family therapy with young children. *Journal of Family Psychotherapy, 14,* 19–31.

Shi, X., & Lu, X. (2007). Bilingual and bicultural development of Chinese American adolescents and young adults: A comparative study. *Howard Journal of Communications, 18,* 313–333.

Shimizu, M., & Pelham, B. (2004). The unconscious cost of good fortune: Implicit and explicit self-esteem, positive life events, and health. *Health Psychology, 23,* 101–105.

Shin, H. B., & Bruno, R. (2003). *Language use and English speaking ability: 2000.* Washington, DC: U.S. Census Bureau.

Shiner, R., Masten, A., & Roberts, J. (2003). Childhood personality foreshadows adult personality and life outcomes two decades later. *Journal of Personality, 71,* 1145–1170.

Shor, R. (2006, May). Physical punishment as perceived by parents in Russia: Implications for professionals involved in the care of children. *Early Child Development and Care, 176,* 429–439.

Shurkin, J. N. (1992). *Terman's kids: The groundbreaking study of how the gifted grow up.* Boston: Little, Brown.

Shuster, L., Rhodes, D., Gostout, B., Grossardt, B., & Rocca, W. (2010). Premature menopause or early menopause: Long-term health consequences. *Maturitas, 65,* 161–166.

Shute, N. (1997, November 10). No more hard labor. *U.S. News & World Report,* pp. 92–95.

Shweder, R. A. (Ed.). (1998). *Welcome to middle age! (And other cultural fictions).* New York: University of Chicago Press.

Shweder, R. A. (2003). *Why do men barbecue? Recipes for cultural psychology.* Cambridge, MA: Harvard University Press.

Sieber, J. E. (2000). Planning research: Basic ethical decision-making. In B. D. Sales & S. Folkman (Eds.), *Ethics in research with human participants.* Washington, DC: American Psychological Association.

Siegal, M. (1997). *Knowing children: Experiments in conversation and cognition* (2nd ed.). Hove, England: Psychology Press/Lawrence Erlbaum (UK), Taylor & Francis.

Siegel, S., Dittrich, R., & Vollmann, J. (2008). Ethical opinions and personal attitudes of young adults conceived by in vitro fertilisation. *Journal of Medical Ethics, 34,* 236–240.

Siegler, R. S. (1994). Cognitive variability: A key to understanding cognitive development. *Current Directions in Psychological Science, 3,* 1–5.

Siegler, R. S. (1998). *Children's thinking* (3rd ed.). Upper Saddle River, NJ: Prentice Hall.

Siegler, R. S. (2007). Cognitive variability. *Developmental Science, 10,* 104–109.

Siegler, R. S. (2012). From theory to application and back: Following in the giant footsteps of David Klahr. In J. Shrager & S. Carver (Eds.), *The journey from child to scientist: Integrating cognitive development and the education sciences.* Washington, DC: American Psychological Association.

Siegler, R. S., & Ellis, S. (1996). Piaget on childhood. *Psychological Science, 7,* 211–215.

Siegler, R. S., & Lin, X. (2010). Self-explanations promote children's learning. In H. S. Waters, W. Schneider, & J. G. Borkowski (Eds.), *Metacognition, strategy use, and instruction.* New York: Guilford Press.

Siegler, R. S., & Richards, D. (1982). The development of intelligence. In R. Sternberg (Ed.), *Handbook of human intelligence.* London: Cambridge University Press.

Sierra, F. (2006, June). Is (your cellular response to) stress killing you? *Journals of Gerontology: Series A: Biological Sciences and Medical Sciences, 61,* 557–561.

Sigman, M., Cohen, S. E., & Beckwith, L. (1997). Why does infant attention predict adolescent intelligence? *Infant Behavior & Development, 20,* 133–140.

Signorella, M., & Frieze, I. (2008). Interrelations of gender schemas in children and adolescents: Attitudes, preferences, and self-perceptions. *Social Behavior and Personality, 36,* 941–954.

Silenzio, V., Pena, J., Duberstein, P., Cerel, J., & Knox, K. (2007, November). Sexual orientation and risk factors for suicidal ideation and suicide attempts among adolescents and young adults. *American Journal of Public Health, 97*(11), 2017–2019.

Silveira, C. M., Andres, A. G., Rodico, G. M., Abadi, A., & Rodriguez, S. M. (2007). Infant with failure to thrive and hepatosplenomeagaly. *Anales de Pediatria, 66,* 201–202.

Silverstein, L. B., & Auerbach, C. F. (1999). Deconstructing the essential father. *American Psychologist, 54,* 397–407.

Silverthorn, P., & Frick, P. J. (1999). Developmental pathways to antisocial behavior: The delayed-onset pathway in girls. *Developmental & Psychopathology, 11,* 101–126.

Simmons, S. W., Cyna, A. M., Dennis, A. T., & Hughes, D. (2007). Combined spinal-epidural versus epidural analgesia in labour. *Cochrane Database and Systematic Review, 18,* CD003401.

Simons, S. H., van Dijk, M., Anand, K. S., Roofthooft, D., van Lingen, R. A., & Tibboel, D. (2003). Do we still hurt newborn babies? A prospective study of procedural pain and analgesia in neonates. *Archives of Pediatrics and Adolescence, 157,* 1058–1064.

Simonton, D. K. (1997). Creative productivity: A predictive and explanatory model of career trajectories and landmarks. *Psychological Review, 104,* 66–89.

Simonton, D. K. (2009). Varieties of (scientific) creativity: A hierarchical model of domain-specific disposition, development, and achievement. *Perspectives on Psychological Science, 4,* 441–452.

Simpkins, S., Parke, R., Flyr, M., & Wild, M. (2006, November). Similarities in children's and early adolescents' perceptions of friendship qualities across development, gender, and friendship qualities. *Journal of Early Adolescence, 26,* 491–508.

Simpson, J. A. (1990). Influence of attachment styles on romantic relationships. *Journal of Personality & Social Psychology, 59,* 971–980.

Simpson, J. A., Collins, W., Tran, S., & Haydon, K. (2007, February). Attachment and the experience and expression of emotions in romantic relationships: A developmental perspective. *Journal of Personality and Social Psychology, 92,* 355–367.

Simson, S. P., Wilson, L. B., & Harlow-Rosentraub, K. (2006). Civic engagement and lifelong learning institutes: Current status and future directions. In L. Wilson & S. P. Simson (Eds.), *Civic engagement and the baby boomer generation: Research, policy, and practice perspectives.* New York: Haworth Press.

Sinclair, D. A., & Guarente, L. (2006). Unlocking the secrets of longevity genes. *Scientific American, 294,* 48–51, 54–57.

Singer, D. G., & Singer, J. L. (Eds.). (2000). *Handbook of children and the media.* Thousand Oaks, CA: Sage Publications.

Singer, L. T., Arendt, R., Minnes, S., Farkas, K., & Salvator, A. (2000). Neurobehavioral outcomes of cocaine-exposed infants. *Neurotoxicology & Teratology, 22,* 653–666.

Singer, M. S., Stacey, B. G., & Lange, C. (1993). The relative utility of expectancy-value theory and social cognitive theory in predicting psychology student course goals and career aspirations. *Journal of Social Behavior and Personality, 8,* 703–714.

Singh, S., & Darroch, J. E. (2000). Adolescent pregnancy and childbearing: Levels and trends in developed countries. *The Canadian Journal of Human Sexuality, 9,* 67–72.

Siniatchkin, M., Jonas, A., Baki, H., van Baalen, A., Gerber, W., & Stephani, U. (2010). Developmental changes of the contingent negative variation in migraine and healthy children. *The Journal of Headache and Pain, 11,* 105–113.

Sinnott, J. D. (1997). Developmental models of midlife and aging in women: Metaphors for transcendence and for individuality in community. In J. Coyle (Ed.), *Handbook on women and aging.* Westport, CT: Greenwood.

Sinnott, J. D. (1998). *The development of logic in adulthood: Postformal thought and its applications.* New York: Plenum.

Siu, A., & Shek, D. (2010). Social problem solving as a predictor of well-being in adolescents and young adults. *Social Indicators Research, 95,* 393–406.

Skinner, B. F. (1957). *Verbal behavior.* New York: Appleton-Century-Crofts.

Skinner, B. F. (1975). The steep and thorny road to a science of behavior. *American Psychologist, 30,* 42–49.

Skinner, J. D., Ziegler, P., Pac, S., & Devaney, B. (2004). Meal and snack patterns of infants and toddlers. *Journal of the American Dietary Association, 104,* S65–S70.

Skinner, M. (2010). Metabolic disorders: Fathers' nutritional legacy. *Nature, 467,* 922–923.

Skoog, T. (2013). Adolescent and adult implications of girls' pubertal timing. In A. Andershed (Ed.), *Girls at risk: Swedish longitudinal research on adjustment.* New York: Springer Science + Business Media.

Skowronski, J., Walker, W., & Betz, A. (2003). Ordering our world: An examination of time in autobiographical memory. *Memory, 11,* 247–260.

Slater, A., & Johnson, S. P. (1998). Visual sensory and perceptual abilities of the newborn: Beyond the blooming, buzzing confusion. In F. Simion & G. Butterworth et al. (Eds.), *The development of sensory, motor and cognitive capacities in early infancy: From perception to cognition.* Hove, England: Psychology Press / Lawrence Erlbaum (UK) Taylor & Francis.

Slater, A., Mattock, A., & Brown, E. (1990). Size constancy at birth: Newborn infants' responses to retinal and real size. *Journal of Experimental Child Psychology, 49,* 314–322.

Sleeboom-Faulkner, M. (2010). Reproductive technologies and the quality of offspring in Asia: Reproductive pioneering and moral pragmatism? *Culture, Health & Sexuality, 12,* 139–152.

Sloan, S., Gildea, A., Stewart, M., Sneddon, H., & Iwaniec, D. (2008). Early weaning is related to weight and rate of weight gain in infancy. *Child: Care, Health and Development, 34,* 59–64.

Sloan, S., Stewart, M., & Dunne, L. (2010). The effect of breastfeeding and stimulation in the home on cognitive development in one-year-old infants. *Child Care in Practice, 16,* 101–110.

Sloane, S., Baillargeon, R., & Premack, D. (2012). Do infants have a sense of fairness? *Psychological Science, 23,* 196–207.

Slonje, R., & Smith, P. K. (2008). Cyberbullying: Another main type of bullying? *Scandinavian Journal of Psychology, 49,* 147–154.

Small, G. W., Moody, T. D., Siddarth, P., & Bookheimer, S. Y. (2009). Your brain on Google: Patterns of cerebral activation during Internet searching. *The American Journal of Geriatric Psychiatry, 17,* 116–126.

Small, G., & Vorgan, G. (2008). *iBrain: Surviving the technological alteration of the modern mind.* New York: Harper Collins.

Smedley, A., & Smedley, B. D. (2005). Race as biology is fiction, racism as a social problem is real: Anthropological and historical perspectives on the social construction of race. *American Psychologist, 60,* 16–26.

Smedley, B. D., & Syme, S. L. (Eds.). (2000). *Promoting health: Intervention strategies from social and behavioral research.* Washington, DC: National Academy of Sciences.

Smetana, J. G. (1995). Parenting styles and conceptions of parental authority during adolescence. *Child Development, 66,* 299–316.

Smetana, J. G. (2005). Adolescent-parent conflict: Resistance and subversion as developmental process. In L. Nucci (Ed.), *Conflict, contradiction, and contrarian elements in moral development and education.* Mahwah, NJ: Lawrence Erlbaum.

Smetana, J. G. (2006). Social-cognitive domain theory: Consistencies and variations in children's moral and social judgments. In M. Killen & J. G. Smetana (Eds.), *Handbook of moral development*. Mahwah, NJ: Lawrence Erlbaum.

Smetana, J. G., Daddis, C., & Chuang, S. (2003). "Clean your room!" A longitudinal investigation of adolescent-parent conflict and conflict resolution in middle-class African American families. *Journal of Adolescent Research, 18,* 631–650.

Smith, B. L. (2012, April). The case against spanking. *Monitor on Psychology*, pp. 60–63.

Smith, C., & Hung, L. (2012). The influence of Eastern philosophy on elder care by Chinese Americans: Attitudes toward long-term care. *Journal of Transcultural Nursing, 23,* 100–105.

Smith, J. M. (2012). Toward a better understanding of loneliness in community-dwelling older adults. *Journal of Psychology: Interdisciplinary and Applied, 146,* 293–311.

Smith, N. A., & Trainor, L. J. (2008). Infant-directed speech is modulated by infant feedback. *Infancy, 13,* 410–420.

Smith, P. K. (1995). Grandparenthood. In M. H. Bornstein (Ed.), *Handbook of parenting*. Hillsdale, NJ: Lawrence Erlbaum.

Smith, P. K., & Drew, L. M. (2002). Grandparenthood. In M. Bornstein (Ed.), *Handbook of parenting*. Mahwah, NJ: Lawrence Erlbaum.

Smith, P. K., Mahdavi, J., Carvalho, M., Fisher, S., Russell, S., & Tippett, N. (2008). Cyberbullying: Its nature and impact in secondary school pupils. *Journal of Child Psychology and Psychiatry, 49,* 376–385.

Smith, R. A., Duffy, S. W., & Tabár, L. (2012). Breast cancer screening: The evolving evidence. *Oncology, 26,* 471–475, 479–481, 485–486.

Smith, R. J., Bale, J. F., Jr., & White, K. R. (2005, March 2). Sensorineural hearing loss in children. *The Lancet, 365,* 879–890.

Smith, S., Quandt, S., Arcury, T., Wetmore, L., Bell, R., & Vitolins, M. (2006, January). Aging and eating in the rural, southern United States: Beliefs about salt and its effect on health. *Social Science & Medicine, 62,* 189–198.

Snowdon, D. A., Kemper, S. J., Mortimer, J. A., Greiner, L. H., Wekstein, D. R., & Markesbery, W. R. (1996, February 21). Linguistic ability in early life and cognitive function and Alzheimer's disease in late life: Findings from the nun study. *JAMA: The Journal of the American Medical Association, 275,* 528–532.

Soares, C., & Frey, B. (2010). Challenges and opportunities to manage depression during the menopausal transition and beyond. *Psychiatric Clinics of North America, 33,* 295–308.

Soderstrom, M. (2007). Beyond babytalk: Re-evaluating the nature and content of speech input to preverbal infants. *Developmental Review, 27,* 501–532.

Soderstrom, M., Blossom, M., Foygel, R., & Morgan, J. (2008). Acoustical cues and grammatical units in speech to two preverbal infants. *Journal of Child Language, 35,* 869–902.

Solberg, P., Kvamme, N., Raastad, T., Ommundsen, Y., Tomten, S., Halvari, H., et al. (2013). Effects of different types of exercise on muscle mass, strength, function and well-being in elderly. *European Journal of Sport Science, 13,* 112–125.

Soldo, B. J. (1996). Cross-pressures on middle-aged adults: A broader view. *Journal of Gerontology: Psychological Sciences and Social Sciences, 51B,* 271–273.

Solomon, W., Richards, M., Huppert, F. A., Brayne, C., & Morgan, K. (1998). Divorce, current marital status and well-being in an elderly population. *International Journal of Law, Policy and the Family, 12,* 323–344.

Somerset, W., Newport, D., Ragan, K., & Stowe, Z. (2006). Depressive disorders in women: From menarche to beyond the menopause. In L. M. Keyes & S. H. Goodman (Eds.), *Women and depression: A handbook for the social, behavioral, and biomedical sciences*. New York: Cambridge University Press.

Sonne, J. L. (2012). Psychological assessment measures. In *PsycEssentials: A pocket resource for mental health practitioners*. Washington, DC: American Psychological Association.

Sonnen, J., Larson, E., Gray, S., Wilson, A., Kohama, S., Crane, P., et al. (2009). Free radical damage to cerebral cortex in Alzheimer's disease, microvascular brain injury, and smoking. *Annals of Neurology, 65,* 226–229.

Sonnentag, S. (2012). Psychological detachment from work during leisure time: The benefits of mentally disengaging from work. *Current Directions in Psychological Science, 21,* 114–118.

Sontag, S. (1979). The double standard of aging. In J. H. Williams (Ed.), *Psychology of women: Selected readings*. New York: Norton.

Soska, K., Adolph, K., & Johnson, S. (2010). Systems in development: Motor skill acquisition facilitates three-dimensional object completion. *Developmental Psychology, 46,* 129–138.

Sousa, D. L. (2005). *How the brain learns to read*. Thousand Oaks, CA: Corwin Press.

Sowell, E. R., Peterson, B. S., Thompson, P. M., Welcome, S. E., Henkenius, A. L., & Toga, A. W. (2003). Mapping cortical change across the human life span. *Nature Neuroscience, 6,* 309–315.

Sowell, E. R., Thompson, P. M., Holmes, C. J., Jerrigan, T. L., & Toga, A. W. (1999). In vivo evidence for post-adolescent brain maturation in frontal and striatal regions. *Nature Neuroscience, 10,* 859–861.

Sowell, E. R., Thompson, P. M., Tessner, K. D., & Toga, A. W. (2001). Mapping continued brain growth and gray matter density reduction in dorsal frontal cortex: Inverse relationships during postadolescent brain maturation. *Journal of Neuroscience, 21,* 8819–8829.

Sparks, M. B. (2008). Inpatient care for persons with Alzheimer's disease. *Alzheimer's Care Today, 9,* 204–210.

Spear, L. (2010). *The behavioral neuroscience of adolescence*. New York: Norton.

Spear, P. D. (1993). Neural bases of visual deficits during aging. *Vision Research, 33,* 2589–2609.

Spearman, C. (1927). *The abilities of man*. London: Macmillan.

Spence, A. P. (1989). *The biology of human aging*. Englewood Cliffs, NJ: Prentice Hall.

Spence, S. H. (1997). Sex and relationships. In W. K. Halford & H. J. Markman (Eds.), *Clinical handbook of marriage and couples interventions* (pp. 73–105). Chichester, England: Wiley.

Spencer, M. B., & Dornbusch, S. M. (1990). Challenges in studying minority youth. In S. Feldman & G. Elliott (Eds.), *At the threshold: The developing adolescent*. Cambridge, MA: Harvard University Press.

Spencer, S. J., Fein, S., Zanna, M. P., & Olson, J. M. (Eds.). (2003). *Motivated social perception: The Ontario Symposium* (Vol. 9). Mahwah, NJ: Lawrence Erlbaum.

Spörer, N., Brunstein, J., & Kieschke, U. (2009). Improving students' reading comprehension skills: Effects of strategy instruction and reciprocal teaching. *Learning and Instruction, 19,* 272–286.

Spraggins, R. E. (2003). *Women and men in the United States: March 2002*. Washington, DC: U.S. Department of Commerce.

Sprecher, S., Sullivan, Q., & Hatfield, E. (1994). Mate selection preferences: Gender differences examined in a national sample. *Journal of Personality and Social Psychology, 66,* 1074–1080.

Sprenger, M. (2007). *Memory 101 for educators*. Thousand Oaks, CA: Corwin Press.

Squatriglia, C. (2007, February 16). Ted Soulis—charitable painter, businessman. *San Francisco Chronicle*, p. B7.

Squeglia, L. M., Sorg, S. F., Schweinsburg, A., Dager, W., Reagan, R., & Tapert, S. F. (2012). Binge drinking differentially affects adolescent male and female brain morphometry. *Psychopharmacology, 220,* 529–539.

Squire, L. R., & Knowlton, B. J. (1995). Memory, hippocampus, and brain systems. In M. S. Gazzaniga (Ed.), *Cognitive neurosciences*. Cambridge, MA: MIT Press.

Srivastava, S., John, O., & Gosling, S. (2003). Development of personality in early and middle adulthood: Set like plaster or persistent change? *Journal of Personality & Social Psychology, 84,* 1041–1053.

Sroufe, L. A. (1994). Pathways to adaptation and maladaptation: Psychopathology as developmental deviation. In D. Cicchetti (Ed.), *Developmental psychopathology: Past, present, and future*. Hillsdale, NJ: Lawrence Erlbaum.

Sroufe, L. A. (1996). *Emotional development: The organization of emotional life in the early years*. New York: Oxford University Press.

Starr, L. (2010). Preparing those caring for older adults to report elder abuse. *The Journal of Continuing Education in Nursing, 41,* 231–235.

Staudinger, U. (2008). A psychology of wisdom: History and recent developments. *Research in Human Development, 5,* 107–120.

Staudinger, U. M., & Baltes, P. B. (1996). Interactive minds: A facilitative setting for wisdom-related performance? *Journal of Personality and Social Psychology, 71,* 746–762.

Staunton, H. (2005). Mammalian sleep. *Naturwissenschaften, 92,* 203–220.

Stearns, E., & Glennie, E. (2006, September). When and why dropouts leave high school. *Youth & Society, 38,* 29–57.

Stedman, L. C. (1997). International achievement differences: An assessment of a new perspective. *Educational Researcher, 26,* 4–15.

Steele, C. J., Bailey, J. A., Zatorre, R. J., & Penhune, V. B. (2013). Early musical training and white-matter plasticity in the corpus callosum: Evidence for a sensitive period. *The Journal of Neuroscience, 33,* 1282–1290.

Steele, C. M. (1997). A threat in the air: How stereotypes shape intellectual identity and performance. *American Psychologist, 52,* 613–629.

Steele, C. M. (2012). Conclusion: Extending and applying stereotype threat research: A brief essay. In M. Inzlicht & T. Schmader (Eds.), *Stereotype threat: Theory, process, and application*. New York: Oxford University Press.

Stein, D., Latzer, Y., & Merick, J. (2009). Eating disorders: From etiology to treatment. *International Journal of Child and Adolescent Health, 2,* 139–151.

Stein, J. H., & Reiser, L. W. (1994). A study of white middle-class adolescent boys' responses to "semenarche" (the first ejaculation). *Journal of Youth and Adolescence, 23,* 373–384.

Stein, Z., Susser, M., Saenger, G., & Marolla, F. (1975). *Famine and human development: The Dutch hunger winter of 1944-1945*. New York: Oxford University Press.

Steinberg, J. (1997, January 2). Turning words into meaning. *The New York Times*, pp. B1–B2.

Steinberg, L. (1993). *Adolescence*. New York: McGraw-Hill.

Steinberg, L., Dornbusch, S., & Brown, B. B. (1992). Ethnic differences in adolescent achievement: An ecological perspective. *American Psychologist, 47,* 723–729.

Steinberg, L., & Monahan, K. C. (2007). Age differences in resistance to peer influence. *Developmental Psychology, 43,* 1531–1543.

Steinberg, L., & Scott, S. S. (2003). Less guilty by reason of adolescence: Developmental immaturity, diminished responsibility, and the juvenile death penalty. *American Psychologist, 58,* 1009–1018.

Steiner, J. E. (1979). Human facial expressions in response to taste and smell stimulation. *Advances in Child Development and Behavior, 13,* 257.

Steinert, S., Shay, J. W., & Wright, W. E. (2000). Transient expression of human telomerase extends the life span of normal human fibroblasts. *Biochemical & Biophysical Research Communications, 273,* 1095–1098.

Steinhausen, H. C., & Spohr, H. L. (1998). Long-term outcome of children with fetal alcohol syndrome: Psychopathology, behavior, and intelligence. *Alcoholism, Clinical & Experimental Research, 22,* 334–338.

Stenberg, G. (2009). Selectivity in infant social referencing. *Infancy, 14,* 457–473.

Steri, A. O., & Spelke, E. S. (1988). Haptic perception of objects in infancy. *Cognitive Psychology, 20,* 1–23.

Stern, G. (1994, November 30). Going back to college has special meaning for Mrs. McAlpin. *Wall Street Journal,* p. A1.

Sternberg, R. J. (1985). *Beyond IQ: A triarchic theory of human intelligence.* New York: Cambridge University Press.

Sternberg, R. J. (1986). Triangular theory of love. *Psychological Review, 93,* 119–135.

Sternberg, R. J. (1987). Liking versus loving: A comparative evaluation of theories. *Psychological Bulletin, 102,* 331–345.

Sternberg, R. J. (1990). *Metaphors of mind: Conceptions of the nature of intelligence.* Cambridge, England: Cambridge University Press.

Sternberg, R. J. (2003a). A broad view of intelligence: The theory of successful intelligence. *Consulting Psychology Journal: Practice & Research, 55,* 139–154.

Sternberg, R. J. (2003b). Our research program validating the triarchic theory of successful intelligence: Reply to Gottfredson. *Intelligence, 31,* 399–413.

Sternberg, R. J. (2005). The triarchic theory of successful intelligence. In D. P. Flanagan & P. L. Harrison (Eds.), *Contemporary intellectual assessment: Theories, tests, and issues.* New York: Guilford Press.

Sternberg, R. J. (2006). A duplex theory of love. In R. J. Sternberg & K. Sternberg (Eds.), *The new psychology of love.* New Haven, CT: Yale University Press.

Sternberg, R. J. (2008). Schools should nurture wisdom. In B. Z. Presseisen (Ed.), *Teaching for intelligence* (2nd ed.). Thousand Oaks, CA: Corwin Press.

Sternberg, R. J., Conway, B. E., Ketron, J. L., & Bernstein, M. (1981). Peoples' conceptions of intelligence. *Journal of Personality and Social Psychology, 41,* 37–55.

Sternberg, R. J., & Grigorenko, E. L. (Eds.). (2002). *The general factor of intelligence: How general is it?* Mahwah, NJ: Lawrence Erlbaum.

Sternberg, R. J., Kaufman, J. C., & Pretez, J. E. (2002). *The creativity conundrum: A propulsion model of creative contributions.* Philadelphia: Psychology Press.

Sternberg, R. J., Wagner, R. K., Williams, W. M., & Horvath, J. A. (1997). Testing common sense. In D. Russ-Eft, H. Preskill, & C. Sleezer (Eds.), *Human resource development review: Research and implications* (pp. 102–132). Thousand Oaks, CA: Sage Publications.

Sterns, H. L., Barrett, G. V., & Alexander, R. A. (1985). Accidents and the aging individual. In J. E. Birren & K. W. Schaie (Eds.), *Handbook of the psychology of aging* (2nd ed.). New York: Van Nostrand Reinhold.

Stevens, J., Cai, J., Evenson, K. R., & Thomas, R. (2002). Fitness and fatness as predictors of mortality from all causes and from cardiovascular disease in men and women in the lipid research clinics study. *American Journal of Epidemiology, 156,* 832–841.

Stevens, N., Martina, C., & Westerhof, G. (2006, August). Meeting the need to belong: Predicting effects of a friendship enrichment program for older women. *The Gerontologist, 46,* 495–502.

Stevens, W., Hasher, L., Chiew, K., & Grady, C. (2008). A neural mechanism underlying memory failure in older adults. *The Journal of Neuroscience, 28,* 12820–12824.

Stevenson, J. (2006). Dietary influences on cognitive development and behaviour in children. *Proceedings of the Nutrition Society, 65,* 361–365.

Stevenson, M., Henderson, T., & Baugh, E. (2007, February). Vital defenses: Social support appraisals of black grandmothers parenting grandchildren. *Journal of Family Issues, 28,* 182–211.

Stewart, A. J., Copeland, A. P., Chester, N. L., Mallery, J. E., & Barenbaum, N. B. (1997). *Separating together: How divorce transforms families.* New York: Guilford Press.

Stewart, A. J., & Vandewater, E. A. (1999). "If I had it to do over again…": Midlife review, midcourse corrections, and women's well-being in midlife. *Journal of Personality and Social Psychology, 76,* 270–283.

Stice, E. (2003). Puberty and body image. In C. Hayward (Ed.), *Gender differences at puberty.* New York: Cambridge University Press.

Stikes, R., & Barbier, D. (2013). Applying the plan-do-study-act model to increase the use of kangaroo care. *Journal of Nursing Management, 21,* 70–78.

Stiles, J. (2012). The effects of injury to dynamic neural networks in the mature and developing brain. *Developmental Psychobiology, 54,* 343–349.

Stipp, S. (2012, January). A new path to longevity. *Scientific American,* pp. 33–39.

Stix, G. (2010). Alzheimer's: Forestalling the darkness. *Scientific American, 302,* 50–57.

Stockdale, M. S., & Crosby, F. J. (2004). *Psychology and management of workplace diversity.* Malden, MA: Blackwell Publishers.

Stolzenberg, S., & Pezdek, K. (2013). Interviewing child witnesses: The effect of forced confabulation on event memory. *Journal of Experimental Child Psychology, 114,* 77–88.

Stone, A. A., Schwartz, J. E., Broderick, J. E., & Deaton, A. (2010). A snapshot of the age distribution of psychological well-being in the United States. *PNAS Proceedings of the National Academy of Sciences of the United States of America, 107,* 9985–9990.

Storfer, M. (1990). *Intelligence and giftedness: The contributions of heredity and early environment.* San Francisco: Jossey-Bass.

Story, M., Nanney, M., & Schwartz, M. (2009). Schools and obesity prevention: Creating school environments and policies to promote healthy eating and physical activity. *Milbank Quarterly, 87,* 71–100.

Stout, H. (2010, May 2). Antisocial networking? *The New York Times,* p. ST-1.

Straus, M. A., & Gelles, R. J. (Eds.). (1990). *Physical violence in American families.* New Brunswick, NJ: Transaction.

Straus, M. A., & McCord, J. (1998). Do physically punished children become violent adults? In S. Nolen-Hoeksema (Ed.), *Clashing views on abnormal psychology: A Taking Sides custom reader.* Guilford, CT: Dushkin/McGraw-Hill.

Straus, M. A., Sugarman, D. B., & Giles-Sims, J. (1997). Spanking by parents and subsequent antisocial behavior of children. *Archives of Pediatrics and Adolescent Medicine, 151,* 761–767.

Straus, M. A., & Yodanis, C. L. (1996). Corporal punishment in adolescence and physical assaults on spouses in later life: What accounts for the link? *Journal of Marriage and the Family, 58,* 825–841.

Strauss, J. R. (2011). Contextual influences on women's health concerns and attitudes toward menopause. *Health & Social Work, 36,* 121–127.

Strauss, J. R. (2013). The baby boomers meet menopause: Fertility, attractiveness, and affective response to the menopausal transition. *Sex Roles, 68,* 77–90.

Streissguth, A. (2007). Offspring effects of prenatal alcohol exposure from birth to 25 years: The Seattle Prospective Longitudinal Study. *Journal of Clinical Psychology in Medical Settings, 14,* 81–101.

Strelau, J. (1998). *Temperament: A psychological perspective.* New York: Plenum Publishers.

Strength, J. (1999). Grieving the loss of a child. *Journal of Psychology & Christianity, 18,* 338–353.

Striano, T., & Vaish, A. (2006, November). Seven- to 9-month-old infants use facial expressions to interpret others' actions. *British Journal of Developmental Psychology, 24,* 753–760.

Strobel, A., Dreisbach, G., Müller, J., Goschke, T., Brocke, B., & Lesch, K. (2007, December). Genetic variation of serotonin function and cognitive control. *Journal of Cognitive Neuroscience, 19,* 1923–1931.

Stroebe, M. S., Hansson, R. O., Schut, H., & Stroebe, W. (2008). Bereavement research: Contemporary perspectives. In M. S. Stroebe, R. O. Hansson, H. Schut, & W. Stroebe (Eds.), *Handbook of bereavement research and practice: Advances in theory and intervention.* Washington, DC: American Psychological Association.

Strohl, M., Bednar, C., & Longley, C. (2012). Residents' perceptions of food and nutrition services at assisted living facilities. *Family and Consumer Sciences Research Journal, 40,* 241–254.

Stromswold, K. (2006). Why aren't identical twins linguistically identical? Genetic, prenatal and postnatal factors. *Cognition, 101,* 333–384.

Strube, M. (Ed.). (1990). Type A behavior [Special issue]. *Journal of Social Behavior and Personality, 5.*

Stutzer, A., & Frey, B. (2006, April). Does marriage make people happy, or do happy people get married? *The Journal of Socio-Economics, 35,* 326–347.

Subotnik, R. (2006). Longitudinal studies: Answering our most important questions of prediction and effectiveness. *Journal for the Education of the Gifted, 29,* 379–383.

Suetta, C., & Kjaer, M. (2010). What are the mechanisms behind disuse and age-related skeletal muscle atrophy? *Scandinavian Journal of Medicine & Science in Sports, 20,* 167–168.

Sugarman, S. (1988). *Piaget's construction of the child's reality.* Cambridge, England: Cambridge University Press.

Suinn, R. M. (2001). The terrible twos—Anger and anxiety: Hazardous to your health. *American Psychologist, 56,* 27–36.

Suitor, J. J., Minyard, S. A., & Carter, R. S. (2001). "Did you see what I saw? Gender differences in perceptions of avenues to prestige among adolescents. *Sociological Inquiry, 71,* 437–454.

Sullivan, M., & Lewis, M. (2003). Contextual determinants of anger and other negative expressions in young infants. *Developmental Psychology, 39,* 693–705.

Sullivan, M. W., Rovee-Collier, C. K., & Tynes, D. M. (1979). A conditioning analysis of infant long-term memory. *Child Development, 50,* 152–162.

Sun, L. H. (2012, April 25). Infant mortality in the district drops to historic low. *Washington Post* B–1.

Sunderman, G. L. (Ed.). (2008). *Holding NCLB accountable: Achieving, accountability, equity & school reform.* Thousand Oaks, CA: Corwin Press.

Super, C. M. (1976). Environmental effects on motor development: A case of African infant precocity. *Developmental Medicine and Child Neurology, 18,* 561–576.

Super, C. M., & Harkness, S. (1982). The infant's niche in rural Kenya and metropolitan America. In L. Adler (Ed.), *Issues in cross-cultural research.* New York: Academic Press.

Supple, A., Ghazarian, S., Peterson, G., & Bush, K. (2009). Assessing the cross-cultural validity of a parental autonomy granting measure: Comparing adolescents in the United States, China, Mexico, and India. *Journal of Cross-Cultural Psychology, 40,* 816–833.

Suro, R. (1999, November). Mixed doubles. *American Demographics,* 57–62.

Sutherland, R., Pipe, M., & Schick, K. (2003). Knowing in advance: The impact of prior event information on memory and event knowledge. *Journal of Experimental Child Psychology, 84,* 244–263.

Swaim, R., Barner, J., & Brown, C. (2008). The relationship of calcium intake and exercise to osteoporosis health beliefs in postmenopausal women. *Research in Social & Administrative Pharmacy, 4,* 153–163.

Swanson, L. A., Leonard, L. B., & Gandour, J. (1992). Vowel duration in mothers' speech to young children. *Journal of Speech and Hearing Research, 35,* 617–625.

Swiatek, M. (2002). Social coping among gifted elementary school students. *Journal for the Education of the Gifted, 26,* 65–86.

Syed, M., & Seiffge-Krenke, I. (2013). Personality development from adolescence to emerging adulthood: Linking trajectories of ego development to the family context and identity formation. *Journal of Personality and Social Psychology, 104,* 371–384.

Szaflarski, J. P., Rajagopal, A., Altaye, M., Byars, A. W., Jacola, L., Schmithorst, V. J., et al. (2012). Left-handedness and language lateralization in children. *Brain Research, 1433,* 85–97. Accessed online, July 18, 2012, http://www.ncbi.nlm.nih.gov/pubmed/22177775

Tajfel, H., & Turner, J. C. (2004). The social identity theory of intergroup behavior. In J. T. Jost & J. Sidanius (Eds.), *Political psychology: Key readings.* New York: Psychology Press.

Takahashi, K. (1986). Examining the Strange Situation procedure with Japanese mothers and 12-month-old infants. *Developmental Psychology, 22,* 265–270.

Takala, M. (2006, November). The effects of reciprocal teaching on reading comprehension in mainstream and special (SLI) education. *Scandinavian Journal of Educational Research, 50,* 559–576.

Tallandini, M., & Scalembra, C. (2006). Kangaroo mother care and mother-premature infant dyadic interaction. *Infant Mental Health Journal, 27,* 251–275.

Tamis-LeMonda, C. S., & Cabrera, N. (1999). Perspectives on father involvement: Research and policy. *Social Policy Report, 13,* 1–31.

Tamis-LeMonda, C. S., & Cabrera, N. (2002). *Handbook of father involvement: Multidisciplinary perspectives.* Mahwah, NJ: Lawrence Erlbaum.

Tamis-LeMonda, C. S., Song, L., Leavell, A., Kahana-Kalman, R., & Yoshikawa, H. (2012). Ethnic differences in mother-infant language and gestural communications are associated with specific skills in infants. *Developmental Science, 15,* 384–397.

Tan, H., Wen, S. W., Mark, W., Fung, K. F., Demissie, K., & Rhoads, G. G. (2004). The association between fetal sex and preterm birth in twin pregnancies. *Obstetrics and Gynecology, 103,* 327–332.

Tanaka, K., Kon, N., Ohkawa, N., Yoshikawa, N., & Shimizu, T. (2009). Does breastfeeding in the neonatal period influence the cognitive function of very-low-birth-weight infants at 5 years of age? *Brain & Development, 31,* 288–293.

Tang, C., Wu, M., Liu, J., Lin, H., & Hsu, C. (2006). Delayed parenthood and the risk of cesarean delivery—Is paternal age an independent risk factor? *Birth: Issues in Perinatal Care, 33,* 18–26.

Tang, W. R., Aaronson, L. S., & Forbes, S. A. (2004). Quality of life in hospice patients with terminal illness. *Western Journal of Nursing Research, 26,* 113–128.

Tang, Z., & Orwin, R. (2009). Marijuana initiation among American youth and its risks as dynamic processes: Prospective findings from a national longitudinal study. *Substance Use & Misuse, 44,* 195–211.

Tangri, S., Thomas, V., & Mednick, M. (2003). Predictors of satisfaction among college-educated African American women in midlife. *Journal of Adult Development, 10,* 113–125.

Tanner, E., & Finn-Stevenson, M. (2002). Nutrition and brain development: Social policy implications. *American Journal of Orthopsychiatry, 72,* 182–193.

Tanner, J. (1972). Sequence, tempo, and individual variation in growth and development of boys and girls aged twelve to sixteen. In J. Kagan & R. Coles (Eds.), *Twelve to sixteen: Early adolescence.* New York: Norton.

Tanner, J. L., Arnett, J., & Leis, J. (2009). Emerging adulthood: Learning and development during the first stage of adulthood. In M. C. Smith & N. DeFrates-Densch (Eds.), *Handbook of research on adult learning and development.* New York: Routledge/Taylor & Francis Group.

Tanner, J. M. (1978). *Education and physical growth* (2nd ed.). New York: International Universities Press.

Tappan, M. B. (1997). Language, culture and moral development: A Vygotskian perspective. *Developmental Review, 17,* 199–212.

Tappan, M. B. (2006, March). Moral functioning as mediated action. *Journal of Moral Education, 35,* 1–18.

Tardif, T. (1996). Nouns are not always learned before verbs: Evidence from Mandarin speakers' early vocabularies. *Developmental Psychology, 32,* 492–504.

Taris, T., van Horn, J., & Schaufeli, W. (2004). Inequity, burnout and psychological withdrawal among teachers: A dynamic exchange model. *Anxiety, Stress & Coping: An International Journal, 17,* 103–122.

Task Force on College Gambling Policies. (2009). *A call to action addressing college gambling: Recommendations for science-based policies and programs.* Cambridge, MA: Division on Addictions at the Cambridge Health Alliance.

Tattersall, M., Cordeaux, Y., Charnock-Jones, D., & Smith, G. S. (2012). Expression of gastrin-releasing peptide is increased by prolonged stretch of human myometrium, and antagonists of its receptor inhibit contractility. *The Journal of Physiology, 590,* 2081–2093.

Tatum, B. (2007). *Can we talk about race? And other conversations in an era of school resegregation.* Boston: Beacon Press.

Taveras, E. M., Rifas-Shiman, S. L., Belfort, M. B., Kleinman, K. P., Oken, E., & Gillman, M. W. (2009). Weight status in the first 6 months of life and obesity at 3 years of age. *Pediatrics, 123*(4), 1177–1183.

Taylor, A., Wilson, C., Slater, A., & Mohr, P. (2012). Self-esteem and body dissatisfaction in young children: Associations with weight and perceived parenting style. *Clinical Psychologist, 16,* 25–35.

Taylor, D. M. (2002). *The quest for identity: From minority groups to Generation Xers.* Westport, CT: Praeger Publishers / Greenwood Publishing.

Taylor, R. J., Chatters, L. M., Tucker, M. B., & Lewis, E. (1991). Developments in research on black families. In A. Booth (Ed.), *Contemporary families.* Minneapolis, MN: National Council on Family Relations.

Taylor, R. L., & Rosenbach, W. E. (Eds.). (2005). *Military leadership: In pursuit of excellence* (5th ed.). Boulder, CO: Westview Press.

Taylor, S., & Stanton, A. (2007). Coping resources, coping processes, and mental health. *Annual Review of Clinical Psychology, 33,* 77–401.

Taylor, S. E. (1991). *Health psychology* (2nd ed.). New York: McGraw-Hill.

Teerikangas, O. M., Aronen, E. T., Martin, R. P., & Huttunen, M. O. (1998). Effects of infant temperament and early intervention on the psychiatric symptoms of adolescents. *Journal of the American Academy of Child & Adolescent Psychiatry, 37,* 1070–1076.

Tellegen, A., Lykken, D. T., Bouchard, T. J., Jr., Wilcox, K. J., Segal, N. L., & Rich, S. (1988). Personality similarity in twins reared apart and together. *Journal of Personality and Social Psychology, 54,* 1031–1039.

Terman, D. L., Larner, M. B., Stevenson, C. S., & Behrman, R. E. (1996). Special education for students with disabilities: Analysis and recommendations. *The Future of Children, 6,* 4–24.

Terman, L. M., & Oden, M. H. (1959). *The gifted group at mid-life: Thirty-five years follow-up of the superior child.* Standord, CA: Standord University Press.

Terracciano, A., Costa, P., & McCrae, R. (2006, August). Personality plasticity after age 30. *Personality and Social Psychology Bulletin, 32,* 999–1009.

Terracciano, A., McCrae, R., & Costa, P. (2009). Intra-individual change in personality stability and age. *Journal of Research in Personality, 27,* 88–97.

Terracciano, A., McCrae, R., & Costa, P. (2010). Intra-individual change in personality stability and age. *Journal of Research in Personality, 44,* 31–37.

Terry, D. (2000, August 11). U.S. child poverty rate fell as economy grew, but is above 1979 level. *The New York Times,* p. A10.

Terzidou, V. (2007). Preterm labour. Biochemical and endocrinological preparation for parturition. *Best Practices of Research in Clinical Obstetrics and Gynecology, 21,* 729–756.

Tessor, A., Felson, R. B., & Suls, J. M. (Eds.). (2000). *Psychological perspectives on self and identity.* Washington, DC: American Psychological Association.

Teutsch, C. (2003). Patient-doctor communication. *Medical Clinics of North America, 87,* 1115–1147.

Tharp, R. G. (1989). Psychocultural variables and constants: Effects on teaching and learning in schools [Special issue: Children and their development: Knowledge base, research agenda, and social policy application]. *American Psychologist, 44,* 349–359.

The Endocrine Society. (2001, March 1). *The Endocrine Society and Lawson Wilkins Pediatric Endocrine Society call for further research to define precocious puberty.* Bethesda, MD: Author.

Thelen, E., & Bates, E. (2003). Connectionism and dynamic systems: Are they really different? *Developmental Science, 6,* 378–391.

Thivel, D., Isacco, L., Rousset, S., Boirie, Y., Morio, B., & Duché, P. (2011). Intensive exercise: A remedy for childhood obesity? *Physiology & Behavior, 102*(2), 132–136.

Thobaben, M. (2010). A drug abuse treatment guide available for home health nurses: The National Institute on Drug Abuse's Principles of Drug Addiction Treatment: A Research-Based Guide. *Home Health Care Management & Practice, 22,* 376–377.

Thoman, E. B., & Whitney, M. P. (1990). Sleep states of infants monitored in the home: Individual differences, developmental trends, and origins of diurnal cyclicity. *Infant Behavior and Development, 12,* 59–75.

Thomas, A., & Chess, S. (1980). *The dynamics of psychological development.* New York: Brunner-Mazel.

Thomas, A., Chess, S., & Birch, H. G. (1968). *Temperament and behavior disorders in children.* New York: New York University Press.

Thomas, C. (2010). Oppositional defiant disorder and conduct disorder. In M. K. Dulcan (Ed.), *Dulcan's textbook of child and adolescent psychiatry.* Arlington, VA: American Psychiatric Publishing, Inc.

Thomas, P., & Fenech, M. (2007). A review of genome mutation and Alzheimer's disease. *Mutagenesis, 22,* 15–33.

Thomas, P., Lalloué, F., Preux, P., Hazif-Thomas, C., Pariel, S., Inscale, R., et al. (2006, January). Dementia patients caregivers quality of life: The PIXEL study. *International Journal of Geriatric Psychiatry, 21,* 50–56.

Thomas, R. M. (2001). *Recent human development theories.* Thousand Oaks, CA: Sage Publications.

Thomas, S. G. (2012, March 3). The gray divorces. *Wall Street Journal,* pp. C1, C2.

Thompson, C., & Prottas, D. (2006, January). Relationships among organizational family support, job autonomy, perceived control, and employee well-being. *Journal of Occupational Health Psychology, 11,* 100–118.

Thompson, R. A., Easterbrooks, M., & Padilla-Walker, L. (2003). Social and emotional development in infancy. In R. Lerner & M. Easterbrooks (Eds.), *Handbook of psychology: Developmental psychology, vol. 6.* New York: Wiley.

Thompson, R. A., & Virmani, E. (2010). Self and personality. In M. H. Bornstein (Eds.), *Handbook of cultural developmental science.* New York: Psychology Press.

Thoms, K. M., Kuschal, C., & Emmert, S. (2007). Lessons learned from DNA repair defective syndromes. *Experimental Dermatology, 16,* 532–544.

Thomsen, L., Frankenhus, W. E., Ingold-Smith, M., & Carey, S. (2011). Big and mighty: Preverbal infants mentally represent social dominance. *Journal of Physiological Science, 61,* 429–435.

Thöni, A., Mussner, K., & Ploner, F. (2010). Water birthing: Retrospective review of 2625 water births. Contamination of birth pool water and risk of microbial cross-infection. *Minerva Ginecologia, 62,* 203–211.

Thornberry, T. P., & Krohn, M. D. (1997). Peers, drug use, and delinquency. In D. M. Stoff, J. Breiling, & J. D. Maser (Eds.), *Handbook of antisocial behavior.* New York: Wiley.

Thorne, B. (1986). Girls and boys together, but mostly apart. In W. W. Hartup & Z. Rubin (Eds.), *Relationships and development.* Hillsdale, NJ: Erlbaum.

Thornton, J. (2004). Life-span learning: A developmental perspective. *International Journal of Aging & Human Development, 57,* 55–76.

Thornton, R. (2010). Verb phrase ellipsis in children's answers to questions. *Language Learning and Development, 6,* 1–31.

Thorvaldsson, V., Hofer, S., Berg, S., Skoog, I., Sacuiu, S., & Johansson, B. (2008). Onset of terminal decline in cognitive abilities in individuals without dementia. *Neurology, 71,* 882–887.

Thurlow, M. L., Lazarus, S. S., & Thompson, S. J. (2005). State policies on assessment participation and accommodations for students with disabilities. *Journal of Special Education, 38,* 232–240.

Tikotzky, L., & Sadeh, A. (2009). Maternal sleep-related cognitions and infant sleep: A longitudinal study from pregnancy through the 1st year. *Child Development, 80,* 860–874.

Time. (1980, September 8). People section.

Timmermans, S., & Buchbinder, M. (2012). Expanded newborn screening: Articulating the ontology of diseases with bridging work in the clinic. *Sociology of Health & Illness, 34,* 208–220.

Tincoff, R., & Jusczyk, P. W. (1999). Some beginnings of word comprehension in 6-month-olds. *Psychological Science, 10,* 172–175.

Tinsley, B., Lees, N., & Sumartojo, E. (2004). Child and adolescent HIV risk: Familial and cultural perspectives. *Journal of Family Psychology, 18,* 208–224.

Tobin, J. J., Wu, D. Y. H., & Davidson, D. H. (1989). *Preschool in three cultures: Japan, China, and the United States.* New Haven, CT: Yale University Press.

Toga, A. W., & Thompson, P. M. (2003). Temporal dynamics of brain anatomy. *Annual Review of Biomedical Engineering, 5,* 119–145.

Toga, A. W., Thompson, P. M., & Sowell, E. R. (2006). Mapping brain maturation. *Trends in Neuroscience, 29,* 148–159.

Tolan, P. H., & Dodge, K. A. (2005). Children's mental health as a primary care and concern: A system for comprehensive support and service. *American Psychologist, 60,* 601–614.

Toldson, I. A., & Lemmons, B. P. (2013). Social demographics, the school environment, and parenting practices associated with parents' participation in schools and academic success among Black, Hispanic, and White students. *Journal of Human Behavior in the Social Environment, 23,* 237–255.

Tomblin, J. B., Hammer, C. S., & Zhang, X. (1998). The association of prenatal tobacco use and SLI. *International Journal of Language and Communication Disorders, 33,* 357–368.

Tomlinson, M., Murray, L., & Cooper, P. (2010). Attachment theory, culture, and Africa: Past, present, and future. In P. Erdman & K.-M. Ng (Eds.), *Attachment: Expanding the cultural connections.* New York: Routledge / Taylor & Francis Group.

Tompson, M., Pierre, C., Boger, K., McKowen, J., Chan, P., & Freed, R. (2010). Maternal depression, maternal expressed emotion, and youth psychopathology. *Journal of Abnormal Child Psychology: An official publication of the International Society for Research in Child and Adolescent Psychopathology, 38,* 105–117.

Tongsong, T., Iamthongin, A., Wanapirak, C., Piyamongkol, W., Sirichotiyakul, S., Boonyanurak, P., et al. (2005). Accuracy of fetal heart-rate variability interpretation by obstetricians using the criteria of the National Institute of Child Health and Human Development compared with computer-aided interpretation. *Journal of Obstetric and Gynaecological Research, 31,* 68–71.

Toomey, R. B., Ryan, C. D., Rafael, M., Card, N. A., & Russell, S. T. (2010). Gender-nonconforming lesbian, gay, bisexual, and transgender youth: School victimization and young adult psychosocial adjustment. *Developmental Psychology, 46,* 1580–1589.

Toporek, R. L., Kwan, K., & Williams, R. A. (2012). Ethics and social justice in counseling psychology. In N. A. Fouad, J. A. Carter, & L. M. Subich (Eds.), *APA handbook of counseling psychology, Vol. 2: Practice, interventions, and applications.* Washington, DC US: American Psychological Association.

Torges, C., Stewart, A., & Nolen-Hoeksema, S. (2008). Regret resolution, aging, and adapting to loss. *Psychology and Aging, 23,* 169–180.

Torvaldsen, S., Roberts, C. L., Simpson, J. M., Thompson, J. F., & Ellwood, D. A. (2006). Intrapartum epidural analgesia and breastfeeding: A prospective cohort study. *International Breastfeeding Journal, 24,* 1–24.

Tracy, M., Zimmerman, F., Galea, S., McCauley, E., & Vander Stoep, A. (2008). What explains the relation between family poverty and childhood depressive symptoms? *Journal of Psychiatric Research, 42,* 1163–1175.

Trainor, L. J. (2012). Predictive information processing is a fundamental learning mechanism present in early development: Evidence from infants. *International Journal of Psychophysiology, 83,* 256–258.

Trainor, L. J., Austin, C. M., & Desjardins, R. N. (2000). Is infant-directed speech prosody a result of the vocal expression of emotion? *Psychological Science, 11,* 188–195.

Trapnell, P. D., & Paulhus, D. L. (2012). Agentic and communal values: Their scope and measurement. *Journal of Personality Assessment, 94,* 39–52.

Traywick, L., & Schoenberg, N. (2008). Determinants of exercise among older female heart attack survivors. *Journal of Applied Gerontology, 27,* 52–77.

Trehub, S. E. (2003). The developmental origins of musicality. *Nature Neuroscience, 6,* 669–673.

Tremblay, A., & Chaput, J. (2012). Obesity: The allostatic load of weight loss dieting. *Physiology & Behavior, 106,* 16–21.

Tremblay, R. E. (2001). The development of physical aggression during childhood and the prediction of later dangerousness. In G. F. Pinard & L. Pagani (Eds.), *Clinical assessment of dangerousness: Empirical contributions.* New York: Cambridge University Press.

Trends in HIV- and STD-related risk behaviors among high school students—United States, 1991-2007. (2008, August 1). *Morbidity and Mortality Weekly Report, 57,* 817–822.

Triche, E. W., & Hossain, N. (2007). Environmental factors implicated in the causation of adverse pregnancy outcome. *Seminars in Perinatology, 31,* 240–242.

Trickett, P. K., Kurtz, D. A., & Pizzigati, K. (2004). Resilient outcomes in abused and neglected children: Bases for strengths-based intervention and prevention policies. In K. I. Maton & C. J. Schellenbach (Eds.), *Investing in children, youth, families and communities: Strength-based research and policy.* Washington, DC: American Psychological Association.

Tronick, E. Z. (1995). Touch in mother-infant interactions. In T. M. Field (Ed.), *Touch in early development.* Hillsdale, NJ: Lawrence Erlbaum.

Tropp, L. (2003). The psychological impact of prejudice: Implications for intergroup contact. *Group Processes & Intergroup Relations, 6,* 131–149.

Tropp, L., & Wright, S. (2003). Evaluations and perceptions of self, ingroup, and outgroup: Comparisons between Mexican-American and European-American children. *Self & Identity, 2,* 203–221.

Trotter, A. (2004, December 1). Web searches often overwhelm young researchers. *Education Week, 24,* 8.

Trzesniewski, K. H., Donnellan, M. B., & Robins, R. W. (2003). Stability of self-esteem across the life span. *Journal of Personality and Social Psychology, 84,* 205–220.

Tsapelas, I., Aron, A., & Orbuch, T. (2009). Marital boredom now predicts less satisfaction 9 years later. *Psychological Science, 20,* 543–545.

Tse, T., & Howie, L. (2005, September). Adult day groups: Addressing older people's needs for activity and companionship. *Australasian Journal on Ageing, 24,* 134–140.

Tucker, J., Martínez, J., Ellickson, P., & Edelen, M. (2008, March). Temporal associations of cigarette smoking with social influences, academic performance, and delinquency: A four-wave longitudinal study from ages 13-23. *Psychology of Addictive Behaviors, 22,* 1–11.

Tucker-Drob, E. M., & Harden, K. (2012). Intellectual interest mediates gene × socioeconomic status interaction on adolescent academic achievement. *Child Development, 83,* 743–757.

Tudge, J., & Scrimsher, S. (2003). Lev S. Vygotsky on education: A cultural-historical, interpersonal, and individual approach to development. In B. Zimmerman (Ed.), *Educational psychology: A century of contributions.* Mahwah, NJ: Lawrence Erlbaum.

Tulving, E., & Thompson, D. M. (1973). Encoding specificity and retrieval processes in episodic memory. *Psychological Review, 80,* 352–373.

Turiel, E. (2006). The development of morality. In W. Damon, R. M. Lerner, & N. Eisenberg (Eds.), *Handbook of child psychology: Vol. 3, Social, emotional, and personality development* (6th ed.). Hoboken, NJ: Wiley.

Turiel, E. (2008). Social decisions, social interactions, and the coordination of diverse judgments. In U. Mueller, J. Carpendale, N. Budwig, & B. Sokol (Eds.), *Social life and social knowledge: Toward a process account of development.* New York: Taylor & Francis Group / Lawrence Erlbaum Associates.

Turiel, E. (2010). Domain specificity in social interactions, social thought, and social development. *Child Development, 81,* 720–726.

Turkheimer, E., Haley, A., Waldreon, M., D'Onofrio, B., & Gottesman, I. I. (2003). Socioeconomic status modifies heritability of IQ in young children. *Psychological Science, 14,* 623–628.

Turner, J. S., & Helms, D. B. (1994). *Contemporary adulthood* (5th ed.). Forth Worth, TX: Harcourt Brace.

Turner-Bowker, D. M. (1996). Gender stereotyped descriptors in children's picture books: Does "Curious Jane" exist in the literature? *Sex Roles, 35,* 461–488.

Turney, K., & Kao, G. (2009). Barriers to school involvement: Are immigrant parents disadvantaged? *Journal of Educational Research, 102,* 257–271.

Turton, P., Evans, C., & Hughes, P. (2009). Long-term psychosocial sequelae of stillbirth: Phase II of a nested case-control cohort study. *Archives of Women's Mental Health, 12,* 35–41.

Twardosz, S., & Lutzker, J. (2009). Child maltreatment and the developing brain: A review of neuroscience perspectives. *Aggression and Violent Behavior, 15,* 59–68.

Twenge, J. M., & Campbell, W. K. (2001). Age and birth cohort differences in self-esteem: A cross-temporal meta-analysis. *Personality and Social Psychology Review, 5,* 321–344.

Tyre, P., & McGinn, D. (2003, May 12). She works, he doesn't. *Newsweek,* pp. 45–52.

Tyre, P., & Scelfo, J. (2003, September 22). Helping kids get fit. *Newsweek,* pp. 60–62.

Uchikoshi, Y. (2006). Early reading in bilingual kindergartners: Can educational television help? *Scientific Studies of Reading, 10,* 89–120.

Uhlenberg, P., Cooney, T., & Boyd, R. (1990). Divorce for women after midlife. *Journal of Gerontology, 45*(1), S3–S11.

Umana-Taylor, A., Diveri, M., & Fine, M. (2002). Ethnic identity and self-esteem among Latino adolescents: Distinctions among Latino populations. *Journal of Adolescent Research, 17,* 303–327.

Umberson, D. J. (2006). Parents, adult children, and immortality. *Contexts, 5,* 48–53.

UNAIDS. (2011). *2011 World AIDS day.* New York: United Nations.

Underwood, M. (2005). Introduction to the special section: Deception and observation. *Ethics & Behavior, 15,* 233–234.

Unger, R. K. (Ed.). (2001). *Handbook of the psychology of women and gender.* New York: Wiley.

Unger, R., & Crawford, M. (1992). *Women and gender: A feminist psychology* (2nd ed.). New York: McGraw-Hill.

Unger, R., & Crawford, M. (2004). *Women and gender: A feminist psychology* (4th ed.). New York: McGraw-Hill.

United Nations Population Division. (2002). *World population ageing: 1950-2050*. New York: United Nations.

United Nations Statistics Division. (2012). *Statistical Annex Table 2.A Health*. Accessed online, July 18, 2012, unstats.un.org/unsd/demographic/products/.%20pdf/Table2A.pdf

United Nations. (2010). *The millennium development goals report 2010*. New York: Author.

United Nations, Department of Economic and Social Affairs, Population Division. (2007). *World Population Prospects: The 2006 Revision, Highlights* (Working Paper No. ESA/P/WP.202). Accessed online, July 12, 2012, http://www.un.org/esa/population/publications/wpp2006/WPP2006_Highlights_rev.pdf

University of Akron. (2006). *A longitudinal evaluation of the new curricula for the D.A.R.E. middle (7th grade) and high school (9th grade) programs: Take charge of your life*. Akron, OH: Author.

Updegraff, K. A., Helms, H. M., McHale, S. M., Crouter, A. C., Thayer, S. M., & Sales, L. H. (2004). Who's the boss? Patterns of perceived control in adolescents' friendship. *Journal of Youth & Adolescence, 33,* 403–420.

Updegraff, K. A., McHale, S. M., Whiteman, S. D., Thayer, S. M., & Crouter, A. C. (2006). The nature and correlates of Mexican-American adolescents' time with parents and peers. *Child Development, 77,* 1470–1486.

Uphold-Carrier, H., & Utz, R. (2012). Parental divorce among young and adult children: A long-term quantitative analysis of mental health and family solidarity. *Journal of Divorce & Remarriage, 53,* 247–266. doi:10.1080/10502556.2012.663272

Urberg, K., Luo, Q., & Pilgrim, C. (2003). A two-stage model of peer influence in adolescent substance use: Individual and relationship-specific differences in susceptibility to influence. *Addictive Behaviors, 28,* 1243–1256.

Urquidi, V., Tarin, D., & Goodison, S. (2000). Role of telomerase in cell senescence and oncogenesis. *Annual Review of Medicine, 51,* 65–79.

U.S. Bureau of Labor Statistics. (2003). *Wages earned by women*. Washington, DC: Author.

U.S. Bureau of the Census. (1997). *Life expectancy statistics*. Washington, DC: Author.

U.S. Bureau of the Census. (1998). *Statistical abstract of the United States* (118th ed.). Washington, DC: U.S. Government Printing Office.

U.S. Bureau of the Census. (2000). *The condition of education. Current Population Surveys, October 2000*. Washington, DC: Author.

U.S. Bureau of the Census. (2001). *Living arrangements of children*. Washington, DC: Author.

U.S. Bureau of the Census. (2002). *Statistical abstract of the United States* (122nd ed.). Washington, DC: U.S. Government Printing Office.

U.S. Bureau of the Census. (2005). *Current population survey*. Washington, DC: U.S. Department of Agriculture, Center for Nutrition Policy and Promotion.

U.S. Bureau of the Census. (2010a). *Current population survey*. Washington, DC: Author. U.S. Department of Agriculture, Center for Nutrition Policy and Promotion.

U. S. Bureau of the Census. (2010b). *Current population survey and annual social and economic supplements*. Washington, DC: Author.

U. S. Bureau of the Census. (2011). *Current population survey and annual social and economic supplements*. Washington, DC: Author.

U.S. Department of Agriculture. (2006). *Dietary Guidelines for Americans 2005*. Washington, DC: Author.

U.S. Department of Education. (2005). *2003–2004 National Postsecondary Student Aid Study (NPSAS:04), unpublished tabulations*. Washington, DC: Author.

U.S. Department of Health and Human Services. (1990). *Health United States 1989* (DHHS Publication No. PHS 90-1232). Washington, DC: U.S. Government Printing Office.

U.S. Department of Health and Human Services, Administration on Children Youth and Families. (2007). *Child Maltreatment 2005*. Washington, DC: U.S. Government Printing Office.

U.S. Department of Health and Human Services, Health Resources and Services Administration, Maternal and Child Health Bureau. (2009). *Child Health USA 2008-2009*. Rockville, MD: U.S. Department of Health and Human Services.

Uylings, H. (2006). Development of the human cortex and the concept of "critical" or "sensitive" periods. *Language Learning, 56,* 59–90.

Vacha-Haase, T., Hill, R. D., & Bermingham, D. W. (2012). Aging theory and research. In N. A. Fouad, J. A. Carter, & L. M. Subich (Eds.), *APA handbook of counseling psychology, Vol. 1: Theories, research, and methods*. Washington, DC: American Psychological Association.

Vaillant, G. E. (1977). *Adaptation to life*. Boston: Little, Brown.

Vaillant, G. E., & Vaillant, C. O. (1981). Natural history of male psychological health, X: Work as a predictor of positive mental health. *The American Journal of Psychiatry, 138,* 1433–1440.

Vaillant, G. E., & Vaillant, C. O. (1990). Natural history of male psychological health, XII: A 45-year study of predictors of successful aging. *American Journal of Psychiatry, 147*(1), 31–37.

Valenti, C. (2006). Infant vision guidance: Fundamental vision development in infancy. *Optometry and Vision Development, 37,* 147–155.

Valles, N., & Knutson, J. (2008). Contingent responses of mothers and peers to indirect and direct aggression in preschool and school-aged children. *Aggressive Behavior, 34,* 497–510.

Van Balen, F. (2005). The choice for sons or daughters. *Journal of Psychosomatic Obstetrics & Gynecology, 26,* 229–320.

Van de Graaf, K. (2000). *Human anatomy* (5th ed., p. 339). Boston: McGraw-Hill.

van den Berg, P., Mond, J., Eisenberg, M., Ackard, D., & Neumark-Sztainer, D. (2010). The link between body dissatisfaction and self-esteem in adolescents: Similarities across gender, age, weight status, race/ethnicity, and socioeconomic status. *Journal of Adolescent Health, 47,* 290–296.

van den Hoonaard, D. K. (1994). Paradise lost: Widowhood in a Florida retirement community. *Journal of Aging Studies, 8,* 121–132.

van der Mark, I., van ijzendoorn, M., & Bakermans-Kranenburg, M. (2002). Development of empathy in girls during the second year of life: Associations with parenting, attachment, and temperament. *Social Development, 11,* 451–468.

van Haren, N. M., Rijsdijk, F., Schnack, H. G., Picchioni, M. M., Toulopoulou, T., Weisbrod, M., et al. (2012). The genetic and environmental determinants of the association between brain abnormalities and schizophrenia: The schizophrenia twins and relatives consortium. *Biological Psychiatry, 71,* 915–921.

van Heugten, M., & Johnson, E. (2010). Linking infants' distributional learning abilities to natural language acquisition. *Journal of Memory and Language, 63,* 197–209.

Van Marle, K., & Wynn, K. (2006). Six-month-old infants use analog magnitudes to represent duration. *Developmental Science, 9,* F41– F49.

van Marle, K., & Wynn, K. (2009). Infants' auditory enumeration: Evidence for analog magnitudes in the small number range. *Cognition, 111,* 302–316.

Van Tassel-Baska, J., Olszewski-Kubilius, P., & Kulieke, M. (1994). A study of self-concept and social support in advantaged and disadvantaged seventh and eighth grade gifted students. *Roeper Review, 16,* 186–191.

van't Spijker, A., & ten Kroode, H. F. (1997). Psychological aspects of genetic counseling: A review of the experience with Huntington's disease. *Patient Education and Counseling, 32,* 33–40.

Vandell, D. L. (2000). Parents, peer groups, and other socializing influences. *Developmental Psychology, 36,* 699–710.

Vandell, D. L. (2004). Early child care: The known and the unknown [Special issue: The maturing of human developmental sciences: Appraising past, present, and prospective agendas]. *Merrill-Palmer Quarterly, 50,* 387–414.

Vandell, D. L., Burchinal, M. R., Belsky, J., Owen, M. T., Friedman, S. L., Clarke-Stewart, A., et al. (2005). *Early child care and children's development in the primary grades: Follow-up results from the NICHD Study of Early Child Care*. Paper presented at the biennial meeting of the Society for Research in Child Development, Atlanta, GA.

Vandell, D. L., Shumow, L., & Posner, J. (2005). After-school programs for low-income children: Differences in program quality. In J. L. Mahoney, R. W. Larson, & J. S. Ecccles (Eds.), *Organized activities as contexts of development: Extracurricular activities, after-school and community programs*. Mahwah, NJ: Lawrence Erlbaum.

Vandello, J., & Cohen, D. (2003). Male honor and female fidelity: Implicit cultural scripts that perpetuate domestic violence. *Journal of Personality & Social Psychology, 84,* 997–1010.

Vanlierde, A., Renier, L., & De Volder, A. G. (2008). Brain plasticity and multisensory experience in early blind individuals. In J. J. Rieser, D. H. Ashmead, F. F. Ebner, & A. L. Corn (Eds.), *Blindness and brain plasticity in navigation and object perception*. Mahwah, NJ: Lawrence Erlbaum.

Vartanian, L. R. (2000). Revisiting the imaginary audience and personal fable constructs of adolescent egocentrism: A conceptual review. *Adolescence, 35,* 639–646.

Vaughan, V., McKay, R. J., & Behrman, R. (1979). *Nelson textbook of pediatrics* (11th ed.). Philadelphia: Saunders.

Vellutino, F. R. (1991). Introduction to three studies on reading acquisition: Convergent findings on theoretical foundations of code-oriented versus whole-language approaches to reading instruction. *Journal of Educational Psychology, 83,* 437–443.

Veneziano, R. (2003). The importance of paternal warmth. *Cross-Cultural Research: The Journal of Comparative Social Science, 37,* 265–281.

Veras, R. P., & Mattos, L. C. (2007). Audiology and aging: Literature review and current horizons. *Revista Brasileira de Otorrinolaringologia (English Edition), 73,* 122–128.

Vereijken, C. M., Riksen-Walraven, J. M., & Kondo-Ikemura, K. (1997). Maternal sensitivity and infant attachment security in Japan: A longitudinal study. *International Journal of Behavioral Development, 21,* 35–49.

Verhoeven, M., Sawyer, M. G., & Spence, S. H. (2013). The factorial invariance of the CES-D during adolescence: Are symptom profiles for depression stable across gender and time? *Journal of Adolescence, 36,* 181–190.

Verkuyten, M. (2003). Positive and negative self-esteem among ethnic minority early adolescents: Social and cultural sources and threats. *Journal of Youth & Adolescence, 32,* 267–277.

Vernon, J. A. (1990). Media stereotyping: A comparison of the way elderly women and men are portrayed on prime-time television. *Journal of Women and Aging, 2,* 55–68.

Verschueren, K., Doumen, S., & Buyse, E. (2012). Relationships with mother, teacher, and peers: Unique and joint effects on young children's self-concept. *Attachment & Human Development, 14,* 233–248.

Veselka, L., Just, C., Jang, K. L., Johnson, A. M., & Vernon, P. A. (2012). The general factor of personality: A critical test. *Personality and Individual Differences, 52,* 261–264.

Vidaver, R. M., Lafleur, B., Tong, C., Bradshaw, R., & Marts, S. A. (2000). Women subjects in NIH-funded clinical research literature: Lack of progress in both representation and analysis by sex. *Journal of Women's Health, Gender-Based Medicine, 9,* 495–504.

Vilhjalmsson, R., & Kristjansdottir, G. (2003). Gender differences in physical activity in older children and adolescents: The central role of organized sport. *Social Science Medicine, 56,* 363–374.

Villarosa, L. (2003, December 23). More teenagers say no to sex, and experts are sure why. *The New York Times*, p. D6.

Vincent, J. A., Phillipson, C. R., & Downs, M. (2006). *The futures of old age*. Thousand Oaks, CA: Sage Publications.

Vingolo, E. M., Salvatore, S., & Limoli, P. G. (2013). MP-1 biofeedback: Luminous pattern stimulus versus acoustic biofeedback in age related macular degeneration (AMD). *Applied Psychophysiology and Biofeedback, 38,* 11–16.

Vink, D., Aartsen, M., Comijs, H., Heymans, M., Penninx, B., Stek, M., et al. (2009). Onset of anxiety and depression in the aging population: Comparison of risk factors in a 9-year prospective study. *The American Journal of Geriatric Psychiatry, 17,* 642–652.

Vizmanos, B., & Marti-Henneberg, C. (2000). Puberty begins with a characteristic subcutaneous body fat mass in each sex. *European Journal of Clinical Nutrition, 54,* 203–206.

Volker, S. (2007). Infants' vocal engagement oriented towards mother versus stranger at 3 months and avoidant attachment behavior at 12 months. *International Journal of Behavioral Development, 31,* 88–95.

Votruba-Drzal, E., Coley, R. L., & Chase-Lansdale, L. (2004). Child care and low-income children's development: Direct and moderated effects. *Child Development, 75,* 396–312.

Vyas, S. (2004). Exploring bicultural identities of Asian high school students through the analytic window of a literature club. *Journal of Adolescent & Adult Literacy, 48,* 12–18.

Vygotsky, L. S. (1926/1997). *Educational psychology.* Delray Beach, FL: St. Lucie Press.

Vygotsky, L. S. (1979). *Mind in society: The development of higher mental processes.* Cambridge, MA: Harvard University Press. (Original works published 1930, 1933, and 1935.)

Wachs, T. D. (1992). *The nature of nurture.* Newbury Park, CA: Sage Publications.

Wachs, T. D. (1993). The nature-nurture gap: What we have here is a failure to collaborate. In R. Plomin & G. E. McClearn (Eds.), *Nature, nurture, and psychology.* Washington, DC: American Psychological Association.

Wachs, T. D. (1996). Known and potential processes underlying developmental trajectories in childhood and adolescence. *Developmental Psychology, 32,* 796–801.

Wada, A., Kunii, Y., Ikemoto, K., Yang, Q., Hino, M., Matsumoto, J., et al. (2012). Increased ratio of calcineurin immunoreactive neurons in the caudate nucleus of patients with schizophrenia. *Progress in Neuro-Psychopharmacology & Biological Psychiatry, 37,* 8–14.

Wade, T. D., Tiggemann, M., Bulik, C., Fairburn, C., Wray, N., & Martin, N. (2008, February). Shared temperament risk' factors for anorexia nervosa: A twin study. *Psychosomatic Medicine, 70*(2), 239–244.

Wade, T. D., & Watson, H. J. (2012). Psychotherapies in eating disorders. In J. Alexander & J. Treasure (Eds.), *A collaborative approach to eating disorders.* New York: Routledge/Taylor & Francis Group.

Wagner, R. K., & Sternberg, R. J. (1985). Alternate conceptions of intelligence and their implications for education. *Review of Educational Research, 54,* 179–223.

Wahlin, T. (2007). To know or not to know: A review of behaviour and suicidal ideation in preclinical Huntington's disease. *Patient Education and Counseling, 65,* 279–287.

Waisbren, S. E., & Antshel, K. M. (2013). Phenylketonuria. In I. Baron & C. Rey-Casserly (Eds.), *Pediatric neuropsychology: Medical advances and lifespan outcomes.* New York: Oxford University Press.

Wakefield, A., Murch, S., Anthony, A., Linnell, J., Casson, D., Malik, M., et al. (1998). Illeal-lymphoid-nodular hyperplasia, non-specific colitis, and pervasive developmental disorder in children. *The Lancet, 351,* 637–641.

Walden, T., Kim, G., McCoy, C., & Karrass, J. (2007). Do you believe in magic? Infants' social looking during violations of expectations. *Developmental Science, 10,* 654–663.

Waldfogel, J. (2001). International policies toward parental leave and child care. *Caring for Infants and Toddlers, 11,* 99–111.

Waldrop, D. P., & Kirkendall, A. M. (2009). Comfort measures: A qualitative study of nursing home-based end-of-life care. *Journal of Palliative Medicine, 12,* 718–724.

Walker, J., Anstey, K., & Lord, S. (2006, May). Psychological distress and visual functioning in relation to vision-related disability in older individuals with cataracts. *British Journal of Health Psychology, 11,* 303–317.

Walker, L. E. (1999). Psychology and domestic violence around the world. *American Psychologist, 54,* 21–29.

Walker, W. A., & Humphries, C. (2005). *The Harvard Medical School guide to healthy eating during pregnancy.* New York: McGraw-Hill.

Walker, W. A., & Humphries, C. (2007, September 17). Starting the good life in the womb. *Newsweek,* pp. 56–57.

Walker-Andrews, A., Krogh-Jespersen, S., Mayhew, E., & Coffield, C. (2013). The situated infant: Learning in context. In M. Legerstee, D. W. Haley, & M. H. Bornstein (Eds.), *The infant mind: Origins of the social brain.* New York: Guilford Press.

Wallerstein, J. S., Lewis, J. M., & Blakeslee, S. (2000). *The unexpected legacy of divorce.* New York: Hyperion.

Wallerstein, J. S., & Resnikoff, D. (2005). Parental divorce and developmental progression: An inquiry into their relationship. In L. Gunsberg & P. Hymowitz (Eds.), *A handbook of divorce and custody: Forensic, developmental, and clinical perspectives.* Hillsdale, NJ: Analytic Press, Inc.

Walter, T. (2012). Why different countries manage death differently: A comparative analysis of modern urban societies. *British Journal of Sociology, 63,* 123–145.

Walters, A., & Rye, D. (2009). Review of the relationship of restless legs syndrome and periodic limb movements in sleep to hypertension, heart disease, and stroke. *Sleep: Journal of Sleep and Sleep Disorders Research, 32,* 589–597.

Walters, E., & Gardner, H. (1986). The theory of multiple intelligences: Some issues and answers. In R. J. Sternberg & R. K. Wagner (Eds.), *Practical intelligence.* New York: Cambridge University Press.

Wamba, N. G. (2010). Poverty and literacy: An introduction. *Reading & Writing Quarterly: Overcoming Difficulties, 26,* 109–114.

Wang, H. J., Zhang, H., Zhang, W. W., Pan, Y. P., & Ma, J. (2008). Association of the common genetic variant upstream of INSIG2 gene with obesity related phenotypes in Chinese children and adolescents. *Biomedical and Environmental Sciences, 21,* 528–536.

Wang, L., Tracy, C., Moineddin, R., & Upshur, R. G. (2013). Osteoporosis prescribing trends in primary care: A population-based retrospective cohort study. *Primary Health Care Research and Development, 14,* 1–6.

Wang, Q. (2004). The emergence of cultural self-constructs: Autobiographical memory and self-description in European American and Chinese children. *Developmental Psychology, 40,* 3–15.

Wang, Q. (2006). Culture and the development of self-knowledge. *Current Directions in Psychological Science, 15,* 182–187.

Wang, Q., Pomerantz, E., & Chen, H. (2007). The role of parents' control in early adolescents' psychological functioning: A longitudinal investigation in the United States and China. *Child Development, 78,* 1592–1610.

Wang, S.-H., Baillargeon, R., & Paterson, S. (2005). Detecting continuity violations in infancy: A new account and new evidence from covering and tube events. *Cognition, 95,* 129–173.

Wang, W. (2012, February 16). *The rise of intermarriage: Rates, characteristics vary by race and gender.* Washington, DC: Pew Research Center.

Ward, R. A. (1984). *The aging experience: An introduction to social gerontology* (2nd ed.). New York: Harper & Row.

Wardle, J., Guthrie, C., & Sanderson, S. (2001). Food and activity preferences in children of lean and obese parents. *International Journal of Obesity & Related Metabolic Disorders, 25,* 971–977.

Warnock, F., & Sandrin, D. (2004). Comprehensive description of newborn distress behavior in response to acute pain (newborn male circumcision). *Pain, 107,* 242–255.

Warshak, R. A. (2000). Remarriage as a trigger of parental alienation syndrome. *American Journal of Family Therapy, 28,* 229–241.

Wasserman, J. D., & Tulsky, D. S. (2005). The history of intelligence assessment. In D. P. Flanagan & P. L. Harrison (Eds.), *Contemporary intellectual assessment: Theories, tests, and issues.* New York: Guilford Press.

Waterhouse, J. M., & DeCoursey, P. J. (2004). Human circadian organization. In J. C. Dunlap & J. J. Loros (Eds.), *Chronobiology: Biological timekeeping.* Sunderland, MA: Sinauer Associates.

Waterland, R. A., & Jirtle, R. L. (2004). Early nutrition, epigenetic changes at transposons and imprinted genes, and enhanced susceptibility to adult chronic diseases. *Nutrition, 20,* 63–68.

Waters, L., & Moore, K. (2002). Predicting self-esteem during unemployment: The effect of gender financial deprivation, alternate roles and social support. *Journal of Employment Counseling, 39,* 171–189.

Watling, D., & Bourne, V. J. (2007). Linking children's neuropsychological processing of emotion with their knowledge of emotion expression regulation. *Laterality: Asymmetries of Body, Brain and Cognition, 12,* 381–396.

Watson, J. B. (1925). *Behaviorism.* New York: Norton.

Watson, J. B., & Rayner, R. (1920). Conditioned, emotional reactions. *Journal of Experimental Psychology, 3,* 1–14.

Watts-English, T., Fortson, B. L., Gibler, N., Hooper, S. R., & De Bellis, M. D. (2006). The psychobiologic of maltreatment in childhood. *Journal of Social Issues, 62,* 717–736.

Wechsler, D. (1975). Intelligence defined and undefined. *American Psychologist, 30,* 135–139.

Wechsler, H., Lee, J. E., Kuo, M., Seibring, M., Nelson, T. F., & Lee, H. (2002). Trends in college binge drinking during a period of increased prevention efforts: Findings from 4 Harvard School of Public Health College Alcohol Study surveys, 1993–2001. *Journal of American College Health, 50,* 203–217.

Wechsler, H., Nelson, T. F., Lee, J. E., Seibring, M., Lewis, C., & Keeling, R. P. (2003). Perception and reality: A national evaluation of social norms marketing interventions to reduce college students' heavy alcohol use. *Journal of Studies on Alcohol, 64,* 484–494.

Weinberg, R. A. (2004). The infant and the family in the twenty-first century. *Journal of the American Academy of Child & Adolescent Psychiatry, 43,* 115–116.

Weinberger, D. R. (2001, March 10). A brain too young for good judgment. *The New York Times,* p. D1.

Weinstock, H., Berman, S., & Cates, W., Jr. (2004). Sexually transmitted diseases among American youth: Incidence and prevalence estimates, 2000. *Perspectives on Sexual and Reproductive Health, 36,* 182–191.

Weiss, R. (2003, September 2). Genes' sway over IQ may vary with class. *Washington Post,* p. A1.

Weiss, R., & Raz, I. (2006, July). Focus on childhood fitness, not just fatness. *Lancet, 368,* 261–262.

Weissberger, G. H., Salmon, D. P., Bondi, M. W., & Gollan, T. H. (2013). Which neuropsychological tests predict progression to Alzheimer's disease in Hispanics? *Neuropsychology, 27,* 343–355.

Weissman, A. S., Chu, B. C., Reddy, L. A., & Mohlman, J. (2012). Attention mechanisms in children with anxiety disorders and in children with attention deficit hyperactivity disorder: Implications for research and practice. *Journal of Clinical Child and Adolescent Psychology, 41,* 117–126.

Weisz, A., & Black, B. (2002). Gender and moral reasoning: African American youth respond to dating dilemmas. *Journal of Human Behavior in the Social Environment, 5,* 35–52.

Weitzman, E., Nelson, T., & Wechsler, H. (2003). Taking up binge drinking in college: The influences of person, social group, and environment. *Journal of Adolescent Health, 32,* 26–35.

Wellings, K., Collumbien, M., Slaymaker, E., Singh, S., Hodges, Z., Patel, D., et al. (2006). Sexual behaviour in context: A global perspective. *The Lancet, 368,* 1706–1738.

Wellman, H., Lopez-Duran, S., LaBounty, J., & Hamilton, B. (2008). Infant attention to intentional action predicts preschool theory of mind. *Developmental Psychology, 44,* 618–623.

Wellman, H. M. (2012). Theory of mind: Better methods, clearer findings, more development. *European Journal of Developmental Psychology, 9,* 313–330.

Wells, B., Peppe, S., & Goulandris, N. (2004). Intonation development from five to thirteen. *Journal of Child Language, 31,* 749–778.

Wells, R., Lohman, D., & Marron, M. (2009). What factors are associated with grade acceleration? An analysis and comparison of two U.S. databases. *Journal of Advanced Academics, 20,* 248–273.

Welsh, T., Ray, M., Weeks, D., Dewey, D., & Elliott, D. (2009). Does Joe influence Fred's action? Not if Fred has autism spectrum disorder. *Brain Research, 1248,* 141–148.

Werker, J. F., Pons, F., Dietrich, C., Kajikawa, S., Fais, L., & Amano, S. (2007). Infant-directed speech supports phonetic category learning in English and Japanese. *Cognition, 103,* 147–162.

Werner, E. E. (1972). Infants around the world: Cross-cultural studies of psychomotor development from birth to two years. *Journal of Cross-Cultural Psychology, 3,* 111–134.

Werner, E. E. (2005). What can we learn about resilience from large-scale longitudinal studies? In S. Goldstein & R. B. Brooks (Eds.), *Handbook of resilience in children.* New York: Kluwer Academic/Plenum Publishers.

Werner, E. E., Myers, M., Fifer, W., Cheng, B., Fang, Y., Allen, R., et al. (2007). Prenatal predictors of infant temperament. *Developmental Psychobiology, 49,* 474–484.

Werner, E. E., & Smith, R. S. (2002). Journeys from childhood to midlife: Risk, resilience and recovery. *Journal of Developmental and Behavioral Pediatrics, 23,* 456.

Werner, L. A., & Marean, G. C. (1996). *Human auditory development.* Boulder, CO: Westview Press.

Wertsch, J. V. (1999). The zone of proximal development: Some conceptual issues. In P. Lloyd & C. Fernyhough (Eds.), *Lev Vygotsky: Critical assessments, Vol. 3: The zone of proximal development.* New York: Routledge.

West, J. H., Romero, R. A., & Trinidad, D. R. (2007). Adolescent receptivity to tobacco marketing by racial/ethnic groups in California. *American Journal of Preventive Medicine, 33,* 121–123.

West, J. R., & Blake, C. A. (2005). Fetal alcohol syndrome: An assessment of the field. *Experimental Biology and Medicine, 230,* 354–356.

Westermann, G., Mareschal, D., Johnson, M. H., Sirois, S., Spratling, M. W., & Thomas, M. S. (2007). Neuroconstructivism. *Developmental Science, 10,* 75–83.

Wethington, E., Cooper, H., & Holmes, C. S. (1997). Turning points in midlife. In I. H. Gotlib & B. Wheaton (Eds.), *Stress and adversity over the life course: Trajectories and turning points* (pp. 215–231). New York: Cambridge University Press.

Wexler, B. (2006). *Brain and culture: Neurobiology, ideology, and social change.* Cambridge, MA: MIT Press.

Whalen, C. K., Jamner, L. D., Henker, B., Delfino, R. J., & Lozano, J. M. (2002). The ADHD spectrum and everyday life: Experience sampling of adolescent moods, activities, smoking, and drinking. *Child Development, 73,* 209–227.

Whalen, D., Levitt, A., & Goldstein, L. (2007). VOT in the babbling of French- and English-learning infants. *Journal of Phonetics, 35,* 341–352.

Wheaton, B., & Montazer, S. (2010). Stressors, stress, and distress. In T. L. Scheid & T. N. Brown (Eds.), *A handbook for the study of mental health: Social contexts, theories, and systems (2nd ed.).* New York: Cambridge University Press.

Wheeldon, L. R. (1999). *Aspects of language production.* Philadelphia: Psychology Press.

Wheeler, S., & Austin, J. (2001). The impact of early pregnancy loss. *American Journal of Maternal/child Nursing, 26,* 154–159.

Whitaker, R. C., Wright, J. A., Pepe, M. S., Seidel, K. D., & Dietz, W. H. (1997, September 25). Predicting obesity in young adulthood from childhood and parental obesity. *New England Journal of Medicine, 337,* 869–873.

Whitbourne, S. K. (2001). *Adult development and aging: Biopsychosocial perspectives.* New York: Wiley.

Whitbourne, S. K. (2007, October). *Crossing over the bridges of adulthood: Multiple pathways through midlife.* Presidential keynote presented at the 4th Biannual Meeting of the Society for the Study of Human Development, Pennsylvania State University, University Park, PA.

Whitbourne, S. K., Jacobo, M., & Munoz-Ruiz, M. (1996). Adversity in the elderly. In R. S. Feldman (Ed.), *The psychology of adversity.* Amherst: University of Massachusetts Press.

Whitbourne, S. K., Sneed, J., & Sayer, A. (2009). Psychosocial development from college through midlife: A 34-year sequential study. *Developmental Psychology, 45,* 1328–1340.

White, K. (2007). Hypnobirthing: The Mongan method. *Australian Journal of Clinical Hypnotherapy and Hypnosis, 28,* 12–24.

Whitebread, D., Coltman, P., Jameson, H., & Lander, R. (2009). Play, cognition and self-regulation: What exactly are children learning when they learn through play? *Educational and Child Psychology, 26,* 40–52.

Whiting, B. B., & Edwards, C. P. (1988). *Children of different worlds: The formation of social behavior.* Cambridge, MA: Harvard University Press.

Whiting, J., Simmons, L., Havens, J., Smith, D., & Oka, M. (2009). Intergenerational transmission of violence: The influence of self-appraisals, mental disorders and substance abuse. *Journal of Family Violence, 24,* 639–648.

Wickelgren, W. A. (1999). Webs, cell assemblies, and chunking in neural nets: Introduction. *Canadian Journal of Experimental Psychology, 53,* 118–131.

Widaman, K. (2009). Phenylketonuria in children and mothers: Genes, environments, behavior. *Current Directions in Psychological Science, 18,* 48–52. Available online at http://search.ebscohost.com

Widom, C. S. (2000). Motivation and mechanisms in the "cycle of violence". In D. J. Hansen (Ed.), *Nebraska Symposium on Motivation Vol. 46, 1998: Motivation and child maltreatment* (Current theory and research in motivation series). Lincoln: University of Nebraska Press.

Wielgosz, A. T., & Nolan, R. P. (2000). Biobehavioral factors in the context of ischemic cardiovascular disease. *Journal of Psychosomatic Research, 48,* 339–345.

Wiggins, M., & Uwaydat, S. (2006, January). Age-related macular degeneration: Options for earlier detection and improved treatment. *Journal of Family Practice, 55,* 22–27.

Wilcox, A., Skjaerven, R., Buekens, P., & Kiely, J. (1995, March 1). Birth weight and perinatal mortality: A comparison of the United States and Norway. *JAMA: The Journal of the American Medical Association, 273,* 709–711.

Wilcox, H. C., Conner, K. R., & Caine, E. D. (2004). Association of alcohol and drug use disorders and completed suicide: An empirical review of cohort studies [Special issue: Drug abuse and suicidal behavior]. *Drug & Alcohol Dependence, 76,* S11–S19.

Wilcox, S., Castro, C. M., & King, A. C. (2006). Outcome expectations and physical activity participation in two samples of older women. *Journal of Health Psychology, 11,* 65–77.

Wilcox, T., Woods, R., Chapa, C., & McCurry, S. (2007). Multisensory exploration and object individuation in infancy. *Developmental Psychology, 43,* 479–495.

Wildberger, S. (2003, August). So you're having a baby. *Washingtonian,* pp. 85–86, 88–90.

Wiley, T. L., Nondahl, D. M., Cruickshanks, K. J., & Tweed, T. S. (2005). Five-year changes in middle ear function for older adults. *Journal of the American Academy of Audiology, 16,* 129–139.

Wilfond, B., & Ross, L. (2009). From genetics to genomics: Ethics, policy, and parental decision-making. *Journal of Pediatric Psychology, 34,* 639–647. Available online at http://search.ebscohost.com

Wilkes, S., Chinn, D., Murdoch, A., & Rubin, G. (2009). Epidemiology and management of infertility: A population-based study in UK primary care. *Family Practice, 26,* 269–274.

Williams, J., & Ross, L. (2007). Consequences of prenatal toxin exposure for mental health in children and adolescents: A systematic review. *European Child & Adolescent Psychiatry, 16,* 243–253.

Williams, K., & Dunne-Bryant, A. (2006, December). Divorce and adult psychological well-being: Clarifying the role of gender and child age. *Journal of Marriage and Family, 68,* 1178–1196.

Willis, S. L. (1985). Educational psychology of the older adult learner. In J. E. Birren & K. W. Schaie (Eds.), *Handbook of the psychology of aging* (2nd ed.). New York: Van Nostrand Reinhold.

Willis, S. L. (1996). Everyday problem solving. In J. E. Birren, K. W. Schaie, R. P. Abeles, M. Gatz, & T. A. Salthouse (Eds.), *Handbook of the psychology of aging* (4th ed.). San Diego: Academic Press.

Willis, S. L., Martin, M., & Rocke, C. (2010). Longitudinal perspectives on midlife development and change. *European Journal of Ageing, 7,* 131–134.

Wills, T., Sargent, J., Stoolmiller, M., Gibbons, F., & Gerrard, M. (2008). Movie smoking exposure and smoking onset: A longitudinal study of mediation processes in a representative sample of U.S. adolescents. *Psychology of Addictive Behaviors, 22,* 269–277.

Wilson, B., Smith, S. L., Potter, W. J., Kunkel, D., Linz, D., Colvin, C. M., et al. (2002). Violence in children's television programming: Assessing the risks. *Journal of Communication, 52,* 5–35.

Wilson, G. T., Grilo, C. M., & Vitousek, K. M. (2007). Psychological treatment of eating disorders [Special Issue: Eating disorders]. *American Psychologist, 62,* 199–216.

Wilson, M. N. (1989). Child development in the context of the black extended family. *American Psychologist, 44,* 380–385.

Wilson, S. L. (2003). Post-Institutionalization: The effects of early deprivation on development of Romanian adoptees. *Child & Adolescent Social Work Journal, 20,* 473–483.

Wines, M. (2006, August 24). Africa adds to miserable ranks for child workers. *The New York Times,* p. D1.

Winger, G., & Woods, J. H. (2004). *A handbook on drug and alcohol abuse: The biomedical aspects.* Oxford, England: Oxford University Press.

Wingfield, A., Tun, P. A., & McCoy, S. L. (2005). Hearing loss in older adulthood: What it is and how it interacts with cognitive performance. *Current Directions in Psychological Science, 14,* 144–147.

Winsler, A. (2003). Introduction to special issue: Vygotskian perspectives in early childhood education [Special Issue]. *Early Education and Development, 14,* 253–269.

Winsler, A., Feder, M., Way, E., & Manfra, L. (2006, July). Maternal beliefs concerning young children's private speech. *Infant and Child Development, 15,* 403–420.

Winterich, J. (2003). Sex, menopause, and culture: Sexual orientation and the meaning of menopause for women's sex lives. *Gender & Society, 17,* 627–642.

Winters, K. C., Stinchfield, R. D., & Botzet, A. (2005). Pathways fo youth gambling problem severity. *Psychology of Addictive Behaviors, 19,* 104–107.

Wisborg, K., Kesmodel, U., Bech, B. H., Hedegaard, M., & Henriksen, T. B. (2003). Maternal consumption of coffee during pregnancy and stillbirth and infant death in first year of life: Prospective study. *British Medical Journal, 326,* 420.

Wisdom, J. P., & Agnor, C. (2007). Family heritage and depression guides: Family and peer views influence adolescent attitudes about depression. *Journal of Adolescence, 30,* 333–346.

Witvliet, M., van Lier, P., Cuijpers, P., & Koot, H. (2010). Change and stability in childhood clique membership, isolation from cliques, and associated child characteristics. *Journal of Clinical Child and Adolescent Psychology, 39,* 12–24.

Woelfle, J. F., Harz, K., & Roth, C. (2007). Modulation of circulating IGF-I and IGFBP-3 levels by hormonal regulators of energy homeostasis in obese children. *Experimental and Clinical Endocrinology Diabetes, 115,* 17–23.

Wolfe, M. S. (2006, May). Shutting down Alzheimer's. *Scientific American,* 73–79.

Wolfe, W., Olson, C., & Kendall, A. (1998). Hunger and food insecurity in the elderly: Its nature and measurement. *Journal of Aging & Health, 10,* 327–350.

Wolfson, A. R., & Richards, M. (2011). Young adolescents: Struggles with insufficient sleep. In M. El-Sheikh (Ed.), *Sleep and development: Familial and socio-cultural considerations*. New York, : Oxford University Press.

Wolinsky, F., Wyrwich, K., & Babu, A. (2003). Age, aging, and the sense of control among older adults: A longitudinal reconsideration. *Journals of Gerontology: Series B: Psychological Sciences & Social Sciences, 58B,* S212–S220.

Wood, L., & Howley, A. (2012). Dividing at an early age: The hidden digital divide in Ohio elementary schools. *Learning, Media and Technology, 37,* 20–39.

Wood, R. (1997). Trends in multiple births, 1938-1995. *Population Trends, 87,* 29–35.

Wood, S., Portman, T., Cigrand, D., & Colangelo, N. (2010). School counselors' perceptions and experience with acceleration as a program option for gifted and talented students. *Gifted Child Quarterly, 54,* 168–178.

Wood, W., & Eagly, A. (2010). Gender. In S. T. Fiske, D. T. Gilbert, & G. Lindzey (Eds.), *Handbook of social psychology, Vol. 1* (5th ed.). Hoboken, NJ: Wiley.

Woodhouse, S. S., Dykas, M. J., & Cassidy, J. (2012). Loneliness and peer relations in adolescence. *Social Development, 21,* 273–293.

Woods, R. (2009). The use of aggression in primary school boys' decisions about inclusion in and exclusion from playground football games. *British Journal of Educational Psychology, 79,* 223–238.

Woodspring, N. (2012). Review of 'Agewise: Fighting the new ageism in America.' *Health: An Interdisciplinary Journal for the Social Study of Health, Illness and Medicine, 16*(3), 343–344. doi:10.1177/1363459311423335

Worden, J. W. (1998). *Children and grief: When a parent dies*. New York: Guilford Press.

World Bank. (2012). *World development indicators 2012 (WDI)*. Washington, DC: Author.

World Factbook. (2009). *Estimates of infant mortality*. Available online at https://www.cia.gov/library/publications/the-world-factbook/rankorder/2091rank.html

World Factbook. (2012). *Estimates of infant mortality*. Accessed online, 2012, https://www.cia.gov/library/publications/the-world-factbook/rankorder/2091rank.html

World Health Organization. (2007). *Male circumcision: Global trends and determinants of prevalence, safety and acceptability*. Paris: Author.

Worrell, F., Szarko, J., & Gabelko, N. (2001). Multi-year persistence of nontraditional students in an academic talent development program. *Journal of Secondary Gifted Education, 12,* 80–89.

Wortman, C. B., & Silver, R. C. (1990). Successful mastery of bereavement and widowhood: A life-course perspective. In P. B. Baltes & M. M. Baltes (Eds.), *Successful aging: Perspectives from the behavioral sciences*. Cambridge, England: Cambridge University Press.

Wright, J. C., Huston, A. C., Reitz, A. L., & Piemyat, S. (1994). Young children's perceptions of television reality: Determinants and developmental differences. *Developmental Psychology, 30,* 229–239.

Wright, J. C., Huston, A. C., Truglio, R., Fitch, M., Smith, E., & Piemyat, S. (1995). Occupational portrayals on television: Children's role schemata, career aspirations, and perceptions of reality. *Child Development, 66,* 1706–1718.

Wright, M., Wintemute, G., & Claire, B. (2008). Gun suicide by young people in California: Descriptive epidemiology and gun ownership. *Journal of Adolescent Health, 43,* 619–622.

Wright, R. (1995, March 13). The biology of violence. *New Yorker,* pp. 68–77.

Wroolie, T., & Holcomb, M. (2010). Menopause. In B. L. Levin & M. A. Becker (Eds.), *A public health perspective of women's mental health*. New York: Springer Science + Business Media.

Wrosch, C., Bauer, I., & Scheier, M. (2005, December). Regret and quality of life across the adult life span: The influence of disengagement and available future goals. *Psychology and Aging, 20,* 657–670.

Wu, P., Hoven, C. W., Okezie, N., Fuller, C. J., & Cohen, P. (2007). Alcohol abuse and depression in children and adolescents. *Journal of Child & Adolescent Substance Abuse, 17,* 51–69.

Wu, P., Robinson, C., & Yang, C. (2002). Similarities and differences in mothers' parenting of preschoolers in China and the United States. *International Journal of Behavioral Development, 26,* 481–491.

Wyer, R. (2004). The cognitive organization and use of general knowledge. In J. Jost & M. Banaji (Eds.), *Perspectivism in social psychology: The yin and yang of scientific progress*. Washington, DC: American Psychological Association.

Wyra, M., Lawson, M. J., & Hungi, N. (2007). The mnemonic keyword method: The effects of bidirectional retrieval training and of ability to image on foreign language vocabulary recall. *Learning and Instruction, 17,* 360–371.

Xiaohe, X., & Whyte, M. K. (1990). Love matches and arranged marriages: A Chinese replication. *Journal of Marriage and the Family, 52,* 709–722.

Xing, X., Tao, F., Wan, Y., Xing, C., Qi, X., Hao, J., et al. (2010). Family factors associated with suicide attempts among Chinese adolescent students: A national cross-sectional survey. *Journal of Adolescent Health, 46,* 592–599.

Yagmurlu, B., & Sanson, A. (2009). Parenting and temperament as predictors of prosocial behaviour in Australian and Turkish Australian children. *Australian Journal of Psychology, 61,* 77–88.

Yaman, A., Mesman, J., van IJzendoorn, M., Bakermans-Kranenburg, M., & Linting, M. (2010). Parenting in an individualistic culture with a collectivistic cultural background: The case of Turkish immigrant families with toddlers in the Netherlands. *Journal of Child and Family Studies, 19,* 617–628.

Yan, J., Li, H., & Liao, Y. (2010). Developmental motor function plays a key role in visual search. *Developmental Psychobiology, 52,* 505–512.

Yan, Z., & Fischer, K. (2002). Always under construction: Dynamic variations in adult cognitive microdevelopment. *Human Development, 45,* 141–160.

Yang, C. D. (2006). *The infinite gift: How children learn and unlearn the languages of the world*. New York: Scribner.

Yang, R., & Blodgett, B. (2000). Effects of race and adolescent decision-making on status attainment and self-esteem. *Journal of Ethnic & Cultural Diversity in Social Work, 9,* 135–153.

Yang, Y. (2008). Social inequalities in happiness in the U.S. 1972–2004: An age-period-cohort analysis. *American Sociological Review, 73,* 204–226.

Yardley, J. (2001, July 2). Child-death case in Texas raises penalty questions. *The New York Times*, p. A1.

Yell, M. L. (1995). The least restrictive environment mandate and the courts: Judicial activism or judicial restraint? *Exceptional Children, 61,* 578–581.

Yildiz, O. (2007). Vascular smooth muscle and endothelial functions in aging. *Annals of the New York Academy of Sciences, 1100,* 353–360.

Yim, I., Glynn, L., Schetter, C., Hobel, C., Chicz-DeMet, A., & Sandman, C. (2009). Risk of postpartum depressive symptoms with elevated corticotropin-releasing hormone in human pregnancy. *Archives of General Psychiatry, 66,* 162–169.

Yinger, J. (Ed.). (2004). *Helping children left behind: State aid and the pursuit of educational equity*. Cambridge, MA: MIT Press.

Yip, T., Sellers, R. M., & Seaton, E. K. (2006). African American racial identity across the lifespan: Identity status, identity content, and depressive symptoms. *Child Development, 77,* 1504–1517.

Yonker, J. E., Schnabelrauch, C. A., & DeHaan, L. G. (2012). The relationship between spirituality and religiosity on psychological outcomes in adolescents and emerging adults: A meta-analytic review. *Journal of Adolescence, 35,* 299–314.

York, E. (2008). Gender differences in the college and career aspirations of high school valedictorians. *Journal of Advanced Academics, 19,* 578–600.

York, G. S., Churchman, R., Woodard, B., Wainright, C., & Rau-Foster, M. (2012). Free-text comments: Understanding the value in family member descriptions of hospice caregiver relationships. *American Journal of Hospice & Palliative Medicine, 29,* 98–105.

Yoshinaga-Itano, C. (2003). From screening to early identification and intervention: Discovering predictors to successful outcomes for children with significant hearing loss. *Journal of Deaf Studies & Deaf Education, 8,* 11–30.

You, J.-I., & Bellmore, A. (2012). Relational peer victimization and psychosocial adjustment: The mediating role of best friendship qualities. *Personal Relationships, 19,* 340–353.

Young, G., & Teitelbaum, J. (2010). Brain drain: Using the deep venous system to declare brain death. *The Canadian Journal of Neurological Sciences/ Le Journal Canadien Des Sciences Neurologiques, 37,* 429–430.

Young, S., Rhee, S., Stallings, M., Corley, R., & Hewitt, J. (2006, July). Genetic and environmental vulnerabilities underlying adolescent substance use and problem use: General or specific? *Behavior Genetics, 36,* 603–615.

Youniss, J., & Haynie, D. L. (1992). Friendship in adolescence. *Journal of Developmental and Behavioral Pediatrics, 13,* 59–66.

Yousafzai, A. K., Yakoob, M. Y., & Bhutta, Z. A. (2013). Nutrition-based approaches to early childhood development. In P. Britto, P. L. Engle, & C. M. Super (Eds.), *Handbook of early childhood development research and its impact on global policy*. New York: Oxford University Press.

Yu, C., Hung, C., Chan, T., Yeh, C., & Lai, C. (2012). Prenatal predictors for father-infant attachment after childbirth. *Journal of Clinical Nursing, 21,* 1577–1583.

Yu, M., & Stiffman, A. (2007). Culture and environment as predictors of alcohol abuse/dependence symptoms in American Indian youths. *Addictive Behaviors, 32,* 2253–2259.

Yuan, A. (2012). Perceived breast development and adolescent girls' psychological well-being. *Sex Roles, 66,* 790–806.

Zacchilli, T. L., & Valerio, C. (2011). The knowledge and prevalence of cyber bullying in a college sample. *Journal of Scientific Psychology*.

Zafeiriou, D. I. (2004). Primitive reflexes and postural reactions in the neurodevelopmental examination. *Pediatric Neurology, 31,* 1–8.

Zahn-Waxler, C., & Radke-Yarrow, M. (1990). The origins of empathic concern. *Motivation and Emotion, 14,* 107–130.

Zahn-Waxler, C., Shirtcliff, E., & Marceau, K. (2008). Disorders of childhood and adolescence: Gender and psychopathology. *Annual Review of Clinical Psychology, 4,* 275–303.

Zalenski, R., & Raspa, R. (2006). Maslow's hierarchy of needs: A framework for achieving human potential in hospice. *Journal of Palliative Medicine, 9,* 1120–1127.

Zalsman, G., Oquendo, M., Greenhill, L., Goldberg, P., Kamali, M., Martin, A., et al. (2006, October). Neurobiology of depression in children and adolescents. *Child and Adolescent Psychiatric Clinics of North America, 15,* 843–868.

Zampi, C., Fagioli, I., & Salzarulo, P. (2002). Time course of EEG background activity level before spontaneous awakening in infants. *Journal of Sleep Research, 11,* 283–287.

Zarit, S. H., & Reid, J. D. (1994). Family caregiving and the older family. In C. B. Fisher & R. M. Lerner (Eds.), *Applied developmental psychology*. New York: McGraw-Hill.

Zauszniewski, J. A., & Martin, M. H. (1999). Developmental task achievement and learned resourcefulness in healthy older adults. *Archives of Psychiatric Nursing, 13,* 41–47.

Zeanah, C. (2009). The importance of early experiences: Clinical, research and policy perspectives. *Journal of Loss and Trauma, 14,* 266–279.

Zeedyk, M., & Heimann, M. (2006). Imitation and socio-emotional processes: Implications for communicative development and interventions. *Infant and Child Development, 15,* 219–222.

Zeiders, K. H., Umañ-Taylor, A. J., & Derlan, C. L. (2013). Trajectories of depressive symptoms and self-esteem in Latino youths: Examining the role of gender and perceived discrimination. *Developmental Psychology, 49,* 951–963.

Zelazo, P. D., Muller, U., Frye, D., & Marcovitch, S. (2003). The development of executive function in early childhood. *Monographs of the Society for Research in Child Development, 68,* 103–122.

Zelazo, P. R. (1998). McGraw and the development of unaided walking. *Developmental Review, 18,* 449–471.

Zemach, I., Chang, S., & Teller, D. (2007). Infant color vision: Prediction of infants' spontaneous color preferences. *Vision Research, 47,* 1368–1381.

Zettergren, P. (2003). School adjustment in adolescence for previously rejected, average and popular children. *British Journal of Educational Psychology, 73,* 207–221.

Zhang, J. (2010). Vygotsky's thinking: Its relevance to learning and education. *Mind, Culture, and Activity, 17,* 188–190.

Zhe, C., & Siegler, R. S. (2000). Across the great divide: Bridging the gap between understanding of toddlers' and older children's thinking. *Monographs of the Society for Research in Child Development, 65*(2, Serial No. 261).

Zheng, Y. (2010). One-child policy and child mental health. In M. E. Garralda & J.-P. Raynaud (Eds.), *Increasing awareness of child and adolescent mental health.* Lanham, MD: Jason Aronson.

Zhu, J., & Weiss, L. (2005). The Wechsler Scales. In D. P. Flanagan & P. L. Harrison (Eds.), *Contemporary intellectual assessment: Theories, tests, and issues.* New York: Guilford Press.

Ziegler, D., Piguet, O., Salat, D., Prince, K., Connally, E., & Corkin, S. (2010). Cognition in healthy aging is related to regional white matter integrity, but not cortical thickness. *Neurobiology of Aging, 31,* 1912–1926.

Ziegler, M., Danay, E., Heene, M., Asendorpf, J., & Bühner, M. (2012). Openness, fluid intelligence, and crystallized intelligence: Toward an integrative model. *Journal of Research in Personality, 46,* 173–183.

Zigler, E. F., & Finn-Stevenson, M. (1995). The child care crisis: Implications for the growth and development of the nation's children. *Journal of Social Issues, 51,* 215–231.

Zimmer-Gembeck, M. J., & Gallaty, K. J. (2006). Hanging out or hanging in? Young females' socioemotional functioning and the changing motives for dating and romance. In A. Columbus (Ed.), *Advances in psychology research, Vol. 44.* Hauppauge, NY: Nova Science Publishers.

Zirkel, S., & Cantor, N. (2004). 50 years after *Brown v. Board of Education*: The promise and challenge of multicultural education. *Journal of Social Issues, 60,* 1–15.

Zisook, S., & Shear, K. (2009). Grief and bereavement: What psychiatrists need to know. *World Psychiatry, 8,* 67–74.

Zolotor, A., Theodore, A., Chang, J., Berkoff, M., & Runyan, D. (2008). Speak softly—and forget the stick corporal punishment and child physical abuse. *American Journal of Preventive Medicine, 35,* 364–369.

Zuckerman, G., & Shenfield, S. D. (2007). Child-adult interaction that creates a zone of proximal development. *Journal of Russian & East European Psychology, 45,* 43–69.

Zuckerman, M. (2003). Biological bases of personality. In T. Millon & M. J. Lerner (Eds.), *Handbook of psychology: Personality and social psychology, Vol. 5.* New York: Wiley.

Zwelling, E. (2006). A challenging time in the history of Lamaze international: An interview with Francine Nichols. *Journal of Perinatal Education, 15,* 10–17.

Glossary

abstract modeling the process in which modeling paves the way for the development of more general rules and principles. (p. 187)

acceleration special programs that allow gifted students to move ahead at their own pace, even if this means skipping to higher grade levels. (p. 228)

accommodation changes in existing ways of thinking that occur in response to encounters with new stimuli or events. (p. 113)

achieving stage the point reached by young adults in which intelligence is applied to specific situations involving the attainment of long-term goals regarding careers, family, and societal contributions. (p. 319)

acquisitive stage according to Schaie, the first stage of cognitive development, encompassing all of childhood and adolescence. (p. 319)

activity theory the theory suggesting that successful aging occurs when people maintain the interests, activities, and social interactions with which they were involved during middle age. (p. 428)

addictive drugs drugs that produce a biological or psychological dependence in users, leading to increasingly powerful cravings for them. (p. 264)

adolescence the developmental stage that lies between childhood and adulthood. (p. 254)

adolescent egocentrism a state of self-absorption in which the world is viewed from one's own point of view. (p. 272)

adult day-care facilities a facility in which elderly individuals receive care only during the day, but spend nights and weekends in their own homes. (p. 430)

affordances the action possibilities that a given situation or stimulus provides. (p. 110)

age stratification theories the view that an unequal distribution of economic resources, power, and privilege exists among people at different stages of life. (p. 425)

ageism prejudice and discrimination directed at older people. (p. 401)

agentic professions occupations that are associated with getting things accomplished, such as carpentry. (p. 348)

aggression intentional injury or harm to another person. (p. 188)

Ainsworth Strange Situation a sequence of staged episodes that illustrate the strength of attachment between a child and (typically) his or her mother. (p. 137)

alcoholics persons with alcohol problems who have learned to depend on alcohol and are unable to control their drinking. (p. 264)

Alzheimer's disease a progressive brain disorder that produces loss of memory and confusion. (p. 409)

ambivalent attachment pattern a style of attachment in which children display a combination of positive and negative reactions to their mothers; they show great distress when the mother leaves, but upon her return they may simultaneously seek close contact but also hit and kick her. (p. 138)

amniocentesis the process of identifying genetic defects by examining a small sample of fetal cells drawn by a needle inserted into the amniotic fluid surrounding the unborn fetus. (p. 47)

androgynous a state in which gender roles encompass characteristics thought typical of both sexes. (p. 177)

anorexia nervosa a severe eating disorder in which individuals refuse to eat, while denying that their behavior and appearance, which may become skeletal, are out of the ordinary. (p. 259)

anoxia a restriction of oxygen to the baby, lasting a few minutes during the birth process, which can produce cognitive defects. (p. 70)

Apgar scale a standard measurement system that looks for a variety of indications of good health in newborns. (p. 70)

applied research research meant to provide practical solutions to immediate problems. (p. 31)

artificial insemination a process of fertilization in which a man's sperm is placed directly into a woman's reproductive tract by a physician. (p. 60)

assimilation the process in which people understand an experience in terms of their current stage of cognitive development and way of thinking. (p. 113)

associative play play in which two or more children actually interact with one another by sharing or borrowing toys or materials, although they do not do the same thing. (p. 179)

Attachment the positive emotional bond that develops between a child and a particular individual. (p. 137)

attention deficit hyperactivity disorder (ADHD) a learning disorder marked by inattention, impulsiveness, a low tolerance for frustration, and generally a great deal of inappropriate activity. (p. 206)

auditory impairment a special need that involves the loss of hearing or some aspect of hearing. (p. 205)

authoritarian parents parents who are controlling, punitive, rigid, and cold, and whose word is law. They value strict, unquestioning obedience from their children and do not tolerate expressions of disagreement. (p. 181)

authoritative parents parents who are firm, setting clear and consistent limits, but who try to reason with their children, giving explanations for why they should behave in a particular way. (p. 181)

autobiographical memory memories about one's own life. (pp. 165, 419)

autonomy having independence and a sense of control over one's life. (p. 288)

autonomy-versus-shame-and-doubt stage the period during which, according to Erikson, toddlers (aged 18 months to 3 years) develop independence and autonomy if they are allowed the freedom to explore, or shame and self-doubt if they are restricted and overprotected. (p. 142)

avoidant attachment pattern a style of attachment in which children do not seek proximity to the mother; after the mother has left, they seem to avoid her when she returns as if they are angered by her behavior. (p. 138)

Babbling making speechlike but meaningless sounds. (p. 125)

Bayley Scales of Infant Development a measure that evaluates an infant's development from 2 to 42 months. (p. 122)

behavior modification a formal technique for promoting the frequency of desirable behaviors and decreasing the incidence of unwanted ones. (p. 16)

behavioral genetics the study of the effects of heredity on behavior. (p. 44)

behavioral perspective the approach that suggests that the keys to understanding development are observable behavior and outside stimuli in the environment. (p. 15)

bereavement acknowledgment of the objective fact that one has experienced a death. (p. 462)

bicultural identity Maintaining one's original cultural identity while integrating oneself into the dominant culture. (p. 218)

bilingualism the use of more than one language. (p. 214)

bioecological approach the perspective suggesting that levels of the environment simultaneously influence individuals. (p. 20)

blended families remarried couples who have at least one stepchild living with them. (p. 245)

body transcendence versus body preoccupation a period in which people must learn to cope with and move beyond changes in physical capabilities as a result of aging. (p. 423)

bonding close physical and emotional contact between parent and child during the period immediately following birth. (p. 71)

boomerang children young adults who return, after leaving home for some period, to live in the homes of their middle-aged parents. (p. 387)

brain death a diagnosis of death based on the cessation of all signs of brain activity, as measured by electrical brain waves. (p. 447)

Brazelton Neonatal Behavioral Assessment Scale (NBAS) a measure designed to determine infants' neurological and behavioral responses to their environment. (p. 103)

bulimia an eating disorder characterized by binges on large quantities of food, followed by purges of the food through vomiting or the use of laxatives. (p. 259)

Burnout a situation that occurs when workers experience dissatisfaction, disillusionment, frustration, and weariness from their jobs. (p. 392)

career consolidation according to Vaillant a stage that is entered between the ages of 20 and 40, when young adults become centered on their careers. (p. 346)

case studies studies that involve extensive, in-depth interviews with a particular individual or small group of individuals. (p. 27)

centration the process of concentrating on one limited aspect of a stimulus and ignoring other aspects. (p. 160)

cephalocaudal principle the principle that growth follows a pattern that begins with the head and upper body parts and then proceeds down to the rest of the body. (p. 93)

cerebral cortex the upper layer of the brain. (p. 96)

cesarean delivery a birth in which the baby is surgically removed from the uterus, rather than traveling through the birth canal. (p. 78)

chorionic villus sampling (CVS) a test used to find genetic defects that involves taking samples of hairlike material that surrounds the embryo. (p. 47)

chromosomes rod-shaped portions of DNA that are organized in 23 pairs. (p. 41)

chronological (or physical) age the actual age of the child taking the intelligence test. (p. 220)

classical conditioning a type of learning in which an organism responds in a particular way to a neutral stimulus that normally does not bring about that type of response. (pp. 15, 84)

cliques groups of from 2 to 12 people whose members have frequent social interactions with one another. (p. 292)

cognitive development development involving the ways that growth and change in intellectual capabilities influence a person's behavior. (p. 5)

cognitive neuroscience approaches the approach that examines cognitive development through the lens of brain processes. (p. 18)

cognitive perspective the approach that focuses on the processes that allow people to know, understand, and think about the world. (p. 17)

cohabitation couples living together without being married. (p. 340)

cohort a group of people born at around the same time in the same place. (p. 8)

collectivistic orientation a philosophy that promotes the notion of interdependence. (p. 175)

communal professions occupations that are associated with relationships, such as nursing. (p. 348)

companionate love the strong affection for those with whom our lives are deeply involved. (p. 334)

concrete operational stage the period of cognitive development between 7 and 12 years of age, which is characterized by the active, and appropriate, use of logic. (p. 209)

conservation the knowledge that quantity is unrelated to the arrangement and physical appearance of objects. (p. 161)

constructive play play in which children manipulate objects to produce or build something. (p. 179)

contextual perspective the theory that considers the relationship between individuals and their physical, cognitive, personality, and social worlds. (p. 20)

continuing-care community a community that offers an environment in which all the residents are of retirement age or older. (p. 430)

continuity theory the theory suggesting that people need to maintain their desired level of involvement in society in order to maximize their sense of well-being and self-esteem. (p. 428)

continuous change gradual development in which achievements at one level build on those of previous levels. (p. 9)

controversial adolescents children who are liked by some peers and disliked by others. (p. 294)

cooperative play play in which children genuinely interact with one another, taking turns, playing games, or devising contests. (p. 179)

coping the effort to control, reduce, or learn to tolerate the threats that lead to stress. (p. 314)

coregulation a period in which parents and children jointly control children's behavior. (p. 243)

correlational research research that seeks to identify whether an association or relationship between two factors exists. (p. 25)

creativity the combination of responses or ideas in novel ways. (p. 322)

critical period a specific time during development when a particular event has its greatest consequences and the presence of certain kinds of environmental stimuli are necessary for development to proceed normally. (p. 10)

cross-sectional research research in which people of different ages are compared at the same point in time. (p. 33)

crowds larger groups than cliques, composed of individuals who share particular characteristics but who may not interact with one another. (p. 292)

crystallized intelligence the accumulation of information, skills, and strategies that people have learned through experience and that they can apply in problem-solving situations. (p. 223)

crystallized intelligence the accumulation of information, skills, and strategies that people have learned through experience and that they can apply in problem-solving situations. (p. 370)

cultural assimilation model the model in which the goal was to assimilate individual cultural identities into a unique, unified American culture. (p. 217)

cycle of violence hypothesis the theory that the abuse and neglect that children suffer predispose them as adults to abuse and neglect their own children. (pp. 183, 390)

decentering the ability to take multiple aspects of a situation into account. (p. 209)

decision/commitment component according to Sternberg the third aspect of love that embodies both the initial cognition that one loves another person and the longer-term determination to maintain that love. (p. 334)

defensive coping coping that involves unconscious strategies that distort or deny the true nature of a situation. (p. 315)

dementia the most common mental disorder of the elderly, it covers several diseases, each of which includes serious memory loss accompanied by declines in other mental functioning. (p. 408)

dependent variable the variable that researchers measure to see if it changes as a result of the experimental manipulation. (p. 29)

developmental quotient an overall developmental score that relates to performance in four domains: motor skills, language use, adaptive behavior, and personal–social. (p. 122)

difficult babies babies who have negative moods and are slow to adapt to new situations; when confronted with a new situation, they tend to withdraw. (p. 143)

discontinuous change development that occurs in distinct steps or stages, with each stage bringing about behavior that is assumed to be qualitatively different from behavior at earlier stages. (p. 10)

disengagement theory the period in late adulthood that marks a gradual withdrawal from the world on physical, psychological, and social levels. (p. 427)

disorganized–disoriented attachment pattern a style of attachment in which children show inconsistent, often contradictory behavior, such as approaching the mother when she returns but not looking at her; they may be the least securely attached children of all. (p. 138)

dizygotic twins twins who are produced when two separate ova are fertilized by two separate sperm at roughly the same time. (p. 42)

DNA (deoxyribonucleic acid) molecules the substance that genes are composed of that determines the nature of every cell in the body and how it will function. (p. 41)

dominance hierarchy rankings that represent the relative social power of those in a group. (p. 241)

dominant trait the one trait that is expressed when two competing traits are present. (p. 43)

Down syndrome a disorder produced by the presence of an extra chromosome on the 21st pair; once referred to as mongolism. (p. 45)

easy babies babies who have a positive disposition; their body functions operate regularly, and they are adaptable. (p. 143)

ego transcendence versus ego preoccupation the period in which elderly people must come to grips with their coming death. (p. 423)

egocentric thought thinking that does not take into account the viewpoints of others. (p. 161)

ego-integrity-versus-despair stage Erikson's final stage of life, characterized by a process of looking back over one's life, evaluating it, and coming to terms with it. (p. 422)

elder abuse the physical or psychological mistreatment or neglect of elderly individuals. (p. 441)

embryonic stage the period from 2 to 8 weeks following fertilization during which significant growth occurs in the major organs and body systems. (p. 59)

emerging adulthood according to Arnett the period from the end of teenage years through early 20's in which people are still sorting out their options for the future. (p. 332)

emotional intelligence the set of skills that underlie the accurate assessment, evaluation, expression, and regulation of emotions. (p. 321)

emotional self-regulation the capability to adjust emotions to a desired state and level of intensity. (p. 188)

empathy an emotional response that corresponds to the feelings of another person. (p. 136)

empathy the understanding of what another individual feels. (p. 188)

empty nest syndrome the experience that relates to parents' feelings of unhappiness, worry, loneliness, and depression resulting from their children's departure from home. (p. 386)

enrichment an approach through which students are kept at grade level but are enrolled in special programs and given individual activities to allow greater depth of study on a given topic. (p. 228)

episiotomy an incision sometimes made to increase the size of the opening of the vagina to allow the baby to pass. (p. 69)

Erikson's theory of psychosocial development the theory that considers how individuals come to understand themselves and the meaning of others'—and their own—behavior. (p. 142)

euthanasia the practice of assisting people who are terminally ill to die more quickly. (p. 457)

evolutionary perspective the theory that seeks to identify behavior that is a result of our genetic inheritance from our ancestors. (p. 22)

executive stage the period in middle adulthood when people take a broader perspective than earlier, including concerns about the world. (p. 320)

experiment a process in which an investigator, called an experimenter, devises two different experiences for participants. (p. 29)

experimental research research designed to discover causal relationships between various factors. (p. 25)

expertise the acquisition of skill or knowledge in a particular area. (p. 372)

expressive style a style of language use in which language is used primarily to express feelings and needs about oneself and others. (p. 128)

extrinsic motivation motivation that drives people to obtain tangible rewards, such as money and prestige. (p. 349)

fantasy period according to Ginzberg, the period, lasting until about age 11, when career choices are made, and discarded, without regard to skills, abilities, or available job opportunities. (p. 347)

fast mapping instances in which new words are associated with their meaning after only a brief encounter. (p. 169)

female climacteric the period that marks the transition from being able to bear children to being unable to do so. (p. 360)

fertilization the process by which a sperm and an ovum—the male and female gametes, respectively—join to form a single new cell. (p. 58)

fetal alcohol effects (FAE) a disorder caused by the pregnant mother consuming substantial quantities of alcohol during pregnancy, potentially resulting in mental retardation and delayed growth in the child. (p. 66)

fetal alcohol syndrome (FAS) a disorder caused by the pregnant mother consuming substantial quantities of alcohol during pregnancy, potentially resulting in mental retardation and delayed growth in the child. (p. 66)

fetal monitor a device that measures the baby's heartbeat during labor. (p. 78)

fetal stage the stage that begins at about 8 weeks after conception and continues until birth. (p. 59)

fetus a developing child, from 8 weeks after conception until birth. (p. 60)

field study a research investigation carried out in a naturally occurring setting. (p. 30)

first-year adjustment reaction a cluster of psychological symptoms, including loneliness, anxiety, withdrawal, and depression, relating to the college experience suffered by first-year college students. (p. 325)

fluid intelligence intelligence that reflects information processing capabilities, reasoning, and memory. (p. 222)

fluid intelligence reflects information processing capabilities, reasoning, and memory. (p. 370)

formal operational stage the period at which people develop the ability to think abstractly. (p. 269)

fragile X syndrome a disorder produced by injury to a gene on the X chromosome, producing mild to moderate mental retardation. (p. 45)

functional death the absence of a heartbeat and breathing. (p. 446)

functional play play that involves simple, repetitive activities typical of 3-year-olds. (p. 179)

gender constancy the awareness that people are permanently males or females, depending on fixed, unchangeable biological factors. (p. 177)

gender identity the perception of oneself as male or female. (p. 177)

gender schema a cognitive framework that organizes information relevant to gender. (p. 177)

gender the sense of being male or female. (p. 144)

generalized slowing hypothesis the theory that processing in all parts of the nervous system, including the brain, is less efficient as we age. (p. 405)

generation gap a divide between parents and adolescents in attitudes, values, aspirations, and world views. (p. 289)

generativity-versus-stagnation according to Erikson, the stage during middle adulthood in which people consider their contributions to family and society. (p. 377)

genes the basic unit of genetic information. (p. 40)

genetic counseling the discipline that focuses on helping people deal with issues relating to inherited disorders. (p. 46)

genetic programming theories of aging theories that suggest that our body's DNA genetic code contains a built-in time limit for the reproduction of human cells. (p. 412)

genotype the underlying combination of genetic material present (but not outwardly visible) in an organism. (p. 43)

germinal stage the first—and shortest—stage of the prenatal period, which takes place during the first 2 weeks following conception. (p. 59)

gerontologists specialists who study aging. (p. 400)

gifted and talented children who show evidence of high performance capability in areas such as intellectual, creative, artistic, leadership capacity, or specific academic fields. (p. 228)

glaucoma a condition in which pressure in the fluid of the eye increases, either because the fluid cannot drain properly or because too much fluid is produced. (p. 357)

goodness-of-fit the notion that development is dependent on the degree of match between children's temperament and the nature and demands of the environment in which they are being raised. (p. 143)

grammar the system of rules that determine how our thoughts can be expressed. (p. 170)

Grief the emotional response to one's loss. (p. 462)

habituation the decrease in the response to a stimulus that occurs after repeated presentations of the same stimulus. (p. 85)

handedness the preference of using one hand over another. (p. 159)

hardiness a personality characteristic associated with a lower rate of stress-related illness. (p. 315)

heterozygous inheriting from parents different forms of a gene for a given trait. (p. 43)

holophrases one-word utterances that stand for a whole phrase, the meaning of which depends on the particular context in which they are used. (p. 126)

home care an alternative to hospitalization in which dying people stay in their homes and receive treatment from their families and visiting medical staff. (p. 460)

homogamy the tendency to marry someone who is similar in age, race, education, religion, and other basic demographic characteristics. (p. 337)

homozygous inheriting from parents similar genes for a given trait. (p. 43)

hospice care care provided for the dying in institutions devoted to those who are terminally ill. (p. 460)

humanistic perspective the theory that contends that people have a natural capacity to make decisions about their lives and control their behavior. (p. 19)

hypothesis a prediction stated in a way that permits it to be tested. (p. 25)

identity achievement the status of adolescents who commit to a particular identity following a period of crisis during which they consider various alternatives. (p. 283)

identity diffusion the status of adolescents who consider various identity alternatives, but never commit to one or never even consider identity options in any conscious way. (p. 283)

identity foreclosure the status of adolescents who prematurely commit to an identity without adequately exploring alternatives. (p. 283)

identity-versus-identity-confusion stage the period during which teenagers seek to determine what is unique and distinctive about themselves. (p. 281)

imaginary audience an adolescent's belief that his or her own behavior is a primary focus of others' attention and concerns. (p. 272)

in vitro fertilization (IVF) a procedure in which a woman's ova are removed from her ovaries, and a man's sperm are used to fertilize the ova in a laboratory. (p. 61)

independent variable the variable that researchers manipulate in an experiment. (p. 29)

individualistic orientation a philosophy that emphasizes personal identity and the uniqueness of the individual. (p. 175)

industry-versus-inferiority stage according to Erikson the period from age 6 to 12 characterized by a focus on efforts to attain competence in meeting the challenges presented by parents, peers, school, and the other complexities of the modern world. (p. 230)

infant mortality death within the first year of life. (p. 78)

infant-directed speech a type of speech directed toward infants, characterized by short, simple sentences. (p. 130)

infantile amnesia the lack of memory for experiences that occurred prior to 3 years of age. (p. 121)

infertility the inability to conceive after 12 to 18 months of trying to become pregnant. (p. 60)

information processing approaches the model that seeks to identify the ways individuals take in, use, and store information. (p. 18, 271)

initiative-versus-guilt stage according to Erikson, the period during which children aged 3 to 6 years experience conflict between independence of action and the sometimes negative results of that action. (p. 175)

institutionalism a psychological state in which people in nursing homes develop apathy, indifference, and a lack of caring about themselves. (p. 431)

instrumental aggression aggression motivated by the desire to obtain a concrete goal. (p. 189)

intellectual disability a disability characterized by significant limitations both in intellectual functioning and in adaptive behavior, which covers many everyday social and practical skills. (p. 227)

intelligence quotient (or IQ score) a score that accounts for a student's mental *and* chronological age. (p. 221)

intelligence the capacity to understand the world, think with rationality, and use resources effectively when faced with challenges. (p. 220)

intimacy component according to Sternberg the component of love that encompasses feelings of closeness, affection, and connectedness. (p. 334)

intimacy-versus-isolation stage according to Erikson, the period of postadolescence into the early 30s that focuses on developing close, intimate relationships with others. (p. 332)

intrinsic motivation motivation that causes people to work for their own enjoyment, for personal rewards. (p. 349)

intuitive thought thinking that reflects preschoolers' use of primitive reasoning and their avid acquisition of knowledge about the world. (p. 162)

Kaufman Assessment Battery for Children, Second Edition (KABC-II) an intelligence test that measures children's ability to integrate different stimuli simultaneously and to use sequential thinking. (p. 221)

Klinefelter's syndrome a disorder resulting from the presence of an extra X chromosome that produces underdeveloped genitals, extreme height, and enlarged breasts. (p. 46)

labeling theory of passionate love the theory that individuals experience romantic love when two events occur together: intense physiological arousal and situational cues suggesting that the arousal is due to love. (p. 334)

laboratory study a research investigation conducted in a controlled setting explicitly designed to hold events constant. (p. 31)

Language the systematic, meaningful arrangement of symbols, which provides the basis for communication. (p. 125)

language-acquisition device (LAD) a neural system of the brain hypothesized to permit understanding of language. (p. 129)

lateralization the process in which certain cognitive functions are located more in one hemisphere of the brain than in the other. (p. 155)

learning disabilities difficulties in the acquisition and use of listening, speaking, reading, writing, reasoning, or mathematical abilities. (p. 206)

learning theory approach the theory that language acquisition follows the basic laws of reinforcement and conditioning. (p. 128)

least restrictive environment the setting that is most similar to that of children without special needs. (p. 226)

life events models the approach to personality development that is based on the timing of particular events in an adult's life rather than on age per se. (p. 377)

life expectancy the average age of death for members of a population. (p. 413)

life review the point in life in which people examine and evaluate their lives. (p. 425)

lifespan development the field of study that examines patterns of growth, change, and stability in behavior that occur throughout the entire life span. (p. 5)

living wills legal documents designating what medical treatments people want or do not want if they cannot express their wishes. (p. 457)

longitudinal research research in which the behavior of one or more participants in a study is measured as they age. (p. 31)

low-birthweight infants infants who weigh less than 2,500 grams (around 5 1/2 pounds) at birth. (p. 76)

mainstreaming an educational approach in which exceptional children are integrated to the extent possible into the traditional educational system and are provided with a broad range of educational alternatives. (p. 226)

male climacteric the period of physical and psychological change relating to the male reproductive system that occurs during late middle age. (p. 362)

maturation the predetermined unfolding of genetic information. (p. 11)

memory the process by which information is initially recorded, stored, and retrieved. (p. 210)

menarche the onset of menstruation. (p. 256)

menopause the cessation of menstruation. (p. 361)

mental age the typical intelligence level found for people at a given chronological age. (p. 220)

metacognition the knowledge that people have about their own thinking processes, and their ability to monitor their cognition. (p. 272)

metalinguistic awareness an understanding of one's own use of language. (p. 213)

metamemory an understanding about the processes that underlie memory, which emerges and improves during middle childhood. (p. 211)

midlife crisis a stage of uncertainty and indecision brought about by the realization that life is finite. (p. 378)

mild intellectual disability intellectual disability in which IQ scores fall in the range of 50 or 55 to 70. (p. 227)

mnemonics formal strategies for organizing material in ways that make it more likely to be remembered. (p. 375)

moderate intellectual disability intellectual disability in which IQ scores range from 35 or 40 to 50 or 55. (p. 227)

monozygotic twins twins who are genetically identical. (p. 42)

moral development the changes in people's sense of justice and of what is right and wrong, and in their behavior related to moral issues. (p. 187)

moratorium the status of adolescents who may have explored various identity alternatives to some degree, but have not yet committed themselves. (p. 283)

multicultural education a form of education in which the goal is to help minority students develop confidence in the culture of the majority group while maintaining positive group identities that build on their original cultures. (p. 219)

multifactorial transmission the determination of traits by a combination of both genetic and environmental factors in which a genotype provides a range within which a phenotype may be expressed. (p. 49)

multimodal approach to perception the approach that considers how information that is collected by various individual sensory systems is integrated and coordinated. (p. 110)

myelin protective insulation that surrounds parts of neurons—which speeds the transmission of electrical impulses along brain cells but also adds to brain weight. (pp. 96, 155)

nativist approach the theory that a genetically determined, innate mechanism directs language development. (p. 129)

naturalistic observation a type of correlational study in which some naturally occurring behavior is observed without intervention in the situation. (p. 27)

neglected adolescents children who receive relatively little attention from their peers in the form of either positive or negative interactions. (p. 294)

neonates the term used for newborns. (p. 69)

neuron the basic nerve cell of the nervous system. (p. 94)

nonorganic failure to thrive a disorder in which infants stop growing due to a lack of stimulation and attention as the result of inadequate parenting. (p. 105)

normative-crisis models the approach to personality development that is based on fairly universal stages tied to a sequence of age-related crises. (p. 377)

norms the average performance of a large sample of children of a given age. (p. 103)

obesity body weight more than 20 percent higher than the average weight for a person of a given age and height. (p. 153)

object permanence the realization that people and objects exist even when they cannot be seen. (p. 115)

onlooker play action in which children simply watch others at play, but do not actually participate themselves. (p. 179)

operant conditioning a form of learning in which a voluntary response is strengthened or weakened by its association with positive or negative consequences. (pp. 16, 85)

operations organized, formal, logical mental processes. (p. 160)

osteoporosis a condition in which the bones become brittle, fragile, and thin, often brought about by a lack of calcium in the diet. (pp. 357, 403)

overextension the overly broad use of words, overgeneralizing their meaning. (p. 127)

parallel play action in which children play with similar toys, in a similar manner, but do not interact with each other. (p. 179)

passion component according to Sternberg the component of love that comprises the motivational drives relating to sex, physical closeness, and romance. (p. 334)

passionate (or romantic) love a state of powerful absorption in someone. (p. 334)

peer pressure the influence of one's peers to conform to their behavior and attitudes. (p. 295)

perception the sorting out, interpretation, analysis, and integration of stimuli involving the sense organs and brain. (p. 108)

peripheral slowing hypothesis the theory that suggests that overall processing speed declines in the peripheral nervous system with increasing age. (p. 405)

permissive parents parents who provide lax and inconsistent feedback and require little of their children. (p. 181)

personal fables the view held by some adolescents that what happens to them is unique, exceptional, and shared by no one else. (p. 273)

personality development development involving the ways that the enduring characteristics that differentiate one person from another change over the lifes pan. (p. 6)

personality the sum total of the enduring characteristics that differentiate one individual from another. (p. 142)

phenotype an observable trait; the trait that is actually seen. (p. 43)

physical development development involving the body's physical makeup, including the brain, nervous system, muscles, and senses, and the need for food, drink, and sleep. (p. 5)

placenta a conduit between the mother and fetus, providing nourishment and oxygen via the umbilical cord. (p. 59)

plasticity the degree to which a developing structure or behavior is modifiable due to experience. (p. 96)

pluralistic society model the concept that American society is made up of diverse, coequal cultural groups that should preserve their individual cultural features. (p. 218)

polygenic inheritance inheritance in which a combination of multiple gene pairs is responsible for the production of a particular trait. (p. 44)

postformal thought thinking that acknowledges that adult predicaments must sometimes be solved in relativistic terms. (p. 319)

postmature infants infants still unborn 2 weeks after the mother's due date. (p. 78)

practical intelligence according to Sternberg, intelligence that is learned primarily by observing others and modeling their behavior. (p. 321)

pragmatics the aspect of language that relates to communicating effectively and appropriately with others. (p. 170)

preoperational stage according to Piaget, the stage from approximately age 2 to age 7 in which children's use of symbolic thinking grows, mental reasoning emerges, and the use of concepts increases. (p. 160)

presbycusis loss of the ability to hear sounds of high frequency. (p. 358)

presbyopia a nearly universal change in eyesight during middle adulthood that results in some loss of near vision. (p. 357)

preterm infants infants who are born prior to 38 weeks after conception (also known as premature infants). (p. 66)

primary aging aging that involves universal and irreversible changes that, due to genetic programming, occur as people get older. (p. 403)

primary appraisal the assessment of an event to determine whether its implications are positive, negative, or neutral. (p. 313)

primary sex characteristics characteristics associated with the development of the organs and structures of the body that directly relate to reproduction. (p. 256)

principle of hierarchical integration the principle that simple skills typically develop separately and independently but are later integrated into more complex skills. (p. 94)

principle of the independence of systems the principle that different body systems grow at different rates. (p. 94)

private speech speech by children that is spoken and directed to themselves (p. 170)

profound intellectual disability intellectual disability in which IQ scores fall below 20 or 25. (p. 228)

prosocial behavior helping behavior that benefits others. (p. 187)

proximodistal principle the principle that development proceeds from the center of the body outward. (p. 93)

psychoanalytic theory the theory proposed by Freud that suggests that unconscious forces act to determine personality and behavior. (p. 13)

psychodynamic perspective the approach that states behavior is motivated by inner forces, memories, and conflicts that are generally beyond people's awareness and control. (p. 13)

psychological maltreatment abuse that occurs when parents or other caregivers harm children's behavioral, cognitive, emotional, or physical functioning. (p. 184)

psychoneuroimmunology (PNI) the study of the relationship among the brain, the immune system, and psychological factors. (p. 313)

psychophysiological methods research that focuses on the relationship between physiological processes and behavior. (p. 28)

psychosexual development according to Freud, a series of stages that children pass through in which pleasure, or gratification, is focused on a particular biological function and body part. (p. 13)

psychosocial development according to Erikson, development that encompasses changes both in the understandings individuals have of themselves as members of society and in their comprehension of the meaning of others' behavior. (pp. 13, 174)

psychosomatic disorders medical problems caused by the interaction of psychological, emotional, and physical difficulties. (p. 314)

puberty the period during which the sexual organs mature. (p. 255)

race dissonance the phenomenon in which minority children indicate preferences for majority values or people. (p. 175)

rapid eye movement (REM) sleep the period of sleep that is found in older children and adults and is associated with dreaming. (p. 98)

realistic period the third stage of Ginzberg's theory, which occurs in early adulthood, when people begin to explore specific career options, either through actual experience on the job or through training for a profession, and then narrow their choices and make a commitment. (p. 347)

recessive trait a trait within an organism that is present, but is not expressed (p. 43)

redefinition of self versus preoccupation with work role the theory that those in old age must redefine themselves in ways that do not relate to their work roles or occupations. (p. 423)

reference groups groups of people with whom one compares oneself. (p. 292)

referential style a style of language use in which language is used primarily to label objects. (p. 128)

reflexes unlearned, organized involuntary responses that occur automatically in the presence of certain stimuli. (pp. 82, 101)

reintegrative stage the period of late adulthood during which the focus is on tasks that have personal meaning. (p. 320)

rejected adolescents children who are actively disliked, and whose peers may react to them in an obviously negative manner.. (p. 294)

relational aggression nonphysical aggression that is intended to hurt another person's psychological well-being.. (p. 180)

resilience the ability to overcome circumstances that place a child at high risk for psychological or physical damage.. (p. 185)

responsible stage the stage where the major concerns of middle-aged adults relate to their personal situations, including protecting and nourishing their spouses, families, and careers.. (p. 320)

rhythms repetitive, cyclical patterns of behavior.. (p. 97)

sample the group of participants chosen for the experiment. (p. 30)

sandwich generation couples who in middle adulthood must fulfill the needs of both their children and their aging parents. (p. 387)

scaffolding the support for learning and problem solving that encourages independence and growth. (p. 167)

schemas organized bodies of information stored in memory. (p. 374)

scheme an organized patterns of functioning that adapt and change with mental functioning. (p. 113)

scientific method the process of posing and answering questions using careful, controlled techniques that include systematic, orderly observation and the collection of data. (p. 25)

scripts broad representations in memory of events and the order in which they occur. (p. 165)

secondary aging changes in physical and cognitive functioning that are due to illness, health habits, and other individual differences, but are not due to increased age itself and are not inevitable. (p. 403)

secondary appraisal the assessment of whether one's coping abilities and resources are adequate to overcome the harm, threat, or challenge posed by the potential stressor. (p. 313)

secondary sex characteristics the visible signs of sexual maturity that do not directly involve the sex organs. (p. 256)

secular trend a pattern of change occurring over several generations. (p. 256)

secure attachment pattern a style of attachment in which children use the mother as a kind of home base and are at ease when she is present; when she leaves, they become upset and go to her as soon as she returns. (p. 138)

selective optimization the process by which people concentrate on selected skill areas to compensate for losses in other areas. (p. 429)

selective optimization with compensation the process by which people concentrate on particular skill areas to compensate for losses in other areas. (p. 372)

self-awareness knowledge of oneself. (p. 135)

self-care children children who let themselves into their homes after school and wait alone until their caretakers return from work; previously known as *latchkey children*. (p. 244)

self-concept a person's identity, or set of beliefs about what one is like as an individual. (p. 175)

self-esteem an individual's overall and specific positive and negative self-evaluation. (p. 231)

senescence the natural physical decline brought about by aging. (p. 306)

Sensation the physical stimulation of the sense organs. (p. 108)

sensitive period a point in development when organisms are particularly susceptible to certain kinds of stimuli in their environments, but the absence of those stimuli does not always produce irreversible consequences. (pp. 10, 96)

sensorimotor stage (of cognitive development) Piaget's initial major stage of cognitive development, which can be broken down into six substages. (p. 114)

separation anxiety the distress displayed by infants when a customary care provider departs. (p. 134)

sequential studies research in which researchers examine a number of different age groups over several points in time. (p. 33)

severe intellectual disability intellectual disability in which IQ scores range from 20 or 25 to 35 or 40. (p. 228)

sex cleavage sex segregation in which boys interact primarily with boys and girls primarily with girls. (p. 292)

sexually transmitted infection (STI) an infection that is spread through sexual contact. (p. 266)

sickle-cell anemia a blood disorder that gets its name from the shape of the red blood cells. (p. 46)

skilled-nursing facilities a facility that provides full-time nursing care for people who have chronic illnesses or are recovering from a temporary medical condition. (p. 431)

slow-to-warm babies babies who are inactive, showing relatively calm reactions to their environment; their moods are generally negative, and they withdraw from new situations, adapting slowly. (p. 143)

small-for-gestational-age infants infants who, because of delayed fetal growth, weigh 90 percent (or less) of the average weight of infants of the same gestational age. (p. 76)

social competence the collection of social skills that permit individuals to perform successfully in social settings.. (p. 238)

social development the way in which individuals' interactions with others and their social relationships grow, change, and remain stable over the course of life. (p. 6)

social problem-solving the use of strategies for solving social conflicts in ways that are satisfactory both to oneself and to others.. (p. 239)

social referencing the intentional search for information about others' feelings to help explain the meaning of uncertain circumstances and events. (p. 135)

social speech speech directed toward another person and meant to be understood by that person. (p. 170)

social support assistance and comfort supplied by another person or a network of caring, interested people. (p. 439)

social-cognitive learning theory learning by observing the behavior of another person, called a model. (p. 16)

socialized delinquents adolescent delinquents who know and subscribe to the norms of society and who are fairly normal psychologically. (p. 296)

sociocultural theory the approach that emphasizes how cognitive development proceeds as a result of social interactions between members of a culture. (p. 21)

speech impairment speech that deviates so much from the speech of others that it calls attention to itself, interferes with communication, or produces maladjustment in the speaker. (p. 206)

Stanford-Binet Intelligence Scales, Fifth Edition (SB5) a test that consists of a series of items that vary according to the age of the person being tested. (p. 221)

state the degree of awareness an infant displays to both internal and external stimulation. (p. 97)

states of arousal different degrees of sleep and wakefulness through which newborns cycle, ranging from deep sleep to great agitation. (p. 86)

status the evaluation of a role or person by other relevant members of a group (p. 238)

Status the evaluation of a role or person by other relevant members of a group or society. (p. 349)

stereotype threat obstacles to performance that come from awareness of the stereotypes held by society about academic abilities. (p. 329)

stillbirth the delivery of a child who is not alive, occurring in fewer than 1 delivery in 100. (p. 78)

stimulus-value-role (SVR) theory the theory that relationships proceed in a fixed order of three stages: stimulus, value, and role. (p. 333)

stranger anxiety the caution and wariness displayed by infants when encountering an unfamiliar person. (p. 133)

Stress the physical and emotional response to events that threaten or challenge us. (p. 313)

stuttering substantial disruption in the rhythm and fluency of speech; the most common speech impairment. (p. 206)

sudden infant death syndrome (SIDS) the unexplained death of a seemingly healthy baby. (pp. 99, 448)

survey research a type of study where a group of people chosen to represent some larger population are asked questions about their attitudes, behavior, or thinking on a given topic. (p. 28)

synapse the gap at the connection between neurons, through which neurons chemically communicate with one another. (p. 94)

synaptic pruning the elimination of neurons as the result of nonuse or lack of stimulation. (p. 96)

syntax the way in which an individual combines words and phrases to form sentences. (p. 169)

Tay-Sachs disease a disorder that produces blindness and muscle degeneration prior to death; there is no treatment. (p. 46)

telegraphic speech speech in which words not critical to the message are left out. (p. 127)

temperament patterns of arousal and emotionality that are consistent and enduring characteristics of an individual. (pp. 49, 142)

tentative period the second stage of Ginzberg's theory, which spans adolescence, when people begin to think more practically about the requirements of various jobs and how their own abilities might fit with them. (p. 347)

teratogen a factor that produces a birth defect. (p. 63)

thanatologists people who study death and dying. (p. 452)

theoretical research research designed specifically to test some developmental explanation and expand scientific knowledge. (p. 31)

theories broad explanations, and predictions about phenomena of interest. (p. 13)

theory of mind knowledge and beliefs about how the mind works and how it affects behavior. (p. 136)

transformation the process in which one state is changed into another. (p. 161)

triarchic theory of intelligence Sternberg's theory that intelligence is made up of three major components: componential, experiential, and contextual. (pp. 224, 321)

trust-versus-mistrust stage according to Erikson, the period during which infants develop a sense of trust or mistrust, largely depending on how well their needs are met by their caregivers. (p. 142)

ultrasound sonography a process in which high-frequency sound waves scan the mother's womb to produce an image of the unborn baby, whose size and shape can then be assessed. (p. 46)

underextension the overly restrictive use of words, common among children just mastering spoken language. (p. 127)

undersocialized delinquents adolescent delinquents who are raised with little discipline or with harsh, uncaring parental supervision. (p. 296)

uninvolved parents parents who show almost no interest in their children and indifferent, rejecting behavior. (p. 181)

universal grammar Noam Chomsky's theory that all the world's languages share a similar underlying structure. (p. 129)

very-low-birthweight infants infants who weigh less than 1,250 grams (around 2.25 pounds) or, regardless of weight, have been in the womb less than 30 weeks. (p. 76)

visual impairment a difficulty in seeing that may include blindness or partial sightedness. (p. 205)

wear-and-tear theories of aging the theory that the mechanical functions of the body simply wear out with age. (p. 412)

Wechsler Intelligence Scale for Children, Fourth Edition (WISC-IV) a test for children that provides separate measures of verbal and performance (or nonverbal) skills, as well as a total score. (p. 221)

wisdom expert knowledge in the practical aspects of life. (p. 426)

X-linked genes genes that are considered recessive and located only on the X chromosome. (p. 44)

zone of proximal development (ZPD) according to Vygotsky, the level at which a child can *almost*, but not fully, perform a task independently, but can do so with the assistance of someone more competent. (p. 167)

zygote the new cell formed by the process of fertilization. (p. 40)

Credits

Photo Credits

Cover Page COVER Robert Adrian Hillman/Alamy; Oleksii Telnov/Alamy; Oleksii Telnov/Alamy.

Front Matter Page viii BananaStock/Getty Images; p. ix Rubberball/Mike Kemp/Getty Images; p. x Jupiterimages/Thinkstock; p. xi absolut/Fotolia; p. xvii baobao ou/Flickr/Getty Images; p. xxv Robert S. Feldman.

Chapter 1 Page 4 67photo/Alamy; p. 7 DPA/The Image Works; p. 12 Bettmann/Corbis; p. 13 Bettmann/CORBIS; p. 15 Jon Erikson/The Image Works; p. 16 Hulton Archive/Archive Photos/Getty Images; p. 17 Monty Brinton/CBS Photo Archive/Getty Images; p. 18 Du Cane Medical Imaging Ltd./Science Source; p. 21 Ami Parikh/Shutterstock; p. 22 Nina Leen/Time Life Pictures/Getty Images; p. 28 Stegerphoto/Peter Arnold/Getty Images; p. 31 Bob Daemmrich/PhotoEdit, Inc.; p. 36 Ariel Skelley/Blend Images/Corbis; p. 37 (top, left) Mel Yates/Cultura/Getty images; (top, right) Jim Esposito/Photodisc/Getty Images; (bottom, right) Photodisc/Getty Images; (bottom, left) Asia Images Group/Getty Images.

Chapter 2 Page 41 (top, left) Don W. Fawcett/Science Source; (centre) CNRI/Science Photo Library/Science Source; (right) LAURENT/BSIP SA/Alamy; p. 46 Bill Longcore/Science Source; p. 47 Saturn Stills/Science Source; p. 50 Michael Shaw/The New Yorker Collection/www.cartoonbank.com; p. 53 shock/Shutterstock; p. 55 Tibor Hirsch/Science Source; p. 59 (left) Science Source; (centre) Science Pictures Ltd./Science Source; (right) Photo Researchers; p. 61 William Hamilton/The New Yorker Collection/www.cartoonbank.com; p. 66 Chris Harvey/Stone/Getty Images; p. 68 Al Goldis/AP Images; p. 71 (top) Jennie Woodcock; Reflections Photolibrary/Encyclopedia/CORBIS; (bottom) Joe McDonald/Encyclopedia/Corbis; p. 72 Jiang Jin/Purestock/Alamy; p. 73 Molly Schlachter/Pearson Education; p. 77 Sally and Richard Greenhill/Alamy; p. 79 Ruth Jenkinson/MIDIRS/Science Source; p. 83 (top) nyul/Fotolia; (bottom) wong sze yuen/Shutterstock; p. 88 Andersen Ross/Blend Images/Getty Images; p. 89 (top, left) Photodisc/Getty Images; (top, right) Mark Andersen/Rubberball/Getty Images; (bottom, left) Ljupco Smokovski/Fotolia; (bottom, right) get4net/Fotolia.

Chapter 3 Page 92 The Image Works; p. 96 Matlung, Bilo, Kuba, & van Rijn, 2011. Forensic Sci Med Pathol. 2011 December; 7(4): 355–363; p. 97 JUSTIN GUARIGLIA/National Geographic Creative; p. 102 (left) Laura Elliott/Jupiter Images; (centre) Dorling Kindersley; (right) Petit Format/Science Source; p. 104 poco_bw/Fotolia; p. 106 Mike Twohy/The New Yorker Collection/www.cartoonbank.com; p. 108 (bottom) PhotoEdit; (top) Vanessa Davies/Dorling Kindersley, Ltd.; p. 109 Owen Franken/Encyclopedia/Corbis; p. 110 Ruth Jenkinson/Dorling Kindersley LTD; p. 111 Ruth Jenkinson/Dorling Kindersley, Ltd.; p. 112 Alain Schroeder/ONOKY/Getty Images; p. 113 Bill Anderson/Science Source; p. 116 Aphichart/Shutterstock; p. 117 Irven DeVore/Anthro-Photo; p. 122 Atlaspix/Alamy; p. 125 DPA/The Image Works; p. 127 Erin Moroney LaBelle/The Image Works; p. 128 (left) Vanessa Davies/Dorling Kindersley, Ltd.; (centre) Giacomo Pirozzi/Panos Pictures; (right) Earl & Nazima Kowall/Documentary Value/Corbis; p. 132 Sky View/Digital Vision/Getty Images; p. 133 (top, left) Courtesy Dr. Carroll Izard; (top, right) Courtesy Dr. Carroll Izard; (centre, left) Courtesy Dr. Carroll Izard; (centre, right) Courtesy Dr. Carroll Izard; (bottom, right) Gary Conner/Photolibrary/Getty Images; p. 134 Vanessa Davies /Dorling Kindersley, Ltd.; p. 139 Keith Brofsky/Brand X Pictures/PictureQuest; p. 140 Larry Williams/Flirt/Corbis; p. 144 Imagestopshop/Alamy; p. 146 Merrill Education; p. 148 BananaStock/Getty Images; p. 149 (top, left) Photodisc/Getty Images; (top, right) Rubberball/Mark Andersen/Getty iamages; (bottom, left) Ljupco Smokovski/Fotolia; (bottom, right) Asia Images Group/Getty Images.

Chapter 4 Page 152 (top) baobao ou/Flickr/Getty Images; (bottom) Jeff Greenberg/PhotoEdit, Inc; p. 154 Duris Guillaume/Fotolia; p. 155 Science Photo Library/CMSP; p. 158 (top) Eva Vargyasi/fotolia; (bottom) Skjold Photographs; p. 160 Vladimir Godnik/Beyond Fotomedia GmbH/Alamy; p. 164 Ann Purcell/Science Source; p. 165 Rob Crandall/SCPhotos/Alamy; p. 166 Sovfoto; p. 174 David R. Frazier Photolibrary, Inc./Alamy; p. 176 (top) SergiyN/Fotolia; (bottom) Will Faller; p. 178 Jeff Greenberg/The Image Works; p. 179 Jonathan Nourok/PhotoEdit; p. 180 Bruce Eric Kaplan/The New Yorker Collection/www.cartoonbank.com; p. 181 Tony Freeman/PhotoEdit; p. 183 AP Photo/Cindy Loo/Department of Social Services; p. 184 Come Alive New Testament Church, ho/AP Images; p. 187 Stanley Fellerman/Spirit/Corbis; p. 188 Catherine Ursillo/Science Source; p. 189 Jonathan Nourok/PhotoEdit; p. 190 Albert Bandura; p. 194 baobao ou/Flickr/Getty Images; p. 195 (top, left) Jim Esposito/Photodisc/Getty Images; (top, right) Photodisc/Getty Images; (bottom, left) Asia Images Group/Getty Images; (bottom, right) Mel Yates/Cultura/Getty images.

Chapter 5 Page 198 Jennie Woodcock/Bubbles Photolibrary/Alamy; p. 199 (top) Jeff Greenberg/The Image Works; (bottom) Terje Lillehaug/Alamy; p. 200 Christopher Weyant/The New Yorker Collection/www.cartoonbank.com; p. 201 Barbara Stitzer/PhotoEdit, Inc; p. 203 Leila Cutler/Alamy; p. 205 Pascal Deloche/Godong/Photononstop/Glow Images; p. 208 Con Tanasiuk/Design Pics Inc/Alamy; p. 210 Morgan Lane Photography/Shutterstock.com; p. 212 Marmaduke St. John/Alamy; p. 216 Earl & Nazima Kowall/Corbis; p. 217 Wellcome Department of Cognitive Neurology/Science Source; p. 218 Elizabeth Crews; p. 221 Bob Daemmrich/The Image Works; p. 225 Kevin R. Morris/Documentary Value/Corbis; p. 227 BL/BSIP/SuperStock; p. 230 stefanolunardi/Shutterstock.com; p. 231 Dann Tardif/LWA/Corbis; p. 232 Robert Brenner/PhotoEdit; p. 233 Kayte Deioma/PhotoEdit, Inc; p. 237 vitalinko/Fotolia; p. 238 Monkey Business/Fotolia; p. 241 Peter Byron/PhotoEdit, Inc; p. 244 Comstock Royalty Free Division; p. 245 Denise Hager, Catchlight Visual Services/Alamy; p. 247 (left) Photo Collection Alexander Alland, Sr./Historical/Corbis; (right) Zhang Chaoqun/Xinhua/Photoshot/Newscom; p. 250 Rubberball/Mike Kemp/Getty Images; p. 251 (top, left) Jim Esposito/Photodisc /Getty Images; (top, right) Photodisc/Getty Images; (bottom, left) Asia Images Group/Getty Images; (bottom, right) Mel Yates/Cultura/Getty images.

Chapter 6 Page 254 Dmitriy Shironosov/Shutterstock; p. 256 (left) Sherry Lewis; (right) Sherry Lewis; p. 259 imac/Alamy; p. 260 AP Photo/Ed Andrieski; p. 261 (top) John Berry/Syracuse Newspapers/The Image Works; p. 263 om & Dee Ann McCarthy/Corbis; p. 264 McQueeny, Tim Schweinsburg, Brian C. Schweinsburg, Alecia D. Jacobus, Joanna Bava, Sunita Frank, Lawrence R. Tapert, Susan F.; Alcoholism: Clinical and Experimental Research, Vol 33(7), Jul, 2009. pp. 1278-1285; p. 268 White House Photo/Alamy; p. 270 Kevin Radford/SuperStock; p. 272 H. John Maier Jr./Time Life Pictures/Getty Images; p. 273 Roz Chast/The New Yorker Collection/www.cartoonbank.com; p. 279 Tony Freeman/PhotoEdit, Inc.; p. 280 Alex Gregory/The New Yorker Collection/www.cartoonbank.com; p. 283 Marilyn Humphries/The Image Works; p. 285 Peter Byron/PhotoEdit; p. 286 ZUMA Wire Service/Alamy; p. 289 Szefei/Shutterstock; p. 292 Steve Skjold/Alamy; p. 294 Richard T. Nowitz/Photo Researchers, Inc.; p. 296 Jim Smith/Photo Researchers, Inc; p. 300 Rhoda Sidney/Pearson Education; p. 302 David De Lossy/Photodisc/Getty Images; p. 303 (top, left) Photodisc/Getty Images; (top, right) Photodisc/Getty Images; (bottom, left) get4net/Fotolia; (bottom, right) Ljupco Smokovski/Fotolia.

Chapter 7 Page 306 Felix Mizioznikov/Shutterstock; p. 307 (top, right) Christopher Bissell/The Image Bank/Getty Images; p. 309 (top, left) Beck Diefenbach/Reuters/Landov; p. 310 (bottom) Tribune Media Services TMS Reprints; p. 311 (top, right) Anthony Magnacca/Merrill Education; p. 314 (top, left) Lon C. Diehl/PhotoEdit, Inc; (top, right) Andre Blais/Shutterstock; p. 317 (bottom, right) Rough Guides/Dorling Kindersley, Ltd.; p. 318 (bottom, left) Kaiser/Caro/Alamy; p. 323 (top, right) Ariel Skelley/Corbis; p. 325 (centre, right) Mike Booth/Alamy; p. 326 (top, right) Lisa F. Young/Alamy; (bottom, left) Michael Pole/Corbis; p. 330 (bottom, right) Arrow Studio/Fotolia; p. 334 (top, left) Altrendo Images/Getty Images; p. 337 (centre, right) Stockbyte/Getty Images; p. 338 (top, right) Bill Aron/PhotoEdit, Inc; p. 339 (bottom, right) DAJ/amana images inc./Alamy; p. 341 (centre, right) Robert Weber/The New Yorker Collection/www.cartoonbank.com; p. 342 (bottom, left) iofoto/Fotolia; p. 345 (top, right) William Haefeli/The New Yorker Collection/www.cartoonbank.com; p. 347 (top, right) Annie Griffiths Belt/Encyclopedia/Corbis; p. 350 (top, right) Rhoda Sidney/The Image Works; p. 352 AntonioDiaz/Shutterstock; p. 353 (top, left) Photodisc/Getty Images; (top, right) Sheer Photo, Inc/Stockbyte/Getty Images; (bottom, left) PhotoAlto Agency RF Collections/Laurence Mouton/Getty images; (bottom, right) Tom Grill/Corbis.

Chapter 8 Page 356 CandyBox Images/Fotolia; p. 357 (top, right) Dylan Ellis/Corbis; p. 359 (bottom, right) Auremar/Fotolia; p. 363 (bottom, right) Antonia Reeve/Photo Researchers, Inc; p. 367 (top, right) Yuri Arcurs/Fotolia; p. 368 (top, left) Ebby May/Stone/Getty Images; p. 370 (bottom, left) Franck Boston/Fotolia; p. 372 (centre, left) Tony Freeman/PhotoEdit, Inc; p. 376 (top, right) Robynmac/Fotolia; p. 379 (top, left) martin moxter/imagebroker/Alamy; p. 381 (top, left) Michael J. Doolittle/The Image Works; p. 386 (top, left) Vibe Images/Fotolia; p. 388 (top, left) Barbara Smaller/The New Yorker Collection/www.cartoonbank.com; p. 389 (top, right) Denise Hager, Catchlight Visual Services/Alamy; p. 392 (bottom, left) Larry Dale Gordon/The Image Bank/Getty Images; p. 393 (centre, right) Exactostock/SuperStock; p. 396 (bottom, centre) Jupiterimages/Thinkstock; p. 397 (top, left) Asia Images Group/Getty Images; (top, right) Sheer Photo, Inc/Stockbyte/Getty Images; (bottom, left) Rubberball/Mark Andersen/Getty Images; (bottom, right) Ljupco Smokovski/Fotolia.

Chapter 9 Page 400 (centre, right) Gravicapa/Shutterstock; p. 402 (top, left) Monkey Business Images/Shutterstock; p. 404 (top, left) Guy Drayton/Getty Active/Dorling Kindersley Ltd.; (top, right) Caroline Wood/Stone/Getty Images; p. 406 (top, left) Pearson Education; p. 408 (top, left) Mke Guastella/AP Images; p. 409 (top, right) Dr. M. Goedert/Science Source; p. 410 (top, left) Bookheimer, S. Y., Strojwas, M. H., Cophen, M. S. Saunders, A. M., Pericak-Vance, M. A., Mazziotta, J. C., & Small, G. W. (2000, August 17). Patterns of brain activation in people at risk for Alzheimer's disease. New England Journal of Medicine, 343, 450-456. Copyright 2003 Massachusetts Medical Society. All right reserved; p. 411 (top, right) Warren Price Photography/Shutterstock.com; p. 413 (top, right) Simon Fraser/Photo Researchers,Inc; p. 416 (bottom, right) Yellow Dog Productions/Digital Vision/Jupiter Images; p. 419 (top, right) Russell Gordon/Danita Delimont Agent/Alamy/Alamy; p. 420 (top, left) Stockbroker/MBI/Alamy; p. 421 tina7si/Fotolia; p. 423 (bottom, left) Rhoda Sidney/The Image Works; p. 424 (top, right) Roz Chast; p. 426 (centre, left) BJI/Blue Jean Images/Getty Images; p. 430 (top, left) Elizabeth Crews Photography; p. 431 (bottom, left) Jupiter Images; (bottom, right) Pearson Education; p. 433 (top, right) MBI/Alamy; p. 437 (bottom, left) Photodisc/Getty Images; p. 442 Kevin Woodrow/Fotolia; p. 443 (top, centre) Fuse/Getty Images; (top, right) Photodisc/Getty Images; (centre, left) get4net/Fotolia; (centre, right) Ljupco Smokovski/Fotolia.

Chapter 10 Page 446 (top, right) Lisa F. Young/Fotolia; p. 449 (centre, right) Tracy Whiteside/Shutterstock; p. 451 (top, left) Anne-Marie Palmer/Alamy Limited; p. 453 Mediscan/Medical-on-Line/Alamy; p. 456 (bottom, centre) Mark Richards/PhotoEdit; p. 461 (centre, right) Stockbyte/Getty Images; (bottom, right) yuanann/Shutterstock; p. 463 (top, right) AP Photo/Jerome Delay; p. 464 (bottom, right) keith morris/Alamy; p. 466 (centre) absolut/Fotolia; p. 467 (top, centre) PhotoAlto/Laurence Mouton/; (top, right) Fuse/Getty Images; (centre, left) Rubberball/Mark Andersen/Getty Images; (centre, right) Tom Grill/Corbis.

Text Credits

Chapter 1 Page 4, Falco, 2012; ICMRT, 2012; p. 15, Watson, J. B. (1925). Behaviorism. New York: Norton.; p. 24, Herodotus; p. 30, figure 1-3, Based on an experiment by Leyens et al. (1975) Effects of movie violence on aggression in a field setting as a function of group dominance and cohesion. Journal of Personality and Social Psychology.

Chapter 2 Page 42, figure 2-2, Martin, J. A., Hamilton, B. E., Sutton, P. D., Ventura, S. J., Menacker, F., & Munson, M. L. (2005). Births: Final data for 2003. National Vital Statistics Reports, 54, Table J, p. 21.; p. 45, figure 2-5, International Human Genome Sequencing Consortium. (2001).

Initial sequencing and analysis of the human genome.Nature, 409, 860–921.; p. 45, table 2-1, From McGuffin, P., Riley, B., & Plomin (2001, Feb. 16). Toward behavioral genomics, Science, 291, 1232–1249.; p. 53, figure 2-6, Bouchard, T. J., & McGue, M. (1981). Familial studies of intelligence: A review. Science, 212, 1055–1059.; p. 54, figure 2-7, Tellegen, A., Lykken, D. T., Bouchard, T. J., Jr., Wilcox, K. J., Segal, N. L., & Rich, S. (1988). Personality similarity in twins reared apart and together. Journal of Personality and Social Psychology, 54, 1031–1039.; p. 56, figure 2-8, Irwin I. Gottesman, excerpt from Schizophrenia Genesis: The Origins of Madness. New York: W. H. Freeman, 1991.; p. 58, figure 2-9, Moore, K. L., & Persaud, T. V. N. (2003). Before we were born (6th ed.). Philadelphia: Saunders.; p. 61, figure 2-11, Reproductive Medicine Associates of New Jersey, 2002.; p. 64, figure 2-12, Moore, K. L. Before We Were Born: Basic Embryology and Birth Defects. FL: W. B. Saunders, 1998.; p. 71, table 2-3, From Apgar, V., A proposal for a new method of evaluation in the newborn infant, Current Research in Anesthesia and Analgesia, 32, 1953, p. 260.; p. 71, Copyrighted by Pearson Education, Upper Saddle River, NJ; p. 75, Copyrighted by Pearson Education, Upper Saddle River, NJ; p. 75, figure 2-14, The World Factbook, 2007; p. 77, figure 2-15, National Center for Health Statistics, 1997; p. 79, figure 2-16, International Cesarean Awareness Network, 2004; p. 80, figure 2-17, Child Health USA 2009.; p. 86, table 2-6, Adapted from Carol O. Eckerman et al. (1992) Very low birth weight newborns and parents as early as social partners. In S.L. Friedman and M. D. Seligman (eds) the Psychological Development of Low-Birth Weight Children.

Chapter 3 Page 93, figure 3-1, Cratty, Bryant, Perceptual and Motor Development in Infants and Children., 2nd Ed., Copyright © 1979 Pearson Education, Inc.. Reprinted and Electronically reproduced by permission of Pearson Education, Inc., Upper Saddle River, New Jersey.; p. 95, figure 3-3, Adapted from Van De Graaff. Human anatomy, 2/e Copyright © 1988 Reprinted by permission of The McGraw-Hill Companies, Inc.; p. 95, figure 3-4, From THE POSTNATAL DEVELOPMENT OF THE HUMAN CEREBRAL CORTEX, Vol I–VIII by Jesse LeRoy Conel, Cambridge, Mass.: Harvard University Press, 1939.; p. 98, table 3-2, Thoman, E. B., & Whitney, M. P. (1990). Sleep states of infants monitored in the home: Individual differences, developmental trends, and origins of diurnal cyclicity. Infant Behavior and Development, 12, 59–75. Reprinted by permission of Elsevier.; p. 99, figure 3-6, Dr. Howard P. Roffwarg et al. REM sleep through the lifespan. Ontogenic development of the human sleep-dream cycle. Science, April, 1966, 29,152, 604–619. Copyright © 1966 Reprinted with permission.; p. 99, figure 3-7, American SIDS Institute, based on data from the Center for Disease Control and the National Center for Health Statistics, 2004. WWW.SIDS.org; p. 102, table 3-4, Adapted from William Frankenburg et al. The Denver II: A major revision and restandardization of the Denver Screening Test, PEDIATRICS 89, Copyright © 1992 by the American Academy of Pediatrics. Reprinted by permission.; p. 103, figure 3-8, Frankenburg, W. K., Dodds, J., Archer, P., Shapiro, H., & Bresnick, B. (1992). The Denver II: A major revision and restandardization of the Denver Developmental Screening Test. Pediatrics, 89, 91–97. Copyright © 1992 by the American Academy of Pediatrics. Reproduced by permission.; p. 107, William James 1890/1950; p. 109, figure 3-10, R.L. Fantz. "The origin of form perception" Scientific American, 1961.; p. 122, table 3-7, Bayley Scales of Infant Development (BSID). Pearson, 1969.; p. 126, figure 3-14, Bornstein, Marc and Lamb, Michael. Development in Infancy: An Introduction, 3/e. McGraw-Hill, 1992.; p. 126, Dromi, E. (1987). Early lexical development. Cambridge, England: Cambridge University Press. & O'Grady, W., & Aitchison, J. (2005). How children learn language. New York: Cambridge University Press.; p. 128, table 3-8, Adapted from R. Brown & C. Fraser, 1963.; p. 131, Doman, G., & Doman, J. (2002). How to teach your baby to read. Wyndmoor, PA: Gentle Revolution Press.; p. 134, figure 3-16, INFANCY: ITS PLACE IN HUMAN DEVELOPMENT by Jerome Kagan, Richard P. Kearsley, and Phillip R. Zelazo. Cambridge, Mass.: Harvard University Press, 1978.; p. 146, figure 3-18, NICHD, 2006.

Chapter 4 Page 153, figure 4-1, National Center for Health Statistics in collaboration with the National Center for Chronic Disease Prevention and Health Promotion, 2000.; p. 156, figure 4-3, From Fischer & Rose (1995) Concurrent cycles in the dynamic development of brain and behavior. Newsletter of the Society for Research in Development Copyright © 1995 Reprinted with permission.; p. 166, Tharp, R. G. (1989). Psychocultural variables and constants: Effects on teaching and learning in schools. American Psychologist, 44 [Special issue: Children and their development: Knowledge base, research agenda, and social policy application], 349–359.; p. 169, Schatz, M. (1994). A toddler's life. New York: Oxford University Press.; p. 170, figure 4-7, Adapted from Berko, J. (1958). The child's learning of English morphology.Word, 14, 150–177. Journal of the International Linguistic Association. Reproduced by permission.; p. 171, figure 4-8, U.S. Department of Education, National Center.; p. 182, table 4-1, From Corbin, A Textbook of Motor Development, 1e. McGawHill, 1973.; p. 183, figure 4-9, U.S. Department of Health and Human Services, Administration on Children, Youth and Families, 2007.; p. 184, table 4-2, "Growing Speech Capabilities" from THE LANGUAGE INSTINCT by STEVEN PINKER. WILLIAM MORROW, 1994.; p. 185, figure 4-10, Scientific American, 2002.

Chapter 5 Page 200, figure 5-1, CDC, 2009.; p. 202, figure 5-2, Adapted from Cratty, B. J., PERCEPTUAL AND MOTOR DEVELOPMENT IN INFANTS AND CHILDREN, 3rd ed. Pearson Education, 1986.; p. 207, figure 5-3, Shaw, P., Eckstrand, K., Sharp, W., Blumenthal, J., Lerch, J. P., Greenstein, D., Classen, L., Evans, A., Giedd, J., & Rapoport, J. L. (2007). Attention-deficit/hyperactivity disorder is characterized by a delay in cortical maturation. Proceedings of the National Academy of Sciences, 104, 19649–19654. Reproduced by permission.; p. 208, figure 5-4, Adapted from Dasen et al. (1979) Cross-cultural training studies of concrete operations. In L. H. Edenberger et al. Cross-Cultural Contributions to Psychology. Taylor & Francis, 1979.; p. 214, figure 5-5, Modern Language Association, www.mla.org/census_map,2005. Based on data from U.S. Census Bureau, 2000. Reprinted by permission of the Modern Language Association of America.; p. 218, figure 5-7, U.S. Census Bureau, 2000.; p. 223, figure 5-9, Gardner's Eight intelligences. In Walters & Gardiner (1986) The theory of multiple intelligences: some issues and answers. In R. J. Sternberg and R. Wagner Practical Intelligence.; p. 230, Kotre, J., & Hall, E. (1990). Seasons of life. Boston: Little, Brown.; p. 234, table 5-1, Kohlberg. Handbook of Socialization Theory and Research. Rand McNally.; p. 237, Damon, W. (1983). Social and personality development. New York: Norton.; p. 239, figure 5-10, EDUCATIONAL PSYCHOLOGY by K. A. Dodge. Taylor & Francis Informa UK Ltd., 1985; p. 241, Goodwin, M. H. (1990). Tactical uses of stories: Participation frameworks within girls' and boys' disputes. Discourse Processes, 13, 33–71. Besage, V. E. (2006). Understanding girls' friend-ships, fights and feuds: A practical approach to girls' bullying.; Maidenhead, Berkshire: Open University Press/McGraw-Hill Education.

Chapter 6 Page 255, figure 6-1, Cratty, B. (1986). Perceptual and motor development in infants and children (3rd ed.). Copyright © 1986. Reprinted and Electronically reproduced by permission of Pearson Education, Inc., Upper Saddle River, New Jersey.; p. 257, figure 6-2, Tanner, J. M. (1978). Education and physical growth (2nd ed.). New York: International Universities Press.; p. 261, figure 6-3, Sowell, E. R., Thompson, P. M., Holmes, C. J., Jerrigan, T. L., & Toga, A. W. (1999). In vivo evidence for post-adolescent brain maturation in frontal and striatal regions. Nature Neuroscience, 10, 859–861. Copyright © 1999 by Nature Publishing. Reproduced by permission.; p. 263, figure 6-4, Johnston, L. D., Bachman, J. G., & O'Malley, P. M. (2009). Monitoring the future study. Lansing: University of Michigan.; p. 264, figure 6-5, Nelson, T., & Wechsler, H. (2003). School spirits: Alcohol and collegiate sports fans. Addictive Behaviors, 28, 1–11.; p. 264, figure 6-7, Alan Guttmacher Institute, 2004.; & Weinstock, H., Berman, S., & Cates, W., Jr. (2004). Sexually transmitted diseases among American youth: Incidence and prevalence estimates, 2000. Perspectives on Sexual and Reproductive Health, 36, 182–191.; p. 275, figure 6-8, Adapted from National Governors Association, 2008.; p. 277, figure 6-9, Pew Internet & American Life Project Surveys, 2009.; p. 279, Anton Merced; p. 280, Harter, S. (1990). Issues in the assessment of self-concept of children and adolescents. In A. LaGreca (Ed.), Through the eyes of a child. Boston: Allyn & Bacon.; p. 281, table 6-2, "Figure of Erikson's Stages of Personality Development," from CHILDHOOD AND SOCIETY by Erik H. Erikson. W. W. Norton & Company, Inc, 1950.; p. 283, table 6-3, Marcia, J. E. "Identity in Adolescence" in J. Adelson (ed.), HANDBOOK OF ADOLESCENT PSYCHOLOGY. John Wiley & Sons, 1980.; p. 287, figure 6-10, Boehm, K. E., & Campbell, N. B. (1995). Suicide: A review of calls to an adolescent peer listening phone service. Child Psychiatry & Human Development, 26, 61–66.; p. 290, figure 6-11, PRIMEDIA/Roper National Youth Survey, 1999.; p. 291, figure 6-12, From Reed Larson et al., Developmental Psychology. Copyright © 1996 by the American Psychological Association. Reproduced with permission.; p. 294, table 6-4, Suitor, J. J., Minyard, S. A., & Carter, R. S. "'Did you see what I saw?' Gender differences in perceptions of avenues to prestige among adolescents," Sociological Inquiry, 71, 437–454. Blackwell Publishing, 2001.; p. 298, figure 6-14, Morbidity and Mortality Weekly Report, 2008.; p. 300, figure 6-15, National Vital Statistics Report, Vol. 57, 2009.

Chapter 7 Page 308, figure 7-1, Blair et al., "Physical fitness and all-cause mortality: A prospective study of healthy men and women." Journal of the American Medical Association, 262 (1989), pp. 2395–2401. American Medical Association, 1989.; p. 308, figure 7-2, United Nations Survey on Crime Trends, 2000.; p. 311, figure 7-3, Centers for Disease Control and Prevention, 2010.; p. 315, table 7-1, Cohen, S., Kamarck, T., & Mermelstein, R. "A global measure of perceived stress." Journal of Health and Social Behavior, 24, 385–396. American Sociological Association, 1983.; p. 316, table 7-2, Benson, H. (1993). The relaxation response. In D. Goleman & J. Guerin (Eds.), Mind–body medicine: How to use your mind for better health. Yonkers, NY: Consumer Reports Publications.; p. 320, figure 7-5, Schaie, K. W. (1977–1978). Toward a stage of adult theory of adult cognitive development. Journal of Aging and Human Development, 8, 129–138.; p. 321, Wagner, R. K., & Sternberg, R. J. (1985). Alternate conceptions of intelligence and their implications for education. Review of Educational Research, 54, 179–223.; p. 322, figure 7-6, JOURNAL OF GERONTOLOGY by W. Dennis. The Gerontological Society of America, 1966.; p. 324, figure 7-7, The Condition of Education 2004, National Center for Education Statistics, 2004.; p. 326, Sadker, M., & Sadker, D. (1994). Failing at fairness: How America's schools cheat girls. New York: Scribner's.; p. 327, figure 7-8, Benton, S.A., Robertson, J. M., Tseng, W-C., Newton, F. B., & Benton, S. L. (2003). Changes in counseling center client problems across 13 years. Professional Psychology: Research and Practice, 34, 66–72.; p. 327, figure 7-9, CIRE (Cooperative Institutional Research Program of the American Council on Education). (1990). The American freshman: National norms for fall 1990. Los Angeles: American Council on Education.; & Astin, A., Korn, W., & Berg, E. (1989). The American Freshman: National norms for Fall, 1989. Los Angeles: University of California, Los Angeles, American Council on Education.; p. 331, table 7-4, Colarusso & Nemiroff, 1981.; p. 333, figure 7-10, Rephrasing the Question, from National Opinion Research Center [NORC]). (1998). Race and friends. Chicago, IL: General Social Survey. Reprinted with permission from NORC.; p. 335, table 7-6, Buss, D. M., et al. (1990). International preferences in selecting mates: A study of 37 cultures. Journal of Cross-Cultural Psychology, 21, 5–47.; p. 336, figure 7-11, Janda, HUMAN SEXUALITY, 1E. Wadsworth, 1980.; p. 339, Cowan, C. P., & Cowan, P. A. (1992). When partners become parents. New York: Wiley.; p. 340, figure 7-13, U.S. Bureau of the Census, 2011.; p. 341, figure 7-14, Population Council Report, 2009. Courtesy of the Population Council.; p. 344, figure 7-16, Bureau of Labor Statistics, 2012.; p. 348, Unger, R., & Crawford, M. (1992). Women and gender: A feminist psychology (2nd ed.). New York: McGraw-Hill.; p. 349, figure 7-17, U.S. Bureau of the Census, 2011.

Chapter 8 Page 359, figure 8-1, From "The Benefits of Exercise," from A. G. DiGiovanna, Human Aging: Biological Perspectives. Copyright © 1994 The McGraw-Hill Companies, Inc. Reprinted with permission.; p. 360, figure 8-2, SEX IN AMERICA by Robert T. Michael, John H. Gagnon, Edward O. Laumann, and Gina Kolata. LITTLE, BROWN & COMPANY, 1994.; p. 364, figure 8-3, USA WEEKEND Magazine, August 1997.; p. 365, table 8-1, Ochsner Clinic Foundation, 2003.; p. 365, figure 8-4, Adapted from Baum (1994) Behavioral, biological, and environmental interactions in disease processes. In Blumenthal, et al. New Research Frontiers in Behavioral Medicine. Proceedings of the National Conference, Washington, DC.; p. 379.; p. 371, figure 8-5, K. W. Schaie, "Longitudinal Studies of Adult Psychological Development," Guilford Press, 1985.; p. 378, table 8-2, Based on Transformations, by R. L. Gould & M. D. Gould, 1978, New York: Simon & Schuster.; p. 380, figure 8-6, Costa, P. T., Jr., & McCrae, R. R. (1989). Personality continuity and the changes of adult life. In M. Storandt & G. R. VandenBos (Eds.), The adult years: Continuity and change. Washington, DC: American Psychological Association.; p. 383, figure 8-7, Rollins and Cannon (1974) Marital satisfaction over the family life cycle: A re-evaluation. JOURNAL OF MARRIAGE AND FAMILY, 36, 271–282. Blackwell Publishing, 1974.; p. 389, figure 8-10, "The Battered Woman Syndrome," by Lenore Walker, 1984.; p. 390, Findlen, 1990.

Chapter 9 Page 401, figure 9-1, Adapted from U.S. Bureau of the Census, 2008.; p. 401, figure 9-2, United Nations Population Division, 2002.; p. 403, table 9-1, "The Myths of Aging" from Palmore, E. B. (1982). THE FACTS ON AGING QUIZ. New York: Springer.; p. 405, figure 9-3, National Highway Traffic Safety Administration, 1994.; p. 407, Feldman, Robert. Development Across the Life Span, 7e. Pearson Education, Upper Saddle River, NJ.; p. 410, figure 9-5, US Census Bureau; p. 413, figure 9-6, U.S. Bureau of the Census, 1997.; p. 415, figure 9-7, Anderson, R. N. (2001). United States life tables, 1998. National vital statistics reports (Vol. 48, No. 18). Hyattsville, MD: National Center for Health Statistics.; p. 418, figure 9-8, Changes in Intellectual Functioning from Schaie, K. W. (1994). "The course of adult intellectual development." p. 307. American Psychologist, 49, 304–313. Copyright © 1994 by the American Psychological Association. Reproduced with permission.; p. 419, People. Time, Inc. September 8, 1980, p. 57.; p. 419, figure 9-9, Rubin, D. C. (1986). Autobiographical memory. Cambridge, England: Cambridge University Press.; p. 420, figure 9-10, Charness, N., & Boot, W. R. (2009). Aging and information technology use: Potential and barriers. Current Directions in Psychological Science, 18, 253–258.; p. 422, Pappano, L. (1994, November 27). The new old generation. Boston Globe Magazine, 18–38.; p. 432, figure 9-11, U.S. Bureau of the Census, 2005.; p. 436, figure 9-12, Administration on Aging, 2006.; p. 437, Doress, P. B., Siegal, D. L., & The Midlife and Old Women Book Project. (1987). Ourselves, growing older. New York: Simon & Schuster.; p. 438, figure 9-13, Federal Interagency Forum on Age Related Statistics, 2000.; p. 440, table 9-2, Based on Hamon & Blieszner, 1990.

Chapter 10 Page 448, Kastenbaum, R. (1985). Dying and death: A life-span approach. In J. E. Birren & K. W. Schaie (Eds.), Handbook of the psychology of aging. New York: Van Nostrand Reinhold.; p. 454, figure 10-1, Kübler-Ross, E. (Ed.). (1975). Death: The final stage of growth. Englewood Cliffs, NJ: Prentice-Hall.

Name Index

Note: Page numbers in *italics* indicate tables and illustrations.

Aaronson, L. S., 460
AARP, *406*, 408, 436, 461
Abadie, V., 109
Abbot-Smith, K., 170
Abdo, C., 362
Abele, A., 392
Aber, J. L., 32
Abma, J. C., 300
Aboud, F. E., 241
Abramson, L., 286
Abreu, R., 5
Accardo, P., 52
Acierno, R., 441
Acker, J., 404
Ackerman, B. P., 132
Acocella, J., 12
ACOG, 73
Adair, L., 105
Adak, M., 183
Adams, G. R., 279
Adams Hillard, P. J., 65
Adams, K. B., 428
Adams, M., 143, 336
Adams, P., 281, 336
Adebayo, B., 325
Administration on Aging, 401, 430, 431, *436*
Adolfsson, R., 419
Adolph, K., 108
Adolph, K. E., 108
Afifi, T., 183, 244
Agnor, C., 286
Agrawal, A., 51
Ah-Kion, J., 280
Ahmed, E., 240
Ahn, S., 246, 345
Ahn, W., 136
Aho, A., 448
Aiello, J., 350
Aiken, L. R., 463
Ainsworth, M. D. S., 137, 138
Aitchison, J., 125
Aitken, R. J., 58
Akasaka, T., 414
Akhtar, S., 450
Akmajian, A., 125
Aksan, N., 142
Akshoomoff, N., 19
Alan Guttmacher Institute, 266
Albers, L. L., 79
Albert, D., 262
Alberts, A., 270, 272, 273
Albrecht, G. L., 311
Alderfer, C., 225
Aldwin, C., 404
Ales, K. L., 64
Alexander, B., 72
Alexander, G. M., 83
Alexander, R. A., 364
Alexandersen, P., 361
Alfonso, V. C., 223
Alfons, V., 436
Alfred, M., 7
Alipuria, L. L., 285
Alisky, J. M., 410
Allam, M. D., 109
Allen, B., 184
Allen, J., 294, 458
Allen, L., 63
Allen, N. B., 258
Alleva, E., 96
Alley, A., 125
Allison, B., 282
Allison, C. M., 256
Allison, D. B., 49, 200
Al-Namlah, A. S., 170
Aloise-Young, P. A., 295
Alonso, R. S., 368
Al-Owidha, A., 209
Alpass, F., 434
Alston, P., 452
Altholz, S., 206
Alwin, D. F., 425
Aly, H., 67
Alzheimer's Association, 410
Amato, P., 244, 384
Ambrose, H. N., 139, 189
American Academy of Pediatrics, 74, 84, 106, 107, 131, 157, 158, 185, 202, 203
American Association of Neurological Surgeons, 96
American Association on Intellectual and Developmental Disabilities, 227
American College of Medical Genetics, 74
American College of Sports Medicine, 307
American College Testing Program, 324
American Heart Association, 366
American Psychological Association, 36, *291, 418*
American SIDS Institute, *99*
Amitai, Y., 67
Amler, R. W., 154
Ammerman, R. T., 183
Amodio, D., 314
Amsterlaw, J., 136, 180
Anand, K. J. S., 110
Andelin, A., 438
Andersen, S.L., 204
Anderson, B., 463
Anderson, C. A., 191
Anderson, D., 171
Anderson, D. R., 366
Anderson, E., 246
Anderson, G., 81
Anderson, T., 385
Andersson, M. A., 323
Anders, T. F., 99
Andreoni, J., 357
André-Pueyo, A., 27
Andrew, L., 288
Andrew, M., 316
Andrews, G., 180
Angleitner, A., 48
Ani, C., 105
Ankrum, J. W., 167
Ansaldo, A. I., 155
Ansberry, C., 438
Anssens, A., 419
Anstey, K., 406
Anstey, K. J., 403
Antonishak, J., 294
Antonucci, T. C., 386
Antshel, K. M., 43
APA, 389
APA Reproductive Choice Working Group, 62
Apostoleris, N. H., 241
Apperly, I., 213
Appleyard, K., 338
Apter, A., 258
Arai, J., 51
Araujo, M. A., 412
Archer, J., 189
Archer, P., 102, *103*
Archer, S. L., 282
Arcus, D., 55
Arendtsz, A., 275
Arenson, K. W., 286
Arguin, M., 155
Ariès, P., 12
Arim, R. G., 258
Armstrong, J., 10, 83
Armstrong, K., 368
Armstrong, P., 348
Armstrong-Stassen, M., 434
Arnautovska, U., 286
Arnett, J., 7, 304, 330, 332
Arnett, J. J., 290, 291
Arnold, J., 377
Arnold, R. M., 450, 457
Arnsten, A., 207
Aro, H., 244
Aron, A., 384
Aronson, J., 225
Artal, R., 67
Arts, J. A. R., 273
Aschbacher, K., 313
Asch, D. A., 457
Asendorpf, J. B., 135
Asher, S. R., 239
Askham, J., 436
Aslin, R. N., 126
Astin, A., *327*
Ata, R. N., 280
Atchley, R. C., 428, 434, 451
Atkins, D. C., 385
Atkinson, T. M., 420
Atkins, S. M., 271
Atwood, M. E., 157
Auerbach, C. F., 139
Augestad, K. M., 457
Aujoulat, I., 239
Auman, C., 419
Austin, C. M., 86
Austin, E., 321
Austin, J., 448
Avia, M. D., 48
Avinun, R., 188
Avlund, K., 439
Axia, G., 110
Axinn, W. G., 297
Aydiner, F., 61
Aylward, G. P., 122
Ayoola, A., 80
Ayoub, N. C., 72
Azar, B., 284
Azuma, S. D., 65

Babu, A., 431
Bacchus, L., 67
Bäckman, L., 419
Badenhorst, W., 86
Bader, A. P., 74
Bade, U., 144
Badger, S., 291
Baer, J. S., 66
Bahna, S., 208
Bährer-Kohler, S., 393
Bahrick, L., 110
Bahrick, L. E., 110
Bailey, E., 206
Baillargeon, R., 117, 136, 163
Baker, J., 246, 260, 345
Baker, P., 300
Baker, R. C., 235
Baker, S. A., 214
Baker, T., 265
Baker-Ward, L., 165
Bakker, A., 393
Balaiah, D., 299
Balakrishnan, V., 166
Bal, E., 19
Bale, J. F. Jr., 205
Ballas, S., 16
Ball, K., 406
Ball, M., 393
Balsam, R. H., 15
Baltes, M. M., 429, 431
Baltes, P., 372, 426, 429
Baltes, P. B., 11, 429
Bamaca, M., 219
Bammel, G., 428
Bandura, A., 16, *23*, 187, 188, 190
Baptista, T., 23
Barber, A. D., 155
Barberá, E., 177
Barber, B., 254
Barber, S., 80
Barbier, D., 71
Barboza, G., 240
Barer, B. M., 435
Barker, E., 285
Barker, E. D., 240
Barner, J., 357, 404
Barnes, H. V., 172
Barnes, J. C., 11, 45
Barnett, D., 131
Barnett, J., 265
Barnett, R. C., 343, 377, 394
Baron-Cohen, S., 60, 176
Barrera, M., 449
Barrett-Connor, E., 81
Barrett, G. V., 364
Barrett, T., 103
Barr, H. M., 66
Barr, R. A., 127
Barry, L. M., 326
Barthelemy, C., 141
Barton, J., 204
Barton, L. J., 430
Barusch, A., 434
Basak, C., 418
Basseches, M., 319
Bass, S., 248
Bastian, B., 191
Bates, E., 97
Bates, J. E., 128
Battin, M., 457
Baudonniere, P., 135
Bauer, I., 427
Bauer, P., 165
Bauer, P. J., 121
Baugh, E., 389, 440
Baulac, S., 409
Bauld, R., 362
Baum, A., *365*
Bauman, K. E., 293
Baumann, U., 377
Baumrind, D., 181
Bava, S., 264, *264*
Bayer, J. K., 258
Bayley, N., 370
Beach, S., 441
Beal, C. R., 240, 241
Beals, K., 338
Bearce, K., 121
Bearman, P., 300
Becker, B., 294
Becker, G., 430, 432
Becker, J. B., 257
Becker, M., 439
Beck, M., 362
Beckman, M., 262
Beckwith, L., 123
Bednar, C., 411
Beeber, L. S., 185
Beer, T., 457
Beets, M., 264
Begeer, S., 180
Begeny, J., 227
Beggs, A. H., 448
Begley, S., 51, 73
Begum, N., 438
Behrman, R., 42
Behrman, R. E., 153, 203, 248
Beilby, J. M., 206
Beisert, M., 86
Belcastro, E. G., 167
Belcher, J. R., 246
Belkin, L., 42, 226
Bell, A., 298
Bellavia, G., 342
Belle, D., 244
Bellinger, D., 63
Bell, I. P., 404
Bellissimo, A., 154
Belliveau, R. A., 448
Bellmore, A., 333
Belschak, F., 240
Belsky, J., 146, 171, 255
Bempechat, J., 275

Bender, H., 232
Benelli, B., 213
Benenson, J. F., 241
Bengtson, V. L., 245, 388
Benini, F., 110
Benjuya, N., 405
Bennani, L., 357
Bennett, J., 260
Benson, E., 133
Benson, H., 316
Benton, S. A., 327, *327*
Ben-Zeev, T., 329
Berendes, H., 64
Berends, M., 293
Berenson, P., 265
Berg, E., *327*
Bergelson, E., 119, 130
Bergen, H., 286
Bergenn, V. W., 155
Berger, L., 244
Bergin, C., 187
Berg, M., 158
Bergman, A., 138
Bergman, K. E., 76
Bergmann, R. L., 76
Bergman, Y. S., 402
Bergstrom, M. J., 428
Berish, D. E., 420
Berkey, C. S., 69
Berkman, R., 430
Berko, J., 169
Berlin, L., 338
Berlin, L. J., 138
Berman, J. S., 464
Berman, S., *266*
Bermingham, D. W., 428
Bernadel, L., 203
Bernard, J., 336, 337, 385
Berndt, T. J., 237, 292, 297
Bernier, A., 138
Bernstein, E., 384
Bernstein, N., 300
Berridge, C., 207
Berry, A., 96
Berry, G. L., 171
Berscheid, E., 333, 334
Bertel, T., 295
Bertera, E. M., 389
Bertin, E., 135
Bertoncini, J., 126
Besage, V. E., 241
Besharov, D. J., 385
Betz, A., 419
Bewley, S., 67
Beyene, Y., 430, 432
Bhattacharya, A., 154
Bhattacharya, S., 79
Bhutta, Z. A., 200
Bialystok, E., 214
Biddle, B. J., 275
Biderman, A., 431
Bielak, A. M., 371
Bierman, K. L., 239
Bigelow, A., 134
Bigelow, A. E., 71
Bionna, R., 316
Birch, H. G., 144
Birch, L. L., 200
Bird, C. M., 420
Bird, G., 342, 386, 437
Birkelund, E., 366
Birlouez-Aragon, I., 414
Biro, F., 281
Bischof-Köhler, D., 188
Bishop, D. I., 440
Bishop, D. V. M., 206
Bishop, J., 440
Bjorklund, D. F., 22, 23
Black, B., 236
Black, K., 236, 290
Black, M., 245
Black, M. M., 122
Blagosklonny, M. V., 414
Blair, C., 225
Blair, P., 99
Blair, S. N., *308*
Blake, C. A., 227
Blake, G., 203
Blake, J., 126, 238
Blakeley, E., 386
Blakemore, J., 176
Blakemore, S., 260
Blakeslee, S., 384
Blanchette, P. L., 451
Blank, H., 166
Blankinship, D. G., 276
Blass, E. M., 85
Blewitt, P., 167
Blieszner, R., 440
Block, S. D., 455
Blodgett, B., 281
Blom, I., 138
Bloom, B., 203
Bloom, C., 375
Blount, B. G., 130
Blumenthal, S., 184
Blumstein, P., 437
Blum, T. C., 349
Bober, S., 179
Bodell, L. P., 260
Bodner, E., 402
Boeckx, C., 129
Boehm, K. E., 287
Boerner, K., 406, 463, 464
Bogat, G., 186
Bogle, K. A., 297
Bohlmeijer, E., 425
Bohlmeijer, E. T., 425
Bohnert, K., 8
Boivin, M., 182
Boles, T., 21
Bolger, N., 338
Bollier, T., 328
Bolman, C., 240
Bonacquisti, A., 66
Bonanno, G. A., 8, 463, 464
Bond, M. H., 214
Boneva, B., 277
Bonichini, S., 110
Bonke, B., 48
Bonoti, F., 452
Bookstein, F. L., 63
Booth, C., 139
Boot, W. R., *420*, 421
Borden, M. E., 171
Borge, A. I. H., 240
Bornstein, M. H., *126*, 127, 176, 179
Bornstein, R. F., 13
Borse, N. N., 203
Bos, C. S., 206
Bos, H., 32, 300
Boshuizen, H. P. A., 273
Boswell, M. K., 245
Botzet, A., 277
Bouchard, T. J. Jr., 52, 53, *53*, 54
Bougatsos, C., 368
Bourgeois, N., 189
Bourne, V., 155
Bourne, V. J., 155
Boutwell, B. B., 11
Bowen, C., 387
Bowers, A. J., 278
Bowers, K. E., 403
Bower, T. G. R., 113
Bowman, M., 131
Boyatzis, C. J., 176, 284
Boyd, R., 139, 436
Boyle, M., 212
Bracey, J., 219
Bracken, B., 228, 231
Bradbury, T. N., 341
Bradlee, M., 201
Bradley, R. A., 72
Bradshaw, D., 337
Bradshaw, M., 54
Brady, S. A., 217
Brainerd, C., 210
Braithwaite, V., 240
Brandone, A. C., 163
Brandon, T., 265
Branje, S., 289
Branje, S. J. T., 243
Brant, M., 203
Branum, A., 77
Brassard, M. R., 184
Braun, K. L., 451
Brawley, L., 307
Bray, G. A., 200, 259
Brazelton, T. B., 103, 104, 185
Bredesen, D., 409
Breen, A., 280
Breheny, M., 362
Brehm, S. S., 338
Bremner, G., 80
Breslau, N., 8
Bresnick, B., 102, *103*
Brickman, A. M., 405
Bridges, J. S., 144
Bridgett, D., 49
Briere, J. N., 183
Brinker, J. K., 425
Brion, S., 31
Broadbent, R., 277
Brody, D., 256
Brody, N., 52
Broesch, T., 135
Brohaugh, B., 402
Bromberger, J. T., 394
Bronfenbrenner, U., 20
Brook, C., 175
Brooks-Gunn, J., 32, 80, 225
Brook, U., 259
Brosh, H., 218
Brouns, M., 457
Brown, B. B., 276, 292
Brown, C., 357, 404
Brown, C. P., 266
Brown, D. L., 286
Brown, E., 83, 228
Browne, A., 390
Browne, C., 426
Browne, K., 177, 389
Brown, E. L., 180
Brownell, C., 135, 237
Browning, C. R., 259
Brown, J., 177, 389
Brown, J. D., 175
Brown, J. S., 279
Brown, J. V., 66
Brownlee, S., 200
Brown, L. M., 282
Brown, R., 127, *128*, 362
Brown, S., 384, *385*
Brown, S. A., 292
Brown, S. P., 30
Brownstone, D., 265
Brown, W. M., 65
Brubaker, T., 436
Bruck, M., 165
Bruckner, H., 300
Brugman, G., 426
Bruin, M., 183
Bruno, R., 214
Brunstein, J., 212
Brunswick, N., 206
Bruskas, D., 247
Bryan, A., 54
Bryant, C. D., 451, 461
Bryant, J., 170
Bryant, J. A., 170
Bucciarelli, A., 8
Buchanan, C. M., 257
Buchbinder, M., 74
Buchmann, C., 325
Bucht, G., 419
Budd, K., 412
Buehler, C., 295
Buehler, J., 65
Buehl, M., 276
Buigas, R., 18
Buitelaar, J., 65
Bullinger, A., 113
Bull, M., 154
Bull, R., 180
Bumpass, L., 385
Bumpus, M. F., 289
Bunch, K., 180
Burbach, J., 56
Burd, L., 66
Bureau of Labor Statistics, 343, *344*, 348
Burgaleta, M., 214
Burgess, K. B., 292
Burgess, N., 420
Burgess, R. L., 333
Burk, W. J., 239, 333
Burman, J., 18
Burnett, P., 231
Burnett-Wolle, S., 429
Burnham, M., 97, 98
Burns, D. M., 411
Burns, M. S., 179
Burock, D., 235
Burrus-Bammel, L. L., 428
Burton, A., 464
Burton, L., 60, 176
Burt, S., 51
Burt, V. L., 408
Bushfield, S., 80
Bushnell, C., 361
Busick, D., 153
Buss, A. H., 22
Buss, D. M., 22, 335, 336, 385
Butler, K. G., 205
Butler, R. J., 78
Butler, R. N., 425, 431
Butterworth, G., 117
Butterworth, M. R., 332, 439
Butzer, B., 384
Buyse, E., 175
Buysse, A., 244
Buysse, D. J., 97
Byrd-Craven, J., 439
Byrd, M., 60
Byrne, A., 345
Byrnes, M. L., 206
Byun, S., 275

Cabrera, N., 131, 139, 171
Cacciatore, J., 80, 448
Cahill, K., 11
Cain, B. S., 436
Cain, D. W., 172
Caine, E. D., 286
Caino, S., 255
Calarco, K., 66
Caleb Alexander, G., 266
Calhoun, F., 66
Callahan, P. M., 409
Callister, L. C., 70
Caltran, G., 83
Calvert, S. L., 177
Calzada, E. J., 182
Camarota, S. A., 395
Cameron, P., 389
Cami, J., 264
Campbell, A., 176, 402
Campbell, D., 73
Campbell, F., 171
Campbell, L., 384
Campbell, N. B., 287
Campbell, W. K., 232
Camras, L., 133
Canals, J., 103
Candy, J., 176
Cannella, C., 411
Cannon, T., 56
Cannon, T. D., 56
Cantin, V., 358
Cantor, N., 218
Caplan, L. J., 127
Cappeliez, P., 425
Caputi, M., 187
Cardenas, J., 218
Cardman, M., 274
Carey, B., 180
Carey, S., 165
Carlin, J. B., 258
Carlson, A., 342
Carmelley, K., 337
Carnegie Task Force, 343
Carnell, S., 105
Caron, A., 136
Carpendale, J. I., 283

Carpenter, B. N., 428, 438
Carpenter, J., 386
Carpenter, L., 266
Carrera, E., 70
Carrere, S., 341
Carrère, S., 344
Carroll, J. S., 139
Carroll, M. D., 200
Carr, P. B., 329
Carson, R. G., 156
Carstensen, L., 428
Carstensen, L. L., 428
Carswell, H., 179
Carter-Saltzman, L., 53
Carter, S. F., 409
Carton, A., 350
Carver, C., 455
Carver, L., 135
Casalin, S., 49
Casanueva, C., 67
Cascalho, M., 414
Case, R., 18, 163, 271
Caserta, M., 314
Casey, B. J., 96, 261
Cashdollar, N., 427
Cashon, C. H., 83, 119
Cashwell, C. S., 340
Caskey, R., 266
Casper, M., 266
Caspi, A., 56, 142
Caspi, J., 243
Cassidy, J., 138, 294, 338
Castel, A., 420
Castle, N., 441
Castro, C. M., 366
Castro, J., 84
Castro-Schilo, L., 115
Catell, R. B., 222
Cates, W. Jr., *266*
Cath, S., 246
Cattani, A., 125
Cauce, A., 54, 247
Cauce, A. M., 246
Cauffman, E., 295
Caughlin, J., 342
Cavallini, A., 108
Cavanagh, K., 154
Ceci, S., 165
Ceci, S. J., 327
Celano, M. P., 203
Center for Communication & Social Policy, 26
Centers for Disease Control, 266, 342, 448
Centers for Disease Control and Prevention, 311
Cerella, J., 405
CFCEPLA, 387
Chabrol, H., 260
Chadwick, A., 179
Chaffin, M., 183
Chahal, H. H., 201
Chaikelson, J., 428
Chaker, A. M., 430
Chall, J. S., 216
Chamberlain, P., 248
Chamorro-Premuzic, T., 52
Chan, B. K., 368
Chan, D. W., 279
Chang, I. J., 182
Chang, L., 259
Chang, S., 83
Chanoine, V., 206
Chao, R. K., 182, 289
Chaplin, T., 286
Chapman, J., 428
Chaput, J., 311
Charles, E., 110
Charles, G. T., 53
Charles, S., 428
Charles, S. T., 428
Charness, N., *420*, 421
Chase-Lansdale, L., 172
Chasnoff, I. J., 65
Chassin, L., 265, 387
Chasteen, A. L., 374
Chasteen, A. L., 374
Chatterji, M., 276
Chattillion, E. A., 437
Chaudhary, N., 105
Cheah, C., 181
Chein, J., 262
Chelebowski, R. T., 362
Chen, C., 10, 410
Chen, D., 386
Chen, E., 203, 314
Chen, H., 182
Chen, H. S., 414
Chen, J., 7, 223
Chen, S., 279
Chen, S. X., 214
Chen, T., 7
Cherlin, A., 386
Cherney, I., 211
Cherry, K., 437
Chess, S., 143, 144
Cheung, A. H., 204
Chien, S., 83
Childers, J., 31
ChildStats.gov., 145
Chiodo, L. M., 66
Chisolm, T., 406
Chitty, L. S., 63
Chiu, C., 175, 210
Chiu, H., 181
Chiu, M. M., 275
Chlup, D., 7
Choi, H., 437
Chomsky, N., 129
Chou, J. L., 386
Choy, C. M., 67
Christakis, D., 191
Christian, L. M., 313
Christiansen, C., 361
Christine, J., 125
Chronis, A., 207
Chuang, S., 290
Chung, O. B., 344
Chung, S. A., 412, 414
Cialdini, R., 27
Cianciolo, A. T., 321
Ciarrochi, J., 280
Cicchetti, D., 184, 204
Cillessen, A., 239
Cirulli, F., 96
Claiborne, L., 166
Claire, B., 286
Clark, A., 129
Clark, B. F. C., 411
Clarke, A. R., 265
Clarke, E., 409
Clarke-Stewart, A., 258
Clark, J. E., 157
Clark, K. B., 232
Clark, M., 377
Clark, M. P., 232
Clark, M. S., 439
Clark, R., 80, 373
Clauss-Ehlers, C., 317
Claxton, L., 103
Clearfield, M., 144
Cliff, D., 394
Clinton, J. F., 342
Closson, L., 294
Cloutier, S., 67
Clubb, P. A., 165
Cnattingius, S., 64, 76
Coall, D. A., 440
Coats, E. J., 239
Cobbe, E., 426
Cochin, S., 141
Cockrill, K., 62
Cogan, L. W., 80
Cohen, D., 134, 391
Cohen, D. J., 204
Cohen-Fridel, S., 402
Cohen, J., 279
Cohen, L. B., 83, 119
Cohen, P., 389
Cohen, S., 314
Cohen, S. E., 123
Cohn, R. M., 425
Cohrs, J., 392
Cokley, K., 275
Colarusso, C. A., *331*
Colburne, K., 144
Colby, A., 236, 433
Colcombe, S., 419
Colcombe, S. J., 405
Cole, D. A., 279
Cole, M., 63
Coleman, H., 406
Coleman, H. L., 285
Coleman, M., 385, 386
Coleman, P., 425
Colen, C., 300
Cole, P., 189
Cole, S. A., 138
Coles, C., 66
Coles, C. D., 66
Coley, R. L., 172
College Board, 274
Collins, A., 62
Collins, J., 218
Collins, W., 288, 297, 461
Collishaw, S., 185
Colombo, J., 85
Colom, R., 27
Coltrane, S., 143, 343
Colwell, M., 179
Combs, J., 260
Committee on Children, Youth and Families, 147
Commons, M. L., 270
Compton, R., 154
Comunian, A. L., 425
Condly, S., 186
Condry, J., 144
Condry, S., 144
Conel, J. L., *95*
Conger, D., 325
Conley, C. S., 323
Connell-Carrick, K., 158
Conner, K., 286
Conner, K. R., 286
Connidis, I., 436
Connor, R., 393
Conn, V. S., 357
Conry-Murray, C., 176
Consedine, N., 428
Consolacion, T., 299
Conte, J. M., 434
Conway, C. C., 239
Conway, G., 175
Conway, M., 428
Cook, E., 295
Cook, J. L., 373
Cook, T. D., 295
Cooney, T., 436
Cooper, D., 313
Cooper, H., 379
Cooper, P., 123, 140
Copen, C. E., 300
Corballis, P., 154
Corbett, M., 154
Corbin, C. B., *157*
Corbin, J., 139
Corcoran, J., 300
Corely, T., 66
Corna, M. F., 100
Cornforth, S., 20
Cornish, K., 45
Cornish, K. M., 45
Corr, C., 449, 455
Corr, D., 455
Corrow, S., 108
Cortese, S., 207
Costa, P., 380, 422
Costa, P. T. Jr., 48, 398. *398*, 422
Costello, E., 104, 258
Costigan, K. A., 62
Cotrufo, P., 257
Cotter, R. F., 69
Coulson, C. C., 79
Couperus, J., 96
Courage, M., 171
Courage, M. L., 121
Courtney, E., 260
Cousins, W., 377
Couture, G., 184
Couzin, J., 63, 204
Cowan, C. P., 339
Cowan, F., 60, 71, 76
Cowan, P. A., 339
Cowley, G., 409
Cox, C., 60, 389
Coyl, D. D., 139
Coyne, J., 26
Craik, F., 417, 420
Cramer, M., 80
Crandall, C. S., 166
Crandall, R., 20
Crane, E., 45
Cratty, B., *93*, 157, *254*
Craven, R., 175
Crawford, D., 342
Crawford, M., 144, 257, 348, 349, 404, 437
Crawley, A., 171
Credé, M., 326, 402
Creswell, C., 123
Crewe, S., 389
Crick, N., 189, 191
Crimmins, E., 450
Crisp, A., 259
Critser, G., 259
Crockett, L. J., 233
Croen, L. A., 32
Crosby, F. J., 349
Crosland, K., 226
Crosnoe, R., 428
Cross, T., 228
Cross, T. B., 175, 242
Cross, W. E., 175, 242
Crouter, A. C., 243, 289
Crowl, A., 246, 345
Crowley, B., 386
Crowne, K., 321
Crowther, M., 440
Cruz, N., 208
Cuervo, A., 414
Cuijpers, P., 292
Culver, V., 461
Cumming, G. P., 361
Cummings, E., 427
Curlette, W., 35
Curnow, C., 307
Currier, J. M., 464
Cwikel, J., 260
Cyna, A., 72
Czaja, S. J., 421

Dabelko, H., 431
Daddis, C., 290
Dagher, A., 366
Dagys, N., 262
Dahl, E., 366
Dahl, R., 262
Dai, D., 281
Dalbert, C., 394
Dale Aagard, S., 386
Daley, K. C., 99
Daley, M. F., 158
Dalton, T. C., 155
D'Ambrosio, B., 167
Damon, W., 236, 237
Daniel, S., 286
Daniels, E. A., 202
Daniels, H., 167
Daniels, M., 53
Dardenne, B., 328
Dare, W. N., 67
Darnall, R., 448
Darnton, N., 343
Dar, R., 117
Darroch, J. E., 298
Dasen, P., 117, 210
Dasen, P. R., 210, 291
Davenport, B., 189
Davey, M., 186, 457
Davidov, B. J., 7, 219
Davidson, A. L., 295
Davidson, D. H., 173
Davidson, T., 391
Davies, S., 436
Davis, A., 45, 245

Davis, C., 463
Davis, D., 337
Davis, L., 276
Davison, G. C., 330
Davis, R. R., 80
Davis, T. S., 246
Daxinger, L., 51
Day, D. O., 183
Deakin, M. B., 338
Dean, R. S., 155
Dearing, E., 146, 172
Deary, I., 371, 405
Deary, I. J., 372, 380
Deater-Deckard, K., 11
Deaux, K., 347, 395
de Bono, S., 357
de Boysson-Bardies, B., 126
Deb, S., 183
Decarrie, T. G., 117
DeCasper, A. J., 85, 86
deCastro, J., 411
Deccache, A., 239
Decety, J., 188
De Clercq, A., 272
DeCoursey, P. J., 97
DeCourville, N., 315
de Dios, A., 7
Deeg, D., 408
DeFrancisco, B., 121
DeGenova, M. K., 425
de Geus, E., 226
Degnen, C., 426
de Graag, J. A., 97
DeHaan, L. G., 284
Dehaene-Lambertz, G., 129
Dehue, F., 240
De Jesus-Zayas, S. R., 18
de Jong, M., 425
Delahaij, R., 316
Delamater, J., 298
DeLamater, J. D., 298
de Lauzon-Guillain, B., 141
Delfabbro, P., 277
DeLisi, L., 19
Dellatolas, G., 159
Dellatolas, G. G., 170
Delle Fave, A., 382
Dell, M. L., 284
DeLoache, J. S., 119
Demaree, H. A., 367
De Marini, D. M., 45
De Meersman, R., 366
Dement, W. C., 99, 99
Demers, R. A., 125
Demetriou, A., 18
De Meyer, G., 409
Demick, J., 317
Demir, M., 438
De Mol, J., 244
Démonet, J. F., 206
Deng, C., 211, 348
Denizet-Lewis, B., 297
Denney, R. L., 18
Dennis, W., 322, *322*
Denollet, J., 366, 367
Denton, M., 436
de Oliveira, A., 5
de Onis, M., 104
DeParle, J., 342
DePaulo, B. M., 345
Derevensky, J., 277
Der, G., 405
Derlan, C. L., 232
Dernetz, V., 139
de Rosnay, M., 135
Derryberry, D., 142
Deruelle, F., 404
Dervic, K., 286
de Schipper, E. J., 147
Désiréa, L., 409
Desjardins, R. N., 86
Desoete, A., 272
de Souza Rezende, G., 5
de St. Aubin, E., 14
Destounis, S., 368
Dette, D., 392
Dette-Hagenmeyer, D. E., 394
Deurenberg, P., 199
Deurenberg-Yap, M., 199
DeVader, S. R., 76
Deveny, K., 176
Devlin, B., 53
De Volder, A. G., 96
de Vries, B., 462
deVries, R., 160
Dey, A. N., 203
DeYoung, C., 45
Diambra, L., 97
Diamond, L., 299, 338
Diamond, L. M., 332, 439
Diaz, V., 80
Dick, D., 56
Dickens, W., 225
Dickinson, D., 217
Diego, M., 28, 67, 78, 110
Diener, E., 381, 382
Dietrich, K., 154
Dietz, W., 200
Dietz, W. H., 105
DiGiovanna, A. G., 357
Dildy, G. A., 64
Dimmitt, C., 272
DiNallo, J. M., 67
Dinero, R., 337
Dion, K. K., 334
Dion, K. L., 334
Diop, A. M., 426
DiPietro, J. A., 62
DiPrete, T., 325
Dishion, T., 290
Dittman, M., 8
Dittrich, R., 62
Diveri, M., 232
Dixon, L., 389
Dixon, W. E. Jr., 129, 419
Dmitrieva, J., 291
Dobson, A., 438
Dobson, V., 83
Dodds, J., 102, *103*
Dodge, K. A., 204, 239, 292
Dodson, C., 211
Doka, K., 455
Doman, G., 131
Doman, J., 131
Dombrovski, A. Y., 450
Dombrowski, S., 76
Domenech-Rodriguez, M., 247
Dominguez, H. D., 85
Domsch, H., 85, 123
Donat, D., 217
Dondi, M., 83
Donini, L., 411
Donlan, C., 164
Donleavy, G., 236
Donnellan, M. B., 279
Donnerstein, E., 191
Doolittle, A., 461
Doress, P. B., 437
Dornbusch, S., 276
Dornbusch, S. M., 293
Dorn, L., 258
Douglas, D., 184
Douglass, A., 172
Douglass, R., 105
Doumen, S., 175
Doussard-Roosevelt, J. A., 76
Downs, D., 67
Downs, M., 388
Doyle, R., 77, 340, 385
Dozor, A. J., 154
Draper, T., 338
Dreman, S., 341
Drew, L. M., 246, 388
Driscoll, A. K., 233
Driver, J., 345
Driver-Linn, E., 327
Dromi, E., 126
Drouin, M., 295
Druzin, M. L., 64
Dryfoos, J. G., 291
Duarte, F. S., 409
DuBois, D. L., 293
Dubois, J., 129
Dudding, T. C., 69
Dudenhausen, J. W., 76
Duenwald, M., 61
Duffy, S. W., 368
Duijts, L., 106
Dumith, C., 259
Dumont, M., 328
Duncan, G. J., 80, 225
Duncan, J. R., 100
Dunford, B. B., 393
Dunkel, C. S., 13
Dunlap, G., 226
Dunne-Bryant, A., 385
Dunne, L., 107
Dunn, M., 264
Duong, H., 262
DuPaul, G., 207
Dupper, D. R., 240
Durbin, D., 154
Durbin, J., 436
Duriez, B., 283
Dweck, C., 175
Dwyer, K., 179
Dykas, M. J., 294
Dynda, A. M., 225
Dyson, A. H., 27

Eagly, A., 336
Eagly, A. H., 336, 348
Eaker, E. D., 367
Earl, J., 434
Easton, J., 22
Eaton, W. O., 157
Eberling, J. L., 420
Ebner, N., 372
Eccles, J., 254
Eccles, J. S., 257
Ecenbarger, W., 266
Eckerd, L., 452
Eckerman, C. O., 86, *86*, 140
Edgerley, L., 80
Edison, S. C., 121
Edwards, C. P., 179, 240
Edwards, M., 276
Edwards, S., 179
Ehrensaft, M., 389
Ehrlich, K., 362
Eichelsheim, V., 291
Eichstedt, J., 144
Eiden, R., 66
Eid, M., 140
Eilers, A., 128
Einspieler, C., 159
Eisenberg, N., 182, 187, 192, 239
Ekeberg, Ø., 450
Elder, G., 388
Elder, G. H. Jr., 279, 428
Eley, T., 285
Elkind, D., 270, 272, 273, 286, 449
Elkins, D., 20
Elliott, K., 183
Elliott, M., 386
Elliott, S., 384
Ellis, B., 22
Ellis, B. H., 299
Ellis, B. J., 256
Ellis, L., 175, 177
Ellison, C., 54
Ellison, S., 360
Ellis, S., 210
Ellman, L., 56
Elman, J., 19
Elmore, A., 246
Elmore, J. G. J., 368
Emery, C. F., 366
Emery, R. E., 258
Emmert, S., 412
Emslie, C., 415
Emslie, G. J., 204
The Endocrine Society, 257
Endo, S., 140
Endrass, T., 358
England, P., 325
Engler, J., 327
Ennett, S. T., 293
Enright, E., 384, 385
Ensenauer, R. E., 48
Epel, E., 412
Epperson, S. E., 328
Epstein, B., 408
Epstein, L., 262
Erber, J., 372
Erdley, C. A., 437
Erickson, D., 130
Erickson, K. I., 405
Erikson, E. H., 142
Erlandsson, K., 77
Erngrund, K., 419
Erwin, P., 238
Eshel, N., 261
Espenschade, A., 201
Essex, M. J., 436
Estell, D. B., 241
Etezadi, J., 428
Ethier, L., 184
Evans, C., 80
Evans, G. W., 247
Evans, P. L., 437
Evans, R., 439
Evans, T., 139
Everhart, D. E., 367
Everson, M., 389
Ewan, J., 73
Ezzo, F., 183

Fabbri, C., 44
Faber, A., 245
Fabes, R., 176
Fagan, J., 225
Fagan, M., 31
Fagioli, I., 98
Fagundes, C. P., 332, 439
Fainsilber-Katz, L., 341
Fais, L., 130
Faith, M. S., 49, 200
Falck-Ytter, T., 140
Falco, M., 4
Fane, B., 175
Fane, B. A., 65
Fanger, S., 27
Fantz, R. L., 108, *109*
Farley, F., 273
Farmer, T. W., 294
Farré, M., 264
Farroni, T., 85, 135
Farr, R. H., 246
Farzin, F., 110
Fayers, T., 267
Fazio, F., 206
Fazzi, E., 108
Federal Interagency Forum on Aging-Related Statistics, 145, 146, 411, 432, *438*
Feigelman, W., 448
Feigenson, L., 121
Feig, L., 51
Feinberg, T. E., 408
Feldhusen, J., 31
Feldman, D., 5
Feldman, D. C., 394
Feldman, J., 123, 165
Feldman, J. F., 123
Feldman, R., 7
Feldman, R. S., 162, 189, 239
Feldstein, S., 139
Fell, J., 5
Felson, R. B., 175
Fenech, M., 409
Fennema, E., 329
Fenwick, J., 70
Fenwick, K., 109
Fenwick, K. D., 109
Ferguson, D. L., 293
Ferguson, F., 321
Ferguson, R., 402
Fergusson, D., 265
Fergusson, D. M., 62
Fergusson, E., 388
Ferholt, B., 21
Fernald, A., 83, 128, 130

Fernald, L., 105
Fernyhough, C., 166, 170
Ferrucci, L., 408
Feshbach, S., 26
Fetchenhauer, D., 240
Fetterman, D. M., 277
Fiedler, N. L., 154
Field, M. J., 153, 203
Fields, D. L., 349
Field, T., 28, 78, 86, 110
Field, T. M., 422
Fifer, W. P., 85, 86
Figley, C. R., 383
Filippi, M., 155
Fincham, F. D., 384
Finch, C., 413
Finch, C. E., 412
Findlen, B., 390
Fine, M., 232
Fine, M. A., 244, 245
Fingerhut, L. A., 366
Finkelhor, D., 277, 448
Finkelstein, D. L., 73
Finkelstein, Y., 65
Fink, M., 414
Finley, G., 245
Finlon, K., 133
Finn-Stevenson, M., 104, 173
First, J. M., 218
Firth, H. V., 63
Fiscella, K., 366
Fischer, K., 18, 428
Fischer, K. W., 117, *156*
Fischer, T., 244
Fisch, H., 60
Fiset, V., 460
Fisher, C., 70
Fisher, C. B., 31, 35
Fish, J. M., 225
Fiske, S. T., 328, 374, 402
Fitzgerald, D., 108
Fitzgerald, P., 299
Fivush, R., 165, 176
Flanagan, C., 244
Flanagan, D. P., 223
Flanigan, J., 395
Flashman, J., 325
Flavell, J. H., 10, 210
Fleischhaker, W., 19
Fleming, M., 277
Fletcher, A. C., 296
Fling, B. W., 371
Flom, R., 110
Florsheim, P., 334
Flouri, E., 185
Floyd, R. G., 224
Flynn, E., 180
Flynn, J., 225
Foehr, U., 248, 277
Fogel, A., 80, 134
Fok, M. S. M., 78
Folbre, N., 342
Folkman, S., 35, 313
Fontes, S., 403
Foorman, B. R., 217
Foote, A., 66
Foote, W. E., 311
Forbes, S. A., 460
Ford, J. A., 264
Forman, M., 64
Foroud, A., 103
Fossett, M. A., 337
Foster, P., 152
Fothergill-Bourbonnais, F., 460
Fowers, B. J., 7, 219
Fowler, J. W., 284
Fozard, J. L., 405
Fraenkel, P., 377
Francis, A. N., 56
Franck, I., 265
Franco, J. L., 409
Franic, S., 204
Frank, E., 463
Frankel, L., 27
Frankenburg, W. K., 102, *103*
Franklin, C., 80
Frank, L. R., 264, *264*
Frank, M. C., 130
Fraser, C., *128*
Frawley, T., 177
Frayling, T., 51
Frazier, L. M., 61
Frederickson, N., 275
Freedman, A. M., 360
Freedman, D. G., 102
Freeman, E., 362
Freeman, H., 139
Freeman, J. M., 79
French, S., 312
Freneau, P., 386
Freud, S., 13, *13*, 14, 137, 189, 299
Freund, A., 372
Frey, B., 341, 362
Friborg, O., 317
Frick, P. J., 296
Fridlund, A. J., 84
Friedlander, L. J., 297
Friedman, D. E., 172
Friedman, S., 258
Friedman, W., 413
Friel, L. V., 245
Frieze, I., 177
Friston, J. J., 141
Frith, C. D., 141
Fritz, C., 345
Fritz, G., 158
Frome, P., 348
Fromholt, P., 419
Fryar, C. D., 200
Fryberg, S., 218
Fry, C. L., 426
Fu, G., 235
Fugate, W. N., 377
Fulcher, M., 345
Fuligni, A., 233, 289
Fuligni, A. J., 233, 276, 284
Fuligni, A. S., 233
Fulton, J., 409
Funk, L., 439
Furman, W., 290, 297
Furrow, J., 385
Furstenberg, F. F. Jr., 340
Fuso, A., 410
Fu, X., 336

Gabelko, N., 229
Gagnon, J. H., 298, 299, 360
Gagnon, S. G., 122
Gaillard, A., 316
Galambos, N., 285
Galaz-Fontes, J. F., 270
Galea, S., 8, 450
Galinsky, E., 181
Gallaty, K. J., 297
Galler, J., 105
Gallistel, C., 164
Gallistel, C. R., 120
Gallup Poll, 342
Galvin, S. L., 79
Gamboz, J., 260
Gamino, L. A., 455
Ganchrow, J. R., 85
Gandour, J., 130
Gangestad, S., 11
Ganley, C. M., 239
Ganong, L., 386
Ganzini, L., 457
Gao, D., 201
Garcia, C., 21
Garcia-Moreno, C., 389
Garcia-Portilla, M., 361
Gardner, H., 223, *223*
Gardner, P., 387
Garlick, D., 97
Gartrell, N., 32
Gartstein, M., 104
Garzarolli, B., 159
Gattringer, T., 404
Gatz, M., 428
Gaulden, M. E., 64
Gaultney, J. F., 296
Gauthier, S., 410
Gauvain, M., 270
Gavin, L. A., 290
Gavin, T., 411
Gawande, A., 406
Gaylor, E., 97, 98
Gazmararian, J. A., 67
Geesey, M., 80
Geller, P. A., 66
Gelles, R. J., 183
Gelman, R., 64, 120, 163
Gelman, S., 136
Gelman, S. A., 176
General Social Survey, *333*
Genest, M. T., 167
Genevro, J. L., 455
Gentile, D., 191
Georgieff, M. K., 60
Gerard, C. M., 99
Gerber, M. S., 345
Geronimus, A., 300
Gerrard, M., 330
Gershkoff-Stowe, L., 31
Gershoff, E. T., 182, 183
Gerstorf, D., 450
Gertler, P., 80
Gerton, J., 285
Gesell, A. L., 104, 122
Geurts, T., 440
Gewirtz, J. L., 235
Ghaemi, S., 204
Ghanem, H., 362
Gharibi, T., 412
Ghazi, A., 413
Ghimire, D. J., 297
Ghisletta, P., 11, 371
Ghule, M., 299
Giannopoulus, C., 428
Giarrusso, R., 436
Gibbons, F., 292, 330
Gibbs, N., 63, 64
Gibson, A., 109
Giedd, J. N., 332
Gielen, U. P., 425
Gifford-Smith, M., 237
Gijselaers, W. H., 273
Gilbert, L. A., 171
Gilbert, S., 286
Gilchrist, L., 301
Giles-Sims, J., 184
Gillath, O., 345
Gillespie, A. I., 373
Gillespie, N. A., 54
Gillham, A., 15
Gillham, J., 286
Gillies, R., 212
Gilligan, C., 235, 282
Gilliland, A. L., 67
Gillmore, M., 301
Gilmer, D., 404
Gilmore, C. K., 164
Gino, F., 462
Ginsberg, R., 385
Ginsberg, S., 270, 272, 273
Ginty, F., 357
Ginzberg, E., 347
Giordano, P., 297
Gitlin, L., 431
Glanz, J. M., 158
Glanz, K., 201
Glaser, D., 96
Glatt, S., 414
Gleason, M., 338
Gleitman, L., 126
Gleitman, L. R., 129
Glennie, E., 278
Glick, P., 328
Gliga, T., 108
Glover, V., 60, 71, 76
Gluhoski, V., 463
Goble, M. M., 259
Godbey, G., 394, 429
Godefroy, O., 358
Goede, I., 289
Goetz, A., 22
Goh, J. X., 327
Goldberg, A., 246, 345
Goldberg, A. E., 129
Goldberg, G. R., 357
Goldberg, J., 69
Goldfarb, Z., 74
Goldfield, G. S., 201
Golding, J., 388
Goldin-Meadow, S., 163
Goldman, L., 457
Goldman, R., 84
Goldney, R. D., 458
Goldscheider, F. K., 436
Goldschmidt, L., 66
Goldsmith, D., 7
Goldsmith, S. K., 285
Goldson, E., 57
Goldsteen, K., 386
Goldstein, L., 126
Goldstein, M. H., 119
Goldstein, S., 186
Goldston, D., 286
Goleman, D., 327
Golensky, M., 206
Golinkoff, R., 217
Golombok, S., 299
Göncü, A., 21
Goode, E., 158, 204
Goodison, S., 414
Goodlin-Jones, B., 97, 98
Goodman, G., 165
Goodman, G. S., 165
Goodman, J. S., 349
Goodson, B.., 32
Goodwin, C. L., 366
Goodwin, M. H., 241
Goold, S. D., 450, 457
Goorabi, K., 406
Gopinath, B., 358
Gopnik, A., 120, 131, 261
Gorchoff, S., 283, 386
Gordon, K., 384
Gordon, N., 156
Gorman, A., 395
Gorman, B., 448
Gormley, W. T. Jr., 172
Gosselin, P., 134
Gostin, L., 459
Goswami, U., 165
Gottesman, I., 52, 56
Gottesman, I. I., 56, *56*
Gottlieb, G. L., 101
Gottman, J., 390
Gottman, J. M., 341, 344
Gottschling, J., 381
Goulandris, N., 213
Gould, H., 62
Gould, M. S., 286
Gould, R. L., 378, *378*
Gould, S. J., 82
Gow, A., 439
Goyette-Ewing, M., 244
Grabner, R. H., 372
Graddol, D., 214
Grad, O., 286
Grady, D., 361, 368
Graham, I., 69
Graham, J. E., 313
Granic, I., 290
Granié, M., 153
Grant, C., 153
Grantham-McGregor, S., 105
Gray, C., 217
Gray-Little, B., 281
Gredler, M. E., 167, 212
Green, A., 311
Greenberg, D., 419
Greenberg, J., 13, 439
Greenberg, L., 260
Green, C., 373
Greene, K., 273
Greene, S., 246
Green, K., 209
Green, M., 315
Green, M. H., 349
Green, R., 300
Greenwood, D. N., 200

Greenwood, H., 48
Gregory, K., 104
Gregory, S., 298
Grela, B., 169
Griffin, M. J., 264
Griffith, D. R., 65
Griffiths, M., 277
Grigorenko, E., 321
Grigorenko, E. L., 221
Grilo, C. M., 260
Grimes, V., 65
Grissmer, D., 103
Grønhøj, A., 290
Groome, L. J., 63, 97
Grossmann, I., 321
Grossmann, K. E., 140
Gross, R. T., 76
Grothaus, L., 362
Grunbaum, J. A., 285, 286
Grundy, E., 387
Grusec, J. E., 16
Gruszczynska, E., 314
Guadalupe, K. L., 246
Guarente, L., 414
Guasti, M. T., 170
Guerra, N. F., 247
Guerrero, A., 275
Guerrero, S., 175
Guerrini, I., 63
Guidine, P., 5
Guiltinan, J., 362
Guindon, M., 425
Guiney, H., 358
Gullotta, T. P., 279
Gump, L. S., 235
Gumz, A., 10
Gunter, B., 177
Gupta, A., 44
Gupta, U., 333
Guralnik, J. M., 408
Güre, A., 258
Gurewitsch, E. D., 62
Guricci, S., 199
Gurin, P., 218
Gurling, H., 63
Gurung, R., 309
Gutek, G. L., 172
Guthrie, C., 200
Guttmacher Institute, *266*, 298
Guttmann, J., 244
Guzman, R., 217

Haas-Thompson, T., 452
Haber, D., 425
Hack, M., 77
Haddock, S., 343
Haedt, A., 260
Haeffel, G., 45
Hafdahl, A. R., 281
Hagerman, R., 45
Hagerty, R. G., 450
Hahn, E., 31, 381
Haines, J., 311
Haith, M. H., 108, 110
Halberda, J., 163
Haleem, M., 414
Haley, D., 120
Haley, W., 464
Halford, G., 180
Halgunseth, L. C., 247
Halkier, B., 28
Hallal, P., 259
Hall, E. G., 201
Halliday, M. A. K., 127
Hall, J. J., 155
Halperin, S., 420
Halpern, D. F., 225
Hamel, L. M., 153
Hamilton, B. E., 42, 300
Hamilton, B. S., 300
Hamlin, J. K., 136
Hammer, C. S., 67
Hammer, T. J., 235
Hamon, R. R., 297, 440
Hane, A., 139
Hannover, B., 276
Hanson, D. R., 56
Hanson, J. D., 80
Hanson, L., 460
Hanson, R., 437
Hansson, R. O., 428, 438
Harden, B., 185
Harden, K., 226, 275
Harder-Kasten, A., 427
Hardy, L. T., 139
Hare, T. A., 260
Harkness, S., 99
Harlow-Rosentraub, K., 420
Harmell, A. L., 437
Harnish, R. M., 125
Harper, D. A., 73
Harris, A., 59
Harris, B., 81
Harris-Britt, A., 67
Harris, J., 54
Harris, J. R., 233, 237
Harris, K. A., 99
Harris, M., 256
Harrison, K., 260
Harris, P. L., 116
Harris, T., 408
Hart, B., 27
Hart, C., 200
Hart, D., 235, 237
Harter, S., 231, 280, 281
Hart-Johnson, T., 218
Hartley, D., 51
Hartmann, B., 64
Hartshorne, T. S., 438
Hart, S. N., 184
Hartup, W. W., 333
Harvey, J., 383
Harvey, J. H., 244, 245
Harway, M., 389
Harz, K., 256
Haslett, A., 334
Hastings, P. D., 187
Hatfield, E., 334, 336
Hatton, C., 225, 226
Hauck, Y., 70
Haugaard, J. J., 183
Hau, K. T., 231
Hauser, S., 44
Hausmann, A., 260
Havighurst, R. J., 428
Hawkins-Rodgers, Y., 248
Hay, D., 179
Hayden, T., 42
Hayflick, L., 412, 413
Hayne, H., 211
Haynes, C. W., 76
Haynie, D. L., 291
Hayslip, B., 386, 437
Hayslip, B. Jr., 440
Hayward, M., 450
Hazan, C., 337
Hazen, N., 27
Heaton, T., 336
Heaven, P., 280
Hebíková, M., 48
Heckhausen, J., 381
Heflinger, C., 263
Hefner, V., 260
Heilbronner, N. N., 287
Heimann, M., 10, 86
Heinemann, G. D., 437
Held, B., 389
Helenius, H., 67, 342
Hellström, A., 158
Helmes, E., 402
Helms, D. B., 450
Helmsen, J., 189
Helms, J. E., 7
Helmuth, L., 426
Helson, R., 283, 377, 386
Helsper, E. J., 203
Hencke, R. W., 117
Henderson, C. E., 440
Henderson, S., 65
Henderson, T., 389, 440
Hendren, S., 366
Hendrick, C., 344
Hendrick, S., 344
Hendrie, H. C., 410
Henis-Korenblit, S., 413
Hen, R., 405
Henretta, J., 387
Henry, G. T., 276
Henry, R., 436
Henry, W. E., 427
Henschel, S., 183
Hensley, P., 463
Henson, R., 295
Herbenick, D., 360
Herdt, G. H., 254
Herman-Kinney, N. J., 264
Hermida, R. C., 408
Hernandez, D. J., 233
Hernandez-Reif, M., 28, 78, 110, 135
Herrnstein, R. J., 53, 225
Hertelendy, F., 69
Hertwig, R., 440
Hertzberg, V. S., 74
Hertzog, C., 394, 418
Hertz-Pannier, L., 129
Hespos, S. J., 120
Hessling, R., 408
Hess, T., 419
Hess, T. M., 374, 419
Hesterberg, K., 54
Hetherington, E., 246
Hetherington, E. M., 244
Hetrick, S. E., 286
Heubusch, K., 386
Heuven, E., 393
Hewstone, M., 242, 293
Heyes, C., 139
Heyman, R., 183
HHL, 406
Hickey, L., 15
Hickey, P. R., 110
Hickey, T., 439
Hietala, J., 56
Higgins, D., 184
Hill, B. D., 223
Hill, H. H., 109
Hillman, J., 411, 412
Hill, R. D., 428
Hilmert, C., 314
Hilton, J., 385
Himes, C., 437
Hines, M., 65, 83, 175
Hinrichsen, V. L., 32
Hinson, J. T., 374
Hirsch, B. J., 293
Hirschl, T. A., 432
Hirschtritt, M. E., 204
Hirsh-Pasek, K., 127, 217
Hirst, K. P., 81
Hitchcock, J., 96
Hitlin, S., 279
Hjelmstedt, A., 62
Ho, B., 388
Hobdy, J., 386
Hocking, D. R., 45
Hocutt, A. M., 226
Hodges, E. A., 374
Hoehl, S., 135
Hoelter, L. F., 297
Hoessler, C., 374
Hoeve, M., 181, 296
Hoeymans, N., 404
Hofer, M. A., 137
Hoff, E., 215, 275
Hofferth, S., 244
Hofferth, S. L., 80
Hoffman, L., 254
Hogg, K., 154
Hohmann-Marriott, B., 340
Holahan, C., 428
Holbert, D., 452
Holcomb, M., 362
Holden, G. W., 182
Holland, A. S., 345
Holland, C., 225
Holland, J. L., 347
Holland, J. M., 438, 464
Holland, J. W., 131
Holland, N., 175
Hollenstein, T., 290
Holloway, S. D., 275
Holmes, C. S., 379
Holmes, E. R., 426
Holmes, L. D., 426
Holmes, M. E., 428
Holowaka, S., 155
Holsey, C., 203
Holstein, B., 439
Holt, L., 155
Holzman, L., 212
Homae, F., 120
Hooker, K., 386
Hooks, B., 10
Hooven, C., 341
Hopkins, B., 104, 405
Hopkins-Golightly, T., 70
Horiuchi, S., 413
Hornor, G., 139
Horowitz, A., 406
Horwitz, B. N., 53
Horwood, L. J., 62
Hoseinabadi, R., 406
Hossain, N., 66
Houdé, O., 28
House, J. S., 342
House, S. H., 155
Houts, R., 342
Howard, A., 392
Howell, E., 81
Howell, P., 81, 206
Howe, M., 171
Howe, M. J., 220
Howe, M. L., 121
Howes, C., 181
Howes, O., 56
Howie, L., 431
Howieson, N., 139
Howley, A., 248
Hoyer, W., 420
Hoyme, H., 227
Hoy-Watkins, M., 276
Hoy, W. G., 461
Hsu, C., 79
Huang, A., 412
Huang, C. T., 86, 111
Huang, D. C., 259
Huang, J., 451
Hubbs-Tait, L., 154
Hubel, D. H., 108
Hubert, L., 348
Hubley, A. M., 258
Hübscher, R., 167
Huddleston, D. E., 405
Hudson, J. A., 166
Hueston, W., 80
Hugdahl, K., 119
Hughes, J., 256
Hughes, P., 80
Hughett, K., 179
Huh, S. Y., 106
Huijbregts, S., 7
Huizink, A., 65
Hülür, G., 450
Humiston, S., 366
Hummel, P., 110
Humphrey, J. H., 157
Humphrey, L., 368
Humphries, C., 65
Humphries, M. L., 73
Humphry, R., 179
Hungi, N., 211
Hung, L., 426
Hunter, J., 299
Hunter, N., 66
Hunter, S., 449
Hunter, T., 163
Hunt, K., 415
Hunt, M., 24, 298
Huntsinger, C. S., 173
Hurst, A., 51
Hussain, I., 86
Huston, T., 342
Huston, T. L., 333, 341

Hust, S., 177
Hutchinson, D., 292
Hutchison, K., 54
Hutchison, S., 18
Hutton, P. H., 12
Huurre, T., 244
Hyde, J., 256
Hyde, J. S., 256, 286, 298, 329, 343, 360, 377, 394, 411
Hyssaelae, L., 67

Ialongo, N., 189
Ialongo, N. S., 260, 285
Ickovics, J., 65
Iecovich, E., 431
Iglesias, J., 96
Ihle, A., 366
Iida, M., 338
Ilies, R., 45
Impett, E., 338
Ingersoll, E. W., 97
Ingoldsby, B. B., 297
Ingraham, E., 72
Ingram, D. K., 414
Inhelder, B., 267
Innamorati, M., 286
Insel, B. J., 286
Insel, P. M., 310
International Cesarean Awareness Network, *79*
Inzlicht, M., 329
Irland, J. M., 73
Isaacs, K. L., 155
Isay, R. A., 299
Ishi-Kuntz, M., 247
Ishizuka, B., 361
Ispa, J. M., 247
Iverson, T., 402
Iwano, S., 372
Izard, C. E., 132, 133
Izard, V., 163

Jachimowicz, V., 431
Jack, F., 211
Jackson, M., 59
Jackson, P. L., 188
Jacobi, C., 259
Jacobo, M., 405
Jacobs, B. A., 45
Jacobson, N., 390
Jacobus, J., 264, *264*
Jager, R., 406
Jahoda, G., 210, 270
Jalonick, M. C., 153
James, J., 256
James, W., 107
Janda, L. H., 336
Janevic, T. T., 79
Jang, K., 54
Janicke, D. M., 200
Jankowski, J., 123, 165
Jankowski, J. J., 123
Janssen, S., 413
Janusek, L., 313
Jarvin, L., 427
Jaswal, V., 211
Jaworski, M., 52
Jay, M., 340
Jayne, K., 135
Jehlen, A., 276
Jelalian, E., 200
Jelicic, H., 231
Jensen, B., 233
Jensen, L. A., 285
Jernigan, M., 7
Jetten, J., 191
Jeynes, W., 246
Jiao, S., 243
Ji, G., 243
Ji-liang, S., 439
Jimenez, J., 217
Jindal, V., 358
Jing, Q., 243
Jirtle, R. L., 52
Joe, S., 286
John, O., 283, 386
Johnson, A. M., 299
Johnson, D. C., 460
Johnson, D. J., 173
Johnson, E., 109
Johnson, J., 260
Johnson, K., 128
Johnson, L., 448
Johnson, N., 203
Johnson, N. G., 257
Johnson, S., 108, 137
Johnson, S. L., 49, 200
Johnson, S. P., 83, 135
Johnson, V., 263, 412
Johnson, W., 380
Johnson, W. G., 78
Johnston, L. D., 263, 264, 265
Johnston, N., 154
Joiner, T. E., 260
Joiner, T. E. Jr., 20
Joliot, M., 28
Jones, A., 20
Jones, D. E., 72
Jones, H., 66, 86, 207
Jones-Harden, B., 247
Jones, R. M., 261, 373
Jonsson, T., 409
Jopp, D. S., 394
Jordan, A., 277
Jordan, J., 448
Jordan-Young, R. M., 60
Jorgensen, G., 236
Jose, O., 436
Joseph, H., 286
Joshi, B., 299
Joyce, A. S., 438, 463
Joy, E. A., 67
Juby, H., 244
Judas, M., 260
Judge, T. A., 45
Jung, M., 307
Junkkari, H., 244
Jurimae, T., 201
Jusczyk, P. W., 125

Kacapyr, E., 394
Kadue, D. D., 433
Kagan, J., 49, 55, 124, *134*, 142
Kahneman, D., 382
Kahn, J. H., 408
Kahn, J. P., 367
Kahn, R. L., 408, 434
Kail, R., 210
Kail, R. V., 117, 271
Kaiser, L. L., 63
Kalb, C., 59, 61, 153
Kaltiala-Heino, R., 258
Kalynchuk, L., 314
Kamijo, K., 411
Kaminaga, M., 258
Kamm, M. A., 69
Kanazawa, S., 109
Kandler, C., 323
Kaneda, H., 407
Kann, L., 285
Kan, P., 169
Kantrowitz, E. J., 179
Kao, G., 233, 241
Kapadia, S., 291
Kaplan, H., 34, 104
Kaplanski, J., 405
Kaprio, J., 56
Kapur, S., 56
Karabulut, E., 434
Karagianni, P., 76
Karelitz, T. M., 427
Karlson, H., 184
Karmaus, W., 154
Karmiloff-Smith, A., 123
Karney, B. R., 341, 342
Karnilowicz, W., 289
Karniol, R., 177
Karp, J., 390
Karsdal, M. A., 361
Kart, C. S., 404
Kartman, L. L., 425
Kaslow, F. W., 383
Kasl, S. V., 428, 463
Kassner, C. T., 460
Kastenbaum, R., 448, 450, 455
Kate, N. T., 342
Kathmann, N., 358
Kato, K., 11
Katsurada, E., 182
Katzer, C., 240
Katz, S., 411
Kaufman, J. C., 221, 323
Kaunonen, M., 448
Kayton, A., 74
Kearsley, R., *134*
Keating, D., 270
Kecskes, I., 215
Kedziora-Kornatowski, K., 414
Kee, D., 115
Keefer, B. L., 104
Keehn, D., 232
Keel, P. K., 200, 260
Keene, J. R., 389
Keen, R., 103
Kehl, K. A., 452
Keitel, M., 59
Keith, P. M., 436
Kelber, S., 410
Kelber, S. T., 342
Kelch-Oliver, K., 245
Keller, H., 182, 344
Kelley, G., 411
Kelley, M., 342
Kelly, G., 297
Kelly, J., 139, 244
Kelly-Weeder, S., 60
Kemmelmeier, M., 218
Kemper, S., 357
Kendall, A., 411
Kennedy, K., 404
Kennell, J. H., 74
Kenrick, D. T., 338
Kenyon, C., 413
Kern, R., 35
Kerns, K., 139
Kerr, M., 333
Kershaw, T., 65
Keski-Rahkonen, A., 260
Kesselring, T., 18
Ketelaar, L., 188
Khachaturian, A. S., 409
Khachaturian, Z. S., 409
Kiang, L., 284
Kiecolt-Glaser, J. K., 313
Kiecolt, K. J., 337
Kieffer, C. C., 140
Kieschke, U., 212
Killen, M., 241
Killoren, S. E., 243
Kilmann, P., 341
Kilner, J. M., 141
Kim-Cohen, J., 317
Kim, E. H., 452
Kim, H. I., 135
Kim, H. S., 315
Kim, J., 395
Kim, J. K., 13
Kim, J.-S., 388
Kim, J.-Y., 243
Kimm, S., 259
Kimoto, T., 96
Kim, T. C., 14
Kimura, K., 405
Kincl, L., 154
King, A., 428
King, A. C., 366
King, D., 277
Kinney, D. A., 264
Kinney, H. C., 63, 100
Kinnunen, U., 392
Kinsey, A. C., 299
Kirby, J., 246
Kirchengast, S., 64
Kirkendall, A. M., 452
Kisilevsky, B. S., 86
Kitamura, C., 130
Kitasaka, T., 372
Kitayama, S., 175
Kit-fong Au, T., 267
Kiuru, N., 292
Kjaer, M., 404
Kjølseth, I., 450
Klass, P., 119
Klebanov, P. K., 225
Klein, M. C., 72
Klemencic, N., 154
Klenke-Hamel, K. E., 336
Klerman, L., 172
Kliegel, M., 384
Klier, C. M., 81
Klimstra, T. A., 285
Klitzman, R. L., 48
Kloep, M., 7
Klohnen, E., 377
Kluger, J., 204
Klump, K. L., 51
Klute, C., 292
Knafo, A., 290
Kneile, L. A., 212
Knickmeyer, R., 60, 176
Knorth, E. J., 248
Knottnerus, G., 154
Knutson, J., 189
Kobrynski, L. J., 203
Kochanska, G., 142, 144
Kodl, M., 265
Koehoorn, M., 256
Koenen, K., 8
Koenig, A., 184
Koenig, L. B., 54
Kogan, C. S., 45
Koglin, U., 189
Kohlberg, L., 177, 233, 433
Kohler, F. W., 179
Kohnert, K., 169
Kohut, S. A., 110
Koivisto, M., 155
Kokko, K., 392
Kolata, G., 61, 298, 299, 360
Kolodny, R. C., 412
Kontos, S., 181
Kooijman, A., 357
Koopmans, S., 357
Koot, H., 292
Koppelman, F. S., 203
Koren, G., 65
Koretz, D., 276
Korfmacher, J., 73
Korn, W., *327*
Koroukian, S. M., 79
Korte, J., 425
Koshmanova, T., 22
Koska, J., 199
Koss, M. P., 390
Kostka, T., 431
Kostovic, I., 260
Kotch, J., 389
Kothari, N., 206
Kotler, J. A., 177
Kotre, J., 82, 230, 237
Kovelman, I., 214
Kradin, R. L., 314
Kramer, A. F., 405
Krampe, R., 429
Krause, N., 232
Krcmar, M., 169
Kretch, K. S., 108
Krishnamoorthy, J. S., 200
Kristensen, P., 411
Kristjansdottir, G., 202
Kroger, J., 209, 282, 283
Krogh, L., 113
Krohn, M. D., 296
Krojgaard, P., 117
Kross, E., 321
Krueger, J., 381
Krulewitch, C. J., 79
Kübler-Ross, E., 453, 454
Kuczmarski, R. J., *153*
Kuczynski, L., 144
Kudo, Y., 361

Kuebli, J., 165
Kuhl, P. K., 130, 131
Kuhn, D., 210, 271
Kunkel, D., 171
Kunzmann, U., 426
Kupek, E., 77, 152
Kupersmidt, J. B., 292
Kupper, L., 67
Kupper, N., 367
Kurdek, L. A., 338, 341, 345
Kurtines, W. M., 235
Kurtz-Costes, B., 275
Kurtz, D. A., 185
Kus-Appough, 340
Kuschal, C., 412
Kutner, J. S., 460
Kwan, K., 35
Kwant, P. B., 414

Laas, I., 20
Labouvie-Vief, G., 271, 318
Lacerda, F., 164
Lacharite, C., 184
Lachmann, T., 203
Lackey, C., 389
LaCoursiere, D., 81
LaCroix, A., 362
Ladd, G. W., 238
Laflamme, D., 144, 344
LaFromboise, T., 285
Lafuente, M. J., 97
Lahiri, D. K., 410
Lain, D., 433
Lally, M. M., 280
Lamaze, F., 72
Lambe, M. P., 76
Lambert, S. F., 285
Lambiase, A., 358
Lamb, M. E., *126*, 140, 173
Lambrinoudaki, I., 361
Lam, C., 130
Lamkin, D., 375
Lamm, B., 344
Lamm, H., 334
Lamon, S. J., 329
Lamont, J. A., 360
Lamorey, S., 244
Lamprecht, M., 231
Lam, S., 182
Lam, V., 176
Landau, B., 126
Landers, D., 307
Landgraff, C., 295
Landhuis, C., 201
Landis, M., 384
Landy, F., 434
Lane, D., 292
Lane, J. D., 180
Lane, K. A., 327
Lang, A., 66
Lange, C., 349
Langer, E., 419
Langille, D., 65
Langlois, E., 66
Lansford, J. E., 183, 241, 244, 245
Lappin, S., 129
Larsen, K. E., 72
Larsen, L., 402
Larsen, S. F., 419
Larson, N., 311
Larson, R. W., 290, *291*
Lasenby-Lessard, J., 154
Laska, M. N., 259
Laskey, M. A., 357
Lassonde, K. A., 402
Latzer, Y., 260
Lauer, J. C., 386
Lauer, R. H., 386
Lau, I., 210
Lau, M., 297
Laumann, E. O., 298, 299, 360
Lauter, J. L., 59
Lavallee, M., 210
Lavers-Preston, C., 440
Lavezzi, A. M., 100
Lavoi, N. M., 202
Law, A., 15
Law, D. M., 240
Lawrence, E., 345
Lawson, M. J., 211
Lay, K., 179
Lazarus, J. H., 81
Lazarus, R. S., 313
Lazarus, S. S., 276
Leach, P., 172
Leadbeater, B., 285
Leadbeater, B. J., 32
Leaper, C., 177
Lease, A., 238
Leathem, J., 429
Leathers, H. D., 152
Leathers, S., 342
Leavitt, L. A., 57
LeBuffe, P., 186
Le Corre, M., 165
Lecours, A. R., 202
Lecusay, R., 21
Lederberg, A. R., 27
Lederhos, C., 383
Lee, A. M., 201
Lee, B. H., 203
Lee, C. C., 126, 421
Lee, E., 452
Lee, E.-H., 388
Lee, K., 109
Lee, M., 343, 441
Leenaars, A. A., 455
Leen-Feldner, E. W., 258
Lee, R. M., 233
Lee, S., 210, 228
Lees, N., 267
Lefkowitz, E. S., 267
Legato, M., 60
Legerstee, M., 86
Le, H., 21, 30
Lehman, D., 175
Lehr, U., 426
Leis, J., 304, 330
Leis-Newman, E., 62
Leman, P., 176
Le Masurier, G., 67
Lemery-Chalfant, K., 49
Lemmons, B. P., 276
Lemoine, C. C., 159
Lemonick, M. D., 257
Lenhart, A., 277, 295
Leonard, L. B., 130, 206
Leondari, A., 452
Leon, I., 176
Lerner, J. W., 206
Lerner, R. M., 31, 231
Lesner, S., 406
Lester, B. M., 104
Lester, D., 286
Leuba, G., 410
Leung, C., 289
LeVay, S., 299
Levendosky, A., 186
Levenson, R. W., 436
Leverone, D., 408
Leversen, J. R., 405
Levine, R. V., 335, 394
Levine, S. C., 145
Levin, R. J., 298
Levin, S., 218
Levinson, D. J., 378, 424
Levitt, A., 126
Levy, B. L., 419
Levy, B. R., 402, 428
Levy-Shiff, R., 344
Lewis, B., 60
Lewis, C. C., 146
Lewis, J., 19
Lewis, J. M., 384
Lewis, M., 132
Lewis, M. I., 431
Lewis, M. J., 66
Lewis, R., 386
Lewis, V., 362
Lewkowicz, D., 110
Leyens, J. P., 29, *30*
Liang, H., 285
Liang, J., 232, 427
Liao, Y., 357
Libert, S., 414
Licciardi, F., 59
Lichter, D. T., 336
Lickliter, R., 110
Lidz, J., 129, 163
Liechty, J., 200
Lieven, E., 200
Light, L. L., 419
Li, G. R., 414
Li, H., 357
Li, J., 275
Li, K., 428
Lilja, G., 73
Lillis, T., 383
Limoli, P. G., 406
Lin, C., 181
Lindau, S., 266, 411
Lindemann, B. T., 433
Lindenberger, U., 11
Lindsay, G., 227
Lindsay, M., 65
Lindsey, E., 179
Lindstrom, H., 394
Ling, R., 295
Lin, H., 79
Lin, I-Fen., 384, *385*
Lin, K., 169
Linn, R. L., 276
Lino, M., 342
Li, N. P., 336
Lin, X., 117
Liou, T., 259
Liou, Y., 259
Lipnevich, A. A., 223
Lipp, A., 62
Lipsitt, L., 101
Lipsitt, L. P., 85, 109
Lipsitt, L. R., 317
Li, Q., 240, 325
Li-qing, Z., 439
Li, S., 22, 45, 51, 307, 325
Lisabeth, L., 361
Lister, J., 406
Little, R. E., 78
Litzinger, S., 384
Liu, H., 384
Liu, J., 79
Liu, L., 362
Liu, N., 314
Livingstone, S., 203
Li, Y., 67, 292
Lloyd, K. K., 172
Lluis-Font, J. M., 27
Lobo, R. A., 361
Locke, C. R., 246
Lock, R. D., 393
Loeb, S., 146
Loehlin, J., 226
Loehlin, J. C., 182
Loessl, B., 262
Loewen, S., 18
Loewenstein, D., 421
Logsdon, R., 411
Lohaus, A., 85, 123
Lohman, D., 224, 228
Lohr, M., 301
London, B., 235
Lonetto, R., 449
Long, B. L., 373
Long, J., 276
Longley, C., 411
Long, M., 325
Longmore, M., 297
Lopez, G. E., 218
Lopez, M. F., 85
Lord, S., 406
Lorenz, K., 189
Losonczy-Marshall, M., 144
Lourenco, F., 96
Lourenco, O., 210
Love, A., 179
Love, J. M., 146, 147, 172
Lovrin, M., 204
LoVullo, S., 16
Lowenstein, J., 166
Low, J., 121
Lowrey, G. H., 155
Lowry, R., 285
Lubinski, D., 222
Lucas, R., 382
Lucas, R. E., 382, 385
Lucassen, A., 48
Lucas, S. R., 293
Ludden, A. B., 280
Ludden, J., 387
Ludlow, V., 107
Luhmann, M., 377
Luke, B., 77
Luke, M. A., 337
Lu, L., 344
Luminet, O., 239
Luna, B., 260
Lundberg, I., 212
Lundblad, B., 158
Lund, R., 439
Luo, B., 427
Luo, C., 262
Luo, L., 420
Luong, G., 53
Luo, Q., 263
Luszcz, M. A., 403
Luthar, S., 294
Lutzker, J., 184
Lu, X., 285
Lyall, S., 340
Lye, T. C., 420
Lynch, M. E., 66
Lynne, S., 258
Lynn, R., 123
Lynskey, M., 51
Lyon, G. J., 46
Lyon, M. E., 286
Lyons, N. P., 235

Maassarani, R., 134
Mabbott, D. J., 156
MacCann, C., 223
Macchi Cassia, V., 85
Maccoby, E. E., 146, 181
MacDonald, W., 350
MacDorman, M. F., 79, 80
Machado, A., 210
Machado, L., 358
Maciejewski, P. K., 455
Macionis, J. J., 384, 425
MacKillop, J., 54
MacWhinney, B., 129
Maddi, S. R., 316
Madsen, P. B., 300
Maes, M., 81
Maes, S. J., 244
Magai, C., 428, 438
Magne, R., 141
Mahn, H., 22, 167
Mäkinen, M., 280
Makino, M., 260
Makishita, H., 358
MaKuc, D. M., 366
Malchiodi, C. A., 20
Malcuit, G., 144, 344
Maller, S., 225
Malling, H. V., 45
Mallis, M., 176
Mallon, G. P., 299
Mancini, A. D., 463, 464
Mangan, P. A., 405
Mangiatordi, A., 227
Mangweth, B., 260
Manlove, J., 301
Mann, C. C., 200
Manning, M., 227
Manning, W., 297
Mansson, D., 388
Manstead, A. S. R., 333
Mao, A., 98
Marceau, K., 285
March, J. S., 204
Marcia, J. E., 282–283

Marcovitch, S., 116
Marcus, A. D., 343
Marcus, D., 409
Marcus, S., 286
Mardon, S., 262
Marean, G. C., 109
Marinellie, S. A., 212
Marin, T., 203, 314
Markell, K., 452
Markison, S., 407
Markman, H., 340
Markova, G., 86
Marks, N., 437
Markus, H. R., 175
Marlier, L., 109
Marolla, F., 49
Marron, M., 228
Marschark, M., 205
Marschik, P., 159
Marshall, B., 411
Marshall, N. L., 147
Marsh, H. W., 175, 231
Marsland, K. W., 173
Martel, M., 154
Martens, B., 227
Marti-Henneberg, C., 256
Martikainen, P., 463
Martin, A., 125, 246
Martina, C., 438
Martin, C. E., 299
Martin, C. L., 176, 177
Martin, D., 48, 340
Martineau, J., 141
Martinelli, P., 419
Martinez, G., 300
Martinez-Torteya, C., 186
Martin, G., 286
Martin, J. A., 42, 181
Martin, M., 340, 379
Martin, M. H., 15
Martin, P., 340
Martin, R., 76
Martin, S., 67
Martin, T., 385
Masalha, S., 7
Masataka, N., 127, 130
Mascher, J., 7
Mashburn, A. J., 276
Masling, J. M., 13
Maslow, A. H., 20
Masocco, M., 286
Massaro, A., 67
Masten, A., 142
Master, S., 314
Masters, W. H., 412
Mastora, A., 452
Mather, M., 428
Mathews, G., 175
Mathews, H. L., 313
Matlin, M., 257
Maton, K. I., 32
Matriano, E., 219
Matson, J., 16
Matsuda, Y., 130
Matsumoto, D., 7
Matsunaga, K., 358
Matthews, K. A., 394
Matthiesen, A. S., 73
Mattison, J. A., 414
Mattock, A., 83
Mattos, L. C., 358
Mattson, M., 414
Mattson, S., 66
Matturri, L., 100
Matula, K., 122
Maughan, B., 388
Mausbach, B. T., 437
Maxmen, A., 402
Maxson, S. C., 44
Mayes, L., 66, 242
Mayes, R., 66
Mayes, T. L., 204
Maynard, A., 117, 209, 272
Mayseless, O., 138
Mazoyer, B., 28
McAdams, D. P., 14
McArdle, E. F., 457
McBride-Chang, C., 275
McBrier, D. B., 349
McCabe, M., 184
McCabe, M. P., 257, 259
McCall, R. B., 98
McCardle, P., 215
McCarthy, B., 385
McCartney, K., 146, 172
McCarty, K. N., 452
McCarty, M., 103
McCauley, K. M., 361
McClelland, D. C., 221
McConnell, V., 440, 441
McCord, J., 184
McCormick, C. B., 272
McCourt, M., 154
McCoy, S. L., 407
McCracken, J., 207
McCrae, R., 380, 422
McCrae, R. R., 48, 398. *398*, 422
McCrink, K., 120
McCrory, E., 206
McCullough, M. E., 31
McCutcheon-Rosegg, S., 72
McDaniel, A., 385
McDonald, K. A., 366
McDonnell, L. M., 216
McDonough, L., 128
McDowell, D., 237
McDowell, M., 256
McElhaney, K., 294
McElwain, N. L., 345
McFadden, J. R., 378
McFadden, S. H., 438
McGadney-Douglass, B., 105
McGeary, J., 54
McGinn, D., 393
McGinnis, E., 179
McGough, R., 206
McGue, M., 45, *53*
McGuffin, P., *44*
McGugin, R., *373*
McGuinness, D., 307
McGuire, J. K., 300
McGuire, S., 243
McHale, J. P., 344
McHale, S. M., 243, 289
McKay, R. J., 42
McKhann, G. M., 405
McKinlay, A., 402
McKinlay, J. B., 412
McKown, C., 242
McLachlan, H., 459
McLaughlin, D., 438
McLean, K., 280
McLoyd, V. C., 246
McMurray, B., 126
McNulty, J. K., 342
McQueeny, T., 264, *264*
McVittie, C., 402
McWhirter, D. P., 299
McWilliams, N., 15
Meade, C., 65
Mead, M., 219
Mealey, L., 145
Medeiros, R., 409
Medina, A., 383
Medina, J. J., 403
Mednick, M., 392
Mednick, S. A., 322
Meece, J. L., 275
Meeus, W., 289
Mehta, C. M., 240
Meijer, A. M., 344
Meins, E., 138, 170
Meisinger, E., 238
Meister, H., 406
Mellet, E., 28
Meltzoff, A. N., 86, 111, 131
Melville, K., 342, 386, 437
Melzer, D., 51
Melzer, I., 405
Menacker, F., 42
Mendle, J., 258
Mendoza, C., 228
Menezes, A., 259
Meng, Z., 133
Menlove, F. L., 16
Menna-Barreto, L., 97
Menna, R., 139, 189
Mennella, J. A., 66
Mensah, F. K., 258
Menzel, J., 408
Mercer, J. R., 225
Merick, J., 260
Merlo, L., 131
Mermelstein, R., 265
Mero, R. P., 342
Merrick, J., 277
Merrill, D. M., 387
Mertesacker, B., 144
Mervis, J., 32, 172
Mesle, F., 413
Messer, D., 171
Messer, S. B., 15
Mester, R., 286
Meyer, M., 437
Mezey, G., 67
Mezuk, B., 45
Mezulis, A., 286
Miao, X., 211
Michael, R. T., 298, 299, 360
Michaels, M., 386
Michels, V. V., 48
Michnick-Golinkoff, R., 127
Microwsky, J., 386
Mieler, W., 406
Miesnik, S., 79
Mikulincer, M., 138, 337, 338
Miles, L., 59
Miles, R., 60, 71, 76
Milevsky, A., 232
Miller, A. J., 340
Miller, C. A., 271
Miller, E. M., 33, 65
Miller, G., 203, 314
Miller, J., 226, 406
Miller, P. C., 182
Miller, P. H., 166
Miller, R., 436
Miller, S. A., 180
Miller, T. L., 455
Millsap, R. E., 422
Mills, E., 84
Mills, J., 439
Mimura, K., 96
Minzenberg, M., 19
Mirecki, R. M., 386
Mirsky, J., 260
Mishna, F., 240
Mishra, R. C., 210
Misri, S., 81
Mistry, J., 117
Mitchell, D., 85
Mitchell, E., 85, 100
Mitchell, E. S., 377
Mitchell, K., 277
Mitchell, S., 8
Mittal, V., 56
Mittendorf, R., 69
Miwa, K., 372
Mix, C., 386
Miyaki, K., 140
Modi, N., 60, 71, 76
Moffitt, T. E., 56
Mohajeri, M., 410
Moher, M., 121
Möhler, E., 183
Mohr, B. A., 412
Mok, A., 219
Molina, J. C., 66, 85
Mols, F., 366
Monahan, C. I., 185
Monahan, K., 295
Monahan, K. C., 295
Monastra, V., 56
Monk, C., 60
Monoi, S., 276
Montazer, S., 313
Montemayor, R., 279
Montgomery-Downs, H., 98
Moon, C., 85
Moore, G., 49
Moore, K., 393
Moore, K. L., 58, *64*
Moore, L., 201
Moore, M., 86
Moore, R., 437
Moore, R. L., 334
Morales, J. R., 247
Morange-Majoux, F. F., 159
Moran, S., 223
Moran, T., 80
Morelli, G. A., 7
Moreno-Torres, I. I., 170
Morfei, M. Z., 386
Morgan, C. A., 109
Morice, A., 80
Mori, K., 372
Morikawa, H., 128
Morita, J., 372
Morley, J. E., 404
Morris, G., 165
Morris, J., 45
Morris, M. W., 219
Morris, P., 345
Morrissey, T., 146
Morris, W. L., 345
Morrongiello, B., 109, 154
Morrongiello, B. A., 109
Morry, M., 333
Morse, S. J., 270
Mortensen, C., 27
Moser, K., 393
Moss, M., 433
Motschnig, R., 20
Mottl-Santiago, J., 73
Mottus, R., 380
Moyer, M. S., 439
Mruk, C. J., 230
Mueller, E., 140
Mueller, M., 388
Muenchow, S., 173
Muilenburg, J., 265
Mulder, E., 65
Müller, U., 18
Munch, J., 203, 314
Munoz-Ruiz, M., 405
Munro, K. J., 109
Munsey, C., 240
Munson, M. L., 42
Munzar, P., 264
Murcia, G., 225
Murguia, A., 309
Murphy, B., 239
Murphy, C., 407
Murphy, F. A., 62
Murphy, M., 46
Murphy, P., 276
Murphy, S., 448
Murray, C., 53, 225
Murray-Close, D., 189
Murray, L., 123, 140
Murray, R. M., 76
Murray, S., 342
Murstein, B. I., 333
Mussner, K., 72
Muzio, J. N., 99, *99*
Myers, A., 411
Myers, D., 405
Myers, R. H., 48
Myklebust, B. M., 101
Myrtek, M., 367

Nabe, C., 455
Nadel, S., 19
Nagda, B. R. A., 218
Nagle, R. J., 122
Naglieri, J., 186
Nagy, E., 86
Nagy, M., 449
Naik, A., 368
Naimark, B., 411
Nakagawa, M., 140
Nam, S., 436
Nangle, D. W., 437

Nanney, M., 200
Nappi, R., 360
Nash, A., 171
Nash, A. S., 171
Nass, C., 373
Nassif, A., 177
Natan, B. M., 431
Nation, M., 263
Navalta, C. P., 204
Navarro, M., 388
Nazzi, T., 126
Neal, T., 155
Needham, A., 103
Needleman, H. L., 63
Negy, C., 233
Neiderhiser, J. M., 182
Neimeyer, R. A., 464
Neisser, U., 121
Nelson, A. R., 66
Nelson, C., 96
Nelson, H. D., 368
Nelson, K., 128, 165
Nelson, L., 291
Nelson, L. J., 139
Nelson, N., 144
Nelson, T., 264, 402
Nemiroff, R. A., *331*
Nesheim, S., 65
Nestler, E. J., 51
Netter, S., 232
Neubauer, A. C., 372
Neugarten, B. L., 424
Neumark-Sztainer, D., 311
Newland, L. A., 139
Newman, R., 86
Newsom, C. A., 205
Newsom, E., 430, 432
Newston, R. L., 436
Newton, K., 362
Ng, F. F., 182
Ngini, L., 210
Ngo, B., 219
Ng, T. H., 394
Nguyen, H., 21
Nguyen, S., 176
Ng, W., 28
Nicholas, H., 28
Nicholson, L. M., 259
Niederhofer, H., 60
Niehorster, S., 326
Nieto, S., 219
Nigg, J. T., 154
Nihart, M. A., 155
Nikkola, I., 448
Nikolas, M., 51, 154
Nilsson, L., 419
Nilsson, L. G., 419
Nisbett, R. E., 225
Nisker, J., 48
Nissen, E., 73
Noakes, M. A., 241
Nobuyuki, I., 358
Nockels, R., 267
Nolan, R. P., 367
Nolen-Hoeksema, S., 463
Noonan, C. W., 203
Noonan, D., 203
Noonan, K., 76
Noone, J., 434
Nordenmark, M., 434
Nordin, S., 407
Norgate, S., 51
Normand, M. T., 170
North, M. S., 402
Norton, A., 167
Norton, M. I., 462
Nosarti, C., 76
Nugent, J. K., 104
Nyberg, L., 419
Nyiti, R. M., 210
Nykl, L., 20
Nylen, K., 80

Oakeshott, P., 267
Oakes, L., 113
Oberlander, S. E., 245
Oblinger, D. G., 276
O'Connor, M., 67
O'Connor, P., 439
Ocorr, K., 414
Oddo, M., 70
Oden, M., 370
Oden, M. H., 228
Odic, D., 163
Oehler, J. M., 86, *86*
Ogbu, J. U., 275
Ogden, C. J., *153*
Ogden, C. L., 200
Ogle, B. M., 414
O'Grady, W., 125
Ogrodniczuk, J. S., 438, 463
O'Hara, M., 80
O'Hara, R., 330
Ohgi, S., 103
Ohta, H., 103
Oishi, S., 382
Okada, M., 96
Okie, S., 207
Oksenberg, J., 44
O'Leary, S. G., 185
Olejnik, S., 238
Olivardia, R., 258
Oliveira, A., 403
Oliver, B., 31
Olness, K., 63
Olsen, S., 277
Olson, C., 411
Olson, E., 72
Olszewski-Kubilius, P., 228
O'Malley, C., 180
Ondersma, S. J., 184
Onishi, K. H., 125
Onwuteaka-Philipsen, B., 457
Opfer, V. D., 276
Ophir, E., 373
Oppenheim, D., 7
Orbuch, T., 384
Orbuch, T. L., 342
Ordovas, J., 200
Oretti, R. G., 81
Orford, J., 393
Ormont, L. R., 315
Ornelas, I. J., 233
Orthel, H., 438
Ortiz, S. O., 225
Orwin, R., 263
Osborne, J. W., 434
Osofsky, J., 183
Ostendorf, F., 48
Osterholm, E. A., 60
Ostrov, J., 189, 191
Oswal, A., 256
O'Toole, M. L., 67
Otsuka, Y., 109
Ott, C., 410
Otto, K., 394
Ownby, R. L., 421
Owsley, C., 406
Oxford, M., 301
Oyserman, D., 218
Ozawa, M., 244

Pacala, J. T., 406
Pachana, N., 438
Padilla, I., 452
Padilla-Walker, L., 139
Padilla-Walker, L. M., 139
Paik, A., 360
Paisley, T. S., 67
Pajkrt, E., 63
Pajulo, M., 342
Palardy, G., 238
Palfai, T., 420
Palmore, E. B., 402, *402*
Paludi, M. A., 297
Palusci, V. J., 184
Pandina, R., 263
Pandolfo, P., 409
Pan, J., 262
Papadopoulos, T., 277
Papini, D. R., 13
Pappano, L., 422
Papp, T., 215
Parisse, C. C., 170
Park, A., 200
Park, C. L., 8
Parke, R., 237
Parke, R. D., 139
Parker, J. G., 241
Parker, K., 287
Parker, S. T., 17
Park, H., 275
Park, K. A., 179
Park, N., 431
Park, S., 275
Parks, C. A., 345
Parks, C. D., 425
Parlee, M. B., 333
Parnell, T. F., 183
Pascalis, O., 123
Pasman, H., 457
Passos, G. F., 409
Paterson, D. S., 448
Paterson, S., 117
Patterson, C., 245, 246
Patterson, C. J., 246, 345
Patton, G. C., 258
Patz, R. J., 183
Paulesu, E., 206
Paulhus, D. L., 348
Pauli-Pott, U., 144
Paul, K., 393
Pavlov, I. P., 83
Paxton, S., 260
Payne, A., 179
Peach, H. D., 296
Pearson, C., 260
Peck, R. C., 423
Pedersen, N. L., 11
Pedersen, S., 240, 367
Peeters, M., 239
Pelham, B., 313
Pellicano, E., 180
Peltzer, K., 299
Pengpid, S., 299
Penido, A., 5
Pennak, S., 371, 417
Penningroth, S., 377
Penninx, B., 408
Pennisi, E., 41
Peplau, L., 338
Peppe, S., 213
Pe-Pua, R., 289
Percy, K., 437
Pereira, A. C., 405
Pereira, G., 5
Perez-Brena, N. J., 289
Pérez-Ló, F. R., 361
Perfetti, C. A., 217
Perner, J., 121
Perreault, A., 460
Perreira, K. M., 233
Perrine, N. E., 295
Perron, M., 134
Perry, W. G., 319
Persaud, T. V. N., 58
Persson, G. E. B., 188
Pesetsky, D., 217
Petanjek, Z., 260
Peterman, K., 140
Petermann, F., 189
Peters, B., 461
Peters, E., 419
Petersen, A., 258
Peterson, C., 431
Peterson, D. M., 283
Peterson, J., 45
Peterson, M., 350, 392
Peterson, R. A., 30, 309
Petitto, L. A., 155, 214
Petkoska, J., 434
Petras, H., 189
Petrides, K., 275
Petrie, R., 357
Petrou, S., 77, 152
Pettit, J. W., 20
Pettit, R. W., 182
Pezdek, K., 165
Phelan, P., 295
Philippot, P., 189
Phillips, D., 454
Phillips, J., 406
Phillips, M. L., 371
Phillipson, C. R., 388
Phinney, J. S., 281, 285, 293
Phipps, M., 300
Piaget, J., 17, 113, 187, 267
Picard, A., 266
Picavet, H. S., 404
Pietromonaco, P. R., 200
Pietroski, P., 163
Pietsch, J. H., 451
Pilgrim, C., 263
Pillai, V., 300
Piller, I., 214
Pine, K., 171
Pine, K. J., 171
Ping, R., 163
Pink, J., 223, 371
Piolino, P., 419
Pipe, M., 165
Piper, W. E., 438, 463
Pittman, L. D., 245
Pizzigati, K., 185
Platsidou, M., 18
Platt, J. L., 414
Plienegger, J., 159
Plomin, R., 31, *44*, 49, 227, 285
Ploner, F., 72
Poest, C. A., 157
Polatti, F., 360
Polkinghorne, D. E., 27
Pollack, W., 280
Pollak, S., 155
Polyak, D., 138
Pomares, C. G., 109
Pomerantz, E., 182
Pomerantz, E. M., 182
Pomerleau, A., 144, 344
Pomeroy, W. B., 299
Pompili, M., 286
Ponirakis, A., 258
Ponton, L. E., 297
Poortman, A., 440
Pope, A. L., 340
Pope, H., 258
Porges, S. W., 109
Porter, M., 79
Posey, D., 425
Posner, J., 172
Poss, J. E., 19
Posthuma, D., 226
Poulin-Dubois, D., 136, 144
Poulton, R., 56
Powell, R., 420
Power, M., 71, 311
Powles, D. L., 62
Prater, L., 275
Prechtl, H., 159
Prechtl, H. F. R., 102
Preciado, P., 333
Prediger, R. D., 409
Premack, D., 136
Prentice, A., 357
Prescott, C., 56
Prescott, M., 450
Pressley, M., 271
Pretez, J. E., 323
Previti, D., 384
Prezbindowski, A. K., 27
Price, C. S., 32
Price, R., 52
Price, R. J. Jr., 67
Priddis, L., 139
Prigerson, H., 410
Prigerson, H. G., 455, 463
Prime, D. J., 358
Prince, M., 77
Prinstein, M. J., 239
Prior, J., 256
Proctor, C., 265
Proctor, R., 231

Prohaska, V., 235
Prokos, A. H., 389
Propper, C., 49
Prottas, D., 350
Puchalski, M., 110
Pulkkinen, L., 392
Pungello, E., 171
Puntambekar, S., 167
Purdy, S. C., 109
Pushkar, D., 428
Putney, N. M., 388
Pyke, K., 336

Qian, Z.-C., 336
Quas, J., 165
Quick, V., 311
Quilty, L., 45
Quinnan, E. J., 285
Quinn, M., 266
Quinn, P., 109, 124
Quintana, S. M., 175, 242

Raag, T., 176
Rabain-Jamin, J., 130
Rabin, R., 107
Rabkin, J., 449
Radke, H. M., 191
Radwan, S., 223
Raeburn, P., 260
Raeff, C., 289
Rafalovich, A., 66
Raggi, V., 207
Ragland, J., 19
Rakison, D., 113
Rakison, D. H., 113
Rakoczy, H., 427
Ramaswamy, V., 187
Ramey, C., 171
Ramsay, J. R., 334
Ramsay, L., 179
Rancourt, D., 239
Randall, W. L., 426
Rando, T. A., 464
Ranganath, C., 19
Rankin, J., 292
Rank, M. R., 432
Ransjö-Arvidson, A. B., 73
Rantanen, J., 392
Rao, V., 391
Rapee, R., 292
Rapin, I., 158
Rapkin, B. D., 428
Rapp, M., 429
Rapson, R. L., 334
Raschke, D., 179
Raspa, R., 20
Ratanachu-Ek, S., 105
Rattan, S. I. S., 411
Rattenborg, K., 343
Rautava, P., 67
Ravanipour, M., 412
Rawson Swan, K. T., 378
Ray, E., 139
Ray, L., 54
Rayner, K., 217
Rayner, R., 84
Razani, J., 225
Razani, L., 407
Raz, I., 201
Raz, N., 404
Raz, S., 70
Read, J. P., 264
Reale, B., 79
Rebok, G. W., 406
Reddy, V., 125
Redman, J., 117
Reed, R. K., 72
Reed, S., 362
Reeve, H. K., 22
Reeves, N. L., 414
Reichenberg, A., 76
Reichenberg, M., 212
Reichert, F., 259
Reid, J. D., 437
Reifman, A., 225
Reinisch, J. M., 299
Reinke, S. S., 48
Reiser, L. W., 257
Reis, S., 227
Reiss, D., 182
Reissland, N., 134
Rembis, M., 22
Remien, R., 449
Renier, L., 96
Renner, L., 390
Renzulli, J., 227
Reschly, D. J., 225, 226
Rescorla, L., 125
Resnick, B., 411
Resnick, M. D., 290
Resnikoff, D., 244
Ressner, J., 447
Resta, R., 46
Rethorst, C., 307
Reuter, E., 372
Reuters Health eLine, 16
Revonsuo, A., 155
Reyna, V. F., 273
Reynolds, A. J., 172
Reynolds, C. A., 428
Reynolds, C. F. III, 463
Reznik, I., 286
Rhoades, G., 340
Rhodes, R., 460
Rhule, D., 32
Ribordy, F., 121
Ricciardelli, L. A., 257, 259
Rice, F. P., 333
Richards, D., 211
Richards, M., 262
Richards, M. H., 293
Richards, M. P. M., 256
Richardson, A., 286
Richardson, G., 66
Richardson, G. A., 66
Richardson, K., 51, 53
Richert, R., 27, 131
Richmond-Rakerd, L. S., 48
Richtel, M., 248, 277, 295
Rick, S., 184
Riddell, R. P., 110
Ridder, E. M., 62
Rideout, V., 170, 171, 248, 277
Rieffe, C., 188
Riesch, S., 290
Riley, B., *44*
Riley, K. E., 8
Riley, L., 387
Rimm, A. A., 79
Rinaldi, C., 239
Rinaldi, C. M., 241
Ritchie, L., 431
Ritter, R. R., 455
Ritzen, E. M., 257
Rivera, S., 110
Robbins, L. B., 153
Robbins, M. W., *184*
Robb, M., 27, 131
Roberto, K. A., 440
Roberts, B., 377
Roberts, B. W., 381
Roberts, C., 262, 386
Roberts, D., 248, 277
Roberts, J., 142
Roberts, M. C., 257
Roberts, R. D., 223
Roberts, R. E., 170, 262
Roberts, S., 340, 387
Robinson, A. J., 123
Robinson, C., 182
Robinson, E., 213
Robinson, G. E., 52
Robinson, J. P., 394
Robins, R. W., 232, 279
Robitaille, A., 425
Rochat, P., 134, 135, 136
Roche, T., 247
RochLocours, L. A., 155
Rocke, C., 379
Rockney, R., 158
Rodgers, R., 260
Rodkin, P. C., 241
Rodnitzky, R. L., 19
Rodrigue, K., 404
Rodriguez, R., 440
Roecke, C., 437
Roeder, K., 53
Roehrig, M., 311
Roelofs, J., 139
Roeltgen, D., 46
Roepke, S. K., 437
Roeyers, H., 272
Roffwarg, H. P., 99, *99*
Rogan, J., 22
Rogers, A. G., 282
Rogers, C. R., 20
Rogers, S., 86
Roggeveen, A. B., 358
Rogoff, B., 7
Rogosch, F., 184
Rohleder, N., 313
Roll, S., 235
Rolls, E., 156
Romero-Moreno, R., 437
Romero, R. A., 265
Romero, S. T., 79
Ron, P., 439
Roos, S., 455
Roper Starch Worldwide, 341
Rose, A. J., 239, 241
Rosenbach, W. E., 271
Rosenberg, M., 244
Rosenblatt, P. C., 465
Rosen, R. C., 360
Rosenthal, G. E., 73
Rose, P., 342
Rose, R., 56
Rose, R. J., 8
Rose, S., 123, 165, 207, 211
Rose, S. A., 123
Rose, S. P., *156*
Ross, C. E., 386
Ross, D., 190
Rossetti, A. O., 70
Rossi, S., 127
Ross, J., 46
Ross, L., 48, 66
Rossman, I., 357
Rossouw, J. E., 362
Ross, S., 190
Rote, W. M., 290
Rothbart, M., 142
Rothbaum, F., 140, 289
Rothbaum, R., 67
Roth, C., 256
Roth, D., 117
Roth, W. T., 310
Rotigel, J. V., 229
Rotman, T., 344
Rounds, J., 348
Rovee-Collier, C., 109, 120, 121
Rovee-Collier, C. K., 121
Rowe, J. W., 408, 434
Rowley, S., 241
Rozalski, M., 226
Rubert, M., 421
Rubin, D. C., 419, *419*
Rubin, K. H., 292, 344
Rubinow, D. R., 362
Ruble, D., 176, 177
Ruble, D. N., 176, 177
Rudd, L. C., 172
Rudy, D., 247
Ruff, H. A., 110
Ruffman, T., 117
Runyan, D., 96
Rupp, D., 402
Rurup, M., 457
Rush, S. C., 276
Russell, D., 408
Russell, S. T., 233, 299, 300
Rust, J., 177
Rutter, M., 11, 296
Ryan, A. M., 241
Ryan, B. P., 206
Ryan, D., 246
Rye, D., 364

Saad, L., 342, *343*
Saar, M., 201
Sabbagh, M., 410
Sabeau-Jouannet, E., 130
Sack, C., 123
Sacks, M. H., 316
Sadava, S., 315
Sadeghi, N., 156
Sadeh, A., 97
Sadker, D., 326, 328, *328*
Sadker, M., 326, 328, *328*
Saenger, G., 49
Saewyc, E., 21
Saiegh-Haddad, E., 213
Saini, M., 240
Saito, Y., 450
Saklofske, D. H., 317
Sales, B. D., 35
Sallis, J., 201
Salthouse, T., 223, 370, 371, 374
Salthouse, T. A., 307, 371, 374, 405, 417, 418, 420
Saltzburg, S., 246
Salvatore, S., 406
Salzarulo, P., 98
Samet, J. H., 45
Sammel, M., 362
Sammons, M., 204
Sampson, P. D., 66
Sanchez, Y. M., 285
Sandberg, J. F., 244
Sander, C., 70
Sanderson, S., 200
Sanders, S., 299, 410
Sandis, E., 401
Sandomierski, M., 154
Sandoval, J., 226, 452
Sandrin, D., 110
Sang, B., 211
Sangree, W. H., 426
Sankar, J., 241
Sanna, L., 425
Sanson, A., 182
Santesso, D., 28
Santini, D. L., 64
Santomero, A., 171
Sapolsky, R., 247
Sapyla, J. J., 204
Saraswathi, T., 117
Sargent-Cox, K. A., 403
Sarlet, M., 328
Sassler, S., 340
Sauer, J., 166
Saul, S., 77
Saunders, J., 276
Savage-Rumbaugh, E. S., 129
Savina, C., 411
Savin-Williams, R., 338
Savin-Williams, R. C., 297, 338
Sawatzky, J., 411
Sawicki, M. A., 67
Sawyer, M. G., 285
Sawyer, R., 323
Saxon, T. F., 172
Sayer, A., 332
Sayil, M., 258
Scalembra, C., 77
Scarr, S., 53, 56, 173
Scelfo, J., 207
Schachar, R., 207
Schachner, D., 345
Schachter, E. P., 15
Schaeffer, C., 189
Schaie, K. W., 319, *320* , *371, 418*
Schaie, W. K., 371, 417
Schall, B., 109
Schaller, M., 166, 175
Scharrer, E., 177
Schatz, M., 168
Schaufeli, W., 393
Schechter, D., 139
Schecklmann, M., 259

Schecter, T., 65
Scheibner, G., 429
Scheier, M., 427, 455
Schellenbach, C. J., 32
Scheltens, P., 410
Schemo, D. J., 217, 228, 275
Scherf, K. S., 260
Schick, K., 165
Schieman, S., 349
Schildmann, E., 459
Schildmann, J., 459
Schiller, J. S., 203
Schipper, L., 22
Schirrer, J., 109
Schlechter, M., 232
Schlosser, F., 434
Schlottmann, A., 117
Schmidt, J., 275
Schmidt, L., 28
Schmidt, M., 67
Schmidt, M. E., 171
Schmidt, P. J., 362
Schmitt, E., 285
Schmitt, M., 384
Schmuckler, M., 116
Schnabelrauch, C. A., 284
Schneider, C. M., 386
Schneider, E. L., 401
Schneider, W., 271, 272
Schoenmakers, I., 357
Schofer, J. L., 203
Schofield, E., 123
Schoklitsch, A., 377
Scholte, R., 239
Schonert-Reichl, K. A., 239
Schoppe-Sullivan, S., 143, 344
Schreiber, G. B., 200
Schreiber, M., 358
Schuetze, P., 66
Schultz, A. H., 82
Schultz, J., 282
Schultz, R., 307
Schumer, F., 463
Schutt, R. K., 25
Schwartz, I. M., 298
Schwartz, M., 200
Schwartz, P., 272, 437
Schwartz, S., 245
Schwartz, S. H., 290
Schwarz, T. F., 266
Schweinhart, L. J., 172
Schweinsburg, A. D., 264, *264*
Schweinsburg, B. C., 264, *264*
Schwenkhagen, A., 361
Scollon, C. N., 382
Scott, A., 452
Scott, S. S., 261
Scott, W. D., 377
Scrimsher, S., 166, 167
Sears, R. R., 228
Seaton, E. K., 332
Seaton, S. E., 76
Sebanc, A., 179
Seçkin, G., 315
Sedgh, G., 62
Sedikides, C., 337
SEER, 368
Segal, J., 207
Segall, M. H., 270
Segal, N. L., 52
Segalowitz, S. J., 158
Segal, Z., 207
Seibert, A., 139
Seidenberg, M. S., 217
Seidman, S., 412
Seier, W. L., 166
Seiffge-Krenke, I., 7
Seiler, E., 426
Selfhout, M., 333
Seli, E., 61
Seligman, M., 286
Seligman, M. E. P., 239
Selig, S., 439
Sellers, R. M., 332
Semerci, Ç., 235
Sener, A., 434
Senju, A., 136
Seppa, N., 427
Serbin, L., 144, 390
Serretti, A., 44, 57
Servin, A., 145, 176
Sesser, S., 266
Settersten, R., 427
Sexton, M., 60
Seymour, J., 460
Shackelford, T., 22
Shaffer, L., 297
Shafto, C. L., 125
Shalev, I., 414
Shamloul, R., 362
Shanahan, L., 243
Shanahna, L., 243
Shangguan, F., 223
Shannon, J., 131
Shapiro, A., 345, 384
Shapiro, A. F., 344
Shapiro, H., 102, *103*
Shapiro, L., 217
Shapiro, L. R., 166
Share, H., 406
Sharf, R. S., 393, 394
Sharma, M. M., 109
Sharma, N., 105
Shaunessy, E., 228
Shaver, P., 337, 345
Shaver, P. R., 138, 337, 338
Shaw, B., 232
Shaw, D. S., 244
Shaw, M. L., 217
Shaw, P., *207*
Shaywitz, B. A., 217
Shea, J., 361
Shea, K. M., 78
Shear, K., 438, 463
Shek, D., 239, 277
Sheldon, K. M., 20
Shellenbarger, S., 145
Shenfield, S. D., 166
Sherman, D., 315
Sherman, E., 425
Sherman, S., 45
Shernoff, D., 275
Shields, C. C., 167, 212
Shields, M. K., 248
Shih, K., 343
Shi, J., 223
Shi, L., 179
Shimizu, M., 313
Shimura, Y., 130
Shiner, R., 142
Shin, H. B., 214
Shirley, L., 176
Shirtcliff, E., 285
Shi, X., 285
Shneidman, E. S., 455
Shopper, M., 246
Shore, R. J., 440
Shor, R., 183
Shpak, V., 367
Shreve, T., 233
Shumow, L., 172
Shurkin, J. N., 228
Shuster, L., 361
Shuster, T., 280
Shute, N., 73
Shweder, R. A., 380
Sieber, J. E., 35
Siegal, M., 162
Siegel, S., 62
Siegfried, N., 84
Siegler, R., 117, 271
Siegler, R. S., 117, 164, 165, 210, 211
Sierra, F., 413
Sigman, M., 123, 267
Sigmundsson, H., 405
Signorella, M., 177
Silenzio, V., 300
Silliman, E. R., 205
Silveira, C. M., 109
Silver, R. C., 437
Silverstein, L. B., 139
Silverthorn, P., 296
Simcock, G., 211
Simion, F., 83
Simmons, S. W., 73
Simonsick, E. M., 408
Simons, R., 330
Simons, S. H., 110
Simonton, D. K., 322, 392
Simpkins, S., 237, 333
Simpson, J. A., 337, 338
Simson, S. P., 420
Sinclair, D. A., 414
Singer, D. G., 26, 171
Singer, J. L., 26, 171
Singer, M. S., 349
Singh, P., 333
Singh, S., 298
Siniatchkin, M., 203
Sinnott, J. D., 318, 319, 320
Siu, A., 239
Skinner, B. F., 16, 128
Skinner, J. D., 105
Skinner, M., 51
Skoglund, R. R., 440
Skoog, T., 258
Skowronski, J., 419
Slack, K., 390
Slade, L., 117
Slade, M. D., 428
Slater, A., 83, 109
Sleeboom-Faulkner, M., 42
Slep, A. M., 183
Sloane, S., 136
Sloan, S., 107
Slone, M., 117
Slonje, R., 240
Small, B., 464
Small, G., 295
Small, G. W., 373
Smedley, A., 7
Smedley, B. D., 7, 364, 367
Smetana, J. G., 289, 290
Smith, B. L., 184, 332
Smith, C., 426
Smith, D., 449
Smith, G., 260
Smith, J. M., 437
Smith, M., 109
Smith, N. A., 86
Smith, O., 367
Smith, P. K., 240, 246, 388
Smith, R. A., 368
Smith, R. J., 205
Smith, R. S., 186
Smith, S., 407
Smith, V., 239
Sneed, J., 332
Snidman, N., 55
Snijders, T. B., 333
Snowdon, D. A., 410
Snyder, L. B., 8
Snyder, P., 66
Soares, C., 362
Soderstrom, M., 130
Solarz, A. L., 32
Solberg, P., 405
Soldo, B. J., 388
Solem, P., 402
Solity, J., 217
Solomon, S., 240
Solomon, W., 436
Somerset, W., 362
Somerville, L. H., 261
Sonne, J. L., 122
Sonnen, J., 413
Sonnentag, S., 393
Sontag, S., 404
Sonuga-Barke, E., 440
Sosa, B. B., 166
Soska, K., 108
Sosunov, A. A., 405
Sousa, D. L., 217
Sowell, E. R., 260, *261*, 307
Sparks, M. B., 410
Sparrow, J. D., 185
Spear, L., 258
Spear, L. P., 66
Spearman, C., 222
Spear, N. E., 66
Spear, P. D., 357
Spehar, B., 109
Spelke, E. S., 111, 164
Spence, A. P., 357
Spencer, M. B., 293
Spencer, P. E., 205
Spence, S. H., 285, 384
Sperduti, M., 419
Spieker, S., 139
Spiker, D., 76
Spinath, F. M., 381
Spohr, H. L., 66
Spörer, N., 212
Spraggins, R. E., 432
Sprecher, S., 336
Sprott, R., 278
Squeglia, L. M., 264
Srivastava, S., 377, 381
Sroufe, L. A., 133, 181
Stacey, B. G., 349
Stalvey, B., 406
Stanley, S., 340
Stanton, A., 314
Starr, L., 441
Starr, R. H., 245
State, M., 44
Stattin, H., 333
Stattin, M., 434
Staudinger, U., 426
Staudinger, U. M., 11
Staunton, H., 98
Stearns, E., 278
Stedman, L. C., 275
Steele, C. J., 10, 96
Steele, C. M., 329
Stefanatos, G., 46
Steffen, V. J., 348
Steihaug, S., 450
Steinberg, L., 261, 262, 276, 290, 295
Stein, D., 260
Steiner, J. E., 85, 109
Steiner, P., 295
Steinhausen, H. C., 66
Stein, J. H., 257
Stein, P., 366
Stein, Z., 49
Stenberg, G., 135
Stephens, C., 362, 434
Steri, A. O., 111
Sternberg, J., 224, 225, 321
Sternberg, R., 224, 321, 334
Sternberg, R. J., 220, 221, 224, 321, 323, 333, 427
Stern, E., 372
Stern, L., 105
Sterns, H. L., 364
Stevens, J., 307
Stevens, N., 333, 438
Stevenson, J., 60, 71, 76, 208
Stevenson, M., 389, 440
Stevens, W., 420
Stewart, A., 226, 463
Stewart, A. J., 379, 386
Stewart, M., 107
Stice, E., 258
Stiffman, A., 21
Stikes, R., 71
Stiles, J., 96
Stinchfield, R. D., 277
Stipp, S., 414
Stix, G., 409
Stockdale, M. S., 349
Stoll, S., 200
Stolzenberg, S., 165
Stone, A. A., 381
Storfer, M., 53
Story, M., 200
Stout, H., 295
Straus, M. A., 183, 184, 389
Strauss, J. R., 361, 362
Streissguth, A., 66
Strelau, J., 143
Strength, J., 448
Striano, T., 135

Strobel, A., 19
Stroebe, M. S., 464
Strohl, M., 411
Strohmeier, A., 159
Stromswold, K., 129
Strough, J., 240
Strube, M., 367
Stubblefield, P., 73
Sturm, L., 427
Stutzer, A., 341
Subotnik, R., 31
Suenaga, Y., 372
Suetta, C., 404
Sugarman, D. B., 184
Sugarman, S., 270
Suinn, R. M., 314
Suitor, J. J., 294, *294*
Sullivan, M., 132
Sullivan, M. W., 121
Sullivan, Q., 336
Suls, J. M., 175
Sumartojo, E., 267
Sunderman, G. L., 276
Sundsoy, P., 295
Sun, L. H., 75
Super, C. M., 99, 104
Supple, A., 289
Suro, R., 336
Susman, E., 258
Susser, M., 49
Sussman, D., 300
Sutherland, R., 165
Sutton, P. D., 42
Swaim, R., 357, 404
Swain, J., 312
Swanson, L. A., 130
Swee-Hin, T., 219
Sweeney, J. A., 260
Sweet, J., 385
Swiatek, M., 228
Swingley, D., 119, 130
Syed, M., 7
Syme, S. L., 364, 367
Szaflarski, J. P., 155
Szarko, J., 229

Tabares, A., 345
Tabares, J., 225
Tabár, L., 368
Taff, S. A., 278
Tajfel, H., 232
Takahashi, K., 140
Takala, M., 212
Takeuchi, D., 246
Tallandini, M., 77
Tamis-LeMonda, C., 131
Tamis-LeMonda, C. S., 117, 139, 171
Tanaka, J., *373*
Tanaka, K., 106, 130
Tanaka, M. L., 373
Tang, C., 79
Tangney, J., 26
Tango, T., 361
Tangri, S., 392
Tang, W. R., 460
Tang, Z., 263
Tan, H., 77
Tanner, E., 104
Tanner, J., 255
Tanner, J. L., 304, 330
Tanner, J. M., *257*
Tanzi, R. E., 412
Tappan, M. B., 166, 236
Tardiff, K., 450
Tardif, T., 127
Tarin, D., 414
Taris, T., 393
Tasker, F., 299
Tatarelli, R., 286
Tate, J. D., 293
Tattersall, M., 69
Tatum, B., 232, 233
Taveras, E. M., 105
Tavernise, S., 342
Taylor, A., 232
Taylor, B., 146, 172
Taylor, D. M., 246
Taylor, J. M., 235
Taylor, M. G., 176
Taylor, R. J., 411
Taylor, R. L., 271
Taylor, S., 314, 315
Taylor, S. E., 313, 374, 450
Taylor, T., 99
Teerikangas, O. M., 144
Teitelbaum, J., 447
Tellegen, A., 54, *54*
Teller, D., 83
Templeton, J., 254
Tenenbaum, J. B., 130
ten Kroode, H. F., 48
Tepper, I., 259
Terman, D. L., 225
Terman, L. M., 228
Terracciano, A., 380, 422
Terry, D., 80
Terzidou, V., 69
Terzioglu, R., 434
Tessier, F., 414
Tessor, A., 175
Teutsch, C., 453
Thach, B., 100
Thach, B. T., 99
Tharp, R. G., 166
Thelen, E., 97
Theokas, C., 206
Thies, W., 409
Thivel, D., 259
Thobaben, M., 264
Thøgersen, J., 290
Thomae, H., 426
Thoman, E. B., 97, *98*
Thomas, A., 143, 144
Thomas, C., 296
Thomas, E. B., 98
Thomas, H., 85, 123
Thomas, P., 403, 409, 410
Thomas, R. M., 12
Thomas, S. G., 384
Thomas, V., 392
Thompson, C., 350
Thompson, D. M., 375
Thompson, E. G., 448
Thompson, P. M., 260, 307
Thompson, R. A., 139, 231
Thompson, S. J., 276
Thompson, W. W., 32
Thomsen, L., 136
Thoms, K. M., 412
Thomson, A., 63
Thomson, D., 228
Thöni, A., 72
Thornberry, T. P., 296
Thorne, B., 240
Thornton, J., 318
Thornton, R., 213
Thorvaldsson, V., 450
Thurlow, M. L., 276
Tikotzky, L., 97
Time, 419
Timmermans, S., 74
Tincoff, R., 125
Tinsley, B., 267
Tobin, J. J., 173
Todd, B., 155
Toga, A. W., 260, 307
Tolan, P. H., 204
Toldson, I. A., 276
Tomasello, M., 170
Tomasian, J., 239
Tomblin, J. B., 67
Tomlinson, M., 140
Tomlinson, T., 439
Tompson, M., 81
Tongsong, T., 60
Toomey, R. B., 300
Toporek, R. L., 35
Torges, C., 463
Torvaldsen, S., 73
Toscano, J. C., 126
Trachtenberg, F. L., 448
Tracy, M., 247
Trainor, L., 28
Trainor, L. J., 86, 123
Trapnell, P. D., 348
Trehub, S. E., 109
Trelease, J., 280
Tremblay, A., 311
Tremblay, R. E., 189
Triche, E. W., 66
Trickett, P. K., 185
Trinidad, D. R., 265
Trisel, B., 79
Tronick, E. Z., 34
Tropp, L., 232, 293
Trotter, A., 277
Trzesniewski, K. H., 232, 279
Tsang, J., 31
Tsapelas, I., 384
Tse, T., 431
Tucker-Drob, E., 223, 371
Tucker-Drob, E. M., 275
Tucker, J., 265
Tudge, J., 166, 167
Tuerk, A. S., 121
Tulsky, D. S., 220
Tulving, E., 375
Tun, P. A., 407
Turiel, E., 235
Turkheimer, E., 226, 258
Turk, J., 45
Turnbull, D., 72
Turner-Bowker, D. M., 177
Turner, J. C., 232
Turner, J. S., 450
Turney, K., 233
Turton, P., 80
Twardosz, S., 184
Twenge, J. M., 232
Tyne, K., 368
Tynes, D. M., 121
Tyre, P., 207, 393
Tzourio- Mazoyer, N., 28

Uçanok, Z., 258
Uchikoshi, Y., 171
Ueno, K., 130
Uhlenberg, P., 436
Ujiie, T., 133
Umana-Taylor, A., 219, 232
Umañ-Taylor, A. J., 232, 289
Umberson, D. J., 384
Underwood, M., 35
Unger, R., 144, 257, 348, 349, 404, 437
Unger, R. K., 280
United Nations, 63
United Nations Population Division, 401, *401*
United Nations Statistics Division, 70
University of Akron, 32
Unvä-Moberg, K., 73
Updegraff, K. A., 243, 279, 289
Uphold-Carrier, H., 244
Urberg, K., 263
Urquidi, V., 414
Urquiza, A., 183
U.S. Bureau of Labor Statistics, 348
U. S. Bureau of the Census, 145, *214,* 217, *218,* 245, 285, 324, 340, *340,* 345, *349,* 413
U.S. Department of Education, 325
U.S. Department of Health and Human Services, Administration on Children Youth and Families, *183*
Uttley, L., 109
Utz, R., 244
Uwaydat, S., 408
Uylings, H., 10, 96
Uylings, H. B. M., 260
Uzelac, S., 272

Vaccaro, B., 135
Vacha-Haase, T., 428
Vagenas, D., 438
Vaillant, C. O., 231, 346
Vaillant, G. E., 231, 346, 378
Vaish, A., 135
Vaizey, C. J., 69
Valente, S. M., 299
Valenti, C., 109
Valerio, C., 277
Valiente, C., 182
Valkonen, T., 463
Valles, N., 189
Van Balen, F. (2005)., 42
van Dam, K., 316
Vandell, D., 140
Vandell, D. L., 146, 172, 237
Vandello, J., 391
van den Berg, P., 280
van den Hoonaard, D. K., 437
van den Wittenboer, G. L. H., 344
van der Heide, A., 457
van der Mark, I., 136
van der Zwaag, B., 56
Vandewater, E., 170, 171
Vandewater, E. A., 379
van Erp, T. G. M., 56
van Gundy, K., 349
van Haren, N. M., 56
van Heugten, M., 109
van Horn, J., 393
Vanlierde, A., 96
van Lier, P., 292
Van Marle, K., 120
Van Tassel-Baska, J., 281
van Teijlingen, E., 79
van Tilburg, T. G., 440
van't Spijker, A., 48
Vaquera, E., 241
Vartanian, L. R., 273
Vastfjall, D., 419
Vaughan, V., 42
Vaughn, S. S., 206
Vazquez, A., 343
Vellutino, F. R., 217
Vendemia, J. C., 341
Veneziano, R., 139
Ventura, J. A., 300
Ventura, S. J., 42
Veras, R. P., 358
Vereijken, C. M., 140
Verhoeven, M., 285
Verhulst, S. J., 122
Verkuyten, M., 281
Vernon-Feagans, L., 343
Vernon, J. A., 402
Vernon, P., 54
Verny, T. R., 67
Verschueren, K., 175
Veselka, L., 53
Vichi, M., 286
Vidaver, R. M., 366
Viechtbauer, W., 381
Vilhjalmsson, R., 202
Villarosa, L., 300, 342
Vincent, J. A., 388
Vingolo, E. M., 406
Vink, D., 408
Virmani, E., 231
Viswanathan, M., 214
Vitaro, F., 240
Vitousek, K. M., 260
Viviani, V., 108
Vizmanos, B., 256
Vlahov, D., 8, 450
Vodanovich, S., 402
Vohringer, P. A., 204
Volker, S., 134
Vollmann, J., 62
Vollnik, T., 240
von Eye, A., 186
von Kluge, S., 60
von Wedel, H., 406
Vorgan, G., 295
Votruba-Drzal, E., 172
Vouloumanos, A., 125
Vragovic, O., 73
Vyas, S., 218
Vygotsky, L. S., 21, 166, 212, 224

Wachs, T. D., 49
Wada, A., 56
Wade, T. D., 260
Waggoner, R., 130
Wagner, A. D., 373
Wagner, R. K., 321
Wahlin, T., 48
Waisbren, S. E., 43
Wakefield, A., 67
Wake, M., 258
Walch, T., 260
Walden, T., 86, 117
Waldfogel, J., 80
Waldrop, D. P., 452
Walker-Andrews, A., 111
Walker, C., 73
Walker, J., 406
Walker, L. E., 389
Walker, W., 419
Walker, W. A., 65
Wallace, R. B., 408
Wallerstein, J., 244
Wallerstein, J. S., 384
Wall, M., 311
Walster, E., 334
Walters, A., 364
Walters, E., *223*
Walter, T., 461
Walton, K. E., 381
Wamba, N. G., 275
Wang, H. J., 259
Wang, L., 357, 404, 405
Wang, Q., 175, 182
Wang, S.-H., 117
Wardell, J. D., 264
Ward, J. V., 235
Wardle, J., 200
Ward, L. M., 358
Ward, R. A., 428
Ward, T. J., 203
Warkentin, V., 135
Warnock, F., 110
Warren, K., 66
Warshak, R. A., 386
Wartella, E., 27, 131, 170, 171
Wasserman, J. D., 220
Waterhouse, J. M., 97
Waterland, R. A., 52
Waterman, A. S., 282
Waters, L., 393
Watling, D., 155
Watson, H. J., 260
Watson, J. B., 15, 16, 23, 84
Watts-English, T., 184
Weaver, S., 386
Weber, A., 383
Webster, P. S., 342
Wechsler, D., 220
Wechsler, H., 264, *264*
Weidman, R., 438, 463
Weikart, D. P., 172
Wei, L., 334
Weinberger, D. R., 261
Weinberg, M. S., 298
Weinberg, R. A., 31, 71
Weinstock, H., *266*
Weintraub, E. S., 32
Weissberger, G. H., 409
Weiss, L., 221
Weissman, A. S., 207
Weissman, D., 154
Weiss, R., 201, 225
Weisz, A., 236
Weisz, B., 63
Weitzman, E., 264
Welkley, D. L., 246
Wellings, K., 299
Wellman, H., 136, 180
Wellman, H. M., 180
Wells, B., 213
Wells, J., 259
Wells, R., 228
Welsh, T., 141
Weng, C., 330
Werker, J. F., 130
Werner, E., 142
Werner, E. E., 104, 186, 317
Werner, L. A., 109
Wertsch, J. V., 167
Wessells, R. J., 414
West, A., 385
Westerhausen, R., 119
Westerhof, G., 425, 438
Westerhof, G. J., 425
Westermann, G., 156
West, J. H., 265
West, J. R., 227
Westra, T., 104
Wethington, E., 379
Wexler, B., 11
Weyandt, L., 207
Whalen, C. K., 206
Whalen, D., 126
Whaley, S., 67
Wheaton, B., 313
Wheeldon, L. R., 169
Wheeler, S., 448
Whishaw, I. Q., 103
Whitaker, R. C., 200
Whitbourne, S. K., 332, 402, 404, 405, 408, 414, 428
Whitebread, D., 179
White, H., 263
White, K., 72, 108
White, K. R., 205
Whitelaw, E., 51
Whiteman, S. D., 243
Whitham, E. A., 204
Whiting, B. B., 240
Whiting, J., 390
Whitney, M. P., *98*
Whittingham, K., 139
Whyte, M. K., 334
Wickelgren, W. A., 226
Widaman, K., 43
Widdicombe, S., 402
Widom, C. S., 183
Widström, A., 62
Widström, A. M., 73
Wiefferink, C., 188
Wielgosz, A. T., 367
Wiesel, T. N., 108
Wiesmann, U., 334
Wiggins, M., 408
Wilcox, A., 80
Wilcox, A. J., 78
Wilcox, H. C., 286
Wilcox, S., 366
Wilcox, T., 111
Wildberger, S., 63
Wiley, T. L., 358
Wilfond, B., 48
Wilhelm, B., 388
Wilkening, F., 117
Wilkes, S., 60
Willford, J., 66
Willheim, E., 139
Williams, A., 5
Williams, B., 450, 457
Williams, J., 66, 86
Williams, J. R., 157
Williams, K., 385
Williams, M. A., 69
Williams, R. A., 35
Williams, T., 276
Williams, W. M., 327
Willis, S., 373
Willis, S. L., 319, 325, 371, 379, 417
Willott, J., 406
Wills, T., 265
Wilson, B. L., 78
Wilson, C., 449
Wilson, G. T., 260
Wilson, J. F., 350, 392
Wilson, L., 246
Wilson, L. B., 420
Wilson, M. N., 357
Wilson, P., 171
Wilson, S. L., 28
Winans, D., 276
Winder, S., 73
Wines, M., 12
Winger, G., 63
Wingfield, A., 407
Winsler, A., 167, 170
Winslow, E. B., 244
Wintemute, G., 286
Winterich, J., 361
Winters, K. C., 277
Wipfli, B., 307
Wisborg, K., 67
Wisdom, J. P., 286
Wismer Fries, A., 155
Witt, D. D., 157
Wittenborn, A., 245
Witvliet, M., 292
Woelfle, J. F., 256
Wolak, J., 277
Wolf, D., 437
Wolfe, W., 411
Wolfson, A. R., 262
Wolinsky, F., 431
Wong, J., 225
Wong, M., 295
Woodburn, E., 133
Wood, D., 180
Woodhouse, S. S., 294
Wood, L., 248
Wood, R., 42
Wood, S., 228
Woods, J. H., 63
Woodspring, N., 402
Woods, R., 239
Wood, W., 336
Worell, J., 257
World Bank, 342
World Factbook, 75, *75*, 415
World Health Organization, 83
Worrell, F., 229
Wortman, C. B., 437, 463, 464
Wright, J. C., 171, 177
Wright, M., 286
Wright, M. F., 292
Wright, R., 34
Wright, S., 232
Wroolie, T., 362
Wrosch, C., 427
Wu, B., 291
Wu, D. Y. H., 173
Wu, L., 448
Wu, M., 79
Wu, P., 182, 286
Wyer, R., 271
Wynn, K., 120, 136
Wyra, M., 211
Wyrwich, K., 431

Xiaohe, X., 334
Xing, X., 286

Yagenska, O., 367
Yagensky, A., 367
Yagmurlu, B., 182
Yakoob, M. Y., 200
Yamaguchi, M. K., 109
Yaman, A., 182
Yang, C., 182
Yang, C. D., 129
Yang, R., 281
Yang, X., 386
Yang, Y., 429
Yan, J., 357
Yan, T., 439
Yan, Z., 18
Yardley, J., 81
Yasunaga, A., 405
Yee, C., 314
Yeh, C., 181
Yell, M. L., 226
Yeo, G., 256
Yetkin, C. E., 61
Yildiz, O., 404
Yim, I., 81
Yinger, J., 217
Yin, L., 76
Yip, L., 79
Yip, T., 284, 332
Yodanis, C. L., 389
Yonker, J. E., 284
Yoon, H., 244
Yoo, S. H., 7
York, E., 326
York, G. S., 460
Yoshikawa, H., 233
Yoshinaga-Itano, C., 205
You, J.-I., 333
Young, G., 447
Young, J., 414
Young, K., 183
Young, K. N., 206
Young, S., 263
Youniss, J., 291
Yousafzai, A. K., 200
Yuan, A., 257
Yu, A. P., 157
Yu, C., 143
Yueh, B., 406
Yu, H. C., 295
Yu, M., 21

Zacchilli, T. L., 277
Zafeiriou, D. I., 102
Zahn-Waxler, C., 285
Zaidman-Zait, A., 239
Zakar, T., 69
Zalenski, R., 20
Zalsman, G., 285
Zampi, C., 98
Zanjani, F. A. K., 319
Zarit, S. H., 437
Zauszniewski, J. A., 15
Zdzieborski, D., 154
Zea, M. C., 309
Zeanah, C., 96
Zeedyk, M., 86
Zehnder, S., 177
Zeiders, K. H., 232
Zelazo, P., 116
Zelazo, P. D., 210
Zelazo, P. R., 101, *134*
Zemach, I., 83
Zeruth, J., 276
Zhang, B., 455
Zhang, J., 166, 262
Zhang, W., 289
Zhang, X., 67
Zhang, Z., 45
Zhe, C., 165
Zheng, X., 7
Zheng, Y., 243
Zhu, J., 221
Zhu, X. D., 414
Ziegler, D., 404
Ziegler, M., 223
Zigler, E. F., 173
Zimmer-Gembeck, M. J., 297
Zimmerman, F., 191
Zimmerman, J., 431
Zinni, D., 434
Zirkel, S., 218
Zisook, S., 438, 463
Zolotor, A., 183
Zubenko, G. S., 463
Zuberi, J., 65
Zuckerman, G., 166
Zuckerman, M., 53
Zwelling, E., 72

Subject Index

Note: Page numbers in *italics* indicate tables and illustrations.

Abortion, 62
Abstract modeling, 187
Abuse. *See specific types*
Academic disidentification, 329
Acceleration, 228
Acceptance, dying stage, 454
Accommodation, 17, 113
Achievement testing, 276
Achieving stage, of development, 319
Acquisitive stage, of development, 319
Active lifespan, 411
Activity level, 142
Activity theory, 428
Acute battering incident, 389
Adaptation, widowhood stage, 438
Addictive drugs, 264
ADHD. *See* Attention deficit hyperactivity disorder (ADHD)
Adolescence
  cognitive development, 269–273
  dating, 297
  death in, 449
  defined, 254
  identity questioning, 279–287
  overview, 252–253
  physical maturation, 254–262
  pregnancy in, 300–301
  psychological disorders in, 285–287
  relationships, 288–296
  school performance, 274–278
  sexual behavior, 297–299
  threats to well-being, 262–267
Adolescent egocentrism, 272–273
Adoption, 51
Adult day-care facilities, 430
Adulthood. *See also* Early adulthood; Late adulthood; Middle adulthood
  developmental tasks of, *331*
Advice, expert, 34
Affordances, 110
Age
  college attendance and, 325
  creativity and, *322,* 322–323
  discrimination, 433–434
  frequency of sexual intercourse and, *360*
  of mother, 63–65
  wisdom and, 425–427
Age-graded influences, 8
Ageism, 401–402
Agentic professions, 348
Age of viability, 76
Age-related macular degeneration (AMD), 406
Age stratification theories, 425
Aggression, preschoolers, 187–192
Aging
  approaches to, 412–414
  coping with, 424–425
  illness and, 410–411
  internal, 404–405
  myth and reality, 401–402, *403*
  outward signs of, 403–404
  personality development and, 421–429
  postponing, 414–415
  successful, 427–429
AIDS (acquired immune deficiency syndrome), 65, 267
Ainsworth Strange Situation, 137–138
Alcohol
  mother's use of, 66–67
Alcoholics, 264
Alleles, 43
Alzheimer's disease, *45,* 409–410
Ambivalent attachment pattern, 138
Americans with Disabilities Act (1990), 311
Amniocentesis, 47, *47*
Anal stage, 13
Androgens, 144, 176, 255
Androgynous, 177
Anecdotal evidence, 34
Anesthesia, for childbirth, 73
Anger, dying stage, 453–454
Anorexia nervosa, 259–260
Anoxia, 70
Antidepressants, children and, 204
Apgar scale, 70
Applied research, 31
Arthritis, 408
Artificial insemination, 60
Assimilation, 17, 113
Assisted living, 430
Assisted suicide, 457
Associated factors, 26
Associative play, 179
Attachment, 137–139, 337–338
Attention deficit hyperactivity disorder (ADHD), 206–208
Auditory impairments, 205
Authoritarian parents, 187
Authoritative parents, 181, 182, 232
Autism, 18, 180
Autobiographical memory, 165, 419
Automatization, 120
Autonomous cooperation stage, 187
Autonomy, in adolescence, 288–289
Autonomy-*versus*-shame-and-doubt stage, *14,* 142
Autostimulation, 99
Avoidant attachment pattern, 138
Awake states, *98*
Axon, 94

Babbling, 125
Babinski reflex, *101*
Back-to-sleep guideline, 99
Bargaining, dying stage, 454
Bayley Scales of Infant Development, *122,* 123–124
Beginnings of thought, *114,* 116
Behavior
  modification, 16
  moral, 235
  relatedness and, 50–52
  teaching, 181–182
Behavioral genetics, 22, 43–45
Behavioral perspective, 15–17
Behavioral states, *98*
Bell curves, intelligence, 225
Benevolent sexism, 328
Bereavement, 462–465
  defined, 462
Beta amyloid precursor protein, 409
Bicultural identity, 218–219, 285
"Big Five" personality traits, 380–381, 422
Bilingual education, 213–215
Bilingualism, middle childhood, 214
Binet's Intelligence Test, 220–224
Binge drinking, 264
Binge eating, 259
Bioecological approach, 20–21
Biological factors, memory changes and, 420
Bionic solution, 414
Birth
  approaches to, 71–73
  from fetus to neonate, 70–71
  labor, 69–70
Birth complications
  Cesarean deliveries, 78–79
  infant mortality and still birth, 79–80
  overview, 75
  postmature babies, 78
  postpartum depression, 81
  preterm babies, 76–78
Bisexuality, adolescence, 299–300
Blastocyst, 59
Blended families, 245
Blindness, 205
Bodily kinesthetic intelligence, *223*
Body growth
  adolescence, 254–262
  early adulthood, 306–309
  infancy, 92–100
  middle adulthood, 356–358
  middle childhood, 198–201
  preschool years, 152–154
Body image
  adolescence, 257
Body proportions, *60,* 94
Body transcendence *versus* body preoccupation, 423
Bonding, 71
Boomerang children, 387–388
Bottlefeeding, *vs.* breastfeeding, 106–107
Boys
  depression and, 285
  early *vs.* late maturation in, 257–258
  puberty in, 257
  self-esteem in, 280
Bradley method, 72
Brain death, 447
Brain development
  ADHD and, *207*
Brain, development and, 94–97
Brain growth
  adolescence, 260–262
  preschool years, 155–156
Brain scans, Alzheimer's patients, *410*
Braxton-Hicks contractions, 69
Brazelton Neonatal Behavior Assessment Scale (NBAS), 103
Breastfeeding, *vs.* bottlefeeding, 106–107
Breech position, 79
Bulimia, 259–260
Bullying, middle childhood, 240
Burnout, 392–393

Calories, restricting, 414
Cancer, 367–368
Career consolidating, 346
Careers
  early adulthood, 346–350
  middle adulthood, 392, 393–394
Case studies, 27–28
Cataracts, 406
Catecholamines, 79
Causal relationships, 25
Cause and effect, 29–31
Centration, 160
Cephalocaudal principle, 93
Cerebellum, 156
Cerebral cortex, 96, 156
Cervix, 69
Cesarean deliveries, 78–79
Change, measurement of, 31–33
Chemotherapy, 367
Chiao shun, 182
Chicken pox, 65
Child abuse, 183–185
Child-care
  centers, 171–172
  infant, 145–147
  providers, selection of, 147
Childhood, death in, 448–449
Children, late adulthood, 439
Chlamydia, 266–267
Chorionic villus sampling (CVS), 47
Chromosomal abnormality, *61*
Chromosomes, 40–41
Chronic disease, middle adulthood and, 364
Chronological age, 220–221
Chronosystems, 21
Cilia, 358
Circular reactions, *114,* 115–116
Circumcision, 83–84
Classical conditioning, 15, 84–85
Cliques, adolescence, 292
Cocaine, 66
Code-based approaches to reading, 217
Cognitive approaches, preschool years, 177–178, 192
Cognitive development, *6*
  adolescence, 269–273
  brain growth and, 155–156
  defined, 5
  early adulthood, 317–329
  infancy, 118–124, 131
  late adulthood, 416–421
  middle adulthood, 369–375
  middle childhood, 208
  overview, 112
  preschool years, 160–164
Cognitive-developmental theory, 177
Cognitive neuroscience approaches, 18–19
Cognitive perspective, 17–19, *23*
Cohabitation, 339–341
Cohort, defined, 8, 33
Cohort effects, 8–9, 370, 417
Collagen, 403
Collectivism, 21
Collectivistic orientation, 175
College
  early adulthood, 323–329
  late adulthood, 420
Commitment, adolescent development, 282
Communal professions, 348
Companionate grandparents, 388
Companionate love, 334
Competence, during middle adulthood, 371–372
Compliant agents, 136
Complicated grief, 438, 463
Componential aspects of intelligence, 224, 321
Comprehension, linguistic, 125, *126*
Computerized axial tomography (CAT) scan, 28
Conception, *41,* 58
Concrete operational thought, 209–210
Conflict, marital, 341–342
Conformity, adolescence, 295
Conjunctive stage, 284
Conservation, 161, *162*
Conservation training, 210
Constructive play, 179
Consummate love, 335, *335*
Contextual components of intelligence, 224, 321
Contextual perspective, 20–22, *23*
Continuing-care community, 430
Continuity theory, 428
Continuous change, 9

Control group, 29
Control strategies, 211
Controversial adolescents, 294
Conventional morality, *234,* 235
Conversational skills, middle childhood, 213
Cooperative learning, 212
Cooperative play, 179
Coordination of secondary circular reactions, *114,* 115
Coparenting teams, 344
Coping, defined, 314
Coping with stress, 314–317
Coregulation, 243
Coronary heart disease, 366–367
Corpus callosum, 155, *185*
Correlational research, 26–29
Correlation coefficient, 26–28
Corticotropin-releasing hormone (CRH), 69
Creativity, early adulthood, 322–323
CRH. *See* Corticotropin-releasing hormone (CRH)
Crisis, adolescent development, 281–282
Crisis intervention education, 452
Critical period, 10
Cross-race friendships, 241–242
Cross-sectional research, 33
Cross-sectional studies, 33, 370
Crowds, adolescence, 292
Crystallized intelligence, 223, 370–371
C-sections. *See* Cesarean deliveries
Cultural assimilation model, 217–218, 284
Cultural tools, 167
Culture
  attachment and, 140
  autonomy and, 289
  childhood growth and, 199
  childrearing practices and, 182
  cognitive development and, 210
  conception of death and, 451
  defined, 219
  development and, 7
  differences in grieving, 461
  education and, 219
  health care and, 309
  infant-directed speech and, 130
  infant mortality and, 80
  influence on development, 6, 7, 17–18
  middle age and, 380
  morality and, 235
  motor development and, 104
  parent-child conflicts during adolescence and, 291
  physical arousal and, 55
  reflexes and, 101–102
  treatment of those in late adulthood and, 426
  violence and, 390–391
Cyberspace, adolescence and, 276–277
Cycle of violence hypothesis, 183–184, 390

Daily life, of late adulthood, 430–434
Dating, adolescence, 297
Death
  in adolescence, 449
  causes and reactions, 447–451
  choosing, 446
  confronting, 453–460
  defining, 446–447
  differing conceptions of, 451
  education, 451–452
  grief and bereavement, 460–465
  in infancy and childhood, 448–449
  in late adulthood, 450
  in middle adulthood, 450
  overview, 444–445
  of spouse, 437–438
  in young adulthood, 449–450
Death education for members of helping professions, 452
Death penalty, adolescents and, 261–262
Decentering, 209
Decision/commitment component, 334
Defended personalities, 425
Defensive coping, 315
Dementia, 408
Demographics
  of higher education, 324
  of late adulthood, 401
Dendrites, 94
Denial, dying stage, 453
Dependent variable, 29
Depression
  adolescent, 285–286
  dying stage, 454
  pregnancy and, 65
Depth perception, 108
DES (diethylstilbestrol), 65
Development. *See also specific types, e.g., cognitive development, and specific stages, e.g., late adulthood*
  influence of culture, ethnicity, and race on, 7
  nature *vs.* nurture, 9–12, 50–52
Developmental change, 31–33
Developmental norms, 103–104
Developmental quotient (DQ), 122
Developmental research, 31–33
Developmental stake, 439
Developmental tasks, adulthood, 331
Development of self, 135
Deviation IQ scores, 221
Dialectical thinking, 319
Diaries, research and, 28
Diet, of mother, 63
Difficult babies, 143
Digital divide, 277
Disabilities, early adulthood, 311–312
Discipline, 181–182, *185*
Discontinuous change, 10
Discrimination, gender, 348–349
Disenchantment stage, retirement, 433–434
Disengagement theory, 427
Disintegrated personalities, 424
Disorganized-disoriented attachment pattern, 138
Disorganized personalities, 424
Diversity, 217–218
Division of labor, marriage and, *344*
Divorce
  late adulthood, 436
  middle adulthood, 384–386
  in middle childhood, 244–245
  statistics, 340, 341, *341*
Dizygotic twins, 42, 52
DNA (deoxyribonucleic acid), 41
Domestic violence, 389–391
Dominance hierarchy, 241
Dominant characteristics, 43
Dominant trait, 43
Do Not Resuscitate (DNR), 456–459
Double standard, 298, 404
Doula, 72
Down syndrome, 45, 64, 227
Drugs, illegal, in adolescence, 263–264, 265
Drug therapy, 414
Drug use, of mother, 65–66
Dual-earner couples, 343
Dualistic thinking, 319
Dual spinal-epidural, 73
Durable power of attorney, 457
Dying. *See also* Death
  process of, 453–455, *454*
Dynamic assessment, 224
Dyslexia, *45,* 206

Early adulthood, 304–306
  cognitive development, 317–329
  college, 323–329
  developmental tasks of, 331
  intelligence, 321–323
  physical development, 306–309
  physical limitations and challenges, 310–312
  relationships in, 331–345
  social and personality development, 330–351
  stress and, 312–318
  work, 346–350
Early childhood education, 171–173
Early development
  basics of genetics, 42–43
  genes and chromosomes, 40–41
  genetic counseling, 46–48
  genetic information transmission, 43–45
  inherited and genetic disorders, 45–46
  multiple births, 41–42
  sex determination, 42
Early maturation, 257–258
Early onset Alzheimer's disease, *45*
Easy babies, 143
Eating disorders, in adolescence, 258–260
Economics, of late adulthood, 432–433
Ectoderm, 59
Education for All Handicapped Children Act (1975), 226
Ego, 13
Egocentric thought, 161–162
Egocentrism, in adolescence, 272–273
Ego-integrity-*versus*-despair stage, *14,* 422
Elder abuse, 441
Electroencephalogram (EEG), 28
Embryo, 59
Embryonic stage, 59
Embryoscopy, *47*
Emerging adulthood, 332
Emotional insulation, 315
Emotional intelligence, 321
Emotional self-regulation, 189
Emotion-focused coping, 314
Emotions, in infancy, 132–135
Empathy, 136, 188
Empty love, 334, *335*
Empty nest syndrome, 386
Encoding, 119–120, 210
Endoderm, 59
"English-only" legislation, 214
Enrichment, 229
Environment(s)
  brain development and, 96–97
  influence of genes on, 56–57
  influence on personality, 53–55
  memory and, 419
  nature *vs.* nurture, 10, 50–52
  psychological disorders and, 55–56
  role of, 49–50
Environmental events, 10
Epidural anesthesia, 73
Episiotomy, 69
Episodic memories, 419
Erectile dysfunction, 362
Erikson's psychosocial theory, 13–14
  autonomy *vs.* shame and doubt, *14,* 142
  ego integrity *versus* despair, *14*
  evaluating, 15
  generativity *versus* stagnation, *14*
  identity *vs.* role diffusion, *14*
  industry *vs.* inferiority, *14,* 230–231
  initiative *vs.* guilt, *14*
  intimacy *versus* isolation, *14*
  stages in, *14*
  trust *vs.* mistrust, *14,* 142
Erikson's psychosocial theory
  ego integrity *versus* despair, 422
  generativity *versus* stagnation, 377–379
  intimacy *versus* isolation, 332
  personality development and, 281–282
Estrogens, 255
Ethgender, 281
Ethics
  infertility treatments and, 62
  research and, 34–35
  sex determination and, 42
Ethnic identity, 284–285
Ethnicity
  adolescent segregation and, 293
  depression and, 285
  development and, 7
  health and, 366
  identity and, 284–285
  influence on development, 7–9
  life expectancy and, 415
  preschool years, identity, and, 175
  reflexes and, 101–102
  school achievement and, 275–276
Ethology, 22
Eustachian tubes, 153
Euthanasia, 457
Evolutionary perspective, 22–23, *23*
Executive stage, of development, 320
Exercise
  early adulthood, 307
  middle adulthood, *359*
  middle childhood, 207
Exosystems, 20
Experiential components of intelligence, 224, 321
Experimental group, 29
Experimental research, 26
Experiments, cause and effect, 29–31
Expert advice, 34
Expertise, middle adulthood, 372–373
Explicit memory, 121
Expressive style, 128
Extinguished, behavior, 16
Extrinsic motivation, 349
Extroversion, 53
Eye-blink reflex, 101
Eyewitness testimony, of children, 165–166

Facial expressions, in infancy, 132–133, 134–135
FAE. *See* Fetal alcohol effects (FAE)
False belief task, 180
False consensus effect, 264
False labor. *See* Braxton-Hicks contractions
False memories, 165–166
False negatives, 368
False positives, 368
Familial retardation, 227
"Familiarity breeds rigidity," 322
Family child-care centers, 172
Family life, 145
  adolescence, 288–296
  late adulthood, 439–441
  middle childhood, 243–248
  preschoolers, 180–181
Family resemblance, environment and, 52
Family size, 342–343
Fantasy period, career choice, 347
FAS. *See* Fetal alcohol syndrome (FAS)
Fathers
  attachment and, 139–140
  influence on prenatal environment, 67
Fatuous love, 335, *335*
Female climacteric, 360
Female reproductive organs, *58*
Fertility rate, 342
Fertilization, 58
Fetal alcohol effects (FAE), 66
Fetal alcohol syndrome (FAS), 66, 227
Fetal blood sampling (FBS), *47*
Fetal development monitoring techniques, *47*
Fetal monitors, 79
Fetal stage, 59–60
Fetus, 60, 70–71

Field study, 30–31
Filter explanation, 336
Fine motor skills
infancy, 102–103
middle childhood, 202
preschool years, 158–159
First habits, *114,* 115
First sentences, 127–128
First stage of labor, 69–70
First-trimester screen, 46
First words, 126–127
First-year adjustment reaction, 325
Fitness, early adulthood, 307
Fixation, 13
Fluid intelligence, 222, 370–371
Food, adolescence and, 258–260
Forensic developmental psychology, 165–166
Formal operational stage, adolescence, 269–271
Fragile X syndrome, 45, *47*
Fraternal twins. *See* Dizygotic twins
Free radicals, 414
Free will, 20
Freud's psychoanalytic theory, 13, *14,* 15
Friendships
across races, 241–242
adolescence, 288–296
development of, 178–180
early adulthood, 333
gender and, 246, 240–241
late adulthood, 438
middle childhood, 237–242
Full inclusion, 227
Functional ages, 400
Functional death, 446
Functionality, 163
Functional magnetic resonance imaging (fMRI) scan, 28, *28*
Functional play, 179
Funerals, 461

Gag reflex, *101*
Gamete intrafallopian transfer (GIFT), 61
Gametes, 41, 43
Gays and lesbians
adolescents, 299–300
early adulthood relationships, 338
families, 246
as parents, 345
Gender
adolescent relations, 292–293
behavior and, 144–145
career choices and, 348–349
college attendance and, 325
college performance and, 326–328
depression and, 285
differences in self-esteem, 279–281
early *vs.* late maturation and, 257–258
friendships and, 240–241
health and, 366
life expectancy and, 415
moral development and, 235–236
preschooler identity development, 176–178
schooling and, 215–216
self-esteem and, 280
Gender constancy, 177
Gender gap, in college attendance, 325
Gender identity, preschoolers, 176–178
Gender schema, preschoolers, 177
Generalized slowing hypothesis, 405
Generation gap, 289
Generativity-*versus*-stagnation stage, *14,* 377–379
Genes, 41–42, 56–57
Genetic counseling, 46–48
Genetic disorders, 45–46
Genetic information transmission, 43–45
Genetic programming theories of aging, 412
Genetics
basics of, 42–43
behavioral, 46–47
cultural differences in, 53
influence on personality, 55
philosophical outlook and, 55
psychological disorders and, 55–56
transmission of genetic information, 43–45
Genital herpes, 267
Genital stage, 13
Genome mapping, 44
Genotypes, 43, 49–50
Germinal stage, 59
Germ line therapy, 48
Gerontologists, 400
GIFT. *See* Gamete intrafallopian transfer (GIFT)
Gifted and talented students, 228
Gilligan's moral development theory, 235–236
Ginzberg's career choice theory, 347
Girls
depression and, 285
early *vs.* late maturation and, 257–258
moral development in, 235–236
puberty in, 256–257
self-esteem in, 280
Glass ceiling, 349
Glaucoma, 357, 406
Goal-directed behavior, 115
Gonorrhea, 65, 267
Goodness-of-fit, 143
Grammar, 170
Grandchildren, late adulthood, 440–441
Grandparenting, 388–389
Grief, 462–465
counseling, 464
defined, 462
helping children cope with, 465
normal *vs.* unhealthy, 463
Grief and mourning, widowhood stage, 438
Grief counseling, 464
Grieving, 461
Gross motor skills
infancy, 102
middle childhood, 201–202, *202*
preschool years, 157
Group homes, 247

Habituation, 85
Hair cells, 358
Handedness, preschoolers, 159
Happiness, across lifespan, 382–383
Hardiness, coping and, 315
Health
early adulthood, 307–309, 310–311
late adulthood, 407–415
middle adulthood, 363–368
middle childhood, 202–203
of mother, 65
preschool years, 153–154, 158
Health care
culture and, 309
late adulthood and, 433
preventative screening recommendations, *365*
Health-care proxy, 457
Hearing
development of, 109
late adulthood, 406–407
loss, 205
middle adulthood, 358
newborns and, 83
Height
adolescence, *255*
early childhood, 199
infancy, *93*
middle adulthood, 357
preschool years, *153*
Helicopter parents, 387
Hemispheres, of brain, 60
Hemophilia, 44
Heredity
intelligence, 52–53
physical traits, 52
Heteronomous morality, 187
Heterosexuality, adolescence, 299–300
Heterozygous, 43
Higher education, early adulthood, 323–329
History-graded influences, 8
Holland's personality type theory, 347–348
Holophrases, 126
Home care, 460
Homogamy, 336
Homosexuality. *See also* Gays and lesbians
adolescence, 299–300
Homozygous, 43
Honeymoon period, retirement stage, 434
Hormone therapy (HT), 361–362
Hospice care, 460
Hostile sexism, 328
Human cell, *41*
Human genomes, 44–45
Humanistic perspective, 19–20, *23*
Human papilloma virus (HPV), 266
Huntington gene identified, 45
Husband-coached childbirth, 72
Hypertension, 407, 408
Hypnobirthing, 72
Hypothesis, 26

ICI. *See* Intracervical insemination (ICI)
Id, 13
Identical twins. *See* Monozygotic twins
Identity, 163, 281–282
Identity achievement, 283
Identity diffusion, 283
Identity foreclosure, 283
Identity-*versus*-identity-confusion stage, 281
Illegal drugs, in adolescence, 263–264, 265
Illness
aging and, 410–411
preschool years, 153–154, 158
terminal, 459–460
Imaginary audience, 272
Imitation, 16
Immigrants
employment for, 395
self-esteem of children, 232–233
Immune system, 314
Implicit memories, 121, 419
Imprinting, 137
Incipient cooperation stage, 187
Independent variable, 29
Individual differences, 6
Individualism, 21
Individualistic orientation, 175
Individuative-reflective stage, 284
Industry-*versus*-inferiority stage, *14,* 230–231
Infancy
cognitive development, 118–124, 131
death in, 448
developing roots of social ability, 132–135
development of senses, 107–112
differences among infants, 141–148
emotions in, 132–135
forming relationships, 137–141
growth and stability, 92–100
life cycles of, 97–99
memory during, 122–123
motor development, 100–107
nutrition in, 104–106
roots of language, 124–132
Infant attachment, 137
Infant-directed speech, 130
Infantile amnesia, 121
Infant-infant interaction, 140–141
Infant mortality, *75,* 80
Infatuated love, 334, *335*
Infertility, 60–62
Infidelity, 384, 390
Information processing approaches, 18
adolescence, 271–272
in infancy, 118–124
middle childhood, 210–211
preschool years, 164–168
Information processing deficits, 419
Information processing perspective, 271–272
Inherited disorders, 46
Initiative-*versus*-guilt stage, *14,* 174
Instinct, aggression and, 189
Institutionalism, 431
Instrumental aggression, 189
Integrated personalities, 425
Integration, 241–242
Intellectual development, middle childhood, 209–215
Intellectual disability, 227
Intelligence
alternative conceptions of, 222–224
defined, 220
early adulthood, 318, 321–323
environment and, 52–53
individual differences in, 121–124
late adulthood, 417–418
measuring, 221, *222*
middle adulthood, 370–372
middle childhood, 219–230
Intelligence quotient (IQ)
alternative conceptions of, 222–224
in Binet's test, 220–221
genetics and, 53
group differences in, 224–226
Intelligence tests, 220–224
Interactional synchrony, 139
Interactionist approaches, 129–130
Interconnectedness of influences on development, 21
Internal aging, 404–405
Internet
adolescence and, 277
bullying and, 240
late adulthood and, 420–421
middle childhood safety and, 203
preschoolers and, 175, 170–171
Interpersonal intelligence, *223*
Intimacy component, 334
Intimacy, early adulthood, 332
Intimacy-*versus*-isolation stage, *14,* 332
Intonation, 213
Intracervical insemination (ICI), 61
Intraocular lens implants, 406
Intrapersonal intelligence, *223*
Intrinsic motivation, 349
Intuitive thought, 162–163
In vitro fertilization (IVF), 4, 61
Involved grandparents, 388
Irritability, 142
IVF. *See* In vitro fertilization (IVF)

Job satisfaction, 349–350
Judgments, moral, 235
Juvenile delinquency, adolescence, 296

Karyotype, 46
Kaufman Assessment Battery for Children, Second Edition (KABC-II), 221
Keyword strategies, 211

Klinefelter's syndrome, 46
Kübler-Ross's theory of death and dying, 453–455
Kwashiorkor, 105

Labeling theory of passionate love, 334
Labor, 69–70
Laboratory study, 31
Labor, division of, marriage and, *344*
LAD. *See* Language-acquisition device (LAD)
Lamaze classes, 72
Language
characteristics of, 125
defined, 125
developmental origins, 128–130
development in middle childhood, 209–215
fundamentals of, 125–128
of infant-directed speech, 130
overview, 125
thought and, 160
Language-acquisition device (LAD), 129
Lanugo, 71
Latchkey children, 244
Late adulthood
daily life of, 430–434
death in, 450
developmental tasks in, *331*
economics of, 432–433
health and wellness in, 407–415
intelligence, 417–418
memory in, 419–421
overview, 398–400
personality development and successful aging, 422–429
physical development, 400–407
relationships in, 435–441
social networks, 438–439
technology and learning in, 420–421
Late maturation, 258
Late-onset Alzheimer's disease, *45*
Lateralization, 155
Lead poisoning, 154
Learned helplessness, 239, 431
Learning disabilities, 206
Learning, late adulthood, 420–421
Learning theory approaches, language acquisition, 128–129
Least restrictive environment, 226
Leisure, middle adulthood, 394
Leptin, 255
Lesbians. *See* Gays and lesbians
Levinson's final season, 423–424
Life events
cognitive development and, 323
models, 377
Life expectancy, 414–415
Life review, 425
Lifespan development
age ranges, 5–6
approaches to, *6*
behavioral perspective on, 15–17, *23*
cognitive perspective on, 17–19, *23*
cohort influences on, 8
contextual perspective on, 19–20, *23*
effect of infant child care on, 145–147
evolutionary perspective on, 22–23, *23*
humanistic perspective on, 19, *23*
nature *vs.* nurture, 9–12
psychodynamic perspective on, 13–15, *23*
research methods, 25–28
scope of field, 5–8
topical areas in, 5
Liking, 334, *335*
Limbic system, *184*
Linguistic intelligence, *223*
Living arrangements, for late adulthood, 430–432
Living wills, 457, *458*
Logical mathematical intelligence, *223*
Logical operations, 209
Longevity genes, 414
Longitudinal research, 31–32
Longitudinal studies, 31–32, 370
Long-term memory, 374
Love
combinations of, *335*
early adulthood, 333–338
faces of, 334
Loving contrition stage, of abuse, 389
Low-birthweight infants, 76, 77–78

Macrosystems, 20
Macula, 406
Mainstreaming, 226
Major depression, 285
Male climacteric, 362
Malnutrition, in infancy, 105
"MAMA" cycle, 283
Mammograms, 368
Marasmus, 105
Marcia's identity development theory, 282–283
Marijuana, 65
Marriage
early adulthood, 339–342
late adulthood, 435–438
middle adulthood, 383–384
relationships, 382–391
Marriage gradient, 336, 385
Masturbation, adolescence, 298
Maturation, 11
early *vs.* late, 257–258
Maturation reform, 325
Meconium, 82
Media
aggression and, 190–191
learning from, 170–171
Meiosis, 41
Memory
late adulthood, 419–421
middle adulthood, 374–375
Memory capabilities
in infancy, 120–121
middle childhood, 210–211
preschoolers, 165–166
Menarche, 256–257
Menopause, 361, 362
Mental age, 220
Mental disorders, late adulthood, 408–410
Mental representation, *114,* 116
Mental retardation, 227
Mesoderm, 59
Mesosystems, 20
Meta-analysis, 30
Metacognition, 272
Metalinguistic awareness, middle childhood, 213
Metamemory, 211
Microsystems, 20
Middle adulthood
cognitive development, 369–375
death in, 450
developmental tasks in, *331*
health in, 363–368
memory in, 374–375
overview, 354–355
personality development, 376–382
physical development, 356–359
sexuality in, 359–362
work and leisure, 392–395
worried of, *364*
Middle childhood
body growth, 198–201
exercise, 207
family life in, 243–248
friendships in, 237–242
information processing in, 210–211
intellectual and language development, 209–215
intelligence, 219–230
motor development and safety, 201–204
overview, 196
schooling, 215–219
self development, 230–236
special needs children, 205–208
Midlife crisis, 378–379
Midwives, 72
Mild intellectual disability, 227
Mirror neurons, 140
Miscarriage, 62
Mnemonics, 375
Models, 187
Moderate intellectual disability, 227
Monozygotic twins, 42, 52
Moral development
middle childhood, 233–236
preschool years, 186–192
Moratorium, 283
Moro reflex, 101, *101, 102*
Morphemes, 125
Motherese, 130
Mothers
age of, 63–65
alcohol and tobacco use by, 66–67
attachment and, 139–140
depression and, 65
diet of, 63
drug use by, 65–66
health of, 65
Motor development
cultural dimensions of, 101–102, 104
early adulthood, 307–309
infancy, 102–104
infant reflexes, 101–102
middle childhood, 201–204
nutrition and, 104–106
overview, 100
preschool years, 156–159
Mourning, 461–464
Multicultural education, 219
Multifactorial transmission, 49
Multigenerational families, 245, 388
Multimodal approach to perception, 112–113
Multiple births, 41–42
Mumps, 65
Murder, early adulthood, 308
Musical intelligence, *223*
Myelin, 60, 96, 155
Myelination, 260

Nativist approaches, 129
Naturalist intelligence, *223*
Nature *vs.* nurture, 9–12, 50–52
NBAS. *See* Brazelton Neonatal Behavior Assessment Scale (NBAS)
Need for belongingness, 333
Negative correlation, 27
Neglect, 181
Neglected adolescents, 294
Neonatal jaundice, 82
Neonates, 70–71
Neo-Piagetian theory, 18
Nervous system, 94–97
Neurons, 59, 94
Neuroticism, 53
Neurotransmitters, 94
Newborn medical screenings, 73–74
Newborns
early learning capabilitie, 84–85
male, circumcision of, 83–84
overview, 83–84
physical competence, 82
sensory capabilities, 83
social competence, 85–87
New York Longitudinal Study, 143
No Child Left Behind Act (2002), 276
Nonhuman animal studies, 50
Non-normative life events, 8
Nonorganic failure to thrive, 105
Nonverbal decoding, 135
Nonverbal encoding, 132
Normative-crisis models, 377
Norms, 103–104, 292
Numbers, preschoolers' understanding of, 164–165
Nurture *vs.* nature, 9–12, 50–52
Nutrition
adolescence, 258–260
early adulthood, 310
infancy, 104–106
middle childhood, 200
preschool years, 153

Obesity
adolescence, 259
early adulthood, 311
infancy, 105–106
middle childhood, 200
preschool years, 153
Object permanence, 115, *116*
Obstetricians, 72
Oldest old, 400
Old old, 400
Onlooker play, 179
Operant conditioning, 16, 85
Operations, 160
Oral stage, 13
Orienting response, 85
Orphanages, 247
Osteoporosis, 357, 403
Overextension, 127–128
Ovulation, 58, 60
Ovum, 40
Oxytocin, 69

Pain-reducing drugs, for childbirth, 73
Pain, sensitivity to, 110
Parallel play, 179
Parenthood, early adulthood, 342–345
Parents, adolescent conflict with, 290–291
Partial sightedness, 205
Partner choice, early adulthood, 335–337
Passionate (or romantic) love, 334
Passion component, 334
Passive-dependent personalities, 424
Passive euthanasia, 457
Peck's developmental tasks, 423
Peer pressure, adolescence, 295
Peers, in adolescence, 282, 291–293
Perception, 108
Perception of time, 405
Perimenopause, 361
Peripheral slowing hypothesis, 405
Permissiveness with affection, 298
Permissive parents, 181
Perry's approach to postformal thinking, 319
Personal fables, 273, 449
Personality aspects, 13
Personality development, *6*
adolescence, 278
defined, 6
early adulthood, 330–351
genetic and environmental influences on, 53–55
infancy, 141–148
late adulthood and, 422–429
middle adulthood, 376–382
middle childhood, 237–248
preschool years, 174
Phallic stage, 13
Phenotypes, 43, 49–50
Phenylketonuria (PKU), 43
Philosophical outlook, genetics and, 55
Phonemes, 125, 212

Phonological recoding skills, 216
Phonology, 125
Physical abuse, 183–184, 389–391
Physical age, 220–221
Physical competence, of newborns, 82
Physical development, *6*
defined, 6
early adulthood, 306–318
infancy, 93
late adulthood, 400–407
middle adulthood, 356–359
middle childhood, 198–201
overview, 93
preschool years, 152
Physical disabilities, early adulthood, 311–312
Physical disorders, late adulthood, 408–410
Physical growth
infant nervous system and brain, 94–97
major principles of, *94*
Physical limitations and challenges, early adulthood, 311–312
Physical traits, environment and, 52
Piagetian theory, 17–18
evaluating, 17–18, 119–120, 163, 215–216, 271
formal operations in adolescence, 269–271
infant cognitive development, 112–118
key elements of, 113
middle childhood cognitive development, 209–210
to preoperational thinking, 160–164
sensorimotor period, 114–116
view of moral development, 187
Pincer grasp, 103
Placenta, 59
Plasticity, 418
of brain, 96
Play
categorizing, 179
social aspects of, 179–180
Pleasure principle, 13
Pluralistic society model, 217–218, 284
Pollyanna principle, 419
Polygenic inheritance, 44
Polyphasic activities, 367
Popularity
adolescence, 294
middle childhood, 238–239
Positive correlation, 27
Postconventional morality, 234, *234,* 235
Postformal thinking, 271, 319
Postmature infants, 78
Postpartum depression, 81
Potty training, 158
Poverty
family life and, 247
in late adulthood, 432–433
Practical intelligence, 321
Pragmatics, 170, 213
Preconventional morality, 234, *234*
Prefrontal cortex, 260, 261
Pregnancy
adolescence, 300–301
problems in, 60–62
Prelinguistic communication, 125
Prenatal growth and change
developmental threats, 63–68
fertilization, 58
pregnancy problems, 60–62
stages of, 59–60
Prenatal testing, 46–47
Preoperational stage, 160–164
Preparation, widowhood stage, 437
Preparatory depression, 454
Presbycusis, 358
Presbyopia, 357
Preschools, 172
worldwide, *173*
Preschool years
body growth, 152–154
brain growth, 155–156
cognitive development, 160–164
moral development and aggression, 187–192
motor development, 56–159, 156–159
overview, 150
self-concept, 175
social aspects, 178–186
Preterm infants, 76–78
Preventive health-care screening recommendations, *365*
Primary aging, 403
Primary appraisal, of stress, 313
Primary circular reactions, *114,* 115
Primary sex characteristics, 256
Principle of hierarchical integration, 94
Principle of independence of systems, 94
Private speech, 170
Problem-focused coping, 314
Production, linguistic, 125, *126*
Profound intellectual disability, 228
Prolonged grief disorder, 463
Prosocial behavior, 187
Prostate gland, 362, 368
Prostate-specific antigen (PSA), 368
Proximodistal principle, 93
Psychoanalytic theory, 13
Psychodynamic perspective, 13–15, *23*
Psychological closeness, friendships and, 238
Psychological disorders
in adolescence, 285–287
genetics and environment and, 55–56
late adulthood, 408–410
middle childhood, 203–204
Psychological maltreatment, 184
Psychological moratorium, adolescence and, 282
Psychoneuroimmunologists, 364
Psychoneuroimmunology (PNI), 313
Psychophysiological methods, 28
Psychosexual development, 13
Psychosocial development, 13, 174–175, 230–231
Psychosomatic disorders, 314
Puberty, 255–258
Public policy, research and, 32
Punishment, 16
Purging, 259

Qualitative research, 27

Race
awareness of, in preschool years, 175
depression and, 285
development and, 7
family life and, 246–247
higher education and, 324
identity and, 284–285
infant mortality and, 79
influence on development, 7
life expectancy and, 415
segregation, adolescence and, 293
self-esteem and, 232–233, 280–281
Race dissonance, 175
Racial differences
in IQ, 225
in school achievement, 275–276
Racial identity, 284–285
Radiation therapy, 367
Random assignment, 29
Rapid eye movement (REM) sleep, 98
RDS. *See* Respiratory distress syndrome (RDS)
Reaction range, 44
Reaction time
late adulthood, 405
middle adulthood, 358
Reactive attachment disorder, 138
Reactive depression, 454
Reading, middle childhood, 216–217
Realistic period, career choice, 347
Reality principle, 13
Reasoning, 187
Recessive characteristics, 44
Recessive trait, 43
Reciprocal teaching, 213
Reciprocal transaction, 22
Redefinition of self *versus* preoccupation with work role, 423
Reference groups, 292
Referential style, 128
Reflexes, infants, 82, 101–102
Reinforcement, 16
Reintegrative stage, of development, 320
Rejected adolescents, 294
Related factors, 25
Relatedness, behavior and, 50–52
Relational aggression, 189
Relationships
adolescence, 288–296
early adulthood, 331–345
forming, 137–141
late adulthood, 435–441
middle adulthood, 382–391
middle childhood, 237–242
Religion, adolescence and, 284
Remarriage, 385–386
Reminiscence, 425
Remote grandparents, 388
Reorientation, retirement stage, 434
Replacement level, 342
Replicated research, 30
Reproductive organs, female, *58*
Research
ethics and, 34–35
experiments, 29–32
theories, hypotheses, and correlational studies, 25–28
Research setting, 30–31
Residential treatment centers, 247
Resilience, 185–186
coping and, 315, 317
Respiratory distress syndrome (RDS), 76
Responsible stage, of development, 320
Restrictive play, 241
Reticular formation, 156
Reticular information, 156
Retirement, 434, 436–437
Retirement routine stage, 434
Retrieval, 119–120, 211
Reversibility, 209
Role ambiguity, 245
Role stage, relationships, 333
Romantic love, 334–335
Rooting reflex, 82, *101, 102,* 110
Routine death education, 452
Rubella, 10, 65

Safe sex, 268
Safety, middle childhood, 201–204
Samples, 30
Sandwich generation, 387
Scaffolding, 167
Schaie's stages of development, 319–320
Schemas, 374–375
Schemes, 17, 113
Schizophrenia, *45,* 55–56
School
disidentification with, 329
worldwide, 215–216
School child care, 172
School performance, adolescence, 274–278
Scientific evidence, 34
Scientific method, 25
Scripts, 165
Seasons of life theory, 378
Secondary aging, 308, 403
Secondary appraisal, of stress, 313
Secondary circular reactions, *114,* 115
Secondary sex characteristics, 256
Secular trend, 256
Secure attachment pattern, 138
Selective optimization, 429
with compensation, 372
Self-absorption, in adolescence, 272–273
Self-actualization, 20
Self-awareness, 135
Self-care children, 244
Self-concept
adolescence, 279
preschoolers, 175
Self-control, language and, 213
Self, development of, 230–236
Self-esteem
adolescence, 279–281
middle childhood, 232–233
Self-fulfilling prophecy, 239
Self-identity, adolescence, 279–287
Semantic memories, 419
Semantics, 125
Senescence, 306, 403
Sensation, 108
Sense of self, preschool years, 174–178
Senses, development of
early adulthood, 306–307
hearing, 109
late adulthood, 406–407
middle adulthood, 357–358
multimodal perception, 110–111
overview, 107–108
pain sensitivity, 110
smell, 109
taste, 109
touch, 110
vision, 108–109
Sensitive period, 10, 96
Sensorimotor stage, cognitive development, 114–116
Sensory capabilities, of newborns, 83
Sensory difficulties, middle childhood, 205–206
Sensory memory, 374
Separation anxiety, 133–134
Sequential studies, 33
Severe intellectual disability, 228
Sex cells, 41
Sex cleavage, 292
Sex determination, 42
Sex segregation, middle childhood, 240–241
Sexual intercourse, 298–299
frequency of per age range, *360*
Sexuality
adolescence, 297–301
late adulthood, 411–412
middle adulthood, 359–362
Sexually transmitted infections (STI), 60, 266–367
Shaken baby syndrome, 96
Shaping, 129
Short-term memory, 211, 374, 419
Sibling rivalry, 243
Sickle-cell anemia, 46
SIDS. *See* Sudden infant death syndrome (SIDS)
Sight, newborns and, 84
Simple reflexes, *114,* 115
Singlehood, early adulthood, 345
Single-parent families, 245
Skilled-nursing facilities, 431
Sleep deprivation, adolescence, 262
Sleep states, *98*
Slow-to-warm babies, 143
Small-for-gestational-age infants, 76
Smell
development of, 109
late adulthood, 407
newborns and, 83

Smiling, 134
Smoking, in adolescence, 265
Sociability
attachment to mother and father, 139–140
development of self, 135
emotions in infancy, 132–135
forming social bonds, 137–139
infant-infant interaction, 140–141
social referencing, 135
theory of mind, 136
Social clocks, *334*
Social-cognitive learning theory, 16
Social comparison, adolescence, 292
Social competence
middle childhood, 238, 242
newborns and, 85–87
Social constructions, defined, 6
Social development, *6*
adolescence, 278
defined, 6
in early adulthood, 330–351
late adulthood, 435–441
middle adulthood, 376–382
middle childhood, 237–248
preschool years, 174
Social identity theory, 233
Socialized delinquents, 296
Social learning approaches, preschool years
aggression and, 189–190
gender-related behavior and, 177
morality and, 192–193
Social lives, of preschoolers, 178–186
Social networking sites
grieving and, *464*
late adulthood and, 421
Social networks, late adulthood, 438–439
Social problem-solving, 239
Social referencing, 135
Social smiles, *133,* 134
Social speech, 170
Social support, 315, 438–439
Societal pressures, in adolescence, 282
Sociocultural events, 8
Sociocultural-graded influences, 8
Sociocultural theory, Vygotsky's, 21–22
Socioeconomic status (SES)
intelligence and, 418
school performance and, 275
self-esteem and, 280–281
Solid foods, 107
SOMPA. *See* System of Multicultural Pluralistic Assessment (SOMPA)
Sonoembryology, *47*
Sonogram, *47*
Sound localization, 109, 358
Spatial intelligence, *223*
Special needs children, 205–208, 226–229
Speech capabilities, preschoolers, 170
Speech impairments, 206
Sperm, 40, 58
Spermarche, 257
Spirituality, adolescence and, 284
Spontaneous mutation, 45
Spousal abuse, 389–391
dealing with, 390
Spouse
caring for, 437
death of, 437–438
Stability *versus* change in personality, 379–382
Stanford-Binet Intelligence Scales, Fifth Edition (SB5), 221
Startle reflex, *101, 102*
States, *98*
States of arousal, 86
Status
career choice and, 350
defined, 349
middle childhood, 238
Stepping reflex, *101*
Stereotype threat, 329
Sternberg's triangular theory, 334–335
STI. *See* Sexually transmitted infections (STI)
Stillbirths, 79–80
Stimulus stage, relationships, 333
Stimulus-value-role (SVR) theory, 333
Storage, 119–120, 211
Stranger anxiety, 133–134
Strength, middle adulthood, 357
Stress
consequences of, 313
coping with, 314–317
defined, 313
early adulthood, 312–318
middle adulthood, 364–366
origins of, 313
Stress-related hormones, 79
Study of Early Child Care and Youth Development, 146
Stuttering, 206
Subcortical levels, 96
Subcultural groups, 218
Subjective well-being, 381
Sucking reflex, 82, *101*
Sudden infant death syndrome (SIDS), 99–100, 448
Suicide
adolescent, 286–287
antidepressants and, 204
by elderly people, 450
prevention of, 287
Superego, 13
Surrogate mother, 61–62
Survey research, 28
Swallowing reflex, 82
Swimming reflex, 101, *101*
Symbolic function, 160
Synapses, 94
Synaptic pruning, 94–96
Syntax, 212
Syphilis, 65, 267
System of Multicultural Pluralistic Assessment (SOMPA), 226

Taste
development of, 109
late adulthood, 407
newborns and, 83
Tay-Sachs disease, 46
Teaching, of desired behavior, 181–182
Teenage pregnancies, 300–301
Telegraphic speech, 127
Television, 170–171, 190–191, 201, 206
Telomeres, 412
Telomere therapy, 414
Temperament, 49, 142–144
Tension-building stage, of abuse, 389
Tentative period, career choice, 347
Teratogen, 63
Terminal decline, 450
Terminal illness, 459–460
Termination, retirement stage, 434
Tertiary circular reactions, *114,* 115–116
Testing, achievement, 276
Testosterone, 360, 362
Thanatologists, 452
Theoretical research, 31
Theories, 12, 25
Theory of mind, 136, 180
Third stage of labor, 69
Thought, language and, 160
Time-outs, 185
Time, perception of, 405
Tobacco
in adolescence, 265
mother's use of, 66–67
Toilet training, 158
Touch
development of, 110
newborns and, 83
Traits, 42–43, 54
Transformation, 161
Transgendered individuals, 299
Transition, 70
Transplants, 414
Transverse position, 79
Treatment group, 29
Triangular theory, of love, 334–335
Triarchic theory of intelligence, 224, 321
Trichomoniasis, 266
Trust, friendships and, 238
Trust-*versus*-mistrust stage, *14,* 142
Turner syndrome, 46
Twins, 41–42, 52, 54. *See also* Dizygotic twins; Monozygotic twins
Type A behavior pattern, 367
Type B behavior pattern, 367

Ultrasound sonography, *47*
Umbilical cord, 60
Unconscious part, of personality, 13
Underextension, 127
Undersocialized delinquents, 296
Unemployment, 393
Uninvolved parents, 181
Universal grammar, 129
Uterus, 58, 60

Value stage, relationships, 333
Variables, in experiments, 29
Vernix, 71
Very-low-birthweight infants, 76–77
Victimization, middle childhood, 240
Violence
cultural roots of, 390–391
early adulthood, 308
middle adulthood, 389–391
in preschoolers, 187–192
Virginity pledges, 300
Vision
development of, 108–109
late adulthood, 406
middle adulthood, 357–358
Visual acuity, 357
Visual cliff, 108
Visual impairment, 205
Visual-recognition memory, *122,* 123
Vocabulary, middle childhood, 212
Voluntary active euthanasia, 457
Voluntary responses, 85
Vygotsky's approach
evaluating, 168
middle childhood cognitive development, 211–212
preschoolers' cognitive development, 166–168
sociocultural theory, 21–22

Walking epidural, 73
Weaning, 107
Wear-and-tear theories of aging, 412
Wechsler Intelligence Scale for Children, Fourth Edition (WISC-IV), 221, *222*
Weight
early adulthood, *311*
early childhood, 199, *200*
infancy, *93*
middle adulthood, 357
preschool years, *153*
Wellness, late adulthood, 407–415
Whole language approach to reading, 217
Widowhood, 437–438
Wisdom, 426–427
Women
career choices and, 348–349
preventative screening health care recommendations, *365*
Work
early adulthood, 346–350
late adulthood, 433–434
middle adulthood, 392–395
Working memory, 211
Worries, middle adulthood, *364*

X-linked genes, 44

Young adulthood, death in, 449–450
Young old, 400

ZIFT. *See* Zygote intrafallopian transfer (ZIFT)
Zone of proximal development (ZPD), 167, 212
ZPD. *See* Zone of proximal development (ZPD)
Zygote intrafallopian transfer (ZIFT), 61
Zygotes, 40

1. C
2. A
3. A
4. B
5. D
6. A
7. A
8. D
9. D
10. B
11. D
12. A
13. B
14. B
15. B
16. C
~~17. D~~ A
18. D
19. A
20. B
21. A
22. D
23. C
24. ~~B~~ A
25. B
26. B
27. D
28. B
29. A
30. B
31. A
32. A
33. D
34. C